THE VICTORIA HISTORY
OF THE
COUNTIES OF ENGLAND

A HISTORY OF
MIDDLESEX

VOLUME IX

THE VICTORIA HISTORY
OF THE
COUNTIES OF ENGLAND

EDITED BY C. R. ELRINGTON

THE UNIVERSITY OF LONDON

INSTITUTE OF

HISTORICAL RESEARCH

Oxford University Press, Walton Street, Oxford OX2 6DP
Oxford   New York   Toronto
Delhi   Bombay   Calcutta   Madras   Karachi
Petaling Jaya   Singapore   Hong Kong   Tokyo
Nairobi   Dar es Salaam   Cape Town
Melbourne   Auckland

and associated companies in
Beirut   Berlin   Ibadan   Nicosia

Oxford is a trademark of Oxford University Press

Published in the United States by
Oxford University Press, New York

British Library Cataloguing in Publication Data
A History of the county of Middlesex.—(The Victoria
history of the counties of England)
Vol. 9
Hampstead and Paddington Parishes
1. London. Middlesex, history
I. Baker, T. F. T.
(Thomas Francis Timothy) 1935–
II. University of London
(Institute of Historical Research)
III. Series
942.1'8
ISBN 0 19 722772 4

Printed in Great Britain
by Bigwood & Staple Ltd., Bridgwater, Somerset

INSCRIBED TO THE

MEMORY OF HER LATE MAJESTY

QUEEN VICTORIA

WHO GRACIOUSLY GAVE THE TITLE TO

AND ACCEPTED THE DEDICATION

OF THIS HISTORY

A HISTORY OF THE COUNTY OF MIDDLESEX

EDITED BY T. F. T. BAKER

VOLUME IX

HAMPSTEAD AND PADDINGTON PARISHES

PUBLISHED FOR

THE INSTITUTE OF HISTORICAL RESEARCH

BY

OXFORD UNIVERSITY PRESS

1989

Distributed by Oxford University Press until 1 January 1992
thereafter by Dawsons of Pall Mall

CONTENTS OF VOLUME NINE

PAGE

Dedication v

Contents ix

List of Illustrations xi

List of Maps xiii

Middlesex Victoria County History Committee xiv

Editorial Note xv

Classes of Documents in the Public Record Office used xvi

Classes of Documents in the Greater London Record Office used . . . xvii

Note on Abbreviations xviii

Topography . . . . Architectural investigation by A. P. BAGGS

    Ossulstone Hundred (*continued*)

        Hampstead . . . By DIANE K. BOLTON; Public Services, Churches, Roman Catholicism, Protestant Nonconformity, Judaism, Education, and Charities by PATRICIA E. C. CROOT; Hampstead Heath, Social Activities, Trade and Industry, and part of Communications by T. F. T. BAKER . . . 1

            Communications 3

            Settlement and Growth 8

                Hampstead Town 15

                Frognal and the Central Demesne 33

                West End 42

                Kilburn, Edgware Road, and Cricklewood . . . 47

                Belsize 51

                St. John's Wood 60

                Chalcots 63

                North End, Littleworth, and Spaniard's End . . . 66

                Vale of Health 71

                Childs Hill 73

                Hampstead Heath 75

            Social and Cultural Activities 81

            Manor and Other Estates 92

            Economic History

                Agriculture 111

                Woods 121

                Mills 122

                Fairs 123

                Trade and Industry 123

            Local Government

                Manorial Government 130

                Parish Government to 1837 132

                Local Government after 1837 135

            Public Services 138

            Churches 145

CONTENTS OF VOLUME NINE

		PAGE
Roman Catholicism	. . . .	152
Protestant Nonconformity	. . . . . .	153
Judaism .	. . . .	158
Buddhism	. . . .	159
Sikhism .	. . . .	159
Other Faiths	. . . .	159
Education	. . . .	159
Charities for the Poor	. . . . . .	169
Paddington	. . . By T. F. T. BAKER . . .	173
Communications .	. . . .	174
Growth		
Settlement and Building to *c.* 1800	. . . . .	181
Building after *c.* 1800 .	. . . . .	182
Paddington Green	. . . . . .	185
Tyburnia	. . . . . .	190
Westbourne Green	. . . . . .	198
Bayswater	. . . . . .	204
Maida Vale	. . . . . .	212
Queen's Park and St. Peter's Park	. . . .	217
Social and Cultural Activities	. . . . . .	221
Manors and Other Estates	. . . . . .	226
Economic History		
Agriculture	. . . .	233
Nurseries and Market Gardens	. . . .	235
Woods	. . . . . .	235
Trade and Industry	. . . . . .	236
Local Government		
Manorial Government .	. . . . .	241
Parish Government to 1837	. . . . .	241
Local Government after 1837	. . . . .	243
Public Services	. . . .	246
Churches	. . . .	252
Roman Catholicism	. . . .	259
Protestant Nonconformity	. . . . . .	260
Greek Orthodox Church	. . . . . .	264
Judaism .	. . . .	264
Education	. . . .	265
Charities for the Poor	. . . . . .	271
Index .	. . . .	273
Corrigenda to Volumes I, III–VI, and VIII	. . . . .	302

LIST OF ILLUSTRATIONS

For permission to reproduce material in their possession, thanks are rendered to: City of London, Guildhall Library; the Greater London Record Office (Photograph Library); London Borough of Camden, Swiss Cottage Library; the National Monuments Record (N.M.R.) of the Royal Commission on Historical Monuments (England); Westminster City Archives, Marylebone Library; Mr. David Sullivan. The coats of arms were drawn by Patricia A. Tattersfield.

Borough of Hampstead: coat of arms . . . . *page* 136
London Borough of Camden: coat of arms . . . . „ 137

Plates between pages 140 and 141

HAMPSTEAD

1. Holly Bush Hill in the early 19th century. From a pencil drawing in Swiss Cottage Library
2. High Street in 1881. From a watercolour by J. P. Emslie in Swiss Cottage Library
3. Hampstead Wells from the Heath in 1745. From an etching by John Chatelaine in Swiss Cottage Library
4. Pond Street in 1745. From an etching by John Chatelaine in Swiss Cottage Library
5. The Vale of Health in 1804. From an engraving, after a drawing by F. J. Sarjent, in Swiss Cottage Library
6. North End in 1822. From a lithograph by T. M. Baynes in Swiss Cottage Library
7. Jack Straw's Castle in 1830. From a drawing by G. S. Shepherd in Swiss Cottage Library
8. Dancing on Hampstead Heath in 1899. From a drawing by Phil May in Swiss Cottage Library
9. Primrose Hill tunnel: the London entrance in 1837. From a coloured aquatint by W. H. Budden in Guildhall Library
10. Kilburn High Road and turnpike gate in 1860. From a photograph in Swiss Cottage Library
11. Rosslyn House in 1896. From a watercolour by J. P. Emslie in Swiss Cottage Library
12. Buckland Crescent, nos. 9 to 19. Photograph, 1937, in Swiss Cottage Library
13. Admiral Saumarez's house c. 1830. From a watercolour in Swiss Cottage Library
14. Heath Mount School c. 1830. From a watercolour by G. S. Shepherd in Swiss Cottage Library
15. Greenhill, Prince Arthur Road. From *Building News*, 3 Jan. 1879, in Swiss Cottage Library
16. Redington Lodge, Redington Road. From a cutting of 1887 in Swiss Cottage Library
17. Annesley Lodge, Platt's Lane. From a cutting of 1896 in Swiss Cottage Library
18. Fitzjohn's Avenue, no. 1. From a cutting of 1883 in Swiss Cottage Library
19. The Old Parish Church c. 1740. From a watercolour in Guildhall Library
20. St. John's Parish Church and Church Row c. 1830. From a pen and wash drawing by Mrs. L. Garne in Guildhall Library
21. St. Stephen's Church, Rosslyn Hill, interior. Photograph, 1965, in N.M.R.
22. St. John's Parish Church, interior. Photograph, 1892, in N.M.R.
23. St. Stephen's Church, Rosslyn Hill. Photograph, 1965, in N.M.R.
24. St. Saviour's Church, Eton Road. Photograph, in N.M.R.
25. Holy Trinity Church, Finchley Road. Photograph, 1964, in N.M.R.
26. St. John's Chapel, Downshire Hill. Photograph, in N.M.R.
27. St. Peter's Church, Belsize Park. Photograph, 1960, in N.M.R.
28. Old Mansion, no. 94 Frognal, in 1780. From a watercolour in Swiss Cottage Library
29. Heathlands, Littleworth, c. 1800. From an engraving in the possession of Mr. David Sullivan
30. Frognal Hall c. 1890. From a watercolour by J. P. Emslie in Swiss Cottage Library
31. Vane House in 1813. From an engraving by W. Davison in Guildhall Library

LIST OF ILLUSTRATIONS

PADDINGTON

32. Westbourne Place *c.* 1796. From an anonymous watercolour in D. Lysons, *Environs of London*, iii (pt. 2), p. 330: grangerized copy in Guildhall Library

33. Palace Court, no. 2. Photograph, 1892, in N.M.R.

34. Paddington Green: Mr. Symmons's House *c.* 1796. From an anonymous watercolour in D. Lysons, *Environs of London*, iii (pt. 2), p. 330: grangerized copy in Guildhall Library

35. St. Sophia's Orthodox Cathedral, Moscow Road. Photograph, in N.M.R.

36. Westbourne Green and Bayswater *c.* 1830. From C. and G. Greenwood, *Map of London*, in Westminster City Archives

37. Paddington Green and Tyburnia *c.* 1830. From C. and G. Greenwood, *Map of London*, in Westminster City Archives

38. Paddington Station, the Canal Basin, and Westway. Photograph, 1982, by Aerofilms Ltd.

39. Paddington Station *c.* 1892. Photograph, in Westminster City Archives

40. Blomfield Road, the Canal, and Delamere Terrace. Photograph, 1967, in Greater London Record Office (Photograph Library)

41. Tyburnia from the south-west. Photograph, 1981, by Astral Aerial Surveys Ltd.

42. Paddington Green in 1827. From a pencil sketch by E. W. Cooke in Guildhall Library

43. Paddington Canal Basin in 1801. From a coloured aquatint by H. Milbourne in Guildhall Library

44. Whiteley's Store, Queensway. Photograph, 1967, in Greater London Record Office (Photograph Library)

45. Eastbourne Terrace, office blocks. Photograph, 1969, in Greater London Record Office (Photograph Library)

46. St. Mary's Hospital in 1847. From a lithograph by G. Hawkins in Westminster City Archives

47. Bayswater Chapel in 1818. From an aquatint published by Edward Orme in Guildhall Library

48. St. Mary's Parish Church *c.* 1796. From an ink and wash drawing in Guildhall Library

49. The Old Parish Church in 1750. From an etching by John Chatelaine in D. Lysons, *Environs of London*, iii (pt. 2), p. 332: grangerized copy in Guildhall Library

50. St. Augustine's Church, Kilburn Park Road. Photograph, 1965, in N.M.R.

51. Holy Trinity Church, Bishop's Bridge Road. Photograph, 1964, in N.M.R.

52. St. Mary's Magdalene's Church, Woodchester Street. Photograph, 1968, in N.M.R.

53. Westbourne Grove *c.* 1895. Photograph, in N.M.R.

54. Lancaster Gate, nos. 104 to 109. Photograph, 1961, in Greater London Record Office (Photograph Library)

Borough of Paddington: coat of arms . . . . *page* 245
City of Westminster: coat of arms . . . . ,, 245

LIST OF MAPS

All the maps except those on pages 14–15 and 184–5 and plates 36–7 were drawn by K. J. Wass of the Department of Geography, University College, London, from drafts prepared by T. F. T. Baker, D. K. Bolton, and P. E. C. Croot.

Ossulstone Hundred. From C. G. Greenwood's *Map of Middlesex* (1819) . . *page* 1

The Holborn Division. From C. G. Greenwood's *Map of Middlesex* (1819) . ,, 2

Hampstead: Communications. From O.S. Map 6″, Mdx. XI. SE., XVI. NE., XVII. NW. (1894 edn.) and London Transport maps . . . . . ,, 4

Hampstead in 1762. From S.C.L., Manor Map (1762) . . . . ,, 10

Hampstead: Settlement and Growth. From building leases and L.C.C. *Municipal Map of London* (1913) . . . . ,, 12

Hampstead: Evolution of Settlement, 1844–1904. Parts of O.S. Maps 1″ (1844, 1877, 1904 edns.) . . . . *pages* 14–15

Hampstead Town and Frognal in 1762. From S.C.L., Manor Map (1762) . . *page* 21

Belsize Leases in 1808. From deeds and estate maps . . . . ,, 54

Hampstead: Manor and Estates. From deeds and estate maps . . . ,, 94

Westbourne Green and Bayswater in 1830. Part of C. and J. Greenwood's *Map of London* (1830) . . . . *plate* 36

Paddington Green and Tyburnia in 1830. Part of C. and J. Greenwood's *Map of London* (1830) . . . . ,, 37

Paddington: Communications. From O.S. Map 6″, Mdx. XVI. NE., SE. (1894 edn.) and London Transport maps . . . . *page* 176

Paddington c. 1750. From Church Commissioners' map of lands of Sir John Frederick (1742) and Rocque, *Map of London* (1741–5) . . . ,, 180

Paddington: Evolution of Settlement, 1844–1904. Parts of O.S. Maps 1″ (1844, 1877, 1904 edns.) . . . . *pages* 184–5

Paddington: Estates c. 1830. From G. Gutch, *Plan of Paddington* (1828) . . *page* 227

EDITORIAL NOTE

THE present volume is the second to have been compiled for the Committee formed in 1979 to complete the Middlesex History. The Committee is financed by the seven London Boroughs whose areas make up what may be called inner Middlesex. An eighth local authority, the Greater London Council, was represented until its abolition in 1986. The Committee has continued, under the chairmanship of Dr. David Avery, to support and supervise the Middlesex editorial staff, which has remained unchanged since 1978. The University of London gratefully acknowledges the help of the Committee and the generosity of the London Boroughs which it represents.

The structure and aims of the Victoria History as a whole are outlined in the *General Introduction* (1970). The contents of the first seven volumes of the Middlesex History are listed and indexed in outline in a booklet, *The Middlesex Victoria County History Council, 1955–84,* which also describes the work of the precursor of the present Middlesex Victoria County History Committee.

Those who have provided information for the volume or commented on parts of the text are named in the footnotes, and they are sincerely thanked for their help. Particular mention may be made here of the valuable contributions of Mr. H. V. Borley and Mr. R. M. Robbins, C.B.E., who read the sections of the text dealing with communications, of Sir John Summerson, C.H., Mr. M. Holmes, Mr. C. W. Ikin, and Mr. D. Sullivan, who read parts of the article on Hampstead, and of Mr. R. A. Bowden, who read the article on Paddington.

CLASSES OF DOCUMENTS
IN THE PUBLIC RECORD OFFICE
USED IN THIS VOLUME
WITH THEIR CLASS NUMBERS

Chancery

		Proceedings
C	2	Series I
C	3	Series II
C	5	Six Clerks Series, Bridges
C	6	Collins
C	7	Hamilton
C	8	Mitford
C	9	Reynardson
C	10	Whittington
C	54	Close Rolls
C	60	Fine Rolls
C	66	Patent Rolls
C	78	Decree Rolls
C	93	Proceedings of Commissioners of Charitable Uses, Inquisitions, and Decrees
C	94	Surveys of Church Livings
		Inquisitions post mortem
C	142	Series II

Court of Common Pleas

CP 25(1)	Feet of Fines, Series I
CP 25(2)	Series II

Exchequer, King's Remembrancer

E 126	Decrees and Orders, Series IV
E 133	Depositions taken before the Barons of the Exchequer
E 159	Memoranda Rolls
E 179	Subsidy Rolls, etc.

Exchequer, Augmentation Office

E 305	Deeds of Purchase and Exchange
E 317	Parliamentary Surveys
E 318	Particulars for Grants of Crown Lands

Exchequer, Lord Treasurer's Remembrancer's and Pipe Offices

E 358	Miscellaneous Accounts

Ministry of Education

ED 3	Educational Returns, London
ED 7	Public Elementary Schools, Preliminary Statements
ED 15	Private Schools not recognized for Grant or Efficiency, Returns

ED 21	Public Elementary School Files
ED 35	Secondary Education: Institution Files

Registry of Friendly Societies

FS 2	Indexes to Rules and Amendments, Series I

Home Office

HO 107	Population Returns
HO 129	Ecclesiastical Returns

Board of Inland Revenue

IR 29	Tithe Apportionments

Justices Itinerant, Assize and Gaol Delivery Justices, etc.

JUST 1	Eyre Rolls, Assize Rolls, etc.

Ministry of Agriculture, Fisheries, and Food

MAF 20	Manor Files
MAF 68	Agricultural Returns: Parish Summaries

Ministry of Health

MH 13	Correspondence

Prerogative Court of Canterbury

PROB 11	Registered Copies of Wills proved in P.C.C.

Office of the Registrar General

RG 9	Census Returns, 1861
RG 10	1871
RG 11	1881
RG 31	Registers of Places of Worship

Court of Requests

REQ 2	Proceedings

Special Collections

SC 6	Ministers' and Receivers' Accounts
SC 11	Rentals and Surveys, Rolls

Court of Star Chamber

STAC 8	Proceedings, Jas. I

Court of Wards and Liveries

WARD 5	Feodaries' Surveys

SELECT LIST OF
CLASSES OF DOCUMENTS IN THE
GREATER LONDON RECORD OFFICE
USED IN THIS VOLUME
WITH THEIR CLASS NUMBERS

A/KE	King Edward's Hospital Fund for London, records
BRA	British Records Association
Cal. Mdx. Sess. Bks.	Calendar of Sessions Books, 1638–1752
E/MW/H	Maryon Wilson Estate Records, Hampstead
M/81	Manorial Records, Hampstead
MAB	Metropolitan Asylums Board, records
MBW	Metropolitan Board of Works, records
MC/R	Clerk of the Peace, registers
MJ/SBB	Sessions Books
MR/FB	Registers of Freeholders
MR/LMD	Music and Dancing Licences
MR/LV	Licensed Victuallers' Lists
MR/RH	Places of Worship
MR/TH	Hearth Tax Assessments
P81	Parish Records, Hampstead
P87	Parish Records, Paddington
Pa. B.G.	Paddington Board of Guardians, records
SBL	School Board for London, records
TA	Tithe Awards
WCS	Westminster Commissioners of Sewers, records

NOTE ON ABBREVIATIONS

Among the abbreviations and short titles used the following may require elucidation, in addition to those noted in the Victoria History's *Handbook for Editors and Authors* (1970):

Archit. of Lond.	E. Jones and C. Woodward, *A Guide to the Architecture of London* (1983)
B.L.	British Library (used in references to documents transferred from the British Museum)
Bacon, *Atlas of Lond.* (1886)	*Ordnance Atlas of London and Suburbs*, ed. G. W. Bacon (1886)
Baines, *Rec. Hampstead*	*Records of the Manor, Parish, and Borough of Hampstead*, ed. F. E. Baines (1890)
Barratt, *Annals*	T. J. Barratt, *The Annals of Hampstead* (3 vols. 1912)
Booth, 'Archives'	J. Booth, 'Extracts from Archives of the Metropolitan Borough of Paddington' (TS. 1930 in Marylebone library)
Booth, *Life and Labour*	C. Booth, *Life and Labour of the People in London* (17 vols. revised edn. 1902–3). Survey begun 1886
Booth's Map (1889)	*Charles Booth's Descriptive Map of London Poverty, 1889* (London Topographical Society 1984)
C.C.C.	Council for the Care of Churches (formerly Council for Places of Worship)
C.H.R.	*Camden History Review* (1973 to date)
C.U.L.	Cambridge University Library
Calamy Revised	*Calamy Revised*, ed. A. G. Matthews (1934)
Clarke, *Lond. Chs.*	B. F. L. Clarke, *Parish Churches of London* (1966)
Colvin, *Brit. Architects*	H. Colvin, *Biographical Dictionary of British Architects, 1600–1840* (1978)
Cruchley's New Plan (1829)	[G. F.] *Cruchley's New Plan of London and Its Environs* (1829)
D.S.R.	District Surveyors' Returns. In G.L.R.O.
E.C.R.	Eton College Records
Freshfield, *Communion Plate*	E. Freshfield, *Communion Plate of the Parish Churches in the County of London* (1895)
Ft. of F. Lond. & Mdx.	*Calendar to the Feet of Fines for London and Middlesex*, ed. W. J. Hardy and W. Page (2 vols. 1892–3)
G.L.C.	Greater London Council
G.L.R.O.	Greater London Record Office. Contains the collection of the former Middlesex Record Office (M.R.O.)
Guildhall MSS.	City of London, Guildhall Library. Contains registers of wills of the commissary court of London (London division) (MS. 9171), bishops' registers (MS. 9531), diocesan administrative records (MSS. 9532–9560), registers of nonconformist meeting houses (MS. 9580), court books of Paddington (MS. 10465), and records of the bishop of London's estates, including material transferred by the Church Commissioners and from St. Paul's cathedral library
Gunnis, *Sculptors*	R. Gunnis, *Dictionary of British Sculptors 1660–1851* (1951)
H.H.E.	*Hampstead & Highgate Express*
Hampstead One Thousand	J. Richardson, *Hampstead One Thousand, A.D. 986–1986* (1985)
Harvey, *Westm. Abbey*	B. Harvey, *Westminster Abbey and its Estates in the Middle Ages* (1977)
Hennessy, *Novum Rep.*	G. Hennessy, *Novum Repertorium Ecclesiasticum Parochiale Londinense* (1894)
Hist. Lond. Transport	T. C. Barker and M. Robbins, *History of London Transport* (2 vols. 1975)
Hist. Mon. Com. *W. Lond.*	Royal Commission on Historical Monuments, *Inventory of the Historical Monuments in London*, ii, *West London* (H.M.S.O. 1925)
Images of Hampstead	S. Jenkins and J. Ditchburn, *Images of Hampstead* (1982)
Insurance Plans	Insurance plans of London, mostly 40' to 1", pub. by Chas. E. Goad Ltd. from 1886. Revisions, to 1925 and to 1970, for parts of Hampstead (Kilburn) and Paddington in Guildhall Library; original and revised plans for Paddington, with modern key, in Marylebone library

Kennedy, *Manor of Hampstead*	J. Kennedy, *The Manor and Parish Church of Hampstead* (1906)
L.B.	London Borough
L.C.C.	London County Council
L.C.C. *Lond. Statistics*	L.C.C. *London Statistics* (26 vols. 1905–6 to 1936–8, beginning with vol. xvi). Followed by ibid. new series (2 vols. 1945–54 and 1947–56) and by further new series from 1957
Lond. Encyc.	*The London Encyclopaedia*, ed. B. Weinreb and C. Hibbert (1983)
Lysons, *Environs*	D. Lysons, *Environs of London* (4 vols. 1792–6 and Supplement 1811)
M.B.	Metropolitan Borough
M.B.W.	Metropolitan Board of Works
M.L.R.	Middlesex Land Registry. The enrolments, indexes, and registers are at the Greater London Record Office
M.M. & M.	May, May & Merrimans, Gray's Inn. Records include court books of Hampstead from 1706
McDonald, 'Paddington'	F. N. McDonald, 'A History of Paddington'. MS. (part TS.) in Marylebone library
Mackeson's Guide	C. Mackeson, *A Guide to the Churches of London and Its Suburbs* (1866 and later edns.)
Mdx. County Rec.	*Middlesex County Records* [1550–1688], ed. J. C. Jeaffreson (4 vols. 1886–92)
Mdx. County Rec. Sess. Bks. 1689–1709	*Middlesex County Records, Calendar of the Sessions Books 1689 to 1709*, ed. W. J. Hardy (1905)
Mdx. Sess. Rec.	*Calendar to the Sessions Records* [1612–18], ed. W. le Hardy (4 vols. 1935–41)
Middleton, *View*	J. Middleton, *View of the Agriculture of Middlesex* (1798)
Mudie-Smith, *Rel. Life*	R. Mudie-Smith, *Religious Life of London* (1904)
New Lond. Life and Labour	H. Llewellyn Smith and others, *New Survey of London Life and Labour* (9 vols. 1930–5). Survey undertaken 1928
Newcourt, *Rep.*	R. Newcourt, *Repertorium Ecclesiasticum Parochiale Londinense* (2 vols. 1708–10)
Newton, *Map of Hampstead* (1814)	J. and W. Newton, map in Park, *Hampstead*, facing p. 1
Norden, *Spec. Brit.*	J. Norden, *Speculum Britanniae : Middlesex* (facsimile edn. 1971)
P.N. Mdx. (E.P.N.S.)	*Place-Names of Middlesex* (English Place-Name Society, vol. xviii, 1942)
Park, *Hampstead*	J. J. Park, *The Topography and Natural History of Hampstead* (1818)
Pevsner, *Lond.* ii	N. Pevsner, *Buildings of England : London except the Cities of London and Westminster* (1952)
Potter Colln.	British Museum, Department of Prints and Drawings, Potter Collection of North London Topography
Reeder, 'Capital Investment'	D. A. Reeder, 'Capital Investment in the Western Suburbs of Victorian London' (Leicester Univ. Ph.D. thesis, 1965)
Rep. on Bridges in Mdx.	*Report of the Committee of Magistrates Appointed to make Enquiry respecting the Public Bridges in the County of Middlesex* (1826). Copy in G.L.R.O.
Rep. Com. Eccl. Revenues	*Report of the Commissioners Appointed to Inquire into the Ecclesiastical Revenues of England and Wales* [67], H.C. (1835), xxii
Rep. Cttee. on Returns by Overseers, 1776	*Report of the Select Committee on Returns by Overseers of the Poor, 1776*, H.C., 1st ser. ix
Robins, *Paddington*	W. Robins, *Paddington : Past and Present* (1853)
Rocque, *Map of Lond.* (1741–5)	J. Rocque, *Exact survey of the cities of London, Westminster, and the borough of Southwark, and the country near ten miles around* (1746, facsimile edn. 1971)
S.C.L.	Swiss Cottage Library
Saint, 'Hampstead Walk'	A. Saint, 'Hampstead Walk' (descriptions for walks by the Victorian Society, 1978)
T.L.M.A.S.	Transactions of the London and Middlesex Archaeological Society (1856 to date). Consecutive numbers are used for the whole series, although vols. vii–xvii (1905–54) appeared as N.S. i–xi
Thompson, *Hampstead*	F. M. L. Thompson, *Hampstead, Building a Borough, 1650–1964* (1974)
Thorne, *Environs*	J. Thorne, *Handbook to the Environs of London* (1876) [alphabetically arranged in two parts]

NOTE ON ABBREVIATIONS

W.A.M.	Westminster Abbey Muniments
Wade, *More Streets*	C. Wade, *More Streets of Hampstead* (1973)
Wade, *Streets of Hampstead*	C. Wade, *The Streets of Hampstead* (1984)
Wade, *W. Hampstead*	C. Wade, *The Streets of West Hampstead* (1975)
Walker Revised	*Walker Revised*, ed. A. G. Matthews (1948)

OSSULSTONE HUNDRED

(continued)

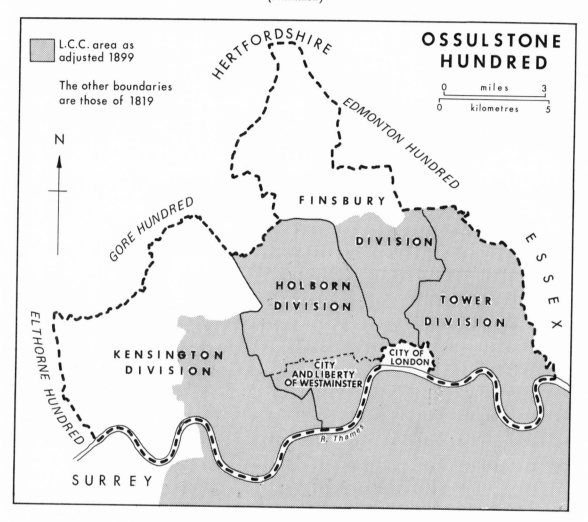

HOLBORN DIVISION
HAMPSTEAD

HAMPSTEAD,[1] known for its left-wing intellectuals and, as 'Appy 'Ampstead, as the playground of London's East End,[2] lies with its south-western corner 3.2 km. north of Marble Arch. A compact parish estimated at 2,070 a. in 1831 and containing 2,265 a. (*c.* 917 ha.) in 1931,[3] it is diamond shaped, *c.* 3.2 km. in length and breath. The boundaries of the parish were described in 10th-century charters.[4]

The genuine charter of King Edgar, *c.* 970, gives only four boundary marks: Watling Street or Edgware Road forming the south-western boundary with Willesden, the cucking pool apparently on Watling Street at the western angle, Sandgate, which has been identified with North End near the northern angle, and Foxhanger.[5] If Foxhanger was Haverstock Hill, a suggestion that seems likely, the whole

[1] The article was written in 1986–7.
[2] Below, growth, Hampstead Heath.
[3] *Census*, 1831, 1931.
[4] Below, manor and other est. The A.-S. boundaries

are discussed in *T.L.M.A.S.* vi. 560–70; *P.N. Mdx.* (E.P.N.S.), 221–2.
[5] M. Gelling, *Early Charters of Thames Valley* (1979), p. 111, no. 226.

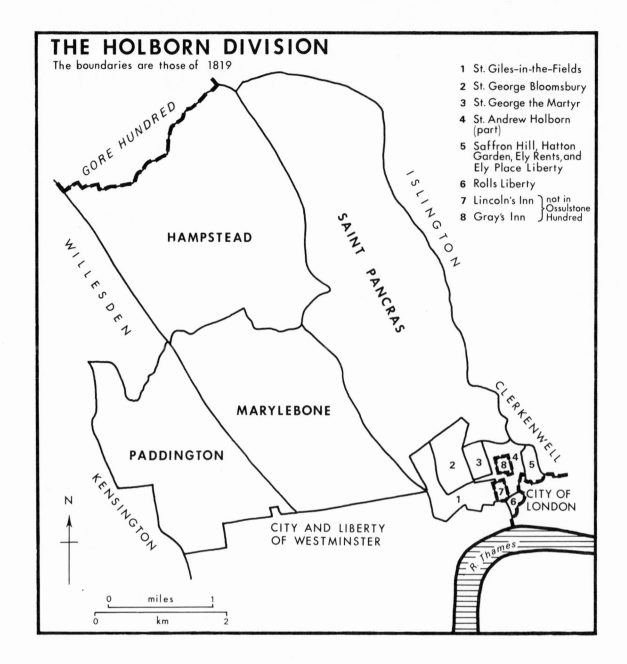

THE HOLBORN DIVISION

The boundaries are those of 1819

1 St. Giles-in-the-Fields
2 St. George Bloomsbury
3 St. George the Martyr
4 St. Andrew Holborn (part)
5 Saffron Hill, Hatton Garden, Ely Rents, and Ely Place Liberty
6 Rolls Liberty
7 Lincoln's Inn ⎤ not in
8 Gray's Inn ⎦ Ossulstone Hundred

GORE HUNDRED

WILLESDEN

HAMPSTEAD

SAINT PANCRAS

ISLINGTON

CLERKENWELL

MARYLEBONE

PADDINGTON

KENSINGTON

2   3   8   4   5

1   7   6   CITY OF LONDON

CITY AND LIBERTY OF WESTMINSTER

R. Thames

N

0   miles   1
0   km   2

east side of the later parish was excluded. The charter attributed to King Æthelred gives more detail: from Sandgate the boundary ran east to Bedegar's *styvic leage*, possibly a hog or cattle run, thence to Deormod's *wic* or farm, to Middle Hampstead, and along the hedge to the rush *leage*. Parts of the boundary and hedge were visible in 1986 and there is every indication that the north-eastern boundary with St. Pancras has since remained constant. The south-eastern boundary with St. Pancras and Marylebone ran westward to the barrow, probably Barrow Hill at Primrose Hill, then to Stangrafe (? Stonepit) and Watling Street. Dense woodland along the north-western and south-eastern bound-

aries and common ownership of estates on either side of them led to ambiguity, for example at Childs Hill and St. John's Wood. The Templars, who held St. John's Wood, denied any connexion with Hampstead. When the wood was cleared, the parish boundary ran through the middle of fields and there were disputes with St. Marylebone and St. Pancras over its course, especially at Primrose Hill, in 1751, 1821, and 1843.[6] Boundaries were determined by the manor court in 1632, by the churchwardens in 1671, and by the vestry by the 18th century.[7] Some 70 boundary stones were needed in 1824.[8] When Hampstead metropolitan borough was created under the Local Government Act, 1899, adjustments were

[6] Vestry mins. 9 Apr. 1751; 8 Aug. 1821; 27 July 1843. Vestry mins. are in S.C.L.: below, local govt.

[7] Ibid. *passim*; G.L.R.O., E/MW/H/I/2311B; P81/ JN1/1A.   [8] Vestry mins. 30 Sept. 1824.

made to the south-eastern boundary, the main effect of which was to straighten the line along Greville Place and Boundary Road.[9]

London Clay, which covers all the parish, is capped in the north-east by Claygate Beds and Bagshot sands, producing the sands, gravel, and elevation of Hampstead Heath.[10] From 30 m. in the south-west, the ground rises to 133 m. near Jack Straw's Castle.[11]

Before it was drained and ponds were created, much of the heath was marshy.[12] Springs and streams fringed the heath, arising especially at the junction of sand and clay.[13] A few streams flowed north, to become tributaries of the Brent, but most became feeders for the three main southward-flowing rivers, the Holborn or Fleet in the east,[14] the Tyburn, of which the main source was Shepherd's Well, and the Westbourne in the west, fed by branches arising in Frognal and on Telegraph Hill and joining at the site of Kilburn priory to become Kilburn brook[15] (also called Ranelagh sewer or Bayswater rivulet).[16] The boundary stream mentioned in the Anglo-Saxon charters gave its name to the Slade[17] and flowed westward as a tributary of the Brent, but had dried up by the 17th century.[18]

COMMUNICATIONS. Watling Street or Edgware Road, often called Kilburn Street or Road,[19] was the Roman road to St. Albans and beyond. Almost parallel to it on the east was a route leading north through Hampstead town and over the heath to Hendon; in the 16th century and later it was sometimes identified as Watling Street.[20] The boundary described in the charter of *c.* 970 and the discovery of a medieval costrel in Holly Hill in 1876 suggest that the route, if not Roman, was old,[21] although its precise course was not established until the 18th century.[22] The road was usually called Hampstead Street or the highway to Hampstead or London.[23] Its most southerly section was called Haverstock (Harberstocke) Hill by 1575[24] and the

next section Red Lion or Rosslyn Hill after the inn and house of those names.[25] High Street, so named (*alte strate*) in 1633,[26] the next section, originally included the part called, after 1831, Heath Street.[27] The northernmost section, which by the 19th century was called North End Hill[28] or Road[29] and in the 20th North End Way, passed through North End and Golders Green. Branching from the main route at Jack Straw's Castle, a second road, by 1862 called Spaniard's Road,[30] led from Hampstead town to Highgate through Cane Wood (Kenwood). It existed by *c.* 1672 and was mentioned in 1695.[31]

Roads crossing North End Way and Edgware Road *c.* 1672[32] indicated a west–east route, which was in use by the mid 18th century,[33] running from Walm Lane in Willesden,[34] through Shoot Up Hill or Mill Lane, Blind Lane, Fortune Green, and Platt's Lane to Childs Hill and thence along the edge of the heath. By 1862 the route near the heath had dwindled to a footpath and Blind Lane had disappeared.[35] By the mid 18th century West End Lane led from Edgware Road at Kilburn through West End to Fortune Green, and Cole Lane and Frognal Lane linked West End respectively with Shoot Up Hill and Frognal.[36] By 1679 Belsize Lane[37] and by 1714 Upper Chalcot (later England's) Lane existed as access roads.[38]

The usual complaints about the state of the roads led to bequests for repairs in the 15th and 16th centuries.[39] Hampstead benefited from the John Lyon and Edward Harvist charities for the whole of Edgware Road and from the turnpike trust set up in 1710. Under the Metropolis (Kilburn and Harrow Roads) Act, 1872, Edgware Road was disturnpiked and administration of the relevant charities passed to the local authorities and their successors, including Hampstead metropolitan borough and Camden L.B.[40] Hampstead Road Trust was established by Act in 1717 initially for 21 years but extended and varied by numerous Acts, to keep in repair the road from Stone's End to Highgate gatehouse and Hampstead, presumably Hampstead Lane and Spaniard's

[9] *Census*, 1901; A. R. Colville, *Lond.: Northern Reaches* (1951), 91; Stanford, *Libr. Map of Lond.* (1891 edn.), sheet 5; L.C.C. *Municipal Map of Lond.* (1913).

[10] Geol. Surv. Map 6", drift, Lond. sheets I. NE., II. SW., IV. NE., V. NW. (1920 edn.).

[11] O.S. Map 1/10,000, TQ 28 SE., NE. (1974–6 edn.).

[12] e.g. rush lea, mentioned in Æthelred's charter; below, growth, Vale of Health; bogs on W. side of heath: Park, *Hampstead*, 30.

[13] Geol. Surv. Map 6"; below, growth, Hampstead Heath.

[14] *T.L.M.A.S.* iv. 97–123.

[15] Ibid. vi. 244–77, map facing p. 285; B.L. Maps, King's Libr. XXX. 7. a.

[16] *Rep. on Bridges in Mdx.* 152.

[17] *V.C.H. Mdx.* vii. 177. Cf. field names (Lr. and Upper Slads) on NE. border: S.C.L., Man. Map and Fieldbk. nos. 485–6.

[18] G.L.R.O., E/MW/H/I/2311B.

[19] W.A.M. 32363; G.L.R.O., P81/JN1/15.

[20] J. Norden, *Map of Mdx.* (1593); J. Ogilby, *Map of Mdx.* [*c.* 1672]; Camden, *Brit.* (1806), ii. 87; M. Drayton, *Poly-Olbion*, ed. J. W. Hebel (1933), iv, Song xvi, line 254; W. F. Grimes, *Excavation of Rom. and Modern Lond.* (1968), 40–1.

[21] *Cart. Sax.* ed. Birch, iii, p. 693; Barratt, *Annals*, i. 7.

[22] Below, growth, North End.

[23] e.g. Guildhall MS. 9171/3, f. 175v.; P.R.O., PROB 11/24 (P.C.C. 16 Thower, will of John Blenerhasset); Park, *Hampstead*, 277.

[24] *Cal. Pat.* 1572–5, 550.

[25] Newton, *Map of Hampstead* (1814); Wade, *Streets of Hampstead*, 67.

[26] G.L.R.O., E/MW/H/2.

[27] Wade, *Streets of Hampstead*, 59.

[28] Stanford, *Libr. Map of Lond.* (1862 edn. with additions to 1865), sheet 1.

[29] O.S. Map 1/2,500, Lond. VII (1870 edn.).

[30] Stanford, *Libr. Map of Lond.* (1862 edn. with additions to 1865), sheet 1.

[31] Ogilby, *Map of Mdx.* [*c.* 1672]; *Mdx. County Rec. Sess. Bks. 1689–1709*, 131.

[32] Ogilby, *Map of Mdx.* [*c.* 1672], which does not delineate the roads between the crossings.

[33] Rocque, *Map of Lond.* (1741–5), sheet 12; S.C.L., Man. Map.

[34] *V.C.H. Mdx.* vii. 179.

[35] Stanford, *Libr. Map of Lond.* (1862 edn. with additions to 1865), sheet 1.

[36] Rocque, *Map of Lond.* (1741–5), sheet 12; S.C.L., Man. Map; S.C.L., D 121.

[37] S.C.L., D 136.

[38] W.A.M. Map 12450.

[39] Guildhall MS. 9171/3, f. 175v.; P.R.O., PROB 11/24 (P.C.C. 16 Thower, will of John Blenerhasset); PROB 11/58 (P.C.C. 20 Carew, will of Sir Ric. Rede); *N. & Q.* 10th ser. viii. 464.

[40] *V.C.H. Mdx.* vii. 178–9, 254; Colville, *Lond.: Northern Reaches*, 95; *Endowed Chars. Lond. III*, H.C. 252, pp. 127–8 (1900), lxi.

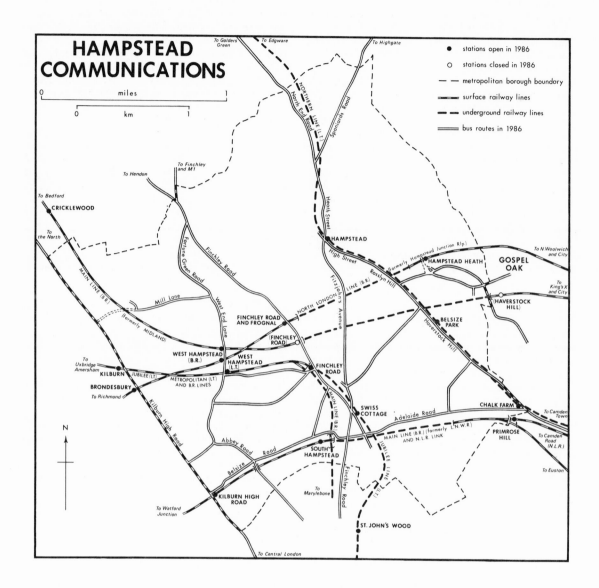

Road. The trustees used gravel from the heath and in 1719 levelled a hill there.[41] There was a tollhouse on Spaniard's Road near the inn, which in 1966 was given by the brewers to the G.L.C. and became part of the heath.[42]

There were abortive attempts in 1778 and 1819 to build a new north–south route through the centre of Hampstead parish. The Finchley Road Act was passed in 1826 and the new turnpike road was completed in 1835.[43]

Until 1769, in accordance with an agreement between the lords of Hampstead and Mapesbury (Willesden) manors, Hampstead paid 5s. a year towards the repair of a brick bridge on Edgware Road,[44] presumably Kilburn bridge.[45] In 1826 Kilburn brook was culverted in West End Lane and the Fleet was culverted near the southern of the heath ponds and at the eastern end of Pond Street.[46]

Regular transport between Hampstead and Holborn or Covent Garden, for the City, and Tottenham Court Road, for the West End, was advertised by John Duffield, who leased Hampstead wells in 1700. Guards were sought for the passengers in 1718[47] and Hampstead stage coaches were often robbed in the 1720s.[48] In *Clarissa Harlowe*, whose plot was set some 20 years before its publication in 1747, the fleeing heroine chose the coach to Hampstead as being 'so ready a convenience'.[49] A coach ran from the Black Swan, Holborn, and another from James Street, Covent Garden, in 1740 and 1755, apparently only once a day. By 1768 there were 2 daily journeys from James Street, 5 in summer and 2 in winter from Holborn bars, and 2 from Chiswell Street, Moorfields.[50]

The service remained too infrequent for daily business travel until the late 18th century, when the number of return journeys by short-stage coach rose, from 14 in 1770 to 18 in 1793 and 43 in 1799. About 43 journeys were still made in 1815.[51] Hampstead was the terminus for 10 coaches from the City, together making 17 return journeys a day, in 1825,[52] when most of them started from the Bird in Hand at the top of High Street. With the services to London's west end, there were perhaps 40 daily journeys in all.[53] In 1826–7 Hamilton & Clarke's coaches ran hourly to the Blue Posts in Tottenham Court Road and the Mansion House, and Mary Woodward's to Covent Garden, Oxford Street, and Tottenham Court Road. The earliest left at 8.0 a.m.[54] but the frequency of mid-day services sug-

gests that most passengers were not bound for an office.[55] Coaches provided the only public conveyance to London until the mid 1830s.[56] Thirteen short-stage coaches ran to Tottenham Court Road or Holborn, or, less often, to Charing Cross, in 1838–9, when all were owned by Alexander Hamilton, who also ran omnibuses.[57] Hamilton still provided a half-hourly coach service, calling at Jack Straw's Castle and so presumably coming from north of the parish, in 1845.[58] Local journeys could be made by hackney coaches, which obstructed High Street in 1783.[59] Sedan chairs survived until *c.* 1841, when there were also three stables for the hire of hackney coaches.[60]

Eight omnibuses[61] made 20 return journeys from Hampstead to the City in 1834. There were 7 omnibuses in all in 1838–9, owned chiefly by Hamilton, and perhaps 24 by 1856, when most were acquired by the Compagnie Générale des Omnibus de Londres (later the London General Omnibus Co. or L.G.O.C.).[62] The route from Hampstead was that of the coaches, from the Bird in Hand down High Street and Haverstock Hill to Chalk Farm, where the Adelaide and Britannia taverns were popular boarding points, and thence to Camden Town.[63] By 1838–9 one of the omnibuses ran along Edgware Road to Kilburn and in 1856 as many as ten, along Finchley Road, served Swiss Cottage, where the Atlas line had been inaugurated *c.* 1850. Less than half of Hampstead's *c.* 800 commuters could have been carried by public road transport in the 1850s.[64] Perhaps many were like a man who rode daily to his City counting house in 1845 and complained at having to pay three turnpike tolls.[65] Omnibuses also had to pay tolls, until the removal of the metropolitan commissioners' only turnpike gate within Hampstead, at Haverstock Hill, in 1864.[66]

Omnibus routes were pushed farther north with the spread of building and opening of suburban railway stations after 1855. By 1880 they not only stretched along Kilburn High Road to Brondesbury but also served Kilburn and West Hampstead by way of Abbey Road and the area north of Swiss Cottage by way of Finchley Road as far as Finchley Road station. Later omnibuses were extended along Finchley Road to meet others from Edgware Road along West End Lane, continuing north to Childs Hill in Hendon. In the populous south part of the parish they ran east–west from Chalk Farm along Adelaide and Belsize roads to Kilburn station.[67]

[41] Park, *Hampstead*, 260–3; G.L.R.O., Cal. Mdx. Sess. Bks. xii. 10, 13, 25.
[42] *The Times*, 16 Sept. 1929, 1b; 28 Oct. 1966, 8d.
[43] Park, *Hampstead*, 260–2 n.; Thompson, *Hampstead*, 110–24; *Gtr. Lond.* ed. J. T. Coppock and H. C. Prince (1964), 106; *V.C.H. Mdx.* v. 3.
[44] G.L.R.O., E/MW/H/I/1938, 2280.
[45] Treated under Willesden: *V.C.H. Mdx.* vii. 180.
[46] *Rep. on Bridges in Mdx.* 152–3.
[47] *Images of Hampstead*, 29–30.
[48] Cuttings, attributed to 1721 and later (on card index in S.C.L.).
[49] S. Richardson, *Clarissa Harlowe*, v, letters viii, x.
[50] *Complete Guide to Lond.* ed. J. Osborn (1740, 1749, 1755); *Baldwin's New Complete Guide to Lond.* (1768).
[51] Thompson, *Hampstead*, 56–7. Dirs. give slightly differing figures, e.g. *P.O. Dir. Lond.* (1815) and *Kent's Lond. Dir.* (1815).
[52] *Hist. Lond. Transport*, i. 391.
[53] *Hampstead One Thousand*, 95; Thompson, *Hampstead*, 56.

[54] *Pigot's Com. Dir.* (1826–7). For departures from Lond. see *Cary's New Itinerary* (1817).
[55] Thompson, *Hampstead*, 57.
[56] Baines, *Rec. Hampstead*, 222.
[57] *Hist. Lond. Transport*, i. 398.
[58] *P.O. Dir. Six Home Counties* (1845).
[59] Vestry mins. 18 June 1783.
[60] Baines, *Rec. Hampstead*, 223. A private sedan chair was in use until 1853: G. W. Potter, *Random Recollections of Hampstead* (1907), 29.
[61] For the distinction between short-stage coaches and omnibuses, see *Hist. Lond. Transport*, i. 14–22.
[62] Thompson, *Hampstead*, 56; *Hist. Lond. Transport*, i. 95, 398, 409.
[63] Thompson, *Hampstead*, 58 (map); Baines, *Rec. Hampstead*, 221.
[64] Thompson, *Hampstead*, 55–7, 58 (map); Baines, *Rec. Hampstead*, 222.
[65] *The Times*, 27 Jan. 1845, 7b.
[66] M. Searle, *Turnpikes and Toll-bars* (1930), i. 194–5; ii. 691.
[67] Thompson, *Hampstead*, 58 (map).

Services also became more frequent: in 1890 the L.G.O.C.'s yellow cars left High Street every 18 minutes and the Adelaide, Haverstock Hill, every 10 minutes, while light or dark green Atlas cars left Swiss Cottage and red or light blue cars left Kilburn at still shorter intervals. Less frequently, omnibuses ran from Kilburn to Willesden green and on 'rural routes' from Swiss Cottage to Hendon and Finchley, although they did not extend north of Hampstead village across the heath.[68] On the opening of Hampstead tube station the service from High Street to Oxford Street, one of the oldest in London, was twice briefly rerouted to run to Bayswater, by way of Swiss Cottage, and then to Kilburn, before returning to its original line and finally closing in 1907.[69]

Horse trams, owned by London Street Tramways, reached Kentish Town in 1871 and Southampton Road on the Hampstead boundary, by way of Prince of Wales and Malden roads, in 1880. A line was opened to the foot of Highgate West Hill and another from Southampton Road across the boundary and along Fleet Road to South End green in 1887.[70] A large stables and depot were built near the terminus, along Fleet Road and with an entrance from Cressy Road.[71] In 1901 the L.C.C., which had taken over London Street Tramways' systems within the county, added a one-way extension from South End green back to Southampton Road along Agincourt Road, so forming a loop.[72] The lines to and from South End green were electrified in 1909.[73]

Opposition to trams, as a working-class form of transport,[74] prevented them from penetrating farther into the parish. The line to South End green, which, with the depot, provided much local employment, was popular with trippers to the heath.[75] Tradesmen and gentry combined, however, in 1881 to resist proposals for cable trams up Haverstock Hill and through the heart of Hampstead village to Jack Straw's Castle. A standing committee of residents drew attention not only to the threat to property values but to the steepness and narrowness of the streets, until the scheme was rejected in 1883,[76] the year before cable trams were introduced up Highgate Hill.[77] Renewed proposals were successfully resisted in 1885.[78]

The L.C.C. in turn hoped for tramways to Jack Straw's Castle and thence back along East Heath Road to Hampstead Heath station in 1899, but by that date a further objection was that they would be made unnecessary by the proposed tube line.[79] Along the Willesden boundary there were no trams in Kilburn High Road, although they operated farther north, from Cricklewood, and eastward along Cricklewood Lane almost to the Hampstead boundary at Childs Hill.[80] In 1874 the vestry opposed a projected Edgware Road and Maida Vale Tramway Co.[81] and in 1911 the L.C.C. decided not to lay tramlines from Marble Arch to Cricklewood, partly because Hampstead council gave a high estimate of the cost of road widening.[82] Plans for an extensive network of tramways, along Adelaide and Finchley roads, were also dropped after opposition from the council, ground landlords, and residents.[83]

Trolleybuses replaced the trams which ran to South End green, by way of the Agincourt Road circle, in 1938. Operating from London Transport's Highgate depot, they made way for motorbuses in 1961.[84]

Motorbuses had replaced horse omnibuses by 1911, when their routes included one which ended, like the tramway, at South End green.[85] Hampstead village and the heath remained free of public road transport[86] until an east–west service from Finsbury Park to Golders Green, entering the parish at the Spaniards and turning away towards North End at Jack Straw's Castle, was started in 1922, despite many objections.[87] Motorbuses also ran north from Adelaide Road across Belsize Park to the upper part of Haverstock Hill, whence they continued as far as Pond Street, South End Road, and Downshire Hill. A Sunday service along Downshire Hill drew further protests in 1928.[88] No motorbuses ran north of Pond Street c. 1950, when the routes were otherwise similar to those of 1930.[89] There was successful resistance in 1957 and 1962 to a proposed service from Swiss Cottage to Golders Green by way of Hampstead village, where the streets were too narrow for double-deckers, despite the lack of any public transport across that part of the borough other than the North London railway.[90] A single-decker service through the village was finally opened in 1968, followed by a circuitous service farther south from Cricklewood by way of Swiss Cottage to Pond Street and thence to Archway station in 1972.[91]

The first railway in the parish was part of the main line from Euston built in 1837 by the London & Birmingham Railway Co., which from 1846 formed part of the London & North Western Railway (L.N.W.R.). The line crossed southern Hampstead and ran beneath Primrose Hill in a much admired stone tunnel, whose turretted entrance front was designed by W. H. Budden. At first the nearest station was by the main goods yards across the

[68] *Hampstead Year Bk.* (1888); Baines and Scarsbrook, *Hampstead Local Guide* (1896); Baines, *Rec. Hampstead*, 221–2.
[69] *The Times*, 12 July 1907, 14f; *N. & Q.* 10th ser. viii. 157, 396–7; S.C.L., H 388.3.
[70] Thompson, *Hampstead*, 58 (map), 363; *Hist. Lond. Transport*, i. 185, 258 (maps).
[71] O.S. Map 1/2,500, Lond. XXVII (1896 edn.).
[72] Thompson, *Hampstead*, 365; *Hist. Lond. Transport*, i. 270; *Hampstead One Thousand*, 95.
[73] *Hist. Lond. Transport*, ii. 100 (map).
[74] Thompson, *Hampstead*, 364.
[75] Ibid. 365; *Hampstead One Thousand*, 95; Baines, *Rec. Hampstead*, 222.
[76] *The Times*, 8 Dec. 1881, 11c; S.C.L., H 388.4; Thompson, *Hampstead*, 364.   [77] *V.C.H. Mdx.* vi. 107.
[78] Vestry mins. 8 Jan., 5 Mar. 1885.

[79] Thompson, *Hampstead*, 364; S.C.L., H 388.4.
[80] *Hist. Lond. Transport*, ii. 100 (map); L.C.C. *Municipal Map of Lond.* (1913).
[81] Vestry mins. 8 Jan. 1874.
[82] *H.H.E.* 13 May 1911, 6g.
[83] Ibid. 7 Jan. 1911, 5b; 21 Jan. 1911, 5f; 28 Jan. 1911, 5b; 11 Feb. 1911, 5b.
[84] *Hist. Lond. Transport*, ii. 300 (map); S.C.L., H 388.
[85] *Hist. Lond. Transport*, ii. 158, 169 (map).
[86] L.C.C. *Municipal Map of Lond.* (1913).
[87] *The Times*, 1 Apr. 1922, 10d; 13 Apr. 1922, 14c; L.C.C. *Municipal Map of Lond.* (1930).
[88] *The Times*, 13 July 1928, 13e; L.C.C. *Municipal Map of Lond.* (1930).
[89] S.C.L., H 388.3 (plan of bus and train svces. c. 1950).
[90] *H.H.E.* 24 Aug. 1962, 1a.
[91] S.C.L., H 388.3 (cuttings).

boundary at Chalk Farm.[92] Although the company was not initially interested in suburban traffic, its desire to reach the docks led it to promote the East & West India Docks & Birmingham Junction Railway, incorporated in 1846 and renamed the North London Railway (N.L.R.) in 1853, which in 1851 extended its line westward from Camden Town to meet the L.N.W.R. line at Hampstead Road station (renamed Chalk Farm in 1862 and Primrose Hill in 1950). The N.L.R. proved popular for travel to the City[93] and could be used by passengers from Hampstead's first station, opened in 1852 in Belsize Road by the L.N.W.R. as Kilburn; it was rebuilt in 1879, with a second entrance in Kilburn High Road, as Kilburn & Maida Vale, was closed in 1917 but reopened in 1922, with only the High Road entrance, and in 1923 was renamed Kilburn High Road. The company opened a second Hampstead station on the new tracks in 1879, when its original main line was quadrupled. The station, at the west end of the Primrose Hill tunnel, was called Loudoun Road;[94] it was closed in 1917 but reopened in 1922 as South Hampstead.[95]

Congestion near Camden Town led the L.N.W.R. to promote the Hampstead Junction Railway (H.J.R.),[96] which in 1860 opened a northerly bypass through Gospel Oak and the central part of Hampstead to rejoin the main line at Willesden. The company was managed by the N.L.R. from 1864 and absorbed by the L.N.W.R. in 1867. Stations in the parish were opened in 1860 at Hampstead Heath, Finchley Road (from 1880 Finchley Road & Frognal) and Edgeware [sic] Road (renamed Edgware Road and Brondesbury in 1872, Brondesbury (Edgware Road) in 1873, and Brondesbury in 1883).[97] The line was tunnelled between Hampstead Heath and Finchley Road and came to be known as part of the Broad Street to Richmond line, the N.L.R. having secured more direct access to the City by means of its Broad Street terminus in 1865.[98] Trains ran every 15 minutes from Hampstead Heath to the City from its opening, first to Fenchurch Street and from 1865 to Broad Street.[99] West End Lane station (from 1975 West Hampstead) was opened in 1888.[1]

From 1868 the Midland Railway, which previously had made use of the Great Northern Railway's terminus at King's Cross, ran trains from Bedford to its own terminus at St. Pancras. The line entered the parish at Childs Hill, passed southeastward beneath the H.J.R.'s line to a second station called Finchley Road (closed 1927) and thence through a long tunnel and Haverstock Hill station (beyond the boundary, in Lismore Circus;

closed 1916) towards Kentish Town. The Midland's local service quickly proved successful,[2] being served by suburban trains which went on to the City by way of the Metropolitan line at King's Cross, besides main line trains to St. Pancras. West End (from 1950 West Hampstead, Midland) station was opened in 1871; it had previously been a halt, built to serve a yard and sidings, and remained profitable only because of the freight traffic.[3]

Meanwhile, south of the parish, the Metropolitan in 1863 had opened London's first Underground railway from Farringdon Street to Paddington, by way of Baker Street. In 1865 the Metropolitan & St. John's Wood Railway Co., promoted and in 1882 absorbed by the Metropolitan, was authorized to construct a feeder northward from Baker Street to Hampstead, where it was to cross High Street by a bridge and terminate at Willow Road. The line never reached the village, where it would have made a powerful impact, because of financial difficulties. A single track, running only as far as Swiss Cottage, was opened in 1868 but there were no through services from the City between 1869 and 1907. A double-tracked extension to Willesden Green was opened, however, in 1879, with stations at Finchley Road, West Hampstead, and, on the Willesden side of the high road, at Kilburn, and in 1882 a double track was completed to Swiss Cottage.[4] In 1888 there was a frequent service from Swiss Cottage to Baker Street, for both the City and (by omnibus) the West End, and a half-hourly service to Willesden Green and beyond.[5] The line was electrified in 1905.[6] Under London Transport's new works programme of 1935, a stretch of the Bakerloo line was built in a tube beneath the Metropolitan line from Baker Street to Finchley Road, where it took over two of the Metropolitan tracks to Wembley Park and its branch to Stanmore.[7] The new Bakerloo line opened in 1939, the Metropolitan's station at Swiss Cottage being replaced in 1940 by one designed by Stanley Heaps. Alterations were carried out at Finchley Road, where the platforms were reconstructed in 1939, and at West Hampstead in 1938.[8] After further work in the 1970s, the Stanmore line, renamed the Jubilee line with its own extension south of Baker Street into the West End, was inaugurated in 1979, when new entrances and a ventilation tower were built at Swiss Cottage.[9]

Hampstead's 19th-century railways ran east and west, except the Underground line through Swiss Cottage. None crossed the comparatively empty northern half of the parish, which required a tunnel under the heights. A railway, albeit less objectionable than tramways, was successfully resisted as

[92] H. P. White, Gtr. Lond. (Regional Hist. of Rlys. of Gt. Britain, iii (1963)), 118, 121; Wade, More Streets, 53; Images of Hampstead, 138 and illus. 463–8; below, plate 9.
[93] White, Gtr. Lond. 74–5; M. Robbins, N. Lond. Rly. (1974), 2–3.
[94] C.H.R. vii. 16–17; inf. from Mr. H. V. Borley.
[95] C. R. Clinker, L.N.W.R. Chronology, 1900–60 (1961), 25, 31.
[96] Para. based on White, Gtr. Lond. 77–8; Robbins, N.L.R. 5.
[97] J. E. Connor and B. L. Halford, Forgotten Stations of Gtr. Lond. (1972), 7–8.
[98] C.H.R. vii. 16–17.   [99] Robbins, N.L.R. 16–17.
[1] C.H.R. vii. 16–17; H. V. Borley, Chronology of Lond. Rlys. (1982), 91.

[2] White, Gtr. Lond. 146–8, 152.
[3] C.H.R. vii. 17–18; Connor and Halford, Forgotten Stations, 15.
[4] Hist. Lond. Transport, i. 128; A. A. Jackson, Lond.'s Metropolitan Rly. (1986), 41–2; White, Gtr. Lond. 135; Thompson, Hampstead, 303.
[5] Hampstead Year Bk. (1888).
[6] A. E. Bennett and H. V. Borley, Lond. Transport Rlys. (1963), map at back.
[7] C. E. Lee, Sixty Years of the Bakerloo (1966), 23.
[8] White, Gtr. Lond. 139; Bennett and Borley, Lond. Transport Rlys. 22, 28; C.H.R. vii. 19; L. Menear, Lond.'s Underground Stations (1983), 91, 93, 96, 138, 140.
[9] O. Green and J. Reed, Lond. Transport Golden Jubilee Bk. (1983), 177; Menear, Underground Stations, 119, 140.

early as the 1860s, when it was alleged that work would affect the drainage and so harm the vegetation of the heath.[10] After the Charing Cross, Euston, & Hampstead Railway had been authorized to build a tube railway from Charing Cross to Heath Street in 1893, nothing was done until its powers passed to the American Charles Tyson Yerkes, who formed the Underground Group.[11] There was more enthusiasm for his proposed line to Hampstead, a village still 'singularly cut off from the west end of London', than for his planned extension 'burrowing mole-like under the heath and throwing up stations to mark its track'.[12] In the event the longer line, to a rural crossroads at Golders Green but without a station on the heath, was opened in 1907 as the Hampstead Tube. There were stations called Chalk Farm, at the foot of Haverstock Hill, Belsize Park, and Hampstead, at the corner of High Street and Heath Street. All were designed by Leslie W. Green in the dark-red glazed bricks used for all surface stations in the group, and at Hampstead the platforms were 192 ft. below the surface, the deepest in London. After the Hampstead Tube had been linked with the City & South London Railway Co. under an Act of 1913, the line was known as the Edgware, Highgate & Morden line and later as the Morden–Edgware line. It formed part of the L.P.T.B.'s Northern line from 1937.[13]

A station to serve the summit of the heath, near Jack Straw's Castle, had been planned by Yerkes but opposed both by Hampstead vestry and the local preservationists.[14] Its site was accordingly moved to a point just across the boundary, where platforms but not access shafts were built for a station whose intended name was changed from North End to Bull and Bush. The station, which never opened, was used for storage of archives in the First and Second World Wars.[15]

For commuters, the early railways have not retained their importance. Soon after 1900 the N.L.R. was menaced by competition from the electrified Metropolitan line through Swiss Cottage, from the Hampstead Tube, and from the electrification of the tramways.[16] A similar loss of traffic by the Midland led to the closure of Haverstock Hill and Finchley Road stations.[17] By 1962 the Broad Street to Richmond line, which still provided a quarter-hourly service through Hampstead Heath, was under threat. West Hampstead (Midland) station, where glass had been replaced by wooden shutters during the Second World War, was a 'gloomy ruin', whose little used hourly diesel service contrasted with busy traffic through the Bakerloo line's West Hampstead. The Broad Street line, however, was valued as a route across the borough by residents west of Finchley Road. Since use was not concentrated at the daily rush hours, its steady service was reputedly

profitable,[18] although trains were reduced to run every 20 minutes from 1962. The service was re-routed to provide electric trains from North Woolwich to Richmond (the North London link), with peak-hour connexions from Camden Town and elsewhere to Broad Street, in 1985.[19]

SETTLEMENT AND GROWTH. Finds on Hampstead Heath, including many Mesolithic flint tools, pits, postholes, and burnt stones, indicate a community of hunter-gatherers of *c.* 7000 B.C.[20] Cinerary urns and grave goods of 90–120 A.D. were found near Well Walk in 1774, suggesting a nearby Roman dwelling or road.[21] Continuous habitation, however, dated from Anglo-Saxon times, when the name Hampstead indicated a single farm-site, presumably in a woodland clearing.[22] Fragments of pottery possibly dating from the 5th–7th centuries were found on the heath but were too small to furnish evidence of settlement. Charcoal-burning took place on the heath in the 10th century.[23]

The charter attributed to King Æthelred mentions one dwelling (Deormod's *wic*) on the eastern border.[24] Domesday Book recorded only 1 villein, 5 bordars, and 1 serf and, although there were presumably *famuli* on the demesne and probably also on Ranulf Peverell's subinfeudated hide, it is unlikely that any other category of inhabitant was omitted.[25] Probably during the 12th century there was considerable increase both in the population and in the cultivated area. There were 41 tenants and another 4 tenants of the Hyde by 1259[26] and 54 by 1281.[27] Some tenants may have held only land and it was not until 1312 that the holdings were described.[28] There were then 40 customary dwellings and six freehold houses in addition to the demesne farm. The manorial demesne farmland occupied the centre of the parish, with woodland and heath to the north and north-east. The freehold estates, most of them held by religious houses, were on the edges of the parish, in areas originally largely woodland. Most of the customary land and dwellings were in Hampstead town and Pond Street, south and east of the heath, with smaller settlements at West End and Kilburn, and one tenement at Frognal. The location of the church suggests that its primary function was to serve the manor, although it was not far from the town well and High Street.

Hampstead, on high ground visible from London, may always have represented health to the overcrowded citizens. In 1349 the abbot of Westminster fled there to escape the Black Death, which he probably brought with him.[29] In 1524 Londoners sought safety on Hampstead's heights from a threatened flooding[30] and in the late 16th century topographers

---

[10] *The Times*, 25 June 1900, 9*b*.
[11] C. E. Lee, *Sixty Years of the Northern* (1967), 10–12.
[12] *The Times*, 25 June 1900, 9*b*.
[13] Lee, *Sixty Years of the Northern*, 7 sqq.; Menear, *Underground Stations*, 46–7.
[14] *Hampstead One Thousand*, 102.
[15] Lee, *Sixty Years of the Northern*, 16.
[16] White, *Gtr. Lond.* 79–80.
[17] Ibid. 152–3.
[18] *H.H.E.* 24 Aug. 1962, 1*a*; White, *Gtr. Lond.* 81; inf. from Mr. H. V. Borley.
[19] Brit. Rail timetable (1985–6); inf. from Mr. Borley.
[20] Inf. from Mrs. D. H. Lorimer, Hendon and Dist.

Arch. Soc.; *The Times*, 12 May 1977, 2*h*; 7 July 1977, 4*a*.
[21] *Gent. Mag.* xlvi. 169; Park, *Hampstead*, 11–12; *V.C.H. Mdx.* i. 65, 71.
[22] *P.N. Mdx.* (E.P.N.S.), 111.
[23] Inf. from Mrs. Lorimer.
[24] B.L. Stowe Ch. 33; *T.L.M.A.S.* 560–1, 568.
[25] *V.C.H. Mdx.* i. 122–3.
[26] W.A.M. 32360.
[27] Ibid. 32361.
[28] C.U.L., Kk.V.29, ff. 30v.–36.
[29] *Flete's Hist. Westm. Abbey*, ed. J. A. Robinson (1909), 128; below.
[30] Barratt, *Annals*, i. 51.

remarked on the fine views and 'very healthful air'.[31] In the plague of 1603 Sir William Waad, who lived at Belsize, wrote of people coming from town and dying under hedges, 'whereof we have experience weekly here at Hampstead'.[32] During the great plague in 1665, trust in clear air on hills brought throngs from London to Hampstead town, where there were 260 deaths in 100 houses.[33]

By 1653 Hampstead had acquired an additional attraction, when doggerel advertised 'Air and Hill and Well'.[34] In 1683, however, the earl of Arran was pleased that the duchess of Ormond was leaving Hampstead: 'for I do by no means think that a wholesome air, there being a bog very near as I remember'.[35] Most people, however, delighted in the air on the heath[36] and agreed with the earl of Oxford in 1720 that Hampstead was a very good place for air and yet within the reach of the best physicians.[37]

The Black Death may have contributed to the concentration of customary holdings among fewer tenants, the most important of whom, by the mid 15th century, were Londoners. Fewer names in rentals from the late 14th century did not, however, necessarily reflect a smaller population, for the inhabitants may have been undertenants.[38] By 1548 Hampstead had 147 communicants,[39] and in 1642 178 males took the protestation oath.[40] As outsiders, particularly Londoners, acquired property, the old inhabitants became landless labourers, employed in the brickfields, or as launderers, servants, or tradesmen. In the early 16th century Hampstead was said to be chiefly inhabited by washerwomen, who served the nobility and London citizens.[41] In 1653 Hampstead pleaded poverty on the grounds that 'divers houses' were occupied by citizens who paid their taxes in London and many inhabitants were poor wage-earning labourers at the tilekilns, while their wives washed clothes for Londoners.[42]

Cheap lodgings were available for people like Sir Martin Frobisher's wife and children, who were said to be starving in Hampstead c. 1577.[43] Most of the newcomers were more prosperous: merchants, courtiers, lawyers, writers, and artists, who often bought or rented a house, initially only for the summer. In 1661 John Woodward sought exemption from the office of constable because he lived in Hampstead only during the three or four summer months[44] and in 1674 the manor house was leased to a man who stayed there six weeks a year.[45] As late as 1724 Defoe observed that in winter Hampstead had nothing to recommend it.[46]

In 1648 poor inhabitants complained that Londoners were taking their houses for the sake of the air in the summer.[47] As more substantial houses

were built for the newcomers on the copyholds and on some of the freehold estates, several, for example, being built in Belsize, indigenous inhabitants tended to move to the heath. Some may have been squatters but most sought grants of the waste, which became copyhold, on which they built small cottages, having in 1648 established their right to do so without needing 4 a. in support.[48] There was one grant of waste, in Pond Street, in 1607 and one in 1654; c. 20 grants, possibly more, were made between 1654 and 1690, another 20 in the next decade, 30 in 1700, and 60 between 1700 and 1720.[49] Some of the earliest inclosures, at Cloth Hill and Boad's Corner (New End), were made during the Civil War and not recorded, presumably because of disorders and because the lord of the manor was on the losing side. Other early inclosures were probably forgotten after court rolls were destroyed in a fire c. 1684. There was another period of disorganization between 1720 and 1737, when rival courts were held and records of grants by Ditchfield, the deputy of one of the contending stewards, were lost.[50]

Settlement spread during the 17th century from Hampstead town across the heath, northward to Cloth Hill and Littleworth, eastward to Boad's Corner and New End, and westward to East End and Frognal. Settlements grew up about the same time at the northern end of the heath, at North End and Spaniard's End and, during the 18th century, at the Vale of Health. Growth in the older hamlets of West End and Kilburn, although not on the heath, was at least partly at the expense of roadside waste. There were 78 cottages in 1646[51] and nearly 100 in 1664, made up of 57 dwellings not charged for hearth tax and another 40 with one or two hearths.[52] In 1674 130 dwellings had two or fewer hearths[53] and in 1762 70 dwellings were described as cottages.[54] The increase in the number of dwellings, therefore, was mainly of larger houses, which gradually replaced first the old cottages and then the newer ones on the waste. A few places in the old town, notably west of High Street, which became an area of crowded yards, and the low-lying New End, long remained the homes of the poor. Most of the copyholds, however, fell into the hands of newcomers, either as owners or occupiers. Hampstead was the home of several prominent parliamentarians during the Civil War, probably because of its connexion with London merchants. In 1664 they still occupied the six largest houses, each with 16 or more hearths, except that Belsize House was occupied by the royalist Daniel O'Neill. Also on the Belsize estate were houses occupied by Serjeant John Wilde, the parliamentarian, and by Thomas Hawley, a London mercer of unknown political affiliation. To

[31] Camden, *Brit.* (1806), ii. 87; Norden, *Spec. Brit.* 22–3.
[32] F. P. Wilson, *Plague in Shakespeare's Lond.* (1927), 94–5.
[33] W. G. Bell, *Great Plague in Lond. in 1665* (1951), 93, 185.
[34] Quoted in *Images of Hampstead*, 26; below, social.
[35] Hist. MSS. Com. 36, *Ormonde*, vii, p. 39.
[36] Below, Hampstead Heath.
[37] Hist. MSS. Com. 29, *Portland*, v, p. 602.
[38] G.L.R.O., E/MW/H40. Rentals listed only head tenants.
[39] *Lond. and Mdx. Chantry Certificates, 1548*, 135.
[40] H.L., Mdx. Protestation Returns.
[41] Park, *Hampstead*, 242.
[42] Barratt, *Annals*, iii, App. 5, p. 364.

[43] *D.N.B.*
[44] G.L.R.O., Cal. Mdx. Sess. Bks. iii. 115.
[45] Below, Frognal.
[46] Defoe, *Tour*, ed. Cole (1927), i. 384.
[47] S.C.L., uncat. doc. 1648.
[48] Ibid.
[49] G.L.R.O., E/MW/H, old no. 26/23 (Snoxell's case 1746).
[50] *H.H.E.* 25 May 1979; S.C.L., Hoare v. Wilson, observations on behalf of plaintiffs, exhib. to Michelwright's affidavit, p. 33.
[51] Barratt, *Annals*, iii, App. 3, pp. 359–61.
[52] G.L.R.O., MR/TH/2, mm. 29d.–30d.
[53] P.R.O., E 179/143/370, m. 43d.
[54] S.C.L., Man. Map and Fieldbk.

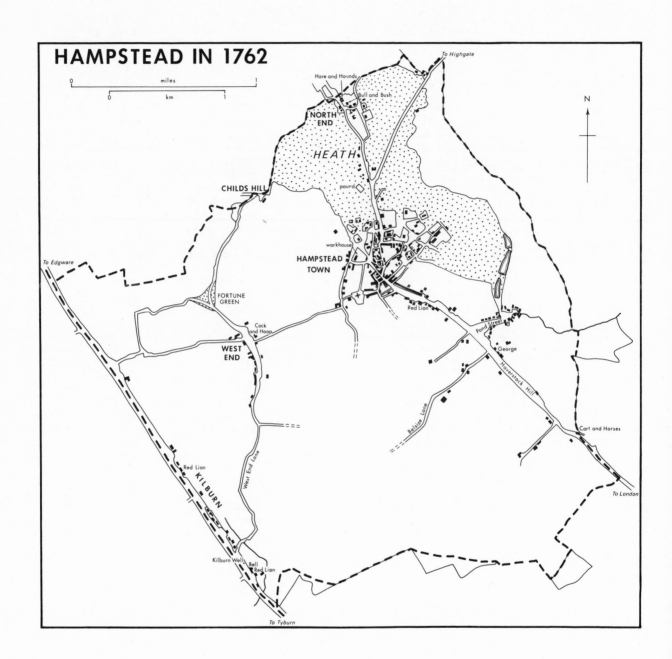

HAMPSTEAD IN 1762

miles

km

the north all the large houses on Slyes estate were occupied by parliamentarians: Col. John Owen and the widow of Harry Vane; the widow of John Towse (d. 1645), grocer and colonel, lived in the Old Mansion at Frognal. Of a total of 161 houses in 1664, 6 had 11–15 hearths, 17 had 6–10 hearths, and 35 had 3–5.[55] By 1674 the total had increased to 225 houses, Belsize House had been rebuilt and was by far the largest, with 36 hearths, and one house had 23 hearths and another had 20; there were six with 11–15, 29 with 6–10, and 54 with 3–5 hearths.[56] By 1704 there were 267 copyhold dwellings, of which 64 were specified as having been taken from the heath.[57]

With the commercial exploitation of the wells from 1698, more visitors wanted lodgings. In 1710 a German observed that 'many drive out from London and some spend all summer there'.[58] For a brief period Hampstead and, a little later, Belsize were the height of fashion, but as early as 1709 the nearness of London brought 'so many loose women in vamped-up old clothes to catch the City apprentices, that modest company are ashamed to appear'.[59] Although in 1735 'the meaner sort' were discouraged from settling there,[60] the town continued to grow, attracting the middle class rather than the fashionable. The petition for a new church in 1747 gave as its reason that the town was a place of great resort, especially in the summer.[61] Hampstead in 1709 was a large village with many pleasant lodgings[62] and by 1724 it had 'increased to that degree, that the town almost spreads the whole side of the hill'.[63] There was some terraced housing, notably in Church Row, which was probably speculative, but most building was of one or two houses, 'good substantial carpenters' jobs'.[64] There were between 500 and 600 families in the parish c. 1730[65] and about 500 houses and cottages by 1762.[66]

During the later 18th century some inns closed and some larger houses were divided or tenemented. More of the wealthy, including lawyers, merchants, bankers, and politicians, moved into the newer areas of settlement, Upper Terrace, Littleworth, Frognal, and North End. In Littleworth, for example, the total number of dwellings declined as villas in extensive grounds replaced the crowded cottages. By 1774 the heath was described as adorned with many gentlemen's houses,[67] and during the late 18th and early 19th centuries villas were built on several freehold and copyhold estates, including Bartrams, Belsize, and West End, and on the demesne at Frognal. There were 686 houses in 1795,[68] 842 inhabited houses in 1811, and 1,180 in 1831.[69] In 1814 Hampstead's permanent residents formed a 'select, amic-

able, respectable, and opulent neighbourhood'.[70] Although Hampstead had ceased to be a spa, it continued to attract visitors and permanent residents anxious for their health. During the 19th century its reputation increased, as London became more polluted. In 1833 residents could enjoy 'pure air, lovely scenery, and retired and beautiful walks', while taking part in the amusements of the capital and in summer receiving an influx of genteel Londoners.[71] In 1816, however, the far-famed salubrity of Hampstead was said to have led speculators to encumber it with tenements far beyond the need of the population. Many streets diverged from the 'great thoroughfare' (presumably the London road), crowded with ill-constructed and unoccupied buildings, intended as lodgings for invalids.[72] In 1826 there was a 'vast and increasing number of small houses' and nearly half the houses were rated at less than £10. Since rates were not collected from them, there was until 1827, when the owners were rated, an inducement for the owners, mostly bricklayers and carpenters, to build small houses. There were still many small dwellings in 1834.[73]

Hampstead town, with its copyholds, was, together with the heath and the demesne, the area mainly affected after 1821 by the restrictions of Sir Thomas Maryon Wilson's will.[74] The wholesale development of estates,[75] as opposed to small-scale building, was largely on freehold land to the south, adjacent to districts outside the parish, where building had already recently taken place. Wholesale exploitation on the Belsize estate began on the Bliss estate in 1815 and increased after an Act in 1842 enabled church lands to be let on building leases. It began on the Kilburn priory estate in 1819 and accelerated during the 1840s and 1850s. An Act enabling 99-year building leases to be granted on the Chalcots estate of Eton College was passed in 1826, followed by much building, especially in the 1840s and 1850s. The construction of the Finchley New Road in 1829 stimulated building on the St. John's Wood estate, which followed agreements in 1838 and 1845. The numbers of houses in the parish rose from 1,411 in 1841 to 2,653 in 1861 and 4,348 in 1871.[76]

The rate of building quickened from the 1860s, partly as a result of the opening of railway stations, which particularly affected West End and central Kilburn. Another factor was the lifting of the restrictions of Sir Thomas Maryon Wilson's will after the death of his son in 1869. The central demesne area was then opened up for development and the copyhold estates on the edges of Hampstead were similarly developed in the 1870s. The tide of building

[55] G.L.R.O., MR/TH/2, mm. 29d.–30d.; V. Pearl, *Lond. and Outbreak of Puritan Revolution* (1961), 325; below, Hampstead town; Belsize.
[56] P.R.O., E 179/143/370, m. 43d. Three entries are illegible.
[57] G.L.R.O., E/MW/H/I/2311A.
[58] *Lond. in 1710, from Travels of Zacharias Conrad von Uffenbach*, ed. W. H. Quarrel and M. Mare (1934), 120.
[59] J. Macky, *Journey through Eng.* (5th edn. 1732), i. 89; below, social.
[60] R. Seymour, *Survey of Lond. and Westm.* (1735), ii. 870.
[61] Park, *Hampstead*, 217.
[62] Macky, *Journey through Eng.* i. 89.
[63] Defoe, *Tour*, i. 384.
[64] J. Summerson, *Georgian Lond.* (1945), 255.

[65] Guildhall MS. 9550.
[66] i.e. 480 listed in S.C.L., Man. Map and Fieldbk., which omits Belsize, where there were about 18 hos.: below, Belsize.
[67] *Ambulator* (1774), 76.
[68] Lysons, *Environs*, ii. 542.　　[69] *Census*, 1811, 1831.
[70] Park, *Hampstead*, 242.
[71] *Corresp. of Wm. Ellery Channing and Lucy Aikin, 1816–42*, ed. A. L. le Breton (1874), 163–4.
[72] Brewer, *Beauties of Eng. & Wales*, x (4), 190.
[73] Vestry mins. 4 Jan. 1826, 20 Dec. 1827; *Rep. Com. Poor Laws*, H.C. 44, p. 99i (1834), xxxv.
[74] Below, Hampstead town; Hampstead Heath.
[75] Classified as the fourth type of suburban growth: Summerson, *Georgian Lond.* 255.
[76] *Census*, 1841–71.

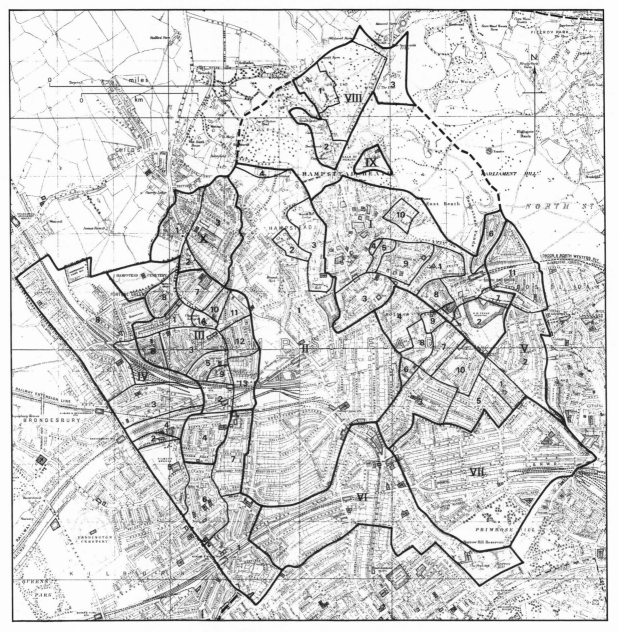

HAMPSTEAD: SETTLEMENT AND GROWTH

The estates (with the date of the earliest building lease in brackets) are:

I *Hampstead Town*: 1 Coleman (1812), 2 Bartrams (1867), 3 Greenhill (1869), 4 Gardnor (1871), 5 Gayton (1871), 6 South Hill Park (1871), 7 Salter (1872), 8 Hampstead Hill Gdns. (*c.* 1873), 9 Carlile (1875), 10 Wells (1876)

II *Frognal and the Central Demesne*: 1 Manorial demesne (1875), 2 Oak Hill (formerly demesne) (1850s), 3 Copyhold, 4 Formerly waste

III *West End*: 1 Land Co. of London (Hillfield) (1868), 2 British Land Co. (West End Ho.) (*c.* 1872), 3 Potter (1873), 4 Nicoll (West End Park) (1877), 5 Ripley (Gilberts) (1881), 6 Land Bldg. Investment & Cottage Improvement Co. (Earlsfield) (1883), 7 National Standard Land Mortgage & Investment Co. (Flitcroft) (1886), 8 Flitcroft (1886), 9 Sandwell Ho. (1893), 10 Woodbine Cottage (1896)

IV *Kilburn*: 1 Kilburn Priory (1819), 2 Nicoll (Little) (1865), 3 British Land Co. (Gilberts) (1869), 4 United Land Co. (Gilberts) (1869), 5 Little (1879), 6 Powell-Cotton (Liddell) (1866), 7 Powell-Cotton (Kilburn Woods) (1874), 8 Powell-Cotton (Shoot Up Hill) (1880)

V *Belsize*: 1 Bliss (1815), 2 Lund (St. John's Park) (1852), 3 Belsize Park (1855), 4 Rosslyn Ho. (1855), 5 Bliss (1864) 6 Todd (1865), 7 Todd (1869), 8 Belsize Court (1880), 9 Rosslyn Grove (1883), 10 Hillfield (1883), 11 South End farm (1878)

VI *St. John's Wood*

VII *Chalcots*

VIII *North End, Littleworth, and Spaniard's End*: 1 North End, 2 Littleworth, 3 Spaniard's End

IX *Vale of Health*

X *Childs Hill*: 1 Burgess (Temple), 2 Burgess (Childs Hill estate after 1855), 3 Teil (Childs Hill estate)

washed northward, reaching Childs Hill by the end of the century, with no estate untouched. In the mid 1950s it was estimated that 69 per cent of Hampstead's buildings had been put up between 1870 and 1916, compared with 20 per cent before 1870 and 11 per cent after 1916.[77] The numbers of dwellings rose to 9,517 in 1891 and 11,976 in 1911.[78]

Most of the 19th- and early 20th-century houses were a mixture of builders' vernacular and architect-designed, the latter mainly in the better-class districts. There were many on the Fitzjohn's and Greenhill estates of the 1870s and later among the northern demesne houses around Redington Road, but virtually none in West Hampstead or Kilburn. Among architects who built in Hampstead, including several who built houses for themselves or their relatives, were Ewan Christian, Richard Norman Shaw, C. F. A. Voysey, Reginald Blomfield, and Basil Champneys. Hundreds of builders, mostly local men, worked on a small scale from pattern books. Among more substantial builders were Daniel Tidey, Charles Bean King, Batterbury & Huxley, William Willett, father and son, E. J. Cave, and Thomas Clowser. In spite of the many different builders, the general impression was of homogeneity, dictated by the style current at the time, from the stuccoed, classical, or Italianate houses of the south part of the parish, to the red-brick, spiky, gabled Gothic or comfortable large-windowed 'Queen Anne' of the central and north parts.[79]

The houses throughout the period were mostly occupied by middle-class families. In 1831 Hampstead contained 356 capitalists, bankers, professionals, and 'other educated men' and 14 per cent of the female population were servants. In 1861 it housed 92 solicitors, 46 barristers, 132 merchants, and 23 stockbrokers. There were 102 coachmen, 56 grooms or horsekeepers, and 147 gardeners, and 2,559 women, 21 per cent of the female population, were servants.[80] By the end of the 1880s Hampstead, 'one of the largest and most prosperous' of London's residential suburbs, had a higher proportion of upper-class and servants, 25.5 per cent and 16.3 per cent respectively, than any other place in London except Brompton. All building was for the rich, rents were high and, with a few exceptions, all areas in Hampstead were becoming more wealthy.[81] An analysis of the occupations of the population[82] confirms that view. Of the male population, professional men and merchants increased from nearly 11 per cent in 1851 to 18 per cent in 1911,[83] and gentry, independents, and annuitants of both sexes similarly increased.[84] A surplus of unmarried but marriageable women was accounted for by servants, whose numbers, indicated by the ratio of women to men, were a sign of the relative wealth of the parish. From 57–8 per cent in the early 19th century, the ratio increased to 61.6 per cent in 1862 and remained c. 61 per cent until 1931.[85] The highest point was reached in the period before the First World War, when 26–7 per cent of all females over the age of 10 were domestic servants.[86] In 1901 in the wealthy Central ward females formed 68 per cent of the total population and in Kilburn, the poorest area, 54.6 per cent.[87]

Professional men and gentlemen were dominant in directing Hampstead's affairs, although in the 1870s and 1880s tradesmen, especially in the old town, were influential, and in 1874 Hampstead was castigated for backwardness in cultural and civic matters. By c. 1900 professional men and gentry from the newer areas were in control and there was a revival in cultural and intellectual life.[88]

Writers had visited or settled in Hampstead at least since the early 18th century, attracted, like others, by the air and rural peace or by the company and entertainments associated with the wells and Belsize.[89] Later, at the time of the romantic movement, the wild beauty of the heath itself became the chief attraction.[90] Hampstead was an especial favourite with artists and writers, many of them young and radical, who could still find relatively cheap lodgings in Hampstead town, the Vale of Health, or North End. There were other, more staid and, in their day, celebrated people like George Romney, Joanna Baillie, and the publishers Longman, but it was Constable and Leigh Hunt and his circle who established Hampstead's reputation as an intellectual centre. Lesser writers and artists, mostly fashionable ones throughout the 19th century, moved in to the newer estates or Church Row. Thomas Batterbury, who lived in Parkhill Road, of the firm Batterbury & Huxley, built artists' studios on the Belsize and Chalcots estates,[91] a group of architects established themselves in Church Row in the 1870s, and architects designed studio houses for artists on the expensive demesne estates and at Greenhill. At the end of the 1880s Hampstead included an influential colony of workers in art, science, and literature.[92] The number of authors, editors, artists, architects, musicians, and actors rose from 42 men and 7 women in 1851, to 1,033 men and 679 women in 1911, an increase from 0.66 per cent to 3.7 per cent of the occupied population.[93]

The wealth and culture were not found everywhere. About 1890, in spite of improvements which had cleared away the worst slums, Hampstead town was still the area with the highest proportion of families in poverty, 28 per cent. In the district east of Haverstock Hill, which included South End, 27.5 per cent of families were in poverty, partly accounted for by a blight on building near the smallpox hospital, which itself increased the death rate in the 1870s in an otherwise very healthy parish.

[77] L.C.C. *Lond. Statistics*, N.S. i. 161.
[78] *Census*, 1871–1911.
[79] Pevsner, *Lond.* ii. 184.
[80] *Census*, 1831, 1861.
[81] Booth, *Life and Labour*, i(1), 252; iii(1), 213–14; *Notes on Soc. Influences*, 17, 25.
[82] Table based on census returns in Thompson, *Hampstead*, 438–42.
[83] Ibid. categories 2 and part of 4.
[84] Ibid. category 7.
[85] *Census*, 1801–1931; Booth, *Life and Labour, Notes on Soc. Influences*, 22.

[86] Only the censuses for 1851, 1861, 1901, and 1911 give occupations. For 1851 and 1861, the age limit was 20, which probably excluded many servants, distorting the ratio.   [87] *Census*, 1901.
[88] Thompson, *Hampstead*, 396–8, 411–12, 419.
[89] e.g. Swift, Pope, Steele, Johnson.
[90] Below, Hampstead Heath. And see J. T. Smith, *Nollekens and his Times* (1949), 52–3.
[91] *C.H.R.* viii. 19–21.
[92] A. Saint, *Ric. Norman Shaw* (1976), 153, 155; Booth, *Life and Labour*, i (1), 252.
[93] Thompson, *Hampstead*, 438–42.

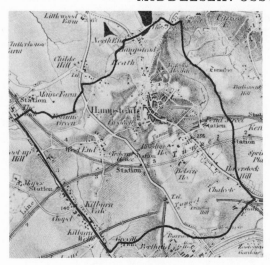
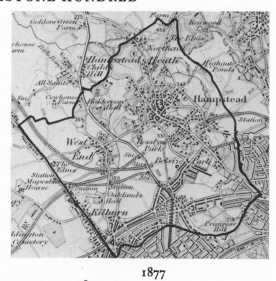

1844   1877

HAMPSTEAD: EVOLUTION OF SETTLEMENT, 1844–1904
(scale 1 in. to 1 mile)

About 1890 20.2 per cent of families in Kilburn were in poverty. The increase in the numbers of wealthy residents caused a rise in rents, and clearances in the old town led the poor to move to Gospel Oak, in St. Pancras, or to West Hampstead and Kilburn, where rents were lower. Other immigrants, from poor parts of London and from Ireland, were competing for rooms there in houses which, though small, were beginning to be divided.[94] Thus developed a cleavage between the wealthy east and the increasingly poor and crowded west parts of Hampstead. Some 10.3 per cent of its inhabitants were living more than two to a room in 1898[95] and the number of houses let in lodgings rose from 199 in 1906 to 405 in 1920.[96]

A certain cosmopolitanism had been apparent since the 16th century, when Londoners owning property and probably living in Hampstead included people whose names indicated Jewish or European origins.[97] There were some 200 refugees from the French revolution[98] and six Jewish households in Belsize in 1868, while Kilburn had enough Irish by 1879 to lead to the opening of a Roman Catholic church.[99] In the late 19th century foreignborn inhabitants came mainly from Germany, France, or the United States;[1] c. 1890 an influx of Jews and Bohemians, especially in West Hampstead, tended to replace the older families.[2]

The arrival of foreigners and urbanized Jews may have furthered the growth, from the late 19th century, of purpose-built flats, and the division of houses into flats and, increasingly, into bed-sitting rooms or lodging houses. By 1931 there were 14,758 separate dwellings.[3] The division of houses spread from West Hampstead to the large, middle-class houses of Belsize, Chalcots, and St. John's Wood.

The trend, intensified after the First World War, was to smaller families and more separate households: between 1911 and 1931 the population grew by only 4 per cent but the number of households by 27 per cent. Although domestic servants dwindled from 27 per cent of the total female population in 1901 to 19 per cent in 1931, there were still 10,348 servants in 1931. Meanwhile the ratio of servants to households almost halved, from 81.4 servants to every 100 households in 1901 to 47 in 1931.[4] Most people rented their homes and many moved on after the short leases expired: in 1895 it was estimated that 4,000 out of 12,000 voters had left the district between electoral registrations.[5] The turnover was still greater after the First World War, partly because use of the motor car hastened migration by some of the wealthy to the country. As others moved to the upper part of the old town or the grand houses hear the heath, 'a tide of multi-occupation swept in' across the formerly smart southern estates, which began to deteriorate, physically and socially. Houses in Belsize Avenue halved in value between the 1880s and the 1920s and 1930s.[6] The number of houses let in lodgings had increased to 1,295 by the end of 1930[7] and a drab existence in bed-sitting rooms, described by George Orwell,[8] became more common during the 1930s. There were patches of poverty but, while the general social and economic level of Hampstead declined, real poverty held only 1.4 per cent of its population in 1930, the lowest for any London borough.[9] Overcrowding, defined as more than two persons to a room, was the lot of 6.5 per cent of the population in 1921 and 4.1 per cent in 1931.[10]

In 1921 Hampstead was still favoured by prosperous businessmen.[11] It also attracted the

[94] Booth, *Life and Labour*, i (2), 28, App. 16–17; iii (1), 213–14; Thompson, *Hampstead*, 400, 405.
[95] G. L. Gomme, *Lond. in Reign of Victoria* (1898), 240.
[96] L.C.C. *Lond. Statistics*, xvii. 110; xxvii. 68–9.
[97] e.g. 'stranger' in Hampstead in 1559: *Rets. of Aliens in Lond. 1523–71* (Huguenot Soc. x), i. 256; Wachter fam.: P.R.O., PROB 11/336 (P.C.C. 1671, f. 70, will of Susanna Wachter).
[98] Park, *Hampstead*, 236.
[99] Thompson, *Hampstead*, 387–8.
[1] *Census*, 1871–1921.

[2] Booth, *Life and Labour*, iii (1), 207.
[3] *Census*, 1931.
[4] Ibid. 1911–31; Thompson, *Hampstead*, 426–7.
[5] P. Thompson, *Socialists, Liberals and Labour* (1967), 72.
[6] Thompson, *Hampstead*, 428, 431.
[7] L.C.C. *Lond. Statistics*, xxxv. 78–9.
[8] Below, Hampstead town.
[9] *New Lond. Life and Labour*, vi. 423.
[10] H. Quigley and I. Goldie, *Housing and Slum Clearance in Lond.* (1934), 200.   [11] *Census*, 1921.

1904

intelligentsia, who formed 2.6 per cent of the occupied population in 1921 and 2.8 per cent in 1931.[12] Hampstead was then about to see a flowering in the arts, which made the 1930s 'the most significant and influential period in its history'.[13] A group of leading British artists and writers, who came especially to the Mall studios in Belsize and to the Downshire Hill area, attracted European refugees, mainly painters but also psychoanalysts, scientists, architects, Viennese booksellers, and German Jewish cabaret artists.[14] Hampstead consequently remained in the forefront of the arts until their practitioners were dispersed by the war.

The percentage of foreign-born residents rose from 4.9 in 1921 to 6.4 in 1931 and 16.4 in 1951. Of those, mainly Jews, most came from Germany, others from Poland, Austria, and Russia. In 1951 those born in the Irish Republic comprised 4.7 per cent of the population, although the number of those in Kilburn with Irish ancestry was evidently much higher. Those born in the Commonwealth overseas formed 2.9 per cent, a proportion which had risen to 7.9 per cent by 1961.[15]

During the Second World War air raids killed 200 people, destroyed 407 houses, and damaged another 13,000.[16] Maintenance was neglected and the deterioration apparent before 1939 continued into the 1950s. In 1951 the Church Commissioners sold off many of their freeholds, which had long been declining in value. Bed-sitting rooms multiplied and the population became still more fluid, with one-third leaving every year.[17] In 1955 Hampstead had the highest suicide rate in England and Wales, which was explained by the loneliness of so many people who had left home for London.[18] In 1961 almost half of all dwellings were unfurnished and privately rented and, in spite of the virtual disappearance of servants, there were still 27,000 un-

married girls, compared with 31,000 in 1931. Hampstead metropolitan borough was one of the first, albeit on a modest scale, to build houses or flats. Its activity in that field greatly increased after the Second World War. There were 2,989 local authority dwellings by 1961, when the total housing stock was 29,468,[19] and 3,660 by 1965, when Hampstead became part of Camden L.B.[20] Blocks of flats, some built by the borough and the L.C.C., others by private developers, have transformed much of Hampstead, particularly the south and west parts. The flats, aesthetically controversial, have relieved the overcrowding, which rose from 0.71 persons to a room in 1931 to 0.81 in 1951, being as much as 0.92 in Kilburn ward. By 1961 the ratio was 0.75 to a room and by 1971 0.66.[21]

Except in Well Walk, where the last of the wells buildings were demolished, Hampstead town survived the war with its old buildings intact and later escaped the wholesale transformation of some other areas. The best houses had never lost their desirability and by the mid 1950s speculators were buying up houses on some of the dingier streets and selling them to the better off. In 1961 most of the 5,467 owner-occupied dwellings, 18.5 per cent of the whole, were in Hampstead town and the more attractive areas to the north.[22] Throughout the 1960s and 1970s, as redevelopment grew more obtrusive, Victorian houses were rehabilitated in increasing numbers, first in Hampstead town and then in the surrounding estates. Although many dwellings were still bed-sitting rooms, more and more houses came to be occupied again by middle-class families, many of the large houses having been divided. At the end of the 1970s the contrast between west and east remained: council flats and large families, often of Irish or more recent immigrant origin, characterized the west, conservation areas with young and prosperous inhabitants the east.[23] By the late 1980s property in most of Hampstead was expensive. Residents included many people prominent in the arts and popular entertainment.

The population doubled from 4,343 in 1801 to 8,588 in 1831, and had increased to 19,106 by 1861, 45,452 by 1881, and 82,329 by 1901. The increase had slowed by 1931 to 88,947 and, after dropping to 58,000 in 1941 during the war, increased, partly by immigration, to 95,131 in 1951 and 98,844 in 1961, before dropping to 89,910 in 1971.[24]

HAMPSTEAD TOWN. The earliest settled area was probably Hampstead town, on the southern slopes of the heath, near the manor and church and on each side of the road to Hendon, later called Hampstead High Street. The principal parish well, Kingswell, in the heart of the old town and probably associated with the town pond west of High Street, in which a woman drowned in 1274,[25] gave its name to the Kingswell family (fl. 1281–1319) whose freehold

[12] Thompson, *Hampstead*, 438–42.
[13] C. H. Stanton, 'Microcosm of a committed decade', *Country Life*, 11 Nov. 1976, pp. 1420 sqq. And see *C.H.R.* viii. 19–21; *Hampstead in the Thirties, a Committed Decade*, exhib. 1974–5, cat. (S.C.L.).
[14] e.g. Agnes Bernelle: radio talk 27 Dec. 1986.
[15] *Census*, 1931–61.
[16] *Hampstead 1939–45* (Camden History Soc. 1977).
[17] Thompson, *Hampstead*, 428, 431.
[18] *The Times*, 25 July 1955, 4f.
[19] *Census*, 1961; Thompson, *Hampstead*, 432.

[20] E. Wistrich, *Local Govt. Reorganisation: First Years of Camden* (1972), 202.
[21] *Census*, 1931–71.   [22] Ibid. 1961.
[23] Camden Boro. Plan, *Hampstead and Belsize Area*, Spr. 1975, Area 4; *W. Hampstead and Kilburn*, Spr. 1975, Area 5.
[24] *Census*, 1801–1971. In 1981 the figs. for Hampstead were inc. among those for Camden L.B.
[25] P.R.O., JUST 1/538, f. 19d.; *Cal. Close*, 1392–6, 136–8; below, other ests., Kingswell. For the well in 'Hampstead street' in 1619, see G.L.R.O., E/MW/H/1.

property lay between High Street and the demesne on the west. Nearby was the copyhold Slyes and Popes.[26] There was a group of medieval customary tenements in Pond Street, so named by 1484[27] after another pond which was filled in in 1835 to form South End Green.[28] Four tenants were surnamed atte Pond on the earliest rental (1259)[29] and other medieval tenements, those of the Aldenhams and Bertrams, were in Pond Street.[30]

By the 15th century many of the customary tenements had passed to London merchants and gentry,[31] some of whom began to occupy or lease them, especially for the summer or in old age.[32] The country retreats in an area appreciated c. 1593 for its air and beautiful views[33] were especially favoured by the Londoners' wives, who often lived out their widowhood in houses originally acquired for the income from their rents.[34] Such people replaced the medieval houses of timber and wattle and daub with brick houses, often of considerable size. One was the curiously named Chicken House on the east side of High Street, which contained glass commemorating a visit by James I and the duke of Buckingham in 1619. Another house, perhaps of the early 17th century and with some classical features, stood on the west side of High Street, farther north.[35] Queen Elizabeth House, presumably nearby, was traditionally that monarch's hunting lodge but was later acknowledged to be of much more recent date.[36] The parsonage house on the east side of High Street opposite Church Lane, the site of the present no. 28, had apparently been built by 1660[37] and was assessed for 7 hearths in 1674.[38] Nearby was a brick house which by 1660 had lately replaced three tenements and was assessed in 1664 for 10 hearths. It descended from William Pitchford[39] to his daughter, wife of Richard Hodilow, a London goldsmith (d. 1698).[40] Pitchford also owned Popes meadow, which passed to his second daughter Anne, wife of Isaac Honywood,[41] and became part of the Honywood, later Carlile, estate, which surrounded the Chicken House.[42] Carlile House had been built by 1692.[43] Two mansion houses were new-built on the east side in High Street in 1698.[44]

On the west side, stretching from Church Lane southward to the Belsize estate, was the medieval customary holding of Slyes. In addition to the capital messuage there was, by 1621 and probably earlier, another house, almost certainly that later called Vane House, if the well found during rebuilding after the Second World War was 16th-century.[45] Both were leased out by 1621.[46] In the mid 17th century, in addition to Slyes itself, there was, at the northern end of the estate, a house occupied by Thomas Hussey, a London grocer, which was assessed in 1664 for 14 hearths[47] and occupied in 1675 by William, Lord Paget (d. 1678); a second house had been 'recently' built south of it by 1675.[48] At the southern end of the estate there was one large house, that later called Vane House opposite the Chicken House. In 1664 the two largest houses in the parish, which were listed next to each other, were assessed to Lady Vane for 24 hearths and to Col. John Owen for 20 hearths.[49] Contemporary memoirs stated that Sir Henry Vane was arrested in 1660 at 'his house in Hampstead near London'[50] and local piety in 1795 identified it with that then called Vane House.[51] More probably, however, Owen occupied in 1664 the house which he certainly possessed in 1681, namely Vane House.[52] Vane's house, therefore, may well have been Slyes itself. By 1686 Slyes had become two houses, occupied by the copyholder William Johnson, a London herbalist, and by a tenant respectively.[53]

Many inns appeared in High Street during the 17th century. The King of Bohemia's Head, mentioned in 1680,[54] a mid-17th century building at no. 14, on the east side, may have originated during the period of enthusiasm for Frederick V, count palatine, after 1619.[55] The White Lion on the east side was temporarily suppressed in 1641 but a 'very considerable new building' had been erected on the site by 1671.[56] The name did not occur after the 17th century and the inn may be identifiable with the King's Arms, so named from 1721, which probably dated from the 17th century and stood opposite Perrin's Court.[57] The King's Head, mentioned from 1721, later called the King William IV, on the west side at the junction with Church (Perrin's) Lane, is probably identifiable with the Queen's Head sited on the Kinghall estate and described as much decayed in 1667. It was extended and a bowling green added c. 1683.[58] On the east side the George existed south of the junction with Pond Street by 1666,[59]

[26] Below, other est.
[27] P.R.O., PROB 11/8 (P.C.C. 6 Milles, will of John Watno).
[28] Wade, More Streets, frontispiece, 25.
[29] W.A.M. 32360. One tenant, Gallota, probably took her name from the town pond.
[30] G.L.R.O., E/MW/H/1 (1621); for Bertrams, below, other est.
[31] e.g. John Watno: P.R.O., PROB 11/8 (P.C.C. 6 Milles); Sir Thos. Sandes: G.L.R.O., E/MW/H/1 (1621).
[32] e.g. Wm. Rollinson, vintner (d. 1678): P.R.O., PROB 11/358 (P.C.C. 116 Reeve); Thos. Hawley, mercer (d. 1687): ibid. 365 (P.C.C. 5 North).
[33] Camden, Brit. (1806), 87; Norden, Spec. Brit. 22.
[34] e.g. Mary, wid. of John Towse, alderman: P.R.O., PROB 11/336 (P.C.C. 1671, f. 70); w. and daus. of Basil Hearne, Lond. gent.: P.R.O., C 7/150/19; C 7/333/28.
[35] Park, Hampstead, 266–7; S.C.L., Man. Map and Fieldbk. nos. 53 (Chicken Ho.), ?353.
[36] Park, Hampstead, 271; N. & Q. 3rd ser. ii. 446.
[37] G.L.R.O., E/MW/H/5; S.C.L., Man. Map and Fieldbk. no. 71; Hist. Mon. Com. W. Lond. 41.
[38] P.R.O., E 179/143/370, m. 43d.
[39] G.L.R.O., MR/TH/2, m. 29d.; E/MW/H/5.
[40] P.R.O., PROB 11/445 (P.C.C. 1698, f. 122).
[41] Ibid. 346 (P.C.C. 1674, f. 109, will of Anne Pitchford).
[42] S.C.L., Man. Map and Fieldbk. nos. 47–52.
[43] Below, other est.
[44] S.C.L., D 43.
[45] S.C.L., H 362.73/Royal Soldiers' Daughters' Home (Brief Hist. Royal Soldiers' Daus. Sch. in Hampstead, 1855–1963).
[46] Below, other est.
[47] G.L.R.O., MR/TH/2, m. 29d.; S.C.L., D 125.
[48] G.L.R.O., E/MW/H/7; Complete Peerage, s.v. Paget.
[49] G.L.R.O., MR/TH/2, m. 29d.
[50] Memoirs of Edm. Ludlow, 1625–72, ed. C. H. Firth (1894), ii. 339–46.
[51] Park, Hampstead, 268–71 and illus.
[52] G.L.R.O., E/MW/H/6; below, other est. Owen's lands abutted Belsize in 1679; S.C.L., D 136.
[53] G.L.R.O., E/MW/H/8.
[54] City Mercury, 17 Mar. 1680, quoted in Barratt, Annals, i. 195.
[55] Hist. Mon. Com. W. Lond. 41.
[56] G.L.R.O., Cal. Mdx. Sess. Bks. i (A), p. 86; MJ/SBB 241, p. 35; P.R.O., C 7/502/3; C 10/97/52.
[57] G.L.R.O., E/MW/H/1/2178; S.C.L., Man. Map and Fieldbk. no. 74; Hampstead One Thousand, 22, 154.
[58] S.C.L., Man. Map and Fieldbk. no. 366; P.R.O., C 7/213/20; Hampstead One Thousand, 154.
[59] G.L.R.O., E/MW/H/6.

the White Hart by 1684,[60] and the Three Tuns by 1685.[61]

Building in High Street was on ancient, mainly customary, tenements which were divided and underset but probably did not stretch farther north than the junction with Heath Street, which in 1680 formed a broad green, over 100 ft. wide, extending from the heath.[62] Development northward and eastward was on the heath, technically waste although Hampstead manor court did not recognize wastehold tenure and land taken from the waste became copyhold, indistinguishable from the ancient customary tenure.[63] The heath was used for many purposes other than pasturing: Cloth Hill, for example, recalled laundering, and there were also diggers of gravel or brickearth and herbalists.[64] They enclosed usually small areas of heath and put up cottages and sheds in a haphazard way. The passages to such enclosures and the spaces between them became roads and squares which, with the steep and uneven nature of the ground, accounted for the bizarre street pattern of Hampstead town. Since roads were unpaved the distinction between them and the surrounding waste, especially on the fringes of settlement, was vague. The process was illustrated in 1762 in the routes round Squire's Mount, which was to become Cannon Place and Lane and Well Road.[65] Only after 1737 were all enclosures recorded, since early records were destroyed and many enclosures originated in squatting during periods of unrest.

One such encloser was Robert James (d. 1618).[66] In 1619 one of his daughters, Mary, wife of Robert Dixon, succeeded her brother Robert in the copyhold,[67] described in 1637 as seven cottages at the north end of the town at East End on the waste or heath.[68] East End or Ostend was the first name of Fenton House in Hampstead Grove, which is dated 1693.[69] There was a windmill nearby from the beginning of the century[70] and in 1666 Robert Dixon conveyed the seven cottages, with land called the Millhill, to a brickmaker.[71] Millhill near Ostend, where there were grants of waste in the 1680s,[72] was presumably Windmill Hill, named in 1709.[73]

In 1646 Robert James's other daughter, Susan Nutting, conveyed parcels of her close next the heath called Boad's, Boar's, or Board's Corner, east

of Heath Street, to several men, mostly 'poor tilemakers', who in 1648 successfully petitioned to be allowed to erect cottages without the statutory 4 a. Most of them also received confirmation at the manor court for their cottages, six of which had been built in 1646.[74] There was a brick clamp nearby[75] and one at least of the petitioners, Thomas Roberts, seems to have prospered, leasing Donningtons as a brickmaker in 1655[76] and acquiring more waste around his house in 1672.[77] By 1679 Roberts had two houses in what by then was called New End.[78] Most 17th-century building in New End was of cottages but there was a new brick house by 1694 when, with five cottages, it was owned by Fortune Mountague, widow;[79] another two cottages had been built on the estate by 1704.[80] The White Bear carries a panel dated 1704[81] and the Duke of Hamilton's Head, though first named in 1721, probably originated as a cottage c. 1700. A shop was added c. 1718 and the conversion to an inn probably occurred soon afterwards.[82] In 1710 34 quit rents, mostly for dwellings, were paid for New End.[83]

Building on the waste between East End and New End proceeded during the 17th century. In 1662 Thomas Goulding, a blacksmith, was granted a cottage and forge which he had recently built,[84] presumably at Goulding's or Golden Yard, west of Heath Street.[85] Holly Hill House, in a hollow on the west side of Holly Hill, supposedly dated from 1665[86] and cottages existed by 1669 'next to the well, under the place called Cloth Hill'.[87] Cloth Hill, where cottages and a carthouse were built in the 1680s,[88] appears to have stretched from Holly Hill to the high ground called the Mount, west of Heath Street, where two houses, later no. 6, were built in 1694.[89] The Crown was one of several houses there in the 1690s.[90]

The beginning of the growth of Hampstead town, whose pure air had been acknowledged from the 16th century and mineral waters since the mid 17th century, is traditionally dated to 1698 when the Wells charity was founded.[91] Commercial exploitation of the waters was well advanced by c. 1700 when both the Flask public houses existed, the fashionable Upper Flask (originally called the Upper Bowling Green House) at the northern part of Heath Street and the Lower Flask in Flask Walk near High

[60] Ibid. P81/JN1/1A; S.C.L., Man. Map and Fieldbk. no. 67.
[61] G.L.R.O., P81/JN/1A; S.C.L., Man. Map and Fieldbk. no. 63.
[62] C.H.R. xi. 20.
[63] There was some attempt to distinguish the ancient capital tenements by describing them as heriotable.
[64] e.g. John Chapman in 1686: G.L.R.O., E/MW/H/8. Waste was granted in 1709 on condition it was used as a herb gdn.: ibid. H, old no. Box L (abs. of leases 1680–1731).
[65] S.C.L., Man. Map.
[66] P.R.O., PROB 11/131 (P.C.C. 30 Meade).
[67] G.L.R.O., E/MW/H/1.
[68] Ibid. 3.
[69] No connexion with Ostend, Belgium, as stated in Fenton Ho. (Nat. Trust guide). And see Archit. of Lond. 41.
[70] Below, econ., mills.
[71] G.L.R.O., E/MW/H/6. The brickmaker was Thos. Roberts: cf. below.
[72] G.L.R.O., E/MW/H/8.
[73] Ibid. H, old no. Box L (abs. of leases 1680–1731).
[74] G.L.R.O., E/MW/H/4; S.C.L., uncat. deed; Barratt, Annals, iii, App. 3, p. 361.

[75] G.L.R.O., E/MW/H/6 (1665).
[76] S.C.L., D 40.
[77] G.L.R.O., E/MW/H/6.
[78] Ibid. 7.
[79] Ibid. H, old no. 33/5 (copyhold admissions).
[80] Ibid. H/I/2311A.
[81] Hist. Mon. Com. W. Lond. 41.
[82] P.R.O., C 78/1750, no. 3; G.L.R.O., E/MW/H/I/2123, 2311A; Hampstead One Thousand, 154.
[83] G.L.R.O., E/MW/H/I/2123, 2311A.
[84] Ibid. H/5.
[85] In 1711 in the 'Great Street in Hampstead': P.R.O., C 8/494/8; Wade, Streets of Hampstead, 26.
[86] Date on bldg.: H. J. K. Usher, C. D. Black-Hawkins, G. J. Carrick, An Angel Without Wings: Hist. of Univ. Coll. Sch. 1830–1980 (1981), 97; C.H.R. vi. 12–13.
[87] G.L.R.O., E/MW/H/6.
[88] Ibid. 7, 8.
[89] Wade, Streets of Hampstead, 26; Hampstead One Thousand, 44.
[90] G.L.R.O., E/MW/H/I/1946; M.M. & M., Lib. D, p. 111.
[91] Hampstead One Thousand, 29; below, social; pub. svces.

Street. The expansion after the Long Room was opened was rapid. Well Walk with its social activities pushed settlement farther eastward, and inns, shops, and lodging houses sprang up throughout Hampstead town to cater for invalids taking the waters and for more active visitors. In 1724 Hampstead had grown 'from a little country village to a city', where the popularity of both the place and the diversions had 'raised the rate of lodgings and that increased buildings'.[92]

Among inns of the period were the Haunch of Venison, on the east side of High Street c. 1729–31[93] and a coffee house in 1730, which became the Bird in Hand at no. 39, licensed from 1771.[94] Many houses were built in High Street in the early 18th century (nos. 25, 26, 36 on the east side, nos. 68–75, 79–85 on the west); the most important was the Green Hill, at the corner with Prince Arthur Road,[95] later called Stanfield House after the artist Clarkson Stanfield (1793–1867), who lived there from 1847 to 1865.[96] The houses on the west side of High Street were on the Slyes estate. The former capital messuage was converted into four tenements between 1712 and 1721.[97] When the estate was split in the 1750s, the southern portion of the messuage seems to have been rebuilt and extended as Mount Grove (the Rookery); the other tenements can probably be identified with Stanfield House and its neighbours.[98] Vane House, described as enchanting and elegant in 1751,[99] was embellished with 16th-century painted glass by Bishop Joseph Butler (1692–1752), the theologian, who lived there from 1749, and after his death was divided, his offices being made into a house occupied by Alderman George Nelson in 1762, when the owner Andrew Regnier occupied the main portion.[1] On the east side of High Street, Norway or Burford House had been built by 1754 when its occupier Thomas Osborne, a London bookseller, held a party there, followed by a duck-shoot on the heath and entertainment at the Long Room. The house stood back from High Street,[2] behind Flask Walk, where a terrace of shops, nos. 1–7, was built in the early 18th century and Thomas Gardnor built the house named after him c. 1736.[3] Nos. 22–4 Rosslyn Hill, on old customary land fronting the east side of the main street, half-way between the Chicken House and Pond Street, had been built by

1762 but probably not by 1702, the date displayed on plaques. The initials on one may refer to Zechariah Morrell, an early 18th-century minister of Rosslyn Hill chapel.[4]

There were c. 24 houses in Pond Street in the first decade of the 18th century,[5] including nos. 33–5[6] and the 'large convenient house' which had lately been occupied by Alderman Sir Thomas Lane (d. 1708).[7] Lane had three houses in Pond Street,[8] probably identifiable with three existing in 1654, one on the site of the medieval Aldenhams, the others called the White House and the Lower White House; they passed to John Lane in 1673,[9] although he had held a lease of Aldenhams before that and had been assessed on 9 hearths.[10] Already containing several substantial houses in the 17th century, Pond Street gained in importance from the wells, as it was the route by which early carriage visitors reached Well Walk, to the disgust of traders in High Street. In 1745 Pond Street was depicted as spacious and elegant, containing most of the houses existing in 1762 on the north side; they included nos. 17 and 17A,[11] probably the 'handsome new house' built by Edward Snoxell on the site of an ancient one soon after 1740.[12] In what was later Rosslyn Hill, south of the junction with Pond Street, a second house stood by the 1740s north of the ancient Bartrams, set back from the main road and approached through a grove railed in from the waste.[13] Two houses were built on the waste near the George by 1756[14] and another two by 1758.[15]

Two houses in Heath Street (nos. 92 and 94) were built c. 1700 and two (nos. 60 and 62) in the early 18th century.[16] A house was built on the site later occupied by Guyon House (no. 98) probably between 1722 and 1740 by William Knight.[17] On the western side of the road Caroline House and Holly Cottage (nos. 11 and 12 the Mount) were built in the mid 18th century.[18] East of Heath Street, growth proceeded at New End, nos. 10–14 being a terrace of 1725 and, in the southward extension from the original road, no. 30 being early 18th-century;[19] nearby was the Fox and Goose, recorded in 1726.[20] In New End Square (in fact a triangle) the most important building was Burgh House, named after a 19th-century owner and earlier called Brook House, built in 1703 by Henry and Hannah Sewell,

[92] Defoe, *Tour*, i. 383–5, quoted in Thompson, *Hampstead*, 22.
[93] G.L.R.O., E/MW/H, old no. Box L (abs. of leases 1680–1731); S.C.L., D 123, 157.
[94] G.L.R.O., MR/LV5/31; LV7/45; LV8/64; S.C.L., Man. Map and Fieldbk. no. 82; *Hampstead One Thousand*, 154.
[95] Hist. Mon. Com. *W. Lond.* 41–2; Pevsner, *Lond.* ii. 195.
[96] G. H. Cunningham, *Lond.: Comprehensive Survey* (1931), 341.
[97] Below, other est.
[98] M.M. & M., Lib. E, pp. 365–6; Lib. D, pp. 262–3; S.C.L., Man. Map and Fieldbk. nos. 375, 368–9, 372, 374.
[99] Barratt, *Annals*, i. 290–1.
[1] Park, *Hampstead*, 269, 271; *D.N.B.*, s.v. Butler; S.C.L., Man. Map and Fieldbk. nos. 378, 381.
[2] *Hampstead One Thousand*, 33–5; S.C.L., Man. Map and Fieldbk. no. 78.
[3] Wade, *Streets of Hampstead*, 40–1; S.C.L., Man. Map and Fieldbk. no. 85.
[4] Wade, *Streets of Hampstead*, 68; S.C.L., Man. Map and Fieldbk. nos. 42–3. The ho. had been divided into two by 1762.
[5] G.L.R.O., E/MW/H/I/2311A, 2123.
[6] Pevsner, *Lond.* ii. 200.
[7] Park, *Hampstead*, 313; Barratt, *Annals*, i. 189.
[8] G.L.R.O., E/MW/H/I/2311A.
[9] Ibid. H/4 (1654); H/6 (1670, 1672, 1673).
[10] Ibid. H/5 (1662); MR/TH/2, m. 29d.
[11] *Images of Hampstead*, 29, 76 nos. 191, 194; Wade, *More Streets*, 28; S.C.L., Man. Map and Fieldbk. nos. 30–40; below, plate 4.
[12] G.L.R.O., E/MW/H, old no. 26/23 (Snoxell's case 1746).
[13] Rocque, *Map of Lond.* (1741–5), sheet 12; S.C.L., Man. Map and Fieldbk. nos. 11–11½.
[14] G.L.R.O., E/MW/H/I/2178, s.v. Vincent; S.C.L., H 711, Isaac Messeder bk. of plans, prop. of Robt. Vincent; Man. Map and Fieldbk. nos. 5–6.
[15] G.L.R.O., E/MW/H/I/2178, s.v. Ash; S.C.L., Man. Map and Fieldbk. no. 4.
[16] Pevsner, *Lond.* ii. 191.
[17] M.M. & M., Lib. C, p. 229; S.C.L., Man. Map and Fieldbk. no. 130.
[18] *Archit. of Lond.* 41; Pevsner, *Lond.* ii, 190–1; Hist. Mon. Com. *W. Lond.* 40; S.C.L., Man. Map and Fieldbk. no. 302.
[19] Wade, *Streets of Hampstead*, 41–2.
[20] S.C.L., Man. Map and Fieldbk. no. 144; G.L.R.O., MR/LV4/28.

wealthy Quakers, and greatly extended after 1720 by Dr. William Gibbon, physician to Hampstead wells. From 1743 it was occupied by Nathaniel Booth, later Lord Delamer (d. 1770).[21] On the western side of New End Square nos. 16–20 were built in the early 18th century.[22] At no. 40, the southern corner with Flask Walk, the Hawk had been built by 1748.[23]

Elm Row, the next street northward off the east side of Heath Street, was presumably called after the line of trees there in 1762.[24] On the north side a terrace was built c. 1720[25] and on the south Elm Lodge, variously ascribed to c. 1700 and c. 1732, faced southward to New End.[26] At the eastern end of Elm Row was Hampstead Square, described in 1725 as having been, 60 years previously, a 'high hill and a sandpit so that there could not be any way through'.[27] Lawn House (no. 12) was built at the Elm Row end and Vine House (no. 6), a five-bayed house at the northern corner, probably before 1709;[28] no. 1, also of five bays, adjoined the northern terrace of Elm Row and was probably built c. 1720,[29] as was the neighbouring no. 2. Opposite Vine House nos. 7–9 (in 1986 Newman Hall homes for the aged) were built c. 1730.[30] Eastward from Hampstead Square, Cannon Place led to Squire's Mount, named after Joshua Squire (d. 1717), a London factor, who acquired waste near an old well in 1714 and built a residence there.[31] Squire was succeeded by his two daughters, one of whom married Thomas Lane (d. 1773), master of Chancery. By 1750 two other houses had been added with Lord Blessington as the tenant.[32] In 1762 Lane occupied the largest, northern house.[33] The two southern houses were later reunited as Chestnut Lodge.[34] Since a terrace of cottages, nos. 1–5 bearing a plate 'Squires Mount Croft 1704', did not exist in 1762, the plate may have come from the stabling of Squire's Mount.[35] Cannon Hall (no. 14 Cannon Place), named from cannons brought by Sir James Cosmo Melville, who occupied it after 1838, was built c. 1720 and originally called Rous's Buildings, probably after Joseph Rous, who succeeded John Duffield as lessee of the Wells estate.[36] The name Cannon Hall probably referred to the whole estate, which extended to Well Road and Christchurch Hill and in 1762 included three other houses, the early 18th-century Providence Corner (formerly Holly Hedge Cottage) and Cannon Cottage[37] and the later Cannon Lodge (no. 12 Cannon Place), then two houses.[38] In 1762 Cannon Hall was occupied by Sarah Holford, widow, who had leased it from 1752 and probably from before 1745 when a print of the Long Room 'from Mrs. Holford's garden' was published. The family later gave its name to Holford Road, a wide, tree-covered piece of waste in 1762.[39] To the north, on the edge of the heath, lay no. 22 East Heath Road (Grove House, later Holford or Heathfield House, Melville Hall, and finally Ladywell Court), in 1762 a 'capital messuage' with stabling, a greenhouse, and 1½ a. owned and occupied by Thomas Webb.[40] In 1762 the most northerly dwelling set back from the east side of Heath Street, was a pair of houses opposite Whitestone pond,[41] which existed by the mid 1740s[42] and were probably the early 18th-century Gangmoor.[43]

The eastern extremity of the town was on the Wells charity estate on either side of Well Walk, where 100 trees had been planted by 1700[44] and there were two houses, a dancing room, shops, and stables by 1704.[45] The dancing room was presumably the Great Room or first Long Room, on the south side, and Wells House was built next to it probably before 1722 for gambling.[46] Although the wells had lost their fashionable cachet by 1725, when Joseph Rous converted the first Long Room to a chapel, building continued and by 1734, when Alexander Pope visited them, a second Long Room had been built on the north side of Well Walk, outside the Wells charity estate.[47] By 1762 there were three houses, a cottage, Wells House, the chapel, the Green Man, and various outbuildings on the estate,[48] and two large buildings west of it, the second Long Room and a ballroom.[49] A single house, later called the Pryors, stood on the heath east of the Wells estate by the 1740s.[50]

The wells also influenced building on the west side of Heath Street. Most of the 17th-century building at Cloth Hill had been of cottages but in the early 18th century many were replaced by larger houses or stabling.[51] Residents included Anne, Lady Crew, later countess of Torrington (d. 1719).[52]

[21] C.H.R. ii. 35–6; inf. at ho. (1985); Archit. of Lond. 42.
[22] Wade, Streets of Hampstead, 39.
[23] Ibid.; G.L.R.O., E/MW/H/I/2178; S.C.L., Man. Map and Fieldbk. no. 160.
[24] S.C.L., Man. Map.
[25] Nos. 1, 3, and 5: Wade, Streets of Hampstead, 44. In 1762 the terrace was not continuous: S.C.L., Man. Map.
[26] Archit. of Lond. 43; Pevsner, Lond. ii. 191; Wade, Streets of Hampstead, 45; S.C.L., Man. Map and Fieldbk. no. 175.
[27] G.L.R.O., E/MW/H/I/1928.
[28] Wade, Streets of Hampstead, 44; Archit. of Lond. 43; Pevsner, Lond. ii. 191; S.C.L., Man. Map and Fieldbk. nos. 171, 189.
[29] All owned in 1762 by Peter Flower: S.C.L., Man. Map and Fieldbk. nos. 176–80; Pevsner, Lond. ii. 191.
[30] Separated by a passage, Stamford Close: S.C.L., Man. Map and Fieldbk. nos. 186–7; Wade, Streets of Hampstead, 44.
[31] M.M. & M., Lib. A, pp. 229, 303.
[32] Ibid. Lib. D, p. 179; Lib. F, pp. 56–8.
[33] S.C.L., Man. Map and Fieldbk. nos. 219–20.
[34] Wade, Streets of Hampstead, 43; O.S. Map 1/2,500, TQ 2686 (1954 edn.).
[35] Wade, Streets of Hampstead, 43.

[36] Ibid.; Pevsner, Lond. ii. 192; Trans. Hampstead Antiq. and Hist. Soc. (1898), 32; Colville, Lond.: Northern Reaches, 60; S.C.L., Man. Map and Fieldbk. no. 193.
[37] S.C.L., Man. Map and Fieldbk. no. 196; Wade, Streets of Hampstead, 39.
[38] S.C.L., Man. Map and Fieldbk. nos. 194–5; Wade, Streets of Hampstead, 43.
[39] Images of Hampstead, 33; C.H.R. vi. 12; S.C.L., Man. Map.
[40] S.C.L., Man. Map and Fieldbk. no. 191; C.H.R. vi. 12–13.
[41] S.C.L., Man. Map and Fieldbk. no. 222.
[42] Rocque, Map of Lond. (1741–5), sheet 12.
[43] Wade, Streets of Hampstead, 45.
[44] Barratt, Annals, i. 181.
[45] G.L.R.O., E/MW/H/I/2311A.
[46] Hampstead One Thousand, 31; below, social.
[47] Hampstead One Thousand, 31–3; below, plate 3.
[48] S.C.L., Man. Map and Fieldbk. nos. 204–16.
[49] Ibid. no. 202.
[50] Ibid. no. 218; Rocque, Map of Lond. (1741–5), sheet 12; Hampstead One Thousand, 43.
[51] M.M. & M., Lib. D, pp. 111, 269–70.
[52] Ibid. p. 241; G.L.R.O., E/MW/H/I/2311A, 2123; Complete Peerage, s.v. Torrington.

Some handsome houses joined Fenton House at East End in the wooded area of the heath, appropriately called the Grove. Two were in the part called, after 1949, Admiral's Walk. One was built in 1700 by Charles Keys (d. 1753), a vintner, who called it Golden Spikes, probably after the symbol of the masonic lodge which met there between 1730 and 1745. Later called the Grove by Fountain North, a naval captain who lived there from c. 1775 to 1811, it was confused in prints with the residence of Admiral Matthew Barton (d. 1795), who lived elsewhere in Hampstead, and given the misleading name Admiral's House. Grove Lodge was built next to it at about the same time.[53] On the eastern side of the part called, after 1937, Hampstead Grove, were the earlier 18th-century Old Grove House (no. 26), with a wing added c. 1730 and, adjoining it to the north by 1762, New Grove House[54] (no. 28), supposedly on the site of one of the windmills.[55] Mount Vernon House, originally called Windmill Hill House, was built on the site of the other windmill between 1725 and 1728 by William Knight, a Hampstead timbersmith.[56] A terrace of tall houses was built at Windmill Hill c. 1730, later called Windmill Hill House (not the original house of that name), Bolton House, and Volta House, which in 1923 retained original panelling and 'hair-powdering closets'.[57] Enfield House, joining the terrace to the east, did not exist in 1762.[58] A terrace of houses built c. 1740 on the edge of the heath gave its name to Upper Terrace House, an 18th-century mansion, by 1762.[59] Capo di Monte, where Sarah Siddons lived in 1804–5, was one of three houses standing by 1762 at the corner of Upper Terrace and Judges Walk.[60]

The area west of High Street, made up of ancient copyhold and freehold, began to be built over in the early 18th century. Richard Hughes of Holborn was buying land on the west side of 'the great street of Hampstead' in 1710.[61] He began building on the Kinghall estate, where a bowling green had replaced the orchard, probably in the 17th century, before he acquired the freehold in 1713. One house may have been built by 1707 and by 1713 Hughes had built eight on the south side of what by 1728 was called Church Row, apparently all at one time[62] and as a speculation stimulated by the success of the wells.

As freehold they were omitted from the survey of 1762, when the north side of Church Row had ten houses of various dates from the early 18th century.[63] Hughes probably also built at least 13 houses on the eastern extension of Kinghall, tenanted in 1730 mostly by tradesmen, including John Perrin, chandler, who may have given his name to Perrin's Court in the centre of the area, although, as freehold, it too was ignored in 1762.[64] North of Church Row the Yorkshire Grey had been built by 1723[65] and cottages called Evans Row probably faced it c. 1730.[66] In 1757 the inn and 14 houses occupied by a brickmaker, clockmaker, carpenter, apothecary, and others were 'late freehold'[67] but in 1762 they were described as copyhold (one alehouse, two houses, and 11 cottages).[68] To the east, by 1762, was a crowded area of courtyards and alleys built on the customary tenement of Popes and possibly, in its northern reaches, on the wide green that had formed an extension of the heath in 1680.[69] The alley later called Oriel Court after Oriel House (itself not yet built) existed,[70] as did Bradley's Buildings, then called Bradley Row, possibly after William Bradley, who had interests in property there in 1762.[71] There were two large houses, Windmill Hill (later Mount Vernon) House and another, traditionally the farmhouse of the windmill, on the site later occupied by nos. 15–19 Holly Hill, at Windmill Hill[72] and between it and Oriel Court,[73] there were 27 houses, two carpenters', a smith's, and two butchers' shops, a brewhouse, and the Still (licensed in 1751),[74] the Cock (1730),[75] and the Three Horseshoes (1721),[76] besides two coach houses, ten stables, summerhouses, and hogstyes on less than 4 a. On the western side of High Street, south of Church Lane,[77] there were ten houses, a carpenter's shop and a smithy, the King's Head,[78] three coach houses, and several stables and cowhouses on nearly 12 a. Several mansions, including Vane House (then divided into two)[79] and Slyes,[80] kept that part of Hampstead town relatively spacious.

On the east side of High Street in 1762, there were five houses and the George south of Pond Street.[81] In Pond Street[82] there were 34 houses, 5 cottages, a butcher's shop, the White Horse (1721),[83] four coach houses, two chaisehouses, and numerous stables. In High Street, between Pond Street and

[53] C.H.R. ix. 2–3; Archit. of Lond. 44; Wade, Streets of Hampstead, 27–8; S.C.L., Man. Map and Fieldbk. nos. 269–70; M.M. & M., Lib. G, pp. 380–2.
[54] S.C.L., Man. Map and Fieldbk. nos. 306, 304; Wade, Streets of Hampstead, 28; Hist. Mon. Com. W. Lond. 40; Archit. of Lond. 41; Pevsner, Lond. ii. 193.
[55] Trans. Hampstead Antiq. and Hist. Soc. (1898), 34.
[56] M.M. & M., Lib. B, p. 296; Lib. D, p. 413; Lib. F, pp. 15–16, 44; S.C.L., Man. Map and Fieldbk. no. 415.
[57] S.C.L., Man. Map and Fieldbk. nos. 289–91; Wade, Streets of Hampstead, 30; The Times, 20 Oct. 1923, 7d.
[58] S.C.L., Man. Map.
[59] Ibid. nos. 274, 271; Wade, Streets of Hampstead, 31.
[60] S.C.L., Man. Map and Fieldbk. no. 273; Wade, Streets of Hampstead, 31.
[61] M.L.R. 1710/3/44–5, 134.
[62] Ibid. 1713/3/6–7; 1728/6/251; Images of Hampstead, 40; Archit. of Lond. 40, 43; Pevsner, Lond. ii. 195.
[63] Pevsner, Lond. ii. 195; S.C.L., Man. Map and Fieldbk. nos. 385–94; below, plate 20.
[64] M.L.R. 1730/6/144–6; S.C.L., Man. Map.
[65] G.L.R.O., MR/LV3/104.
[66] Ibid. LV5/22, licensee John Evans; E/MW/H, old no. 27/15 (sales parts. 1791).

[67] M.L.R. 1757/2/352.
[68] S.C.L., Man. Map and Fieldbk. nos. 395–9.
[69] Cal. Close, 1392–6, 136; C.H.R. xi. 20; above.
[70] S.C.L., Man. Map at no. 363; Wade, Streets of Hampstead, 62, 64.
[71] S.C.L., Man. Map and Fieldbk. no. 352.
[72] Ibid. nos. 415, 333; Wade, Streets of Hampstead, 25.
[73] S.C.L., Man. Map and Fieldbk. nos. 333–65.
[74] i.e. Black Boy and Still: ibid. no. 340; G.L.R.O., MR/LV7/3. Also called Green Man and Still: S.C.L., H 711, Isaac Messeder, plans of prop. of Robt. Vincent, 1773.
[75] S.C.L., Man. Map and Fieldbk. no. 354; G.L.R.O., MR/LV5/30.
[76] S.C.L., Man. Map and Fieldbk. no. 360; Hampstead One Thousand, 154.
[77] S.C.L., Man. Map and Fieldbk. nos. 366–84.
[78] Ibid. no. 366.
[79] Ibid. nos. 378, 381.
[80] Ibid. no. 375.
[81] Ibid. nos. 4–7.
[82] Ibid. nos. 11–40.
[83] S.C.L., Man. Map and Fieldbk. no. 21; Hampstead One Thousand, 154.

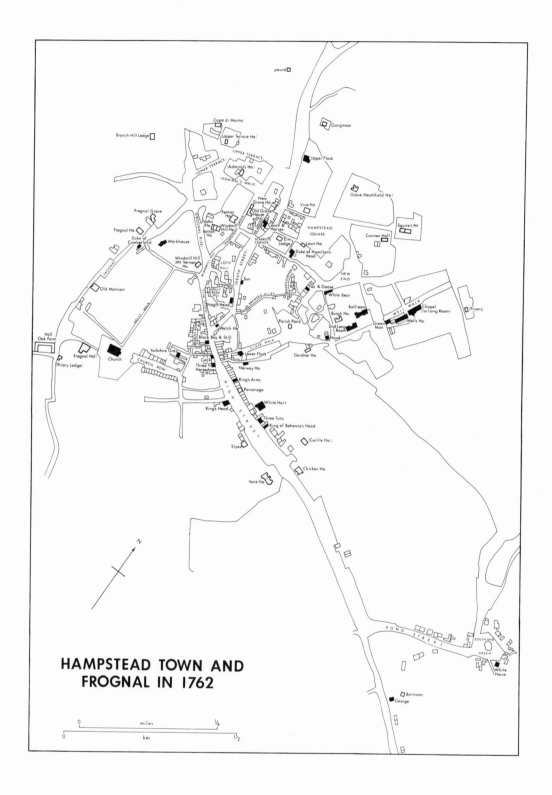

**HAMPSTEAD TOWN AND
FROGNAL IN 1762**

Flask Walk,[84] there were 38 houses, 4 cottages, a butcher's and 2 other shops, a school, a meeting house, 3 public houses (the Three Tuns, the White Hart, the King's Arms), and numerous stables and coach houses, especially in and around Flask Walk. Between Flask Walk and Streatley Place (then called Brewers Alley)[85] there were 24 houses, 2 cottages, 5 shops including a smith's, cooper's, carpenter's, and tallow chandler's, the Lower Flask,[86] a coach house, a chaisehouse, and 2 stables, forming a more working-class area. It included the parish pond,[87] which had presumably replaced that in High Street c. 1700. There was no sign of the bowling green which had been part of the Lower Flask's attractions in 1705.[88] There were few buildings on the north side of Streatley Place but they were densely packed at Boad's Corner, both at the eastern end of the road, where there were 7 houses and 4 sheds on 14 perches,[89] and along the southern side of the road, later itself confusedly called New End, from Heath Street to New End. In the whole quarter, described as from Brewers Alley to Scarrotts Corner (probably the corner of Heath Street and New End) and New End,[90] there were 28 houses, one of them a 'capital house' with a coach house and large garden, 2 cottages, 3 shops including a plumber's and a cooper's, 3 stables, the Sun (1756),[91] and the Fox.[92] In New End quarter, comprising the southward extension of the modern New End and New End Square,[93] there were 6 houses, including Burgh House, 4 cottages, 4 coach houses, 2 stables, a workshop, the Hawk, and the (White) Bear.[94] To the east lay the Hampstead wells quarter, consisting of 5 houses, a cottage, a coach house, 4 stables, the Green Man, the Long Room, a drinking room, the chapel, and Wells House.[95] In the area north of the road called New End, stretching north of what later became East Heath Road,[96] there were 34 houses, 2 cottages, a workshop, 6 coach houses, 6 stables, and the Duke of Hamilton. Except in the square bounded by Heath Street, Elm Row, and Hampstead Square, where buildings were crowded together, it was a spacious area of quite large houses on the edge of the heath.

On the west side of Heath Street, in the tongue of land bounded on the west by Holly Hill and Hampstead Grove,[97] buildings were mostly concentrated at the southern end and around The Mount Square. There were 54 houses, 3 cottages, 2 coach houses, 10 stables, the Coach and Horses, the Nag's Head, 7 shops including 2 smiths', a baker's, and a butcher's, and several sheds, one for a brickmaker. West of Hampstead Grove as far as Fognal Rise

(then called the road to Childs Hill) and stretching northward to Judges Walk and Upper Terrace[98] were 21 houses, a cottage, 4 coach houses, and 8 stables. Like the area on the opposite side of Heath Street, it was a neighbourhood of large houses and gardens.

In all, Hampstead town contained c. 327 houses, 35 cottages, 20 shops, and 19 public houses in 1762.[99]

The later 18th century saw a decline in the wells and consequently the closure of some inns, although Hampstead's attractions as a permanent residence increased. By 1810 there were more than 500 dwellings in Hampstead town,[1] many of them fine new houses. Among High Street inns which closed were the Haunch of Venison after 1731, the White Hart probably by 1762, the King's Arms between 1770 and 1800, and the Three Tuns between 1773 and 1800.[2] Houses built possibly on their sites were nos. 27, 30–1, 45–6 High Street, all on the eastern side.[3] The Chicken House had become a lodging house by 1754 when Samuel Gale, the antiquary, died there[4] and after being licensed in the 1760s and 1770s as a public house acquired a dubious reputation.[5] In Pond Street nos. 17–21 were probably built in the late 18th century.[6] The street housed the Venetian ambassador in 1774, several fashionable doctors later, and Baron John Dimsdale from c. 1807 to 1815. An attempt to exploit a new spa in 1803 was a failure.[7]

Several substantial houses were built on the broad piece of waste south of Pond Street, later called Hampstead Green. By 1800 there were two brick houses in place of the old Bartrams. Between 1799 and 1814 most of the land and houses nearby was bought by Charles Cartwright, who between 1806 and 1809 replaced the relatively new capital messuage with the large, irregularly shaped house called Bartrams, behind the George.[8] In 1815 the lord of the manor agreed that Cartwright should let part of Lower Bartrams to his cousin William Winfield to build himself a 'substantial house' there, Belle Vue or Bartram Park, south of the existing 18th-century Belle Vue houses. In 1825 the George and most of Bartrams estate passed to trustees for Winfield. John Moore, a captain in the East India service, who lived in the northernmost of the Belle Vue houses, acquired the house and former waste north of the George which Cartwright had bought in 1799.[9] Although not on Bartrams copyhold, the house was usually called Bartram House.[10]

On the west side of High Street, Vane House was still divided in two in 1787, when it was sold to

[84] S.C.L., Man. Map and Fieldbk. nos. 42–91.
[85] Ibid. nos. 92–120.
[86] Ibid. no. 94.
[87] Site in 1986 occupied by hos. between Lutton and Murray terraces.
[88] P.R.O., C 5/354/30.
[89] S.C.L., Man. Map and Fieldbk. nos. 148–54.
[90] Ibid. nos. 121–47.
[91] Ibid. no. 125; Hampstead One Thousand, 154.
[92] S.C.L., Man. Map and Fieldbk. no. 144.
[93] Ibid. nos. 155–66.   [94] Ibid. nos. 160, 166.
[95] Ibid. nos. 201–18.
[96] Ibid. nos. 167–200, 219–20.   [97] Ibid. nos. 294–332.
[98] Ibid. nos. 265–77, 283–93.
[99] The no. of hos. is approx. because those in the freehold area were omitted from the 1762 survey and have been estimated from other sources.

[1] Poor rate bk. 1800.
[2] G.L.R.O., E/MW/H/I/2280; MR/LV8/64; LV10/89; S.C.L., H 711, Messeder, Bk. of Plans 1773.
[3] Wade, Streets of Hampstead, 31, 65–6.
[4] D.N.B.
[5] G.L.R.O., MR/LV7/45; LV8/64; E. Walford, Old and New Lond. (1878), v. 485.
[6] Pevsner, Lond. ii. 200.
[7] Wade, More Streets, 28; G.L.R.O., E/MW/H, old no. 27/15 (sales parts. 1813); poor rate bks. 1807, 1810, 1815. Dimsdale was not the doctor, Thos. Dimsdale (d. 1800), who treated Cath. the Gt.; below, social.
[8] M.M. & M., Lib. L, pp. 305–12; ho. unfinished in 1810, completed by 1813: poor rate bks.
[9] M.M. & M., Lib. L, pp. 305–12, 443; poor rate bk. 1826.
[10] Pigot's Dir. Mdx. (1840); P.R.O., HO 107/1492/3.

James Pilgrim (d. 1813).[11] Pilgrim modernized it, possibly in 1789, a date inscribed with the unidentified initials IRW on the leads, reorienting the main house and giving it a classical façade and portico.[12] It has been suggested that Admiral Matthew Barton lived there in the 1790s.[13] Farther north, there were 16 houses by 1767 on the freehold around Perrin's Court,[14] probably including nos. 74-6 High Street.[15] On the adjoining copyhold to the north was property acquired in 1757 and 1761 by George Bussee, a carpenter,[16] who in 1762 possessed one house on the north side of Church Row, which he occupied himself,[17] and four houses east of Little Church Row.[18] By his death in 1792 he had three houses, one of them probably Oriel House, which faced Church Row, and nine cottages in Crockett's Court.[19] In 1791 land adjoining the house on the eastern corner of Perrin's (then Church) Lane was offered as suitable for erecting a row of small houses[20] and nos. 14-26, at the western end, were built in the early 19th century.[21] Still farther north, at the southern corner of the lane to Bradley's Buildings, an old, possibly 16th-century, house was ruinous by 1777 and had been replaced by new houses by 1814.[22] Church Row housed the writers Anna Letitia Barbauld (1743-1825) and her niece Lucy Aikin (1781-1864) at no. 8 c. 1800 and Hampstead's historian John James Park (d. 1833) and his father Thomas (1759-1834), the antiquary, at no. 18 c. 1814.[23]

Some houses and cottages were built in the later 18th century in Holly Mount and in Holly Bush Hill, where Romney's House originated as the stables of no. 6 the Mount or Cloth Hill, which the artist George Romney (1734-1802) bought in 1796. Before he left Hampstead in 1799, he converted the stables into a house (Prospect House) and studio. His son sold the house in 1801, whereupon it was converted into assembly rooms and its stables into the Holly Bush tavern.[24] Bentham House, next to no. 6 the Mount, nos. 12 and 14 Holly Hill (Granary House), and no. 1 Holly Bush Hill (Alpine Cottage) were all built about the same time.[25]

In Heath Street the Sun closed in the late 1760s[26] and the Upper Flask became a private house in the 1750s, the home from 1769 of George Steevens (1736-1800), the commentator on Shakespeare.[27]

Building on the west side of Heath Street included nos. 113-25 (odd), a 'pretty informal group of two-storeyed Georgian cottages',[28] which may have existed in 1762 as 'four messuages with a workshop',[29] no. 93 (Conduit House), late 18th-century, and nos. 83-89 (odd), early 19th-century.[30] On the east side nos. 112 and 114 may have existed in 1762;[31] no. 96 and no. 98 (Guyon House), the latter a large house named after a prominent Hampstead family, are late 18th-century; nos. 70-84 (even) and no. 118 (Mansfield Cottage) are of the same or slightly later date.[32]

In the area west of Heath Street, Netley Cottage (no. 10 Lower Terrace) was built by 1779; of nos. 1-4, forming an irregular range, nos. 1 and 4 may have existed in 1762.[33] Nos. 10-16 The Mount Square were built on the site of stabling and nos. 4-14 Hampstead Grove on the site of a 'walled ground with temple', all in 1762 part of Amy Cary's Old Grove House estate.[34] Amy Cary (d. 1769) was the widow of a London merchant and one of her neighbours was Lady Riddell.[35] Other local residents included the Holfords, a merchant family: Josiah (d. 1817) lived in 1775 at Windmill Hill House, before moving in 1776 to no. 22 Church Row and in 1782 to Holly Hill House, and Charles (d. 1838) at Upper Terrace House from 1799 to 1830.[36] Fenton House was bought in 1793 by Philip Fenton (d. 1807), a Riga merchant, whose son James was probably responsible for its Regency alterations inside.[37] Admiral's House was altered by Fountain North, whose additions included bulwarks, port-holes, and other features of a man-of-war, and who in 1805 bought and demolished the Grove for incorporation into his garden.[38] The neighbouring house to the west, Grove Lodge,[39] where priest's vestments were discovered,[40] may be identifiable with Grove House, 'on an eminence on the verge' of the heath, which was the residence of a French refugee, the marquis de Villedeuil, in 1792.[41] From c. 1781 to c. 1800 Gen. Charles Vernon leased Windmill Hill House, later called Mount Vernon,[42] previously the home of the surgeon William Peirce (d. 1772).[43] The author Joanna Baillie (1762-1851) lived from 1791 at Bolton House, where she was visited by leading literary figures.[44] John Constable (1776-1837), who painted Admiral's House, lived at no. 2 Lower Terrace from

[11] M.M. & M., Lib. G, pp. 228-9.
[12] Ibid. J, pp. 542-56; Baines, Rec. Hampstead, 65-6; Park, Hampstead, 270-1. The initials may relate to the owner John Regnier (d. 1780) and his mother Wigge, an occupier in 1787; below, plate 31.
[13] Wade, Streets of Hampstead, 69.
[14] G.L.R.O., E/MW/H/I/1941.
[15] Wade, Streets of Hampstead, 43.
[16] M.M. & M., Lib. D, pp. 372, 439-40.
[17] S.C.L., Man. Map and Fieldbk. no. 386.
[18] Ibid. nos. 362-3.
[19] M.M. & M., Lib. G, pp. 413, 473-9; Wade, Streets of Hampstead, 58, 62.
[20] G.L.R.O., E/MW/H, old no. 27/15 (sales parts. 1791).
[21] Wade, Streets of Hampstead, 63.
[22] Park, Hampstead, 266.
[23] Wade, Streets of Hampstead, 71-2; D.N.B.
[24] S.C.L., D 138 (i-xix); C.H.R. v. 2-3; Archit. of Lond. 41; Pevsner, Lond. ii. 194; Wade, Streets of Hampstead, 25-6; below, social; plate 1.
[25] Pevsner, Lond. ii. 191; Wade, Streets of Hampstead, 25.
[26] Hampstead One Thousand, 154; G.L.R.O., MR/LV8/64.

[27] Hampstead One Thousand, 41-2; M.M. & M., Lib. D, pp. 193, 430; D.N.B.   [28] Pevsner, Lond. ii. 191.
[29] S.C.L., Man. Map and Fieldbk. no. 295.
[30] Wade, Streets of Hampstead, 60.
[31] Ibid.; poss. identifiable with S.C.L., Man. Map and Fieldbk. nos. 180-1.
[32] Pevsner, Lond. ii. 191; Wade, Streets of Hampstead, 59-60.
[33] Pevsner, Lond. ii. 194; Wade, Streets of Hampstead, 32; S.C.L., Man. Map and Fieldbk. nos. 176-7.
[34] Wade, Streets of Hampstead, 27; S.C.L., Man. Map and Fieldbk. nos. 296, 307.
[35] M.M. & M., Lib. E, pp. 319-20.
[36] C.H.R. vi. 12-13.
[37] Fenton Ho. (Nat. Trust booklet, 1984), 6.
[38] C.H.R. ix. 2-3; cf. above.
[39] Wade, Streets of Hampstead, 27-8.
[40] N. & Q. 11th ser. ix. 348.
[41] G.L.R.O., E/MW/H, old no. 27/15 (sales parts. 1792).
[42] Wade, Streets of Hampstead, 29; vestry mins. 10 Nov. 1781; 39 & 40 Geo. III, c. 35 (Local and Personal).
[43] M.M. & M., Lib. F, pp. 15-16, 44; N, p. 249.
[44] Wade, Streets of Hampstead, 30-1; D.N.B.

1821 until 1823, when he moved to Stamford Lodge on the eastern side of Heath Street.[45]

Constable's first home in Hampstead, which he rented in 1819, was Albion Cottage, one of a group east of Heath Street, opposite Whitestone pond.[46] Fronting what was later called Whitestone Lane was the early 18th-century Gangmoor, which in 1762 formed two houses. Adjoining it was a Regency house called successively Heath House, the Lawn, and Whitestone House.[47] To the south fronting East Heath Road were, by 1829, several smaller houses, including Albion Cottage and Bellmoor, where Sir John Jackson, director of the East India Co., died in 1820.[48]

East Heath Road, which defined the limits of the heath to the north-east, did not exist in 1762 but two cottages (nos. 14 and 15), traditionally used by shepherds, were built at the north-west end in 1770.[49] Foley House at the junction with Well Walk, although locally reputed to be late 17th-century, was built after 1762.[50] It may be identifiable with three houses built between 1771 and 1773 by Edward Helling, a Holborn glazier, on a site described as bounded east and north by the heath, south by Upper Wells Walk, and west by the Cross Walk.[51] In 1786 Henry White, a local builder, had recently built East Heath Lodge and South Heath as a pair at the junction of East Heath Road and Heathside, then located as at Pollard Hill near the brick clamps.[52] Two smaller houses to the west, called Heathside, were added probably by 1814.[53]

A lane belonging in 1762 to Honywood[54] started as a broad tract from the junction of Flask and Well walks opposite the Long Room and ran to join a track along the line of East Heath Road. Besides being a farm lane it was probably used by visitors taking the air on the heath.[55] In the 1740s it was shown, perhaps inaccurately, as running farther north than in the 19th century.[56] The road, called Willow Road after willows planted there in 1845,[57] was by 1785 a public road from the bottom of Pond Street across the heath towards the Long Room.[58] In 1786 Henry White was permitted to make an open coach road across the heath southward from his new houses at Heathside to Willow Road.[59] His road was presumably part of that later known as East Heath Road. By 1814 a few houses had been built at the northern end of Willow Road.[60] The north-west

part of Christchurch Hill in the mid 18th century formed a broad space between enclosures[61] and the south-east extension to Willow Road, earlier called Green Man Lane, existed by 1800;[62] no. 14 was 'late Georgian',[63] no. 26 (Sunnybank) early 19th-century,[64] and there was a building, perhaps Willow Place, at the south-east end by 1814.[65]

In the old established area east of Heath Street, the Fox and Goose closed after 1773,[66] the Hawk became a private house between 1770 and 1800,[67] and the second Long Room (later called Weatherall House) had become one by c. 1803, when it was leased by Thomas Weatherall, a Cheapside haberdasher, to a linendraper from Fleet Street.[68] Nos. 36–40 (even) Well Walk were built on the site of Wells House in the early 19th century.[69] The Lower Flask, never so fashionable as the Upper Flask, survived in an area which became yet more working-class. In the early 19th century workers' cottages (nos. 35–47, odd) were built in Flask Walk, with no. 48 opposite and some shops (nos. 2 and 4); Thomas Gardnor built the terrace, nos. 53–67 (odd) on the site of the parish pond in 1811 and no. 75 (Rose Mount) was built in 1812.[70] In 1800, when a workhouse was opened on the south side of New End, the site was 'like the bottom of a punch bowl . . . being every way surrounded by houses and very closely too, all above one another'.[71] To the south off Brewhouse Lane, Hitchman's Buildings were built c. 1814.[72]

In the late 18th and early 19th century Sir Thomas Maryon Wilson (d. 1821) and his mother Dame Jane (d. 1816) encouraged building on copyhold land by waiving their right to arbitrary fines on every death and alienation in favour of fixed fines for a specified term. In 1811 they made such an agreement with Thomas Gardnor, who had built small houses, Gardnor's Place, by 1815, on garden ground off Flask Walk.[73] A larger development took place to the east, with the effect of extending the limits of Hampstead town.

In 1811 the vestry bought the 2½-a. field on the east side of Holly Walk for a churchyard, which it made from only the southern portion.[74] It sold the rest which became the site of Prospect Place, stuccoed, weatherboarded, semi-detached houses traditionally built by French refugees, of Benham's Place, nine terraced cottages built in 1813 by

[45] C.H.R. i. 23.
[46] Ibid.
[47] Wade, Streets of Hampstead, 45; Pevsner, Lond. ii. 192; S.C.L., Man. Map and Fieldbk. no. 222; Cruchley's New Plan (1829).
[48] Cruchley's New Plan (1829); Images of Hampstead, 86, illus. 222; Barratt, Annals, iii: 282.
[49] Wade, Streets of Hampstead, 46.
[50] Rocque, Map of Lond. (1741–5), sheet 12; S.C.L., Man. Map and Fieldbk. no. 215.
[51] M.L.R. 1773/3/94.
[52] S.C.L., Man. Map and Fieldbk. no. 217; ibid. D 47–8; M.M. & M., Lib. G, p. 199; Pevsner, Lond. ii. 196; Archit. of Lond. 44; O.S. Map 5', Lond. II. 90 (1936 edn.).
[53] Newton, Map of Hampstead (1814); Wade, Streets of Hampstead, 46.
[54] S.C.L., Man. Map and Fieldbk. no. 161½.
[55] Chatelain, 'Prospect of Long Rm. from Heath' (1745), in Hampstead One Thousand, 32.
[56] Rocque, Map of Lond. (1741–5), sheet 12; T. Milne, Land Use Map of Lond. (1800) (Lond. Topog. Soc. 1975–6); Newton, Map of Hampstead (1814). Cf. exit in

relation to Hampstead ponds. The course is not depicted on the 1762 map.
[57] Wade, Streets of Hampstead, 49.
[58] M.M. & M., Lib. G, p. 148.
[59] Ibid. p. 199.
[60] Newton, Map of Hampstead (1814).
[61] Rocque, Map of Lond. (1741–5), sheet 12; S.C.L., Man. Map.
[62] Milne, Land Use Map of Lond. (1800).
[63] Pevsner, Lond. ii. 191.
[64] Wade, Streets of Hampstead, 42–3.
[65] Newton, Map of Hampstead (1814); J. Wyld, Map of Lond. and Environs (1848).
[66] Hampstead One Thousand, 154.
[67] G.L.R.O., MR/LV8/64; LV10/89; Barratt, Annals, i. 193.
[68] S.C.L., D 114; Hampstead One Thousand, 31.
[69] Wade, Streets of Hampstead, 36–7.
[70] Ibid. 40–1; S.C.L., Man. Map.
[71] Park, Hampstead, 288.
[72] Poor rate bks. 1813, 1815.
[73] Thompson, Hampstead, 124–5, 127.
[74] Vestry mins. 27 Oct. 1811.

William Benham, a High Street grocer,[75] and of Holly Place, a recessed terrace built in 1816 with the Roman Catholic chapel of St. Mary in the centre.[76] The Roman Catholic connexion went back at least to 1796, when the Abbé Morel first held services in Oriel House.[77]

The largest development in the early 19th century was on copyhold land east of the London road, between Pond Street and the built up area around Flask Walk.[78] In 1809 Samuel Gambier acquired most of the medieval estates called Searsfield, which since the 16th century had been linked with Bartrams, and Popes, which had been held by the Honywood family since the 17th century. In 1811 he conveyed 14 a. forming a compact block stretching from the London road to East Heath Road and South End Road, to William Coleman, a Kentish developer.[79] In 1812 Coleman agreed to pay the lord of the manor a fine based on a fixed rate per acre in lieu of the traditional two years' value. Coleman wanted to let on building leases[80] and, having mortgaged the original 14 a., obtained from Gambier the rest of the Honywood estate, another 15 a. adjoining it on the north, together with the mansion and meeting house.[81] By 1813 the western part of Downshire Hill and Keats Grove, originally called Albion Grove and then John Street, had been driven eastward from the London road to East Heath Road and at least some of the land divided into building plots, several subleased to William Woods.[82] Coleman had not paid for his latest acquisition by 1814, when Gambier's widow was in immediate need, and he sold the Honywood house and some 4 a. to Edward Carlile, who acquired another 9 a. in 1816 after Coleman's bankruptcy.[83] Building proceeded on Coleman's remaining estate. By 1814 there were a few houses at the eastern end, the most desirable because of its views over the heath.[84]

In 1815–16 the antiquary Charles Wentworth Dilke (1789–1864) and a retired St. Petersburg merchant Charles Armitage Brown (1786–1842) built for themselves a semi-detached pair called Wentworth Place (later Lawn Cottage, Lawn Bank, and finally Keats House). John Keats lived in Brown's house from 1818 to 1820, where he wrote much of his best work and met Fanny Brawn, whose mother was the tenant of Dilke's house.[85] After Coleman's bankruptcy, his interest was conveyed in 1817 to William Woods, who designed and built the church and probably most of the houses on the estate. In 1818 Keats wrote of the 'half-built houses

opposite'.[86] Downshire Hill had probably been extended to Willow Road by 1819, when the Freemasons' Arms was built at the junction between them. By 1826 building was apparently complete on the northern side, where there were 18 houses between the public house and the junction with John Street; on the southern side were St. John's church, opened in 1823 in the angle with John Street, and at least five houses (nos. 39–43). Houses had also been built fronting East Heath Road at the end of John Street (Albion Grove House and a baker's shop) and off the London road (Sydney House).[87] Building was complete on all frontages by 1829,[88] many of the later houses being the work of William Kerrison.[89] An early inhabitant was John Constable, who moved from Heath Street in 1826 to no. 2 Langham Place, Downshire Hill, 'almost opposite the new church'. In 1827 he moved again, to no. 40 Well Walk, where he remained until his death.[90]

The exploitation of copyhold lands for building was in abeyance during the lordship (1821–69) of Sir Thomas Maryon Wilson, who could make agreements only of less than 21 years.[91] Activity was therefore small-scale, largely rebuilding or infilling. New Grove House was 'stuccoed and Tudorized' c. 1840[92] and nos. 16–24 Holly Hill replaced a stable and garden between 1846 and 1850.[93] In Heath Street nos. 69–73 and 77–81 (odd) on the west side and Claremont Terrace (nos. 86–90 even) on the east were built in the mid 19th century.[94] A terrace called Willow Cottages (nos. 33–41 Willow Road) was built between 1852 and 1862.[95] One large house was the Logs (nos. 17–20 Well Road), built in 1868 to the design of J. S. Nightingale in yellow, red, and black brick, later described as 'a formidable atrocity'[96] and a 'wonderful uncertainty between Gothic and Italian'.[97]

Three cottages were built in New End Green (1848), three houses in Church Lane (1851), two in Perrin's Place (1846), and single houses in Lower Terrace (1846), Upper Terrace (1847 by Hugh Jackson), Flask Walk (1847 and 1851), on the charity estate in Well Walk (1850), Golden Yard (1851), and Willow Place (1852).[98] Building did not keep pace with demand, however, and the mid 19th century saw social decline. The working classes were said in 1848[99] to be living in alleys and courts[1] without drainage or water supply. Overcrowding, with many families living in single rooms, was general and rents were high. There were several lodging houses and many of the former residences, including

---

[75] Wade, *Streets of Hampstead*, 30; datestone; *Archit. of Lond.* 42.
[76] Pevsner, *Lond.* ii. 195; datestone; *Archit. of Lond.* 45.
[77] Barratt, *Annals*, i. 294; below, Rom. Cathm.
[78] Thompson, *Hampstead*, 125–6.
[79] M.M. & M., Lib. L, pp. 273–6.
[80] Ibid. p. 631; M.L.R. 1817/5/285.
[81] M.M. & M., Lib. J, pp. 304, 357.
[82] Ibid. pp. 419–20.
[83] Ibid. pp. 486, 494–6; S.C.L., D 133.
[84] Newton, *Map of Hampstead* (1814); Thompson, *Hampstead*, 126.
[85] *Keats Ho., Hampstead. A Guide* (1980), *passim*; *Archit. of Lond.* 45.
[86] Wade, *Streets of Hampstead*, 55.
[87] G.L.R.O., E/MW/H, old no. 27/15 (sales parts. 1826); Wade, *Streets of Hampstead*, 52–6; below, churches and plate 26.
[88] *Cruchley's New Plan* (1829).
[89] S.C.L., Hampstead manor min. bk. (1824–39), pp. 11, 103–5; (1839–43), p. 27.   [90] *C.H.R.* i. 23.
[91] Thompson, *Hampstead*, 127.
[92] Pevsner, *Lond.* ii. 193.
[93] S.C.L., Man. Map and Fieldbk. no. 332; Wade, *Streets of Hampstead*, 25.
[94] Wade, *Streets of Hampstead*, 59–60.
[95] Wyld, *Map of Lond. and Environs* (1848); Stanford, *Libr. Map of Lond.* (1862 edn. with additions to 1865); Wade, *Streets of Hampstead*, 49; P.R.O., HO 107/1492.
[96] Pevsner, *Lond.* ii. 196; Potter Colln. 19/133.
[97] Quoted in Wade, *Streets of Hampstead*, 37.
[98] D.S.R.
[99] S.C.L., H 331.833 file, Metrop. Assoc. for Improving Dwellings of Industrial Classes, 1848.
[1] e.g. Bradley's Bldgs., Johnson's Yd., Crockett's Ct., Yorkshire Grey Yd., Perrin's Ct., Pilgrim's Ct., Watson's Yd., Murray Ct., mostly off High St.: P.R.O., HO 107/1492.

the Chicken House, Oriel House, Vine House, and South End House, were tenemented.[2] In 1848 the inhabitants of the Frognal demesne houses met at the home of Robert Prance to establish a branch of the Metropolitan Association for Improving the Dwellings of the Industrial Classes. In spite of basing their appeal for funds on fear of the contemporary European revolutions,[3] nothing apparently resulted. It was not until 1857 that Hampstead acquired a block of model dwellings, New Buildings or Court, built north of Flask Walk by the Jackson brothers, lawyers, of Upper Terrace; a reading room and ten more dwellings were added in 1871.[4]

Philanthropy helped to produce not only the model dwellings but several other institutions in the town. One of the largest buildings was the workhouse, rebuilt in 1847 and later considerably extended.[5] The dispensary, also in New End, opened in 1853,[6] Christ Church school opened in 1855 and the main buildings of Hampstead Parochial school west of Bradley's Buildings were built between 1856 and 1862.[7] The Royal Soldiers' Daughters' Home moved from one of the Belsize houses to part of Vane House in 1855 and a large purpose-built home on the southern part of Slyes estate in 1858.[8] The Royal Sailors' Daughters' Home, which had similarly grown out of the Crimean War, moved from Frognal to a new building, later called Monro House, designed by Edward Ellis in 1869 at no. 116 Fitzjohn's Avenue on the freehold Kinghall estate.[9] Several of the older residences were taken over by institutions. No. 28 Church Row housed a Roman Catholic school in the 1850s, a home for the rescue of young women in the 1860s, and a female servants' home in the 1870s.[10] Burgh House was from 1858 to 1881 the headquarters of the Royal East Middlesex Militia, which also built a barracks in Willow Road in 1863. In 1862 the Hampstead Volunteers took over Well Walk chapel, the Anglicans having departed in 1852 for Christ Church, built on what had been part of Hampstead Square.[11] Many early chapels were built in the town, partly because wealthy Roman Catholics and nonconformists provided sites and partly because only Anglican places of worship were permitted on the newly built Chalcots (Eton College) and Belsize (Westminster abbey) estates.[12]

A group of 'good Georgian houses'[13] south of the junction of the London road (Rosslyn Hill) with Pond Street included one occupied by Basil George Woodd in 1835 and another, Tensleys, the home of the historian Sir Francis Palgrave (1788–1861) from 1834 and of the architect S. S. Teulon from 1864 to 1868. Palgrave's son Francis Turner (1824–97), the poet, referred to the 'pretty, old-fashioned house at Hampstead'.[14] The next house to the south, Bartram House or Upper Bartrams, was leased from c. 1849 to Sir Rowland Hill (1795–1879), the postal pioneer, who in 1852 bought it with 2½ a.[15] Bartrams was occupied from 1851 to c. 1861 by Lord Sidney Godolphin Osborne (1808–89), the philanthropist.[16] In 1867 the house, the George, and 12 a. were enfranchised and offered for sale, mostly as building land.[17] The house was bought as a convent by the Sisters of Providence, who added an orphanage, school, and chapel in 1878 and 1887 in a Gothic style designed by C. G. Wray.[18] The rest of the estate was purchased by the Metropolitan Asylums Board for a smallpox hospital.[19] Bartram Park, a large house with double bay windows behind, set in 10 a. in the southern part of the copyhold Bartrams estate, was occupied by the Winfield family until c. 1851 and by John Fleming, a Baltic merchant, in 1860–1.[20] The Winfields sold the estate in 1867 to the Midland Railway Co.,[21] which in 1875 offered for sale 2½ a. and the house,[22] which became a girls' industrial home, called Tre Wint.[23]

In 1851[24] Carlile and Burgh houses were inhabited, respectively, by a Manchester warehouseman and the Revd. Allatson Burgh, vicar of St. Lawrence Jewry. Burgh, the owner since 1822, published *Anecdotes in Music* and reputedly added a music room, but by 1854 the house was very dilapidated.[25] In 1838–9 Eliza Chester (d. 1859), a retired actress, purchased both Wentworth Place houses, converted them into one, which she called Lawn Cottage, and added a drawing room; she lived there until 1849.[26] Sir James Cosmo Melville, secretary to the East India Co., had been at Cannon Hall since 1838[27] and two houses on the eastern borders of the town, the Pryors and Foley House, were associated with the Hoare family. Thomas Marlborough Pryor (d. 1821), a brewer who gave his name to the house, married Hannah (d. 1850), daughter of the elder Samuel Hoare. Their son Robert lived at the Pryors until 1863 and their daughter married Charles, son of Edward Toller and himself a lawyer, and lived in Foley House.[28] Grove

[2] P.R.O., HO 107/1492 *passim.*
[3] S.C.L., Metrop. Assoc. for Improving Dwellings etc.
[4] D.S.R.; *C.H.R.* ix. 7; Wade, *Streets of Hampstead,* 31, 40.
[5] Wade, *Streets of Hampstead,* 42; Pevsner, *Lond.* ii. 190; below, local govt. after 1837.
[6] D.S.R.; below, pub. svces.
[7] Wade, *Streets of Hampstead,* 42, 63; below, educ., pub. schs.
[8] *Brief Hist. Royal Soldiers' Daus. Sch. in Hampstead 1855–1963* (pamphlet in S.C.L., H 362.73, Royal Soldiers Daus. Home); Potter Colln. 19/135.
[9] Wade, *Streets of Hampstead,* 69–70; *The Times,* 18 Jan. 1869, 11d.
[10] Wade, *Streets of Hampstead,* 73.
[11] Ibid. 39; *Hampstead One Thousand,* 58–60; below, churches.
[12] Thompson, *Hampstead,* 387–9; below, Rom. Cathm.; prot. nonconf.
[13] Barratt, *Annals,* iii. 9, 264.
[14] Poor rate bks. 1835, 1860, 1864, 1868, 1875; P.R.O., HO 107/1492/3; *D.N.B.*; Baines, *Rec. Hampstead,* 551;

G. F. Palgrave, *Fras. Turner Palgrave* (1899), 4.
[15] Barratt, *Annals,* ii. 271–2; poor rate bks. 1826, 1835, 1860, 1864, 1875; *D.N.B.*; *Home Counties Dir.* (1845).
[16] Poor rate bk. 1860; P.R.O., HO 107/1492/3; *Census,* 1861; *D.N.B.*
[17] M.M. & M., Lib. Q, p. 407; Potter Colln. 19/89.
[18] S.C.L., Illus. Colln. LGE, Bartrams; H 728.3, Bartrams, plan; D.S.R.
[19] Below, pub. svces.
[20] Poor rate bks. 1826, 1835, 1860, 1864, 1868; P.R.O., HO 107/1492/2; *Census,* 1861.
[21] M.M. & M., Lib. Q, p. 385.
[22] S.C.L., H 728.3, file Folios/Bartram Pk., sales parts. 1875.
[23] Wade, *More Streets,* 40.
[24] Based upon Census, 1851: P.R.O., HO 107/1492.
[25] *C.H.R.* ii. 35–6.
[26] *Keats Ho. Guide* (1980); *C.H.R.* iv. 23–4.
[27] Wade, *Streets of Hampstead,* 43.
[28] *C.H.R.* ix. 2–3; *Memoirs of Sam. Hoare* (1911), ed. F. R. Pryor, p. xii, fam. tree. For the Hoares, below, s.v. North End etc.

House (Holford or Heathfield House) was occupied from 1830 by Charles Holford (d. 1838) and his wife Mary Anne (d. 1861), Edward Toller's daughter.[29] Edward Toller, a City lawyer, had leased Grove House from the Holfords until 1830, when he moved to the house confusedly called the Grove (Admiral's House), where he and his daughters lived until 1848. Later occupants were Edward Browell, of the Lord Chamberlain's office, the architect Sir George Gilbert Scott (1811–78) from 1856 to 1864, and from 1865 the family of Henry Sharpe (d. 1873), a merchant who had lived in Heath Street since 1834.[30]

Barristers living in the town included Thomas Turner at Fenton House in the 1840s and 1850s and Philip Le Breton at Milford House in John Street in the 1860s, both allies of the Hoares in opposition to Sir Thomas Maryon Wilson's plans for Hampstead.[31] There were several other lawyers in 1851, especially in Upper and Lower Terrace, Pond Street, Downshire Hill, and John Street. Old and New Grove houses were occupied by a glass merchant and a surgeon respectively, and Gardnor House by a china dealer. There were many merchants, some manufacturers, and numerous fund-holders. High Street and Heath Street housed many shopkeepers and craftsmen, and the crowded courts on either side were the homes of labourers, coachmen, gardeners, and laundresses. There was a wide sprinkling of artists and authors, Church Row, for example, housing, in addition to several schools, the painter John R. Herbert (1810–90) and an author. Gangmoor was from 1862 the home of the engraver W. J. Linton (1812–98) and his wife the writer Eliza (1822–98) and later of the artist and novelist George Du Maurier (1834–96), before he moved to Church Row in 1870.[32] Ford Madox Brown (1821–93), whose painting 'Work' was of excavations in the Mount, Heath Street, lodged in 1852–3 at no. 33 High Street.[33] After their marriage in 1860 Dante Gabriel Rossetti (1828–82) and Lizzie Siddal lived in Spring Cottage, Downshire Hill, which Rossetti thought 'pretty well beyond civilization'. Tennyson often visited Rose Lodge, no. 40 New End Square, his mother's home in the 1860s.[34]

Enfranchisement at the copyholder's suit had been possible since 1852, but few sought it before Sir Thomas Maryon Wilson's death in 1869. Building activity thereafter mostly followed enfranchisements, of which there were many between 1870 and 1877.[35] On the Slyes and Kinghall estate, combined under the name Greenhill, building was contemplated before 1869, possibly because it adjoined Belsize.[36] The Erringtons enfranchised the copyhold in 1868[37] and

the first building went up in the corner between Church Lane and Church Place in 1869.[38] Two houses were built at Greenhill in 1871 and by 1872 Church Place had been extended as Greenhill Road (after 1892 Fitzjohn's Avenue). Mount Grove disappeared when Prince Arthur Road was driven through the site and a Wesleyan chapel erected in 1872 on the south-east corner.[39] Vane House survived as the Royal Soldiers' Daughters' Home and Stanfield House became a subscription library in 1884.[40] By 1874 all the roads on the estate, Ellerdale (then Ellerdale and Manners roads), Prince Arthur (then Prince Arthur and Lingard roads), and the eastern portion of Arkwright Road, were laid out and many of the houses built, mostly substantial detached or semi-detached. The westward continuation of Arkwright Road, with land on either side divided into 16 plots, was planned. Most houses were completed by 1880.[41] Among them was no. 75 Fitzjohn's Avenue, a Gothic villa designed for the painter Paul Falconer Poole (1807–79) by T. K. Green, who also designed several houses in Prince Arthur Road and Arkwright Road, including the Gothic no. 1 and nos. 2 and 4 for the artist F. W. Topham (1808–77) and no. 2 Ellerdale Road, 'a defiantly Gothic house' built for himself c. 1890. Several houses in Ellerdale Road have a sunflower motif, including no. 6 which Richard Norman Shaw built for himself in 1875 and occupied until his death in 1912.[42]

Development began on several copyhold estates on the eastern side of the London road in the early 1870s. Gardnor Road off Flask Walk was developed in 1871–2 by Charles Till.[43] Land adjoining it to the east and south belonged in 1870 to a barrister, George Nathan Best of Norfolk, who probably named Gayton Road and Crescent after the Norfolk village; they were built from 1871 by George Potter, father of the Hampstead historian.[44] Duddingtons, most easterly of the copyhold estates, between South End Green and East Heath Park, was enfranchised and laid out as South Hill Park in 1871.[45] Some 76 houses had been built there by 1875,[46] mostly by Joseph Pickett, lessee of South End farm,[47] and by one Sharp, presumably Charles Smithee Sharp, a local builder.[48] Also bordering Belsize were Hodges, where development was closely associated with Belsize, and Bartrams which, being mostly owned by the Metropolitan Asylums Board and the Midland Railway, was insulated from residential building.[49]

North of Pond Street was a small estate owned by George Crispin, where Hampstead Hill Gardens had been built by 1873,[50] when there were six houses, all occupied by artists. Most of the houses, nos. 3–21

[29] C.H.R. vi. 12–13.
[30] Ibid. ix. 2–3.
[31] Thompson, Hampstead, 169, 184, 188–9.
[32] G. H. Cunningham, Lond.: Comprehensive Survey (1931), 315; Wade, Streets of Hampstead, 45.
[33] C.H.R. ii. 16–17.
[34] Wade, Streets of Hampstead, 39, 55.
[35] Thompson, Hampstead, 300–1.
[36] Ibid. 298, 301.
[37] M.M. & M., Lib. Q, pp. 527–30.
[38] i.e. Sailors' Orphans' Home, above.
[39] D.S.R.; below, prot. nonconf.
[40] Wade, Streets of Hampstead, 61; below, pub. svces.
[41] D.S.R.; S.C.L., H 912.421/1874, Greenhill est. plan 1874.

[42] Wade, Streets of Hampstead, 66, 70–1; Thompson, Hampstead, 298; A. Saint, Ric. Norman Shaw (1976), 413; Archit. of Lond. 35; below, plate 15.
[43] S.C.L., Man. Map and Fieldbk. no. 84; D.S.R.
[44] D.S.R.; Wade, Streets of Hampstead, 49; E. F. Oppé, Hampstead, Lond. Town (1951), 6.
[45] M.M. & M., Lib. Q, pp. 209–11; Hampstead One Thousand, 83.   [46] D.S.R.
[47] Below, Belsize.
[48] S.C.L., D 119.
[49] Above; below, Belsize.
[50] Thompson, Hampstead, 128. Owned in 1762 by Edw. Snoxell: S.C.L., Man. Map and Fieldbk. nos. 40–1; J. Summerson, 'Lond. Suburban Villa', Archit. Rev. civ. 71.

(odd) and 2–6 (even), were designed for gentleman artists by Batterbury & Huxley from 1876 as 'rose-red villas' with rubbed-brick ornaments.[51] On the same estate houses were built fronting Rosslyn Hill.[52] In 1873 the contractor John Culverhouse[53] was allowed to enclose waste on the south side of Willow Road, from Willow Cottages to Downshire Hill. The strip was enfranchised and conveyed in 1875 to the British Land Co., which also acquired the Carlile estate, enfranchised in 1873, between Gayton Road and Crescent, Willow Road, and Downshire Hill.[54] All the roads (Denning, Willoughby, Kemplay, and Carlingford roads and Rudall Crescent) had been laid out on the estate by 1878,[55] and houses there and on the Willow Road frontage were complete by 1886. Among the last to be built, in 1890, were nos. 54–66 Rosslyn Hill, where the Chicken House had been demolished c. 1880.[56] Carlile House made way for Willoughby Road in 1876.[57]

At the northern end of Hampstead town William Shepherd, a local builder, bought the Heathfield or Holford estate in 1875. He built nos. 7–25 Cannon Place (originally called Heathfield Gardens) in 1875–7 and began building in Holford Road in 1876. Batterbury & Huxley designed a studio house, no. 1 Cannon Place, in 1879. Friedrich von Hügel, the theologian, lived in no. 4 Holford Road from 1882 to 1903. High Close on the western side of the road, was built by W. H. Murray in 1884.[58]

The Hampstead charities took part in building during the 1870s and 1880s. In 1873–4 the trustees of the Wells charity enfranchised their property, containing 19 buildings, mostly houses in Well Walk. In 1876 they acquired a site in Crockett's Court, where they built a block of artisans' dwellings called Wells Buildings.[59] For their older estate Henry Simpson Legg drew up a plan in 1876. Charles Bean King, of Church Row, built nos. 16–22 Christchurch Hill in 1877–8 and nos. 15 and 17 Well Walk in 1879 and, together with Allison & Foskett, built on the south side of Well Road in 1879–81.[60] In 1881 Legg designed nos. 21–7 Well Walk (until 1924 called Foley Avenue) on the site of Foley House's garden as a speculation for Edward Gotto of the Logs, and the architect Ewan Christian built for himself an elaborate house called Thwaitehead (later Klippan House) at no. 50 Well Walk and another house, no. 8 East Heath Road. Alfred Hackworth was the builder of nos. 11 and 13 Well Walk in 1884. The Wells trustees laid out Gainsborough Gardens on the southern side of Well Walk in 1883, when E. J. May built nos. 3 and 4, said to be the first houses with hot air heating. Legg designed almost half the houses; nos. 11–14 were designed by Horace Field in the early 1890s. As part of that development, the

first Long Room was demolished in 1882, although Wellside, 'good Queen Anne work', was not built on the site until 1892. In 1885 the trustees of the combined Wells and Campden charities bought land in Flask Walk, where in 1888 they built public baths, and in 1886 they bought land in Holly Bush Vale, where they built Campden Buildings.[61] By 1898 the trustees owned 48 houses, the baths and washhouses, and two blocks of artisans' dwellings, Wells Buildings (73 tenements) and Campden Buildings (65 tenements).[62]

Campden Buildings were designed for those displaced by a town improvement scheme. Development on the Greenhill and manorial Fitzjohn's Avenue estates had drawn attention to the defects of the area to the north, where narrow twisted roads and overcrowded courts blocked access to High Street and Heath Street. In 1883 the Metropolitan Street Improvement Act authorized redevelopment of the whole area at the joint expense of the local authority and M.B.W. In 1888 High Street was widened, Fitzjohn's Avenue (then Greenhill Road) was extended to meet Heath Street, and soon afterwards Crockett's Court, Bradley's Buildings, and other slums, including Oriel House and other tenemented houses, were replaced by Oriel Place, shops, and tenement blocks. Among the blocks were Greenhill flats (1904) in Perrin's Court, Hampstead Mansions (nos. 15–21 Heath Street) with a terracotta façade dated 1888, and Express Mansions (nos. 23–7 Heath Street), designed by Keith Young for Express Dairies in 1889. To the north a drill hall (later the Everyman theatre) was built in Holly Bush Vale in 1888[63] and to the east no. 24 Heath Street was built for the Liberal Club in 1889.[64] Many of the shops and flats in Heath and High streets were built from 1887 by E. J. Cave, a prolific builder in Hampstead.[65] Norman Shaw designed Moreland hall, near the drill hall, in 1893,[66] and in 1898 the 'improvements', which had already destroyed the eastern end of Church Row, replaced old houses on the north side with Gardnor Mansions, a change deplored at the time.[67]

South End Green, which had been formed in 1835 when the pond at the east end of Pond Street was filled, was transformed by the London Street Tramways Co.'s extension to a terminus there. In 1886 the street was widened and run across the green; houses, including Clifton House, were demolished. The isolated village at the eastern end of Pond Street had already been affected by the crowds of trippers at Hampstead Heath station after 1860, and by building at South Hill Park and on the Pickett's Farm estate to the east. From 1887 the old houses and cottages were replaced by red-brick shops and flats, including Maryon Terrace. One of the early

[51] D.S.R.; Wade, *More Streets*, 29; Thompson, *Hampstead*, 266–7; *Archit. of Lond.* 48.
[52] Datestone.
[53] *C.H.R.* x. 13–17; below, econ., ind.
[54] S.C.L., D 133; below, other est.
[55] *Metropol. Improvement Map No.* 46 (1878).
[56] D.S.R.; Wade, *Streets of Hampstead*, 49–52, 67; Stanford, *Libr. Map of Lond.* (1891 edn.).
[57] S.C.L., Carlile Ho. file, photo.
[58] D.S.R.; Wade, *Streets of Hampstead*, 43–5; Thompson, *Hampstead*, 383.
[59] Wade, *Streets of Hampstead*, 64; *Endowed Chars. Lond. III*, H.C. 252, pp. 98–100 (1900), lxi.
[60] D.S.R.; Wade, *Streets of Hampstead*, 43; A. Saint,

'Hampstead Walk' (notes for Victorian Soc.), 1.
[61] *Endowed Chars. Lond.* 106–8; Char. Com. Scheme 1971, schedule of prop.; Wade, *Streets of Hampstead*, 34, 36–7, 46, 61; D.S.R.; *Survey of Lond.* ix. 370; Saint, 'Hampstead Walk', 1.
[62] *Endowed Chars. Lond.* 112–13, 117.
[63] Thompson, *Hampstead*, 316–17; Wade, *Streets of Hampstead*, 61–4; P. J. Edwards, *Hist. Lond. Street Improvements, 1855–97* (1898), 111, plan xlv; below, social.
[64] Datestone.
[65] D.S.R.
[66] Wade, *Streets of Hampstead*, 63.
[67] Ibid. 71; *N. & Q.* 9th ser. ii. 5; *Mdx. & Herts. N. & Q.* iv. 95, 149.

19th-century houses, Russell House, survived, with alterations made in 1890 by Voysey.[68] In Heath-hurst Road, north of the green, 29 houses were built between 1897 and 1899.[69] The area south of South End Green and Pond Street came to be filled with buildings belonging to the smallpox hospital.[70] Sir Rowland Hill had led the opposition to the hospital; in 1884 his executors sold Bartram House to the Metropolitan Asylums Board, which pulled it down in 1902. After an exchange the land became, in 1906, the site of Hampstead General hospital, which had demolished Tensleys and the other house to the north.[71]

There had been small-scale building, rarely of more than four houses, in the old town, in Heath Street, Flask Walk, and New End, from the late 1870s.[72] In 1876 the second Long Room was transformed into Weatherall House, with a Tudor-style front, and in 1882 George Price built nos. 2–14 Well Walk 'with cheerful crowstepped gables' on the site of the barracks.[73] A tuberculosis hospital, in the style of a French château, was built in Mount Vernon in 1879 and later extended, and considerable extensions were made to the workhouse.[74] There was a rebuilding of frontages on the east side of Rosslyn Hill in the 1890s, with the bank at the corner of Pilgrim's Lane built by Horace Field in a 'Queen Anne' style in 1896. The police station at the corner with Down-shire Hill was designed in 1913 by J. Dixon Butler, near no. 1B Downshire Hill, built as a postal sorting office in 1891.[75] New End schools were built in 1905–6 and the Friends' meeting house in Heath Street in 1907.[76] In 1880 the local historian Thomas Barratt, a partner in Pears, the soap manufacturers, combined four of the houses opposite Whitestone pond into one house, called Bellmoor after one of them.[77] The large Tudor (later Hawthorne) House was built in Lower Terrace in 1882 by Ernest George & Peto for W. J. Goode, who had made his fortune from selling china.[78] Charles Bean King built nos. 1–6 Windmill Hill in 1894–6 and Thomas Garner designed Moreton, a large house on the west side of Holly Walk, for Frederick Sidney in 1894.[79] The Pryors was demolished in 1902 and replaced in 1908 by flats of the same name, designed in 'Edwardian baroque' by Hall & Waterhouse.[80]

Early flats in Hampstead town included Albany Flats in Flask Walk in 1893, followed by Hampstead Hill Mansions in Downshire Hill (1896), Northcote House and Mansions at the corner of Heath Street and Hampstead Square (1897–8), and Streatley Flats in Streatley Place (1898).[81] The last were built by Herbert Marnham, Baptist, philanthropist, and later

mayor, who was also responsible for Grove Place Flats, 28 'model dwellings for artisans', built c. 1914 on the site of the wells' bathhouse, and for the adjoining nos. 57 and 59 Christchurch Hill.[82] Heath Mansions, between Hampstead Grove and the Mount, Heath Street, were built in 1903.[83] The building of flats was particularly resented as the 'march of the unsentimental builder', threatening to engulf old Hampstead.[84]

Poverty had long existed in old Hampstead c. 1890.[85] Most of it was concentrated on each side of High Street, in Crockett's Court and other yards, and in Flask Walk, Gardnor Road, and New End, where many houses were tenemented. The inhabitants in 1881 belonged to a greater variety of occupations than in 1851, with many small craftsmen among them. There were a lot of bricklayers, presumably employed by builders such as George Potter in Gayton Road, James Burford at Norway House with 50 men, and Thomas Clowser in High Street with 30.[86] Removal of the worst slums in the 1880s did not eliminate squalor. In 1903 New End was a 'rather depressed neighbourhood' and Silver Street and Golden Square (later the Mount and The Mount Square), between Heath Street and Hampstead Grove, had 'nothing in their present appearance, except irony, to suggest the etymology of their names'.[87] In 1881 High Street and Heath Street were dominated by tradesmen and the rest of old Hampstead town was still a predominantly middle-class mixture of professional and commercial interests. Most of the grand houses were still in private hands, if sometimes less distinguished ones than formerly. Gardnor House was occupied by an architect, Wentworth House by a barrister, Bartram House by Sir Rowland Hill's widow, Tensleys by a solicitor,[88] and New Grove House from 1874 to 1895 by George Du Maurier.[89] Burgh House was occupied from 1884 by a stained glass painter, from 1898 by a novelist, and from 1906 by an expert on miniature portraits.[90] Before its demolition the Pryors housed the painter Walter Field (1837–1901), whose relative Horace Field, the architect, lived at Chestnut Lodge (the western part of Squire's Mount) from c. 1891.[91] Others in the older parts of Hampstead town included R. L. Stevenson in 1873 at Abernethy House, Mount Vernon, then a lodging house, Sir Henry Cole (1808–82), a founder of the Victoria and Albert Museum, at no. 3 Elm Row in 1879–80, the poet W. J. Cory (1823–92) at no. 25 Cannon Place, and the composer Sir Henry Walford Davies (1869–1941) at no. 15 in the 1880s and 1890s.[92]

Of the newer areas, Downshire Hill and Keats

[68] Wade, *More Streets*, 19, 21–7; *Hampstead One Thousand*, 93–4; D.S.R.
[69] D.S.R.
[70] Below, pub. svces.
[71] G.L.R.O., MAB 2417; 1026, pp. 42, 69; 1038; ibid. PH/HOSP/3/64; Wade, *More Streets*, 35; O.S. Map 1/2,500, Lond. XXVII (1906 edn.); I.16 (1915 edn.).
[72] D.S.R.
[73] Saint, 'Hampstead Walk', 1.
[74] D.S.R.; Pevsner, *Lond.* ii. 190; below, pub. svces.; local govt.
[75] D.S.R.; Wade, *Streets of Hampstead*, 67–8.
[76] *Hampstead One Thousand*, 57; Saint, 'Hampstead Walk', 1.
[77] Cunningham, *Lond.: Comprehensive Surv.* 314–15; Oppé, *Hampstead, Lond. Town*, 6.
[78] Wade, *Streets of Hampstead*, 32.

[79] Ibid. 29, 31; D.S.R.
[80] Wade, *Streets of Hampstead*, 46; D.S.R.
[81] D.S.R.
[82] Wade, *Streets of Hampstead*, 19, 39, 41–2.
[83] *Kelly's Dir. Hampstead and Childs Hill* (1903–4).
[84] *Mdx. & Herts. N. & Q.* iv. 95.
[85] Booth, *Life and Labour*, iii (1), 207.
[86] P.R.O., RG 11/168/6/12/1.
[87] C. White, *Sweet Hampstead* (1903), 98.
[88] P.R.O., RG 11/168/6/10/1; RG 11/168/6/12/1. For High Street in 1881, below, plate 2.
[89] Wade, *Streets of Hampstead*, 28, 73; Cunningham, *Lond.: Comprehensive Surv.* 139.
[90] *C.H.R.* ii. 28–31, 35–6.
[91] Wade, *Streets of Hampstead*, 46; Saint, 'Hampstead Walk', 1.
[92] Wade, *Streets of Hampstead*, 29, 43, 44.

Grove were still in 1881 respectably middle-class and contained one novelist, but there were also tradesmen, commercial travellers, a pawnbroker, and several lodging houses.[93] By the end of the First World War the neighbourhood seemed 'a bit run down'.[94] In 1881 the terraces of the Gayton and Carlile estates housed a mixture of tradesmen, clerks, merchants, manufacturers, and professional people, and included some tenementation and lodging houses in Gayton Road. There was also a photographer, an artist, and one 'literary' man in Gayton Road, an author in Kemplay Road, the historian James Gairdner (1828–1912) in Carlingford Road, and an architect in Denning Road. Ernest Bell, a publisher, lived at Saxon House, Willoughby Road,[95] and was presumably related to Edward Bell, who lived at the Mount, Heath Street, in the 1900s.[96] By 1900 the Carlile estate had declined and become lower middle-class.[97]

At South Hill Park, the opportunity to create an upper-class district on a fine site facing the heath was lost when a large number of 'tasteless' and inward-facing houses was packed into the elongated estate.[98] In 1881 they housed a mainly middle-class population, including merchants, brokers, manufacturers, several builders (James Pickett, Charles Sharp, and Alfred Leammell), an architect, and two artists.[99] South End Green, however, was predominantly working-class, partly because trippers using the railway station turned the green into a resort of tearooms and souvenir shops. Other factors were the building of the smallpox hospital and the advent of trams.[1]

By c. 1900 the old established gentry had left Hampstead town. After the apathy of the 1870s, intellectual and cultural life became more vigorous during the 1890s, while remaining largely conventional.[2] In the 1870s Church Row housed a group of architects important in the shift of style from High Victorian to late Gothic. In 1872 George Gilbert Scott the younger (d. 1897) moved to no. 26 Church Row, next to George Du Maurier. G. F. Bodley (1827–1907), to whom Scott was related by marriage, lived at no. 24, and Thomas Garner (1839–1906) at no. 20. The three shared a drawing office in a mews and founded Watts & Co., producing wallpaper, furniture, and metalwork to their designs. Scott's pupil Temple Lushington Moore (1856–1920) lived at no. 6 Downshire Hill from 1884 and at no. 46 Well Walk from 1892.[3] Gardnor's house was bought in the 1890s by Henry Holiday (1839–1927), the stained-glass painter, who had lived in Hampstead since 1872 and set up his glassworks in the later no. 20 Perrin's Walk, possibly the site of the architects' drawing office.[4] Scott's house was the home of Lord Alfred Douglas from 1907 to 1910 and Du Maurier's,

no. 27, of the musician Cecil Sharp (1859–1924), director of the Hampstead Conservatoire, from 1915 to 1918. The novelists H. G. Wells lived at no. 17 from 1909 to 1912 and Compton Mackenzie at no. 28 in 1910. Virginia Woolf, who with her husband Leonard visited no. 28 after 1908, when it was the office of the Women's Co-operative Guild, described the 'immaculate and moral heights of Hampstead' with its 'uncompromising and high minded' inhabitants.[5]

There was a similar concentration of notables at Well Walk: early socialists Henry Hyndman (1842–1921) and Henry Brailsford (1873–1958) lived at nos. 13 and 32 respectively. Marie Stopes, the birth control pioneer, came to no. 14 in 1909, and Max Beerbohm and John Masefield lived at nos. 12 and 13 respectively during the First World War. In 1917 D. H. Lawrence and Frieda stayed with their friends, the Radfords, also poets, at no. 32.[6] H. H. Asquith, later prime minister, lived at no. 12 Keats Grove from 1877 to 1887, contemporary with the philologist Henry Sweet (1845–1912) at no. 118 Heath Street from 1879 to 1887 and the newspaper owner Alfred Harmsworth, later Viscount Northcliffe (1865–1922), at no. 99 South End Road from 1882.[7] Gordon Craig (1872–1966), the stage designer, and Martin Shaw, the composer, shared rooms at no. 8 Downshire Hill c. 1900.[8]

By the First World War nearly all the available land had been built over, leaving room only for in-filling or rebuilding. Bartram Park had been demolished by 1915 and houses were built on the site after the war by Frederick Bristow.[9] Sir Edwin Lutyens extended Upper Terrace Lodge in the 1920s.[10] A house was built in Hampstead Grove in 1920, no. 15 Church Row was built to blend in with its 18th-century neighbours in 1924, and six neo-Georgian houses were built fronting Hampstead Grove (1936). Flats replaced some of the stables in Church (later Perrin's) Walk in 1934, a neo-Georgian studio, Richford Lodge, by Edward Maufe, was built in Admiral's Walk in 1931–2, and one house was built in Windmill Hill in 1937.[11]

On the newer estates two houses were squeezed into plots in Keats Grove in 1924, another was built on the north side and six were built on the south (Keats Close) in 1927, some early 19th-century houses in Downshire Hill made way for flats,[12] and a controversial façade by Michael Bunney was given to no. 13.[13] On the Carlile estate two houses were squeezed into Kemplay Road in 1927 and three replaced the library in Worsley Road in 1932. Howard Sugden was the main builder on the Greenhill estate, where three houses were built at the junction of Prince Arthur Road and Fitzjohn's Avenue in 1933, and seven at the junction of Ellerdale and

[93] P.R.O., RG 11/168/6/10/1.
[94] *C.H.R.* vii. 14.
[95] P.R.O., RG 11/168/6/11/1; 12/1; *D.N.B.*
[96] Oppé, *Hampstead, Lond. Town*, 36; *Kelly's Dir. Hampstead and Childs Hill* (1903).
[97] Thompson, *Hampstead*, 373.
[98] Ibid. 307–8.
[99] P.R.O., RG 11/168/7/9/1.
[1] Thompson, *Hampstead*, 301, 326; *Hampstead One Thousand*, 93–4.
[2] Thompson, *Hampstead*, 408, 410, 419.
[3] *C.H.R.* vii. 2–7.
[4] Ibid.; vi. 24–7; cf. O.S. Map 1/2,500, TQ 2685 (1970 edn.).

[5] Wade, *Streets of Hampstead*, 72–3.
[6] Ibid. 34, 36–7.
[7] Ibid. 56–7, 60.
[8] Ibid. 53.
[9] O.S. Map 1/2,500, Lond. XXVII, XXXVII (1896 edn.); I.16 (1915 edn.); D.S.R.
[10] Wade, *Streets of Hampstead*, 32.
[11] D.S.R. The 1936 hos. were described as Heathmount, Heath St. They backed on Heath St.
[12] Probably 1929–31, for which D.S.R. not available. No. 13A was blt. on site of demolished bldg. in 1935.
[13] *Hampstead in the Thirties, a Committed Decade*, exhib. 1974–5, catalogue (S.C.L.); *The Times*, 22 Nov. 1935, 11d; 6 Dec. 1935, 12c.

Arkwright roads and opposite, in Arkwright Road, between 1935 and 1937. Sir Clough Williams-Ellis (1883–1978), who from 1929 to 1939 lived at Romney's house, which he much altered, and enlarged Whitestone House (formerly the Lawn) in Whitestone Lane in 1934, also built the four houses of Ellerdale Close in 1934.[14] The largest and most obtrusive development was the Greenhill flats, which replaced the Wesleyan chapel at the corner of High Street and Prince Arthur Road in 1935.[15] Old buildings demolished included Norway House on the east side of High Street, replaced by a garage in 1931,[16] the early 19th-century Heath Cottage in South End Road in 1938,[17] and a row of cottages, replaced by nos. 1–3 Willow Road, built in reinforced concrete in 'the contemporary style in an uncompromising form' by Ernö Goldfinger in 1938.[18] A Tudor-style block of flats called Bellmoor replaced Barratt's 19th-century house in 1929.[19]

Institutions which took over private houses included ASLEF, the railway union, which in 1921 bought no. 9 Arkwright Road, the home from 1909 of the millionaire Sir Joseph Beecham.[20] In 1922 Queen Mary's maternity home replaced Upper Heath (formerly the Upper Flask) with a neo-Georgian building designed by B. Kitchin and F. Danby Smith.[21] In 1927 University College school replaced the 17th-century Holly Hill House, which it had occupied since the 1890s.[22] Hampstead Magistrates' Court was built in Downshire Hill next to the police station in 1934.[23]

Local opposition, led by Sir Gerald Du Maurier, prevented road-widening which would have destroyed the Mount in Heath Street, although it failed to preserve some of old Hampstead.[24] Smaller families and a lack of servants led to the conversion of several cottages into middle-class residences, while larger houses were abandoned or divided. Burgh House, for example, which had been occupied from 1925 to 1937 by a bank director and a diplomat, was thereafter empty. The wealthy tended to move to the newer districts or to 18th-century houses on the edge of the heath, leaving most of Hampstead town to flats, many of them shabby.[25] The faded gentility of the 1930s was caught by Vita Sackville-West in her novel, *All Passion Spent*. In 1930 the whole area between New End and Gayton Road east of High Street, and around Perrin's Court and Holly Bush Vale on the west, was occupied by 'skilled workers or similar', as was South End Green.[26] The worst slums lay to the east, in the Belsize part of South End Green, but George Orwell wrote dismissively of the locality of the bookshop over which he lived, at the corner of the green and Pond Street, in his semi-autobiographical *Keep the Aspidistra Flying* of 1936. Willow (Willowbed)

Road was 'not definitely slummy' but depressing; it 'contrived to keep up a kind of mingy, lower-middle class decency', and two-thirds of the houses advertised apartments. Keats Grove was satirized as Coleridge Grove: 'Literary associations of the wrong kind hung heavy upon it', and decaying early 19th-century houses, so highly desirable in the 1980s, had an atmosphere of outmoded 'culture'.[27] Ten years before, D. H. Lawrence, who had lodged at no. 30 Willoughby Road, had similarly shown 'how depressing and void he found the 18th-century charm of Hampstead'.[28]

In their reaction to conventional, 'establishment' Hampstead, Orwell and Lawrence were expressing a parallel local tradition, that of the avant-garde and usually politically left-wing intellectual, which became dominant in the 1930s and was especially associated with the Downshire Hill and Keats Grove area, as also with Belsize.[29] The movement was rooted in the early 20th century. Henry Woodd Nevinson (1856–1941), journalist and essayist, from a family resident in Rosslyn Hill House, lived in Keats Grove, where his son C. R. W. Nevinson (1889–1946), the painter, was born. Another journalist and essayist Robert Lynd (1879–1949) lived at no. 9 Gayton Road c. 1908 before he married a Hampstead poet, Sylvia Dryhurst; they lived at no. 14 Downshire Hill until 1918 and then at no. 5 Keats Grove until the 1930s, giving literary dinner parties attended by people like J. B. Priestley and Rose Macaulay.[30] Katherine Mansfield (1888–1923) and John Middleton Murry (1889–1957) lived from 1918 to 1921 at no. 17 East Heath Road, a house they called 'the Elephant'. Roger Fry (1866–1934), artist and art critic, was at no. 22 Willow Road from 1903 to c. 1908 and subsequently in Pond Street. Mark Gertler (1891–1939), the painter, worked at the Penn Studios behind no. 13 Rudall Crescent from 1915 to 1932 and at no. 1 Wellmount Studios from 1932 to 1933. He lodged in various houses: no. 41 Pilgrim's Lane, no. 19 Worsley Road (1926–30), no. 22 Kemplay Road (1932), and no. 53 Haverstock Hill (1933–6).[31] Gertler and Nevinson were among the artists who met at no. 14A Downshire Hill, which was used as studios during the First World War by the Carline family, who lived at no. 47 from 1914 to 1936. Hilda Carline married Stanley Spencer and her brother Richard (1896–1980), the painter and writer, was co-founder of the Hampstead Artists' Council in 1944. The house later became the headquarters of the Artists' Refugee Committee. Sir Roland Penrose (d. 1984), the art expert, who lived at no. 21 Downshire Hill from 1935 until 1939 and subsequently at no. 36, was also responsible for bringing refugees to Hampstead, including many expelled after the closure of the

[14] D.S.R.; Wade, *Streets of Hampstead*, 26, 45, 71.
[15] D.S.R.; Wade, *Streets of Hampstead*, 66.
[16] *The Times*, 31 Oct. 1974, 18h.
[17] Ibid. 23 Nov. 1938, 8e.
[18] D.S.R.; Pevsner, *Lond.* ii. 196–7; *Archit. of Lond.* 50; Wade, *Streets of Hampstead*, 49.
[19] *The Times*, 8 Oct. 1929, 11d; Oppé, *Hampstead, Lond. Town*, 6, 30.
[20] Wade, *Streets of Hampstead*, 70.
[21] Ibid. 60; Pevsner, *Lond.* ii. 192.
[22] D.S.R.; Wade, *Streets of Hampstead*, 25; below, educ.
[23] Wade, *Streets of Hampstead*, 55.
[24] *The Times*, 25 Mar. 1933, 4g; 27 July 1933, 17b; 22 Nov. 1935, 11d; 6 Dec. 1935, 12c.

[25] *C.H.R.* ii. 36; Thompson, *Hampstead*, 428; *New Lond. Life and Labour*, vi. 423.
[26] *New Lond. Life and Labour*, vii, maps 8, 10, 11.
[27] G. Orwell, *Keep the Aspidistra Flying* (1954), 10, 30, 83.
[28] Quoted in Wade, *Streets of Hampstead*, 50.
[29] Para. based on *Hampstead in the Thirties, a Committed Decade*; *Country Life*, 11 Nov. 1976, pp. 1420 sqq. For Belsize, below.
[30] Wade, *Streets of Hampstead*, 52–3; *Hampstead One Thousand*, 149–50; L. Macneice, *The Strings are False* (1965), 165.
[31] Wade, *Streets of Hampstead*, 46, 51; *Hampstead One Thousand*, 147, 150–1.

Bauhaus in 1933. In the 1930s a vigorous branch of the Left Book Club met in Keats Grove, where no. 4A housed the poets Geoffrey Grigson and then Louis Macneice (1907–63), and no. 7 Downshire Hill housed the writer Edwin Muir (1887–1959) and no. 35 the physicist J. D. Bernal (1901–71).[32] C. E. M. Joad (1891–1953), the writer and teacher, lived in an 'ugly but comfortable' house, no. 4 East Heath Road, which he shared during the war with Kingsley Martin, editor of the *New Statesman*.[33] Mary Llewelyn Davies, champion of the Women's Co-operative Guild, lived at no. 26 Well Walk from 1926 to 1935 and J. C. M. Garnett (1880–1958), the educationist, was at no. 21.[34]

Others who lived in Hampstead town during the period between the wars included the writer Salvador de Madariaga (1886–1978) at no. 14 Willoughby Road from 1916 to 1921, the Egyptologist Sir Flinders Petrie (1853–1942) at no. 5 Cannon Place from 1919 to 1935, and the writers John Galsworthy (1867–1933) at Grove Lodge in Admiral's Walk from 1918, Eleanor Farjeon (1881–1965) at no. 20 Perrin's Walk from 1920, and Mary Webb (1881–1927) at no. 12 Hampstead Grove from 1923.[35] E. V. Knox (1881–1971), editor of *Punch*, was at no. 34 Well Walk from 1922 to 1945, and there were two more generations of Du Mauriers, Sir Gerald (1873–1934), the actor-manager, at Cannon Hall and his daughter Daphne, the novelist, at Cannon Cottage in Well Road in the 1930s.[36] Inhabitants in the 1930s included the writers J. B. Priestley, at no. 27 Well Walk and Evelyn Underhill (1875–1941) at no. 12 Hampstead Square,[37] the artist Charles Ginner (1878–1958), one of the founders of the Camden Town Group, at no. 61 High Street, and the cartoonist David Low (1891–1963), who had a studio at no. 13A Heath Street.[38] Among musicians were Sir Thomas Beecham (1879–1961) at the Bellmoor flats, Sir Arthur Bliss (1891–1975) at East Heath Lodge, and Sir William Walton (1902–83) at no. 10 Holly Place (Holly Berry Lane) c. 1939.[39] Actresses included Fay Compton (1894–1978) at no. 22 Well Walk, Flora Robson at no. 37 Downshire Hill after 1936, and Anna Neagle at no. 14 Holly Hill in the late 1930s.[40] Sir Geoffrey Harmsworth, Bt., the newspaper director, was at no. 1 Mount Vernon.[41]

Hampstead town suffered little from bombing during the Second World War. The worst damage was on 2 a. bounded by Well Walk, New End Square, and Christchurch Hill, where only five houses survived and casualties included the second

Long Room and ballroom.[42] In 1948 the council opened two blocks of 24 flats, called Carnegie House, designed by A. & J. Soutar, and built on a ½-a. site in New End previously occupied by a Baptist chapel and some 15 houses.[43] It then began to clear the bombed site, despite local opposition, leaving only Burgh House, surrounded by the various wings of Wells House, 64 'tactfully Georgianizing' municipal flats designed by C. H. James and opened in 1950.[44] The council built a few houses in Flask Walk and Kemplay Road in the 1950s[45] and Henderson Court, old people's flats, in Fitzjohn's Avenue in 1966.[46]

Most building was done in the 1960s and especially the 1970s by private developers. Mayer Hillman designed offices for the *Hampstead and Highgate Express* in Perrin's Court and Boissevain & Osmond no. 13 Admiral's Walk c. 1960.[47] Trinity Presbyterian church was pulled down in 1962 and replaced by nos. 1A–C Hampstead High Street and Essex Court. Ten years later the church hall fronting Willoughby Road was replaced by Trinity Close.[48] On the opposite side of High Street, Vane House and the orphanage of the Royal Soldiers' Daughters' Home were demolished between 1970 and 1972; the home moved to no. 65 and two closes were built, Vane with 21 houses and Mulberry with 12.[49] Ted Levy, Benjamin & Partners designed Kingswell, a double tier of shops, maisonettes, and offices around a pedestrian piazza at the junction of Heath Street and Back Lane in 1972.[50] The same firm was later responsible for Maryon Mews, small-scale brick housing at South End Green.[51] Off the eastern side of High Street Old Brewery Mews were designed by Dinerman, Davidson & Partners in 1973[52] and the 1¾-a. site of the Blue Star garage, formerly Norway House, was replaced after 1974 by Spencer Walk, a mixture of shops, flats, and studios by Ian Fraser and John Roberts.[53] On the west side in 1974 J. E. Jolly designed a post office to replace motor showrooms and offices.[54] In Flask Walk nos. 30–6 replaced the Salvation Army hall and in 1973 Gerson Rottenberg designed Lakis Close on the north side for a Greek developer.[55] In 1975 flats called Village Mount were built on the site of 19th-century flats in Perrin's Court, and Arthur West House, designed by Stefan Zins, was opened as a hostel at no. 79 Fitzjohn's Avenue.[56] In 1978 Pollard, Thomas & Edwards built Field Court for the council at the corner of Fitzjohn's Avenue and Arkwright Road and Michael Hopkins designed a 'stunning glass structure' at no. 49A Downshire Hill.[57] Houses built

[32] Wade, *Streets of Hampstead*, 53–4; *Hampstead One Thousand*, 112, 148, 151.
[33] Wade, *Streets of Hampstead*, 46.
[34] Ibid. 36.
[35] Ibid. 28–9, 44, 46, 50, 63.
[36] Ibid. 37, 39, 43.
[37] Ibid. 36, 44, 70.
[38] Ibid. 61, 65.
[39] Ibid. 30, 46.
[40] Ibid. 26, 36, 43, 54.   [41] Ibid. 29.
[42] *The Times*, 6 Nov. 1944, 5g; 8 Nov. 1944, 5d.
[43] Wade, *Streets of Hampstead*, 42; *Builder*, 15 Oct. 1948; S.C.L., H 711.13, Council Housing Reps., Hampstead Boro. *Rep. on Housing* (1948).
[44] *The Times*, 3 Nov. 1944, 5g; 15 Feb. 1945, 2d, 6; 22 June 1945, 2b; Pevsner, *Lond.* ii. 191; Wade, *Streets of Hampstead*, 34; Hampstead Boro. *Rep. on Housing* (1951).
[45] Wade, *Streets of Hampstead*, 40, 51.

[46] Ibid. 69; S.C.L., P.B. Housing, Camden Gen. file, MS. list of Camden housing est. (1971).
[47] Wade, *Streets of Hampstead*, 63–4; Saint, 'Hampstead Walk', 1.
[48] Wade, *Streets of Hampstead*, 50, 67.
[49] Ibid. 68–9; *H.H.E.*, 13 Feb. 1970; 1 May 1970; 24 Nov. 1972 (S.C.L., H 724.3 Vane Ho. file).
[50] Wade, *Streets of Hampstead*, 59; *The Times*, 13 July 1970.
[51] *Hampstead One Thousand*, 140, 143.
[52] Ibid. 143; Wade, *Streets of Hampstead*, 67.
[53] Wade, *Streets of Hampstead*, 66; *The Times*, 31 Oct. 1974, 18b.
[54] Wade, *Streets of Hampstead*, 66.
[55] Ibid. 40.
[56] Ibid. 63, 70.
[57] Ibid. 55, 70; *Hampstead One Thousand*, 141, 143; *Archit. of Lond.* 53.

in South Hill Park by architects for themselves were nos. 80–90 (even), 'good examples of the short-lived English brutalism', by Howell & Amis in 1956, no. 31 by Michael Brawn in 1961, and no. 78 by Brian Housden in 1968.[58]

Gentrification became much more prevalent after the Second World War. About 1955 the Communist party was complaining that speculators were buying up working-class houses. In 1964 old people were being given notice to quit, Georgian cottages were available only for the very rich, and the demand was extending to poor areas like New End Square and Flask Walk.[59] By 1975 ordinary small shops were being replaced by specialist shops in what by then was called Hampstead village, a conservation area.[60]

The retreat of the working classes left yet more houses for people prominent in the arts and entertainment. They included the artist David Bomberg (1890–1957) at no. 12 Rosslyn Hill and the art historian Kenneth Clark, later Baron Clark (1903–83), at Capo di Monte and then at Upper Terrace House in the 1940s[61] and many others in the 1950s.[62] The poet Edith Sitwell (1887–1964) lived in a flat in Greenhill from 1961 and died at no. 20 Keats Grove.[63] Other figures of the 1960s were the economist Thomas Balogh, Baron Balogh (1905–85), at Wellside, Well Walk, the politician Anthony Greenwood, Baron Greenwood of Rossendale (1911–83), at no. 38 Downshire Hill, and the architect Sir Frederick Gibberd (1908–83) at no. 49 Holford Road.[64] Residents in the 1970s included the politicians Sir Frank Soskice, later Lord Stow Hill (1902–79), at no. 19 Church Row, Norman St. John Stevas, and Timothy Wentworth Beaumont, Baron Beaumont of Whitley, and the writers Marghanita Laski, Kingsley Amis and Elizabeth Jane Howard,[65] John Le Carré, and Melvyn Bragg. Ben Nicholson, the painter, died at no. 2B Pilgrim's Lane in 1982[66] and John Braine, the novelist, in a basement room 'off Downshire Hill' in 1986. 'Boy George', the singer, had a home in Well Walk which was the centre of a drugs scandal in 1986.[67]

In 1905 the architect Thomas Graham Jackson, whose family lived in Upper Terrace, wrote that old Hampstead retained, with its shady groves, 'curious little steep alleys ending in flights of steps upwards or downwards, raised paths with white handrails, and some of the tiniest little band-boxes of houses that ever were seen, with miniature gardens in proportion'.[68] The same was true in 1986, especially of the area west of Heath Street. Much of the northern part on the east, Squire's Mount, Elm Row and Hampstead Square, and Well Walk, was similarly

unspoilt. In spite of redevelopment, many grand houses remained, some, like Fenton, Burgh, and Keats houses, open to the public. Former working-class streets like Back Lane and Flask Walk contained attractive residences and shops, while Downshire Hill, with its mixture of stuccoed classical and Gothick, had regained its original splendour.[69] Most recent changes have been sympathetic to the 18th- or early 19th-century houses. Even in High Street and Heath Street, full of boutiques, restaurants, and antique shops, the more garish style of shop-front has been avoided.[70] Most jarring notes are late 19th-century: the château-like National Institute for Biological Standards and Control (formerly Mount Vernon hospital), and the terracotta and red-brick flats in Church Row, otherwise virtually untouched, and Downshire Hill.

FROGNAL AND THE CENTRAL DEMESNE. Frognal was mentioned in the early 15th century as a customary tenement and in 1740 Frognal field was the eastern abutment of Northfield, part of the demesne.[71] By the 17th century there were several cottages and houses at Frognal;[72] by then the name probably indicated the road leading from the church and manor farm northward to the heath, between the demesne on the west and Hampstead town on the east. By the end of the 18th century the name also applied to the houses built on the site of the manor farm buildings in Frognal Lane, and by the mid 19th century to the northern part of the demesne. The road, Frognal, was extended southward in 1878.

The 15th-century tenement was probably the 'house called Frognal',[73] which lay on the west side of the road, probably on the site later occupied by Frognal House. There were two houses or cottages there by the beginning of the 18th century, held by brothers, John and Thomas Smith. Thomas, a bricklayer, had divided his into two.[74] All the property had passed to John Padmore, gentleman, of St. Giles-in-the-Fields by 1741, when he acquired waste near the house lately built there,[75] presumably Frognal House, no. 99 Frognal.[76] In 1762 the estate, which also included Upper Frognal Lodge (no. 103) and a pair of houses to the south, was held by Padmore's nephew John Padmore Perry (d. 1764).[77] Another house, on the east side of the road, was leased by a London draper, Charles Purrett, to Robert James in 1616. It was occupied by John Towse (d. 1645) and by a London goldsmith Richard Hodilow (d. 1698).[78] It was assessed for 16 hearths in 1664 and was rebuilt c. 1700 and, with additions, is identifiable with the Mansion or Old Mansion (no. 94), a nine-bayed brick house.[79] Two more

[58] Archit. of Lond. 50–2.
[59] S.C.L., H 331.833 Housing file, Hampstead Communist party, Homes for Hampstead [c. 1955]; Guardian, 30 May 1964.
[60] Camden Boro. Plan, Hampstead and Belsize Area, Spr. 1975, Area 4.
[61] Wade, Streets of Hampstead, 31, 53, 68.
[62] Ibid. 30, 51, 73.
[63] Ibid. 42, 56.
[64] Ibid. 36, 39, 45, 54–5.
[65] Ibid. 40, 43–4, 52, 71–2; S.C.L., cuttings.
[66] Ibid. 50, 52.
[67] Lond. Standard, 29 Oct. 1986; S.C.L., cuttings.
[68] Quoted in Saint, 'Hampstead Walk', 1.
[69] Illus. in Wade, Streets of Hampstead, 47.
[70] Photo. exhib. at Burgh Ho.
[71] W.A.M. 32356–7.

[72] e.g. G.L.R.O., E/MW/H/3 (1637); 4 (1649); 8 (1685); 10 (1691).
[73] All other property was described as 'at Frognal'.
[74] G.L.R.O., E/MW/H/I/2311A; M.M. & M., Lib. A, pp. 34, 203; B, p. 276; P.R.O., C 7/257/21; C 10/444/59.
[75] M.M. & M., Lib. C, pp. 1–2; D, pp. 93–5.
[76] S.C.L., Man. Map and Fieldbk. no. 424; Pevsner, Lond. ii. 199.
[77] S.C.L., Man. Map and Fieldbk. nos. 423, 426; M.M. & M., Lib. D, pp. 93–5; E, p. 73; Barratt, Annals, iii. 300.
[78] P.R.O., C 2/Jas. I/P7/10; G.L.R.O., G/MW/H/2 (1636); 7 (1680); M.M. & M., Lib. A, p. 298; C, pp. 3–5; Topographer and Genealogist, ed. J. G. Nichols, ii. 54–8.
[79] G.L.R.O., MR/TH/2, m. 30; S.C.L., Man. Map and Fieldbk. no. 408; Pevsner, Lond. ii. 199; S.C.L., Town and Country Planning, 52nd List of Bldgs. (1974); below, plate 28.

houses had been built on the estate by 1731[80] and another one by 1762, when the property was held by Richard Westfield or Wastfield (d. 1765) of Lincoln's Inn.[81] Other 16th- or 17th-century buildings included three cottages, on the east side of the road, which were converted to a coach house and workhouse by 1729.[82] Nearby, at the southern junction with Mount Vernon, Grove Cottage (no. 110) has been dated to the 17th century, with the adjoining no. 108 slightly later.[83] An early inn, called successively the Three Pigeons, Pilgrim, and Duke of Cumberland's Head, stood in front of, but was not identifiable with, nos. 108 and 110.[84] By the mid 1740s[85] there were two houses at the southern end of Frognal. Set back from the road in $1\frac{1}{2}$ a., adjoining the churchyard, was Frognal Hall, which probably existed by 1646 and can be identified with the attorney-general's house visited by Pepys in 1668.[86] It may have been rebuilt by the architect Isaac Ware, who owned it from 1759 to 1765.[87] The southernmost house was that later called Priory Lodge, opposite Frognal Lane, which has been identified with the 'small house just beyond the church', alluded to by Samuel Johnson, where his wife lodged for the country air according to Boswell and where Johnson wrote most of the *Vanity of Human Wishes*, published in 1749.[88] Barton Booth, Robert Wilks, and Colley Cibber may have had summer lodgings at Frognal, though probably not, as stated in 1816, in the workhouse building.[89]

On the west side of Frognal only the estate associated with Frognal House was ancient copyhold, the rest being either ancient demesne to the south or waste, part of the heath, to the north. In 1741 the architect Henry Flitcroft (1697–1769) acquired from Thomas Watson-Wentworth, earl of Malton, a house dating from 1700 or earlier on what was then heath, a coach house and stable and another cottage, and himself obtained further grants of adjoining waste, including the lime walk illustrated by William Collins.[90] He probably built Frognal (later Montagu) Grove on the site (nos. 105 and 107); no. 109 was formed from the stabling.[91] Flitcroft is also credited with building the house to the north, variously called Bleak Hall, Judges Bench House, and

Branch Hill Lodge.[92] On pieces of waste next to Northwood well, buildings had been erected by a lessee, Henry Popple, between 1731 and 1739. They included a house by 1745, when the property passed to Thomas, later Sir Thomas, Clarke (d. 1764), Master of the Rolls.[93] In 1762, therefore, there were 16 copyhold houses in Frognal. A pair of cottages (nos. 104 and 106) was evidently built soon afterwards.[94]

Many important lawyers lived in late 18th-century Frognal. From 1772 until 1794 or later Frognal Grove was the home of Edward Montagu, master in Chancery,[95] and from *c.* 1810 to 1813 of Richard Richards, chief justice of Chester.[96] Branch Hill Lodge was left by Clarke in 1764 to his patron Thomas Parker, earl of Macclesfield (d. 1795), who leased it to Thomas Walker, Master in Chancery, and then to Lord Loughborough, who lived there before he moved to Belsize in 1792.[97] Stephen Guyon (d. 1779), a merchant, lived in Frognal Hall, which by 1791 was the home of Sir Richard Pepper Arden (1745–1804), Master of the Rolls, later Lord Alvanley and Lord Chief Justice of the Common Pleas. He was leased 6 a. of adjacent demesne land, part of which he later bought and all of which was occupied by his widow for some years.[98]

In 1792 Frognal was praised for its 'salubrity of air and soil, in the neighbourhood of pleasure and business'.[99] As early as 1762 some 43 a. of demesne were leased to copyhold tenants who used them as pleasure grounds.[1] In 1674 the manor house was leased to a Londoner, Benoni Honywood, who occupied it for only six weeks a year, subletting the land and part of the house.[2] From 1757 and probably earlier the manor house was divided and although one half was used as a farmhouse, the other may always have been a dwelling house detached from the farmland.[3] By 1774 the eastern part, leased to John Foster, had been made by him into two distinct houses, each with its own stabling.[4] Foster lived in one until 1783, when the two were converted into a single house, occupied from 1785 until 1803 by the Revd. Charles Grant (d. 1811), the curate, and, after the manorial court met there in 1802, was called the Manor House.[5] In 1785 the western part

[80] M.M. & M., Lib. C, pp. 38–9.
[81] Ibid. Lib. E, p. 129; S.C.L., Man. Map and Fieldbk. nos. 406–7.
[82] S.C.L., Man. Map and Fieldbk. nos. 414, 416–17; M.M. & M., Lib. F, pp. 15–16, 44; *Hampstead One Thousand*, 85; below, local govt.
[83] Pevsner, *Lond.* ii. 199; S.C.L., Town and Country Planning, 52nd List of Bldgs. (1974).
[84] S.C.L., Man. Map and Fieldbk. nos. 410–12; G.L.R.O., MR/LV3/104; LV4/28; *Hampstead One Thousand*, 154; Wade, *Streets of Hampstead*, 16.
[85] Rocque, *Map of Lond.* (1741–5).
[86] Below, Man. and other est. (Jacksfield).
[87] S.C.L., Man. Map and Fieldbk. nos. 427–8; M.M. & M., Lib. C, p. 117; D, p. 438; E, p. 126; Park, *Hampstead*, 341.
[88] S.C.L., Man. Map and Fieldbk. no. 429? [no. missing on map]; J. Boswell, *Life of Johnson* (1969), 137, 169; *Trans. Hampstead Antiq. and Hist. Soc.* (1899), 24; Park, *Hampstead*, 334.
[89] Brewer, *Beauties of Eng. & Wales*, x(4), 198.
[90] M.M. & M., Lib. E, pp. 293–4; G.L.R.O., E/MW/H, old no. Box L; Wade, *Streets of Hampstead*, 17; *Complete Peerage*, s.v. Malton.
[91] S.C.L., Man. Map and Fieldbk. nos. 418–22; S.C.L., Town and Country Planning, 52nd List of Bldgs. (1974); Pevsner, *Lond.* ii. 199; *Images of Hampstead*, 56.

[92] Barratt, *Annals*, ii. 74–5.
[93] M.M. & M., Lib. B, p. 22; C, pp. 18–22, 214; D, p. 37; E, p. 129; S.C.L., Man. Map and Fieldbk. no. 278.
[94] S.C.L., Town and Country Planning, 52nd List of Bldgs. (1974).
[95] G.L.R.O., E/MW/H/I/2178; Hist. MSS. Com. 43, *15th Rep. VII, Ailesbury*, pp. 251, 261–2.
[96] Park, *Hampstead*, 337–9; poor rate bks. 1810–15.
[97] Park, *Hampstead*, 272; G.L.R.O., E/MW/H/I/2178.
[98] M.L.R. 1806/2/484–8; Park, *Hampstead*, 341, 355; S.C.L., Man. Fieldbk. no. m.
[99] G.L.R.O., E/MW/H, old no. 27/15 (sales parts. 1792).
[1] Most (33½ a.) was leased to Thos. Clarke of Branch Hill Lodge: S.C.L., Man. Map and Fieldbk. nos. m–o, t–bb.
[2] G.L.R.O., Cal. Mdx. Sess. Bks. v (1673–7), 41–2.
[3] Edw. Snoxell jr. held on lease all the ho. and Hall Oak and Belsize farms in 1729 but may have sublet part: S.C.L., D 25. In 1757 Wm. Bovingdon leased both farms and the man. ho. except part once let to Snoxell: G.L.R.O., E/MW/H, old no. 31/8 (lease 1757). In 1762 Snoxell occupied E. part of ho. and bldgs., Bovingdon the W.: S.C.L., Man. Map and Fieldbk. nos. a, e (Snoxell); A, E (Bovenden, *sic*). And see G.L.R.O., E/MW/H, old no. 31/8 (leases 1769, 1772). [4] G.L.R.O., E/MW/H/I/1938.
[5] Poor rate bks. 1774–1804; G.L.R.O., E/MW/H/I/ 2276/29.

of the very dilapidated manor house was leased to Thomas Pool on condition that he carried out considerable repairs.[6] Pool probably began work on the eastern end, apparently preserving the carcase of the old building; he borrowed £300 from the lord of the manor; which perhaps led to an inscription on a datestone, 'erected by Sir T. S. Wilson bt. 1785'.[7] Two houses had been built by 1797: no. 23, which was occupied from 1798 by John Ogilvie, an army agent who spent heavily on completing the building, which he leased directly from 1801[8] until his bankruptcy in 1804,[9] and the house to the west of it, later nos. 19 and 21 Frognal Lane. Pool himself occupied the western house and at great expense had completed it by 1800 when he sold it to George Stacey, a Holborn chemist, who then obtained a direct lease from the lord.[10] Pool moved to 'another messuage opposite' on which he spent money between 1798 and 1800 and which was presumably no. 40 Frognal Lane, later called Manor Lodge after the manorial courts held there.[11] In 1810 Pool (d. 1813) was leased the house with its surrounding 5 a. and outbuildings on the southern side of Frognal Lane, formerly occupied by farm buildings only.[12]

John Metcalf, who bought no. 23 in 1804, also acquired some 27 a. of demesne land leased to Ogilvie, on which by 1806 he built a 'new white house', later called Frognal Park, set well back from Frognal Lane, north-west of the other houses.[13] Frognal Park, in parkland and possibly the largest of the Frognal houses, passed in 1809 to Joseph Blunt, a solicitor, and between 1826 and 1831 to John F. Menet,[14] whose widow Louisa subleased the estate in 1849 to Henry Hucks Gibbs, a merchant.[15] Metcalf subleased no. 23 in 1805 to Jeremy Bentham's brother Sir Samuel (1757–1831), naval architect and engineer, who had superintended shipbuilding in Russia, where he had been made a general. He obtained a direct lease in 1813 but left England again in 1814;[16] the house was empty in 1820. In the mid 1820s it was occupied by John Innos and during the 1830s by Miss Anne Hetherington.[17] It was leased to Henry B. Fearon, a wine merchant and one of the founders of London University, in 1841 and occupied throughout the 1850s and most of the 1860s by his widow.[18]

Between 1810 and 1814 a timber cottage, later called Manor Cottage, was built on the south side of Frognal Lane, east of Manor Lodge.[19] It was mostly occupied by undertenants of the demesne farm, including a newsman of Tottenham Court Road in 1817,[20] a New Bond Street hatter in 1851[21] and the manorial bailiff in 1872–3.[22] In 1815 Manor Lodge was occupied by John Thompson (d. 1843), a retired auctioneer, called Memory Thompson for his phenomenal knowledge of London. In 1817 he relinquished the house and c. 4 a. of the 8 a. of demesne leased to him, which were leased, together with the demesne farmland, to William Baker in 1819 and Robert Stone, a Marylebone stablekeeper, in 1834. The house was sublet and from 1843 to 1871[23] was occupied by George Chater, a wholesale stationer, who obtained a direct lease in 1848 and extended the house in 1849.[24] Thompson retained 4 a. on which he had built a new house by 1818, called by 1834 the Priory or Frognal Priory. He had added a lodge by 1820.[25] The house, on an elevated site with extensive views, had Gothic crenellations, Renaissance windows, Dutch gables, turrets, and a cupola. It was filled with furniture claimed by Thompson to have belonged to Cardinal Wolsey and Elizabeth I and drew many visitors.[26] Thompson was still the occupier in 1840 but by 1851 the house had passed, under his will, to Barnard Gregory (1796–1852), editor of the *Satirist*, whose title was successfully disputed by Thompson's relations, the McCullochs.[27]

On the northern side of Frognal Lane the Manor House, later no. 59 Frognal, was occupied from 1804 to 1817 by Thomas Norton Longman (1771–1842), the publisher, whose father lived in Mount Grove.[28] The house changed hands several times until it was occupied 1834–41 by Robert M. Kerrison, a doctor[29] and 1842–81 by Matthew Thomas Husband, a leather merchant from Regent's Park, who rebuilt it probably soon after he took the lease.[30] William Carr, a solicitor to the Excise, replaced George Stacey at nos. 19 and 21 Frognal Lane in 1807, obtained a

---

[6] G.L.R.O., E/MW/H, old no. 31/8 (lease 1798). Cf. estimate of repairs needed: ibid. old no. 33/16 (Notes 1783–4).
[7] Ibid. E/MW/H/I/2280. The payment of £3 4s. 6d. for 'taking down the manor house' was presumably for only a partial dismantling.
[8] Ibid. old no. 31/8 (leases 1798, 1801); poor rate bks. 1796–1804.
[9] S.C.L., D 228.
[10] G.L.R.O., E/MW/H, old no. 31/8 (lease 1800).
[11] Ibid.
[12] Ibid. old no. 31/9 (lease 1810). Pool was rated for all his prop. in a lump sum. Only in 1814, after his d., was the ho. rated separately: poor rate bks. 1800–14.
[13] Poor rate bks. 1803–20; G.L.R.O., E/MW/H, old no. 21/18 (rental 1820).
[14] Poor rate bks. 1808–34; G.L.R.O., P81/JN 1/14/10; Thompson, *Hampstead*, 120.
[15] P.R.O., HO 107/674/12; G.L.R.O., E/MW/H, old no. 31/3 (lease 1839; covenant to sublease 1849).
[16] G.L.R.O., E/MW/H, old no. 31/8 (dorse of lease 1801); poor rate bks. 1805–14; *D.N.B.* Fam. lived in Hampstead ho. 1807–14: B. D. Jackson, *Geo. Bentham* (1906), 6.
[17] Poor rate bks. 1815–34; G.L.R.O., P81/JN1/14/10; *Pigot's Dir. Mdx.* (1840); Thompson, *Hampstead*, 120.
[18] G.L.R.O., E/MW/H, old no. 31/3 (lease 1841); P.R.O., HO 107/1492/3; ibid. RG 9/92/10; W. Howitt,

Northern Heights of Lond. (1869), 152.
[19] G.L.R.O., E/MW/H, old no. 31/9 (lease 1810; agreement to lease 1814).
[20] Ibid. 31/1 (agreement to let 1817).
[21] Ibid. 31/4 (lease 1851).
[22] Ibid. 26/4 (lease 1873); poor rate bks. 1872–3.
[23] Poor rate bks. 1814–71; G.L.R.O., E/MW/H, old no. 31/1 (agreement to let 1817); 31/9 (lease 1819); 31/2 (lease 1834; consent to underlet 1834); 38/17/17; B.L., Potter Colln. 19/84.
[24] G.L.R.O., E/MW/H, old no. 31/2 (letter by Stone 1848); 31/3 (lease 1848); P.R.O., HO 107/1492/13; D.S.R.
[25] G.L.R.O., E/MW/H, old no. 31/9 (lease 1819); 21/18 (rental 1820); poor rate bks. 1815–20.
[26] Howitt, *Northern Heights*, 152; *Images of Hampstead*, 54–5; Thompson, *Hampstead*, 120–1.
[27] *Pigot's Dir. Mdx.* (1840); P.R.O., HO 107/1492/13; H.H.E. 8 Aug. 1874 (cutting in G.L.R.O., E/MW/H, old no. 26/46); *D.N.B.* s.v. Gregory.
[28] Poor rate bks. 1804–17; P. Wallis, *At the Sign of the Ship 1724–1974* (1974), 15; above, Hampstead town.
[29] Poor rate bks. 1817–20, 1826–34; *Pigot's Dir. Mdx.* (1840); P.R.O., HO 107/674/12.
[30] G.L.R.O., E/MW/H, old no. 31/3 (lease 1842); 31/4 (lease 1863); P.R.O., HO 107/1492/13; ibid. RG 9/92/10; RG 10/192/12; RG 11/167/7/1B; Baines, *Rec. Hampstead*, 547.

direct lease in 1812, and lived there until 1829 or later.[31] Carr, with his large and sociable family, entertained Joanna Baillie and Maria Edgeworth. The latter often stayed with the family several times between 1819 and 1822, in a 'delightful airy bedchamber' with a bow window.[32] From 1833 to 1841 the house was occupied by James Gordon Murdoch.[33] In 1841 the house, with 6 a. of grounds, was leased to William James Ferguson, who assigned the lease in 1845 to Robert Prance (d. 1869),[34] a stockbroker and magistrate.[35]

A cottage called the Salt Box was built on demesne land on the edge of the heath north of Branch Hill Lodge between 1789 and 1808[36] and was replaced by a house called the Grange probably by 1834.[37] In 1799 the earl of Macclesfield's son sold Branch Hill Lodge to a wealthy merchant, Thomas Neave, who became a baronet in 1814. Neave enlarged the house, which he filled with stained glass from convents plundered during the French Revolution in addition to the glass taken from the Chicken House.[38] To his 4 a. of copyhold land Neave added 9 a. of demesne freehold, which he purchased in 1807 and 1815; he was leased another 21½ a. of demesne from 1808.[39] He sold Branch Hill Lodge, which later briefly housed Lord Byron's widow and was purchased with 14 a. in 1867 by a city wine merchant, and built two houses to the west on former demesne land, Oak Hill Lodge, where he was living by 1840, and Oak Hill House. He later moved to his family seat at Dagnam Park, Romford, taking his glass collection with him,[40] and the Frognal estate passed to his third son Sheffield Neave, a director of the Bank of England, possibly as part of Sheffield's marriage settlement in 1851.[41] By 1850, however, Sheffield was already associated with a local builder, Thomas Clowser, in building two houses in Branch Hill field, possibly Sandfield Lodge and another large house on the borders of the Neave estate, near the Grange, which existed by 1870. Clowser built another 10 in the next two years in what he called Oak Hill Park estate after the new road running from Frognal to Oak Hill House and Lodge.[42] George Smith (1824–1901), founder of the *Dictionary of National Biography*, lived from 1863 to 1872 in Oak Hill Lodge, where he entertained leading writers and artists. Florence Nightingale was a frequent visitor to Oak Hill Park, where Manley Hopkins, an authority on maritime law, lived in the 1850s with his family, including Gerard, the future poet.[43] The actor-manager Herbert Beerbohm Tree (1852–1917) later lived at the Grange which he left in 1891 because of the difficulties of travel to 'such a remote country spot'.[44]

There were few changes in old Frognal. The dilapidated old workhouse was taken down soon after 1800.[45] Between 1819 and 1844 John Hodgson considerably enlarged Priory Lodge with a bay-windowed extension[46] and on the west side, north of the demesne houses, Bay Tree Cottage existed by 1841.[47] In 1811 Frognal was a 'hamlet of handsome residences', surrounded by groves and gardens 'of an extent begrudged by builders in these modern days'.[48] In 1824 arguments against the proposed new road made particular reference to the houses occupied by Carr, Blunt, Innes (*sic*), and Thompson, the few gentlemen's houses valued for their privacy and the views which they or their grounds commanded.[49] When the Finchley Road was built through the middle of the demesne between 1826 and 1835, it destroyed the exclusivity and converted the farmland into ripe building land, which the lord of the manor, Sir Thomas Maryon Wilson, was eager to exploit. He was thwarted by the will of his father, Sir Thomas (d. 1821), which left him unable to grant building leases, and by local defenders of the heath who opposed his private bills.[50] The demesne became available only after his death in 1869, when building was further delayed, mainly because the new lord Sir John (d. 1876) and his son Spencer needed to resolve their differences in order to break the terms of the entail. In 1873 they agreed to divide the estate, allocating to Spencer frontages along Finchley Road, and on two proposed new roads, Priory Road and Fitzjohn's Avenue, on all of which it was planned to build, and land in the north. Apart from Spencer, whose grandiose plans ultimately prevailed in Fitzjohn's Avenue, the main influence in shaping the estate was F. J. Clark, the land agent who advised the Maryon Wilsons to build the main roads and sewers themselves and to release the land for building in an orderly manner.[51]

Some of the earliest building on the demesne estate was along Finchley Road.[52] To the south, building was already completed on the St. John's Wood estate up to the boundary with the Maryon Wilson estate. Much of the demesne west of Finchley Road was occupied by railways, with a station called Finchley Road opened on each of the three lines, in 1860, 1869, and 1879, respectively.[53] In 1872 Holy Trinity church was built on the east side of Finchley Road on a site given by Sir John Maryon Wilson[54] and six cottages were built in 1873 on the Finchley Road brickfield, which had been leased to

[31] Poor rate bks. 1806–29; G.L.R.O., E/MW/H, old no. 21/8 (rental 1820).
[32] *Maria Edgeworth, Letters from Eng. 1813–44*, ed. C. Colvin (1971), pp. xxii, 189–91, 300, 303, 315.
[33] Poor rate bks. 1833–4; P.R.O., HO 107/674/12.
[34] G.L.R.O., E/MW/H, old no. 31/3 (lease 1841); 26/86 (consent to assign lease 1845); tombstone in chyd.: inf. from Dr. Stella Tristram.
[35] P.R.O., HO 107/1492/13; ibid. RG 9/92/10.
[36] G.L.R.O., E/MW/H/I/2280; H, old no. 31/8 (lease 1808).
[37] Ibid. H, old no. 21/18 (rental 1820); poor rate bk. 1834; O.S. Map 1/2,500, Lond. VII (1870 edn.).
[38] Park, *Hampstead*, 272; G.L.R.O., E/MW/H/I/2178; Burke, *Peerage* (1904), s.v. Neave.
[39] G.L.R.O., E/MW/H, old nos. 31/7 (sale 1807); 33/7 (release 1815); 31/1 (lease 1808).
[40] Thompson, *Hampstead*, 129; Barratt, *Annals*, i. 107; i. 77; *The Times*, 8 May 1867, 6e.

[41] S.C.L., D 228–9; Burke, *Peerage* (1904), s.v. Neave.
[42] D.S.R.; O.S. Map 1/2,500, Lond. VII (1870 edn.).
[43] *D.N.B.*; Barratt, *Annals*, iii. 30, 301; Wade, *Streets of Hampstead*, 18.
[44] Wade, *Streets of Hampstead*, 24; G.L.R.O., E/MW/H, old no. Locker 24 (rental 1890–1900).
[45] Below, local govt.
[46] Barratt, *Annals*, i. 259; E. F. Oppé, *Hampstead, Lond. Town* (1951), 39. [47] P.R.O., HO 107/674/12.
[48] Abraham, quoted in *Images of Hampstead*, 56.
[49] Quoted in Thompson, *Hampstead*, 120.
[50] Thompson, *Hampstead*, 130, 132–8, 181; below, Hampstead Heath.
[51] Thompson, *Hampstead*, 308–10, 323; V. Cedar, 'Urban Development in Camden 1840–90' (TS. thesis, 1978, in S.C.L.).
[52] Thompson, *Hampstead*, 323.
[53] Above, communications.
[54] Wade, *More Streets*, 67; below, churches.

John Culverhouse in 1871.[55] Holy Trinity Vicarage was built in 1877 and a skating rink in 1880, and 29 houses and at least five shops were built in Finchley Road from Swiss Cottage northward in the early 1880s and another 19 houses at the end of the decade. In 1891 another five shops were built and five houses altered into shops; the Midland Railway built six coal offices.[56]

Spencer Maryon Wilson's second area of development was in the south-west, where it joined the Upton and Cotton estates. Land was exchanged between the Maryon Wilson estate and Col. Cotton and Priory Road, extending northward from the Upton estate, was begun in 1874.[57] Plots were for sale in Priory (then called Canfield) Road in 1875[58] and 51 mostly detached houses were built between 1877 and 1882.[59]

As early as 1871 F. J. Clark had suggested a new road direct to Hampstead and in 1872 Spencer Maryon Wilson was hoping to create a 'truly imposing road'. In 1875 he contracted with John Culverhouse, who since 1871 had been the tenant at will of the two main demesne farms, to make Fitzjohn's Avenue, from College Crescent off Finchley Road to Greenhill Road, and to plant ornamental trees. Most of the building land on either side was let under a single agreement to Herbert and Edward Kelly, speculative builders, although some plots were sold to individuals who commissioned architects.[60] Applications to build 70 houses in Fitzjohn's Avenue were made between 1877 and 1879; nos. 45 and 61 were built in 1878, the latter a low building with Dutch gables, designed by Richard Norman Shaw for the fashionable painter Edwin Long (1829–91). No. 47, designed by George Lethbridge, dated from 1880, as did nos. 53 and 55 (the Tower), which had 25 rooms; no. 6 (Three Gables) was built in 1881 by Shaw for the portrait painter Frank Holl (1845–88). In 1883 no. 1 (Oakwood Hall) was designed by J. J. Stevenson in red brick in a neo-Dutch style and a drill hall was built for the Hampstead Volunteers near the junction with College Crescent.[61]

Spencer Maryon Wilson's insistence on a tree-lined boulevard with large houses proved to be justified. Fitzjohn's Avenue was compared with Paris and was described by *Harpers* magazine in 1883 as 'one of the noblest streets in the world'. Its early inhabitants included Lloyds underwriters, shipowners, auctioneers, silk manufacturers, a wine merchant, a director of Hull Docks, an Arctic explorer, and an Islamic scholar. It was particularly popular with successful artists, who included John Pettie (1839–93) at the Lothians and Paul Falconer

Poole (1807–79)[62] at Uplands (no. 75), built by T. K. Green and described as 'elephantine Gothic with bargeboarded gables'.[63] The artists' houses were opened on Show Sunday, attracting, according to the novelist Sir Max Pemberton (1863–1950),who lived at no. 56, those who 'should have been a source of inspiration . . . to the makers of fashion-plates'. Another resident was the author James Cotter Morison (1832–88), who entertained Henry James and George Meredith at no. 30.[64]

The last of the areas of demesne land allocated to Spencer Maryon Wilson in 1873 was in the north, bordering the heath and the Branch Hill and Oak Hill estates.[65] Seven houses were built at Branch Hill between 1873 and 1877, most of them on land belonging to Basil Woodd Smith of Branch Hill Lodge, where there had been rebuilding to S. S. Teulon's designs in 1868.[66] They probably included Combe Edge in Oak Hill Way, an old footpath from Branch Hill to Oak Hill Park, which was built in 1874 and first owned by the author Elizabeth Rundle Charles (1828–96), and Oak Tree House, Redington Gardens, designed in 1874 by Basil Champneys for Henry Holiday (1839–1927), the stained-glass painter, on land at Branch Hill Park.[67] Another house was built in Oak Hill Park in 1873.[68] Probably the success of those houses prompted the construction on Spencer's demesne land of Redington Road, a long road curving from Frognal round Oak Hill Park to the northern part of West Heath Road. In 1875 land was offered in lots at the Frognal end. In 1876 nos. 2 and 4, 'a wonderfully subtle pair', were designed by Philip Webb and no. 6, 'unrepentantly Gothic', by T. K. Green as St. John's Vicarage. No. 12 (Wellesley House), 'curiously old-fashioned Italianate', was built in 1878. Building thereafter was slow, no. 35 (Redington Lodge) by Horace Field being built in 1887 and no. 16 (One Oak) designed by A. H. Mackmurdo in 1889. Among those who lived in the road was the sculptor Sir Hamo Thornycroft (1850–1925) at no. 16.[69] John Lewis (d. 1928), the store owner, had built Spedan Tower, a large house, on the site of Sandfield Lodge by 1889.[70]

From the late 1870s building spread beyond Spencer Maryon Wilson's allocation on the demesne lands. The first major development was in the south-west, which lack of height and the vicinity of Kilburn made less desirable and houses were middle-class but more crowded than those farther north or east.[71] Several roads, named after Maryon Wilson estates in other counties, ran from Finchley Road to Priory Road, linking with roads on the Cotton estate. Building began from the east end with 20 houses by Charles Kellond in Goldhurst Terrace, the most

55 D.S.R.; Cedar, 'Urban Dev.'.
56 D.S.R.
57 Thompson, *Hampstead*, 319–20.
58 G.L.R.O., E/MW/H, old no. 27/15 (sales parts. 1875).
59 D.S.R.; Stanford, *Libr. Map of Lond.* (1891 edn.), sheet 5.
60 Thompson, *Hampstead*, 308, 313, 317–18; G.L.R.O., E/MW/H, old no. 27/15 (sales parts. 1875); Cedar, 'Urban Dev.'.
61 Wade, *More Streets*, 69–70; Pevsner, *Lond.* ii. 202; *Hampstead One Thousand*, 83, 86; A. Saint, *Ric. Norman Shaw* (1976), 158–9, 418, 425; *Archit. of Lond.* 47; *Building News*, 18 Feb. 1881 (Potter Colln. 19/134); below, plate 18.
62 Thompson, *Hampstead*, 312; Cedar, 'Urban Dev.';

Wade, *More Streets*, 68–9; *D.N.B.*
63 Pevsner, *Lond.* ii. 202.
64 Wade, *More Streets*, 69–70; *D.N.B.*
65 Cedar, 'Urban Dev.'.
66 Wade, *Streets of Hampstead*, 33; D.S.R.; Pevsner, *Lond.* ii. 199.
67 Wade, *Streets of Hampstead*, 18, 21; *C.H.R.* vi. 24–7; *D.N.B.*   68 D.S.R.
69 Ibid.; G.L.R.O., E/MW/H, old no. 27/15 (sales parts. 1875); Saint, 'Hampstead Walk', 1; Wade, *Streets of Hampstead*, 20–1; Thompson, *Hampstead*, 323; *D.N.B.*; below, plate 16.
70 *Kelly's Dir. Hampstead and Highgate* (1889–90); Wade, *Streets of Hampstead*, 22.
71 Thompson, *Hampstead*, 319–20.

southerly of the roads, in 1879 and another 50 there between 1880 and 1885; 101 houses, some flats, and a riding school were added between 1886 and 1900, mostly by T. K. Wells of Kentish Town. The middle road was Canfield Gardens, where six houses were built in 1881, 30 between 1885 and 1886, mansion flats in 1886 and 1889, and three shops in 1897. The northern road, near the Metropolitan railway line, was Broadhurst Gardens, where 116 houses were built between 1882 and 1894. Fairhazel Gardens (originally called North End Road) crossed the three roads to link with Loudoun Road in St. John's Wood; five houses were built there in 1879 and 1881 and another 31 houses and three blocks of flats between 1886 and 1896. Eleven stables and six houses were built in Canfield Place, backing on Finchley Road station, in 1884–5 by Ernest Estcourt and James Dixon, who also, with Wells, built Canfield and Greencroft gardens, which by 1891 reached Fairhazel Gardens from its eastern junction with Goldhurst Terrace; some 68 houses and Rutland House flats were built in Greencroft Gardens, after 1891 extended to Priory Road, between 1886 and 1897. Compayne Gardens, which extended from its eastern junction with Canfield Gardens, reached Fairhazel Gardens by 1891 and Priory Road by 1913; 77 houses and three blocks of flats were built there between 1886 and 1894 by local builders, James Tomblin and E. Michael. Tomblin also built most of the 29 houses erected between 1893 and 1897 in Aberdare Gardens, the last road in the area, which ran from its western junction with Goldhurst Terrace to Fairhazel Gardens. Building was complete throughout the area by 1913.[72] Except the mews Canfield Place, which was 'fairly comfortable', the whole district was middle-class c. 1890.[73] Residents included Mme. Bergman-Osterberg, pioneer of physical education, at no. 1 Broadhurst Gardens in the 1880s, and Walter Sickert, the painter, at no. 54 from 1885 to 1894.[74] Cecil Beaton recalled a more exotic atmosphere at no. 74 Compayne Gardens, called Santa Cruz c. 1900 when it housed the Bolivian consul general. Another exotic inhabitant was Frederick Rolfe, author and self-styled Baron Corvo, at no. 69 Broadhurst Gardens.[75]

The south-west demesne estate was bounded by Finchley Road and the railway line. To the north, in Lithos Road, squeezed in between the railway lines, 20 houses were built between 1882 and 1887 and another 14 houses, two blocks of flats, and a power station between 1892 and 1896. Eight stables and five houses were built in the parallel Rosemont Road between 1893 and 1897. There was no building in Lymington Road, which ran between Finch-ley Road and West End Lane north of the railway lines, until 1899, when 10 houses were built; shops were added in 1911.[76]

East of Finchley Road spacious houses were built, mostly in the 1880s, on the former Belsize farm lands on either side of Fitzjohn's Avenue:[77] 13 houses were built in Netherhall Terrace (later Gardens) from 1879 to 1888, 30 in Maresfield Gardens from 1881 to 1886, 3 in Nutley Terrace from 1885 to 1887, and 2 in Daleham Gardens in 1888.[78] South Hampstead High school was opened at the southern end of Maresfield Gardens in 1882 and Herbert Henry Asquith, then an M.P., lived at no. 27 from 1887 to 1892. In Netherhall Gardens a second house was designed for Edwin Long by Richard Norman Shaw at Kelston (no. 42) in 1888. Batterbury & Huxley were responsible for St. Kilda (no. 6) c. 1882 and Sidney and Beatrice Webb moved into no. 10 after their marriage in 1892.[79] The area, all former demesne land, where building was complete by 1891, was classified as upper middle- and middle-class and wealthy.[80]

Frognal Priory, 'very far in ruin' in 1869,[81] and let to John Culverhouse in 1871, was demolished in 1876[82] and the old road, Frognal, had been extended southward beyond Arkwright Road by 1878[83] and reached Finchley Road soon afterwards. Basil Champneys (1842–1935) built himself a house (no. 42 Frognal Lane) on the site of farm buildings on the Priory estate in 1881. A red-brick four-square house, 'very snug and solid', it was called Manor Farm and, from 1894, Hall Oak and was occupied by the architect until his death.[84] Two houses were built in 'Frognal Road' in 1881 and 20 in Frognal between 1882 and 1890, mostly by Sharp.[85] They included, on the west side, another Gothic house called Frognal Priory, designed by Richard Norman Shaw for Edwin Tate and built in 1881–2,[86] and no. 39, tile-hung in the style of a Surrey Weald cottage with a studio across the top, designed in 1885 by Norman Shaw for Kate Greenaway (1846–1901), the illustrator, who died there.[87]

The break-up of Thompson's Priory estate opened up the area south of Frognal Lane to development. Arkwright Road was extended from the Greenhill estate westward to Finchley Lane and six houses were being built there in 1878.[88] Fourteen houses were built in Lindfield Gardens in 1884 and 1890–2, one house was built in Frognal Lane, west of Manor Lodge, in 1877, and Langland Gardens had been constructed, though as yet no houses built, by 1891.[89]

In old Frognal no. 99 housed the Sailors' Orphan Girls' Home from 1862 until 1869[90] and Montagu

[72] Ibid. 320; Wade, *W. Hampstead*, 54–5; D.S.R.; Stanford, *Libr. Map of Lond.* (1891 edn.); L.C.C. *Municipal Map of Lond.* (1913).
[73] Booth, *Life and Lab.* map.
[74] Wade, *W. Hampstead*, 53.
[75] Ibid. 52–4; C. Beaton, *My Bolivian Aunt* (1971), 24, 29.
[76] D.S.R.; L.C.C. *Municipal Map of Lond.* (1913).
[77] Below, econ., for Belsize farm.
[78] D.S.R.; Thompson, *Hampstead*, 321.
[79] Wade, *More Streets*, 71; Saint, *Norman Shaw*, 162, 431; S.C.L., Town and Country Planning, 52nd List of Bldgs. (1974).
[80] Booth, *Life and Lab.* map; Stanford, *Libr. Map of Lond.* (1891 edn.).
[81] Howitt, *Northern Heights*, 152.

[82] Potter Colln. 18/9; *Images of Hampstead*, 54–5; Cedar, 'Urban Dev.'.
[83] G.L.R.O., E/MW/H, old no. 26/86 (agreement to lease 1878).
[84] D.S.R.; Pevsner, *Lond.* ii. 199; *D.N.B.*; *Kelly's Dir. Hampstead and Highgate* (1888–9, 1894); *Kelly's Dir. Hampstead and Childs Hill* (1934).
[85] D.S.R.
[86] Ibid.; Saint, *Norman Shaw*, 425; Stanford, *Libr. Map of Lond.* (1891 edn.).
[87] *C.H.R.* ii. 24–6; *Archit. of Lond.* 35; Saint, *Norman Shaw*, 159–61, 429.
[88] G.L.R.O., E/MW/H, old no. 26/86 (agreement to lease 1878); D.S.R.
[89] D.S.R.; Stanford, *Libr. Map of Lond.* (1891 edn.).
[90] Below, educ., priv. schools.

Grove was enlarged in the 1860s by the architect G. E. Street, whose family had acquired it through marriage.[91] Of the demesne houses, Frognal Park was leased from 1856 to after 1896 to James Anderson, a shipowner,[92] who by 1861 had rebuilt it after a fire.[93] No. 23, the Ferns, was leased from 1868 to William Dunlop Anderson, a colonial broker, who made alterations in 1883 and whose widow obtained the freehold in 1889.[94] The adjoining house, nos. 19 and 21, which by the 1890s was called Maryon Hall, was the home of Reginald Prance, a stockbroker, from 1871 until 1894, when he moved to the Ferns.[95] In 1896 Francis Tasker of Bedford Row converted Maryon Hall into two dwellings, with separate doorways.[96] Frognal Hall was occupied c. 1878–c. 1890 by Julius Talbot Airey but by c. 1903 it housed a school.[97] George Hornblower built nos. 79–87 Frognal (the Oaks), including an Italianate watch tower for no. 79, for E. P. Musman in 1902.[98] In 1878 Frognal was described as a beautiful suburban village, full of gentlemen's seats.[99] In 1903 it still had an air of affluence but was overlooked by 'many-windowed, scarlet-faced mansions' and had lost its 'aimless paths and trees'.[1] Building had covered most of the frontage to the road, old as well as new, and was encroaching on the large private gardens.[2] Alexander Gray bought the Old Mansion on the east side of old Frognal c. 1889, laid out an **L**-shaped road, Frognal Gardens, through the grounds, and commissioned James Neale, a former pupil of Street. He added a wing to the old house, and designed no. 100 Frognal and five houses in Frognal Gardens, built by the local firm Allison & Foskett from 1890 to 1896. They included no. 18 (Frognal End), built in 1892 for the novelist and antiquary Sir Walter Besant (1836–1901). Two houses were added in the rear in 1907.[3] Frognal House was in a dangerous state in 1896 but presumably was repaired, and Frognal Mansions flats were built by Palgrave & Co. next to it together with an astronomical observatory in 1897.[4] In 1895 the architect Sir Reginald Blomfield (1856–1942) built no. 51 Frognal for himself and the adjoining no. 49, occupied by William Morris's typographer, Thomas Cobden-Sanderson (1840–1922), south of the junction with Frognal Lane.[5] In 1906–7 Arnold Mitchell designed University College school, 'an impressive group of Edwardian baroque buildings' just south of Priory Lodge.[6] At the Finchley Road end of Frognal nos. 2–16, 'huge but coarse Queen Anne pairs' were built in 1889–91[7] and most of the 25 houses and four blocks of flats built in Frognal between 1891 and

1896 were by E. H. & H. T. Cave. The same firm was responsible for most of the 38 houses, blocks of flats, and 16 shops built in Finchley Road between 1893 and 1897 and the 10 houses and 15 shops in 1905, for the flats at the junction with Arkwright Road in 1896, and for 17 houses in Frognal Lane in 1897–8; 17 houses and some flats built in Langland Gardens from 1895 to 1897 and 4 houses built in Lindfield Gardens in 1895 were probably part of the same development.[8]

Edward Michael built three houses in Frognal Lane in 1898–9, one of them at the junction with Chesterford Gardens. That road, for which an application was made in 1896, crossed the grounds of Frognal Park from Frognal Lane to Redington Road; nine houses were built there from 1897 to 1900 and another two in 1905; C. H. B. Quennell may have designed nos. 5–11.[9]

Building spreading northward along Finchley Road was virtually complete on the eastern side and, mostly as shops, had reached beyond Lymington Road on the western by 1913. In 1899 six houses and a block of flats were built at the junction with West Hampstead Avenue (later Heath Drive), a new road skirting the demesne from Finchley Road to Redington Road; 20 houses and a block of flats were built there between 1897 and 1900 and another four between 1905 and 1907, mostly designed by C. H. B. Quennell. Nearby six houses were built in Redington Road and four in Branch Hill Park between 1905 and 1908;[10] no. 66 Redington Road was built in 1910 for William Garnett, education adviser to the L.C.C.[11] New roads included Bracknell Gardens, between Heath Drive and Frognal Lane, where 23 houses were built between 1905 and 1912, Barby (later Oakhill) Avenue, between Bracknell Gardens and Redington Road, where 10 houses were built between 1907 and 1909, Templewood Avenue, between Heath Drive and West Heath Road, where 13 houses, including some handsome ones by Quennell, were built between 1910 and 1912, and Redington Gardens, from Templewood Avenue to Redington Road, laid out in 1911 where four houses were built in 1913.[12] The large new houses were said to 'bristle with . . . respectable establishment figures'.[13] They also included the photographer and designer Cecil Beaton (1904–80), who was born at no. 21 Langland Gardens, a 'small, tall red-brick house of ornate but indiscriminate Dutch style', and lived from 1911 to 1922 at no. 1 Templewood Avenue. The literary forger Thomas Wise (1859–1937) lived at no. 25 Heath Drive from 1910 and the writer Leonard

[91] Wade, *Streets of Hampstead*, 17.
[92] G.L.R.O., E/MW/H, old no. 31/3 (consent to assign underlease 1856); H, old no. Locker 24 (rental 1890–1900); *Kelly's Dir. Hampstead and Highgate* (1896).
[93] G.L.R.O., E/MW/H, old no. 31/4 (lease 1861).
[94] Ibid. old no. 31/6 (lease 1868); D.S.R.; sales parts. 1933: inf. from Dr. Stella Tristram.
[95] P.R.O., RG 10/192/12; G.L.R.O., E/MW/H, old no. 26/46 (lease 1874); old no. Locker 24 (rental 1890–1900).
[96] S.C.L., Town and Country Planning, 52nd List of Bldgs. (1974).
[97] Baines, *Rec. Hampstead*, 547; C. White, *Sweet Hampstead* (1903), 74; below, plate 30.
[98] Saint, 'Hampstead Walk', 1; A. S. Gray, *Edwardian Archit.* (1985), 216.
[99] E. Walford, *Old and New Lond.* (1878), v. 501.
[1] White, *Sweet Hampstead*, 83.
[2] Thompson, *Hampstead*, 339.

[3] D.S.R.; Wade, *Streets of Hampstead*, 18; *Builder*, 13 June 1891 (Potter Colln. 19/130); Saint, 'Hampstead Walk', 1.
[4] D.S.R.; Saint, 'Hampstead Walk', 1.
[5] Wade, *Streets of Hampstead*, 16; *D.N.B.*; Gray, *Edwardian Archit.* 114, says that Blomfield and Cobden-Sanderson blt. a pair, nos. 51 and 53, for themselves in 1886, but the pair was nos. 49 and 51: O.S. Map 1/2,500, TQ 2685 (1970 edn.).
[6] *Archit. of Lond.* 35; below, educ., priv. schools.
[7] Saint, 'Hampstead Walk', 1.
[8] D.S.R.; *C.H.R.* ix. 12.
[9] D.S.R.; Saint, 'Hampstead Walk', 1. L.C.C. *Municipal Map of Lond.* (1913).
[10] L.C.C. *Municipal Map of Lond.* (1913); D.S.R.
[11] Wade, *Streets of Hampstead*, 21.   [12] Ibid.; D.S.R.
[13] Wade, *Streets of Hampstead*, 32; O.S. Map 1/2,500, Lond. I. 16 (1915 edn.); TQ 2585 (1955 edn.).

Huxley (1860–1933) at no. 16 Bracknell Gardens from *c.* 1917; Leonard's son Aldous, the novelist, was there from 1917 to 1920.[14]

After the First World War building continued in all areas, usually as infilling. Four houses were squashed in between Fitzjohn's Avenue and Spring and Shepherd's paths in 1922, another house (no. 1) was added to Fitzjohn's Avenue in 1925, and five others were built behind existing houses from 1936 to 1938; 11 houses were added to Maresfield Gardens in 1920, from 1925 to 1928, and in 1937–8. Another six were built in Redington Road between 1920 and 1927, including the neo-Georgian no. 81, designed by Sir Edward Maufe, and Hill House (no. 87), a red-brick house 'in the style of Mies van der Rohe', designed in 1938 by Oliver Hill with gardens by Christopher Tunnard.[15] Individual houses were built in Heath Drive in 1922 and 1933 and on former heath in West Heath Road in 1927 and 1932, the latter, Sarum Chase, 'unashamed Hollywood Tudor'.[16] In Bracknell Gardens a few houses were built in 1920, 1928, and 1936 and flats in 1937. Greenaway Gardens was built in 1914 through the grounds of Frognal Park, which was demolished soon afterwards; the new road had six houses by 1920, four more in 1923–4, and another one in 1934.[17]

Priory Lodge and Frognal Hall, threatened in 1899,[18] finally succumbed in the 1920s. They were replaced by nos. 96–98 Frognal and nos. 3–9 Frognal Gardens, by E. B. Musman, in 1923 and by Frognal Way, which has been described as the 'showpiece of interwar Hampstead housing' and also as exhibiting styles ranging from neo-Georgian to Hollywood Spanish–Colonial and South African Dutch.[19] The first house was built there in 1924 and at least five others were added from 1928 to 1935, including no. 7 by Oswald Milne, no. 13 by C. H. B. Quennell, no. 11 in 1925 by Albert Farmer, no. 5 in 1930 by Adrian Gilbert Scott for himself, no. 4 in 1934, no. 20 in 1934 for Gracie Fields, the singer, and no. 9, the Sun House, by Maxwell Fry in 1935.[20] The last, Fry's first London building, and an 'object lesson in façade composition', was one of the most important embodiments of the modern, international movement of the 1930s in Hampstead. Houses were also built on the east side of Frognal, between University College school and Frognal Way, in 1934. No. 66, north of Frognal Way, was designed by Connell, Ward & Lucas and built in 1937 of reinforced concrete 'in the extreme idiom of the day' as an attempt to 'épater les bourgeois'.[21] Unlike most of the new houses, which were 'charming', it was considered out of character with the district's brick and Georgian architecture.[22] On the western side of Frognal,

Frognal Priory was replaced in 1937 by Frognal Close, six large semi-detached houses but in a modern style by E. L. Freud, Sigmund's son.[23] The Manor House, the easternmost of the demesne houses in Frognal Lane, was demolished in 1938 and three houses (nos. 59, 61, and 63 Frognal) were built by D. E. Harrington, the architect who lived at no. 61, to complete the frontage, no. 65 having been built by the owner, Miss W. B. Acworth, in 1934.[24]

The remaining large area of open ground lay between Finchley Road, Lymington Road, and the western boundary of the estate. Alvanley Gardens had been constructed there by 1922 and, although a cricket ground on the western side survived, *c.* 15 houses were built between 1922 and 1927. On the western side of Finchley Road, backing on Alvanley Gardens, nos. 341–59 (odd) and Dunrobin Court existed by 1930 and other blocks were built in 1934 (probably Mandeville and Hillside Courts).[25] Farther south, a major change from 1934 to 1938 was the rebuilding of nos. 191–217 Finchley Road to house John Barnes and St. John's Court flats.[26] On the east side of Finchley Road, Palace Court was built in 1926 south of the junction with Frognal Lane, Frognal Court in 1934 at no. 160, and Bracknell Gate at the junction of Frognal Lane and Bracknell Gardens in 1933.[27]

In 1930 the area had a few warehouses and workshops near the railway west of Finchley Road and was inhabited by skilled workers 'or similar', while the rest of the district around Frognal was middle-class and wealthy.[28] It still had distinguished residents like the politician John Sinclair, Lord Pentland (1860–1925) at no. 18 Frognal Gardens, the civil engineer Sir Owen Williams (d. 1969) at no. 16 Redington Road, both in the 1920s, Ramsay Mac-Donald, the prime minister, at no. 103 Frognal 1925–37, and Morris Ginsberg (1889–1970), the sociologist, at no. 35 Redington Road in the 1930s.[29] Publishers, long attracted to Hampstead, included Sir Geoffrey Faber (1889–1961) at no. 1 Oak Hill Park in the 1930s and 1940s and Sir Stanley Unwin (1884–1968), who lived opposite him from the 1930s and formed a company to buy the war-damaged Victorian houses in Oak Hill Park from the Neave family; he failed, and built no. 4 for himself.[30] Musicians included Sir Edward Elgar (1857–1934) at no. 42 Netherhall Gardens 1912–21, Cecil Sharp at no. 4 Maresfield Gardens 1918–24, and the conductor Warwick Braithwaite in Fitzjohn's Avenue *c.* 1935.[31] Stephen Spender, the poet, grew up at no. 10 Frognal, at the Finchley Road end, in an 'ugly house in the Hampstead style, as if built from a box of bricks', and from 1942 to 1944 lived in a flat next to the fire station in Maresfield Gardens, where he

[14] Wade, *Streets of Hampstead*, 19–22; *D.N.B.*
[15] D.S.R.; Wade, *Streets of Hampstead*, 21; Pevsner, *Lond.* ii. 197; *Archit. of Lond.* 36.
[16] Pevsner, *Lond.* ii. 197; Thompson, *Hampstead*, 338. D.S.R. for 1929–31 are missing, so there may have been more.
[17] D.S.R.; *Kelly's Dir. Hampstead and Childs Hill* (1913–15, 1920).
[18] *N. & Q.* 9th ser. iii. 228, 415.
[19] Quoted in Wade, *Streets of Hampstead*, 16; Pevsner, *Lond.* ii. 199.
[20] D.S.R.; Wade, *Streets of Hampstead*, 16; Saint, 'Hampstead Walk', 1; *C.H.R.* vii. 2–7.
[21] *Hampstead in the Thirties, a committed decade*, exhib. 1974–5, catalogue (S.C.L.); Pevsner, *Lond.* ii. 199;

Archit. of Lond. 36–7; A. Service, *Architects of Lond.* (1979), 191; D.S.R.
[22] *The Times*, 30 Oct. 1935, 10d; 22 July 1936, 11d; 19 Aug. 1938, 10e.
[23] D.S.R.; *Archit. of Lond.* 36.
[24] D.S.R.; local inf.; *Kelly's Dir. Lond.* (1960).
[25] D.S.R.; L.C.C. *Municipal Map of Lond.* (1930); O.S. Map 1/2,500, TQ 2585 (1955 edn.).
[26] D.S.R.; below, econ., trade and ind.
[27] D.S.R.; O.S. Map 1/2,500, TQ 2585, 2684 (1955 edn.).
[28] *New Life and Labour*, vii, maps 8, 10, 11.
[29] Wade, *Streets of Hampstead*, 17, 19, 21; *D.N.B.*
[30] Wade, *Streets*, 18; S. Unwin, *Truth about a Publisher* (1960), 253, 261–2.   [31] Wade, *More Streets*, 70–1.

and the writer William Sansom (1912–76) were temporary firemen. Other writers included Rafael Sabatini (d. 1950) at no. 27 Fitzjohn's Avenue in the 1920s and Stella Gibbons (b. 1902) at no. 67 1930–2. The last home of the Victorian artist Henry Holiday (d. 1927) was no. 18 Chesterford Gardens and the fashionable painter Philip de László (1869–1937) lived and worked at no. 3 Fitzjohn's Avenue from 1922.[32] The demesne estate, which included part of cosmopolitan Swiss Cottage, housed its share of political refugees in the 1930s, among them the Austrian painter Oskar Kokoschka (1886–1980), in Mandeville Court, no. 383 Finchley Road, in 1938[33] and the psychoanalyst Sigmund Freud (d. 1939) at no. 20 Maresfield Gardens from 1938. Freud's daughter Anna, a children's psychoanalyst who opened a clinic there in 1952, maintained his rooms intact until her death in 1980; the house was opened as the Freud Museum in 1986.[34] Gen. Charles de Gaulle lived from 1942 to 1944 in no. 99 Frognal.[35]

Not all the writers and artists could afford expensive houses. Stella Gibbons lived in one room and many large houses were converted to flats or bed-sitting rooms. Others housed institutions, like Havelock Hall, the Baptist training college on the corner of Fitzjohn's Avenue and Akenside Road in the 1920s, which later became the Marie Curie hospital. In Fitzjohn's Avenue no. 7 became a hostel for mothers and babies in 1933, no. 33 a foster home in 1937, and no. 47 a school in 1947.[36]

Among the areas badly damaged during the Second World War was Broadhurst Gardens, where 168 council flats were planned in 1948 although work was not begun until 1953 and completed in 1956, the architect being Richard Nickson.[37] The council acquired a few large houses in Fitzjohn's Avenue, which it converted into flats during the 1950s and 1960s.[38] The most controversial post-war development was at Branch Hill, a sparsely populated area where the L.C.C. decided to purchase 13 a. in 1951. It retreated in the face of local and government opposition, since most of those waiting for council houses in Hampstead could be accommodated in the Chalcots developments and there was a possibility of adding the Branch Hill Lodge grounds to the heath. In 1965 Lord Glendyne sold the house and 11 a., described as the last important open site in Hampstead village, to Camden L.B. for the house to become an old people's home and with a covenant limiting building in the grounds to semi-detached houses. The council, anxious to house those on its St. Pancras waiting list, produced in 1978 a scheme for 42 houses designed by Gordon Benson and Alan

Forsyth, built in concrete in pairs with flat roofs and stepped brick paths, possibly 'the most expensive council houses ever built'.[39] Plans for the redevelopment of a 50-a. site bounded by Finchley Road, Lymington Road, West End Lane, and Broadhurst Gardens, most of which lay within the old demesne estate, were announced in 1963 by the Second Covent Garden Property Co., with Hampstead council as the comprehensive development authority. The existing railway lines and warehouses were to continue, alongside private and council flats to house 6,000.[40] In 1987 the original shabby Finchley Road frontage remained but a new stone-clad L.E.B. building replaced the old power station in 1975[41] and in the late 1970s Norfolk Mansions was built in Lithos Road and a housing estate of red-brick terraces grouped around new roads, Dresden Close and Wedgwood Walk, was built south of Lymington Road.[43] The death of Sir Percy Maryon-Wilson in 1965 provoked political conflict when freeholds of the area to the south, between Broadhurst and Fairhazel Gardens and Goldhurst Terrace, became available. Camden L.B.'s wish to buy them, supported by a tenants' association, was twice vetoed by the government, and in 1972 they were sold to Bryston Property Group.[43]

At the southern end of Fitzjohn's Avenue, St. Thomas More church was built in 1953, next to nos. 3–7, Holy Cross convent.[44] No. 6 was demolished c. 1965 and, with Marie Curie hospital's laboratories, was replaced by the Tavistock clinic, while the hospital, at the corner with Akenside Road, was replaced in 1969 by flats built for the Medical Research Council.[45]

Most of the private, and expensive, modern rebuilding has been in the northern part. Michael Lyell's design in the early 1960s of five seven-storeyed blocks containing 65 'luxury' flats on the Oak Hill Park estate, which replaced the 19th-century houses, won a Civic Trust award.[46] Oak Tree House in Redington Gardens had, by the 1980s, been converted to council flats.[47] In 1984 some 26 detached houses, designed by Ted Levy Benjamin, were built by Barratt in Grange Gardens on the site of the Grange.[48] Beaumont Gardens, neo-Georgian houses, also off West Heath Road, were built at the same time by Sutherland Paris Developments for a mainly foreign market.[49] In 1985–6 48 houses and flats, designed by Bickerdike Allen Simovic, were built on the site of Spedan Tower.[50] In 1987 the future of no. 9 West Heath Road, a 'strange and obsessive building', built in 1963 by James Gowan for Chaim Schreiber (d. 1983) of the furniture firm,

[32] S. Spender, *World Within World* (1951), 26, 279; Wade, *Streets of Hampstead*, 15, 20; Wade, *More Streets*, 69–71; D.N.B. [33] Wade, *W. Hampstead*, 59.
[34] *The Times*, 26 July 1986, 6b; Wade, *More Streets*, 70–1.
[35] Wade, *Streets of Hampstead*, 17.
[36] Wade, *More Streets*, 69–70.
[37] *Hampstead 1939–45* (Camden History Soc. 1977); S.C.L., H 711.13, Council Housing Reps., Hampstead Boro. *Rep. on Housing* (1948, 1954); S.C.L., P.B. Housing, Camden Gen. file, MS. list of Camden Housing est. (1971).
[38] Hampstead Boro. *Rep. on Housing* (1954); *The Times*, 16 Nov. 1960, 7b; S.C.L., H 331.833 Housing file, Metrop. Boro. of Hampstead, *Municipal Housing Est.* [c. 1962].
[39] Hampstead Communist party, *Homes for Hampstead*

[c. 1955]; *The Times*, 12 Nov. 1951, 2d; 24 Apr. 1953, 2f; 17 Apr. 1965, 5a; 12 Sept. 1978; *Hampstead One Thousand*, 138–9; *Archit. of Lond.* 37.
[40] *Contract Jnl.* 2 May 1963.
[41] Inf. from Lond. Electricity 1987.
[42] *Kelly's Dir. Lond.* (1975, 1980); local inf.
[43] H.H.E. 24 June 1966; 2 June 1972; *Hampstead News*, 10 Feb. 1967 (S.C.L., H 333.3 Manor of Hampstead file); *The Times*, 22 Jan. 1975, 3e.
[44] Wade, *More Streets*, 69, 71.
[45] Ibid. 70; Saint, *Norman Shaw*, 425; below, pub. svces.
[46] *The Times*, 16 Nov. 1960, 7b; Wade, *Streets of Hampstead*, 18.
[47] Wade, *Streets of Hampstead*, 21, 33.
[48] Inf. from Bickerdike Allen Partners.
[49] *Observer*, 4 Nov. 1984.
[50] Inf. from Bickerdike Allen Partners.

was in doubt.[51] Elsewhere conversions of large houses to flats continued, the Fairhazel Gardens area being noted for the number of young, professional, and often single people who moved in during the 1970s.[52]

The central area, lacking large council estates, has undergone less change than some other parts of Hampstead. It continued to attract those involved in the arts, like Kathleen Ferrier (1912–53), the contralto, at Frognal Mansions, no. 97 Frognal, from 1942, Dennis Brain (1921–57), the horn player, at no. 37 Frognal, and Tamara Karsavina Diaghilev, the ballerina, at no. 108 Frognal in the 1950s, E. V. Knox (1881–1971), the editor of *Punch*, at no. 110 Frognal from 1945,[53] Hesketh Pearson, the biographer, at no. 14 Priory Road from 1950 to 1956,[54] and several more recent writers. No. 3 Oakhill Avenue, the home of the singer Elisabeth Schwarzkopf and her husband Walter Legge, was in 1960 the headquarters of the Philharmonia Orchestra.[55] Anton Walbrook, the actor, died at no. 69 Frognal in 1967[56] and Peggy Ashcroft, the actress, had in 1987 lived at Manor Lodge in Frognal Lane since the 1950s.[57] Politicians included Hugh Gaitskell (1906–63), who lived at no. 10 Frognal in the 1940s and as Chancellor of the Exchequer in 1950, and Henry Brooke, Hampstead's M.P. and Home Secretary (later Baron Brooke of Cumnor) who lived at no. 45 Redington Road 1962–4. Sir Bernard Spilsbury (1877–1947), the pathologist, died at no. 20 Frognal and Melanie Klein (1882–1960), the Viennese-born psychoanalyst, lived her last years at no. 16 Bracknell Gardens.[58] She exemplified the European connexion established in the 1930s, which contributed so much to the atmosphere described by John Mortimer, the barrister and author, who lived in Swiss Cottage in the 1950s and 1960s: 'a sort of late Viennese melancholy, promoted by the large number of middle-aged refugees who sat drinking *Kaffee mit Schlag* in the Finchley Road tea-rooms ... On summer evenings the crumbling terraces would come to life with the sound of exiled string quartets'.[59] In 1975 Compayne Gardens was 'distinctly cosmopolitan', with a Polish Jewish ex-serviceman's association at no. 71A and Maccabi House, a former Russian embassy, at no. 73.[60] No. 12A Greenaway Gardens was sold for use by the high commissioner of Trinidad and Tobago in 1970 and many houses in Templewood Avenue and Gardens had become ambassadorial residences about the same time.[61] The Sun House in Frognal Way belonged to the

Indian high commission in the 1980s, when the high price of property increased the cosmopolitan character of the area, many wealthy residents coming from America, the Middle East, Africa, or Europe.[62]

WEST END. The mid 13th-century le Rudyng, a name which indicates a woodland clearing, was by 1534 called West End,[63] because of its position in relation to the central demesne lands. West End was then the name of a freehold estate, later called Thorplands, belonging to Kilburn priory. There was a house on the estate by 1646 and possibly by 1244[64] and although none of the copyhold tenements at West End can be traced back to 1312, the fact that several were heriotable suggests their origin in the Middle Ages.[65] The road junction at which West End lies appears to be later than the hamlet but West End Lane and Mill Lane (Shoot Up Hill Lane and Cole Lane), although not named until later, probably existed as access in the Middle Ages since they formed the boundaries of several ancient estates.[66] In 1644 Hillfield abutted on Northwood apparently without Frognal Lane, called West End Lane in the 18th century, separating them but presumably there was always a route from West End hamlet to the parish church.[67]

Several houses in West End were mentioned in the early 17th century[68] and by the mid century London merchants were building larger ones. Richard Gibbs, a goldsmith, acquired Hillfield on the east side of West End (or Kilburn) Lane, north of Jacksfield, together with two houses in 1644.[69] One may have been the decayed brick house purchased from Gibbs before 1663 by the father of Matthew Blueh, a Chancery clerk.[70] The Hillfield estate was held by another Londoner in 1685[71] and the house was 'new fronted and much beautified and another house built' after 1703 by Henry Binfield.[72] Both houses, with their coach houses, were owned by Mary Binfield in 1762.[73] One was West End Hall and the other possibly Treherne House.[74]

In 1655 William Hitchcock, merchant tailor, conveyed a new house, described in 1687 as a mansion house on the west side of West End Lane, to William Bennett, another London merchant, and north of it another house was held by three generations of Wachters, London merchants, possibly Jews, from c. 1649 to 1686.[75] Bennett's house was probably the White House, which passed to Norwich Salisbury by 1692 and to Richard Limbrey in 1743. In 1762 Limbrey owned and occupied a brick house

[51] *Observer*, 26 Oct. 1986; *Daily Telegraph*, 4 Sept. 1987; *Hampstead One Thousand*, 143; *Archit. of Lond.* 37.
[52] Camden Boro. Plan, *W. Hampstead and Kilburn*, 1975, Area 5.
[53] Wade, *Streets of Hampstead*, 15–17; *D.N.B.*
[54] Wade, *W. Hampstead*, 52.
[55] Wade, *Streets of Hampstead*, 21; *Kelly's Dir. Lond.* (1960).
[56] Wade, *Streets of Hampstead*, 17, 19; Wade, *More Streets*, 72.
[57] *Daily Mail*, 17 Aug. 1987, p. 15.
[58] Wade, *Streets of Hampstead*, 16, 19–21.
[59] J. Mortimer, *Clinging to the Wreckage* (1982), 148; *C.H.R.* xi. 24–5.
[60] Wade, *W. Hampstead*, 153.
[61] Wade, *Streets of Hampstead*, 20–1.
[62] Local inf.
[63] P.R.O., E 318/Box 38/2042; *P.N.Mdx.* 203.
[64] Below, other est. (Kilburn priory, Thorplands).

[65] e.g. Jacksfield, Earlsfield, and three est. at Catemead (Gilberts): G.L.R.O., E/MW/H/42; and see Treherne Croft: below, other est.
[66] Above, communications; below, map of manor and est.
[67] G.L.R.O., E/MW/H/3; Rocque, *Map of Lond.* (1741–5), sheet 12.
[68] e.g. ho. of Thos. Crisp, 1614: *Mdx. Sess. Rec.* ii. 26–7; ho. of Rose Smith, 1621; G.L.R.O., E/MW/H/1; ho. of Ric. Clerk, 1631: ibid. 2.
[69] G.L.R.O., E/MW/H/3.   [70] P.R.O., C 5/565/83.
[71] G.L.R.O., E/MW/H/8.
[72] Ibid. H, old no. Box L.
[73] S.C.L., Man. Map and Fieldbk. nos. 444–8.
[74] Below, other est.
[75] G.L.R.O., E/MW/H/5 (1655); 8 (1686); P.R.O., PROB 11/386 (P.C.C. 1687, f. 2, will of Wm. Bennett); 373 (P.C.C. 66 Drax, will of Abraham Wachter); Barratt, *Annals*, iii, App. 3, pp. 361–3.

and coach house opposite Jacksfield, the most southerly house in West End.[76] The house and stabling north of it, owned by Armine Snoxell in 1762, was probably Wachter's, later Sandwell House.[77] There was a house at Colemead, north of Shoot Up Hill Lane and west of Fortune Green Lane, by 1707.[78] The Black Lion stood on the west side of West End Lane by 1721 and the Cock and Hoop almost opposite, north of the junction with Frognal Lane, by 1723.[79] In 1710 West End had 14 rent-paying tenements and by 1762 there were 19 houses, 18 cottages, and 2 inns, in West End, mostly on the west side of West End Lane and Fortune Green Lane.[80]

By 1800 West End was a hamlet of cottages and seats set in parkland. The White House had by 1774 been replaced by West End House, which, as a result of the straightening of West End Lane, stood back from the road.[81] The property, with other West End estates, passed in 1796 to Maria Beckford,[82] whose family, which included William Beckford (1709–70), lord mayor of London, had occupied a house nearby since 1762 or earlier.[83] The house was occupied by Miss Beckford from c. 1807 to 1810, by the marchioness of Headfort from c. 1815 to 1825,[84] and by the Hon. Henry Frederick Compton Cavendish in 1842.[85] Another resident by 1800 was Germain Lavie, J.P.,[86] who was lessee of Lauriston Lodge and some 11 a., part of Gilberts estate, from 1806.[87] The house, later occupied by Sir William Woods, Garter King-at-Arms, was of red brick with stained-glass windows and a fine entrance.[88] The engraver Josiah Boydell (1752–1817) was lessee of land in West End in 1783[89] and by 1807 was occupying a house and coach house. Boydell was a tenant of Jeremy Jepson Ripley, who built a house and coach house after 1814, possibly that with a large garden north of Lauriston Lodge. Admiral James Saumarez, Baron de Saumarez (1757–1836), lived in one of the West End houses.[90]

West End Hall was owned 1796–1807 by the family of the Hon. Richard Walpole, M.P., in 1807 by Lord Walpole, and 1815–89 by John Miles and his wife, benefactors of West End.[91] Two other substantial houses in 1807, occupied by Thomas Kesteven and Mrs. Mears,[92] were probably Treherne House and Flitcroft's farmhouse.[93] There

were c. 16 houses and 9 cottages in 1810 and another four modest houses by 1815.[94] Between 1762 and 1814 houses were built on Fortune Green and fronting Frognal Lane, Mill Lane, and Fortune Green Lane,[95] the last being Cholmley Lodge, a two-storeyed stuccoed house.[96] At the southern end of the hamlet, on the west side of West End Lane, Charles Spain bought 5 a. of the Little estate[97] and between 1829 and 1838 built York Villa.[98] That house was renamed or replaced by Oaklands Hall, an elaborate Gothic mansion, occupied in the 1860s by Donald Nicoll, a merchant.[99] Two white Italianate houses were built in the 1860s by the Greenwood brothers, contractors working on the Midland railway: Sandwell House near Lauriston Lodge and Canterbury House opposite, on Jacksfield.[1]

In 1812 James Leigh Hunt moved to a cottage at West End, attracted by a district so quiet that the inhabitants of West End Hall claimed to have heard the cannon at Waterloo.[2] A proposal to bring Finchley Road to West End Lane in 1824 failed and the new road, east of the hamlet, had little immediate effect.[3] The only building was of a few houses at New West End, on the east side of Finchley Road, in the 1840s.[4] A National school and cottage for the schoolmistress was built on the north side of the village, on part of the grounds of Cholmley Lodge, in 1844.[5] In 1851 West End was a hamlet mainly of agricultural labourers, gardeners, craftsmen, and tradespeople for daily needs, with an innkeeper and two beershop keepers and a schoolmistress; the few gentry included Rear-Admiral Sir George Sartorius (1790–1885) of West End House, a retired ironfounder, a surgeon, some civil servants, and a clergyman.[6] Industry, in the form of Thomas Potter's foundry on the south-west side of West End Green, arrived in the 1860s, followed by Potter's Buildings or West Cottages for its workers.[7]

The transformation of West End came with the building of three railway lines south of the village, crossing West End Lane. Large sections of several estates were sold to the railway companies: in addition to the lines themselves, sidings, yards, and rubbish tips occupied much space and the remaining farm- and parkland was cut into segments, determining the subsequent street pattern. The Hampstead Junction Railway, built by 1857, ran along the

[76] S.C.L., Man. Map and Fieldbk. no. 451; D 1j; G.L.R.O., E/MW/H/I/2304; 2311A; H/11.
[77] S.C.L., Man. Map and Fieldbk. no. 453.
[78] G.L.R.O., E/MW/H, old no. Box L; S.C.L., Man. Map and Fieldbk. no. 476; S.C.L., D 3(a).
[79] *Hampstead One Thousand*, 154; G.L.R.O., MR/LV3/104; M 81/1; S.C.L., Man. Map and Fieldbk. nos. 468, 440.
[80] G.L.R.O., E/MW/H/I/2123; S.C.L., Man. Map and Fieldbk. nos. 431–81.
[81] S.C.L., D 1i; S.C.L., Man. Map; Newton, *Map of Hampstead* (1814).
[82] S.C.L., D 1d.
[83] S.C.L., Man. Map and Fieldbk. no. 466; *Hampstead One Thousand*, 87–8.
[84] Poor rate bks. 1807, 1810–15; Thompson, *Hampstead*, 122; Wade, *W. Hampstead*, 17; *D.N.B.* s.v. Wm. Beckford.
[85] S.C.L., D 19.
[86] 39 & 40 Geo. III, c. 35 (Local and Personal).
[87] M.M. & M., Lib. J, pp. 473–80; poor rate bks. 1807, 1810–15.
[88] Wade, *W. Hampstead*, 20.
[89] S.C.L., D 3c; *D.N.B.*
[90] Poor rate bk. 1807; M.M. & M., Lib. J, pp. 473–7,

map; Q, pp. 62–4, 533–5, map; O.S. Map 1/2,500, Lond. XV (1879 edn.). For Ripley, below, other est. (Gilberts); S.C.L., LR West End; below, plate 13.
[91] Poor rate bks. 1807, 1810–15, 1826, 1834; Wade, *W. Hampstead*, 11, 14.
[92] Poor rate bks. 1807–15.
[93] M.M. & M., Lib. I, p. 90.
[94] Poor rate bks. 1810–15.
[95] Newton, *Map of Hampstead* (1814).
[96] *Images of Hampstead*, 149; S.C.L., LR Cholmley Lodge.
[97] M.M. & M., Lib. L, p. 225; below, other est.
[98] *Cruchley's New Plan* (1829); tithe map.
[99] *Images of Hampstead*, 150; poor rate bk. 1864.
[1] Wade, *W. Hampstead*, 16; O.S. Map 1/2,500, Lond. XV (1879 edn.).
[2] Wade, *W. Hampstead*, 9, 11.
[3] Thompson, *Hampstead*, 121–2.
[4] D.S.R.; J. Wyld, *Map of Lond. and Environs* (1848).
[5] Wade, *W. Hampstead*, 29–30.
[6] P.R.O., HO 107/1492/5; *D.N.B.*
[7] Below, econ., ind.; O.S. Map 1/2,500, Lond. XV (1879 edn.); S.C.L., H 728.3/West Cottages, West End La. file.

southern boundary of West End House. The Revd. William Dunbar, who lived in Scotland, sold the estate to a speculator, Charles Bischoff, the owner in 1863 when the second railway line, the Midland, was proposed. The Midland line, opened in 1868, passed along the northern boundary of West End House, which in 1857 became a girls' laundry training school and later accommodated railway workers before its demolition in the late 1890s. Before 1873 Bischoff sold the estate to the British Land Co., which constructed Iverson Road, where four cottages were built in the West End portion in 1872, and developed the land to the west, in Kilburn, but most of the West End section was occupied by railway land.[8] The Midland Railway bought the eastern section of the estate and built coal offices in Iverson Road in 1890–1 and Heysham Terrace (nos. 202–20) on the site of West End House in 1897.[9]

Coincidentally the next estate to be developed, like West End House, had belonged to the Beckfords, although it had followed a different descent since the 1840s. Consisting of c. 15 a. north of Mill Lane and west of Fortune Green Lane, it was sold in 1865 to the Real Property Co. and in 1868 to the Land Co. of London, which laid out Hillfield Road and Aldred Street in building plots.[10] Development was slow. Two houses and a temporary church were built in Mill Lane, east of the junction with Aldred Road, in 1874 and one plot fronting Mill Lane, sold in 1875, was built on by 1878.[11] Premises for Field Lane boys' industrial school were built on the north side of Hillfield Road in 1877.[12] Sustained building began in 1878 and by 1890 some 88 houses, by various builders, had been erected in Hillfield Road; 16 were built in 1888 in Aldred Road by Cossens, who lived there, and the Pavement, nos. 41–83 (odd), was built in Mill Lane. In 1908 Berridge House opened next to the industrial school, at the junction of Hillfield Road and Fortune Green Lane, as the National Society's training college for teachers of domestic subjects.[13]

Most of the land north of West End Green and around Fortune Green belonged to the Flitcroft estate, 20 a. of which were sold to the parish in 1875 for a cemetery, thereby holding back housing in the area for a decade.[14] Apart from the Hillfield Road estate, the only building was on a small estate west of Finchley Road, owned in 1841 by Francis Lovel, where between 1870 and 1878 Charles Cannon, a dye merchant who lived at Kidderpore Hall, converted an old footpath into Cannon Hill, and West House and Wellesley House were built west of the junction of Finchley Road and West End Lane.[15]

The period of greatest development was in the 15 years from 1879, beginning with the opening of the

third railway, the Metropolitan & St. John's Wood, with a station in West End Lane (West Hampstead). Stations on the other two lines opened in 1880 and 1888.[16] The first to exploit the railway was Donald Nicoll, M.P. and owner of a gentlemen's outfitter's in Regent Street, who leased Oaklands Hall from Charles Spain from 1861 to 1872 and owned portions of the Little estate to the north and west, together forming a 23-a. estate which he called West End Park. Nicoll was a director of the Metropolitan and St. John's Wood railway from 1864 to 1872 and, in anticipation of its plans, laid out a road (Sherriff, then called Nicoll, Road) on the line later taken by the railway, for which he received substantial compensation. He then sold West End Park to the London Permanent Building Society, which was connected with Alexander Sherriff, a fellow M.P. and railway director, who gave his name to the northernmost road on the estate.[17]

Forty-two houses were built between 1877 and 1879 in Lowfield Road, adjoining Nicoll's development in Palmerston Road in Kilburn. Building began in West End Park itself in 1879, when houses were under construction in all the roads (Sherriff, Hemstal, Kylemore, and Gladys roads) except Hilltop Road, where they were not begun until 1883. Various builders, mostly local and including James Tavener, Reeder of Maygrove Road, and Haines of Sherriff Road, were working on c. 186 houses and 3 studios in 1893. Some houses at the eastern end of the estate were detached but most were terraced and cramped. St. James's church was built in 1887 and the Beacon, 'the exact representation of a ruin on the coast of England', at the junction of West End Lane with Hemstal Road about the same time. It was itself replaced by St. James's Mansions in 1894. Oaklands Hall was occupied by Sir Charles Murray until 1878, when it was offered for sale, and in 1883 houses were built in Dynham and Cotleigh roads on its site. Mostly local builders, including A. Rathbone of Mill Lane and Julia Bursill, had erected 123 terraced houses there by 1893, in addition to completing the frontage on West End Lane.[18] A library was built in Cotleigh Road in 1901.[19]

On the west side of West End Lane, north of Nicoll's estates, the land between the three railway lines was still largely untouched but beyond them building spread during the 1880s. Thomas Potter, owner of Thorplands, 13 a. south of Mill Lane, stretching westward from the junction with West End Lane, where he lived in Poplar House,[20] built c. 15 houses fronting Mill Lane between 1873 and 1877 and the Elms and the Cedars next to the green by 1878.[21] New roads were constructed in the late 1870s and 346 houses were built between 1882 and

[8] Thompson, *Hampstead*, 342–3; *C.H.R.* vii. 16–17; G.L.R.O., E/MW/H, old no. 37/12 (enfranchisement 1857); Stanford, *Libr. Map of Lond.* (1862 edn. with additions to 1865), sheet 5; D.S.R.; S.C.L., LP West End La., pamphlet on Girls' Laundry, inc. illus. of West End Ho.; Baines, *Rec. Hampstead*, 48.
[9] Wade, *W. Hampstead*, 32; D.S.R.
[10] S.C.L., D 117.
[11] Ibid.; D.S.R.; *Metrop. Improvement Map No. 46* (1878).
[12] Reformatory and Refuge Union, *Classified List of Saving Institutions* (1912), 16.
[13] D.S.R.; Wade, *W. Hampstead*, 28, 62.
[14] Wade, *W. Hampstead*, 31, 62.
[15] Ibid. 64; P.R.O., IR 29/21/24, no. 82; O.S. Map

1/2,500, Lond. VI (1870 edn.); *Metrop. Improvement Map* (1878); Stanford, *Libr. Map of Lond.* (1891 edn.).
[16] Thompson, *Hampstead*, 342–3.
[17] Ibid.; *C.H.R.* vii. 18–20; P.R.O., IR 29/21/24, nos. 108–9; poor rate bk. 1864, vol. 2, nos. 73–4.
[18] D.S.R.; Hutchings and Crowsley, *Hampstead and Highgate Dir.* (1874, 1878); Wade, *W. Hampstead*, 18–19, 39; Stanford, *Libr. Map of Lond.* (1891 edn.), sheet 5; O.S. Map 1/2,500, TQ 2584 (1955 edn.).
[19] Wade, *W. Hampstead*, 41.
[20] Poor rate bk. 1880 (vol. 4, no. 2765); Hutchings and Crowsley, *Hampstead and Highgate Dir.* (1874); for Thorplands, below, other est.
[21] D.S.R.; Wade, *W. Hampstead*, 13; Hutchings and Crowsley, *Hampstead and Highgate Dir.* (1878).

1894 in Sumatra, Solent, Holmdale, Glenbrook, Pandora, and Narcissus roads, mostly by J. I. Chapman of Solent Road, G. W. Cossens of Mill Lane, Jabez Reynolds of Holmdale Road, and James Gibb of Dennington Park Road. Another 28 houses and a Methodist church were built on the estate fronting Mill Lane in 1886-7 and seven blocks of flats in West End Lane on what was called the Cedars estate in 1894. Some 49 houses were built, mostly by Reynolds, in the last road on the estate, Inglewood Road on the site of Poplar House, in 1893-4. Welbeck Mansions, flats notable for their ironwork balconies, were built north of Inglewood Road, on the site of Potter's foundry, in 1897.[22] The London General Omnibus Co. built stables and a depot c. 1901 on ground previously used for tennis at the north-eastern corner of the estate, which later became a post office garage. A fire brigade station, by 'O. Fleming and/or C. C. Winmill . . . in Voysey manner', was built c. 1901 at the northern end of West End Lane.[23] Holmdale Mansions were built in Holmdale Road in 1904 and Cavendish Mansions at the east end of Mill Lane about the same time, when the Cedars, which had become a school, was demolished.[24]

South of Potter's estate was the Ripley estate, originally part of Gilberts, with its house at West End Lane still occupied in 1874 by Thomas Ripley, and Lauriston Lodge, which survived until the late 1890s.[25] About 1881 Dennington Park Road was constructed on the line of Sweetbriar Walk, the old path to Lauriston Lodge, and 58 houses were built there and in Kingdon Road, possibly named after a speculator Emmeline Kingdon, between 1883 and 1888, mostly by James Gibb. A synagogue was built at the eastern end of Dennington Park Road in 1891. Three blocks of flats, named Dene Mansions after Little Dene, home of the Ripley family, replaced Lauriston Lodge in 1904.[26] Farther east, fronting West End Lane, was the Sandwell House or Park estate, where in 1893-4 the last big house on the western side of West End Lane made way for flats (Sandwell and Victoria mansions) along West End Lane and Sumatra Road and for 10 houses in a new road, Sandwell Crescent.[27]

Fronting Mill Lane west of Potter's estate was the Earlsfields estate, reduced by the Midland railway to a triangle of land which was sold to the Land Building Investment and Cottage Improvement Co. Terraced houses in varied styles presumably indicating the builders, E. Garrett and William Brown, both of Ravenshaw Street, J. C. Wallas of Belsize Road, and Rathbone of Croydon, were crammed into Ravenshaw and Glastonbury streets and Broomsleigh and Dornfell roads between 1883 and

1887. Another 10 were built in Broomsleigh Road in 1890 and two in Ravenshaw Street in 1894.[28]

Land companies were probably responsible for similar activity on the Flitcroft estate. Although the name Parsifal Road was approved in 1883,[29] no houses went up there until the 1890s but Hackney or New College, a brick building with majolica dressings designed by W. P. Manning, was built at the eastern end in 1887.[30] The National Standard Land Mortgage and Investment Co. constructed Ingham and Burrard roads between Fortune Green Road and Finchley Road in 1885 and 64 small terraced houses were constructed there between 1886 and 1892 by Rathbone, Gray, Pulling, Brown, and other builders, while much of the frontage on Fortune Green Road and Finchley Road was covered with houses and shops. A Congregational church was built at the junction of Burrard and Finchley roads in 1894. Between 1890 and 1897 c. 13 larger detached or semi-detached houses were built in Parsifal Road.[31] A land company was probably also involved in building lower middle-class terraces on the rest of the Flitcroft estate south of the cemetery and west of Fortune Green, where fear of the cemetery outweighed the advantage of adjacent open space. W. H. Suttle, of Agamemnon Road, was the main builder of 155 houses in Agamemnon, Ajax, Ulysses, and Achilles roads between 1886 and 1896.[32] In 1895 Lyncroft Gardens was constructed through the site of Woodbine Cottage, former home of the Eleys and later of the society beauty, Mrs. Laura Thistlethwayte, at the south-eastern corner of the Flitcroft estate. E. J. Cave, one of the district's most prominent builders, built 21 houses and four blocks of flats there in 1896-7. In 1898 Emmanuel church moved from its mission church in Aldred Road to the corner of Lyncroft Gardens and West End Green, next to the recently closed Cock and Hoop. The site was sold to Cave, who became bankrupt in 1900, whereupon H. A. Rayner, a speculative builder from Croydon, acquired it, demolished the inn, and in 1902 built Alexandra Mansions on the site. Cave had been involved in work on the neighbouring Cannon Hill estate where Marlborough, Buckingham, and Avenue mansions were built in the triangle formed by Cannon Hill, Finchley Road, and West End Lane in 1896-1900.[33]

The eastern side of West End Lane, with its three large houses, remained unchanged almost until 1900. There was one road, Blackburn Road, named after a local builder, by 1869, where Joseph Sloper's engineering works were established in 1872, but Sloper failed to exploit it and the works remained isolated between the railway lines.[34] Maj.-Gen. Sir

[22] D.S.R.; Wade, *W. Hampstead*, 20-1; O.S. Map 1/2,500, Lond. XXVII (1894-6 edn.); Stanford, *Libr. Map of Lond.* (1891 edn.), sheet 5. The southern part of Sumatra and Pandora rds. belonged to the neighbouring Ripley est.

[23] Wade, *W. Hampstead*, 13, 28; O.S. Map 1/2,500, TQ 2585 (1955 edn.); D.S.R.; *Kelly's Dir. Hampstead and Childs Hill* (1900, 1902).

[24] D.S.R.; *Kelly's Dir. Hampstead and Childs Hill* (1902, 1905).

[25] P.R.O., IR 29/21/24, nos. 101-4; M.M. & M., Lib. Q, pp. 533-5; Hutchings and Crowsley, *Hampstead and Highgate Dir.* (1874); O.S. Map 1/2,500, Lond. XXXVII (1894-6 edn.). For possible views of hos., see S.C.L.,

LR West End, Adm. Saumarez's ho.; LP Folios, At West End by J. J. Ripley; West End by C. Miles 1841.

[26] D.S.R.; Wade, *W. Hampstead*, 20.   [27] D.S.R.

[28] Ibid.; Wade, *W. Hampstead*, 21.

[29] The opera was first performed in 1882.

[30] Pevsner, *Lond.* ii. 189; Wade, *W. Hampstead*, 59.

[31] D.S.R.; Wade, *W. Hampstead*, 63; O.S. Map 1/2,500, TQ 2585 (1955 edn.).

[32] D.S.R.; Wade, *W. Hampstead*, 31. The northern part of Agamemnon Rd. was named Penelope Road in 1891: Stanford, *Libr. Map of Lond.* (1891 edn.), sheet 1.

[33] D.S.R.; Wade, *W. Hampstead*, 13, 63-4; *C.H.R.* ix. 9-12; O.S. Map 1/2,500, TQ 2585 (1955 edn.).

[34] Wade, *W. Hampstead*, 17; *C.H.R.* vii. 19; D.S.R.

C. Crauford Fraser, who had entertained the prince of Wales at West End Hall, died in 1896 and the house and 12 a. were sold for development in 1897. The adjacent Treherne and Canterbury houses were evidently disposed of at the same time and apparently Honeybourne, Fawley, and Lymington roads and Crediton Hill (originally Road) were laid out on the combined estates about 1897.[35] Building began in 1897 with two large blocks of flats, presumably Canterbury and Lymington mansions, on the site of Canterbury House. In 1899 houses were built in Lymington and Crediton roads and two blocks were erected at 'the corner of West End Lane and Crediton Road', probably Fawley and Crediton mansions on each side of Fawley Road. One builder, A. Davis, applied to build 21 houses in Honeybourne, Crediton, and Fawley roads in 1900 and by 1913 building on the combined estate was complete, mostly fair-sized semi-detached houses but including shops fronting West End Lane and Yale and Harvard courts, built c. 1903 in Honeybourne Road.[36] To the south, offices were built at the junction of West End Lane and Blackburn Road in 1905.[37]

In the period from the late 1870s to the 1890s West End, hitherto a village with grand houses, became increasingly working-class. At the end of the 1880s some big houses remained, classified as wealthy, upper middle-, and middle-class, but on the western side of West End Lane a 'fair proportion' of people with good, ordinary earnings was mixed with the middle class and residents in the West End Park estate were only 'fairly comfortable'. Most houses in West Hampstead, where building was 'still fast increasing', were for the 'better class of artisans, clerks, railway men, policemen, travellers and a few professional men'.[38] Railways influenced the timing and character of West End's growth but probably more important was the fact that West End Lane formed a boundary between large estates on the east and small and fragmented ones to the west.[39] The few sizeable estates to the west had tended to break up before the railway lines divided them and reduced them still further, the owners being content to take the immediate profit of selling to a land company or speculative builder.

Although West End was said to be within the area where old families made way for Jews and a 'Bohemian element',[40] it housed few artists and writers. Alfred Harmsworth, later Viscount Northcliffe, came to no. 31 Pandora Road in 1888 and in 1890 founded the Pandora Publishing Co. Another publisher, Arthur Waugh, lived at no. 11 Hillfield Road, where his author sons Alec and Evelyn were born in 1898 and 1903 respectively.[41] Sir Henry Walford Davies, the composer, lived at no. 21 Fawley Road from 1901 to 1911.[42]

Almost all the building in the period between the two world wars was in the north. Cholmley Lodge was demolished in 1921, and 17 blocks of flats were built fronting Mill Lane, Aldred, Hillfield, and Fortune Green roads between 1922 and 1927.[43] The industrial school in Hillfield Road closed in 1932 and its building was taken over by the adjacent Domestic Science College in 1934,[44] while in 1938 a new building by Lawrence of Bristol west of Hackney College in Finchley Road was opened for the New College displaced from Swiss Cottage.[45] The only other building was of small blocks of shops and flats (Queen's Mansions) north of no. 222 West End Lane and at the junctions of Finchley Road with West End Lane in 1927 and with Burrard Road in 1932, of flats in Sherriff Road and Holmdale Road in 1936, and of an office block at nos. 158–60 West End Lane in 1938.[46]

In 1930 all the area east of West End Lane and Fortune Green Road was classified as middle-class and wealthy, as was most of the area on the west side north of the railway lines and the eastern part of West End Park. The rest of West End Park, however, and most of the land companies' estates were inhabited by skilled workers and the like and were overcrowded.[47] Inhabitants included E. C. Bentley (1875–1956), the novelist, at no. 28 Lymington Road in the 1920s and Naum Gabo, the sculptor, at no. 101 Cholmley Gardens from 1938 to 1946. Nigel Balchin, the novelist, died in 1970 in Marlborough Mansions, Cannon Hill.[48]

West End suffered during the Second World War, although not so badly as to necessitate large-scale rebuilding. Bombed sites included nos. 76–86 Sumatra Road and nos. 9–17 Solent Road, which were replaced by an open space and clinic, and on the corner of Dennington Park Road where a library was built in 1954.[49] The council opened a terrace of eight three-storeyed houses on one bombed site in Agamemnon Road in 1952 and completed four flats in Gladys Road in 1953, when it started on eight dwellings in Broomsleigh Street and 18 fronting Dennington Park Road and West End Lane.[50] The demolition of Broomsleigh and Ravenshaw streets and Sumatra Road was urged c. 1955, because of bad drainage and neglected houses.[51] They had been overcrowded in the 1930s but survived in the 1980s. An ambitious scheme of 1963 for wholesale redevelopment along the three railway lines from Finchley Road to West End Lane had not been effected near West End by 1987.[52] The Kingsgate general improvement area, planned in 1969, included the sites south of the railway and west of West End Lane, originally Nicoll's estate, but there had been little rebuilding in the West End section by 1984. As in many areas the main post-war trend

[35] Thompson, *Hampstead*, 344; Wade, *W. Hampstead*, 14, 16, 65; *Hampstead Advertiser*, 7 May 1896 (S.C.L., Newton Cuttings Bk., p. 83).
[36] D.S.R.; L.C.C. *Municipal Map of Lond.* (1913); O.S. Map 1/2,500, TQ 2584, 2585 (1955 edn.); *Kelly's Dir. Hampstead and Childs Hill* (1902, 1905).
[37] D.S.R.
[38] Booth, *Life and Labour*, i (1), 16; iii (1), 208; map.
[39] Thompson, *Hampstead*, 376–7.
[40] Booth, *Life and Labour*, iii (1), 207.
[41] Wade, *W. Hampstead*, 21, 31.
[42] Ibid. 64.
[43] D.S.R.; Wade, *W. Hampstead*, 29.

[44] J. Tucker, *Emmanuel Ch., West End* (1981), 60.
[45] Wade, *W. Hampstead*, 59.
[46] D.S.R.
[47] *New Lond. Life and Labour*, iv, map of overcrowding; vii, maps 8, 10, 11.
[48] Wade, *W. Hampstead*, 29, 64, 66.
[49] *Hampstead, 1939–45* (Camden History Soc. 1977); Wade, *W. Hampstead*, 20–1; O.S. Map 1/2,500, TQ 2584 (1955 edn.).
[50] Hampstead Boro. *Rep. on Housing* (1952, 1954).
[51] Hampstead Communist party, *Homes for Hampstead* [c. 1955].
[52] *Contract Jnl.* 2 May 1963.

was towards the refurbishing and conversion of old houses to flats, with young, single people replacing families.[53] Other changes included the conversion of the Congregational church at the corner of Finchley and Burrard roads to a synagogue in 1947 and the building of a community centre by Seifert in Dennington Park Road for the synagogue there in 1964.[54] In 1966 the Domestic Science college moved to Tottenham and Berridge House was demolished, to be replaced in 1972 by a police station.[55]

KILBURN, EDGWARE ROAD, AND CRICKLEWOOD.

The name Kilburn, used c. 1134 as Cuneburna, the royal or possibly cow's stream,[56] was applied to the priory built beside the stream and later to the whole neighbourhood on both sides of Edgware Road. The western portion, in Willesden parish, has been treated elsewhere.[57] Before c. 1134 there was a hermitage, probably on Edgware Road, where Kilburn priory was built shortly afterwards.[58] By 1535 the priory buildings included a mansion and a 'hostium', which may have been the priory's guesthouse,[59] possibly the origin of the Red Lion, traditionally said to date from 1444. The mansion 'opposite the hostium' may have stood on the site later occupied by the Bell, said to date from c. 1600,[60] which was part of a freehold estate probably once belonging to Kilburn priory but detached from the other priory lands by 1704.[61] At the northern end of Edgware Road a substantial dwellinghouse was built in 1522 on the Hospitallers' estate, presumably Shoot Up Hill Farm south of the junction with Mill Lane.[62]

A 13th-century family surnamed de Kilburn presumably lived there,[63] and in 1296 John de Kilburn sold his house and 20 a. to the lord of the manor.[64] The tenement was still in the lord's hand, leased out in 1312, but none of the other customary estates described then can be located in Kilburn, although John of Eton, who had a piece of land in 1312, later held a house and land in Kilburn Street.[65] There was a house in Kilburn Lane, the southern part of West End Lane, in 1598[66] and a cottage at Shoot Up Hill, associated with the western, copyhold, portion of Earlsfield, in 1632.[67] There was at least one cottage in 'Kilburn Street' or high road in 1637.[68] By 1646 there were at least 10 houses and 5 cottages in the area, including the farmhouses of the Shoot Up Hill, Gilberts, and Liddell estates.[69] The house on the Little estate, assessed for five hearths,[70] was

leased to Thomas Green, an alehouse keeper, in 1653 and 1667[71] and by 1674 was occupied by Walter Green, a farmer.[72] The Black Lion, built on the waste bordering the Little estate north of the farmhouse, displays the date 1666.[73]

By 1714 a medicinal well had been discovered and exploited near the Bell, which by 1733 opened gardens and a great room for the 'politest companies' in a pale imitation of Hampstead wells.[74] The Kilburn wells did not, in contrast to Hampstead town, stimulate building and by 1762 there were still only 10 houses, 7 cottages, a tollhouse, a smith's shop, and 3 public houses on Edgware Road.[75] Any 17th-century building in Kilburn Lane had gone by the 1740s and the cottages on Earlsfield in Mill Lane disappeared between the 1740s and 1762.[76] Although Edgware Road shared with Haverstock Hill the combination of accessibility to London with a rural setting,[77] it did not attract gentry and London merchants in the same way, possibly because it lacked the height to give fine views.

Building during the 18th century included the rebuilding of the old farmhouse on the Liddell estate and the construction of 5 cottages by 1771 and then their replacement by a new brick house by 1807.[78] Most of the building was of cottages on waste along Edgware Road bordering the Liddell and Little estates.[79] More extensive building began on the Kilburn priory estate, which bordered St. John's Wood in St. Marylebone, where development was already well in hand by 1819 when Fulk Greville Howard (formerly Upton) bought it. In the same year he made an agreement with John Gelsthorp and Henry Jay, carpenters from Marylebone and Kilburn respectively, to build on plots fronting an existing farm lane (Abbey Lane) running south from West End Lane, with the intention of granting 99-year leases once the houses were completed. The builders were small men with little capital and their houses were small, pairs joined by a single storey. Gelsthorp, who also built a range of stables, went bankrupt in 1821 and Jay in 1825 and the plots were sold by auction to investors.[80] Howard made an agreement in 1819 with George Pocock, a surveyor who lived on the Marylebone side of Edgware Road, to take a field on the parish border and build residences for the gentry. He laid out Greville Place, then in Marylebone, with plots for detached and semi-detached villas, six or seven of which had been built by the time building ceased in 1825.[81] A group of

---

[53] Camden Boro. Plan, *W. Hampstead and Kilburn*, Spr. 1975, Area 5. For Kingsgate, below, Kilburn.
[54] Wade, *W. Hampstead*, 20, 59.
[55] Ibid. 62.
[56] *P.N. Mdx.* (E.P.N.S.), 112.
[57] *V.C.H. Mdx.* vii.
[58] Below, other est.
[59] *Valor Eccl.* (Rec. Com.), i. 432.
[60] *Images of Hampstead*, 152.
[61] G.L.R.O., E/MW/H/I/2311A, s.v. John Aldridge. Cf. ibid. 2123, 2178, s.v. Halton Vear (Vere); S.C.L., Man. Map and Fieldbk. nos. 533–5, freehold.
[62] B.L. Cott. MS. Claud. E. vi, ff. 235v.–236; below, other est.
[63] e.g. Wm. and Ric. in 1259; W.A.M. 32360; Maud in 1281: ibid. 32361.
[64] Ibid. 32359.
[65] Ibid. 32357; C.U.L., Kk. V. 29, ff. 30v., 34.
[66] G.L.R.O., E/MW/H/1, s.v. 1598, 1600.
[67] Ibid. 2; below, other est.

[68] Thos. Bassill d. seised of 6 cottages. The location of the other 5 is uncertain: G.L.R.O., E/MW/H/3.
[69] Barratt, *Annals*, iii, App. 3, pp. 359–64; below, other est.
[70] G.L.R.O., MR/TH/2, m. 29d.; P.R.O., E 179/143/370, m. 43d.
[71] G.L.R.O., Cal. Sess. Bks. ii, p. 52; MJ/SBB 241, p. 35.
[72] P.R.O., E 179/143/370, m. 43d.; G.L.R.O., MR/FB/1/20; E/MW/H/12, s.v. 1693.
[73] Wade, *W. Hampstead*, 36.
[74] *Images of Hampstead*, 152; below, social.
[75] S.C.L., Man. Map and Fieldbk. nos. 482–535. The Black Lion was then called the Red Lion: ibid. no. 507.
[76] Ibid. nos. 494–5; Rocque, *Map of Lond.* (1741–5), sheet 12.   [77] Cf. *Images of Hampstead*, 152.
[78] M.M. & M., Lib. E, p. 423; L, pp. 102–25.
[79] Newton, *Map of Hampstead* (1814).
[80] Thompson, *Hampstead*, 76–7, 84–6; S.C.L., D 14.
[81] Thompson, *Hampstead*, 86–7.

houses called Prospect Place had been built fronting Edgware Road south of the junction with West End Lane, and a field lane linking West End Lane with Edgware Road near the parish boundary had been turned into a private road, later called Kilburn Priory, by 1829.[82] Howard's ambitions had not, however, been realized. As a wealthy man Howard could afford to wait until the demand for houses revived but his experience may have been responsible for the behaviour of Samuel Ware, the surveyor and architect of the duke of Portland's London estate.[83] Ware, who already owned property elsewhere in Hampstead, bought the Little estate in 1822[84] and began almost immediately to sell off pieces of it.[85] By 1841 he had leased the remaining 12 a. bordering Edgware Road to five or more tenants, one a nurseryman but the others including a solicitor, who occupied Oak Lodge. The Grange, possibly in existence by 1841, was occupied by a retired coachbuilder, Thomas Peters, by 1851.[86] Sidney Terrace existed at the north of the estate by 1842, as did Royston Hall on the Gilberts estate.[87]

Building began again on the Kilburn priory estate in 1843 when Howard made an agreement with William Cullum, a china manufacturer, who had built four substantial houses by 1846 when Howard died.[88] In 1845 Howard made an agreement with James Carter, a Maida Vale builder, who laid out Springfield Lane (originally Goldsmith's Place, Osborne Terrace, and Bell Terrace), built Greville (originally Manchester) Mews and two-storeyed tenements (Manchester Place) backing the stables and the Bell and Red Lion, and built some more 'classy' houses in Springfield Villas (later Kilburn Priory). Carter was still building in 1849 but in 1851 he was superseded by George Duncan, a substantial developer from Grove End Road on the Eyre estate, with whom Col. Arthur Upton, heir to the Kilburn priory estate on Howard's death in 1846, made a building agreement for 15½ a. In Kilburn Priory, Priory Road, and St. George's Road, Duncan built mostly pairs of good-class villas, with some terraces of shops in Belsize Road, extended westward from the Eyre estate, a public house in West End Lane and a church, St. Mary's, built in Abbey Road in 1856. Some 69 houses were built in Kilburn between 1845 and 1850 and another 200 were added between 1851 and 1857, mostly by Duncan and, after 1854, by his son John Wallace Duncan, but about a third by a number of small builders on underleases. The Duncan houses, Italianate and three-storeyed, were mostly north of the L.N.W.R. railway, built through the middle of the estate in 1837, and some of the occupants used Kilburn station, opened on it in 1852. The main access to

London was by horse omnibus along Edgware Road. Some larger houses were built on higher ground in Greville and Mortimer roads, laid out in 1853. By 1860 building was almost complete on the estate.[89]

There was little growth elsewhere in the area before 1860. At Shoot Up Hill new farm buildings replaced old ones, which were converted to a cottage, and a new lodge was built c. 1852. One house was built in Cricklewood in 1853[90] and the Bell was rebuilt in 1863.[91] David Tildesley, a Paddington ironmonger, filled some of the gaps on the Kilburn priory estate, in St. George's Road and Alexandra Road, in 1867.[92]

The estate most directly affected by the railways was Gilbert's across which the Hampstead Junction railway was built in 1860. The railway company acquired some 6½ a. from Gilberts, then held by Thomas H. Ripley, in 1864–5, and another 10 a. were sold to the Midland Railway Co. in 1867.[93] Royston Hall was replaced by some five houses in 1871–2. The rest of the estate was enfranchised in 1868[94] and sold by 1869 to land companies. The British Land Co., which bought the portion north of the Hampstead Junction railway, obtained approval in 1869 for the formation of Iverson, Loveridge, and Maygrove roads and Ariel Street.[95] Station Road, where six houses were built in 1874–5, may have been an early name for Iverson Road. By 1878 all four roads had been laid out between the railway lines and c. 70 houses and a Baptist chapel built;[96] another 195 houses had been added by 1882. In 1879 at the east end of the estate John Edward Medley of St. John's Wood, who had bought the plot in 1872, built 11 houses in Medley Road.[97] The portion of the Gilberts estate south of the railway was sold to the United Land Co. which in 1869 obtained approval for Netherwood, Kelson, and Linstead streets, named after directors of the company.[98] Netherwood Street was originally called Royston Road, after Royston Hall, which made way for it. Some 80 houses were built on the estate between 1871 and 1880. In 1880–1 a board school and a mission hall were built in Netherwood Street.[99] Adjoining the Gilberts estate to the south was the Little estate, the northern part of which had been sold off in 1827.[1] By 1862 it, together with other parts of the estate to the east, was in the hands of Donald Nicoll.[2] He built Palmerston Road in 1865, which was linked to the United Land Co. estate. Building, of cramped terraces as on the land company estates, was almost complete by 1871.[3]

Although plans were drawn up in 1855 to develop the Powell-Cotton Shoot Up Hill estate, they were delayed by uncertainty over the course of the railway.[4] The earliest development on the family's

[82] *Cruchley's New Plan* (1829).
[83] Thompson, *Hampstead*, 88, 130.
[84] M.M. & M., Lib. K, pp. 603–5; P, pp. 502–12.
[85] Ibid. Lib. L, pp. 92–6, 225, 267–9, 467–8; M, pp. 19–21.
[86] Ibid. P, pp. 502–12; P.R.O., IR 29/21/24, nos. 113–16; HO 107/1492/7. The Grange and Oak Lodge were not the same bldg., as in Wade, *W. Hampstead*, 37.
[87] *Laurie's Plan of Lond.*, Westminster (1842).
[88] Thompson, *Hampstead*, 254.
[89] Ibid. 254–9; D.S.R.; Wade, *W. Hampstead*, 43. For Kilburn in 1860, below, plate 10.   [90] D.S.R.
[91] Wade, *W. Hampstead*, 36.
[92] Thompson, *Hampstead*, 259.
[93] M.M. & M., Lib. Q, pp. 99–100, 158–60, 399–401.

[94] Ibid. pp. 536–9.
[95] Thompson, *Hampstead*, 371–2.
[96] D.S.R.; *Metrop. Improvement Map No. 46* (1878).
[97] D.S.R.; Wade, *W. Hampstead*, 32.
[98] M.M. & M., Lib. Q, pp. 536–9; Wade, *W. Hampstead*, 36.
[99] D.S.R.; *Metrop. Improvement Map No. 46* (1878).
[1] M.M. & M., Lib. L, pp. 467–8.
[2] Ibid. Lib. P, pp. 502–12, map; Q, pp. 536–9, map; above, West End.
[3] Wade, *W. Hampstead*, 36; *Metrop. Improvement Map No. 46* (1878); no entries for Palmerston Rd. from 1871: D.S.R.
[4] Thompson, *Hampstead*, 375; Wade, *W. Hampstead*, 23.

estates began in the south, north of the existing L.N.W.R. line and adjacent to the built-up areas of the Kilburn priory estate. In 1866 plans were approved for a number of roads on the Powell-Cotton's Liddell estate, mostly named after places in Kent near the Powell-Cotton family seat of Quex Park: Quex, Birchington, and Mutrix roads. A Roman Catholic church and Wesleyan and Unitarian chapels were built in Quex Road in 1868–9[5] and at least 55 houses were built on the estate between 1871 and 1885.[6] In 1874 building spread to the eastern part of the Powell-Cotton estates at Kilburn Woods, which lay between West End Lane and the Maryon Wilson estate. By agreement Col. Henry Cotton laid out Canfield (later Priory) Road on the boundary between the estates and some 45 houses were built there between 1877 and 1882. Acol Road was laid out to link with the development to the east. Between 1874 and 1886 parallel roads were laid out to the north and 56 mostly detached and semi-detached houses built in Acol Road (1877–9), Woodchurch Road (1878–9), Cleve Road (1882–6), and Chislett Road (1884–8, later the western section of Compayne Gardens), and 19 stables in Acol Mews (1879) and West Hampstead Mews (1886–7).[7]

On the western side of West End Lane, on the Powell-Cotton (Liddell) estate north of Quex Road, the Chimes, a large house built in the 1860s by E. W. Pugin for the painter John Rogers Herbert (1810–90), for some time insulated the area from further building.[8] Building spread northward from Quex Road west of the Chimes. Kingsgate Road, named after another place in Kent, stretched northward to the estate border by 1875 and 77 houses were built there between 1878 and 1888.[9] On the remnants of the adjoining Little estate a new lodge and house were built at Oak Lodge in 1877.[10] A road, Eresby Road, was planned across the southern part of the Little estate between Edgware Road and Kingsgate Road in 1879[11] and 26 houses were built there between 1883 and 1885; houses and shops were built by R. Rose on the Oak Lodge estate in 1881. Eleven houses were built in Smyrna Road, on the Liddell estate, opposite Eresby Road, in 1883 and two roads to the north, Gascony and Messina avenues, were constructed across both estates; 130 houses were built there between 1881 and 1887.[12] Of the Little estate, only the Grange and nursery lands remained untouched.[13]

Stables and workshops were built in Kingsgate Mews and Place from 1886 and another 30 houses and 6 shops were added in Kingsgate Road 1892–6, 12 houses in Eresby Road 1891–2, and 49 houses in Mazenod Avenue 1891–6 and flats (presumably Priory Court) 1899–1900. The last were probably part of the development on the site of the Chimes which was given over to the builders in the late 1890s. A block of flats (Douglas Mansions) was built

at the corner of West End Lane and Quex Road in 1896 and another three blocks there (King's Gardens) in 1897.[14]

Five houses were built behind the Bell in 1871. Houses, workshops, and shops were built fronting Edgware Road on all the estates from 1872. Some were on the Shoot Up Hill estate, south of the farmhouse, by 1878, and George Verey, lessee of the farm, was responsible for building houses there in 1881. H. B. Oldrey of Albert Works, Kilburn, rebuilt the Red Lion and built some houses and shops in Kilburn High Road in 1890 and three houses in Kilburn Priory in 1893.[15]

The Liddell and Little estates were built by several local builders including Henry Stock of Gascony Avenue and J. Bursill. The Powell-Cottons controlled the development of the Shoot Up Hill estate, where Kentish names predominated. Fordwych Road, from Mill Lane to Maygrove Road, defined the eastern boundary of the estate, and was linked to Edgware Road by Garlinge Road, planned in 1880, and Dandelion (later St. Cuthbert's) Road, planned in 1882. Between 1880 and 1892 some 147 houses, a church, and a school were built in the new roads. The principal builder was Joshua Parnell of Fordwych Road. Another 12 houses were built fronting Shoot Up Hill between 1890 and 1894. In 1911 permission was given for Kingscroft Road on the site of Shoot Up Hill Farm and the Elms; 7 houses were built there before 1914.[16]

In the 1890s building on the Powell-Cotton estate spread north of Mill Lane.[17] Fordwych Road was extended north of the lane by 1892 and most of the 57 houses built in the road between 1892 and 1907 were probably in the northern section.[18] The new roads, named after Kentish places or places abroad visited by Maj. Percy Powell-Cotton, were Minster Road (30 houses between 1891 and 1900), Gondar Gardens (52 houses between 1892 and 1896 and 5 blocks of flats in 1899), Westbere Road (30 houses and a school between 1893 and 1904), Sarre Road (25 houses between 1896 and 1904), Skardu Road (48 houses in 1897), Manstone Road (15 houses in 1899–1900), and Rondu Road (6 houses in 1900). At the northern end of the estate c. 23 shops and dwellings were built in the Parade, Cricklewood, and in Richborough Road in 1885 and between 1892 and 1899. Most of those in Richborough Road and Ebbsfleet Road, named in 1893, were presumably built 1901–3.[19] Some 22 houses were built in Somali Road between 1904 and 1908 and 6 in Menelik Road in 1913. By 1913 the only land left unbuilt was on the northern borders of the Powell-Cotton estate and at Kilburn Grange, which was acquired as a public park in 1911.[20]

There was a greater proportion of the 'fairly comfortable, good ordinary earnings' category in Kilburn c. 1890 than in any other district of Hampstead. The

[5] Wade, W. Hampstead, 38.   [6] D.S.R.
[7] Ibid.; Thompson, Hampstead, 319–20; S.C.L., H 912.421 file 1875, plan of bldg. site Canfield Rd. 1875.
[8] Wade, W. Hampstead, 18.
[9] D.S.R.; Wade, W. Hampstead, 39.
[10] M.M. & M., Lib. P, pp. 502–12; D.S.R.
[11] Wade, W. Hampstead, 39.
[12] D.S.R.
[13] Stanford, Libr. Map of Lond. (1891 edn.), sheet 5.
[14] D.S.R.

[15] Ibid.; Metrop. Improvement Map No. 46 (1878); poor rate bks. 1864.
[16] D.S.R.; Wade, W. Hampstead, 23–5.
[17] Para. based on D.S.R.; Wade, W. Hampstead, 25–6.
[18] Only the W. side of the road, N. from opposite St. Cuthbert's ch., remained empty in 1891: Stanford, Libr. Map of Lond. (1891 edn.), sheet 5.
[19] D.S.R. not available.
[20] L.C.C. Municipal Map of Lond. (1913); The Times, 6 July 1912, 10f.

most spacious and therefore high-class area was the Powell-Cottons Kilburn Woods estate, designated middle-class and well-to-do, with one street, Cleve Road, upper middle- and middle-class. There was one other upper middle-class area, Greville Road, an extension of the Marylebone part of the Kilburn priory estate. Most of the Hampstead section of that estate, together with the southern part of the Powell-Cottons' Liddell estate, was middle-class but the mews and industrial sections of both estates were of lower status, as was the housing on the land companies' estates in the centre. Although most houses were terraced and, by Hampstead standards, densely packed, the pressure of population and increasing rents led to some division among families and the taking of lodgers. In 1887 severe weather and unemployment caused great suffering to the poor in Kilburn. Booth noted the social decadence of the whole area, the lack of religious attendance, the arrival of the Jews, and the prevalence of the artistic and Bohemian element.[21] The biggest increase, however, was in the Irish and, compared with elsewhere in Hampstead, the artistic element was meagre. H. G. Wells taught from 1889 to 1890 at a school in Mortimer Road (later Crescent),[22] and there were studios at no. 1 Woodchurch Road and nos. 24–6 Greville Road belonging to Seymour Lucas (1882–1904) and Goscombe John (1860–1952) respectively.[23]

Building resumed on the northern borders of the borough on the Powell-Cotton estate after 1918, with some 70 houses being built in Westbere, Somali, Menelik, and Asmara roads between 1922 and 1928. Almost all the building of the 1930s was of flats on the sites of earlier houses. On the Kilburn Woods estate it included no. 17 Acol Road in 1932, Acol Court at the junction with West End Lane in 1934, Kingswood Court to the south in 1935, Cleve House in Cleve Road in 1935, and Embassy House at the junction of Cleve Road and West End Lane in 1936–7. On the Kilburn priory estate Hillsborough Court, a neo-Tudor block decorated with heraldic motifs in stone, was built for Greville Estates in Mortimer Crescent in 1933 and Ascot Lodge was built at the corner of Greville Road and Place in 1939. Between 1934 and 1938 Fordwych, Hillcrest, and Kendal courts and Warwick Lodge were built on the sites of nos. 50–64 Shoot Up Hill, on either side of Mill Lane.[24] In 1935 the Westcroft estate, 290 houses, was built by Douglas & Wood for Hampstead council just over the border in the Hendon part of Cricklewood.[25]

By 1930 the United Land Co.'s estate at Netherwood Street and Palmerston Road was occupied by unskilled labourers and contained some poverty and overcrowding. There was overcrowding to a lesser extent on the adjacent British Land Co.'s estate which, together with the southern part of the Liddell estate and parts of the Kilburn priory estate, was mostly occupied by skilled workers.[26] The cosmopolitan and Irish elements continued to grow in the area, which did not particularly attract European artist refugees. Artists in the district between the wars included the painters Sir Frank Dicksee (1853–1928) at no. 3 Greville Place and David Bomberg (1890–1957), the cubist and vorticist, at no. 10 Fordwych Road 1930–3 before moving to Lymington Road, then to Greville Place, and finally to Belsize. John Drinkwater (1882–1937), the poet, lived at North Hall, Mortimer Crescent, from 1934. Harry St. John Philby (1885–1960), diplomat and traveller, lived with his family, including the future spy Kim, at no. 10 Acol Road from 1930 to 1949.[27]

Bomb-damage was widespread during the Second World War, possibly because the railways were an obvious target.[28] It combined with overcrowding in densely packed back-to-back houses to necessitate extensive rebuilding. The first post-war borough council estate was Kilburn Priory or Gate, which started in 1948 with plans for 94 flats on 2½ a. off Kilburn Priory near the southern border. The first 60 flats were opened in 1951, the rest, designed by J. B. K. Cowper, in 1957. In 1953 Sidney Boyd Court, three blocks containing 80 flats, was opened on the east side of West End Lane, between Woodchurch and Acol roads.[29] Forty-three dwellings were under construction in Springfield Lane, Kilburn, in 1954.[30] At the other end of the district the Templar House estate, 112 flats by Frank Scarlett on 3½ a. at Shoot Up Hill, between Garlinge and St. Cuthbert's roads, which had been cleared for flats before the war, was opened in 1954.[31] On a smaller scale were flats in Garlinge Road, designed in 1967–9 by David Hyde-Harrison[32] and old people's homes, designed on a hexagonal system, on 1 a. at the corner of Priory and Woodchurch roads in 1967.[33] In 1969 the whole of the area bounded by Edgware Road, West End Lane, and the railway lines was made a general improvement area.[34] The first phase, a council estate called Florence Cayford, later Webheath, designed by the borough architect Sidney Cook, was opened in two stages, in 1970 and 1972, to house 400 people on a site cleared of the notorious slums in the Netherwood Street and Palmerston Road area.[35] In 1975 on the Kingsgate estate to the south 146 new houses were built in the area south of Gascony Avenue and west of Kingsgate Road, and there was building in Smyrna Road.[36]

In 1947 the L.C.C. announced a scheme for 104

[21] Booth, *Life and Lab.* map; i (1), 16–17; iii (1), 207, 214; *The Times*, 26 Mar. 1887, 4*e*; Thompson, *Hampstead*, 259, 378–9. [22] *C.H.R.* x. 2–4.
[23] Wade, *W. Hampstead*, 41, 43.
[24] D.S.R.; O.S. Map 1/2,500, TQ 2485, 2584 (1955 edn.).
[25] W. Barnes, *Century of Camden Housing* [1972] (S.C.L., P.B. Housing Gen.); O.S. Map 1/2,500, TQ 2485 (1955 edn.); *The Times*, 9 Nov. 1956, 6*f*.
[26] *New Lond. Life and Labour*, i. 423; iv, map of overcrowding; vii, maps 8, 10, 11.
[27] Wade, *W. Hampstead*, 23–5, 41–3; *D.N.B.*
[28] *Hampstead 1939–45* (Camden History Soc. 1977).
[29] Hampstead Boro. *Rep. on Housing* (1948, 1949, 1952); S.C.L., P.B. Housing, Camden Gen. file, MS. list of Camden housing est. (1971); O.S. Map 1/2,500, TQ 2584 (1955, 1973 edns.).
[30] Hampstead Boro. *Rep. on Housing* (1954).
[31] *The Times*, 5 Nov. 1954, 6*b*; Hampstead Boro. *Rep. on Housing* (1948, 1952); Wade, *W. Hampstead*, 25; D.S.R.
[32] MS. list of Camden housing est. (1971).
[33] *Architect and Bldg. News*, 29 Nov. 1967 (Guildhall, Noble Colln. BH 3/P & T 1967).
[34] Camden Boro. Plan, *W. Hampstead and Kilburn*, Spr. 1975, Area 5.
[35] MS. list of Camden housing est. (1971); Wade, *W. Hampstead*, 36; *Hampstead News*, 20 Sept. 1969 (S.C.L. H 728.3/West End file).
[36] Camden Boro. Plan, *W. Hampstead and Kilburn*, Spr. 1975, Area 5; MS. list of Camden housing est. (1971); *Kelly's Dir. Lond.* (1976, 1980).

flats in Kilburn Vale. The estate, south of West End Lane, which involved the demolition of some of the earliest building in the area in Kilburn Vale and Abbey Lane, was opened *c.* 1951. In 1948 the L.C.C. began clearing the area between Greville Road and Mortimer Place and Crescent, which it replaced with the Mortimer Crescent estate, eight small-scale, brick blocks of flats, which were opened *c.* 1955.[37] A second phase of the Kilburn Vale estate, north of West End Lane, bound by Mutrix and Quex roads and involving the demolition of the eastern part of Birchington Road, was completed by 1984.[38] In 1984 two estates in the area belonged to the Cicely Davies housing association, 16 flats in converted houses at nos. 6 and 8 Woodchurch Road, and 70 flats on the Priory Road estate.[39]

A high proportion of the population, especially in Kilburn, lived in council houses. There was said to be a 40 per cent increase in the number of homes in West Hampstead and Kilburn between 1966 and 1971, and overcrowding fell: it had been 0.96 per room in Kilburn ward and 1.45 in Priory ward in 1921, was 0.92 and 0.88 respectively in 1951, and was 0.78 and 0.70 respectively in 1971. The improvement was, however, aided by a decline in population from 26,286 in the two wards in 1921 to 24,085 in 1971. After the war immigrants were numerous: the Irish still came and there were West Indians and Indians and Pakistanis, all of whom tended to have larger families than average, a characteristic noted in Kilburn ward in 1971. Nevertheless, the proportion of households (4,200) to population (10,181) in Kilburn ward was less than in Hampstead Town ward and there were many people living singly.[40]

In spite of the large-scale redevelopment, traces remained in 1987 of most of the phases of the area's history. The Bell and Red Lion, though rebuilt in 1863 and 1890 respectively,[41] still stood on their original sites, as did the Black Lion, rebuilt in 1898 and a listed building. Also listed were the early 19th-century nos. 1–5 Greville Place and nos. 24 and 26 Greville Road, remnants of the earliest building estates on the Kilburn priory estate, and nos. 13–19 (odd) Greville Place and no. 37 Greville Road, from the mid 19th century.[42] Edgware Road contained examples, mostly of terraces fronted by shops, from every decade from the 1860s. As building spread northward the earlier stucco and stock brick gave way to the red-brick terraced and semi-detached houses of the northern Powell-Cotton estate. The northern area at Cricklewood was homogeneous, entirely residential except for the shops in Edgware

Road, but Kilburn was a mixture of elegant stuccoed Regency villas, Victorian stock-brick terraces, mansion flats of the 1890s, post-1945 council blocks, small-scale industry, and shops. In Kilburn High Road the fish shops, public houses, and small factories and shops selling exotic vegetables and saris reflected the successive waves of immigrants that have given Kilburn its cosmopolitan flavour.

BELSIZE.[43] The Belsize estate, with its frontage on both sides of Haverstock Hill, was an early magnet for merchants and others who wanted a country house within easy reach of London. Apart from the manor house of Belsize, there was one house on the estate by 1549, probably on the eastern side of Haverstock Hill, near the southern boundary of the parish.[44] It was associated with brickmaking by 1557, by which date there were two other houses, one of them a new house belonging to Philip Cockram (or Cokerham), a London mercer.[45] Cockram's house apparently existed in 1664, when it was assessed for 5 hearths.[46] On the west side of the main road a house was built by Sir Isaac Wake (d. 1632), a courtier. Screened by a grove, and standing back from the road, it was described as a fine seat with its views and walks of pines and firs.[47] The house, which was assessed at 17 hearths, one of the largest in the parish, in 1664,[48] had passed by 1646 to John Wilde, Chief Baron of the Exchequer and parliamentarian, who died there in 1669.[49] It was inherited by his daughter and her husband Charles West, Baron De La Warr (d. 1687),[50] who sold it *c.* 1683 to a London citizen, probably John Coggs, a goldsmith to whom the lease was assigned after 1685 and who rebuilt the house in 1686. The lease was assigned to Thomas Ketteridge, upholsterer,[51] and the under-lease sold in 1711 to William Paget, Baron Paget (d. 1713), listed as occupier in 1714, when the house was set in formal gardens.[52]

Several other houses existed on the estate on the western side of Haverstock Hill by 1646. One, occupied by John Mascall,[53] who was still there in 1650,[54] was probably the house south of the Avenue which was occupied in 1679 by Thomas Butler[55] and in 1714 was called the Blue House.[56] Another, leased with 16 a. to Benjamin Rutland, was probably the farmhouse at the south end of the estate at the junction of the London road with what was later called England's Lane[57] in 1679; it was occupied by John Newman and in 1714 by Thomas Stringfield.[58] At the northern end of the estate Ambrose Turner occupied in 1646 a 'fair mansion house'[59] which was

[37] *The Times*, 28 June 1947, 3*b*; 21 Feb. 1948, 2*c*; *Kelly's Dir. Lond.* (1950, 1952, 1954, 1955); O.S. Map 1/2,500, TQ 2584 (1955 edn.).
[38] *Kelly's Dir. Lond.* (1980, 1985); personal observation, 1984.
[39] St. Marylebone Housing Assoc. *Ann. Rep.* (1984), 9.
[40] *Census*, 1921–71; Camden Boro. Plan, *W. Hampstead and Kilburn*, Spr. 1975, Area 5.
[41] Wade, *W. Hampstead*, 35–6.
[42] S.C.L., Town and Country Planning, 52nd List of Bldgs. (1974).   [43] See also below, other est. (Belsize).
[44] W.A.M. 16476; P.R.O., C 2/Jas. I/W 10/29.
[45] W.A.M. 16475. For the position of the tilekiln, see survey 1679: S.C.L., D 136–7, no. 3.
[46] Occupied by John Marsh: G.L.R.O., MR/TH/2, m. 29d.; P.R.O., C 54/3553, no. 33.
[47] Thompson, *Hampstead*, 19, quoting J. Aubrey, *Brief*

Lives, ed. A. Powell (1949), 318.
[48] G.L.R.O., MR/TH/2, m. 29d.
[49] Barratt, *Annals*, iii, App. 3, pp. 359–61; *D.N.B.*
[50] P.R.O., E 179/143/370, m. 43d.; S.C.L., D 136–7, no. I; *Complete Peerage*, s.v. De La Warr.
[51] Aubrey, *Brief Lives*, 318; W.A.M. 16501.
[52] P.R.O., C 10/519/57; W.A.M. 16545; W.A.M. Map 12450, no. 17; *D.N.B.*
[53] Barratt, *Annals*, iii, App. 3, pp. 359–61.
[54] P.R.O., C 54/3553, no. 33.
[55] S.C.L., D 136–7, no. a.
[56] W.A.M. Map 12450, no. 2; W.A.M. 16545.
[57] Barratt, *Annals*, iii, App. 3, pp. 359–61; P.R.O., C 54/3553, no. 33.
[58] S.C.L., D 136–7, no. c; W.A.M. Map 12450, no. 1.
[59] Barratt, *Annals*, iii, App. 3, pp. 359–61; P.R.O., C 54/3553, no. 33.

assessed in 1664 at 7 hearths[60] and between 1679[61] and 1714 replaced by four houses, a shop and stable and a timber roughcast house in the extreme north,[62] which by 1730 housed the Red Lion.[63] In 1650 a dwelling had been formed from outbuildings belonging to the manor house[64] but it was presumably swept away in the rebuilding of the 1660s.

A large house, assessed at 16 hearths, was built between 1650 and 1664 on the north side of Belsize Lane.[65] Thomas Hawley or Haley (d. 1681), the London mercer who lived there, left it to his nephew to sell.[66] In 1714 it was called the White House and untenanted. Hawley may have built one or more houses nearby, which in 1714 were leased to Mrs. Hall.[67] Two more houses had been built by 1679. One, approached by a tree-lined walk from Wilde's house, lay on the western border of the estate and was then occupied by Mrs. Lister.[68] Although Elizabethan coins found under the floor and ring-dating of a Spanish chestnut in the avenue, blown down in 1884, suggested that the house was late 16th-century, it is not identifiable with any of those described in 1650 and is more likely to have been built c. 1667, the date of leaden cisterns on the site.[69] In 1685 it was leased to Richard Mulys of St. James, Westminster, who replaced the old house, which included a pigeon house, with a brick and slated mansion erected by a Westminster carpenter and a Hampstead bricklayer, whose work he found unsatisfactory.[70] It was probably that house which was later described as four-square, with a high mansard roof and square corner-turrets with pyramidal roofs. The chimney piece was carved by a pupil of Grinling Gibbons.[71] The house, called Mulys,[72] was occupied in 1714 by Mrs. Mulys[73] and in 1723 by William Fellows, underlessee of Thomas Ketteridge, who was obliged by the terms of his lease to pay for new buildings and repairs.[74] John Harris, a goldsmith, was the tenant of the second new house to have been built by 1679, south of the junction of Belsize Lane and the London road.[75] Capt. Edward Harris spent a considerable sum in new buildings and repairs and had two houses by 1714.[76]

All the buildings on the eastern side of the London road, with the possible exception of a barn, had apparently gone from the Belsize estate by 1679.[77]

An inn, called the Load of Hay or the Cart and Horses, stood on the roadside waste at the southern boundary by 1712.[78]

Between 1679 and 1714 the number of houses, excluding the manor house, increased from 6 or possibly 8 to 14;[79] by 1808 there were 22.[80] Apparently the whole estate suffered from the notoriety of Belsize House in the 1720s and 1730s[81] but in the later 18th century it again attracted outsiders of rank. Only three new houses were built between 1714 and 1750. One stood before 1723 on an orchard on Harris's estate on the south side of Belsize Lane at the point where the lane turned south-west.[82] In 1808 it was a 'Chinese-built cottage residence' (later Belsize Cottage).[83] The inhabitants of Hampstead subscribed c. 1734 to build a house for a poor cobbler,[84] which can probably be identified with a house and workshop on the waste on the east side of Haverstock Hill in 1762.[85] A 'neat timber and tiled' farmhouse, later called Holyland, Pickett's, or South End Farm, was built at South End Green probably by the 1740s.[86] Of the older houses, Wilde's was occupied by a Mr. Cartwright of St. James's in 1723 when over 100 trees in front were cut down by order of the bailiff of Hampstead manor.[87] It was let to a doctor in 1726 but had reverted to the lessee, Ketteridge, by the 1740s. It may have already fallen into decay and was almost certainly smaller than in the mid 17th century.[88] Mulys, later called Grove House, Shelford Lodge, and Rosslyn House, was occupied by the Fellows family from c. 1723 to c. 1777.[89]

A second house had probably been built on Wilde's estate by 1757.[90] One existed on the site later occupied by Rosslyn Lodge by 1774[91] and another small one adjoining Wilde's by 1779.[92] Wilde's house was occupied by Sarah Ketteridge until 1770 when, as 'an old messuage', it was leased to John Stokes, probably a lawyer, who built a new house, coach house, and stables on the site.[93] In 1800 Stokes subleased to Thomas Roberts,[94] who in 1808 occupied a brick mansion (Rosslyn Grove), essentially the late 18th-century building standing in 1986, with stabling and pleasure grounds, 2½ a. in all.[95] Rosslyn Lodge was rebuilt, probably between 1799 and 1802,[96] and was described in 1808 as new,

[60] G.L.R.O., MR/TH/2, m. 29d.
[61] Ho. occupied by John Turner: S.C.L., D 136–7, no. N.
[62] W.A.M. Map 12450, nos. 8–11.
[63] G.L.R.O., MR/LV5/30.
[64] Occupied by Hugh Bishop: P.R.O., C 54/3553, no. 33.
[65] P.R.O., C 54/3553, no. 33; G.L.R.O., MR/TH/2, m. 29d.
[66] S.C.L., D 136–7, no. Q; P.R.O., PROB 11/365 (P.C.C. 5 North).
[67] W.A.M. Map 12450, nos. 26–7. The 1679 survey mentioned 'hos.'
[68] S.C.L., D 136–7, no. Y.
[69] Also marked 'H.A.': Baines, Rec. Hampstead, 67–70; Howitt, Northern Heights, 209; P.R.O., C 54/3553, no. 33.
[70] P.R.O., C 8/387/25.
[71] Howitt, Northern Heights, 193, 209; Baines, Rec. Hampstead, 70.
[72] S.C.L., D 231.
[73] W.A.M. Map 12450, no. 23.
[74] W.A.M. 16499, 16501.
[75] Ibid. 16480; S.C.L., D 136–7, no. 8; G.L.R.O., MR/FB/1/198–9.
[76] W.A.M. 16501; W.A.M. Map 12450, no. 16.
[77] S.C.L., D 136–7.
[78] Oxford Literary Guide to Brit. Isles, ed. D. Eagle and H. Carnell, 189; S.C.L., Man. Map and Fieldbk. no. 1.

[79] S.C.L., D 136–7; W.A.M. Map 12450.
[80] Ch. Com. Deed 146072.
[81] Below, social.
[82] W.A.M. Map 12450, no. 13; W.A.M. 16499.
[83] Occupied by Marnie: Ch. Com. Deed 146073, no. 4 (after no. 5).
[84] W.A.M. 16519–20.
[85] S.C.L., Man. Map and Fieldbk. no. 2.
[86] Ch. Com. Deed 146072, no. 9; Rocque, Map of Lond. (1741–5), sheet 12.
[87] W.A.M. 16499.
[88] Ibid. 16506; Rocque, Map of Lond. (1741–5), sheet 12.
[89] W.A.M. 16499, 16517A; G.L.R.O., E/MW/H/1/1938.
[90] 'Messuages' in possession of Sarah Ketteridge lay s. of Gravel field: W.A.M. 16517A. Although the 1714 and 1723 maps (W.A.M. Map 12450; W.A.M. 16499) mark several bldgs., they could be coachhos. and stables.
[91] Poor rate bks. extracted in S.C.L., H 728.3/Rosslyn Lodge file.
[92] Occupied by Marchant fam.: poor rate bks.
[93] W.A.M. 16515, 16517A; M.L.R. 1770/3/239: cf. W.A.M. 16499; O.S. Map 1/2,500, Lond. VII (1870 end.).
[94] W.A.M. 16599.
[95] Ch. Com. Deed 146072, no. 3; S.C.L., Town and Country Planning, 52nd List of Bldgs. (1974), s.v. no. 11 Rosslyn Hill.
[96] Ho. empty 1799–1802: poor rate bks.

with four bedrooms, a double coach house, and gardener's house.[97] The small brick house next to Rosslyn Grove was in 1808 still occupied by a member of the Marchant family.[98]

The Blue House was rebuilt with stabling between 1761 and 1773 by the undertenant William Horseley, a merchant.[99] In 1808 it was occupied, with other buildings, a plantation, and pleasure grounds, by Thomas Pryor (d. 1821), who had been given it by his father-in-law Samuel Hoare (d. 1825) on his marriage in 1802; the Pryors later moved to Hampstead town.[1] The White House on the north side of Belsize Lane was in 1747 occupied by Sir Thomas Burnet (d. 1753), a judge of the Common Pleas.[2] In 1808, when occupied by George Todd, it had outbuildings, pleasure grounds, plantations, fishponds, and 7 a.[3] Nearby were two modest brick houses,[4] probably late 17th-century and rebuilt before 1735,[5] one of which was in bad repair. In 1747 one had been occupied by a surgeon and the other by George Errington, a copyholder in Hampstead town, who subleased to Andrew Regnier, a tailor from St. Martin-in-the-Fields, another copyholder, who in 1753 assigned the lease to a coffin-plate chaser from St. Sepulchre's.[6] On the south side of Belsize Lane, James Inglish, a Hampstead gentleman, in 1773 subleased Harris's house (later Elm House) to a merchant of Bucklersbury,[7] who probably rebuilt it.[8] In 1808 it was occupied by Benjamin Hanson Inglish and was a mansion with a bow window and had two coach houses. Adjoining it to the north was the brick house later called Belsize Lodge.[9]

At the southern end of the Belsize estate the farmland became detached during the 18th century from the farmhouse and barn at the junction with England's Lane.[10] By 1808 only the barn belonged to the farmer. The farmhouse had become two houses, part brick and part lath and plaster. Probably after 1773 a house, occupied in 1808 by a doctor, was built at the western end of England's Lane.[11] On the east side of Haverstock Hill a 'neat brick dwelling' was built c. 1770 next to the cobbler's house, which by 1808 was a decayed timber building, divided into three.[12] At the northern end of the estate the timber Red Lion survived until 1868[13] but the other houses, of brick and timber, were replaced between 1752

and 1808 by four brick residences, each with a coach house and two of them tenanted in 1808 by Dobson Willoughby and Sir Richard Phillips.[14] Mulys or Shelford Lodge was occupied in 1789 by the Revd. Mr. Addison[15] and in 1792 was leased to Alexander Wedderburn, Lord Loughborough, Lord Chancellor and later earl of Rosslyn. He added a large oval room which held the library and disguised the shape of the original house, renamed Rosslyn House. Rosslyn left in 1803[16] and in 1808 the house, a newly planted orchard, and 21 a., were occupied by Robert Milligan (d. 1809), a West India merchant. There were also houses for a gardener and a coachman.[17]

In 1808 the Belsize estate was split into nine leasehold estates, largely based upon the traditional underleases and focussed on single houses.[18] Until the 1850s Belsize was an area of country houses set in parkland. By 1815 George Todd, a former undertenant and one of the purchasers of 1808, had at great expense replaced the White House and the two neighbouring houses with a 'very capital mansion' called Belsize House, containing a library and conservatory, and with two coach houses and fine grounds.[19] Described in 1841 as a stuccoed Grecian villa with a stone portico and two lodges,[20] it was later called Belsize Court and occupied from 1833 by Matthew Forster (d. 1869), a London merchant and M.P.[21] It remained a seat until 1880 and was not demolished until 1937.[22] On the opposite side of Belsize Lane, but on the same estate, Belsize Cottage or Hunter's Lodge was built shortly before 1820 for William Tate, a merchant and undertenant, on the site of the 'Chinese' cottage of 1808.[23] Described in 1841, when it was occupied by another merchant James Lang, as a Gothic cottage villa,[24] it survived in 1986. At the eastern end of Todd's estate, Elm House and Belsize Lodge were replaced c. 1875 by Ivy Bank, which survived until 1911.[25]

John Lund, who bought Forsyth's estate on the eastern side of Haverstock Hill, built Haverstock Lodge for himself in 1819;[26] it survived until the First World War.[27] There was little building on the three estates leased to Thomas Roberts. South End Farm continued as a farmhouse and Rosslyn House was sold in 1816 to the undertenant and remained in parkland until it was demolished between 1896 and 1909. Occupiers included Sir Francis Freeling,

[97] Occupied by Hen. Cooke: Ch. Com. Deed 146072, no. 3.
[98] Ch. Com. Deed 146072, no. 3.   [99] W.A.M. 16417e.
[1] Ch. Com. 146072, no. 6; C.H.R. iii. 10; Memoirs of Sam. Hoare, ed. F. R. Pryor, 30.
[2] M.L.R. 1747/3/69.
[3] Ch. Com. Deed 146072, no. 4.
[4] Occupied by Price and Bright: Ch. Com. Deed 146072, no. 4.
[5] S.C.L., D 136-7, no. Q; W.A.M. 12450; M.L.R. 1735/1/197.
[6] M.L.R. 1747/3/69; 1753/1/231.
[7] Ibid. 1773/3/99.
[8] Both Elm Ho. and Belsize Lodge (below) were reblt. after 1723: W.A.M. 16499. Cf. O.S. Map 1/2,500, Lond. VII (1870 edn.).
[9] Occupied by Mercer: Ch. Com. Deed 146072, no. 4 (after 5).
[10] W.A.M. 16517A; below, econ.
[11] W.A.M. 16517A; Ch. Com. Deed 146072, no. 7. There were 2 more hos. to the W., presumably at Chalcots.
[12] W.A.M. 16519-20; 16610, nos. 23-4; Ch. Com. Deed 146072, no. 8.

[13] W.A.M. RCO 32; Barratt, Annals, i. 195.
[14] W.A.M. 16517A; Ch. Com. Deed 146072, no. 1.
[15] Poor rate bk.
[16] S.C.L., D 231; N. & Q. 8th ser. ix. 381-2; Hampstead One Thousand, 81; below, plate 11.
[17] Ch. Com. Deed 146072, no. 2.
[18] Below, other est. (Belsize); map of Belsize leases.
[19] Ch. Com. Deed 146073; Thompson, Hampstead, 97-8. Todd spent c. £15,000: G.L.R.O., E/MW/H, old no. 38/17/18; poor rate bks. 1813-15.
[20] G.L.R.O., E/MW/H, old no. 27/15 (sales parts. 1841).
[21] W.A.M., RCO 32 (agreement 1856); Ch. Com. Deeds 240253, 240264.
[22] Thompson, Hampstead, 288; Wade, More Streets, 33.
[23] Ch. Com. Deeds 146073, 240254; G.L.R.O., E/MW/H, old no. 38/17/1, 18; Wade, More Streets, 74, illus.
[24] G.L.R.O., E/MW/H, old no. 27/15 (sales parts. 1841).
[25] S.C.L., LH Folios/Ivy Bank (photo. before 1875); card index.
[26] W.A.M. 16617; poor rate bks. 1818-20.
[27] Below.

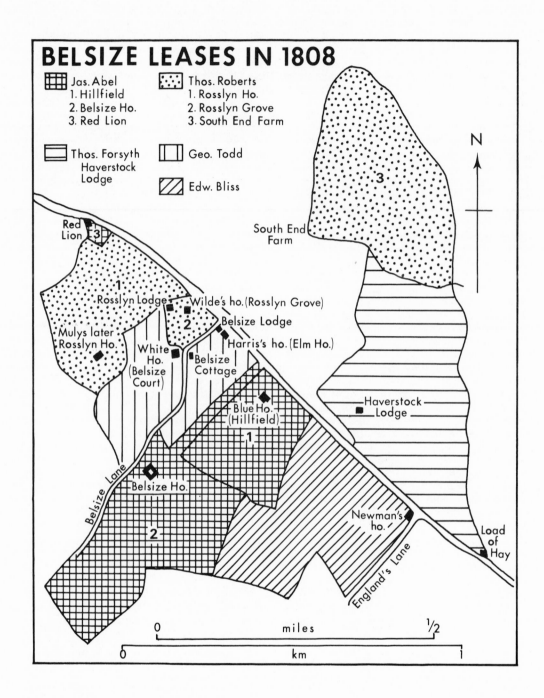

BELSIZE LEASES IN 1808

Jas. Abel
1. Hillfield
2. Belsize Ho.
3. Red Lion

Thos. Roberts
1. Rosslyn Ho.
2. Rosslyn Grove
3. South End Farm

Thos. Forsyth
Haverstock Lodge

Geo. Todd

Edw. Bliss

N

Red Lion 3

South End Farm

1

Rosslyn Lodge Wilde's ho.(Rosslyn Grove)

2 Belsize Lodge

Mulys later Rosslyn Ho.
White Ho. (Belsize Court) Harris's ho. (Elm Ho.)

Belsize Cottage

Blue Ho. (Hillfield) Haverstock Lodge

1

Belsize Lane

Belsize Ho.

2

Newman's ho.

England's Lane Load of Hay

0 miles ½

0 km 1

secretary to the General Post Office *c.* 1814,[28] Lt.-Gen. Sir Moore Disney 1816–23, the dowager countess of Galloway 1835–41, the Soldiers' Daughters' Home 1855–8, and Charles H. L. Woodd from 1861 to his death in 1893. It was probably Woodd who removed a colonnade on the west side of the house and transferred the portico and main entrance from the east to the north side.[29] Rosslyn Grove remained the house of Roberts and his family until 1835 or later, and Rosslyn Lodge was leased from 1832 to 1874 to Arthur Johnstone Blackwood but occupied in 1851 by Count Edward Zohrab, a Turkish diplomat.[30] One new house was built on the Rosslyn Grove estate between 1808 and 1817, on the north corner of Belsize Lane and the London road.[31]

On James Abel's largest estate (Belsize Park), centred on Belsize House itself, there were by 1841, in addition to the main house, a large Gothic lodge with four coach houses, and a bailiff's house in Belsize Lane.[32] Blue House, on his Hillfield estate, was rebuilt or enlarged, probably by his undertenant, the wine merchant Basil George Woodd, before 1841, when it was called Heathfield House and had a 'modern' elevation, a stuccoed front, a library, and six bedrooms.[33] Since the value quadrupled between 1841 and 1857 Woodd probably improved the house which he then called Hillfield; it survived until 1928.[34] Between 1864 and 1868 he built a second large house, Woodlands, at the southern end of what had become his freehold estate, for his son Robert Ballard Woodd.[35]

The only estate to be exploited early as a building venture was that of Edward Bliss on the west side of Haverstock Hill, north of England's Lane. Bliss, a self-made man, began developing the 14 a. fronting Haverstock Hill soon after 1815. In addition to the single and paired villas like Devonshire House, probably built by Basil Woodd in 1826, there were terraces like the Grecian-style Haverstock Terrace (in 1986 nos. 26–38 Belsize Grove), built in 1825–6, and Devonshire Place. Almost all the 38 houses on the estate had been built by 1830, with stabling and occupied by 'persons of quality'. Bliss made the land available, on underleases to his lease for lives, both to individuals and to speculators like George Crane of Cheltenham, who built Bedford, Oak, and Gilling lodges in addition to Haverstock Terrace.[36]

In 1842 an Act enabled Church lands to be let on long building leases and in 1851 the opening of Hampstead Road station prompted William Lund, lessee of the Forsyth estate, to secure a 99-year building lease in 1852.[37] Setting aside *c.* 8 a. around

his home, Haverstock Lodge, Lund planned an estate called St. John's Park on the other 38 a. His initial scheme, for parallel curving roads from Haverstock Hill to his boundary at the Fleet, linked by four cross roads, was soon modified, with Lawn Road replacing a lake intended for his own grounds. There were to be *c.* 280 buildings, consisting of 133 semi-detached villas on *c.* 29 a. and terraces, shops, and mews on the low-lying land by the river.[38] Building began from the Haverstock Hill end and by 1862 Park (later Parkhill) Road and Fleet Road, as yet unnamed, were laid out, together with the south-western half of Lawn Road and Upper Park Road. About 60 houses had been built on those roads and fronting Haverstock Hill, where the houses were called St. John's Park Villas. Most were substantial and 'unobtrusively classical', of grey brick and stucco, many built by Richard Batterbury of Camden Town, the chief speculative builder.[39] Church (after 1937 Tasker) Road and Lower Cross (after 1934 Garnett) Road had been laid out by 1862 but no houses built.[40] Residents were described in a guidebook of the 1860s on Haverstock Hill as 'City men such as stockbrokers, merchants, and commercial agents'.[41]

In 1852 Charles James Palmer, a Bloomsbury solicitor, bought the lease of the Belsize House estate (Belsize Park), one of Abel's leases and the largest of the country house estates, with the intention of building.[42] The land lay between the two London roads, Haverstock Hill and the new Finchley Road,[43] and the decision of the chapter of Westminster to retain control of the Avenue prompted Palmer to orientate the layout towards Finchley Road, with access through College Crescent, where houses had been built in 1849.[44] In 1853 Palmer proposed to demolish the manor house and build, under a 99-year building lease, a church in a square with detached and semi-detached houses and stables to the north, forming a secluded estate of five, mostly large, houses to the acre.[45] The formal building lease was not drawn up until 1855,[46] by which time Palmer, who had been paying high rent, was ready to allow modifications of the plan by the principal builder Daniel Tidey, a Sussex-born man who lived in one of his own houses in Belsize Park. In haste to secure the wealthiest clients, Tidey started work in 1855 from the western end, fronting the existing Belsize Lane, followed by Belsize Park and Buckland Crescent, in all of which he built large stuccoed town houses, where Palmer had planned the service quarter.[47] In 1863 Belsize Park had 'labyrinths of streets that will ultimately bear

---

[28] Park, *Hampstead*, 272.
[29] Poor rate bks.; Barratt, *Annals*, ii. 91–4; Howitt, *Northern Heights*, 209; *N. & Q.* 8th ser. ix. 382; Thompson, *Hampstead*, 292.
[30] S.C.L., H 728.3/Rosslyn Lodge file; poor rate bks. 1805–35; P.R.O., HO 107/1492/3.
[31] Occupied by Watts: W.A.M. 16610; O.S. Map 1/2,500, Lond. VII (1870 edn.).
[32] G.L.R.O., E/MW/H, old no. 27/15 (sales parts. 1841).
[33] Ibid.; Thompson, *Hampstead*, 95–6.
[34] Thompson, *Hampstead*, 95–7, 340; O.S. Map 1/2,500, Lond. VII (1870 edn.).
[35] Thompson, *Hampstead*, 294; poor rate bks. 1864, 1868.
[36] Thompson, *Hampstead*, 98–100, 107; Pevsner, *Lond.* ii. 200; Stanford, *Libr. Map of Lond.* (1862 edn. with additions to 1865), sheet 6.

[37] Thompson, *Hampstead*, 262–3; Ch. Com. Deed 142560.
[38] W.A.M. Maps 12532, 12534.
[39] Thompson, *Hampstead*, 265–6; Stanford, *Libr. Map of Lond.* (1862 edn. with additions to 1865), sheet 6.
[40] Weller's map (1862) in Wade, *More Streets*, 76.
[41] Quoted in D. J. Olsen, *Growth of Victorian Lond.* (1976), 241.
[42] Below, other est. (Belsize).
[43] J. Wyld, *Map of Lond. and Environs* (1848).
[44] D.S.R.
[45] Ch. Com. Deed 142526; file 7143, pt. 1/2; Thompson, *Hampstead*, 273–4, 283.
[46] Ch. Com. Deed 142527.
[47] Ch. Com. file 7143, pt. 1/2; Thompson, *Hampstead*, 274–9; below, plate 12. Dan. Tidey lived in Buckland Cres.: P.R.O., RG 9/93/17.

comparison with Belgravia'.[48] The eight- or ten-bedroomed houses were built for the wealthy professional and commercial class rather than for aristocratic occupation. In 1858 only 50 houses had been built; very few were occupied and those only by persons 'of very limited incomes'.[49] By 1864 there were more than 100 families on the estate although few kept carriages, there being only one block of 12 stables at Belsize Lane. By the 1870s, however, there were some 120 stables, an average of one to four houses, more than in other parts of Hampstead.[50]

In 1853 Henry Davidson agreed to exchange his lease for lives of the Rosslyn House estate for a 99-year building lease, which was drawn up in 1855. Probably fearing that the market would be saturated by building on the neighbouring Maryon Wilson land, Davidson hoped to demolish Rosslyn House and cover the whole estate with detached and semi-detached houses, like those in Belsize Park and with access from Haverstock Hill.[51] Progress was slower than expected, partly because of competition in Hampstead town and Belsize Park and partly because of reluctance to build above Hampstead Junction Railway's tunnel. In 1859 Davidson sold Rosslyn House and the south-western part of the estate to Charles Henry Lardner Woodd, who kept it as a country house until his death in 1893. On the rest of the estate Thurlow, Lyndhurst, and Eldon roads and Windsor Terrace had been laid out by 1862 and c. 40 houses built by 1864, mostly fronting Haverstock Hill.[52] Demand for the houses, of similar value to those in Belsize Park,[53] rose during the 1860s and more had been built by 1870.[54]

In 1864 the chapter of Westminster bought out the lessee's interest in the 24 a. of undeveloped backland on the Bliss estate and transferred it to Daniel Tidey on a 99-year building agreement.[55] Tidey destroyed the exclusivity of Belsize Park by extending its roads southward into Bliss's estate and by 1866 had drawn up a plan for the two estates, linked to Chalcots estate.[56] He began building in England's Lane in 1865 and by 1870 had pushed St. Margaret's Road (later Belsize Park Gardens) into Bliss's estate.[57] He was building in Stanley (after 1939 Primrose) Gardens in 1871.[58]

In 1857 the chapter had acquired full control over the portion of Todd's lease north of Belsize Lane and in 1865 it made an agreement with Tidey for the western 4½ a.[59] He constructed Prince Consort Road (later Belsize Crescent) as a northern extension of the Belsize Park estate and in 1869 subleased it to William Willett, another important builder in Hampstead. Tidey had constructed over 250 houses

on the three Belsize estates by 1870, when he went bankrupt.[60]

By 1870 all the Belsize estates were socially homogeneous, with mainly detached and semi-detached houses in a classical or Italianate style, broken only by small groups of mews.[61] There were many barristers, merchants, stockbrokers, fundholders, and clerks, ranging from senior civil servants to more lowly commercial clerks on Lund's estate. In 1861 residents included an author in Haverstock Place, a sculptor in Devonshire Place, and two architects in College Terrace.[62] The artist William Dobson (1817–98) lived in Eldon House in Eldon Grove from c. 1861 to 1883, the publisher Charles Knight (1791–1873) at no. 7 Eldon Grove from 1864–1870, and the artist Clarkson Stanfield (1793–1867) at no. 6 Belsize Park from 1865 to 1867; the dramatist G. W. Lovell (1804–78) died at no. 18 Lyndhurst Road.[63]

In 1869 Richard Pierce Barker exchanged his lease for lives of the portion of Todd's estate south of Belsize Lane for a building lease and planned a new road, Ornan Road.[64] The northern 5 a. were occupied by Belsize Cottage and Elm House, subleased until 1884, but the other 7½ a., Ornan Road and the northern side of Belsize Avenue, was to be developed for high-class detached and semi-detached houses. Building, mostly by William Willett, proceeded on both sides of Belsize Avenue from 1871 and in Ornan Road from 1878.[65]

Activity continued throughout the 1870s under the several building leases. Belsize Park was virtually built up by 1878, with the development of Lancaster Road (later Grove), as was the whole of Tidey's 4½-a. extension north of Belsize Lane. On Bliss's estate only the western section remained, where Lancaster Road, Lamboll Road, and Lamboll Place had been constructed but ew houses built. Building was nearly complete on the northern part of the Rosslyn House estate, where it continued into the 1880s, 42 houses, for example, being built in Stanley Gardens between 1879 and 1882.[66]

The chief builder after Tidey's bankruptcy was William Willett (1837–1913), helped, probably from 1881, by his son William (1856–1915), the originator of 'daylight saving'.[67] A fashionable builder in Kensington from 1876, the elder Willett opened an office in Belsize Court after 1873 and, having built some cramped houses in Belsize Crescent, put up large houses in Belsize Avenue.[68] In 1880 he obtained a 99-year lease of 12 a. of the Belsize Court estate,[69] where from 1886 he built Lyndhurst Gardens and Wedderburn Road.[70] The Willetts' houses were solidly constructed and set a new artistic standard

[48] *Builder*, xxi. 767, quoted in Olsen, *Victorian Lond.* 196.
[49] W.A.M., RCO 32 (letter to dean and chapter).
[50] Thompson, *Hampstead*, 277–80.
[51] Ibid. 288–90; Ch. Com. Deeds 142569–70.
[52] Thompson, *Hampstead*, 290–2; Weller's map (1862) in Wade, *More Streets*, 76.
[53] e.g. rental valued at £90–£150 for hos. in Lyndhurst, Eldon, and Thurlow rds. on Rosslyn Ho. est., at £90–£110 for Buckland Villas and Cres., £110 for Belsize Pk., £100 for Belsize Sq. and £130 for Belsize Pk. Gdns. on Belsize Pk. est. in 1868: rate bk.
[54] O.S. Map 1/2,500, Lond. VII (1870 edn.).
[55] Ch. Com. Deed 152554; W.A.M., RCO 32; Thompson, *Hampstead*, 279, 286.
[56] Ch. Com. Deed 142582.
[57] Ibid. 142581; file 33405, pt. 1; W.A.M., RCO 32; O.S.

Map 1/2,500, Lond. XV (1870 edn.); *Archit. of Lond.* 46.
[58] Wade, *More Streets*, 45; D.S.R.
[59] Ch. Com. Deeds 142574, 240259; W.A.M., RCO 32.
[60] Thompson, *Hampstead*, 276–88.
[61] Olsen, *Victorian Lond.* 242.
[62] P.R.O., RG 9/91/8/1–3; RG 9/93/14–17.
[63] Wade, *More Streets*, 31–2, 44, 80; *D.N.B.*
[64] Ch. Com. Deed 240263; Thompson, *Hampstead*, 293.
[65] Thompson, *Hampstead*, 293; 27 hos. were blt. in Belsize Ave. 1871–4: D.S.R.
[66] *Metrop. Improvement Map no. 46* (1878); D.S.R.; *Archit. of Lond.* 46.
[67] Inf. from Mr. A. Saint; *D.N.B.*
[68] Thompson, *Hampstead*, 344–6; *Survey of Lond.* xlii. 153–4.   [69] Ch. Com. file 60576, pt. 1/2.
[70] Stanford, *Libr. Map of Lond.* (1891 edn.); D.S.R.

for speculative architecture. In contrast with the classicism of Tidey's, they were red-brick and varied in design, many of them by the Willetts' own architects Harry B. Measures and, after 1891, Amos Faulkner.[71]

In 1881 the Rosslyn Grove estate, whose freehold had reverted to the Church Commissioners, was leased to Congregationalists who in 1883 built a church on the corner of Lyndhurst Road and Haverstock Hill, retained Rosslyn Grove as a manse, and sold the southern part of the estate; Rosslyn Gardens (later nos. 4–26 Belsize Lane) was built there about the same time.[72] On his Hillfield estate, by then freehold, Basil Thomas Woodd gave a site for the vestry hall in 1878 and built houses fronting Belsize Avenue in 1883.[73]

In the 1880s and early 1890s the entire Belsize estate west of Haverstock Hill was occupied by people classified as living 'in comfort'. Mews, in Lancaster Road, north of England's Lane, and especially in the centre of Belsize Lane, were occupied by the 'fairly comfortable', such as coachmen, gardeners, tradesmen, and craftsmen, but most of Belsize Park was 'upper middle- and middle-class, wealthy' and the other estates to north and south were 'middle-class, well-to-do'.[74] Inhabitants included Cornelius Walford (1827–85), the writer on insurance and owner of 30,000 rare books in two adjoining houses at Belsize Park Gardens, the composer Martin Shaw (1875–1958) at no. 18 Belsize Lane probably in the 1890s, the writer Lytton Strachey (1880–1932) at no. 67 Belsize Park Gardens from 1907 and at no. 6 from 1914, and, in his youth, the newspaper proprietor Harold Harmsworth, later Viscount Rothermere (1868–1940), in Wedderburn Road.[75]

It was the area on the eastern side of Haverstock Hill, Lund's St. John's Park, however, that was noted in the 1880s and 1890s for good houses occupied by artists and professional people,[76] probably mainly because of the Mall studios, built by Thomas Batterbury behind Park Road in 1872.[77] Artists who used them included Robert Macbeth (1848–1910), from 1875 to 1879, who lived in Park Road in 1873, and Sir George Clausen (1852–1944) c. 1879. Thomas Danby (1817?–86), the landscape painter, lived at no. 44 Upper Park Road from 1869 to 1882 and Arthur Rackham (1867–1939), the illustrator, at no. 54A Parkhill Road in 1903. The author Henry Morley (1822–94) lived at no. 8 Upper Park Road from 1858, and Thomas Wise, the forger, lived at no. 23 Downshire Crescent from 1901 to 1911.[78] The district, from Haverstock Hill north to just beyond Church (Tasker) Road, was 'well-to-do, middle-class'.[79] The area to the north, however, consisted of modern roads occupied by 'decent artisans', large

tram stables at South End, and streets near Fleet Road housing transport workers and labourers.[80]

Lund's plans for the northern part of the Haverstock Lodge estate were distorted from the start, partly because the river Fleet's unsavoury condition prevented the establishment of a middle-class shopping quarter, partly because of refusals to build above the St. Pancras tunnel extension of the Midland railway, completed in 1866 just south of Lower Cross Road. The final blight was the opening in 1870 of the smallpox hospital on the Bartrams site.[81] Building virtually stopped until c. 30 houses and 12 stables were built between 1879 and 1885 in Park, Upper Park, and Lawn roads. By that date the social status of the estate had started to decline and workshops were built at the Grange, Park Road, in 1883–4. Terraces, a mission house, and a working men's club were built in the late 1870s and 1880s in Fleet Road and in 1893 a resident of Upper Park Road recorded the tenementation of houses at the north end of the street to 'objectionable people'.[82]

In 1872 the dean and chapter of Westminster became aware of building next to their South End farm and agreed with Joseph Salter, the owner of Hodges, to straighten the boundary and enable him to make a road (Cressy Road) and sewer preparatory to development.[83] The scheme was delayed by the effects of the smallpox hospital, and some partly built houses were taken down.[84] In 1878 the chapter made a building agreement with Joseph Pickett, the tenant of South End farm, and John Ashwell, a Kentish Town builder, for the 15½ a. north of the Hampstead Junction Railway.[85] The area, farther from the smallpox hospital and on higher ground next to the heath, proved more attractive and South Hill Park Road (later Parliament Hill Road) and Nassington Road were laid out in 1878 and 90 houses built between 1879 and 1892. The planned extension of the roads into Lord Mansfield's lands in St. Pancras was halted by the addition of Parliament Hill Fields to the heath in 1889. Tanza Road was made instead, to connect the existing roads, and building began there in 1890.[86] Ashwell withdrew in 1881 and Pickett (d. 1893), who by then described himself as a master builder and lived in South Hill Park, was under-financed and built cheaply, mostly semi-detached and terraced tall but cramped red-brick houses for the middle class. In 1881 the eight existing houses in South Hill Park Road contained a commercial traveller, a teacher, an annuitant, a clerk, and a lodging house.[87] Richard Garnett (1835–1906), writer and president of the Hampstead Antiquarian and Historical Society, lived at no. 27 Tanza Road from 1899.[88]

In 1880 Thomas E. Gibb, a developer from Kentish Town and trustee of Salter's estate,

[71] Thompson, *Hampstead*, 346–7; inf. from Mr. Saint.
[72] Thompson, *Hampstead*, 292; Wade, *More Streets*, 73; Ch. Com. file 60576, pt. 1/2; Barratt, *Annals*, iii. 104–5; *Archit. of Lond.* 46.
[73] Thompson, *Hampstead*, 340.
[74] Booth, *Life and Labour*, i (2), 16; map, NW. sheet; P.R.O., RG 11/169/7/13/1.
[75] Wade, *More Streets*, 31–2, 80; *Hampstead One Thousand*, 144, 148, 152; *D.N.B.*
[76] Booth, *Life and Labour*, i (2), 16.
[77] *C.H.R.* viii. 19–21; *Archit. of Lond.* 46.
[78] Wade, *More Streets*, 47–9; *Hampstead One Thousand*, 146–7, 149–51, 153.

[79] Booth, *Life and Labour*, map.
[80] Ibid. i (2), 16; iii (1), 213.
[81] Thompson, *Hampstead*, 268–9; below, pub. svces.
[82] Thompson, *Hampstead*, 270–1; D.S.R.
[83] Thompson, *Hampstead*, 351–2; Ch. Com. Map 13305; Survey CC 7, pp. 13–23.
[84] Ch. Com. file 62499, pt. 1.
[85] Ibid. 45820, pt. 2.
[86] Thompson, *Hampstead*, 353; D.S.R.
[87] Thompson, *Hampstead*, 353–4; P.R.O., RG 11/168/7/9/1.
[88] Wade, *More Streets*, 49; *Hampstead One Thousand*, 147.

purchased some 3½ a. of South End farm, adjoining Salter's land on the south-west. In 1881 he took a 99-year lease on the remaining 11 a. of farmland, the rest having been sold to the railway and the London school board, and undertook to build 120 small houses at 'the lower end of middle-class respectability'. He planned to cover both Salter's freehold estate and the southern part of South End farm and agreed to construct a sewer which would also serve Pickett's northern portion of the estate.[89] Gibb laid out Cressy (sic), Agincourt, and Lisburne roads and began brickmaking on the Salter estate, but the smallpox hospital unexpectedly reopened and, indeed, expanded. Patients were brought along Fleet Road and the area deteriorated even further. No one would take houses and for years the only buildings in the new roads were two houses, a school chapel, the board school, factories, and a steam laundry. In 1886 the Church Commissioners, recognizing the social change, allowed Gibb to build 215 houses on the 11 a.; Constantine Road was planned, as a direct route from Gospel Oak and Kentish Town to South End Green and the heath, and building began in 1887. By 1894, when Gibb died, 113 houses had been built in Constantine, Agincourt, and Lisburne roads. Gibb's interest passed to Francis Thomas Binnington, a Hampstead surveyor, who subleased to Robert Thorpe and John Sanders, local men who had built for Gibb and Pickett. By 1898 another 153 houses had gone up, in Constantine, Cressy, and Mackeson roads.[90]

Most of the remaining large houses marooned in their gardens disappeared in the 1890s. The Ivy Bank (Elm House) estate south of Belsize Lane was for sale in 1893[91] and building was taking place in the grounds from 1894, including Ornan and Rosslyn Court, large flats in Ornan Road (1896). The house, which was occupied from 1897 to 1911 by Alfred Ridley Bax, F.S.A., and his sons, the composer Sir Arnold (1883–1953) and author and playwright Clifford, was replaced in 1911 by Beaulieu (later Perceval) Avenue.[92] The last houses were built there in 1924 and six semi-detached ones were built on the site fronting Haverstock Hill in 1925.[93] In 1896 the executors of C. H. L. Woodd sold Rosslyn House to speculators, who by 1909 had completed houses in Lyndhurst and Wedderburn roads on the site.[94] In 1890 the Church Commissioners bought out the leasehold interest on the 14 a. of Bliss's estate next to Haverstock Hill,[95] where developers demolished the few houses at the back and constructed Antrim Road, mainly on nursery land; flats and a library were built there from

1896.[96] On the eastern side of Haverstock Hill, Downshire Crescent was driven in 1897 through the grounds of Haverstock Lodge, where most housing was completed by 1913. Some houses were built in Lawn Road on the eastern side of the estate in 1911. Haverstock Lodge had gone by 1916 and 10 houses were built on the site in Downshire Crescent and Lawn Road between 1922 and 1924.[97] Almost opposite, Woodlands was replaced soon after Robert Ballard Woodd's death in 1901 by Glenloch, Glenmore, Glenilla, and Howitt roads.[98]

The main change after the First World War was the growth of flats, both in the conversion of houses[99] and in the building of blocks. The first purpose-built block, one of the earliest in London, was Manor Mansions of 1884, on the site of no. 48 Belsize Park Gardens.[1] Few houses were demolished before the Second World War but several were converted for institutions. Although most of the Belsize estates were still classified in 1930 as middle-class and wealthy,[2] there had been some social decline. There was more demand for lower middle- and working-class houses in areas which had previously seemed unattractive, like the northern part of Lund's estate. In 1905–6 Hampstead borough council had bought a site there, in Lower Cross (later Garnett) Road, where it built Park Buildings, three blocks of flats.[3] A similar site was Pickett's Farm and adjacent land, where in 1920 the borough built several large blocks containing 140 flats, South End Close.[4] In 1932 Glenloch Investment Co. began building on a site acquired from the Lund estate near Park Buildings, where it put up 51 small houses in Lawn, Lower Cross, and Upper Park roads between 1932 and 1934.[5] The area to the north was still the poorest: Fleet Road was both overcrowded (more than 1 person to a room) and inhabited by unskilled labourers, and the area from there to the railway, on Gibb's estate, was inhabited by 'skilled workers or similar'.[6]

On the west side of Haverstock Hill, Glenloch Investment Co. was responsible for the Woodlands estate, where houses were still being built in Glenilla Road in 1923–4 and blocks of flats were put up, Glenloch Court in 1927 and Banff House and Howitt Court in 1932.[7] In 1929 a 'comparatively modern' house on Todd's estate at the junction of Haverstock Hill and Ornan Road was replaced by a 'great garage' which, it was feared, would change the character of the area.[8] It proved to be symptomatic, followed by a rash of flats which transformed Haverstock Hill and its vicinity. Bell Properties Trust was responsible for building flats on the remaining vacant land on Bliss's 14 a.: Gilling Court

[89] The nominal purchaser was Mrs. Salter: Ch. Com. file 45820, pt. 1/2; 62499, pt. 1; Thompson, *Hampstead*, 356–9.
[90] Thompson, *Hampstead*, 357–61; Stanford, *Libr. Map of Lond.* (1891 edn.); D.S.R.
[91] S.C.L., H 942.14 (Newton cuttings bk. p. 29).
[92] Wade, *More Streets*, 39; Thompson, *Hampstead*, 426; S.C.L., card index; *D.N.B.* s.v. Bax; D.S.R.
[93] Thompson, *Hampstead*, 427 n.; D.S.R.
[94] Wade, *More Streets*, 30; O.S. Map 60″, Lond. II. 100 (1893, 1909 edns.); D.S.R.
[95] Ch. Com. Survey CC 7, p. 8.
[96] O.S. Map 60″, Lond. VI. 10 (1895, 1916 edns.); D.S.R.
[97] O.S. Map 60″, Lond. VI. 10 (1916 edn.); L.C.C. *Municipal Map of Lond.* (1913, 1930); Thompson, *Hamp-*

stead, 340; D.S.R.
[98] Woodd's wid. was there in 1902; *Kelly's Dir. Lond.* (1902); Wade, *More Streets*, 39–40; J. Tucker, *Emmanuel Ch., West End* (1981), 12; D.S.R.
[99] D.S.R.
[1] Thompson, *Hampstead*, 426.
[2] *New Lond. Life and Labour*, vii, maps 8, 10, 11.
[3] Thompson, *Hampstead*, 424–5.
[4] Ibid. 429; Ch. Com. Map 13305; O.S. Map 1/2,500, Lond. I. 16 (1934–6); S.C.L., H 711.13, Council Housing Reps., Hampstead Boro. *Rep. on Housing* (1951).
[5] D.S.R.
[6] *New Lond. Life and Labour*, iv, map of overcrowding; vi. 423; vii, maps 8, 10, 11. [7] D.S.R.
[8] *The Times*, 2 Oct. 1929, 11e; O.S. Map 1/2,500, TQ 2785 (1965 edn.).

(1932) and Holmfield Court (1933) in Belsize Grove and two blocks of shops and flats fronting Haverstock Hill north of the junction with Belsize Grove in 1934.[9] The site of Hillfield, reduced by the building of the vestry hall in 1878[10] and of 18 houses in Belsize Avenue in 1900[11] to a narrow strip of backland, was sold in 1928 to Hillfield Estates, which demolished the old house and, against fierce local opposition, built a cinema and two blocks of flats (Hillfield Court and Mansions, 1934) fronting Haverstock Hill and three blocks on the backland (Tudor Close, 1935).[12] In 1937 John Laing, the construction firm which bought Belsize Court, the last of the seats in spacious grounds, extended Wedderburn Road eastward to Belsize Lane, replacing the house by seven blocks of flats called Belsize Court.[13]

On the east side of Haverstock Hill, Lawn Road flats (1934), garages behind no. 126 Haverstock Hill (1934), and Garnett House in Garnett Road (1939) filled vacant sites on the Haverstock Lodge estate. Parliament Court flats were built in Parliament Hill next to the railway in 1937 on the South End Farm estate.[14]

Walter Sickert (1860–1942) was at the Mall studios before 1919 and Cecil Stephenson (1889–1965) had a studio there from 1919 to 1965. Harold Brighouse, author of *Hobson's Choice*, lived at no. 67 Parliament Hill from 1919 to 1959, John Drinkwater (1882–1937), the poet, lived at no. 10 Belsize Square in 1921–2, Jerome K. Jerome (1859–1927), the writer, moved to no. 41 Belsize Park in 1924, and Frederick Delius (1862–1934), the composer, was in Belsize Park Gardens, probably in the early 1920s. Ramsay MacDonald lived at no. 9 Howitt Road from 1916 to 1925.[15]

It was during the 1930s that Belsize contributed most to the artistic and intellectual life of Hampstead and, indeed, of England.[16] Artists associated with the Mall studios included Dame Barbara Hepworth (1903–75) from 1927 to 1939, her first husband John Skeaping and second Ben Nicholson from 1931 to 1939, and Henry Moore, who lived at no. 11A Parkhill Road from 1929 to 1940. They were members of Unit One, a group of artists and architects founded in 1933 by Paul Nash (1889–1946), who lived at no. 3 Eldon Grove from 1936 to 1939. Sir Herbert Read, the poet and art critic, who lived in 1934–5 at the Mall studios, which he described as a 'nest of gentle artists', published the group's manifesto, a theory of modern style. Another centre was no. 37 Belsize Park Gardens, meeting place of MARS, an architectural group, and home of Jack Pritchard, who founded Isokon, a firm making modern furniture designed by people like Walter

Gropius and Marcel Breuer, refugees who brought a European dimension to the abstract design movement in the arts. Others included Piet Mondrian, the Dutch painter, who stayed with the Pritchards before moving to no. 60 Parkhill Road (1938–41). Pritchard also commissioned Wells Coates in 1934 to build the Isokon or Lawn Road flats, partly to house artistic refugees, on a site which he owned. Built in concrete in a functional style, the flats came to be recognized as 'a milestone in the introduction of the modern idiom into London'.[17] They contained a restaurant called the Isobar, designed by Breuer and run independently, with Philip Harben as chef, 'the nearest thing that Hampstead had to an artists' club'.[18] Among residents were the painter and writer Adrian Stokes (1902–72), the Bauhaus architect Walter Gropius, the Constructivist sculptors the Hungarian László Moholy-Nagy and the Russian Naum Gabo.[19] Gabo, together with Nicholson and the architect Leslie Martin, edited *Circle*, another publication on modern architecture, the majority of whose contributors lived in Hampstead. Most artists left in 1939, many for Cornwall, and Henry Moore was bombed out in 1940.

Writers in Belsize in the 1930s did not form a group with shared ideals like the artists and architects. Nicholas Monsarrat (1910–79) was an early inhabitant of the Isokon flats and Agatha Christie (1890–1976) lived there in 1945. Stella Gibbons was at no. 33 Upper Park Road from 1933–6, James Agate (1877–1947), the drama critic, at Antrim Mansions just before the Second World War, Henry W. Nevinson (1846–1941), the essayist, at no. 4 Downshire Crescent from 1939, and William Empson (b. 1906), the poet, at no. 160 Haverstock Hill in 1940.[20]

Belsize, like other areas, suffered damage in the Second World War, especially on the Lund estate.[21] The main problem after the war was to provide accommodation, for those bombed out and those who previously had been living in overcrowded conditions. The council requisitioned some large houses which it converted to flats but the main drive was to build flats on the few empty sites and on cleared sites, mostly on the Haverstock Lodge estate. Wood Field and Barn Field, 92 flats built as Georgian terraces, were opened in 1949 on 2½ a. cleared of houses between Upper Park Road and Parkhill Road. Troyes House, with 25 flats, was built in 1952 at the south-east end of Lawn Road on the site of a bombed out convent.[22] Fleet Road, half of which was scheduled under the London Plan for commercial use, was very dilapidated and overcrowded,[23] and in 1963 work began on the south side, adjoining

[9] O.S. Map 1/2,500, TQ 2684 (1955 edn.); D.S.R.
[10] At the corner of Belsize Ave. and Haverstock Hill: below, local govt.
[11] D.S.R.
[12] Thompson, *Hampstead*, 340; *Kelly's Dir. Lond.* (1935–6); O.S. Map 1/2,500, TQ 2684 (1955 edn.); *The Times*, 23 Nov. 1934, 9g; 23 Sept. 1935, 14c; 17 Oct. 1935, 11c; 23 Oct. 1935, 11c; 30 Oct. 1935, 10d; D.S.R.
[13] O.S. Map 1/2,500, Lond. VII (1870 edn.); TQ 2684 (1955 edn.); D.S.R.
[14] O.S. Map 1/2,500, TQ 2785 (1965 edn.); for Lawn Rd. flats, below.
[15] Wade, *More Streets*, 44, 49, 78, 80; *Hampstead One Thousand*, 110, 146, 152; *D.N.B.*
[16] Following two paras. based on *C.H.R.* viii. 19–21; *Country Life*, 11 Nov. 1976, pp. 1420 sqq.; *Hampstead*

One Thousand, 110–12, 148, 150, 151.
[17] Pevsner, *Lond.* ii. 200; *Hampstead One Thousand*, 111, 140; P. Kidson, P. Murray, P. Thompson, *Hist. Eng. Archit.* (1979), 330; *Archit. of Lond.* 49; J. Pritchard, *View From A Long Chair* (1984), 13–16, 22, 78–96, passim.
[18] Pritchard, *View*, 17–18, 92; *Country Life*, 11 Nov. 1976, p. 1420.
[19] Pritchard, *View*, 17, 86–90.
[20] *Hampstead One Thousand*, 147, 150; Wade, *More Streets*, 45, 47–8.
[21] *Hampstead 1939–45* (Camden History Soc. 1977).
[22] S.C.L., H 711.13, Hampstead Boro. *Rep. on Housing* (1948–52, 1954); *The Times*, 9 Apr. 1945, 2c; 7 Dec. 1945, 8b.
[23] S.C.L., H 331.833, Housing file, Hampstead Communist party, *Homes for Hampstead* [c. 1955].

the council flats of Garnett Road, where the Victorian terraces and shops were replaced by blocks named after Hampstead citizens (Siddons, Stephenson, and Palgrave), while at about the same time Du Maurier and Cayford houses were built at the northern end of Lawn Road.[24] Low-rise council housing was built at the eastern end of Fleet Road between 1967 and 1977.[25] In 1970 the large garage built in 1929 at the junction of Haverstock Hill and Ornan Road was replaced by the Post House hotel.[26] The Lawn Road Community workshops were built at the Fleet Road end in the 1980s.

In 1986, apart from the municipal and commercial area of Fleet Road, small repair shops in some mews, shopping parades in Haverstock Hill, and the increasingly smart shopping quarters of Belsize Village and England's Lane, Belsize was residential, divided between mainly Victorian housing, often subdivided, and blocks of flats, some late 19th-century but mostly dating from the 1930s or later. Many houses, in Belsize Park and elsewhere, had been replaced from the 1960s by usually modest blocks of flats and groups of small houses such as those built in 1961 at Belsize Park Mews and Village Crescent in Belsize Lane.[27] Among the most recent were the impressive Tower Close on the site of Eldon House, off Lyndhurst Road,[28] and St. Crispin's Close between South End Close and the railway. Parts of Fleet Road were still run down, the Isokon flats, which had been bought by Camden L.B. in 1972,[29] were looking decidedly seedy, and the area around Garnett Road and Fleet Road was working-class. The rest of the Belsize estate, on both sides of Haverstock Hill, was middle-class, its status raised in many cases by gentrification visible in repairs and repainting. By 1975 the stuccoed villas of Belsize Park and around Park Hill Road formed two conservation areas, the houses mostly divided into flats and bed-sitters with young, often professional occupants.[30]

Two houses remained in 1986 from before 1808: Rosslyn Grove (no. 11 Rosslyn Hill), dating from soon after 1770, brick with a symmetrical façade and pedimented attic, and Rosslyn Lodge, built c. 1800 as a double-fronted stuccoed villa with a Doric portico, later altered,[31] which escaped an attempt to build on its site in 1973.[32] Hunter's Lodge, built by 1820, a 'stuccoed, castellated Gothic house', stood in Belsize Lane[33] and nos. 129–33 Haverstock Hill and nos. 26–38 Belsize Grove, a handsome stuccoed terrace, survived from before 1830 on the Bliss estate.[34]

ST. JOHN'S WOOD. The Hampstead portion of the

St. John's Wood or Eyre estate, low-lying and not easily accessible, never attracted seats as Belsize had done[35] and even the farm buildings lay on the Marylebone side of the border. The Eyre family was, however, always anxious to promote building and in 1794 a plan was drawn up on the model of Bath, with a crescent, circus, and square. The plan was never executed, probably blighted by the French wars, but from 1802 development on the Eyre estate was directed by John Shaw, a young architect inspired by the town-planning ideals of the late 18th century. In 1803–4 he exhibited views of a projected circus and in 1807 building began on the Marylebone portion.[36] In 1819 Col. Eyre began the first of several attempts to promote the construction of a public road through his estate, ultimately successful in the Finchley Road Act of 1826. Finchley New Road and Avenue Road, the southern part of which existed by 1824, thrust northward into the Hampstead portion of Eyre's land and were built by 1829.[37] Swiss Cottage tavern was built at the apex of the two roads by 1841.[38] At the western end of the estate Abbey Road was driven northward by 1829.[39]

Building spread northward in the salient formed by the Finchley and Avenue roads. A building agreement was made in 1838[40] and in 1841 the vestry was discussing the boundary with Marylebone at Avenue Road and St. John's Wood Road (probably St. John's Wood Park) where houses were being erected.[41] Several houses, called Regent's Villas, stood in the Hampstead section of Avenue Road by 1842.[42] There was a second agreement in 1845, followed by a burst of building activity in the later 1840s and 1850s. Between 1845 and 1852, 33 houses were built in Finchley Road, 13 in the road parallel to it, St. John's Wood Park, 16 in Avenue Road, 28 in Boundary Road, the east–west road joining them at the southern boundary, and 13 in College Crescent to the north, bordering the Belsize estate. Except for the last, which were stuccoed terraces with iron balconies built by W. Wartnaby, most houses were detached, even imposing, built in small groups by a number of builders: C. C. Cook, E. Thomas & Son, Thomas Clark, and Wartnaby.[43] The buildings included the school for the blind, built in 1848 at the southern junction of College Crescent and Avenue Road and enlarged in 1864, 1878, and 1912; of brick with stone dressings, it had an Italianate central block with two wings.[44] The North Star public house was opened at the northeast tip of the estate in 1850 and, enclosed by the curve of College Crescent, the New College of Independent Dissenters, for training ministers, was

[24] Wade, *More Streets*, 23; O.S. Map 1/2,500, TQ 2785 (1965 edn.); *Kelly's Dir. Lond.* (1964–5).
[25] *Archit. of Lond.* 52.
[26] Wade, *More Streets*, 39; below, econ., ind.
[27] *Sunday Times*, 16 Apr. 1961 (S.C.L., H 728.3 file/ Belsize Pk. Mews).
[28] *Kelly's Dir. Lond.* (1981, 1986).
[29] Wade, *More Streets*, 47.
[30] Camden Boro. Plan, *Hampstead and Belsize Area*, Spr. 1975, Area 4.
[31] S.C.L., Town and Country Planning, 52nd. List of Bldgs. (1974).
[32] S.C.L., H 728.3/Rosslyn Lodge file (cuttings: *H.H.E.* 6, 13 Apr., 7 Sept. 1973).
[33] Pevsner, *Lond.* ii. 200.
[34] Wade, *More Streets*, 40, 44.

[35] Thompson, *Hampstead*, 110.
[36] Ibid. 66; J. Summerson, 'Beginnings of an Early Victorian Suburb' (MS. of lecture 20 Feb. 1958).
[37] Thompson, *Hampstead*, 110–24; *Cruchley's New Plan* (1829); Wade, *More Streets*, 58.
[38] *Map of Marylebone* (1832); *Laurie's Plan of Lond., Westm.* (1842); P.R.O., HO 107/674/2; below, social.
[39] Newton, *Map of Hampstead* (1814); *Cruchley's New Plan* (1829).
[40] Thompson, *Hampstead*, 247.
[41] Vestry mins. 15 July 1841.
[42] *Laurie's Plan of Lond., Westm.* (1842).
[43] D.S.R.; Thompson, *Hampstead*, 248; J. Wyld, *Map of Lond. and Environs* (1848).
[44] P.R.O., C 54/16950, no. 11; S.C.L., H 371.911, Lond. Soc. for Blind, *Rep. 1928–9.*

opened in 1851 in a building designed in an early Tudor style by J. T. Emmett. He also designed the college's Gothic chapel, opened soon afterwards to the south, at the junction of Avenue Road and Adelaide Road.[45] Immediately south of the blind school a large house, Sunnyside (later St. Columba's hospital), with a Greek Doric porch, was built by 1862 and possibly in 1847.[46] St. Paul's church was built on the western side of Avenue Road in 1859.[47]

In 1851 the estate, like Chalcots and Belsize, housed mainly the professional and commercial classes: merchants, an Italian banker, retired manufacturers, people of private means, and some tradesmen, almost all with several servants. Coachmen, grooms, and servants were housed in Regent's Villa Mews. The writer James Buckingham (1786–1855) lived in Avenue Road,[48] where William Collins, the landscape painter, had lived at no. 20 from 1839–40. William's son Wilkie set one of the scenes of his novel *The Woman in White*, published in 1862 but based on childhood recollections, at the turnpike at Swiss Cottage.[49]

The character of new housing, to serve a slightly lower social level, began to change after 1851, with westward expansion along roads parallel with the railway and at the western end around Abbey Road and its side-roads.[50] Apart from Adelaide Road, the St. John's Wood portion of which was later called Hilgrove Road,[51] the westward-thrusting roads were Boundary Road and Belsize Road, where 41 houses were built in 1851–2, some by Robert Yeo, who was later to build at Chalcots. Yeo also built some of the 17 houses of those years in Victoria (later Fairfax) Road, which ran from Finchley Road to Belsize Road at the north end of the estate; another 19 were built at the same time in Albion (later Harben) Road, between Victoria and Adelaide roads. Bridge (later Loudoun) Road, with 8 houses, ran from the northern group across the railway to Boundary Road and St. Marylebone. At the western end of the estate 19 houses were built in Abbey Road, and 4 in Belgrave Road and Boundary Mews were begun.[52] By 1862 most of the area between Avenue Road and Bridge Road was built up with detached and semi-detached houses.[53]

West of Bridge (Loudoun) Road the land sloped to a shallow trough before rising again beyond the Eyre estate. The slope, together with the narrowness of the remaining sites imposed by the railway and estate boundary, contributed to higher-density, mostly terraced housing.[54] On the northern boundary two stables were built at Victoria (Fairfax) Mews in 1852, and North End Road (later Fairhazel Gardens) provided access by 1855.[55] Eventually there were 57 stables there, for omnibus horses, and

Britannia Terrace, in Belsize Road, and Victoria (Fairfax) Road were built during the later 1850s and early 1860s for the stable staff and drivers and conductors. A similar development took place in the south-west at the opposite end of the estate, with stabling and terraces in Bolton and Holtham roads (1858–66), Belgrave Gardens, Alexandra Mews, and part of Boundary Road. With transport assured, close-packed middle-class housing followed in the centre, especially in Boundary Road, in Springfield Road to the south, and in Alexandra Road (built after the marriage of the Prince of Wales in 1863) and Belsize Road to the north.[56] By 1866 building was virtually complete.[57]

In 1871–2 five houses were built in Belsize Road, 14 in Alexandra Road, and one in Bolton Road, followed by one house and six stables in Boundary Mews in 1873. A few more houses were built in Abbey and Boundary roads in 1880.[58] In 1881 the mews were still overwhelmingly inhabited by stablemen and the like, although the streets surrounding them also housed small craftsmen, clerks, agents, and tradesmen, while professional people and businessmen occupied the other roads.[59] By the end of the 1880s, the mews, off Fairfax Road, Loudoun Road and in the south-west, were no longer service areas on the edge of the housing, which had moved beyond them, but pockets classified as 'fairly comfortable, good ordinary earnings'. The earliest developed area, Finchley Road and roads to the east, were 'wealthy, upper middle- and middle-class', while the rest of the estate was 'well-to-do, middle-class'.[60] Inhabitants included Lillie Langtry, a cousin of the local politician Philip Le Breton, who lived in Leighton House in Alexandra Road in the 1870s, the Harmsworth family at no. 94 Boundary Road from 1874 to 1888, and Herbert Spencer, the philosopher, at no. 64 Avenue Road from 1889 to 1897.[61] Samuel Palmer, of the biscuit firm, lived at no. 40 College Crescent, a large house called Northcourt built in 1881.[62]

By 1900 lodging houses and institutions had begun to take over some of the larger houses. In Avenue Road, for example, Sunnyside was taken for the Friedenheim hospital (later St. Columba's) in 1892; the Home Treatment of Disease by Diet was at no. 7, the Yoga School at no. 12, and the Theosophical Society at no. 19 c. 1903.[63] In 1908 nine shops were built in the corner between Finchley and Fairfax roads.[64] The general social status of the estate had declined by 1930. One mews, by then called Fairfax Place, was singled out as one of the worst parts of the borough for overcrowding. The other mews areas, Loudoun Road Mews and the south-west, were occupied by 'skilled workers and similar', but so,

[45] D.S.R.; *Hampstead Annual, 1905–6*, 120, 123, 127; Wade, *More Streets*, 59, 67.
[46] Below, pub. svces.; Pevsner, *Lond.* ii. 201–2; Stanford, *Libr. Map of Lond.* (1862 edn. with additions to 1865), sheet 5.
[47] Below, churches.
[48] P.R.O., HO 107/1492/5–6; *D.N.B.*
[49] Wade, *More Streets*, 59. For the turnpike, see *Map of Marylebone* (1832).
[50] Thompson, *Hampstead*, 248.
[51] St. John's Wood hos. indistinguishable from those in Chalcots in D.S.R.　　　　　　　　　　[52] D.S.R.
[53] Stanford, *Libr. Map of Lond. and Suburbs* (1862 edn. with additions to 1865), sheet 5; Wade, *W. Hampstead*, 51.

[54] Thompson, *Hampstead*, 248–9.
[55] D.S.R.; vestry mins. 15 Jan. 1855.
[56] Thompson, *Hampstead*, 248–53; Wade, *W. Hampstead*, 49.
[57] O.S. Map 1/2,500, Lond. XV (1866 edn.).
[58] D.S.R.
[59] P.R.O., RG 11/173/7/1/11.
[60] Booth, *Life and Labour*, maps.
[61] Wade, *W. Hampstead*, 47, 49; Wade, *More Streets*, 59.
[62] Wade, *More Streets*, 68.
[63] Ibid. 59; L.C.C. *Mun. Map of Lond.* (1913); below, pub. svces.
[64] D.S.R.

too, were the whole of Belsize Road, much of Alexandra Road, and part of Hilgrove Road. The rest was still middle-class and wealthy.[65]

The Hampstead portion of St. John's Wood did not feature in the artistic flowering of the 1930s but it housed the Hungarian film producer Sir Alexander Korda at no. 81 Avenue Road from 1933 until 1939.[66] The estate shared in the flat-building of the decade. The first major project was the building of 14 blocks by A. Clarke on the south side of Belsize Road from 1932 to 1936. From 1933 flats replaced the old houses in St. John's Wood Park and Avenue Road, including in the south near St. Stephen's church, a district transferred to Hampstead by boundary changes, the Poplars estate (1934) and Avenue Close (1935, by Stanley Hall, Easton & Robertson); some houses were also built in Avenue Road in 1935–8.[67] At the northern end of the estate New College and much of College Crescent were pulled down in 1934 and replaced by Northways, two concrete blocks of flats and shops by London & City Real Estate.[68] The whole of the Swiss Cottage site between Finchley Road and Avenue Road was redeveloped with the building in 1937 of the Odeon cinema and, after 1938, of Regency Lodge flats by R. Atkinson, 'good, though a trifle stodgy'.[69]

There was extensive rebuilding after 1945, mostly for local authority housing. The whole area suffered war damage[70] and houses were dilapidated through tenementation and neglect. About 1955 the Communist party designated Bolton Road a black spot and described the Belsize Road area as overcrowded, with damp and crumbling houses; there were said to be 2,372 people in 369 houses.[71] The L.C.C. acquired land for housing 4,000 people on the west side of Finchley Road in both Hampstead and Marylebone in 1946, arousing fierce objections by its threat to the middle-class character of the neighbourhood.[72] The whole area around Finchley Road and Avenue Road was transformed by flats and public buildings, mostly in the 1960s. Centre Heights, a concrete and glass block designed by Douglas Stephen and Panos Koulermos and containing shops, offices, and flats, was built on the west side of Finchley Road in 1961.[73] Two special schools, F. D. Roosevelt and John Keats, were opened in 1957 and 1958 respectively, on the west side of Avenue Road.[74] St. John's Wood Park Investment Co. built on 9 a. facing Boundary Road and St. John's Wood Park c. 1955[75] and two thirteen-storeyed blocks and ter-

raced housing were erected on each side of Boundary Road between St. John's Wood Park and Finchley Road in 1962.[76]

Redevelopment of the site previously occupied by the school for the blind, St. Columba's hospital, and the New College Chapel, all on the east side of Avenue Road, was considered in 1957. A scheme for a civic centre was published in 1959 by the architect, Basil Spence, and part of it, the library and the adjoining swimming baths, was opened in 1964.[77] In 1962 Hampstead theatre opened on a site north of the library that had been intended for civic buildings.[78] At the southern end of Avenue Road, St. Paul's church was replaced by the Polygon flats in the early 1960s.[79] During the same period a large council estate was built on the west side of Finchley Road, stretching from Boundary Road northward to Belsize Road and centred on Hilgrove Road from which it took its name.[80] Adjoining it on the north was the Harben council estate, planned between 1954 and 1959 by Norman & Davison for 170 flats.[81] The work, which included building five blocks in Harben Road, itself truncated by the Hilgrove development, and two new closes, Naseby and Marston, north of Fairfax Road, was not carried out until the late 1960s.[82]

In 1954 the borough council planned a modest 22 dwellings in Abbey Road.[83] In the 1960s, in conjunction with the L.C.C., it rebuilt the entire western portion of the estate, west of Abbey Road, from which the new development took its name; high-rise blocks obliterated the street pattern of the old service area. Later phases, by the borough architect S. A. G. Cook, dated from 1970 and 1973 and included a multi-storeyed car park, shops, a community centre, and health centre in Belsize Road.[84] Two large developments in the 1970s have transformed the centre of the area. The G.L.C. built the Ainsworth estate east of Abbey Road, north of Boundary Road, mostly by 1970.[85] Private rebuilding in Alexandra Road aroused considerable opposition and Camden L.B.'s architectural department took it over in the mid 1970s. Alexandra Road west of Loudoun Road made way for pedestrian walks and stepped concrete housing.[86] Other recent construction has been of pastiche Georgian or Victorian houses in Fairfax Road and the eastern part of Belsize Road and in Hilgrove Road and of striking blocks of flats and offices: no. 133 (Cresta House) Finchley Road (before 1985),[87] no. 100 Avenue Road by Levy Benjamin Horvitch (1986),[88] and the glass

[65] New Lond. Life and Labour, i. 423; vii, maps 8, 10, 11.
[66] Wade, More Streets, 59.
[67] Pevsner, Lond. ii. 202; D.S.R.
[68] D.S.R.; Wade, More Streets, 67.
[69] D.S.R.; Archit. of Lond. 45; Pevsner, Lond. ii. 201; below, social.
[70] Hampstead 1939–45 (Camden History Soc. 1977).
[71] S.C.L., H 331.833 Housing file, Hampstead Communist party, Homes for Hampstead [c. 1955].
[72] Ibid.; The Times, 4 Oct. 1947, 6b.
[73] Archit. of Lond. 51.
[74] Wade, More Streets, 59; below, educ.
[75] Hampstead Communist party, Homes for Hampstead [c. 1955]. [76] The Times, 18 Oct. 1962, 23a.
[77] Ibid. 17 Dec. 1957, 9d; 21 Feb. 1959, 9b; 22 Nov. 1960, 20; 10 Nov. 1964, 6e; Archit. of Lond. 51; below, pub. svces.
[78] Hampstead One Thousand, 138; below, social.
[79] Wade, More Streets, 58–9; Kelly's Dir. Lond. (1960, 1965).

[80] Kelly's Dir. Lond. (1960, 1965); O.S. Map 1/10,000, TQ 28 SE. (1974 edn.).
[81] S.C.L., H 711.13, Council Housing Reps., Hampstead Boro. Rep. on Housing (1954); P. B. Housing, Camden Gen. file, MS. list of Camden housing est. (1971); W. Barnes, Century of Camden Housing [1972].
[82] Kelly's Dir. Lond. (1965, 1970); Official Street Plan of Camden [1980].
[83] Hampstead Boro. Rep. on Housing (1954).
[84] Thompson, Hampstead, 253; O.S. Map 1/10,000, TQ 28 SE. (1974); S.C.L., P. B. Housing, Camden Gen. file, MS. list of Camden housing est. (1971); Architectural Design, 3/1972.
[85] MS. list of Camden housing est. (1971); Wade, W. Hampstead; Kelly's Dir. Lond. (1970).
[86] Hampstead One Thousand, 136; C. McKean and T. Jestico, Guide to Modern Bldgs. in Lond. (1976), 38; Architects Jnl. 8 Sept. 1978.
[87] Kelly's Dir. Lond. (1980, 1985).
[88] Inf. from Levy Benjamin Horvitch Ltd.

and red painted building at the corner of Finchley Road and Eton Avenue (1986).

No part of the St. John's Wood estate in Hampstead was included in a conservation area in 1975[89] and only the Swiss Cottage public house, itself much altered, was among listed buildings.[90] The overwhelming impression in 1986 was made by flats, especially by large-scale schemes dating from after 1945. Surprisingly some of the mid-19th century houses remained, including a dilapidated but handsome terrace in Belgrave Gardens, transferred from Hampstead to St. Marylebone, and a terrace with shops on the western side of Abbey Road on the southern border. Other survivals were mainly on the better built eastern side of the estate, including most of the north side of Belsize Road and nos. 11–15 (odd) on the south side at the east end, the southern side of Hilgrove Road east of Loudoun Road as far as its turning southward, and several houses in Fairfax Road. Except for the high Gothic red-brick pair, nos. 22 and 24 Hilgrove Road, all the houses were stock brick and stuccoed in a classical or Italianate style similar to those of Belsize or Chalcots.

CHALCOTS. Until the 19th century, the only building on the Hampstead portion of the Chalcots estate, apart from the two farmhouses in England's Lane,[91] was Steele's Cottage, where Sir Richard Steele the essayist stayed in 1712 to evade his creditors. The house, which stood on a mound on the west side of Haverstock Hill and was depicted, among others, by Constable, was also where Sir Charles Sedley, the poet and wit, had died in 1701.[92] As the White House, it gave its name to the surrounding field but by 1755 it was described as a cottage.[93] In 1811 there were only six houses on the whole estate.[94]

The first proposals to develop the estate[95] were made in the early 1820s, though not by Eton itself,[96] prompted by the building boom nearby, especially around Regent's Park to the south. On the advice of its London solicitor, the college appointed John Shaw, the developer of St. John's Wood, as surveyor and in 1826 obtained an Act to grant 99-year building leases.[97] Shaw refrained from drawing up a scheme for the whole estate not because planned development was no longer the fashion but because the market for such projects had collapsed. Instead in 1827 and 1829 he drew up schemes similar to that taking place on Bliss's estate to the north for the 15 a. fronting Haverstock Hill, involving half-acre plots for detached or semi-detached villas. In 1830 the college constructed some 100 yd. of a road, which it called Adelaide Road, presumably after the queen, but no speculator was attracted, partly because the market was temporarily saturated and partly because

the London & Birmingham Railway, first projected in 1831 and opened in 1838, made the area less attractive. A small-scale builder, William Wynn, built houses fronting Haverstock Hill in 1830, a few others were erected by a Holborn plumber, and a cowkeeper replaced his cottage by a 'substantial lodge', but there were still no buildings beyond the Haverstock Hill frontage by 1840. Throughout the 1830s Eton considered ambitious plans for the southern part of the estate, at Primrose Hill, for a giant mausoleum, a cemetery full of classical buildings, and a botanical garden, which ended in 1842 in the acquisition of the hill for public recreation.[98]

John Shaw the younger (1803–70), who had succeeded his father as surveyor in 1832, favoured treatment of the entire estate, but the college rejected the last chance, offered in 1839 by William Kingdom, a builder also active in Paddington.[99] Later development was piecemeal, dependent upon small-scale opportunist schemes. Although Shaw drew up a general plan in 1840, the course of the streets was determined by the builders. It was Shaw who insisted on linking the Eton estate with St. John's Wood so that early building, once the Haverstock Hill frontage was completed, was concentrated on Adelaide Road, which was driven through to Avenue and Finchley roads by 1848.[1]

William Wynn had by 1842 built 41 houses fronting Haverstock Hill and in the eastern section of Adelaide Road. He put up only a few houses a year and subleased to other builders. One of them was Samuel Cuming, a Devonshire carpenter who evolved an integrated business, following the trend set on a much larger scale by Cubitt, employing some 80 men by 1851 and dying in 1870 a wealthy man. In 1843 he obtained his first building agreement from the college, for eight plots along Adelaide Road, followed later by four others. Cuming built 104 houses between 1845 and 1852,[2] mostly stuccoed pairs, three-storeyed above a basement, in a plain late Georgian style in Adelaide Road, but including a few Gothic specimens on the north side. In Provost Road and Eton Villas, he built gabled pairs of two storeys and attic above a basement, with Tuscan eaves to give the 'villa' effect.

In 1851 Cuming lived in one of his own houses in Bridge Road (later Bridge Approach), a short road south of Adelaide Road. Of the 117 householders living in his houses, 35 per cent were employed in manufacture and trade, 19 per cent were in the professions, 15 per cent were of independent means, 14 per cent were clerical workers, and another 14 per cent in artistic or literary occupations. The last included a portrait painter at no. 4 Provost Road and Alfred Clint (1807–83), marine painter, at no. 7. In

[89] Camden Boro. Plan, *Hampstead and Belsize Area*, Spr. 1975, Area 4; *W. Hampstead and Kilburn*, Spr. 1975, Area 5.
[90] S.C.L., Town and Country Planning, 52nd list of bldgs. (1974).
[91] Below, other est.
[92] *Images of Hampstead*, 117–19; Park, *Hampstead*, 309–10.
[93] E.C.R. 54/164, no. 9; 54/173; S.C.L., Man. Map and Fieldbk. no. 544.
[94] Thompson, *Hampstead*, 108.
[95] Following section based on Summerson, 'Beginnings of an Early Victorian Suburb' (MS. of lecture 1958); D. J. Olsen, 'House upon house, est. dev. in Lond. and Shef-

field', *Victorian City*, i, ed. H. J. Dyos and M. Wolff, 333–57; Thompson, *Hampstead*, 216–44.
[96] The registrar infuriated developers by his consistent procrastination. The college finance system, which gave fellows the benefit from fines on the renewal of leases but not from rents, worked against building development.
[97] 7 Geo. IV, c. 237 (Private, not printed).
[98] *Images of Hampstead*, 134–6; F. Barker and R. Hyde, *Lond. As It Might Have Been* (1982), 75, 142–4; below, other est.
[99] *Survey of Lond.* xxxvii. 278; below, Paddington, Bayswater.
[1] J. Wyld, *Map of Lond. and Environs* (1848).
[2] D.S.R.

Eton Villas, John Jackson (1819–77), the portrait engraver, was at no. 3 and Ewan Christian (1814–95), the architect, at no. 6. William Dobson (1817–98), the artist, and Samuel Birch (1813–85), the egyptologist, were in Chalcot Villas in Adelaide Road, at nos. 5 and 17 respectively.[3]

The houses in Adelaide Road, which were pushing westward from the junction with Church (later Eton) Road in 1848,[4] had reached the Eyre estate by 1853. After early plans for houses with mews remained unfulfilled, an omnibus service was opened in 1856 along the road, serving a neighbourhood without the extremes of wealth and poverty found in some other districts. In 1856 Cuming extended building at the western end of the estate, on King Henry's Road, which ran south of and parallel to Adelaide Road, on link roads between them, King's College Road and Merton Rise, and on Winchester and Harley roads, which formed the western front of the estate. Most houses were semi-detached Italianate villas but there were also a terrace of shops and a public house in King's College Road, built in 1858 by Robert Yeo, a builder on the Eyre estate, to whom Cuming subleased. By 1862 Adelaide Road formed a band of building through the centre of the estate with side roads and groups of houses at either end. It was more complete in the east,[5] where building included Eton Road with St. Saviour's church (1856) and Wellington House, designed by Alfred Stevens for his own occupation but incomplete at his death in 1875. He lived from 1865 next door at no. 9 Eton Villas, using the abandoned temporary church on the site as a studio; there he modelled the Wellington monument for St. Paul's cathedral.[6] Primrose Hill Road was planned by Cuming in 1858 as a link between England's Lane, the northern boundary of the estate, and Regent's Park Road to the south. During the 1860s building took place there as it did on all the existing roads and on Fellows Road, another east–west road running north of Adelaide Road by 1864.[7]

The two men who most shaped the early development of Chalcots, John Shaw and Samuel Cuming, retired in the 1860s. On the direction of George Pownall, Shaw's successor, Steele's Cottage was demolished in 1867 and replaced by 1870 by a 'very respectable row of shops'[8] in Haverstock Hill and by the new Steele's Road, in which 22 houses, 9 studios, and 7 stables were built between 1871 and 1879.[9] At the east end were the mews and beyond them were ordinary stock-brick terraces. Among detached houses opposite them on the north side were five (nos. 35–9) built by Thomas Batterbury & W. F. Huxley for individual artists, including no. 37 for Frederick Barnard, a *Punch* illustrator, no. 38 for

Edwin Hayes (1819–1904), the marine painter, in 1873, and no. 35 for J. D. (later Sir James) Linton, the landscape painter. Dating from between 1872 and 1875 and in styles proceeding from Gothic to 'Queen Anne', they illustrated a significant moment of change in English taste. To the east, the much altered nos. 31 and 32 were built by J. M. Brydon, who lived briefly at no. 31.[10]

In 1868 Pownall applied for several new roads.[11] In Albert Park, at the south-eastern end of the estate, 16 houses were built in Primrose Hill Road between 1871 and 1873 and two in 1879; 13 were built in Oppidans Road, constructed off it in 1868, between 1872 and 1874 and another 10 between 1878 and 1879. The last road in the area, Ainger Road, existed by 1869 and 38 houses, three stables, and a workshop were built there in 1878–9. Apart from Oppidans Mews, built in 1884, the estate, of grey-brick terraces, was complete by the end of the 1870s.[12] Most houses in King Henry's Road, semi-detached villas in stock brick with Corinthian porches, were of the 1860s[13] but 16 were built between 1871 and 1873.[14]

Some 40 grey-brick houses, with unusually high basements and in pairs but very close together, were built in Fellows Road by 1870,[15] starting from the eastern end. Between 1873 and 1878 another 45 were built there, and in 1879 Roberts Bros. applied to build 24 more. Almost half the road was completed by the end of the 1870s.[16] At the western end of the estate, called Eton Park, 9 houses were built in Winchester Road and 11 stables in Winchester Mews between 1871 and 1873, although most of the small houses there had been built in 1867. Mews were also built in 1871 at Eton Place off Adelaide Road.[17] Elsworthy Road, one of those listed by Pownall in 1868, was started from Primrose Hill Road at the southern edge of the estate, where St. Mary's church (1872) and 35 houses (1875–81) were built.[18]

Most of the roads applied for in 1868 were in the north part of the estate but by 1878 houses existed only in Adamson Road, at the western end; Bursars Road (later Eton Avenue), the largest, had not been completed.[19] In Crossfield Road, which adjoined Adamson Road to the east, 17 houses were built in 1880–1, and in Chalcot Gardens, off England's Lane, six in 'Queen Anne' style.[20] In 1881 William Willett the elder made a building agreement with Eton for the north-western 15 a. of the estate where he undertook to erect 200 houses by 1900, reduced in 1885 to 140 houses, shops, and stables.[21] Although he did not complete that number, he was responsible for 37 houses in Fellows Road in 1882–5, 20 in Adamson Road in 1882–4, 4 in Strathray Road in 1884, and 20 in Eton Avenue in 1886–93.[22] Willett's red-brick houses were popular at the time,[23] although later

[3] P.R.O., HO 107/1492/1, analysed by Summerson, op. cit.
[4] Wyld, *Map of Lond.* (1848).
[5] Stanford, *Libr. Map of Lond.* (1862 edn. with additions to 1865), sheet 6.
[6] *C.H.R.* iii. 18.
[7] P.R.O., C 54/18990, m. 26.
[8] *Hampstead and Highgate Dir.* (1870).
[9] D.S.R.
[10] J. Summerson, 'The Lond. Suburban Villa', *Archit. Rev.* civ. 68–9, 71; *C.H.R.* viii. 19–21; inf. from Mr. A. Saint.
[11] Thompson, *Hampstead*, 244.
[12] Ibid. 243 n.; D.S.R.; Wade, *More Streets*, 57;

Metrop. Improvement Map No. 46 (1878).
[13] Wade, *More Streets*, 53.
[14] D.S.R.
[15] Wade, *More Streets*, 63.
[16] D.S.R.; *Metrop. Improvement Map No. 46* (1878).
[17] D.S.R.; Wade, *More Streets*, 63.
[18] D.S.R.; Thompson, *Hampstead*, 244; *Metrop. Improvement Map No. 46* (1878).
[19] Thompson, *Hampstead*, 244; *Metrop. Improvement Map No. 46* (1878).
[20] D.S.R.
[21] Thompson, *Hampstead*, 347.
[22] D.S.R.
[23] Thompson, *Hampstead*, 347–8.

seen as 'airless excrescences'.[24] The earlier ones were designed by H. B. Measures and those after 1891 by A. F. Faulkner.[25] Among the few buildings not by Willett were the Hall school in Crossfield Road, designed by E. R. Robson, architect to the London school board, and no. 69 Eton Avenue, designed by Frederick Walker for John Collier (1850–1934), the painter, in Flemish Renaissance style, both built in 1890.[26] The Villa Henriette, no. 35 Eton Avenue, was built in 1895 in an elaborate style with stepped gables, turret chimney, dogs, and dragons.[27] The central portion of Eton Avenue was built between 1900 and 1910, nos. 10–14 in the style of Norman Shaw and nos. 28–32 on the north and nos. 11 and 27–39 on the south being by Faulkner.[28]

In 1883 Willett made a building agreement for the site of the Elms and West Croft, two large houses on the site of Upper Chalcots Farm at the west end of England's Lane.[29] Another eight houses were built nearby in 1882–3 in Chalcot Gardens,[30] where additions were later made to no. 16 by C. F. A. Voysey.[31] In 1890 Eton made an agreement with William Willett the younger for 11 a. in the south-western corner of the estate, used as a cricket ground. The Willetts extended Elsworthy Road, forming a loop with the new Wadham Gardens, which they linked to Avenue Road on the west and the existing roads on the north. The site, bordering Primrose Hill but within easy reach of public transport, was highly sought after. By 1903, when the elder Willett retired, the firm had built more than 100 houses, designed by Faulkner, behind privet hedges rather than garden walls and forming a neglected precursor of Hampstead Garden Suburb.[32] By 1913 building was complete throughout the Chalcots estate.[33]

In spite of early efforts to exclude mews, there were several: Steele's, Oppidans, Winchester, and King's College mews and Eton Place. By the end of the 1880s they were classified as 'fairly comfortable' and housed, besides the coachmen, tradespeople serving a community which was classified as middle-class and even, in Eton Avenue and Strathray Gardens, upper middle-class and wealthy.[34] Besides the artists in Steele's Road, King Henry's Road had Arthur Boyd Houghton (1836–75) at no. 162 from 1866,[35] a succession of artists at no. 22 from 1873, and studios at no. 151A.[36] In Adelaide Road the ceramic artist William De Morgan (1839–1917) lived at no. 91 in 1855, the painter Frank Topham (d. 1924) was at no. 43 from 1862 to 1868, followed by his father Francis Topham (1808–77), the water-colourist, in 1870, and the engraver William Holl (1807–71) was at no. 174 in 1870–1 after being at no. 28 Studios, King Henry's Road, in 1869–70. Wych-

combe studios, north of Steele's studios, housed Robert Macbeth at no. 2 from 1880 to 1884, Arthur Rackham at no. 6 in 1900, and Charles Orchardson at no. 3 in 1903–4.[37] The Winchester public house in Winchester Road was a meeting place of artists and writers from 1867, and in 1885 seven houses in Eton Road were occupied by artists.[38] Other artists included Robert Bevan (d. 1925) at no. 14 Adamson Road from 1901, Arthur Rackham at no. 16 Chalcot Gardens 1903–20, Duncan Grant at no. 143 Fellows Road c. 1910, and Stanley Spencer for a short time in Adelaide Road.[39] Among musicians were Cecil Sharp at no. 183 Adelaide Road 1905–11, the conductor Sir Henry Wood at no. 4 Elsworthy Road 1905–37, the singers Dame Clara Butt at Compton Lodge, no. 7 Harley Road, 1901–29, and Adelina Patti (d. 1919) at no. 8 Primrose Hill Road, and Frederick Delius at no. 4 Elsworthy Road at the end of the First World War. Marie Lloyd, the music-hall star, was at no. 98 King Henry's Road in 1906.[40] Frances Buss (d. 1894), the educationalist, lived at Myra Lodge at the corner of King Henry's Road and Primrose Hill Road from 1868 and Mary Webb (d. 1927), the writer, lived for a short while before 1923 in Adelaide Road.[41]

The social changes associated with the First World War reinforced a tendency to convert large houses to flats or for institutions. By 1905, for example, Adelaide Road housed the Huguenot Home for French Governesses (no. 96), the Adelaide Home for Charity Organization Society Pensioners (no. 165), the Christian Social Union (no. 102), and the Jewish Domestic Training Home (no. 113).[42] In 1918–19 Bedford College took over some houses in Adamson Road, which after 1925 formed a hall of residence called Bedford College House.[43] In 1927 Eton Avenue housed the London Academy of Music, Hampstead Ethical Institute, and the London Society for Teaching and Training the Blind.[44] In 1930 the whole area was still classified as middle-class and wealthy, except for patches in Bridge Road and King's College Road at either end of Adelaide Road where mews and small houses were occupied by 'unskilled labourers above the poverty line'.[45]

There was virtually no new building during the 1920s but large blocks of flats were erected during the 1930s, despite protests by Hampstead council and the Ratepayers' Association that there were already far too many flats in the borough.[46] Eton Court was built in Eton Avenue after 1926.[47] An application to build flats on the corner of Haverstock Hill and England's Lane was made in 1936, although apparently they were not built until 1947,[48] Els-worthy Court was built on the corner of Primrose

[24] Quoted in Olsen, *Victorian City*, i. 336.
[25] Inf. from Mr. Saint.
[26] Wade, *More Streets*, 62; S.C.L., Town and Country Planning Act 1971, 52nd List of Bldgs. 1974; *Archit. of Lond.* 47.
[27] Wade, *More Streets*, 61.
[28] Thompson, *Hampstead*, 348; Pevsner, *Lond.* ii. 201. Two hos. were built in 1904. The others were presumably in 1901–3, for which returns are not available: D.S.R.
[29] Thompson, *Hampstead*, 347.
[30] D.S.R.
[31] *Archit. of Lond.* 48.
[32] Thompson, *Hampstead*, 348–50; D.S.R.; inf. from Mr. Saint.
[33] L.C.C. *Municipal Map of Lond.* (1913).
[34] Booth, *Life and Labour*, map; Wade, *More Streets*, 55.
[35] *C.H.R.* iv. 2–4.

[36] Wade, *More Streets*, 55.
[37] *Hampstead One Thousand*, 146, 148–51, 153; *Archit. of Lond.* 47.
[38] Wade, *More Streets*, 63–4.
[39] Ibid. 46, 53, 62–3.
[40] Ibid. 53, 55, 57–8; *Hampstead One Thousand*, 146, 152.
[41] Wade, *More Streets*, 53–5; *Hampstead One Thousand*, 153.
[42] Wade, *More Streets*, 53; *Kelly's Dir. Lond.* (1905).
[43] Wade, *More Streets*, 62; *V.C.H. Mdx.* i. 345.
[44] *Kelly's Dir. Lond.* (1927).
[45] *New Lond. Life and Labour*, vii, maps 8, 10, 11.
[46] *The Times*, 27 Nov. 1935, 16d; 6 Aug. 1936, 6c.
[47] D.S.R.; flats appeared between 1927 and 1930: *Kelly's Dir. Lond.* (1927, 1930).
[48] D.S.R.; *Kelly's Dir. Lond.* (1936–47).

Hill Road and Elsworthy Road in 1937, when major rebuilding began on the Haverstock Hill frontage.[49] John Shaw's first development had been on a very spacious site bounded by Haverstock Hill, Eton Road, (Eton) College Road, and Adelaide Road. When the leases began to fall in during the 1930s, villas in their long gardens were replaced by six-storeyed, five-wing brick blocks in neo-Georgian style, designed by Toms & Partners and called Eton Place, Hall, and Rise respectively.[50]

One of the houses demolished in 1937 was no. 53 Haverstock Hill, where the artist Mark Gertler lived from 1933 to 1936.[51] Although Steele's and Wychcombe studios did not have the importance of the Mall studios in Belsize, Chalcots housed some of the people associated with the artistic flowering of the 1930s. C. R. W. Nevinson, the painter, was at no. 1 Steele's Studios in 1939 and among the refugees the painter Oscar Kokoschka was at no. 45A King Henry's Road from 1939 and the psychoanalyst Sigmund Freud and his daughter Anna made their first home in Britain at no. 39 Elsworthy Road in 1938. The writer Helen Waddell lived at no. 32 Primrose Hill Road, a 'large, damp house', from 1933 until 1965, the composer Sir Arnold Bax was at no. 155 Fellows Road from 1934 to 1939 and the actress Gladys Cooper was at no. 35 Elsworthy Road in 1939. During the 1960s Elizabeth Lutyens, the composer, and Ernest Read, the musicologist, lived at no. 13 and no. 151 King Henry's Road respectively. Sir John Summerson was at no. 1 Provost Road from 1938, before moving to a flat at Eton Rise and then to no. 1 Eton Villas.[52]

Chalcots was badly damaged during the Second World War[53] and as early as 1945 the borough council agreed to the compulsory purchase of a 2-a. bombed site between King Henry's and Oppidans roads where, in 1951, it opened Primrose Hill Court, 102 council flats in five- and seven-storeyed blocks designed by Douglas & Wood;[54] Constable House, a five-storeyed neo-Georgian block designed by Louis de Soissons, was built at the eastern end of Adelaide Road in 1953–4.[55] In 1954 the council began work on 80 flats, designed by D. H. McMorran, in the Fellows Road estate, a site at the east end of Fellows Road, bounded by Adelaide and Primrose Hill roads. Andrews and Higginson houses were opened there between 1960 and 1963, followed by Hutchison, Johnson, and Cleaver houses between 1965 and 1970 and Mary Wharrie between 1970 and 1976. On the north side of Fellows Road, Hancock Nunn House was opened between 1960 and 1963 and Godolphin

House between 1963 and 1965.[56] Hill View flats were built in Primrose Hill Road 1960–3.[57] The nearby Clive hotel was also rebuilt[58] and Alfred Stevens's house in Eton Villas was replaced by flats in 1964.[59]

The largest post-war redevelopment scheme, called the Chalcots estate and published in 1964, was for 33 a. centred on Adelaide Road between Winchester Road on the west and Primrose Hill Road on the east. Eton made 5 a. in the north available to the council for terraces and tower blocks. Building started at the west end in 1965 on blocks of 23 storeys, designed by Dennis Lennon & Partners in consultation with S. A. G. Cook and called Dorney, Bray, Burnham, and Taplow after villages near Eton. One block, Blashford, was in the east. Most blocks were finished by 1970, the whole group forming a striking example of Le Corbusier's 'Plan Voisin'. Private developers built houses and low-rise flats, mostly in the 1970s, on the southern part of the estate, grouped around new roads and closes off King Henry's and Fellows roads.[60] At the western end Swiss Cottage Holiday Inn replaced no. 162 King Henry's Road[61] and at the eastern end Steele's Mews were redeveloped as groups of small houses around courtyards from 1969.[62] At the southern end the Whitton council estate was built in Oppidans Road by Thomas McInerney & Sons in 1970 and Meadowbank flats replaced Oppidans Mews c. 1971.[63] One of the most recent developments is Beaumont Walk, built c. 1978, a precinct of light-brown brick houses of unusual design, north of Adelaide Road, next to Constable House.[64]

In 1975 Eton Villas and Elsworthy Road were conservation areas, with a 'spacious suburban atmosphere'.[65] Almost the whole of Eton Villas and Provost Road consisted of listed buildings, pairs or groups of stucco villas approved by John Shaw in the 1840s.[66] Elsworthy Road, of a later period, was a bizarre mixture of Tudor England, Gothic France, and Moorish Spain. Rebuilding in Adelaide Road exhibited the 1960s' taste for high-rise concrete and glass rectangles and the equally uniform low-rise housing of the 1970s. Almost all other parts of Chalcots in 1986 were a mixture of 19th-century housing, much of it being repainted, and blocks of flats, dating from the 1930s or later, usually of a scale and materials to harmonize with the villas.

NORTH END, LITTLEWORTH, AND SPANIARD'S END.[67] Sandgate, one of the Anglo-Saxon boundary points, has been plausibly located at North End[68] and probably represented a gap in the surrounding

[49] D.S.R.; O.S. Map 1/2,500, TQ 2784 (1954 edn.).
[50] D.S.R.; Thompson, *Hampstead*, 227; inf. from Sir John Summerson.
[51] Wade, *More Streets*, 42.
[52] Ibid. 55, 57–8, 63; *Hampstead One Thousand*, 146, 149–51; inf. from Sir John Summerson.
[53] *Hampstead 1939–45* (Camden History Soc. 1977).
[54] *The Times*, 21 Sept. 1945, 2g; S.C.L., Hampstead Boro. *Rep. on Housing* (1949, 1952); O.S. Map 1/2,500, TQ 2784 (1954 edn.); W. Barnes, *Century of Camden Housing* [1972] (S.C.L., P.B. Housing Gen.).
[55] *Kelly's Dir. Lond.* (1953–4); O.S. Map 1/2,500, TQ 2784 (1954 edn.).
[56] S.C.L., H 711.13 Council Housing, Metrop. Boro. of Hampstead, *Mun. Housing Est.* [*c.* 1962]; *Kelly's Dir. Lond.* (1960, 1963, 1965, 1970, 1976); S.C.L., P.B. Housing, Camden Gen. file, MS. list of Camden housing est. (1971).
[57] *Kelly's Dir. Lond.* (1960, 1963).

[58] Wade, *More Streets*, 63; below, econ., ind.
[59] *C.H.R.* iii. 18 sqq.
[60] *The Times*, 5 May 1964, 8g; 29 Aug. 1964, 4b; 10 Mar. 1965, 19a; 4 Nov. 1965, 6; Wade, *More Streets*, 51, 53, 55, 64; *Kelly's Dir. Lond.* (1965, 1970, 1976); MS. list of Camden housing est. (1971).
[61] *C.H.R.* iv. 2–4; below, econ., ind.
[62] Wade, *More Streets*, 46.
[63] MS. list of Camden housing est. (1971); *Kelly's Dir. Lond.* (1970, 1972).
[64] *Kelly's Dir. Lond.* (1977, 1979).
[65] Camden Boro. Plan, *Hampstead and Belsize Area*, Spr. 1975, Area 4.
[66] S.C.L., Town and Country Planning, 52nd list of bldgs. (1974).
[67] Much of the material for the following subsection, especially that relating to the 18th and early 19th cents., has been supplied by Mr. David Sullivan.
[68] *T.L.M.A.S.* vi. 560–70.

woodland. The wood, Wildwood, part of Eton College's Wyldes estate in Hendon, probably originally extended across to the northern slopes of Hampstead Heath[69] and by 1632 it marked the parish boundary.[70] Until *c.* 1730 the ancient route across the heath to Hendon took a sharp westward turn, before turning north again. Its twists were presumably imposed by obstacles, probably dense woodland, at the location marked as Wildwood Corner *c.* 1672.[71] About 1730 a cutting was made through the heath west of the old route, creating the modern North End Way (formerly Road), a more direct route to Hendon.[72]

In the late 16th century there was a wayside cottage at the northern end of the heath.[73] Cottages were mentioned on the northern part of the heath in 1666[74] and at Wildwood Corner in 1679 and 1685.[75] By the end of the century houses around a pond where the road turned west and on both sides of the road where it turned north again formed a village called North End. The house belonging to Thomas Tidd, wheelwright, who had lived in the area since 1666, was termed a 'mansion house' in 1692.[76] By 1710 there were 10 people paying 19 quit rents for 18 houses and cottages, and 2¾ a., almost all taken from the heath, at 'over the heath or North End'.[77] The copyholders included William Trott, a London draper,[78] and Joseph Keble (1632–1710), the barrister and essayist, who for the sake of the air had bought a small estate, where he lived for part of the week.[79]

Two of the 18 houses were recently built cottages at 'le Parkgate', later called Spaniard's End, at the north-east end of the heath and parish.[80] The only other building in the area was Mother Huff's, an inn later called the Shakespeare's Head, on the edge of the demesne land fronting Spaniard's Road.[81] The house, where Mother Huff claimed in 1728 to have been for 50 years, was recorded in 1680 and may have been the New inn marked on the road through Cane Wood (Kenwood) to Highgate *c.* 1672.[82]

At the other side of the heath, where Heath Road branched into North End Way and Spaniard's Road, was Jack Straw's Castle. The inn may not have been as early as the possibly mid 16th-century brick foundations.[83] In 1670 Henry Skerrett was licensed to enclose 2 a. of heath, between the road to Hendon on the east and an old gravel pit, as a bowling green

to entertain guests. There were new buildings there in 1673, a house and a cottage next to the bowling green by 1686,[84] and three cottages by 1711. They were then held by John Fletcher, an innholder who lost them through financial difficulties to the brewer John Vincent.[85] The three cottages were called Jack Straw's Castle in 1713, when Vincent acquired waste nearby.[86] Cottages were built nearby in the late 17th and the early 18th century, some by squatters.[87] In 1690 Silvester Killett owned a cottage next to the bowling green; in 1714 his family gave the cottage for the use of the poor.[88]

There was modest growth during the early 18th century, with a few country houses appearing among the cottages. In North End the Bull and Bush, licensed from 1721,[89] may have originated in the estate belonging to the Tidds in the 17th century;[90] although the story of Hogarth's residence there was probably apocryphal, the inn attracted artists and writers in his day.[91] A second inn, the Hare and Hounds, was licensed from 1751.[92] Robert Dingley (d. 1742), a City goldsmith, acquired a small house in North End in 1727 and a grant of waste in 1738. He left the estate to his younger son Charles, who made a fortune out of trade with Russia and by 1769 had bought buildings and pieces of waste in Hampstead[93] in 17 separate lots.[94] In 1762, when North End contained 17 houses, 3 cottages, and 2 inns, Dingley's house, called in turn Wildwoods, North End, and Pitt House, was set in 2½ a., mostly on the southern side of the village, and included a coach house, stabling, garden, grotto, wilderness, and four other houses.[95] Politically ambitious, Dingley invited William Pitt the elder to North End in 1763. Asserting that no ague was ever known there, he made considerable alterations, building a new wing and a gymnasium for Pitt's children by 1766, when Pitt first moved in. Pitt returned during his illness in 1767 but Dingley, put up as a candidate to oppose Wilkes, died in 1769 after being beaten up by the mob.[96]

In 1770 one of two new brick houses on the eastern side of North End, later called Hollybush Hill, was occupied by a wine merchant.[97] In 1781, with another house to the south called Myrtle, later Byron, Cottage or Lodge, it was bought by John Bland (d. 1788), a City banker.[98] In 1787 the eastern portion

[69] *V.C.H. Mdx.* v. 21.
[70] G.L.R.O., E/MW/H/I/2311B.
[71] Ogilby, *Map of Mdx.* (*c.* 1672).
[72] S.C.L., Man. Map and Fieldbk. no. 250; new rd. on Rocque, *Map of Lond.* (1741–5), sheet 12; below, plate 6.
[73] A. Farmer, *Hampstead Heath* (1984), 9.
[74] G.L.R.O., E/MW/H/6.
[75] Ibid. 7–8.
[76] Ibid. 11; ibid. MR/FB/1/115.
[77] Ibid. E/MW/H/I/2123, 2311B.
[78] S.C.L., J 45, extracts from ct. rolls 1607–1843, s.v. 1695.
[79] Park, *Hampstead*, 313–14; *D.N.B.*
[80] M.M. & M., Lib. A, p. 48.
[81] G.L.R.O., E/MW/H, old no. Box L (abs. of leases 1680–1731); H, old no. 31/8 (lease 1767); S.C.L., Man. Map and Fieldbk. no. mm. As demesne freehold it was not listed in the 1704 and 1710 rentals.
[82] *Hampstead One Thousand*, 23; Ogilby, *Map of Mdx.* (*c.* 1672).
[83] Article by Jas. Bristow, 29 Mar. 1963, in S.C.L., H 728.5, Jack Straw's Castle.
[84] G.L.R.O., E/MW/H/6 (1673); 8 (1686).
[85] P.R.O., C 5/635/49; below, econ., ind.
[86] *Post-Boy*, 25–8 July 1713, quoted in Barrett, *Annals*,

i. 195; M.M. & M., Lib. A, p. 203.
[87] Article by D. Sullivan in *H.H.E.*, 25 May 1979.
[88] G.L.R.O., E/MW/H/9; S.C.L., D 134; below, local govt. There were Killetts in Hampstead by 1664: G.L.R.O., MR/TH/2, m. 30.
[89] *Hampstead One Thousand*, 154.
[90] G.L.R.O., E/MW/H/6 (1666); 8 (1689); 11 (1692); Mary Tidd surrendered property in 1743 to Peter Pierson, owner of Bull and Bush: S.C.L., Hampstead manor min. bk. (1742–82), pp. 19, 201.
[91] G. H. Cunningham, *Lond.: Comprehensive Survey* (1931), 472–3.
[92] *Hampstead One Thousand*, 154.
[93] Article on Dingley by P. Venning and D. Sullivan in *H.H.E.* 19 May 1978; extracts by Oppé in S.C.L., Hampstead manor min. bk. (1742–82).
[94] G.L.R.O., E/MW/H/I/2178. His quit rents totalled £5 7s. 3d.
[95] S.C.L., Man. Map and Fieldbk. nos. 230–50.
[96] *H.H.E.* 19 May 1978.
[97] S.C.L., Man. Map and Fieldbk. no. 231; Hampstead manor min. bk. (1742–82), pp. 306–7.
[98] S.C.L., Man. Map and Fieldbk. no. 230; Hampstead manor min. bk. (1742–82), p. 459; F. G. Hilton Price, *Handbk. of Lond. Bankers* (1890), 13.

of Dingley's estate, where a cottage had been demolished in 1786, passed to Bland by bequest.[99] Most of Dingley's estate, including Pitt House, was bought in 1787 by Abraham Robarts, another banker, who sold it in 1807 to John Vivian, solicitor to the Excise.[1] Robarts and Vivian apparently occupied Pitt House. Byron Cottage was occupied by the judge Sir Robert Dallas (1756–1824) c. 1810,[2] by the Quaker philanthropist Sir Thomas Buxton (1786–1845) and his wife Hannah, sister-in-law of Samuel Hoare the younger, before 1820,[3] and by the marchioness of Lansdowne in 1823.[4] Hope Cottage, a weatherboarded cottage near the Bull and Bush, housed the painter John Linnell in 1822 and, after he had moved to Wyldes, his friend the painter, William Collins. Both were visited by fellow artists, including Blake, Varley, Morland, and Palmer, attracted, according to William Collins's son Wilkie, the novelist, 'by some of the prettiest and most varied inland scenery'.[5]

In 1734 John Turner, a rich draper or tobacconist from Fleet Street, built at Parkgate a house called the Firs, after the clump of trees which he planted on the heath and which were to be painted by Constable and others.[6] By 1762 it was one of five houses at what was called Spaniard's quarter.[7] Another was Parkgate, on the boundary, then occupied by John Sanderson, architect of the parish church.[8] Spaniards inn, which gave its name to the district, lay just over the border.[9] About 1788 Heath End House was built on the site of three of the houses of 1762,[10] next to Saunderson's house, which was purchased about the same time by Thomas Erskine (1750–1823), later Lord Chancellor.[11] Erskine created a stuccoed house, which he called Evergreen Hill (later Erskine House), with a covered porch and very large upper windows for a room designed as a banqueting hall to entertain George III.[12] Humphry Repton worked on the grounds, which were stocked with Scottish fir trees from Kew.[13] Erskine bought a piece of demesne land fronting Kenwood Lane in 1804, which became an extension of his garden, linked by a tunnel under the road. He took leases in 1806 of the former Shakespeare's Head, where the Elms was built by 1851, and in 1811 of more demesne.[14] He left c. 1819 and by 1834 his house was occupied by Sir Nicholas Conyngham Tindal (1776–1846), chief justice of the Common Pleas,[15] who may

have been responsible for building by 1848 another house on the east side of Spaniard's Road, north of the Elms.[16] Charles Bosanquet (1769–1850), a governor of the South Sea Co., then lived at the Firs, where his brother Sir John (1773–1847), the judge, died.[17]

Small plots were taken from the heath near Jack Straw's Castle during the 18 years from c. 1720 when the stewardship of the manor was in dispute, and in 1737 several people had to regularize their titles to land in the area by then called Littleworth.[18] Most were local tradesmen or craftsmen like the harness-maker Samuel Hatch or the tallow chandler John Ayres,[19] of whose cottages one illustrated at the end of the century may have been typical.[20] By 1720, however, the gentry had begun to move in. Three cottages, part of John Fletcher's estate, had been converted to two houses, one of which was occupied by William Brooks, gentleman,[21] and in 1734 was a good brick house, about half way over the heath, with a view over nine or ten counties.[22] The house was part of lands acquired from 1720 by Joseph Rous (d. 1731), a London gentleman,[23] and in 1744 it was sold, with adjacent parcels enclosed from the waste, to Christopher Arnold, a goldsmith and partner in Hoare's bank, who was granted more waste in the same year.[24] By 1762 Arnold had a house and stabling in 1½ a. bounded by North End Way and Spaniard's Road, the whole later called the Heath or Heath House.[25] Another cottage built before 1738, the most northerly of the Littleworth group, was enlarged, probably by Lewis Allen after 1749.[26] By 1762 Littleworth consisted of Heath House on the east side of the Hendon road,[27] Jack Straw's Castle and nine cottages, on the west side,[28] and a house and two cottages a little to the north, also on the west side.[29]

Jack Straw's Castle, popular both with visitors to the wells and with travellers,[30] was important in publicizing the attractions of the locality, with ease of access from London, proximity to the heath, and wide views. As a consequence Littleworth, the hamlet of humble cottages, was transformed into an area of villas set in extensive grounds and lost its former name, often being called simply the Heath.[31] In 1764 the painter William Oram bought an existing plot, where by 1770 he had built a brick house and stabling.[32] In 1777 his widow conveyed the house to

[99] i.e. on E. side of North End Ave., S. of his existing property: S.C.L., Man. Map and Fieldbk. nos. 247–8; S.C.L., Hampstead manor min. bk. (1783–1809), pp. 68, 77–8.
[1] S.C.L., Hampstead manor min. bk. (1783–1809), pp. 8, 405; Park, *Hampstead*, 358; Hilton Price, *Lond. Bankers*, 142.
[2] S.C.L., Hampstead manor min. bk. (1809–24), p. 393; poor rate bk. 1810; *D.N.B.* s.v. Dallas.
[3] C. White, *Sweet Hampstead*, 292; *D.N.B.*
[4] S.C.L., Hampstead manor min. bk. (1809–24), p. 393.
[5] Barratt, *Annals*, ii. 20; *Images of Hampstead*, 62.
[6] Wade, *Streets of Hampstead*, 80; *Hampstead One Thousand*, 89.
[7] S.C.L., Man. Map and Fieldbk. nos. 224–6.
[8] *Hampstead One Thousand*, 46.
[9] Below, social.
[10] S.C.L., Man. Map and Fieldbk. no. 226.
[11] Wade, *Streets of Hampstead*, 79.
[12] *Survey of Lond.* ix. 365; *Hampstead One Thousand*, 92.
[13] *C.H.R.* xi. 4–9; *The Times*, 20 Oct. 1808, 4b.
[14] G.L.R.O., E/MW/H, old nos. 31/7 (sale 1804); 8 (lease 1806); 9 (lease 1811); Wade, *Streets of Hampstead*, 79; P.R.O., HO 107/1492/9.

[15] Cunningham, *Lond.: Comprehensive Surv.* 660; poor rate bk. 1834; *D.N.B.*
[16] J. Wyld, *Map of Lond. and Environs* (1848).
[17] *D.N.B.*
[18] S.C.L., Hoare v. Wilson, observations on behalf of plaintiffs, exhibits, p. 33.
[19] M.M. & M., Lib. B, p. 5.
[20] Farmer, *Hampstead Heath*, 30.
[21] M.M. & M., Lib. B, p. 29.
[22] J. Soame, *Hampstead Wells* (1734), 26–7.
[23] M.M. & M., Lib. B, pp. 5, 15, 22–3, 29; C, pp. 18–22.
[24] S.C.L., Hampstead manor min. bk. (1742–82), pp. 29, 37; *H.H.E.* 25 May 1979.
[25] S.C.L., Man. Map and Fieldbk. no. 264; Barratt, *Annals*, ii. 180; Farmer, *Hampstead Heath*, 26.
[26] S.C.L., Hampstead manor min. bk. (1742–82), pp. 35, 73, 75.
[27] S.C.L., Man. Map and Fieldbk. no. 264.
[28] Ibid. nos. 254–8, 260–3.
[29] Ibid. nos. 251–2.
[30] Below, social and plate 7.
[31] e.g. in rate bks. and dirs.
[32] S.C.L., Man. Map and Fieldbk. no. 253; Hampstead manor min. bk. (1742–82), pp. 206, 302; *D.N.B.*

Francis Willes, in 1784 knighted for secret service work as a decipherer.[33] Willes (d. 1828) bought the adjoining plots, including the poor cottages, and acquired grants of waste to make a total of over 2 a., centred on the house later called Heathlands.[34]

In 1775 Jane Hemet *alias* Mrs. Lessingham, actress and mistress of Sir William Addington, a magistrate, was granted 2 a. of waste at Gibbet Hill, west of the road to North End, where she employed the builder Bradley to erect a house. Henry White, another builder, led protestors who, claiming that she was not a copyholder and was not entitled to the grant, filled in the excavations. In 1776 she overcame the technicality by buying a cottage at Littleworth and succeeded in building Heath Lodge in the centre of the heath,[35] a three-storeyed cube with a central semicircular bay and flanking two-storeyed wings designed by James Wyatt on the model of a villa in Italy.[36] Mrs. Lessingham (d. 1783) left the house to Thomas Harris (d. 1820), manager of Covent Garden theatre, but it was occupied by William, Lord Byron (d. 1798), the poet's great-uncle, in 1784.[37]

Near Heath Lodge, the northernmost of the Littleworth houses of 1762[38] was three-storeyed with a semicircular bay extending to the roof;[39] it was advertised in 1779 as lately built.[40] In 1807 the house (the Hill, Hill House, or the Whinns) was given to Samuel Hoare the younger (d. 1847) by his father Samuel the elder (d. 1825), who in 1790 had left Stoke Newington for the healthy elevation of Heath House.[41] The elder Samuel's father had become a partner in Bland, Barnett & Co., the banking firm of John Bland of North End, c. 1722.[42] The Hoares were Quaker, later Anglican, bankers, prominent in the anti-slavery movement and familiar with many leading politicians and literary figures. George Crabbe often visited Heath House and Tennyson and Wordsworth met for the first time at the Hill in 1845. For a century the family played an important part in Hampstead's history, supporting churches and schools and other causes, and leading the battle over the heath against Sir Thomas Maryon Wilson.[43]

Thomas Pool, who acquired Jack Straw's Castle in 1774, built two brick houses in 1788, which c. 1820 were converted into one house south of the inn, called successively Heath View, Earlsmead, and Old Court House.[44]

Two adjacent cottages behind Jack Straw's Castle came to be occupied by John, after 1806 Baron, Crewe (d. 1829) and his wife Frances and by Lady Camelford. At what became Crewe Cottage, Frances Crewe (d. 1818), the celebrated beauty and Whig hostess, from c. 1792 to c. 1807 entertained Fox, Burke, Sheridan, Reynolds, Canning, the princess of Wales, and Fanny Burney and her father.[45] Her interests included helping refugees from the French revolution and she may have been influential in attracting many to Hampstead, including the marquis de Cincello, who c. 1800 lived in a house near Hill House, later called Cedar Lawn.[46] Camelford Cottage was occupied c. 1799 by Anne (d. 1803), widow of the politician Thomas Pitt (1737–93), first Baron Camelford and nephew of William Pitt, who had stayed in North End. The house passed to her son Thomas (1775–1804), the duellist, who was killed in 1804, and was afterwards occupied by her son-in-law William Wyndham Grenville, Baron Grenville (1759–1834), who also acquired Crewe Cottage c. 1807. Grenville was resident in Hampstead during the period when he headed the Ministry of All the Talents, which saw the abolition of the slave trade. He left c. 1813, when both Crewe and Camelford cottages were empty.[47]

Between 1805 and 1820 Samuel Sotheby, 'bookseller of the Strand', a founder of the auctioneering firm, acquired several of the old cottages and adjacent plots of waste and built the house later called Fern Lodge. He became bankrupt in 1829 and again in 1841, when he lost his Hampstead estate.[48]

The combined population for North End and Littleworth increased from 108 in 1801 to 307 in 1851 and 416 in 1871.[49] North End remained predominantly a village of agricultural labourers, gardeners, and laundresses,[50] and in 1839 had the second highest concentration of laundries in the parish.[51] There were a few tradesmen, like William Ambridge the grocer in 1851, whose family had lived in Hampstead since the 17th century and owned property in North End since the 18th.[52] The two inns survived and a school had been built, largely through the support of John Gurney Hoare, in 1849 on the western edge of North End.[53] In 1841 Pitt House was occupied by a clergyman who kept a boarding school and in 1851 there was another boarding school in North

[33] S.C.L., Hampstead manor min. bk. (1742–82), p. 411; *H.H.E.* 25 May 1979.
[34] S.C.L., Man. Map and Fieldbk. nos. 254, 258; Hampstead manor min. bk. (1824–39), p. 133; below, local govt.; below, plate 29.
[35] S.C.L., Hampstead manor min. bk. (1742–82), pp. 386, 394; Farmer, *Hampstead Heath*, 33–6.
[36] Barratt, *Annals*, ii. 201; cutting 1813 in S.C.L., H 728.3, files, Heath Lodge.
[37] S.C.L., Hampstead manor min. bk. (1783–1809), p. 24. Edwin C. Harris, 'one of the sons of Jane Hemet' surr. all claims in 1813: ibid. (1809–24), p. 99; Park, *Hampstead*, Corrections, p. xxxvi; *D.N.B.*; *Complete Peerage*, s.v. Byron.
[38] S.C.L., Man. Map and Fieldbk. no. 251.
[39] *Images of Hampstead*, 84, illus. 218.
[40] S.C.L., Hampstead manor min. bk. (1742–82), p. 346; inf. from Mr. Sullivan.
[41] S.C.L., Hampstead manor min. bk. (1783–1809), p. 152; *V.C.H. Mdx.* viii. 165.
[42] Hilton Price, *Lond. Bankers*, 13.
[43] Barratt, *Annals*, ii. 176–7, 182; *C.H.R.* ix. 18–19; below, Hampstead Heath.
[44] S.C.L., Hampstead manor min. bk. (1742–82), p.

375; (1783–1809), p. 91; *H.H.E.* 25 May 1979.
[45] S.C.L., Hampstead manor min. bk. (1783–1809), pp. 262–3; (1809–24), p. 133; F. Burney, *Jnls. and Letters*, ed. J. Hemlow (1972–5), i. 193–213; iii. 75–6, 112, 141; iv. 313; v. 207, 389.
[46] S.C.L., rate bk. 1800; Hampstead manor min. bk. (1809–24), pp. 10–11; *C.H.R.* x. 5–6; *Corresp. of Edm. Burke*, ed. P. J. Marshall and J. A. Woods (1968), vii. 421; A. Edwards, *Fanny Burney*, 100.
[47] S.C.L., Hampstead manor min. bk. (1783–1809), pp. 257, 262, 408–10; (1809–24), p. 94; poor rate bks. 1810, 1813; *D.N.B.* s.v. W. W. Grenville, Thos. Pitt; *H.H.E.* 25 May 1979.
[48] S.C.L., Man. Map and Fieldbk. nos. 255–7; Hampstead manor min. bk. (1783–1809), pp. 343, 433; (1824–39), p. 171; (1839–43), p. 95; T, p. 237; *H.H.E.* 25 May 1979.
[49] Census returns analysed by Mr. Sullivan.
[50] For North End in 1822 see Barratt, *Annals*, ii. 62.
[51] Barratt, *Annals*, ii. 268; below, econ., ind.
[52] P.R.O., E 179/143/370, m. 43d.; G.L.R.O., E/MW/H/I/2123, 2311A; S.C.L., Man. Map and Fieldbk. no. 240.
[53] Wade, *Streets of Hampstead*, 77; below, educ.

End Lodge. A solicitor lived in one of the Hollybush houses in 1841, a barrister in Gothic Cottage in 1851, and solicitors in North End Lodge and Stowe House in 1871. Wildwood Lodge, a mid 19th-century *cottage orné*, belonged to Queen Victoria's dentist before 1869[54] and to a provision merchant in 1871, when Myrtle Lodge housed a lamp manufacturer. The poet Coventry Patmore (1823–96) lived in Elm Cottage *c.* 1862,[55] and the author Dinah Maria Mulock (Mrs. Craik, 1826–87) in Wildwood Cottage from 1857 to 1864.[56]

Wildwood Grove, near the northern border, was a terraced row begun in the 1860s. The local builder, T. Clowser, was permitted to build four houses there in 1871 and another six stood there and in Wildwood, probably Wildwood Terrace, by 1882. A new school house was built in 1872[57] and by 1875 there were 77 houses and cottages in North End, including a few over the border in Hendon.[58] A house was built at the Hare and Hounds in 1879, additions were made to the Bull and Bush in 1885, and Ambridge Cottages were extended by a further three in 1887.[59] By 1890 one house in Wildwood Terrace had become a convalescent home, a lieutenant-colonel lived in Stowe House, and two Hoare sisters lived in North End, as they still did in 1911. Most of North End was still cottages in 1890 and there were several laundries, although a new feature was the number of tea gardens.[60] Presumably visitors included hikers and cyclists, in addition to those attracted by the Bull and Bush, celebrated in a music-hall song.[61]

On the east side of North End Avenue a second North End House had been built by 1913[62] and in 1923 Brandon House and Wyldeways were built north of it.[63] Myrtle Lodge, farther north again, had been renamed Byron Cottage after Fanny Lucy, Lady Byron and later Lady Houston (1857–1936), the thrice married ex-chorus girl and patriot, who went to live there in 1908.[64] One small block of flats, the Limes, was built between the two inns in 1935.[65] Pitt House, in 1869 a two-storyed building with a central doorway and a side bay,[66] was later enlarged by the addition of a billiard room and in 1899 Sir Harold Harmsworth, later Viscount Rothermere, bought it and added a storey, also moving the Georgian doorcase to the side bay. He sold it in 1908 and it was occupied during the First World War by Valentine Fleming, M.P., and his sons the writers Ian (d. 1964) and Peter (d. 1971), and from 1924 to 1939 by the earl of Clarendon.[67]

At Spaniard's End, Heath End House was occupied by Sir William Parry (1790–1855), the Arctic explorer, and from 1889 to 1912 by Canon Samuel Barnett (1844–1913), the social reformer, and his wife Dame Henrietta (1851–1936), founder of Hampstead Garden Suburb. In 1895 they lent the house, which they called St. Jude's Cottage, to the painter James Whistler (1834–1903) and in 1903 they took over Erskine House for a convalescent home. The whole estate was acquired by Sir Hall Caine (1853–1931), the novelist, who demolished Erskine House in 1923. From 1894 to 1908 the Elms was the home of Sir Joseph Joel Duveen (1843–1908), the art dealer.[68] The house to the north was demolished between 1891 and 1913.[69] A new house, called Mount Tyndale, was built in the 1920s and occupied in 1938 by Viscount Knollys.[70]

The advertisement for Old Court House in 1839, a detached residence with extensive views, suitable for a 'family of respectability', could have applied to any of the houses along North End Way. Old Court House was used as an estate office during the 1850s and 1860s although there is no evidence that courts were held there[71] but the other houses continued as substantial family homes. In 1841 the inhabitants included merchants at Fern and Heath lodges, a banker at Hill House, a clergyman at Camelford Cottage, a solicitor at Crewe Cottage, and several described as 'independent'. A major-general lived in Fern Lodge in 1851[72] and his widow and daughter were still there in 1890. From 1872 until 1890 or later Heathlands was the home of Hugh M. Matheson, the Far Eastern merchant.[73] By 1890 Sir Richard Temple, Bt., had built Heath Brow on the site of Crewe Cottage.[74] The elder Samuel Hoare's widow Hannah (d. 1856) lived in Heath House which remained with the family until *c.* 1911 but was leased by 1876. It was occupied from 1888 by Sir Algernon Borthwick, later Baron Glenesk (1830–1908), the newspaper proprietor, and by 1911 by Edward C. Guinness, Viscount and later earl of Iveagh (1847–1927), the philanthropist. When he left for Kenwood in 1919, Guinness was succeeded by his third son the statesman Walter Edward Guinness, later Baron Moyne (1880–1944).[75] The second residence of the Hoares, Hill House, was occupied after the younger Samuel's death successively by his sons John Gurney (d. 1876) and Francis until 1895. In 1896 Sir Samuel Hoare, Bt., John Gurney's son, sold it to George Fisher, who rebuilt the house.[76] He sold it in 1904

[54] Wade, *Streets of Hampstead*, 77.
[55] Barratt, *Annals*, ii. 184.
[56] Cunningham, *Lond.: Comprehensive Surv.* 471; *D.N.B.*
[57] *Census*, 1871; D.S.R.
[58] Hutchings and Crowsley, *Hampstead Dir.* (1875).
[59] D.S.R.
[60] *Kelly's Dir. Hampstead and Highgate* (1889–90); *Memoirs of Sam. Hoare*, ed. F. R. Pryor (1911), p. xii.
[61] *Images of Hampstead*, 59; below, social.
[62] Stanford, *Libr. Map of Lond.* (1891 edn.), sheet 1; L.C.C. *Municipal Map of Lond.* (1913).
[63] D.S.R.; L.C.C. *Municipal Map of Lond.* (1930); O.S. Map 1/2,500, TQ 2586 (1955 edn.).
[64] Wade, *Streets of Hampstead*, 78; Debrett, *Peerage and Baronetage* (1976), s.v. Byron.
[65] D.S.R.; *Kelly's Dir. Hampstead and Childs Hill* (1938).
[66] *Images of Hampstead*, 63, illus. 118. According to W. Howitt, *Northern Heights* (1869), 90, the ho. had been 'raised another storey' by the present occupier, but his own photograph shows only two.

[67] *Images of Hampstead*, 63, illus. 119–22; Barratt, *Annals*, ii. 60; S.C.L., H 728.3 file, Pitt Ho.; *The Times*, 11 Nov. 1908, 4*f*; 18 Nov. 1908, 22*e*; Wade, *Streets of Hampstead*, 78.
[68] Wade, *Streets of Hampstead*, 79–80; Oppé, *Hampstead: Lond. Town*, 44.
[69] Stanford, *Libr. Map of Lond.* (1891 edn.), sheet 1; L.C.C. *Municipal Map of Lond.* (1913).
[70] L.C.C. *Municipal Map of Lond.* (1930); *Kelly's Dir. Hampstead and Childs Hill* (1920, 1938).
[71] S.C.L., H 728.3 files, Court Ho.; below, local govt.
[72] Census returns analysed by Mr. Sullivan.
[73] *Hampstead Dir. and Guide* (1854); Hutchings and Crowsley, *Hampstead and Highgate Dir.* (1876); *Kelly's Dir. Hampstead and Highgate* (1889–90); *H.H.E.* 25 May 1979.
[74] Barratt, *Annals*, iii. 286.
[75] *Memoirs of Sam. Hoare*, p. xii, fam. tree; Wade, *Streets of Hampstead*, 76; Hutchings and Crowsley, *Hampstead and Highgate Dir.* (1876); *D.N.B.*
[76] *Memoirs of Sam. Hoare*, p. xii; Barratt, *Annals*, ii. 182.

to William H. Lever, later Viscount Leverhulme (1851–1925), the soap manufacturer, who made further additions, including a ballroom and art gallery, and acquired the neighbouring Heath Lodge in 1911 and Cedar Lawn in 1914. Heath Lodge was demolished and Thomas Mawson designed grounds for the combined estate. Cedar Lawn, which served as a hospital during the First World War and subsequently as a maternity home, was demolished in 1922. In 1925 the whole estate was bought by Lord Inverforth (1865–1955), the shipowner, and the new house named Inverforth House.[77]

Much of North End was destroyed or damaged by a parachute mine during the Second World War. The Hare and Hounds was rebuilt in 1968. Pitt House, used by the army and then left empty, was sold in 1948 to an investment company, which demolished it in 1952 and replaced it with a house of the same name; the L.C.C. acquired 3 a. of the garden in 1954.[78] Building after 1945 was discreet and North End kept its quiet village atmosphere in the 1980s. The Old Bull and Bush, although largely rebuilt in the 1920s, retained two 18th-century bay windows and one venetian window. Behind it, an early 18th-century pair, nos. 1 and 3 North End, remained, as did Wildwood, dating from the 18th century and tile-hung in the late 19th century. Byron Cottage and the Gothic Wildwood Lodge also survived.[79] Michael Ventris (1922–56), the architect and decipherer of Linear B, built no. 19 North End Avenue in the 1950s. Sir Nikolaus Pevsner (d. 1983), the architectural historian, lived at no. 2 Wildwood Terrace from 1936, next to Geoffrey Grigson the poet at no. 3 in 1938. Sir Donald Wolfit (1902–68), the actor manager, lived at no. 5 Wildwood Grove in the 1950s.[80]

At Spaniard's End the Firs was divided in the 1950s into three houses called the White House, the Chantry, and Casa Maria, the third being formed from the billiard room. The outbuildings were converted into other dwellings. Heath End House survived under the name Evergreen Hill, next to a wing of the old Erskine House.[81] The Elms housed St. Columba's hospital from 1957 and was then owned, but rarely inhabited, by Barbara Hutton, the Woolworth heiress. In 1981 it was sold for a large sum to the president of the United Arab Emirates but it remained unoccupied and in 1987 was sold to developers, the Holly Corporation.[82]

The greatest change has been in North End Way, in the area once called Littleworth. In 1941 a second land-mine destroyed Heathlands and Heath Brow and damaged Jack Straw's Castle and Heath House.[83] The house was repaired, occupied from 1971 by Peter King, the publisher, and, despite its sale in 1977 to a property developer,[84] survived in the 1980s as a 'large, square, somewhat grim-looking Georgian house of brown brick'.[85] The inn was rebuilt in 1962.[86] In 1948 the Hampstead Heath Protection society bought the site of Fern Lodge and presented it to the L.C.C., which itself compulsorily purchased the site of Heathlands in 1951, the combined ground being opened to the public as part of the heath in 1955. The L.C.C. bought the site of Heath Brow in 1953 as a car park for visitors to the heath, and in 1955 part of the former garden of Heath Lodge, which it opened to the public in 1963. Lord Inverforth left his estate in 1955 to Manor House hospital.[87] Old Court House survived, a square building with a central portico and wings, dating from the early 18th century and refaced later in the century;[88] it was converted to old people's flats in the 1960s.[89]

THE VALE OF HEALTH. East of the road across the heath to Spaniard's was an area of bog[90] called Gangmoor, described towards the end of her life by the sculptor Joseph Nollekens's wife (d. 1817) as 'a stagnate bottom, a pit in the heath'.[91] There Samuel Hatch, a harness maker presented for building a shop on the highway at Jack Straw's Castle and dumping his hides, built a workshop and in 1714 was granted a piece of waste.[92] By 1720 he had a cottage at what was subsequently called Hatch's or Hatchett's Bottom.[93] In 1762 a single enclosure, approached by an unfenced track from Heath Street, contained a barn, stable, and cowshed, for which ground rent was payable to the lord of the manor, and possibly a cottage next to a small pond, which may have been Hatch's cottage and was not listed as copyhold.[94] In 1777 the Hampstead Water Co. enlarged the pond and drained the marshy ground, and three cottages were built there for the poor in 1779,[95] to replace those which passed into private ownership at the increasingly fashionable Littleworth. Thomas Naylor, the occupier of the enclosure of 1762, had tan pits at Hatch's Bottom in 1777.[96] The enclosure, which was leased by the lord of the manor like demesne, had by 1808 become the site of a varnish factory.[97] A chimneysweep had by then built a cottage adjoining it to the north, possibly Chestnut Cottage, which was later rented from the lord by a chimneysweep.[98] The place was also used for laundering and in 1839 the Vale had the highest number of clothes posts in the parish.[99]

[77] Wade, *Streets of Hampstead*, 76; Oppé, *Hampstead: Lond. Town*, 42; inf. supplied by Mr. Sullivan; O.S. Map 1/1,056, Lond. II. 79 (1935 edn.).
[78] Wade, *Streets of Hampstead*, 77; C. W. Ikin, *Hampstead Heath* (1985), 27; *The Times*, 17 Jan. 1948, 2g; 3 Feb. 1948, 2b; *Images of Hampstead*, 63, 66.
[79] S.C.L., Town and Country Planning, 52nd List of Bldgs. (1974); Pevsner, *Lond.* ii. 192; O.S. Map 1/2,500, TQ 2686, 2687 (1953–4 edn.).
[80] Wade, *Streets of Hampstead*, 77–8; *Kelly's Dir. Hampstead and Childs Hill* (1938).
[81] Wade, *Streets of Hampstead*, 79–80.
[82] Ibid. 80; *Daily Telegraph*, 3 Dec. 1981; 4 July 1987.
[83] *The Times*, 29 Mar. 1941, 2d; 31 Mar. 1941, 6; Ikin, *Hampstead Heath*, 27.
[84] *The Times*, 9 Apr. 1977, 3b.
[85] S.C.L., Town and Country Planning, 52nd List of Bldgs. (1974); Barratt, *Annals*, ii. 69, 180.

[86] Below, social.
[87] Ikin, *Hampstead Heath*, 27–8.
[88] S.C.L., Town and Country Planning, 52nd List of Bldgs. (1974).
[89] Wade, *Streets of Heampstead*, 75.
[90] Marked on 1680 map: *C.H.R.* xi. 21.
[91] J. T. Smith, *Nollekens and His Times* (1949), 52.
[92] D. Sullivan, article on Littleworth in *H.H.E.* 25 May 1979.
[93] M.M. & M., Lib. C, pp. 18–22. Hatch's Bottom still identifiable: C. W. Ikin, *Hampstead Heath*, 16.
[94] S.C.L., Man. Map and Fieldbk. no. 223.
[95] H. C. Bentwich, *Vale of Health on Hampstead Heath* (1968), 15, 23; below, local govt.
[96] G.L.R.O., E/MW/H/I/1938.
[97] Ibid. H, old no. 31/8 (leases 1787, 1808).
[98] Ibid. H. old no. 21/18 (rental 1820); 26/34 (rental 1871); *C.H.R.* x. 18.
[99] Barratt, *Annals*, ii. 268; below, econ. ind.

The name the Vale of Health, recorded in 1801, may have originated as a euphemism which was exploited or as a new name invented in a deliberate attempt to change the image of the place. Such an attempt might have been made by John Rudd, a builder, who acquired most of the grants of waste made during the later 18th century and probably built the seven houses and two cottages which were sold at his death in 1801.[1] The enclosure recorded in 1762 was subleased in 1808 to William Woods, a carpenter, who had built two cottages there by 1810.[2] The middle-class element became increasingly important from the early 19th century. In 1801 the attractions of the area included 'unbounded prospects' of Kent and the river Thames, and screening, presumably by trees and the lie of the land, from north winds.[3] By 1821 the inhabitants, petitioning for the removal of the poor houses, observed that the neighbourhood had 'greatly increased in respectability' through the 'improvement of property'.[4] Sir Samuel Romilly (1757–1818), the law reformer, retired to a cottage in the Vale.[5] In 1815 James Leigh Hunt (1784–1859), on his release from prison for libelling the Prince Regent, went to live in the Vale where he stayed until 1819, returning again for a brief period in 1820–1. His home became the centre for most of the leading literary figures of the day, including Byron and Shelley, who were supposed to have shared a cottage there, where they inscribed lines on a window.[6] The Vale, with its modest but picturesque cottages surrounded by the heath, was the perfect setting for the romantic poets, and Hunt's circle was important in establishing the literary and politically radical tradition later associated with Hampstead.[7] During the period 1825–32 the poets Samuel Taylor Coleridge and George Crabbe visited the Vale and the publisher Charles Knight (1791–1873) lived there 1830–5, as from 1831 did his friend Matthew Davenport Hill (1792–1872), lawyer and radical M.P. and brother of Rowland. Knight and Hill together established the *Penny Magazine* in 1832 and formed the Society for the Diffusion of Useful Knowledge.[8] Prince Esterhazy was said to have taken a house in the Vale in 1840.[9]

The hamlet grew from 4 houses and 10 cottages in 1815[10] to 18 houses in 1851, of which 5 were larger houses. In 1841 the population of 112 included 5 gentry and 26 domestic servants. The population dropped to 87 in 1851 possibly because some of the larger houses were used as country retreats: several were empty or occupied only by caretakers. Although described in 1852 as a 'range of indifferently white-washed cottages ... relieved by clothes-props and lines', the Vale became increasingly desirable, both for permanent residents and visitors, especially after the opening of the Hamp-

stead Junction Railway in 1860.[11]

Several cottages at the northern end of the Vale have been claimed as Hunt's home, which cannot be certainly identified and was probably one of the northern group of 2 houses and 10 cottages which had belonged to Rudd, passed to the Munyard family, and was enfranchised in 1860 when it included Vale Lodge and House, Woodbine, Pavilion, and Rose cottages, and four cottages which had been turned into tea rooms. Helen, countess of Dufferin (1807–67), a granddaughter of Richard Sheridan and herself a poet, lived in Pavilion Cottage at some time between 1848 and 1860. Although the Munyards retained the ownership of nine houses in the Vale in the 1890s, Thomas Munyard lived in Munich and Henry Milton, who was his tenant in 1860, may have been responsible for building on the estate. Milton (d. 1883), described as a carpenter in 1851, 'proprietor of houses' in 1861, and retired builder by 1871, owned 8 houses in 1861 and 15 in 1881.[12]

To the south-west four pieces of waste, granted between 1791 and 1807, had been acquired by Donald Nicoll (d. 1872) who obtained their enfranchisement in 1858.[13] In 1856 Nicoll bought the freehold site, where the parish poorhouses had stood, probably nearby. The existing buildings were demolished and nos. 1–6 Heath Villas built in 1862 by Culverhouse with high Gothic gables; farther east the Suburban hotel (also called the Vale of Health tavern) with towers and battlements and accommodation for 2,000 was built in 1863, nos. 7–12 Heath Villas by 1868, and the Hampstead Heath hotel, between the two groups of villas, by 1869. Separating the new buildings from the pond to the east were grottos and arbours which, like the tea gardens, boats and fairground, provided for the crowds of summer visitors.[14]

The buildings called the Villas on the Heath were built at the southern end of the Munyard estate during the 1860s. George Samuel Jealous lived at no. 1 by 1869: a radical, with interests in the co-operative movement, temperance, vegetarianism, ragged schools, and the Peace Society, he acquired the *Hampstead and Highgate Express* and is credited with stimulating the interest of the Harmsworth family in printing. Alfred Harmsworth, a lawyer, went to live in Rose Cottage in 1870 with his three sons Alfred, later Viscount Northcliffe, Harold, later Viscount Rothermere, and Cecil, later Baron Harmsworth (d. 1948). In 1893 Ernest Rhys, editor of Everyman's Library, rented Rose Cottage, which in 1895 he renamed Hunt Cottage, believing it to have been Leigh Hunt's house.[15]

A few houses were built to the west and south in 1870 but building on the waste ended in 1872 when the M.B.W. bought the heath. Copyholders and

[1] G.L.R.O., E/MW/H, old no. 27/15 (sales parts. 1801). For the Vale in 1804, below, plate 5.
[2] G.L.R.O., E/MW/H, old no. 21/18 (rental 1820).
[3] Ibid. 27/15 (sales parts. 1801); cf. illus. 1804: *Hampstead One Thousand*, 53.
[4] G.L.R.O., P81/JN1/15, s.v. 3 Sept. 1801. For the Vale in 1825, see Phillips, *Shepherd's Lond.* plate 16.
[5] D.N.B.
[6] Bentwich, *Vale of Health*, 34–7; Cunningham, *Lond.: Comprehensive Surv.* 756–7; G.L.R.O., E/MW/H, old no. 27/15 (sales parts. 1836).
[7] Thompson, *Hampstead*, 28.
[8] Bentwich, *Vale of Health*, 39, 41–2; Cunningham,

Lond.: Comprehensive Surv. 757.
[9] W. Besant, *Survey of Lond.* ix (1911), 364.
[10] Poor rate bk. 1815.
[11] Bentwich, *Vale of Health*, 47–51; C.H.R. x. 17–18.
[12] Bentwich, *Vale of Health*, 54–7; C.H.R. x. 17–18; J. Wyld, *Map of Lond. and Environs* (1848); G.L.R.O., E/MW/H, old no. Locker 24 (rental 1890–1900).
[13] G.L.R.O., E/MW/H, old no. 37/8 (enfranchisement 1858).
[14] Bentwich, *Vale of Health*, 58–62; *Images of Hampstead*, 73; O.S. Map 1/2,500, Lond. VII (1870 edn.); below, social.
[15] Bentwich, *Vale of Health*, 63–6; C.H.R. x. 17–18.

freeholders could still build on their estates, so the Vale grew within the existing confines.[16] Between 1875 and 1887 the 19 houses built[17] included nos. 1–6 the Gables in the north in 1883 and Hollycot in the south, one of the last built; from 1906 to 1913 J. L. Hammond (1872–1949) and his wife Barbara, the social historians, lived at Hollycot. By 1890 there were 53 houses in the Vale.[18]

The two hotels failed as speculative ventures. The large Vale of Health tavern, originally intended as a hotel and sanatorium, was sold in 1876, became associated with the fair, was let as flats, and c. 1900 became a hotel again on a smaller scale, with the upper rooms let as studios. In 1877 the smaller Hampstead Heath hotel passed to Henry Braun, who opened it as the Athenaeum club, the members including many foreigners and political radicals. In 1882 the upper half of the building was let to the Salvation Army and in 1883 there were complaints about the noise and ugliness of the Vale, a compound of the swings and roundabouts, accompanied presumably by quantities of drink, with Salvation Army processions. Another hotel was opened next to the Athenaeum in the late 1880s but it had closed by 1903 and was replaced by Byron Villas. The Athenaeum, which had become an Anglo-German club by 1908, closed in 1914 and was used as a factory.[19]

Although the Vale of Health was described in 1911 as vulgarized by its tavern, tea gardens, merry-go-rounds, and slot machines,[20] it continued to attract distinguished inhabitants. Rabindranath Tagore (1861–1941), the Indian poet and mystic, lived at no. 3 Villas on the Heath in 1912, the author D. H. Lawrence (1885–1930) and his wife Frieda at no. 1 Byron Villas in 1915, Cyril Joad, the philosopher and broadcaster, at no. 4 the Gables in 1923–4, and the writers Edgar Wallace (d. 1932) at Vale Lodge, John Middleton Murry at no. 1A the Gables in 1926, and Stella Gibbons at Vale Cottage in 1927–30. Sir Compton Mackenzie (1883–1972), who lived at Woodbine Cottage from 1937 to 1943, summed up the attraction of the Vale for writers: 'village life half an hour from Piccadilly Circus was a continuous refreshment and stimulus'. The artist Sir Muirhead Bone (1876–1953) lived at no. 1 the Gables in 1907 and among others who used the studios in the Vale of Health hotel were Henry Lamb, who painted his portrait of Lytton Strachey there in 1912, Stanley Spencer from 1914 to 1927, and Sir William Coldstream in the 1930s.[21]

The Vale of Health studios closed in 1939.[22] In-habitants since the Second World War include Norman Bentwich (1883–1971), the exponent of Jewish ideals, and his wife Helen (d. 1972), chairman of the L.C.C. and the Vale's historian, who lived in Hollycot from 1931, Sir Leon Bagrit (1902–79), the Russian-born industrialist, and Sir Paul Chambers (1904–81), the banker, at Vale Lodge in the 1950s, and Alfred Brendel, the pianist, at North Villa in the 1970s.[23] Since 1945 the Vale has changed less than any other district in Hampstead. Luxury flats (the Athenaeum) replaced the old Athenaeum in 1958 and Spencer House (flats) replaced the Vale of Health hotel in 1964.[24] The changes did not alter the generally village-like atmosphere of the Vale, with its narrow streets, isolated on the heath. Listed buildings included the early 19th-century group from Rudd's estate, Vale House, Cottage, and Lodge, North and South Villas, Hunt Cottage, and the weatherboarded (possibly 18th-century) Woodbine and Old cottages; Chestnut Cottage to the west, from before 1812, with the Vivary and Lavender cottages opposite, which were probably built either in 1845 by William Hooper or in 1846 by H. Hill; the Villas on the Heath, dating from the 1860s, and Byron Villas, from 1903.[25]

CHILDS HILL. A district on both sides of the Hendon–Hampstead border,[26] Childs Hill took its name from Richard le Child, who in 1312 held a customary house and 30 a., probably on the Hendon side. A similar estate was held at the same time by Richard Blakett,[27] who gave his name to Blacketts well,[28] which in 1632 was one of the boundary markers in the area[29] and in 1801–2 was disputed in ownership.[30] By the mid 18th century the Hampstead part of Childs Hill was divided in two by the road later called Platt's Lane, which ran from West End and Fortune Green to the heath, Hampstead town, and Hendon. It was entirely occupied by two estates, both of which may have originated as land of the Templars. A farmhouse on the edge of the heath in the north part of the larger estate[31] had apparently become detached from the farmland before 1811, when it was enlarged by Thomas Platt as a 'pleasing and unostentatious' brick house set in well wooded grounds.[32]

The arrival of the Finchley road lessened the area's isolation. A house called Temple Park was built on the smaller Temples estate probably in the 1830s by Henry Weech Burgess, a prosperous Lancastrian. About the same time farm buildings were erected on Platt's estate fronting Platt's Lane.[33] In

[16] Bentwich, *Vale of Health*, 67; *C.H.R.* x. 17–18.
[17] D.S.R.
[18] Bentwich, *Vale of Health*, 67, 85; Wade, *Streets of Hampstead*, 81.
[19] Bentwich, *Vale of Health*, 67–84; below, social.
[20] Besant, *Survey of Lond.* ix. 364.
[21] Bentwich, *Vale of Health*, 86–93; Wade, *Streets of Hampstead*, 80–2.
[22] Bentwich, *Vale of Health*, 88.
[23] Wade, *Streets of Hampstead*, 81–2; *D.N.B.* s.v. Bentwich, Bagrit; *Who's Who* (1981), s.v. Chambers; *Dict. Business Biog.* (1984), i, s.v. Chambers.
[24] Bentwich, *Vale of Health*, 12, 83–4; Wade, *Streets of Hampstead*, 80–1.
[25] S.C.L., Town and Country Planning, 52nd List of Bldgs. (1974); Pevsner, *Lond.* ii. 192; Wade, *Streets of Hampstead*, 81–2; D.S.R.; Map on notice bd. at Vale. For Chestnut Cottage, above.

[26] For the part in Hendon, see *V.C.H. Mdx.* v.
[27] C.U.L., Kk. V. 29, f. 34; cf. W.A.M. 32406, 32563; below, econ.
[28] Stanford, *Libr. Map of Lond.* (1862 edn. with additions to 1865), sheet 1. Sometimes Plackets well: G.L.R.O., E/MW/H/I/2178.
[29] G.L.R.O., E/MW/H/I/2311B.
[30] Vestry mins. 22 Sept. 1801, 29 Mar., 20 Apr. 1802; below, pub. svces.
[31] Below, other est., Temples and Childs Hill; Rocque, *Map of Lond.* (1741–5), sheet 12; S.C.L., Man. Map and Fieldbk. nos. 568–70, A 571–81.
[32] Brewer, *Beauties of Eng. & Wales*, x (4), 201; C. White, *Sweet Hampstead*, 93. The rateable value of the ho. doubled between 1810 and 1813: poor rate bks. 1810, 1813; below, other est.
[33] P.R.O., IR 29/21/24, nos. 58A–59, 60–61A; *Cruchley's New Plan* (1829).

1843, on the western portion of Childs Hill estate, T. Howard built Kidderpore Hall, a stuccoed Greek revival house with a slightly projecting colonnade, side pediments, and a semicircular bay, for John Teil, an East India merchant with tanneries in the district of Calcutta from which the house took its name.[34] The grounds became a private park and two lodges were added, one on the Finchley road in 1849,[35] the other on Platt's Lane in the late 1860s.[36] On a field of Platt's estate which jutted westward south of Teil's estate, four houses fronting Finchley Road were built in the 1840s in the district called New West End.[37] By 1870 the farm buildings at Platt's Lane had been replaced by a house.[38] Two cottages were built in Platt's Lane by P. Bell of West End in 1875 and 13 houses, mostly by George Pritchard, between 1884 and 1886.[39]

Some 9½ a. of Henry Weech Burgess's estate had become a brickfield by 1864[40] and Temple Park had become the Anglo-French College by 1873.[41] A few houses had been built in what became Burgess Hill by 1878[42] and in 1880 Weech Road was constructed between Fortune Green Road and Finchley Road on the portion of Teil's estate purchased by the Burgesses in 1855.[43] Four houses were built there in 1880 and another 12 in 1887 by A. R. Amer and Becket. In 1886 there was building at the Anglo-French college. In 1890 Kidderpore Hall was acquired by Westfield College, which made considerable additions to it in 1904–5, and the rest of the estate given over to the builders. Building, mostly of detached or semi-detached houses fronting Platt's Lane, Finchley Road, Kidderpore Avenue, and Cecilia Road (later Kidderpore Gardens), was complete by 1913.[44] C. F. A. Voysey designed Annesley Lodge, no. 8 Platt's Lane, an L-shaped, roughcast house with sloping buttresses, 'astonishingly ahead of its date', for his father in 1896 on the corner with Kidderpore Avenue. Next to no. 14 Kidderpore Avenue, built in 1901 by the artist George Swinstead, was St. Luke's church, designed by Basil Champneys in 1898. At the southern end of the road was no. 4, built in 1900 in a highly decorated Tudor style.[45]

In 1886 Joseph Hoare, son of Samuel and brother of John Gurney Hoare, died after living for some 40 years at Childs Hill House, to which he added a storey. Although not pulled down until c. 1904, Childs Hill House was empty by c. 1897 when build-

ing began on the estate.[46] Between 1897 and 1913 Ferncroft, Hollycroft, and Rosecroft avenues were laid out and mostly semi-detached houses were built by George Hart. There were also several detached houses designed by C. H. B. Quennell, nos. 7 and 20 Rosecroft Avenue, designed in 1898, and Phyllis Court, no. 22, designed in 1905. Quennell designed several houses on the neighbouring demesne estate and Sir Guy Dawber, one of the architects of the nearby Hampstead Garden Suburb, was responsible for no. 46 Hollycroft Avenue, built in 1907.[47] At much the same time building was proceeding on the Burgess Park (Temples) estate: the same builder, George Hart, was responsible for Briardale Road and Clorane Gardens, where the houses were built between 1900 and 1910.[48] In 1905 on the Burgess Park estate 18 houses were built in Finchley Road, possibly including nos. 601 and 603 designed by Voysey, and by 1913 building was complete in Burgess Hill, Ardwick Road, and Weech Road and two houses had been built in Ranulf Road.[49] In 1901 a small piece on the western side of the Burgess Park estate was added to the cemetery.[50] A few years before, two houses had been built in Fortune Green Road on the estate facing the cemetery by undertakers. One, no. 128, noted for its Graeco-Egyptian stucco pastiche, survived.[51] All Souls Unitarian church was built to the south at the junction with Weech Road in 1903 and Burgess Park Mansions to the north about the same time.[52]

The cemetery did not blight development to the north and east as it had to the south and west, possibly because building north and east was necessarily later. Whereas in the 19th century proximity to cemeteries was disliked, by the 20th the open space in a built-up district was regarded as an asset.[53] The whole of the Childs Hill area was classed in 1930 as middle-class and wealthy.[54] There was building on all sites by the opening of the First World War and the only development between the wars was in Ranulf Road, where 13 houses were built by 1920 and the rest by 1930,[55] at Westfield College to which additions were made in 1920–3,[56] and at the corner of Fortune Green and Weech roads, where a block of flats, Weech Hall, replaced the Unitarian chapel in 1937.[57]

During the Second World War bombing destroyed several houses on the Burgess Park estate, including some in Ardwick Road[58] and two of Voysey's houses,

[34] Wade, *Streets of Hampstead*, 22; Pevsner, *Lond.* ii. 189; Barratt, *Annals*, ii. 251.
[35] D.S.R.
[36] Stanford, *Libr. Map of Lond.* (1862 edn. with additions to 1865), sheet 1; O.S. Map 1/2,500, Lond. VII (1870 edn.).
[37] D.S.R.; *Laurie's Plan of Lond., Westm.* (1842); J. Wyld, *Map of Lond. and Environs* (1848).
[38] Stanford, *Libr. Map of Lond.* (1862 edn. with additions to 1865), sheet 1; O.S. Map 1/2,500, Lond. VII (1870 edn.).
[39] D.S.R.
[40] Rate bk. 1864; below, econ., ind.
[41] Wade, *W. Hampstead*, 59.
[42] *Metrop. Improvement Map No. 46* (1878).
[43] Wade, *W. Hampstead*, 63; G.L.R.O., E/MW/H, old no. 27/15 (sales parts. 1855).
[44] D.S.R.; L.C.C. *Municipal Map of Lond.* (1913); Wade, *Streets of Hampstead*, 22.
[45] D.S.R.; A. Service, *Architects of Lond.* (1979), 151–2; Pevsner, *Lond.* ii. 186, 198; O.S. Map 1/2,500, TQ 2585 (1955 edn.); Wade, *Streets of Hampstead*, 22; below,

plate 17.
[46] *C.H.R.* ix. 18–19; C. White, *Sweet Hampstead*, 93; Thompson, *Hampstead*, 344; *Kelly's Dir. Hampstead and Highgate* (1889–90, 1900).
[47] D.S.R.; Wade, *Streets of Hampstead*, 23; Pevsner, *Lond.* ii. 197; A. S. Gray, *Edwardian Archit.* (1985), 299; O.S. Map 1/2,500, TQ 2586 (1969 edn.).
[48] D.S.R.; Wade, *Streets of Hampstead*, 23.
[49] D.S.R.; Gray, *Edwardian Archit.* 265; L.C.C. *Municipal Map of Lond.* (1913).
[50] Wade, *W. Hampstead*, 62.
[51] Ibid. 63; S.C.L., Town and Country Planning, 52nd List of Bldgs. (1974).
[52] *Kelly's Dir. Hampstead and Childs Hill* (1900, 1905); below, prot. nonconf.
[53] Thompson, *Hampstead*, 376.
[54] *New Lond. Life and Labour*, vii, maps 8, 10, 11.
[55] *Kelly's Dir. Hampstead and Childs Hill* (1920, 1939); L.C.C. *Municipal Map of Lond.* (1930).
[56] *V.C.H. Mdx.* i. 359.
[57] D.S.R.; Wade, *W. Hampstead*, 63.
[58] *Hampstead 1939–45* (Camden History Soc. 1977).

nos. 601 and 603 Finchley Road, which were replaced by houses designed by R. Seifert.[59] A new block was added to Westfield College in 1962[60] but from 1945 until the 1980s Childs Hill remained essentially unchanged. Inhabitants have included Thomas Masaryk, later first president of Czechoslovakia, at no. 21 Platt's Lane during the First World War, Leslie Brooke (d. 1940), the illustrator and father of Hampstead's M.P. Henry, at no. 28 Hollycroft Avenue, and Jonas Wolfe, cinema pioneer, at no. 4 Kidderpore Avenue during the 1940s. The musical Craxton family owned no. 14 Kidderpore Avenue from 1945 and during the 1960s James Gunn (d. 1965), the portrait painter, lived at no. 7 Kidderpore Avenue.[61]

HAMPSTEAD HEATH. The modern Hampstead Heath is normally considered to be the entire open space of c. 800 a.,[62] most of it added to the original heath bordering Hampstead town, the administration of which passed from the L.C.C. to the G.L.C.[63] It stretches from Highgate Road across northwestern St. Pancras and the northern part of Hampstead, and at two points reaches well beyond the Hendon boundary. Less than half of the area lies within Hampstead, as is recognized by the restricted use of the name Hampstead Heath on many maps.[64] The origins of the lands added on the east side of the heath, Parliament Hill, Parliament Hill Fields, and Kenwood, belong to the history of St. Pancras; those of the north-westerly additions, the Golders Hill estate and Hampstead Heath Extension, to that of Hendon.[65]

The first part of the heath to be taken into public ownership, the kernel of the existing open space, was itself smaller than the waste of the medieval manor of Hampstead. Much of Hampstead town was built on encroachments or inclosures from the heath, which lay to its north and east. In 1703 c. 27 a., supporting more than 50 houses, were noted as having been taken, leaving c. 313 a. as 'remains of the heath unimproved'. The deductions noted took no account of many established copyholds which probably represented inroads made much earlier. By the time that encroachments ceased on its purchase by the M.B.W. in 1871, the heath had been further reduced[66] to c. 220 a.[67] The town had spread north of New End and west of Heath Street in the early 18th century.[68] Other losses had been to outlying settlements described above, notably Hatch's Bottom (later the Vale of Health) and Littleworth (later Heath Brow), or to private residences such as the Firs near the

Spaniards inn and Heath Lodge in North End Road (later Way).[69] Most of the later grants were very small: 219, covering 37½ a., were made between 1799 and 1870.[70] The practice of permitting inclosures in return for annual payments to the lord without the homage's consent was a grievance in 1806.[71]

The heath in 1871, although divided by nothing more than roads or tracks consisted of sections with well established local names.[72] East Heath lay east and north-east of the town, around the Vale of Health, and south-east of Spaniard's Road. It formed an irregular strip, being separated from the St. Pancras boundary by c. 60 a. of manorial freehold known as East Park and by part of Lord Mansfield's Elms estate. North or Sandy Heath filled most of the triangle between Spaniard's and North End roads, and West Heath most of that between North End Road and West Heath Road; together they covered c. 150 a. The vague description of Upper, as opposed to Lower, Heath was sometimes given to the high ground of Sandy and East heaths and possibly of West Heath.[73]

The physical appearance of the heath was owed chiefly to the fact that its summit was a sandy ridge, running from Highgate to Hampstead, resting on a belt of sandy clay, which protruded at the edges and was underlain by water-resistant London Clay. Rainwater penetrated the sand only to be forced out by the clay, creating a landscape much of which easily dried out but which had many springs and, partly as a result of man-made excavations, swampy hollows.[74]

Although there had been a Mesolithic settlement and some Neolithic cultivation of West Heath, the medieval heath was left mainly as rough moorland, in contrast to the demesne farmland south and west of Hampstead town. Divided from St. Pancras by Whitebirch wood, which the lord cleared in the 17th century for farmland which became East Park, the heath was of value to the commoners for their grazing, gathering, and digging rights.[75] It was first recorded as 'a certain heath' in 1312, when it supplied brushwood normally worth 2s. a year,[76] and was called Hampstead Heath in 1543, when its springs were to supply London,[77] and in 1545, when hunting and hawking were forbidden over a wide area in order to preserve game for the king.[78] It was also known as Hampstead Heath to the herbalist John Gerard (1545–1612), who in 1597 described plants which he had found there, some native to marshes and others to 'dry mountains which are hungry and barren'.[79] Such a varied habitat within easy reach of

[59] Gray, *Edwardian Archit.* 265.
[60] *V.C.H. Mdx.* i. 359   [61] Wade, *W. Hampstead*, 22–3.
[62] Varying acreages have been given: below. 804 a. is the figure in C. W. Ikin, *Hampstead Heath* (1985), 32.
[63] Maps showing the heath in 1680 and 1871 and successive purchases under the M.B.W. and L.C.C. are in A. Farmer, *Hampstead Heath* (1984), 6, 105, 142–3. For revised maps, see Ikin, *Hampstead Heath* (1985), 8, 16–17.
[64] e.g. O.S. Map 1/10,000, TQ 28 NE. (1976 edn.).
[65] Farmer, *Hampstead Heath*, 37–47, 132, 135–7, 140–1; *V.C.H. Mdx.* v. 11, 21.
[66] Thompson, *Hampstead*, 13–14, 16–17, 23; G.L.R.O., E/MW/H/I/2311A; above, settlement and growth.
[67] Baines, *Rec. Hampstead*, 145. Thompson's figure, 240 a., may inc. land near Telegraph Hill retained by the lord and freed from rights of common.
[68] *C.H.R.* xi. 20–1 (inc. earliest map of heath, 1680, in S.C.L.); Farmer, *Hampstead Heath*, 16; above, growth,

Hampstead town.
[69] Above, growth, Vale of Health; North End.
[70] Thompson, *Hampstead*, 140.
[71] G.L.R.O., M/81/6 (mins. of mtgs. of copyholders), 3 Mar. 1806.
[72] Para. based on Thompson, *Hampstead*, 13 (map), 155; Farmer, *Hampstead Heath*, 61; C. W. Ikin, *Hampstead Heath* (1971), 6.
[73] Called North Heath by Thompson, who estimates E. Heath as c. 90 a. and N. and W. heaths as c. 150 a.: Thompson, *Hampstead*, 102, 155.
[74] Farmer, *Hampstead Heath*, 12.
[75] Ibid. 7–8; below, econ., agrarian; woods.
[76] Kennedy, *Man. of Hampstead*, 118–19.
[77] 35 Hen. VIII, c. 10; below, pub. svces.
[78] *Tudor Royal Proclamations*, ed. P. L. Hughes and J. F. Larkin, i (1964), 356.
[79] J. Gerard, *Herball* (facsimile edn. 1974), ii. 971, 1199.

London attracted many later plant hunters: Gerard's editor Thomas Johnson (d. 1644) described an expedition made in 1629[80] and the Apothecaries' Company in 1734 was said to have seldom failed to come for its spring 'herbarizing feast'.[81]

Changes were effected over the centuries by tree felling and later by planting, which included John Turner's firs near the Spaniard's inn from the 1730s[82] and controversial municipal attempts at improvement from the late 19th century.[83] Other changes, which came to appear natural, resulted from exploitation of the water resources and of the soil.

For all its springs, the heath until the end of the 17th century had no large ponds. Nothing was done under the Act of 1543 for London's water until the lord mayoralty of Sir John Hart, 1589–90, whom Gerard accompanied to view the springs and who 'attempted' some unspecified works.[84] Hampstead ponds began as a string of reservoirs of the Hampstead Water Co., which was established to supply London in 1692. They were made by damming Hampstead brook, one of the sources of the Fleet, just as Highgate ponds were made from a more easterly source in St. Pancras. There were two ponds on Lower Heath by 1703[85] and in 1745,[86] three by 1786, and four by 1810.[87] The New River Co.'s rights in the smallest and southernmost one, whose drainage was sought by the residents of South Hill Park, were acquired in 1892 by the L.C.C., which filled it in, to provide a grassy approach to the heath from the nearby railway station.[88] The Vale of Health pond was dammed when the supply system was extended in 1777.[89] Leg of Mutton pond on West Heath was probably dammed as part of a plan, reported in 1816, to employ the poor; the nearby Sandy Road was sometimes known as Hankins's folly, after further relief work was carried out under Thomas Hankins, surveyor of the highways 1823–4.[90] The pond was marked simply as a reservoir in 1891, although already known by its modern name.[91] Viaduct pond, crossed by a viaduct begun in 1844 and finished in 1847, was on Sir Thomas Maryon Wilson's freehold and created as part of his abortive preparations to build there.[92] Whitestone pond was originally a small dew pond, called the horse pond and later after a milestone; in 1875 it was enlarged and lined by the vestry and by 1890 artificially supplied with water. Some small ponds on the edge of

the heath near the town disappeared after the building of the covered reservoir near Whitestone pond in 1856.[93] Branch Hill pond was filled in c. 1889.[94]

Fine sand, not found farther east at Highgate, was estimated in 1813 to cover Hampstead Heath to an average depth of 10 ft.[95] Digging and quarrying were carried on from the Middle Ages: a pilgrim's flask was found in the bed of a sandpit at Holly Hill,[96] in 1597 a gravel pit lay near the beacon,[97] and in 1680 there was a sandpit at Branch Hill.[98]

The lord sold large quantities of sand and gravel to the Islington turnpike trustees in the early 18th century.[99] One Anderson had leave to dig loam and sand on the heath in 1787[1] but the conditions in the lease were not kept: the steward threatened prosecution in 1806 and the copyholders who had prompted him to do so recorded that pits begun by the late Alexander Anderson had not been filled up and that David Anderson ought to make smooth and sow a slope near 'the second pond'. They pointed out that payments to the lord for digging would be small in comparison with a fall in the value of the copyholds, since the pits were dangerous and 'the whole face of the heath is become so mutilated that the prospect of beauty is nearly destroyed'.[2]

Not all depredations could be blamed on the lord. There were presentations for unauthorized digging in 1773[3] and a suit for trespass was brought by Sir Thomas Wilson in 1781 against Lady Riddell, who claimed a tenant's immemorial right to dig for the improvement of a copyhold. Further actions in 1801 and 1802 led to a judgement in 1806 that the taking of turves, while it might be a custom, would be unreasonable if it tended towards the destruction of the common.[4] The sand was of a quality to be used by both builders and iron founders. Digging continued, bringing the lord payments on 20 cart loads a day c. 1811 and on 7 or 8 loads in 1813.[5] Its effects at Branch Hill pond on the edge of West Heath were depicted by Constable in 1821. On Sandy Heath they were so marked that Spaniard's Road was described as a lofty causeway in 1823, although the heath still rose in places on either side, as it no longer did in 1856.[6] Old workings were not necessarily eyesores: the mixture of vegetation with patches of bright red and yellow sand was admired in 1823,[7] picnickers enjoyed the ridges and hollows,[8] Dickens thought that a few made an improvement,[9] and later they were often seen as picturesque.[10]

[80] Farmer, *Hampstead Heath*, 10.
[81] J. Soame, *Hampstead Wells* (1734), 27.
[82] Farmer, *Hampstead Heath*, 31; *Images of Hampstead*, 68, illus. 145–7.
[83] Below.
[84] Gerard, *Herball*, i. 466.
[85] Farmer, *Hampstead Heath*, 15–16.
[86] Rocque, *Map of Lond.* (1741–5), sheet 12, which, however, marks Highgate ponds as Hampstead ponds.
[87] Baines, *Rec. Hampstead*, 208.
[88] *Images of Hampstead*, 79; L.C.C. *Ann. Rep. 1894–5*, 69.
[89] Farmer, *Hampstead Heath*, 16; above, growth, Vale of Health.
[90] Baines, *Rec. Hampstead*, 208; Farmer, *Hampstead Heath*, 54; vestry mins. 22 Sept. 1823.
[91] Baines, *Rec. Hampstead*, 208; Stanford, *Libr. Map of Lond.* (1891 edn.), sheet 1.
[92] Farmer, *Hampstead Heath*, 72; below.
[93] Baines, *Rec. Hampstead*, 208; *Images of Hampstead*, 78, 85; below, pub. svces.
[94] 'Last winter': Baines, *Rec. Hampstead*, 214.

[95] Park, *Hampstead*, 45.   [96] Barratt, *Annals*, ii. 214.
[97] Gerard, *Herball*, ii. 1061.
[98] *C.H.R.* xi. 20–1. For brickmaking, below, econ., ind.
[99] Barratt, *Annals*, ii. 215.
[1] G.L.R.O., E/MW/H/I/2280.
[2] Ibid. M/81/6 (mins. of mtgs. of copyholders), 12 May, 24 Nov. 1806, 16 Nov. 1807.
[3] S.C.L., Hampstead manor min. bk. (1742–82), pp. 357, 361.
[4] G.L.R.O., M/81/8, 2 Dec. 1801, 27 Mar. 1802, 3 Mar. 1806.
[5] *Images of Hampstead*, 95; *N. & Q.* 12th ser. i. 46; Park, *Hampstead*, 45. Casters could mould the wet sand, which dried hard but fell loose at a tap: inf. from Mr. Ikin.
[6] Farmer, *Hampstead Heath*, 57, 92–3; *Images of Hampstead*, 95.
[7] V. de Soligny [i.e. P. Patmore], *Letters on Eng.* ii (1823), 266–7.
[8] *Images of Hampstead*, illus. 250 (lithograph of 1856).
[9] Ikin, *Hampstead Heath*, 21.
[10] e.g. H. Clunn, *Face of Lond.* (1951), 354.

The most thorough excavations, an episode in the struggle to preserve Hampstead Heath, followed the sale by Sir Thomas Maryon Wilson of ¼ a. of sand and ballast in strips along Spaniard's Road to the Midland Railway Co. in 1866–7. The company, which could not obtain materials from farther afield until it had completed its tunnels, paid a stiff price and in places delved 25 ft. deep.[11] Exploitation ceased when the heath became public property, until in 1939 large pits were dug near the Vale of Health and on Sandy Heath for the filling of sandbags. The new pits were filled with rubble at the end of the war and their sites thereafter marked only by a different flora.[12]

The heath was of value not only for its natural resources but from its mere situation, as a commanding height near London. It was the site of a beacon, erected as part of an early warning system by 1576,[13] and later was used both for military manoeuvres and firing practice.[14] The county elections were held there from 1681 to 1701[15] and in 1836.[16] It was also associated with highwaymen, from the late 17th until the early 19th century, and long remembered for having been chosen for the exemplary display of the body of Francis Jackson, who was hanged in 1674.[17] The gibbet probably stood at the top of the hill leading down to North End, although the 'gibbet elms' depicted in the 19th century were farther down the slope.[18]

A healthy situation and fine outlook were appreciated earlier than the heath's own scenery. In 1709 one of the assets of the newly fashionable spa was 'a fine heath to ride out and take the air on'[19] and in the 1720s Defoe praised the air, although too rarefied, and prospects in fine weather.[20] In 1734 the ground's rapid drying out made it a pleasant place for walks[21] and later the views were often illustrated[22] and praised.[23] The heath's interest, however, was still seen to lie in its composition and resources rather than its scenic beauty by Hampstead's first historian, J. J. Park, in 1813.[24]

The heath and, by association, much of its neighbourhood, appeared in a more romantic light from the early 19th century. Some of the appreciative language, as in the protests against digging in 1806,[25] expressed little more than the copyholders' concern for agreeable surroundings and assured property values. The more romantic view was soon pioneered by Leigh Hunt, who arrived in 1812 and wrote the first of his five sonnets To Hampstead, invoking its

'sweet upland', while in prison in 1813. The heath itself was a major, although not the only, local source of Hunt's inspiration.[26] Shortly after his release he settled in 1816 at the Vale of Health, where Shelley, who particularly admired the sunsets, Keats, and Byron were among his visitors.[27]

The poets were soon followed by painters, notably Constable, who probably knew Hampstead from c. 1812[28] and stayed first near Whitestone pond in 1819, John Linnell from 1822, and William Collins from 1823.[29] A newspaper attack on the plan of 1816 for poor relief, as the work of 'tasteless improvers', celebrated the heath's artistic appeal; it praised not only the panorama but the 'bold inequalities' of the foreground, claiming that, like Shakespeare and Newton, it was the property of Europe.[30] Constable, whose first, serene, views were probably done before 1819, came to occupy a succession of second homes in Hampstead.[31] He soon found his main inspiration in the heath's openness to the elements: he studied the sky, whose moods the land merely reflected, and in 1829 included a sandpit on East Heath among four mezzotints of his works engraved by David Lucas, an experiment which led to the reproduction of other views in 1830–1 and later.[32] The heath thus became, in literary and artistic circles, a recognized beauty spot. Its attractions can only have been enhanced by the growing contrast between its breezy heights and the grime of London, as recalled in 1835 by Wordsworth.[33]

More important, for the future of the heath, was its popularity with day trippers. As early as 1829, when battle was first joined to prevent building, a writer from Gray's Inn stressed the need for all classes to escape from noise and dirt to one of the few remaining 'lungs of the metropolis'. His hope that a public asset might be preserved, if only for the sake of private rights, found support in the House of Commons and in a well known cartoon by George Cruikshank, showing the advance of bricks and mortar.[34] The general good was again emphasized in 1844: Lord Chief Justice Denman, supporting the local property holders, declared that thousands of Londoners daily enjoyed the heath during the fine months.[35] The claim was perhaps exaggerated. Eighteenth-century races had presumably attracted outsiders but many early sporting contests concerned only local or visiting teams, while parties, as opposed to individual walkers, may have been drawn more by the inns and pleasure gardens than by the heath it-

[11] Thompson, Hampstead, 192–3, plate 7.
[12] Ikin, Hampstead Heath, 21.
[13] Farmer, Hampstead Heath, 10.
[14] Below, social.
[15] Hist. Parl., Commons, 1660–90, i. 309; Lewis, Topog. Dict. Eng. (1831), ii. 305.
[16] Lond. Gaz. 27 Dec. 1836, p. 2643.
[17] Baines, Rec. Hampstead, 225; Images of Hampstead, 59.
[18] A bearing to the gibbet is given in the field bk. of 1680: C.H.R. xi. 20–1.
[19] J. Macky, Journey through Eng. (5th edn. 1732), i. 89. The description is repeated in Camden, Magna Brit. (1738), iv. 45.
[20] Defoe, Tour, i. 384.
[21] Soame, Hampstead Wells, 27.
[22] e.g. views across heath by Chatelain, 1745: Images of Hampstead, illus. 6, 10.
[23] Lond. & Its Environs Described, iii (1761), 134; Lysons, Environs, ii. 527.

[24] Park, Hampstead, which has chap. on nat. hist.; Thompson, Hampstead, 151.
[25] Above.
[26] Poetical Works of Leigh Hunt, ed. H. S. Milford (1923), 235–7. His Description of Hampstead followed in 1815.
[27] Thompson, Hampstead, 153–4; Works of Shelley, ed. H. B. Forman, viii (1880), 118; above, growth, Vale of Health.
[28] C. Wade, Constable's Hampstead (1976), 2.
[29] Thompson, Hampstead, 152.
[30] Above; Farmer, Hampstead Heath, 54.
[31] Wade, Constable's Hampstead, 3, 9–11; above, growth, Hampstead town.
[32] Images of Hampstead, 89–91, illus. 234–9.
[33] Extempore Effusion upon the Death of Jas. Hogg (pub. 1835).
[34] The Times, 17 June 1829, 3b; Thompson, Hampstead, 144–5, plate 4.
[35] Thompson, Hampstead, 165.

self.[36] Donkey riders, numerous from the 1820s or earlier, were often shown as middle-class in the 1850s.[37] There were also, however, crowds of humbler visitors and even all-night revellers.[38] Together with riders and picnickers, they had attracted cartoonists before the Hampstead Junction railway made the heath accessible to thousands of poorer families who lived beyond walking distance.[39]

The opening of Hampstead Heath station in 1860[40] assured the heath's future as a playground for London's East Enders. There followed yet more published accounts and illustrations of popular pastimes,[41] including copies of Watkin Williams's song 'Hampstead is the Place to Ruralise' c. 1863.[42] An informal fair presumably had already benefited from the closure in the 1850s of Bartholomew, Camberwell, and Greenwich fairs;[43] it was held near the Vale of Health, where the first hotel was built in 1863 in order to profit from the crowds brought by the railway.[44] The trend was encouraged by Sir Thomas Maryon Wilson, who, in his campaign against the gentry, licensed an ice-cream vendor to build a wooden refreshment room at the foot of Downshire Hill in 1861 and assigned a large site for a fair ground in 1865.[45] The writer William Howitt complained in 1869 that Sunday evening revellers swarming homeward down Haverstock Hill could be heard from his house in Highgate.[46] Such popularity was perhaps decisive in the parliamentary battle to prevent building.[47]

Acquisition as a public open space was followed closely by the Bank Holidays Act, 1871, which created three holidays in months when it was possible to enjoy the heath. Enormous crowds gathered, as on Whit Monday 1872, when the fair covered the whole of East Heath to Spaniard's Road, from which height carriage visitors could look down on the working class at play.[48] Damage, particularly fires among the furze, and rowdiness were often a problem in the 1870s, when there might be 30,000 visitors at the August holiday and 50,000 on a fine Whit Monday.[49] Violence was also a problem at the bonfires and processions held from before 1850 on Guy Fawkes day, until in 1880 a committee was set up to regulate them.[50] Numbers reached 100,000 in the 1880s, although that estimate for 1880 included trippers to Parliament Hill Fields, which were not yet part of the heath.[51] The crowds were thickest in the south-east corner near the station, where in 1892 nine people died in a rush to escape from the rain. 'Appy 'Ampstead became a nationally known phrase in the 1890s, when celebrated in a song by Albert Chevalier and in the cartoons of Phil May.[52] The heath was the L.C.C.'s most popular open space in

1899[53] and bank holiday pleasures at other London parks were mere 'modifications' of those at Hampstead in 1901.[54]

The scene had grown more respectable by 1910, when there were fewer assaults and thefts at what had become gigantic children's parties'. Attendance records were broken on Easter Monday, always the heath's busiest day, with an estimated 200,000; on the following August holiday, 50,000 came by railway alone.[55] In 1920 Queen Alexandra drove slowly by, to view Easter Monday's 'traditional festivities and licence', and promenaders still thronged Spaniard's Road on a fine Sunday.[56] The survival of the fair ensured the heath's continuing popularity during and after the Second World War.[57]

The public acquisition of the heath in 1871 ended more than forty years of uncertainty.[58] Sir Thomas Maryon Wilson, restricted by his father's will to granting leases of no more than 21 years on his Hampstead property, sought wider powers through successive estate Bills, all of which were defeated. His proposals alarmed substantial local residents, who successfully presented them to a wider public as threats to an increasingly popular heath. The battles in the press and parliament left Sir Thomas, a stubborn and irascible man, with a long lasting reputation as a would-be despoiler. Only in the 1970s, in the most detailed account, was it pointed out that Sir Thomas was singularly unfortunate in meeting such powerful opposition. His story showed the rights of property, at a time when they were normally paramount, being overridden in the name of the public interest. It also showed how motives could be disguised by confusing the issues of the copyholders' rights, the lord's freehold, and public enjoyment of the heath.

Sir Thomas's first estate Bill was withdrawn from the House of Commons in 1829, after local opposition and a campaign in the press on the need to preserve open space. In reality his desire to obtain the power to grant 99-year building leases on all his Hampstead lands did not arise from plans for the heath as it then existed, where the copyholders could insist on their rights of pasturage, but for his 60 a. of exclusive freehold which were later known as East Heath Park or East Park. Building there, along the St. Pancras boundary, would have hemmed in the heath and threatened the views of many Hampstead gentry and of Lord Mansfield from Kenwood. Lord Mansfield therefore joined the opposition and in 1830 helped to defeat a second, modified, Bill in the House of Lords. It was probably the House's first division on an estate Bill, all the more notable for taking place in an unreformed parliament. Despite

[36] Below, social.
[37] Ibid.; e.g. *Images of Hampstead*, illus. 278.
[38] *Images of Hampstead*, illus. 280 (servants' outing illus. by Phiz); A. Mayhew, *Paved With Gold* (1858), 144–8, 195.
[39] *Images of Hampstead*, illus. 278, 280–1, 283–4; above, communications.   [40] Above, communications.
[41] *Images of Hampstead*, illus. 275, 277.
[42] Ibid. illus. 279.
[43] Farmer, *Hampstead Heath*, 112.
[44] Below, econ., ind.
[45] Thompson, *Hampstead*, 175; Farmer, *Hampstead Heath*, 114.
[46] W. Howitt, *Northern Heights of Lond.* (1869), 94–5.
[47] Thompson, *Hampstead*, 169.
[48] Farmer, *Hampstead Heath*, 114.

[49] *H.H.E.* 10 June, 12 Aug. 1876; Walford, *Old and New Lond.* v. 453.
[50] *N. & Q.* 11th ser. iv. 526; Bentwich, *Vale of Health*, 79.
[51] Farmer, *Hampstead Heath*, 114; *H.H.E.* 3 Apr. 1880.
[52] Farmer, *Hampstead Heath*, 114–16, 120; D. Cuppleditch, *Phil. May* (1981), 76; below, plate 8.
[53] L.C.C. *Ann. Rep. 1898–9*, 127.
[54] G. R. Sims, *Living Lond.* (1901), ii. 119.
[55] *The Times*, 29 Mar. 1910, 4a, b; 2 Aug. 1910, 8c.
[56] Ibid. 6 Apr. 1920, 7a; C. R. Smith, *Hampstead As It Was*, i (1981), 15.
[57] Smith, *Hampstead As It Was*, i. 19; F. R. Banks, *Penguin Guide to Lond.* (1968), 489.
[58] Following 3 paras. based on Thompson, *Hampstead*, 132–209.

Sir Thomas's disavowals of plans for the heath itself, a third estate Bill had to be withdrawn in 1843 and a fourth, to permit the sale of all his Hampstead property, was defeated in 1844. A fifth Bill was defeated in 1853 and a sixth, concerned only with land along Finchley Road, in 1854. When a seventh Bill was overtaken by the Leases and Sales of Settled Estates Act of 1856, making it easier to change strict settlements, an unprecedented clause was inserted to debar Sir Thomas, as a previous applicant, from taking advantage of the new law.[59] Further debates followed in 1857, 1859, and 1860, as lawyers' attempts to remove the clause were frustrated by metropolitan M.P.s, whose constituents were making increasing use of the heath.

When the struggle began there was small likelihood of reaching a fair and logical solution by buying the heath with public funds. In 1853, however, the vestry, ahead of its time, resolved that it was in the interests of both the parish and the metropolis that the government should buy the heath 'with such portions of the adjoining ground as are essential to its beauty'.[60] The proposal was made after public discussion of a plan by C. R. Cockerell to lay out a park on the enlarged heath, which would have come to resemble Regent's Park.[61] Public purchase was urged on both the M.B.W. and the government in 1856 by the reformed vestry, which in 1857 promoted an unsuccessful Bill. The climate changed in the 1860s, as threats to other open spaces led to the conferment of new powers on the M.B.W. by the Metropolitan Commons Act, 1866.[62] The Act was a result of pressure by the Commons Preservation Society under George Shaw-Lefevre, which included Gurney Hoare, Philip Le Breton, and other Hampstead campaigners among its members. In Hampstead the danger was acute. Sir Thomas's only obtrusive building had been of the viaduct begun in 1844,[63] which was to bring a road to East Park and which came to be misrepresented as a design against the heath,[64] although both the viaduct and the intended 28 villas were on his exclusive freehold.[65] In 1861, however, he threatened to commercialize the heath, a process which he began by building on the summit and selling the sand along Spaniard's Road. East Park was also despoiled, by brickfields.[66] He went on to reject compromise offers not to oppose building on his land along Finchley Road in return for the abandoning of plans for East Park. In consequence a Hampstead Heath Protection Fund was established under Gurney Hoare, to defray the expenses of a suit which was started against Sir Thomas in Chancery in 1866 and was ended only by his death in 1869. The ability of his brother and heir Sir John to break the restrictive settlement, which renewed the danger, and the inflamed state of public feeling then compelled the M.B.W. to buy the heath for a stiff but not extortionate price.

The Hampstead Heath Act, 1871, authorized the M.B.W.'s purchase of nearly all that survived from the original common,[67] (East, North-West or Sandy, and West heaths), which was ceremonially taken over early in 1872.[68] A few small additions were soon made, including Judges' Walk,[69] and in 1879 its estimated 240 a. made Hampstead Heath the largest of the M.B.W.'s open spaces after Blackheath.[70] The Act did not allay all the fears of those who had resisted building, since the right to lay roads across the heath had been reserved in the sale, which did not include East Park or other adjacent lands. It would still have been possibly to hem in East Heath with buildings, as shown by the construction of South Hill Park between the lower ponds and Parliament Hill Fields. Fortunately for preservationists, the Maryon Wilsons concentrated their resources on the area around Fitzjohn's Avenue.[71] Meanwhile the Act had secured an inviolable core of open space for public recreation and set a precedent by sanctioning its purchase with public funds.

The story of the heath after 1871 was one of its expansion and of the changes which were brought about by public ownership. Expansion was largely in response to the spread of housing north and west of the heath, where open country survived in the 1880s, and its full value became apparent only as the ring of building was completed in the 20th century.[72]

The first move towards extending the heath came in 1884 with the establishment of a local society's open spaces committee, with C. E. Maurice as secretary.[73] Its aim was to acquire East Park, where building was likely to be most obtrusive, and c. 200 a. from the neighbouring southern part of Lord Mansfield's Kenwood estate. The committee, stressing social and sanitary needs, soon won support from such reformers as Lady Burdett-Coutts and Octavia Hill. A Hampstead Heath Extension committee was then formed, with the duke of Westminster as chairman; it was ready to pay the market price and, through Shaw-Lefevre, reached agreement with the landowners. The Hampstead Heath Enlargement Act, 1886, amended in 1888,[74] allowed the application of public and charitable funds, after Hampstead vestry, which supported the extension committee,[75] had voted a contribution, followed by St. Pancras. The M.B.W. adopted the Act shortly before its own extinction in 1889, leaving a monument as important as the Thames Embankment in the form of a heath doubled in size by the addition of East Park, Parliament Hill and Fields, and part of Lord Mansfield's Elms estate.

The next addition was that of the 36-a. Golders Hill estate, at North End but in Hendon parish[76] and adjoining West Heath. Funds were sought in 1897 for the purchase of 20 a. and in 1898 for the whole estate, although it was saved from speculators only when the local historian Thomas Barratt bid beyond the guaranteed total. Barratt conveyed his contract to the guaranteeing committee, which, strengthened

[59] 19 & 20 Vic. c. 120, clause 21.
[60] Vestry mins. 22 June 1853.
[61] Farmer, *Hampstead Heath*, 75 and illus.
[62] 29 & 30 Vic. c. 122.
[63] Above.
[64] e.g. Barratt, *Annals*, ii. 205.
[65] Farmer, *Hampstead Heath*, 71 and illus.
[66] Below, econ., ind.
[67] 34 & 35 Vic. c. 77 (Local). Land near Telegraph Hill was left to Sir John and other small pieces were omitted.

[68] *H.H.E.* 20 Jan. 1872.
[69] Ikin, *Hampstead Heath* (1971), 24.
[70] *M.B.W. Rep.* (1879), 43.
[71] Thompson, *Hampstead*, 196, 202, 209, 307–10.
[72] Ibid. 335.
[73] Para. based on ibid. 325–33; Farmer, *Hampstead Heath*, 123–7.
[74] 50 Vic. c. 41 (Local); 51 & 52 Vic. c. 151 (Local).
[75] Vestry mins. 16 July, 19 Nov. 1885.
[76] *V.C.H. Mdx.* v. 11.

by the duke of Westminster and Shaw-Lefevre, recouped its expenses after a public appeal; the L.C.C. promised £12,000 and Hampstead vestry £10,000.[77] The property was conveyed in 1898 to trustees appointed by the committee and in 1899 to the L.C.C.,[78] whose parks committee drew attention to the damage which might have been done if building had been allowed to press too close, as at Clapham common.[79]

Similar arguments, and a similar mixture of public and private contributions, secured the addition of c. 80 a. in Hendon, adjoining Sandy Heath.[80] The campaign to buy the land, which was part of Eton college's Wyldes farm, was stimulated by plans for a tube railway under the heath, with a station at North End and the consequent prospect of building. Hampstead Heath Extension council was formed in 1903 by Henrietta Barnett, with Shaw-Lefevre as president, and public contributions were permitted by an Act of 1905.[81] Although support from the L.C.C. and Hampstead borough council was inadequate, Hampstead bearing a much smaller proportion of the cost than in 1898, the 80 a. were bought in 1907. They came to be known as the Heath Extension, while the rest of Wyldes farm was taken for Hampstead Garden Suburb.[82]

The last major additions, on the east side of the heath, resulted from the break-up of Lord Mansfield's estate, first projected in 1914. The Kenwood Preservation Council in 1922 raised money to buy 100 a., of which 9 a. east of Millfield Lane were resold to the owners of Caen Wood Towers and Beechwood subject to a ban on building. Ken wood itself and the lakes south of the mansion, 32 a., were also bought, vested in the L.C.C., and in 1925 opened by George V. Kenwood House and 75 a. around it were saved from the builders by the earl of Iveagh (d. 1927), who settled them on himself for life. He installed art treasures and left the mansion in trust as a picture gallery, which was opened in 1928. The grounds were left to the L.C.C., as part of the heath.[83] Kenwood House was taken over by the L.C.C. in 1949.[84]

In 1925 the Paddock, 1¾ a. at North End, was bought from Lord Leverhulme's executors with subscriptions.[85] Further small but important additions followed the Second World War as a result of bombing, demolitions, or changes of use. They included the sites of Fern Lodge and Heathlands north of Jack Straw's Castle in 1948 and 1951, the gardens of Pitt House, 3 a. when the Elms became a hospital, the Hill gardens of Heath Lodge, and in 1967 the tollhouse at the Spaniards.[86] The many changes helped to account for slight variations in the figures given for the acreage. In 1937 the heath, including the Extension and Golders Hill Park, was estimated by the L.C.C. at 287.5 a., Parliament Hill at 270.5 a., and Kenwood at 195.2 a., a total of 753.2 a.[87] In 1951

the heath was said to be 290.5 a. and the other two areas were unchanged. In 1971 the G.L.C.'s estimated total was 802 a.[88]

The appearance of the heath continued to cause concern after the possibility of direct private exploitation had been eliminated. One controversy was about the moorland character of the old heath, in which it differed from most of London's open spaces and from the additions made after 1871, which were either farmland or parkland. Another was about the threat from traffic across the heath and from inappropriate buildings overlooking it. Neither question was finally laid to rest.

Some landscaping was needed, if only to repair the harm done by digging, which had made much of the ground 'one collection of dangerous and unsightly pits'. The Times, regretting the M.B.W.'s six-month delay in producing any measures of ornamentation or regulation, looked forward to a tasteful conversion into 'one of the most exquisite parks in the world'.[89] Philip Le Breton, however, as chairman of the parks committee, favoured the restoration of natural beauty, which also met his colleagues' desire to economize.[90] By 1875, with the scars of excavation largely grown over, the M.B.W. won praise for a judicious neglect which had not made the heath 'prim or park-like'.[91]

The success of resistance to the plans of public authorities may have owed much to the prominence of many of the heath's local defenders. The L.C.C., warned by Octavia Hill in 1890 against attempted improvements, adopted schemes for tree planting, in 1894, and tidying up, both of which brought petitions signed by distinguished protesters.[92] Critics were told that the need to provide shelter for visitors must affect views from some houses but were assured that it was desired to preserve the rusticity of West Heath and that gorse cutting was pruning.[93] The Hampstead Heath Protection society was formed in 1897, with the aim of co-operating with the L.C.C.; further planting was prevented, although thinning was not conceded until 1918.[94] An action group was formed in 1978 to stir up what had become the Heath and Old Hampstead Protection society, after the G.L.C. in its turn had been accused of wanting to turn the wilder parts into a typical park.[95]

The threat from new roads and obtrusive buildings was lessened by the acquisition of East Park in 1889, which made it possible for access roads reserved in the Act of 1871 to be left as no more than tracks. The L.C.C. at first hoped to make wider ways, with cinders from the dismantled East Park brickfields, but retreated after protests by Octavia Hill and others.[96] Sandy Road, skirting West Heath and bisecting Sandy Heath from West End Lane to the Spaniards, was closed to motor traffic in 1924 and thereafter formed two bridle paths.[97] The main roads across the old heath, Spaniard's and North End

[77] Barratt, Annals, ii. 221–6.
[78] Ibid. 225–6; inf. from Mr. C. W. Ikin.
[79] L.C.C. Ann. Rep. 1898–9, 127.
[80] Para. based on Thompson, Hampstead, 336–7; Farmer, Hampstead Heath, 134–7.
[81] 5 Edw. VII, c. 206 (Local).
[82] V.C.H. Mdx. v. 13.
[83] Farmer, Hampstead Heath, 140–1; Survey of Lond. xvii. 114, 131; inf. from Mr. Ikin.
[84] L.C.C. Lond. Statistics, N.S. i. 145.
[85] The Times, 25 Sept. 1925, 14d.
[86] Farmer, Hampstead Heath, 144; Ikin, Hampstead

Heath (1985), 32.
[87] L.C.C. Lond. Statistics, xli, map of open spaces.
[88] Ibid. N.S. i. 156; inf. from Mr. Ikin.
[89] The Times, 12 Dec. 1871, 8f.
[90] Farmer, Hampstead Heath, 107.
[91] Thorne, Environs, 292.
[92] Farmer, Hampstead Heath, 130.
[93] L.C.C. Ann. Rep. 1895–6, 67; 1896–7, 91.
[94] Ikin, Hampstead Heath (1971), 18.
[95] The Times, 25 Apr. 1978, 20e.
[96] Farmer, Hampstead Heath, 130.
[97] Ikin, Hampstead Heath (1971), 23.

roads, were kept free of public transport services until 1922.[98] A proposal to demolish the tollhouse opposite the Spaniards in 1961 was successfully resisted, partly on the grounds that it would lead to more and faster traffic.[99]

Tall or incongruous buildings overlooking the heath had caused alarm since William Howitt's attack on the 'Tower of Babel' bulk of the castellated hotel in the Vale of Health.[1] The flats called the Pryors, in East Heath Road, were similarly criticized in 1903. Projected seven-storeyed flats at Bellmoor were limited by the L.C.C., to make them four-storeyed, in 1929, but there was a possibility of new blocks at the Old Court House and Heath Brow, near Jack Straw's Castle, in 1938. The L.C.C.'s London development plan of 1951 would have permitted bigger buildings around the heath, only to be disallowed by the government, and redevelopment on the bombed site at Heath Brow was averted by its purchase for a car park.[2] The acquisition of such plots as the Hill gardens brought further protection. Vigilance was still needed in 1984, however, when fears sprang mainly from plans for houses in the grounds of Witanhurst, on the Highgate side of the heath.[3]

In the 1960s Hampstead Heath's 'romantic abrupt scenery, a bit like the hilly parts of Shropshire', was thought to give maximum effect in the smallest area.[4] It continued to be praised in the 1980s for its variety and in particular for its wildness.[5] Its future management was uncertain, after the abolition of the G.L.C. in 1986. Proposals for a division between Camden, Barnet, and Haringey L.B.s were unwelcome to local residents and to the Heath and Old Hampstead society, as was management by the City of London to Camden and by Camden to the government. Other possibilities were for the London Residuary Body, temporarily in charge, to be succeeded by a joint committee from three local authorities, or by a new authority, or a local trust.[6]

SOCIAL AND CULTURAL ACTIVITIES. There were three alehouses in Hampstead in 1552[7] and three after suppressions by the justices in 1630.[8] Victuallers were often prosecuted for keeping disorderly houses in the 17th century,[9] when offences included Sunday drinking in 1641[10] and a quarrel resulted in death in 1653.[11] Alehouses nonetheless multiplied: after several had been suppressed at the

petition of the minister and others, a further nine innkeepers remained to be investigated in 1667.[12] Licences for Hampstead and Paddington were to be renewed only if one of the justices lived nearby in 1673.[13]

Since Hampstead was not on a major road from London, it lacked large hostelries for travellers.[14] The number of inns rose with the exploitation of the wells and of Belsize House but thereafter remained fairly constant throughout the 18th century. Thirty-four alehouse keepers were licensed in 1723,[15] 30 in 1726,[16] 37 in 1730,[17] 34 in 1751, 1760, and 1770, and 27 in 1800.[18] They included the licensees of two coffee houses in 1730[19] and, soon afterwards, of the Long Room connected with the wells.[20] Most of the identifiable inns were in Hampstead town, but a few were on the road from Camden Town or on the heath, and at North End, West End, or Kilburn.

New inns were built to serve the 19th-century suburbs.[21] In 1845 there were 25 inns listed under Hampstead and another 5, of which 3 were on the Hampstead side of High Road, under Kilburn.[22] By 1872 there were 44 in all, including 2 called hotels and a few across the St. Pancras boundary towards Kentish Town.[23] In 1889, despite the disappearance of some old names as a result of the 'town improvements',[24] there were still 44 inns listed.[25]

Many 18th-century inns, in addition to those connected with the wells and their attendant attractions, were resorts of Londoners. The popular Chalk Farm tavern or Stag and Hounds, often treated under Hampstead, stood just inside St. Pancras parish.[26] Mother Huff's tavern was recorded on the heath, near the Elms, in 1680 and was mentioned in a play printed in 1706. It had different licensees in 1723 and 1730, although Mother Huff herself in 1728 had moved only recently to the Hoop and Bunch of Grapes at North End.[27] The Chicken House, opposite Vane House, in 1807 was an old building said by tradition to have been visited by James I and to have been a hunting lodge of James II;[28] it may have been licensed only for a few years c. 1760–70.[29] On the heath Jack Straw's Castle and the Spaniards, both of them in 1807 'known to every citizen of London', were popular by the mid 18th century. Jack Straw's Castle, apparently of 17th-century origin and thought to bear a generic name for a farmworker rather than to commemorate the rebel, was probably the 'Castle on the heath' mentioned in *Clarissa Harlowe*.[30] The Spaniards, a tollgate inn astride the

[98] Above, communications.
[99] S.C.L., H 728.5/Spaniards.
[1] Howitt, *Northern Heights*, 94.
[2] Ikin, *Hampstead Heath* (1971), 21.
[3] Farmer, *Hampstead Heath*, 144, 167; *V.C.H. Mdx.* vi. 138.
[4] I. Nairn, *Nairn's Lond.* (1966), 217.
[5] e.g. *Images of Hampstead*, 17.
[6] *Camden Mag.* Sept. 1986, 11.
[7] *Mdx. County Rec.* i. 11.
[8] *Cal. S.P. Dom.* 1631–3, 525.
[9] e.g. *Mdx. Sess. Rec.* ii. 340; iii. 33, 64; Cal. Mdx. Sess. Rec. i. 84; ii. 34.
[10] Cal. Mdx. Sess. Bks. iA. 86.
[11] Ibid. ii. 52.
[12] Ibid. iv. 47.
[13] Ibid. iv. 194.
[14] Thompson, *Hampstead*, 5.
[15] G.L.R.O., MR/LV3/104.
[16] Ibid. MR/LV4/28-9.
[17] Ibid. MR/LV5/30-1.
[18] Ibid. MR/LV7/3; MR/LV7/45; MR/LV8/64; MR/LV10/89.
[19] Ibid. MR/LV5/31.
[20] Ibid. MR/LV7/3 et seq.; below.
[21] e.g. on Eton college's est.: Thompson, *Hampstead*, 229–30. For individual inns, see also above, growth, s.v. dist.
[22] *P.O. Dir. Six Home Counties* (1845).
[23] *P.O. Dir. Lond. Suburbs, North* (1872).
[24] *H.H.E.* 11 Jan. 1908, 6c; Wade, *Streets of Hampstead*, 61, 63.
[25] *Kelly's Dir. Hampstead & Highgate* (1889–90).
[26] *C.H.R.* vi. 2–5; *Images of Hampstead*, 127, 132.
[27] S.C.L., H 728.5/General; H 728.5/Mother Huff's; Thos. Baker, *Hampstead Heath* (1706), act II, scene 1; G.L.R.O., MR/LV3/104; MR/LV5/30.
[28] S.C.L., H 728.5/General; Woodward, *Eccentric Excursions*, 14; *Images of Hampstead*, 43.
[29] G.L.R.O., MR/LV7/45; MR/LV8/64.
[30] Woodward, *Eccentric Excursions*, 13; *Images of Hampstead*, 82; *Home Counties Mag.* i. 89–93; above, growth, North End.

Finchley boundary at the entrance to the bishop of London's estate, perhaps had an early proprietor of Spanish origin. Its pleasure gardens, with an artificial mound and mechanical tableaux, were depicted by Chatelaine in 1750.[31]

The Lower Flask, in Flask Walk, rebuilt in 1873–4 as the modern Flask tavern,[32] and the Upper Flask, in Heath Street,[33] owed their names, if not their existence, to the exploitation of the wells. Both figured in *Clarissa Harlowe*, the Lower Flask as 'a place where second-rate persons are to be found, occasionally in a swinish condition'.[34] In contrast the Upper Flask brought Hampstead its most influential and distinguished gatherings, earning a comparison with Parnassus,[35] by serving as a summer meeting place of the Whig grandees' Kit-Cat club. On the club's dissolution *c.* 1720 the Upper Flask continued as a tavern until the 1750s, when it became the residence later called Upper Bowling Green House, which made way in 1921 for Queen Mary's maternity hospital.[36] Closer to the springs, in Well Walk, was the Green Man, licensed in 1751, perhaps connected with an earlier Whitestone tavern and demolished in 1849 to make way for the Wells hotel (later tavern).[37]

A well was publicized as early as 1653.[38] The depiction of a well and bucket on tokens of 1669 and 1670, with inscriptions recording 'the well in Hampstead', perhaps referred merely to a shop near the village well or to a tavern, rather than to the sale of medicinal waters.[39] Celia Fiennes, however, likened the water from a Hampstead spring to that of Tunbridge Wells or Bath in 1697 and visited Hampstead in 1698 probably in order to sample it.[40] Chalybeate springs were included in the 6 a. conveyed to the parish by Susannah Noel in 1698[41] and were immediately exploited by the new Wells trustees, who in 1700 advertised that flasks were on sale at several places in London.[42] Water was also distributed locally by a widow, Elizabeth Keys, although she was excluded with other vendors under an agreement of 1701, leasing the land and all springs except the upper or head spring to John Duffield. Inhabitants were free to drink or take away the waters every morning, while Duffield, in addition to his rent, was to undertake building work.[43]

Although the head spring was near Bath pond (later in the garden of Willow House) and was retained by the trustees, the main well was some 100 yards lower down the hill. There, the slope being less steep, Duffield laid out the amenities of a spa, along the southern side of a promenade, Well Walk.

The chief building was the Great Room, for assemblies, with its east end partitioned off as a pump room, where a basin held the waters. Concerts and dances were first advertised for the summer of 1701. The Great Room stood at the entrance to the modern Gainsborough Gardens and soon afterwards there were also a row of raffling shops, for bets, a tavern, and Well Walk chapel, all to the west. To the south were gardens, with an ornamental pond and a bowling green. Duffield's enterprise allowed the world of fashion to combine the quests for health and pleasure. So successful was he that in 1705, the year of Beau Nash's first visit to Bath, a comedy called *Hampstead Heath* was played at Drury Lane. London was shown as deserted in favour of Hampstead, where 'the cards fly, the bowl runs, the dice rattle'.[44]

Soon afterwards the entertainments began to deteriorate, perhaps mainly because rough crowds could easily make the journey from London. The music was interspersed with popular entertainments,[45] including acrobatics and comic turns, and by 1709 there were complaints about swindlers and prostitutes.[46] Duffield raised money by conveying much of his interest to William Luffingham, to whom in 1719 he made a new 21-year lease without the consent of the lord or the trustees. Expedients failed to halt the decline, which was hastened by highway robberies, by complaints from the inhabitants, and by the sudden rise to popularity of Belsize.[47] Defoe *c.* 1724 found that ladies who valued their good name were avoiding Hampstead, although there were still many visitors.[48] The conversion of the Great Room into a chapel of ease by Luffingham's sublessee William Hoar in 1725[49] marked the end of the first and most colourful phase in the history of the wells.

A briefer and more lurid fame was enjoyed by Belsize House,[50] where in 1710 Lord Chesterfield's tenant Charles Povey opened Sion chapel, offering cheap weddings with no further charge if couples should dine in the gardens. The chapel closed *c.* 1720[51] when Povey subleased Belsize to James Howell, a speculator soon satirized as 'the Welsh ambassador'. A ballroom was lavishly furnished,[52] concerts and walks in the grounds were announced, in 1721 a visit was paid by the prince and princess of Wales, and for one deer hunt in 1722 there was an attendance of between 300 and 400 carriages. The attractions of promiscuity, racing, and gambling quickly enabled Belsize, renamed the Wilderness, to outrival Vauxhall. In 1722, however, Howell was

[31] *Images of Hampstead*, 69 and illus.
[32] Wade, *Streets of Hampstead*, 40.
[33] Not in Flask Walk, as stated in Pevsner, *Lond.* ii. 196.
[34] Richardson, *Clarissa Harlowe*, letter x; S.C.L., H 728.5/Flask.
[35] R. Blackmore, *The Kit-Cats, a Poem* (1708).
[36] Wade, *Streets of Hampstead*, 43; G.L.R.O., MR/LV3/104; MR/LV7/3; above, growth, Hampstead town.
[37] G.L.R.O., MR/LV7/3; S.C.L., H 728.5/General; board on bldg.
[38] Above, settlement and growth.
[39] *C.H.R.* v. 18–19, correcting *Trade Tokens in 17th Cent.* ed. G. C. Williamson, ii (1891), 818. The last Eng. tokens were dated 1674.
[40] *Journeys of Celia Fiennes*, ed. C. Morris (1949), 121, 198.
[41] Below, charities, Wells char.
[42] Rest of para. and following 2 paras. based on G. W. Potter, *Hampstead Wells* (Camden History Soc. reprint, with additions, 1978), *passim*. See also W. Wroth, *Lond.*

Pleasure Gdns. of 18th Cent. (1896), 178–9; *Images of Hampstead*, 28–30; Wade, *Streets of Hampstead*, 34; Thompson, *Hampstead*, 20–2.
[43] Below, charities, Wells char.
[44] Baker, *Hampstead Heath*, act I, scene 1.
[45] *C.H.R.* iii. 13.
[46] J. Macky, *Journey through Eng.* (5th edn. 1732), i. 88–9; *Lond. in 1710, from Travels of Zacharias Conrad von Uffenbach*, ed. W. H. Quarrell and M. Mare (1934), 120.
[47] G.L.R.O., Cal. Mdx. Sess. Bks. xii. 118; xiii. 11–12; below.
[48] Defoe, *Tour*, i. 385.
[49] Below, churches.
[50] Para. based on Wroth, *Pleasure Gdns.* 189–92; *Images of Hampstead*, 115–16; Thompson, *Hampstead*, 35–7.
[51] Below, churches (Sion chapel). Thorne, Wroth, Potter, and others mistakenly connected Sion chapel with Hampstead wells.
[52] Defoe, *Tour*, i. 384–5.

publicly accused of profiting from a 'scandalous lewd house', and unlawful gaming was suppressed. Fashionable patrons thereupon moved away, although entertainments, including music and athletics, continued at least until 1745, when a foot race was advertised. The mansion was then left empty until its rebuilding.[53]

Meanwhile an attempt had been made to revive the appeal of Hampstead wells. After litigation, which had been started in 1726 over arrears claimed from Luffingham and others by the parish overseers, the trustees were reconstituted in 1730. The raffling shops disappeared but the bowling green survived, while the fountain and basin were probably moved to the Wells house, a small building by the tavern. Such a move would have brought them nearer a second Long Room on the north side of a westerly extension of Well Walk, next to Burgh House.[54] In 1734 John Soame, who ascribed the waters' first popularity to Dr. Gibbon (d. 1725) of Burgh House, dedicated a treatise to the wells' new proprietor John Mitchell. Himself a physician of Hampstead, Soame considered its waters far more efficacious than those in fashion at Islington.[55] Further building took place in 1735, probably by Henry Vipand as part of the Long Room's structure, and a separate ballroom was put up a little to the east.[56] The village was then ranked, after Scarborough, Bath, and Tunbridge Wells, as one of the politest places in England.[57] The physician John Arbuthnot (1667–1735) spent half his mornings at the Long Room in 1734, when Alexander Pope visited him,[58] but Hampstead thereafter prospered as a sedate middle-class resort rather than as a fashionable spa.[59] Assemblies continued to be held in the 1770s, when the young Samuel Rogers danced with 'a great deal of good company'[60] and the heroine of *Evelina* endured some ill-bred attentions at a ball in the Long Room, a place 'without any sort of singularity and merely to be marked by its length'.[61] The Long Room was licensed for public entertainments from 1751 or earlier until 1802, the licensee from 1769 to 1781 being a vintner, Robert Simmonds.[62] It was still used for musical recitals in 1800.[63]

Later efforts to publicize the curative properties of the waters were made by two doctors, John Bliss and Thomas Goodwin. The first in 1802 praised the waters of Hampstead, which allegedly had been growing in reputation again over the past twenty years, and of Kilburn.[64] The second in 1804 had recently discovered a saline or purgative spring, like those at Cheltenham, near Pond Street.[65] Neither advertisement had much success. The village soon

afterwards acquired its own assembly rooms in Holly Bush Hill, leaving the Long Room to become part of a private residence, Weatherall House, and the ballroom to become Lasted Lodge; both buildings were replaced by municipal flats in 1948.[66] The waters had fallen into disuse by the mid 19th century,[67] although a local guidebook claimed that they were still sampled by visitors, as a tonic for general debility.[68] A fountain on the south side of Well Walk, in front of a house replaced by nos. 42 and 44, remained active until it was affected by drainage work. A new fountain, 'recently erected' in 1876 on the north side at the foot of Well Passage, thereafter supplied a trickle of mildly chalybeate water, attempts to provide a more lavish flow being frustrated by warnings about impurities.[69] It no longer supplied water in 1986.

Kilburn wells were merely an 18th-century adjunct of the much older Bell inn. The chalybeate spring in Abbey field was encased in a brick reservoir dated 1714 but apparently not exploited until 1742, after Hampstead's waters had become known. The Bell's proprietor advertised his extended gardens, refurbished house, and great room for polite public entertainments in 1773. Visitors were given an 'eminent physician's' account of the waters but little was recorded of their use, which had ceased by 1814. The brick reservoir survived the rebuilding of the Bell in 1863 but had been built over, behind the corner of Belsize Road, by 1896.[70]

The 19th-century Hampstead assembly rooms,[71] near the top of Holly Bush Hill, consisted of the house built by George Romney, which was acquired by Maria Elizabeth Rundell, a widow whose husband had been leased an older house by Romney. Having acquired all Romney's adjacent properties, Mrs. Rundell in 1806 conveyed them to trustees for the assembly rooms, apart from her own residence, which was sold separately. The trustees in 1807 leased a cottage and stables for 21 years to Thomas Lovelock, who was to put up a new building,[72] thereby creating the Holly Bush tavern as an appendage of the assembly rooms. The rooms, which were not managed by the innkeeper, included a ballroom and card room.[73] They remained in use, latterly more as a public hall than as an elegant social centre, until the opening of the new vestry hall in 1878, thereafter being taken over by the Constitutional club.[74]

Kilburn town hall and assembly rooms were opened by a speculator, Thomas Bate, in 1876. His ornate Gothic building at the west end of Belszie Road included two halls, to seat 800 and 250, and

[53] Below, manor.
[54] Potter, *Hampstead Wells*, 53, 63, 70–1.
[55] J. Soame, *Hampstead Wells* (1734), pp. iii, vii, ix, xii–xiii, 29, 34.
[56] Potter, *Hampstead Wells*, 72–3; Wroth, *Pleasure Gdns.* 181; *Images of Hampstead*, 31–2.
[57] R. Seymour, *Survey of Lond. and Westm.* (1735), ii. 870.
[58] *Corresp. of Alex. Pope*, ed. G. Sherburn, iii (1956), 434.
[59] e.g. adverts. in S.C.L., H 728.5/Long Room.
[60] *Table-Talk of Sam. Rogers*, ed. M. Bishop (1952), 70.
[61] F. Burney, *Evelina*, ii, letter xix.
[62] S.C.L., H 728.5/gen.; G.L.R.O., MR/LV7/3; MR/LV10/89; MR/LMD1/7, 9–19.
[63] *Hampstead Annual, 1899*, 83.

[64] J. Bliss, *Experiments on Medicinal Waters of Hampstead and Kilburn* (1802), 11.
[65] T. Goodwin, *Account of Neutral Saline Waters Recently discovered at Hampstead* (1804), 1, 3, 5–6.
[66] *Images of Hampstead*, 35; *Home Counties Mag.* xi. 7–15; *C.H.R.* ii. 36.
[67] Lewis, *Topog. Dict. Eng.* ii (1849), 391.
[68] *Shaw's Hampstead Dir. and Almanack* (1854), 30.
[69] Thorne, *Environs*, 281; Potter, *Hampstead Wells*, 80–1, 96–100.
[70] Park, *Hampstead*, 63; Wroth, *Pleasure Gdns.* 194–5; *Images of Hampstead*, 152.
[71] Para. based on S.C.L., H 728.5/Holly Bush (esp. letter of E. F. Oppé on hist. of rooms).
[72] Lease in S.C.L., D 138.
[73] Plan in ibid.; also trustees' min. bk. and acct. bk.
[74] Below.

was intended for dances, exhibitions, and public meetings. It also housed a club from 1877 until it was taken over for the Theatre Royal.[75]

Tea gardens, with their attendant amusements, remained popular for most of the 19th century. The Spaniards, where Charles Dickens placed the arrest of Mrs. Bardell in *The Pickwick Papers* of 1836,[76] still had its gardens and bowling green, although without the mound and other embellishments, in 1876.[77] It was the subject of controversy in the early 1960s after a proposal by Finchley council to demolish the tollhouse on the east side of the road in order to improve the flow of traffic. An early victory for conservationists was marked in 1967 by the building's conveyance to the G.L.C. and its repair by the Hampstead Heath and Old Hampstead Protection Society.[78] Jack Straw's Castle in 1837 still had its tea gardens and in 1876 had for long been favoured by artists and writers.[79] They included Washington Irving c. 1824[80] and Dickens, who from 1838 often read manuscripts to his friends over dinner there.[81] By 1914 it was associated with theatrical figures, boxers, and many local clubs.[82] As a three-storeyed building with bay windows, it was given a castellated addition soon after 1834; after damage in 1941 it was rebuilt to a controversial design by Raymond Erith and Quinlan Terry, with white weatherboarding and battlements, in 1962.[83]

The garden of the Bell at Kilburn, with grottoes and summerhouses, was popular c. 1840, when patrons could watch the trains speed by.[84] At North End the Bull and Bush, dated traditionally from c. 1645 but probably from c. 1700, in 1876 furnished a rare example of 'the old Hampstead tavern garden'; the inn was reconstructed in 1924, a few older windows being retained.[85] The Wells tavern in 1876 also had tea gardens, although much smaller than those of its predecessor the Green Man.[86] At the Vale of Health there were tea gardens, scornfully described by Dickens, from 1841 or earlier until the Second World War.[87]

Other inns had particular attractions. In Haverstock Hill the Load of Hay, so named by 1723[88] although said once to have been called the Cart and Horses, had a varying reputation. Its boisterous landlord Joe Davis (d. 1806) was widely caricatured in prints and patronized by the nobility,[89] whereas Washington Irving remembered it for its rowdy Irish haymakers.[90] In 1863 the Load of Hay was re-

built and from 1965 until 1974 it was called the Noble Art in honour of the Belsize boxing club and of a gymnasium behind used by the British Boxing Board of Control.[91] The Swiss Cottage tavern had a former pugilist, Frank Redmond, as its first landlord in the early 1840s and became famous as the starting point for foot races along Finchley Road. After much alteration a new building was finished by 1966; it was in the original style, that of an alpine chalet, made popular after the opera Le Chalet was performed in Paris in 1834.[92] Nearby the Britannia in Fairfax Road, built by 1872, was used by many sports clubs early in the 20th century. A new building was opened on the other side of a roundabout, at the corner of Hilgrove Road, in 1971.[93]

A playhouse, recently built and presumably patronized by visitors to the wells, was suppressed in 1709 at the instance of the vicar and other inhabitants. Further suppression, however, was needed in 1710[94] and again in 1723. Plays thereafter were probably performed only by amateurs until in 1805 'Gyngell's theatre of mirth and mechanism' appeared at the Square, in a booth. A new theatre was advertised in 1817 at the assembly rooms, where, although no permanent theatre was established, concerts took place at least once a month until 1829.[95] Music and dancing were licensed at several inns with tea gardens: at the Bell in Kilburn High Road from 1840 or earlier,[96] at Jack Straw's Castle from 1856,[97] and at the Bull and Bush, made famous through 'Down at the old Bull and Bush' sung by Florrie Ford, from 1867.[98] Entertainments were also licensed at the Yorkshire Grey off High Street, demolished during the 'town improvements',[99] the Duke of Hamilton at New End, the Cock and Hoop at West End, closed in 1896 after a temperance workers' campaign,[1] and mid 19th-century taverns in south Hampstead: the Eton in Adelaide Road, the North Star in College Villas Road (later College Crescent), and the Prince Arthur in Boundary Road.[2]

The Theatre Royal, Kilburn, was opened in 1886 in the place of Kilburn town hall, which itself had been licensed for music and dancing. It was altered in 1895, to hold 514, was known by 1903 as the Kilburn Empire Theatre of Varieties, no. 256 Belsize Road,[3] and was still a theatre of varieties in 1910, although used also as a cinema, later called the Kilburn Palace, by 1909.[4] Nearby the New Empire

[75] *H.H.E.* 28 Oct. 1876; *Kilburn Times*, 18 Nov. 1876, 5c; 23 Dec. 1876, 5b; below.
[76] C. Dickens, *Pickwick Papers*, cap. xlvi.
[77] Thorne, *Environs*, 284.
[78] S.C.L., H 728.5/Spaniards.
[79] S.C.L., H 728.5/Jack Straw's Castle (sales parts.); Thorne, *Environs*, 284.
[80] W. Irving, *Tales of a Traveller* (Longman's 1896), 127–8.
[81] e.g. *Letters of Chas. Dickens*, ed. M. House, G. Storey, and K. Tillotson (1965–74), i. 353; ii. 144, 200, 205; iii, 15, 94, 123, 425.
[82] *H.H.E.* 3 Jan. 1914, 3b.
[83] *Images of Hampstead*, 82–3; C. McKean and T. Jestico, *Guide to Modern Bldgs. in Lond.* (1976), 39; S.C.L., H 728.5/Jack Straw's Castle; *The Times*, 10 Aug. 1962, 6b; *H.H.E.* 23 Nov. 1962, 1d.
[84] *Osborne's Lond. and Birmingham Rly. Guide* [1840],86; C. Barman, *Early Brit. Rlys.* (1950), illus. 5.
[85] Thorne, *Environs*, 284; S.C.L., H 728.5/Bull and Bush; Pevsner, *Lond.* ii. 193.
[86] Thorne, *Environs*, 281.

[87] Bentwich, *Vale of Health*, 50.
[88] G.L.R.O., MR/LV3/104.
[89] *Gent. Mag.* lxxvi. 287.
[90] Irving, *Tales of a Traveller*, 126.
[91] Wade, *More Streets*, 41; S.C.L., H 728.5/Load of Hay.
[92] *Images of Hampstead*, 125–6; Pevsner, *Lond.* ii. 201; S.C.L., H 728.5/Swiss Cottage.
[93] Wade, *W. Hampstead*, 50; S.C.L., H 728.5/Britannia.
[94] *Mdx. County Rec. Sess Bks. 1689–1709*, 346; G.L.R.O., Cal. Mdx. Sess. Sess. Bks. x. 24–6.
[95] *N. & Q.* n.s. xvii. 168–9.
[96] G.L.R.O., MR/LMD 2/9 and card index.
[97] Ibid. LMD 9/344 and card index.
[98] Ibid. LMD 26/14 and card index; S.C.L., H 728.5/ Bull and Bush.
[99] D. Howard, *Lond. Theatres and Music Halls* (1970), 268; S.C.L., H 728.5/General.
[1] Howard, *Lond. Theatres*, 49, 70; *C.H.R.* ix. 9.
[2] Howard, *Lond. Theatres*, 82, 160, 182.
[3] Ibid. 127; *P.O. Dir. Lond.* (1903).
[4] *P.O. Dir. Lond.* (1910, 1912); D.S.R.; below.

Theatre of Varieties was built in 1907 as a music hall and circus at nos. 9–11 the Parade, Kilburn High Road. An ornate three-storeyed building, topped by a balustrade, urns, and a central statue, it seated 1,913[5] and contained animal traps and pits which survived its conversion into a full-time cinema, the Kilburn Empire, in 1928.[6] Kilburn was so popular as a place of entertainment that on the sale of the Grange (formerly Oak Lodge) in 1910 Sir Oswald Stoll proposed a Coliseum on the lines of his London theatre in St. Martin's Lane, only to be baulked by Hampstead borough council.[7]

Concerts and plays by Hampstead societies took place in several halls in the late 19th century, including the assembly rooms, advertised in 1872 as being for the first time under the same management as the Holly Bush hotel.[8] Later the new vestry hall, the new drill hall in Holly Bush Vale, and Hampstead Conservatoire at Swiss Cottage were often used,[9] although Hampstead dramatic society staged its productions in London theatres.[10]

The Everyman theatre was opened by Norman MacDermott, with help from private contributors, in 1920. A conversion of the Holly Bush Vale drill hall, which had come to be used as a 'shady palais de whist', it had a steeply raked floor and seating for 300. After an experimental three months of repertory there were longer runs of new plays,[11] whose success made the Everyman a hunting ground for commercial managers.[12] Despite furthering many theatrical careers, including that of Noel Coward in the first performance of his *Vortex*,[13] MacDermott was always short of money: the building work had been expensive and Hampstead's residents did not provide many of the bookings. New partners took control in 1926 and there was a temporary closure in 1929, followed by the establishment of a guild with Sir Gerald Du Maurier as president and in 1931 of the Everyman theatre club. The lease was nonetheless sold for the building's conversion into a drama school and then into a cinema, which opened in 1933.[14]

The Embassy theatre was opened in 1928, when the premises of Hampstead Conservatoire were adapted by Andrew Mather. After two changes of control and the establishment of a playgoers' association in 1930, the Embassy school of acting opened there in 1932. After war damage, the building was reopened in 1945, with a capacity of 678, and sold to the Central School of Speech and Drama in 1956. There were 338 students in 1986, when public performances were held in a theatre seating 278.[15]

German Jewish refugees opened the Little Theatre at no. 37A Upper Park Road in 1940.[16] Hampstead Theatre Club spent its first season, 1959–60, at Moreland hall behind the Everyman cinema.[17] Served by a permanent company called Theatre West, the club moved in 1962 to a prefabricated civic theatre, seating 160, at Swiss Cottage.[18] The site, next to the new library, was proposed in 1965 by Camden L.B. as a home for the National Youth Theatre, which later opened in Euston Road (St. Pancras).[19] Each show at Hampstead theatre was individually casted in 1986, when there was seating for 173 and all Camden residents were honorary members of the club.[20] The small New End theatre used no. 27 New End, formerly a mortuary, from c. 1975 until 1986.[21]

A moving picture show, as distinct from magic lantern shows in the basement of the drill hall, was recalled as having been held c. 1901 at the Y.M.C.A.'s premises in Willoughby Road.[22] Early open-air shows took place on Hampstead Heath, to judge from photographs of 'Biddall's Electric Show' and of a booth labelled 'Queen's Cinematograph'.[23] The ornate Frognal Bijou Picture Palace, opposite Finchley Road station at no. 156, was opened in 1911 with seating for 240.[24] The cinema, which was distinct from Keith Prowse & Co.'s Bijou hall at no. 167 Finchley Road, survived residents' protests against Sunday opening.[25] From 1921 it was in turn called O'Dett's picture house, the Frognal, the Casino, next to a dance hall of the same name, and the New Frognal, which had closed by 1933.[26] Kilburn Electric Palace was opened in 1910 at no. 10 Kilburn High Road,[27] where it survived in 1911 and 1912. Kilburn Picture Palace and Theatre of Varieties, which had been built as a theatre, continued as the Kilburn Palace at no. 256 Belsize Road until 1941.[28] A Biograph theatre was open at no. 236 Kilburn High Road from 1911 to 1913. It was replaced by Kilburn Grange cinema, seating 1,300 and with a dome over its entrance at the corner of Messina Avenue, in 1914. The building was a cinema in 1977 but housed a night club, the National, from 1978.[29]

In Hampstead town no. 64 Heath Street was converted into a cinema for the New Eldorado Co. in 1910.[30] The El Dorado functioned as 'a crooked little cinema by the side of Cornick's yard' in 1913[31] and presumably was renamed Hampstead Electric Palace, at no. 64 Heath Street from 1914 to 1916.[32] Hampstead Picture Playhouse, a 'luxurious hall' in

[5] Thompson, *Hampstead*, 259; Howard, *Lond. Theatres*, 126–7. Licensed as Kilburn Vaudeville theatre: *The Times*, 2 Nov. 1907, 14e.
[6] D. Atwell, *Cathedrals of the Movies* (1981), 43–4; below.
[7] Wade, *W. Hampstead*, 37; *The Times*, 26 Nov. 1910, 14f.   [8] *H.H.E.* 23 Nov. 1872.
[9] e.g. *Hampstead Rec.* 21 Sept., 5 Oct. 1889; below.
[10] e.g. *H.H.E.* 23 Feb. 1895, 5f; *Hampstead Social Review*, Mar. 1905; *H.H.E.* 5 Mar. 1910, 5.
[11] N. MacDermott, *Everymania: Hist. of Everyman Theatre* (1975), 12–13, 15, 21, 27, 100.
[12] *Official Guide to Hampstead* [1925].
[13] Wade, *Streets of Hampstead*, 61. Lists of plays and actors, 1920–6, in MacDermott, *Everymania*, 124–32.
[14] MacDermott, *Everymania*, 27, 29, 79, 100; Howard, *Lond. Theatres*, 83; below.
[15] Howard, *Lond. Theatres*, 78; S.C.L., H 792/Embassy theatre; inf. from acting principal.
[16] Inf. from Agnes Bernelle.
[17] *The Book of Hampstead*, ed. M. and I. Norrie (1968), 82, 121.
[18] *H.H.E.* 23 Nov. 1962, 1d; 21 Dec. 1962, 1b.
[19] S.C.L., H 792/Nat. Youth theatre.
[20] Inf. from artistic dir.
[21] *P.O. Dir. Lond.* (1975 and later edns.).
[22] *H.H.E.* 9 Jan. 1959, 4f.
[23] Smith, *Hampstead As It Was*, 18; S. Nowell-Smith, *Edwardian Eng.* (1964), pl. xxiv b.
[24] *H.H.E.* 15 Apr. 1911, 7b; *Hampstead and St. John's Wood Advertiser*, 20 Apr. 1911, 5b.
[25] *Hampstead and St. John's Wood Advertiser*, 27 Apr. 1911, 11e; 4 May 1911, 5b; 25 May 1911, 11e.
[26] *P.O. Dir. Lond.* (1921 and later edns.).
[27] *The Times*, 22 Apr. 1910, 12f.
[28] *P.O. Dir. Lond.* (1911 and later edns.).
[29] Ibid.; Atwell, *Cathedrals of the Movies*, 18, 21; S.C.L., H 791.43/Kilburn Grange Cinema.   [30] D.S.R.
[31] *H.H.E.* 9 Jan. 1959, 4f.
[32] *P.O. Dir. Lond.* (1914–16).

Pond Street, drew large audiences in 1914.[33] Called the Playhouse after the Second World War and the Classic from 1966, it was altered in 1968, when it was the oldest cinema in Hampstead,[34] and was refurbished as Cannon 1, 2, and 3 in 1986. The borough's best known cinema opened in 1933, after the Everyman theatre had been acquired and converted by James Fairfax-Jones, a solicitor.[35] As a specialist cinema, showing mainly foreign films, the Everyman remained open in 1986.

The Kilburn Empire, a full-time cinema from 1928, was renamed the Essoldo c. 1950 and survived until 1971. Alterations then spared only the stage area, the exterior being clad in sheet metal and a small cinema, the Classic, built inside the auditorium.[36] As a result the most imposing relic of Kilburn High Road's places of entertainment was the former Gaumont State cinema, opened in 1937 on the Willesden side and serving in 1986 as a bingo club.[37]

The Odeon, Haverstock Hill, south of the town hall, was designed in 1934 by T. P. Bennett & Son and taken over before its completion by Oscar Deutsch. It had a lavishly decorated auditorium and served as Deutsch's chief London advertisement until his opening in 1937 of the Odeon, Leicester Square.[38] Closure followed the sale of the lease by the Rank Organization in 1972.[39] The Odeon, Swiss Cottage, immediately south of the Swiss Cottage tavern, was opened in 1937. A plain brick building, it was designed in the Birmingham office of Harry Weedon and was unlike most of London's Odeon cinemas.[40] Its total seating of 1,740 was reduced by nearly half in 1973, on its conversion into three cinemas, which remained open in 1986.[41]

Horses were raced in 1732 at Hampstead, where in 1733 a three-day August meeting on the heath was advertised, each race to consist of several circuits around 'the mile course'.[42] The course was said to have been on the later West Heath, probably starting at the foot of Flagstaff Hill and reaching to North End.[43] As late as 1853 a road across the top of the heath was a 'race ground' on Sundays, although probably only in reference to donkey drivers.[44] The hiring of donkeys and pony chaises caused concern by 1825, when the vestry was advised against prosecution, since no wilful damage was done.[45] There were said to be 100 donkeys daily on the heath in 1836. Soon their popularity inspired cartoonists and attracted Charles Dickens and even, in the early 1850s, Karl Marx, who rode with more fervour than

skill.[46] The M.B.W. sought sites for donkey stands when it took over in 1872; 45 were built near the Vale of Health and 60 at the foot of Downshire Hill. Residents soon petitioned against Sunday rides, in 1873 the drivers' noisy plying for trade led to their being licensed,[47] and in 1876 their alleged unkindness contributed to the establishment of a Hampstead branch of the R.S.P.C.A.[48] Few drivers were left by 1907, when they were remembered as gipsylooking people who married only among themselves.[49] Horses continued to be exercised on the heath: there were many summonses for 'furious riding' and in 1882 the M.B.W. was accused of neglecting the north-west part of the heath, which was supposed to be maintained for riders.[50]

Many other sports were practised casually on the heath, until in 1882 the M.B.W. set apart 80 a. and banned playing on West Heath. The board claimed that its Act of 1877, authorizing the regulation of all games, nullified the protection of traditional rights which had been enshrined in the Hampstead Heath Act, 1871. The vestry protested, however, and G. W. Potter staged a cricket match, which led to litigation ending in the vestry's victory in 1883.[51]

Cricket was played in 1794 by Hampstead and Kentish Town against Highgate 'on Highgate common', in 1796 by Hampstead and Highgate against the Middlesex Thursday club at Lords, and in 1802 against the M.C.C. on Hampstead Heath.[52] Batsmen also played trap-ball south of Jack Straw's Castle, without authority, in 1833.[53] An unauthorized booth was set up on the heath, by the landlord of the Green Man, for a cricket match in 1840.[54] The ground in a hollow on West Heath, where G. W. Potter's team defied the M.B.W., was laid out in 1822.[55] Another early ground lay possibly near East Heath Road behind the Pryors but more probably was the Trap-ball ground, at the end of Well Walk opposite Foley House, which was gradually abandoned after a footpath had been cut across it on the draining of a swamp near the Vale of Health pond. Hampstead Albion cricket club, formed in 1837, reestablished in 1861, and afterwards called Hampstead United, still played on the Trap-ball ground in 1876,[56] as did other teams,[57] but there was little room for players there in 1907.[58]

The Eton and Middlesex cricket ground was created at the north-west foot of Primrose Hill c. 1858 by Samuel Cuming, perhaps partly to add to the attractions of the district which he was building up. It was approached at first along the line of

[33] H.H.E. 3 Jan. 1914, 5b; 18 Apr. 1914, 6e.
[34] P.O. Dir. Lond. (1914 and later edns.); S.C.L., H 792/Cinemas.
[35] S.C.L., H 792/Everyman.
[36] Atwell, Cathedrals of the Movies, 43–4; P.O. Dir. Lond. (1949, 1950); above.
[37] Atwell, Cathedrals of the Movies, 97, 99; V.C.H. Mdx. vii. 208.
[38] Atwell, Cathedrals of the Movies, 146.
[39] S.C.L., H 791.43/Odeon, Haverstock Hill.
[40] Attwell, Cathedrals of the Movies, 153–4; Archit. of Lond. 49.
[41] S.C.L., H 791.43/Odeon, Swiss Cottage.
[42] Park, Hampstead, 250; S.C.L., Hampstead Heath, cuttings box.
[43] Potter, Random Recollections, 28–9.
[44] The Times, 13 Apr. 1853, 7f.
[45] Vestry mins. 6 July 1825.
[46] Farmer, Hampstead Heath, 108–12; Images of Hampstead, illus. 273, 277–8, 281–2; B. Nicolaievsky and O.

Maenchen-Helfen, Karl Marx (1973), 258. In A. Mayhew, Paved With Gold (1858), 135–40, the hero worked as a donkey boy.
[47] H.H.E. 20 Jan., 10 Feb. 1872; The Times, 14 Apr. 1873, 9c; Farmer, Hampstead Heath, 112.
[48] H.H.E. 22 Jan. 1876.
[49] Potter, Random Recollections, 10.
[50] Thompson, Hampstead, 391; H.H.E. 12, 27 May 1876; The Times, 20 Jan. 1882, 12b.
[51] The Times, 18 May 1882, 6f; Baines, Rec. Hampstead, 156–9.
[52] Monro, Hampstead C.C. 15, 18–19.
[53] G.L.R.O., E/MW/H/I/1437c.
[54] Diary of heath keeper (1834–40) in S.C.L.
[55] Monro, Hampstead C.C. 25–6; Baines, Rec. Hampstead, 158.
[56] Monro, Hampstead C.C. 21–4; Hampstead Almanack (1863).
[57] H.H.E. 13, 27 May 1876.
[58] Potter, Random Recollections, 90.

Elsworthy Rise but was shifted westward towards the south end of Harley Road in the 1870s, as Elsworthy Road was started.[59] Several metropolitan and suburban clubs used the ground in 1890, when it was about to make way for Wadham Gardens.[60]

A mid 19th-century Hampstead cricket club existed by 1851 and may also have been known as Adelaide or Adelaide Road club. It was limited to 60 members and had a field on the north side of England's Lane which was built over in 1870, whereupon the club closed or amalgamated. A 'tradesmen's cricket field' lay west of the club's 'subscription' field in 1865.[61]

A succeeding Hampstead cricket club originated as the third St. John's Wood club in 1867,[62] using the Eton and Middlesex ground until 1870. It moved near St. Mary's church in Belsize Road and became St. John's Wood (Hampstead) cricket club in 1871, when it probably absorbed the nearby Belsize club. The name was changed to Hampstead in 1877 after a move to Lymington Road, where a ground was leased from the lord of the manor. A pavilion was to be built in 1879 and was replaced by a large clubhouse after the freehold had been bought in 1924.[63] Hampstead cricket club limited its numbers to 200 full and 50 lawn tennis members in 1880.[64] It was considered the most important of the local recreative clubs by 1890, having already witnessed the highest score yet made,[65] and in 1949 was claimed to have produced more fine players than any other non-county club in England.[66]

Other cricket clubs included the Spaniard's, started in 1870, and the North End, both active in 1872, and Hampstead United and Park (Hampstead) in 1876.[67] The Alert started its fourth season in 1880, when there were also the Heath Nondescripts, Adelaide, and Haverstock United clubs.[68] Hampstead Alert, playing at Gospel Oak, Crescent and Haverstock clubs, on the Eton and Middlesex ground, Hampstead Montrose, and the wandering Hampstead Nondescripts existed in 1890.[69] Maitland cricket club, established in 1899, played on Parliament Hill and on the heath until 1915.[70] In 1907 the heath, much of which was too hilly for cricket, might accommodate as many as six matches at the same time on a Saturday afternoon.[71]

Hockey was played as early as 1874, by a Hampstead team against Richmond, but perhaps only intermittently until 1890. A hockey section of Hampstead cricket club, which had played at Lymington Road, became independent in 1894 as Hampstead hockey club, hiring a ground at Acton and from 1895 until 1939 at Richmond. Well known players, some of whom joined from the cricket club, made Hampstead London's leading hockey side before the First World War. After its re-establishment in 1950, the club first used grounds at Cricklewood, then at Boston Manor, Brentford, and from 1959 Hornsey cricket club's grounds at Crouch End.[72]

Lawn tennis was presumably played at Hampstead cricket club in 1878, when the proposed admission of lady members for tennis was defeated. Tennis players paid separate subscriptions by 1880 and more land was leased for them, at the west end of the ground, in 1881. Five hard courts were provided for the cricket club's flourishing tennis section on the building of the new clubhouse in 1925.[73]

Cumberland lawn tennis club, founded in 1880 in Regent's Park, from 1903 played at Alvanley Gardens. A company was formed in 1922 in order to buy the freehold, which adjoined the cricket ground in Lymington Road, and a clubhouse was built in the 1920s and later enlarged. In 1927 the Cumberland inaugurated an annual tournament, which was open to any player until 1985 and remained one of the season's earliest outdoor events in the annual preparations for Wimbledon.[74] There were 1,300 members, half of them full tennis members, and 11 tennis and 4 squash courts in 1986.

Several other clubs existed in the 1920s and 1930s, when lawn tennis was very popular.[75] In 1930, in addition to courts at the Imperial sports ground in Blackburn Road, there were eight clubs off Haverstock Hill, besides a Hampstead hard court lawn tennis club nearby in Glenloch Road; all save one survived in 1939.[76] Seven clubs played near the reservoir in Gondar Gardens, West Hampstead, by 1925 and six in 1930; they included clubs from Gospel Oak and Paddington.[77]

Hampstead athletic club was formed in 1880 and active in 1905.[78] Belsize boxing club was also formed in 1880, to help protect local ladies, and trained for nearly 50 years across the Marylebone boundary at the Eyre Arms. As perhaps the oldest amateur boxing club in the country, it was revived in 1965 on being allowed to use the British Boxing Board of Control's new gymnasium behind the Load of Hay.[79] A widely illustrated mid 19th-century gymnasium on Primrose Hill was at the southern side, outside the parish,[80] but a gymnasium adjoined Hampstead's first public baths, opened in 1887.[81] The Wigmore Harriers, for cross-country running, were established in 1885 and had their headquarters at Jack Straw's Castle in 1925.[82] The Hampstead Harriers were founded in 1890.[83]

Belsize and Hampstead were among the county's ten leading rugby football clubs which declined to join the new Football Association in 1863.[84] The

[59] Thompson, *Hampstead*, 243, 348–9; Stanford, *Libr. Map of Lond.* (1862 edn. with additions to 1865), sheet 6; ibid. (1891 edn.), sheet 6; above, growth, Chalcots.
[60] *Cricket and Lawn Tennis Clubs Dir.* (1890–1); Thompson, *Hampstead*, 348–9.
[61] Monro, *Hampstead C.C.* 2–4; Stanford, *Libr. Map of Lond.* (1862 edn. with additions to 1865), sheet 6.
[62] An older St. John's Wood club had amalgamated with the M.C.C.: Monro, *Hampstead C.C.* 13.
[63] Ibid. 7–8, 11.   [64] *H.H.E.* 12 June 1880.
[65] Baines, *Rec. Hampstead*, 297.
[66] Monro, *Hampstead C.C.* 32, 138–9.
[67] *H.H.E.* 4, 18 May 1872; 13 May, 3 June 1876.
[68] Ibid. 20 Mar., 8 May, 17 July, 7 Aug. 1880.
[69] *Cricket and Lawn Tennis Clubs Dir.* (1890–1).
[70] S.C.L., H 796.358/Cricket.

[71] Potter, *Random Recollections*, 91.
[72] C. Greenhalgh, *Hampstead Hockey Club, 1894–1969* (1969), 1–3, 7, 20–24.
[73] Monro, *Hampstead C.C.* 29–30, 32.
[74] Wade, *W. Hampstead*, 66; inf. from club manager.
[75] *Official Guide to Hampstead* [1925].
[76] *Hampstead Blue Bk.* (1939); *Kelly's Dir. Hampstead and Childs Hill* (1930, 1939).
[77] *P.O. Dir. Lond. County Suburbs* (1925, 1930).
[78] *H.H.E.* 3 Jan. 1880; *Hampstead Social Rev.* Apr. 1905, 48.   [79] S.C.L., H 728.5/Load of Hay.
[80] *Images of Hampstead*, 137; Stanford, *Libr. Map of Lond.* (1862 edn. with additions to 1865), sheet 6.
[81] Below, pub. svces.
[82] *Official Guide to Hampstead* [1925].
[83] *V.C.H. Mdx.* ii. 302.   [84] Ibid. 277.

Rugby Football Union in 1875 included the Belsize club, with a ground 'at the back of Belsize Road' and dressing room at the Britannia, and Hampstead, with a ground near Heath Street and dressing room at the Roebuck.[85] Hampstead Wanderers rugby football club was established by 1895 and active in 1910.[86]

Hampstead football club originated in 1887 as the Crescent club, playing on fields near St. Mary's church. After moves to Neasden, north Paddington, Brondesbury, and Queen's Park, it first entered for the English Cup and played on Kensal Rise athletic ground, for the season of 1896–7. The name was changed to Hampstead Crescent in 1891 and, to proclaim itself the leading local club, which regularly fielded four teams, to Hampstead in 1897.[87] Hampstead Druids was started in 1892, playing on the old Eton and Middlesex cricket ground, then at Willesden, at Neasden, and from 1897–8 at Willesden Junction.[88] Both clubs were reported in *Hampstead Football News*, a monthly paper with unpaid contributors and distributed by members of the teams, from 1897 until 1899.[89]

Football was also played by an earlier Crescent club and South Hill Park club in 1876, both with grounds at Clapton and both apparently short lived.[90] Rosslyn Park played in 1880[91] and, as did a Haverstock team, in 1889.[92] Hampstead's 'old rivals', West Hampstead, had a new ground at Willesden Green in 1898.[93] Clubs active in 1910 included Hampstead, Hampstead Druids, both of them members of the Amateur Football Association, Kilburn, Kilburn Marlborough, Hampstead Corporation Athletic, Hampstead Grove, and West Hampstead.[94] Hampstead's ground was at Claremont Road, Cricklewood, in 1930.[95]

Skaters traditionally used ponds on the heath. A club formed in 1867 skated on Viaduct pond from *c.* 1876 until *c.* 1890, when it moved to a private pond near the Spaniards.[96] Whitestone pond, the most easily frozen, was often used when other ponds were patrolled as unsafe.[97]

Belsize skating rink, partly covered and with a refreshment room, was opened in Lancaster Road (later Grove), Belsize Park, by Stanley and Walter Bird in 1876, but temporarily closed because of litigation over the use of patented skates.[98] Hampstead skating rink, on the west side of Finchley Road at Swiss Cottage, was opened soon afterwards.[99] Both rinks were refused music and dancing licences, on the grounds that they might be turned into music

halls.[1] The first apparently was short lived. The second in 1882 was to be rebuilt as a clubhouse, adjoining shops along Finchley Road and with a rink behind. It also offered lawn tennis, since the lessee P. R. Conron complained of courts on the nearby grounds of Hampstead cricket club. The site of the Swiss Cottage rink was taken in 1887 for the municipal baths.[2]

Roller skating was newly popular in 1910, when Hampstead Roller Skating Pavilion ended its first season at the council's Finchley Road baths and Hampstead Palace roller skating club, with a rink in a former tram depot in Cressy Road, held its first annual dinner.[3] The Cressy Road rink was placed under a freshly formed Hampstead skating club in 1911, when the rival establishments continued to advertise.[4]

A cycling club, the Clarence, was described as the oldest of its kind in Hampstead in 1890, when the Pegasus cycling club was formed and when there was a Belsize tricycle club[5] which dated from 1882.[6] Hampstead cycling club held its third annual dinner in 1895.[7] The Clarence and the Pegasus had their headquarters at the Railway hotel, West End, and the Red Lion, Kilburn High Road, in 1905, when there was also a Hampstead Freemasons' social and cycling club.[8]

Hampstead golf club was established in 1893. It was leased a nine-hole course at Winnington Road, Finchley, which it later extended and bought and where it remained in 1986. A clubhouse was burnt down in 1929 and replaced in 1933.[9] Hampstead school of golf, which also had a tennis ground, was in Harben Road in 1939.[10]

Open-air bathing, chiefly in the fourth or most northerly of the Hampstead ponds, caused accidents and scandal.[11] Nearly 39,000 bathers were reported in 1875[12] and *c.* 1,600 a day in 1876, when the vestry asked the M.B.W. to ban them or make the pond safe.[13] The L.C.C. had recently deepened the pond and built a bathing shelter in 1894.[14] Women were allowed to use it, and also Parliament Hill (Highgate) pond, on one day a week by 1905; having been excluded from Parliament Hill, they could use it twice weekly in 1930, shortly before several days were assigned for mixed bathing.[15]

Other sports clubs included ones for swimming and badminton, at the Finchley Road baths, and for lacrosse, playing at Edgware, in 1914.[16] Squash courts were built by Hampstead cricket club in the

[85] *Football Calendar* (1875), 79, 83.
[86] 16th ann. dinner: *H.H.E.* 29 Jan. 1910, 7.
[87] *Hampstead Football News*, 1 Jan. 1898, 4; 1 Mar. 1898, 3.
[88] Ibid. 1 Nov. 1898, 9.
[89] Ibid. 1 Nov. 1898, 12; *passim*.
[90] *H.H.E.* 1 Jan., 9 Dec. 1876.
[91] Ibid. 28 Feb. 1880.
[92] *Hampstead Record*, 19 Oct. 1889.
[93] *Hampstead Football News*, 1 Nov. 1898, 6.
[94] Cricket Press Ser. *Football Dir.* (1910–11).
[95] *H.H.E.* 27 Dec. 1930, 5.
[96] *Hampstead Year Bk.* (1888); Baines, *Rec. Hampstead*, 297.
[97] e.g. *H.H.E.* 5 Jan. 1895, 3*a*; 12 Jan. 1895, 3*a*.
[98] Ibid. 15 Jan., 1 Apr., 3 June 1876.
[99] Ibid. 25 Mar., 19 Aug. 1876.
[1] Ibid. 21 Oct. 1876.
[2] G.L.R.O., E/MW/H/67/1–18; *Hampstead and Highgate Dir.* (1886–7); Wade, *W. Hampstead*, 57. Bird's rink

was not the one in Finchley Rd., as stated in Thompson, *Hampstead*, 412.
[3] *H.H.E.* 23 Apr. 1910, 5; 4 June 1910, 6; D.S.R.
[4] *H.H.E.* 28 Jan. 1911, 7*a*, 7*f*; 15 Apr. 1911, 6*f*, 7*d*.
[5] *Hampstead Social Rev.* Mar. 1905; Baines, *Rec. Hampstead*, 298.
[6] *Hampstead Year Bk.* (1888).
[7] *H.H.E.* 9 Feb. 1895, 7*c*.
[8] *Hampstead Social Rev.* Apr. 1905, 43.
[9] *V.C.H. Mdx.* vi. 63, 74; *H.H.E.* 8 Mar. 1930, 6; inf. from Mr. R. L. Glover.
[10] *Kelly's Dir. Hampstead and Childs Hill* (1939).
[11] *The Times*, 24 July 1872, 10*c*.
[12] Vestry mins. 28 Oct. 1875.
[13] *H.H.E.* 10 June 1876.
[14] L.C.C. *Ann. Rep. 1893–4*, 72.
[15] L.C.C. *Lond. Statistics*, xvi. 149; xxxv. 143; xxxix. 160.
[16] Baines and Scarisbrook, *Local Guide and Almanac* (1914).

1920s.[17] Hampstead squash and rugby fives club opened c. 1933 at no. 81 Belsize Park Gardens, in purpose-built premises, with social facilities, which were taken over in 1967, 1983, and by Ragdale health club in 1985.[18] A bowling green was also maintained by Hampstead cricket club until 1939.[19] From 1880 Hampstead lawn billiards and skittle club played pell mell or lawn billiards, a game reputedly introduced from Flanders at the Restoration, at the Freemasons' Arms, which was reputed c. 1953 to have England's last surviving court.[20]

Military events took place in the 18th century on Hampstead Heath, as in 1716 when horsemen of the county militia mustered there[21] and in 1750 when new cannon were fired for practice.[22] A little known corps of light cavalry was formed at Hampstead under a captain who was commissioned in 1796, but apparently it trained with troops from other parishes rather than locally.[23] The earliest infantry corps, the Loyal Hampstead Association, was formed in 1798 under the engraver Josiah Boydell and disbanded in 1802. After a proposal that Hampstead, Marylebone, and Paddington should together furnish one division, Hampstead Loyal Volunteers were formed in 1803, again under Boydell. They numbered c. 500 men in 8 companies in 1807–8 and were disbanded in 1813.[24] Their target ground on East Heath by 1808 was used by companies from outside the parish, to the anger of residents.[25]

A new volunteer force was recruited in 1859, training in the paddock of J. Gurney Hoare's house, the Hill, and in the winter in the Holly Bush assembly rooms. It joined corps from Highgate and Hornsey to form the 2nd Administrative Battalion of the Middlesex Rifle Volunteers in 1860 and was officially entitled the 3rd Middlesex (Hampstead) Rifle Volunteers in 1862. The corps was enlarged to two companies in 1860 and, after drilling in different schoolrooms, took a lease of the former pump room and chapel in Well Walk in 1862. It was reduced to one company and a subdivision in 1864, having attracted little support in Kilburn, and failed to raise a detachment in Hendon in 1866. Popular shooting matches were held regularly at Childs Hill, where a range was opened in 1860, and the house next to the drill hall was taken as a club room in 1877. The Hampstead corps ended its separate existence in 1880, on becoming A and B companies (Hampstead Detachments) of the 3rd Middlesex Rifle Volunteers,[26] later the 1st and in 1908 the 7th Volunteer Battalion of the Duke of Cambridge's Own (Middlesex Regiment).[27] After the surrender of the drill hall for demolition in 1881 the Hampstead detachment had smaller premises in High Street, in 1886 suitable

only as a club.[28] A hall had been built in Holly Bush Vale by 1890 and was shared with the East Middlesex Militia, becoming the Everyman theatre in 1920.[29]

Hampstead monthly dinner club, the oldest of the primarily social clubs, was founded at the end of 1784. The diners, who contributed to a poor box, met at the Long Room in Well Walk, occasionally at the Red Lion or the Bull and Bush, and from 1807 in the new assembly rooms, where they were supplied by the landlord of the Holly Bush. Bets were sometimes laid and celebrations held to mark national events. Ballotting was introduced for members in 1788 and those elected in 1799 included the Lord Chancellor (Lord Loughborough), the Master of the Rolls (later Lord Alvanley), and Spencer Perceval. The last dinner, after the club had lost much of its prestige, was held in 1859.[30]

Hampstead Conversazione society met monthly during the winter at the assembly rooms from 1846 until 1872. In addition to lectures, it provided art exhibitions which for limited periods were open free to all residents.[31]

The Athenaeum club, which, despite its name, was social rather than literary, in 1877 occupied the hotel which had been built c. 1869 near the Vale of Health tavern.[32] The owner Henry Braun was convicted of selling alcohol without a licence in 1880, when he claimed that 1,200 'members' had been added during the past year.[33] Although the Salvation Army used part of the building in 1882, Braun remained in 1886. His establishment presumably continued as the Anglo-German club, with 500 English and 700 German members in 1908, when unlicensed sales were again reported, until the First World War.[34]

Philanthropic work was begun by the Philo-Investigists, a group of townsmen formed in 1781 for discussions 'to improve the understanding and mend the heart'. Funds were collected for charity, leading to the foundation in 1787 of a Sunday school, from which Hampstead parochial school was formed.[35]

An amicable society met at the King's Head in 1796.[36] Hampstead parochial benefit society, foreshadowed in suggestions published by the vestry in 1799, was established in 1802. Intended 'to place charity on the basis of industry', it was claimed to differ from all other benefit societies in being sustained by the chief inhabitants, who subscribed from 1 to 10 guineas a year and were called guardians, and by members who paid three classes of contributions.[37] A female friendly society had been established by 1814, offering similar sickness, death, and pension benefits.[38] It may have been absorbed into

[17] Monro, Hampstead C.C. 139.
[18] Inf. from Mr. Bill Ashford.
[19] Monro, Hampstead C.C. 139.
[20] H.H.E. 15 May 1880; Hampstead Past and Present [c. 1953]; Wade, More Streets, 17.   [21] S.C.L., card index.
[22] S.C.L., Hampstead Heath cuttings box.
[23] Hampstead Annual (1905–6), 42. See also E. T. Evans, Rec. of 3rd Mdx. Rifle Volunteers (1885), passim.
[24] Hampstead Annual (1905–6). 28–40; S.C.L., H 356.14/Volunteers.
[25] G.L.R.O., M/81/6 (mins. of mtgs. of copyholders), 18 July 1808 sqq.
[26] Hampstead Annual (1906–7), 41–57.
[27] V.C.H. Mdx. vi. 159.
[28] Hampstead and Highgate Dir. (1885–6); H.H.E. 4 Dec. 1886, 5d.

[29] Baines, Rec. Hampstead, 280; C.H.R. iii. 31; above.
[30] Hampstead Annual (1898), 127–35; Potter, Random Recollections, 56.
[31] Potter, Random Recollections, 56–7; H.H.E. Dir. and Almanac (1870).
[32] Above, growth, Vale of Health; below, econ., ind.
[33] Bentwich, Vale of Health, 68–70, 72; S.C.L., H 367/ Athenaeum.
[34] Below, prot. nonconf.; Bentwich, Vale of Health, 73–5, 83.
[35] Park, Hampstead, 290–1; below, educ.
[36] P.R.O., FS 2/7/800.
[37] Park, Hampstead, 295–9. The soc. had earlier been described by Thos. Goodwin, its physician, in Account of Neutral Saline Waters (1803), 103–11.
[38] Park, Hampstead, 299.

the older society, which met at the assembly rooms in 1844.[39] Hampstead benevolent society, which apparently superseded the benefit society, may have been a separate foundation. In 1848, in its nineteenth report, the benevolent society recorded that it had relieved 846 applicants during the year; all relief was in kind, in the form of food, sheets or blankets, and weekly orders to tradesmen for food or fuel.[40] The society, which urged Sunday worship on recipients, survived in 1854 and was presumably the benefit society which met at the Flask in 1863 and was dissolved in 1869.[41] Hampstead Charity Organization society was established in 1868, to co-ordinate relief work, and later helped to secure municipal grants. It was renamed in 1907, when there were 56 associated agencies, and in 1938. Its successor, Camden Council of Social Service, staffed citizens' advice bureaux in 1985.[42]

Hampstead Bible society, auxiliary to the British and Foreign Bible Society, was founded in 1816. It had William Wilberforce as vice-president from 1826 and still flourished in 1890.[43] A local branch of the Church Missionary Association was founded in 1829 and one for the Society for the Propagation of the Gospel in Foreign Parts in 1845.[44] Hampstead Temperance society had well attended meetings in 1872[45] and Hampstead Vigilance society, to promote public morality, existed by 1888.[46]

Mutual aid associations spread, some being branches of national bodies. The Independent Order of Odd Fellows established their first lodge, at the Flask, in 1830, the Freemasons had a lodge from 1853, and the Ancient Order of Foresters a court from 1858.[47] Hampstead savings bank was opened in 1848 and had 677 depositors by 1854.[48] It was presumably the penny bank at no. 1 Wells Buildings, High Street, in 1885.[49] The South End provident society, at the White Bear, and the Gardeners' philanthropic society were both established in 1849.[50] Many other friendly societies met in public houses: the United Brothers, Birmingham, and the St. John's Wood and Kilburn Provident Investment society were both recorded in 1845,[51] the Friends of Labour loan society in 1861,[52] with branches for Kilburn in 1864 and Maitland Park in 1866, and four more loan or building societies for Kilburn and branches of the Star Bowkett building society between 1864 and 1867.[53] Hampstead working men's club opened at a reading room in the New Buildings in 1872[54] and South Hampstead working men's club was in Fleet Road by 1880.[55]

A subscription library opened as Hampstead public library of general literature and elementary science in 1833 in Flask Walk, whence it moved in 1840 to no. 91 High Street. Its first committee included several Unitarians and there were eminent shareholders, but support declined in the 1840s with competition from the circulating libraries. The books, from which controversial works were excluded, were moved to an existing reading room in Heath Street in 1849 and came near to being sold after failures to revive support in 1872 and 1877. A new committee introduced graduated subscriptions, took rooms at Cavendish House, High Street, in 1882, and, as membership rose, obtained a lease of Green Hill House, renamed Stanfield House, at the corner of Prince Arthur Road, in 1885. Free lending started in 1887[56] and the library and reading rooms were opened free on Sundays in 1889, when lecture rooms were also available.[57] As Hampstead public or sub-scriptional library and literary institution, it thus was a forerunner of the municipal libraries opened in the 1890s.[58] It survived at Stanfield House until 1966, when the Christian Scientists, who had had reading rooms there since 1953, took over the building.[59]

Mid 19th-century Hampstead was not noted for its public intellectual and artistic life. Residents were accused in 1874 of failing to maintain a literary and scientific institution, presumably in reference to the vicissitudes of the subscription library, and to support any private venture to amuse or instruct them.[60] More energy was spent on such practical aims as holding down the rates[61] or restricting the spread of building. The Commons Preservation Society, whose agitation led to the Metropolitan Commons Act, 1866, included among its original members Gurney Hoare and Philip Le Breton, the two leading campaigners to save the heath.[62] A local cultural group, the Kyrle society, appointed a sub-committee to safeguard the heath, although a permanent Hampstead Heath Protection society was not formed until 1897.[63] An amateur musical society met at private houses in 1876.[64]

Activities multiplied in the 1880s. Hampstead choral society gave its first classical season in 1879[65] and Hampstead vocal society performed by 1890.[66] Hampstead musical club entertained at Jack Straw's Castle, Hampstead string band at dances in the drill hall,[67] and Rosslyn Hill brass band, founded as early as 1866, on summer Saturday evenings on the heath.[68] Hampstead Conservatoire of Music and

[39] G.L.R.O., MC/R 2, f. 12.
[40] S.C.L., H 361/Benevolent Soc.
[41] *Shaw's Hampstead Dir. and Almanack* (1854); *Hampstead Almanack* (1863); P.R.O., FS 2/7/2668.
[42] R. Colville, *Northern Heights* (1951), 70–1; *Bk. of Hampstead*, 18–19.
[43] Baines, *Rec. Hampstead*, 295–6.
[44] *Hampstead Almanack* (1863).
[45] *H.H.E.* 20 Jan. 1872.
[46] *Hampstead Year Bk.* (1888); Baines, *Rec. Hampstead*, 295.
[47] *Hampstead Almanack* (1863); *H.H.E. Dir. and Almanac* (1870).
[48] *Shaw's Hampstead Dir. and Almanack* (1854).
[49] Hutchings and Crowsley, *Hampstead and Highgate Dir.* (1885–6).
[50] *Hampstead Almanack* (1863).
[51] G.L.R.O., MC/R 2, ff. 16, 73.
[52] Ibid. 3, f. 86.
[53] Ibid. 4, ff. 5, 12, 24–5, 53, 57, 65, 69, 73, 79.

[54] *H.H.E.* 23 Nov. 1872.
[55] Ibid. 10 Jan. 1880; *P.O. Dir. Lond. County Suburbs, North* (1898).
[56] *Hampstead Annual, 1898*, 22–9; *Hampstead Year Bk.* (1888).
[57] *Hampstead Record*, 12 Oct. 1889, advert.
[58] Thompson, *Hampstead*, 415–17; below, pub. svces.
[59] I. Norrie, *Hampstead, Short Guide* (1973), 29; below, prot. nonconf.
[60] Thompson, *Hampstead*, 411.   [61] Below.
[62] Thompson, *Hampstead*, 188–90; above, growth, Hampstead Heath.
[63] Thompson, *Hampstead*, 189; S.C.L., H 942/14 Newton cuttings bk. (large).
[64] *H.H.E.* 8 Apr. 1876.
[65] *Hampstead Record*, 21 Sept. 1889, advert.
[66] Baines, *Rec. Hampstead*, 295.
[67] *Hampstead Record*, 5 Oct., advert.; 26 Oct. 1889.
[68] *H.H.E.* 8 Aug. 1874, advert.; Baines, *Rec. Hampstead*, 295.

School of Art was founded in 1885 and promoted modern English composers in 1890. With Cecil Sharp as director from 1896 to 1905, it was used for lectures and concerts:[69] West Hampstead Choral and Orchestral society performed in 1900, for its ninth season, and Sharp gave his first lecture on folk song there in 1903.[70] By 1906 the conservatoire had been amalgamated with the London Academy of Music.[71] Hampstead Mandoline and Guitar orchestra was founded in 1904 and New West End (Hampstead) orchestra in 1905.[72]

Hampstead Dramatic society had its first season in 1879 and Hampstead Art society, exhibiting at the town hall, in 1894.[73] Hampstead Chess club existed by 1885, as did Belsize Chess club in 1888, and met at Stanfield House until the 1950s.[74]

Scholarly enthusiasm also grew. Hampstead Antiquarian and Historical society was founded in 1897 and first met, at the town hall, in 1898. Sir Walter Besant was president and the local historians Thomas Barrett and G. W. Potter were members.[75] Publication of learned articles in the society's *Transactions* from 1898 to 1904–5 and more literary ones in its *Hampstead Annual* from 1897 to 1905–6 quickly made Hampstead appear superior to other suburbs in the richness of its historical associations.[76] Hampstead Astronomical and Scientific society was founded in 1899, having been given a telescope which it placed on a site on East Heath granted by the L.C.C.[77] The society, which met at Stanfield House, was divided into astronomical, photographic, and natural history sections. It opened an observatory and meteorological station on top of the covered reservoir near the summit of the heath in 1909.[78] The shorter lived Hampstead Selborne and Archaeological society also met at Stanfield House by 1910.[79]

Debating and political societies were formed, in addition to such pressure groups as the ratepayers' association and committees to protect amenities.[80] A meeting chaired by the vicar resolved that a local Conservative association was to be set up in 1835, with Viscount Stormont as president and Sir Thomas Maryon Wilson among its vice-presidents. Although probably abortive or short lived, it was claimed as a forerunner of the later Conservative association.[81] The Sylvan Debating club held an annual dinner in 1872.[82] Hampstead Parliamentary Debating society was founded in 1883 and met weekly during the winter at the vestry hall until 1888, with 500 or more members. The society was moribund, for lack of a Conservative opposition, in 1890 but revived in 1891 as the Hampstead Parliament, which reproduced the procedure of the House of Commons.[83] It met at the blind school, Swiss Cottage, in 1910 and 1939 and,[84] as 'the oldest local parliament in the kingdom', at the town hall c. 1953, shortly before its dissolution.[85]

Hampstead Constitutional club opened in the former assembly rooms in Holly Bush Hill in 1886.[86] It was founded by Conservatives of Town ward to combine social entertainment with politics and in 1898, with over 400 members, was 'what a really militant Unionist club should be'.[87] The premises were sold in 1928, with the adjoining inn, and converted into the private Romney House.[88] Kilburn and West Hampstead Constitutional club, at the corner of Kingsgate and Dynham roads, was planned in 1886 and open by 1888.[89] The Conservative association was at no. 4 College Villas (later no. 36 College Crescent) by 1888, with a habitation of the Primrose League, and remained there in 1986.[90]

Hampstead Liberal association in 1880 was formally separated from a branch of the Middlesex Liberal Association which had also served Willesden.[91] Hampstead Liberal club was also formed in 1880, at no. 13 High Street,[92] and was at no. 1 Downshire Hill in 1885, no. 31 High Street in 1888, and no. 24 Heath Street from 1889.[93] Hampstead Liberal and Radical association, a recent amalgamation of separate bodies in 1886,[94] met at no. 9 Swiss Terrace in 1890.[95] The Liberal union was at no. 16 Upper Park Road and Kilburn Liberal club, largely social, in Belsize Road by 1888, when the Social Progressive club, 'a socialist organization', had rooms at no. 2 Perrin's Court.[96] Lectures at Oriel hall, Heath Street, were organized by the local branch of the Fabian Society in 1908.[97] Hampstead Liberal association and Hampstead Labour party, both of which had several later changes of address, were in Heath Street and Mill Lane respectively in 1925.[98]

In 1925 it was claimed that no other part of London was so intensely organized as Hampstead for intellectual and social clubs.[99] They so multiplied that by 1952 there were 9 roughly classified as general or literary, including Hampstead Parliament and the subscription library. Five more were devoted to art or films, 8 to ballet or drama, 12 to music, 13 to politics, and at least 26 to sports. Among over 60 others were Hampstead Scientific society, with its

[69] Wade, *More Streets*, 61; *The Times*, 23 May 1890, 5c; M. Karpeles, *Cecil Sharp* (1967), 21–2.
[70] *St. John's Wood, Kilburn, and Hampstead Advertiser*, 22 Feb. 1900, 5d; Karpeles, *Cecil Sharp*, 46.
[71] *The Times*, 21 Dec. 1906, 9f.
[72] *H.H.E.* 30 Apr. 1910, 3; 19 Apr. 1930, 5.
[73] Ibid. 5 Mar. 1910, 5; 21 May 1910, 4; Baines and Scarisbrook, *Local Guide and Almanac* (1914).
[74] *H.H.E.* 30 Apr. 1910, 5; *Hampstead Year Bk.* (1888); *Hampstead Past and Present* [c. 1953].
[75] *Hampstead Annual, 1898*, 136–9; *Images of Hampstead*, 18.
[76] *Bk. of Hampstead*, 173–4; *Home Counties Mag.* i. 271.
[77] *Hampstead Annual, 1899*, 113–14.
[78] Baines and Scarisbrook, *Local Guide and Almanac* (1914); *H.H.E.* 1 Jan. 1910, 3; 19 Mar. 1910, 5.
[79] *H.H.E.* 22 Jan. 1910, 5.
[80] e.g. groups to oppose tramways: above, communications.
[81] *H.H.E.* 26 Jan. 1895, 5e, 7d.
[82] Ibid. 23 Nov. 1872.

[83] Baines, *Rec. Hampstead*, 285–6; Baines and Scarisbrook, *Local Guide and Almanac* (1914).
[84] *H.H.E.* 12 Feb. 1910, 3; *Hampstead Blue Bk.* (1939).
[85] *Hampstead Past and Present* [c. 1953]; *Bk. of Hampstead*, 19.
[86] *H.H.E.* 18 Dec. 1886, 5c.
[87] Baines, *Rec. Hampstead*, 297; S.C.L., H 363/Constitutional club.
[88] S.C.L., H 728.5/Holly Bush.
[89] *H.H.E.* 4 Dec. 1886, 5d; *Hampstead Year Bk.* (1888).
[90] *Hampstead Year Bk.* (1888); *P.O. Dir. Lond.* (1900 and later edns.).
[91] *H.H.E.* 26 June 1880.
[92] Ibid. 29 May, 12 June 1880; 26 June 1886, 3a.
[93] *Hampstead and Highgate Dir.* (1885–6); *Hampstead Year Bk.* (1888); datestone.
[94] *H.H.E.* 26 June 1886, 3c.
[95] Baines, *Rec. Hampstead*, 295.
[96] Ibid.; *Hampstead Year Bk.* (1888).
[97] *H.H.E.* 19 Mar. 1908, 6a.
[98] *Official Guide to Hampstead* [1925 and later edns.].
[99] Ibid. [1925].

observatory, Hampstead Heath and Old Hampstead Protection society, and many branches of national organizations.[1] Lectures and exhibitions were held in 1953 by Hampstead Artists' council, founded in 1944, and Hampstead Literary circle, while many societies formed a federation called Music and Arts in Hampstead, through which they received municipal sponsorship.[2]

More recent organizations included the Hampstead Historical society, followed by the Camden History society, which was founded in 1970 with help from Camden L.B. and which published the annual *Camden History Review* from 1973.[3] Camden Arts centre, with an exhibition gallery and teaching centre, was opened by the council in Arkwright Road after the central library's move to Swiss Cottage.[4] It housed Hampstead Artists' council, Camden Arts trust, and Arkwright Arts trust in 1986.[5] Local preservation or welfare groups, with constitutions dating from the 1970s, included the Vale of Health society and the Adelaide, Boundary, Hampstead, Primrose Hill, and West Hampstead community associations in 1986.[6]

The weekly *Hampstead and Highgate Express* was founded at Hampstead in 1860.[7] Known as the 'Ham and High' and vigorously independent, it was edited for *c.* 35 years from 1862 by George Jealous, whose neighbour's schoolboy son Alfred Harmsworth, later Viscount Northcliffe, wrote for the newspaper *c.* 1880.[8] Ownership passed to trustees in the 1930s, then to the Goss family, and in 1964 from Arthur Norman Goss to Home Counties Newspapers, of Luton. For many years the paper was produced at Hampstead's only printing works in the former Baptist chapel, Holly Bush Hill. The staff moved in 1961 to new offices in Perrin's Court, where, although printing was done at Luton, it remained in 1986.[9]

The weekly *Hampstead Record*[10] in its opening leader in 1889 pointed out that the only established local newspaper was shared with another district[11] but itself was renamed the *Hampstead and Highgate Record and Chronicle* in 1918 and the *Camden and Hampstead and Highgate Record and Chronicle* in 1963, before incorporation with the *Hackney Gazette*. Parts of Hampstead were covered from 1868 by the *Kilburn Times*, still published from Kilburn Lane, Willesden, in 1986, and from 1880 by the *South Hampstead Advertiser*, which continued under different titles, including *St. John's Wood, Kilburn, and Hampstead Advertiser* and *Hampstead News*, until its incorporation with the *Camden Journal* in

1971. Shorter lived newspapers included the *Kilburn News* from 1882 to 1883, the *Kilburn Post* and its successor the *Post* from 1886 to 1901, and the *Hampstead Gazette* in the 1920s and 1930s.

MANOR AND OTHER ESTATES. In a charter of *c.* 974 King Edgar (d. 975) granted 5 hides (*cassati*) in Hampstead, defined by their boundaries, to his faithful servant Mangoda for life.[12] None of the Westminster charters is quite what it purports to be. The so-called charter of 986 recording the grant to the abbey of the same 5 hides (*mansiunculae*) by King Æthelred the Unready (d. 1016) before 986, while not in itself a genuine charter, was a record made at Westminster during the grantor's lifetime.[13] The charters of confirmation, by Æthelred in 998 and by Edward the Confessor in 1065 and 1066, are generally agreed to be spurious, the last two probably the work of Prior Osbert de Clare before 1139. Nevertheless a genuine grant almost certainly lay behind the fabrications[14] and by 1086 Westminster abbey held the manor of *HAMPSTEAD* as 5 hides.[15]

Henry I (in 1133) and Stephen confirmed a grant by Westminster to Richard de Balta of 'land of the fee of Westminster of Hampstead' for rent of £2 a year and Abbot William de Humez (1214–22) assigned the £2 rent 'from the manor of Hampstead' to the abbey's kitchen.[16] It is not clear whether the grant was of the whole manor or of an estate within it, similar to the 1 hide held under the abbey by Ranulf Peverell in 1086.[17] During the reign of Henry II, however, the whole manor seems to have passed into the hands of Alexander de Barentyn,[18] the king's butler and kinsman of Richard Ilchester, bishop of Winchester, pluralist, and supporter of the king, who was associated with Barentyn's acquisition of property belonging to other religious houses.[19] Barentyn had been succeeded by 1203 by his son Richard, who died in debt soon after 1210[20] leaving his estates in confusion and probably fragmented. His brother Thomas had to surrender his estate at Yeoveney[21] and it may have been as a result of that transaction that Ralph of Yeoveney was the lord of 1½ virgate in Hampstead held of him by Constantine son of Alulf in 1222–3[22] and of 50 a. held of him by Alice of Westminster in 1225.[23] Most of the estate passed to Richard de Barentyn's niece (*neptem*) and heir Sibyl and her husband Andrew de Grendon,[24] who in the 1220s and 1230s held a messuage and 2

[1] S.C.L., H 062/Societies (duplicated list, spring 1952). Lists also exist for 1959–61.
[2] *Hampstead Past and Present* [*c.* 1953]; *Bk. of Hampstead*, 19.
[3] *Images of Hampstead*, 20.
[4] Norrie, *Hampstead, Short Guide*, 13.
[5] Inf. from Camden Arts Centre.
[6] Char. Com. files.
[7] *Willing's Press Guide* (1896). The earliest surviving copies of *H.H.E.* are 1872.
[8] *Bk. of Hampstead*, 109; *D.N.B.*; *H.H.E.* 21 Aug. 1880.
[9] *Bk. of Hampstead*, 108–9.
[10] Para. based on B.L. Newspaper Cat.; *Willing's Press Guide* (1896 and later edns.).
[11] *Hampstead Record*, 21 Sept. 1889.
[12] The charter is dated 978: P. H. Sawyer, *A.-S. Charters* (1968), p. 256, no. 805; M. Gelling, *Early Charters of Thames Valley* (1979), p. 111, no. 226.
[13] B.L. Stowe Ch. 33; *O.S. Facsimiles*, iii. 34; inf. from

Dr. P. Chaplais, who believes the document was written by the scribe of W.A.M. X and of the Bosworth Psalter. Cf. *A.-S. Eng.* ii (1973), 173–87.
[14] Sawyer, *A.-S. Charters*, no. 894; pp. 310–11, no. 1043; p. 407, no. 1450; Gelling, *Early Charters*, pp. 112–14, 117, nos. 229, 231, 241–3; Harvey, *Westm. Abbey*, 22.
[15] *V.C.H. Mdx.* i. 122, nos. 38–9.
[16] Westm. Domesday, f. 120v.; *Reg. Regum Anglo-Norm.* ii. 262, no. 1758.
[17] *V.C.H. Mdx.* i. 122.
[18] Below, other est. (Chalcots).
[19] W.A.M. 659–60. For Ilchester see *D.N.B.*; D. Knowles, *Episcopal Colleagues of Thos. Becket*, 38, 92 n., 134.
[20] *Cur. Reg. R.* iii. 11, 111; *V.C.H. Suss.* iv. 192–3.
[21] Barratt, *Annals*, i. 27–8.
[22] *Rot. Litt. Claus.* (Rec. Com.), i. 562b.
[23] *Cur. Reg. R.* xii. 167.
[24] *Cal. Close*, 1227–31, 267.

carucates as two-thirds of a 3-carucate holding. The other third was held in 1231–2 by Joscelin of Chichester and his wife Aubrey, possibly the aunt who inherited Thomas de Barentyn's estate in West Stoke (Sussex).[25] In 1230 Gilbert of Hendon, tenant of the neighbouring manor of Hendon, unsuccessfully challenged Andrew and Sibyl de Grendon's title.[26]

In 1231–2 the abbot of Westminster was content merely to register his claim to the 3-carucate estate[27] but Abbot Richard of Crokesley (1246–58) made a more determined effort. He sued Andrew de Grendon in 1253 for his messuage and 2 carucates,[28] presumably successfully because when he instituted his anniversary in 1256 and endowed it with the rents and profits of the manors of Hampstead and West Stoke (another Barentyn acquisition) he asserted that he had acquired them by his own efforts.[29] In 1267, in response to a plea by the abbey that the anniversary imposed an unfair burden on it, the pope reduced the endowment to £6 13s. 4d. from the issues of Hampstead manor,[30] comparable to a year's assized rents.[31] It is unlikely that Abbot Crokesley succeeded in regaining all the abbey's rights in Hampstead, for two undated charters made grants in free alms to the abbey of a grove and the lands and services of several tenants, including the Knights Templars, and it was not until the abbacy of Crokesley's successor Richard of Ware (1258–83) and probably after 1275 that Robert le Baud quitclaimed all right in the manor and vill of Hampstead.[32] The abbey administered the manor directly from 1259[33] and, although it continued to make grants at farm,[34] it did not again lose its rents.

Following the surrender of the abbey in 1540, Hampstead manor formed part of the endowment made by the Crown to the new bishopric of Westminster.[35] When the bishopric was dissolved in 1550 its estates reverted to the Crown, which granted Hampstead manor, together with Northolt and Down Barns, to Sir Thomas Wroth (d. 1573) of Durants, Enfield, gentleman of the Privy Chamber.[36] The manor descended[37] to Sir Thomas's son, Sir Robert (d. 1606), and Sir Robert's son, Sir Robert, who died in 1614 leaving the manor to his brother and other trustees, each called John Wroth, to sell to discharge his debts and legacies. In 1620 they sold it to Sir Baptist Hicks, moneylender to the king and London mercer, who became Viscount Campden (d. 1629) and whose heir was his daughter Juliana. Her husband, Sir Edward Noel, Viscount Campden (d. 1643), was a royalist, as was his son and successor Baptist (d. 1682), who had compounded for his estates in 1646. The manor descended to his son Edward (d. 1689), created earl of Gainsborough, and to Edward's son Wriothesley Baptist, who died without issue in 1690. The title and estate passed to a cousin Baptist Noel (d. 1714), who sold Hampstead manor in 1707[38] to Sir William Langhorne (d. 1715) of Charlton (Kent), a former governor of Madras and wealthy East India merchant. Under Langhorne's will the manor passed to his nephew William Langhorne Games (d. 1732) with 14 remainders.[39] After Games's death the manor passed to the 14th tenant in tail, Margaret (d. 1745), widow of Joseph Maryon and a Langhorne descendant. Her son John Maryon (d. 1760) devised the manor to his niece Margaretta Maria (d. 1777), widow of John Weller, and then to her daughter Jane (d. 1818), wife of General Sir Thomas Spencer Wilson, Bt. (d. 1798). Their son Sir Thomas Maryon Wilson (d. 1821) left the manor for life to his son, also Sir Thomas Maryon Wilson (d. without issue 1869) with remainder to a younger son, Sir John Maryon Wilson (d. 1876). It descended to Sir John's son, Sir Spencer Maryon Wilson (d. 1897) and to his son, Sir Spencer Pocklington Maryon Maryon-Wilson (d. 1944), in whose lifetime the manorial rights lapsed.[40] The demesne lands were inherited by his brother, the Revd. Canon Sir George Percy Maryon-Wilson (d. 1965), who was succeeded by his cousin, Sir Hubert Guy Maryon Maryon-Wilson, with whose death in 1978 the baronetcy became extinct. The estate passed to Shane Hugh Maryon Gough, Viscount Gough, grandson of Sir S. P. M. Maryon-Wilson.[41]

Small pieces on the edge of the demesne were sold off, mostly in the early 19th century.[42] In 1804 the northernmost part of the demesne lands east of the heath were sold to Lord Erskine[43] and by 1841 his successor, the earl of Mansfield, owned 20 a. of former demesne land there as an extension of his Kenwood estate.[44] In 1804 Church field (2½ a.) at Frognal, on the eastern border of the main block of demesne lands, was sold to the trustees of the will of Richard Arden, Lord Alvanley.[45] In 1807 Thomas Neave, later Sir Thomas Neave, Bt., purchased 4. a. of demesne land on the western edge of the heath.[46] Further sales were prevented until 1869 under the terms of the will of Sir Thomas Maryon Wilson (d. 1821) and even when the death of the second Sir Thomas in 1869 released the land, little was sold. Some building plots at Fitzjohn's Avenue were offered for sale in 1875 but most of the estate was developed on building leases. The largest portion sold was East Heath Park (56 a.), which in 1889 was

[25] Cur. Reg. R. xi. 98; xvi. 175; P.R.O., CP 25(1)/146/8/98; V.C.H. Suss. iv. 192–3.
[26] Cal. Close, 1227–31, 334, 559; P.R.O., CP 25(1)/146/8/98.
[27] P.R.O., CP 25(1)/146/8/98.
[28] Cal. Close, 1251–3, 442.
[29] Westm. Domesday, ff. 115v.–17.
[30] Ibid. ff. 116v.–18; Harvey, Westm. Abbey, 391.
[31] e.g. £6 11s. 6d. in 1259: W.A.M. 32360.
[32] Westm. Domesday, f. 115 and v. The grants were made to 'Abbot Ric.'. Le Baud may have been a descendant of Ric. de Balta: see above. For the dating after 1275, below, other est., Temple.   [33] W.A.M. 32360, 32399.
[34] e.g. 1289: Westm. Domesday, f. 119v.
[35] L. & P. Hen VIII, xv, p. 24; xvi, pp. 242–4.
[36] Cal. Pat. 1550–3, 6; V.C.H. Lond. 447; V.C.H. Mdx. iv. 114; P.R.O., E 305/G/22.

[37] Para. based on Barratt, Annals, i. 64–5, 111–26; fam. tree by Mrs. G. E. Gosling in S.C.L., H 333.3 Manor of Hampstead.
[38] P.R.O., CP 25(2)/946/6 Anne East.
[39] S.C.L., D 8.
[40] Burke, Peerage and Baronetage (1949).
[41] Debrett, Peerage and Baronetage (1976, 1980); Who's Who (1983); H.H.E. 24 June 1966.
[42] For the topography of the demesne, below, econ. and map of manor and est.
[43] G.L.R.O., E/MW/H, old nos. 31/7 (sale 1804); 31/8 (lease 1806).
[44] P.R.O., IR 29/21/24, nos. 2–4.
[45] M.L.R. 1806/2/484–5; G.L.R.O., E/MW/H, old no. 27/15 (sales parts. 1843).
[46] G.L.R.O., E/MW/H, old no. 31/7 (sale 1807); S.C.L., D53; Thompson, Hampstead, 128–9.

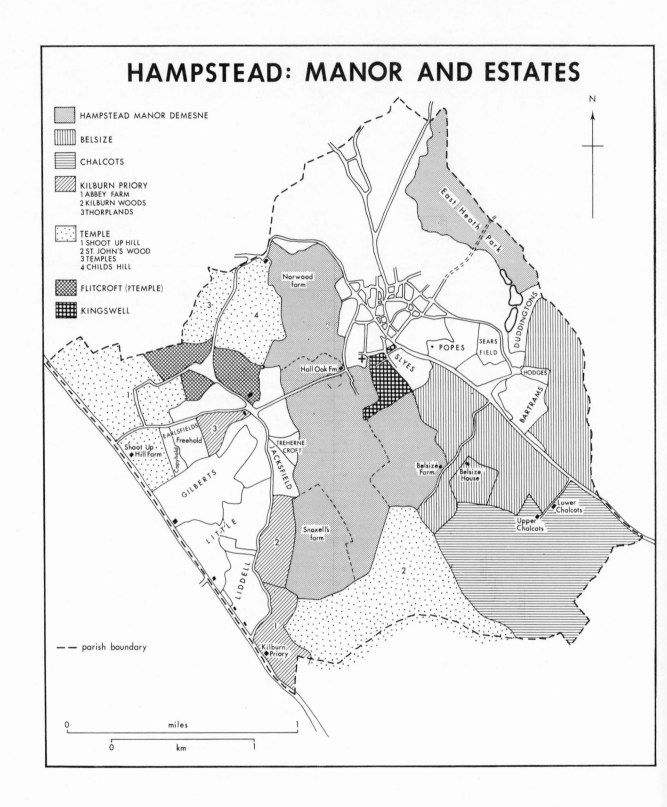

HAMPSTEAD: MANOR AND ESTATES

N

HAMPSTEAD MANOR DEMESNE

BELSIZE

CHALCOTS

KILBURN PRIORY
1 ABBEY FARM
2 KILBURN WOODS
3 THORPLANDS

TEMPLE
1 SHOOT UP HILL
2 ST. JOHN'S WOOD
3 TEMPLES
4 CHILDS HILL

FLITCROFT (?TEMPLE)

KINGSWELL

East Heath Park

Norwood farm

DUDDINGTONS

POPES

SEARS FIELD

Hall Oak Fm.

SLYES

HODGES

BARTRAMS

EARLSFIELDS
Freehold

TREHERNE CROFT

Shoot Up
Hill Farm

Copyhold

JACKSFIELD

Belsize
Farm.

Belsize
House

GILBERTS

Snoxell's
farm

Lower
Chalcots

Upper
Chalcots

LITTLE

LIDDELL

Kilburn
Priory

– – parish boundary

0   miles   1

0   km   1

added to the heath, already acquired by the M.B.W.[47] In 1972 some freeholds were sold to Bryston Property Group (London).[48]

A messuage formed part of the 3-carucate holding of Sibyl and Andrew de Grendon in 1231,[49] a kitchen and sheepcote were mentioned in 1259[50] and from 1272 to 1322 the grange buildings included an oxhouse, a sheepcote, a dairy, a cowhouse, a henhouse, and a granary, most of them of plaster and wattle.[51] A hall (*aula*), first mentioned in 1285,[52] was distinct from the grange and included a screens passage (1285) and a solar (1347).[53] The position of Hall Grove and Hall Field, first mentioned in 1379 and 1470 respectively,[54] suggests that the medieval hall was at Frognal and probably on the site of the later Hall Oak Farm, at the junction of Frognal and West End Lane.[55] It was called the 'manor place of Hampstead' in 1543–4[56] and Manor House or Hampstead Hall in 1619.[57] None of the post-Reformation owners lived at the manor house, which became a farmhouse, leased out with part of the demesne lands. The lessee subleased part of the house in 1674, when he was assessed for 6 hearths and his undertenant for 4.[58] The manorial buildings seem to have remained divided throughout the 18th century. In 1762 the farmhouse of what by then was called Hall Oak farm, formed, with a barn, two stables, a coach house, and a cowhouse, three sides of a yard on the north side of West End (later Frognal) Lane, with another barn on the south side. The western buildings were occupied by the largest demesne tenant, William Bovingdon, the eastern by Edward Snoxell.[59] The house, of which no illustration is known,[60] was described in the late 18th century as a low, ordinary building in farmhouse style but containing a very capacious hall,[61] which suggests that the medieval hall may have survived. Snoxell's eastern portion of the house and buildings had passed by 1774 to John Foster who converted them into two houses, later replaced by another house. Bovingdon's portion needed considerable repairs in 1783 and in 1785 it was leased with demesne farmland to Thomas Pool, who, before he renewed the lease in 1798, had begun erecting the Frognal houses on the site.[62]

The tithes of Hampstead went to the rector of Hendon until Hendon church was appropriated by the abbot and convent of Westminster in 1478.[63]

When the Crown granted Hampstead manor to the bishop of Westminster in 1541 the chapel and tithes of the parish were annexed, and successive lords of the manor were also impropriators of the great and small tithes. In 1650 part of the great tithes were let at £45 a year, the remainder being valued at £30 a year. The small tithes were valued at £10 a year and let to the incumbent.[64] In 1731 the lord let the tithes of corn, grain, and hay for 21 years at £30 a year, but excluded tithes payable from the demesne.[65] From 1784 Sir Thomas Spencer Wilson successfully sued occupiers of land in Kilburn, who claimed that the land as part of Kilburn priory was tithe-free like Belsize manor;[66] a modus of 2s. 6d. an acre was charged for the years 1764–8, and 4s. an acre thereafter.[67] Most occupiers of titheable lands paid a composition of 4s. an acre until 1786, when Wilson raised it to 5s.[68] The great tithes were commuted for £398 4s. in 1841, when there were said to be no small tithes payable for any lands in the parish. Sir Thomas Maryon Wilson was impropriator of the tithes of all the 1,739 a. titheable except for 5 a. held by Sir Thomas Neave, Bt.[69]

The so-called manor of Belassise, Belseys, or *BELSIZE*, whose name means 'beautifully sited', was first named in 1334–5,[70] but appears to have originated in the 1 hide of land of the *villani* which Ranulf Peverell held in Hampstead of the abbot of Westminster in 1086.[71] In 1259 there were 4 tenants 'of the hide' (*de Hyda*), one of whom was Gilbert le Kanep.[72] Since Gilbert was one of those whose services Robert le Baud granted to Abbot Richard,[73] it is probable that Robert was lord of the hide. About 1260 Robert granted a house, 40 a., and 1½ a. of wood for 6d. a year rent to William the linendraper.[74] By 1272 the abbey had regained possession of Gilbert's estate,[75] which in 1286 it leased to Gerin of St. Giles for 10s. a year.[76] Gerin was perhaps the same as Gerin or Gervin Linendraper, who had evidently succeeded William the linendraper by 1281 and in 1293 successfully defended his title to a house, 46 a. of land, and 2 a. of wood in Hampstead.[77] In 1296 Gerin of St. Giles also had the lease from John at Lofte of Agardesfield, on the eastern side of Haverstock Hill and later identifiable as part of Belsize,[78] and c. 1299 he conveyed a large estate to Luke of Hedham (or Stedham). Part of it appears to

[47] Thompson, *Hampstead*, 130, 165, 195, 317–18, 329–30; G.L.R.O., E/MW/H, old no. 27/15 (sales parts. 1875).
[48] *H.H.E.* 2 June 1972.
[49] P.R.O., CP 25(1)/146/8, no. 98.
[50] W.A.M. 32360.
[51] Ibid. 32367, 32393, 32396, 32384, 32397, 32375
[52] Ibid. 32384.
[53] Ibid. 32394, 32494.
[54] Ibid. 32500, 32356.
[55] Rocque, *Map of Lond.* (1741–5), sheet 12; S.C.L., Hampstead Man. Map and Fieldbk. nos. A, a.
[56] Act for repairing conduits of London, 35 Hen. VIII, c. 10: Park, *Hampstead*, 71–3.
[57] *Mdx. County Rec.* ii. 148.
[58] i.e. Benoni Honywood and Hen. Twyford: P.R.O., E 179/143/370, m. 43d.; G.L.R.O., Cal. Mdx. Sess. Bks. v (1673–7), pp. 41–2.
[59] S.C.L., Man. Map and Fieldbk. nos. A–E, a–e. There is a clearer sketch map of the site in S.C.L. 89.3, FROGNAL, Manor Ho. The 1762 survey wrongly names Thos. Bovenden as tenant. Wm. Bovingdon leased from 1757 the demesne together with the 'capital messuage or tenement . . . commonly called the Manor ho.' except the part occupied by Snoxell: G.L.R.O., E/MW/H, old no. 31/8 (lease 1757).

[60] *Images of Hampstead*, 52.
[61] Park, *Hampstead*, 125.
[62] Holborn Libr., Hampstead poor rate bks. 1774–1814; G.L.R.O., E/MW/H, old no. 33/16 (notes 1783–4); 31/8 (lease 1798). For Frognal hos., above, growth, Frognal.
[63] Below, churches.
[64] *Home Counties Mag.* i. 220.
[65] S.C.L., D 37.
[66] P.R.O., E 133/137/18, 24, 27; E 126/33, East. 25 Geo. III, no. 2.
[67] Ibid. E 126/33, Trin. 26 Geo. III, no. 5.
[68] Ibid. E 133/137/24.
[69] Ibid. IR 29/21/24.
[70] E. H. Pearce, *Monks of Westminster* (1916), 83.
[71] *V.C.H. Mdx.* i. 122–3.
[72] W.A.M. 32360.
[73] Westm. Domesday, f. 115 and v.
[74] P.R.O., CP 25(1)/147/21, no. 414.
[75] W.A.M. 32367.
[76] Westm. Domesday, ff. 119v.–120.
[77] W.A.M. 32361; Barratt, *Annals*, i. 30.
[78] W.A.M. 32359, 16475. Agnes at Lofte had been a tenant of le Baud's. 'Hagadesfeld' was in the hands of Westm. by 1272: Westm. Domesday, f. 115 and v.; W.A.M. 32367.

have passed to Martin de la Rokele, who in 1311–12 sold a house, a carucate, and 4 a. of wood to Roger le Brabazon, a judge.[79]

In 1312 Roger had two free tenements, a house and 40 a., held at a rent of 10s. 6d., and the tenement of John son of Gerin of St. Giles, which he held for John's life at 19s. a year rent and which reverted to Westminster at John's death.[80] On his deathbed in 1317 Roger granted to Westminster abbey a house and 57 a. which he held of the abbey at a rent of 10s. 6d. The grant was to endow a daily mass and anniversary for himself and Edmund, earl of Lancaster, and his wife Blanche.[81] In 1318 an estate was created for the prior of Westminster from all Brabazon's lands on condition that he found a chaplain and chantry to fulfil the obit, responsibility for which was placed on the 'church of St. Mary in the Fields', a possession of the prior of Westminster.[82] In 1360, in recognition of the considerable benefactions made to the abbey by the then prior, Nicholas of Litlington, his estate of Belsize was discharged from all rents and services due to Hampstead manor.[83]

Belsize absorbed land from other estates. East field, which in the 1290s was part of the demesne of Hampstead manor,[84] was leased to the prior in 1322[85] and 1347,[86] and by 1500 it was described as parcel of Belsize manor and identified as the block of land east of the London road.[87] A customary tenement belonging to John le Lord, who probably died in the Black Death, was by 1354 leased to the prior[88] and may be identifiable with Lord's meads, part of Belsize in 1650.[89]

Belsize, like Hampstead manor, was surrendered to the king on the dissolution of Westminster abbey in 1540[90] but it did not form part of the endowment of Westminster bishopric. In 1542 it was among the endowments of the newly constituted dean and chapter of Westminster,[91] confirmed by Elizabeth I in 1560 after being returned to the restored monastic chapter in 1556. It was from Elizabeth's charter, which established the dean and chapter as a corporation, that Westminster subsequently claimed its title.[92] In 1642 the royalist dean was driven out and the Cromwellian Col. Downes was said to have 'gotten possession' of the estate.[93] By Act in 1649 the rent from Belsize and other abbey estates was assigned to Westminster school.[94] In 1650 parliamentary trustees sold Belsize to Richard Mills and John Birdhall, citizens of London.[95] It was returned to the dean and chapter at the Restoration and remained with them until most of it was vested in the Church Commissioners in 1869 and the rest in 1888.[96] Some 20 a. were sold to Basil George Woodd in 1857,[97] 8 a. to Hampstead Junction Railway Co. in 1859,[98] 3½ a. to Thomas E. Gibb in 1880, and the freehold of the rest, mostly to the sitting tenants of individual houses, between 1948 and 1981, mostly in the 1950s.[99]

A 99-year lease of Belsize in 1549 by the dean and chapter to Richard Goodrich (Goodwike) was conveyed to Armagil Waad (Wade), clerk of the council, 'the English Columbus', and man of letters, in 1557.[1] Waad (d. 1568) bequeathed the lease to his son William (d. 1623),[2] also clerk of the council, lieutenant of the Tower, and diplomat, who was knighted in 1603. He left his property to his son James, a minor, subject to his widow's right of residence.[3] In 1633 James surrendered his interest to his mother Anne, who obtained a 21-year lease in 1634[4] and another in 1642 when she married Col. Thomas Bushell and mortgaged Belsize to raise money for the king's cause.[5] She died soon afterwards, possibly in 1643 when the undertenants were instructed to pay their rents to the Hampstead parliamentarian, Serjeant John Wilde.[6] In 1651 she was said to have 'passed away her whole interest' in the estate to her son-in-law John Holgate, who was listed as farmer of Belsize from c. 1644 to 1653 and who 'purchased the inheritance of the contractors'.[7]

In 1650 Armenigilda Mordaunt, daughter of Sir William and Anne Waad, occupied the house and some of the estate[8] but the dean and chapter rejected a request by Thomas Bushell for a renewal of the lease in 1660.[9] Instead they leased it in 1661 for 21 years to Daniel O'Neill, another royalist but one whose great wealth made him a more desirable tenant.[10] O'Neill (d. 1664) left the lease to his widow Katharine, who had been married twice before. When she died in 1667 she left Belsize to Charles Henry Kirkhoven, Lord Wotton, her son by her second husband, who obtained a lease for lives from the dean and chapter in 1667.[11] After Wotton's death without issue in 1683 Belsize passed to Philip Stanhope, earl of Chesterfield (d. 1714), Katharine's son by her first husband, who obtained a new lease in 1683.[12] Chesterfield's son, Philip, Lord Stanhope,

[79] P.R.O., CP 25(1)/148/36, no. 289; 149/41, no. 71.
[80] C.U.L., Kk. V. 29, f. 31v.; Cal. Pat. 1317–21, 220.
[81] Cal. Pat. 1313–17, 663; P.R.O., C 143/122, no. 11. For Brabazon D.N.B.
[82] Probably St. Martin-in-the-Fields: Cal. Pat. 1317–21, 220; Barratt, Annals, i. 30–2; below, churches.
[83] B.L. Cott. MS. Faust. A. iii, f. 341.
[84] W.A.M. 32381, 32374, 32403.
[85] Ibid. 32406.
[86] Ibid. 32494.
[87] Ibid. 16471.
[88] Ibid. 32495, 32357.
[89] P.R.O., C 54/3553, no. 33.
[90] Above.
[91] L. & P. Hen. VIII, xvii, pp. 391–6.
[92] Cal. Pat. 1555–7, 349; 1558–60, 397; W.A.M. 16527.
[93] P.R.O., C 54/3553, no. 33.
[94] C.J. vii. 59.
[95] W.A.M. 16618.
[96] Lond. Gaz. 13 Aug. 1869, pp. 4524–47; Eccl. Com. 42nd Rep. (1890), App. pt. II, p. 7. Belsize Ho. (Ct.) leased in 1861 to Mat. Forster was exempt in 1869.
[97] Ch. Com. Deed 240259.
[98] Ibid. 142580; file 45820, pt. 1 (letter 1872).
[99] Ibid. Survey CC 7, pp. 28–31, 445–58; Thompson, Hampstead, 356–7, 431–2.
[1] P.R.O., E 159/357, rot. 532; D.N.B. s.v. Waad. Following paras. based on Park, Hampstead, 137 sqq.; Barratt, Annals, i. 75–100, 137–8.
[2] P.R.O., PROB 11/52 (P.C.C. 6 Lyon).
[3] Ibid. 142 (P.C.C. 116 Swan).
[4] W.A.M. Lease bk. XIV, ff. 338v.–40.
[5] Cal. S.P. Dom. 1660–1, 246.
[6] C.J. iii. 142.
[7] Ibid. vii. 59; W.A.M. 42497; Barratt, Annals, iii. 359–64; below, St. John's Wood.
[8] P.R.O., C 54/3553, no. 33; Mdx. Pedigrees (Harl. Soc. lxv), 33.
[9] Cal. S.P. Dom. 1660–1, 246.
[10] W.A.M. Lease bk. XVI, f. 173; D.N.B.
[11] P.R.O., PROB 11/315 (P.C.C. 124 Bruce); W.A.M. Lease bk. XVIII, ff. 32v.–34. Thenceforth all leases were for lives.
[12] P.R.O., PROB 11/323 (P.C.C. 53 Carr); Complete Peerage, s.v. Chesterfield; W.A.M. Lease bk. XXI, f. 252.

renewed the lease in 1707[13] and again in 1715, as earl of Chesterfield.[14] His son, author of the *Letters*, was the owner from 1726 to 1773, renewing the lease in 1733, 1751, and 1769.[15] Trustees to whom he devised Belsize for his cousin and heir, Philip, obtained new leases in 1774 and 1786.[16]

In 1807 the earl of Chesterfield (d. 1815) obtained an Act to enable him to sell his interest in Belsize.[17] It was purchased by a syndicate of four, Thomas Roberts, who was already an undertenant of Belsize, James Abel, Thomas Forsyth, and Germain Lavie. They divided the estate into lots, kept the best parts, and sold the rest.[18] In 1808 the dean and chapter made nine separate leases,[19] still for lives and at the same rent, precisely divided. James Abel took three leases, of Belsize House and 45 a. surrounding it, of a house at Haverstock Hill and 19 a. (Hillfield), and of the Red Lion, another four houses, and 3 a.[20] Thomas Roberts took three leases, of Shelford Lodge (Rosslyn House) and 21 a., of three houses and 5 a. next to Haverstock Hill (Rosslyn Grove), and of a small timber farmhouse and 40 a. (South End farm).[21] Thomas Forsyth, of St. Marylebone, took one lease, of a house, three dilapidated tenements, and 45 a. south of South End farm (Haverstock Lodge).[22] Germain Lavie, who lived at West End, did not take a lease.[23] The two remaining leases were of five houses and 26 a. on either side of Belsize Lane, to George Todd, a Baltic merchant who was already an undertenant of the estate[24] and of three houses and 38 a. at the southern end of the estate, to Edward Bliss (d. 1844) of Tower Hill.[25]

James Abel disposed of his lease of the Red Lion and other houses, which in 1809 were divided among three lessees.[26] Abel (d. 1817) left his other property to his son-in-law Edward Harvey but in 1822 Hillfield was sold to William Francklin of Lincoln's Inn, the underlessee, to pay off James's debts. Francklin (d. 1826) left it to his sister Martha, who sold it in 1834 to John Wright, banker of Covent Garden, who mortgaged it in the same year to Catherine Blount. Wright & Co., a private bank, failed in 1840 and Hillfield (or Heathfield House) was sold by Catherine Blount in 1841 to Basil George Woodd, a wine merchant of New Bond Street, who was already an underlessee.[27] In 1857 Woodd obtained the freehold of Hillfield in exchange with the dean and chapter for the Belsize Court estate. On his death in 1872 Hillfield was inherited by Woodd's sons Basil Thomas and Robert Ballard (d. 1901) and the estate was not given over to the builders until the 1890s

and 1900s.[28]

In 1830 Edward Harvey sold the main Belsize House estate to the undertenant John Wright, with whose other property it was sold in 1841 to Sebastian Gonzalez Martinez, a wine merchant. He sold it in 1852 to Charles James Palmer, a Bloomsbury solicitor, who in 1855 exchanged the old lease for lives for a 99-year building lease. About 5½ a. on either side of the Avenue, the access road to Belsize House, was excluded from the lease to give the dean and chapter entrance to their other estates. Palmer had submitted a complete plan for building on the estate in 1853, but was in financial difficulties in 1855, and the dean and chapter converted the lease of the whole estate into separate 99-year leases for each house, as it was completed, to Palmer's nominee, usually the builder Daniel Tidey.[29]

Thomas Roberts sold Shelford Lodge (Rosslyn House) and 21 a., which the dean and chapter leased in 1816 to Lt.-Gen. Sir Moore Disney, the occupier. Disney sold the estate in 1823 to Henry Davidson (d. 1827), whose son, another Henry Davidson, a West India merchant, obtained a new lease in 1846.[30] Building started on the northern part of the estate in 1853. In 1859 Davidson sold Rosslyn House to Charles Henry Lardner Woodd, another of Basil George's sons, and further parts of the estate to him in 1863 and 1869, some 8 a. in all. In 1869 he sold the rest of the estate, 13 a. covered with houses, to W. J. Blake.[31]

Roberts renewed his lease of the Rosslyn Grove estate in 1816 and left it to his wife Mary for life with remainder to his daughters and grandson. In 1828, after his death, a new lease was made to James Campbell,[32] Roberts's son-in-law or grandson, who was still the owner in 1860.[33] The third lease, of South End farm, then called Holyland after the undertenant of 1808, was held by Roberts's daughter Sarah and her nephew, James Campbell, in 1859 when they conveyed their interest in 8 a. and the original farmhouse to Hampstead Junction Railway Co.[34] The lease of 1808 was not renewed and in 1872 the dean and chapter, discovering the reversion to them through the death in 1868 of the last surviving life, leased the remaining 32 a. to the occupier, Joseph Pickett, as a yearly tenant.[35] A building agreement to lease 15½ a. on a 99-year lease from 1878 was made to Pickett and Ashwell, and by 1880 other parts of the estate had been sold to the London school board and neighbours.[36]

Thomas Forsyth's lease passed, on his death in

---

[13] W.A.M. Lease bk. XXVII, f. 114.
[14] Ibid. XXIX, f. 80.
[15] Ibid. XXXIV, f. 573; XXXIX, ff. 184v.–186v.; XLIV, f. 313.
[16] Ibid. XLVI, f. 25; L, ff. 146–50; W.A.M. 16540; *Complete Peerage*, s.v. Chesterfield.
[17] Chesterfield Est. Act, 47 Geo. III, c. 58 (Local and Personal), copy in W.A.M. 16595.
[18] Thompson, *Hampstead*, 91.
[19] The preamble to the first lease says 8 leases but there are 9 extant: W.A.M. Lease bk. LVII, f. 65. For partics. and valuation made in 1808, for the 9 leases, see Ch. Com. Deed 146072.
[20] W.A.M. Lease bk. LVII, ff. 65–72v.
[21] Ibid. ff. 72v.–78.
[22] Ibid. ff. 82v.–84.
[23] Thompson, *Hampstead*, 91.
[24] W.A.M. Lease bk. LVII, ff. 78–80v.
[25] Ibid. ff. 80v.–82v.
[26] Ibid. ff. 116v.–122v.

[27] W.A.M., RCO 32 (abs. of title of B. G. Woodd); Thompson, *Hampstead*, 95; G.L.R.O., E/MW/H, old no. 27/15 (sales parts. of Belsize Pk. etc. 1841).
[28] Thompson, *Hampstead*, 287–8, 339–40; W.A.M., RCO 32 (agreement 1857); Ch. Com. Deed 240259; below for Belsize Ct.
[29] Ch. Com. Deed 142527; file 7143, pts. 1, 2; Thompson, *Hampstead*, 275, 283.
[30] W.A.M. Lease bks. LVIII, ff. 286–287v.; LXIV, ff. 259–61; Ch. Com. Deeds 142564–7; P.R.O., HO 107/1492/8/3.
[31] Thompson, *Hampstead*, 95, 292–3; Barratt, *Annals*, 249.
[32] Ch. Com. Deed 142556; W.A.M. Lease bk. LXI, ff. 79–81.
[33] Poor rate bk. 1860.
[34] Ch. Com. Deeds 142580, 146072.
[35] Ibid. 270200; file 45820, pt. 1; Map 13305; Survey CC 7, pp. 13–23; Thompson, *Hampstead*, 94, 351–3.
[36] Ch. Com. file 45820, pts. 1, 2.

1810, by will to his widow, Jane, who sold it in 1817 to John Lund (d. 1843), a warehouseman of Westminster, who built Haverstock Lodge there and in 1828 purchased 3 a. of adjoining copyhold. His son, William T. B. Lund, succeeded to the estate and in 1852 exchanged the lease for lives for a 99-year building lease and proceeded to develop the estate, which he called St. John's Park.[37]

By 1817, when he renewed his lease for life,[38] George Todd (d. 1829) had replaced an old mansion with a new one, Belsize Court (at first called Belsize House, although the main estate house still existed), which was sold with 10 a. in 1841 to Basil George Woodd and returned to the dean and chapter in 1857 as part of their exchange with Woodd. The dean and chapter let 4½ a. on a building agreement to Daniel Tidey in 1865 but Belsize Court, set in the remaining land, stayed a country seat until 1880. Todd's son, also George, sold the other 16 a. south of Belsize Lane, in 1835 to John Wright, and on Wright's bankruptcy in 1841 James Sharp Giles (d. 1854), underlessee of part of the estate, acquired the lease. Giles's son Peter sold it in 1862 to Richard Pierce Barker, who surrendered the lease for a building agreement in 1869.[39]

Edward Bliss, who made his wealth in Portugal and acquired considerable estates in England, renewed his lease of his 38-a. farm in 1812, 1837, and 1840.[40] Bliss (d. 1845) left his Belsize estate to trustees for his nephew Henry Aldridge, who took the surname Bliss and later the Portugese titles of Baron de Bliss and Baron Barreto. The trustees renewed the lease in 1848, and in 1854 the dean and chapter, having discovered that Edward Bliss had built houses on 14 a., made a new lease for the 24 a. not built on. In 1864 the chapter bought out the leasehold interest of the 24 a. and later made a regular building agreement for it. It was only in 1890 that the Ecclesiastical Commissioners bought out Barreto's interest in the 14 a.[41]

A house formed part of the Brabazon estate in 1312 and was conveyed with it to Westminster abbey in 1317.[42] It may have been built of brick on a much larger scale in 1496.[43] Although they subleased part of Belsize,[44] the Waads retained the house, set amid parkland. In 1568 the house contained 24 rooms, including the hall, long gallery, great chamber, and two counting houses.[45] In 1650 there were still remains of a moated site, a wooded park, and a walk[46] but the house had evidently suffered from the poverty of the royalists and depredations during the Commonwealth. The house and garden were 'built with vast expense' by Daniel

O'Neill (d. 1664); the house, which contained a fine gallery,[47] formed four sides around a courtyard. The east front, from which the north and south ranges projected, faced a brick court and was approached from the London road by a wooded avenue. A gravel walk along the west side may have been the remnant of a 'highway to St. John's Wood' that had been mentioned in 1650. The stabling and kitchen garden lay to the north and formal gardens to the south, at a lower level than the house and centred on a fountain; there was a cherry orchard to the west. The whole area, 25½ a., was enclosed by a brick wall.[48] O'Neill's building seems to have enlarged the house from 16 hearths to 36, though he died in the year that the assessment of 16 hearths was made.[49] It was a Dutch Renaissance building with a central tower and entrance, two storeys, and dormer windows.[50] Pepys, who in 1668 was particularly enthusiastic about the orange and lemon trees, considered the gardens 'too good for the house . . . the most noble that ever I saw'.[51] Evelyn, in 1676 more impressed by the contents of the house, notably the porcelain and Indian cabinets, thought the gardens 'large, but ill kept; yet woody and changeable; the mould a cold weeping clay, not answering the expense'.[52]

Lord Wotton was resident at Belsize from 1673 or earlier to 1681, but after the lease passed to the earls of Chesterfield in 1683 the house and 25¼ a., besides the farmland, were let to undertenants.[53] By 1714, when the 25¼ a. were called the Wilderness, they were in the hands of the notorious Charles Povey,[54] a coal merchant, who was accused in that year of having ruined Belsize by cutting down timber and demolishing outbuildings and of selling thousands of bricks from the walls and all the pipes and lead that 'played the waterworks' and of having filled in the fountain. Povey, a belligerent man who published pamphlets against all who offended him, claimed that he had found the mansion house and outhouses 'little more than a heap of rubbish', the land overrun with briars and weeds, and the walls ready to fall down. He had spent £2,200 on repairs, replaced the old pipes, and renewed the walls so that everything was in good order. Chesterfield was threatened with a pamphlet if he insisted on taking Povey to law.[55] In 1717 Belsize was 'now turned into a public house'[56] and in 1718 Povey, a rabid protestant, claimed that he had sacrificed £1,000 a year by refusing to lease the house and park, which included a newly erected chapel, to the French ambassador. Hurt that his gesture was not appreciated by the government and that his offer of the house to the prince of Wales was not acknowledged, Povey in

[37] Ibid. Deed 142560; W.A.M. 16617; W.A.M. Map 125342; Thompson, *Hampstead*, 97, 262–4.
[38] W.A.M. Lease bk. LIX, ff. 12–14.
[39] Ch. Com. Deeds 146073, 240254–9, 240263, 240261; W.A.M., RCO 32 (valuation 1857); Thompson, *Hampstead*, 97–8, 279–80, 287–8, 293; G.L.R.O., E/MW/H, old no. 27/15 (sales parts. of Belsize Pk. etc. 1841).
[40] W.A.M. Lease bks. LVIII, ff. 57v.–58v.; LXII, ff. 321v.–323v.; LXIII, ff. 201–3; Thompson, *Hampstead*, 98–9.
[41] W.A.M., RCO 32 (abs. of title 1864 and accompanying docs.); Ch. Com. Deeds 142550–4; Survey CC 7, pp. 8–11; Thompson, *Hampstead*, 99–101.
[42] C.U.L., Kk. V. 29, f. 31v.; *Cal. Pat. 1313–17*, 663.
[43] W.A.M. 16470; Thompson, *Hampstead*, 8; but see below, econ., ind.

[44] e.g. in 1557: W.A.M. 16475.
[45] P.R.O., E 159/357, rot. 532.
[46] Ibid. C 54/3553, no. 33.
[47] *Diary of John Evelyn*, ed. E. S. de Beer, iv. 92; above.
[48] S.C.L., D 136–7 (map and survey 1679); P.R.O., C 54/3553, no. 33.
[49] G.L.R.O., MR/TH/2, m. 29d.; P.R.O., E 179/143/ 370, m. 43d.
[50] *Images of Hampstead*, 115, cat. nos. 341–6.
[51] *Diary of Sam. Pepys*, ed. R. Latham and W. Matthews, ix. 281.
[52] *Diary of John Evelyn*, iv. 92.
[53] Park, *Hampstead*, 154, 156.
[54] W.A.M. Map 12450.
[55] W.A.M. 16483, 16486, 16546.
[56] Ibid. 16495.

1720 opened Belsize as a place of entertainment.[57] In 1726 Chesterfield's agent claimed that the 'Great House' was far from having brought any profit for more than 40 years.[58] In 1733 the dean and chapter permitted Chesterfield to pull down and replace the present ruinous manor house.[59] In 1744 Chesterfield subleased the old house and $25\frac{1}{2}$ a. to Joshua Evans on condition that he built a new house of four rooms on each floor.[60] Evans had built it by 1746[61] as a plain building of three storeys and basement, with six bays and a stepped and porticoed entrance on its main front.[62]

Spencer Perceval, whose wife was the daughter of Sir Thomas Wilson, lord of Hampstead manor, rented Belsize House, the park, and other land, 45 a. in all, from 1797 to 1808. He considered it 'a rambling old place' and 'a miserable hole', spent considerable sums on it, and planted trees of all kinds but remained dissatisfied.[63] In 1808 the three-storeyed house had a hall, dining room, library, 3 drawing rooms, 6 bedrooms, 6 chambers, a dressing room, and a nursery.[64] By the 1840s the house had become a more complex building than that illustrated in 1800,[65] probably through alterations by Perceval and later tenants. In 1841 it was described as an elegant Gothic mansion and included a Gothic conservatory, vineries, aviaries, and a Grecian temple.[66] After the break-up of the estate in 1808 the house and parkland were occupied by tenants until 1853 when they were given over to the builders; the site of the house is the junction of Belsize Avenue, Belsize Park, and Belsize Park Gardens.[67]

CHALCOTS, first named in 1253,[68] originated in a grant, confirmed by the king in 1204 and 1242, by Alexander de Barentyn to the leper hospital of St. James, Westminster, of 1 hide in Hampstead.[69] The hospital's title was threatened by the abbot of Westminster's efforts to recover Hampstead from the heirs of the Barentyns[70] but was confirmed in 1258, when the abbot granted the hospital a house, a carucate, and 40 a. of wood in Hampstead in free alms, to be held of Westminster for £2 a year.[71] The £2 rent was paid for what in 1312 was described as a free holding of 80 a. of land and wood.[72] In 1448 Henry VI endowed his foundation of Eton College with the property of the hospital of St. James, the grant to take effect when Thomas Kempe ceased to

be warden of the hospital. Eton held Chalcots from 1449 when Kempe became bishop of London.[73] St. George's chapel, Windsor, received the revenues 1463-7 while Eton was incorporated with it.[74] When Henry VIII, covetous of the site of the hospital, exchanged property with Eton in 1531, Chalcots was expressly reserved to the college.[75] In 1842 Eton acquired 32 a. of Crown land in Eton in exchange for 53 a. of the southern portion of Chalcots, which became Primrose Hill public open space.[76] The rest of Chalcots was covered in housing in the course of the 19th century. During the 1950s and early 1960s the college sold almost half its freeholds to the sitting tenants but in 1985 it retained the freehold of some 75 a., the western portion of the estate.[77]

As with Belsize, lessees replaced the institutional freeholders as the effective owners of the estate. Chalcots was leased by 1450 to John Rye,[78] to William Amy in 1481,[79] to Thomas Leckhampton for 20 years from 1481,[80] and from 1514 was leased together with Wyldes in Hendon,[81] to Thomas and William Kempe for 21 years[82] and in 1531 to William Kempe for 21 years.[83] The timber, which was reserved in the earlier leases, was leased in 1538 to John Slanning[84] who in 1556, when a lease to run from 1573 was made to him, was already in possession of the rest of Chalcots and Wyldes.[85] Slanning (d. 1558) left the lease to his kinsman Henry Cliff.[86] In 1579-80 a lease was made to the queen to run after the expiry of Slanning's lease in 1593[87] but before 1583 the lease was held by Richard Loftis, whose widow Helen (d. c. 1590) brought it to Bartholomew Quyny, clothworker (d. c. 1593), whom she married c. 1583. In 1594 Quyny's widow and daughters were in dispute with friends of Helen, to whom Quyny had mortgaged the estate.[88] In 1615-16 Eton leased Chalcots and Wyldes for 21 years to Philip Barrett[89] (d. 1630), who left it to his wife Elizabeth.[90] The college made 21-year leases in 1632 to William Watkins[91] and from 1639 until 1676, usually at 7-year intervals, to Sir Thomas Allen (d. 1681) of Finchley.[92] Sir Thomas's son Edward took a lease in 1683, and in 1692, probably after his death, the estate was leased to Sir William Rawlinson (d. 1703) of Hendon. Rawlinson's heir was his daughter Elizabeth, wife of Giles Earle (d. 1759), the wit and politician,[93] and in 1720 the lease

[57] Park, *Hampstead*, 156-9. The chapel may have been blt. at the NW. corner of the ho.: cf. 1679 and 1714 maps: S.C.L., D 136; W.A.M. Map 12450; above, social.
[58] He was pleading for a lower fine on the renewal of the lease: W.A.M. 16501.
[59] W.A.M. Lease bk. XXXIV, f. 577 and v.
[60] W.A.M. 16517A.
[61] M.L.R. 1746/1/455.
[62] Walford, *Old and New Lond.* v. 492.
[63] H.M.C., N.R.A. Rep. Perceval Papers IV, nos. 124, 319; D. Gray, *Spencer Perceval* (1963), 38; Barratt, *Annals*, ii. 55; W.A.M. 16595.
[64] Ch. Com. Deed 146072.
[65] Walford, *Old and New Lond.* v. 492.
[66] G.L.R.O., E/MW/H, old no. 27/15 (sales parts. 1841). *Images of Hampstead*, cat. no. 347, does not confirm the 'Gothic' style.
[67] Thompson, *Hampstead*, 95-6, 275; *Shaw's Hampstead Dir.* (1854).
[68] *Cal. Close, 1251-3*, 323.
[69] *Rot. Chart.* (Rec. Com.), i. 117b; *Cal. Chart. R. 1226-57*, 269.
[70] *Cal. Close, 1251-3*, 323; *1254-6*, 60.
[71] P.R.O., CP 25(1)/147/20, no. 391.
[72] W.A.M. 32360-1, 32363, 32357*; C.U.L., Kk. V. 29,

f. 31v.
[73] *T.L.M.A.S.* xx. 51; *V.C.H. Lond.* i. 545.
[74] *V.C.H. Bucks.* ii. 167-8; *V.C.H. Lond.* i. 545.
[75] *L. & P. Hen. VIII*, v, pp. 201, 276, 287-8.
[76] 5 & 6 Vic. c. 78; Thompson, *Hampstead*, 222.
[77] Inf. from Eton Coll. ests. manager, 1985.
[78] E.C.R. 61/RR/A/66.
[79] Ibid. 16/ST. JAS/3, m. 1.
[80] Ibid. 54/163, vol. 13, p. 117.
[81] *V.C.H. Mdx.* v. 21.
[82] E.C.R. 54/163, vol. 13, p. 160.
[83] Ibid. vol. 14, p. 10.
[84] Ibid. p. 36; 61/BI/G/26.
[85] Ibid. 54/163, vol. 15, p. 12; Hist. MSS. Com. 39, *15th Rep. II, Hodgkin*, pp. 259-60.
[86] P.R.O., PROB 11/41 (P.C.C. 63 Noodes).
[87] E.C.R. 54/163, vol. 15, p. 152.
[88] P.R.O., C 3/252/75.
[89] E.C.R. 54/163, vol. 16, p. 140.
[90] P.R.O., PROB 11/158 (P.C.C. 76 Scroope).
[91] E.C.R. 54/163, vol. 17, pp. 57, 114.
[92] Ibid. pp. 128, 198; vol. 18, pp. 40, 154, 253; vol. 19, p. 71; for the Allens, *V.C.H. Mdx.* vi. 57.
[93] E.C.R. 54/163, vol. 19, pp. 177, 236, 262; *V.C.H. Mdx.* v. 6; *D.N.B.* s.v. Giles Earle. Eliz. d. young.

was held in trust for their children, William Rawlinson Earle and Eleanor Earle, who held it in 1755.[94] About that time, however, the lease was renewed to William Rawlinson Earle (d. 1771) alone[95] and it passed under William's will to his son Giles (d. 1811),[96] to whom leases were renewed in 1775, 1790, 1797, and 1804.[97] In 1818 and 1825 Giles's widow Margaret (d. 1827) renewed the lease, which was held in 1829 by trustees of her will and later by mortgagees.[98] Thomas Clarke, Earle's solicitor, was the lessee in the early 1830s and leases were made in 1839 to Charles Bowyer and in 1840 to John S. Hulbert.[99] In 1867 Ramsay Robinson Clarke was the lessee as mortgagee of Giles Clarke Earle.[1] Eton obtained a private estate Act in 1826 enabling it to grant 99-year building leases and, as parts of the estate were leased for building, starting with the eastern area next to Haverstock Hill, the Chalcots estate in the main lease shrunk. There were still 120 a. of grassland at Chalcots in 1871.[2]

A house formed part of the Chalcots estate in 1258[3] and wages paid to a tiler and plasterer in 1481 were presumably for work on farm buildings.[4] The estate contained various messuages in 1594,[5] although 'Chalcote' was a single site in woodland in 1593.[6] By 1646 the estate was divided among five undertenants, two of whom had houses,[7] presumably Chalcot or Upper Chalcot and Lower Chalcot or Low Chalcot as recorded c. 1672.[8] By 1720 the 212-a. estate was equally divided into two compact farms centred on the two farmhouses, Upper Chalcots at the west end of Upper Chalcots Lane (later England's Lane after an undertenant) and Lower Chalcots on the south side of the same lane.[9] In 1756 all the buildings were said to be in a good state and the estate to be extremely well tenanted.[10] There were still two farms in 1774[11] but by 1797 most of the land was in the hands of Thomas Rhodes,[12] who had Upper Chalcots (c. 101 a.) from 1791 and in 1802 and 1841 had 165 a.[13] Lower Chalcots had ceased to be a farmhouse by 1839, when it was leased with only 2½ a. to Charles Adey, a solicitor.[14] In 1851

there was only one Chalcots, occupied by a lawyer,[15] although both were marked on a map of 1862.[16] Upper Chalcots, called Chalcots, survived in 1873 but had disappeared by 1878.[17] A third farmhouse, south of the parish boundary at Chalk Farm, was sometimes wrongly confused with Lower Chalcots.[18]

KILBURN PRIORY was founded in 1134 and endowed by Herbert, abbot of Westminster, with the site of Godwin's hermitage in Kilburn on the Hampstead side of Edgware Road, 'all the land of that place', and rents.[19] In 1243–4 the priory acquired 14 a. and 1s. 6d. rent in Hampstead from Robert son of Nicol,[20] an endowment probably identifiable with its later 18-a. West End estate, described in 13th- and 14th-century rentals as freehold called le Rudyng held of Westminster for 13s. (later 13s. 4d.) rent.[21] By 1535 the priory received nearly £11 from property in Hampstead and Kilburn, which may have included 40 a. in south-east Willesden.[22] Kilburn was dissolved in 1536 and in the same year Henry VIII granted the site and the demesne and other lands in Kilburn, Hampstead, and Kilburn wood to the Knights Hospitallers of St. John of Jerusalem in exchange for other estates.[23]

After the dissolution of the Knights Hospitallers in 1540 the king took the rents, including £1 a year from Robert Radcliffe, earl of Sussex (d. 1542), for the site of the priory. In 1547 the whole estate was granted to John Dudley, earl of Warwick,[24] who sold it in the same year to the Taverner brothers, Richard, Robert, and Roger.[25] Richard Taverner conveyed it in 1550 to John Lamb (d. 1550),[26] whose son Richard died in 1557 leaving infant daughters and coheirs, Joan (d. 1567) and Mary (d. 1571), who married Edward Josselyn.[27] The estate was conveyed in 1584 to Henry Josselyn.[28] He sold it in the same year to Sir Henry Gate (d. 1589), to whom he may have been connected by marriage,[29] and his wife Katharine. In 1590 Gate's son Edward conveyed it to Arthur Atye.[30]

By his will proved 1604 Atye left all his estates to his wife Judith (who later married Sir John Dormer

[94] E.C.R. 54/163A, 168; S.C.L., D 59.
[95] E.C.R. 54/172. [96] Ibid. 180; S.C.L., D 62.
[97] S.C.L., D 63; E.C.R. 16/CHA/3, 4; *Trans. Hampstead Antiq. & Hist. Soc.* (1902–3), 156.
[98] E.C.R. 16/CHA/5, 7; Thompson, *Hampstead*, 217.
[99] E.C.R. 16/CHA/12, 14; Thompson, *Hampstead*, 108, 225.
[1] *Trans. Hampstead Antiq. & Hist. Soc.* (1902–3), 156.
[2] Thompson, *Hampstead*, 217, 244; Summerson, 'Beginnings of an Early Victorian Suburb' (MS. of lecture 1958).
[3] P.R.O., CP 25(1)/147/20, no. 39.
[4] E.C.R. 16/ST. JAS./3, m. 2d.
[5] P.R.O., C 3/252/75.
[6] J. Norden, *Map of Mdx.* (1593).
[7] Barratt, *Annals*, iii, App. 3, pp. 359–61.
[8] Ogilby, *Map of Mdx.* [c. 1672].
[9] E.C.R. 51/6, nos. 56, 73; 54/163A; cf. S.C.L., Man. Map and Fieldbk., nos. 549, 564.
[10] E.C.R. 54/174.
[11] Ibid. 183; S.C.L., Oppé, Extracts from Rate Bks., poor rate 1774, ff. 7–19. [12] E.C.R. 54/184.
[13] S.C.L., D 64–5; *T.L.M.A.S.* xii. 310–13; P.R.O., IR 29/21/24, nos. 175–85.
[14] E.C.R. 16/CHA/11; P.R.O., IR 29/21/24, no. 174; ibid. HO 107/674/1.
[15] P.R.O., HO 107/1492/2. The only farmer in England's Lane occupied North Hall Cottage, E. of Lower Chalcots.
[16] Stanford, *Libr. Map of Lond. and Suburbs* (1862 edn. with additions to 1865).

[17] O.S. Map 6″, Mdx. XVI (1873 edn.); Hutchings and Crowsley, *Hampstead and Highgate Dir.* (1873); *Metrop. Improvement Map No. 46* (1878).
[18] *Images of Hampstead*, 127. Cf. Laurie's Plan of Lond., *Westm.* (1851).
[19] Dugdale, *Mon.* iii. 426. The date, given as c. 1130 in *V.C.H. Mdx.* i. 178 and 1139 in C. N. L. Brooke and G. Keir, *Lond. 800–1216*, 330, was temp. Bp. Gilbert (the Universal 1128–34), Abbot Herbert (1121–c. 1136): Harvey, *Westm. Abbey*, preface; and Prior Osbert de Clare (from 1134): *Letters of Osbert de Clare*, ed. E. W. Williamson (1929), 16, 19.
[20] P.R.O., CP 25(1)/147/13, no. 222.
[21] W.A.M. 32336–1, 32363; C.U.L., Kk. V. 29, f. 31v.
[22] *Valor Eccl.* (Rec. Com.), i. 432; *V.C.H. Mdx.* vii. 214.
[23] Park, *Hampstead*, 190.
[24] Ibid. 196; P.R.O., E 318/Box 38/2042; *Cal. Pat.* 1547–8, 253.
[25] *Cal. Pat.* 1547–8, 222; M. C. Rosenfield, 'Disposal of Property of Lond. Monastic Hos.' (Lond. Univ. Ph.D. thesis, 1961), 297.
[26] Lysons, *Environs*, ii. 531; P.R.O., C 142/91, no. 52.
[27] P.R.O., C 142/145, no. 59; C 60/386, nos. 53, 62; B.L. Harl. MS. 758, f. 149v.
[28] Unlikely to have been the son of Mary, who was only 16 in 1570.
[29] Dorothy Gate, Sir Hen.'s sister, married Sir Thos. Jocelyn: *Familiae Minorum Gentium*, iii (Harl. Soc. xxxix), 996.
[30] P.R.O., PROB 11/73 (P.C.C. 48 Leicester); ibid. IND 16943 s.v. East. 32 Eliz.

and died in 1618) with remainder to his son Robert. Robert (d. 1612) on his marriage in 1608 to Jane, daughter of John St. John, settled the reversion of what was called the manor of Hampstead on himself and his wife. In 1621, after Robert's widow had married Sir Charles Pleydall, the marriage of his daughter Eleanor, then aged 13, was sold to Sir John Dormer, who married her to Sir William Roberts (d. 1662), her powerful Willesden neighbour.[31] In 1636 John St. John, trustee of the 1608 marriage settlement, conveyed two thirds of the Kilburn priory estate to Eleanor, the other third presumably being held by Jane Pleydall.[32] Eleanor's estate, though probably not the Pleydall third, was sold to Edward Nelthorpe, a London merchant, either directly by her in 1663[23] or after a sale in 1663 to Edward Kelyng, who resold to speculators John King and Edward Jenkinson in 1673, who resold to Nelthorpe.[34] Nelthorpe died in 1680 and his property, which included copyhold, was divided between his son Edward (d. 1720) and his daughter Mary (d. 1756), wife of Thomas Liddell, who inherited her brother's portion and whose son Henry (d. 1771) was succeeded by his nephew Richard Middleton of Denbighshire.[35] Middleton divided his estates: he sold *ABBEY FARM*, 46½ a., of which 33 a. and the site of the priory lay in Hampstead, in 1773 to Richard Marsh, the underlessee,[36] and 31 a., formerly Kilburn woods, in 1774 to John Powell of Fulham,[37] who had bought Shoot Up Hill farm from Middleton in 1773.[38]

In 1818 Richard Marsh's son Richard was said to be the owner of Abbey farm[39] although a conveyance, possibly as part of a marriage settlement, was supposedly made by Richard Marsh in 1794 to Daniel Chapman and his daughter Ann and in 1819 Daniel Chapman and Ann Marsh, widow, conveyed the farm to Fulk Greville Howard.[40] Howard (formerly Upton), through his wife a great landowner, concluded building agreements within a few months of buying the Kilburn estate.[41] The estate passed on his death in 1846 to his nephew, Col. Arthur Upton, and it was under him that building was completed.[42]

The other part of the Kilburn estate, formerly *KILBURN WOODS*,[43] was combined with 29 a. of copyhold (Liddell) to form a 60-a. estate on either side of West End Lane. John Powell (d. 1783) devised his estates for life to his nephew Arthur Annesley Roberts, who changed his surname to Powell and died in 1814. He was succeeded, under

his uncle's will, by his brother John Roberts, who changed his name to John Powell Powell.[44] Powell died in 1849 and his estates were held by trustees under his will, for the use of his nephew, Col. Henry Perry Cotton, who also inherited his uncle's house at Quex Park, Isle of Thanet, and who was still in possession in 1874.[45] In 1894 the estate descended to Maj. Percy Horace Gordon Powell-Cotton, a grandson of Col. Cotton.[46]

In 1535, besides the site of the priory with its dovecotes and other buildings, there was a mansion opposite the church door,[47] which may have been the chapel house mentioned later in the 16th century[48] and possibly the building still standing in 1722.[49] Sir William Roberts, who also owned the Shoot Up Hill estate, had a house and 30 a. in hand and 4 houses and 138 a. divided among six tenants.[50] In 1764 the Kilburn estate included a farmhouse for Abbey farm and another one for John Pawlett's farm,[51] which stood on his copyhold land on Edgware Road north of West End Lane.[52] In 1773 Abbey farm included the site on which the capital messuage of the priory 'lately stood', the Red Lion, and a cottage.[53] The last remnants of the priory buildings were removed in 1790 although foundations were still visible.[54]

At least some of the Kilburn priory estate appears to have become detached from the main estate in the 16th or 17th centuries, perhaps because boundaries became confused during the ownership of the Hospitallers and the Atyes, who had other estates in the area, and complicated divisions were caused by several surviving widows' dowries. In 1559 Edward Bacon was licensed to alienate lands in Kilburn late of the Hospitallers to Robert Cripps, who in turn was licensed to alienate them in 1564 to William Bubbington.[55] Since John Bacon had been an undertenant of the Kilburn priory estate in 1547, when he held a tenement and lands in Kilburn for £1 a year,[56] Edward Bacon's estate was probably a detached part of the priory's lands.

THORPLANDS, in 1762 an 18-a. freehold estate with a house at West End, was almost certainly the medieval Rudyng.[57] It had been leased to William Wylde in 1534 and was part of the lands granted to Warwick in 1547,[58] but it had become detached from the main estate by the mid 17th century, perhaps in 1636. A Mr. Thorpe held it at least from 1646 to 1653.[59] John Thorpe (d. 1687) left his freehold lands at Kilburn to trustees for his grandson, John Thorpe.[60] It was presumably the grandson who sold

[31] Ibid. C 66/1777, no. 13; ibid. PROB 11/105 (P.C.C. 6 Hayes); ibid. WARD 5/30, nos. 431–2; Atye pedigree in *Mdx. Pedigrees* (Harl. Soc. lxv), 153; *V.C.H. Mdx.* vii. 217.
[32] P.R.O., C 66/2724, m. 30.
[33] Park, *Hampstead*, 201.
[34] Thompson, *Hampstead*, 83.
[35] G.L.R.O., E/MW/H/17; M.M.& M., Lib. B, pp. 20, 33; D, pp. 328–9; E, p. 423; F, p. 23.
[36] M.L.R. 1773/2/89–90; P.R.O., IR 29/21/24.
[37] M.L.R. 1774/4/283.
[38] Ibid. 1773/1/174.
[39] Park, *Hampstead*, 202.
[40] Thompson, *Hampstead*, 83 n. 3; M.L.R. 1819/5/625. There is no record of the 1794 conveyance (alluded to in abs. of title 1824) in M.L.R.
[41] Thompson, *Hampstead*, 76–7, 84.
[42] Ibid. 254.
[43] Identified in P.R.O., E 133/137/27.
[44] M.M. & M., Lib. G, pp. 56–8; J, pp. 499, 556–9.

[45] Ibid. Lib. O, pp. 175, 206–13; P.R.O., PROB 11/2095 (P.C.C. 1849, f. 465); Thompson, *Hampstead*, 319.
[46] S.C.L., D 165; Wade, *W. Hampstead*, 25.
[47] *Valor Eccl.* (Rec. Com.), i. 432; for the priory, *V.C.H. Mdx.* i. 181.
[48] P.R.O., C 142/91, no. 52; C 60/386, no. 53.
[49] Park, *Hampstead*, 202; *Images of Hampstead*, nos. 507–11.
[50] Barratt, *Annals*, iii, App. 3, pp. 359–61.
[51] M.L.R. 1764/5/405.
[52] S.C.L., Man. Map and Fieldbk., no. 525; below, Liddell est. Cf. M.L.R. 1774/4/283.
[53] M.L.R. 1773/2/89.
[54] B.L. Maps, Kings XXX 7.a.
[55] *Cal. Pat.* 1558–60, 131; 1563–6, 131.
[56] P.R.O., E 318/Box 38/2042.
[57] S.C.L., Man. Map; above.
[58] P.R.O., E 318/Box 38/2042.
[59] Barratt, *Annals*, iii. 359–64.
[60] P.R.O., C 8/554/90.

the estate to John Dee (d. 1721), who was succeeded by his cousin Elizabeth, wife of Thomas Draper.[61] In 1762 the estate was described as tithe-free freehold owned by 'Mr. Draper'.[62] When Elizabeth Draper died in 1771, her copyhold property descended to her son John[63] but the freehold estate was held in 1767 and 1771 by Mrs. Robinson and later by Thomas Fentham.[64] John Thomas Fentham was the owner in 1841[65] and Thomas Potter in the 1860s and 1870s when building began.[66] There was a house on the estate possibly by 1244, probably by 1534, and certainly from 1646.[67]

Several grants created the *TEMPLE* estate, which lay in two main blocks on the western side of the parish, one in the north, which was sometimes associated with the Hendon estates of the Knights Templars, and one in the south, linked to Lisson manor in Marylebone. Though not recorded in the 1185 inquest,[68] the estate may have originated in Henry II's reign since 'Hamstede' was included in John's charter of 1199 among the gifts of his father to the Temple.[69] The Templars almost certainly had the northern estate by 1239, when they were said to hold 1 hide of the Barentyn estate 'from the parson of Hendon'. The name of the rector of Hendon at that date is unknown and probably the allusion was to Westminster abbey, which owned the Hendon advowson and was Hampstead's overlord.[70] From 1259 the Templars held a freehold estate in Hampstead from Westminster abbey for £1 a year rent,[71] which can be identified at the Dissolution with the northern estate, later called Shoot Up Hill.[72] By the 14th century the estate had a frontage of 100 perches (1,650 ft.) to Edgware Road[73] and in 1470 it formed the western boundary of Northfield wood, part of the manorial demesne.[74]

The Templars acquired part of the southern estate before 1237 when Otes (Otho) son of William gave them some land and wood in free alms. In 1238 he granted them the whole manor of Lisson (Lilleston).[75] In 1243 Hamon son of Roger granted them 80 a. in free alms in Lisson, Hampstead, and Hendon.[76] The services of the master of the Temple were among those surrendered by Robert le Baud to Westminster abbey;[77] in 1275 Robert claimed 140 a. of wood in Hampstead against the master, who asserted that the Hampstead wood formed part of Lisson park.[78] It is not known where the disputed wood lay but there is no evidence that the southern estate, later St. John's Wood, acknowledged overlordship of Hampstead manor. Woodland was appar-

ently not included in the survey of 1308 when the Hampstead and Hendon estates were members of Lisson and only 49 a. of arable was mentioned at Hampstead.[79]

In 1312 the pope dissolved the order of the Temple and transferred its possessions to the Knights Hospitallers of St. John of Jerusalem.[80] The Hospitallers, who had possessed a house at Hampstead in 1223,[81] took over the Temple estate there and in 1327 Lisson manor was described as including 100 a. of arable and 3 a. of meadow in Hampstead, held in 1332 by William Langford for life.[82] In 1338 Lisson manor was held by Sir William of Cleeve for life and the Shoot Up Hill estate, by then severed from Lisson manor, was part of Clerkenwell bailiwick and leased out at £2 a year.[83] In 1522 the prior of St. John leased to John Barne, tiler of Hampstead, the Shoot Up Hill estate, which he called the 'manor and farm of Hampstead', together with all the hospital's land in Willesden and Hendon lately held by Edward and Anne Moore.[84] By 1540 Barne had assigned his 50-year lease to Thomas Bland.[85] The 1522 lease was for £11 a year and in 1535 'Hampstead' was valued at £11 a year, while the St. John's Wood estate was presumably included in Lisson bailiwick.[86]

The Hospitallers were dissolved in 1540,[87] and in 1546 the 'lordship and manor of Hampstead' was granted to Sir Roger Cholmeley.[88] On Cholmeley's death in 1565 the estate, then called the farm at *SHOOT UP HILL*, was divided into moieties, one held by his daughter Elizabeth, widow of Leonard Beckwith and wife of Christopher Kenn, the other by John Russell, the 14 year-old son of his other, dead, daughter Frances.[89] In 1566 Elizabeth (d. 1583) and Christopher Kenn conveyed their moiety to trustees. From Elizabeth's heir Roger Beckwith (d. 1586) the reversion descended to his sister Frances, wife of George Harvey, and then to Frances, wife of Henry Slingsby and daughter of Roger's other sister, Elizabeth Vavasor.[90] In 1595 Henry Slingsby was licensed to alienate a moiety of the 'manor of Hampstead' and considerable lands and houses in Hampstead, Willesden, and Hendon to Sir Arthur Atye and his wife Judith,[91] who were already in possession of the Kilburn priory estate.[92]

Sir John Russell died in 1593 seised of the other moiety, which passed to his widow Elizabeth for life, his son Thomas being then a minor.[93] In 1590 Russell had entered into a recognizance, possibly a mortgage or pre-nuptial settlement, with Robert

[61] M.M. & M., Lib. B, p. 43; M.L.R. 1751/3/27.
[62] S.C.L., Man. Map and Fieldbk. p. 62.
[63] M.M. & M., Lib. E, p. 424.
[64] G.L.R.O., E/MW/H/I/1941–3.
[65] P.R.O., IR 29/21/24, nos. 84–7.
[66] Above, growth, West End.
[67] P.R.O., CP 25(1)/147/13/222; E 318/Box 38/2042; Barratt, *Annals*, iii. 359–64.
[68] It may, however, have existed: *Rec. of Templars in Eng. in 12th cent.* ed. B. A. Lees (1935), p. lxxxv.
[69] *Rot. Chart.* (Rec. Com.), i. 3.
[70] *Cur. Reg. R.* xvi. 175; *V.C.H. Mdx.* v. 33.
[71] W.A.M. 32360–1, 32363; C.U.L., Kk. V. 29, f. 32.
[72] P.R.O., E 318/7/270, mm. 3–4.
[73] B.L. Cott. MS. Nero E. VI, f. 74v.
[74] W.A.M. 32356.
[75] B.L. Cott. MS. Nero E. VI, f. 73 and v.
[76] P.R.O., CP 25(1)/147/13, no. 205.
[77] Westm. Domesday, f. 115 and v.
[78] P.R.O., JUST 1/538, f. 6; B.L. Cott. MS. Nero E.

VI, f. 74 and v.
[79] P.R.O., E 358/20, m. 3d.
[80] M. McKisack, *Fourteenth Cent.* (1959), 292.
[81] *Cur. Reg. R.* xi. 109–10.
[82] B.L. Cott. MS. Nero E. VI, f. 74v.
[83] *Kts. Hospitallers in Eng.* (Camd. Soc. [1st ser.], lxv), 95, 173.
[84] B.L. Cott. MS. Claud. E. VI, ff. 235v.–236.
[85] P.R.O., SC 6/Hen. VIII/2402, m. 8d.
[86] *Valor Eccl.* (Rec. Com.), i. 403.
[87] *V.C.H. Mdx.* i. 196.
[88] *L. & P. Hen. VIII*, xxi (1), p. 687.
[89] *Lond. Inq. p.m.* 1561–77 (Brit. Rec. Soc. xxvi), 43. Cholmeley's will, giving the whole estate to Eliz., was apparently ignored: P.R.O., PROB 11/48 (P.C.C. 24 Morrison).
[90] *Lond. Inq. p.m.* 1577–1603 (Brit. Rec. Soc. xxxvi), 140.
[91] P.R.O., C 66/1432, m. 14.   [92] Above.
[93] *Lond. Inq. p.m.* 1577–1603, 210.

North, the lessee of Shoot Up Hill farm and in 1594 Thomas Russell married Anne North. In 1595 North was licensed to alienate the moiety to Sir Arthur Atye and his wife Judith, subject to Elizabeth Russell's life interest which continued in 1621[94] but had been extinguished by 1636. The Atyes' rights in both moieties of Shoot Up Hill descended with the main Kilburn estate[95] until 1773, when Richard Middleton sold Shoot Up Hill, then 112 a. in the north-west corner of Hampstead parish, to John Powell of Fulham.[96] Thereafter the estate descended with Powell's Kilburn estate.[97] It was built up after 1880.[98]

There is unlikely to have been a dwelling house on the Temple estate earlier than the one which the prior of the Hospitallers was said in 1522 to have made at his own expense, a substantial dwelling house with a barn, stable, and tilehouse.[99] It was probably on the site of the later Shoot Up Hill Farm, which certainly existed by the 1580s,[1] on Edgware Road just south of its junction with Shoot Up Hill Lane.[2] The farm buildings remained until the early 20th century.[3]

The Lisson manor portion of the Hospitallers' estate, which included south-west Hampstead, followed, as *ST. JOHN'S WOOD*, a separate descent after the Dissolution. It was administered by John Conway and, after 1542, by Sir Henry Knyvett as Crown land.[4] In 1547 it was granted to Edward Seymour, duke of Somerset.[5] Queen Mary gave it back briefly to the reconstituted Knights Hospitallers in 1558.[6] Her successor leased it c. 1583 to Arthur Atye, who was later to build up a large estate on either side of Edgware Road, but in 1594 she granted a 40-year lease to Sir William Waad, to run from the expiry of Atye's lease in 1639, and for the next 150 years St. John's Wood was closely associated with Belsize. Sir William (d. 1623) left the lease to his son James although there is no indication that he ever enjoyed it. St. John's Wood was administered as part of the Belsize estate occupied by Anne Waad during her lifetime. In 1644 James and Philip Cage, her son-in-law and administrator, sold the lease to her other son-in-law, John Holgate, who was still in possession in 1649.[7] In 1650 John Collins of Great Stanmore, who claimed that Holgate had assigned the lease to him, purchased at least part of the estate from the parliamentary commissioners, who had seized it as Crown land. At the Restoration he maintained that he had tried to delay payment so that he

'could pay it to his rightful sovereign', but his application for a new lease in 1660 failed.[8] In 1663 Henry Bennet, later earl of Arlington, successfully applied for the lease, which in 1666 was confirmed in possession or reversion.[9] In the same year Bennet sold his rights to Katharine, countess of Chesterfield (d. 1667), who devised the reversionary leasehold of St. John's Wood, together with the lease of Belsize, to her son Charles Henry, Lord Wotton. In 1673 Charles II granted Wotton the freehold of the whole of St. John's Wood, then 492 a., of which c. 150 a. lay in Hampstead.[10] Thereafter the estate followed the same descent as Belsize until 1732 when the earl of Chesterfield, who had already mortgaged it, sold St. John's Wood to Henry Samuel Eyre (d. 1754), a London wine merchant.[11] The estate passed to Eyre's nephew Walpole Eyre (d. 1773) and, on the death of Walpole's widow Sarah in 1823, to their son Col. Henry Samuel Eyre (d. 1851), who had 144 a. in Hampstead in 1838. He left it in trust for his brother Walpole and nephew George John Eyre (d. 1883), the latter being in possession by 1864. It then passed to Walpole's son the Revd. Henry Samuel Eyre (d. 1890), who left it in equal portions to his five children.[12] The family, which was one of the first to develop its estate for building, still owned the land in 1972.[13]

It is probable that parts of the Temple estate, like parts of Kilburn priory's, became detached. One such portion was almost certainly *TEMPLES*, so named by 1632,[14] 24 a. on the Hendon border. It was probably wrongly classified as copyhold in 1762,[15] being apparently freehold in 1714, when owned by Elizabeth Baker,[16] and in 1716, when held by trustees for Thomas Marsh.[17] In 1767 and 1784 it was freehold belonging to 'esquire Mead'[18] and in 1798 it was 'late Ashurst'.[19] It may be identifiable with 23 a. rated to B. Eyles in 1819 and A. P. Johnson in 1826.[20] It had passed by 1837 to Henry Weech Burgess (d. 1903) who was succeeded by his son Maj. Ardwick Burgess.[21]

Since the medieval Temple estate extended as far as the manorial demesne, it almost certainly included the estate at *CHILDS HILL*, called in 1784 Hogmans farm,[22] 57 a. of freehold land held in 1762 and 1771 by William Pritchard Ashurst.[23] In 1731 Ashurst had succeeded his father, Sir William Ashurst, to copyhold estates which Sir William had acquired from John and Mary Fletcher in 1694[24] and it is possible that Childs Hill followed the same

[94] P.R.O., C 2/Jas. I/B 31/1; ibid. WARD 5/30, no. 432; ibid. C 66/1432, m. 14; Par. Reg. (microfilm in S.C.L.).
[95] Above; Park, *Hampstead*, 200–1; Thompson, *Hampstead*, 83; P.R.O., C 66/2724, m. 30.
[96] M.L.R. 1773/1/174; S.C.L., Man. Map and Fieldbk.
[97] Above. [98] Above, growth, Kilburn.
[99] B.L. Cott. MS. Claud. E. VI, ff. 235v.–236.
[1] P.R.O., C 2/Jas. I/B 31/1.
[2] S.C.L., Man. Map and Fieldbk. no. 491; R. Morden, *Map of Mdx.* (1701).
[3] Wade, *W. Hampstead*, 25; G.L.R.O., E/MW/H, old no. 37/3 (enfranchisement 1854).
[4] A. M. Eyre, *St. John's Wood* (1913), 7–8.
[5] *Cal. Pat.* 1547–8, 131.
[6] Ibid. 1557–8, 313; Eyre, *St. John's Wood*, 8.
[7] P.R.O., E 317/Mdx. 56; ibid. PROB 11/142 (P.C.C. 116 Swan); above, Belsize. In 1651 it was claimed that the lease to Waad dated from 1584: P.R.O., C 10/11/41.
[8] P.R.O., C 10/11/41; S. J. Madge, *Domesday of Crown Lands* (1938), 214, 267–8.
[9] P.R.O., C 5/436/55; Eyre, *St. John's Wood*, 12–13.

[10] *Cal. Treas. Bks.* 1672–5, 44, 94–5, 493. The par. boundary passed through the middle of fields: S.C.L., D 136–7; ibid. Man. Map and Fieldbk.; M.L.R. 1732/5/753.
[11] M.L.R. 1730/5/251; 1732/5/753–5.
[12] Eyre, *St. John's Wood*, 31–2; P.R.O., IR 29/21/24; S.C.L., D 230.
[13] H. P. Clunn, *Lond. Marches On* (1947), 120–1; G. Bebbington, *Lond. Street Names* (1972), 127.
[14] G.L.R.O., E/MW/H/I/2311B.
[15] S.C.L., Man. Map and Fieldbk. nos. 568–9.
[16] M.L.R. 1714/1/189–92.   [17] Ibid. 1716/5/142.
[18] G.L.R.O., E/MW/H/I/1941; H, old no. 33/16.
[19] Ibid. old no. 31/8 (lease to Pool 1798).
[20] Poor rate bks. 1819, 1826.
[21] Bebbington, *Lond. Street Names*, 64; P.R.O., IR 29/21/24, nos. 60–1.
[22] G.L.R.O., E/MW/H, old no. 33/16.
[23] S.C.L., Man. Map and Fieldbk. nos. A 572–81; G.L.R.O., E/MW/H/I/1941–2.
[24] M.M. & M., Lib. C, p. 164; Index to Ct. Rolls, roll 13, p. 1.

descent. It probably passed to William Smith in 1774 and was held by Hugh Smith in 1798.[25] The estate was apparently divided soon afterwards and the house and surrounding 6 a. were held by Enoch Hodgkinson from c. 1801 to 1810, then by Thomas Platt, and, probably after 1829, by his son Thomas Pell Platt (d. 1852), the orientalist,[26] who in 1841 owned the eastern 33½ a., of which he occupied 6½ a.[27] Platt's representatives were still the owners in 1880 and the estate was sold for building in 1896.[28] The western part of the estate lost some land to Finchley Road and the remaining 20½ a. was purchased in 1840, possibly from Stephen Beadle, who had a 21-a. farm in the area in 1834, by John Teil, an East India merchant. A strip of land was sold to the West Middlesex Waterworks Co. before 1855, when Teil was dead and the rest of the estate was put up for sale. The portion west of Finchley Road was bought by the son of the owner of the neighbouring Temple estate and the rest, 15½ a. and Kidderpore Hall, by Charles Cannon (d. 1876), a dyer. His daughters inherited the estate, which they sold in 1890 for building, except for the house and 2½ a., purchased by Westfield College.[29]

KINGSWELL or KINGHALL was a freehold estate lying east of the manorial demesne and defined by its abutments in 1393 and 1713.[30] It can probably be traced to 1259 when Roger de la Methe paid 1s. rent for an estate later held by Geoffrey de Kingswell.[31] In 1281 Geoffrey de Kingswell paid 4s. 5½d. rent as a tenant from the Hide, and another 10d. and two geese presumably for another holding;[32] he was alive in 1296[33] but by 1312 had been succeeded by Robert de Kingswell, who then held a freehold estate consisting of a house and 16 a. for the annual rent of 5s. 8d., two geese, and one chicken.[34] Robert was apparently still a tenant of Westminster in 1319[35] but by 1346 the estate had escheated to the lord because rent was not being paid.[36] By 1372 Thomas son of William Wright (or Wight) held the house and 12 a. and William Robin 4 a.[37] In 1393 Thomas Wright conveyed his portion, described as Kingswell garden, a croft called Combe, and More Kingswellfield, to William and Alice Gibb, who acquired 6 a. called Little Kingswellfield from William and Christine Ford at the same time.[38] William Gibb was farmer of the adjoining manorial demesne from 1381 to 1411[39] and, probably after 1418, 'Wrythes', together with Popes, which lay north of it, was held by Alice Gibb.[40] By 1472 Kingswell was one of the many holdings in the hands of 'Master' Watno,[41] probably John Watno, who by will proved 1484 left his 'place called Kingswell' together with 'an orchard, two closes and a grove lying thereto' to his son Thomas.[42] In 1621 it was in the hands of Sir William Waad (d. 1623) of Belsize and it passed to his son James, being called Kinghall in 1633 and described as a farm and three closes (20 a.) of pasture.[43] It descended, heavily mortgaged,[44] to James's son William and, by 1713, to William's sister Anne Baesh, a widow, who conveyed it in that year to Lancelot Lee, a London linendraper, and Lancelot Baugh of Lincoln's Inn.[45] In 1717 they conveyed it to Richard Hughes of Holborn, who also acquired all the mortgagors' interests.[46] Involved in the transaction of 1717 was Charles Humphreys of Hatton Garden and in 1730 the estate was in the hands of his widow Sarah,[47] who devised it by will dated 1755 to trustees. In 1757 they sold it to Robert Cary (d. 1777),[48] who was succeeded by his daughters Amy Anne, Lucy Elizabeth (who apparently married brothers, Adam and Thomas Askew), and Mary, who sold the bulk of the estate, by then called Shepherd's Close, in 1797 to Jonathan Key, stationer of Paternoster Row.[49] About the same time individual houses built in the early 18th century on the south side of Church Row at the north end of the estate were sold off to the occupiers.[50] In 1797 Key sold 4 a. to George and Thomas Goodwin.[51] That part was devised by the will of George Goodwin to Harriet and Emma Parkinson, wives respectively of the Revd. Thomas Wynter Mead and Charles Trueman, who sold it in 1845 to George Henry Errington.[52] The rest of the estate passed by will of William Cade Key, dated 1823, to Rose, wife of the Revd. Barrett Edward Lampet, who sold it to Errington in 1846.[53] Errington retained it until the development of all his estates in the 1870s.[54]

There was a house on the estate by 1312,[55] which may have long been associated with the lessees of the manorial demesne.[56] The farmhouse was replaced by the south side of Church Row in the early 18th century.[57] By 1730 a barn had been built next to the lane[58] which later became Fitzjohn's Avenue, and by 1870 it was called Mount Farm though perhaps containing no dwelling.[59] It disappeared in the building development of the 1870s.

The 50-a. estate at Fortune Green and West End,

[25] G.L.R.O., E/MW/H/I/2178; H, old no. 31/8 (lease to Pool 1798).
[26] Vestry mins. 22 Sept. 1801, 20 Apr. 1802; poor rate bks. 1810, 1813, 1826, 1834; G.L.R.O., M/81/4; C.H.R. x. 7–9; D.N.B. s.v. Thos. Pell Platt.
[27] P.R.O., IR 29/21/24, nos. 32, 53–4, 55a, 56a, 58a, 59.
[28] Rate bk. 1880; above, growth, Childs Hill.
[29] P.R.O., IR 29/21/24, nos. 55–8, 79; G.L.R.O., E/MW/H, old no. 27/15 (sales parts. 1855); rate bks. 1834, 1880; Wade, Streets of Hampstead, 341.
[30] Cal. Close, 1392–6, 136–7; M.L.R. 1713/3/6.
[31] W.A.M. 32360.   [32] Ibid. 32361.
[33] Ibid. 32359.
[34] C.U.L., Kk. V. 29, f. 32.
[35] Cal. Pat. 1317–21, 465.
[36] W.A.M. 32494.
[37] Ibid. 32357, 32363.
[38] Cal. Close, 1392–6, 136–8.
[39] Below, econ.
[40] W.A.M. 32357 (section labelled unyeld) dated by d. of Rog. Aldenham: Guildhall MS. 9171/2, f. 380.
[41] W.A.M. 32357*.

[42] P.R.O., PROB 11/8 (P.C.C. 6 Milles).
[43] Est. described as an abutment of Slyes (below): G.L.R.O., E/MW/H/1 (1621).
[44] P.R.O., PROB 11/142 (P.C.C. 116 Swan); C 7/39/29; C 5/46/67; C 5/496/76.
[45] M.L.R. 1713/3/6–7.
[46] Ibid. 1718/3/16–18.
[47] Ibid. 1730/6/144.
[48] Ibid. 1757/2/328–9; 1758/1/275.
[49] Ibid. 1797/1/220.
[50] Ibid. 1796/6/201; 1797/1/475, 722.
[51] Ibid. 1797/1/332.
[52] Ibid. 1845/9/174; S.C.L., D 234A.
[53] M.L.R. 1846/4/63–64.
[54] Above, growth, Hampstead town.
[55] C.U.L., Kk. V. 29, f. 29.
[56] Cf. Wm. Gibb and Rob. James (lessee before 1652: P.R.O., C 5/496/76), possibly a member of the fam. which leased the man. in the 16th cent.: below, econ.
[57] M.L.R. 1713/3/6; above, growth, Hampstead town.
[58] M.L.R. 1730/6/144.
[59] O.S. Map 1/2,500, Lond. VII (1870 edn.).

called *FLITCROFT* after its owner in the 18th century,[60] was then a copyhold of Hampstead manor, though its position and the fact that no heriots were demanded suggest that its origins may have been as part of the Temple estate. The core of Flitcroft was land left by Rachel Farby in 1626 to William Clark (d. 1630). William's son Richard was succeeded in 1644 by his son William,[61] who had a house and 28 a. in 1646[62] and was succeeded in 1651 by his sister Mary (d. 1652), the wife of Ralph Everett. In 1677 Everett sold his life interest to Gerald Conyers, who had already acquired the reversion from Richard Clark's sisters.[63] Tristram and Gerald Conyers in 1684 sold two houses in West End and 38 a. of meadow or pasture to James Shuter and his wife Elizabeth.[64] In 1722 Elizabeth died as a widow with that holding and a house and 8½ a. acquired by her father Charles Tilford (or Titford) before 1671.[65] She was succeeded by her daughters Elizabeth (d. 1728) and Rebecca (d. 1724), and their estate, including three cottages and 12 a. at West End left in 1709 by Charles Tilford's wife Rebecca to Rebecca Shuter (her granddaughter), was held by trustees under the younger Elizabeth Shuter's will until sold by court order in 1755. The buyer was the agent for the architect Henry Flitcroft (or Fleetcroft), who was admitted in 1756.[66] Flitcroft (d. 1769) was succeeded by his son Henry,[67] who died a lunatic in 1826. The estate descended to the latter's grand nephew Joseph Walmsley (d. 1836) and, in accordance with the latter's will, to Thomas Bruce Wavell, subject to trusts.[68] Wavell's son Thomas Brooke Wavell succeeded when his father died intestate in 1866, and he conveyed his estates to Mary Ann, wife of John Vining Porter.[69] The 20 a. north of Fortune Green was sold to the parish for a cemetery in 1874 and the rest of the estate was given over to the builders in the 1880s.[70]

There was a farmhouse at West End by the mid 17th century.[71]

An estate lying between Edgware Road and West End and consisting in 1762 of 54½ a.,[72] copyhold of Hampstead manor, was called from the 17th century *GILBERTS*, presumably after a former owner, perhaps the 13th-century Gilbert Gers or Ters, whose estate escheated to the lord by the late 1280s.[73] It was called Cate Mead farm in 1704 and Church Path farm in the late 18th century.[74] It can be traced to

John Badger (d. 1644), a Londoner who held it in 1638[75] and whose son Thomas had a house, a cottage, and 40 a. in Hampstead in 1646.[76] In 1647 Thomas sold the estate to Thomas Tyler (d. 1655) and his wife Judith (d. 1664), who possessed 50 a. in 1649;[77] their son Joseph surrendered the estate in 1677 to his son William. William died in 1681, followed shortly afterwards by his wife and infant daughter, and his estates passed by will to his father in trust for his sister Judith and her infant son Brune Ryves.[78] Joseph Tyler conveyed the estate to trustees in 1686 to pay an annuity to the beneficiaries. In 1700, with the approval of Brune Ryves, the surviving trustee conveyed the reversion to the use of Clement Petit of London,[79] who was admitted in 1706.[80] His son James succeeded in 1717[81] and sold the estate in 1729 to Sarah Bucknell, who paid three heriots, suggesting that the estate was an amalgamation of three ancient customary holdings.[82] Sarah's daughter Sarah (d. 1753), wife of Thomas Ripley of Westminster, succeeded in 1750 and left the estate by will to her stepson Thomas Ripley (d. 1770).[83] His son, the Revd. Thomas Ripley of Fulham, succeeded in 1780[84] and on his death in 1814 the estate was divided between his two sons. The western 46 a., including a house and cottage on Edgware Road, passed to his eldest son the Revd. Thomas Hyde Ripley, while the other 11 a., together with stables and sheds at West End, passed to Jeremy Jepson Ripley.[85] Thomas's son, Thomas E. T. Ripley, succeeded to his father's estate in 1865 and to his uncle's in 1864.[86] The estate was depleted by the sale of c. 6½ a. to the Hampstead Junction Railway Co. in 1864 and of 10 a. to the Midland Railway Co. in 1867,[87] and the rest was enfranchised in 1868.[88]

South of Gilberts in 1762 was a 43-a. copyhold estate centred on a farmhouse on Edgware Road and then owned by John *LITTLE*.[89] No heriots were asked for it so it may have originated in Kilburn priory or the Temple estate. It can probably be identified with the estate held by Sir Henry Herbert in 1646 and 1649, when it consisted of a house and 36 a. and three cottages, all in the hands of tenants. By 1653 it had apparently passed to a Mr. Plummer.[90] John Plummer, who held it in 1678,[91] was succeeded in 1719 by his son Walter.[92] Walter sold the estate in 1736 to William Orton (d. 1738), who left it to his sister Anne (d. 1786) and her husband John Little

[60] S.C.L., Man. Map and Fieldbk. nos. 430–6.
[61] M.M. & M., Index to Ct. Rolls, roll 2, ff. 1, 4; roll 3, f. 13.
[62] Barratt, *Annals*, iii, App. 3, pp. 359–61.
[63] P.R.O., C 8/121/155; M.M. & M., Index, roll 4, ff. 10, 12; roll 5, ff. 6, 11; roll 7, f. 4a.
[64] M.M. & M., Index, roll 7, f. 17a.
[65] Ibid. Lib. B, pp. 85, 87.
[66] Ibid. Lib. A, pp. 69–70; Lib. B, pp. 65, 117–18, 169–73, 293, 302–3; Lib. D, pp. 344–5.
[67] Ibid. Lib. E, pp. 293–4.
[68] Ibid. Lib. L, pp. 414, 437–40, 480, 519–20; Lib. M, pp. 112–18, 586–94.   [69] Ibid. Lib. Q, pp. 329–34.
[70] Thompson, *Hampstead*, 375; Wade, *W. Hampstead*, 31, 63.
[71] Barratt, *Annals*, iii, App. 3, pp. 359–61; M.M. & M., Lib. B, pp. 85, 87; G.L.R.O., E/MW/H, old no. Box L (abs. of leases 1680–1731).
[72] S.C.L., Man. Map and Fieldbk. nos. 496–503.
[73] W.A.M. 32360–1, 32375–6.
[74] G.L.R.O., E/MW/H/I/2311A; H, old no. 31/8 (lease to Pool 1798).
[75] M.M. & M., Index to Ct. Rolls, roll 3, m. 3; G.L.R.O., E/MW/H/I/2109.

[76] Barratt, *Annals*, iii, App. 3, pp. 359–61.
[77] Ibid. App. 4, pp. 361–3; P.R.O., C 8/95/209; ibid. C 9/4/149; ibid. C 78/1283, no. 6; ibid. PROB 11/249 (P.C.C. 1655, f. 345); G.L.R.O., E/MW/H/I/2114.
[78] P.R.O., C 7/587/124. Ryves was listed as owner in 1704: G.L.R.O., E/MW/H/I/2311A.
[79] G.L.R.O., E/MW/H/19, m. 6.
[80] M.M. & M., Lib. A, pp. 8–14, 22–3.
[81] Ibid. Lib. B, p. 286.
[82] Ibid. pp. 326–7, 339–40.
[83] Ibid. Lib. D, pp. 169–70, 260–1; G.L.R.O., E/MW/H/I/2178.
[84] M.M. & M., Lib. F, pp. 443–5.
[85] Ibid. Lib. J, pp. 473–80.
[86] Ibid. Lib. Q, pp. 62–4, 175, 227.
[87] Ibid. pp. 99–100, 158–60, 399–401.
[88] Ibid. 533–9.
[89] S.C.L., Man. Map and Fieldbk. nos. 509–18.
[90] Barratt, *Annals*, iii, App. 3–5, pp. 359–64. The rental value and the tenants reinforce the identification. Cf. Thos. & Walter Green: G.L.R.O., MR/TH/2, m. 29d.; P.R.O., E 179/143/370, m. 43d.
[91] G.L.R.O., E/MW/H/I/2114.
[92] M.M. & M., Lib. A, p. 331.

(d. 1778). Their son Richard (d. 1796) gave the estate by will to his sister Dorothy, who married John Mills Jackson of Southampton in 1810.[93] They sold the estate in 1822 to Samuel Ware, the architect and manager of the duke of Portland's London estate.[94] Between 1823 and 1829 Ware sold most of the estate piecemeal, the largest portion, 17 a., to Henry Aglionby Aglionby (d. 1854) in 1829,[95] and by 1841 his estate was confined to the 12 a. bordering Edgware Road.[96] That part passed on Ware's death in 1860 to his nephew Charles Nathaniel Cumberlege. Kilburn Grange was built on the estate.[97]

The 29-a. copyhold and heriotable estate at Kilburn held in 1762 by *LIDDELL*,[98] and confusingly called Abbey Farm in 1704,[99] had belonged to Thomas Pawlett (d. 1656), who in 1646 had a copyhold and freehold estate of a house, four cottages, and 50 a., and probably to John Pawlett in 1640.[1] Thomas Pawlett left the copyhold to his wife for life with remainder to his daughters Margaret and Elizabeth.[2] In 1674 Margaret, then wife of Francis Painter, conveyed her moiety to Edward Nelthorpe, who already possessed the Kilburn priory and Shoot Up Hill estates,[3] and in 1676 Elizabeth, then wife of Richard Arthur, conveyed hers to Elizabeth Ireton for life, with remainder in 1687 to Mary Nelthorpe.[4] Nelthorpe's widow Mary was in possession of both moieties by 1704[5] but had apparently died by 1713, when the estate was divided between his children Edward (d. 1720) and Mary (d. 1756), wife of Thomas Liddell. The estate descended with the Kilburn Woods portion of the Kilburn priory estate, being sold to John Powell in 1774.[6]

In 1674 the estate included a tilekiln house and 5 cottages; a house had been added by 1698. The tilekiln house had fallen down by 1756.[7]

Between Thorplands on the east and Shoot Up Hill on the west lay several fields called *EARLSFIELDS*. Pastureage sold in 'Erlesfeld' was listed among the issues of the manor in 1322.[8] It is unlikely that Earlsfield was part of the original manorial demesne because of its position. It may have originated in assarted land that was later leased or granted out or it may have been tenant land which had escheated to the lord. In 1632 John Kemp leased a cottage at Shoot Up Hill and two crofts called Earlsfield (6 a.). They, together with two cottages and a small close at Kilburn, passed on John's death in 1643 to his brother Francis Kemp of Willesden,[9] who owned three dwellings and 6 a., all leased to tenants, in 1649 and 1653.[10] In 1657 Francis conveyed the property to Charles Ramsbury,[11] who had conveyed it by 1678 to Samuel Walter.[12] It was held in 1704 and 1710 by a widow Waters (or Walter)[13] and from c. 1750 to c. 1820 by the Greenhill family, by which time the estate was identifiable as two fields south of Mill Lane, forming a long strip of 7 a., copyhold and heriotable. It passed to Samuel Hoare (d. 1847) and his son Joseph, who sold it to the Midland Railway Co. c. 1867.[14] The other two long fields to the east were freehold, comprising a house and 14 a. in 1705, when Robert Winter conveyed them to John Skinner.[15] The freehold estate passed to Richard Wilson in 1709, to Rebecca Osgood by 1743, to Osgood Gee in 1754, and to Edward Snoxell (d. 1766), lessee of the main demesne farm in 1759.[16] In 1764 it was the subject of a marriage settlement between Snoxell's son Armine and Jenny, daughter of Edward Nicoll.[17] Armine died young, however,[18] and from 1766 it was held by Jane Snoxell (later Mrs. Hill) and later by John Foster (d. 1785), whose executors were in possession in 1798.[19] It had passed to Edward Houlditch by 1810,[20] and was held by Richard Houlditch in 1841,[21] and by his executors in 1864.[22]

A customary holding called *BARTRAMS* (Bertrams or Bartrums) derived its name from a family which held customary and heriotable property in Hampstead from 1259 to 1347.[23] In 1312 Stephen Bertram held a house and 15 a.[24] The holding had passed to John Sleigh by 1371 and then passed to his son John (d. 1420), who held two other customary holdings.[25] It was part of the estate for which Anthony Sands paid five heriots on the death of Robert Sands, probably his father, in 1530.[26] In 1576 Thomas Sands succeeded his father Anthony to four houses or cottages and c. 50 a., mostly around Pond Street. Thomas's widow Margaret held the estates from his death in 1593 to 1621, when their daughter Frances, wife of Sir Thomas Savile, succeeded and

[93] Ibid. Lib. C, pp. 124, 194, 205–6; Lib. F, pp. 367, 369–72; Lib. G, p. 536; Lib. H, pp. 246–8; Lib. J, pp. 167–8.
[94] Ibid. Lib. K, pp. 603–5; Thompson, *Hampstead*, 129–30; Colvin, *Brit. Architects*, 867.
[95] M.M. & M., Lib. L, pp. 92–6, 225, 267–9, 467–8; Lib. M, pp. 19–21, 38; Lib. N, pp. 466, 522; S.C.L., D 69.
[96] P.R.O., IR 29/21/24, nos. 113–16.
[97] M.M. & M., Lib. P, pp. 502–12; Thompson, *Hampstead*, 130.
[98] S.C.L., Man. Map and Fieldbk. nos. 520–7; M.M. & M., Lib. E, p. 423.
[99] Presumably because the est. included Kilburn woods, originally priory land: above; G.L.R.O., E/MW/H/I/2311A.
[1] Barratt, *Annals*, iii, App. 3, pp. 359–61; G.L.R.O., E/MW/H/I/2109.
[2] P.R.O., PROB 11/259 (P.C.C. 1656, f. 375).
[3] G.L.R.O., E/MW/H/6; above.
[4] G.L.R.O., E/MW/H/8; M.M. & M., Index to Ct. Rolls, roll 7, m. 3.
[5] M.M. & M., Index, roll 7, m. 9; G.L.R.O., E/MW/H/I/2311A.
[6] M.M. & M., Lib. B, pp. 20, 33; Lib. D, pp. 328–9; Lib. F, p. 119; above, Kilburn priory.
[7] G.L.R.O., E/MW/H/6 (1674); H/17 (1698); M.M. & M., Lib. E, p. 423.

[8] W.A.M. 32406.
[9] G.L.R.O., E/MW/H/1; H/3.
[10] Barratt, *Annals*, iii, App. 4–5, pp. 361–4.
[11] G.L.R.O., E/MW/H/5.
[12] Ibid. H/I/2114. Ramsbury held the rest of the est., cottages and Huntslane abutting Catesmead, presumably at West End, until 1684: ibid. H/7.
[13] G.L.R.O., E/MW/H/I/2311A, 2123.
[14] Ibid. H/42; S.C.L., Man. Map and Fieldbk. nos. 494–5.
[15] S.C.L., D 121.
[16] M.L.R. 1709/1/188; 1714/6/6; 1743/2/477; 1754/3/188; 1759/1/194–5; S.C.L., Man. Map.
[17] M.L.R. 1764/1/136.
[18] He d. in 1761 so the 1764 settlement must have been recording an earlier transaction: S.C.L., H 283/St. John's Par. Ch. recording tombstones.
[19] G.L.R.O., E/MW/H/I/1941–3, 2178; H, old no. 31/8 (lease to Pool 1798); par. reg. (microfilm in S.C.L.).
[20] G.L.R.O., E/MW/H, old no. 30.
[21] P.R.O., IR 29/21/24, no. 88.
[22] Poor rate bk. 1864.
[23] W.A.M. 32360–1, 32494.
[24] C.U.L., Kk. V. 29, f. 32.
[25] W.A.M. 32363; Guildhall MS. 9171/3, f. 49v.; below.
[26] W.A.M. 33279.

sold them to John Needham and Edward Marsh.[27] When Needham, a London haberdasher, died in 1641, he divided Bartrams between his daughters.[28] Catherine (d. 1692) received Upper Bartrams, which passed to Joseph Needham (d. 1736),[29] to Joseph's son Joseph and, in 1744, to the latter's grandson John Thornhill, who sold it in 1746 to Ralph Farr Winter (d. 1753). Ralph's brother Joshua,[30] who held the estate as a house and c. 10 a. in 1762,[31] was succeeded in 1768 by his son Ralph,[32] who sold it to Elizabeth Baldwin in 1777.[33] Upper Bartrams, together with a house south of Pond Street, was later divided among five members of the Creed family, who between 1800 and 1809 sold their shares to Charles Cartwright.[34]

John Needham left Lower Bartrams to his other daughter Anne,[35] although there is no evidence that she held it. It may have been included in the 25 a. owned in 1646 by 'Mr.' Needham and leased to Edward Marsh.[36] In 1676 the reversion to Lower Bartrams was conveyed by Thomas Marsh to William Astley, who sold it in 1700 to Theodore Drage.[37] Drage had acquired possession before his death in 1737 when it was inherited by his son Dr. William Drage.[38] All William Drage's property passed by will in 1765 to his friend William Harrison (d. 1781) and descended to Harrison's nephew Edmund Horrex,[39] who sold Lower Bartrams to Charles Cartwright in 1810. Cartwright (d. 1825) left the reunited Bartrams to his cousin William Winfield.[40] Winfield sold 3 a. at the southern end in 1828 to John Lund, lessee of the neighbouring Belsize estate,[41] and the rest passed on his death in 1840 to his widow Anne, and on hers in 1855 to William's father Charles Henry Winfield (d. 1864).[42] In 1867 Winfield's son and heir, Lt. Col. Charles Henry Winfield, sold nearly 10 a. to the Midland Railway Co. and obtained the enfranchisement of the rest.[43] The estate was put up for sale in that year when most of it, 8 a., was bought by the Metropolitan Asylums Board, which opened a smallpox hospital there in 1870.[44]

There was a single house on the Bartrams estate from 1312,[45] at Hampstead Green south of Pond Street, just north of the George.[46] From 1641, when the estate was split between Upper and Lower Bartrams, the house descended with the first. Between 1762 and the end of the century the old house was replaced by two brick houses. Charles Cartwright in turn replaced one with another, the large irregularly shaped house called Bartrams, c. 1810.[47] It was purchased in 1867 by the Sisters of Providence as a convent and replaced by a modern block in 1967.[48]

HODGES, a heriotable copyhold estate east of Bartrams, was probably identifiable with Hoggis, a close and garden held c. 1472 by Richard Kemp.[49] It was part of Anthony Sands's estates in 1530[50] and descended with Bartrams until 1641, when John Needham left it to his widow Mary (d. 1662).[51] In 1682 their son John sold Hodges, then described as a house and 7 a. in Pond Street, to John Turner, who left it in 1688 to his son Richard.[52] It was bought by John Dee and his wife Margaret in 1703 and passed in 1721 to John's cousin Elizabeth (d. 1771), wife of Thomas Draper. In 1772 their son John sold it to John Bond, who sold it in 1774 to William Key. George Goodwin purchased Hodges in 1779 from Key's creditors[53] and sold it in 1789 to Horatio Sharp (d. 1792), whose trustees sold it in 1792 to Charles Cartwright.[54] Cartwright left it in 1825 to his uncle Charles Henry Winfield and after 1855 Hodges descended with Bartrams.[55]

ALDENHAMS, named after the family which held it from 1281,[56] was a small heriotable customary estate on the north side of Pond Street. In 1312 William Aldenham held a house and 4 a.[57] Although the family still held land in Hampstead in the 15th century, Aldenhams was one of the estates held by 'Master' Watno c. 1472[58] and by Anthony Sands in 1530. It was among the property sold in 1621 by Frances Savile to Edward Marsh,[59] who in 1646 held 11 a., subleased to three tenants.[60] Edward had been succeeded before 1650 by his son John, who in 1654 sold the estate to Alexander Ratcliff of London, who was succeeded in 1670 by his son Alexander.[61] His estate was divided, probably in the late 17th century, and Aldenhams, by 1704 consisting of two houses and 3 a.,[62] passed from Susannah to Thomas Cumber and then to S. Bromwich, Blandine Marsh, and Marsh Dickenson, who in 1762 owned three houses and 3 a. Soon afterwards Aldenhams was sold to the lessee, Richard Norris, and descended to Christopher and, in the early 19th century, to Richard Norris. It was held by trustees after his death and in the 1860s was enfranchised and partly sold to Hampstead Junction Railway.[63]

SEARSFIELD, 8 a. of copyhold north of Aldenhams, may have originated in the estate held

27 G.L.R.O., E/MW/H/1, m. 7; M.M. & M., Index to Ct. Rolls, roll 1, mm. 7–8.
28 Guildhall MS. 9052/10, f. 83.
29 M.M. & M., Index, roll 11, m. 2; ibid. Lib. C, p. 132.
30 Ibid. Lib. C, p. 132; D, pp. 9–12, 56, 268.
31 S.C.L., Man. Map and Fieldbk. nos. 8–10.
32 M.M. & M., Lib. E, pp. 268, 282–7.
33 Ibid. Lib. F, pp. 296–8.
34 Ibid. Lib. L, pp. 305–12.
35 Guildhall MS. 9052/10, f. 83.
36 Barratt, Annals, iii, App. 3, pp. 359–61.
37 M.M. & M., Index, roll 7, m. 3; roll 19, m. 1.
38 Ibid. Lib. C, pp. 140–1.
39 M.M. & M., Lib. E, p. 113; Lib. F, p. 512.
40 Ibid. Lib. J, pp. 113, 163; Lib. L, pp. 305–12.
41 Ibid. Lib. L, pp. 576–7; above, Belsize.
42 M.M. & M., Lib. N, pp. 137, 211; Lib. O, pp. 537, 581; Lib. Q, p. 67.
43 Ibid. Lib. Q, pp. 125–33, 385, 407.
44 Potter Colln. 19/89; below, pub. svces.
45 C.U.L., Kk. V. 29, f. 32.
46 S.C.L., Man. Map and Fieldbk. no. 8.

47 M.M. & M., Lib. L, pp. 305–12; poor rate bks. 1810, 1813.
48 Below, Rom. Cathm.
49 W.A.M. 32357*.
50 G.L.R.O., E/MW/H/1 (1621).
51 Guildhall MS. 9052/10, f. 83; M.M. & M., Index, roll 5, m. 10.
52 M.M. & M., Index, roll 7, m. 12; P.R.O., C 7/337/43.
53 M.M. & M., Lib. B, p. 43; Lib. E, p. 424; Lib. F, pp. 29, 129–30, 372–7.
54 Ibid. Lib. G, pp. 293–423, 456–9.
55 Ibid. Lib. L, pp. 312, 443.
56 W.A.M. 32361.
57 C.U.L., Kk. V. 29, f. 34v.
58 W.A.M. 32357*.
59 G.L.R.O., E/MW/H/1 (1621).
60 Barratt, Annals, iii, App. 3, pp. 359–61.
61 P.R.O., C 7/125/74; G.L.R.O., E/MW/H/3 (1654); H/6 (1670).
62 G.L.R.O., E/MW/H/I/2311A.
63 Ibid. H 40; S.C.L., Man. Map and Fieldbk. nos. 36–8.

in 1259 and 1281 by Asketin Pond, whose daughter Cecily sold part at least in 1296 to William Aldenham, who held 3½ a. of it in 1312. As Ponders it was held by 'Master' Watno c. 1472[64] and as Sarisfeld it was part of Anthony Sands's estates in 1530. It descended with Aldenhams until 1682 when it was acquired by Daniel Lodington, who in 1704 held a house and 10 a.[65] Lodington's seven children sold it to William Drage in 1732 and it descended with Lower Bartrams until 1809, when Edmund Horrex sold Searsfield to Samuel Gambier, who conveyed 8½ a. in 1811 and 2½ a. in 1812 to William Coleman. It formed part of the Downshire Hill estate built up after 1815.[66]

DUDDINGTONS or Donningtons, in 1576 10 a. of pasture, once called Bedyngs, and 4 a. of wood,[67] was a copyhold but not heriotable estate stretching along the borders of the Belsize estate from Pond Street to the heath.[68] It was one of the estates held by 'Master' Watno c. 1472[69] and by the Sands family in the 16th century and was among the lands sold by Frances Savile in 1621 to Edward Marsh,[70] who surrendered it in 1638 to William Marsh, a London tailor, who held it in 1655.[71] John Marsh surrendered it to Thomas Hussey of London in 1663;[72] it had passed to Peter Hussey by 1678[73] and from Nathaniel to Sarah Hussey in 1698. Joseph Ashton, the owner by 1704,[74] died in 1728 seised of three closes containing 14 a. called Duddingtons, together with three houses in High Street, including the White Hart and c. 6 a. His widow Mary and daughter were admitted for life[75] but his nephew Henry Ashton claimed the estate under his uncle's will in 1729 and died seised of it in 1731, when he was succeeded by his son Robert. There were nine houses, including the Crown and Haunch of Venison besides the White Hart by then.[76] By 1754 Robert was described as a lunatic and the estate was being administered by his sister Mary and her husband John Merry,[77] and in 1776 Mary, then a widow, inherited on Robert's death.[78] Mary (d. 1802) was succeeded by her niece Margaret Merry, who sold Duddingtons but not the rest of the estate to Thomas Rhodes (d. 1856) in 1804.[79] Rhodes was succeeded by his grandson Thomas William Rhodes,[80] who sold nearly 3 a. to the Hampstead Junction Railway Co. in 1860 and obtained the enfranchisement of the rest in 1865.[81] In 1871 Rhodes began developing the estate, which he called South Hill Park.[82]

SLYES, a copyhold estate on the west of High Street, bounded by Church (Perrin's) Lane and the Kingswell and Belsize estates, probably took its name from the Sleigh (Slegh) family, which included two Johns, father and son, who held the office of manorial beadle and rent-collector from 1375 to 1412.[83] It may be identifiable with the estate held by Gallota atte Pond in 1259,[84] by William Woodsore (or Wodesour) in 1281,[85] and by Philip Woodsore in 1312. It was then described as a house and 13½ a. held for an annual rent of 2s. 8d., four geese, and three chickens.[86] In 1372 Philip Woodsore's holding was in the hands of John Mareys, William Aldenham, and the elder John Sleigh, who also held two tenements probably near Pond Street.[87] The younger John Sleigh, described as of London, died in 1420[88] and in 1459 Roger Aldenham and Richard Kemp paid an annual rent of 2s. 8d. for crofts, messuages, and lands.[89] In 1462 Aldenham conveyed to Kemp a croft and an adjoining garden in 'Kingwell Street in length next to the king's highway'.[90] By 1530 Slyes was one of the heriotable estates held by Anthony Sands and it descended with his other holdings to Frances, wife of Sir Thomas Savile, in 1621. It was then described as two houses and appurtenances in Hampstead town called Slyes, with two orchards, gardens, and three closes (8 a.) of meadow.[91] In 1623 Henry Fleetwood claimed that Savile had agreed to sell the estate to him[92] but there is no evidence that he acquired any part of the estate, which was probably broken up about that time.

Part of Slyes had passed by 1648 to Richard Brown, a London merchant who in that year leased a customary messuage in Hampstead Street 'against the common well' with gardens and orchards (2 a.) to a London vintner, who in 1658 assigned the lease to Thomas Hussey (d. 1671), a London grocer.[93] In 1675 Thomas's son and heir Peter, by then in possession of the copyhold, conveyed the house next the common well, together with another, to Basil Herne.[94] The property, which seems to have lost one house to John Cubbidge by 1704, descended from father to son, each called Basil Herne, on their respective deaths in 1729 and 1774.[95]

In 1652 Brown's land abutted a copyhold house called Slyes together with two closes (6 a.) which was sold by Robert Marsh of Hendon to Michael Sparkes (d. 1655), a London stationer, and his wife Isabel.[96] Under Isabel's will the estate, consisting of two

[64] W.A.M. 32357*, 32359–61; C.U.L., Kk. V. 29, f. 34v.
[65] G.L.R.O., E/MW/H/1 (1621); H/I/2311A; M.M. & M., Lib. C, p. 55.
[66] M.M. & M., Lib. C, p. 59; Lib. E, p. 113; Lib. J, pp. 273–6, 357, 631; S.C.L., Man. Map and Fieldbk. nos. 45–6.
[67] G.L.R.O., E/MW/H/1 (1621). Mentioned in 1650 as an abutment of Belsize: P.R.O., C 54/3553, no. 33.
[68] S.C.L., Man. Map and Fieldbk. nos. 565–7.
[69] W.A.M. 32357*.
[70] M.M. & M., Index to Ct. Rolls, roll 1, mm. 7–8.
[71] S.C.L., D 40, 129.   [72] Ibid. D 148.
[73] Ibid. D 23; G.L.R.O., E/MW/H/I/2114.
[74] M.M. & M., Index to Ct Rolls, roll 17, mm. 2–3; G.L.R.O., E/MW/H/I/2311A.
[75] M.M. & M., Lib. B, pp. 293–4.
[76] Ibid. pp. 307–9; Lib. C, p. 31; S.C.L., D 123, 157.
[77] M.M. & M., Lib. D, pp. 302–3.
[78] Ibid. Lib. F, pp. 252–3.
[79] Ibid. Lib. H, pp. 472–4; Lib. I, p. 68; P.R.O., IR 29/21/24, nos. 19–20.

[80] M.M. & M., Lib. O, pp. 604, 622.
[81] Ibid. Lib. P, p. 269; Lib. Q, pp. 209–11; S.C.L., D 66.
[82] Thompson, Hampstead, 307–8.
[83] W.A.M. 32497–32531.
[84] Ibid. 32360.   [85] Ibid. 32361.
[86] The only holding at that rent: C.U.L., Kk. V. 29, f. 34v.
[87] W.A.M. 32357.
[88] Guildhall MS. 9171/3, f. 49v.
[89] Only 1 other holding at that rent: Dorset R.O., D 396/M/81.
[90] W.A.M. 32358.
[91] G.L.R.O., E/MW/H/1 (1621).
[92] P.R.O., C 3/349/5.
[93] S.C.L., D 125; P.R.O., PROB 11/336 (P.C.C. 1671, f. 61).
[94] G.L.R.O., E/MW/H/7.
[95] M.M. & M., Lib. F, pp. 94, 106; S.C.L., Man. Map and Fieldbk. no. 368.
[96] G.L.R.O., E/MW/H/4(1652); H/5(1655); P.R.O., C 5/375/80.

houses and two fields, passed in 1671, after the death of her second husband Robert Davies, to her cousin Susan, wife of William Johnson, a London herbalist.[97] Johnson was still the owner in 1704 but by 1710 the estate had passed to John Cubbidge, who in 1704 held a house and 5 p. of land and who in 1706 was granted a shop and some waste at the town pond, adjoining his house. In 1704 the property there, apparently from north to south belonged to John Cubbidge, Basil Herne (with a house and 32 p.), William Johnson, and John Hibbert (Hubbard). It seems, therefore, that Cubbidge had acquired one of Herne's houses which thereafter became part of the 6-a. estate.[98] By 1712 a moiety had passed to John Ward of the Inner Temple and his wife Isabel, possibly Cubbidge's daughter, who conveyed it in that year to Thomas Weedon (d. 1715), a London merchant, and his wife Susanna.[99] They acquired various pieces of waste 'on the hill before the house' and part of the town pond[1] and in 1721 Susanna conveyed the whole 6-a. estate, together with the former waste, to Alexander and Margery Staham,[2] who in turn conveyed it in 1730 to Elizabeth De Cols (or Colls).[3] After her death her nephew and devisee sold the northern portion, just over $2\frac{1}{2}$ a. together with various buildings, to George Errington (d. 1769) in 1753,[4] and the southern portion (c. 3 a.), which included the site of the ancient Slyes house, to Thomas Watson in 1754.[5] Errington's portion descended in the direct line to George (d. 1796), George Henry (d. 1843),[6] and George Henry Errington of Essex, who enfranchised it c. 1870 and merged it with his freehold Kingswell estate.[7] Watson sold his portion in 1759 to Robert Cary (d. 1777), who was already the lessee,[8] and in 1796 Cary's daughters Amy Anne, Lucy Elizabeth, and Mary sold it to Jonathan Key (d. 1805).[9] Key was succeeded by his widow Elizabeth (d. 1818) and then by his son Jonathan Henry (d. 1838). Under the latter's will the estate was divided in the proportion of $\frac{7}{10}$ and $\frac{3}{10}$ between his sons, Sir John Key, Bt., a City of London alderman, and Henry Garrett Key of Brixton.[10]

Col. John Owen, who was assessed for hearth tax in 1664, is unlikely to have been the Welsh Cromwellian of that name[11] but a London grocer who in 1671 owned land[12] previously owned by Richard Brown and who in 1681 conveyed a capital messuage with two crofts (3 a.) called Slyes to Grace Andrews, who conveyed it in 1683 to Henry Pollexfen. Al-

though the ancient capital messuage was on the northern, 6-a. estate, the payment of heriot passed with the southern, 3-a. estate.[13] The latter had passed to William Cope by 1686[14] and to William Hibbert (Hubbert) by 1704, who then had a house and close of just over 4 a.[15] By will dated 1715 Hibbert, a wealthy London skinner, left his copyhold house and appurtenances to his wife Hester for life, with remainder to his daughter Hester (or Esther), wife of Thomas Blunden.[16] After Hester Blunden's death without issue in 1749 the estate passed to her niece Esther, wife of James Lambe,[17] who immediately sold it to Joseph Butler (1692–1752), then bishop of Bristol (later of Durham). Under his will it was sold to Andrew Regnier (d. 1768), a tailor from St. Martin-in-the-Fields,[18] who was succeeded by his son John (d. 1780) and daughters Mary Buffar, widow, and Elizabeth wife of Charles Maddocks Hardey.[19] In 1787 the sisters sold their interest to James Pilgrim (d. 1813), who directed by will that the estate was to be sold. Most was purchased in 1815 by John Morice in trust for John Peter De Roure (or Rowe) and his wife Mary, who lived there[20] and were succeeded by Thomas Roper. The estate was sold by John Moore Roper to Henry Littleton Powys (who later added Keck to his surname), enfranchised in 1857, and conveyed to trustees of the Royal Soldiers' Daughters' Home in 1862.[21] A small portion was retained by Charles Pilgrim and enfranchised by his son Charles in 1882.[22]

There was a house on the estate by 1312[23] and there were two by 1621[24] and probably by 1459.[25] One house may have been that of the recusant John Raynes, which was broken into in 1609.[26] The ancient Slyes house stood, according to mid-18th century tradition, in the centre of the estate on the southern part of the 6-a. estate, which was sold in 1754 to Thomas Watson.[27] It was a single dwelling house in 1652[28] but had been divided into two by 1671.[29] Between 1712 and 1721 the house was 'new built and expanded and converted to four tenements'.[30] It was later converted to three tenements[31] and in 1762 was again a single house, occupied by the owner Robert Cary together with a coach house, stables, a dairy, a summer house, two gardens, and a pleasure ground, very much a gentleman's seat.[32] It can probably be identified with the Rookery (also called Mount Grove or Greenhill), which was occu-

[97] G.L.R.O., E/MW/H/6(1671); H/8(1686).
[98] Ibid. E/MW/H/I/2311A, 2123; M.M. & M., Lib. A, pp. 14–15.
[99] M.M. & M., Lib. A, pp. 169, 264.
[1] Ibid. pp. 176, 233, 313.
[2] Ibid. Lib. B, p. 37.
[3] Ibid. Lib. D, p. 287.
[4] Ibid. pp. 262–3; Lib. E, p. 319; S.C.L., Man. Map and Fieldbk. nos. 369–73.
[5] M.M. & M., Lib. D, p. 287.
[6] S.C.L., Hampstead manor min. bk. (1783–1809), p. 226; (1839–43), p. 134.
[7] G.L.R.O., E/MW/H/211; above, Kingswell.
[8] M.M. & M., Lib. D, pp. 400–1.
[9] Ibid. Lib. F, pp. 307, 326–9, 416, 495; Lib. H, pp. 177–9, 189–92.
[10] Ibid. Lib. I, p. 220; S.C.L., Hampstead manor min. bk. (1809–24), p. 279; (1824–39), p. 435; (1839–43), p. 3.
[11] Who d. in 1666: D.N.B.
[12] G.L.R.O., E/MW/H/6.
[13] Ibid. 7.
[14] Ibid. 8.
[15] Ibid. E/MW/H/I/2311A.
[16] P.R.O., C 78/1796, no. 10; S.C.L., D 122.
[17] M.M. & M., Lib. D, p. 150.
[18] Ibid. pp. 168, 257; S.C.L., Man. Map and Fieldbk. nos. 378–84.
[19] M.M. & M., Lib. E, pp. 244–5; F, p. 474.
[20] Ibid. Lib. G, pp. 228–9; J, pp. 499, 542–56.
[21] S.C.L., Hampstead manor min. bk. (1824–39), p. 397; H 362.73/Royal Soldiers' Daughters' Home (deed 1862).
[22] G.L.R.O., E/MW/H/40.
[23] C.U.L., Kk. V. 29, f. 34v.
[24] G.L.R.O., E/MW/H/I.
[25] Dorset R.O., D 396/M/81.
[26] G.L.R.O., Cal. Mdx. Sess. Rec. ii. 61; below, Rom. Cathm.; Wm. Raynes, also a recusant, was the tenant in 1621: G.L.R.O., E/MW/H/I.
[27] M.M. & M., Lib. D, pp. 400–1.
[28] G.L.R.O., E/MW/H/4 (1652).
[29] Ibid. 6 (1671).
[30] M.M. & M., Lib. B, p. 37.
[31] Ibid. Lib. D, pp. 400–1; Lib. E, pp. 365–6.
[32] S.C.L., Man. Map and Fieldbk. nos. 375–7.

pied by the publisher Thomas Norton Longman (d. 1842) and was demolished in 1870, to be replaced in turn by a Wesleyan chapel and in the 1930s by the Greenhill flats.[33]

POPES, also called the Honywood or Carlile estate, of 16 a. in 1762,[34] took its name from a family which held land in Hampstead by 1296.[35] Heriot was paid after the death of Christopher Pope in 1355[36] and in 1393 Popes garden, probably held by William and Alice Gibb, was a northern abutment of Kingswell garden.[37] In the early 15th century Alice Gibb paid rent for a tenement called Popes,[38] which probably formed part of the houses and lands held by John Gibb the younger in 1459.[39] By will dated 1516 John Gibb left his house and three closes on the south and west and one called East Popes field to his stepson William Smith.[40] The east and west components of the estate had apparently separated by 1621, when the name was applied exclusively to the east part.[41] By 1660 Popes meadow (8 a.) and a brick house bought from Robert Foster were left to Anne Pitchford by her husband William.[42] Anne died in 1674 and the meadow, though not the house, passed to her daughter Rebecca, wife of Isaac Honywood (d. 1721).[43] In 1704 Isaac Honywood had an estate of two houses and four closes totalling 17 a.,[44] which descended in turn to Isaac's sons Edward (d. 1727) and Isaac (d. 1740).[45] Isaac's son (d. 1764), an eminent London banker[46] left the estate to his fourth cousin Sir John Honywood, Bt. (d. 1806).[47] In 1809 Sir John's son Sir John Courtenay Honywood, Bt., conveyed it to Samuel Gambier, first commissioner of the Navy, who sold 5 a. in 1811[48] and the rest in 1812 to William Coleman.[49] Coleman became bankrupt and in 1814 4 a. were bought by Edward Carlile,[50] to be followed by the rest in 1816. Carlile (d. 1833) left the estate for the use of his wife Elizabeth (d. 1838), his son James (d.s.p. 1859), and the children of his daughter Janette Anne, who married Benjamin Edward Willoughby (d. 1854) in 1833. The estate was enfranchised in 1873 and sold to the British Land Co. in 1875.[51]

The medieval Popes house probably lay near Popes garden and was therefore west of High Street and north of Kingswell.[52] Anne Pitchford's house

was assessed at 10 hearths in 1664. The Elizabethan Chicken House was on the Honywood estate. In 1674 Mrs. Honywood, presumably Rebecca, occupied the 23-hearth Slyes house, possibly while the main Honywood residence, later called Carlile House, was being built.[53] In 1692 the dissenting meeting house, between the Chicken House and Carlile House, was first recorded as at the dwelling of Isaac Honywood, who had two houses in 1704.[54] Fraser Honywood had a 'handsome edifice' in 1755.[55] It was probably rebuilt and by the 19th century was a stuccoed, rectangular building of three storeys and basement, with a two-storeyed bay at the side. It was demolished in 1876.[56]

JACKSFIELD, a heriotable copyhold of 8 a. at West End, bordering the demesne,[57] was mentioned in 1387.[58] It was held by Nicholas Fletcher (fl. 1397), by William Hunt (d. 1439),[59] and later by Edward Westby and by John Gilling (d. 1475), parish clerk of St. Sepulchre, who left it to his kinsman Thomas Gilling for life, and then to be sold for charity.[60] It was held in 1646 by Martin Dawson, who owned, *inter alia*, three houses and 8 a.[61] By will proved 1662 Dawson left his copyhold property to his wife Susan,[62] but he had incurred debts as a royalist and she apparently lost the property between 1664[63] and 1668 when it was held by Sir Geoffrey Palmer, Bt. (d. 1670), attorney-general. Palmer left it to his daughter Frances, wife of John De La Fontayne, who conveyed it in 1686 to Anthony Keck.[64] Anthony was succeeded in 1696 by Francis Keck,[65] whose estate in 1704 consisted of an 8-a. close (Jacksfield) and a house and $1\frac{1}{4}$ a. of orchard (Frognal Hall) and 4 a. of demesne land adjoining the churchyard, which he leased.[66] Francis was succeeded in 1730 by his seven sisters or their heirs, who in 1735 conveyed all the estate to Joseph Stanwix or Stanwick, on whose death in 1747 it passed by will to his widow Mary, with remainder to his daughters Mary, wife of James Battin, and Jane, wife of Robert Slaughter.[67] Mary conveyed her share to Jane, who in 1765 conveyed Jacksfield to John Taylor, butcher, who in turn conveyed it in 1769 to Christopher Fowler. Thence it passed in 1771 to Thomas Boone and in 1775 to Thomas Wildman. Wildman (d. 1796) left it in trust for Maria Beckford.[68] It passed

[33] *Hampstead One Thousand*, 81–2; Barratt, *Annals*, iii. 27–8, 270; P. Wallis, *At the Sign of the Ship, 1724–1974* (1974), 13–15, 19; S.C.L., Hampstead manor min. bk. (1809–24), p. 279; G.L.R.O., E/MW/H/211.
[34] S.C.L., Man. Map and Fieldbk. nos. 47–53.
[35] W.A.M. 32359.
[36] Ibid. 32496.
[37] *Cal. Close R.* 1392–6, 136.
[38] W.A.M. 32357.
[39] Dorset R.O., D 396/M/81.
[40] Guildhall MS. 9171/9, f. 10.
[41] G.L.R.O., E/MW/H/1 (1621).
[42] Ibid. (1660); 7 (1675).
[43] Ibid.; P.R.O., PROB 11/346 (P.C.C. 1674, f. 109).
[44] G.L.R.O., E/MW/H/I/2311A.
[45] Ibid. H, old no. Box L (abs. of leases 1680–1731).
[46] Ibid. H/I/2140; *Lond. in Miniature* (1755), quoted in Barratt, *Annals*, i. 268.
[47] G.L.R.O., E/MW/H/I/2178; poor rate bks. 1767, 1779, 1800; *Topographer and Genealogist*, ed. J. G. Nicols, ii. 54–6, 190–1.
[48] Burke, *Peerage* (1890); M.M. & M., Lib. J, pp. 273–6; *H.H.E.* 24 Aug. 1951.
[49] M.M. & M., Lib. J, pp. 357 sqq.
[50] Ibid. pp. 486, 494–6.
[51] S.C.L., D 133, 247.

[52] *Cal. Close R.* 1392–6, 136.
[53] G.L.R.O., MR/TH/2, mm. 29d.–30; P.R.O., E 179/143/370, m. 43d.; above, growth, Hampstead town.
[54] G.L.R.O., E/MW/H/I/2311A; S.C.L., Man. Map and Fieldbk. nos. 43 (Chicken Ho.), 51 (Carlile Ho.); *Rosslyn Hill Chapel 1692–1973* (1974), 17, 19; below, prot. nonconf.
[55] *Lond. in Miniature* (1755).
[56] S.C.L., Carlile Ho. file, photo. c. 1870.
[57] G.L.R.O., E/MW/H/42; S.C.L., Man. Map and Fieldbk. nos. 449–50.
[58] W.A.M. 32508.
[59] Ibid. 32362, 32519; *Cal. of Wills in Ct. of Husting, Lond. 1258–1688*, ed. R. R. Sharpe, ii (2), 486.
[60] W.A.M. 32357*; Dorset R.O., D 396/M/81; Guildhall MS. 9171/6, f. 133.
[61] Barratt, *Annals*, iii, App. 3, 359–61.
[62] P.R.O., PROB 11/309 (P.C.C. 139/1662).
[63] *Cal. Cttee. for Money*, i. 290; ii. 1090; P.R.O., C 6/20/47; G.L.R.O., MR/TH/2, m. 30.
[64] G.L.R.O., E/MW/H/6 (1668); 8 (1686); P.R.O., PROB 11/333 (P.C.C. 81 Penn).
[65] M.M. & M., Lib. B, p. 338.
[66] G.L.R.O., E/MW/H/I/2311A.
[67] M.M. & M., Lib. B, p. 338; C, p. 117; D, pp. 117–19.
[68] Ibid. Lib. D, p. 438; S.C.L., D 1 (a–d, i, m).

in 1800 to Richard Howard, earl of Effingham, as devisee of Maria Beckford and, on his death in 1818, by will to Samuel March Phillips, who was the owner in 1841. In 1858 it passed to one Walters, who enfranchised it.[69]

The house associated with Jacksfield by 1646 was probably Frognal Hall.[70] It was presumably one of two houses owned by Susan Dawson in 1664: she occupied one with 11 hearths and another with 10 hearths was empty.[71] In 1668 Pepys visited Sir Geoffrey Palmer 'in the fields by his old route and house'.[72] In 1761 Frognal Hall was detached from the Jacksfield estate, and during the 18th century became part of the West End House estate. Canterbury House was built on Jacksfield in the 1860s.[73]

TREHERNE CROFT, a triangular-shaped 4-a. close north of Jacksfield,[74] originated as customary land taken into the lord's hand for default of rent, possibly as a result of the Black Death. It was leased to Geoffrey le Fowler 1353–5,[75] to Thomas Bolton 1372–6,[76] to John Gibbs 1408–9,[77] then to Thomas Gibbs and to John Gilling and Hugh Penne in 1459.[78] John Gilling (d. 1475), left it, with Jacksfield, to his kinsman Thomas Gilling[79] and it was later held, also with Jacksfield, by Edward Westby.[80] It was a copyhold again by 1580 when William Jurden and his wife conveyed it to Richard Weeks, gentleman, and his wife Jane. Jane left her husband and married Edward Fust, by whom she had a son, Richard, who leased Treherne Croft and other property to John Wroth, kinsman of the lord of the manor.[81] A Fust was apparently still the owner in 1660.[82] By 1704 Treherne Croft was associated with Hillfield, the close to the north, and was held by Charles Herriott,[83] who conveyed the estate, a house, garden, and nearly 17 a. in three closes, to Henry Binfield in 1720.[84] The Binfields retained the estate until the end of the 18th century[85] but by 1841 Treherne Croft had become detached from the land to the north and was owned by Robert Shout.[86]

Treherne House had been built by 1762,[87] possibly by 1720.[88] It was probably rebuilt in the late 18th or early 19th century when it became a grand house, having a seven-bayed main section with attics and central porch and a large bay-windowed wing. In 1825 it was occupied by S. H. Binns[89] and in 1841 by the owner, Robert Shout. The house survived until the 1890s.[90]

ECONOMIC HISTORY. AGRICULTURE. Most, $3\frac{1}{2}$ of the 5 hides of the pre-Conquest Hampstead estate, belonged in 1086 to the manorial demesne, which had 1 ploughteam and 1 serf. The other $1\frac{1}{2}$ was villein land, but 1 hide of it was held by Ranulf Peverell who had $\frac{1}{2}$ ploughteam, while of the remaining $\frac{1}{2}$ hide, where 1 *villanus* had 1 virgate and 5 bordars the other, there was 1 villein ploughteam. There was room for one further ploughteam presumably on the demesne. The woodland, for 100 pigs, was small, especially since the 5 hides did not correspond with Hampstead's acreage in 1931 (2,265 a.), but that was probably because wood for pigs described mast-bearing oak and beech and most of Hampstead's woodland was birch and heath. The whole manor, worth 50s. in 1086, had halved in value since 1066.[91]

During the period of confusion and alienation in the 12th and 13th centuries a considerable amount of the demesne was lost to freehold estates. Belsize may have originated in the Peverell holding[92] but the estates held in free alms, Chalcots, Kilburn priory, and the Temple, evidently came from manorial demesne. Together with one 16-a. secular holding (Kingswell) they covered nearly half of the parish.[93] By 1312 there were 285 a. of manorial demesne in addition to an unspecified amount of woodland and at least 340 a. of customary land.[94]

For about a century from the mid 13th century, Westminster abbey exploited its Hampstead demesne directly through a reeve or *serviens*.[95] There were from 5 to 10 *famuli* who were paid in grain: two ploughmen, a carter, a shepherd, a cowherd, often a harrower, a dairyman or girl, a boy to keep the woods in summer and lead the reapers in autumn, and sometimes a neatherd, a keeper of lambs, a driver, a housemaid, a swineherd, and a greyhound keeper. A miller and a smith were also employed on the demesne and carpenters and building workers were hired as needed. Other work was performed as customary labour or hired for the job. The demesne occupied the heart of Hampstead manor and parish, centred on the grange farm which was probably at Frognal. In 1312 the demesne contained 204 a. of profitable (*lucrabilis*) land, which has been interpreted as arable. The largest portion, 87 a., lay in Summer Leas in the south-west, while there were 61 a. in Homefield, presumably near the grange, 11 a. in Pirley field in the south-east, and smaller

[69] M.M. & M., Lib. K, p. 281; G.L.R.O., E/MW/H/42; P.R.O., IR 29/21/24.
[70] Barratt, *Annals*, iii, App. 3, pp. 359–61; above, growth, Frognal.
[71] G.L.R.O., MR/TH/2, m. 30.
[72] *Diary of Sam. Pepys*, ed. R. Latham and W. Matthews, ix. 281; G.L.R.O., E/MW/H/6 (1668). Pepys went on to Belsize Ho., an easier journey from Frognal than from West End.
[73] S.C.L., Man. Map and Fieldbk. nos. 449–50; M.M. & M., Lib. K, p. 281; Wade, *W. Hampstead*, 10, 16–17.
[74] S.C.L., Man. Map and Fieldbk. no. 446.
[75] W.A.M. 32495–6.
[76] Ibid. 32357, 32497.
[77] Ibid. 32529.
[78] Dorset R.O., D 396/M/81.
[79] Guildhall MS. 9171/6, f. 133.
[80] W.A.M. 32357*. Westby was the farmer of the man. and collector of rents in 1497–8: Dorset R.O., D 396/M/81.
[81] P.R.O., C 5/605/139; C 8/31/36.
[82] G.L.R.O., E/MW/H/5.
[83] Ibid. E/MW/H/I/2311A.

[84] Ibid. H, old no. Box L (abs. of leases 1680–1731).
[85] Ibid. H/I/2178: H, old no. 31/8 (lease 1798, schedule of titheable land).
[86] P.R.O., IR 29/21/24, nos. 132–3.
[87] S.C.L., Man. Map and Fieldbk. no. 448.
[88] G.L.R.O., E/MW/H, old no. Box L (abs. of leases 1680–1731); above, growth, West End.
[89] Thompson, *Hampstead*, 119–20 and plate 11.
[90] Ibid. 343–4; P.R.O., IR 29/21/24, nos. 132–3; Wade, *W. Hampstead*, 16.
[91] *V.C.H. Mdx.* i. 122–3, nos. 38–9. Cf. Nuthurst (probably hazel) and Whitebirch (silver birch): below, woods.
[92] Above, other est.
[93] i.e. 900 a. or 950 a., inc. the Flitcroft est., as assessed in 1762: S.C.L., Man. Map and Fieldbk.; cf. map of manor and est.
[94] C.U.L., Kk. V. 29, ff. 30v.–36.
[95] Following paras. based on man. accts. 1271–1355: W.A.M. 32367–76, 32381–5, 32393–406, 32493–6. Most accts. were from Mic.–Mic. Dates are from the second year: see T. Z. Titow, *Eng. Rural Soc. 1200–1350* (1969), 28.

amounts in other named shots and crofts.[96] Other evidence suggests that Pirley was much larger[97] and the three may have originally formed a three-field system. By the later 13th century, however, recorded acreages of arable crops were much lower, suggesting a two-field system with half the arable fallow at any one time. Acreages mentioned are 24 a. of rye in 1271, 60 a. of wheat in 1272, 70 a. of oats in 1273, and 52 a. of oats in 1286. In 1347 103 a. were under crops: 66 a. of oats (31 a. in Homefield, 25 a. in Summer Leas, and 10 a. in Pirley), 33 a. of wheat (26 a. in Homefield and 7 a. in Summer Leas), and 4 a. of peas in Homefield. All the usual grains were grown but, while the amounts produced each year fluctuated, oats were by far the most important crop. In the 1270s and 1280s there was an average yield of 63 qr. of oats, compared with 15 qr. of wheat, 12½ qr. of rye, and 6 qr. of barley. From 1290 rye was usually grown with maslin. Small amounts of peas and beans, 1–2½ qr., were also grown. The yield from all crops was low, especially for wheat where sometimes the whole crop was used for seed, and frequently grain was bought or acquired from other Westminster manors. The oats were used as provender for the oxen and horses, the other grains for the *famuli* and boonworkers. Any surplus was sold or sent to other Westminster manors.

In 1312 the arable was valued at 4d. an acre, amounting to £3 8s. Permanent meadow for mowing, of which there were only 28 a., was worth 4s. an acre or £5 12s. Most of it, 14 a., was in Summer Leas, while there were 4½ a. in Pirley and 4½ a. in Homefield.[98] Throughout the late 13th century and early 14th about 25 a. were regularly mown but the hay never fetched more than £3 10s.[99] Pasture included 11 a. mostly in Homefield, for which no value was given, 34½ a. in Northfield (23 a.) and Pirley (11 a.) worth 5d. an acre or 14s. 4½d., and 7 a. of fallow land worth 2d. an acre or 1s. 2d. All the meadows and pastures were commonable from 29 September to 25 March. There was common pasture throughout the year in some woods, named as Northwood, Nuthurst, and Sheppenbrighull, all probably in the northern part of the demesne. No value was given.[1]

In the 1270s most of the pasture was presumably used by the demesne animals, only 4s. a year being received from pasture sold to the Templars. In 1286 pasture fetched £1 4s. 11d. and throughout the 1280s and 1290s the annual income from pasture sold was between £1 and £2 13s. Possibly extra pasture was obtained by clearing the woods and heath, and Eastfield, later part of Belsize, was mentioned as demesne pasture in 1297. In the 14th century the sale of pasture seems to have been less profitable. No winter pasture was sold in 1303 because it was used by the demesne animals and in 1322 there were no buyers for several pastures. There was a lot of hedging around the demesne fields in the late 14th and early

15th century, especially in the 1380s, mostly to 'save young wood', possibly from grazing animals.[2]

In 1259 the demesne stock consisted of 2 carthorses, 12 stots, 8 oxen, a bull, 18 cows, 9 other cattle, 320 sheep, 4 geese, 12 capons, and 6 chickens.[3] From 1270 to 1299 it averaged 2 carthorses, 4 stots, 7 oxen, a bull, 12 cows, and 15 other cattle, with little variation from year to year. The cows were farmed out from 1297, the farmer paying £4 1s. 1d. a year for their milk and calves. The oxen were used for ploughing, the horses and stots for carting, and profit was obtained from the sale of butter, cheese, excess animals, and the skins of dead animals. The profits from sheep, potentially much greater, were more erratic. There were 376 sheep in 1271 and the numbers increased to 511 in 1279 but by 1283 they had fallen to 131, increasing again to 231 in 1286. In that year, however, the flock was devastated by disease,[4] falling to 62 in 1287. It never really recovered and ceased to be an item in the accounts in 1297–9. In 1314 there were 220 and in 1347 124. The sheep were kept mainly for their wool, most of which was sent to Westminster, as was their cheese.

Other profits of the demesne listed in 1312 were, besides the furze and wood,[5] manure, valued at 3s.,[6] an item which never appeared on the manorial accounts, and the apples and herbage from the gardens and courtyards valued at 3s. 8d. Herbage was usually included in the accounts with other pasture and the profit from apples was erratic, varying when it occurred at all from 1s. 2d. (1288) to 7s. (1292). One barrel of cider was produced in 1297. The tenants rendered 8 or 10 geese at the feast of St. Peter in Chains (1 Aug.), 42 or more chickens at Christmas, and 110 or more eggs at Easter, which were usually sent to the cellarer at Westminster or sold. From the mid 1280s geese and chickens were also kept at the grange and a henhouse was mentioned in 1289. Pigs were listed on the demesne only from 1298.

Leasing became increasingly important in the economy of the demesne. In the 1270s, apart from the farm of the manorial mill,[7] some 4s. a year was obtained from the sale of pasture, an item which had risen to over £1 a year by the mid 1280s and over £2 by the mid 1290s. From 1297 the demesne cows were farmed out at 5s. a cow, and from 1298 escheated tenant land and Eastfield were farmed out, although there appears to have been difficulty in finding lessees in the early 14th century. The Black Death, which presumably devastated the *famuli* and manorial officials besides the abbot and Westminster monks who fled to Hampstead in a vain attempt to avoid it,[8] accelerated the drift to leasing. In 1350 all the land, meadow, and pasture of the demesne, together with 2 oxen, a bull, and 15 cows, were leased to Richard Hanningham for 5 years at £10 a year, while Eastfield and some escheated tenant land was leased to the prior of Westminster and ultimately became part

[96] C.U.L., Kk. V. 29, ff. 30v.–31; Harvey, *Westm. Abbey*, 430; Kennedy, *Man. of Hampstead*, App. VIII. Kennedy consistently misreads 80 in rom. numerals as 24.
[97] e.g. 180 perch of hedge was made round Pirley in 1412: W.A.M. 32531. The 4 closes called Pirley fields in 1729 totalled 38 a.: S.C.L., D 25.
[98] C.U.L., Kk. V. 29, f. 30v.–31.
[99] Some may have been used on the grange or sent to Westm. but if so it was never entered on the accounts.
[1] C.U.L., Kk. V. 29, ff. 30–31v.

[2] There was c. 3,471 perch of hedging c. 1377–1412.
[3] W.A.M. 32360.
[4] Almost all the ewes were sterile and oil was purchased for scabby sheep.
[5] Below, woods.
[6] *Aysiamenta domorum necessarium*, rendered in the 1606 translation of Hendon's survey as 'easements of cowhos.': *T.L.M.A.S.* xii. 580. [7] Cf. below.
[8] *Flete's Hist. Westm. Abbey*, ed. J. A. Robinson (1909), 128–30; 26 monks died.

of Belsize. The reeve continued to administer the woods, rents, and other manorial dues. Westminster still received £10 a year from Hampstead manor in 1370[9] and by 1376, when the demesne was leased with its meadow, pasture, and stock to John Brown, the rent was £13 6s. 8d. and the rents, profits from woods, and other dues were then collected by a bedell, John Sleigh, who continued in office until 1393, when he was succeeded by his son, also John Sleigh (d. 1420).[10] Brown was succeeded in 1381 by William Gibb, who leased the demesne for 20 years at £14 a year. Gibb continued as farmer until 1411 when the demesne, but not the stock, was leased to William Winter for £12. The stock, 2 oxen, a bull, and 15 cows, was sold or sent to other Westminster estates.[11] From 1497, when the lessee was also the collector of rents and issues of the courts, the lessees were Edward Westby (1497–1500),[12] Bartholomew Westby, baron of the Exchequer (1513–20),[13] and John James (1521–41).[14] With the possible exception of the last two, all the known lessees also held customary tenements and came from Hampstead families.[15]

In the 1270s and 1280s the Templars rented pasture in the demesne.[16] In 1308 on their Hampstead estate, which was administered as part of their manor of Lisson, 14 a. were sown with peas and 35 a. with oats, and oxen were kept.[17] The estate, having passed to the Hospitallers, was in 1327 described as including 100 a. of arable and 3 a. of meadow in Hampstead, part of Lisson manor leased for life to William Langford.[18] In 1338 the southern portion of the estate, later St. John's Wood, was presumably still part of Lisson manor, which was leased for life to William de Cliff, while the northern, later the Shoot Up Hill estate, was part of Clerkenwell bailiwick and leased at the will of the prior.[19] In 1522 the Shoot Up Hill estate, together with the Hospitallers' lands in Willesden and Hendon, was leased to John Barne,[20] who by 1540 had assigned his 50-year lease to Thomas Bland.[21]

The Chalcots estate was apparently administered directly by the master of St. James's hospital in 1296, when he was distrained for harbouring his servants who had trespassed in the demesne corn.[22] It was leased by 1450 to John Rye[23] and by 1481 to William Amy;[24] in 1481 Chalcots was leased to Thomas Leckhampton for 20 years.[25] From 1514 it

was leased together with Wyldes in Hendon[26] to Thomas and William Kempe for 21 years;[27] William Kempe renewed the lease for 21 years in 1531.[28]

After the demesne was leased, Westminster abbey's control of Hampstead evidently passed to the prior, and the prior's estate, Belsize, became the centre of the administration of the whole manor.[29] The prior apparently still had Belsize in hand c. 1486 and in 1496[30] but in 1500 Eastfield (then in four closes) and Fishers croft, the portion of Belsize east of the London road, were leased to William Griffen, a London butcher, for three years.[31] The same land was leased for 12 years to Robert Cheeseman and John Palmer, both gentlemen of Kentish Town, in 1518,[32] and by 1539 the whole estate was leased to William Wrench.[33]

Excluding the free tenants,[34] there were 35 tenants paying rent of £2 18s., 40 hens, and 11 geese in 1259, and 44 tenants paying £3 17s. 3½d. in 1281. In 1312 there were 41 customary tenants paying £4 3s., 8 geese, 45 hens, and 113 eggs.[35] Two other holdings were in the hands of the lord: Alwinesfield, 16 a. held for 3s. 8d. rent, had been surrendered to the lord in 1295 by John Lyon because of his inability to pay the rent and services, and a house and 20 a. held for 4s. 10d. had been sold by John de Kilburn in 1296 to the lord, who sold the house in 1298.[36] Both holdings were leased during the 14th century.[37] Alwinesfield was still leased in 1459[38] and although Kilburn's holding, then called Pagesfield after Robert Page, the lessee for most of the 14th century, was held as customary land in the early 15th century,[39] it may have later reverted to the lord and become part of the demesne by 1704.[40] There were 51 customary holdings in 1312, and although reckoning in virgates was obsolete by then[41] it was apparently still the basis of most of the existing holdings. There were two probable virgate holdings, each a house and 30 a. held for 3s. 10d. rent by Richard Blakett and Richard le Child respectively. The rents and services of those two ought to have been accounted for under Hendon,[42] and although they were not listed in the Hendon survey of 1321 they were in 1349.[43] The place names Childs Hill and Blacketts well indicate that their holdings were on the boundaries of Hampstead and Hendon.[44] By 1322 rent was no longer being received in Hampstead for either holding and Blakett's tenement was sold to Henry le

[9] W.A.M. 19864.
[10] Ibid. 32497–531; Guildhall MS. 9171/3; f. 49v.
[11] W.A.M. 32497–531.
[12] Dorset R.O., D 396/M/81; P.R.O., SC 6/Hen. VII/400.
[13] Westm. Lease bk. II, ff. 52v.; W.A.M. 33269, f. 24.
[14] Westm. Lease bk. II, ff. 174 and v., 287 and v.; P.R.O., SC 6/Hen. VIII/2415, m. 17.
[15] W.A.M. 32357, 32357*; Dorset R.O., D 396/M/81.
[16] W.A.M. 32367, 32394, 32384, 32376.
[17] P.R.O., E 358/20, m. 3d. The wheat and rye in Hampstead were not separately recorded.
[18] B.L. Cott. MS. Nero E. vi, f. 74v.
[19] Kts. Hospitallers in Eng. (Camd. Soc. [1st ser.], lxv), 95, 173.
[20] B.L. Cott. MS. Claud. E. vi, ff. 235v.–6.
[21] P.R.O., SC 6/Hen. VIII/2402, m. 8d.; above, other est. (Temple).   [22] W.A.M. 32359.
[23] E.C.R. 61/RR/A/66.
[24] Ibid. 16/ST. JAS/3, m. 1.
[25] Ibid. 54/163, vol. 13, p. 117.
[26] V.C.H. Mdx. v. 21.
[27] E.C.R. 54/163, vol. 13, p. 160.
[28] Ibid. vol. 14, p. 10.

[29] W.A.M. 32357, 32509, 32499; Dorset R.O., D 396/M/81.
[30] W.A.M. 16470, 32274.   [31] Ibid. 16471.
[32] Ibid. 16472.
[33] Ibid. RCO 32.
[34] Not named as such but identifiable in 1259 as the Templars, Kilburn priory, the brothers of Chalcot, Rog. de la Methe, and the tenants of the Hide: W.A.M. 32360; in 1281 as master of the New Temple, Kilburn priory, Chalcot, Geof. Kingswell, and Maud of Kilburn and the holding of 'Kanep' (the last two linked with the Hide): W.A.M. 32361.
[35] C.U.L., Kk. V. 29, ff. 32–5.
[36] W.A.M. 32359, 32374, 32401, 32403.
[37] Ibid. 32494, 32529.
[38] Dorset R.O., D 396/M/81.
[39] W.A.M. 32362.
[40] G.L.R.O., E/MW/H/I/2311A.
[41] Harvey, Westm. Abbey, 206.
[42] C.U.L., Kk. V. 29, f. 34.
[43] W.A.M. 32563.
[44] T.L.M.A.S. xii. 547 sqq.; Stanford, Libr. Map of Lond. and Suburbs (1862 edn. with additions to 1865); above, growth, Childs Hill.

Scrope, who held the manor of Hodford and Cowhouse in south Hendon.[45] It is probable, therefore, that the two customary Hampstead holdings became absorbed into that manor and that the parish boundary was later adjusted.

There was one holding of a house and 24 a. and 14 possibly derived from half virgates, each being a house and between 10–20 a.; the house had become detached from another and was held by an undertenant. There were 13 holdings of less than 10 a., each with a house, in one case with 2 houses, and 7 houses with no land. Two of the latter were undersets and one other was held together with 7½ a. from other holdings. There were nine holdings of land only, usually small amounts, some underset and some probably assarts. Rents bore little relation to the size of tenement, the highest, 6s. 8d. and 4s. 8d., being paid for holdings of 10 and 11 a. respectively. Almost all the holdings with land paid hens and eggs as rent while those with only a house paid only a few pence.

One tenement of a house and 12 a. was lost as a result of the Black Death, being leased to the prior of Westminster and absorbed into Belsize.[46] Another, Arnoldsland, was in the hands of the lord in 1354[47] but later was granted out again. The main effect of the Black Death was to concentrate the customary holdings in fewer hands. By 1372 26 tenants held 55 tenements. The increased number of tenements is accounted for by the fragmentation and recombination of existing holdings rather than the creation of new ones. The total rent was £4 2s. 2d.[48] From 1376 to 1412 rents were a fixed item of £9 0s. 4¼d., of which the assised rents formed £8 0s. 0¼d., the remainder being composed of tallage and medsilver.[49] By 1459 a distinction had been made between so-called assised rents (in 1539 described as paid by free tenants although it included tallage) totalling £6 3s. 10¾d. and customary rents, totalling £4 6s. 11¾d., then paid by 19 tenants. The greatest concentration of property was in the hands of Walter Hunt, who paid £1 10s. 4½d. rent.[50] He was the son of William Hunt (d. 1439), a London butcher whose Hampstead estate was centred on his house in Kilburn.[51] In 1472 there were 21 tenants paying £10 7s. 6½d. a year for 38 holdings which were either customary or held at farm; the farmed tenant land had in 1459 comprised 7 holdings farmed for 19s. a year.[52]

Most customary tenants whose holdings in 1312 possibly derived from half-virgates owed a total of 15 works each: harrowing, carting dung, hoeing, haymaking, carting hay, and autumn boonworks: reaping and carting corn and oats. In addition they owed a day's

ploughing each for the winter and spring sowing if they possessed a plough. Fifteen tenants owed those services, one owed twice as many, and another half as many.[53] The two probable virgate holdings owed similar but lighter services which were probably performed in Hendon, each owing a day's harrowing, hoeing, haymaking, and carting corn, 4 days' reaping, and a day's ploughing if he possessed a plough. In addition he had to thresh 2 bu. of rye or wheat and 5 bu. of oats. Two tenants each with a house and 5 a. owed week-work, one day's work each week except for the weeks of Christmas, Easter, and Whitsun, and one with 16 a. from which the house had been separated owed 16 works in autumn. The week-work (also called small or manual works) was defined in detail in 1297 and included harrowing, hoeing, reaping, collecting and spreading manure, planting beans, hedging, and cutting and collecting stubble.[54] The works performed never, except for the week-works, corresponded with those owed. In 1312 they were 35 harrowing, 25½ carting dung, 1 hoeing, 83½ haymaking, 16½ carting hay, 37 reaping and 34 carting corn, and 114 manual works, valued at £1 15s. 4¼d. The ploughing works were not included. In 1274 there were 13 ploughmen at the boon ploughing and £2 15s. 2¼d. was paid on the equivalent of 158½ reapers, but it is not clear whether the expense was in food and drink for boon-reapers or in wages for hired men.[55] In 1289 the reaping was performed by at least 28 boonworkers besides the *famuli*, and 8 hired reapers.[56] In 1297, when works were separately listed, 18 autumn boonworks were commuted.[57] By 1299 the commuted works were 18 autumn boonworks, 8 ploughing, 63 carting, and 2 threshing works.[58] In 1322 £1 0s. 10½d. was obtained from the sale of 32 hoeing, 67 carrying, 37 reaping, 8 autumn, and 27 winter manual works.[59] By 1347 commuted works, which included all the manual works, brought in £1 11s.[60] After the demesne was leased in 1350 all the works were commuted, except 85 haymaking works which were granted to the lessee.[61] The value of commuted works had crystallized at £1 9s. 2d. by 1459 and so remained until 1539.[62]

Customary tenants had to pay a common tallage at Martinmas. In 1281 the amounts paid by 32 tenants varied from ½d. to 2s. and totalled £1 0s. 7½d.[63] The total fell from £1 5s. in 1271 to £1 2s. 2d. in 1312 and 19s. from 1376 to 1412.[64] As 'unyeld', it was paid by 24 tenants in the early 15th century.[65] By 1459 it had dropped to 15s. 8¾d., which was explained by the annexation of tenements by Belsize,[66] and it was thereafter included in the figure for assised rents.[67] Other payments demanded from

45 W.A.M. 32406; *V.C.H. Mdx.* v. 4, 18.
46 W.A.M. 32495; above, other est.
47 W.A.M. 32495.
48 W.A.M. 32357.
49 Ibid. 32497–32531.
50 Ibid. 33269–79; ibid. RCO 32 (copy of ministers' acct. 1539); Dorset R.O., D 396/M/81.
51 W.A.M. 32362; *Cal. of Wills in Ct. of Husting, Lond. 1258–1688*, ed. R. R. Sharpe, ii (2), 486; Guildhall MS. 9171/5, f. 10.
52 W.A.M. 32357*; Dorset R.O., D 396/M/81.
53 C.U.L., Kk. V. 29, ff. 32–35v. The 15 tenants included 11 with a ho. and 10–20 a., 1 with a ho. and 24 a., 3 with a ho. and 3½–7 a. The tenant owing twice the svces. had a ho. and 18 a., the tenant owing half had a ho. and 3½ a.
54 W.A.M. 32403.

55 i.e. 12 reapers for 6 days, 8 for 6 days, 10 for 3 days, 7 for 1 day, 3 for ½ day: W.A.M. 32393.
56 Ibid. 32375.
57 Ibid. 32403.
58 Ibid. 32401.
59 Ibid. 32406.
60 Ibid. 32494.
61 Ibid. 32495.
62 Ibid. 33269–79; ibid. RCO 32 (copy of acct. 1539); Dorset R.O., D 396/M/81.
63 W.A.M. 32361.
64 Ibid. 32399, 32405–6, 32497–32531; C.U.L., Kk. V. 29, f. 35v.   65 W.A.M. 32357.
66 Dorset R.O., D 396/M/81.
67 Ibid.; W.A.M. 33269–79; ibid. RCO 32 (1539 mins.' acct.).

customary tenants in 1312 were a 4s. fine on Hockday Monday, which did not appear in the accounts, pannage for pigs at Martinmas, which averaged 3s., and medsilver (?meadsilver), 10d. at Midsummer from the two tenants who owed week work.[68] From 1384 chevage of 6d. and a capon was demanded from one of those tenants, as a neif.[69] Two other neifs paid chevage from 1386.[70]

The neifs were members of families long associated with Hampstead: Aldenham (1281–1529), Pond or Ponder (1259–1386), and Roke or Rook (1281–1387).[71] Other peasant families were Woodward (1259–1384), Brown (1281–1397), Sturgis or Turgis (1259–1372), Bycok (1281–1372), and Bertram (1259–1347).[72] Some early surnames probably originated as descriptive terms for *famuli*: Shepherd (1281–96), Forester (1281–1322), Woodward (1259–1384), and Herd (or Cowherd) (1259–1322).[73] Although surnames tended to change more quickly in the late 14th and 15th century, John Rye, the granger in 1347,[74] may have been a forebear of John Rye of Hampstead, a tax-commissioner in Middlesex in 1449, lessee of Chalcots in 1450, and the holder of several customary lands in 1459.[75] The Kemp family was active in Hampstead and Kilburn from the early 15th to the early 18th century.[76] An early 15th-century tenement was called after the prolific Marsh family,[77] of which lasted into the early 19th century, of which branches were copyholders and underlessees of Belsize and Kilburn.[78]

Except possibly for the demesne, there is no evidence of any open-field system in Hampstead. The holdings, customary as well as freehold, seem to have consisted of crofts, some of which can be identified.[79] Most of the holdings described in 1312 would have been too small to support subsistence if they were primarily arable.[80] Little is known of agriculture on the customary land. The goods of one tenant, confiscated in 1271, included 6½ qr. of oats, 1½ qr. of barley, an ox, 3 carthorses, 2 cows, and 4 bullocks.[81] Animals played an important part in the peasant economy, particularly since tenants had the right of common pasture on the demesne. One, probably free, tenement of 9 a. in the 13th century had the right of common for 60 sheep, 12 cattle, and 16 pigs wherever the animals of the abbey were allowed. Heriots of an ox, horses, cattle and, less usually, sheep, were paid in kind until c. 1400; they had apparently been commuted into a money payment by the 1530s.[82] Ewe lambs were bequeathed in the will of one customary tenant in 1418.[83] The rents in

kind showed that numbers of geese and hens were kept.[84] Pannage was paid for between 15 and 72 pigs in the 13th century but the numbers had dropped to 9–18 by the mid 14th century.[85] Payments were no longer made by c. 1400.

Only one of the major freehold estates, Chalcots, did not change hands at the Dissolution and the Temple estate fragmented into at least two and possibly five estates. The local effect was probably slight because all the estates were then leased and most of the lessees continued under the new lay owners who were as much absentee landlords as the religious they replaced. On the two estates still owned by institutions, Chalcots by Eton and Belsize by the dean and chapter of Westminster, the lessees themselves from the 17th century became absentee landlords. Many estates were underleased and most were divided into small farms.

There were 296 a. of demesne farmland in 1646,[86] little changed since 1312, but the acreage increased as the woodland was cleared, probably in the 1650s or 1660s. The Upper Dell, a field in the north in what had been Northwood, had been leased before 1665.[87] In 1687 70 a. in three closes called Northwood were leased.[88] By 1704 they formed the 76-a. Northwood farm (later called Norwood), divided into 19 small closes.[89] Whitebirch, an area of woodland, presumably of silver birches, on the east side of the heath, had begun to be cleared by 1663[90] and parcels of it, described as 'late wood', were leased in the 1680s.[91] By 1762 it formed 81 a. of demesne farmland, later called East Park.[92] In 1704 the demesne farmland was said to total 481 a.,[93] probably an exaggeration since the more accurate survey of 1762 gives 464 a.[94] The demesne estate described in the tithe award of 1841 totalled 416 a.,[95] the reduction caused by the area taken for the demesne houses, by the pieces sold off in the late 18th and early 19th century, and by land lost to the Finchley Road. More land was taken for railways in the 1860s and farmland shrank as building on the demesne spread after 1860 and East Park was incorporated in the heath in 1889. Even before the loss to building, parts of farmland had been leased for other purposes, like brickfields, and the value fell from £5 an acre in 1819 to less than £3 in 1870.[96]

In 1646 the demesne was leased to 16 tenants, the largest of whom held 166 a., and the next, a baker who had died by 1664 possessed of a great personal estate, held 40 a.[97] The boundaries of the leasehold estates were fluid and in 1649 there were 17 tenants:

[68] C.U.L., Kk. V. 29, ff. 33v., 35–6.
[69] W.A.M. 32505.
[70] Ibid. 32507.
[71] W.A.M. 32360–1, 32507–8, 33277, f. 21.
[72] W.A.M. 32360–1, 32357, 32494, 32505, 32518.
[73] W.A.M. 32360–1, 32374, 32406, 32504; *Cal. Close*, 1381–5, 564–5.
[74] W.A.M. 32494.
[75] *Cal. Fine R.* 1445–52, 127; E.C.R. 61/RR/A/66; Dorset R.O., D 396/M/81.
[76] W.A.M. 32357; Guildhall MS. 9171/4, f. 61; P.R.O., E 179/143/370, m. 43d.; G.L.R.O., E/MW/H/I/2311A.
[77] W.A.M. 32357.
[78] S.C.L., D 40, 137; Barratt, *Annals*, iii, App. 3–5. M.L.R. 1819/5/625; W.A.M. 16595, 16533.
[79] e.g. Kingswell: *Close R.* 1392–6, 136–8; cf. mans. and other est.
[80] Titow, *Eng. Rural Soc. 1200–1350*, 78 sqq.
[81] W.A.M. 32399.
[82] Ibid. 33279.

[83] Guildhall MS. 9171/2, f. 380.   [84] Above.
[85] Tenants paid 1d. for every pig over 1 year, ½d. for younger ones: C.U.L., Kk. V. 29, f. 36.
[86] Barratt, *Annals*, iii, App. 3, pp. 359–61.
[87] P.R.O., PROB 11/318 (P.C.C. 128, 1665, will of Mat. Warner).
[88] G.L.R.O., E/MW/H, old no. box L (abs. of leases 1680–1731).
[89] Ibid. H/I/2311A.
[90] S.C.L., D 148.
[91] G.L.R.O., E/MW/H, old no. box L (abs. of leases 1680–1731).
[92] S.C.L., Man. Map and Fieldbk. nos. hh–zz, ab, ac.
[93] G.L.R.O., E/MW/H/I/2311A.
[94] S.C.L., Man. Map and Fieldbk. nos. A–Z, a–z, aa–zz, ab, ac.
[95] P.R.O., IR 29/21/24.
[96] Thompson, *Hampstead*, 305.
[97] Barratt, *Annals*, iii, App. 3, pp. 359–61; P.R.O., C 6/49/86.

three holding between 48 a. and 56 a. each, the rest much smaller parcels.[98] In 1704 the increased demesne was divided into 10 farms and three smaller estates[99] and by *c.* 1732 there were some 14 leases, dividing the demesne among 12 tenants.[1] There were 11 tenants in 1762, two of them substantial farmers, the rest holding less than 40 a. each, of which the largest was used by Thomas Clarke as parkland for his copyhold estate.[2] There were 16 tenants in 1777,[3] 21 in 1820,[4] and 19 in 1841,[5] but several held land as parks or gardens attached to houses at Frognal or beside the northern part of the heath.

The principal farm was presumably always centred on the manor house, by 1729 called Hall Oak farm.[6] In 1674 the lessee subleased all the land and part of the house.[7] A second farm, *c.* 60 a. in the south-west, was leased to Edward Snoxell in 1687 and was to remain with the Snoxell family until 1766.[8] There were no buildings on the estate and it seems to have formed one farm in conjunction with Kilburn Woods estate, which was leased to the same tenant after 1766, John Pawlett and, from 1772, James Baker,[9] and probably in 1646.[10] To the south-east was the 63-a. Belsize farm, so called by 1729 presumably because of its proximity to the Belsize estate; it was formed from several smaller estates, one of which had been held in 1687 with part of Belsize, and leased to a salesman from St. Sepulchre's in 1711.[11] There were farm buildings fronting Belsize Lane by *c.* 1732[12] and a cottage by 1842, but usually the farm was combined with Hall Oak farm and in the 1830s it was held with 64 a. of the Belsize estate.[13] Northwood farm was in 1704 rented by two men who had houses on the edge of the heath, at Cloth Hill or Frognal. It had been divided by *c.* 1732 and still further by 1762.[14]

The lessees of Belsize were resident and retained a personal estate around the mansion house until 1683.[15] In 1650 Belsize was estimated at 200 a., divided among seven tenants, including the family of the lessee.[16] In 1679, after the rebuilding of the main house and laying out of the gardens, it contained 235 a., of which 59 a. were kept in hand by the lessee and the rest was divided among nine undertenants.[17] The Belsize House estate, no longer occupied by the lessee, had shrunk to 25 a. by 1714 when the whole estate was divided among 14 under-

lessees,[18] and there were 28 underlessees, mostly occupiers of a house only, by 1808, when the estate was broken up.[19] The part of the estate east of the London road had been leased separately since before the Dissolution. In 1557 a house and *c.* 85 a. were subleased to Philip Cockram (or Cokerham), a London mercer,[20] in whose family they remained until the 1620s or later,[21] although part of it was subleased to others.[22] By 1650 61 a. in two blocks east of the London road were leased to John Marsh[23] and they remained with the Marshes until well into the 18th century, probably initially run from their copyhold farm in Pond Street.[24] By 1800 the northern block formed a 40-a. farm called after its occupiers, Holyland (John Holyland, *c.* 1800–26), Pickett (Joseph Pickett, *c.* 1851–93), and South End farm. The southern block, 46 a. and a barn, was by 1800 leased to William Rothery but with the split-up of the estate in 1808 it became the parkland of Haverstock Lodge.[25]

Farm boundaries in the western part of Belsize were less constant and most of the land served as parks and gardens for the country houses wihch were built there from an early period.[26] The only farm to survive in 1808 was represented in 1650 by 20 a. in the south subleased to Benjamin Rutland who farmed from a house at the corner of the London road and England's Lane.[27] By 1679 the farm, then 49 a. subleased by John Newman, had taken in land to the north.[28] It was subsequently subleased to Thomas Stringfield,[29] Anthony (1725) and Thomas Grove (1749–73),[30] and Thomas Allaly, cowkeeper of New Road, Tottenham Court Road (1779–1807). As the Bliss estate, it was the first part of the Belsize estate to be systematically built up after 1808.[31]

There is no evidence that the lessee of Chalcots was resident. From 1556 or earlier the estate was underleased[32] and by 1720 the 212-a. estate was divided into two farms, of roughly equal size, called Upper and Lower Chalcots, farmed from farmhouses to the west and south respectively of England's Lane,[33] until they were reunited *c.* 1797.[34]

During the 17th century St. John's Wood was finally cleared for farmland, which was divided among several lessees.[35] In 1679 it comprised some 176 a. in Hampstead, divided among four lessees, the largest of whom had 111 a., as part of 185 a. run

[98] Barratt, *Annals*, iii, App. 4, pp. 361–3.
[99] G.L.R.O., E/MW/H/I/2311A.
[1] S.C.L., D 25–38.
[2] Ibid. Man. Map and Fieldbk. nos. A–Z, a–z, aa–zz, ab, ac. For Clarke, above, growth, Frognal.
[3] G.L.R.O., E/MW/H/I/1938.
[4] G.L.R.O., E/MW/H, old no. 21/18 (rental 1820).
[5] P.R.O., IR 29/21/24, nos. 5–18, 31, 33–7, 40–6, 50–2, 130–1, 134–58, 162–3.   [6] S.C.L., D 25.
[7] G.L.R.O., Cal. Mdx. Sess. Bks. v (1673–7), pp. 41–2.
[8] G.L.R.O., E/MW/H, old no. box L (abs. of leases 1680–1731); S.C.L., D 34; Man. Map and Fieldbk. nos. g–l; H 283/St. John's par. ch., tombs in ch.
[9] e.g. G.L.R.O., E/MW/H, old no. 31/8; ibid. H/I/ 1938; P.R.O., E 133/137/27.
[10] Wm. Crewes held 34 a. of demesne and 12 a. from Sir Wm. Roberts: Barratt, *Annals*, iii, App. 3, pp. 359–61.
[11] S.C.L., D 25; G.L.R.O., E/MW/H, old no. box L (abs. of leases 1680–1731).
[12] G.L.R.O., E/MW/H/I/1929; S.C.L., Man. Map and Fieldbk. no. N.
[13] G.L.R.O., E/MW/H, old no. 31/3 (lease 1842). Held by John Wright: above, other est., Belsize.
[14] G.L.R.O., E/MW/H/I/1929; S.C.L., Man. Map and Fieldbk. nos. p–z, aa–gg.

[15] Above, other est.
[16] P.R.O., C 54/3553, no. 33.
[17] S.C.L., D 137.
[18] W.A.M. Map 12450.
[19] Ch. Com. Deed 240250, 146072.
[20] W.A.M. 167475.
[21] P.R.O., C 3/359/48.
[22] P.R.O., C 2/Jas. I/W 10/29.
[23] P.R.O., C 54/3553, no. 33.
[24] S.C.L., D 136–7; W.A.M. Map 12450; W.A.M. 16501, 16517A; poor rate bk. 1779.
[25] Poor rate bks. 1800–7, 1826, 1834; Ch. Com. Deed 146072; P.R.O., HO 107/1492/3; above, growth, Belsize.
[26] Above, growth, Belsize.
[27] P.R.O., C 54/3553, no. 33.
[28] S.C.L., D 136–7, nos. c–n.
[29] W.A.M. Map 12450.
[30] W.A.M. 16501, 16508, 16517A.
[31] Ibid. 16529, 16595; poor rate bks. 1779–1826; Ch. Com. Deed 146072.
[32] Hist. MSS. Com. 39, *15th Rep. II, Hodgkin*, p. 259.
[33] E.C.R. 54/163A.
[34] Ibid. 184.
[35] P.R.O., E 317/Mdx. 56; ibid. C 3/447/132; C 10/11/ 41; C 5/436/55.

from a farmhouse in Marylebone.[36] In the 1730s there were six or seven lessees on the whole estate.[37] By 1762 almost all the Hampstead section formed a single farm, of 151 a., subleased to John Pye[38] and it continued as a single estate, probably combined with land in Marylebone, where the farmhouse lay.[39] In 1834 it was combined with Abbey farm,[40] the 32-a. estate of Kilburn priory, which had been held by four tenants in 1547,[41] occupied by the owner in 1605[42] and probably in 1646,[43] and leased from 1762 to 1810 to the Marsh family.[44]

Shoot Up Hill farm, 110 a. in 1762, was leased from 1546, mostly to single lessees:[45] John Barne in 1546, Robert North from 1565 to 1595, John Haley from 1762 to 1773, and the Froggart family from 1786 to 1850.[46] Thereafter the farmland was broken up, the farmhouse and most of the remaining farmland being occupied by George Verey until the 1860s.[47] The Kilburn Woods estate was combined with the Liddell copyhold to form a single 60-a. farm from the late 17th century, which was probably at first occupied by its owners[48] but from the mid 18th century was leased and was sometimes farmed with the Snoxells' demesne farm.[49]

There were 39 customary tenants paying £5 10s. a year in quitrents in 1640,[50] a number which had increased to 88 by 1678, when the rents totalled £8 15s. 3d.[51] The rental of 1704 records 140 tenants with 165 holdings occupying 573 a. but included the freehold Shoot Up Hill farm estate (115 a.). Of the rest 51 holdings were on the heath and were mostly houses on land recently taken from the waste.[52] In 1762 there were 189 copyhold tenants with 465 a.; 153 held buildings only, and 23 others had up to 5 a. each, 5 had 6–10 a., 4 had 11–20 a., 1 had 26 a., and 3 had 41–60 a.[53] By 1775 194 people paid £25 13s. 9d. in quitrents.[54] The number rose, largely through grants of waste, to 238 in 1810, 256 in 1826, and 267 in 1851.[55] Thereafter the numbers increased, through enfranchisement. There were 20 enfranchisements between 1854 and 1860,[56] another 69 by 1868, 105 by 1879, and 6 by 1893.[57]

Copyhold land was leased as widely as freehold. In 1646, except for Thomas Pawlett's house and 50 a., only very small acreages were held by copy-

holders, the rest being let to tenants.[58] In 1762 all the estates of more than 5 a. were leased. One leasehold farmer, William Bovingdon (229 a.) at Hall Oak and Belsize farms, had more than 200 a. and one, John Pye, had 151 a. of the St. John's Wood estate in Hampstead, but the other ten farms were of 49–115 a., averaging 78 a. A few held land leased from more than one estate: Edward Finch, for example, farmed the 55-a. Flitcroft estate and other copyhold nearby as a 70-a. farm in Childs Hill and West End.[59] In the early 19th century few farms were of more than 100 a.[60]

After the 16th century farms did not remain long in a single family. A branch of the Marsh family had the lease of Gilberts by 1646[61] and in 1686 and 1700.[62] It moved to the nearby Kilburn priory estate, lessees by 1762 and owners from 1773 to 1818.[63] Three members of the Snoxell family, Edward, a grazier (fl. 1687, 1729), and his presumed sons William (d. 1748) and Edward (d. 1766) were lessees at various times of three of the demesne farms and of farms on the St. John's Wood and Chalcots estates.[64] One of the Edward Snoxells acquired a copyhold close and house in Pond Street in 1740 which he pulled down and replaced with a handsome new one.[65] Before the death of William Snoxell, the family occupied over 400 a. of farmland in Hampstead. The main Hall Oak farm and Belsize farm were leased from 1757 to 1784 to William Bovingdon.[66]

The principal farmer in the late 18th century was Thomas Pool, in the 1770s a grocer who had stables, a warehouse, and a small piece of land in Hampstead town and the lease, since 1774, of Jack Straw's Castle.[67] In 1785 he took the lease of Hall Oak and Belsize farms (229 a.), and in 1786 of 14 a. of demesne land to the north and 81 a. of East Heath,[68] besides 50 a. of copyhold bordering Hall Oak to the west.[69] From 1789 Pool was rated for Snoxell's farm (62 a.), although it was not formally leased to him until 1798.[70] He thus had a total of c. 440 a. Although Pool (d. 1813) described himself in his will as 'farmer', he appears to have devoted his time from the 1780s to building and selling houses at Frognal and Littleworth.[71] The East Heath estate, previously leased to the bricklayer Isaiah Buckhurst, with leave

[36] S.C.L., D 136–7. The bulk of the 492 a. was in Marylebone. Two other lessees held land wholly in Marylebone.

[37] M.L.R. 1730/5/251; 1732/5/753.

[38] S.C.L., Man. Map and Fieldbk.

[39] Subleased to 'Mr. Berks' (1779), Thos. Willan (1807–26): poor rate bks. 1779, 1807, 1826.

[40] Leased by Hen. Cleeve: poor rate bk. 1834.

[41] P.R.O., E 318/box 38/2042.

[42] Ibid. WARD 5/30/431.

[43] Barratt, Annals, iii, App. 3, pp. 359–61.

[44] S.C.L., Man. Map and Fieldbk. p. 63; poor rate bks. 1767, 1800, 1807, 1810.

[45] S.C.L., Man. Map and Fieldbk. nos. 482–93; cf. L. & P. Hen. VIII, xxi (1), p. 687; P.R.O., PROB 11/48 (P.C.C. 24 Morrison, will of Rog. Cholmeley); ibid. STAC 8/116/5; ibid. WARD 5/30/431; M.L.R. 1773/1/174.

[46] Poor rate bks. 1786, 1800, 1826, 1834, 1840; P.R.O., IR 29/21/24, nos. 63–74, 91–7.

[47] Poor rate bks. 1851, 1864; above, growth, Kilburn.

[48] e.g. in 1704: G.L.R.O., E/MW/H/I/2311A; above, man. and other est.   [49] Above.

[50] G.L.R.O., E/MW/H/I/2109.   [51] Ibid. 2113–14.

[52] G.L.R.O., E/MW/H/I/2311A.

[53] S.C.L., Man. Map and Fieldbk.; the freeholds Shoot Up Hill and Chalcots were wrongly included as copyhold.

[54] G.L.R.O., E/MW/H/I/2178.

[55] Ibid. 2224, 2231, 2256.

[56] Ibid. H, old no. 34 (list of enfranch. 1854–60).

[57] P.R.O., MAF 20/89–92.

[58] Barratt, Annals, iii, App. 3, pp. 359–61. Of the freehold, 60 a. of demesne wood was in hand and Sir Wm. Roberts kept a ho. and 30 a. in hand.

[59] S.C.L., Man. Map and Fieldbk., naming Wm. Bovingdon as Thos. Bovenden.

[60] Park, Hampstead, 134.

[61] Barratt, Annals, iii, App. 3, pp. 359–61.

[62] P.R.O., C 7/587/124; G.L.R.O., E/MW/H/19.

[63] S.C.L., Man. Map and Fieldbk. p. 63; above, man. and other est.

[64] S.C.L., D 25–6, 34, 59; ibid. H 283/St. John's par. ch., tombs in ch.; M.L.R. 1732/5/753; G.L.R.O., E/MW/H, old no. box L (abs. of leases 1680–1731).

[65] G.L.R.O., E/MW/H, old no. 26/23 (Snoxell's case 1746).

[66] G.L.R.O., E/MW/H, old no. 31/8 (lease, 1757); poor rate bk. 1784–5.

[67] G.L.R.O., E/MW/H/I/2178; ibid. MR/FB/14–15 (freeholder lists); poor rate bk. 1779.

[68] G.L.R.O., E/MW/H, old no. 31/8 (leases 1798); poor rate bks. 1784–6.

[69] Poor rate bk. Dec. 1786; G.L.R.O., E/MW/H, old no. 31/8 (lease 1798, schedule of tithes).

[70] Poor rate bks. 1789–98; G.L.R.O., E/MW/H, old no. 31/8 (lease 1798).

[71] Above, growth, Frognal, North End, etc.

to dig sand and gravel on the heath,[72] seems to have been valued as a source of bricks and was usually leased to those interested in building.

Pool's property was put up for sale in accordance with his will.[73] William Baker, lessee of the combined Kilburn woods and Liddell copyhold farm since 1810, acquired 50 a. of Pool's land, probably Snoxell's farm, in 1813 and in 1819 obtained a lease of 268 a. of demesne land, the combined farmland of Hall Oak south of Frognal Lane and of Belsize and Snoxell's farms, run from Manor Lodge and the farm buildings to the south, which had been the farmhouse at least since 1810.[74] Baker spent much on fencing and manuring the demesne farm, which had been neglected by Pool,[75] and although the lands were divided and leased to others in 1834 Baker ran Manor farm as an undertenant from 1848 to 1852, when it was leased to Frederick Willis until 1864.[76] Belsize farm had been detached from Manor farm in 1834, leased to John Wright of Belsize House until 1841,[77] and in 1848 to John Culverhouse.[78] Culverhouse, who described himself as farmer of New End, took out yearly tenancies of Belsize farm and Manor farm in 1865 and the Culverhouses continued to take leases of the diminishing demesne farmland into the 1890s. They were also contractors and made bricks on demesne land west of Finchley road and in East Park.[79]

The influence of London was apparent in agricultural leases as in other aspects of Hampstead's economy. Of the estates nearest to London, John Slanning, the lessee, was said in 1556 to have let Chalcots to London butchers and innholders[80] and the southernmost part of the Belsize estate was leased in 1557 to a London mercer, whose family had subleased part of it to another citizen by 1616.[81] Parts of Chalcots were subleased to residents of St. Giles-in-the-Fields in 1676, of St. Martin-in-the-Fields in 1749, and of St. Pancras in 1769 and 1791.[82] The last was Thomas Rhodes, farmer, of Hampstead Road, who from 1797 until the 1840s farmed both Upper and Lower Chalcots as a large-scale stock and dairy farmer. It was presumably a member of the same family who farmed Duddingtons until the building of South Hill Park in the 1870s.[83] In 1772 James Baker, stablekeeper of New Bond Street, took the lease of Snoxell's farm[84] and Samuel Carr, coach-master of Oxford Street, applied for land in Hampstead, for hay and grazing.[85] He held c. 10 a. of demesne by 1777[86] and he, and later Henry Carr, leased the combined Kilburn Woods and Liddell farm from 1786 to 1807.[87] Another stablekeeper, Robert Stone, of Marylebone, leased Manor farm from 1834 to 1848.[88]

The needs of London were important in determining what the farms grew. The general trend, as throughout Middlesex, was away from the mixed farming of the Middle Ages to grassland. There is some indication that many customary holdings were predominantly grass even in the Middle Ages. The holdings around Pond Street were entirely meadow or pasture, except where wood remained, by 1593.[89] At Belsize the annual render of 100 loads of hay and 10 qr. of oats reflected pre-Reformation farming[90] and there were only 5 a. of arable compared with 186 a. of meadow and pasture there in 1650.[91] Kinghall consisted of 20 a. of pasture in 1652[92] and there were 165 a. of meadow and pasture and only 18 a. of arable at Chalcots in 1683.[93] The six closes of Gilberts, equally divided between arable and meadow in 1647, were wholly grassland by 1686.[94] Of 289 a. of demesne leased in 1687, 124 a. were specified as meadow or pasture, 66 a., including Snoxell's farm, were presumably arable, and 99 a. were not described.[95] Of 353 a. of demesne leased in 1729 and 1730, 229 a. were meadow or pasture, 63 a. were arable, and 62 a. (Snoxell's farm) were unspecified. The core of Hall Oak farm was, at least from the late 17th century, grassland, while the more recently reclaimed woodland on the edge of the heath was arable before it too became grassland.[96]

The depiction in the 1740s of considerable arable in the west, at St. John's Wood and Belsize,[97] is unreliable. Before 1773 there had been at least 15 a. and possibly another 39 a. of arable at Shoot Up Hill farm[98] and c. 10 a. were sown with wheat at the 60-a. Kilburn farm c. 1774.[99] St. John's Wood was, however, entirely grassland in 1732[1] and all 112 a. of Lower Chalcots were meadow in 1752.[2] A visitor to Hampstead in 1748, presumably using the London road, commented on the great number of inclosures nearly all laid as meadows.[3] Out of the 1,331 a. described in 1762,[4] 75 a. were arable, 18 a. pasture, and the rest described as meadow, although this pre-

[72] G.L.R.O., E/MW/H/I/1938.
[73] S.C.L., cutting in cat. advertising auction, 1813; P.R.O., PROB 11/1543 (P.C.C. 210, 1813, will of Thos. Pool).
[74] Poor rate bks. 1810–19; G.L.R.O., E/MW/H, old no. 31/9 (lease, 1819).
[75] G.L.R.O., E/MW/H, old no. 38/17/2, 17; Thompson, *Hampstead*, 114.
[76] G.L.R.O., E/MW/H, old no. 27/15 (sale cat. 1848); 31/2 (letter 1848); 31/4 (lease 1851); rate bks. 1848–64.
[77] G.L.R.O., E/MW/H, old no. 31/2 (lease 1834); above, other est. (Belsize).
[78] G.L.R.O., E/MW/H, old no. 31/3 (agreement to lease 1848); below, ind.
[79] Ibid. 26/86 (agreements to lease 1865, 1879); 26/34 (rental 1871); Locker 24 (rental 1890–1900); Thompson, *Hampstead*, 305; C.H.R. x. 13–18; below, ind.
[80] Hist. MSS. Com. 39, *15th Rep. II, Hodgkin*, p. 259.
[81] W.A.M. 167475; P.R.O., C 2/Jas. I/W 10/29.
[82] S.C.L., D 58–9, 61, 64; E.C.R. 54/180.
[83] E.C.R. 54/184; poor rate bk. 1842; P.R.O., IR 29/21/24, nos. 175–85; Thompson, *Hampstead*, 108, 218, 298; above, growth, Hampstead town; other est. (Duddingtons).
[84] G.L.R.O., E/MW/H, old no. 31/8 (lease 1772).

[85] Thompson, *Hampstead*, 11.
[86] G.L.R.O., E/MW/H/I/1938.
[87] Ibid. H, old no. 31/8 (lease 1798, schedule of tithes); poor rate bks. 1786, 1789, 1800, 1807.
[88] G.L.R.O., E/MW/H, old no. 31/2 (lease 1834, letter from Stone 1848).
[89] G.L.R.O., E/MW/H/I.
[90] W.A.M. Lease bk. XVIII, ff. 32v.–34.
[91] P.R.O., C 54/3553, no. 33.
[92] Ibid. C 9/4/149.
[93] E.C.R. 54/181.
[94] P.R.O., C 7/587/124; C 9/4/149.
[95] G.L.R.O., E/MW/H, old no. box L (abs. of leases 1680–1731).
[96] S.C.L., D 25–36.
[97] Rocque, *Map of Lond.* (1741–5), sheets 11, 12.
[98] M.L.R. 1773/1/174.
[99] P.R.O., E 126/33, East. 25 Geo. III, no. 2; E 133/137/27.
[1] M.L.R. 1732/5/753.
[2] S.C.L., D 59.
[3] *Kalm's Visit to Eng. 1748*, trans. J. Lucas (1892), 47, 49.
[4] S.C.L., Man. Map and Fieldbk. Excludes the heath, Belsize, St. John's Wood, and Kilburn priory est.

sumably included grazing land. Most of the arable, 52 a., was on the demesne, concentrated in the north near Childs Hill and on Belsize farm, where there had been 38 a. of arable in 1729.[5] The rest of the arable was at Chalcots (18 a.) and on Shoot Up Hill farm (5 a.). Chalcots was entirely grassland in 1769 but had 10 a. of arable in 1779.[6] Abbey farm and Shoot Up Hill farm were entirely under grass by 1773[7] and in 1787 Belsize lands were being laid down to grass.[8]

The estimate in 1798 of 100 a. arable in the parish is almost certainly too high.[9] The land was said to be meadow in 1794,[10] a few arable fields were depicted in St. John's Wood and Chalcots in 1800,[11] and in 1801 there were only 12 a. of arable and the farmers paid little attention to anything but grass.[12] In 1811 the land was almost entirely grass farms.[13] No arable was recorded in 1841[14] or after 1867.[15]

The grassland was partly used to pasture animals. Copyholders believed they had the right to depasture cattle on the waste without stint but the numbers were limited by the amount their own lands would support during the winter.[16] There are many references to cattle among goods in the 16th and 17th centuries,[17] but only one to sheep,[18] although Robert James's 4 hogs, recorded in 1604,[19] may have been sheep. Six oxen and 6 kine were bequeathed with the lease of Chalcots in 1558[20] and stock at Belsize in 1568 included 9 kine, 3 heifers, a bull, 6 hogs, and 3 young pigs, but not, apparently, any sheep unless they were the 4 'waymlings' and one 'curtall' also listed.[21] About 1620 28 horses were pastured at Shoot Up Hill farm[22] and stablekeepers and coachmasters were lessees during the 18th and 19th centuries. Pigs were kept in small domestic premises as well as on farms. Nine pigstyes were recorded in 1762,[23] and hogs were apparently kept in the churchyard in 1805.[24] Pigs, sheep, and goats were running at large in 1807 and in 1829 the vestry undertook to prosecute owners of unringed pigs found in the town.[25]

Most farming was of grassland, a mixture of hay, dairying, and short-stay stock-keeping.[26] Butchers who leased land included the Londoners at Chalcots in the 16th century,[27] Philip Cater of Pond Street, who leased demesne east of the heath in 1687 and 1704,[28] and John Tayler, who leased 15 a. at West End in 1762, Jacksfield in 1765, Thorplands in 1766, and 54 a. of Gilberts by 1770.[29] Hampstead butchers leased demesne lands and cattle sheds on the southwest side of the heath in the 1860s and on what was left of Snoxell's farm in 1879.[30]

Six cowhouses, two dairies, and a milkhouse were recorded in 1762,[31] including two cowhouses on the demesne, one in the north and one at Hall Oak Farm, where there was a cowhouse and calfpen in 1783.[32] A cowhouse and piggery were included among farm buildings at Manor Farm c. 1826.[33] Much meadow was 'attached to the villas of private gentlemen',[34] who kept two or three horses and cows,[35] and several included cowhouses on their property. There were cowhouses on the Belsize country estates of Spencer Perceval, George Todd, Sir Richard Phillips, and Thomas Pryor in 1808 and two cowhouses and a piggery besides a stable attached to Todd's new house (Belsize Court) in 1817.[36] Belsize Park included a cowhouse and boxes for 12 hunters in 1841 and Frognal Hall, described as the residence for a prominent man, included a cowhouse and piggery in 1843.[37] There was a cowhouse in Brewhouse Lane in 1791, a dairy in Perrin's Court in 1807, and a newly erected cowhouse for 22 cows at North End in 1820.[38] Among the best of the 19th-century dairy farms was South End farm; in other parts, notably Kilburn, cows were kept in bad conditions.[39]

The hay crop depended on the supply of manure. In 1796 the high state of cultivation and 'very great' crops of hay at Chalcots were attributed mainly to its contiguity to London, whence manure was easily obtained.[40] In 1748 the length of grass was attributed to yearly manuring.[41] Some 50 a. out of 60 a. at the Kilburn Woods farm c. 1774 produced hay at a rate of 1½ loads an acre.[42] At Belsize in 1787 the grasslands were said to be mown once or twice a year and then depastured by sheep or cattle.[43] In 1814 farming was said to be dependent on the supply of hay for the London market. On higher ground the meadow was cut once and manured every three years. The later math of the lower ground was especially good for suckling sheep and house lambs.[44] Thomas Pool's goods in 1813 included four fine ricks of hay,[45] and John Wright's in 1842 included grass growing on 46 a. besides 150 loads of hay, 5 cows, 2 calves, 31 sheep, pigs, poultry, pheasants, 4 cart-

[5] S.C.L., D 25. [6] Ibid. D 61; E.C.R. 54/180.
[7] M.L.R. 1773/1/174; 2/89–90.
[8] P.R.O., E 133/137/24.
[9] Middleton, *View*, 560.
[10] Foot, *Agric. of Mdx.* 9.
[11] T. Milne, *Land Use Map of Lond.* (1800).
[12] P.R.O., HO 67/16.
[13] H. Hunter, *Hist. of Lond. and Environs* (1811), ii. 89.
[14] P.R.O., IR 29/21/24.
[15] Ibid. MAF 68, *passim*.
[16] Park, *Hampstead*, 128.
[17] e.g. Guildhall MS. 9171/15, f. 332; ibid. 16, f. 13v.; *Mdx. County Rec.* i. 250; ibid. ii. 7–8; P.R.O., PROB 11/292 (P.C.C. 1659, f. 326, will of John Franklin); PROB 11/295 (P.C.C. 1659, f. 492); ibid. C 7/213/20; C 10/414/14.
[18] In 1616: *Mdx. Sess. Rec.* iii. 220.
[19] *Mdx. County Rec.* ii. 7–8.
[20] P.R.O., PROB 11/41 (P.C.C. 63 Noodes, will of John Slannyng). [21] P.R.O., E 159/357, rot. 532.
[22] P.R.O., STAC 8/116/5.
[23] S.C.L., Man. Map and Fieldbk. nos. 87, 94, 97, 118, 237, 240, 277, 331, 358.
[24] Vestry mins. 18 Dec. 1805.
[25] Ibid. 22 Oct. 1829; G.L.R.O., M/81/6.
[26] Thompson, *Hampstead*, 10.   [27] Above.

[28] G.L.R.O., MR/FB/1/20, 73–4; E/MW/H, old no. box L (abs. of leases 1680–1731); H/I/2311A.
[29] Ibid. H/I/2178; S.C.L., Man. Map and Fieldbk. nos. 355, 477–81; S.C.L., D 1(a); M.L.R. 1766/7/446.
[30] G.L.R.O., E/MW/H, old nos. 31/4 (lease 1865 to Thos. Cunnington); 31/6 (agreement to lease 1867 to Chas. H. Fry); 26–86 (agreement to lease 1879 to Ric. Coles).
[31] S.C.L., Man. Map and Fieldbk. nos. A, z, 22, 218, 263, 368–9, 375, 402.
[32] G.L.R.O., E/MW/H, old no. 33/16 (est. of repairs 1783).   [33] Ibid. 27/15 (plan).
[34] Brewer, *Beauties of Eng. & Wales*, X (4), 186.
[35] Park, *Hampstead*, 134.
[36] Ch. Com. Deeds 146072–3.
[37] G.L.R.O., E/MW/H, old no. 27/15 (sales parts. 1841, 1843).
[38] Ibid. (sales parts. 1791, 1807, 1820).
[39] S.C.L., C. F. J. Lord, 'Rec. of Sanitary Experience 1827–89' (MS.).
[40] Quoted in Thompson, *Hampstead*, 12.
[41] *Kalm's Visit to Eng.* 49.
[42] P.R.O., E 133/137/27.   [43] Ibid. 24.
[44] Park, *Hampstead*, 133.
[45] S.C.L., cutting in cat. (1813).

and 12 riding-horses, and a donkey and its foal.[46] When the lessee left Manor farm in 1848, grass with after-pasture to be mown twice or grazed on 190 a. of very productive meadow producing crops of 'herby grass' were put up for sale.[47] When the demesne was let on a yearly tenancy in the late 19th century as a way of releasing land for building, the agreement was for the grass crop and grazing of grassland not occupied for building.[48]

In 1867,[49] of 661 a. under crops, 637 a. were grassland. In 1874 the acreage under crops was 878 a., of which 620 a. were grassland for hay and 184 a. permanent pasture. Of 505 a. of farmland in 1890, 334 a. were permanent pasture and 141 a. hay. By 1900 there were only 115 a. left, entirely divided between grass for mowing (66 a.) and pasture (49 a.), and by 1914 there were 5 a. for mowing and 12 a. of pasture. There were 268 cattle, mostly milk cows, recorded in 1867, 409 in 1874, 183 in 1883, and 179 in 1890. No figures were given for 1900 but probably all cattle had gone by then, as cowhouses, of which there were five in 1890–1, had disappeared by 1905.[50] There were 201 sheep in 1867, 328 in 1874, 300 in 1890, 305 in 1900, and 800 in 1914, when they were probably kept on the heath. There were 156 pigs in 1867, 196 in 1874, 40 in 1883, and 23 in 1890. In 1867 there were 2 a. of clover and 2 a. of potatoes, mangolds, and vetches, probably all grown for animal feed. In 1874 there were 50 a. of clover, 9 a. of vetches, and 8 a. of roots, reduced by 1883 to 3 a., 1 a., and 3 a. respectively. There were 21 a. of clover in 1890 but all the other crops had gone.

Nearly three quarters of the working population of Hampstead was engaged in agriculture c. 1614.[51] Agriculture employed 199 persons in 1801 and 191 families in 1811, less than 17 per cent of the population. There were 161 such families (11 per cent) in 1821 and 80 (5 per cent) in 1831.[52] The 80 families included 1 farmer employing labourers, 8 not employing labourers, and 90 agricultural labourers. In 1851 the bulk of the demesne farmlands were combined with the Kilburn Woods and Liddell estate to form a 290-a. farm run from the Liddell farmhouse at Kilburn by William Baker, who employed six labourers. John Culverhouse, who employed seven labourers, farmed the 77-a. Belsize farm from his house in New End Square, the farm buildings in Belsize Lane being occupied by a farm labourer. James Ward, who employed two labourers, farmed 50 a. from North Hall Cottage in England's Lane, presumably one of the buildings belonging to Upper Chalcots. Joseph Pickett employed two labourers at South End farm and Henry Randall farmed 18 a. of

demesne land at Branch Hill with two labourers. There was a self-styled 'farmer' in Heath Street and there were cowkeepers at South End Green, Pond Street, Rosslyn Street, Heath Street, Flask Walk, North End, Church Lane, and Frognal. Shoot Up Hill farm was temporarily empty and there was a farmer's son at Fortune Green. Only 19 labourers were recorded as employed by the Hampstead farmers, and although some of the 78 recorded farmworkers probably worked outside the parish, many were probably unemployed except at mowing time.[53] Haymakers, needed in large numbers only for short periods, were usually itinerant. At haymaking time in 1841.there were more than 170 labourers in barns and huts, mostly on Chalcots, Belsize, Branch Hill, and Manor farms.[54] Casual relief during a wet season of haymaking in 1824 was expensive.[55] There were 56 agricultural labourers in 1861 but nearly all the people described as employed in agriculture from 1861 (384 in 1861, 393 in 1921) were gardeners for the growing number of large houses.[56]

In 1683 the earl of Chesterfield, lessee of Belsize, made a seven-year agreement with a gardener, William Serman (or Surman) of St. Pancras, who was to take the profits in return for maintaining the gardens and orchards, which included 118 quinces, 197 pears, 68 peaches and nectarines, 96 apricots, 115 plums, 63 cherries, and 10 figs. All orange and lemon trees, citrons, the best winter pears, and all fish were reserved for the earl.[57] Gardeners were recorded in the parish in 1697,[58] 1700,[59] 1720,[60] and 1789.[61] Land on the heath was granted in 1709 on condition that it was used as a herb garden.[62] Until the early 19th century there were watercress beds in the streams flowing from the heath.[63]

There was one nursery ground, near the church, in 1762[64] and John Campbell (d. 1804) had a nursery at Haverstock Hill by 1774, property in High Street from 1775, and gardens in Church Row and Frognal from 1779. Campbell's widow retained all the land and buildings until 1820, when most, but apparently not that at Haverstock Hill, passed to George Campbell, presumably his son. Campbell had a nursery in High Street in 1834 and in Heath Street from c. 1840 to 1854.[65] The Haverstock nursery on Belsize land at the junction of Haverstock Hill and England's Lane, was by 1831 run by George Sinton (or Linton), who employed four men by 1851.[66] It survived until the area was built up in the 1890s.[67] There was another nurseryman in Wetherall Place in 1834,[68] who had gone by 1840 when there were three more in Hampstead town.[69] By 1841 there was a 5½-a. nursery, occupied by Andrew Henderson, on the Little estate

---

[46] G.L.R.O., E/MW/H, old no. 31/2 (sale, 1841); 31/3 (auction, 1842).

[47] Ibid. 27/15 (sale cat. 1848).

[48] Ibid. 26/86 (agreement, 1883); ibid. Locker 24 (rental, 1890–1900).

[49] Para. based on agric. rets.: P.R.O., MAF 68/136 (1867, probably incomplete); MAF 68/364 (1874); MAF 68/535 (1877); MAF 68/877 (1883); MAF 68/1276 (1890); MAF 68/1846 (1900); MAF 68/2644 (1914).

[50] L.C.C. Lond. Statistics, i. 544; xvii. 110.

[51] L. Martindale, 'Demography and Land Use in 17th and 18th cent. Mdx.' (Lond. Univ. Ph.D. thesis, 1968), 62.

[52] Census, 1801–31.

[53] P.R.O., HO 107/1492/1–16.

[54] Ibid. HO 107/674/1–13; Census, 1841.

[55] G.L.R.O., P81/JN1/15.   [56] Census, 1801–1931.

[57] P.R.O., C 6/297/119; Cal. Mdx. Sess. Rec. vii (1683–6), p. 110.

[58] G.L.R.O., MR/FB/1/20, 73–4 (John Skerret).

[59] Ibid. 1/198.

[60] D. F. McKenzie, Stationers' Co. Apprentices, 1701–1800, 73.   [61] Ibid. p. 119.

[62] G.L.R.O., E/MW/H, old no. box L (abs. of leases 1680–1731).

[63] C.H.R. xi. 10–14.

[64] S.C.L., Man. Map and Fieldbk. no. 403.

[65] T.L.M.A.S. xxvi (1975), 299; Pigot's Lond. and Provincial Dir. (1834); Pigot's Dir. Mdx. (1840); Home Counties Dir. (1845).

[66] Pigot's Lond. and Provincial Dir. (1834); P.R.O., HO 107/1492/2; Stanford, Libr. Map of Lond. and Suburbs (1862 edn. with additions to 1865), sheet 6; G.L.R.O., P81/JN1/14.

[67] Above, growth, Belsize.

[68] Pigot's Lond. and Provincial Dir. (1834).

[69] Pigot's Dir. Mdx. (1840).

in Edgware Road at Kilburn, which survived in 1891.[70] There was another nursery at Kilburn, by the High Road and Kilburn Priory, from 1855 to 1887.[71] There were nine nurserymen in 1861[72] and some market gardening near South End Green in 1867.[73] Nursery grounds covered 9 a. of the parish and another 1 a. produced beans, peas, and cabbages in 1883. The nursery grounds had shrunk to 3 a., with another 3 a. of orchard and 2 a. of soft fruit, by 1890.[74] There were still nurseries at Haverstock Hill, presumably on the eastern side, belonging to John Russell in 1929,[75] and in 1947 there were two horticultural holdings totalling 1 a., both with glasshouses.[76]

WOODS. In 1312 six demesne woods were listed (Northwood, Nuthurst, Sheppenbrighull, Whitebirch, Brockhole, and Timberhurst). It was estimated that from them and from the hedges enclosing fields an average of 8,000 faggots were sold worth £6 10s. a year.[77] In the years between 1271 and 1355[78] for which figures are available an average of 9,400 faggots were cut annually but only just over a quarter were sold, the rest being sent to Westminster. Nevertheless the sale of faggots made up much of the manorial income, between a tenth and a fifth of the whole, the income, particularly in the 1290s, being higher than the valuation in 1312. In 1298 and 1299 at least 120 trees were cut down for building at Westminster, the small branches and bark being sold at Hampstead. In 1355 charcoal fetched 10s. Between 1376 and 1412[79] an average of nearly 12,000 bavins and faggots were cut each year of which only 2,330, less than a fifth, were sold. The rest were sent to the abbey, mainly as fuel for brewing, baking, and cooking. Over 3,500 perch (19,250 yd.) of new hedges were made both round woods and fields during those years to 'save wood'; probably they were quick hedges which were then cropped, thus sparing existing woods. The hedges may also have protected against animals. Westminster was still taking wood from Hampstead in the 15th century. In 1452 the sick prior was granted 600 faggots and 13 qr. of charcoal a year from Hampstead and Hendon.[80] In 1498 63 loads of polewood, 45 loads of tall wood, 6 loads of long wood, and 11 loads of short faggots were cut of which c. 40 per cent were sold, supplying one eighth of the total demesne revenue.[81]

Although some of the wood sold in the 14th century came from hedges, most of it was from the woods, Hampstead wood, Brockhole, Northwood, Eastwood, and Hallgrove being particularly mentioned.[82] In 1470 the abbey sold for £28 13s. 4d. the

right to take for three years all the wood and underwood growing in Northfield to Thomas Burgeys, vintner of Westminster, and Richard Kemp, yeoman of Hampstead, on condition that they left 52 old standards and 30 new storers (saplings).[83] In 1498, in addition to faggots and other felled wood, £8 10s. was obtained from the sale of a parcel of wood, probably on similar terms to the sale of 1470.[84] Robert Shepherd owed £15 10s. for wood sold to him in 1511–12, too large a sum merely for faggots and bavins.[85] Wood continued to be sold in the 1520s, though in small amounts,[86] and hedges were still planted around demesne woods and fields in the 1530s.[87]

In 1535 the demesne woods were worth £1 on average a year.[88] In 1556 Sir Thomas Wroth, then lord of the manor, was presented for selling 40 a. of wood on the common without the consent of the tenants. He had the right to enclose and sell a quarter but he had sold it all and felled most,[89] presumably part of three woods recorded in 1312 as containing common pasture: Northwood, Nuthurst, or Sheppenbrighull, all probably lying north of the demesne farmlands.[90] In 1641 the bailiff was paid £2 a year to preserve the woods.[91] There were still 60 a. of woodland left on the demesne, kept in hand, in the 1640s.[92] Clearance of the remaining demesne woodland, north of the farmland and east of the heath, was under way in the 1660s[93] and probably complete by the 1680s when leases were made of Northwood and Birchfields, both lately woodland.[94]

Wood was being cut at Belsize at the end of the 15th century.[95] When leases were made in 1500 and 1518 the woods and hedgerows were reserved to the prior.[96] In 1535 the average annual income from the sale of wood there was 10s.[97] The Belsize farmland was formed by clearings which became larger as the bands of woodland between them were narrowed. There was a good deal of woodland on the portion, most of it east of the London road, underleased to Philip Cockram in 1557;[98] there were still 'hawts' (possibly holts or strips of woodland) on the eastern side of the road in 1622[99] but they had been reduced to a strip of less than 1 a. by 1679.[1] There were 9¼ a. of woodland on the whole Belsize estate in 1650.[2] West of the London road Hart wood, 5½ a., remained around fields in 1679, reduced by 1714 to 4¾ a. Another 1¾ a., the wood walks, remained in 1679 of the original woodland but the rest, the chestnut walks and the walk to the house, later called the Avenue, was probably planted as part of the beautifying of the house in the 1660s.[3] Many trees were cut down by underlessees in the 17th and 18th cen-

[70] P.R.O., IR 29/21/24, no. 113; Stanford, *Libr. Map of Lond.* (1891 edn.).
[71] Thompson, *Hampstead*, 259 n.   [72] *Census*, 1861.
[73] Potter Colln. 19/89.
[74] P.R.O., MAF 68/877; MAF 68/1276.
[75] *The Times*, 2 Oct. 1929, 11e.
[76] L. G. Bennett, *Horticultural Ind. of Mdx.* 38.
[77] C.U.L., Kk. V. 29, f. 31v.
[78] W.A.M. 32367–406, 32494–6.
[79] Ibid. 32497–531.
[80] *Cal. Papal Reg.* x. 590–1.
[81] Dorset R.O., D 396/M/81.
[82] e.g. W.A.M. 32504, 32522, 32525.
[83] W.A.M. 32356.
[84] Dorset R.O., D 396/M/81.
[85] W.A.M. 33270, f. 21.
[86] Ibid. 33271, f. 21; 33272, f. 21; 33273, f. 21; 33275, f. 21.

[87] Ibid. 32075, 32099, 32188.
[88] *Valor Eccl.* (Rec. Com.), i. 415.
[89] Hist. MSS. Com. 59, *15th Rep. II, Hodgkin*, p. 260.
[90] C.U.L., Kk. V. 29, f. 31v.
[91] G.L.R.O., E/MW/H/I/2303.
[92] Barratt, *Annals*, iii, App. 3, p. 359; App. 4, p. 361.
[93] e.g. Upper Dell, a field in 1665: P.R.O., PROB 11/318 (P.C.C. 128 1665, will of Matt. Warner); S.C.L., Man. Map and Fieldbk. no. CC; e.g. Whitebirch, field in 1663: ibid. D 148.
[94] G.L.R.O., E/MW/H, old no. Box L (abs. of leases 1680).   [95] W.A.M. 32274.
[96] Ibid. 16471–2.
[97] *Valor Eccl.* (Rec. Com.) i. 410.
[98] W.A.M. 16475.
[99] P.R.O., C 3/359/48.   [1] S.C.L., D 136–7.
[2] P.R.O., C 54/3553, no. D 33.
[3] S.C.L., D 136–7; W.A.M. Map 12450.

turies.[4] There were complaints in 1714, against Fovey and others, of heavy felling within the last three or four years[5] and in 1715 the dean and chapter of Westminster were seeking legal advice about the rights of the lessee and underlessees to take timber other than for necessary repairs. By that date there were said to be no woods other than the wilderness around the house.[6] In 1716 239 trees, oaks, elms, ashes, and chestnuts were felled.[7] One underlessee was warned by the dean and chapter about cutting down timber in 1749,[8] but legal opinion was that the only remedy was for an action of trespass against a stranger since the head lease to Lord Chesterfield included woods.[9] Many trees had been 'wantonly cut down' in 1773.[10] By 1774 there was not enough rough timber on the estate to keep the building and fences in repair.[11]

The southern part of the parish was well wooded in the late 16th and probably into the 17th century.[12] In 1482, for example, 18 cartloads of pole-wood were taken from Chalcots to St. James's hospital, Westminster,[13] and from 1538 rent for Chalcots included 12 loads of wood. From 1481 Eton College reserved the woods when it leased the rest of Chalcots, but the provision may have proved impossible to enforce. In 1556–7 the woods were leased together with the rest of Chalcots to John Slanning,[14] who had recently been presented for cutting down 6 a. of wood there.[15] Some of Chalcots wood, which abutted St. John's Wood and Belsize, remained in 1650 but some had been converted to arable[16] and there was no woodland by 1683.[17] In 1755 although all the woodland had been ploughed up and was mostly pasture much timber remained in the hedges.[18]

St. John's Wood suffered from 1643 to 1645 when Londoners, unable to obtain coal, took wood.[19] There were still 2,000 oak trees left in 1650.[20] When Charles I hunted in Marylebone Park, the hunt extended into the neighbouring St. John's Wood and the first lease of St. John's Wood after the Restoration required the lessee to keep it stocked with deer. In 1666, however, the lessee was allowed to convert the wood to farmland and by 1673 so much wood had been destroyed that the requirement was of little use.[21] By 1679 the estate was entirely farmland.[22]

In 1319 the abbot of Westminster and many of his tenants were accused of breaking into woods at Lisson and Kilburn, removing trees, and allowing their cattle to eat the herbage of the wood.[23] The woods may have belonged to the St. John's Wood estate or to Kilburn priory. The priory in 1535 possessed woods valued at £1 6s. a year,[24] presumably Kilburn woods,[25] which, like all other woods in Hampstead, except those on the heath, had become farmland by 1762.[26]

MILLS. A mill, farmed for £1 a year, formed part of the demesne by 1270.[27] It was a windmill,[28] probably a wooden post mill since a new oak post was provided in 1273.[29] It was blown down in 1294 but repaired.[30] The profits of the demesne were said in 1312 to include a windmill valued at £1 13s. 4d. a year.[31] It was still at farm in 1347 but not in 1353, perhaps because the miller had died in the Black Death.[32] Rent was received from the mill for only part of the year in 1376 because the miller had fled.[33] The mill was farmed to John Cogel from Christmas 1376 and to John Drew in 1390,[34] but Drew defaulted on the rent and the mill was idle for years, being reported in 1399 as empty and unrepaired and thereafter it was omitted from accounts.[35]

There was said to have been a corn mill in 1539, called the Abbot's mill, in a field adjoining the churchyard, where the house called Dr. Johnson's stood. The assumption was that the mill was a water mill, associated with the streams and ponds on the east of Frognal, near the church,[36] and Dr. Johnson's house was presumably Priory Lodge.[37] A mill near the churchyard was mentioned in 1597.[38] That mill was almost certainly the windmill and cottage called the Millhouse, which in 1636 were part of the copyhold Coneyfield, on the east side of Frognal, north of the church and south of Mount Vernon, the estate associated with the Old Mansion, no. 94 Frognal.[39] The mansion had replaced the mill buildings by 1680 and probably by 1664.[40]

Two windmills were illustrated at Hampstead in views of from c. 1593 to 1638.[41] One was the Frognal mill, which had disappeared by c. 1672.[42] The other, described in 1666 as on the waste and in 1704 as on the heath at the 'Upper End and Cloth Hill', had by 1666 given its name to Mill Hill (later Windmill Hill) in East End,[43] and is identifiable with Mount Vernon House, earlier called Windmill Hill House.[44] Millers were recorded in 1614 and 1665.[45] In 1674 the Mount Vernon mill belonged to Philip Cater,

[4] e.g. in 1646: W.A.M. 16478.
[5] W.A.M. 16486, 16546.
[6] Ibid. 16482, 16489.   [7] Ibid. 16492, 16494.
[8] Ibid. 16508.   [9] Ibid. 16511.
[10] Ibid. 16515.   [11] Ibid. 16521.
[12] Norden, *Map of Mdx.* (1593).
[13] E.C.R. 16/ST JAS/3, mm. 1–2d.
[14] Ibid. 54/163, vol. 13, p. 117; vol. 14, p. 36; vol. 15, p. 12.
[15] Hist. MSS. Com. 39, *15th Rep. II, Hodgkin*, p. 260.
[16] P.R.O., C 54/3553, no. 33; ibid. E 317/Mdx. 56.
[17] E.C.R. 54/181.
[18] Ibid. 54/165.
[19] P.R.O., C 10/11/41; ibid. E 317/Mdx. 56.
[20] Ibid. E 317/Mdx. 56.
[21] *Cal. Treas. Bks.* 1672–5, 94–5.
[22] S.C.L., D 136–7.
[23] *Cal. Pat.* 1317–21, 465.
[24] *Valor Eccl.* (Rec. Com.), i. 432.
[25] P.R.O., E 126/33, East. 25 Geo. III, no. 2.
[26] S.C.L., Man. Map and Fieldbk.
[27] W.A.M. 32399.   [28] Ibid. 32393, 32375.
[29] Ibid. 32370.   [30] Ibid. 32372, 32374.
[31] C.U.L., Kk. V. 29, f. 31v.
[32] W.A.M. 32494–5.
[33] Ibid. 32495.
[34] Ibid. 32498, 32511.   [35] Ibid. 32512–20.
[36] *Hampstead Annual* (1905–6), 73–88.
[37] Above, growth, Frognal.
[38] Park, *Hampstead*, 27.
[39] G.L.R.O., E/MW/H/2; S.C.L., Man. Map and Fieldbk. nos. 400–9.
[40] Above, growth, Frognal.
[41] J. Norden, *View of Lond.* (1600) (Lond. Topog. Soc. no. 94); C. J. Visscher, *View of Lond.* (1616) (Lond. Topog. Soc. no. 4); M. Merian, *View of Lond.* (Lond. Topog. Soc. no. 49); J. Howgego, *Printed Maps of Lond. c. 1553–1850* (1978), p. 7, no. 5; cf. Ikin, *Hampstead Heath*, 9.
[42] Ogilby, *Map of Mdx.* [c. 1672].
[43] G.L.R.O., E/MW/H/6 (1666); H/I/2311A, 2123.
[44] S.C.L., Man. Map and Fieldbk. no. 415.
[45] *Mdx. Sess. Rec.* ii. 184; P.R.O., PROB 11/325 (P.C.C. 1667, f. 7, will of John Sell).

who conveyed it in that year to Richard Thornton, miller, who was already the occupier.[46] In 1686 Thornton conveyed it to Richard Snelling[47] and by 1704 it was held by George Love.[48] In 1725 Samuel Love conveyed it to William Knight, a smith, and in 1728, when Knight sold the site, the windmill was described as broken and a house had been built.[49] By 1759 the windmill had gone and the house and locality were called Windmill House and Windmill Hill.[50]

FAIRS. There is no record of a market in Hampstead. By 1712 a four-day summer fair was associated with the Lower Flask tavern.[51] In 1725 constables were ordered to attend the 'fair or pretended fair' held for some years past at Hampstead to prevent disorder, which included drunkenness, swearing, and plays and 'drolls' enacted against the law.[52] In 1746, when fear of Jacobites sharpened official distaste for crowds, the fair was seen as a disturbance of the peace and an encouragement of vice. The fair was apparently held by Joseph Cranfield of Hampstead and included gaming, dancing, and shows at booths.[53] Orders to suppress it were repeated in 1747 and 1748[54] and were presumably eventually successful for in 1814 no one could remember the fair.[55]

In the late 18th century there was a small three-day toy and gingerbread fair in high summer at West End. Ladies added a charity booth[56] and by 1802 it was a genteel affair with booths furnished by the Hampstead ladies with 'the most brilliant and tasteful bijoux' and attended 'by all the beauty and fashion of the place'.[57] Mrs. Barbauld celebrated the fair 'where Charity with Fashion meets'.[58] The fair was associated, however, with the Cock and Hoop and soon began to attract unsavoury elements from London. Following a general public meeting, the fair was presented in 1812 as a great nuisance and the lady of the manor issued instructions that she would not permit the fair at West End or anywhere else.[59] Local tradesmen foiled the first attempts at suppression[60] and the fair became even larger, spilling into a field let out by a cowkeeper, some 50 or 60 booths being erected and much wine, porter, and tea being consumed in 1816.[61] The inhabitants of West End tried unsuccessfully to get the fair removed to Fortune Green in 1816.[62] A clown was killed during a fight with the constables at the public house after the fair in 1817,[63] and in 1819 some 200 ruffians broke up the booths, overwhelmed the local con-

stables, and committed violent robbery, for which at least three of them were hanged.[64] The local West End magistrate Germain Lavie, supported by the manorial court, the vestry, and a separate committee, promoted a military-style operation in 1820 in which 150 police and special constables were deployed to intercept roughs and ensure orderly conduct at the public houses, and anyone erecting booths was to be prosecuted.[65] The fair, though later asserted to have lasted long after 1819 or until c. 1840, attracted no further attention.[66]

There were attempts during the 19th century to hold unofficial fairs. The heath keeper forbade swings and stalls in Pond Street in 1835 and prevented an attempt to show wild beasts from the Tower at White Bear Green in 1837. Some village sports, like sack races, did take place at White Bear Green until c. 1844.[67] After the opening of Hampstead Heath station in 1860 and especially after the Bank Holiday Act of 1871, fairs were provided at a number of places to cater for the London crowds. Booths on the heath were recorded from c. 1865, steam merry-go-rounds and swings were erected on the Carlile estate in Easter 1878, and by the following Easter a fair was being held at South End Green, while swings and other entertainments were provided at the Vale of Health and on East Heath by the 1880s. Fairs on the heath remained popular in the 20th century.[68]

TRADE AND INDUSTRY. Tiles were being made at Belsize between 1483 and 1490.[69] In 1496 Westminster abbey contracted with two brickmakers, from New Brentford and Hertfordshire respectively, to make 400,000 bricks,[70] perhaps for building Belsize House,[71] since Brickfield lay just to its north in 1679.[72] Tiles and bricks were produced, presumably commercially, in 1557 at Kilnfield next to the London road at the south-east corner of the Belsize estate.[73] Production had probably ceased by 1568 as no bricks or tiles were listed with Armagil Waad's property at Belsize.[74] The lease of Belsize in 1634 included tilehouses[75] and in 1646 the tilekiln was found to be four bays of low building with an untiled roof and a quantity of tiles.[76] There was another tilekiln in 1676 on the west side of the London road adjacent to Chalcots, possibly near Chalk Farm just outside Hampstead parish.[77]

The other centre of tilemaking was in Kilburn, like Belsize easily accessible by road from London.

[46] G.L.R.O., E/MW/H/6.   [47] Ibid. 8.
[48] G.L.R.O., E/MW/H/I/2311A.
[49] M.M. & M., Lib. B, p. 296.
[50] Ibid. Lib. D, pp. 413 sqq.
[51] Advert. in *Spectator*, 29 July 1712, quoted in Park, *Hampstead*, 246.
[52] G.L.R.O., Cal. Mdx. Sess. Bks. xiii. 247.
[53] Ibid. xxi. 51–6, 76.
[54] Ibid. 94; xxii. 28.
[55] Park, *Hampstead*, 246.
[56] Barratt, *Annals*, ii. 244–6.
[57] *The Times*, 27 July 1802, 2c.
[58] Quoted in Barratt, *Annals*, i. 299.
[59] G.L.R.O., M/81/6, 7.
[60] Some persons adopted 'injudicious proceedings': Park, *Hampstead*, 256. Cf. verse by tradesmen: G.L.R.O., M/81/7.
[61] *Observer*, 4 Aug. 1816, quoted in *N. & Q.* 12th ser. ii. 170; Barratt, *Annals*, ii. 244–6.
[62] Vestry mins. 25 Apr. 1816.
[63] Newspaper cutting in S.C.L., card index.

[64] Ibid.
[65] G.L.R.O., M/81/7; vestry mins. 13 Aug. 1819; S.C.L., H 394.6 West End Fair (docs. about fair).
[66] V. Hart, 'Popular Celebrations and customs in Hampstead, 1800–1914' (TS. thesis for Dip. in Eng. Local Hist., Portsmouth Polytechnic, 1985, in S.C.L.).
[67] Ibid.; Barratt, *Annals*, ii. 246.
[68] Hart, 'Popular Celebrations'; H. C. Bentwich, *Vale of Health*, 77–8; Thompson, *Hampstead*, 327; *C.H.R.* iv. 13–16; above, growth, Hampstead Heath.
[69] W.A.M. 32274.
[70] Ibid. 16470.
[71] Thompson, *Hampstead*, 8.
[72] S.C.L., D 136–7.
[73] Ibid.; W.A.M. 16475.
[74] P.R.O., E 159/357, rot. 532.
[75] W.A.M. 16476.
[76] Ibid. 16477–8.
[77] S.C.L., D 58, i.e. lease of part of Chalcots 'Hanging Hill field (5 a.) next the tile kiln'. For Hanging field (5½ a.), part of Chalcots in 1720, see E.C.R. 51/6; 54/163A no. 61.

In 1522 the prior of St. John of Jerusalem leased all his manor and farm of Hampstead to John Barne, tiler of Hampstead: the prior had erected a house, barn, and tilehouse at his own expense, except for 3,000 tiles provided by Barne.[78] Other tilemakers of Kilburn were mentioned in the early 16th century,[79] c. 1574 when disputed property included a tilehouse,[80] 1600,[81] and the 1650s when William Freelove, tilemaster of Kilburn, Hampstead, was an underlessee of St. John's Wood.[82] A tilekiln on the Liddell estate had become a private house by 1698.[83] Tilemakers from unidentified places in Hampstead were mentioned in the early 16th century when one sold 1,500 tiles to Henry VIII,[84] c. 1550,[85] 1609,[86] and 1611.[87] In 1609 two Hampstead yeomen were licensed to search all tiles in Middlesex.[88] In 1653, in an attempt to reduce a tax assessment on Hampstead, attention was drawn to its many poor men subsisting only on wages from the tilekilns.[89] There was a brick clamp on the heath in 1665 and a place near the south-east corner of the Wells charity estate was known by 1742 as 'the Brick Lamps'.[90] Bricks were also made at West End in 1793, when they were not to be carted to Edgware Road by way of West End Lane.[91]

Brickmaking expanded and shifted with the demand for housing in the 19th century. The church of St. John, Downshire Hill, opened in 1823, was remembered as having been built in a brickfield, which gave its name to the Lower Heath quarter, the triangle formed by Downshire Hill, Keats Grove, and part of South End Road.[92] In 1834 William Kerrison of Mount Villa Cottage was a brickmaker and builder, as were seven others, mostly in High Street or Flask Walk.[93] New brickfields around Belsize Park posed no threat to public health in 1856,[94] unlike ones in the triangle between Finchley Road and the Midland and Hampstead Junction railways, where in 1858 John Culverhouse dumped refuse and was forbidden to make bricks with contaminated water.[95] Brickfields lay near the Hendon boundary next to Platt's Lane by 1864 and, worked by Culverhouse, between Finchley Road and the railways and on the east side of the heath in 1866; they covered $8\frac{1}{2}$ a., 9 a., and $10\frac{1}{2}$ a. respectively in 1871.[96]

John Culverhouse, also a farmer, in 1842 had leased 7 a. of the lord's freehold on the east side of the heath.[97] He was both a dust contractor and a supplier of road-making materials to the parish in 1857–8,[98] but fulfilled neither contract satisfactorily.[99] His address was Manor Farm in 1874, when he was a vestryman and responsible for four insanitary cottages for brickmakers at East Park.[1] Edward Culverhouse lived at no. 5 Villas on the Heath, one of a row which he built in the 1860s. Alfred Culverhouse tendered for the removal of dust and supplied road materials in 1874. East Park brickfields were occupied by John and Alfred in 1875 and by Alfred and Frederick Culverhouse, also described as farmers, in the 1880s.[2]

Notice to quit the Finchley Road fields was given to John Culverhouse in 1876.[3] Brickmaking on land belonging to the Hampstead Junction Railway Co. near Fleet Road began in the early 1880s but was not profitable; some of the work ceased c. 1882 and the rest was stopped after litigation by the vestry in 1885.[4] All the brickfields had gone by 1896.[5]

Several 19th-century building firms were long lived, although they moved into Hampstead only as housing spread northward.[6] Charles Tavener, a bricklayer, was said to have started his business in 1846. It operated for nearly a century in St. John's Wood and may have been connected with that of Walter Tavener, in Adelaide Road by 1885. C. Tavener & Son was owned by the family for at least three generations,[7] with premises from 1920 to 1971 in Finchley Road and from 1935 a works in Iverson Road which survived in 1986. Richard Densham & Sons, claiming to date from 1850 and also starting in St. John's Wood, were by 1934 in Fortune Green Road, which they left c. 1974. William Littlewood, dating from 1864, was in England's Lane as an ironmonger by 1880 and stayed until 1979. Others included H. R. Bence & Son, dating from 1860, in Ainger Road as Gregory & Bence by 1881 and Winchester Road by 1890 and until 1965, Charles Hankin, dating from 1875, in Downshire Hill by 1880 and until 1959, and Roff & Sons, 'established over a century' in 1951, in Heath Street.

A few auctioneers and estate agents had similarly long existences. Henry Paxon of no. 22 High Street in 1862 claimed to continue there a business which his father had started in 1784. George Paxon had been an auctioneer in High Street in the 1820s, when Francis had been a glazier;[8] George had chaired the vestry in 1803, as churchwarden,[9] and several later

[78] B.L. Cott. MS. Claud. E. VI, ff. 235v.–6.
[79] John Walker: *Lond. Topog. Rec.* xix. 101.
[80] Wm. Tilcock assigned lease to Wm. Bateman, bricklayer: P.R.O., REQ 2/41/36.
[81] P.R.O., PROB 11/95 (P.C.C. 18 Wallopp, will of John Evans).
[82] Ibid. PROB 11/222 (P.C.C. 132 Bowyer); ibid. C 10/11/41.
[83] G.L.R.O., E/MW/H/17; S.C.L., Man. Map and Fieldbk. no. 521.
[84] *Lond. Topog. Rec.* xix. 104.
[85] P.R.O., REQ 2/241/1.
[86] G.L.R.O., Cal. Mdx. Sess. Recs. ii. 34.
[87] Ibid. vii. 169.
[88] Ibid. iii. 73.
[89] Barratt, *Annals*, iii, App. 5, p. 364.
[90] G.L.R.O., E/MW/H/6.
[91] S.C.L., Hampstead manor min. bk. (1742–82), p. 10; ibid. (1783–1809), pp. 166, 185, 388.
[92] S.C.L., H 942.14 (Newton cuttings bk., p. 31); Wade, *Streets of Hampstead*, 52.
[93] *Pigot's Lond. and Provincial Dir.* (1834).
[94] Vestry mins. 25 Mar., 22 Aug., 5 Sept. 1856.
[95] Ibid. 19 Mar. 1858.
[96] Rate bk. (1864); O.S. Map 1/2,500, Lond. VII (1870 edn.); *O.S. Bk. of Ref. to Plan of St. John, Hampstead* (1871), nos. 56, 282, 409.
[97] G.L.R.O., E/MW/H, old nos. 31/3 (lease 1842); 31/6 (lease 1868); *C.H.R.* x. 17–18.
[98] Vestry mins. 27 Mar., 17 July 1857.
[99] Ibid. 11 Sept. 1857, 21 May 1858.
[1] Ibid. 11 June, 2 July 1874.
[2] *P.O. Dir. Lond. Suburban North* (1872); Bentwich, *Vale of Health*, 59; vestry mins. 19 Feb. 1874; *P.O. Dir. Lond.* (1875); *P.O. Dir. Lond. County Suburbs, North* (1880, 1884). Photo c. 1880 in Farmer, *Hampstead Heath*, 124.
[3] G.L.R.O., E/MW/H, old no. 26/86.
[4] Ch. Com. files 45820, pt. 2; 62499, pt. 1; Thompson, *Hampstead*, 359; vestry mins. 4, 18 June, 16 July 1885.
[5] O.S. Map 1/2,500, Lond. XXVII (1896 edn.).
[6] Following two paras. based on *P.O. Dir. Lond.* (1848 and later edns.); *P.O. Dir. Lond. County Suburbs, North* (1880 and later edns.); *Hampstead and Highgate Dir.* (1885–6). Reputed dates of firms' establishments are in *Hampstead Dir.* (1951–2).
[7] *H.H.E.* 20 Aug. 1971, 24d.
[8] *Hampstead Dir. and Almanack* (1862); *Pigot's Com. Dir.* (1826–7).
[9] e.g. vestry mins. 10 Aug. 1803, 14 Mar. 1804 et seq.

members of the family were vestrymen.[10] Potters, advertised as the oldest estate agents in 1936,[11] were founded in the 1830s by George Potter. The firm continued under his son G. W. Potter, who wrote on Hampstead wells, and grandson H. G. Potter (d. 1951)[12] in High Street from 1880[13] and afterwards in Rosslyn Hill and, by 1912, Heath Street until 1983. Ernest Owers & Williams was established in West End Lane in 1879 by Ernest Owers, who later opened offices in Finchley Road and at Golders Green and whose business was bought by W. Charles Williams in 1931. The firm, which later expanded to Mayfair, had only two senior partners during its first hundred years.[14]

Hampstead brewery was established in 1720, according to the firm's later tradition,[15] by John Vincent, who in 1713 had owned Jack Straw's Castle.[16] A leading parishioner, he was allowed by the Wells trustees to draw piped water, which later supplied his brewery behind the King of Bohemia's Head, in High Street. Vincent also acquired much other property, including the George near the corner of Pond Street.[17] His unsettled copyholds passed in 1755 to a younger son Robert, who probably carried on the business with his elder brother Richard, whom he succeeded in 1776.[18] Robert's widow Elizabeth was admitted in 1787 to the brewery, the King of Bohemia's Head, the George, the Black Boy and Still (formerly Coach and Horses) and other property, all of which was mortgaged in 1790 and again in 1797. The brewery was occupied by Messrs. Shepheard and Buckland in 1797,[19] but Elizabeth retained her interest in it until 1812, when she surrendered it to James Buckland, and in the George until 1814.[20] John Buckland worked the brewery c. 1827,[21] Thomas Buckland in 1834 and 1854,[22] and John Tanner Hawkins, under whom it was called the Hampstead brewery, in 1859.[23] The property was enfranchised for Hawkins in 1865.[24] A limited company was formed in 1866, with prominent local shareholders, controlled in 1870 and 1875 by Edward Harris[25] and from c. 1880 by Mure & Co. (known for a few years as Mure, Warner & Co.).[26] Hampstead Brewery had 184 employees in 1928 but closed in 1931 or 1932.[27] The brewhouse was to be repaired in 1834, when held by James Buckland's heirs Elizabeth and Ann Seager Buckland.[28] Rebuilt in 1869

with two shops in front,[29] it was dilapidated in 1959, when used for motor repairs.[30] It was later converted into offices, approached by Old Brewery Mews, whose arched entrance survived in 1986 next to the refronted King of Bohemia.[31]

A brewhouse and dwelling house at the end of Pond Street, near the banks of the Fleet, were held by Michael Combrune in 1746.[32] Combrune, who had been described as a brewer of St. Giles's parish in 1743,[33] published two books on brewing with dedications dated from Hampstead in 1758 and 1762.[34] He acquired many copyholds, being admitted to the Duke of Hamilton's Head and the Fox and Goose in 1753, the Cock and Hoop at West End in 1754, the Bull and Bush at North End in 1763, and the Cock in 1770.[35] He also had a reversionary interest in the Nag's Head, an inn which eventually passed to his daughter Susanna, while Eleanor Combrune, presumably another daughter, was admitted to a half share in the Bear in 1766 and to the Flask, with several other houses, in 1767.[36] Presumably all those inns were supplied from Michael Combrune's brewery, which may not have survived his death in 1773.[37] Eleanor's property passed in 1773 to her son Thomas Gardner and Michael's, on the death of his widow Mary in 1778, to Susanna Combrune.[38] Gideon Combrune was a brewer of Golden Lane (Lond.) in 1797.[39]

Kilburn brewery was run in the mid 19th century by William Verey, a Hampstead resident, and later by Michell & Phillips. It stood on the Willesden side of Kilburn High Road at nos. 289 and 291.[40]

Laundry work, giving rise to the name Cloth Hill, was widespread by the 16th century.[41] Although traditionally associated with Hampstead,[42] claims that it was the main occupation of the first inhabitants of the Vale of Health were an exaggeration.[43] Presumably some washing was done in the pond there, as 10 people had set up a total of 83 clothes posts on the heath at the Vale of Health by 1839, when there were also 58 posts at North End and 33 at West End. The posts, some of which had stood for 20 years, were to be replaced in order to preserve the rights of the lord.[44] Charles Dickens's father John was a lodger with Mrs. Davis, a laundress at North End, in 1834.[45] Another laundress at North End advertised that clothes were dried on the heath

[10] e.g. ibid. 21 Aug., 22 Sept. 1823, 1 Feb. 1828 et seq.
[11] H.H.E. 13 June 1936, 2d.
[12] S.C.L., H 920/Potter.
[13] H.H.E. 5 June 1880.
[14] Inf. from Mr. W. C. Williams.
[15] S.C.L., advert. cutting in card index; H.H.E. 9 Oct. 1920, 5e.
[16] Images of Hampstead, 82.
[17] H.H.E. 9 Oct. 1920, 5e; S.C.L., Hampstead manor min. bk. (1742–82), p. 138 and passim.
[18] S.C.L., Hampstead manor min. bk. (1742–82), pp. 156, 226, 393.
[19] Ibid. (1783–1809), pp. 72, 112–13, 239–42.
[20] Ibid. (1809–24), pp. 37, 48–9, 101.
[21] Pigot's Com. Dir. (1826–7, 1828–9).
[22] Pigot's Lond. & Provincial Dir. (1834); Shaw, Hampstead Dir. & Guide (1854).
[23] Hampstead Dir. & Almanack (1859, 1862).
[24] H.H.E. 9 Oct. 1920, 5e; H.H.E. Dir. (1870); P.O. Dir. Lond. (1875).
[25] P.R.O., MAF 20/89.
[26] P.O. Dir. Lond. County Suburbs, North (1880 and later edns.).
[27] Hampstead One Thousand, 127; P.O. Dir. Lond. County Suburbs (1931, 1932).

[28] S.C.L., Hampstead manor min. bk. (1824–39), p. 335.
[29] S.C.L., advert. cutting in card index; Images of Hampstead, illus. 328 (trade card, 1872, in S.C.L.).
[30] Hampstead News, 27 Mar. 1959, 9a–e.
[31] Images of Hampstead, 112; dates of brewery on King of Bohemia.
[32] Hampstead One Thousand, 51; S.C.L., Hampstead manor min. bk. (1742–82), p. 54.
[33] Hampstead manor min. bk. (1742–82), p. 17.
[34] M. Combrune, Essay on Brewing (1758); idem, Theory and Practice of Brewing (1762).
[35] S.C.L., Hampstead manor min. bk. (1742–82), pp. 122, 135, 202, 298.
[36] Ibid. pp. 166, 260.   [37] Ibid. p. 360.
[38] Ibid. pp. 352–6, 361, 414, 420–1.
[39] Ibid. (1783–1809), pp. 239–42.
[40] P.O. Dir. Six Home Counties (1845); vestry mins. 8 Jan., 29 Mar. 1864; Hutchings and Crowsley, Hampstead and Highgate Dir. (1885–6).
[41] Above, growth, Hampstead town.
[42] Macky, Journey through Eng. i (1732), 89.
[43] Bentwich, Vale of Health, 26–7.
[44] Ibid. 94; Barratt, Annals, ii. 268–9; diary of heath keeper (1834–40) in S.C.L.
[45] Letters of Chas. Dickens, i. 5, 47.

in 1870, when 20 laundries were listed at Hampstead, presumably larger establishments than those of the earlier washerwomen.[46] In 1872, before the M.B.W. had made byelaws for the heath, some of its prettiest parts were usurped by laundresses,[47] but by 1907 only a few clothes could be seen, near North End.[48] Later laundry firms included, in Fleet Road, the Fleet laundry in 1885 and 1895 and, in Fairhazel Gardens, the Belsize Park Laundry Co. in 1885 and the South Hampstead Sanitary Laundry Co. in 1889.[49] Probably the biggest was the Hampstead Model Steam Laundry, on the east side of Cressy Road by 1885 and until 1914 or later.[50]

The iron and brass foundry of Thomas Potter & Sons was established c. 1860 by Thomas Potter of Poplar House,[51] a West End resident by 1854.[52] Twelve cottages called Potter's Buildings (later West Cottages) were under construction by George Potter immediately north of the foundry in 1864,[53] apparently because local hostility made it impossible for his workmen to find other accommodation. There was also hostility to plans for making gas to light the workshops, with the result that a half-built gasometer could be used only as a water tank.[54] Among the foundry's products were metalwork for the outer screen walls of G. E. Street's Law Courts (built 1874–82) and for Welbeck Abbey (Notts.), besides church fittings.[55] A younger Thomas Potter, who lived at the Elms in the 1880s, built on sites north of Poplar House and around Sumatra Road. The foundry had closed by 1894 and was replaced by the flats called Welbeck Mansions.[56]

There was little industry in the central part of the parish, apart from workshops, studios, and other premises used by local tradesmen. Short-lived concerns included, in the early 19th century, a 'small cartridge factory' built by the Eley family of Woodbine Cottage, West End, where village girls were reluctant to work.[57] Presumably it was a forerunner of the cartridge making business of William Eley, established in London by 1838 and later well known as Eley Bros.[58] Isaac Alexander had a biscuit factory in Pond Street in 1859 and 1862.[59] G. S. Jealous in 1870 produced the *Hampstead & Highgate Express* at 'the only printing office in Hampstead' in Holly Mount, where there was still a printer's, Provost & Co., in 1885.[60]

In 1904 Hampstead had 51 factories and 257 workshops, employing 2,988 people.[61] Dressmaking was their main employment, with 1,047 people or nearly 35 per cent of the workforce. It was followed by work in paper and printing with as many as 24.1 per cent, in laundries with 11.9 per cent, and in wood, the largest single employer of men, with 10.9 per cent.[62] The figures, accounting for less than 1 in 27 of the total population, did not include those in domestic service, among whom were coachmen in mews dwellings. Nor did they include inhabitants, chiefly in West Hampstead, who worked as clerks, policemen, travelling salesmen, or in many other relatively humble occupations.[63]

Some industry spread with working-class housing from across the St. Pancras boundary to South End Green.[64] In 1874 the owner of a carpet beating ground in Fleet Road met complaints by claiming that he had been there for 20 years. After Cressy Road had been built for access to the tram depot,[65] the steam laundry was joined in 1894 by Mansell, Hunt & Catty, makers of crackers and doileys, who in 1901 built a subway to the west side of the road, where already there were two piano manufacturers. The tram depot passed in turn to the L.C.C., to British Road Services, and to Camden L.B. as a vehicle maintenance depot; the yellow-brick tramsheds survived in 1986, behind the modern Northern District office of the G.L.C.'s department of mechanical and electrical engineering. One of the piano makers, Francis Lambert, was in Cressy Road until 1927 or later and Mansell, Hunt & Catty remained until the early 1970s, when they were replaced by Camden L.B.'s ambulance station.

Industrial premises close to Kilburn High Road[66] included, at the north-west end of Belsize Road, the Priory works of 1892, and an adjoining area, nos. 252 and 254, next to Kilburn town hall (later the Theatre Royal).[67] Priory works was occupied by the Dunlop Rubber Co. in 1913 and 1918, and later by from two to four firms, few of which stayed for long but which included makers of zip fasteners from the 1930s until the 1970s. The building stood empty in 1986. Next door a depository was used from c. 1896 until c. 1934 by R. C. Barnes & Sons, furniture removers whose main offices were on the west side of Kilburn High Road but who had more premises behind the east side in Kingsgate Road. In 1952 and 1964 the depository was used by W. & S. Williams, who had been established as auctioneers in Birchington Road since the 1930s, but by 1975 it was an audio-visual aids centre.

The main industrial area lay along the railways between Finchley Road and Kilburn High Road. Land in the triangle between the Midland and

[46] *H.H.E. Dir.* (1870).
[47] *The Times*, 24 May 1872, 7e.
[48] Potter, *Random Recollections*, 10.
[49] *Hampstead and Highgate Dir.* (1885–6); *Kelly's Dir. Hampstead and Highgate* (1889–90, 1895).
[50] O.S. Map 1/2,500, Lond. XXVIII (1896 edn.); *Hampstead and Highgate Dir.* (1885–6); *Kelly's Dir. Hampstead and Childs Hill* (1914–15).
[51] Wade, *W. Hampstead*, 13, 21.
[52] Shaw, *Hampstead Dir. and Guide* (1854).
[53] Wade, *W. Hampstead*, 13; vestry mins. 12 Feb., 7 Oct. 1864.
[54] A. E. Barnes, 'Reminiscences of W. End' (MS. and TS. in S.C.L.).
[55] Ibid.; Pevsner, *Lond.* i. 322; Wade, *W. Hampstead*, 13.
[56] Barnes, 'Reminiscences of W. End'; *P.O. Dir. Lond. County Suburbs, North* (1880, 1888, 1894); Wade, *W. Hampstead*, 20–1; above, growth, West End.
[57] Barnes, 'Reminiscences of W. End'.
[58] *Pigot's Lond. Dir.* (1838); *P.O. Dir. Lond.* (1845 and later edns.).
[59] *Hampstead Dir. and Almanack* (1859, 1862).
[60] *H.H.E. Dir.* (1870); *Hampstead and Highgate Dir.* (1885–6).
[61] L.C.C. *Lond. Statistics*, xix. 42–3.
[62] Ibid. xvii. 54, 56, 58.
[63] Booth, *Life and Labour*, i(2), app. pp. 16–17; Mudie-Smith, *Rel. Life*, 132. Detailed employment figs., by occupation, are in *Census*, 1901, table 35.
[64] Para. based on Wade, *More Streets*, 23; *Kelly's Dir. Hampstead and Highgate* (1894–5 and later edns.); *Kelly's Dir. Hampstead and Childs Hill* (1920 and later edns.).
[65] Above, communications.
[66] Para. based on Wade, *W. Hampstead*, 44; *Kelly's Dir. Hampstead and Highgate* (1896 and later edns.); *Kelly's Dir. Hampstead and Childs Hill* (1913–14 and later edns.); *P.O. Dir. Lond.* (1952 and later edns.); insurance plan B 13 (rev. 1925, 1970).
[67] Date on building; Wade, *W. Hampstead*, 44; above, social.

Hampstead Junction railways and Finchley Road, which had formed John Culverhouse's brickfield and dustyard, was bought from the Maryon Wilson estate for a parish stone yard in 1881.[68] The vestry opened its electricity power station there in 1894.[69]

A little to the west[70] by 1885 six coal merchants' and two cement merchants' yards lined the north side of Iverson Road, from Maygrove Road to the Midland's West End station (opened 1871). In 1896 the Anglo-American Oil Co. had a depot in Maygrove Road, where from c. 1904 it adjoined one belonging to the General (later British) Petroleum Co. The extension of the Metropolitan line to West Hampstead in 1879 left a stretch of land between it and the Midland railway, bisected by West End Lane and crossed diagonally by the H.J.R. line. There the wholly industrial Blackburn Road, leading eastward from West End Lane, had been planned by 1885. At first it served only a few small firms, most of them short lived. No. 3, for example, was occupied in turn by a builder's yard, a sawmill, a bicycle maker, a pill maker, and from c. 1935 by the Alliance Plating Works. F. R. Napier, who had opened a plating shop behind West Hampstead fire station in 1919 and later worked for the Alliance, took the site for his Hampstead Plating Works, which was founded in 1940 and survived as a family firm with four employees in 1986.[71] The longest presence was that of J. Sloper & Co., established in London in 1858 as makers of perforating machines, who employed 14–20 people at their Tower Royal works in Blackburn Road in 1986.[72] There were stained glass artists from c. 1888 until c. 1938 at F. W. Noble's, no. 48 Maygrove Road.[73] Mill glass works was founded by G. H. Hill in 1911 and was a small family firm making leaded lights in 1986, when, at no. 84, it was the oldest in Mill Lane.[74]

In 1918 the yards of coal merchants, a builder's merchant, and two wholesale potato merchants stretched along Iverson Road, where they remained in 1939.[75] Beck & Pollitzer Contracts, exhibition specialists founded in 1913 as a branch of an older London transport business, occupied premises on the south side of the road from 1926.[76] The two oil companies left Maygrove Road between 1930 and 1932. F. J. Lewis, who started business as a wooden handrail maker at no. 3 Blackburn Road in 1922 and moved to Exeter Mews, off West Hampstead Mews, in 1928, built a factory, mainly of timber, in 1936[77] in Maygrove Road, where Maygrove Motors also opened in 1936.[78] Beyond the eastern end of Blackburn Road, and listed under it, sites had been taken by 1933 for a depot of Cadbury Bros. and for a warehouse of the Canadian government's exhibition commission. The Post Office, which had opened a telephone exchange at no. 33 College Crescent in

1904 and later took over an exchange opened in 1901 by the National Telephone Co. in Goldhurst Terrace, opened its new Hampstead exchange at no. 361 Finchley Road in 1932.[79]

All seven coal merchants on the north side of Iverson Road in 1964 had gone by 1975, when the neighbourhood had many motor car repair firms.[80] Later changes included closures at the end of Blackburn Road, where the Canadian government's building and its neighbours were included in the West Hampstead trading centre, occupied by over 20 firms in 1986. Workshops for small firms were also provided by Camden L. B. in Liddell Road, in 1984 a new cul-de-sac between Maygrove Road and the railway; there were over 30 sites, not all of which had been filled by 1986. F. J. Lewis enlarged its site in 1950 and built Handrail House, no. 65 Maygrove Road, which it extended in 1960. The building was always shared, other occupants including Brent L.B.'s rent office in 1986, when Lewis's remained a family firm, with c. 36 employees.[81] Maygrove Motors and several more recent firms were established nearby. Among them was Arnold R. Horwell, laboratory and clinical supplies, who from 1983 occupied no. 73 Maygrove Road, having begun trading in 1950 at the founder's flat before moving in 1956 to Cricklewood Broadway and in 1966 to Grangeway, off Kilburn High Road. The firm, with 28 employees, exported to 110 countries in 1986.[82] Second-hand car dealers and repair workshops also congregated off the west side of Finchley Road, around Rosemont Road. The largest industrial premises were probably those of the London Electricity Board, with its rebuilt depot at the end of Lithos Road, and of Beck & Pollitzer Contracts, which employed 170 people in its head office and in designing and making exhibition stands in Iverson Road.[83] British Telecommunications was a major employers, with 350 at its Centre Area exchange at no. 361 Finchley Road and 180 at a telephone service centre which had been opened in 1956 in Blackburn Road.[84]

Domestic service was the largest employment in 1901, when 13,843 people, in addition to those in commercial establishments or charwomen, were indoor servants. Hampstead's 81.4 servants to every 100 families or separate occupiers was the highest proportion in London, slightly exceeding that of Kensington. The fact that six metropolitan boroughs had proportionately more men servants, however, showed Hampstead to be well-to-do rather than very rich or aristocratic.[85]

The hotel and catering trades were comparatively unimportant in the 19th century. The Holly Bush and the Wells hotels, offering every modern comfort in 1859, had replaced earlier inns.[86] The Suburban

---

[68] Thompson, *Hampstead*, 407; above.
[69] Below, pub. svces.
[70] Para. based on *Hampstead and Highgate Dir.* (1885–6); *Kelly's Dir. Hampstead and Highgate* (1894–5 and later edns.); *Kelly's Dir. Hampstead and Childs Hill* (1899 and later edns.).
[71] Inf. from Mr. F. H. Napier, managing dir.
[72] Inf. from Mr. W. F. Steere, dir.; above, growth, West End.
[73] *P.O. Dir. Lond. County Suburbs, North* (1888 and later edns.); *P.O. Dir. Lond.* (1938 and later edns.).
[74] Inf. from Mr. A. G. Hill, Mill Glass Works.
[75] Para. based on *Kelly's Dir. Hampstead and Childs Hill* (1918–19 and later edns.); *P.O. Dir. Lond.* (1934 and later

edns.).
[76] Inf. from Mr. D. J. Cure, Beck & Pollitzer Contracts Ltd.
[77] Inf. from Mr. A. E. Lewis.
[78] Inf. from Mr. K. Munn-Barron.
[79] Inf. from Telecom Technology Showcase.
[80] Para. based on *P.O. Dir. Lond.* (1964 and later edns.).
[81] Inf. from Mr. A. E. Lewis.
[82] Inf. from Mr. A. R. Horwell.
[83] Inf. from Mr. D. J. Cure.
[84] Inf. from Telecom Technology Showcase.
[85] *Census*, 1901; Thompson, *Hampstead*, 50–1; above, settlement and growth.
[86] *Hampstead Dir. and Almanack* (1859).

Hotel Co.'s purpose-built Hampstead Heath hotel, also called the Vale of Health tavern, was rated from 1863; it soon proved unsuccessful, although it was not finally closed, as the Vale of Health hotel, until 1960. Two smaller hotels in the Vale of Health, built *c.* 1869 and in the 1880s, had shorter existences.[87] Twelve hotels were listed in 1889, eight of them in Belsize Park or on the edge of St. John's Wood.[88] Lodgings in 1903 could be found only in the district bordering Kilburn High Road.[89]

The conversion of many large houses after the First World War may have produced more hotels. Two pairs of Italianate villas had formed the 60-bedroom Ormonde hotel in Belsize Grove by 1936, when Grew's hotels at nos. 43 and 45 Fitzjohn's Avenue also had 60 rooms and Hampstead Towers hotel had recently opened in Ellerdale Road.[90] Thirteen residential hotels and 15 guest houses, some with branches in different roads, were listed in 1951, besides 48 restaurants and 57 cafés, snack bars, or tea rooms, many of them in Kilburn High Road.[91] At the corner of Primrose Hill and Fellows roads the Clive Hall hotel, originally the Clive guest house, was rebuilt with six storeys and 60 bedrooms, to the design of Hugh Sprince, and reopened in 1965 as the Clive hotel. It was extended *c.* 1970 and, with 84 bedrooms, awaited further extension as part of the Ladbroke chain in 1986.[92] The Clive was described as the only major hotel in 1970, when the area was seen as attractive to visitors with their own cars, who might not wish to stay in the centre of London. Trusthouse Forte opened the Post House in 1970, on the site of the Vandervells' home in Haverstock Hill. A six-storeyed building designed by the group's own architects, it was at that time Hampstead's largest hotel and had 140 bedrooms, as it still had in 1986. In 1970 there were plans for three more establishments, which in all would provide 1,500 beds in five hotels.[93] One was the Holiday Inn, which was opened in 1973 at the west end of King Henry's Road. The building, designed by Dennis Lennon & Partners, was owned as part of a chain by Commonwealth Holiday Inns of Canada in 1986, when it had 296 bedrooms and was being refurbished to provide more accommodation on the 7th floor.[94]

Shops until the early 19th century were found only in Heath Street or in High Street, whose southern end was known as Rosslyn Street. In 1734 provisions were said to be better and, except meat, cheaper than in London.[95] Food shops included 5 bakers, a confectioner, 2 grocers, and a fishmonger in 1802 and a greengrocer, who was also a carpenter, and a butcher

and a fishmonger in 1805. Two tallow chandlers, two coal merchants, an ironmonger, and a linen draper were among those who met other common needs.[96] By 1826 less essential demands were met by 2 china and glass dealers, 2 booksellers, 4 perfumers and haircutters, 5 straw hat makers, a watchmaker, and an umbrella maker. A few shops had opened in Kilburn High Road but only in the more usual trades.[97]

Hampstead town had several old family firms and many more businesses which continued for long at the same premises with no more than a change of name. Nineteenth-century advertisers had often traded for several decades, although it was not always clear where they had started. In 1888 T. A. Evans & Sons, drapers, claimed to have been established in 1740, Albert Jones, fishmongers, since 1752, and J. Ware & Sons, grocers, since 1815;[98] Jones soon left no. 2 Heath Street, where J. J. Shepherd had been a fishmonger in 1862, but Evans remained at nos. 46 and 47 High Street until *c.* 1913 and Ware was succeeded by another grocer, Edward Lambert.[99] Andrew & Sons, harness makers at no. 75 High Street until 1947 or later, in 1918 traced their origins back to 1765, Jesse Andrew in 1862 having succeeded John Clarke (fl. 1802) and Joseph Clarke (fl. 1845).[1] Foster's, at no. 73 High Street until 1979, was advertised as dating from 1790 but probably originated in Francis Mason's grocery shop of 1774, which passed in turn to John Riddle, John Payne, George Payne Ashby, and by 1885 to James Foster.[2] The Hampstead Pharmacy at no. 29 was opened *c.* 1840[3] by Joseph Lane and managed for 40 years by Edward Blanshard Stamp (d. 1908), whose name was still used in 1983.[4]

Away from Hampstead town, shops were built in terraces on the fringes of the new estates.[5] Such roads included England's Lane, Belsize Park Terrace (later part of Belsize Lane), Upper Belsize Terrace (later Belsize Terrace), and King's College Road by 1870, and parts of Broadhurst Gardens, Fairhazel Gardens, and Fairfax Road by 1885.[6] Meanwhile shops spread along Kilburn High Road, where there were *c.* 30 on the Hampstead side by 1854, besides another 10 at the south end near Kilburn station, forming St. George's Terrace.[7] There were also shops in West End Lane south of West Hampstead station and at the Kilburn High Road ends of many side roads, including Belsize, Quex, Palmerston, and Netherwood roads, by 1885.[8]

Hampstead tradesmen's association was founded in 1898[9] and was soon followed by Kilburn chamber of trade, which in 1911 held its twelfth annual

[87] Bentwich, *Vale of Health*, 58, 61–2, 67, 82–3; above, growth, Vale of Health.
[88] *Kelly's Dir. Hampstead and Highgate* (1889–90).
[89] Mudie-Smith, *Rel. Life*, 132.
[90] H.H.E. 6 June 1936, 8c. [91] *Hampstead Dir.* (1951).
[92] Wade, *More Streets*, 63; S.C.L., H 728.5/Hotels; inf. from gen. manager.
[93] S.C.L., H 728.5/Hotels; Wade, *More Streets*, 39, 55; inf. from gen. manager, Post Ho. hotel.
[94] Inf. from sales manager, Holiday Inn.
[95] Soame, *Hampstead Wells*, 27. For shops in 1762, above, growth, Hampstead town.
[96] *Holden's Triennial Dir.* (1802–4); (1805–7). Names are listed alphabetically among those for Lond.
[97] *Pigot's Com. Dir.* (1826–7).
[98] *Hampstead Year Bk.* (1888), adverts.
[99] *Hampstead Dir. and Almanack* (1862); *P.O. Dir. Lond. County Suburbs* (1913, 1914).

[1] *Kelly's Dir. Hampstead and Childs Hill* (1918–19), advert.; *P.O. Dir. Lond.* (1947); *Hampstead Dir. and Almanack* (1862); *Holden's Triennial Dir.* (1802–4); *P.O. Dir. Six Home Counties* (1845).
[2] *Hampstead One Thousand*, 126; H.H.E. 27 July 1973, 8d.
[3] 1838 according to *H.H.E. Dir.* (1870), advert.; 1842 according to Lane's advert. in *Hampstead One Thousand*, 125.
[4] H.H.E. 1 Feb. 1908, 5a, 6a; Brit. Telecom, *Lond. Postal Area Dir.* (1983).
[5] Thompson, *Hampstead*, 257, 265, 279.
[6] *H.H.E. Dir.* (1870); *Hampstead and Highgate Dir.* (1885–6).
[7] *Hampstead Dir. and Almanack* (1854).
[8] *Hampstead Dir.* (1885–6).
[9] *Hampstead Social Rev.* Mar. 1905; *Kelly's Dir. Hampstead and Childs Hill* (1900).

dinner.[10] By 1901 the borough had 126 general shop-keepers or dealers, a category which excluded many more people employed in shops in a subordinate capacity.[11] West Hampstead tradesmen's association was founded in 1911, initially for the area between Finchley Road and Kilburn High Road.[12] It was called Hampstead chamber of commerce by 1925, when it had a wider membership, and later united with St. Pancras chamber of commerce.[13]

Most of the shops, serving Hampstead town and its neighbourhood, remained small. A few stores, however, expanded in the less exclusive Kilburn High Road.[14] Among them was William Roper's drapery, in an ornate building of 1884[15] next to the Bell and with further premises in Osborne Terrace and later also in Goldsmith Place. Known as Kilburn Bon Marché, it extended its showrooms and rebuilt a block behind in 1900,[16] closing after 1925 and being succeeded by 1932 by a London Co-operative Society's store.[17] David Fearn & Co., another draper, had spread from one shop to include nos. 52, 52A, and 54 Kilburn High Road by 1896, to which nos. 50 and 56 had been added by 1918;[18] it still traded in 1930 but by 1932 had made way for Montague Burton's and British Home Stores.[19]

A few local shops acquired several branches. T. Gurney Randall, who became an alderman, established his butcher's business in 1867, obtained royal warrants, and by 1900 traded in High Street, England's Lane, Haverstock Hill, and King's College Road.[20] John Dudman, a grocer, had branches in Rosslyn Hill, Upper Belsize Terrace, and Belsize Park Terrace in 1889.[21] Randall's business survived in 1940 and Dudman's name was advertised at no. 56 Rosslyn Hill until the 1980s.[22] Among the earliest local branches of multiple stores were those of John Sainsbury at nos. 292 and 294 Kilburn High Road and of Lilley & Skinner at nos. 260 and 262, by 1889. Both firms were also in Hampstead, where the 'town improvements' had provided better sites, by 1894, as were Boots the chemists by 1905. In Finchley Road there were branches of Sainsburys by 1905 and of Boots by 1910. Marks & Spencer had a penny bazaar on the west side of Kilburn High Road from 1907[23] and moved to nos. 66 and 68, on the east side, c. 1930.[24]

Benjamin Beardmore Evans started as a draper in a single terraced house in Kilburn High Road in 1897. Neighbouring houses were soon acquired and

in 1905 nos. 142–54 were converted and nos. 156–60 rebuilt to the design of G. A. Sexton, a local architect who also worked on nos. 50–56 for Fearns. More rebuilding, including no. 162, followed a fire in 1910.[25] B. B. Evans was described as Kilburn's oldest department store in 1962, when it was sold by Tesco Stores to Canadian & English Stores and employed more than 500 people, and as its only department store in 1971.[26] It closed in 1971 and was divided between Safeway at nos. 142–50, a wine merchant's, and Lamerton's furniture shop at nos. 156–62.[27]

The largest department store in the borough was that of John Barnes & Co. in Finchley Road, where in 1870 there had been only a few shops at Swiss Cottage but where there were several near the Metropolitan Railway station by 1885.[28] The company, which started trading in 1900, was described as 'American style' in that, although named after a local trader who had been drowned in 1899, it did not expand from small beginnings but was financed by a syndicate, including directors of Jones Bros. of Holloway and Dickens & Jones of Regent Street. The intention was to profit from the spread of building around Fitzjohn's Avenue by providing a lavishly equipped store, with 37 departments and a workforce of nearly 400.[29] John Barnes, after passing to Jones Bros. in 1922 and Selfridge's in 1926, was considered primarily as serving Hampstead people in 1936, when the mayor declared that the store's rebuilding would make Finchley Road 'the Regent Street of north London'.[30] Part of the premises was leased temporarily to F. W. Woolworth & Co. The John Lewis Partnership, however, which acquired John Barnes in 1940, found the site too cramped and tried vainly to sell it in the 1960s. After local protests at plans to move to Brent Cross in Hendon in the 1970s,[31] part of the Finchley Road building housed a Waitrose supermarket within the John Lewis Partnership in 1986.

The original building, at nos. 191–217, replaced 14 shops and filled a 1-a. island site immediately south of Finchley Road station. It was designed in red brick with stone dressings by A. R. Stenning and contained four storeys, attics, basements, a corner tower and a central tower. There was accommodation for 160 women on the third floor and for the manager and 46 male employees in 8 houses behind.[32] Demolition of the main block began in 1932 and the northern part of its successor was opened in 1936,

[10] Hampstead & St. John's Wood Advertiser, 4 Mar. 1911, 7b.
[11] Census, 1901, table 35.
[12] H.H.E. 8 Apr. 1911, 6d; 15 Apr. 1911, 7d.
[13] Official Guide to Hampstead [1925]; H.H.E. 16 Nov. 1962, 1c.
[14] Insurance plans B 12–17 (rev. 1925, 1970).
[15] Wade, W. Hampstead, 36; datestone.
[16] Hampstead and Highgate Dir. (1885–6); St. John's Wood, Kilburn, & Hampstead Advertiser, 4 Jan. 1900, 8b; 22 Feb. 1900, 8b.
[17] Kelly's Dir. Hampstead and Childs Hill (1920); Kelly's Dir. Kilburn (1931).
[18] Kelly's Dir. Hampstead and Highgate (1896); Kelly's Dir. Hampstead and Childs Hill (1918–19).
[19] Kelly's Dir. Hampstead and Childs Hill (1930, 1932); M. Holmes, 'Work of G. A. Sexton & Sons' (TS. thesis, 1978, in S.C.L.), 26.
[20] Kelly's Dir. Hampstead and Highgate (1895); St. John's Wood, Kilburn, & Hampstead Advertiser, 4 Jan. 1900, 8b; Baines and Scarisbrook, Local Guide and Almanac (1914).
[21] Kelly's Dir. Hampstead and Highgate (1889–90).
[22] Kelly's Dir. Hampstead and Childs Hill (1935); P.O. Dir. Lond. (1940, 1941); Wade, Streets of Hampstead, 67.
[23] Kelly's Dir. Hampstead and Highgate (1889–90, 1894–5); Kelly's Dir. Hampstead and Childs Hill (1905, 1906, 1910–11); Hampstead One Thousand, 85.
[24] P.O. Dir. Lond. (1927, 1934).
[25] Holmes, 'G. A. Sexton', 4–5, 91–110.
[26] H.H.E. 24 Aug. 1962, 3a; Kilburn Times, 16 July 1971, 1f.
[27] Holmes, 'G. A. Sexton', 6.
[28] H.H.E. Dir. (1870); Hampstead and Highgate Dir. (1885–6).
[29] St. John's Wood, Kilburn, & Hampstead Advertiser, 22 Mar. 1900, 5b; The Times, 7 Apr. 1899, 9a.
[30] L. Morison, 'John Barnes Dept. Store and St. John's Ct.' (Open Univ. thesis, 1979, photocopy in S.C.L.), 27; H.H.E. 30 May 1936, 4d.
[31] Morison, 'John Barnes', 36, 44–5; Evg. Standard, 4 Mar. 1974, 10.
[32] St. John's Wood, Kilburn, & Hampstead Advertiser, 22 Mar. 1900, 5b.

the rest being finished by 1938. The new building held the stores on three floors, with five floors containing 96 flats, called St. John's Court, overhead. It was designed by T. P. Bennett, who faced the lower storeys with artificial Portland stone and the upper with multicoloured brickwork.[33] The 'ocean-liner' style has been both criticized for modern clichés[34] and commended for an imposing façade, with horizontal window bands and long balconies carried past rounded corners.[35]

After the Second World War some piecemeal rebuilding included the provision of a long shopping parade north of Swiss Cottage.[36] Most of the shops in Finchley Road, Kilburn High Road, and West End Lane, however, remained in late 19th-century buildings. Occasionally adjoining premises were converted into a single unit, as at nos. 341–7 (odd) Finchley Road: by 1959 they formed motor car showrooms for Scott Cars, which in 1951 had occupied only no. 347, and from 1965 for Alan Day.[37] Heavy traffic in Finchley Road and lack of parking space worried the owners of John Barnes by the 1970s, when several closures were attributed to the opening of Brent Cross shopping centre.[38]

A consumers' group, the first of its kind in London, was set up in 1962, when it was boycotted by Hampstead and St. Pancras chamber of commerce, whose 700 trader members included 75 from Hampstead.[39] The essentially local character of Hampstead's village shops diminished in the 1960s and 1970s, as property values rose and leases expired.[40] By 1974 the centre of Hampstead had lost many of its suppliers of everyday goods. As in other fashionable parts of London, family businesses were giving way to boutiques selling clothes or gifts, to expensive restaurants, antique shops, and offices. Despite residents' protests, a campaign in the press, and greater selectivity by Camden L.B. in permitting changes of use,[41] further changes had taken place by 1983.[42]

LOCAL GOVERNMENT. MANORIAL GOVERNMENT.[43] In 1294 the abbot of Westminster claimed view of frankpledge, assize of bread and of ale, chattels, free warren, and all pleas in Hampstead as a member of Westminster in which he claimed all pleas which the king's sheriff exercised in the county except pleas and outlawry.[44] Courts were held on Hampstead manor by 1271. Free tenants, in 1312 excluding those holding in free alms, owed suit

twice a year at the abbot's court in Hampstead.[45] In 1451 the farmer of Chalcots paid to be excused suit.[46] From the 13th century two principal courts were held each year: a view of frankpledge with court leet initially at Easter but, from the late 15th century, on Whit Monday, and a general court baron in autumn or winter, which, from the 1380s, was invariably in November. Courts were also held at other times. There were, for example, four courts in 1274, 1347, and 1354, six in 1299, and seven in 1298, but from 1378 there were generally only two; in the late 16th and the 17th centuries there was one court with view in May. During the 18th century special courts, for single tenurial transactions, became common.

An estimate in 1312 of £1 10s. as the average annual income from perquisites of court[47] was correct for the 13th and early 14th century although there was wide variation, between 17s. 10d. in 1288 and £3 19s. 5d. in 1290. In the late 14th and early 15th century the average was £2 3s. but it had dropped to £1 14s. in the early 16th century and was over-estimated at £4 6s. 8d. in 1535.[48]

There is only one extant medieval court roll, for 1296.[49] Rolls purporting to be court rolls for 1572–1705[50] are more probably extracts, recording tenurial transactions, and many rolls from before 1690 were destroyed by fire.[51] Court books are complete from 1706.[52]

The court was held at the manor house, presumably in the hall, by the bailiff of Westminster, a monk, but the prior and bailiff held it in 1372[53] and in 1459 the court was held at Belsize.[54] Early 16th-century leases of the manor reserved wards, reliefs, and other perquisites and obliged the lessee to entertain the treasurer, steward, and other officials when he held courts in Hampstead.[55] In 1535 courts, with other profits of the manor, were the responsibility of the treasurer.[56] In 1550 the bishop of Westminster granted the bailiwick of Hampstead for life to William Sybrand.[57]

After the manor passed into lay hands the court was not leased with the rest of the manor but was reserved to the lord, whose steward, by the mid 18th century or earlier, was usually a London lawyer.[58] From 1720 to 1737 there was a dispute over the stewardship during which rival courts made admissions.[59] The bailiff still issued the summons to the courts, some of which from 1731 were held at Jack Straw's Castle, of which the bailiff was then the lessee.[60] By the 19th century the main court, if not

[33] Morison, 'John Barnes', 4, 6–7, 14, 27.
[34] Wade, *W. Hampstead*, 57; Pevsner, *Lond.* ii. 198.
[35] Morison, 'John Barnes', 4, 6.
[36] S.C.L., H 725.21/Shops.
[37] *P.O. Dir. Lond.* (1951 and later edns.).
[38] Morison, 'John Barnes', 44–5.
[39] *H.H.E.* 16 Nov. 1962, 1c.
[40] e.g. ibid. 28 Feb. 1964, 1b, 8f; 29 June 1973, 1a.
[41] *Evg. Standard*, 14 Mar. 1974, 21.
[42] *C.H.R.* xi. 25; *Hampstead One Thousand*, 126.
[43] Subsection based on manorial accts. 1271–1355 (W.A.M. 32367–76, 32381–5, 32393–406, 32494–6); 1375–1412 (W.A.M. 32497–32531); 1497–8 (Dorset R.O., D 396/M/81); 1499–1500 (P.R.O., SC 6/Hen. VII/400); 1519–32 (W.A.M. 33269–79); 1539–41 (P.R.O., SC 6/Hen. VIII/2415, m. 17); ct. rolls (below).
[44] *Plac. de Quo Warr.* (Rec. Com.), 479.
[45] C.U.L., Kk. V. 29, f. 31v.–32; Westm. Domesday, ff. 118v.–20v.
[46] E.C.R. 61/RR/A/66.
[47] C.U.L., Kk. V. 29, f. 36.

[48] *Valor Eccl.* (Rec. Com.), i. 415.
[49] W.A.M. 32359.
[50] G.L.R.O., E/MW/H/1–24.
[51] Ibid. E/MW/H, old no. 26/23 (Snoxell's case 1746).
[52] M.M. & M., Lib. A–S; G.L.R.O., E/MW/H/25–26. There are indexes to the extant rolls and bks. at M.M. & M. and copies of ct. min. bks. 1742–1843 and extracts of ct. rolls 1607–1843 at S.C.L.
[53] e.g. rental made at ct. at Hampstead Jan. 1372 by prior and bailiff: W.A.M. 32357.
[54] Rental made at ct. in Belsize in presence of prior, bailiff, and clerk: Dorset R.O., D 396/M/81.
[55] W.A.M. Lease bk. II, ff. 52v., 174–v., 287–v.
[56] *Valor Eccl.* (Rec. Com.), i. 415.
[57] W.A.M. Lease bk. III, f. 123v.
[58] G.L.R.O., E/MW/H/I/2300–2, 2304; M.M. & M., Lib. A sqq.; *The Times*, 9 May 1868, 1b; 30 June 1909, 14d.
[59] *H.H.E.* 25 May 1979.
[60] G.L.R.O., E/MW/H/I/1930, 2276/29; S.C.L., Man. of Hampstead, notices of cts. 1884, 1900 (H 333.3).

held at the inn, adjourned there for lunch.[61] The main court met at the 'Hall house' in 1685[62] and 18th-century leases preserved the lord's right to hold the court annually in the hall and parlour of the manor house.[63] In 1798, after most of the old manor house had been pulled down, the lease of the site reserved the right to hold an annual court there, as had 'anciently' been done.[64] Thomas Pool, the principal lessee, was obliged to offer his house for the courts but in 1800 he sold it (later nos. 19 and 21 Frognal Lane) and a new lease extinguished the lord's right of entry and with it, presumably, the right to hold courts.[65] Probably Pool's house (Manor Lodge, no. 40 Frognal Lane) was not yet finished and for a few years courts met at the easternmost of the Frognal houses, which therefore took the name Manor House.[66] Pool's house on the south side of Frognal Lane, for which he obtained a lease in 1810,[67] subsequently housed the main Whitsun court, and leases reserved the right to hold courts there.[68] In 1851 the house was called Manor Lodge.[69] Courts still met there in 1934,[70] but enfranchisements had long before reduced the number of copyholders and the public seldom attended.[71]

All courts were mainly and most courts exclusively concerned with tenurial transactions. In 1296 the courts also dealt with trespass, the taking of demesne wood, breaking the assize of bread and of ale, the default of customary works, and leasing without consent. The view of frankpledge considered the common fine, bloodshed, and receiving strangers.[72] Rentals were made at courts in 1372 and 1459,[73] 17th-century courts dealt with boundaries,[74] encroachments, and regulations about the heath,[75] and 18th-century courts punished the obstructors of footpaths.[76] Constables, headboroughs, and aletasters were elected at the view from the 17th to the early 19th century.[77]

A constable was recorded in 1558[78] and by 1608[79] there was one for Hampstead and one for Kilburn.[80] By the end of the 17th century a constable and a headborough or tithingman, who had been recorded in 1641,[81] were chosen for both Upper and Lower Side respectively at the May leet court.[82] The number of headboroughs had increased to nine by 1808 although there were still only two constables.[83]

Special constables were also appointed, a list of over 100 being made in anticipation of a repetition of the violence associated with West End fair in 1819.[84] From the 17th century there were many requests to be excused the office of constable, often on the grounds of non-residence.[85] There were two aletasters in 1683.[86]

Several pounds included one at Hallwick in the late 14th and early 15th century, although they may have been enclosures for demesne cattle rather than manorial pounds for strays.[87] By 1619 the manorial pound was in High (Hampstead) Street.[88] In 1678 it was described as next Basil Herne's house, which suggests a site at the upper end of Slyes, on the west side of High Street. Herne was then granted the site[89] and in 1708 the site of the pound which presumably replaced it was again to be moved to a place assigned by the homage.[90] By 1754 it was near Jack Straw's Castle[91] and despite leave to move it again in 1761[92] it was still there in 1762.[93] In 1787 its removal was presented and a new pound was built in a hollow east of Spaniard's Road opposite Whitestone pond. The jaw bones of a whale formed the supports of the gate until the early 20th century and the high brick walls survived until 1935, when the pound was the responsibility of the L.C.C.[94] The stocks, which by 1672 were maintained by the churchwardens,[95] and were used as late as 1831, stood at the bottom of Flask Walk next to the watchhouse.[96]

Belsize was called a manor in 1360 and released from all services, including presumably suit of court, to the demesne manor.[97] The title of manor continued long afterwards[98] but perquisites of court were not among its resources in 1535[99] and there is no reliable evidence of courts. The grant at the Dissolution to the chapter of Westminster was of the manor of Belsize with its 'wards, reliefs, heriots, ponds, and views'.[1] In the 17th and 18th centuries there were disputes, especially over waste and impounded animals, between the tenants of Belsize and Hampstead manor, in which courts at Belsize were mentioned. Old tenants claimed that a Belsize court was held at a tenant's house, possibly the Red Lion, c. 1680, to which a jury was summoned from Paddington, and that cattle straying into St. John's Wood were impounded at Belsize.[2] Possibly the

[61] *The Times*, 9 May 1868, 1*b*; *N. & Q.* 11th ser. iv. 526–7; x. 7.
[62] G.L.R.O., P81/JN1/1A.
[63] Ibid. E/MW/H, old no. Box L (abs. of leases 1680–1731); S.C.L., D 25.
[64] G.L.R.O., E/MW/H, old no. 31/8 (lease 1798).
[65] Ibid. (lease 1800).
[66] Ibid. H/I/2276/29.
[67] Ibid. H, old no. 31/9 (lease 1810).
[68] e.g. ibid. (lease 1819); 31/2 (draft lease 1834); 31/6 (draft lease 1869).
[69] P.R.O., HO 107/1492/13; R.G. 10/192/12.
[70] G.L.R.O., E/MW/H/I/2309/3.
[71] Barratt, *Annals*, iii. 66; *N. & Q.* 11th ser. x. 7.
[72] W.A.M. 32359.
[73] Ibid. 32357; Dorset R.O., D 396/M/81.
[74] In 1632: G.L.R.O., E/MW/H/I/2311B.
[75] e.g. in 1692, 1693, 1696: G.L.R.O., E/MW/H/I/1946.
[76] M.M. & M., Lib. B, p. 1.
[77] Ibid., J, pp. 1, 81; listed for 1683–1779: G.L.R.O., P81/JN1/1A; S.C.L., A/F/53.
[78] P.R.O., PROB 11/41 (P.C.C. 63 Noodes, will of John Slanning).
[79] G.L.R.O., Cal. Mdx. Sess. Recs. i. 222.
[80] Ibid. vii. 45.
[81] Ibid. Cal. Mdx. Sess. Bks. i (A), 89; iii. 200.

[82] Ibid. i (B), 49–50; E/MW/H/I/1946; M.M. & M., Lib. B, p. 1.
[83] M.M. & M., Lib. J, p. 1.
[84] G.L.R.O., M/81/7; above, econ., fairs.
[85] e.g. 1646: G.L.R.O., Cal. Mdx. Sess. Bks. i (B), 49–50; 1661: ibid. iii. 115; 1674: ibid. v. 41–2.
[86] G.L.R.O., P81/JN1/1A.
[87] W.A.M. 32511, 32515, 32523, 32530.
[88] G.L.R.O., E/MW/H/1.
[89] Ibid. 7.
[90] M.M. & M., Lib. A, pp. 49–50.
[91] G.L.R.O., M/81/1.
[92] Barratt, *Annals*, iii. 350.
[93] S.C.L., Man. Map.
[94] Barratt, *Annals*, i. 16; Stanford, *Libr. Map of Lond.* (1862 edn. with additions to 1865), sheet 1; *The Times*, 25 Sept. 1929, 9*a*, 16; 19 Jan. 1935, 8*d*.
[95] G.L.R.O., P81/JN1/1A.
[96] Barratt, *Annals*, i. 15–16; Baines, *Rec. Hampstead*, 164–5.
[97] B.L. Cott. MS. Faust. A. iii, f. 341.
[98] W.A.M. Lease bks. XIV, f. 338v.; XVIII, f. 32v.; XLVI, f. 25.
[99] *Valor Eccl.* (Rec. Com.), i. 410.
[1] *L. & P. Hen. VIII*, xvii, p. 392.
[2] W.A.M. 16618*; W.A.M. Map 12450, nos. 10, 21.

manorial rights of Lisson were attached to St. John's Wood, then held by the lessees of Belsize. A dispute *c.* 1682 between Lord Wotton, holder of Belsize and St. John's Wood, and the earl of Gainsborough, holder of Hampstead manor, about waste was resolved because they were relations and did not consider it worth a lawsuit.[3] During a further dispute over trees cut down on waste at Belsize in the 1720s, the representative of the chapter searched for court rolls at Belsize[4] but apparently found none.[5] Houses built on waste along the London road caused similar disputes in the 1770s,[6] 1791,[7] 1814,[8] 1817,[9] and 1819, when King's Bench decided that Belsize was a manor.[10] A point repeatedly in dispute was the pound at Belsize, which by the late 17th century[11] had been built by a tenant at the upper end of the lane near Belsize House.[12] In 1817 the pound was at the junction of Belsize Lane and the London road[13] and in 1819 it was admitted that the agent of the lady of Hampstead manor used it for his sheep.[14]

In 1522 the prior of St. John of Jerusalem leased his 'manor of Hampstead', reserving 'wards, marriages, reliefs, escheats, and goods and chattels of felons',[15] and for some time after the Dissolution the Shoot Up Hill estate was termed 'the lordship and manor of Hampstead'.[16] No courts belonging to the estate were held in 1535 in Hampstead, where tenants in the Middle Ages were probably subject to the manorial court at Lisson.[17] It is unlikely that courts were held at Chalcots, although it was termed a 'lordship' in 1640 and 1790.[18]

PARISH GOVERNMENT TO 1837. Administration of obits was in the hands of churchwardens by the mid 16th century,[19] churchwardens for Hampstead first appeared at the bishop's visitation in 1598,[20] and a churchwarden was associated with the manorial constable in organizing the Protestation Returns of 1641–2.[21] The inhabitants of Hampstead were apparently acting in consort in 1648[22] and by 1670, the date of the first extant churchwardens' accounts, the parish had replaced the manor as the main unit of local government, with the two churchwardens as its principal officers.[23] Most 17th- and early 18th-century meetings were designated 'general parish meeting' and although some were called vestries there was apparently no distinction between them. Meetings of both descriptions were usually held in the church and attended by the parish officers and other inhabitants, varying in number between 7 and 17. Some parish meetings were held at inns, usually centrally sited ones like the White Hart or the King of Bohemia's Head. There were generally four meetings a year at the beginning of the 18th century,

when rates were set, officers elected, and decisions taken about poor relief, apprenticing, expelling vagrants, prosecuting robbers, securing a water supply, purchasing surplices and pulpit cloths, and raising subscriptions to relieve distressed people outside the parish, such as French Protestants in 1686 and Turkish slaves in 1700.

There is a gap in the parish records from 1710 to 1746,[24] when the extant vestry minutes begin.[25] By that date all parish meetings were designated vestries and held at the workhouse. Their frequency increased from *c.* 7 a year in the 1740s to 9 by the 1780s, 11 by the first decade of the 19th century, and 17 by the 1820s, but declined sharply to only 8 in 1833. Most vestries attracted between 6 and 11 people although there were larger attendances: of 46 in 1754, 43 in 1759, and 50 in 1805 for the election of new beadles, of 160 in 1793 and 65 in 1819 for the election of the parish lecturer, of 104 in 1836 and 173 in 1842 when feeling was aroused over the poor law union.

From the institution of church trustees in 1744, an alternative authority, of doubtful legality until it was regulated by an Act in 1816–17, was created to deal with the church,[26] while the vestry continued to interest itself in and to some extent to finance church affairs. Although in 1827 the vestry stated that no church rate had ever been levied, rates were levied in 1785 and 1786 for the repair of the organ. In 1781 the vestry instructed the churchwardens to erect a weathercock on the church tower. In 1811 it passed a resolution to remove the organist, and in 1792 and 1819 it clashed with the minister over the right to choose the lecturer.

Apart from the poor, the vestry dealt with charities, boundaries, footpaths, policing, and such disparate problems as 'noxious insects' which infested the trees and hedges in 1782, obstruction by hackney coaches and other carriages in Hampstead town in 1783, and measures necessitated by the Napoleonic wars: enforcing a royal proclamation urging frugality in 1800, raising volunteers in 1805, and supplying boys for ships in 1808. In 1758 the vestry appointed a committee to look into the parish debts; others were set up in 1766 to deal with the course of a new path and in 1775 to draft a bill for lighting and watching the parish. By the 1790s the automatic response of the vestry to any problem was to appoint a committee.

The vestry and its officers were drawn mainly from farmers, tradesmen, and especially innkeepers. Many of the principal inhabitants did not attend[27] and in 1800 the parish obtained a local Act[28] to regulate its poor by setting up a board of guardians.

[3] G.L.R.O., E/MW/H/I/1925.
[4] Ibid.; W.A.M. 16499, 16505.
[5] 'It is said freehold cts. have been held but ct. bks. and rolls or other docs. not extant': W.A.M. 16551.
[6] W.A.M. 16515, 16519–20.   [7] Ibid. 16529–31.
[8] Ibid. 16597–9.
[9] Ibid. 16610.
[10] Ibid. 16612.
[11] Ibid. 16618*.
[12] Ibid. 16501; G.L.R.O., E/MW/H/I/1925.
[13] W.A.M. 16610.
[14] Ibid. 16612.
[15] B.L. Cott. MS. Claud. E VI, ff. 235v.–236.
[16] Above, manor and other est.
[17] *Valor Eccl.* (Rec. Com.), i. 403.
[18] E.C.R. 16/CHA/1; S.C.L., D 63.

[19] *Lond. and Mdx. Chantry Cert.* (Lond. Rec. Soc. xvi), 64.
[20] Park, *Hampstead*, 213.
[21] H.L., Mdx. Protestation Returns (MS. 1641–2), f. 2b.
[22] S.C.L., uncat. doc. 1648.
[23] Rest of para. based on chwdns. accts. 1671–1710: G.L.R.O., P81/JN1/1A.
[24] The records had already been lost by 1793: vestry mins. 7 Jan. 1793.
[25] Following paras. based on S.C.L., vestry mins. (1746–79), (1780–1805), (1805–23), (1823–35), (1835–54), (1854–73).
[26] Park, *Hampstead*, 218–24; 57 Geo. III, c. 71.
[27] *Rep. Com. Poor Laws*, H.C. 44, p. 99f (1834), xxxv, App. B2, pt. 1.
[28] 39 & 40 Geo. III, c. 35 (Local and Personal).

The first board was named as Sir Richard Pepper Arden, Master of the Rolls, Thomas Erskine (later Lord Chancellor), Spencer Perceval (a lawyer and later Prime Minister), Gen. Charles Vernon, and nine other prominent inhabitants, together with the lord or lady of the manor, the resident minister or curate, the churchwardens, overseers, and any resident magistrates. Subsequent guardians had to be inhabitants paying rates of more than £30 a year elected by the existing guardians. The board could appoint its own officers and raise money by annuities or bonds payable out of the poor rates. The guardians also assumed control over charities. In 1834 there were some 60 guardians.[29] Although the Act assumed weekly meetings of guardians in the vestry, by 1816 they usually met once a month at the workhouse, with attendances of 5–14.[30] From 1801, however, they appointed three of their members as visitors, who held weekly meetings at the workhouse, usually also attended by the overseers and often by the curate, Charles Grant, at which the affairs of the poor were dealt with in great detail.[31]

In 1801 the copyholders met at the Long Room to consider their ancient rights to dig turf and soil on the heath. They continued to meet until 1813 or later and to set up committees to watch over threats to rights by the lady of the manor or others.[32] In 1812 the campaign against West End fair was begun by a resolution at the copyholders' meeting to raise the problem at the court leet. The vestry clerk joined the steward of the manor in an appeal to the lady of the manor and the J.P.s to suppress the fair[33] but complaints about it did not appear in the vestry minutes before 1816 and it was not until 1819 that the vestry appointed a committee to deal with it. In 1814, when considering the parish cottages, the vestry noted the opinion of the guardians of the poor and of the court leet. In view of the number of bodies with overlapping authority, it is surprising that there were not more disputes. In 1829 there was a clash between the vestry and the guardians over the treatment and especially the expense of paupers outside the workhouse.

The two churchwardens, one of them selected by the minister, and the two overseers were chosen at the Easter vestry and the two surveyors in December in the early 18th century, in September or October by the 1780s. In the 17th century apparently anyone could be nominated an officer[34] but after Capt. James Shuter was nominated in 1684 but excused on the grounds that his work as captain of trained bands required his presence in London,[35] nominations were confined to a relatively few individuals, many of whom performed all the offices in turn. Edward Snoxell, the demesne farmer, for example, was a headborough in 1686, later becoming an overseer and in 1699 churchwarden, in spite of being illiter-

ate.[36] In 1784, a century after Shuter's case, the vestry resolved that it was 'but reasonable' that the burden of office should be borne indiscriminately and that those who wished to be excused should pay a fine of 10 guineas, whereupon the Hon. Henry Cavendish and Capt. Fountain North were fined for refusing nomination. In 1704 six sidesmen were chosen to assist the churchwardens and an additional, salaried, overseer was appointed in 1782. A request by the magistrates to increase the number of surveyors was turned down by the vestry on the grounds of expense although it did concede them an expense allowance.

In 1704 the parish meeting appointed a beadle to watch out for vagabonds and those who tried to settle without notifying the churchwardens. He was to be salaried and to receive a new hat and coat. The beadle's salary was increased in 1816, 1824, and 1825, when a second beadle, probably a relation of the first, was appointed.[37]

There was a parish clerk by the 1650s.[38] The appointment was in the gift of the minister, who dismissed the clerk in 1778 for indecent behaviour[39] and in 1799 was asked to replace a clerk of 'past and present immoral habits'. The parish clerk was usually excused rates and in 1806, when he was not occupying a rateable house, he was allowed a modest payment for officiating at the burial of paupers. In 1683 a parish meeting agreed to pay Thomas Middleton £2 a year to register all the parochial and manorial officers, draw up the parish accounts, and make a roll of the poor. Although he was not given a title Middleton seems to have been distinct from the parish clerk[40] and was presumably a precursor of the vestry clerk. From 1799 to 1827 the vestry clerk was William Masters, who was succeeded by John Masters, probably his son. From 1832 the vestry clerk was Thomas Toller, son of a lawyer who lived in Admiral's House.[41] From 1828 the vestry clerk was paid £150 a year. From Middleton's appointment until 1779 a record was kept of all the manorial and parochial officers.[42] Churchwardens had kept accounts at least since 1671, which were audited, and their accounts for the overseers and surveyors dating from 1684, probably drawn up by Middleton.[43] In 1705 the churchwardens and surveyors were instructed to bring their accounts to the parish meeting and the constables to keep an account of the watch. In 1753 all parish officers were to produce their accounts for inspection by the vestry before they were submitted to the justices. There were frequent irregularities. The accounts for 1773 and 1775 were not examined until 1780. Vestry minutes were to be kept in the vestry chest in 1793 and in the strong room at the workhouse in 1833. In 1814 a guardians' committee found that one overseer was bankrupt and two were insolvent.[44] In 1815 the

[29] *Rep. Com. Poor Laws*, 99*f*.
[30] G.L.R.O., P81/JN1/15 (mins. of guardians 1816–26).
[31] Ibid. 16–27 (mins. of visitors 1801–37).
[32] G.L.R.O., M/81/6 (mins. of mtgs. of copyholders 1801–13); above, growth, Hampstead Heath.
[33] Ibid. 7 (suppression of fair).
[34] e.g. Jos. Herne, a merchant, was overseer in 1683.
[35] G.L.R.O., P81/JN1/1A; Cal. Mdx. Sess. Bks. vii. 46.
[36] He made his mark in 1702: G.L.R.O., P81/JN1/1A.
[37] i.e. Chas. and John Adams.
[38] P.R.O., PROB 11/264 (P.C.C. 162 Ruthen, will of

Wm. Lewis); PROB 11/277 (P.C.C. 302 1658, will of John Rixton).
[39] i.e. for kissing a bride: *Ann. Reg.* quoted in Barratt, *Annals*, iii. 86.
[40] Wm. Prater (d. 1690) was par. clerk in 1683: P.R.O., PROB 11/386 (P.C.C. 2 1687, will of Wm. Bennett); PROB 11/402 (P.C.C. 189 Dyke, will of Wm. Prater).
[41] *C.H.R.* ix. 2–3.
[42] For 1683–1710 entered on the chwdns. accts.: G.L.R.O., P81/JN1/1A; 1746–79 at back of vestry mins.: S.C.L., vestry mins.
[43] All entered in same bk.: G.L.R.O., P81/JN1/1A.
[44] G.L.R.O., P81/JN1/15.

overseers had not made up their accounts for seven years and in 1825 the churchwardens' accounts had not been produced for ten years. The surveyors, whose accounts were unsatisfactory in 1783, had in 1825 not produced theirs for even longer. In 1826 when the vestry eventually confronted the muddle, reporters from the *Morning Herald* and other newspapers attended meetings where accounts dating from 1800 were presented and it was revealed that Masters, the vestry clerk, had been withholding money and not keeping the accounts. The vestry was persuaded to make more allowances for expenses but by 1829 was regretting the large amount paid out of the poor rate for salaries and parish officers. In 1836, however, it appointed a collector of the highway rate, paid for by a poundage.

There was a rate of 4*d.* in the £ in 1698 and of 1*s.* in the £ for the year 1705. In the late 1720s it was 1*d.* 6*d.*, reduced to 10*d.* by 1731.[45] By the mid 18th century the poor rate was levied four times a year and it was not until 1846 that it was reduced to twice a year. From 1*s.* 6*d.* a year in 1747–77, the rate increased to 2*s.* 3*d.* by 1780–1, but varied little between 3*s.* 4*d.* and 4*s.* in the years from 1804 to 1836. From £1,021 in 1776,[46] the amount raised by the poor rate increased to £1,175 in 1785,[47] £3,320 in 1805, and £5,403 in 1819.[48] Thereafter it fell to £3,537 in 1831[49] but rose again to £6,909 by 1835.[50] By 1812 collection was a considerable problem. A committee was appointed and a paid collector employed but in 1826 there was an increasing number of small houses from which no rates were collected. Although it was then suggested that there should be some sort of composition with the owners, by 1834 rates were still seldom paid for cottages and about one sixth of all rates remained uncollected.[51]

In the 18th century over 90 per cent of the rate was spent directly on the poor, a proportion which contracted to 70 per cent by 1803 and 42 per cent by 1835 as more was spent on salaries, the militia, the police, and other expenses.[52] In the 17th and early 18th centuries most relief was in weekly pensions for widows, although the parish also paid for rent, clothing, sickness expenses, apprenticing, and nursing children. There were 23 people on the pensions list in 1705. The parish owned at least one poorhouse, in Pond Street, by 1670. It had another at New End by 1705, when it decided to move another widow's house, presumably a wooden hovel, from the heath to a position next to it. There was a parish house on the heath south of the old bowling green in 1714.[53] In that year Leonard Killett left the house next to it to the churchwardens for the use of the parish.[54] About 1730 the inhabitants subscribed to building a house on the waste at Belsize for a poor cobbler.[55]

By 1762 the parish owned two cottages on the heath, near Jack Straw's Castle, and had three cottages in Pond Street.[56] In 1778 the vestry permitted Sir Francis Willes to remove the parish houses from the heath, where he wished to enlarge his grounds, and rebuild them in the Vale of Health, which was done by 1779.[57] A similar request was made in 1813 by the purchaser of property next to the Pond Street cottages, and freehold brick cottages were built for the poor at the eastern end of Flask Walk. In 1821 the inhabitants of the Vale of Health petitioned for the removal of the poorhouses there to a 'less respectable' area but a decision was postponed[58] and it was not until 1856 that all the parish houses were offered for sale.[59]

In 1729, alarmed at the cost of the poor, to whom they paid 2*s.* 6*d.* or 3*s.* 6*d.* a head a week, the parishioners took a long lease on an old house at Frognal, near its junction with the road later called Mount Vernon, where they opened a workhouse. For approximately 2*s.* a head a week, it housed, from 1734 to 1739, 14–33 paupers, mainly women and children.[60] A woman housekeeper and later a salaried master and mistress were employed and in 1755 the master was dismissed for neglect. In 1757 the workhouse badly needed repairing and the vestry abandoned it, paying weekly pensions instead, but after a year the lease was renewed and repairs were authorized. Other expenses included an apothecary to attend the sick poor and some education for the workhouse children. The workhouse grew some of its own food and there were various attempts to employ the inmates, in spinning mop yarn in 1788, and in 1797 a workshed was added to the premises. Flax was dressed in 1817, silk in 1822, and men and boys were employed on the roads in 1818.[61] Bad weather and a sharp rise in the price of bread caused great distress in 1795 and the vestry opened a fund to buy bread, rice, meat, potatoes, and coal. In eleven days in July it provided 1,346 people with loaves. At the same time the disrepair of the house at Frognal raised the question of the workhouse again. In 1800, therefore, the new board of guardians was set up to consider the whole question of the poor.

The guardians raised £6,000 by issuing debentures and purchased a house at New End, enlarged it, and opened it as the new workhouse, for many more than the 80 who could be accommodated in the old one.[62] In 1801 there were approximately 130 inmates, a number which fluctuated according to the season but rose to 155 in 1813, when there were also many requiring casual relief, and 174 in September 1814.[63] There were said to be strikingly fewer claims for admittance to the workhouse after the formation

[45] *Acct. of Workhos. in Gt. Britain in 1732* (1786 edn.), 54.
[46] *Abstract of Returns by Overseers of Poor* (1777), p. 101.
[47] *Rep. from Cttee. on Returns made by Overseers of Poor* (1787), p. 142.
[48] *Rep. from Sel. Cttee. on Poor Rates*, H.C. 748, p. 100 (1821), iv.
[49] *Rep. Com. Poor Laws*, H.C. 44, p. 99*f* (1834), xxxv, App. B2, pt. 1.
[50] *Poor Law Com. 2nd Rep.* H.C. 595-II, p. 212 (1836), xxix.
[51] *Rep. Com. Poor Laws*, 99*k*.
[52] Park, *Hampstead*, 285–6; *Poor Law Com. 2nd Rep.* 212.
[53] P.R.O., C 7/155/13.
[54] S.C.L., D 134.
[55] W.A.M. 16519–20.
[56] S.C.L., Man. Map and Fieldbk. nos. 254, 15.
[57] *N. & Q.* 5th ser. ii. 513; vestry mins. 1778; Bentwich, *Vale of Health*, 23.
[58] G.L.R.O., P81/JN1/15.
[59] Ibid. E/MW/H, old no. 27/15 (sales parts. 1856).
[60] *C.H.R.* iv. 28–31; *Acct. of Workhos. in Gt. Britain in 1732* (1786 edn.), 54–5; S.C.L., A/F/49 (Thos. Clowser's weekly jnl. 1734–9); ibid. Man. Map and Fieldbk. no. 414; M.M. & M., Lib. F, p. 44; illus. in Park, *Hampstead*, 287.
[61] G.L.R.O., P81/JN1/15.
[62] *Abstract of Returns by Overseers of Poor* (1777), 101; Park, *Hampstead*, 288–9; *The Times*, 18 Aug. 1900, 10*e*.
[63] G.L.R.O., P81/JN1/16, 18.

of a benefit society in 1802.[64] In 1803, when there were 117 in the workhouse, 140 received permanent and 98 occasional relief outside.[65] There was heavy expenditure on casual relief in 1824 because haymaking had been disrupted by rain. In 1832 the guardians relieved 168 outside the workhouse, compared with 133 within.[66]

LOCAL GOVERNMENT AFTER 1837. In 1837 Hampstead was combined with six other parishes in Edmonton poor law union. The old local guardians continued to exercise financial powers and to employ a clerk and treasurer until 1900, having in 1800 issued debentures bearing interest for 100 years.[67] All other powers relating to its poor passed to a union board, on which Hampstead had six representatives. As the vestry protested at the time, those most eligible for the post of guardian worked in London and could not attend weekly meetings in Edmonton, 8–11 miles away in a direction unserved by public conveyance. Consequently Hampstead was under-represented and the poor were deterred from applying for relief.[68] Hampstead sought separation from Edmonton union in 1841, 1842, and 1844 and succeeded in 1848, after exposing the absurdity by which the Hampstead poor were made to walk daily to and from Edmonton to receive relief of bread and cheese and work in a stoneyard.[69] Hampstead then became a poor law authority in its own right, administered by guardians composed of the minister, overseers, churchwardens, resident magistrates, and 12 elected members who met once a week in the workhouse.[70] Under the Local Government Act of 1894 the guardians, initially 18 and later 21, were elected for wards.[71] In 1861 the guardians employed a master and matron of the workhouse, a medical officer of health, and a relieving officer and his assistant.[72]

Hampstead's workhouse at New End, with accommodation for 200, was used for the old and sick until 1842, when it was replaced by a new central workhouse at Edmonton.[73] The latter proved inadequate and the workhouse at Hampstead was rebuilt and reopened in 1847 for the sick from Hampstead and Hornsey.[74] The workhouse took all indoor paupers from Hampstead after 1848. Infirmary wards were added in 1870 and 1883,[75] giving a total accommodation of 441 by 1906.[76] The number of inmates rose from 259 in 1891 to 352 in 1911.[77] The total number of paupers relieved each year doubled from 1,216 in 1853 to 2,437 in 1888,[78] although the population in-

creased five times.[79] From 1848 Hampstead raised money to enable some of its poor to emigrate to Australia.[80]

The spread of building confronted the vestry with additional problems: the blurring of a boundary in 1841, threats to the heath by the lord of the manor in 1846 and 1853 and by the New River Co.'s plan to build a reservoir in 1854, the need for a better water supply and sewerage system in 1852, the overcrowding of courts and alleys, and the general question of refuse disposal in 1854.[81] Under the Metropolis Management Act of 1855,[82] the old vestry was replaced by a restricted vestry of 33 members elected by householders occupying houses rated at more than £40 a year. The members, one third of whom were elected each year, choose one member as their representative on the M.B.W.[83] Hampstead sent two representatives to the L.C.C., which replaced the M.B.W. under the Local Government Act of 1888.[84] In 1873 Hampstead was divided into four wards: Town with 18 vestrymen, Belsize and Adelaide with 15 each, and Kilburn with 12.[85] By 1885 the numbers of vestrymen had been increased to 21, 18, 15, and 18 respectively[86] and by 1896 a new ward, West End with 12 vestrymen, had been created and the numbers of the others adjusted to 18, 12, 9, and 21.[87] The vestry met at the board room of the guardians in the workhouse until 1878 when a vestry hall and offices were built on the Belsize estate at Haverstock Hill. The red-brick and stone Italianate building, designed by H. E. Kendall, the district surveyor, and Frederick Mew,[88] was extended in 1896.[89]

Before the vestry hall was built, the vestry officers used the workhouse. They consisted of a treasurer, a non-salaried resident banker, of whom the first was John Gurney Hoare, a salaried vestry clerk, a resident solicitor, the first of whom was Thomas Toller, clerk of the old vestry, a medical officer, and a surveyor who was also inspector of nuisances and foreman of roads.[90] Charles Lord, who had come to Hampstead as a medical practitioner in 1827 and had been employed by the poor law guardians, was appointed joint medical officer of health and sanitary inspector and was to be an enlightened force in Hampstead's local government until he retired in 1879.[91] The collection of refuse was contracted out.[92] By 1863 the authority employed two rate collectors and a messenger. The main problem was sewerage and the surveyor's department had acquired a clerk by 1863[93] and three clerks, an assistant surveyor, and

[64] Brewer, *Beauties of Eng. and Wales*, x (4), 209; above, social.
[65] Park, *Hampstead*, 289.
[66] *Rep. Com. Poor Laws*, 99g.
[67] Baines, *Rec. Hampstead*, 247; *The Times*, 18 Aug. 1900, 10e.
[68] Vestry mins. (1835–54); G.L.R.O., P81/JN1/61.
[69] G.L.R.O., P81/JN1/61 (petition to H.C. 1848); vestry mins. (1835–54).
[70] Barratt, *Annals*, i. 46.
[71] G. L. Gomme, *Lond. in Reign of Victoria* (1898), 197; *Kelly's Dir. Hampstead* (1909–10).
[72] *Hampstead Almanack* (1863).
[73] *Poor Law Com. 4th Rep.* H.C. 147, App. D, p. 68 (1838), xxviii; *Poor Rates Returns*, H.C. 63, p. 99 (1844), xl.
[74] S. I. Richardson, *Edmonton Poor Law Union* (Edmonton Hund. Hist. Soc.), 62.
[75] Baines, *Rec. Hampstead*, 238.
[76] L.C.C. *Lond. Statistics*, xvii. 90.
[77] *Census*, 1891, 1911.   [78] Baines, *Rec. Hampstead*, 246.

[79] *Census*, 1851, 1891.
[80] Vestry mins. (1835–54); *Ann. Reps. of Poor Law Bds. 1848* [1024], H.C. p. 79 (1849), xxv; *1850* [1340], H.C. p. 149 (1852), xxiii; *1852* [1625], H.C. p. 133 (1853), 1; *1853* [1797], H.C. p. 180 (1854), xxix.
[81] Vestry mins. (1835–54).
[82] 18 & 19 Vic. c. 120.
[83] Vestry mins. (1855–1900); Thompson, *Hampstead*, 394–5.
[84] Baines, *Rec. Hampstead*, 136–7.
[85] *Lond. Gaz.* 4 Mar. 1873, p. 1371; *Census*, 1881.
[86] *Hampstead and Highgate Dir.* (1885–6).
[87] L.C.C. *Lond. Statistics*, x. 172–5.
[88] *The Times*, 24 Apr. 1878, 4b; Thompson, *Hampstead*, 407–9.
[89] *The Times*, 21 Dec. 1938, 6f.
[90] Vestry mins. (1856); Thompson, *Hampstead*, 401.
[91] C. F. J. Lord, *Rec. of Sanitary Experience, 1827–89* (MS. in S.C.L.); *C.H.R.* iii. 26–9.
[92] Vestry mins. (1856).   [93] *Hampstead Almanack* (1863).

an assistant inspector of nuisances by 1870.[94] From the early 1870s to 1896 a separate burial board was responsible for cemeteries but generally the 1880s and 1890s were decades of expanding activity by the vestry.[95] By 1889 the full board met once a fortnight and there were ten standing committees, Works, Highways, Sanitary, Finance, House, Tree, Mortuary, Records, Hampstead Improvement, and Assessment, which met in all 137 times a year, and ten temporary committees and sub-committees, which included Legal, Hampstead Heath Extension, Local Government Bill, Electrical, and Fortune Green, which met 46 times in the year.[96]

Factions were indicated by an increasing number of amendments to resolutions in the vestry during the 1820s. Radical classes were held in 1836 at the Yorkshire Grey[97] and in 1837 the followers of the Radical Joseph Hume made an unsuccessful bid to have their nominees appointed to the offices of the vestry and elected as guardians. Their policy of support for the Edmonton union and of higher spending was heavily defeated by the conservatives, who elected 'respectable tradesmen'.[98] In 1836 the vestry refused to challenge John Lund's obstruction of a footpath on the grounds that it was not desirable that ratepayers should pay for litigation 'in order to disturb a respectable inhabitant in the occupation of his property'.[99]

After 1855 the vestry was less open: the restriction of the electorate by the property qualification was reinforced by the activities of the Ratepayers' Association, founded in 1858.[1] Of the 33 vestrymen elected in 1855, 43 per cent were 'gentlemen', 30 per cent professional men, and 18 per cent shopkeepers. Over half came from Hampstead town, the new estates being poorly represented until the division into wards in 1873 ensured that local men represented their own areas. John Gurney Hoare died in 1875 and by the 1880s the few families which in earlier days had dominated parish government had mostly gone and local traders had much greater importance. From the 1890s, however, the upper classes, 'gentlemen', professional men, and businessmen, especially those with interests in the City, again became prominent, although they were drawn from areas like Belsize rather than Hampstead town. Among leading figures were Philip Hemery Le Breton, a barrister who lived in Milford House in John Street (Keats Grove) and served on the vestry until 1880, and Sir Henry Harben (d. 1911), chairman of the Prudential Assurance Co., who lived in Fellows Road on the Eton estate, a vestryman from 1874 to 1900 and first mayor of Hampstead.[2] Vestrymen included men interested in the history of Hampstead like F. E. Baines, a post office assistant secretary, who was chairman of 13 vestry committees between 1880 and 1891, and E. E. Newton, a tea merchant, who was a vestryman and town councillor from 1896 to 1914.[3] Hampstead was praised for its 'business-like management' by 'men of high character willing to serve'; party politics were little regarded.[4]

BOROUGH OF HAMPSTEAD. *Azure, a cross argent charged with a mitre and four fleurs-de-lis all gules; and indented chief or fretted gules* [Granted 1931]

Under the London Government Act, 1899, Hampstead parish became a metropolitan borough with a mayor, 7 aldermen, and 42 councillors, 6 for each of 7 wards: Town, Belsize, Adelaide, Central, West End, Kilburn, and Priory. The borough officers were a town clerk and solicitor and his deputy, an engineer and surveyor and his deputy and assistant surveyor, a medical officer of health, a superintendent of roads, an inspector of sewers, an analyst, an accountant and his assistant, a sanitary inspector and five assistant inspectors, a chief electrical engineer and two assistants, a chief librarian, superintendents of baths and the cemetery, and three collectors.[5] The vestry hall became the town hall, which was extended in 1911 to a design by John Murray to house the municipal departments which had grown too large for their offices.[6] By 1938 accommodation had again become inadequate and the council contemplated replacing the existing buildings with a six-storeyed building.[7] The project was interrupted by the war and in the 1950s other buildings at Haverstock Hill held the housing and architect's departments, while the public health department was accommodated at Lancaster Grove and later at Avenue Road.[8] In the mid 1950s a site in the centre of the borough became available at Swiss Cottage.[9] Sir Basil Spence, chosen by the town planning committee, designed a civic centre to include a library, swimming baths, and assembly halls besides a council chamber, committee rooms, and an office block.[10] When the building was opened, however, in 1964, the need for a town hall had disappeared in the merger of the borough in Camden L.B.[11]

The electorate for the metropolitan borough was wider than for the vestry, including all occupiers of property and lodgers. More than 50 per cent of the electorate voted in the first election and 53.2 per cent in 1906, when the range was from 64.9 per cent in Town ward to 39.6 in Kilburn. The proportion declined to 30.4 per cent in 1919 and 27.1 per cent in 1931 but increased again to 43 per cent in 1945

[94] *Hampstead and Highgate Dir.* (1870); Thompson, *Hampstead*, 401 sqq.
[95] Thompson, *Hampstead*, 406 sqq.
[96] Baines, *Rec. Hampstead*, 176–8.
[97] *Lond. Radicalism 1830–43* (L.R.S. v), pp. xx, 88, 143.
[98] *The Times*, 4 Apr. 1837, 2f.
[99] Vestry mins. 7 Jan. 1836.
[1] *Hampstead Almanack* (1863).
[2] Thompson, *Hampstead*, 396–400, 412; *C.H.R.* v. 6–8; ix. 18–19.

[3] Oppé, *Hampstead, a Lond. Town* (1951), 5–6.
[4] Booth, *Life and Lab.* iii (1), 212.
[5] *Kelly's Dir. Hampstead* (1909–10).
[6] *The Times*, 27 July 1911, 14d.
[7] Ibid. 21 Dec. 1938, 6f.
[8] *Hampstead Boro. Dir.* (1951–2, 1959–60).
[9] *The Times*, 23 Sept. 1955, 4g; 17 Dec. 1957, 9d.
[10] Ibid. 24 Jan. 1958, 5a; 21 Feb. 1959, 9b.
[11] Ibid. 10 Nov. 1964, 6e.

and 1953, declining below 40 per cent in the later 1950s and 1960s.[12]

There were 98 candidates, of whom 55 were former vestrymen, for the first election of 1900; 26 of the first 42 councillors were former vestrymen. Although not elected on party lines, the councillors comprised 23 Conservatives, 13 Progressives, and 6 Independents, some promoted by the Ratepayers' Association, the Progressive Committee, and the Central Council for the Promotion of Public Morality.[13] The Non-Political and Progressive Association, active by 1904, chose candidates according to their record or qualifications for public service and in 1906 the Hampstead Middle Class Defence League was formed to 'resist extravagance'.[14] The first woman member of a metropolitan borough council, sponsored by Hampstead Women's Local Government Association, was elected for Belsize ward in 1907.[15] Two of the 25 Progressive councillors in 1903 and three of 13 in 1906 were working-class but thereafter councillors were all drawn from a middle-class background.[16] The first municipal election said to be fought on party lines was in 1906 when 29 Municipal and 13 Progressive candidates were returned, the latter mostly for Kilburn and Town wards.[17] Kilburn continued to return mostly Progressive candidates and was the first to elect Labour candidates, in 1918,[18] and in 1922 there were five Labour councillors, four of them for Kilburn. There continued to be a few Independent and Progressive councillors but most were Municipal Reformers.[19] In 1925 all the councillors were described as Ratepayers Association, Labour candidates failing even in Kilburn.[20] From 1928 to 1934 all councillors were sponsored by the Hampstead Municipal Electors' Association which was opposed to party politics.[21] To oppose its candidates, Hampstead Ratepayers Association was formed in 1934, the earlier ratepayers' association having presumably dissolved. The Labour party alone put forward its own candidates, of which it had 16 in 1937, although only 6, all for Kilburn, were returned in that year.[23]

The Municipal Electors' Association was dissolved in 1945 when the Conservative Association sponsored candidates for the first time. In that election Labour won 14 seats, 5 for West End and 3 for Belsize besides all the Kilburn seats. The Conservatives won all the seats except 2 in 1949 and thereafter dominated the council, although Labour gained seats in a second ward in 1962 and 1964.[23]

In 1965 Hampstead, much against its will, was combined with St. Pancras and Holborn in the London Borough of Camden. Hampstead formed seven

LONDON BOROUGH OF CAMDEN. *Argent, a cross gules charged with a mitre or; on a chief sable, three escallops argent*

[Granted 1965]

wards, represented by 24 councillors. By c. 1980 one ward, Central, had gone and four new ones, Frognal, South End, Fortune Green, and Fitzjohns, had been formed, and Hampstead comprised 11 wards, represented by 59 councillors, out of a total 26 wards. The council and its seven committees met in Camden town hall in Euston Road, where the principal offices were housed, although the departments of the chief engineer, works, including parks, highways and street lighting, and car parks were housed in the old Hampstead town hall in Haverstock Hill.[24] Party politics at a local level became more acrimonious after the union of Conservative Hampstead and Socialist St. Pancras in Camden L.B. Although the Conservatives continued to dominate Hampstead, Labour won overall control of the council in each election except that of 1968.[25]

Hampstead became a parliamentary borough in 1885, one of its early M.P.s being E. Brodie Hoare (1888–1902), from the prominent Hampstead family.[26] Other M.P.s, who were generally long-serving, included J. S. Fletcher 1906–18, a barrister who had been chairman of the board of guardians for 18 years and Hampstead's representative on the L.C.C.,[27] George Balfour 1918–41, engineer and businessman,[28] and Henry Brooke 1950–66, Home Secretary and later Baron Brooke, who served on Hampstead council from 1936 to 1957.[29] Conservatives, under the title Unionist until the Second World War, won all the parliamentary elections except 1966. Labour candidates stood from 1918 and included in 1957 the West Indian David Pitt, later the first black member of the House of Lords.[30]

Parliamentary elections were much better attended than those for the borough. In 1906 a fairly high 82.1 per cent of the electorate voted, a proportion which dropped to 59 per cent in 1935, rose to 68.4 per cent in 1945 and 80.5 per cent in 1950 and

[12] L.C.C. *Lond. Statistics*, xvii. 18; xxvii. 19; xxxv. 17; xli. 24; N.S. i (1945–54), 23; vii. 17; E. Wistrich, *Local Govt. Reorganisation. The First Years of Camden* (1972), 5.
[13] Wistrich, *Local Govt. Reorg.* 5; *The Times*, 3 Nov. 1900, 14b, c.
[14] P. Thompson, *Socialists, Liberals and Labour* (1967), 83, 183; *The Times*, 6 Nov. 1906, 11d.
[15] *The Times*, 23 Nov. 1907, 9f; 13 Dec. 1907, 8e.
[16] Thompson, *Socialists, Liberals and Labour*, 315.
[17] The previous council was said to consist of 42 independents: *The Times*, 3 Nov. 1906, 5b.
[18] *The Times*, 2 Nov. 1909, 12d; 3 Nov. 1909, 10a; 2 Nov. 1912, 11b; 4 Nov. 1912, 11a.
[19] Ibid. 3 Nov. 1922, 16c.
[20] Ibid. 4 Nov. 1925, 9b.
[21] Ibid. 3 Nov. 1928, 7d; 4 Nov. 1931, 6d; 3 Nov. 1934, 7c.
[22] Ibid. 1 Apr. 1935, 11c; 25 Sept. 1937, 12f; 29 Sept.

1937, 14e; 3 Nov. 1937, 19b, c; *Hampstead One Thousand*, 134–5.
[23] *The Times*, 3 Nov. 1945, 2c; 14 May 1949, 2b; Wistrich, *Local Govt. Reorg.* 6.
[24] *Census*, 1971; Camden L.B. *Official Street Plan* [c. 1980]; Camden L.B. *Official Guide* [c. 1980]; *Municipal Yr. Bk.* (1983), 835.
[25] *Hampstead One Thousand*, 141–2; Wistrich, *Local Govt. Reorg.* 65.
[26] Barratt, *Annals*, i. 292.
[27] *The Times*, 17 Jan. 1910, 7a.
[28] *Hampstead One Thousand*, 117.
[29] *Who's Who* (1981).
[30] *The Times*, 18 Jan. 1906, 10b; 17 Jan. 1910, 7a; 30 Nov. 1918, Suppl. ib; 16 Nov. 1922, 7g; 7 Dec. 1923, 6c; 31 Oct. 1924, Suppl. ic; 28 Oct. 1931, 6a; 14 Nov. 1935, Suppl. id; 6 May 1957, 5f; *Hampstead One Thousand*, 135–6.

dropped to just under 70 per cent in the late 1950s and 1960s.[31]

PUBLIC SERVICES. Springs on the heath and southern slopes of the parish provided a plentiful water supply and also formed the tributaries of several London rivers.[32] Ponds were made by the springs to gather the water, and wells were sunk to tap underground streams; in the later 19th century many large houses still had their own well or pump.[33] An Act of 1543 allowed water from the heath to be used to supply the City, leading later to the formation of the Hampstead Water Co., which, however, did not supply Hampstead itself.[34] In 1684 the earl of Gainsborough received permission to pipe water from springs in his manor of Hampstead to the City and suburbs.[35] The chalybeate spring given by his widow to the poor of Hampstead in 1698[36] was probably thought unsuitable for this purpose because of its salts. When, however, the mineral waters were exploited, the vestry retained control over the springhead north-west of the well and in 1700 ordered water from the springhead to be piped into the town, apparently to raise money to relieve the poor rate rather than to meet any scarcity of water. Arrangements were made to lay pipes and contract with householders. In 1705 John Vincent proposed relaying the pipes on a different route, repairing the spring, and drawing on other springs; he was to have a lease of the water, for which he could charge the householders supplied. In the event the supply benefited only Vincent's brewery behind the King of Bohemia's Head and a few neighbouring houses, which were still supplied in 1824.[37]

Until the advent of piped water, public supplies for the town consisted principally of a pond or well, fed by a spring but perhaps not always in the same place. A pond was mentioned in 1274,[38] and both pond and well occurred in surnames and locations from the late 13th to the 15th century.[39] The Act of 1543 included protection for the springs, at the foot of the hill of the heath, which had been enclosed in brick for the use of the inhabitants.[40] Possibly it was the same town pond or well[41] that in 1680 stood at the junction of Heath and High streets,[42] most likely on the west side, and described as in Hampstead Street in 1619 and at the foot of Cloth Hill (later Holly Bush Hill) in 1669.[43] Tokens issued by Dorothy Rippin and Richard Bazell in 1669 and 1670,[44] may refer to this well. It was mentioned again in 1693 as the common well,[45] but in 1706 the town pond and

land around it were granted out as manorial waste and the pond was filled in at the direction of the overseers.[46] It may have been filled in because of contamination from new building on Cloth Hill and because the Revd. Samuel Nalton left money in 1706 to provide a water pump on the heath for the poor and a fountain in the middle of the town.[47] In 1783 the town pump stood at the north end of the narrow part of High Street,[48] near the old pond. Another parish pond existed at the east end of Flask Walk in 1762, possibly fed by the spring that formed a tributary of the river Fleet which rose nearby.[49] It may have been the pond that the vestry ordered to be enlarged in 1787.[50] The Fleet tributary ran along the line of Willow Road to the lowest of the Hampstead ponds and fed watercress beds and wells along its length. A brick conduit and dipping-place, long out of use in 1870, stood near the site of Gayton Road.[51] Another old well called Skirret's well stood on East Heath in 1714, close to the site of the house at Squire's Mount.[52] Parish wells near Whitestone pond, at White Bear green, and at the southern end of High Street were used for watering the roads, but all were closed by 1872.[53]

Other districts had similar water supplies through conduits, pumps, or ponds, fed by springs, or could draw on tributaries of the Kilburn brook (Westbourne), some of which rose south of the manor house and parish church, others south of West End green feeding a stream which ran parallel to Kilburn High Road.[54] In 1543 the right was reserved to the lord to pipe water to the manor-place from springs west of the Hendon road.[55] Several wells served the western half of the parish, although recorded only in the 19th century. Blackett's well at Childs Hill was claimed by the vestry to be a public well in 1802.[56] Wells at North End and on West Heath near Childs Hill supplied laundries and in 1872 were still open, and conduits existed at Branch Hill, Wild Wood Lodge at North End, by West End House, and near Redington Road.[57]

Belsize was supplied by tributaries of the Tyburn, one rising near Belsize House, which it supplied by way of a pond,[58] another in Shepherd's fields, northwest of Rosslyn House, where the public spring was conduited and known by 1829 as Shepherd's well.[59] By 1801 pipes led from that well to a cistern at the bottom of the Grove, Rosslyn Hill, opposite Pond Street whose inhabitants were supplied from it. In 1808 the vestry tried to have other pipes removed, as water was being drawn off to Rosslyn House to the detriment of the public supply in the Grove, but the

[31] L.C.C. *Lond. Statistics*, xvii. 12; xli. 19; N.S. i (1945–54), 11–12; vii. 12.
[32] N. J. Barton, *Lost Rivers of Lond.* (1982), 26, 30, 37.
[33] O.S. Map 1/2,500, Lond. VII (1877 edn.); Baines, *Rec. Hampstead*, 211.
[34] 35 Hen. VIII, c. 10; *C.H.R.* iii. 2.
[35] *Cal. S.P. Dom.* 1684–5, 77, 111, 231; *Cal. Treas. Bks.* 1681–5, 1188.
[36] Below, charities.
[37] G.L.R.O., P81/JN1/1A, 17, 25 Sept. 1700, 28 Apr., 12 May 1701, 7 Sept. 1702, 26 July, 20 Sept. 1705; above, econ., ind.; below, charities.
[38] P.R.O., JUST 1/538, m. 19d.
[39] e.g. W.A.M. 32504, 32358; *Cal. Close*, 1392–6, 136–8; above, other est. (Slyes, Kingswell).
[40] 35 Hen. VIII, c. 10.
[41] Terms used interchangeably as translation of 'fontem'.
[42] S.C.L., MS. survey of Hampstead Heath, 1680.
[43] G.L.R.O., E/MW/H/1, 6. Abutments and size of

grants suggest that the pond area may have stretched to Perrin's Lane.   [44] *C.H.R.* v. 18.
[45] G.L.R.O., E/MW/H/12.
[46] M.M. & M., Lib. A, p. 7.
[47] Kennedy, *Manor of Hampstead*, 71.
[48] Vestry mins. 18 June 1783.
[49] S.C.L., Man. Map; *C.H.R.* xi. 10.
[50] Vestry mins. 21 Oct. 1787.
[51] Potter, *Hampstead Wells*, 15–19.
[52] M.M. & M., Lib. A, pp. 229, 303.
[53] *Return of Public Surface Wells in Metropolis*, H.C. 200, p. 8 (1872), xlix.
[54] *Cruchley's New Plan* (1829).
[55] 35 Hen. VIII, c. 10.
[56] Vestry mins. 29 Mar., 20 Apr. 1802.
[57] Potter, *Hampstead Wells*, 27; *Return of Pub. Surface Wells*, p. 8.
[58] Thompson, *Hampstead*, 104.
[59] *Cruchley's New Plan* (1829).

owner of Rosslyn House claimed that the deficiency was generally due to shortages at the spring.[60] In the mid 19th century the well served residents, principally laundresses, up to a mile away, using water-carriers.[61] By that time, however, piped supplies were arriving. Pipes from Camden Town were extended to the southernmost part of the parish in the 1830s and 1840s. In 1852 both the vestry and the board of guardians were seeking a better supply, by asking the local M.P. to secure the town's inclusion in a Bill for supplying Hendon and West End, and by approaching existing water companies.[62] In 1853 the New River Co. extended pipes from Highgate to the top of the town, with the vestry consenting in 1854 to a reservoir as long as it was not built on the site first chosen, by Jack Straw's Castle; it was built at Hampstead Grove in 1856.[63] The vestry tried unsuccessfully to get the charges for water modified in 1854, claiming that those borne by larger properties were discouraging wider use of piped supplies.[64] In 1866 the West Middlesex Water Co. obtained powers to serve parts of Hampstead, building reservoirs near Kidderpore Hall (in 1868) and near Fortune Green. By 1872 they provided a constant supply to the area between Kilburn High Road and West End, besides a small area east of Finchley Road. By 1884 the company supplied all the parish roughly west of Haverstock Hill and Fitzjohn's Avenue, while the New River served the remainder, though a constant supply was not available until later.[65]

Before the drainage system was constructed from 1859 onwards, Hampstead's sewerage was rudimentary, using cesspools which drained into the soil contaminating water supplies, or into streams and ditches suitable only for surface water.[66] As the town was near the top of a hill, drainage was not seen as a problem until in the 1840s, after cholera had heightened awareness, complaints were made about crowded alleys and courts, which in addition to receiving sewage were piled with refuse.[67] Open ditches around Kilburn and West End were also full of sewage.[68] Though Hampstead came within the jurisdiction of the commissioners of sewers for Holborn and Finsbury, they dealt chiefly with existing water-courses and had more pressing problems with the Fleet. In 1852 the vestry appointed a committee to discuss improvements with the Metropolitan Commissioners of Sewers, who had replaced the district commissioners; a short sewer was built in 1853–4 from South End Green to the Fleet before the M.B.W. came into being and built the metropolitan sewer system.[69]

Under the Metropolis Local Management Act, 1855, the vestry could raise money for building sewers; its surveyor in 1857 proposed to drain the area between North End and Pond Street, 665 a. requiring c. 7 miles of sewers. By 1872 the whole parish drained into the M.B.W.'s system, the eastern part into the high-level 'intercepting' sewer, the Kilburn area into the Ranelagh sewer; 11.5 miles of sewers had been constructed by the vestry, and another 11 miles at private expense.[70]

The vestry also introduced regular collection of household refuse; in 1854 it was recommended that a contractor be employed to collect from all householders once a week. The vestry later employed its own collectors and built a dust destructor on land which it bought in Scrubs Lane, near Willesden Junction (Hammersmith), where all the refuse was burnt.[71]

The parish constable was assisted by a watch of 12 men when apprehending a felon in 1673,[72] and the constable or headboroughs were to warn 6 men to watch with them in 1704 until further notice, possibly for the winter months.[73] In 1707 the constables complained that they had never had the shelter of a suitable watchhouse, and the justices ordered one to be built.[74] Expenses were paid in 1708 for surveying the watchhouse and in 1710 a room under the same roof as the watchhouse and cage was let to a poulterer until needed by the parish.[75] In 1748 the watchhouse was reported to be an obstruction to passengers and in disrepair, and a new one was to be built nearby.[76] Whether or not it was rebuilt, its site was again considered very inconvenient in 1764,[77] when it stood in the roadway in Heath Street near its junction with High Street.[78] By 1795 the watchhouse had been moved to the bottom of Flask Walk,[79] presumably the west end of the green, where it stood with its two dungeons in 1839 shortly before being demolished.[80]

The watch could not prevent highway robberies on the London road, where in 1720 armed patrols protected visitors to the Belsize House pleasure gardens.[81] By 1774 the number of robberies in and around Hampstead warranted a local Act for watching and lighting the town: commissioners were empowered to raise a rate and appoint foot and horse patrols, armed if necessary.[82] An association, established in 1789 to reward those who caught offenders against the property of the subscribers, was revived in 1805.[83] By 1828 the parish had regular day and night patrols and paid a superintendent, 17

[60] Vestry mins. 6 July 1801, 27 Apr. 1808.
[61] S.C.L., H 628.1, cuttings.
[62] Vestry mins. 8, 29 Apr. 1852.
[63] Ibid. 30 Mar. 1854; Thompson, *Hampstead*, 393.
[64] Vestry mins. 23 Feb., 25 May 1854.
[65] F. Bolton, *Lond. Water Supply* (1888), 104, maps facing pp. 72, 110; H. W. Dickinson, *Water Supply of Gtr. Lond.* (1954), 87.
[66] *Return of Vestries on Improvements since 1855*, H.C. 298, pp. 38–9 (1872), xlix; *Rep. of Proc. of Hampstead Vestry to 1858 inc. M.O.H. Reps.* (1858), 18–19.
[67] G. Potter, *Random Recollections of Hampstead* (1907), 20; Baines, *Rec. Hampstead*, 198.
[68] P.R.O., MH 13/261, no. 3774/53.
[69] Vestry mins. 29 Apr. 1852; Metropolitan Com. of Sewers, *Return showing Sewers constructed at expense of Com.* [1855].
[70] Baines, *Rec. Hampstead*, 188; *Return of Vestries on Improvements*, 38–9.
[71] Vestry mins. 27 Apr. 1854; Baines, *Rec. Hampstead*,

199–200. John Culverhouse was a dust contractor: above, econ., ind.
[72] G.L.R.O., Cal. Mdx. Sess. Bks. iv. 187.
[73] G.L.R.O., P81/JN1/1A, 9 Oct. 1704.
[74] *Mdx. County Rec. Sess. Bks. 1689–1709*, 320.
[75] G.L.R.O., P81/JN1/1A, chwdns. accts. Oct. 1708; S.C.L., vestry mins. 20 Mar. 1709.
[76] Vestry mins. 22 June 1748.
[77] Ibid. 31 Oct. 1764.
[78] S.C.L., Man. Map.
[79] Vestry mins. 28 Dec. 1795.
[80] Ibid. 11 Apr. 1839; Baines, *Rec. Hampstead*, 164–5. A plaque on the lock-up in Cannon Lane wrongly calls it the par. lock-up. It was probably privately built, perhaps for J.P.s living nearby who held petty sessions in their hos., and has no known connexion with the par. watch.
[81] Lysons, *Environs*, ii. 534 n.
[82] 15 Geo. III, c. 58 (Priv. Act).
[83] Vestry mins. 16, 29 Apr., 30 June 1805.

watchmen, and 8 patrols; 17 watchboxes were provided.[84]

The establishment of the metropolitan police force brought residents a large bill for building the police stations and other expenses. An unsuccessful deputation told Sir Robert Peel that the force was both oppressively expensive and unnecessary because of the local Act and because the village was off the main thoroughfares.[85] Hampstead became part of S division and a police station was opened at no. 9 Holly Place,[86] moving in 1834 to the corner of Holly Hill and Heath Street.[87] It was replaced c. 1870 by a new station on Rosslyn Hill next to the Soldiers' Daughters' Home,[88] which in turn was replaced in 1913 by a new station and magistrates' court at the corner of Rosslyn Hill and Downshire Hill,[89] still in use in 1986. A station for West Hampstead and Kilburn was opened at no. 90 West End Lane in 1883,[90] being replaced in 1972 by one at no. 21 Fortune Green Road.[91]

The Local Act of 1774 allowed commissioners to levy a lighting rate for the town, which was not to exceed 1s. in the £ on property in lighted districts and 6d. elsewhere.[92] The oil lamps used were quite sparsely positioned, many larger houses still provided their own lights,[93] and the Act did not extend to Kilburn, which was unlit until 1849.[94] In 1823 the Imperial Gas Light & Coke Co. received permission to lay pipes; gas lamps were provided, beginning in High and Heath streets.[95] In 1853 Hampstead had 405 lamps, with a further 54 for the 2 miles of roads in the Kilburn area.[96] In 1872 Imperial Gas supplied 935 lamps and the Western Gas Light Co. 126 lamps.[97] The spread of building made it difficult to supply enough lamps, even in the 1880s; by that time there were nearly 2,000 lamps, supplied by the Gas Light & Coke Co.[98]

Private companies obtained Board of Trade orders for bringing electricity to the parish in 1883 and again in 1892,[99] but nothing was achieved owing to vestry opposition. The vestry, persuaded that it would be profitable to build and run its own electricity undertaking, opened a power station in Stone Yard, Lithos Road, in 1894, in order to supply both private consumers and the public street lamps. Though the scheme was very successful, particularly with private users, so much capital was needed for new generators in 1897 and for more cables that the parish rates received little benefit.[1] Street lamps were converted to electricity from 1909, starting with Adelaide and Upper Avenue roads.[2] The under-

taking remained in the borough's control until nationalization. The power station was replaced with a new building opened in 1975.[3]

Two fire engines were provided by public subscription, but were in disrepair by 1753 because there was nowhere suitable to keep them. The parish officers agreed to take charge of the engines, which were to be lodged in Mr. Sibthorp's coach house, and the overseers of the poor paid for repairs by the maker, Mr. Broadbent, who had an agreement to maintain the engines for ten years. The equipment included copper branch pipes, 20 ft. of suction pipes, 160 ft. of forcing pipes, and 44 leather buckets.[4] The engine pond in Flask Walk, cleansed in 1757, may have been for the use of the fire engines.[5] By 1837 the cost of constant repairs exceeded the value of the two machines and doubts were raised about the legality of poor-rate money being spent on them. The vestry therefore asked the church trustees appointed under the 1827 Local Act to buy one new engine, house it, and defray expenses, as the Act empowered them to do (for the protection of the parish church); the old engines were to be sold and the proceeds given to the trustees.[6] The engine dated 1810 that was stored at Cannon Hall in 1898[7] may have been the one bought by the trustees; it was kept in a shed in Church Row.[8] The trustees raised £200 initially and a further £200 in 1850,[9] but in 1856 the vestry took over responsibility for the engine.[10] In 1863, just prior to the formation of the London Fire Brigade by the M.B.W., the parish engine was in good repair and had one specially appointed keeper.[11] The Kilburn area was served by the Kilburn, Willesden, and St. John's Wood volunteer fire brigade, established after a fire at Shoot Up Hill in 1863, with its headquarters at Bridge Street, Kilburn.[12]

The M.B.W. opened a temporary fire station in a rented house in Belsize Avenue in 1869, and the permanent St. John's Wood station in 1870 near the corner of Adelaide and Finchley roads, its observation tower overlooking most of the parish.[13] Hampstead fire station, designed by George Vulliamy, was opened in 1874 at the corner of Holly Hill and Heath Street on the site of the former police station.[14] The two stations, both in A district,[15] covered the whole parish until 1901, when West Hampstead fire station, no. 325 West End Lane, was opened.[16] In 1915 Belsize station, in Lancaster Grove, was opened to replace the very cramped St. John's Wood station.[17] Hampstead station was closed in 1923,[18] and thereafter the parish was served by two stations once more,

[84] *Rep. Cttee. on Police of Metropolis*, H.C. 533, pp. 348–9, 378–9 (1828), vi.
[85] Vestry mins. 4, 11 Nov. 1830.
[86] E. E. Newton, *Fifty Yrs. of Progress* (1910), 169–70. Plaque on bldg. erroneously refers to Hampstead police force.   [87] Wade, *Streets of Hampstead*, 30.
[88] Ibid.; Newton, *Fifty Yrs.* 170.
[89] *The Times*, 2 Dec. 1913, 4a.
[90] Newton, *Fifty Yrs.* 170.
[91] Wade, *W. Hampstead*, 62.
[92] 15 Geo. III, c. 58 (Priv. Act).
[93] Newton, *Fifty Yrs.* 163.
[94] Baines, *Rec. Hampstead*, 163.
[95] Vestry mins. 21 Aug. 1823; Newton, *Fifty Yrs.* 163–4.
[96] *Return on Paving, Cleansing and Lighting Met. Districts*, H.C. 127, p. 168 (1854–5), liii.
[97] *Return of Vestries on Improvements*, 38–9.
[98] Newton, *Fifty Yrs.* 163; *The Times*, 11 Oct. 1884, 4f.
[99] 46 & 47 Vic. c. 217 (Local); 55 & 56 Vic. c. 220 (Local).

[1] Thompson, *Hampstead*, 413–14.
[2] *H.H.E.* 23 Dec. 1911.
[3] Inf. from Lond. Electricity Bd.
[4] Vestry mins. 27 June 1753.
[5] Ibid. 21 Sept. 1757.
[6] Ibid. 21 Sept., 15 Dec. 1837.
[7] *Trans. Hampstead Hist. Soc.* (1898), 33.
[8] Baines, *Rec. Hampstead*, 168.
[9] Vestry mins. 31 Oct. 1850.
[10] Ibid. 1856, p. 299.
[11] *Return of Amounts Paid to Maintain Fire Engines*, H.C. 322, p. 21 (1864), l.
[12] *V.C.H. Mdx.* vii. 233.
[13] Baines, *Rec. Hampstead*, 166–7.
[14] *H.H.E.* 17 Aug. 1872; *Images of Hampstead*, 110.
[15] *Rep. of M.B.W. 1888*, H.C. 326, p. 735 (1889), lxvi.
[16] Mem. plaque.
[17] Mem. plaque; L.C.C. *Mins. 1911* (1), 289; *1913* (2), 733.
[18] *The Times*, 5 Feb. 1923, 7b.

1. Holly Bush Hill in the early 19th century

2. High Street in 1881

HAMPSTEAD

3. Hampstead Wells from the Heath in 1745. The second Long Room is in the centre, with Burgh House behind and to the left

4. Pond Street from the west in 1745

HAMPSTEAD

5. The Vale of Health in 1804

6. North End in 1822

HAMPSTEAD

7. Jack Straw's Castle in 1830

8. Dancing on Hampstead Heath in 1899

HAMPSTEAD

9. Primrose Hill tunnel: the London entrance in 1837

10. Kilburn High Road and turnpike gate in 1860

HAMPSTEAD.

11. Rosslyn House in 1896

12. Buckland Crescent, nos. 9 to 19

HAMPSTEAD

13. West End: Admiral Saumarez's house *c.* 1830

14. Heath Mount School *c.* 1830

HAMPSTEAD

15. Greenhill, Prince Arthur Road

16. Redington Lodge, Redington Road

HAMPSTEAD

17. Annesley Lodge, Platt's Lane

18. Fitzjohn's Avenue, no. 1

HAMPSTEAD

19. The Old Parish Church from the south-east *c.* 1740

20. St. John's Parish Church and Church Row *c.* 1830

HAMPSTEAD

21. St. Stephen's Church, Rosslyn Hill

22. St. John's Parish Church

HAMPSTEAD

23. St. Stephen's Church, Rosslyn Hill

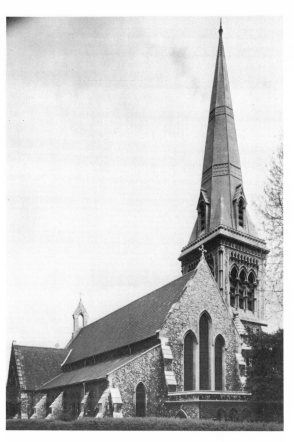

24. St. Saviour's Church, Eton Road

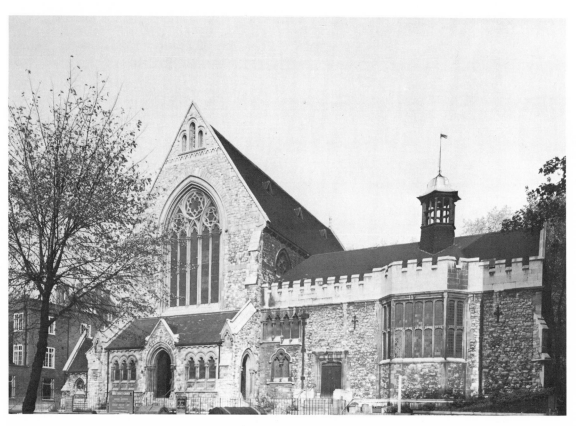

25. Holy Trinity Church, Finchley Road

HAMPSTEAD

26. St. John's Chapel, Downshire Hill

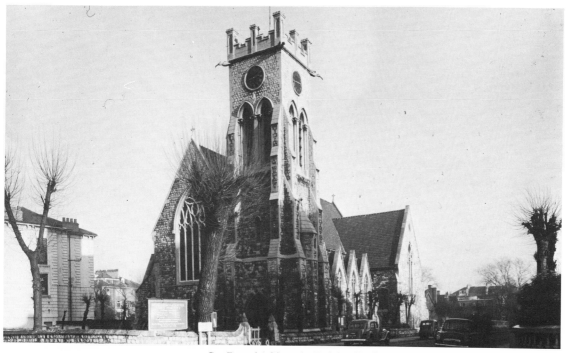

27. St. Peter's Church, Belsize Park

HAMPSTEAD

29. Heathlands, Littleworth, c. 1800

28. Old Mansion, no. 94 Frognal, in 1780

31. Vane House in 1813

30. Frognal Hall c. 1890

HAMPSTEAD

33. Palace Court, no. 2

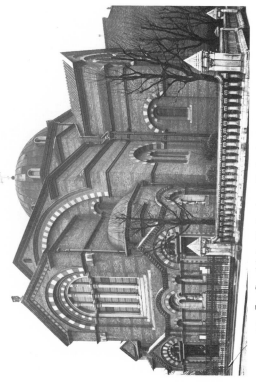

35. St. Sophia's Orthodox Cathedral, Moscow Road

PADDINGTON

32. Westbourne Place c. 1796

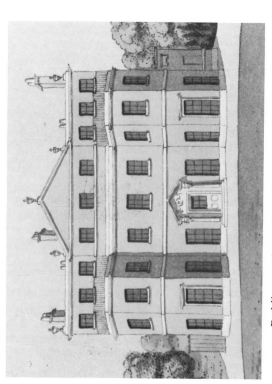

34. Paddington Green: Mr. Symmons's House c. 1796

36. Westbourne Green and Bayswater *c.* 1830

PADDINGTON

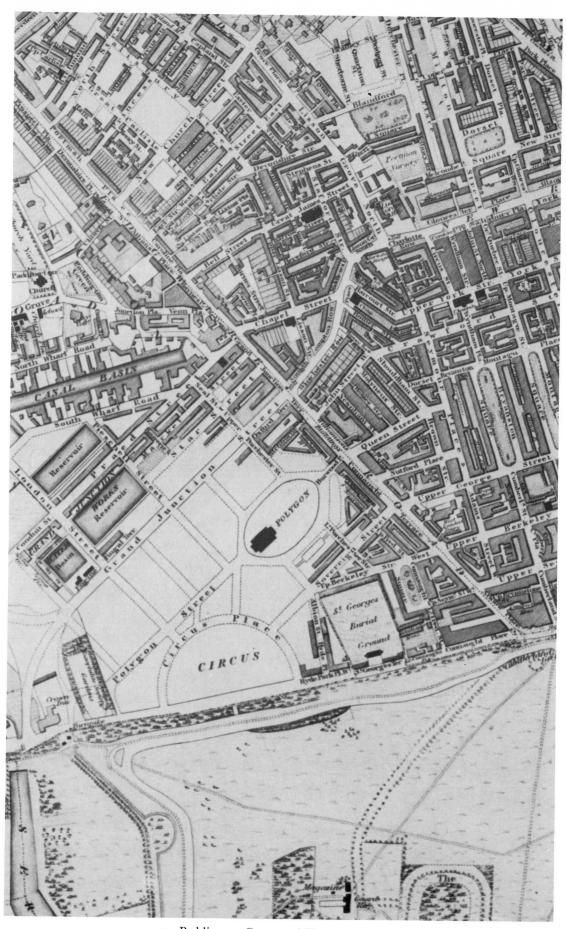

37. Paddington Green and Tyburnia *c.* 1830

PADDINGTON

38. Paddington Station, the Canal Basin, and Westway from the south-east

39. Paddington Station *c.* 1892; the view is inwards

PADDINGTON

40. Blomfield Road, the Canal, and Delamere Terrace from the west

41. Tyburnia from the south-west. St. James's Church, at the end of Sussex Gardens, is in the centre

PADDINGTON

42. Paddington Green in 1827

43. Paddington Canal Basin in 1801

PADDINGTON

44. Whiteley's Store, Queensway

45. Eastbourne Terrace, office blocks

PADDINGTON

47. Bayswater Chapel in 1818

49. The Old Parish Church from the north-west in 1750

46. St. Mary's Hospital in 1847

48. St. Mary's Parish Church from the west c. 1796

PADDINGTON

52. St. Mary Magdalene's Church, Woodchester Street

51. Holy Trinity Church, Bishop's Bridge Road

50. St. Augustine's Church, Kilburn Park Road

PADDINGTON

54. Lancaster Gate, nos. 104 to 109

53. Westbourne Grove, north side, c. 1895

PADDINGTON

West Hampstead covering the north and west parts, and Belsize the south and east.[19]

Hampstead subscription library, founded in 1833, began free lending to working-class readers in 1887, after its move to Stanfield House, and in 1891 provided them with their own reading room.[20] In 1892, after the adoption of the Public Libraries Act, the vestry set up commissioners to provide libraries for other districts; they continued to manage the libraries until c. 1896, when the vestry took over their functions.[21]

The first public library to be opened was a temporary one at no. 48 Priory Road, Kilburn, in 1894, which included lending and reference libraries and reading room. It was superseded in 1902 by a purpose-built branch library in Cotleigh Road.[22] Belsize branch library, Antrim Road, was opened in 1897, with lending and reference sections and a magazine room, and was adapted as an open-access library in 1910. Structural defects led to closure in 1936 and the opening of a new building on the same site in 1937.[23]

The Central library, at the corner of Finchley and Arkwright roads, opened in 1897, was designed by A. S. Tayler as a two-storeyed building in domestic Tudor style. It contained a reference library, reading rooms, and lending library (opened in 1899), and the cost was covered by a gift from Sir Henry Harben. The reference library housed 8,000 volumes of Professor Henry Morley, bought by the vestry in 1896, and a local archive collection was begun by the purchase of a survey of 1680 of the heath. The site allowed room for additions: an extension of 1909 included a children's library, one of the first of its kind in the London area, with a separate entrance in Arkwright Road, and a small exhibition and lecture room; a further extension in 1926 provided a larger lending library and a lecture hall for 220. After severe damage in 1940 and 1945 the adjoining bombed sites were bought for future enlargement, but in 1964 the library closed. Its departments were transferred to the new Swiss Cottage library at no. 88 Avenue Road, an oval-planned building designed by Sir Basil Spence, which in 1986 also housed Camden L.B.'s local history collection and archives covering Hampstead and St. Pancras, besides its reference collection on philosophy and psychology. The old building subsequently became Camden Arts centre, administered by the Arkwright Arts trust with municipal support.[24]

West End, later West Hampstead, branch library was opened in 1901 at the corner of Westbere and Sarre roads, a single-storeyed building with lending, reference, and magazine rooms. The building was destroyed in 1940, and replaced by temporary services in the basement of the Methodist church in Mill Lane and by 1950 in adapted bank premises in Cholmeley Gardens. In 1954 a new library was built as part of a small housing development at the corner of Dennington Park Road and West End Lane.[25]

Heath branch library opened as Worsley Road branch in 1907 in the former school building. In 1931 a new library was opened in the grounds of Keats House to serve also as a museum for the Keats collection formed by Sir Charles Dilke and given to the borough in 1911. Keats House had been in the care of the borough from 1924, after it had been bought by public subscription, and the library was designed to blend with the style and scale of the house. In 1948 the partition between the lending library and reading room was removed and in 1986 part of the Keats memorial library was in Keats House.[26]

A sick relief club and self-supporting dispensary, formed by the Revd. T. Ainger and other leading parishioners, began in 1846 with 53 members. Benefited members, who had to be earning less than 25s. a week and not be receiving poor relief, paid a small weekly sum, while unbenefited members paid large contributions; the club was run by a committee of both groups. By the end of 1846 membership had increased to 332; it was 957 by 1851, when the name was changed to Hampstead Provident Dispensary. The dispensary used rooms in the New End workhouse, for which it paid £20 a year. In 1850 a site at New End was bought with money from the collection taken in 1849 in all Hampstead churches and chapels in thanksgiving for escape from cholera. After a further appeal in 1852, a three-storeyed building was opened on the site in 1853. In addition to the dispensary, it housed the soup kitchen which had been started c. 1844 at the workhouse to sell soup to the poor during two winter months. By the 1870s the dispensary also provided dental treatment. A branch for West Hampstead was opened at no. 33 Mill Lane before 1888. After the National Insurance Act, 1911, the dispensary gradually lost its importance and in 1948 it closed; the building, standing in 1986, was sold in 1950.[27]

Hampstead Health Institute was founded by Thomas Hancock Nunn in 1913 as a memorial to Edward VII, in a building at the corner of Kingsgate and Dynham roads, West Hampstead. St. George's hall, adjoining it, was built 1929–30. Nunn wanted to unite various social services in one centre, then a novel concept: the main object was prevention of disease through hygiene education, but by 1929 the institute also had pre-natal clinics, and dental, oral, ophthalmic, and infant welfare centres, in addition to a social club, becoming the first local community centre. After the N.H.S. introduced similar centres, the building became Kingsgate community centre, run by Camden council.[28]

The Metropolitan Asylums Board bought c. 8 a. of the Bartrams estate in 1868 as the site for the North-western smallpox and fever hospital (also known briefly as Hampstead hospital).[29] Because of a sudden epidemic of relapsing fever, temporary wooden and corrugated iron huts with 90 beds were opened early in 1870, as England's first state hospital.

[19] L.C.C. *Lond. Fire Brigade* [c. 1954], 40–1; G.L.C. *Lond. Fire Brigade* [1979].
[20] *Hampstead Annual* (1898), 29; above, social.
[21] Thompson, *Hampstead*, 417.
[22] S.C.L., H 027.4/Kilburn.
[23] Ibid. H 027.4/Belsize.
[24] Ibid. H 027.4/Central; Camden L.B. *Official Guide* [1980]; *Archit. of Lond.* 51.
[25] S.C.L., H 027.4/West Hampstead; Central.

[26] Ibid. H 027.4/Heath; Central; *N. & Q.* 11th ser. iii. 145–6; iv. 51; *Keats Ho., a Guide* (1980).
[27] S.C.L., H 362.12; plaque on former dispensary bldg.; *Hampstead Year Bk. 1888–91*; *H.H.E. Dir. and Almanac* (1870).
[28] Mem. plaques; *The Times*, 5 Dec. 1913, 11a; 24 Apr. 1929, 13d; 5 Feb. 1930, 11a; Wade, *W. Hampstead*, 39.
[29] G.L.R.O., MAB 1038, report 1884 on right of way.

The hospital closed when the fever had subsided, but reopened at the end of 1870 for an outbreak of smallpox. The addition of a temporary building from the grounds of the London fever hospital, Islington, increased the number of beds to 450. Siting a hospital for infectious diseases in Hampstead aroused great opposition, especially from Haverstock Hill residents led by Sir Rowland Hill (d. 1879), whose property, Bartram House, adjoined the hospital. A select committee of the House of Commons supported the Metropolitan Asylums Board in 1875 but legal battles were settled out of court only in 1883, when the board agreed to buy Bartram House and 3 a. from Sir Rowland's son and move the hospital entrance from Haverstock Hill to Fleet Road. Bartram House was used as a nurses' home and committee rooms before being exchanged in 1901 for land belonging to Hampstead General hospital (below). A report in 1882 and a petition to parliament in 1884–5 finally caused the hospital to stop taking smallpox cases from 1885 and to become a fever hospital only.[30]

Work to turn the temporary buildings into a permanent hospital was started in 1876[31] but was soon halted by the legal proceedings. In 1884 a surveyor suggested that the dilapidated buildings, six fever and two smallpox pavilions linked by a long corridor built c. 1878, with several ancillary buildings, almost all of wood, might be replaced. The acquisition of Sir Rowland's property, which included a field stretching to the houses on the southern edge of South End Green, permitted rebuilding in stages on a larger scale.[32] Five wards were built on the vacant land c. 1887, the original huts being replaced by 11 pavilions c. 1888 and 4 more later.[33] An administration and reception block was built 1893–5.[34] Some houses in Lawn Road near the junction with Fleet Road were bought in 1894 and made way for a new ambulance station, opened in 1897.[35] Additional buildings for isolation wards were built in 1913.[36] An eight-bed clinic for the treatment of cancer by radium was in use from 1928 until the hospital was transferred to the L.C.C. in 1930; at that date the hospital had 410 beds.[37] In 1948 it became the north-western branch of the Royal Free teaching hospital group, with c. 275 beds.[38] Infectious cases were transferred to Coppetts Wood hospital, Hornsey.[39]

Plans to replace the Royal Free hospital, Gray's Inn Road (St. Pancras), with a new building on the site of the North-western fever hospital began in 1954 but only in 1968 did work begin on the building, which would replace the Royal Free group's many scattered units. The new teaching hospital, on a 15-a. site, was designed by Alexander Gray, and the main structure was a cruciform tower of 18 storeys. It was opened in 1974 with 871 beds and became fully operational in 1975. Additional work, including the demolition of Hampstead General, was completed c. 1978.[40]

Hampstead General hospital was founded in 1882 by Dr. W. Heath Strange as Hampstead Home Hospital and Nursing Institute in a house in Parliament Hill Road, taking paying patients only. In 1885, however, when funds were being raised, it was said to have treated 174 patients, mostly poor, and was designed for those who could not obtain care at home but did not want to go into a public hospital. Qualified doctors attended their own patients in the hospital. Adjoining houses were added and by 1888 it occupied nos. 2, 3, and 4 Parliament Hill Road; charges ranged from 7s. to 5 guineas a week. In 1894 the hospital had 29 beds, in 11 wards of which 8 were free; four fifths of those treated were out-patients.[41] Hampstead Jubilee fund, 1897, financed two beds for which Hampstead residents had priority.[42] It was felt that the district needed a general hospital, and in 1901 the site facing Hampstead Green was obtained and appeals were made.[43] The hospital exchanged with the fever hospital part of its land for Bartram House, which was demolished in 1902, and a new building, designed by Keith Downes Young, with 50 beds was opened on the site in 1905.[44] In 1907 it had 60 beds, of which 35 were in use, and treated 446 in-patients and 2,393 out-patients.[45] The same year another voluntary hospital, North West London, nos. 18–24 Kentish Town Road (St. Pancras), agreed to amalgamate with Hampstead General, keeping the Kentish Town building for out-patients. A new out-patients' department was opened at Bayham Street, Camden Town, in 1912.[46] Changes in administration and staffing brought complaints from the Hampstead division of the B.M.A., whose members' role in attending patients was replaced by consultants in the enlarged hospital. Local doctors, who had already protested at the transformation of the cottage hospital into a large general one, felt that a great metropolitan hospital had been created in an area where most of the population could pay for medical attendance rather than attend a hospital.[47] Extensions were made in 1929 with a new operating theatre, dispensary, and casualty department, and in 1936 with X-ray, massage, and pathology departments.[48] In 1945 the hospital had 86 general beds, 31 special beds, 21 pay beds, and 2 operating theatres, and registered 90,000 out-patient visits; there had been a waiting list of 200 in 1938. Amalgamation with Hampstead Children's and the North-western fever was suggested, to provide more beds for maternity and chronic sick and allow New End to be closed.[49] The plans were carried out by including Hampstead General in the Royal Free group in 1948 and the

[30] G. M. Ayers, *Eng.'s First State Hosps. and Met. Asylums Bd. 1867–1930* (1971), 32–6, 51, 53, 57–8, 72–4; A. Powell, *Met. Asylums Bd. and its Work, 1867–1930* (1930), 21, 32, 41; B. Abel-Smith, *Hospitals 1800–1948* (1964), 120–1; *The Times,* 19 Dec. 1883, 9d.
[31] Ayers, *Eng.'s Hosps.* 58.
[32] G.L.R.O., MAB 1038.
[33] Ibid. MBW 1762, no. 70; 1771, no. 72; D.S.R.
[34] Ibid. MAB 1038. [35] Ibid. MAB 2417.
[36] Ibid. MAB 2421; D.S.R.
[37] Ayers, *Eng.'s Hosps.* 199–200, 274.
[38] *Hosp. Year Bk.* (1948), 65.
[39] *V.C.H. Mdx.* vi. 171.
[40] *The Times,* 27 Jan. 1960, 7d; 29 Jan. 1968, 17f; S.C.L.,

47.1315/Royal Free, newscuttings.
[41] *Hampstead Year Bk. 1888–91*; *The Times,* 24 Apr. 1885, 9e; 18 Mar. 1901, 7f; 22 Oct. 1902, 10c.
[42] *C.H.R.* v. 32.
[43] *The Times,* 22 Oct. 1902, 10c.
[44] G.L.R.O., MAB 1025, pp. 91–3; 1026, pp. 42, 69; *The Times,* 18 Dec. 1905, 12e; A. S. Gray, *Edwardian Archit.* 394.
[45] L.C.C. *Lond. Statistics,* xvii. 118.
[46] *The Times,* 1 Aug. 1907, 10a; 3 Apr. 1912, 11a; *P.O. Dir.* (1902).
[47] *The Times,* 19 Oct. 1908, 6b.
[48] Ibid. 8 Nov. 1929, 11f; 1 May 1936, 13c.
[49] Min. of Health, *Hosp. Survey* (1945), 65, 84.

later removal to Hampstead of the Royal Free, which then replaced Hampstead General. Accordingly Hampstead General was demolished in 1975 and the site used for a car park and a small garden dedicated to Heath Strange.[50]

The workhouse and infirmary at New End became a military hospital during the First World War, and received such facilities as an X-ray unit and operating theatre. It was returned to the Hampstead guardians after the war and was thenceforth called New End hospital. In 1929 it was taken over by the L.C.C. and in 1938 was a general municipal hospital with 260 beds, including 26 for children and 19 maternity, and out-patients' and casualty departments. The premises were old and on a restricted site, but the maternity beds in particular were much needed. Management was taken over by the N.W. regional hospital board in 1948, and the X-ray and physiotherapy departments were enlarged. Thyroid surgery was developed from 1932, attracting foreign observers, and by 1955 the world's most modern radio-active iodine isotope unit had been developed in the basement. By 1958 it was under the Archway group hospital management committee, with 221 beds for acute cases. In 1968 the hospital was transferred to the Royal Free teaching hospital group. When the new Royal Free opened in Pond Street in 1974, New End, where a new geriatric unit had been opened in 1972, was left as a geriatric hospital, with 143 beds in 1978 and 127 in 1985. The desire to close it when facilities at Pond Street should be available, first expressed in 1945, was reiterated with the opening of the Royal Free, and in 1986 plans were being completed, amid much opposition.[51]

The North London (later Mount Vernon) Hospital for Consumption and Diseases of the Chest was founded in 1860 in Fitzroy Square (St. Pancras), but moved to an old house at Mount Vernon, Hampstead, in 1864, keeping an out-patients' clinic at no. 41 Fitzroy Square. Apart from two private beds, the hospital took only patients who could not pay for treatment. From 1898 it received grants from the later King Edward's Fund. A building, designed by T. Roger Smith in 17th-century French Renaissance style, was built at Mount Vernon; the western block with 34 beds was started in 1880 and the central block was opened in 1893, making a total of 80 beds, but only 60 were in use in 1898 owing to lack of funds. A temporary extension was built in 1900 and the eastern block was completed in 1903, making a total of 140 beds. Mount Vernon House was leased as a nurses' home. In 1904 a new Mount Vernon hospital was opened at Northwood, where by 1913 it was decided to concentrate its work. The Hampstead building was taken over by the Medical Research Council.[52]

Hampstead Children's hospital, Northcourt, no. 30 College Crescent, was founded in 1875 as the

Hospital and Home for Incurable Children, and was probably the hospital at no. 2 Maida Vale (Marylebone) in 1892. The children were aged up to 16 years. It was incorporated in 1902 and by 1907 had moved to Northcourt. The number of beds was raised in 1910 from 45 to 56. From 1920, by which time some curable cases were taken, the name was changed to Northcourt hospital for sick children. The number of beds was reduced again to 45 by 1938. During the Second World War the hospital was temporarily closed but in 1948 it became part of the Royal Free group and the children were treated elsewhere; the building itself became the Royal Free's preliminary training school.[53]

St. Columba's hospital or home of peace was founded in 1885 as the Friedenheim hospital, after a meeting at the home of a Dr. Schofield, and largely at the expense of Frances Mary Davidson who became the honorary superintendent. It was intended for poor people in the last stages of acute disease and not chronic incurables, although their care did result in some unexpected recoveries. By 1904 a committee had been formed to run the home in place of Miss Davidson. King Edward's Fund agreed to make grants to the home from 1904 as its work relieved other hospitals. It opened first at no. 133 Mildmay Road, Islington, moving in 1892 to Sunnyside, no. 8 Upper Avenue Road (later no. 98 Avenue Road), Swiss Cottage. In 1915 the name was changed to St. Columba's. The home had 50 beds, but only c. 30 were in use in 1938 and 1953. In 1948 the home came under the Paddington group hospital management committee. It moved to the Elms, Spaniard's Road, 1957, where it had 35 beds,[54] but closed in 1981.[55]

Queen Mary's maternity home was founded by the queen to use the residue of funds from Queen Mary's Needlework Guild. The home, for the wives of servicemen, opened in 1919 in temporary premises at Cedar Lawn, North End Road, provided by Lord Leverhulme, who also gave the site for the permanent building at Upper Heath, formerly the Upper Flask inn. The home, with 16 beds, opened in 1922, and patients were charged according to their means. The queen made frequent visits, giving gifts to the staff and her own crochet-work for the cots. She also gave part of the cost of an additional ward and isolation section erected in 1929, bringing the number of beds to 25, and further extensions c. 1937 brought the number to 34 in 1938. In 1946, with demand increasing, the London hospital took over the home at the suggestion of the queen, and under the National Health Service Queen Mary's remained part of the London hospital group, with 38 beds. In 1972 the home was taken over by the Royal Free, which closed the maternity unit c. 1975.[56] In 1986 the building was used as a staff home and community health offices.

Marie Curie hospital, for women cancer patients

[50] Above for North-western, Royal Free; below for Hampstead Children's, New End; Hosp. Year Bk. (1948), 65; The Times, 27 Jan. 1960, 7d; plaque in Heath Strange gdn.; H.H.E. 7 Mar. 1975.
[51] S.C.L., H 362/New End, cuttings; Min. of Health, Hosp. Survey, 65, 102; Hosp. Year Bk. (1958), 125; Hosp. & Health Svces. Year Bk. (1978, 1985); The Times, 3 Mar. 1955, 4f; Evg. Standard, 22 May 1986.
[52] G.L.R.O., A/KE/253/17; S.C.L., H 362/Mount Vernon; V.C.H. Mdx. iv. 133. Illus. and plan in Builder, 25 Dec. 1880.
[53] G.L.R.O., A/KE/249/6; Kelly's Lond. Med. Dict.

(1892), 307; Min. of Health, Hosp. Survey, 65, 90; Hosp. Year Bk. (1948 and later edns.); P.O. Dir. Lond. (1952).
[54] S.C.L., H 362.1/Friedenheim; G.L.R.O., A/KE/257/1; Min. of Health, Hosp. Survey, 58, 98; Hosp. Year Bk. (1947 and later edns.).
[55] Above, growth, North End, Littleworth, and Spaniard's End.
[56] S.C.L., B 47.1314, list of rec. of Queen Mary's mat. home; 47.1314, notes on mat. home; Min. of Health, Hosp. Survey, 92; Hosp. Year Bk. (1948 and later edns.); H.H.E. 7 Feb. 1975.

and, exceptionally, staffed by women, was founded in 1929 at no. 2 Fitzjohn's Avenue, with 30 beds. After destruction in the Second World War, the hospital moved to no. 66 Fitzjohn's Avenue, formerly an annexe of Westminster hospital, where it had 50 beds. It closed in 1967 because the accommodation was unsuited to new developments in radiotherapy, and the work was transferred to Mount Vernon hospital, Northwood. The building was demolished in 1969.[57]

The Hill, a 60-room mansion with 8 a. near North End, was left by Lord Inverforth in 1956 to Manor House hospital, Golders Hill, and as Inverforth House became the women's section of the hospital, with c. 100 beds, and a home for 60–70 nursing staff.[58]

The Tavistock clinic moved in 1967 to a purpose-built five-storeyed building at the corner of Belsize Lane and Fitzjohn's Avenue, gathering together departments from Devonshire and Beaumont streets (Marylebone) and elsewhere. The building also housed the Tavistock Institute of Human Relations and the Child Guidance Training Centre, and provided training in psychology and psychiatry. The Young People's Consultation Centre moved there from King's College Road, Swiss Cottage, where it had opened in 1962.[59]

Hampstead burial board, recently set up at the instigation of the medical officer of health, bought 20 a. at Fortune Green in 1874 to form Hampstead cemetery; c. 11 a. were consecrated in 1876, the remainder was left for non-Anglicans, and a chapel for each portion, designed by Charles Bell in Gothic style, straddled the division. A mortuary was also built there. Another 5 a. were added in 1901 and part was consecrated in 1906. The burial board was reincorporated into the vestry in 1896.[60] In 1889 Chesnut [sic] House, New End, was bought as the site for a mortuary for the town, the single-storeyed building being built in 1890. It remained in use until c. 1968 and later became New End theatre.[61]

The first baths and washhouses for the public were built by the Wells and Campden charity: 14 private baths, a laundry, and a drying-room were opened in Palmerston Road, Kilburn, in 1887, and 9 baths, a laundry, and drying-room in Flask Walk in 1888.[62] Though said to be very much appreciated by the poor, they incurred such financial loss that in 1906 the charity threatened to close them. After much argument over the price and a public inquiry, the council leased the baths in 1908 at a nominal rent.[63] The washhouses continued in use until the 1970s: Palmerston Road baths were closed in 1976 and demolished as part of the rebuilding of the area,

and Flask Walk baths were closed in 1978 and converted into private housing.[64]

The vestry opened its own baths in Finchley Road, opposite the North Star, in 1888 in a building designed by A. W. S. Cooper and Henry Spalding. There were two swimming baths for men, one for women, and 24 private baths; washhouses were not required in that neighbourhood. Success led to the opening of a second bath for women in 1891.[65] New baths, a gymnasium, and squash and badminton courts were built in 1963–4 with the library at Avenue Road, Swiss Cottage, designed by Sir Basil Spence. The Finchley Road building was used thereafter as a warehouse until destroyed by fire in 1972.[66]

Hampstead had 281 a. of open space in 1906, covering 12.4 per cent of the borough. The greatest part was formed by the heath and its extensions, lying on the north and east sides of the borough. The M.B.W. acquired 240 a. of the heath in 1871, most of it in Hampstead, and Golders Hill in 1898, of which 4 a. lay in Hampstead.[67] Inside the southern boundary of the parish lay 34 a. of Primrose Hill,[68] acquired by the Crown in 1842.[69] The borough council owned the remaining 3.5 a. of open space: 0.5 a. formed a playground in Lawn Road, opened in 1887, and the rest lay in the western part of the borough, which was badly provided for. West End Green, 0.75 a., was acquired in 1885, and Fortune Green, 2.25 a., was opened to the public in 1897, both preserved as a result of local agitation.[70] Plans from 1883 to provide Kilburn with a park resulted in the creation of Queen's park (Willesden),[71] which was too far away to benefit West Hampstead, where the sale of Kilburn Grange in 1910 was thought to be the last opportunity to acquire a substantial open space. After much negotiation, the L.C.C. bought 8.5 a., reserving 7 a. for a park, which it maintained; it paid just over a third of the purchase price, Hampstead contributed nearly another third, and the rest came from Willesden U.D.C., Middlesex C.C., and local contributions.[72] Hampstead Green was also preserved as open space: in 1899 a lady bought the green, then a paddock with fine trees belonging to two adjoining houses, to give the vestry the chance to take it over at little or no cost. In 1969 it was handed over to the Royal Free hospital and in 1986 very little remained.[73]

In 1929 public open space totalled 337 a., 14.9 per cent of the borough, and private playing fields covered another 36 a.; the percentage of open space was well above the average for London of 9.7.[74] Even so, Hampstead had only 3.7 a., compared with a recommended 4 a., for each 1,000 of population.[75]

[57] L.C.C. *Lond. Statistics*, xxxv. 2; R. Colville, *Northern Reaches*, 86; *The Times*, 5 May 1966, 15g; 28 Sept. 1966, 1d; S.C.L., H 362/Marie Curie, cuttings.
[58] *The Times*, 17 Feb. 1956, 3 [photo.]; 13 Apr. 1961, 14e.
[59] S.C.L., H 362/Tavistock clinic, cuttings.
[60] Thompson, *Hampstead*, 407; Guildhall MS. 19224/315, files 2, 3; *The Times*, 11 Nov. 1876, 10e; 22 Sept. 1879, 9f.
[61] *Hampstead Year Bk. 1888–91*; datestone; *P.O. Dir. Lond.* (1968).
[62] *Endowed Chars. Lond. III*, H.C. 252, pp. 106–7, 118 (1900), lxi; below, charities; *Hampstead Year Bk. 1889*, 28–9.
[63] S.C.L., Hampstead boro. council mins., vol. 45, pp. 666–7, 698; vol. 46, pp. 489–90, 564, 592, 730, 806; vol. 47, pp. 272, 414–16, 510, 657.
[64] S.C.L., H 725.73, 46.293, 46.284, newscuttings files.

[65] Thompson, *Hampstead*, 412; Gray, *Edwardian Archit.* 157; *The Times*, 17 Feb. 1891, 4c; *Hampstead Year Bk. 1889*, 27.
[66] A. Service, *Architects of Lond.* 198; Camden L.B. *Official Guide* [1980]; S.C.L., H 728.3/Finchley Rd.
[67] Above, growth, Hampstead Heath.
[68] L.C.C. *Lond. Statistics*, xvii. 156–7, 160, 162.
[69] Thompson, *Hampstead*, 221–2.
[70] L.C.C. *Lond. Statistics*, xvii. 17, 160; *C.H.R.* x. 13–17.
[71] *The Times*, 11 May 1885, 7b; 1 Nov. 1886, 9e.
[72] S.C.L., H 942.14, Kilburn scrapbook.
[73] *The Times*, 4 Aug. 1899, 7f; 19 Sept. 1899, 5b; Wade, *More Streets*, 28.
[74] L.C.C. *Survey of Open Spaces and Playing Fields* (1929).
[75] J. H. Forshaw and P. Abercrombie, *County of Lond. Plan* (1943), 43–4, 168.

Despite the acquisition of small pieces of land in garden squares and disused churchyards, most of Hampstead remained poorly provided for, the heath benefiting only the eastern part.

CHURCHES. Hampstead church apparently originated in a chapel built to serve the manor of Hampstead when it lay within Hendon parish. The chapel was first mentioned in the period 1244–8, when it was included in the valuation of the rectory and vicarage of Hendon,[76] as it was again in 1262–3.[77] It may have been founded by the Barentyns when they held the manor from the reign of Henry II until *c.* 1255,[78] because in 1333 the king as guardian of the heir of Gilbert de Barentyn granted the chapel in the manor of Hampstead to Stephen de Duddeley, king's clerk.[79] This grant may have been erroneous or an assertion of right, since the manor had been returned to Westminster abbey in the meantime[80] and had been valued as part of Hendon rectory;[81] the grant probably never took effect.[82]

The process by which Hampstead gained independence from Hendon is uncertain. In 1365 the church and cemetery at Hampstead were dedicated by the bishop of London.[83] The chapel was referred to as a parish church, and its chaplains were called parish priests, in 1382, 1384, 1413, and 1441.[84] The chapel was not mentioned at the institution of the rector of Hendon in 1433,[85] and property was described as being in Hampstead parish in 1470.[86] However, the chapel was not valued in 1535,[87] and no first fruits, tenths, or synodial or other dues were charged;[88] the tithes presumably still went to Hendon, leaving Hampstead in that regard part of Hendon parish. Moreover, in 1461, 1466, and 1477 the rectors of Hendon were instituted to that church with the chapel of Hampstead annexed to it;[89] no wills have been found to indicate whether Hampstead still had its own chaplain who carried out burials there. It is not clear whether the annexation was mentioned because of a new arrangement about the chapel, or because of a desire to check a growing independence at Hampstead. A definite change did occur in 1478 when Westminster abbey, the patron of Hendon, appropriated the rectory and the annexed chapel and became responsible for providing a chaplain at Hampstead. It was probably then that Hampstead became a separate perpetual curacy in the gift of Westminster.[90] The vestiges of Hampstead's dependence on Hendon were represented in 1826 in a clause of the Act for rebuilding Hampstead

church, which protected the rights of the vicar of Hendon.[91]

In 1541 the chapel and its advowson were part of the grant by the Crown to the new bishopric of Westminster,[92] and in 1542–3 the chapel was described as annexed to the manor of Hampstead;[93] both manor and chapel were returned to the Crown by the bishop in 1550.[94] In the same year the chapel with its tithes and emoluments were included in a grant of the manor to Sir Thomas Wroth,[95] who thereby became the lay rector. The advowson was not mentioned but presumably passed to Wroth and succeeding lords, as Baptist Noel, Viscount Campden, held the right to appoint ministers in 1650,[96] and the advowson of the so-called vicarage of Hampstead was included in the sale of the manor and rectory in 1707.[97] In 1801 the Wilson family granted the next presentation to William White for £1,890.[98]

The advowson passed with the manor until 1929, when Sir Spencer Maryon-Wilson sold it together with the advowson of Holy Trinity, Hampstead, to Sir Charles King-Harmon and the Martyrs Memorial Trust for £2,700. The sale, which affected the patronage of four other churches in Hampstead, aroused an outcry since neither the incumbent nor the congregation had been consulted. The parochial church council, fearing that the work of the vicar, H. T. Carnegie, in promoting good relations between Anglicans of different outlooks might be undone, would itself have purchased the advowson. The matter was raised in parliament but was left to a committee of the Church Assembly, leading to the Benefices Measure of 1933. The measure enabled Hampstead parochial church council to buy the advowson in 1935: when King-Harmon refused its offer, the matter went to arbitration and in 1936 the advowson was transferred to the diocesan board of patronage.[99]

No vicarage was created and the incumbents were properly styled perpetual curates until the District Churches Tithes Act Amendment Act, 1868. The tithes great and small of Hampstead, which belonged to the lord of the manor as impropriator, are treated above as part of the manorial estate.[1] In 1548 the rector, the bishop of Westminster, paid £10 a year to a chaplain to serve the cure.[2] By his will of 1629, Baptist Hicks, Viscount Campden, settled a moiety of the tithes of Woodhorn (Northumb.), due to him after the death of the earl of Northumberland, on the church and chapel of Hampstead to maintain an able preacher; the church had to pay half the fee

[76] Guildhall MS. (formerly St. Paul's MS. W.D.9 (Reg. Fulk Basset), f. 85).
[77] *Val. of Norw.* ed. Lunt, 179, 359.
[78] Above, manor.
[79] *Cal. Pat.* 1330–4, 407.
[80] Above, manor.
[81] Above.
[82] Duddeley was not instituted to Hampstead and the widely held belief that he was rector is therefore unfounded.
[83] *Reg. Sudbury* (Cant. & York Soc.), ii. 30.
[84] *Cal. Pat.* 1381–5, 148; *Cal. Close,* 1381–5, 564–5; Guildhall MSS. 9171/2, f. 244v.; 4, f. 61.
[85] Guildhall MS. 9531/4.
[86] W.A.M. 32356.
[87] *Valor Eccl.* (Rec. Com.), i. 403, 415, 422, 439.
[88] e.g. Guildhall MSS. 9550; 9556, f. 51; 9557, f. 27.
[89] Ibid. 9531/7, ff. 76, 103v., 162.

[90] Newcourt, *Rep.* i. 625.
[91] 7 & 8 Geo. IV, c. 91 (Local and Personal).
[92] *L. & P. Hen. VIII,* xvi, pp. 242–4.
[93] P.R.O., SC 11/845.
[94] Ibid. E 305/G/22.
[95] *Cal. Pat.* 1550–3, 6. Wroth may not have come into possession until a little later, possibly 1553: P.R.O., C 142/171, no. 97. The delay may explain why the dean and chapter of Westm. were recorded as rector in 1554: Guildhall MS. 9537/1, f. 73Av.
[96] *Home Counties Mag.* i. 220.
[97] P.R.O., CP 25(2)/946/6 Anne East.
[98] G.L.R.O., E/MW/H/III/32/6.
[99] *The Times,* 25 Mar. 1930, 18d; 27 Mar. 1930, 8b; 7 Apr. 1930, 11e; 9 Apr. 1930, 12b; 20 Dec. 1934, 17e; 26 Nov. 1935, 17d; Guildhall MS. 19224/315, file 1.
[1] P.R.O., C 94/3, m. 11; above, manor.
[2] *Lond. Rec. Soc.* xvi. 64.

farm of £34 13s. 4d. reserved to the Crown.[3] John Sprint, minister 1633–58, let the tithes in 1648 for 3 years at £50 a year, out of which he paid the fee farm. Sprint's other income in 1650 was £50 a year paid as a supplement by Baptist Noel, Viscount Campden, on the instructions of the Committee for Compounding, by which Campden reduced his fine as a delinquent.[4] In the earlier 18th century four successive curates each received a grant from the lord of the manor of the rectory, all tithes except corn and hay, the chancel with the benefit of the seats there, and a dwelling house in Hampstead. In addition they continued to receive the moiety of the Woodhorn tithes, which were let for £120 a year by a lease expiring in 1783, and in 1832 would have given the incumbent £422 10s. from the tithe composition for that year, had they not been abated because of agricultural distress.[5] In 1835 the incumbent received a net income of £887 out of which he paid £80 to his assistant curate.[6]

The lord provided a house and garden worth £5 a year for the incumbent in 1650.[7] In 1757 the lord gave £50 to Dr. Warren towards furnishing his new house at Hampstead, and in 1762 the incumbent inhabited a parsonage house on the east side of High Street, near its southern end,[8] possibly the site of the house of 1650. In 1835 the house was described as unfit for residence: the incumbent was living at Frognal by 1833, but his successor was at the parsonage house, High Street, presumably the house of 1762, in 1851.[9] The house was sold in 1923. No. 14 Church Row was bought in 1924 and was the Vicarage in 1981.[10]

Few medieval parish priests are known. There is no evidence that John de Newport served Hampstead chapel.[11] John Abingdon, parish priest of Hampstead, was required in 1382 to answer for debts, for which he had been summoned in the previous reign (probably the 1370s):[12] John, parish priest of Hampstead, ordered to be released in 1384 after imprisonment at the suit of William Woodward for rape and abduction of his wife and goods, may have been the same man.[13] The only other medieval parish priest known for certain was John Bastard, recorded in 1413.[14] Robert Henry, clerk, pardoned in 1347 for the death of another Hampstead man,[15] and John Cuchow, ordained priest in 1370,[16] may also have served the chapel, since both were described as of Hampstead. A succession of ministers is known from 1545.[17]

From the late 17th century most of the perpetual curates held Hampstead with other livings: Langhorn Warren held livings in Essex and Kent, besides two other rectories at different times for short periods; he was resident in Hampstead for only six months of the year.[18] Of the ministers in the 18th and 19th centuries the most outstanding was Thomas Ainger, incumbent 1841–63 and canon of St. Paul's 1859–63. He was an energetic pastor and poor-law guardian, who enlarged the church, reorganized and rebuilt the schools, and helped to found a dispensary and to provide new churches as the population grew.[19]

The extent of episcopal jurisdiction was often felt to be uncertain, possibly because the incumbents were not instituted by the bishop. In 1709 the parishioners approached the lord to rebuild the chapel, as they believed that the bishop could not grant them a faculty and they could not be helped by a diocesan collection.[20] In 1725, when the incumbent tried to ban preaching in the Wells chapel, it was stated that during the incumbency of Samuel Nalton (1678–1706) the bishop had been refused permission to visit the church and children had been sent to Highgate for confirmation.[21] Hampstead's parish officers, however, attended the bishop's visitations from the earliest recorded in 1554,[22] and there is nothing in the diocesan records to suggest any alternative jurisdiction.

The chapel had lights for St. Mary in 1441[23] and for St. Christopher in 1494.[24] In 1548 the lights on the high altar were kept for 2s. 4d. a year by arrangement with Eton College; there were two small obits.[25] In 1658 John Rixton left 20s. a year to the minister for a sermon in April.[26] In the early 18th century Esther Blondell left annuities worth 40s. in trust for a sermon by the minister on Good Friday.[27] William Pierce left stock in 1771 to provide £24 a year for evening prayer and the litany with a lecture every Friday, with payments for candles, for ringing the bell, and to the clerk for attending; £3 a year was to be spent on bibles and prayer books for the poor.[28] Occasional clashes occurred between minister and parishioners over who was entitled to appoint the lecturer.[29] By the late 18th century services were held twice on Sundays and once on Wednesdays, Fridays, and holy days, besides the lecture and prayers on Friday evening. Communion was held monthly and at the three great festivals, and was fairly well attended.[30]

The medieval chapel was dedicated to ST. MARY, probably following the dedication of Hen-

[3] P.R.O., PROB 11/156 (P.C.C. 101 Ridley).
[4] Ibid. C 94/3, m. 11; Cal. Cttee. for Compounding, ii. 939.
[5] G.L.R.O., E/MW/H/III/32/6.
[6] Rep. Com. Eccl. Revenues, 648.
[7] Home Counties Mag. iii. 317.
[8] G.L.R.O., E/MW/H/III/32/6; S.C.L., Man. Map and Fieldbk.
[9] Rep. Com. Eccl. Revenues, 648; Holborn libr., Hampstead poor rate bk.; P.R.O., HO 107/1492/5.
[10] Guildhall MS. 19224/315, file 1.
[11] As stated in Kennedy, Man. of Hampstead, 13.
[12] Cal. Pat. 1381–5, 148.
[13] Cal. Close, 1381–5, 564–5.
[14] Guildhall MS. 9171/2, f. 244v.
[15] Cal. Pat. 1345–8, 275.
[16] Reg. Sudbury (Cant. & York Soc.), ii. 86.
[17] Hennessy, Novum Rep. 188. To the names given there should be added Peter Prestott [?recte Prescott], 1554, Wm. Prest, 1558, Phil. Heynes, 1563, Wm. Hodge-

son, 1567, Wm. Green, 1574, Edw. Powell, 1580, 1588: Guildhall MSS. 9537/1, f. 73Av.; 3; 4, f. 71; 6, f. 6; 14, f. 71v.; 15, ff. 107v.–108, 332; Wal. Adams, 1658, 1660: Hennessy, Novum Rep. 466; P.R.O., PROB 11/299 (1660), f. 115.
[18] Guildhall MSS. 9550; 9556, ff. 51, 149, 173.
[19] D.N.B.
[20] Trans. Hampstead Antiq. & Hist. Soc. (1898), 37–9.
[21] G.L.R.O., E/MW/H/III/32/6.
[22] Guildhall MSS. 9537/1, f. 73Av.
[23] Ibid. 9171/4, f. 61.
[24] Ibid. 8, f. 67.
[25] Lond. Rec. Soc. xvi. 64.
[26] P.R.O., PROB 11/277 (1658), f. 302.
[27] Endowed Chars. Lond. III, H.C. 252, p. 90 (1900), lxi.
[28] Ibid.
[29] Vestry mins., e.g. 26 Dec. 1792, 7 Jan. 1793, 9, 26 Feb., 22 Apr. 1819.
[30] Guildhall MSS. 9550; 9557, f. 27.

don church, by 1441.[31] It served the whole parish until the early 18th century, when proprietary chapels were opened.[32] The building was demolished in 1745 and is known only from engravings of the church from the south-east published after that date, one of *c.* 1860 after a view by J. E. dated 1640 and several others published from 1750 on. The latter, which are slightly more easterly, are thought to have been taken from a painting made shortly before demolition rather than from the view of 1640, from which they differ in detail though most of the architectural features are the same. The low, rambling building apparently had a 14th-century nave with a steeply pitched tiled roof with dormers, one very large, and a Perpendicular north aisle under a separate roof. The walls were of brick or small stone, with stone dressings. There was a two-storeyed south porch, which had a sundial on a gable in the 18th century, and the main entrance was said to have been at the west end, where there was a bell-tower of wood. In 1640 the tower had a well proportioned steeple-like roof. In the later prints a low roof, making the tower appear squat, and the general air of decrepitude may represent artistic licence, but more probably indicate rebuilding and decay. The later engravings also show a north-west extension, either a porch or a vestry.[33] John Rixton (d. 1658) bequeathed money to repair the belfry, and 20s. a year to repair the north-west side and end of the church.[34] Constant repairs were made during the late 17th century,[35] but in 1709 the minister and inhabitants complained that the chapel had for some time been so ruinous that many stayed away lest it should fall on them. Great sums had been spent but no further repairs were possible.[36] Failure to replace the fabric may have given the impetus for the opening of the proprietary chapels.[37] More repairs were carried out, apparently by Sir William Langhorne, and in 1733 the churchwardens brought bills for repairs to the manorial court for payment.[38]

Only in 1745 was the old church replaced, after the parishioners, advised in 1740 that the cost would be too onerous to leave to the lord,[39] and failing to secure parliamentary funds, raised a subscription and appointed trustees from those who paid £20 or more. The funds included £1,000 given for rebuilding by Sir William Langhorne in 1714, and the deficit was made up by mortgaging the offertory and pew rents. Subscribers were illegally allocated pews and, despite advice in 1777, an Act to legitimize the trustees' activities was not obtained until 1827. The Act vested pew rents in the trustees to pay for the upkeep of the church, making the parish virtually exempt from church rates.[40]

The new church, consecrated in 1747, was dedicated simply to *ST. JOHN*, whom the bishop further identified in 1917 as St. John the Evangelist.[41] The trustees appointed John Sanderson, a local builder, to design and build the new church.[42] It had five bays and a sanctuary of plain London brick with Portland stone dressings in classical style, with an unusual embattled tower at the east end over the sanctuary; part of the spire had to be rebuilt in 1759, and in 1784 the tower was extended and given a taller copper spire. Alterations in 1756 increased the accommodation. The church was entered from the east end by two doors. flanking the tower and opening almost directly to the sanctuary. The tunnel vault of the nave was supported on Ionic columns with galleries between. In 1843-4 Robert Hesketh added transepts, an extension westward, and a new large gallery; reseating increased the accommodation to 1,600, and the interior decoration possibly dated from that time.[43] In 1851 969 of the seats were free and attendance on census Sunday was 1,144 in the morning, 500 in the afternoon, and 900 in the evening.[44] By 1870 a new building was proposed but it was decided to rebuild the tower farther east, allowing room for an extension. In the resulting outcry, the beauty of Church Row and the church as a group was stressed by many leading architects and artists, led by Sir George Gilbert Scott. He proposed a new chancel at the west end built in 1878 to designs by F. P. Cockerell, adding *c.* 400 sittings.[45] The interior was thus turned round; the new sanctuary had a balustraded parapet, and the galleries new open fronts. Decoration of the chancel, with the reredos and choirstalls, was by Thomas G. Jackson, 1878, but much of the chancel decoration was removed in the 1950s.[46] The pulpit is 18th-century. The tomb of the benefactor John Rixton was retained from the old church.

Monuments in the church include those to Charles Duncan (d. 1806), the Hon. Frances Erskine (d. 1809), Louisa Lownds (d. 1811), and Marianne Beresford (d. 1818), all by John Bacon the younger, to Samuel White (d. 1841) by William Graves, to William Bleamire (d. 1803) by Joseph Kendrick, to T. N. Longman (1771–1842) by Christopher Moore, and to George Todd (d. 1829) by Sir Richard Westmacott.[47]

Except for a paten presented in 1701, the communion plate was given in 1747 or later, including three pieces of the early 17th century.[48] Attendance in 1886 was 754 in the morning and 753 in the evening.[49] In 1903 it had fallen slightly to 695 in the morning and 507 in the evening.[50] In 1970 the church used Anglo-Catholic ritual,[51] but by the 1980s it used different rites on alternate Sundays, with the full choir on the first Sunday of each month.

[31] Guildhall MS. 9171/4, f. 61. The ref. in 1318 to the ch. of 'St. Mary in the Fields' (*Cal. Pat.* 1317–21, 220), thought by some writers to refer to Hampstead chapel, is more likely an error for St. Martin-in-the-Fields, appropriated by Westm. in 1275 and assigned to the prior: Harvey, *Westm. Abbey*, 408.
[32] Below.
[33] Potter Colln. 19/67; *Images of Hampstead*, 23–4; above, plate 19.
[34] P.R.O., PROB 11/277 (1658), f. 302.
[35] G.L.R.O., P81/JN1/1A, *passim*.
[36] *Trans. Hampstead Antiq. & Hist. Soc.* (1898), 37–9.
[37] Below.
[38] G.L.R.O., E/MW/H/III/32/6.   [39] Ibid.
[40] Park, *Hampstead*, 217; 7 & 8 Geo. IV, c. 91 (Local

and Personal); P.R.O., HO 129/8/1/1/3.
[41] E. Koch, *Par. Ch. of St. John Hampstead* [1928].
[42] Rest of para. based on ibid.; Clarke, *Lond. Chs.* 77; Pevsner, *Lond.* ii. 185; *Par. Ch. of St. John-at-Hampstead: Short. Hist.* (leaflet from par. ch.).
[43] Barratt, *Annals*, iii. 74; *Images of Hampstead*, 39; above, plate 20.
[44] P.R.O., HO 129/8/1/1/3.
[45] Guildhall MS. 19224/315, file 1.
[46] *Images of Hampstead*, 108; above, plate 22.
[47] Gunnis, *Sculptors*, 30–1, 181, 226, 263, 427.
[48] Freshfield, *Communion Plate*, 24.
[49] *Brit. Weekly*, 19 Nov. 1886, p. 4.
[50] Mudie-Smith, *Rel. Life*, 165.
[51] E. Raymond, *Good Morning, Good People* (1970), 25.

It was also claimed to be one of the few churches which retained English church music as part of worship, with a long established musical tradition. Scholarships were available for choir boys and Hampstead Music Trust was formed to help finance the choir.[52]

The wrought iron gates and railings at the Church Row entrance to the churchyard were bought at the sale of Canons Park, Edgware, in 1747.[53] The churchyard was enlarged in 1755 by a plot on the south side given by John Maryon.[54] Land on the north side of Church Row was bought by trustees appointed under a local Act to provide an additional burial ground in 1811 and was consecrated in 1812.[55] In 1854 burials beneath the church were discontinued, as were those in the churchyard and in the parts of the new burial ground already used, except in private vaults and graves.[56] From 1878 only family vaults that could be opened without disturbance might still be used, and every new coffin had to be enclosed by cemented brickwork.[57] A small strip of the burial ground was sold to the council for road widening in 1908.[58] In 1940 a columbarium or cloister was added to the new burial ground as a site for memorial tablets.[59] Among those buried in the churchyard are John Constable (1776–1837), Henry Cort (1740–1800), inventor of the iron purifying process, John Harrison (1693–1776), inventor of the chronometer, George Du Maurier (1834–96), R. Norman Shaw (1831–1912), and T. F. Tout (1855–1929).

In the early 18th century two unconsecrated chapels were opened. Sion chapel, at Belsize House, was in use from *c.* 1710 to 1720. Although it was said that two sermons were preached there every Sunday, its principal function was to provide cheap weddings for visitors to the gardens, and it was probably not frequented by local residents.[60] Well Walk chapel was converted from the Great Room of the wells in 1725. Although proprietary, it was officially described as a chapel of ease and was hired by the parish when the church was being rebuilt or repaired.[61]

With new building another proprietary chapel, St. John's, Downshire Hill, was opened in 1823. It, too, was considered a chapel of ease to the parish church.[62] Kilburn, where building was spreading along Edgware Road, was served by the parish church and, from 1825, by another proprietary chapel, St. Paul's, Kilburn Square, on the Willesden side.[63] From the 1840s the building of large estates of houses south and west of the old town led to the formation of district parishes.[64] The church was usually among the earliest buildings on an estate, in order to attract middle-class buyers, although occasionally provision lagged behind, as at St. Saviour's where a temporary church was opened in 1848 but the permanent church not until 1856.[65] The first

district church to open, however, Christ Church in 1852, was built to replace the crowded Well Walk chapel. It aroused much opposition from Sir Thomas Maryon Wilson, patron of St. John's, who saw its sponsorship by the Hoares and their friends as an attack on his interests. Sir Thomas wanted, not unreasonably, to keep the old town as the district for St. John's, but about half of its parishioners, including many of the wealthiest, were included in the district of Christ Church, thus substantially reducing the income, derived mainly from fees and offerings, of the incumbent of the parish church.

The other district churches were built without opposition, those on the large new estates being the first to open: St. Saviour's, 1856; St. Mary's, Priory Road, 1856; St. Peter's, Belsize Square, 1859; St. Paul's, Avenue Road, 1864; All Souls', Loudoun Road, 1865; St. Stephen's, Rosslyn Hill, 1869; Trinity (later Holy Trinity), Finchley Road, 1872; St. Mary's, Primrose Hill, 1873. In West Hampstead, where estates were smaller, the provision was different: apart from St. Mary's, Priory Road, only St. Luke's, 1898, was built to serve an estate.[66] Emmanuel, 1885, St. Cuthbert's, 1886, and St. James's, 1888, all originated as mission churches before support could be gathered for a permanent church; in the case of Emmanuel, services had started at West End as early as 1846 in the schoolroom, but it was only in 1875 that a mission church was provided.

Missionary work was much needed only in the relatively poor districts of West Hampstead and Kilburn, where there was such duplication of work by Anglicans and dissenters that in 1902 there were said to be four churches after every poor family.[67] Evangelical Anglicans were on friendly terms with nonconformists, in common resistance to Roman Catholicism, which was especially strong in Kilburn with its Irish immigrants, and ritualism. Antiritualism was exacerbated by two High Church sisterhoods, both called the Kilburn Sisters, which by 1900 had spread over England. One was formed for parochial work but became a nursing order and from 1875 ran St. Peter's Home, a hospital at Mount Greville, Mortimer Road, on the boundary with Marylebone.[68] The second, a teaching order called the Church Extension Association, aroused more hostility, being accused of extravagance and disobedience.[69] Opposition to ritualism and Roman Catholicism led to increased evangelical effort and probably raised church attendances before 1900. In the longer term, however, attendances showed a sharp decline: excluding missions, whose numbers were in any case small, Anglican attendances dropped from 13,515 recorded in 1886 to 9,925 in 1903. Dissenting congregations were more stable: though individual churches showed a slight fall in attendance between 1886 and 1903, the opening of new churches meant that the overall total, excluding mis-

---

[52] *St. John-at-Hampstead Year Bk. 1982–83* (in S.C.L.).
[53] *St. John-at-Hampstead: Short Hist.*; *V.C.H. Mdx.* v. 116.
[54] P.R.O., C 54/5958, no. 17.
[55] 50 Geo. III, c. 71 (Local and Personal); Guildhall MS. 19224/315, file 2; notice at cemetery.
[56] *Lond. Gaz.* 31 Mar. 1854, p. 1016.
[57] Ibid. 25 Jan. 1878, p. 392.
[58] *The Times*, 21 May 1908, 4d.
[59] *Builder*, 3 July 1942, p. 5 (cutting in rec. of C.C.C.).

[60] Below.
[61] Below.
[62] Below.
[63] *V.C.H. Mdx.* vii. 241.
[64] Rest of para. based on Thompson, *Hampstead*, 227–9, 382–4.
[65] Below.
[66] Thompson, *Hampstead*, 386.
[67] Para. based on Booth, *Life and Labour*, iii(1), 208–11.
[68] P.R.O., C 54/17814, no. 1.
[69] Below, Paddington, churches.

sions, rose from 6,503 in 1886 to 7,413 in 1903. Though Roman Catholic attendances also increased in this period, from 694 to 1,599, this was solely due to their advance in Kilburn, and Catholics made up less than 8 per cent of Hampstead's total church attendances in 1903; dissenters represented just under 37 per cent while Anglicans totalled 51 per cent. Among worshippers of all denominations only *c.* 5 per cent were at mission services.[70]

Other C. of E. chs. were:[71]

ALL SOULS, Loudoun Rd.[72] Founded and endowed by Revd. Hen. Robinson Wadmore, asst. at St. John's Wood chapel. Patron H. R. Wadmore (incumbent until 1890), then bp. of Lond. Dist. formed 1865 from St. Paul's, Avenue Rd., St. Mary's, Kilburn, and All Saints', Marylebone. G. F. Terry, V. 1901–9, later canon of Edinburgh, revitalized congregation. His bro. C. J. Terry, V. 1909–19, increased endowment. Attendance 1886: 274 a.m.; 176 evg.; 1903: 294 a.m.; 248 p.m. Ch. fashionable in 1920s when many came from Kensington and Westm. Bldg. of stock brick with bands of red and Bath stone dressings, seating 600, by Jas. F. Wadmore, bro. of V., 1864–5: apsidal chancel, aisled nave with E. bellcot, W. saddleback tower, NW. vestry. Small S. porch 1903. S. aisle, tower, baptistery, porches, and choir vestry, giving 250 more seats, 1905 by Sir Chas. Nicholson, Bt. Consecrated 1905.[73] Apse panelled and filled with oak triptych, by C. G. Hare, 1905. Chancel roof decorated like ancient choir roof of St. Albans abbey. Large oak altar installed as First World War mem. Floor-plan reordered 1965: altar placed in front of chancel steps, font brought forward, former chancel arranged as weekday chapel, baptistery for exhibitions.

CHRIST CHURCH, New End. Founded through application led by Hoare fam. to replace overcrowded Well Walk chapel (q.v.); opposed by Sir Thos. Maryon Wilson as threat to value of par. benefice.[34] Patron trustees. Attendance 1886: 1,137 a.m.; 1,188 evg.; 1903: 497 a.m.; 412 p.m. Bldg. of Kentish rag in Dec. style by S. W. Dawkes 1851–2: chancel with N. tower and spire and S. chapel, aisled nave with N. porch, W. gallery 1860 by Sir Gilb. Scott, member of congregation.[75] Organ by Willis 1857.[76] New N. aisle, extension of N. porch, and conversion of base of tower into vestry, by Ewan Christian *c.* 1881. Organ moved to S. chancel chapel. Seated 1,250 in 1889.[77] Rededicated, after restoration, 1920.[78] Missions held 1903 at Bickersteth mem. hall, built in Grove Pl. 1895,[79] attendance 142 a.m.; 80 p.m.; also at North End sch.,[80] attendance 79 a.m.; 105 p.m. Miss Juliana M. Hoare (d. 1936) used charitable

collns. to support North End mission hall and left *c.* £1,500 to maintain it. Legacy later used for Bickersteth hall,[81] which was converted into nos. 29–31 Grove Pl. 1970.[82]

EMMANUEL, Lyncroft Gdns., West End.[83] Svces. in West End Nat. sch., licensed from 1846,[84] served from par. ch., St. Paul's, Avenue Rd., and temp. ch. in Belsize Lane. In 1851 sch. seated 110 and attendance was 91 evg. Revd. Hen. Sharpe, who held mission svces. at Belsize Lane ch.,[85] was appointed curate-in-charge of West End 1870 and held Sun. evg. svces. at sch. Became part of Trinity par. Mission ch. built by Trinity at corner of Mill Lane and Aldred Rd.,[86] opened 1875, seating 120. Resident curate-in-charge appointed 1876. Ch. enlarged 1884 to seat nearly 400, and consecrated 1885, when dist. assigned. Endowed with £200 p.a. by Church Com. Patron Evangelical trustees.[87] Svces. strongly evangelical from start, less so after Second World War. Attendance 1886: 249 a.m.; 171 evg. Larger attendance 1895–1908 led to perm. ch. 1897. Attendance 1903: 425 a.m.; 340 p.m. Nos. declined from 1930. Bldg. in red brick on basilican plan in Early Eng. style by J. A. Thomas of Whitfield & Thomas: chancel with N. vestry and 4 bays of aisled nave, seating 570, 1897–8; W. end of nave, baptistery, and porches 1903; seated 800 on completion. Tower over NE. porch not built. Repairs to counter subsidence 1923 and 1929. S. chapel renovated 1952 with painting by Frank Salisbury, who also gave panelling for reredos, as mem. to wife; thereafter known as Salisbury chapel. Vestries incorporated into new Vicarage, and new vestry in S. aisle, 1967–8. Mission started at no. 38 Broomsleigh Street 1892; special evangelistic svces. held Sun. evgs. Mission ch. demol. as unsafe 1901. New mission hall replaced nos. 8 and 10 Broomsleigh Street 1905, seating 250 with club and reading rooms on 1st floor; sited away from ch. as possible centre for new par. Evangelistic svces. ended 1923 because of small attendance and social distinction between ch. and mission, but revived 1931 to bring in new residents. Hall and men's institute let to Camden L.B. 1980. E. N. Sharpe, V. 1894–1908, later archdeacon and canon of St. Paul's.

HOLY TRINITY (TRINITY until *c.* 1930), Finchley Rd. Temp. ch. in Belsize Lane licensed 1845; erected by Sir Thos. Maryon Wilson, who paid minister's stipend, although area not built up until much later.[88] In 1851 seated 393; attendance 185 a.m.; 107 aft.; average attendance 230 a.m.; 120 aft. In 1865 Revd. Hen. Sharpe began mission work among navvies working on Belsize rly. tunnel; svces. in brick mission ch., built 1865 opposite no. 101

[70] From figs. in *Brit. Weekly*, 19 Nov. 1886, pp. 2, 4; Mudie-Smith, *Rel. Life*, 165–7.
[71] Inf. about patrons is from *Clergy List*, *Crockford*, and *Lond. Dioc. Bk.* (various edns.); seating and attendance figs. 1851 from P.R.O., HO 129/8/1; attendance figs. 1886 are from *Brit. Weekly*, 19 Nov. 1886, p. 4; attendance figs. 1903 from Mudie-Smith, *Rel. Life*, 165. Liturgical directions are used in all architectural descriptions. The following abbreviations are used, in addition to those in the index: aft., afternoon; Dec., Decorated; demol., demolished; Eng., England or English; evg., evening; mem., memorial; mtg., meeting; perm., permanent; Perp., Perpendicular; temp., temporary; V., vicar.
[72] Para. based on *All Souls S. Hampstead: Souvenir Bk. 1929*; *Par. Mag. of All Souls' Loudoun Rd. Centenary Issue May 1965* (both in files of C.C.C.).

[73] Barratt, *Annals*, iii. 95.   [74] *C.H.R.* ix. 19.
[75] A. Service, *Architects of Lond.* (1979), 122.
[76] C.C.C., Christ Ch., survey 1975.
[77] *Mackeson's Guide* (1889), p. 39.
[78] Clarke, *Lond. Chs.* 77–8.
[79] Wade, *Streets of Hampstead* (rev. edn.), 39.
[80] Barratt, *Annals*, iii. 93.
[81] Char. Com. files.
[82] Wade, *Streets of Hampstead*, 39.
[83] Para. based on J. Tucker, *Emmanuel Ch., West End, Hampstead: Complete Hist.* (1981).
[84] P.R.O., HO 129/8/1/1/2.
[85] Below, Holy Trinity.
[86] P.R.O., C 54/17949, no. 15.
[87] Ibid. C 54/18968, no. 15.
[88] P.R.O., HO 129/8/1/1/1; Thompson, *Hampstead*, 384.

Belsize Lane, also attracted local residents and led to funds for perm. ch.[89] Dist. formed 1873 from St. John's, Hampstead.[90] Patron Evangelical trustees 1887, Maryon-Wilson fam. in reversion 1913, Ch. Pastoral Aid Soc. 1955.[91] Attendance 1886: 823 a.m.; 564 evg.; 1903: 481 a.m.; 470 p.m. Social change and decline in 20th-cent. churchgoing led to financial difficulties, but after Second World War ch. remained a community focus, especially for temp. overseas residents, and co-operated with welfare authorities to help old and sick living alone. Bldg., on site given by Sir John Maryon Wilson, of Kentish rag with Bath stone dressings in Gothic style by Hen. S. Legg: aisled nave 1871–2; chancel, gift of lady impressed by Sharpe's preaching, 1875. Tower and spire not built. Completed ch. seated 1,000.[92] Parochial rooms in Belsize Terr. c. 1900. Hall adjoining S. side of ch. built in similar materials 1902. Ground in front taken for road widening 1964. Private Act to redevelop site 1968: ch. demol. 1976 and svces. held temporarily at no. 295 Finchley Rd. Smaller ch. consecrated 1978, with hall, meeting rooms, and vestries, paid for by leasing rest of site for a small office block and 6-storey block of 24 flats.[93] Temp. mission ch. built at West End 1874, became Emmanuel ch. (q.v.) 1885. Mission ch. built in Fordwych Rd. 1882 became St. Cuthbert's (q.v.) 1886.[94] Mission held in 1903, attendance: 32 p.m.

ST. CUTHBERT, Fordwych Rd., W. Hampstead. Dist. formed 1888 from Holy Trinity (q.v.).[95] Patron ch. trust fund trustees. Attendance 1886: 253 a.m.; 138 evg.; 1903: 218 a.m.; 149 p.m. Iron ch. founded by Trinity, superseded 1882 by brick mission ch., designed by W. C. Street and served by Lond. Diocesan Home Mission 1882–7. Bldg., at right angles to mission ch., of red brick with stone dressings in Early Eng. style by Street 1886: aisled nave consecrated 1887; chancel with 3-sided apse 1903–4; SW. tower not built. Mission ch. became par. hall until demol. 1902 by Midland Rly. Co., which rebuilt it nearer ch. 1903.[96] Proposed to use hall again for svces. and sell site of ch. to housing assoc. 1979. Ch. still standing 1986. Iron mission hall blt. 1894 at Maygrove Rd.,[97] attendance 1903: 95 p.m.

ST. JAMES, Sheriff Rd., West End Lane. Patron trustees. Attendance 1886: 215 a.m.; 208 evg.; 1903: 359 a.m.; 293 p.m. Mission hall by A. W. Blomfield by 1882. Bldg. of red brick with stone dressings in Early Eng. style, seating 1,000, by Blomfield 1887–8: chancel with S. vestry, N. chapel, aisled nave. 18th-cent. wooden figure of St. Jas., possibly Spanish. Mission hall in Netherwood Street by 1900;[98] attendance 1903: 68 p.m.

ST. JOHN, Downshire Hill (proprietary chapel). Probably originally intended as chapel of ease to par. ch., hence dedication.[99] Revd. John Curry offered to pay for bldg. and site if appointed min., so chapel became proprietary and in 1982 was last remaining in Lond.[1] Not consecrated. Chapel bought 1832 by Revd. John Wilcox who established evangelical ministry. Attendance 1851: 1,370 a.m.; 120 aft.; 325 p.m.; exceptionally high due to sermon by abp. of Canterbury. Proposed conversion to dist. par. ch. 1863 rejected but new dist. ch. of St. Steph., Rosslyn Hill (q.v.), blt. and min. of St. John's became 1st V.;[2] many worshippers, however, remained at St. John's. Attendance 1886: 288 a.m.; 262 evg.; 1903: 172 a.m.; 125 p.m. Chapel in financial difficulties 1916, bought by Leslie Wright and leased to congregation at token rent. Patronage vested in C.P.A.S. and chapel safeguarded under Wright's will as long as it should be used for worship.[3] Stuccoed bldg., on copyhold site acquired 1817, in classical style designed and built by Wm. Woods opened 1823:[4] 5-bay nave with no recessed chancel, vestibule staircase each side of W. porch, galleries on 3 sides supported by 2 orders of slim columns, Doric portico and cupola at W. entrance. Evangelical design: prominent pulpit; small communion table backed by inscribed panels; box pews. Seated 1,000 in 1851. Temp. closure for repairs 1896, when svces. in vestry hall. Further repairs 1964–71 and subject of major appeal 1982.[5]

ST. LUKE, Kidderpore Ave. Dist. formed 1896.[6] Patron trustees. Iron ch. built on site of later Vicarage 1896.[7] Bldg. of red brick with stone dressings in Arts and Crafts Perp. by Basil Champneys 1898–9: chancel, aisled nave, W. gallery, asymmetrical W. front, SE. turret.[8] Attendance 1903: 300 a.m.; 280 p.m. Some internal improvements made 1920s.[9]

ST. MARY, Priory Rd., Kilburn. Dist. formed 1863 from St. John's, Hampstead.[10] Patron Ch. Patronage Soc. Briefly one of leading ritualistic chs. in Lond. 1860s.[11] Attendance 1886: 859 a.m.; 585 evg.; 1903: 431 a.m.; 452 p.m. Bldg., near site of Kilburn priory and containing fragment of 15th-cent. brass of nun found nearby, of Kentish rag in Dec. style by F. & H. Francis 1857–62: chancel with N. vestry and S. chapel, aisled nave with transepts, SW. tower and spire. Consecrated 1862. Vestry enlarged 1889. Reredos 1885, with 7 new panels 1902.[12] Clock and bells given by Sam. John Housley and maintained by char. endowed by him 1879.[13]

ST. MARY THE VIRGIN, Primrose Hill Rd. Local residents came to svces. held by Chas. Jas. Fuller, chaplain of boys' home moved 1865 from Euston Rd. (St. Pancras) to corner Regent's Pk. Rd. and

[89] P. R. Butcher, *First Hundred Yrs. Holy Trinity Ch. Hampstead* [1972] (in S.C.L.); Wade, *More Streets*, 75.
[90] *Lond. Gaz.* 11 Feb. 1873, p. 367.
[91] *First Hundred Yrs.*
[92] Clarke, *Lond. Chs.*, 82; *Mackeson's Guide* (1889), 170; *First Hundred Yrs.*; above, plate 25.
[93] *First Hundred Yrs.*; S.C.L., 16/Holy Trinity, ephemera file, copies of par. letters; cutting from *Country Life*, 23 Dec. 1976, p. 1911.
[94] *First Hundred Yrs.*
[95] Para. based on C.C.C., rep. 1979 on redundant ch.; G.L.R.O., P81/CUT/1; Hennessy, *Novum Rep.* 189.
[96] Barratt, *Annals*, iii. 95.　　　　　　　[97] Ibid.
[98] S.C.L., 16/St. Jas. Ch., photocopy of par. mag. 1900.
[99] Para. based on *Short Hist. of St. John's, Downshire Hill, 1823–1973*.

[1] S.C.L., 16/St. John's, Downshire Hill, pamphlet file, *Appeal Newsletter*, Spring 1982.
[2] G.L.C., Historic Bldgs. Paper no. 1, *St. Steph. Rosslyn Hill* [1980].
[3] C.C.C., St. John's Appeal 1969.
[4] Not Cockerell as in Pevsner, *Lond.* ii. 186.
[5] S.C.L., St. John's, *Appeal Newsletters*, 1982; above, plate 26.
[6] Hennessy, *Novum Rep.* 189.
[7] Wade, *Streets of Hampstead* (1972), 20.
[8] Pevsner, *Lond.* ii. 186–7; Clarke, *Lond. Chs.*, 83.
[9] C.C.C., St. Luke's, rep. c. 1926.
[10] *Lond. Gaz.* 13 Jan. 1863, p. 199.
[11] Clarke, *Lond. Chs.* 79.
[12] Ibid. 78–9.
[13] Char. Com. files.

King Henry's Rd. Part of St. Saviour's assigned as mission dist. and iron ch. opened in Ainger Rd. 1867; Eton Coll. gave site for larger ch. Patron 7 trustees inc. provost of Eton and V. of Hampstead. Despite enthusiastic crowds, consecration of perm. ch. refused by John Jackson, bp. of Lond., on grounds of ritualism. Members of guilds carried out all functions of ch. life by 1876. Protests 1877 led bp. to suppress sung celebrations and most ornaments, but ritualism restored after consecration by Jackson's successor 1885. Attendance 1886: 148 a.m.; 133 evg.; 1903: 407 a.m.; 241 p.m. Resistance to Anglo-Cathm. led to emphasis on minutiae in 1930s. Liturgical movement brought more moderate approach under G. B. Timms, V. 1952–65. Par. libr. in N. porch, specializing in religious educ., 1955. United with St. Paul's, Avenue Rd. (q.v.), 1956–7. Bldg. of dark red brick in early French Gothic style, seating c. 750, by Wm. Manning, member of congregation, 1870–2: apsidal chancel with N. and S. vestries, incomplete tower, aisled nave with S. chapel, N. transept, N. porch. Nave and chancel opened 1872; S. aisle with chapel, sacristy, and choir vestry 1892, smaller than Manning's design because part of site had been sold. Interplay of light and shade in interior to increase apparent size.[14] Reredos by Bodley & Garner 1895; restored 1974.[15] Massive rood cross at chancel arch 1914. Percy Dearmer, V. 1901–15, later professor of ecclesiastical art at King's Coll., Lond., and canon of Westm., made St. Mary's well known for music and liturgical reforms: whitewashed interior as foil for ornaments and for ceremonial in wholly English tradition.[16]

St. Paul, Avenue Rd. Dist. formed 1860 from St. John's, Hampstead, and St. Saviour's, with addition 1865.[17] Patron V. of Hampstead. Attendance 1886: 719 a.m.; 367 evg.; 1903: 372 a.m.; 187 p.m. Par. united with St. Mary's, Primrose Hill Rd. (q.v.), 1955. Bldg., seating 870, by S. S. Teulon consecrated 1859: apsidal chancel, N. and S. chapels, galleried transepts, aisled nave, W. front with elaborate 2-storeyed half-hexagonal porch with diagonal flanks adorned with stone caps and turrets. Unusual, much criticized style.[18] Tile reredos by Teulon.[19] Bombed 1940 and svces. held in St. Paul's sch., Winchester Rd. Declared redundant 1956 and demol. 1958; replaced by Polygon flats.[20]

St. Peter, Belsize Pk. Dist. formed 1861 from St. John's, Hampstead.[21] Patron dean and chapter of Westm. Endowed 1861 with £200 p.a. from Belsize ground rents by Westm. abbey.[22] Attendance 1886: 724 a.m.; 334 evg.; 1903: 1,398 a.m.; 125 p.m. Bldg., on site given by Westm., of Kentish rag in Dec. style by W. Mumford: aisled nave and tran-

septs, paid for by F. W. Tremlett, first V., consecrated 1859; chancel with S. vestry, stained glass in W. window, and SW. tower, designed by J. P. St. Aubyn, consecrated 1876. Seated 1,040 in 1889.[23] Extensive repairs with underpinning of foundations 1917.[24] W. and S. galleries removed and chapel added 1927.[25] Sanctuary redesigned 1965. Proposal to put movable altar in front of chancel steps 1985.[26]

St. Saviour, Eton Rd. Worshippers from Haverstock Hill at chapel of Asylum for Relief of Journeymen Tailors, east of Haverstock Hill (St. Pancras), decided 1846 to build ch.;[27] site given by Eton Coll. Work begun 1847 to design of H. E. Kendall jr. but stopped for lack of funds. Iron chapel, seating 574, nearby at corner of Eton Rd. and Eton College Rd., later site of Wellington Ho.,[28] licensed for worship from 1848. Attendance 1851: 300 a.m.; 150 evg. Dist. had 120 hos. in which 27 families were dissenters, but was increasing rapidly 1851.[29] Closed when perm. ch. opened and dist. assigned from St. John's, Hampstead, 1856.[30] Patron V. of Hampstead. Attendance 1886: 398 a.m.; 423 evg.; 1903: 139 a.m.; 126 p.m. Bldg. of Kentish rag in Early Eng. style, seating 800, by E. M. Barry 1855–6: chancel with N. and S. vestries, aisled nave with N. and S. transepts, SW. tower and spire finished 1864. Repairs to walls and foundations 1872. Choir vestry by Ewan Christian 1882; chancel lengthened 1909. Reredos added 1885, screen 1890. Mission room in Fleet Rd., 1889; svces. held there or elsewhere in 1903, attendance: 42 a.m.; 100 p.m.

St. Stephen, Rosslyn Hill. Dist. assigned 1870 from St. John's, Hampstead.[31] United with All Hallows', Gospel Oak (St. Pancras) 1977.[32] Patron V. of Hampstead. Worshippers at St. John's, Downshire Hill, decided 1864 to build dist. ch. Site given by Sir T. Maryon Wilson. Attendance 1886: 752 a.m.; 620 evg.; 1903: 301 a.m.; 242 p.m. Bldg. of purple-red Dunstable brick, with bands of Kentish rag and dressings of rag and granite, in Gothic style with strong French characteristics, seating 1,200, by S. S. Teulon 1866–9: apsidal chancel with N. and S. transepts, massive tower with spires, aisled nave with W. gallery and N., W., and S. porches.[33] Vaulted crypt below. Steeple completed 1871. Peal of 10 bells by Taylors of Loughborough 1872; returned to Taylors 1982.[34] Chapel in S. transept 1905; stalls and screen by Temple Moore 1912.[35] Intended for Low Ch. svces. with broad well-lit nave, but placing of tower E. of nave created long chancel, which led to much decoration; described as one of most moving Victorian interiors. Cost was 3 times that estimated, with rich ornament inside and out.[36] Alabaster roundels 1880, one of Latimer given

[14] St. Mary's, Primrose Hill: Guide and Hist. [booklet 1972]; Hennessy, Novum Rep. 190.
[15] C.C.C., St. Mary's, Primrose Hill.   [16] D.N.B.
[17] Lond. Gaz. 3 Aug. 1860, p. 2872; 21 Nov. 1865, p. 5505.
[18] C.C.C., St. Paul's Avenue Rd., photos. 1946; survey notes; Pevsner, Lond. ii. 187–8; Mackeson's Guide (1889), 138.
[19] Pevsner, Lond. ii. 187–8.
[20] St. Mary's, Primrose Hill, 32–3; C.C.C., survey notes; S.C.L., St. Paul's, notes in index file.
[21] Lond. Gaz. 14 May 1861, p. 2050.
[22] W.A.M., RCO 32, deed.
[23] Ibid. letters; Mackeson's Guide (1889), 144; Clarke, Lond. Chs. 79; above, plate 27.
[24] H. Isenberg, Short Hist. of St. Pet. Belsize Pk. (1979), 8.

[25] Clarke, Lond. Chs. 79; C.C.C., St. Pet., file.
[26] C.C.C., St. Pet., file.
[27] Para. based on St. Saviour's Par. Paper, centenary nos. 1 and 2 (July and Oct. 1956), photocopy in S.C.L.; Clarke, Lond. Chs. 78.
[28] Ibid.; C.H.R. iii. 18.
[29] P.R.O., HO 129/8/1/1/6.
[30] Lond. Gaz. 24 Oct. 1856, p. 3465; above, plate 24.
[31] Ibid. 20 May 1870, p. 2649.
[32] Para. based on G.L.C., Hist. Bldgs. Paper no. 1, St. Steph. Rosslyn Hill.
[33] Pevsner, Lond. ii. 188; Mackeson's Guide, 159; above, plate 23.
[34] C.C.C., St. Steph., cutting from Ringing World, 14 Jan. 1983, 27.
[35] Clarke, Lond. Chs. 80.
[36] C.C.C., St. Steph., rep. 1971; above, plate 21.

by Ewan Christian, member of congregation, in protest against Anglo-Cathm. Glass by Lavers & Westlake, and Clayton & Bell, inc. mem. window to Teulon. Subsidence 1896, 1898, 1901, and serious cracking 1969, when foundations for new Royal Free hosp. dug. Although no further movement found between 1970 and 1981, ch. closed 1977 while new use sought.[37] No firm plans 1985, but diocese criticized for neglect, as most fittings had been stolen or vandalized.[38] Grant by G.L.C. for urgent repairs 1985.[39] Possibly Teulon's best work, set off by sloping site. Denning hall, no. 38 Denning Rd., built for missions 1883, later converted into artists' studios.[40]

SION chapel (proprietary), Belsize. Built at Belsize Ho. by Chas. Povey[41] and open by 1710 when advertised for performance of weddings, with two sermons each Sun. Fees for weddings to be waived for those who had wedding dinner in gdns. 1716.[42] Chapel probably closed by 1720 when Povey left.

WELL WALK or HAMPSTEAD chapel (proprietary). Opened 1725 in Great or Pump Room at Hampstead wells, after alterations started by Wm. Hoar and completed after financial difficulties by Jos. Rous; Mr. Wood presented bell, and Dr. Gibbon communion plate. Chapel, seating c. 370 in 1810, used continuously until Christ Ch. opened 1852 and regarded as chapel of ease to par. ch. although never consecrated. Hired while par. ch. was being rebuilt or repaired, e.g. 1745-7, 1755, 1843.[43] Seated 774 in 1851, when attendance 359 a.m.; 92 aft.; 287 evg.[44] Used as Presb. chapel 1853-62 and H.Q. of 3rd Mdx. (Hampstead) Rifle Volunteers[45] before demol. 1882.[46]

ROMAN CATHOLICISM. Recusants were mentioned in the 16th and 17th centuries: John Phillips in 1583 and 1588;[47] John Sappton in 1592;[48] Francis Holt in 1610; members of the Raynes family and John Woodgate or Widgett in 1613 and 1617;[49] the wife of Anthony Hancock in 1636;[50] John Needham and Thomas Tidd in 1663.[51] No Roman Catholics were reported thereafter until the 1770s, when there were enough to justify the appointment of the Revd. Gerard Robinson in 1778 to serve them. Between 1784 and 1790 at least 12 other priests celebrated mass in Hampstead.[52] The main mass centre was apparently the house of Lucy Nihell or Nihill, member of a well known Roman Catholic family, at Ladywell Court, East Heath Road, in the mid 1780s and at Rosslyn Lodge (later no. 19 Lyndhurst Road) by 1788. Presumably it was the school which she was running by 1790, said to be in the Grove facing Pond Street, Haverstock Hill. From 1789 services included a sung high mass. Some Catholics also attended mass at the house of Thomas Hussey, later bishop of Waterford and Lismore, who lived in Hampstead by 1784 and kept a house there until 1789. There were also said to have been chapels in houses belonging to Thomas Cockburn and Henry Cooke.[53]

Lucy Nihell's school, under Felicity Nihell by 1791, continued to be used for mass in the 1790s. In 1796 Abbé Jean-Jacques Morel, a French emigré, settled in Hampstead and ministered to compatriots, converting into a chapel a room in Oriel House, Little Church Row (later the southern end of Heath Street). It may have been the public chapel 'lately opened' by 1796, with c. 100 worshippers, mentioned in a report to Rome, although its address was not published in the Laity's Directory until 1806.[54] More than 200 French people were said to have stayed in Hampstead at the height of the emigration.[55] In 1814 the congregation was said to number 150,[56] by that time mainly or solely English, who paid for a purpose-built chapel, St. Mary's, Holly Place, which was opened in 1816. Abbé Morel continued as its priest, remaining in Hampstead until his death in 1852.[57]

Apart from a few short-lived chapels in religious houses, it was 50 years before a second mass centre was set up. In 1865 the Oblates of Mary Immaculate came to Kilburn and founded a religious house, with a small temporary church.[58] The area was being rapidly built up and by 1900 the permanent church of the Sacred Heart had a congregation four times the size of St. Mary's, although the total number of Roman Catholic attendances in 1903, 1,599, was less than that of either Congregationalists or Methodists. The Sacred Heart was also well placed to serve the influx of Irish into Kilburn after the Second World War.[59] The small church of St. Mary was not replaced: the south-east part of Hampstead from 1867 was served by St. Dominic's, Haverstock Hill, just outside the boundary, and Swiss Cottage from the 1930s by St. Thomas More's, Maresfield Gardens.[60] The attractions of Hampstead for schools, nursing homes, and other institutions brought many religious orders, several of whose convents are noticed below.[61]

St. Mary's, Holly Pl., originated in congregation of Abbé Morel at Oriel Ho. in 1796.[62] Chapel built as part of small terr. in Holly Walk, at expense of congregation, and dedic. 1816, one of earliest surviving Rom. Cath. chs. in Lond.[63] Seated 300 in 1851; average attendance 500 a.m.; 70 p.m.; 250

[37] C.C.C., St. Steph., rep.
[38] H.H.E. 12 Apr. 1985, 8.
[39] Ibid. 11 Jan. 1985, 1.
[40] Wade, Streets of Hampstead, 51.
[41] Tract by Povey, 1718, quoted by Park, Hampstead, 157-9.   [42] Barratt, Annals, i. 220-2.
[43] Ibid. 217-18; iii. 88; Gent. Mag. lxxxiv (1), 213; Guildhall MSS. 9557, p. 27; 19224/315, file 1.
[44] P.R.O., HO 129/8/1/1/4.
[45] Below, prot. nonconf.; Thorne, Environs, 281.
[46] The Times, 4 Feb. 1882, 5f.
[47] Mdx. County Rec. i. 143; Cath. Rec. Soc. xxii. 123.
[48] Mdx. County Rec. i. 205.
[49] Ibid. ii. 214, 235; Mdx. Sess. Rec. i. 246; iv. 269-71; Cal. Mdx. Sess. Rec. v. 33, 136.
[50] Mdx. County Rec. iii. 139.
[51] Cath. Rec. Soc. vi. 288.

[52] Rest of para. based on Cath. Rec. Soc. l, passim; Lond. Recusant, iv. 29-30; C.H.R. x. 5-6.
[53] Park, Hampstead, 236.
[54] Lond. Recusant, iv. 29-30; G.L.R.O., MR/RH 1/13.
[55] Park, Hampstead, 236.
[56] Lond. Recusant, iii. 16.
[57] Ibid. iv. 30, 74.
[58] Below.
[59] V.C.H. Mdx. i. 143; Mudie-Smith, Rel. Life, 133, 167.
[60] Below.
[61] The following abbreviations are used, in addition to those in the index: dedic., dedicated; demol., demolished; Eng., England or English; reg., registered.
[62] Above.
[63] Para. based on Lond. Recusant, iv. 30, 73-4; Pevsner, Lond. ii. 187; A. Rottmann, Lond. Cath. Chs. (1926), 245-7.

evg.[64] Attendance 1886: 206 a.m.; 65 evg.; 1903: 247 a.m.[65] Nave copied from Morel's former ch. at Verneuil, Normandy; stuccoed front with Tuscan doorway 1830; statue over entrance 1850; interior altered and 2 side altars built 1878. Highly decorated sanctuary in Byzantine style by G. L. Simpson and 2 side chapels and sacristies added 1907.

Oblates of Mary Immaculate first held mass in Kilburn 1865 at no. 1 Greville Rd. Temp. ch. soon built nearby and reg. 1868.[66] Perm. ch. of Sacred Heart of Jesus, Quex Rd., of light brick with stone dressings in Early Eng. style by Pugin & Pugin 1878-9: high roofed, no tower; long wide nave straight into deep chancel. Sanctuary built 1898-9 and ch. consecrated 1909. Priory bldgs. attached; new bldgs. on NE. side of ch. 1965. Attendance 1886: 220 a.m.; 203 evg.; 1903: 1,095 a.m.; 257 p.m.[67] Name changed to Sacred Heart ch. 1970.[68] Former Unitarian ch. in Quex Rd. also reg. by Rom. Caths. 1971.[69]

Temp. ch. of St. Thos. More opened 1938 in Maresfield Gdns. Perm. ch. built beside it 1953, rebuilt in red brick and concrete by Gerard Goalen 1968-9:[70] elliptical plan with ambulatory around, lit by clerestory, with coloured glass over sanctuary and with gallery half way round.

Passionist Fathers, who came to Eng. 1842, opened first Lond. ho. with 4 priests 1848 at Poplar Ho., West End Lane, through help of Bp. (later Cardinal) Wiseman, who wanted missions to Irish poor. Local priests sought help from fathers, who were assigned Rom. Caths. west of Finchley Rd. As ho. was in poor repair, community moved to Hendon 1849.[71]

Sisters of Providence of the Immaculate Conception bought part of Bartrams est. c. 1867:[72] opened private boarding sch. for 25 girls in Belle Vue ho., and orphanage and day sch. for girls in Bartram Ho. Large new block linked to Belle Vue built for 100 additional boarders 1887. Boarding sch. later closed, and day sch. became vol. aided after 1945.[73] Old hos. demol. and 4-storeyed Bartram hostel with chapel built in Rowland Hill Street c. 1967. Convent was Provincial Ho. of order 1986.[74]

Les Dames Anglaises of the Institute of the Blessed Virgin Mary (Bavarian branch) opened St. Mary's convent and sch., England's Lane, by 1880. Moved to no. 47 Fitzjohn's Avenue c. 1927, where sch. continued.[75]

Sisters of Hope (Institute of the Holy Family,

Bordeaux) opened nursing home for retired ladies at no. 20 Quex Road, Kilburn, by 1931 with 8 sisters. Order's Provincial Ho. opened at no. 2 Aberdare Gdns. between 1966 and 1969. Nursing home moved to Cricklewood 1974.[76]

Dominican Sisters ran sch. for young ladies in Chislett Rd. (later Compayne Gdns.), Kilburn, by 1931, until c. 1932.[77]

Sisters of Charity of Saint Vincent de Paul had convent in Chislett Rd. (later no. 88 Compayne Gdns.) from c. 1933. Visited poor and taught in parochial sch., besides running small private sch. By 1949 also ran St. Cath.'s hostel, nos. 80-2 West End Lane, as probation home and hostel for business girls. Moved away late 1960s.[78]

Sisters of Mercy of the Holy Cross founded first ho. in Eng. 1938 at no. 3 Fitzjohn's Avenue, formerly home of Phil. de László, later also taking over nos. 5 and 7. Ran international ho. of studies for girls 1985.[79]

The Society of Jesus opened ho. of studies at Southwell Ho., no. 39 Fitzjohn's Avenue, by 1950.[80]

Sisters of St. Marcellina opened residential sch. for foreign girls c. 1956 at Hampstead Towers, no. 6 Ellerdale Rd., which R. Norman Shaw had designed for himself. Sch. survived 1985.[81]

Missionary Sisters of the Immaculate Heart of Mary opened convent of Our Lady of Good Counsel, no. 172 Haverstock Hill, c. 1966.[82]

Sisters of St. Dorothy opened international hostel for girls at Frognal Ho., no. 99 Frognal, 1968.[83]

PROTESTANT NONCONFORMITY. Ralph Honywood's[84] house on Red Lion Hill, where from 1666 he had a chaplain, was a meeting place for Presbyterians until Red Lion chapel was built close by; the congregation became Unitarian in the mid 18th century.[85] George Whitefield held a meeting on Hampstead Heath, probably near Gospel Oak (St. Pancras), in 1739 to an attentive audience.[86] His anti-Unitarian preaching was said to have inspired the formation of an Independent chapel:[87] as some Anglicans used that name for both the Unitarians and the Methodists,[88] the church that was formed was probably the Calvinistic Methodist one which met in a shed near the later chapel at the east end of Church Row; the chapel stood by 1771, when William Pierce left £10 a year as long as it was used

[64] P.R.O., HO 129/1/1/11.
[65] Brit. Weekly, 19 Nov. 1886, 4; Mudie-Smith, Rel. Life, 166.
[66] Para. based on Rottmann, Lond. Cath. Chs. 250-1; Pevsner, Lond. ii. 188; The Times, 4 June 1878, 8a; G.R.O. Worship Reg. no. 18735.
[67] Brit. Weekly, 19 Nov. 1886, 4; Mudie-Smith, Rel. Life, 166.
[68] G.R.O. Worship Reg. no. 24556.
[69] Ibid. no. 72674.
[70] Ibid. no. 58289; Cath. Dir. (1969); C.C.C., Clarke MSS. xxiii. 116.
[71] Para. based on Poplar Ho., West End Lane, and Passionists (Mt. Argus Historical Papers, 1977), in S.C.L.; V.C.H. Mdx. v. 38.
[72] G.L.R.O., MAB 1038, papers dated 1884; Potter Colln. 19/89.
[73] Hampstead Year Bk. 1889, 29; below, educ., pub. schs. (Rosary R.C.).
[74] G.R.O. Worship Reg. no. 70789; Cath. Dir. (1986).
[75] Cath. Dir. (1880); P. F. Anson, Rel. Orders of Gt. Britain and Irel. (1949), 320; below, educ., private schs.

(St. Mary's convent).
[76] Cath. Dir. (1931 and later edns.); V.C.H. Mdx. vii. 242; inf. from Holy Fam. convent, 1978.
[77] Cath. Dir. (1931 and later edns.).
[78] Ibid. (1933 and later edns.); Anson, Rel. Orders, 209.
[79] Anson, Rel. Orders, 285; Cath. Dir. (1939 and later edns.).
[80] Cath. Dir. (1950 and later edns.).
[81] Ibid. (1956 and later edns.); Service, Architects of Lond. 136-7.
[82] Cath. Dir. (1966 and later edns.).
[83] H.H.E. 8 Nov. 1968; Cath. Dir. (1970 and later edns.).
[84] No Ralph is given in the extensive Honywood genealogies although he is listed in the hearth tax in 1664: G.L.R.O., MR/TH/2, m.30.
[85] Below, Presb. Section based on paras. on individual sects, below.
[86] Geo. Whitefield's Jnls. (1960), 265; Vickers and Young, Meth. Guide to Lond. and SE. 26.
[87] Park, Hampstead (1814), 238.
[88] e.g. Guildhall MS. 9558, f. 443.

for religious services,[89] and was probably built after 1768, when the site was leased for 3 terms of 21 years by the copyholder[90] and assigned to a group of London tradesmen. In 1777 it was assigned to Charles Chandler, clerk, who may have served the chapel. It was bought by the countess of Huntingdon for her Connexion in 1780 but was later used by other Methodists. Wesleyans were meeting in private houses in Golden Square and New End in 1823, and Calvinist Methodists in Kilburn in 1827. Baptists were meeting in a private house in Kilburn in 1798 and in the town by 1811. Scottish Presbyterians met in the town from 1832.

Congregationalists had no place of worship in the parish until after the opening in 1851 of New College at College Crescent, Finchley Road. The college was founded in 1850 to unite Homerton, Highbury, and Coward (Bloomsbury) colleges in order to train nonconformist ministers; it was affiliated to the University of London's school of divinity from 1900.[91] New College chapel, built nearby in 1853, was not part of the college, although closely linked with it. Congregationalists did not secure a chapel nearer the town until the 1880s, partly through the hostility of Anglican landowners.[92] Hackney Theological Seminary (later College) moved to Hampstead in 1887, to a new building in Finchley Road near Parsifal Road, and helped to found West Hampstead Congregational church. In 1924 an Act united Hackney and New colleges as New College, a school of London University training ministers principally for Congregational churches, and in 1934 the College Crescent buildings were demolished, leaving the college at Parsifal Road. In 1977 the college closed and its fine nonconformist library was transferred to Dr. Williams's Library.[93]

Like the Anglicans, nonconformists found only a limited need for missionary or charitable work; Lyndhurst Road Congregational church had to go to Kentish Town (St. Pancras) to start a mission. There was much scope only in Kilburn and West End, where the nonconformists and evangelical Anglicans co-operated and opposed ritualism.[94] The number of chapels and sects in Hampstead remained small until the late 19th century. In 1882 only eight chapels for six sects were registered for worship; in 1903 and 1914 there were 22 chapels for nine sects. Congregationalists were the leading sect in 1903, with 2,351 attendances, followed by Wesleyan Methodists with 1,659, Baptists with 1,543, and Presbyterians with 1,108.[95]

The Salvation Army had arrived in the 1880s, and the Society of Friends and the Brethren by 1903. Other sects appeared only after the Second World War, with the Christian Community, Christian Scientists, and Seventh-day Adventists. Although a few chapels closed or moved early in the century, most closures occurred during or after the Second World War. The three Congregationalist churches had all closed by 1978, three of the four Presbyterian churches by 1970, two of the four Methodist churches by 1971, and two of the three Unitarian churches by 1965. One Baptist chapel moved away but the rest remained open in 1985.

The following abbreviations are used in the accounts of protestant nonconformist churches, in addition to those used in the index: Bapt., Baptist; Cong., Congregationalist; Dec., Decorated; demol., demolished; Eng., England or English; Ind., Independent; Met., Metropolitan; Meth., Methodist; mtg., meeting; perm., permanent; Presb., Presbyterian; reg., registered; temp., temporary; Utd. Ref., United Reformed; Wes., Wesleyan. Attendance figs. 1886 are from *Brit. Weekly*, 19 Nov. 1886, 4; figs. 1903 from Mudie-Smith, *Rel. Life*, 165-6.

PRESBYTERIANS. Ralph Honywood kept ejected min. Dan. Evans at his ho. as chaplain 1666–75.[96] Dissenters, probably Presbs., met at ho. of their preacher Steph. Lobb 1691.[97] Mtg. place for dissenters reg. at ho. of Isaac Honywood 1692;[98] chapel built adjoining stables of Honywood's ho. and rebuilt 1736 as small, square, brick bldg., roughly on site of later Rosslyn hall and reached by drive of ho.[99] Strict orthodoxy was relaxed, probably during ministry of Ric. Amner, 1765–77, and members became Unitarian.[1]

In 1832 Presbs. reg. for worship ho. of John Thompson, physician, on S. side of Pond Street, and room in ho. of Geo. Purden Bennett in Grove Pl., New End.[2]

Trinity Presb. ch. began after report by Presbs.' dist. visitor for Hampstead that Scottish inhabitants needed preaching station 1844.[3] Lond. Presbytery suggested that mtg. be formed to rent premises. Eight men, inc. 5 gardeners, rented Temperance hall in Perrin's Ct., recognized as preaching station. By end of 1845 average attendance 130 a.m.; 80 p.m. Perm. pastor 1846. Hall seated 97 in 1851, when attendance 65 a.m.; 70 evg. Moved to Well Walk chapel 1853. Bldg. dilapidated, so site at no. 2 High Street, corner of Willoughby Rd., bought 1861. Ch. by Campbell Douglas opened 1862; early membership mostly Scottish. Lecture hall enlarged 1882. Attendance 1886: 348 a.m.; 146 evg. Ch. enlarged 1889; seated 596 in 1892, when 256 communicants.[4] Attendance 1903: 119 a.m.; 145 p.m. Demol. 1962 and members joined St. And. Presb. ch., Finchley Rd. Shops built on site and hall converted into Trinity Close 1970s.[5] Mission in Perrin's Ct. started between 1864 and 1869, inc. ragged sch. Cottage mtgs. at New End 1869, and open-air svces. in brickfields and Branch Hill Sq. Mission formed at Dickinson Street hall, Kentish Town (St. Pancras) 1888, moved to no. 73 Carlton Street 1889, and bought no. 114 Carlton Street 1896.

St. Andrew's Utd. Ref. ch., at corner of Finchley Rd. and Frognal Lane, originated as Presb. ch. Site

[89] *Endowed Chars. Lond. III*, H.C. 252, p. 91 (1900), lxi.
[90] M.L.R. 1768/4/512.
[91] *Hampstead Annual*, 1905–6, 118–27.
[92] Thompson, *Hampstead*, 387–8.
[93] A. Cave, *Story of Founding of Hackney Coll.* [1898], 53–4; *Univ. of Lond. Calendar, 1962–63*, 511–12; G. F. Nuttall, *New Coll., Lond., and its Libr.* (1977).
[94] Booth, *Life and Labour*, iii (3), 208; above, churches.
[95] Mudie-Smith, *Rel. Life*, 167.
[96] *Rosslyn Chapel: Short Hist. 1692–1973* (1974),

19; *Calamy Revised*, ed. A. G. Matthews, 185.
[97] *Mdx. County Rec. Sess. Bks. 1689–1709*, 43.
[98] Ibid. 72.
[99] *Rosslyn Hill Chapel*, 26.
[1] *Some Rec. of Presbyterianism in Hampstead, 1662–1912*, ed. J. P. R. Lyell (1912), 3; below. Unitarians.
[2] Guildhall MS. 9580/7, pp. 58–9.
[3] Para. based on *Presbyterianism in Hampstead*.
[4] *Presb. Official Handbk.* (1892), 55.
[5] Wade, *Streets of Hampstead*, 20, 50.

bought 1897 and lecture hall built by 1902, when ch. formed.[6] Svces. in mission hall 1903; attendance: 137 a.m.; 57 p.m. Ch. of Kentish rag in Dec. style by Pite & Balfour 1904; imposing tower and spire.[7]

Oxendon Presb. ch., Haverstock Hill, Chalk Fm., was built 1877.[8] Attendance 1903: 156 a.m.; 121 p.m. Bldg. closed 1970 and sold to Seventh-day Adventists (q.v.).[9]

Cricklewood Presb. ch., Rondu Rd., reg. 1900. Attendance 1903: 187 a.m.; 186 p.m. Closed by 1954.[10]

UNITARIANS. Dissenters, probably Presb., at chapel on Red Lion (later Rosslyn) Hill, had become Unitarian, probably under Ric. Amner.[11] Rochemont Barbauld was min. c. 1787–1802.[12] Nos. said to be decreasing 1790, and only c. 20 in 1810.[13] Jeremiah Joyce, min. 1815–16, was sec. of Unitarian Soc.[14] In 1822 svces. were Unitarian a.m., Wes. Meth. p.m. After unpopular min., nos. rose from handful in 1846 to 600 in 1891. Dr. Brooke Herford, min. 1892–1901, was instrumental in founding Quex Rd. ch. (q.v.). Attendance 1851: 130 a.m.[15] Average attendances 1870s: 300 a.m. Attendance 1886: 195 a.m.; 157 evg.; 1903: 138 a.m.; 65 p.m. Membership only 200 in 1931 and below 100 by 1949. Shared min. 1953–6 with another ch. Chapel of 1736, known as Red Lion Hill mtg. ho. until 1862, rebuilt 1828 because unsafe. Freehold of site bought 1832.[16] Seating increased from 210 in 1851[17] and again by enlargement on SE. side 1856. Land between chapel and Pilgrim's Lane bought 1858 by wealthy members. Ch. of Kentish rag and Bath stone, seating 400, by John Johnson, opened as Rosslyn Hill chapel 1862. Gallery and W. end added 1867, increasing seating to 460; new chancel and side aisle, flanked by vestry and cttee. room, by Thos. Worthington 1885; main entrance moved from Pilgrim's Lane to Rosslyn Hill 1898 when 2 shops were demol. Interior renovated 1966 by architect Kenneth Tayler, former chairman of congregation; foyer at rear for mtgs. Notable stained glass, inc. by Wilson & Hammond 1886, Hen. Holiday, whose works were at no. 20 Church Row,[18] 1887, Wm. Morris and Burne-Jones 1888, and Lavers & Westlake 1889. Adjoining plots bought, those fronting Kemplay Rd. presented to chapel 1898 and used as tennis cts.; 3 cottages in Pilgrim's Pl. bought 1918. Land around chapel sold for building 1950s. Old chapel used for Rosslyn Hill schs. until 1906,

afterwards as Rosslyn hall.

Quex Road Unitarian ch. founded in 1890s, when Brooke Herford of Rosslyn Hill chapel raised funds to buy site and build hall;[19] reg. 1897.[20] Attendance 1903: 36 a.m.; 48 p.m. Ch., designed by T. Chatfeild Clarke as mem. to Herford, opened 1908.[21] Closed 1965 and acquired by Camden L.B. but reg. by Rom. Cath. ch. of Sacred Heart[22] 1971.[23]

Unitarians opened All Souls' Free ch. at corner of Weech and Fortune Green rds. 1903. Closed 1925 and replaced by new ch. at Golders Green (Hendon).[24]

METHODISTS. In 1780 ctss. of Huntingdon bought lease of mtg. ho. at E. end of Church Row, opposite Yorkshire Grey, settling it on local members of her Connexion.[25] Chapel may already have served Calvinistic Meths.[26] Lease renewed for further 42 years 1789.[27] Nos. said to be increasing 1790 and to be c. 150 in 1810.[28] Probably no formal organization until James Wraith became min. c. 1795.[29] Under Jacob Snelgar, who succeeded 1815, membership was 'independent congregation of Calvinistic Dissenters'.[30] Chapel leased 1826 to Wes. Meths.,[31] possibly those who had met at Wm. Larke's ho., no. 8, New End, 1817, and at Jane Blake's ho., New End, 1823.[32] In 1851 congregation was Wes. Meth. Old Connexion; chapel seated c. 160; and attendance was 42 a.m.; 53 evg.[33] Chapel bought by M.B.W. 1886, when congregation, Primitive Meths., moved to temp. premises.[34] Site at corner of Solent Rd. and Mill Lane, W. Hampstead, bought 1886 and bldg. reg. 1890 as Ebenezer Primitive Meth. chapel.[35] Attendance 1903: 63 a.m.; 89 p.m. Chapel closed by 1971[36] and demol. c. 1975.[37]

Wes. Meths. reg. room in premises of J. Milford of Golden Sq. 1823.[38]

Calvinistic Meths. reg. no. 3 Prospect Pl., Kilburn, in possession of Edw. Woodhouse, 1827.[39]

Wes. reg. chapel in Victoria Terr., St. John's Wood (presumably later Fairfax Rd., S. Hampstead), 1850.[40]

Wes. Reformers reg. Temperance hall, Henry Pl., St. John's Wood, 1851.[41]

Wes. Meths. reg. preaching hall in Upton Rd. (later part of Belsize Rd.) from 1861 to 1870;[42] may have been forerunner of Quex Rd. ch.

Quex Rd. Meth. ch., Kilburn, built by Wes. on site bought 1868,[43] reg. 1870.[44] Bldg. of stock brick in Italianate style by J. Tarring; large Corinthian

[6] P.R.O., C 54/20825, no. 3; datestone.
[7] G.R.O. Worship Reg. no. 40193.
[8] Datestone.
[9] Wade, *More Streets*, 42; G.R.O. Worship Reg. no. 24038.
[10] G.R.O. Worship Reg. no. 37748.
[11] Above, Presbs.
[12] Para. based on *Rosslyn Hill Chapel*.
[13] Guildhall MS. 9558, f. 443.
[14] *D.N.B.*
[15] P.R.O., HO 129/8/1/1/12.
[16] Ibid. C 54/10886, no. 5.
[17] Ibid. HO 129/8/1/1/12.
[18] Wade, *Streets of Hampstead*, 21.
[19] *The Times*, 7 Dec. 1908, 5e.
[20] G.R.O. Worship Reg. no. 35911.
[21] *The Times*, 7 Dec. 1908, 5e.
[22] Wade, *W. Hampstead*, 38; above, Rom. Cathm.
[23] G.R.O. Worship Reg. no. 72674.
[24] *V.C.H. Mdx.* v. 42; inf. from chairman, Hoop Lane, 1969; G.R.O. Worship Reg. no. 39995.

[25] M.L.R. 1780/2/207–9.   [26] Above.
[27] M.L.R. 1790/5/54.
[28] Guildhall MS. 9558, f. 493: described as 'Independents adhering to C. of E.'.
[29] Park, *Hampstead*, 239.
[30] Potter Colln. 18/31.
[31] P.R.O., C 54/10356, no. 20.
[32] Guildhall MSS. 9580/4, 5; P.R.O., RG 31/3, nos. 2, 8.
[33] P.R.O., HO 129/8/1/1/7.
[34] *Endowed Chars. Lond. III*, 125.
[35] P.R.O., C 54/19184, no. 9; G.R.O. Worship Reg. no. 32205.
[36] G.R.O. Worship Reg. no. 32205.
[37] Wade, *W. Hampstead*, 28.
[38] Guildhall MS. 9580/5 (unpag.).
[39] Ibid. 9580/6, p. 148.
[40] P.R.O., RG 31/3, no. 24.
[41] Ibid. no. 25.
[42] G.R.O. Worship Reg. no. 18225.
[43] P.R.O., C 54/16909, no. 12.
[44] G.R.O. Worship Reg. no. 19774.

portico.[45] Attendance 1886: 356 a.m.; 400 evg.; 1903: 282 a.m.; 409 p.m. Ch. hall built 1905. Ch. replaced by 1975[46] with small block of flats in Quex Rd. and 2-storeyed ch. in Kingsgate Rd.

Hampstead Wes. ch., corner of High Street and Prince Arthur Rd. Small Wes. congregation held Sun. sch. in ho. in South Hill Pk. from *c.* 1869. Site for ch. bought 1870. Bldg. of red brick with stone dressings, seating 850, by Chas. Bell 1872, with donations from Sir Fras. Lycett and others; gallery added 1878; NW. tower not built. Sch., vestries, and caretaker's ho. 1884. Attendance 1886: 332 a.m.; 297 evg.; 1903: 119 a.m.; 217 p.m. Ch. closed 1934 and demol.[47]

Gospel Oak Meth. ch., Agincourt Rd., originated 1875 in Wes. mtgs. in Lismore Circus (St. Pancras), recognized as mission 1877 and placed under Prince of Wales Rd. ch.[48] Site at corner of Lisburne Rd. bought from Eccl. Com. but only sch. built at first, designed by Chas. Bell[49] and reg. for worship 1882.[50] Had own min. from 1896. Octagonal bldg. of red brick, seating 750, opened 1900. Attendance 1903: 264 a.m.; 368 p.m. Nos. declined after First World War. Ch. incorporated in circuit with former Primitive Meth. chapels in Grafton Rd. (St. Pancras), Mill Lane, and Hendon 1935; Grafton Rd. amalgamated with Gospel Oak 1940. Repairs when transepts made into additional rooms for Sun. sch. 1956 but need for further repairs brought union with Prince of Wales Rd. ch. at Gospel Oak site 1965, with agreement to rebuild. Gospel Oak ch. demol. 1970 and svces. held in sch. hall until new bldg. opened 1971.

BAPTISTS. Mtgs. said to have started 1811 on Holly Bush Hill,[51] where room in ho. of Geo. Hart was reg. for worship 1816.[52] Jas. Castleden invited to be min. 1817; remained until d. 1854; well known preacher and friend of both Thos. Ainger, min. of Hampstead, and Rom. Cath. Abbé Morel. Castleden put up bldg. on Holly Bush Hill, later no. 17 Holly Mount, with residence on ground floor and Bethel Bapt. chapel, opened 1818, above. Membership quickly rose to 80. Strict Bapt. until 1825, when Castleden opened communion svce. to all, whereupon seceders founded Ebenezer Strict Bapt. chapel, New End (below). Ch. dissolved 1862 after Heath Street ch. opened (q.v.), and bldg. was used for other purposes; some members joined New End or Heath Street; others met at Montagu Grove (nos. 103–109 Frognal), residence of Ric. Burdon Sanderson who acted as min. until 1864; 32 members then joined New End ch. Bethel chapel was described as solid and commodious, with galleries, but rather comfortless.[53] In 1851 it seated 450 and attendance was 110 a.m.; 40 p.m.; 150 evg.[54]

Ebenezer Strict Bapt. chapel, Christchurch Passage, New End, originated with 8 members and several adherents who seceded from Bethel chapel (above) 1825.[55] They were offered mtg. room: hos. at New End of Geo. Jackson, reg. 1825, and Jas. Rice Seymour, reg. 1826, may have been for them.[56] Nos. quickly grew and Ebenezer chapel opened 1827 in former schoolroom. In 1851 it seated 170 and attendance was 30 a.m.; 36 evg.[57] Seated 250 by 1890.[58] Attendance 1886: 53 a.m.; 47 evg.; 1903: 29 a.m.; 31 p.m. Chapel compulsorily purchased for Carnegie Ho. flats 1938, whereupon congregation moved to Temple Fortune (Hendon).[59]

Heath Street ch. founded by Jas. Harvey, in gratitude for sick son's recovery in Hampstead; he obtained site 1861, on former nursery, and provided large part of cost of chapel, as local Bapts. poor.[60] Bldg. of brick with prominent ashlar W. front in Dec. style, seating 700,[61] by C. G. Searle 1861; twin spires. First min. was Wm. Brook jr.; ch. formed with 34 members 1862, many from Holly Bush Hill (q.v.). Open-air svces. on Sun. evgs. on heath and in New End, and during week in back streets of town. Membership rose to 226 in 1871, 320 in 1881, 424 in 1904, and peak of 527 in 1913. Attendance 1886: 457 a.m.; 351 evg.; 1903: 253 a.m.; 291 p.m. Nos. reduced by First World War, although 33 members joined after closure of Regent's Pk. ch. 1922, and only 184 in 1952. Joined Lond. Bapt. Assoc. when formed 1865. City missionary supported by a member to work among summer visitors to heath; winter svces. at Childs Hill (Hendon), where mission hall seating 150 opened 1867; chapel opened 1870 seating 450: became independent ch. 1877.[62] Harvey gave adjoining land 1881 where lecture hall built with classrooms and schoolroom. Gymnasium with reading and recreation rooms built on plot in Cornick's Yd. bought by ch. member 1896. Rickett hall built for men's institute 1908. Drummond Street mission, Kentish Town (St. Pancras), built 1865, taken over when Regent's Park ch. closed; became separate Regent's Park Free ch. 1958.

Ebenezer Strict Bapt. chapel, Kilburn Vale (later Hermit Pl.), Belsize Rd., was built 1870 in memory of Thos. Creswick by his sister: he had preached nearby in open air and worked among sick 1859–68; site chosen to be near that of his last sermon.[63] Chapel supported by Mount Zion chapel, St. John's Wood Rd. (Marylebone). Ch. formed 1883. Attendance 1886: 65 a.m.; 54 evg.; 1903: 43 a.m.; 44 p.m. Absorbed membership of Streatley hall, Brondesbury (Willesden) 1925.[64] Still open for worship 1985.

Brondesbury Bapt. chapel, corner of Kilburn High and Iverson rds., was built on site given by Jas. Harvey 1878.[65] Ornate bldg., seating 780, by W. A. Dixon 1878; tower and spire. Ch. formed

[45] Pevsner, *Lond.* ii. 188–9.
[46] Wade, *W. Hampstead,* 38.
[47] *H.H.E.* 11 May 1872; S.C.L., 18.5/Hamp. Wes. Ch. pamphlet file, cutting from *Meth. Recorder,* 4 June 1908; *The Times,* 26 July 1934, 17*f*; 8 Aug. 1935, 6*g*; G.R.O. Worship Reg. no. 21068.
[48] Para. based on S.C.L., 18.5/Gospel Oak Meth. Ch. pamphlet file, *Gospel Oak Meth. Ch.: Centenary 1982.*
[49] Foundation stone.
[50] G.R.O. Worship Reg. no. 26630.
[51] Whitley, *Bapts. of Lond.* 148.
[52] Guildhall MS. 9580/4.
[53] *Bapt. Quarterly,* xxvi. 109–18; F. Buffard, *Heath*

Street Bapt. Ch. Hampstead, 1861–1961 (1961), 6.
[54] P.R.O., HO 129/8/1/1/8.
[55] Para. based on inf. from deacon, Ebenezer Strict Bapt. chapel, Hendon, 1969.
[56] Guildhall MS. 9580/6, pp. 39–40, 76–7.
[57] P.R.O., HO 129/8/1/1/9.
[58] *Bapt. Handbk.* (1890), 196.   [59] *V.C.H. Mdx.* v. 42.
[60] Para. based on Buffard, *Heath Street Bapt. Ch.*
[61] Whitley, *Bapts. of Lond.* 281.
[62] *V.C.H. Mdx.* v. 41.
[63] Mem. stone; P.R.O., C 54/17115, no. 8.
[64] Whitley, *Bapts. of Lond.* 229.
[65] P.R.O., C 54/18124, no. 34.

1879.[66] Attendance 1886: 421 a.m.; 453 evg.; 1903: 221 a.m.; 387 p.m. Membership 468 c. 1912, with 454 in Sun. sch.[67] Ch. closed 1980[68] and demol.; plans for smaller ch. and sheltered flats approved 1979[69] but work not started 1984. Brondesbury hall, nos. 9 and 11 Iverson Rd., built 1884 and mission svces. held there.[70] Attendance 1903: 70 a.m.; 174 p.m. Svces. held there 1984.

CONGREGATIONALISTS. New College chapel, corner of Upper Avenue and Adelaide rds., built near New Coll. but as separate institution.[71] Founded 1853,[72] reg. 1854,[73] it was designed by J. T. Emmett and contained much stained glass, inc. by Alfred East, ch. member. Attendance 1886: 221 a.m.; 128 evg.; 1903: 111 a.m.; 86 p.m. Ch. had 30 members 1939, when known as Avenue Road Cong. ch.,[74] but closed 1941; stained glass windows given to Hendon Cong. ch.[75] Missions in lecture hall and Townsend Cottages 1894.[76]

Congs. reg. temp. ch. in Upton Rd. (later part of Belsize Rd.) 1856,[77] and formed ch. 1858. Perm. bldg. in Greville Pl. (Marylebone) opened 1859.[78]

Lyndhurst Road Cong. ch., Rosslyn Hill,[79] originated in svces. held in iron bldg., Willoughby Rd., by Revd. J. B. French 1876. Supported for 2 years by Lond. Cong. Union until progress ceased and French resigned. Theologian Robt. F. Horton (1855–1934) was persuaded by T. T. Curwen, a Hampstead resident, to preach at Sun. svces. for 6 months in 1879, and for whole of 1880: enthusiastic followers began mission work in Kentish Town and formed ch. with c. 60 members 1880. By 1883 membership 220 and iron ch. often held 600 in space for 440. Eccl. Com. sold 4-a. Rosslyn Grove estate to 4 members,[80] who kept ¾ a. for ch. and sold rest to finance it.[81] Horton became full-time min. 1884, remaining until 1930: influential writer and preacher, whose Sun. night lectures drew many working men. Bldg. an irregular hexagon of deep red brick with majolica dressings in Romanesque style, normally seating 1,500, by Alf. Waterhouse 1884.[82] Lecture hall and sch. added later.[83] Attendance 1886: 857 a.m.; 1,165 evg.; 1903: 888 a.m.; 894 p.m. Membership 1,276 in 1913 but fell to c. 1,000 during First World War and to 613 in 1939.[84] Utd. Ref. ch. from 1972. Closed 1978. Plan to convert ch. into recital room with flats for musicians, in addition to small sch. already there, 1979.[85] Japanese Aikido classes

held there 1985. Mission at Litcham Street, Kentish Town (St. Pancras) from 1882, replaced by Lyndhurst hall, Warden Rd. (St. Pancras), 1889, with new hall 1909; attendance 1903: 54 a.m.; 201 p.m. Also at no. 60 Southampton Rd. (St. Pancras) from 1887.[86]

West Hampstead Cong. ch., no. 527A Finchley Rd., originated in svces. in libr. of Hackney Coll. 1894. Bldg. of red brick with terracotta and moulded brick dressings to match adjacent coll., on central plan and seating 1,125 inc. galleries, by Spalding & Cross 1894. Also sch. hall and libr.[87] Attendance 1903: 162 a.m.; 210 p.m. Closed 1940 and sold to Shomrei Hadath syngagogue 1946.[88]

CATHOLIC APOSTOLIC CHURCH (IRVINGITES). Edw. Irving preached on heath near Mr. Holford's ho. 1832, before his ch. was formed.[89]

Abbey Ho., no. 1 Manchester Terr., Kilburn, reg. 1876 and in use 1882, closed by 1895.[90]

SALVATION ARMY. Athenaeum hall in Vale of Health, seating c. 700, reg. 1882.[91] Seniors used ground-floor hall, juniors first floor. Hall filled for evg. svces. during week and banqueting hall on Sun. Processions across heath stopped because imitated and attacked by ruffians. Hall, lacking financial support, given up 1886.[92]

Mission room in New Bldgs., Flask Walk, reg. 1887, closed by 1896.[93]

In 1903 svces. were held at Oriel hall: attendance 55 a.m.; 121 p.m. Also at the barracks, Ridge Mews: attendance 7 a.m.; 57 p.m.

Salvation Army barracks and hall, Flask Walk, built 1905, reg. 1906. Young people's hall, also Flask Walk, opened 1907. Both had closed by 1971.[94]

SOCIETY OF FRIENDS (QUAKERS). Friends met in Willoughby Rd. 1903: attendance 20 a.m.

Mtg. ho. at no. 120 Heath Street, designed by Fred. Rowntree, built and reg. 1907.[95] Still in use 1985.

BRETHREN. Brethren met at Gospel hall, Fleet Mews, 1903: attendance 19 a.m.; 86 p.m. Also ran gospel mission at no. 192 Broadhurst Gdns. 1902.[96] Attendance 1903: 110 a.m.; 82 p.m.

Single-storeyed hall adjoining no. 158 Mill Lane reg. 1936,[97] closed by 1985.

[66] Whitley, Bapts. of Lond. 281; Wade, W. Hampstead, 36; S.C.L., 18.3/pamphlet file, Brondesbury Bapt. Chapel, copy of Camden L.B. development subcttee. rep. 1979.
[67] Barratt, Annals, iii. 101.
[68] G.R.O. Worship Reg. no. 28550.
[69] S.C.L., Brondesbury Bapt. Chapel, Camden L.B. rep. 1979.
[70] Whitley, Bapts. of Lond. 224, 281.
[71] Para. based on Hampstead Annual, 1905–6, 127.
[72] P.R.O., C 54/14573, no. 7; Cong. Year Bk. (1894), 291.
[73] G.R.O. Worship Reg. no. 4101.
[74] Cong. Year Bk. (1939), 417.
[75] V.C.H. Mdx. v. 41.
[76] Cong. Year Bk. (1894), 291.
[77] G.R.O. Worship Reg. no. 7195.
[78] A. Mearns, Guide to Cong. Chs. of Lond. (1882), 26.
[79] Para. based on R. F. Horton, Autobiog. (1917), passim; A. Peel and J. A. R. Marriott, Robert Forman Horton (1937), passim; R. T. Jones, Congregationalism in Eng. 325–6; Brit. Weekly, 31 Dec. 1886, 16; D.N.B.
[80] Thompson, Hampstead, 388.
[81] Barratt, Annals, iii. 105.
[82] Pevsner, Lond. ii. 188; The Times, 4 July 1884, 4e.
[83] C.C.C., Clarke MSS. xviii. 69.
[84] Peel and Marriott, Horton, 268; Cong. Year Bk. (1939), 417.
[85] S.C.L., 18.2/pamphlet file, Lyndhurst Rd. Utd. Ref. Ch., copy of Camden L.B. rep. 1979.
[86] Horton, Autobiog. 50, 65; Barratt, Annals, iii. 106; Cong. Year Bk. (1895), 301.
[87] Cong. Year Bk. (1894), 172–3; Pevsner, Lond. ii. 189.
[88] Below, Judaism.   [89] C.H.R. vi. 13.
[90] G.R.O. Worship Reg. no. 23106; Return of Chs., Chapels and Bldgs. reg. for worship, H.C. 401, p. 171 (1882), l.
[91] G.R.O. Worship Reg. no. 26260.
[92] Bentwich, Vale of Health (1977), 73–5.
[93] G.R.O. Worship Reg. no. 29842.
[94] Ibid. nos. 41813, 42386; Wade, Streets of Hampstead (1972), 33.
[95] Pevsner, Lond. ii. 188; G.R.O. Worship Reg. no. 42823.
[96] Booth, Life and Labour, iii (1), 216.
[97] G.R.O. Worship Reg. no. 56518.

CHRISTIAN COMMUNITY. Ch. of the Christian Community, no. 32 Glenilla Rd., designed by Kenneth Bayes,[98] built and reg. 1948.[99] Seasons of concerts also held there 1980s.[1]

CHRISTIAN SCIENTISTS. Fourth Ch. of Christ Scientist reg. 1953 on ground floor of Stanfield Ho., Prince Arthur Rd., probably in part behind main ho., called Stanfield hall. Closed 1978,[2] and property thereafter provided income for Ch. Moved to no. 36 Mill Lane,[3] where basement used for worship and ground floor as reading room 1986.

SEVENTH-DAY ADVENTISTS. Sect's Lond. ch. moved from Regent Street to former Oxendon Presb. ch., Haverstock Hill, 1970. Reopened after renovation as Oxendon Adventist ch. 1972.[4]

SPIRITUALISTS. Spiritualist Ch. of the New Revealing, no. 131 West End Lane, reg. 1918, closed by 1925.[5]
Hampstead Spiritual Temple, Willoughby hall, no. 1 Willoughby Rd., reg. 1938 and again 1945, closed by 1954.[6]

OTHER DENOMINATIONS AND UNSPECIFIED MISSIONS. The following were reg. by undesignated Christians: hall in Denning Rd., 1886, closed by 1954; mission room in Vale of Health, 1899–1906; Evangelical hall, no. 158A West End Lane, 1923, closed by 1925; mission rooms over shops at nos. 192–8 Broadhurst Gdns., 1920, closed by 1954; United Sanctuary of the New Day of the Nook, first floor, Windsor Terr., 1938, closed by 1954; Institute of Occult Social Science Religion, ground floor no. 17 Sherriff Rd., 1938, closed by 1954; Parkhill chapel, no. 17 Fleet Rd., 1960, by the evangelical mission formerly at Malden hall, Malden Rd., Kentish Town (St. Pancras) from 1886 and used by Strict Bapt. 1982; Faith Christian Fellowship, no. 339A Finchley Rd., 1982.[7]

JUDAISM. Like other City merchants, many Jews bought houses as country retreats. Daniel Defoe commented in the 1720s that Jews seemed to have a preference for Highgate and Hampstead. Eliezer Isaac Keyser retired to Hampstead in 1812 until his death in 1820, leaving a series of letters about his life there, and Jewish names were recorded occasionally in the late 18th and early 19th century, although there was no place of worship.[8]
More widespread settlement took place from 1870, the newcomers being served by St. John's Wood synagogue, Abbey Road, just south of the parish, from 1876 until Hampstead synagogue opened in

1892. Hampstead was popular with Jewish scholars and intellectuals in the 1880s and 1890s, while many Jews from the City moved into Kilburn in the 1880s and followed the spread of building north and west.[9] From 1905 Kilburn was served by Brondesbury synagogue, Chevening Road (Willesden).[10] The period between the World Wars brought many Jewish refugees from Europe, especially to Swiss Cottage and West Hampstead, and several congregations set up their own synagogues.[11]
Hampstead synagogue, Dennington Park Road, was founded after a meeting of c. 20 members of St. John's Wood synagogue in 1889. A second group held more radical services at West Hampstead town hall from 1890 and then at Kilburn town hall until 1893. Hampstead synagogue, designed by Delissa Joseph, was built in 1892 to accommodate 700. It came under the guidance of the United Synagogue, but concessions were made to the strong desire of Jews in England for reform. The number of seats let rose from 293 in 1893 to 668 by 1900, and membership continued to rise until Hampstead was the largest congregation in the United Synagogue. Seating was increased in the body of the building, by a classroom at the side in 1897, and by further additions in 1900–1. Attendance 1903: 898 a.m. Hebrew and religious classes were started in 1891 at West Hampstead town hall, later moving to the synagogue, with 72 children in 1892 and 200 in 1908. Youth services from 1925 led to the opening of a junior synagogue in 1935. A community centre was built 1962–4 adjoining the synagogue.[12]
North-west London Hebrew Institute, no. 1 Minster Road, Shoot-up Hill, was registered for worship in 1928 and closed by 1954.[13]
The Beth Hamedrash Kehilath Israel synagogue was registered in rooms at no. 6 Minster Road in 1938 and had closed by 1960.[14]
Regent's Park and Belsize Park district synagogue opened at the corner of Eton Road and Eton Villas in 1938 and was affiliated to the United Synagogue. It was rebuilt in 1960 on the same site and renamed South Hampstead district synagogue.[15]
The Adath Yisroel congregation registered Sarah Klausner Memorial synagogue at no. 11 Fairfax Road in 1943. It moved to no. 33 Compayne Gardens in 1945, to no. 31 Broadhurst Gardens in 1947, and no. 10A Cranfield Gardens c. 1974. A constituent member of the Union of Orthodox Hebrew Congregations,[16] it was in use in 1985.
Shomrei Hadath synagogue (Beth Hamedrash), a constituent synagogue of the Federation of Synagogues, was opened 1946 in the former West Hampstead Congregational church, no. 527A Finchley Road,[17] and was in use in 1985.
New Liberal Jewish congregation was established

[98] Wade, *More Streets*, 44.
[99] G.R.O. Worship Reg. no. 62033.
[1] S.C.L., 19.97/pamphlet file, Christian Community Ch.
[2] G.R.O. Worship Reg. nos. 64016, 73841.
[3] Camden L.B., List of Places of Worship, 1982; Char. Com. files.
[4] G.R.O. Worship Reg. no. 72284; Wade, *More Streets*, 42.   [5] G.R.O. Worship Reg. no. 47268.
[6] Ibid. nos. 58158, 61135.
[7] Ibid. nos. 29524, 29602, 36975, 48704, 47976, 57906, 57877, 67998, 76405; Camden L.B., List of places of worship, 1982.

[8] C. Roth, *Essays and Portraits in Anglo-Jewish Hist.* (1962), 242–9.
[9] *Trans. Jewish Hist. Soc.* xxi. 89–90.
[10] *V.C.H. Mdx.* vii. 246.
[11] Below.
[12] S.C.L., Hampstead Syn., cuttings; R. Apple, *Hampstead Synagogue 1892–1967* (1967).
[13] G.R.O. Worship Reg. no. 51430.
[14] Ibid. no. 58288; *Jewish Year Bk.* (1960).
[15] A. Newman, *United Synagogue 1870–1970* (1976), 221–2; G.R.O. Worship Reg. no. 58845.
[16] G.R.O. Worship Reg. nos. 60524, 61124, 61616.
[17] Ibid. no. 61564.

in 1939, and registered a synagogue at no. 30 Buckland Crescent in 1943, moving to its own building at no. 51 Belsize Square in 1951. Renamed Belsize Square synagogue *c.* 1972, it was a constituent of the Union of Liberal and Progressive Synagogues[18] and was in use in 1985.

BUDDHISM. In 1962 the Hampstead Buddhist Vihara was set up at no. 131 Haverstock Hill, to teach Buddhist beliefs, and was registered for worship from 1965.[19]

SIKHISM. The Guru Ram Das Ashram was registered for worship at no. 246 Belsize Road *c.* 1982.[20]

OTHER FAITHS. Theists registered Frognal Bijou Picture Palace, no. 158 Finchley Road, in 1914; closed by 1921.[21]
Zoroastrians registered Zoroastrian House, no. 88 Compayne Gardens, for worship in 1971.[22]

EDUCATION. A charity school for the poor, possibly at the workhouse, existed in 1731, when the Wells charity repaid the parish's debt for fitting it up.[23] The only other assistance for educating the poor before 1787 came from John Stock's charity, by will of 1780, which included annual payments for educating and clothing 6 boys and 4 girls between the ages of about 8 and 14; in 1818 the charity paid for teaching and clothing 10 boys and 6 girls at Hampstead Parochial schools.[24] In 1787 a Sunday school for the poor was started and its success led to provision for day pupils in 1788: at first the 12 boys and 12 girls were taught in private schools but *c.* 10 years later their own schools had been formed, which in 1815 became affiliated to the National Society.[25]

In 1833 Hampstead had two infants' schools, one being at Kilburn, with a total of 159 pupils, and three weekday schools for the poor: the two Hampstead Parochial schools, with 150 boys and 112 girls, and the Roman Catholic school for 25 girls. Kilburn had a day and Sunday school for 45 boys and 40 girls, while another 16 girls received free instruction on Sundays from a lady at her home. Some basic education was also provided at the three recently started Church of England Sunday schools with a total of 282 boys and 202 girls, and at the Baptist Sunday school with 50 pupils and the Wesleyan with 51, both started in the 1820s.[26] By 1846 the Kilburn schools had disappeared, but the infants', Roman Catholic, and Parochial schools had been joined by a day school at West End with 31, a girls' school for 40, North End dame school for 26, and St. John's chapel schools for 76 boys, 40 girls, and 40 infants. In 1846 883 children out of the population of 10,093

received free or almost free education at the National or Church schools, and about 25 at the Roman Catholic school.[27] In 1851, of 1,577 pupils attending day schools, 857 were at public and 720 at private schools. Though the total was equally divided between boys and girls, the majority of boys, 500, attended the public schools, while the majority of girls, 428, attended private schools. Over 700 of the public school pupils went to the 8 National or Church schools, leaving 49 at the R.C. school, 62 at the blind school, 26 boys at a ragged school, and 15 girls at the orphan school. In addition 708 children received some education at the 4 Church and 3 nonconformist Sunday schools.[28]

Until the mid 1870s, new district churches all provided some form of day school, at any rate for infants, as did some of the nonconformist chapels, either singly, as at Rosslyn Hill in the 1860s, or as a combined effort, as at Heath Street in 1862. Church schools opening before 1875 included Christ Church (1855), All Souls (*c.* 1860), St. Mary, Kilburn (1864), St. Paul (1870), St. Saviour (1871), and Holy Trinity (1873). An additional Roman Catholic school was opened in Kilburn in the 1860s.[29] By the time that the London School Board took office the Church, British, and Roman Catholic schools provided accommodation for over 3,000, with only about 1,900 on their rolls.[30] Although two Church schools were not good enough to be recognized as elementary schools, the board did not need to provide a school in Hampstead until 1879 when Fleet Road opened.

Three more schools were opened by the London School Board, all in West Hampstead: Netherwood Street (1881), Broomsleigh Street (1886), and Kingsgate Road (1903). There was great difficulty, however, in obtaining a central site for a school to replace three voluntary schools which had been transferred to the board: Heath Street, Rosslyn Hill, and St. Stephen's. Attempts to purchase sites in Well Walk in 1900 and 1901 caused an outcry,[31] and the Parochial and Christ Church schools waged a vigorous campaign to raise their own numbers and so obviate the need for a new board school. Managers of Church schools grew all the more bitter as competition from board schools, with their much better facilities, increased. The improvements required by the London School Board and Board of Education caused much financial strain on the congregations, which was made worse by the abolition of fees in board schools, as the Church schools could not afford to follow suit.[32] Despite the campaign, which included the publication of the correspondence with the board in a pamphlet distributed to all Hampstead residents,[33] the board eventually compulsorily purchased a site at New End; the school there was opened in 1906 by the L.C.C. The Education Act, 1902, giving support from the rates to Anglican schools, aroused further anger in Hampstead. A branch of the Passive Resistance League was formed,

[18] Ibid. nos. 60422, 63061; *Jewish Year Bk.* (1973, 1986).
[19] Wade, *More Streets*, 40; G.R.O. Worship Reg. no. 69941.
[20] G.R.O. Worship Reg. no. 76513.
[21] Ibid. no. 46179; above, social.
[22] G.R.O. Worship Reg. nos. 72604, 73638.
[23] *Endowed Chars. Lond. III*, H.C. 252, p. 88 (1900), lxi.
[24] Below, charities.
[25] Below, pub. schs. (Hampstead Parochial).
[26] *Educ. Enq. Abstract, 1833*, H.C. 62 (1835), xlii. 93.

[27] Nat. Soc. *Inquiry, 1846–7*, Mdx. 6–7.
[28] *Census*, 1851.
[29] For individual schs., below.
[30] G.L.R.O., SBL 1518.
[31] *The Times*, 6 Nov. 1900, 7*f*; 24 July 1901, 9*f*.
[32] F. Nagy, 'Development of Elem. Sch. Provision and Use of Schs. as Welfare Institutions in Hampstead between 1902 and 1914' (diss. for Teacher's Cert. Exam. 1977, in S.C.L.), 20–3.
[33] Nat. Soc. files, Christ Ch. sch.

with the support of leading nonconformist ministers, but only *c.* 100 received a court summons for non-payment of rates.[34]

More difficulties came with the L.C.C., which inspected the eight surviving non-provided element-ary schools in 1904. Only St. Mary's Roman Catholic school had to be closed, as it gave a serious fire hazard, but two others were restricted to girls and infants, as there were not enough entrances for boys, and the L.C.C. wanted the remaining five to be re-organized for mixed and infants under one head;[35] in most cases, however, reorganization did not take place until well after the First World War. In 1905 elementary school accommodation totalled 5,091 places in the four council schools, with another 612 to come at New End, and 1,906 places in seven non-provided schools. Although the number of places exceeded demand, some schools, such as Fleet Road, were still overcrowded because of their popu-larity or because the distribution of places was uneven.[36]

A graver problem for Church schools was the L.C.C.'s insistence on improvements. Some, such as repairs to drainage systems, were very expensive, particularly for those congregations whose numbers were starting to fall. The Christ Church managers sought advice from the National Society, as they not only had to pay for improvements, but saw a threat from the big new school at New End and therefore wondered if they should close their own school. The society's response was sanguine: the managers should retain their school, as the L.C.C. would have to maintain it if it had the required number of pupils; if they should not be allowed to continue with three departments, they should try with boys only or with girls and infants, as a mixed school would not be morally or educationally good in their district. It was thought that there should be no difficulty in making a smaller school suitable for better-class children. The very existence of a large council school made it important to preserve the Church school, and there was a growing reaction in favour of provision for the middle class.[37]

The National Society's optimism was justified; despite financial problems, and the cramped sites and buildings, all the non-provided schools except All Souls survived in 1986, being popular especially with middle-class parents. One, St. Paul's, moved in 1972 to spacious new premises overlooking Primrose Hill.[38] The need to replace buildings was recognized: in 1974 the North Camden (Hampstead) deanery synod proposed an annual levy on each of Hamp-stead's 15 churches to help finance the maintenance and building costs of the remaining six Church schools.[39]

Council schools also had their problems. Over-crowding remained: the limit of 60 to a class was often exceeded, especially for infants, and the further reductions in size, to 48 for infants and 40 for seniors, were not achieved until 1936.[40] Only one new school, an infants' at Kingsgate Road in 1914,

was opened before the 1950s. In the school plan of 1947 all the existing county primary schools were retained,[41] and one new one, Fitzjohn's, was opened in 1954, with opposition again from Hampstead Parochial where there were still places vacant.[42]

Secondary schools had little chance to become established in Hampstead. Under the London School Board, Fleet Road had had a higher grade school and Kingsgate had taken senior pupils. Neither, how-ever, was accepted by the Board of Education as a higher elementary school, nor, despite its many scholarship successes, was Fleet one of the schools in the L.C.C. area that became a central school after 1910. Pupils had to transfer to schools outside the borough, in St. Pancras or Paddington,[43] a need that was the more surprising because Hampstead children won nearly twice the London average of junior county scholarships to grammar schools.[44]

In the reorganizations of the 1930s, Hampstead Parochial and Harben also took senior pupils, but under the 1947 plan only Harben was to become a secondary school. Another secondary school was opened at Fleet Road in 1955, but closed in the 1960s, and Harben became the annexe to a Padding-ton R.C. secondary school in 1961, so that almost all pupils of secondary age again went outside the parish. A very few elementary-school children won scholar-ships to leading local independent schools which took direct-grant pupils after 1918: Haberdashers' Aske's and University College schools for boys, and South Hampstead High for girls. In 1947 the L.C.C. supported 30 boys at Haberdashers' and 140 girls at S. Hampstead High; University College school no longer applied for grant aid but still took 25 boys supported by the L.C.C.,[45] in order to gain bright pupils.[46] After Haberdashers' moved their boys' school to Hertfordshire in 1961, the L.C.C. opened a comprehensive secondary school in their buildings, but it was so located that it served Hendon and Willesden as much as Hampstead.

As part of Camden, the area joined Westminster in a division of the I.L.E.A. under the London Government Act, 1963.[47] In 1983 Hampstead had five county primary and eight non-provided primary schools, one county secondary school, and four special schools.

Public schools.[48] Except where otherwise stated, basic historical information and figures of accom-modation and average attendance have been taken from: files on Church of England schools at the National Society; P.R.O., ED 3/19; ED 7/75, 81; *Educ. Enq. Abstract, 1833*, H.C. 62, p. 93 (1835), xlii; National Society, *Inquiry, 1846–7*, Mdx. 6–7; *Mins. of Educ. Cttee. of Council, 1849* [1215], H.C. (1850), xliii; *1852–3* [1623], H.C. (1852–3), lxxix; *Rep. of Educ. Cttee. of Council, 1867–8* [4051], H.C. (1867–8), xxv; *1876–7* [C. 1780–I], H.C. (1877), xxix; *1880–1* [C. 2948–I], H.C. (1881), xxxii; *1890–1* [C. 643–I], H.C. (1890–1), xxvii; *Return of Elem. Schs. 1899* [Cd. 315], H.C. (1900), lxv (2);

[34] Nagy, 'Elem. Sch. Provision', 27–8.
[35] Ibid. 32–6.
[36] Ibid. 41, 43.
[37] Nat. Soc. files, Christ Ch.
[38] Below.
[39] Nat. Soc. files, Christ Ch.
[40] Nagy, 'Elem. Sch. Provision', 60, 63.
[41] L.C.C. *Sch. Plan* (1947).
[42] Nat. Soc. files, Hampstead Parochial.
[43] Nagy, 'Elem. Sch. Provision', 80.

[44] J. S. Maclure, *One Hundred Years of Lond. Educ.* (1970), 121.
[45] L.C.C. *Sch. Plan* (1947), 60.
[46] H. J. K. Usher, C. D. Black-Hawkins, G. J. Carrick, *Angel Without Wings: Hist. of Univ. Coll. Sch. 1830–1980* (1981), 74.
[47] *Ann. Abstract of Gtr. Lond. Statistics* (1967).
[48] Private schs. are treated separately below.

Return of Non-Provided Schs. H.C. 178–XXXIII (1906), lxxxviii; *Bd. of Educ., List 21, 1908–38* (H.M.S.O.); L.C.C. *Educ. Svce. Particulars* (1937 and later edns.); L.C.C. (I.L.E.A. from 1965) *Educ. Svce. Inf.*(1951 and later edns.); *Catholic Educ.*(1978).

The following abbreviations are used in addition to those in the index: a.a., average attendance; accn., accommodation; amalg., amalgamated, amalgamation; B, boy, boys; Bapt., Baptist; C.E., Church of England; Cong., Congregationalist; demol., demolished; dept., department; G, girl, girls; J, JB, JG, JM, junior, junior boys, girls, mixed; I, infant, infants; M, mixed; mod., modern; Meth., Methodist; Nat., National; parl., parliamentary; perm., permanent; R.C., Roman Catholic; reorg., reorganized; roll, numbers on roll; S, SB, SG, SM, senior, senior boys, girls, mixed; S.B.L., School Board for London; sch., school; sec., secondary; sep., separate; tech., technical; temp., temporary; vol., voluntary; V., vicar; Wes., Wesleyan. The word 'school' is to be understood after each named entry. Separate departments are indicated by commas: B, G, I; JM, I.

ALL SOULS C.E., Fairhazel Gdns., Belsize Rd. Founded *c.* 1860 in large hay loft in Victoria Mews, Fairfax Rd., granted free of rent by Mr. Yeo. 1871 accn. 72, a.a. 42: instruction poor and sch. mainly refuge for children of omnibus drivers and similar. Wilson fam. conveyed site in Victoria Mews (later Fairfax Pl.) at corner of Fairhazel Gdns. 1871,[49] where one room for 194 BGI built 1872. Financed by vol. contributions, sch. pence, parl. grant. From 73 in 1876, a.a. rose to 125 in 1899, and 173 in 1906. Union with Nat. Soc. 1892. Reorg. for 105 M, 52 I to meet L.C.C.'s improved standards. 1908 a.a. 125 M, 52 I. Lack of space prevented expansion. Bldg. and playground renovated 1927. Roll 1940: 125 M, 40 I. Sch. closed by 1951 as part of L.C.C.'s post-war plans.[50]

BARTRAMS R.C., see Rosary.

BECKFORD PRIMARY, Dornfell Street, Mill Lane, West End. Opened 1886 by S.B.L. as Broomsleigh Street bd. sch. for BGI. Accn. nearly doubled to 1,381 by 1894. By 1895 had cookery and laundry centre and manual training centre.[51] Reorg. between 1927 and 1932 for 630 JM, 368 I, and renamed Beckford. Roll 1940: 693 JM, 364 I. Inc. nursery class 1958. Roll 1986: 358 JM & I.

BERKELEY RD. BD. Temp. sch. opened 1874 for GBI in rooms rented for one year. 1874–5 a.a. 185.

BROOMSLEIGH STREET, see Beckford.

CHRIST CHURCH C.E. PRIMARY, Christchurch Hill, New End. Dist. schs. under construction 1854.[52] I opened in bldg. on Wells char. land; trustees refused a lease in order to preserve right to build, but sch. still there 1892. Site perhaps that vacated by Parochial I sch. Site for B, G schs. conveyed by Fras. Hoare 1855,[53] and schoolroom and classroom built for each with aid of parl. grants. Children not required to learn catechism or attend Sun. sch.[54] I sch. received grant of £250 from Wells char. 1857. Schs. financed by subscriptions, sch. pence, parl. grants. 1868 a.a. 254. Roll 1871: 117 B, 121 G, 104 I. 1880 accn. 393; 1906 accn. 449, but reduced to 372 by 1908; heavy expenditure required by L.C.C. Competition from New End sch., but Nat. Soc. advised sch. reorg. 1917 for 202 M, 130 I. New porch 1919 allowed official recognition of nursery class of 20. Recognized accn. reduced 1922 to 200 M, 96 I. Reorg. 1926 for 296 M, and again between 1932 and 1936 for 294 JM & I. 1937 a.a. 152; 1949 a.a. 207. Roll 1967: 170. Children mainly middle-class and from overseas by 1970s. Parents resisted proposals 1970–2 to merge with Parochial schs. on new site, preferring the 'village school' atmosphere. Decline in nos. during early 1970s reversed 1975. Teacher's ho. in playground converted to maisonnette 1975 and basement used as community centre. Roll 1986: 155 JM & I.

EMMANUEL C.E. PRIMARY (formerly WEST END NAT.), no. 101 Mill Lane. Site conveyed to trustees and enfranchised 1845.[55] Sch. and teacher's ho. 1845, designed by Chas. Miles of West End Hall; opened 1846 with accn. for 146.[56] Roll 1846–7: 14 B, 17 G under one mistress. Bldg. grant from Nat. Soc. Financed by subscriptions and sch. pence which did not cover teacher's salary 1848. Premises and instruction efficient for 95 in 1871, when roll 37. B, 39 G, aged 3 to 11. Single schoolroom with I in gallery 1872; teacher's ho. converted into classroom, making accn. 132, and new ho. built on opposite side of original bldg. 1874. In 1880s a.a. doubled and continued to rise in 1890s. Additional classroom 1886, making accn. 190. Enlargement of 1874 and part of original room replaced 1892, but both new room and I room badly ventilated 1895, when new roof and other repairs needed and lack of staff hampered sch. Dist. then poorest in Hampstead and had difficulty in financing sch. 1899 accn. 248 M & I, a.a. 242. For I and G of all ages by 1914, when inspection found many bldg. defects. G room divided into 3 to increase accn. from 80 to 116, with I room remaining at 93, by 1927. In 1936 36 SG transferred to Netherwood Street and sch. reorg. for 217 JG & I, a.a. 149. Reorg. for JM & I between 1964 and 1970. Former G.P.O. site at no. 160 Mill Lane cleared by 1973 but plans still in abeyance 1986. So overcrowded that over 90 children walked to par. hall in Broomsleigh Street for lunch 1968; 4 rooms for 140 children and only 1 room for head and staff 1970.[57] Roll 1986: 110 JM & I.

FITZJOHN'S PRIMARY, no. 86A Fitzjohn's Ave. Opened 1954 for JM & I, incorporating fine schoolroom and chapel designed by Wm. Munt and built 1858 for Royal Soldiers' Daughters' Home in grounds of Vane Ho.[58] Roll 1986: 202 JM & I.

FLEET PRIMARY, Fleet Rd., Gospel Oak. First bd. sch. in Hampstead, opened 1879 for 1,207 with SM in one bldg. of 8 classrooms, I in another of 2 rooms on same site. Sch. pence. Served quickly growing area; new classroom for 377 1881 and several extensions until 1890s.[59] JM dept. opened 1884. 1890

[49] P.R.O., C 54/17340, no. 34.
[50] A. R. Colville, *Lond. Northern Reaches* (1951), 87.
[51] Nagy, 'Elem. Sch. Provision', 19.
[52] Nat. Soc. files, Hampstead Par.
[53] P.R.O., C 54/14857, no. 14.
[54] *Endowed Chars. Lond. III,* H.C. 252, pp. 132–3 (1900), lxi.
[55] P.R.O., C 54/13176, nos. 5, 6; C 54/13185, no. 15.

[56] Additional inf. from T. S. Jennings, '*Sch. in Mill Lane'—Acct. of Emmanuel Primary Sch. 1845–1972* [n.d.].
[57] *Hampstead News,* 27 Dec. 1968, 17 July 1970; *H.H.E.* 24 Oct. 1969, 13 Apr. 1973; J. Tucker, *Emmanuel Ch., West End, Hampstead* (1981), 83.
[58] *Images of Hampstead,* 113; Wade, *Streets of Hampstead,* 69; below, priv. schs.
[59] Nagy, 'Elem. Sch. Provision', 15.

accn. 1,891. By 1890s known as 'Harrow of the board schools', regularly winning majority of S.B.L. and Wells char. scholarships to sec. schs.; in 1896 won top 2 scholarships for G and top 2 for B out of all pupils' in L.C.C.'s competition.[60] By 1897 had cookery centre, laboratory, manual training centre, and drawing class, and senior part recognized as higher grade sch. By 1900 no longer catered only for poor, drawing children from considerable distance, but after establishment of central schs. did not receive S pupils from other schs.[61] Roll 1940: 520 SM, 424 JM, 408 I. Reorg. by 1951 as Fleet primary for JM, I, and combined JM & I by 1964. Fleet sec. M opened on same site by 1958, but became Fleet Youth Centre by 1964 and Fleet Community Educ. Centre between 1970 and 1976. In 1986 educ. centre was in original bldgs. fronting Agincourt Rd., while JM & I sch. used mod. bldgs. on Fleet Rd. side. Roll 1986: 226 JM & I.

HAMPSTEAD, Westbere Rd., Cricklewood. Opened c. 1961 for SM in former Haberdashers' Aske's B sch. Roll 1983: 1,114 SM, with additional bldgs. on c. 6-a. site and large 6th form.[62] Roll 1986: 1,069 SM.

HAMPSTEAD PAROCHIAL C.E. PRIMARY, Holly Bush Vale.[63] Day sch. for poor founded 1788 by Philo-Investigists Soc.: 12 B and 12 G selected from soc.'s Sun. sch. Funds increased by collections at par. ch. and Hampstead chapel, allowing increase to 58 pupils in 1790. Clothing given from 1789 to Sun. sch. pupils and then to some day pupils. In 1798 soc. known as Sun. Sch. Soc. and teachers had to be members of Reformed Ch. Day B taught reading, writing, and arithmetic; day G reading, knitting, and sewing. B taught at private sch. of Thos. Mitchell, member of soc., until 1806, and then temporarily in Chicken Ho. Early premises for G sch. unknown, but c. 1799 occupied new bldg. in Yorkshire Grey Yard. New B schoolroom built c. 1808 near Fenton Ho., Hampstead Grove. From 1815 schs. governed by Parochial Sch. Soc., which decided on support by vol. contributions and on educ. in accordance with doctrines of C.E., but admission without religious test; sch. was affiliated to Nat. Soc. By 1816 G bldg. dilapidated and sch. moved to new bldg. at corner of Holly Walk and Mount Vernon built with aid of vol. contributions.[64] B moved c. 1815 to Sam. Hoare's schoolroom (later New End Bapt. chapel) until 1826, when new room built with permission of guardians of poor at SE. corner of wkho. gdn. on site held at will from par.[65] with vol. contributions.

I sch. founded 1827 or 1829 in bldg. near Well Walk on site belonging to Wells char.: rent paid to lessees until lease expired 1850; thereafter none demanded. Roll 112 I in 1833, when master had rent-free ho. and salary paid from vol. contributions and sch. pence. B sch. had 150 in 1833, when master received £90 p.a. G sch. had 112; mistress had accn. and £50 p.a. B and G schs. also supported by sch.

pence, vol. contributions, and up to £12 p.a. from John Stock's char. for educating 12 orphan B. Rolls 1846-7: 102 B, 89 G, 153 I.

B and I schs. were in dist. assigned to Christ Ch. 1854. B sch. very dilapidated, so new schs. on freehold site at Bradley's Bldgs. (later Holly Bush Vale) completed 1856,[66] paid for by subscriptions, grants from parl., Wells char., Shakespeare's char., Nat. Soc. Additional land 1862 and 1865;[67] G sch. for 100 built on site c. 1862. B, G & I schs. each had 2 rooms and teacher's ho. 1871; rolls: 125 B, 80 G, 90 I. Subjects inc. history, grammar, geography, needlework, singing. Part of site sold to M.B.W 1887[68] to pay for new I classroom. Mission hall built on part of site 1891-2, with large upper room fitted up for cookery classes for many schs. by 1900. L.C.C. plan for M sch. resisted until 1926 when reorg. for 362 M & I. Falling pop. led to further reorg. 1936 whereby Parochial sch. became SM, with accn. 314, J went to Christ Ch., and I to New End. Roll 1940: 317 SM, before bldg. requisitioned. Reopened 1951 as JM & I vol. aided primary with roll of 299. Roll 1986: 131 JM & I.

HARBEN, Linstead Street, Kilburn. Opened 1881 by S.B.L. as Netherwood Street bd. sch. for c. 600 BGI, 18 classrooms. 1880 accn. increased to 1,587; a.a. 1,056 and 40 at evg. sch. Cookery centre added by 1895.[69] Reorg. between 1927 and 1932 for 360 SB, 360 SG, 426 I, and renamed the Harben. Reorg. 1940 with roll of 440 SM. In 1951 2 schs. formed: Harben sec. for SM, Harben primary for JM & I, but latter closed by 1955. Sec. sch. closed 1961, when bldg. became lower sch. annexe of St. George R.C. comprehensive, Lanark Rd. (Paddington).[70]

HEATH STREET BRITISH.[71] M & I schs. opened 1862 to meet demand for freer type of ch. sch. than C.E. Nat. Met in Heath Street Bapt. ch. schoolroom but controlled by cttee. of several dissenting chs. Over 100 enrolled by end of 1st year. In 1871 M sch. with 300 accn. in 2 rooms gave extensive range of instruction at expense of proficiency; roll 112 B and 58 G under one master. I sch. with 56 accn. in one room gave fairly good instruction; roll 70 under one mistress. Recognized as pub. elem. sch. and received parl. grant from 1872. Also financed by sch. pence (2d.-9d.), collections. Roll 1881: 303; 1886: 400. Evg. classes for S pupils started 1887, teaching drawing, shorthand, French, woodwork. 1890 accn. 508, a.a. 325. Taken over by S.B.L. 1900 when roll 264 M, 156 I, but treated as temp. sch. with accn. 261 M, 127 I. Defended as flourishing sch. by managers of Christ Ch. Nat. 1901. Roll 1906: 230 M, 110 I, when pupils transferred to New End.

HOARE'S, see Mrs. Hoare's; Samuel Hoare's British.

HOLY TRINITY C.E. PRIMARY (formerly TRINITY NAT.), Trinity Walk, Maresfield Gdns. Opened 1873 in former temp. ch. in Conduit Fields (Belsize Lane) with rooms for M, I; roll c. 90. Sch. pence. Site for

---

[60] Thompson, *Hampstead*, 416; Baines, *Rec. Hampstead*, 324-5; Maclure, *One Hundred Yrs. of Lond. Educ.* 57.

[61] Nagy, 'Elem. Sch. Provision', 19, 81.

[62] I.L.E.A. *Changing Schs. at Eleven: Sec. Schs. in City of Westm., Camden* (1983), 14.

[63] Additional inf. from *Endowed Chars. Lond. III*, 128-32; E. V. Knox, *Adventures of a Sch.* [1969].

[64] P.R.O., C 54/16005, no. 7.

[65] G.L.R.O., P81/JN1/15, mins. of guardians, 1 Mar. 1824, 6 Mar. 1826.

[66] P.R.O., C 54/14904, no. 19; 54/15018, no. 11.

[67] Ibid. C 54/16417, nos. 12, 13.

[68] Ibid. C 54/19201, no. 9.

[69] Nagy, 'Elem. Sch. Provision', 19.

[70] Below, Paddington, educ.

[71] Additional inf. from Buffard, *Heath Street Bapt. Ch.* 9, 13-14, 16, 19; P.R.O., ED 21/11581.

perm. sch. granted 1874 by Wilson fam.[72] Sch. built 1876 for 174 M, 70 I, with grants from parl. and Nat. Soc. 1880 a.a. 106. 1890 accn. 284, a.a. 179. After Educ. Act, 1902, large sums spent on improvements; by 1908 accn. reduced to 139 M, 102 I. 1927 accn. 109 M, 80 I. 1936 accn. 206 M & I. Renamed Holy Trinity 1932. Attendance declined from 183 to 157 in 1930s, when ch. had difficulty in financing the sch.; pop. of dist. 80 per cent foreign by 1942. Roll 1940: 176 M, 46 I. 1942 a.a. 150. By 1951 reorg. for JM & I. New classroom built in playground 1978. Roll 1986: 174 JM & I.

KILBURN DAY AND SUN. Founded 1829; in 1833 had 45 B under master, 40 G under mistress. Nothing further known.

KILBURN I. Started 1833 with 47 I; mistress paid from vol. contributions. Nothing further known.

KILBURN R.C., Quex Rd. Opened c. 1868 in 2 rooms of shopkeeper's ho. Roll 1871: 29 B and 34 G all ages under one mistress; I in dark kitchen but premises for 300 being purchased and would probably allow recognition as public elem. sch. 1880 accn. 337, a.a. 200. Not listed among public schs. thereafter, but an R.C. sch. in Mazenod Ave., behind ch., in 1891,[73] on site later used for Mazenod primary (q.v.).

KINGSGATE, Messina Ave., Kilburn.[74] Opened 1903 as Kingsgate Rd. bd. sch. by S.B.L. and intended as higher grade sch., but after disagreement with Bd. of Educ. opened for SM, taking seniors from Netherwood Street. 1908 accn. 452 SM, a.a. 333. Standard not good enough for higher elem. status. I dept. for 366 opened 1914. Reorg. between 1927 and 1932 for 480 JM, 306 I. Roll 1940: 528 JM, 322 I. By 1951 became Kingsgate primary for JM, I. Roll 1986: 171 JM; 197 I.

MAZENOD R.C. PRIMARY, Mazenod Ave., Kilburn. Vol. aided sch. opened 1967 for JM & I, on site used for sch. or annexe since 1947.[75] Roll 1977: 250 JM & I; 1986: 215 JM & I.

MRS. HOARE'S.[76] Hannah Hoare, w. of Sam. (d. 1825), said to have had G sch. c. 1812. Probably that supported by dau. Sarah Hoare in East Heath Rd. and possibly that listed 1846 with 40 G under one mistress and financed by subscriptions. Nothing further known.

NETHERWOOD STREET BD., see Harben.

NEW END PRIMARY, Streatley Pl.[77] Opened by L.C.C. 1906, after much difficulty in obtaining site, for 198 SM, 194 JM, 220 I, replacing Heath Street Brit., St. Steph.'s Nat., and Rosslyn Hill. Tried new system of combining GBI under one head, but without Bd. of Educ.'s sanction, so reorg. for M, I under 2 heads 1910; a.a. 489, but declined steadily to 94 in 1938. 1922 accn. 270 M, 192 I. 1927 accn. 350 M, 192 I. Reorg. 1932 for 336 M & I, and 1936 for 348 JM & I. Roll 1940: 176 JM, 184 I. Became New End primary for JM & I 1951. Roll 1986: 187 JM & I.

NORTH END I, Sandy Rd.[78] Originated in sch. held in mistress's ho. at North End, which had 12 B and 14 G in 1846. Schoolroom built by pub. subscriptions 1840 on land given by lord of manor. Financed by vol. contributions, sch. pence; deficit made up by John Gurney Hoare 1872 and sch. managed by his w. Room for 30 I under one mistress; premises and instruction satisfactory 1871. Reorg. as pub. elem. sch. but apparently did not receive parl. grant and was not maintained by L.C.C. 1903. Closed 1907.

NORTH-WEST LONDON JEWISH, Minster Rd., Cricklewood. Opened 1945 as vol. aided Jewish sch. for JM & I. Moved to Willesden 1958.[79]

ROSARY R.C. PRIMARY, no. 238 Haverstock Hill. Formerly Bartrams R.C. sch. at orphanage run by Sisters of Providence from c. 1867.[80] 1871 accn. 68 and roll 48 G, aged 3 to over 13, of whom 39 boarded at orphanage. Sch. pence. Not recognized as pub. elem. sch. 1871 but received parl. grant from 1876. Accn. increased to 116 by 1880, 250 by 1890, 337 by 1899. Not maintained by L.C.C. until 1921. 1922 accn. 198 G, 74 I; 1937, 158 G, 114 I.[81] After Second World War became Rosary R.C. vol. aided primary for JG & I, reorg. for JM, I by 1969. Roll 1977: 188 JM, 128 I; 1986: 295 JM & I.

ROSSLYN HILL BRITISH, Willoughby Rd.[82] M sch. opened by Rosslyn Hill Unitarian ch. between 1862 and 1869 in former chapel. 1871 accn. 288 in 2 rooms under one master, a.a. 31; evg. sch. 6 hrs. a week for 23 B all ages. Premises and instruction efficient but, unusually, more pupils needed for size of bldg. I sch. in 2 rooms at no. 3 Pilgrim's Pl., Rosslyn Hill, accn. 32, a.a. 19; not recognized as pub. elem. sch. Schs. financed by subscriptions, mainly from chapel members, sch. pence. 1876 a.a. 106. 1880 a.a. 136, beside small evg. sch. Declined to 1890 a.a. 54. Roll 1900: 34 G, 29 I, when taken over by S.B.L. as temp. sch. for M, I. Pupils transferred to New End 1906.

ST. JOHN'S CHAPEL, Downshire Hill. B, G, and I schs. founded by Revd. John Wilcox, min. of chapel, in 1830s at no. 14A Downshire Hill.[83] Roll 1846–7: 76 B under master, 40 G under mistress, 40 I under mistress. Financed by subscriptions, sch. pence, parl. grant. Instruction for B useful 1852, but less so in G sch., partly organized like an I sch. Roll 1871: 46 B, 48 G, 43 I, with separate rooms and teachers. Transferred to St. Steph.'s elem. sch. (q.v.) 1874–5.

ST. MARY, KILBURN, C.E. PRIMARY, West End Lane.[84] Established 1864 in rented premises: I in same bldg. as master's ho., B & G in adjoining bldg. Financed by sch. pence, collections. B & G moved 1868 to bldg. at corner of West End Lane and Kilburn Pl., leased by bp. of Lond., and formed Nat. Sch., with 1 schoolroom, 1 classroom, and mistress's ho.; 1867–8 a.a. 125. New sch. built 1870 on adjoining site, with 2 rooms for B, 2 for GI, 2 classrooms, mistress's ho. Roll 1871: 162 B, 70 G, 80 I. New bldg. for I sch. 1874. Subjects inc. history, grammar,

[72] P.R.O., C 54/17632, no. 40.
[73] Stanford, *Libr. Map of Lond.* (1891 edn.), sheet 5.
[74] Additional inf. from Nagy, 'Elem. Sch. Provision', 77, 79.
[75] Additional inf. from S.C.L., cuttings file 49.41 Mazenod.
[76] P. Fleming, 'Educational Provision in par. of St. John, Hampstead, 1850–70' (Sidney Webb coll. thesis, 1972, in S.C.L.), 34; *H.H.E.* 18 May 1907; Nat. Soc. *Inquiry, 1846–7*, Mdx. 6–7.
[77] Additional inf. from Nagy, 'Elem. Sch. Provision', 56, 59.
[78] Additional inf. from *H.H.E.* 18 May 1907; L.C.C. *Educ. Cttee. Mins.* (1905), 163.
[79] *V.C.H. Mdx.* vii. 251.
[80] Above, Rom. Cathm.   [81] P.R.O., ED 21/57009.
[82] Additional inf. from *Rosslyn Hill Chapel 1692–1973*, 41, 53.
[83] Wade, *Streets of Hampstead*, 53.
[84] Additional inf. from P.R.O., C 54/17169, no. 4; S.C.L., cuttings file 49.42 St. Mary's; P.R.O., ED 21/11583.

geography, singing, drawing, physical science. 1880 accn. 391, a.a. 320. Income 1899 from small endowment (£10 p.a.), sch. pence, parl. grant. 1900 accn. enlarged for 429 BGI, but L.C.C. wanted reduction and sch. for G and I only. By 1906 accn. 348 but still for BGI. 1908 a.a. 365; steady decline thereafter. Reorg. between 1932 and 1936 for 304 M & I, a.a. 321. Roll 1940: 242 M, 85 I. Reorg. by 1951 as vol. aided primary sch. for JM & I. Roll 1986: 160 JM & I. Appeal for new sch. 1984: bldg. to start in Quex Rd. 1989.

St. Mary, Primrose Hill, day, no. 4 Ainger Rd. M sch. for all ages in 2 rooms opened by 1871. Roll 1871: 85, with amateur teachers and mostly from congregation. Inc. evg. sch. with 22 B and 9 G. Not considered efficient or recognized as pub. elem. sch. Nothing further known.

St. Mary R.C., Holly Pl.[85] R.C. day sch. with 25 G established by 1833, financed by vol. contributions. Cath. Poor Sch. Cttee. grant 1849. 19 B and 13 G examined 1851, when rooms too small but new bldgs. planned. Annual parl. grant until 1865, then closed until 1872. Reopened with a.a. 39. 1880 accn. 77, a.a. 60. 1900 accn. 50 M, 27 I and further 20 I in temp. room. Roll 1905: 50 M, 28 I. Closed 1905 because of fire risk, as premises lay behind terraced ho.

St. Paul C.E. primary, Elsworthy Rd., Primrose Hill. St. Paul's Parochial schs. opened in ho. in King's Coll. Rd. Mews, Adelaide Rd., with 40 B on ground floor from 1870, 20 G and 30 I on first floor from 1871. Financed by collections, subscriptions, sch. pence. Recognized as pub. elem. sch. 1872, as new bldg. planned, and received parl. grants. Site in Winchester Rd. leased to V. by Eton Coll. 1873, where sch. built for 104 B, 84 G, 55 I in 3 rooms and 2 classrooms. 1880 a.a. 167. 1899 a.a. 255. 1908 accn. after improvements 201. Reorg. between 1927 and 1932 for 181 M & I. Roll 1940: 137 M, 46 I. Became vol. aided C.E. primary 1951. Bldg. condemned 1913[86] but not replaced until 1972 by sch. in Elsworthy Rd., with 6 classrooms in bungalow style in landscaped grounds; bldg. completed 1976. Roll 1976: 206 JM & I; 1986: 200 JM & I.

St. Saviour I, Fleet Mews, Upper Park Rd., Haverstock Hill. Opened 1871 in rented ho. with 2 rooms for mistress and 2 rooms for 100 I of poor and constantly changing neighbourhood; renewal of 7-year lease depended on success. 1871 a.a. 35, when premises adequate but sch. not recognized. V. tried unsuccessfully to establish perm. ch. sch. opposite site of new Fleet Rd. bd. sch. 1878.[87]

St. Stephen elem. day.[88] M & I sch. started 1870 in 2 rooms in crypt of St. Steph.'s, Rosslyn Hill; financed by vol. contributions, sch. pence, offertories, Nat. Soc. grant. Roll 1871: 44 B and 61 G all ages under 1 mistress, a.a. 72; evg. sch. for 30 B aged 8–16. Premises unsuitable but instruction efficient, and new site nearby obtained 1871. Succeeded St. John's chapel sch. at no. 14A Downshire Hill 1874–5; a.a. 195. Site in Worsley Rd. (later nos. 40–44 Pilgrim's Lane) conveyed to V. 1877, where bldg. for

B Nat. opened. 1880 accn. 554, a.a. 201. I in iron bldg. at South End Green from c. 1886. Financial difficulties led to closure of B sch. 1897, when B sent mainly to Fleet Rd. Permission from Char. Com. to sell premises and build new I sch. near iron sch. 1898 but G & I schs. transferred to S.B.L. 1899. 1900 accn. 130 G & I in Downshire Hill temp. sch. S.B.L. hired former Worsley Rd. sch. for 159 M 1902, retaining 51 I in Downshire Hill. 1905 accn. 159 M, 262 I. Iron bldg. at South End Green became St. Steph.'s Sun. sch. M & I schs. closed 1906, when pupils transferred to New End.

Samuel Hoare's British, New End. Opened by 1811 in bldg. paid for by Hoare, who also paid master's salary and other expenses. Roll 1811: 112 B.[89] After Parochial sch. was united with Nat. Soc. but without religious test, Hoare closed sch. and offered bldg. for Parochial B.[90]

Trinity Nat., see Holy Trinity.

West End Nat., see Emmanuel.

Special schools. Alexandra Priory, Ainsworth Way, Boundary Rd. Opened between 1967 and 1974 in Sans Walk, Clerkenwell, and moved to Ainsworth Way by 1978. For primary and sec. educationally subnormal M, with special care unit. Roll 1986: 53 M.

Frank Barnes primary, Harley Rd., Swiss Cottage.[91] Opened 1978 as primary sch. for 80 M from sch. in Clerkenwell. Designed by G.L.C.'s dept. of architecture to incorporate latest techniques for teaching profoundly deaf, on site allotted 20 years before, where noise and vibration which would have affected hearing aids led to bldg. of special defences on N. side; S. side, adjoining sites of John Keats and Franklin Delano Roosevelt schs., all glazed. Group rooms, polygonal to reduce echoes, for 2 junior groups, 2 I and nursery groups, and group of multiple-handicapped aged 5 to 7. Roll 1986: 38 M.

Franklin Delano Roosevelt, Avenue Rd., Swiss Cottage. Opened 1901 for physically handicapped in Essendine Rd., Paddington, and moved to Hampstead 1957. Roll 1986: 66 M.

Iverson Rd., Kilburn. Opened by 1899, when a.a. 29, as bd. sch. for 40 defective children. Probably replaced by dept. for mentally defective opened at Kingsgate Rd. bd. sch. 1903. Nothing further known.

John Keats, Adelaide Rd., Swiss Cottage. Opened 1958 for delicate M all ages on site shared with Franklin Delano Roosevelt. Roll 1986: 97 M.

Private schools. In 1609 James Hill was licensed to teach in the parish church.[92] Robert Bramwick was presented in 1618 for keeping a school without a licence.[93] George Turner of Kilburn in Hampstead was a schoolmaster whose bequests of books in 1651 indicated a strong interest in the classics.[94] Licensed schoolmasters included Jacob Baileman in 1661, teaching grammar, John Frederick Wagner in 1662, teaching literature, and Theophilus Wragge in 1674,

[85] Additional inf. from Nagy, 'Elem. Sch. Provision', 32, 35; Fleming, 'Educ. Provision', 36; P.R.O., ED 21/371.
[86] Nagy, 'Elem. Sch. Provision', 21.
[87] Fleming, 'Educ. Provision', 75.
[88] Additional inf. from P.R.O., ED 21/11579; Nagy, 'Elem. Sch. Provision', 23; *Endowed Chars. Lond. III*, 135.

[89] Royal Lancasterian Institution for Educ. of Poor, *Rep. of Finance Cttee. and Trustees for 1811* (1812), 22.
[90] Above, Hampstead Parochial.
[91] Para. based on *Architects' Jnl.* 15 Nov. 1978, 929–42.
[92] G.L.R.O., DL/C/339, f. 85v.
[93] *Mdx. Sess. Rec.* iv. 337.

teaching grammar.[95] Lancelot Johnson in 1684 was permitted to plant trees on part of the waste 'for the ease and defence' of the boys in his school.[96] Lewis Vaslet is said to have opened his 'French school' in Hampstead in 1713, moving to Fulham in 1716,[97] but in 1702 a Mr. Vallett, possibly the same man, rented the new vestry room for his scholars.[98] Similar random references to 18th-century schools give little idea of their number or duration; only from the late 19th century can histories be traced.[99]

In 1828 nine boarding schools for young ladies, mainly finishing schools, included one at Kilburn, and eight for boys included two at Kilburn.[1] In 1833 there were eight private day schools, three of them with a total of 22 boys and 29 girls, one with 14 girls and five with 90 boys; 15 boarding schools, nine of them with 144 girls, six with 193 boys; and two day and boarding schools, one with 26 boys and girls, the other with 21 boys.[2] By 1851 there were 39 private day schools for a total of 428 girls and 292 boys, 46 per cent of all day pupils in Hampstead, but with an average roll of only 18, whereas the National Society and other public schools had an average of 71.[3] Fifteen endowed and private schools for boys were listed in 1872, mainly preparing for the Public schools, and some 45 private girls' schools in 1884.[4] Roman Catholics were also well represented, with both boys' preparatory schools and convent boarding schools for girls.[5] H. G. Wells and A. A. Milne recalled Henley House,[6] which was probably fairly typical of the small private schools of the 1880s, when they differed in their strengths according to the proprietor but were similar in their weaknesses: a lack of space and equipment, and an emphasis on career success at the expense of other values. Wells thought that Alfred Harmsworth, a pupil at Henley House, was an example of the failure of such schools to impart moral values.[7] By the late 19th century social decline in districts such as Kilburn was causing closures: J. V. Milne sold Henley House, which provided secondary education, c. 1892, in the belief that only preparatory schools would continue to have any chance of success.[8]

Private schools in Hampstead recorded under the Education Act, 1918, included 24 with 1,270 boys and girls, 5 with 337 girls, and 4 with 165 boys. About 32 other schools applied for inspection and recognition.[9] The system of recognition probably helped to reduce the number of schools, as did removals and the financial depression of the 1930s.[10] Most schools were evacuated in 1939; although a few returned in 1940, others remained away throughout the war and many never returned, their premises having been damaged and the demand much reduced.

After the Second World War, 7 of Hampstead's independent schools were recognized as efficient in 1951. Twenty-two were listed in 1960, of which 10 were recognized, and 14 in 1984, almost all recognized.[11] Although by the 1980s boarders were no longer taken, independent day schools remained relatively numerous for London. Some of the schools, both past and present, are described in alphabetical order below.[12]

Sara and Rita Allen-Olney set up a school for general and higher education of girls in 1886 in St. John's Wood at the Elms, with some pupils from South Hampstead High where Rita had been headmistress.[13] By 1889 they had moved to no. 41 Belsize Park Gardens and in 1891 they moved to the Hall, a new house in Crossfield Road. They took boarding and day girls from the age of 6. In 1905 their school was sold to the Revd. D. H. Marshall, who moved his Belsize preparatory school there, renaming it the Hall school, and carried on the girls' school at no. 18 Buckland Crescent. In 1919, under Mrs. Rosa Money Dawes, the roll was 50–60. The Allen-Olney school prepared day girls and boarders for university entrance and school examinations in 1927 but apparently had closed by 1934.

Burgess Hill school, for day boys and girls aged 5 to 14, was started in Hampstead in 1936 as a modern co-educational primary school. Within two years it had 120 pupils. Weekly meetings involved pupils in many decisions regarding the school. It moved to Cranleigh (Surr.) as a boarding and day school in 1939 and returned to nos. 11, 12, and 13 Oak Hill Park c. 1948,[14] where it remained until c. 1960.

Frognal school, under Miss E. J. Campbell, had 100 girls in 1919, when it was at no. 84 Fitzjohn's Avenue. By 1931 it had moved to no. 104, with an annexe at no. 14 Prince Arthur Road, and management was by a limited company with Miss Campbell continuing as head.[15] It was recognized and took day girls aged 6 to 19; roll in 1929: 189; in 1931: 212. Education was on Public school lines, without too much pressure. A domestic science department was opened at no. 106 Fitzjohn's Avenue for students over 18, with preparation for national certificates. The school closed in 1938, when a member of the staff opened Settrington school (q.v.), with many staff and pupils from Frognal.

Haberdashers' Aske's School for Boys originated as a day school run by the Haberdashers' Aske's charity foundation at Hoxton (Shoreditch) from 1690 until 1898, when it moved temporarily to Cricklewood. In 1903 it moved to a new building in Westbere Road and was recognized. In 1906 the school was thought to be of value in a rapidly expanding neighbourhood but was cramped, with 412

[94] P.R.O., PROB 11/218 (P.C.C. 198 Grey).
[95] G.L.R.O., index of licensed schoolmasters 1627–85.
[96] Ibid. E/MW/H/I/2304.
[97] V.C.H. Mdx. i. 244.
[98] G.L.R.O., P81/JN1/1A, 7 Apr. 1702.
[99] Below.
[1] Boarding Schs. Dir. (1828).
[2] Educ. Enq. Abstract, 93.
[3] Census, 1851: Educ., p. 54.
[4] F. S. de Carteret-Bisson, Our Schs. and Colls. (1872), 273; (1884), 437, 536, 538–42, 658.
[5] For examples, see below.
[6] Below.
[7] H. G. Wells, Experiment in Autobiog. (1934), i. 328–9.
[8] A. A. Milne, It's Too Late Now (1939), 84.

[9] P.R.O., ED 15/23.
[10] Rest of para. based on histories of individual schs.
[11] Min. of Educ. List 70 (1951 and later edns. H.M.S.O.); Truman & Knightley, Schools (1960, 1983/4).
[12] Gen. inf. for these schs. is taken from List 70 (1951 and later edns.); Truman & Knightley, Schs. (1960 and later edns.); Guide to Schs. in Camden (Mar. 1983), pp. 28–30; Public and Prep. Schs. Yearbk. 1984.
[13] Para. based on P. R. Bodington, The Kindling and the Flame: Cent. Review of S. Hampstead High [c. 1976], 12; P. G. Drury-Lowe, Hall Sch. Hampstead 1889–1964 (1964), 5–7, 9; Dir. of Women Teachers (1927), 64; P.R.O., ED 15/23; P.O. Dir. Lond. (1934).
[14] P.R.O., ED 35/5270; P.O. Dir. Lond.
[15] P.R.O., ED 35/5271.

boys in accommodation suitable for 200–300. In 1907 an additional block was proposed for 240, including 50 juniors. The roll was 503 in 1911, of whom about one third came from Hampstead. Teaching so improved between 1906 and 1911 that inspectors foresaw a most efficient and advanced school. It received a direct grant and in 1961 moved to Aldenham (Herts.),[16] when the buildings were taken over by Hampstead school.[17]

The Hall school[18] originated as Belsize school, founded in 1889 by the Revd. Francis John Wrottesley, who with his wife had taken fee-paying pupils at their home, no. 18 Buckland Crescent, since 1881. The Wrottesleys sold their school in 1898 to the Revd. D. H. Marshall, who took over an adjoining house in 1903, when there were 58 boys, including 10 boarders. In 1905 Marshall bought the Allen-Olney girls' school,[19] which his wife continued at Buckland Crescent. Marshall moved the boys to Crossfield Road and renamed the school the Hall. The roll was over 100 in 1909, when he sold the school to G. H. Montauban. It prepared boys aged 5 to 13 for Public schools and won many scholarships. Montauban bought Woodcote, no. 69 Belsize Park, at the corner of Buckland Crescent, in 1916 and opened it in 1917 for boys under 8.[20] The school was recognized from 1919, when Montauban sold the Hall to R. T. Gladstone, retaining the junior school until 1923. In the 1920s the roll increased from 60 to 270. In 1935 ownership passed to a private company. The main building was extended in 1935 and the junior school in 1938. The roll fell to 45 in 1940 but under a new company rose to 170 in 1942. The junior school, evacuated in 1939, reopened in 1942 with 35 boys. The school became a charitable trust in 1952. In 1951 there were 302 boys aged 5 to 15, including 30 boarders, but boarding ceased between 1960 and 1974. In 1983 the school prepared up to 320 boys for Public schools.

Heath Mount school, at the corner of Heath Street and the Grove, was variously said to have been founded in 1795 and 1817.[21] In 1872 it prepared boarders and day boys for the Civil Service, the armed services, and Public schools.[22] It was taken over by J. S. Granville Grenfell in 1895 and had 56 pupils aged 8 to 14 in 1903. In 1921 there were 24 boarders and 65 day boys, mostly from Hampstead. After an adverse inspection had prevented recognition, a dismissed master sought the help of Arthur Waugh, whose son Evelyn he had taught there, to approach the Minister of Education.[23] The school had closed by 1934 and moved to Hertford.[24]

Henley House school, nos. 6 & 7 Mortimer Road (later Crescent), Kilburn, had been unsuccessful before 1878 when John Vine Milne, father of the writer A. A. Milne, bought the goodwill. Numbers rose from c. 6 to 50 boys, aged 8 to 18, including 15 boarders. Milne's family lived in one semi-detached house, the other being adapted for classrooms. H. G. Wells taught English, science, and drawing 1889–90 and admired Milne, although equipment was sparse and the school fell short of its intentions; the honour system for discipline was in advance of its time, and a new approach to mathematics proved successful for university entrance. Alfred Harmsworth was encouraged to start the school magazine in 1878, printed from 1881. Milne moved his school c. 1892 to Westgate-on-Sea (Kent); Henley House continued as a school until c. 1910 under various proprietors.[25]

King Alfred school was opened in 1898 at no. 24 Ellerdale Road by the new King Alfred School Society, to practise modern theories of education. Day boys and girls aged c. 8 to 18 were taught together to at least the age of 14. The school had no religious or political affiliations; discipline depended mainly on the pupils' co-operation and competition was discouraged, although there was preparation for entrance examinations to further education. In 1903 there were 20 girls and 15 boys in classes smaller than at most maintained schools and under a staff better qualified than at most private schools. By 1913 there were 85 pupils and more space was needed, despite the addition of no. 22 Ellerdale Road. The school also needed capital and more older boys. It moved to Hendon in 1919.[26]

Lyndhurst House preparatory school, no. 24 Lyndhurst Gardens, was opened for 150 day boys aged 7 to 13 c. 1950 by Davies Tutors and renamed Lyndhurst House school by 1960. Recognized from 1957, it successfully prepared boys for Public schools in 1983.[27]

North Bridge House school, no. 8 Netherhall Gardens, a mixed preparatory school, was formerly at nos. 23–4 St. John's Wood Park and had 120 pupils by 1960. In 1983 it prepared 320 pupils aged 3 to 13 for Public schools, with juniors at Netherhall Gardens and seniors at Gloucester Gate (St. Pancras).

Peterborough Lodge school, no. 143 Finchley Road, started c. 1898 as a school belonging to A. H. Linford and later occupied a block added to a private house in 1901, standing in 2 a. It was a preparatory school for c. 100 boys aged 5 to 15, including 5 to 10 boarders, and in 1921 had 92 boys, mainly from Hampstead. The school was highly successful in preparation for the Royal Navy and Public schools and was recognized from 1921. Linford also ran Downsend school, Leatherhead (Surr.), which he had opened during the First World War for the boarders from Peterborough Lodge. A branch was opened in 1931 at no. 17 Maresfield Gardens to take c. 90 juniors, aged 5 to 9. In 1937 the lease of the main school expired and the school moved to no. 6 Netherhall Gardens, whose garden adjoined that of the junior school.[28] The whole school amalgamated with Downsend in 1940 and apparently did not return to Hampstead.

[16] V.C.H. Mdx. i. 297; P.R.O., ED 35/1689; Public and Prep. Schs. Yearbk. 1984, 145.
[17] Above, pub. schs.
[18] Para. based on Drury-Lowe, Hall Sch.; P.R.O., ED 35/1690.   [19] Above.
[20] A painting of the ho. by Robt. Bevan, 1917, is in Lond. Mus.
[21] P.R.O., ED 35/1691; Wade, Streets of Hampstead, 60.
[22] Bisson, Schs. and Colls. (1872), 273.
[23] P.R.O., ED 35/1691. Grenfell is said to be the model

for the head in Waugh's Decline and Fall: Wade, Streets of Hampstead, 60.
[24] Wade, Streets of Hampstead, 60; Truman & Knightley, Schs. (1960).
[25] Para. based on Milne, It's Too Late Now, 4–5, 10, 24, 26, 49–50, 55, 84; Wells, Experiment in Autobiog. i. 317–29; P.O. Dir. Lond.
[26] P.R.O., ED 35/1692; V.C.H. Mdx. v. 48.
[27] S.C.L., 49.42 Lyndhurst, cutting.
[28] P.R.O., ED 35/1694, 5276, 5277; P.O. Dir. Lond.

Purcell school, no. 13 Lyndhurst Terrace, formerly the Central Tutorial School for Young Musicians, was recognized from 1972. It had 65 day girls and boys aged 8 to 18 in 1974. It left Hampstead c. 1978.

Queen's House school, no. 69 Fitzjohn's Avenue, opened in 1947 for day girls aged 9 to 18, with education up to university entrance. It was recognized from 1950 and had 83 girls in 1951. It closed c. 1964.

The Royal Soldiers' Daughters' Home, no. 65 Rosslyn Hill, was founded at Rosslyn House in 1855 to relieve the families of soldiers in the Crimea. The trustees bought Vane House and rebuilt it in 1858 to designs by William Munt, incorporating part of the 17th-century house; the grounds of c. 4 a. included part of those of Rosslyn House. The home had been enlarged by 1876, when it had 163 girls with accommodation for 200. Originally intended for destitute war orphans, it later took the daughters of serving or retired soldiers; they were admitted from infancy to 13 and left at 16, able ones being trained to become teachers. From 1924 the school was maintained by the L.C.C., with a roll of c. 110 until the Second World War. Accommodation was reduced from 200 to 145 in 1924. In view of the small numbers in a wide age range, inspectors recommended limiting the school to juniors or sending the girls out to school. The L.C.C. ceased maintenance from 1945, when the governors decided to run an independent all-age boarding school. By 1973, however, and possibly as early as 1951 when they sold the school building to the L.C.C., all the girls were sent to local maintained schools, while the home provided extras such as dancing, drama, music, and riding. A new building was opened in 1970 behind the old, which was replaced by Vane Mews, Vane Close, and Mulberry Close.[29]

The Royal Sailors' Orphan Girls' School and Home was said to have been established in 1829 as a home,[30] which opened in Hampstead in 1862 at Frognal House. In 1869 it moved to a new building at nos. 96–116 Fitzjohn's Avenue, designed by Edward Ellis. In 1871 two rooms for 78 served as a school, attended by 60 girls of all ages, whose subjects included domestic ones. It was recognized as a public elementary school from 1879 and received a parliamentary grant from 1882, when the roll was c. 116, but ceased to receive grants between 1903 and 1908, and in 1919 again became independent. The Home closed in 1957 and was demolished to make way for council flats.[31]

St. Anthony's preparatory school, no. 90 Fitzjohn's Avenue, opened c. 1953 as a Roman Catholic day school for boys aged 6 to 14, preparing them for Public schools. It was recognized from 1956. The roll was 200 in 1960, 275 in 1974, and 280 in 1983. No. 1 Arkwright Road was added to the school c. 1965.[32]

St. Christopher's school was thought to have been founded in 1883. A small Froebel class held by 1889, probably by Mrs. Roberts, soon developed into a preparatory school, Hampstead kindergarten and school at no. 13 Carlingford Road, under Miss Amy Pridham, who was later joined by Miss E. G. Wells; the school embodied the ideas of Pestalozzi and Froebel. It moved in 1898 to no. 16 Hampstead Hill Gardens and had c. 35 junior girls and boys c. 1905. After another move, to no. 20 Hampstead Hill Gardens, the school was carried on from 1912 by Miss Violet H. Wright, who in 1919 moved to no. 32 Belsize Lane, formerly a nursery training college, having taken over Tremarth and Ruskin House schools. Thereafter she took girls up to 18. The school had 112 girls and boys in 1919 and was recognized from 1924. Miss Wright also opened a school of domestic science at the Lodge, no. 2 Rosslyn Hill, in 1924, with accommodation for 8–9 boarders. In the 1930s the lower school took girls and boys aged 4 to 10, and senior girls were prepared for London Matriculation and Oxford School Certificate. In 1937 the juniors moved to no. 20 Lyndhurst Gardens. The school, which was evacuated during the Second World War, was bought by Miss Rosemary Manning and Miss Bell in 1950. It had 19 pupils under 5, 122 aged 5 to 10, and 7 aged 11 to 15 in 1951, and later had c. 180 until the early 1970s. Principally a girls' preparatory school, taking a few small boys, it encouraged parents to send children on to local day schools rather than to boarding schools. The arts, especially music, were emphasized. When Miss Manning decided to retire in 1972, a parent, Dr. David Cohen, bought the property through his family trust and leased it to a board of governors. A new block was opened in 1983, containing 3 classrooms and 2 music rooms. In 1974 the school had 164 girls aged 4 to 12 and in 1984 it took up to 215 day girls aged 5 to 11.[33]

St. Margaret's school, no. 18 Kidderpore Gardens, was started by Miss Elizabeth Tulloch in West Hampstead in 1884 and moved to a pair of semi-detached houses at Oak Hill Park in 1898. Originally a day and boarding school for girls aged 11 and upwards, by 1904 it included a small preparatory class. In 1904 there were 57 girls, prepared for examinations up to university entrance. The school was recognized in 1920, when it had 85 day girls and 11 boarders aged 5 to 18, mostly from Hampstead. It incorporated Threave House school (q.v.) from 1932. After the Second World War the school reopened in Kidderpore Gardens c. 1948 with 72 day girls. From 1954 management was by a company, registered as a charitable trust. By 1974 the roll was 151 girls, aged 7 to 16, and in 1983 it was 145.[34]

St. Mary's convent school was opened by the Dames Anglaises of the Institute of the Blessed Virgin Mary in England's Lane by 1880.[35] In 1919 it had 97 girls. The convent moved to no. 47 Fitzjohn's Avenue c. 1927, where it ran a boarding and day school for girls with a kindergarten and mixed preparatory school in 1949.[36] The school was recognized from 1951. By 1960 it was a Roman Catholic girls' preparatory day school, with a few small boys. In 1974 there were 156 girls aged 4 to 11, and 40

[29] Char. Com. files; P.R.O., ED 21/34812, 57007; C 54/15954, no. 13; Thorne, *Environs*, 287–8; Wade, *Streets of Hampstead*, 68–9.   [30] P.R.O., ED 7/81.
[31] Rest of para. based on P.R.O., ED 3/19; Nat. Soc. files; *Images of Hampstead*, 113; Wade, *Streets of Hampstead*, 17.

[32] *P.O. Dir. Lond.*
[33] S.C.L., 49.42/*St. Chris. Sch. Mag. Cent. Edn. 1883–1983*; cutting 1983.
[34] P.R.O., ED 35/1693; Char. Com. files.
[35] *Cath. Dir.* (1880), 354.
[36] *P.O. Dir. Lond.*; Anson, *Rel. Orders*, 320.

boys aged 4 to 8; in 1983 the maximum roll was 200.

St. Mary's Town and Country school started in 1937 when a small school called St. Mary's was taken over in co-operation with Mrs. Ena Curry, of Dartington Hall, as a progressive educational day school. It continued to be built up at Hereford during the Second World War and the day school reopened in 1945 at no. 38 Eton Avenue, while the boarding school was at Stanford Park near Rugby. Pupils were interchanged between town and country, and from 1951 often used a weekend and summer school at the 16-a. Hedgerley Wood (Bucks.).[37] In 1951 there were 144 girls and boys of all ages including 17 boarders. In 1969 it was proposed to adapt a house in Glenloch Road, formerly used for boarders, for teachers' accommodation and as a laboratory.[38] The school was recognized by 1960; in 1974 it had 186 girls and boys aged 4 to 16. It closed c. 1983.

Sarum Hall school, no. 51 Eton Avenue, started in 1929 when a management company was incorporated. It prepared day girls aged 5 to 14 for Public schools[39] and was recognized from 1934. There were 95 girls aged 5 to 15 in 1951 and 120 in 1984. The school closed in 1986.[40]

Settrington school, no. 24 Lyndhurst Gardens, was started in 1938 by Miss Hilda M. Johnson, a teacher at the former Frognal school, with support from parents there. Numbers were limited to 60 girls, nearly all of them at first from Frognal. Day girls aged 10 to 18 were prepared up to university entrance. The school was recognized in 1939. It closed c. 1950, when the premises were taken over by Davies Tutors as Lyndhurst House.[41]

South Hampstead High school[42] was founded as St. John's Wood High by the Girls' Public Day School Trust in 1876 in a house in Winchester Road. Numbers had reached 197 by 1878 and 302 by 1882, when the school moved to a new building in Maresfield Gardens. Two laboratories, two classrooms, and a fives court were added in 1889. In 1908 the school had 244 girls of all ages and was recognized.[43] In 1921 it acquired no. 1 Maresfield Gardens, formerly the home of Sir Ernest Waterlow, which became a junior school, the studio later being used by the seniors. Extensions including a gymnasium, library, laboratory, and classrooms marked the school's jubilee. In 1927 girls were prepared for examinations up to university entrance.[44] A direct grant was received after 1944, but the junior school remained wholly fee-paying. In 1957, when the total roll was over 500, the juniors moved to no. 12 Netherhall Gardens and the seniors took over Waterlow House. A site adjoining the playground was bought in 1968 and a science block opened there in 1972. In 1976 the school had 160 juniors, aged 5 to 11, and 466 seniors, aged 11 to 18, including a 6th form of 117; numbers were similar in 1984. Despite

its restricted site, the school drew pupils from a wide area of north and west London, with strong support from the Jewish community. A large new building, on the site of Waterlow House, including a theatre and sports hall, was due for completion in 1987.[45]

Stepping Stone school, no. 33 Fitzjohn's Avenue, was opened as a nursery and mixed preparatory school c. 1964[46] and recognized since 1970. It had 193 girls and boys aged 3 to 9 in 1974 and up to 220 in 1983.

Threave House school, no. 7 Heath Drive, was founded in 1886 by the Misses McMillan as a day school for girls aged 7 to 19. In 1903 it occupied a large detached house and was particularly strong in Mathematics, French, German, and Latin, while the life drawing, taught by the head of Sydenham School of Art, was the best which the inspector had seen in a girls' school. In 1903 there were 80 girls. Compulsory religious instruction in 1906 caused the withdrawal of perhaps a third of the pupils, who were Jewish or Roman Catholic. It was recognized in 1919, when the roll was 69 and it could accommodate 75, although in 1930 the inspectors wanted less emphasis on examinations and the introduction of science. The surviving Miss McMillan retired in 1932, whereupon the school was amalgamated with St. Margaret's (q.v.).[47]

University College school[48] was founded in 1830 in Gower Street as part of University College, London. When the college became part of London University in 1907,[49] the school became a separate corporation and moved with c. 200 boys to Hampstead, where the preparatory school was already established.[50] It occupied a neo-Georgian building of brick with stone dressings, designed by Arnold Bidlake Mitchell[51] as three linked blocks accommodating 500. The school was recognized from 1907 but suffered as other schools adopted its nonconformist and liberal traditions. It applied for a direct grant in 1919, providing 25 per cent of the places free, and also received an annual grant from the L.C.C. from 1920 to 1924. The roll, only c. 300 in 1917, had increased to 525 by 1931. Academic standards were affected by the reliance on fee-payers but the curriculum was extended in the period between the World Wars. After the mortgages were paid off the school dispensed with the direct grant and in 1944 became completely independent again, while continuing to offer 25 per cent of the places to boys from primary schools, often those refused assistance by L.C.C. but accepted by Middlesex C.C. After the Second World War, competition for places increased, although the number was kept down to 500 boys, aged 13 to 18; the 6th form was built up and the school became strong in classics. A new laboratory, music room, library, and headmaster's house were paid for through a jubilee appeal in 1957. A brick and glass 6th-form centre, designed

[37] H. A. T. Child (ed.), *The Independent Progressive Sch.* (1962), 136; *P.O. Dir. Lond.*
[38] S.C.L., 49.42/Town and Country sch., cutting.
[39] P.R.O., ED 35/5278.
[40] Inf. from Camden local hist. librarian.
[41] P.R.O., ED 35/5279.
[42] Para. based on *Girls' Public Day Sch. Trust 1872–1972* (1972), 90–1; Bodington, *Kindling and Flame.*
[43] *List of Sec. Schs. in Eng. Recognised as Efficient* [Cd. 4374], p. 40, H.C. (1908), lxxxiii.
[44] *Dir. of Women Teachers* (1927), 63.
[45] *Girls' Sch. Yearbk. 1984, 1986.*
[46] S.C.L., 49.42/Stepping Stone Sch., cutting; *P.O. Dir. Lond.*
[47] Para. based on P.R.O., ED 35/1696, 5282.
[48] Following 2 paras. based on H. H. Bellot, *Univ. Coll. Lond. 1826–1926* (1929), 170, 402; *Univ. Coll. Sch.: Register 1860–1931, with Short Hist.*, 13, 16–21; Usher, Black-Hawkins, Carrick, *Angels Without Wings: Hist. of Univ. Coll. Sch.*
[49] *V.C.H. Mdx.* i. 358.
[50] Below.   [51] Gray, *Edwardian Archit.* 262.

by Michael Foster of T.F.P. Architects,[52] was opened in 1974. The main building was damaged by fire in 1978, the restored hall being reopened by Queen Elizabeth II in 1980, on the school's sesquicentenary.

University College preparatory school was opened in 1891 at Holly Hill House (no. 11 Holly Hill). It had c. 80 boys by 1900, over 100 by 1907, and 250 at its peak in 1921, necessitating the housing of the top forms in the senior school at Frognal. The house was rebuilt for 200 boys in 1926–8 to a design by Sir John Simpson, incorporating woodwork from the old house. James Elroy Flecker, poet, was a master there.[53] In 1984 there were c. 250 boys aged 7 to 13.

Warwick House school, founded in 1883, was at no. 145 King Henry's Road in 1919 with 30 boys[54] and moved to no. 30 Lymington Road c. 1939.[55] It took both boarders and day boys, preparing seniors for examinations up to university entrance and juniors for Public schools. Special provision was made for Jews, Moslems, and Roman Catholics. The school closed c. 1969.[56]

Wykeham House school was established in 1895, probably by a Miss Budd. Miss Ada Wright, a member of staff, took over in 1898 and may have moved to no. 147 Abbey Road, Kilburn, by 1908, and certainly by 1919. The school was recognized in 1920, when it prepared day boys and 5 boarders aged 5 to 13 for Public schools. It closed in 1933.[57]

CHARITIES FOR THE POOR. In the 18th century income from charities was not always used as the donors intended. In 1710 the lord of the manor, Sir William Langhorne, complained that the rents of the Wells charity estate were being used by the parish officers to ease the poor rate.[58] For many years all the income from the other charities was put in one general account by the churchwardens to defray their expenses, about £16 a year, and, up to 1802, to pay for the sacramental bread and wine. After 1806 the accounts were not properly kept, and money was lost when a churchwarden for 1808 died insolvent. The clerk, beadle, sexton, bellringer, and pew openers were among the weekly recipients of bread, although only the clerk (under Cleave's gift) was entitled to a loaf. The local Act of 1800 enabled the guardians to distribute the charities' income, but that was done only from c. 1821, when they also appointed a committee to look into the churchwardens' accounts regarding charities and provided for stricter accounting.[59]

Campden charity. Elizabeth Hicks, Lady Campden, by will dated 1643, bequeathed £200 to buy freehold land worth £10 a year, half of which was to relieve the most needy of Hampstead and half to apprentice boys. In 1644 the parish bought 14 a. in Hendon for £250, the rest of the purchase price coming from £40 bequeathed by a maid to provide every inhabitant of Hampstead, rich or poor, with a

½d. loaf on Good Friday, and £10 given by John Rixton during his lifetime. In 1824 the whole income went into the general charity account and no boy had been apprenticed for 50 years. The charity commissioners declared that ⅗ of the income, £47 14s., should be used for bread, and ⅖, £31 16s., for apprenticing. The proceeds from a small sale of land were invested. New trustees were appointed in 1855, when ⅗ of the income was distributed as cash to poor residents of 3 years' standing not receiving relief. In 1877 the trustees were authorized to sell the land; when the charity was amalgamated with the Wells charity under a Scheme of 1880, it had £7,708 in stock.[60]

Wells charity.[61] In 1698 Susannah Noel, on behalf of her son Baptist, earl of Gainsborough, lord of the manor and a minor, granted 6 a. of Hampstead Heath, including the well of mineral water, to 14 trustees, who were admitted as copyholders at a rent of 5s. a year to use the income for the poor of Hampstead. The trustees leased all the property except the pond or springhead north-west of the mineral spring to John Duffield in 1701 for 21 years at £50 a year, on condition he spent £300 over 3 years improving it, and agreed for a second term for improvements worth £200. In 1710 they agreed on a third term of 21 years for further improvements. The excluded pond or spring was let separately to John Vincent, who undertook to run water into the town, spending £200 on it; in return he was to hold the supply for 21 years at a rent of £15, although no lease was drawn up. In 1707 the trustees had to defend a suit brought by an entrepreneur who claimed that his own water supply to the City from the heath was affected by Vincent's enterprise.[62] In 1710 the new lord challenged the copyhold grant as illegal and claimed that the trustees were misusing the income,[63] while the churchwardens accused them of neglecting the pond and well.[64] In 1729 a Chancery decree established the charity: the estate was to be held of the lord for 5s. a year and a reasonable fine; the lord was to appoint 13 resident copyholders as trustees and to nominate others when the number fell to 5. The lord and trustees presented a Scheme in 1731 to use the arrears of rent and future income: James, son of John Duffield, owed arrears of £575 from 1718; John Vincent, son of the original tenant, owed £322 10s. After costs and fines £412 remained, of which £150 repaid the parish for fitting up the workhouse and charity school; the residue and future income was for apprenticing to trades or domestic service, and other uses for the poor.

John Duffield sold his interest in 1730 to John Mitchell, who was granted leases for the remaining 42 years. In 1734, when the buildings were decayed, Mitchell received a further term of 31 years to run from 1764, in return for spending £200 on repairs and a further 21 years for spending £500 on replacements and building on vacant ground. In 1795 a new

[52] *Building Design*, 26 Oct. 1979, 20–1.
[53] Wade, *Streets of Hampstead*, 25.
[54] P.R.O., ED 15/23.
[55] *P.O. Dir. Lond.*
[56] Ibid.
[57] P.R.O., ED 15/23; ED 35/1700, 5285; *P.O. Dir. Lond.*
[58] P.R.O., C 8/492/56.
[59] *Endowed Chars. Lond. III*, H.C. 252, pp. 85–8 (1900),

lxi, which includes copies of reps. of 1819, 1824, and 1861–3; 39 & 40 Geo. III, c. 35; above, local govt., par. govt.
[60] *Endowed Chars. Lond. III*, 83, 85, 95–6, 101; below, Wells and Campden char.
[61] Account based on *Endowed Chars. Lond. III*, 87–118.
[62] P.R.O., C 7/270/61.
[63] Ibid. C 8/492/56.
[64] Ibid. C 7/1/28.

lease of the property, which in addition to the medicinal spring and 6 a. with its buildings included three small plots granted by the lord in 1789, was made to Anne Frewen and Joseph Baldwin, executors of Charles Frewen, for 21 years at £70, with an agreement for a further 40 years. The additional lease was granted in 1810 to Anne, as Anne Buckner, and included a plot near the garden of Lady Watson; in all the additional plots totalled c. 1¼ a. By 1824 the estate was built up, mostly in Well Walk, and at £800 a year its value was considerably more than the income which the charity was to receive until the lease expired in 1850.

The springhead excluded from the lease of 1701 was auctioned under the Chancery decree of 1729. John Vincent alone made an offer and was granted a lease in 1733 for 33 years from 1731 at £15, to include the banks and pipes which conveyed the water to the lower part of Hampstead town. Additional terms were granted in 1764 and 1785 at the same rent. In 1806 Elizabeth Vincent was granted a 21-year lease for £25 a year, which by 1824 was vested in her executors. The springhead, used only to supply the Vincents' brewery in High Street and a few adjoining houses, was of little value to anyone other than the brewer.

By 1824 the charity also possessed £1,100 stock, bought with rent arrears in 1783–4 and a legacy of £100 from John Peter Blaquiere in 1801; the annual income was £95 in rents and £33 in dividends. The income was spent on apprenticing between 8 and 10 children each year, with premiums of £3 to £7, on clothing children going into service, and on sums of 5s. to £1 for paupers who were old, infirm, or had large families, and did not receive parish relief. The money gifts were made at the workhouse, usually in December, at a meeting advertised by the secretary, who received a salary of £4 4s., beside £1 1s. for each apprenticeship indenture.

In 1850 the property consisted of Foley House, the chapel, the Wells hotel (formerly the Green Man), 11 houses in Well Walk, Willow House, 4 cottages, the springhead, and £1,100 stock. Gross income after the lease expired was £976 in rents and dividends. Sales in 1851 and 1853, to pay for repairs and expenses, and a further purchase in 1855 left a balance of £577 stock. In 1857 a new Scheme provided for managers, who would include the minister of Hampstead, the district incumbents, and three members appointed by the board of guardians. They were to invest £50 a year as a repair fund and £250 as a fund for the copyhold admission fines, and spend up to £250 on apprenticing. Out of the first money received, £250 was to be paid towards the new infants' school and £250 for building Christ Church National schools, so long as both should be open to all poor children without religious restriction. Surplus money was to be invested. In 1857 a small piece of copyhold was bought with the £577 stock and income, and between 1859 and 1873 £907 stock was bought for the repair fund. In 1873–4 the various copyhold parcels were enfranchised, using c. £7,000 stock.

A Scheme in 1875 established 20 trustees, who could spend up to £150 a year on the further education of a boy or girl from a Hampstead elementary school and £150 p.a. on apprenticeships or putting out to service. Accumulated and future income was to be used to improve the dwellings of the poor in Hampstead, or to help the poor in other ways. In 1876 the trustees acquired Crockett's Court, where they built artisans' dwellings. In 1880 the charity was amalgamated with the Campden charity and a new Scheme drawn up.

The Wells and Campden charity. Under the Scheme of 1880, amended in 1885, 1893, and 1897, for the consolidated charity, the 20 trustees were to spend £150 a year, raised to £300 in 1899, on needy pensioners resident in Hampstead for six years and not receiving poor relief; until 1899 preference was to be given to those reduced from better circumstances but thereafter to length of residence. Annual sums of £50, later £200, were to be spent on any dispensary, hospital, or convalescent home, £150 on advancing children in life, and £230 on education above elementary level, including exhibitions of up to £40 a year. The residue was to improve the dwellings of the poor, for which purpose the trustees could buy or fit up houses; they could also provide facilities such as lecture rooms, day nurseries, laundries, and night schools. From 1893 £100 a year could assist any institution giving scientific instruction in technical or industrial work, and from 1897 grants could be made for public open spaces, and £50 a year used to assist emigration to British colonies or moves within the British Isles.

Changes to the property of the amalgamated charities included, in 1881, sales of stock to pay off the loan for Crockett's Court and of the rest of the land in Hendon that was part of Campden's charity, from which £6,500 was invested and £1,200 used to buy 1 r. 6 p. adjoining the Wells estate in 1882. From 1882 the trustees might raise money to put in sewers before making building leases. They bought and enfranchised Mount Cottage in Flask Walk in 1885 and property in Palmerston Road, part of West End Park estate, in 1886, for baths and washhouses on both sites, and in 1886 they bought land in Holly Bush Vale from the M.B.W. for artisans' dwellings. They also contributed £500 towards the purchase of the 265-a. extension to Hampstead Heath.

In 1898 the charity estate consisted of many buildings[65] and c. £2,600 stock. The site of the old well had been lost, as the water flow had been affected by drainage works, and £20 could be spent seeking it. So wide were the charity's functions that committees were formed for apprenticeships, artisans' dwellings, baths and wash-houses, finance, gardens, letting and repair, and pensions. The income was spent on pensions, hospitals and dispensaries, apprenticing and outfitting, and education. Five male and 17 female pensioners received 5s. a week in 1898. During the previous five years £200 a year had been paid to six medical charities serving Hampstead, c. £130 a year for apprenticing and outfits, and c. £107 a year for exhibitions; there were usually two annual exhibitions to children aged 12 to 14, chosen by examination and mainly from board schools, in particular Fleet Road. A subscription of £50 a year to the Hampstead School for Cookery brought the right to nominate to free places there. The artisans' dwellings

---

[65] Above, growth, Hampstead town, for est. in 1898; pub. svces., for baths.

were all in the eastern part of the parish; no block was planned for Kilburn because of difficulties in finding a site.

The educational element of the charity was separated under Schemes of 1899, 1905, and 1924, as the Wells and Campden educational foundation. Its income derived from £2,323 stock and sums of £230 and £100 a year from the main charity; £230 provided children resident in the borough for at least 2 years with exhibitions at institutions higher than elementary, and £100 paid for instruction in technical and industrial work. In 1971 the foundation was amalgamated with the Stock foundation (below).

Hampstead Wells and Campden trust.[66] In 1971 the Hampstead Wells and Campden trust was established by a Scheme which included more recent charities with similar objectives. The charities were brought together into two funds. The first, the Hampstead Relief in Sickness fund, comprised the Hampstead Aid in Sickness fund, Hampstead Aid for Sick Mothers and Children, the charity of James Stewart Henderson for a convalescent home, and the Thomas Hancock Nunn Memorial fund. It was to supply medical items or services which were not readily available from other sources. Any income not so used could be added to the Relief in Need fund (below). In 1985 the fund's assets were worth *c.* £140,000, yielding *c.* £12,000 net, of which £1,600 was applied to the charity in 1985.

The second, the Hampstead Relief in Need fund, comprised the charities of Henry Joseph Ogden and Theresa Thurlow, and the Hampstead Wells and Campden charity. Its objective was to relieve needy residents, generally or individually, through grants of money or by providing items or services. In 1985 the fund held the freehold Well Walk estate (not valued), other properties worth *c.* £1.3 million, and investments and other assets of *c.* £1 million. The net income was *c.* £165,000 in 1985, when *c.* £186,000 was applied to the charity, including part of £376,000 brought forward from previous years.

The trustees also administered the Wells and Campden and Stock education foundation,[67] the Wharrie Cabman's Shelter fund from 1971, and the Hampstead Relief in Sickness charity (which was distinct from the Hampstead Relief in Sickness fund) from 1977. The Wharrie Cabman's Shelter fund was founded by Mrs. Wharrie in 1935 and registered as a charity in 1964. It provided a shelter at Hampstead Green, the residue to be used for other charitable purposes. In 1985 the fund owned the freehold shelter, valued at £2,000, and investments and other assets worth £4,400, with a net income of £656 of which £200 was applied to the charity.

The Hampstead Relief in Sickness charity was the successor to Kilburn and West Hampstead District Nursing Association, which had been founded in 1901 to nurse the sick at home. In 1961 the association had 20 nurses at its nurses' home, nos. 18 and 20 Dennington Park Road, and its income of £16,300 was almost all derived from an L.C.C. grant. In 1967 the home was sold and the proceeds invested. In 1985 the stock was worth *c.* £12,000 and the net income *c.* £2,600, to be applied in grants or pensions to nurses formerly employed by the association or for the same purposes as the Hampstead Relief in Sickness fund.

Stock's charity.[68] John Stock, by will dated 1780, left £1,000, the interest to educate and clothe 10 fatherless children, 6 boys aged 8 to 15 and 4 girls aged 8 to 13, and afterwards put them out as apprentices or covenanted servants, paying £5 with each boy and £2 with each girl. Annual sets of clothing were to include a chocolate coloured coat for boys and a similar gown for girls. The charity was to be administered by a committee of at least five parishioners. By 1784 the fund had increased to £2,000 through the investment of dividends and a donation of £60 from the Wells charity. In 1801 a legacy of £100 stock from J. P. Blaquiere was added, and a committee appointed by the vestry to manage the charity.[69] With savings the fund reached £2,300 in 1819, producing £69 a year for clothing and educating as many children as possible, with occasional apprenticeship fees; 10 boys and 6 girls had received clothing in 1818. The children attended the National school, the boys free of charge, the girls for £1 a year. In 1823 Sir Francis Willes left a rent charge of £13 6s. 8d. to augment the charity, but the bequest was made valid by his legal heir the Revd. Edward Willes only in 1842. The stock stood at £2,600 in 1860 and the income was £71 10s. from dividends and £13 6s. 8d. from the rent charge in 1898, when it was spent on clothing *c.* 30 children every year, two thirds of them boys, from all the parish's elementary schools; the distinctive colours had recently been discontinued. A Ministry of Education Scheme of 1957 applied the income, £65 beside the fee farm rent of £2 14s. 11d., to maintenance or clothing grants for pupils at any level, assistance for school-leavers, and apprenticeships.[70]

In 1971 the charity was amalgamated with the educational part of the Wells and Campden charity as the Wells and Campden and Stock educational foundation, and was administered by the trustees of the Hampstead Wells and Campden trust. The net income of the foundation, £400 in 1985, was to benefit children resident in Hampstead for at least two years, by means of exhibitions at any secondary or higher educational institution, or financial assistance to enter a profession or trade.

Distributive charities.[71] Thomas Charles (d. 1622) of Holborn, clothworker, by will dated 1617, left his four houses in Fetter Lane and all his goods to meet legacies which included 24s. a year to the churchwardens of Hampstead for bread.[72] The money remained unpaid until 1688, when the owners of the houses were ordered to pay the arrears of *c.* £72 and future sums.[73] In 1824 the sum was subject to 3s. land tax. In 1898 the 21s. a year was applied in bread with Rixton's charity (below).

Thomas Cleave, by deed dated 1635, paid £50 for a rent charge of 56s. a year on 2 a. near Battle Bridge, St. Pancras, later Cromer Street, Gray's Inn Road, with which the vicar of Hampstead was to buy 13

[66] Account based on Char. Com. files.
[67] Below, Stock's char.
[68] Account based on *Endowed Chars. Lond. III*, 81, 93–4.
[69] Vestry mins. 3 May 1801.
[70] Char. Com. files.
[71] Account based on *Endowed Chars. Lond. III*, 81–137.
[72] Guildhall MS. 9052/5.
[73] P.R.O., C 93/43, no. 16.

wheaten penny loaves each week and distribute them to 12 poor people and the parish clerk, any surplus to be used for the poor or repair of the church. Income in 1824 was 56s. In 1898 the rent charge was applied with Rixton's charity.

John Rixton, by will dated 1657, charged his four copyhold houses in Hampstead town with the following annual payments: £3 to the churchwardens for 12 penny loaves each Sunday for the poor, especially frequent churchgoers, with the remaining 8s. to the parish clerk to clean Rixton's grave; £1 to the minister for a sermon on 9 April; £1 towards repairing part of the church. In 1759 the houses were chargeable with £7 10s. a year, perhaps in compensation for arrears. Sums for the sermon and the grave were being paid, but not for repair of the church, and £3 18s. was due for bread. In 1898 the property, in High Street, belonged to Henry Wakeford: £5 2s. a year, together with Charles's, Cleave's, and Mallory's charities, was distributed weekly in bread to respectable elderly parishioners, usually 12 women, of whom one third lived in the Kilburn part of the parish.

Henry Waite, by will dated 1720, gave £100 for annual payments to the most needy on the date of his burial. The legacy was reduced to £50 because his assets were too small, and was lent at interest to the trustees of Hampstead church until it was repaid in 1813, when it was invested. The annual income was £2 10s. 11d. in 1824. It was £2 6s. 8d. in 1898, when it was distributed with Marshall's charity.

John Robinson, bishop of London (d. 1723), left £100 to the poor of the parish in which he should die, which was Hampstead. The sum, like Waite's, was lent to the trustees of the church and in 1813 invested. The income was £5 1s. 11d. in 1824. It was £4 13s. 4d. in 1898, when it was distributed with Marshall's charity.

Mary Arnold, by will of 1767, left £100 stock for payments each Christmas day to poor householders. In 1824 the dividends were part of the general distribution on St. Thomas's day. In 1898 the income was £2 15s., distributed with Marshall's charity.

Francis Marshall, by will dated 1772, left £100 stock for payments at Easter to poor householders not receiving alms. In augmentation his widow Rosamond, by will dated 1785, left £100 stock. In 1824 £6 formed part of the general distribution on St. Thomas's day. In 1898 the income of £5 10s. was added to Waite's, Robinson's, and Arnold's charities to produce £15 5s., for 'the annual gifts'. One third was distributed by the churchwarden chosen by the parishioners in Kilburn, in varying amounts, and the rest by the vicar, generally in sums of £1.

Anne Mallory, by will dated 1789, left £100 for 2d. loaves for the poor every Sunday. The income was £3 10s. 2d. in 1824. It was £3 4s. 4d. in 1898, when it was distributed with Rixton's charity.

Elizabeth Shooter, by will dated 1727, left the reversion of a copyhold in Langley (Bucks.), which was valued at c. £5 10s. in 1824, in trust to maintain two widows of Hampstead for life. The land produced a rent of £20 in 1811 and the fund was managed by the vicar of Hampstead. After 1816 small sums were occasionally given to other widows with the agreement of the principal recipients. In

1851 the trustees of the poor of Hampstead were admitted to the property, which in 1898 formed part of a market garden, and £30 less 7s. 7d. quit rent was divided between three widows.

Thomas Rumsey, by will dated 1798, left £1,000 stock in reversion after the deaths of his three daughters to four inhabitants of Hampstead chosen by the vestry, for coals at Christmas for families attending the Anglican church and not receiving parish alms. The stock, £889 after duty, was received by the parish in 1835. Tickets for 2 cwt. of coal were distributed in 1898.

Eliza Anne Hume, by will proved 1856, left £100 stock to repair her tomb and vault every 3 years, the surplus to go to the poor. After duty £90 was received, yielding £2 9s. 4d. in 1898. At the distribution in 1892 £10 10s. was paid to the Hampstead Benevolent Society for work in the eastern part of the parish and £10 10s. was distributed amongst the poor of Kilburn; no part was used for her tomb.

John Clarke, by will proved 1861, left £100 to be distributed with charities at St. Paul's chapel, Kilburn (Willesden). In 1897 the surviving trustees applied for a Scheme, which in 1898 assigned the income to the minister and churchwardens in aid of charities of the district, which included part of Hampstead. The charity then consisted of £192 in stock, and £127 in cash which was to be used towards a parish room. After the demolition of St. Paul's, a Scheme of 1936 assigned the income from the £88 stock to the charities of St. Mary's, Kilburn, in Hampstead. The income in 1964 was £2 12s. 8d.[74]

Isabel Constable, by will dated 1888, left £50 for the repair of her family vault in the churchyard, the surplus to go to the poor. In 1898 the dividends of £1 7s. 8d. were used for annual gifts, similar to Marshall's charity, and no part was spent on the vault.

James Stewart Henderson, by will proved 1933, left £4,000 for payments to the poor of St. Stephen's, Rosslyn Hill. The income in 1961 was £140 and was used for grants, supporting boys at camps and holiday homes, and Christmas gifts to pensioners.[75]

Hampstead Parochial charities. A Scheme of 1983 administered the small charities of Arnold, Charles, Cleave, Constable, Hume, Mallory, Marshall (Francis and Rosamond), Rixton, Robinson, Shooter, and Waite, besides the charity of Elizabeth Blondell for which no details were given. Their assets consisted entirely of stock in 1983, except those of Shooter's charity, which still derived an annual rent of £175. All except Blondell's £56 stock and 26 shares out of 64 making up Rixton's charity were administered together as the Hampstead Parochial charities. The 26 shares were managed separately as John Rixton's Church charity. Half of the income of the Church charity and all the income of Blondell's charity were to be paid to the vicar of St. John's for a sermon on or near Good Friday; the remaining half of the Church charity was to help maintain the parish church. Income from the parochial charities was to relieve the poor in the former metropolitan borough of Hampstead through grants, goods, or services, or grants and subscriptions to organizations.

[74] Char. Com. files.   [75] Ibid.

PADDINGTON

PADDINGTON,[1] apart from containing the G.W.R. Co.'s London terminus and St. Mary's hospital, was notable mainly for contrasting social conditions, with fashionable terraces facing Hyde Park and Kensington Gardens, middle-class avenues around Westbourne Grove and in Maida Vale, and some of London's worst slums along the lines of communication which bisected the parish.

The present account includes Queen's Park, formerly part of a detached portion of Chelsea parish.[2] Paddington was roughly triangular in shape before the addition of Queen's Park and was nearest to London at the south-eastern corner, close to Marble Arch. Marylebone lay to the east, Willesden to the north, Chelsea detached to the north-west, and Kensington to the west. St. Margaret's, Westminster, lay to the south, until its division left Paddington bordered by a detached portion, with part of St. Martin's-in-the-Fields, later St. George's, Hanover Square, farther east. The longest, north-eastern, boundary followed Edgware Road, the Roman Watling Street, for 3.2 km. to Kilburn. The north-west boundary in the north followed the Westbourne stream, which was later straightened along the line of Kilburn Park Road, before turning north-westward towards Willesden Lane, and then ran south and south-eastward through fields to meet the Uxbridge road (later Bayswater Road) nearly opposite Kensington Palace Gardens. The southern boundary mostly followed the Uxbridge road but south of the road it included a rectangular piece of Kensington Gardens[3] and on the north, near Marble Arch, from 1763 it excluded c. 5 a. which were sold by the beneficial lessee of Paddington manor to St. George's, Hanover Square, as a burial ground.[4] The eastern and western halves of the parish were divided by the Westbourne, in part a manorial boundary,[5] and the northern and southern halves by Harrow Road, and later also by the Paddington canal, the G.W.R. line, and the elevated road called Westway.

The inclusion within Paddington of land south of the Uxbridge road antedated the creation of a royal residence at Kensington Palace and annexations to it from 1689 of parts of Hyde Park as Kensington Gardens.[6] Boundary stones between the parishes of St. Margaret's, Kensington, and Paddington were to be placed in Hyde Park in 1658.[7] It was suggested in 1803 that a perambulation of Paddington had failed to include enough of the park.[8] After an attempt to levy rates on the land leased to St. George's parish

for a burial ground, Paddington in 1828 was advised that it had no rights there, despite a breach of faith by St. George's in having allowed houses to be built.[9]

The area of the parish was estimated at 1,220 a. in 1831.[10] After minor changes, including an addition from Kensington Palace's gardens in 1841[11] and a transfer to Willesden in 1883, the acreage was 1,256 in 1891. Under the Metropolis Local Management Act, 1855, Paddington became a civil metropolitan parish within the area of the M.B.W.[12] In 1900, under the London Government Act, 1899, Queen's Park, the northern part of Chelsea detached, was allotted to the new Paddington metropolitan borough, which also acquired the disused St. George's burial ground. Many slight adjustments were made to the Kensington boundary, chiefly eastward to skirt Ledbury Road, southward from Artesian Road to the west end of Westbourne Grove, westward from Hereford Road to Chepstow Place, and eastward again to Ossington Street.[13] Houses at the north-eastern end of Kensington Palace Gardens, with part of the gardens stretching east to the Broad Walk, were also surrendered to Kensington.[14] Paddington metropolitan borough, covering 1,357 a. (c. 550 ha.) in 1911 and 1961, formed the north-western portion of Westminster L.B. from 1965.[15]

The northern two thirds of the parish are covered by London Clay, which also covers the west side as far south as Moscow Road but the east side only to Paddington green. A narrow central tongue of clay, along the line of the Westbourne stream and Gloucester Terrace, stretches south across Bayswater Road to the Serpentine. Taplow Gravel lies in the south-western corner, south of Moscow Road, and more extensive gravel, broken only by a patch of clay beneath Stanhope Street, covers south-eastern Paddington.[16]

The natural contours were said in 1853 to have been obscured by excavations, deposits, and subsidence.[17] Paddington lies on a gentle slope from Hampstead and has its highest point, 120 ft. (36.6 m.) above sea level, in the north-east corner at Maida Hill. The slope is gradual along Edgware Road but more marked along the valley of the Westbourne, where part of Westbourne Grove lies at only 63 ft. There is a slight rise towards Bayswater Road in the south-western part, with Craven Hill and the north-western slope of Notting Hill.[18]

The Westbourne,[19] until the mid 19th century

---

[1] The article was written in 1983–4 and revised in 1985.

[2] Following 2 paras. based on Gutch, *Plan of Paddington* (1828, 1840); Lucas, *Plan of Paddington* (1869); O.S. Maps 1/2,500, Lond. XXIII, XXIV, XXXII, XXXIII (1869–71 edn.); ibid. Lond. XLVII, XLVIII, LIX, LX (1896–7 edn.); ibid. Lond. IV. 7, 8, 11, 12 (1915–16 edn.); ibid. 1/10,000, TQ 28 SE. (1974 edn.).   [3] Below.

[4] Ibid.; Westm. libr., C 770, ff. 203, 220 (St. Geo. Hanover Sq. vestry mins. 19 Feb., 2 May 1763).

[5] Below, manors.

[6] R. Church, *Royal Parks of Lond.* (H.M.S.O. 1965), 18, 25.

[7] Chwdns. acct. bk. (1656–1736), f. 8. Par. rec. are in Marylebone libr.: below, local govt.

[8] Vestry mins. 6 May 1803.

[9] Select vestry mins. 2 Dec. 1828.

[10] Para. based on *Census*, 1831–1961.

[11] 5 & 6 Vic. c. 19.

[12] 18 & 19 Vic. c. 120.

[13] Old and new boundaries are on *Map of Paddington* (1900) in Marylebone libr.

[14] *Survey of Lond.* xxxvii. 151.

[15] Lond. Govt. Act, 1963.

[16] Geol. Surv. Map 6″, drift, Lond. IV. NE., SE. (1920 edn.).

[17] Robins, *Paddington*, 107.

[18] Ibid.; *Bayswater Annual* (1885); O.S. Map 1/10,000, TQ 28 SE. (1974 edn.).

[19] Para. based on N. J. Barton, *Lost Rivers of Lond.* (1962), 37, 96, and map; *T.L.M.A.S.* vi. 272 (map).

usually called the Bayswater rivulet, is a union of streamlets rising on the west side of Hampstead Heath and joining near Kilburn. From the dip in the northern boundary it flows overall in a south-easterly direction across Paddington. Often straightened and culverted, as the Ranelagh sewer, before being built over, its course was still open in 1871 along the later line of Kilburn Park and Shirland roads;[20] farther south, it had disappeared beneath Formosa Road, Ranelagh (later Lord Hill's) Road, the western ends of Bishop's Bridge Road and Cleveland Square, and behind the western side of Gloucester Terrace to Hyde Park, where its valley had been dammed in 1730 to form the Serpentine. Half way along Shirland Road, the Westbourne was joined by a stream which flowed from Kensal Rise across Queen's Park. A small eastern tributary, from Marble Arch to the Serpentine, was sometimes called the Tyburn brook but was not the better known Tyburn, which flowed southward across Marylebone.

COMMUNICATIONS. Roman roads formed the parish's north-eastern and southern boundaries from Marble Arch: Watling Street, later Edgware Road, and the Uxbridge road,[21] whose length to Notting Hill Gate was known by the 1860s as Bayswater Road.[22] In the early 19th century, when both roads were coming to be built up, houses were often described as lying only in a particular stretch, such as Maida Vale and Maida Hill in Edgware Road or Hyde Park Place, Uxbridge Place, and Bayswater Terrace in the Uxbridge road.[23]

Failure to repair the highway and scour the ditches from Tyburn to Kilburn bridge led to indictments of the abbot of Westminster between 1422 and 1440.[24] The Uxbridge road was noted for robberies in the 18th century, when a wall screened travellers from Hyde Park and Kensington Gardens, and was in very bad repair in 1807, although soon afterwards it was improved. It was administered from 1714 by the Uxbridge turnpike trust, while Edgware Road from 1721 was in the charge of the St. Marylebone turnpike trust.[25] The parish paid annual sums in composition by 1738 to the St. Marylebone turnpike trustees and later to the Uxbridge trustees,[26] both bodies being superseded from 1827 by the metropolis turnpike roads commissioners. A gate and toll house of the St. Marylebone trust, previously at the Oxford Street corner of Park Lane, moved to the Paddington angle between the Uxbridge and Edgware roads after the dismantling of the permanent Tyburn gallows in 1759. Gates barred both main roads c. 1790, when they were sketched by Paul

Sandby, but the Edgware Road gate had been moved northward by 1794 and the Uxbridge road gate, with the tollhouse, was given up in 1829. Other gates, which changed in number and position, included one in Edgware Road at Chapel Street in 1799 and the earlier Bayswater gate in the Uxbridge road, east of the Serpentine, which was also sketched by Sandby and survived until 1834, leaving Notting Hill gate as the first out of London. The spread of housing necessitated the placing of many bars across side roads, which were increasingly resented until their abolition under the Metropolis Roads Amendment Act, 1863.[27]

The only way westward across the centre of the parish until the 19th century was a forerunner of the modern Harrow Road,[28] leading from Edgware Road past Paddington green, thence turning north-west and west to cross the stream to Westbourne green, and continuing north-westward to Chelsea detached, Willesden, and Harrow. A charity for repairs was set up by John Lyon in 1582 but the income was withheld by Harrow school on the establishment in 1801 of Harrow Road turnpike trust, to which Paddington paid annual sums in composition.[29] The Paddington branch of the Grand Junction canal, opened in that year,[30] passed under the road near the later Little Venice, where the road was shifted slightly to the north,[31] and also farther west, north of Westbourne green. Under an Act of 1826[32] the turnpike trustees conveyed the eastern stretch of Harrow Road, from Edgware Road to the first canal bridge, to Paddington parish, which was to receive some of the income from Lyon's charity. With the parish's agreement,[33] the stretch between the bridges was conveyed by the metropolitan turnpike roads commissioners to the G.W.R. Co. under an Act of 1837,[34] and was then realigned a little to the north, the work being finished in 1841. A turnpike gate stood at Westbourne green,[35] where a lane ran south to the Uxbridge road, until the realignment; after three moves, the gate survived slightly west of the junction with Great Western Road until the 1860s. Widening of a 700-ft. stretch of Harrow Road at the corner of Edgware Road was completed in 1877. Extending into Willesden, Harrow Road was thought in the 1960s to be the longest road in London to have its buildings numbered consecutively throughout.[36]

Harrow Road and Westbourne green were connected with the Uxbridge road and Bayswater by Westbourne Green Lane,[37] so called in the mid 18th century[38] and probably the Westbourne Lane recorded in 1360.[39] It was known as Black Lion Lane by 1767[40] and in the early 19th century, when parishioners objected to a toll bar maintained by the metropolitan turnpike roads commissioners at its

[20] O.S. Map 1/2,500, Lond. XXIV (1871 edn.).
[21] V.C.H. Mdx. i. 66.
[22] O.S. Map 1/2,500, Lond. XXXIII (1869 edn.).
[23] Gutch, Plan of Paddington (1828, 1840).
[24] W.A.M. 6623.
[25] A. C. Jones, 'Turnpike Roads around Paddington' (TS. 1965 in Marylebone libr.).
[26] Marylebone libr., highway surveyors' accts. (1738–73, 1774–1822).
[27] Jones, 'Turnpike Rds.'. For the St. Marylebone trust in general, see F. H. W. Sheppard, Local Govt. in St. Marylebone, 1688–1835 (1958), 55–70.
[28] Para. based on Jones, 'Turnpike Rds.'.
[29] 41 Geo. III, c. 129 (Local and Personal); highway surveyors' accts. (1774–1822).

[30] Below.
[31] Vestry mins. 22 May 1800; 22 Sept. 1801.
[32] 7 Geo. IV, c. 91 (Local and Personal).
[33] Select vestry mins. 26 Apr. 1836; 19, 26 Jan., 4 Feb. 1837.
[34] 1 Vic. c. 92 (Local and Personal).
[35] E. T. MacDermot, Hist. G.W.R. (1964), i. 23.
[36] Marylebone libr., P 138, cuttings. Finchley Rd., however, had more nos.: P.O. Dir. Lond. (1964).
[37] Following 4 paras. based on Rocque, Map of Lond. (1741–5); Gutch, Plan of Paddington (1828, 1840); Bacon, Atlas of Lond. (1886).
[38] Highway surveyors' accts. (1738–73).
[39] W.A.M. 16446.
[40] Highway surveyors' accts. (1738–73).

junction with the Uxbridge road.[41] A small part near Westbourne green had been built up as Pickering Place by 1828, when its houses backed on another row called Pickering Terrace, which in 1876 was renamed as part of Porchester Road.[42] The southern stretch of Black Lion Lane by 1840 was called Queen's Road, a name extended c. 1911 to cover Pickering Place and changed from the beginning of 1938 to Queensway.[43]

There was a Green Lane near Westbourne green in 1548,[44] presumably the one which in 1591 was to have a stile built at its end.[45] In the 1740s a lane ran west from Westbourne green, in the direction later taken by Westbourne Park Road, and zigzagged north-westward to join Harrow Road at the modern junction with Great Western Road.[46] After the lane had been severed by the Grand Junction canal, over which it had no bridge, the northernmost stretch disappeared while the rest, although described as Green Lane in 1864,[47] fell into disuse. Another Green Lane, so named in 1746, ran northward from Harrow Road into fields, north-west of Paddington green, along the line of Warwick Avenue, but had vanished by the early 19th century.

Among footpaths was one running eastward from the southern end of Westbourne green across Bayswater rivulet to Paddington green in 1746. It was stopped by the canal in 1801 to the anger of the vestry, which insisted that the canal company's road bridge lay too far to the north and in 1803 secured a new footbridge on the original route.[48] The path was called Bishop's Walk in 1828. The eastern end of the path crossed the canal and land acquired for the depot and lines of the G.W.R. Co., which in 1837 undertook to construct a road, including a viaduct over the railway and a bridge over the canal.[49] The new way was called the Bishop's Road, from 1938 renamed Bishop's Bridge Road.[50]

Apart from the roads mentioned above, there were only short local lanes around Paddington green, Westbourne green, and Bayswater until the building up of the bishop of London's estate in the early 19th century. Building began in the south-east corner of the parish, where a grid pattern of roads formed Tyburnia. The grid's axis was Grand Junction Street (later Sussex Gardens), which ran north-eastward and enabled traffic from the Uxbridge road to avoid Oxford Street by cutting across to Edgware Road and the 18th-century New Road (later Marylebone Road).[51] By 1886 building had produced many long straight north–south roads across Bayswater and some still longer avenues were being laid out farther north, in Maida Vale. None, however, was intended as more than a shopping or residential street. The only modern main road consisted of the Marylebone flyover across Edgware Road, opened

in 1967, and the elevated Westway, opened in 1970. Together they linked Marylebone Road with Western Avenue, the eastern end of the new route running parallel with that of a straightened Harrow Road past the south side of Paddington green.[52]

The Westbourne or Bayswater rivulet was crossed by Edgware Road at Kilburn bridge and, on leaving the parish, by the Uxbridge road at Bayswater bridge.[53] Kilburn bridge, supposedly built in the mid 13th century by a prior of Kilburn, in 1826 consisted of a single medieval stone arch which had been widened in brick on either side. The bishop of London, as lord of the manor, had been charged with one quarter of its repairs in 1647[54] but by 1826 its south side was repaired by the St. Marylebone turnpike trust and its north side by the Kilburn Road trust. Bayswater bridge, a single arch of brick, was considered the responsibility of the bishop in 1826, although he had been charged with only half the upkeep in 1647 and the parish had repaired it in 1746.[55] The bishop's lessee in 1753 agreed to pay 20s. a year towards its upkeep and in 1762 compounded with the Uxbridge road turnpike trustees, who rebuilt it in 1824. The only ancient road bridge wholly within Paddington was Westbourne bridge, mentioned in 1402,[56] where the rivulet was crossed by Harrow Road east of Westbourne green. Bridge field, to the south-west, was so named by 1530.[57] In 1826 the bridge was a single arch of brick, supposedly built and, as in 1647, repaired by the bishop, although in 1819 its upkeep had been the subject of negotiations between the parish and the Harrow Road trustees.[58] A little to the south Bishop's Walk was provided in 1817 with a footbridge, for which the vestry was summoned by the court of sewers but which was allowed to remain until replaced by the G.W.R. Co.[59]

In 1795, while work was proceeding on its canal from Brentford to Braunston (Northants.), the Grand Junction Canal Co. was empowered to construct an easterly cut from Bull's bridge in Norwood to Paddington.[60] Some 48 a. were leased in 1798 from the bishop and his lessees[61] and in 1801 the Paddington branch of the Grand Junction canal was opened. Entering the parish slightly south of Harrow Road, the canal was built mainly on a raised embankment. It passed under the road at the northern end of Westbourne green and again at the south end of a pool at the later Little Venice north-west of Paddington green, terminating in a basin south of Harrow Road's junction with Edgware Road. The Harrow Road bridge south of the pool and the Lock bridge, together with a wooden footbridge for Bishop's Walk, were built and in 1826 maintained by the company.[62] There followed the later Westbourne Terrace Road bridge immediately west of the pool,

[41] Select vestry mins. 19 Aug., 2 Dec. 1828.
[42] L.C.C. *Names of Streets* (1901). An earlier Porchester Rd. of 1828 and 1840 was renamed Porchester Terr.
[43] L.C.C. *Names of Streets* (1912, 1955).
[44] *Cal. Pat.* 1548–9, 59.
[45] W.A.M. 16453.
[46] See also Ch. Com. 'Map of 1742'.
[47] MacDermot, *G.W.R.* ii. 7, 628.
[48] Vestry mins. 30 June 1800; 14 May, 22 Sept. 1801; 4 Feb., 27 May 1802; 19 May 1803.
[49] 1 Vic. c. 92 (Local and Personal).
[50] L.C.C. *Names of Streets* (1955).
[51] G. Mackenzie, *Marylebone* (1972).
[52] Marylebone libr., P 138, cuttings; O.S. Map 1/10,000, TQ 28 SE. (1974 edn.); above, plate 38.

[53] Para. based on *Rep. on Bridges in Mdx.* 153–6.
[54] Guildhall MS. 10464A.
[55] Ibid.; highway surveyors' accts. (1738–73).
[56] W.A.M. 16447.
[57] W.A.M., Reg. Book i, f. 264; Ch. Com., 'Map of 1742'.
[58] Guildhall MS. 10464A; vestry mins. 29 Apr. 1819.
[59] Gutch, *Plan of Paddington* (1828); above.
[60] *V.C.H. Mdx.* vii. 104; 35 Geo. III, c. 43.
[61] Guildhall MS. 12601. More land was leased to the co. in 1825: ibid. and plans. Below, manors (Grand Junction Canal Co.).
[62] C. Hadfield, *Brit. Canals* (1979), 126; C. Hadfield, *Canals of E. Midlands* (1970), 118; *Rep. on Bridges in Mdx.* 158; Gutch, *Plan of Paddington* (1828).

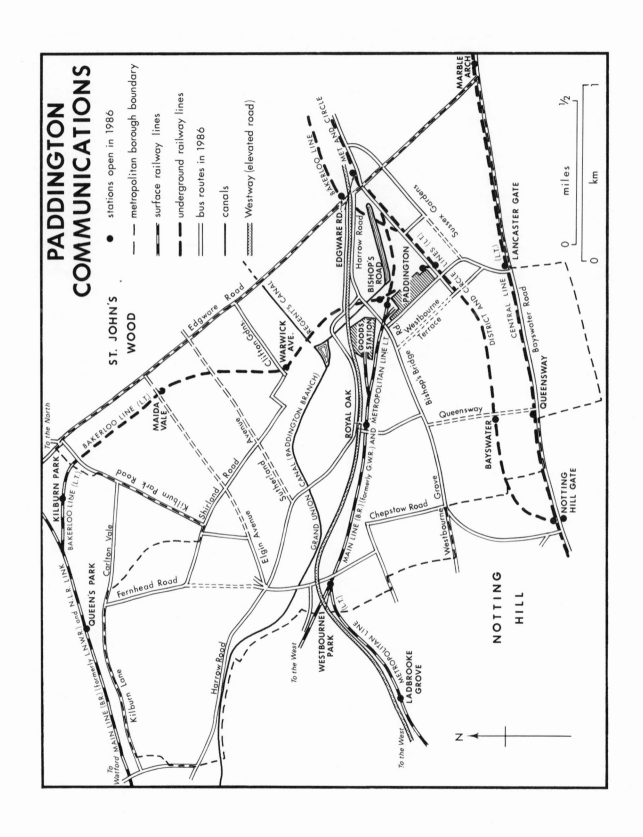

PADDINGTON COMMUNICATIONS

- ● stations open in 1986
- – – metropolitan borough boundary
- ▬ surface railway lines
- ▬▬ underground railway lines
- ▬ bus routes in 1986
- ▬ canals
- ▬ Westway (elevated road)

ST. JOHN'S
WOOD

To the North

BAKERLOO LINE (L.T.)

To Watford MAIN LINE (B.R.) (formerly L.N.W.R.) and N.L.R. LINK

KILBURN PARK

QUEEN'S PARK

BAKERLOO LINE (L.T.)

Kilburn Lane

Carlton Vale

Kilburn Park Road

Shirland Road

Edgware Road

Clifton Gdns.

REGENT'S CANAL

MAIDA VALE

WARWICK AVE.

Elgin Avenue

Sutherland Avenue

Fernhead Road

Harrow Road

CANAL (PADDINGTON BRANCH)

GRAND UNION CANAL

To the West

WESTBOURNE PARK

METROPOLITAN LINE

LADBROOKE GROVE

To the West

MAIN LINE (B.R.) (formerly G.W.R.) AND METROPOLITAN LINE L.T.

ROYAL OAK

GOODS STATION

BISHOP'S ROAD

PADDINGTON

Harrow Road

EDGWARE RD.

BAKERLOO LINE

MET. AND CIRCLE

MARBLE ARCH

Sussex Gardens

CIRCLE LINES (L.T.)

DISTRICT AND CIRCLE

Westbourne Terrace

Bishop's Bridge Rd.

Chepstow Road

Westbourne Grove

Queensway

BAYSWATER

CENTRAL LINE (L.T.)

LANCASTER GATE

Bayswater Road

QUEENSWAY

NOTTING HILL GATE

NOTTING HILL

N

0   ½   miles

0   ½   1   km

176

known also as the weighbridge because tolls for barges were collected near by, and the G.W.R. Co.'s Bishop's Road bridge of *c.* 1838. After housing had spread north-westward the Great Western Road or Carlton bridge was built at the expense of the M.B.W., the vestry, and private subscribers *c.* 1870. Footbridges built by the canal company at the western end of Delamere Terrace and, in Chelsea detached, at Wedlake Street were taken over by the M.B.W. and in 1885 conveyed to the vestries. Paddington metropolitan borough had ten canal bridges, including footbridges and crossings of the Regent's canal, in 1928.[63]

The Regent's canal, passing north of London to the Thames at Limehouse, was authorized in 1812, despite parochial objections.[64] From a pumping station at Little Venice it headed north-east to a tunnel under Edgware Road at Maida Hill, a bridge being built by the Regent's Canal Co. across the canal's western end at what became Warwick Avenue. The first section, from Paddington to Camden Town, was opened in 1816. Running at first mainly through fields,[65] the canals confirmed a division between the northern and southern parts of the parish already marked by Harrow Road and later reinforced by the railway.

The Paddington canal, although built mainly for goods, was used also by passengers. The pool at Little Venice was intended from the start for pleasure boats.[66] Transport to Uxbridge was provided at first by the canal company and then by its lessees, while a private service ran from Paddington to Buckingham. Troops for Liverpool were carried on the canal in 1806 and again in 1822, although regular passenger services ceased *c.* 1810.[67] Later traffic was limited mostly to the summer months and presumably consisted of pleasure trips, as in 1820 when refreshments were offered on a daily passage boat to Greenford and Uxbridge.[68] Cheap summer excursions were increasingly popular in 1853[69] and those along the Regent's canal to Camden Town were said to be quicker than road transport.[70] Other boats occasionally operated throughout the year, conveying both passengers and parcels in 1831.[71]

Summer excursions by former working narrow boat from Little Venice to Camden Town were started by John James in 1951. The trips, with occasional westward excursions to Harlesden, continued in 1983, by which date the British Waterways Board had opened a service from Little Venice to the Zoo.[72] A canalside walk from Harrow Road to Great Western Road, the first Paddington section of one

from Primrose Hill to Ladbroke Grove, was opened in 1972.[73] There was also a walkway along part of the south side of the canal basin by 1985. It was then planned to extend the walk around the 3-a. basin, which was to be used for water sports and as a London terminus for leisure boats.[74]

Paddington has figured prominently in the history of public transport, partly because the New Road through Marylebone was a quick route to the City and partly because the rapid spread of housing on the bishop's estate and around the canal basin in the early 19th century created a demand.[75] In 1780 hired hackney coaches were apparently the only means of conveying passengers from London but by 1798 a coach left Newgate Street for Paddington three times a day, as did another from Fore Street.[76] Twenty short-stage coaches left the City for Paddington daily in 1817, 12 of them from the Mansion House,[77] and 54 short stages provided 158 return journeys, far more than to any other single destination, in 1825.[78]

In 1829 George Shillibeer (1797–1866),[79] 'patron saint of the London omnibus',[80] inaugurated four services daily along the New Road to the Bank. His omnibus, running from Paddington green,[81] soon faced competition until in 1831 operators jointly agreed to limit themselves to 57 vehicles, providing a three-minute service. In 1832, from a headquarters in St. Alban's Place on the Paddington side of Edgware Road, Shillibeer also started a service along Oxford Street to the Bank.[82] Paddington vestry was concerned at obstruction by omnibuses in Edgware Road, particularly outside the Wheatsheaf at the corner of Church Street, where in 1833 there were often 8 or 10 vehicles, whose drivers' rowdy behaviour was said to threaten property values.[83] Omnibuses largely replaced short-stage coaches during the 1830s and, although Shillibeer soon moved away, the two main routes from Paddington to the Bank remained London's busiest in 1838–9: 55 vehicles were then licensed for the New Road and for Oxford Street with a further 13 serving an extension to Maida Hill. The largest firm was Richard Blore & Co., which controlled the London Conveyance Co. with its office in St. Alban's Place.[84] A service from Paddington to Charing Cross, with cheap fares for short distances, started in 1846. After the Great Exhibition of 1851 had left a surplus capacity, cheap fares were offered on several routes, beginning with one from Bayswater to Tottenham Court Road.[85] In 1856 most vehicles were acquired by the Compagnie Générale des Omnibus de Londres,[86] re-registered in 1858 as the London

[63] Marylebone libr., P 136.2, cuttings; G. F. Robinson, 'Waterways of Paddington' (TS. 1928 in Marylebone libr.).
[64] Hadfield, *Brit. Canals*, 126; vestry mins. 2 Mar. 1812.
[65] Hadfield, *Brit. Canals*, 126; *Canals of E. Midlands*, 129–30; *Rep. on Bridges in Mdx.* 157; Gutch, *Plan of Paddington* (1828).
[66] *Original Plan of Termination of Grand Junction Canal* (undated, in Marylebone libr.).
[67] Hadfield, *Brit. Canals*, 120; *Canals of E. Midlands*, 120, 144.
[68] Lysons, *Environs* (Suppl.), 241; *Ambulator* (1820), 251; B.M., Crace xxx. 49, 51.
[69] Robins, *Paddington*, 177.
[70] *Paddington News*, 28 May 1859.
[71] *Ambulator* (1807); *Priestley's Navigable Rivers and Canals* (1831) (1969 edn., intro. C. Hadfield), 312.
[72] Marylebone libr., P 136.2, cuttings; inf. from Mr. A. R. Hopkins, Jason's Trip.
[73] Marylebone libr., P 136.2, cuttings.
[74] *Paddington Basin Draft Planning Brief, 1985* (in Marylebone libr.).
[75] Below, growth.
[76] *Lond. Dir.* (1780, 1798).
[77] J. Cary, *New Itinerary* (1817).
[78] *Hist. Lond. Transport*, i. 5.
[79] D.N.B.
[80] V. Sommerfield, *Lond.'s Buses* (1933), 7.
[81] *Hist. Lond. Transport*, i. 20 and n. The Yorkshire Stingo in Marylebone, sometimes described as the terminus, may have been Shillibeer's depot.
[82] *Hist. Lond. Transport*, i. 19, 22, 24–8, 37–8.
[83] Select vestry mins. 4 Oct. 1831; 7 Feb. 1832; 3 Dec. 1833.
[84] *Hist. Lond. Transport*, i. 38; *P.O. Dir. Lond.* (1844, 1850).
[85] *Hist. Lond. Transport*, i. 60–2.
[86] Ibid. 79, 404–12.

General Omnibus Co. (L.G.O.C.), which had a provender depot at Irongate wharf.[87] The large number of east–west routes soon gave rise to a joke about French visitors who imagined that all Londoners went home at night to Bayswater.[88]

A steam coach was introduced by Walter Hancock's London and Paddington Steam Carriage Co. along the New Road in 1833. One vehicle, the abortive forerunner of the motor omnibus, ran in the summers of 1833 and 1834 and three larger coaches, with no greater success, in 1836.[89] London's first horse tramway, a single track of c. 1 mile along the Uxbridge road to Porchester Terrace, was opened by G. F. Train's Marble Arch Street Rail Car Co. in 1861. The line, which had been temporarily approved by the metropolis turnpike roads commissioners but opposed by Paddington vestry, was closed after six months. Trams provoked resentment in a fashionable area and the raised part of their rails proved an obstruction to other wheeled traffic;[90] no tramways were later laid along either Edgware or Bayswater roads.

The Harrow Road and Paddington Tramways Co., established in 1886, opened a 2½-mile track along Harrow Road from Amberley Road to Harlesden in 1888. A northward branch along Chippenham Road to Carlton Vale was abandoned in 1894, although an annual trip with a horse-car was made until 1910, in order to keep the powers alive.[91] The company's line, unconnected with any other route in 1895, was bought in 1902 by the Metropolitan Electric Tramways Co., a subsidiary of the British Electric Traction Co. Electric trams from Harlesden were introduced in 1906 and extended along Harrow Road to a terminus at Edgware Road in 1910.[92]

Omnibuses, numbering 87 an hour in Harrow Road c. 1904, provided a more comprehensive service than trams. In 1911 the L.G.O.C.'s motorbuses ran straight along Edgware Road to Dollis Hill and Cricklewood. Others turned westward off Edgware Road along Clifton Gardens and Shirland Road, along Harrow Road, and along Praed Street and Westbourne Grove, while three routes led to Shepherd's Bush or beyond along Bayswater Road.[93] All parts of Paddington were served by 1913.[94] The London Passenger Transport Board, responsible for trams and motorbuses from 1933, replaced the trams in Harrow Road with trolleybuses in 1936.[95] The trolleybuses, which ran to a turning circle at Paddington green rather than to Edgware Road, were in turn replaced by motorbuses in 1961–2.[96] London Transport Executive's Westbourne Park Bus Garage, opposite the railway station, was opened in 1981.

Designed to hold 110 buses and with a four-storeyed operations block faced with red brick, it replaced garages in North Kensington and Willesden.[97]

The Great Western Railway Co. was authorized by its Act of incorporation in 1835 to build a rail link between London and Bristol.[98] Broad gauge tracks, which necessitated a separate London terminus, were adopted at the insistence of the company's engineer I. K. Brunel. By agreement with the bishop and his lessees, work began on the easternmost stretch from Acton to Paddington, running through clay cuttings south of the canal, in 1836, although the eastern end and terminus were delayed until an Act of 1837 permitted the alteration of public roads.[99] To avoid delay, a temporary station was built on land intended for a goods depot and was opened in 1838 for journeys as far as Maidenhead (Berks.), trains running through to Reading from 1840 and to Bristol from 1841.[1]

The first Paddington station was approached by London Street, which ran northward from Praed Street and Tyburnia. The front was formed by the new Bishop's Road viaduct, some of whose arches were used for halls, offices, and access ways. The rest of the structure was mainly timber, containing one platform for arrivals and another for departures, to take c. 12 trains a day. Queen Victoria made her first railway journey, from Slough to Paddington, in 1842, and the station had been enlarged to have five platforms, with a carriage shed at the outer end and an engine shed and workshops beyond, by 1845.[2] Compared with other London termini, it was considered both unsightly and inconvenient in 1851.[3]

A second, permanent, terminus was authorized in 1850, on land to the south-east[4] which had already been taken for the wooden buildings of the goods station. Its opening in 1854 was following by the completion of new engine sheds at Westbourne Park in 1855, whereupon the remains of the first station made way for a depot, as originally planned. The permanent station was designed by Brunel, with ornamental details devised by Matthew Digby Wyatt and a colour scheme by Owen Jones.[5] The main building ran along Spring Street (later Eastbourne Terrace), where it was served by a cab route, and was extended southward towards the hotel in 1881 and given an extra storey c. 20 years later. Behind it were 3 parallel roofs of wrought iron and glass, on cast iron columns, interrupted in two places by 'transepts', covering 3 arrival and 3 departure platforms and 5 sidings. The inner platforms formed islands, reached by retractable drawbridges, the space by the track ends being used for turnplates and

[87] Ibid. 95; *P.O. Dir. Lond.* (1863, 1879).
[88] *Bayswater Annual* (1885), which gives routes and fares.
[89] Sommerfield, *Lond.'s Buses*, 4–5; *Hist. Lond. Transport*, i. 44.
[90] *Jnl. Transport Hist.* i (1), 98–100; *Hist. Lond. Transport*, i. 180; *Bayswater Chron.* 27 Mar. 1861.
[91] *Hist. Lond. Transport*, i. 258, 268; inf. from Mr. R. M. Robbins.
[92] *Hist. Lond. Transport*, i. 258; ii. 30, 100.
[93] Ibid. ii. 16, 169.
[94] Tram and motorbus routes on L.C.C. *Municipal Map of Lond.* (1913).
[95] *Hist. Lond. Transport*, ii. 300.
[96] Inf. from Mr. Robbins.
[97] Marylebone libr., P 137, cuttings; O. Green and J. Reed, *Lond. Transport Golden Jubilee Bk.* (1983), 186.

[98] 5 & 6 Wm. IV, c. 107 (Local and Personal).
[99] 7 Wm. IV & 1 Vic. c. 92 (Local and Personal); MacDermot, *G.W.R.* i. 20, 22–4; A. A. Jackson, *Lond.'s Termini* (1969), 304; above.
[1] Jackson, *Termini*, 304.
[2] MacDermot, *G.W.R.* i. 24–5, 45–6, 660–1; Jackson, *Termini*, 304–6; H.-R. Hitchcock, *Early Victorian Architecture in Britain* (1954), i. 506; ii. figs. xv. 15, 16; B.M., prints, Crace xxx. 57.
[3] *Knight's Cyclopaedia of Lond.* (1851), 844; J. Weale, *Lond. Exhibited* (1851), 807.
[4] For environs of both stations, see plan in MacDermot, *G.W.R.* i. 23.
[5] Ibid. i. 44; Jackson, *Termini*, 305–8; Pevsner, *Lond.* ii. 304; L.T.C. Rolt, *Isambard Kingdom Brunel* (1957), 232. For Wyatt's decoration, see Hitchcock, *Early Victorian Archit.* i. 559–60; ii, fig. xvi, 36, 37; above, plate 39.

later for mails.[6] Many changes, including the addition of more platforms, were carried out under Brunel's roof in the 1870s and 1880s, with the removal of carriage sidings and the gradual abandonment of broad gauge track. Enlargements from 1906 involved extension of the roof, in the original style, and of the platforms.[7] By 1921 *c.* 300 trains arrived and left every day.[8] Another major rebuilding, begun in 1930,[9] led to the absorption of the adjoining suburban station at Bishop's Road[10] and the creation of the modern concourse at the south end of the terminus, flanked by administrative blocks completed in 1933 to the design of P. G. Culverhouse.[11] The last scheduled passenger steam train left Paddington in 1965 and extensive track and signal modernization took place in 1967.[12]

Brunel saw his station as primarily an engineering work, 'admitting of no exterior'.[13] Inspired by a forerunner at Munich and by the Crystal Palace, it had one of England's first large station roofs in metal, spanning an area 700 ft. by 238 ft. and at the height of its curves reaching 55 ft. above the platforms.[14] The light and elegant interior became well known from W. P. Frith's 'Paddington Station', painted in 1862. As the G.W.R. served Windsor, an apartment for the queen was designed near platform 1.[15] The station was lit experimentally in 1880 by the Anglo-American Brush Electric Light Corporation and in 1886 by a more lasting system from generators near Westbourne railway bridge, hailed as the first attempt to supply large-scale electric lighting as a rival to gas.[16] Royal patronage, literary references,[17] and associations with long-distance travel to the west country rather than with suburban commuting,[18] earned Paddington a romantic, aristocratic reputation.[19] Paddington was also popular with railway enthusiasts as the last home of broad gauge express trains, which finally ceased to run in 1892.[20] In the 20th century the building, 'an aisled cathedral in a railway cutting',[21] has probably received more praise from architectural writers than any rival terminus.[22]

A hotel for travellers, the Prince of Wales, was opened near the temporary station before 1850. Its success induced a group of G.W.R. Co. shareholders and officials to build the Great Western (later the Great Western Royal) hotel at the southern end of the second station, where it masked the train sheds. Well publicized when it opened in 1854 as London's largest and most sumptuous hotel, it was managed directly by the G.W.R. from 1896[23] and became the headquarters of the company's catering depart-ment.[24] The building was mainly the work of C. P. Hardwick, although nominally that of his father Philip.[25] A stucco-fronted block of 5 storeys with 7-storeyed corner towers, it is perhaps the earliest Victorian example of the influence of French Renaissance and Baroque, notably in the lines of the roof; a central pediment contains allegorical figures by John Thomas.[26] Later additions and alterations had raised the number of bedrooms from 103 to 250 by 1936, when a low wing behind the hotel linked the new office blocks on either side of the station's concourse. Changes in 1936–8 included a new entrance canopy and external refacing.[27]

The G.W.R. Co., with its broad gauge, did not at first contemplate links with suburban lines. Its local traffic was comparatively light, until the 20th-century building up of outer Middlesex and south Buckinghamshire: as late as 1903 only 8 suburban trains arrived daily at Paddington, compared with 136 at Liverpool Street.[28] The company, however, subscribed to the North Metroplitan Railway Co., reincorporated in 1854 as the Metropolitan, for a mixed broad and standard gauge line which was opened in 1863 from Farringdon Street to a station built slightly north-west of the main line terminus and called Bishop's Road. A 15-minute service was worked briefly by the G.W.R., then by the Metropolitan with other companies' help, and from 1864 by the Metropolitan alone. A westward link from Bishop's Road to Hammersmith was provided from 1864 by the Hammersmith and City Railway Co., incorporated in 1861 to build a mixed gauge line which left the main G.W.R. line at Green Lane bridge, from 1866 the site of Westbourne Park station. That line too was worked at first by the G.W.R. and later by the Metropolitan, the two companies jointly acquiring control of the Hammersmith and City line in 1867. Under an Act of 1869, regulating arrangements with the Metropolitan, the G.W.R. laid extra track from Paddington to Westbourne Park. In 1871 it rebuilt the wooden Westbourne Park station and opened Royal Oak station. Suburban trains thus no longer had to use the main line, although they continued to cross it until a subway was built between Royal Oak and Westbourne Park in 1878. Electric traction was introduced in 1906. Bishop's Road station, built in the G.W.R.'s French Renaissance style, was linked by a footbridge to the main line terminus *c.* 1878. After enlargements, the name was abandoned and the platforms were renumbered in 1933 as part of Paddington station.[29]

The parish's first Underground railway was that

[6] Jackson, *Termini*, 307 and plan, 314; Pevsner, *Lond.* ii. 305; H. P. White, *Gtr. Lond.* (*Regional Hist. of Rlys. of Gt. Britain,* iii (1963)), 112.
[7] Jackson, *Termini*, 313–19.
[8] Bingham, *Official Guide to Paddington* [1921].
[9] Jackson, *Termini*, 319.
[10] Below.
[11] Jackson, *Termini*, 319, 321; Pevsner, *Lond.* ii. 305.
[12] Marylebone libr., P 135, cuttings.
[13] Rolt, *Brunel*, 231.
[14] Jackson, *Termini*, 306–7. Newcastle Central, opened 1850, had a roof 614 ft. by 184 ft.: J. C. Bruce, *Handbk. to Newcastle on Tyne* (1863), 119.
[15] Jackson, *Termini*, 311; Pevsner, *Lond.* ii. 305.
[16] Jackson, *Termini*, 314.
[17] e.g. R. Usborne, *Wodehouse at Work* (1976 edn.), 137.
[18] Below.

[19] White, *Gtr. Lond.* 113.
[20] Jackson, *Termini*, 313.
[21] J. Betjeman, *Lond.'s Historic Rly. Stas.* (1972), 108.
[22] e.g. I. Nairn, *Nairn's Lond.* (1966); G. Stamp and C. Amery, *Victorian Bldgs. of Lond. 1837–87* (1980), 43–4.
[23] Jackson, *Termini*, 308, 311; Marylebone libr., P 137, cuttings.
[24] MacDermot, *G.W.R.* ii. 269.
[25] Hitchcock, *Early Victorian Archit.* i. 211.
[26] Ibid. 211–13; N. Taylor, *Monuments of Commerce* (R.I.B.A. 1968), 49, 56; Jackson, *Termini*, 308; Pevsner, *Lond.* ii. 304.
[27] Jackson, *Termini*, 321.
[28] *Hist. Lond. Transport*, i. 53, 58; Jackson, *Termini*, 319–20.
[29] Jackson, *Termini*, 311–12, 320; T. B. Peacock, *Gt. Western Suburban Svces.* (1948), 13, 17, 19, 47; A. A. Jackson, *Lond.'s Metropolitan Rly.* (1986), 26, 40.

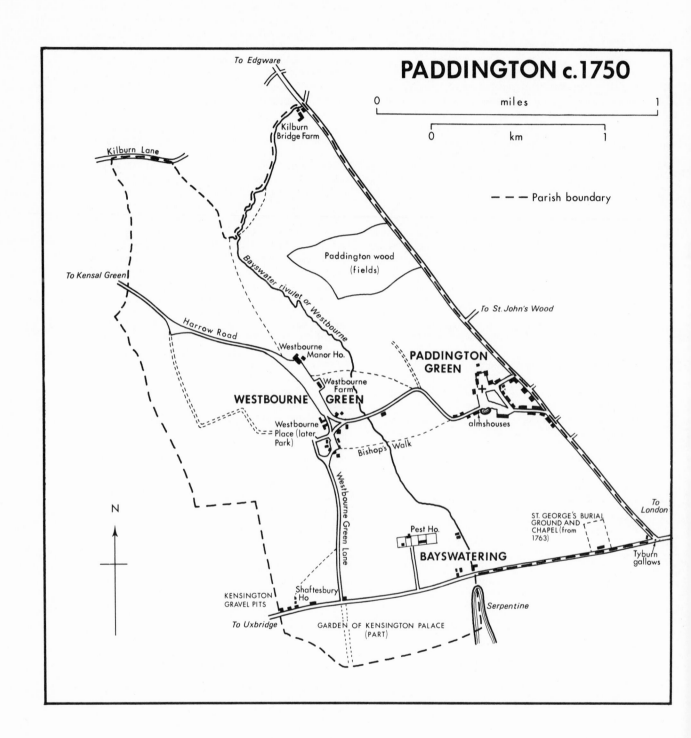

PADDINGTON c.1750

0   miles   1

0   km   1

– – – Parish boundary

To Edgware

Kilburn
Bridge Farm

Kilburn Lane

Paddington wood
(fields)

To Kensal Green

Bayswater rivulet or Westbourne

Harrow Road

To St. John's Wood

Westbourne
Manor Ho.

PADDINGTON
GREEN

Westbourne
Farm
GREEN

WESTBOURNE

Westbourne
Place (later
Park)

almshouses

Bishop's Walk

N

Westbourne Green Lane

To
London

Pest Ho.

ST. GEORGE'S BURIAL
GROUND AND
CHAPEL (from
1763)

BAYSWATERING

Tyburn
gallows

KENSINGTON
GRAVEL PITS

Shaftesbury
Ho

To Uxbridge

GARDEN OF KENSINGTON PALACE
(PART)

Serpentine

of the Metropolitan, whose forerunner, the North Metropolitan, had originally been called the Bayswater, Paddington, and Holborn Bridge Railway Co. The first plans, to bring the line as far as Westbourne Terrace, had been altered to provide for a terminus on the Marylebone side of Edgware Road, to placate Paddington vestry.[30] Later, however, it was decided to continue west along Praed Street to a station of that name in front of the G.W.R. terminus and to join the main line itself by a north-westward branch under South Wharf Road to Bishop's Road. Trains from Farringdon Street started in 1863 and were to be extended westward to South Kensington, under an Act of 1864, as part of an 'inner circuit'. Work proved expensive because of compensation to property owners and included the building of a well known pair of false house fronts in Leinster Gardens, where the line passed under the road. The stretch from Praed Street junction through Bayswater to Gloucester Road was opened in 1868.[31] On the completion of the 'circle' line in 1884, trains at first were run alternately by its two owners, the Metropolitan and the Metropolitan District or District railway companies. Later District trains ran on the inner rail and Metropolitan trains, clockwise, on the outer rail. Electric trains were introduced in 1905 by the Metropolitan, which soon afterwards took over the sole working of the 'Inner Circle'.[32] A subway between Praed Street and the terminus was built only in 1887.[33] Praed Street station was renamed Paddington in 1948 and Bayswater was called Bayswater (Queen's Road) for Westbourne Grove from 1922 until 1933.[34] Their design has been attributed to the Metropolitan's engineer John Fowler (later a baronet), whose white-brick stations, in a vaguely Italian Renaissance style, survived with minor alterations in 1986.[35]

Along the southern edge of the parish a tube railway, from the Bank to Shepherd's Bush, was opened by the Central London Railway Co. in 1900. There were stations at Marble Arch, on the Marylebone side of Edgware Road, at Lancaster Gate, and at Queen's Road, which was renamed Queensway in 1946, by which time the railway was part of the L.P.T.B.'s Central line.[36] Lancaster Gate station was rebuilt beneath the Royal Lancaster hotel in the 1960s, but Queensway has remained a little altered example of the original stations designed by H. B. Measures.[37]

A link with south London was provided by the Baker Street and Waterloo Railway Co., early nicknamed the Bakerloo, whose tube reached Great Central (later Marylebone) and Edgware Road stations in 1907. The company was absorbed by the

London Electric Railway Co. in 1910.[38] Enticed westward by the G.W.R. Co., the tube was extended to Paddington in 1913 and headed north-westward through the parish, with stations at Warwick Avenue and Maida Vale, to reach Queen's Park in Willesden by 1915. Its trains were running to Watford, on tracks of the London and North Western Railway, by 1917.[39] The Bakerloo's only surface station in Paddington, Maida Vale, survived in 1986 with its facing of glazed red bricks in the style of Leslie Green.[40]

Under the Post Office (London) Railway Act, 1913,[41] a tube line for the carriage of mails was opened to a western terminus beneath Paddington main line station in 1927.[42]

GROWTH. SETTLEMENT AND BUILDING TO c. 1800. Although both Edgware and Bayswater roads were of Roman origin, the earliest evidence of settlement lies in the name Padintune, Padda's *tun* or farm,[43] in a charter of Westminster abbey ostensibly of 959 but compiled after the Conquest.[44] Not mentioned in Domesday Book, Paddington was an estate whose profits had been assigned to the abbey's almonry by the mid 12th century.[45] It formed a vill within St. Margaret's parish, as did Westbourne and Knightsbridge, in 1222,[46] when its chapel[47] presumably served only the eastern part of the later Paddington parish. Neither courts nor a manor house were recorded during the Middle Ages. Paddington's tenants were still listed with those of Knightsbridge c. 1225,[48] and Westbourne tenants from the 14th century or earlier were subject to courts which normally met at Knightsbridge.[49] Paddington's church or chapel, close to the highway about half way along the parish's north-eastern boundary, probably came to attract worshippers from the Westbourne part of Knightsbridge manor, who otherwise had to travel to St. Mary Abbot's, Kensington.

The medieval settlements, at Paddington green, Westbourne green, and along the Uxbridge road, were small. Twenty people were assessed for subsidy in 1524[50] and there were 74 communicants in 1548.[51] Paddington, like Marylebone, contributed comparatively little towards county assessments in 1608 and 1636.[52] Seventy people were assessed for hearth tax in 1664, 52 being listed as in Paddington and the rest in Westbourne green,[53] and in the early 18th century the parish was described as very small.[54] In the 1740s the chief settlement was around Paddington green and along the nearby stretch of Edgware Road, opposite Lisson green in Marylebone, with smaller groups of houses to the west around Westbourne green and

[30] *Hist. Lond. Transport*, i. 104–5, 107.
[31] Ibid. 108, 115, 122, 136, 149, 152; White, *Gtr. Lond.* 83, 91.
[32] C. E. Lee, *Metropolitan Dist. Rly.* (1956), 30.
[33] Jackson, *Termini*, 312.
[34] J. E. Connor and B. L. Halford, *Forgotten Stations of Gtr. Lond.* (1972), 5, 12.
[35] L. Menear, *Lond.'s Underground Stations* (1983), 9; by an 'unknown and uninspired' architect, according to Jackson, *Lond.'s Metropolitan Rly.* 53.
[36] *Hist. Lond. Transport*, ii. 45, 145; Connor and Halford, *Forgotten Stations*, 12.
[37] Menear, *Lond.'s Underground Stations*, 37, 40.
[38] C. E. Lee, *Sixty Years of the Bakerloo* (1966), 10, 13, 17–19.
[39] Ibid. 19, 21; Jackson, *Termini*, 313.
[40] Menear, *Lond.'s Underground Stations*, 48.
[41] 3 & 4 Geo. V, c. 116 (Local).
[42] W. G. Carter, *Post Office (London) Rly.* (P.O. Green Papers, 1937), 4.
[43] *P.N. Mdx.* (E.P.N.S.), 132.
[44] *Cart. Sax.* ed. Birch, iii, p. 265; F. E. Harmer, *A.-S. Writs* (1951), 338.
[45] Below, manors.
[46] Harvey, *Westm. Abbey*, 45; text in H.F. Westlake, *St. Marg. Westm.* (1914), 231.
[47] Below, churches.
[48] Harvey, *Westm. Abbey*, 105.
[49] Below, local govt.
[50] Robins, *Paddington*, 180.
[51] *Lond. and Mdx. Chantry Certificates, 1548*, 73.
[52] *Mdx. County Rec.* ii. 103; iii. 63.
[53] G.L.R.O., MR/TH/2, mm. 30d.–31r.
[54] Newcourt, *Rep.* i. 703; *Magna Brit.* (1724), iii. 50.

at Bayswatering, where the Westbourne was crossed by the Uxbridge road. A pest house stood in the fields later covered by Craven Hill, and there were isolated buildings at the Tyburn and Kilburn ends of Edgwater Road and at the western end of the Uxbridge road.[55]

Apart from building next to St. George's burial ground,[56] little further change took place until the 1790s.[57] Painters appreciated the rural scenery in the 1780s[58] and there were estimated to be only 340 houses in 1795.[59] Most of the parish was grassland, providing hay for the cowkeepers who supplied London with milk.[60] Rural charms were enhanced by their contrast with the threatening spread of housing north-westward from London. An Act of 1763 applied new building regulations to Paddington, along with Marylebone, St. Pancras, Chelsea, and the city of Westminster,[61] and by 1792 Paddington was considered as united to the metropolis.[62] In 1795 it was hard to believe that the parish adjoined that of St. George, Hanover Square, Paddington's emptiness being ascribed to the fact that much of the land was in ecclesiastical hands. Already, however, activity in neighbouring parishes was making itself felt: nearly 100 wooden 'cottages', presumably not included in the total number of houses, had sprung up within the last four years along Edgware Road, for artificers working in London.[63]

BUILDING AFTER c. 1800. Acts of 1795, authorizing the Grand Junction Canal Co. to cut its Paddington branch[64] and the bishop of London and trustees for his lessees, the Morshead and Thistlethwayte families,[65] to build on what came to be called the Paddington Estate, opened the parish to London's sprawl. The bishop was to inclose c. 5 a. of waste and make a new lease for 99 years, the trustees could sublease up to 200 a. to builders for 98 years, and the bishop was to approve house plans and receive a third of the profits.[66] Later building Acts in 1804 allowed subleasing by private contracts, as an alternative to auctions, and the sale of brickearth or gravel[67] and in 1805 clarified the rents that might be charged.[68] Further Acts in 1808 led to negotiations with the City of London over water pipes which crossed the intended building land[69] and in 1812 authorized their purchase from the City.[70] An Act of 1826 'put the keystone into this expensive legislative arch', permitting the subleasing of up to 400 a.[71]

Approved building was slow to start: near the

Tyburn turnpike the almost empty west side of Edgware Road contrasted with the Marylebone side in 1799,[72] although there was more housing along the Uxbridge road, and Paddington still had only 324 houses in 1801.[73] Delay may have been caused at first by the scarcity of capital during the war years. More lasting causes were probably drainage problems[74] and a policy of subleasing small amounts to mostly local builders, in order to ensure a high standard of housing. The success of the policy was ultimately shown, both in the grandeur of the first new houses in Connaught Place c. 1807 and in the elegance of the terraces put up over the next thirty years.[75] Thus there arose a fashionable suburb, Tyburnia, in the previously open south-eastern corner of Paddington between Edgware Road and the Uxbridge road.

In contrast to the slow realization of plans for Tyburnia, there took place a rapid growth of labourers' shacks. In 1806 and again in 1808 the agents of the Paddington Estate promised to let no more land for cottages, but in 1809 squalor caused mounting concern and in 1811 it was admitted that the ban on new leases had led to denser building on existing plots.[76] In 1811, when Paddington had 879 inhabited houses and a population of 4,609,[77] the vestry complained that 500 small tenements were inhabited by 2,107 people, of whom 948 had arrived during the past year,[78] and in 1812 the fringe of Tyburnia had acquired an evil reputation.[79] Several of the huts, near Edgware Road opposite George Street, were known in 1812 as Tomlins Town.[80] Most of them probably proved short lived, having been built on plots leased for only 4 or 5 years[81] and being liable to demolition at six months' notice. They were often rebuilt nearby, however, with the result that in 1816 there were perhaps 690 on the Paddington side of Edgware Road and many more in Marylebone.[82]

The need to control housing was also made urgent by the construction of the Grand Junction canal. Negotiations with the canal company were in train at the time of the bishop's first building Act, when it was clear that industrial growth would take place around the proposed basin south of Paddington green.[83] The canal was said to have attracted the labourers, many of them Irish, who were still squatting on the bishop's land in both Paddington and Marylebone in 1816.[84] Its construction set a limit to the northward spread of Tyburnia, marked by Grand

[55] Ch. Com., 'Map of 1742'; Rocque, *Map of Lond.* (1741–5), sheet 11.
[56] Below, Tyburnia.
[57] Ch. Com., 'Plan of 1790'.
[58] *Reminiscences of Hen. Angelo*, i (1828), 230–1.
[59] Middleton, *View*, 329; below, econ.
[60] Lysons, *Environs*, iii. 336.
[61] 4 Geo. III, c. 14.
[62] *Ambulator* (1792).
[63] Lysons, *Environs*, iii. 330, 336–7.
[64] Above, commun.
[65] Below, manors.
[66] 35 Geo. III, c. 83 (Priv. Act); summarized in Robins, *Paddington*, 75–84.
[67] 44 Geo. III, c. 63 (Local and Personal, not printed); Robins, *Paddington*, 84–5.
[68] 45 Geo. III, c. 113 (Local and Personal); Robins, *Paddington*, 85–6.
[69] 48 Geo. III, c. 142 (Local and Personal); Robins, *Paddington*, 86–7; below, pub. svces.
[70] 52 Geo. III, c. 193 (Local and Personal).

[71] 6 Geo. IV, c. 45 (Private); Robins, *Paddington*, 93.
[72] R. Horwood, *Plan of Cities of Lond. and Westm.* (1799).
[73] *Census*, 1801.
[74] D. A. Reeder, 'Capital investment in western suburbs of Victorian Lond.' (Leic. Univ. Ph.D. thesis, 1965), app. A, p. viii.
[75] *Study of Urban Hist.* ed. H. J. Dyos, 262; below, growth, Tyburnia.
[76] Vestry mins. 2 Dec. 1808; 4 Apr. 1809; 19 Jan. 1811.
[77] *Census*, 1811.
[78] Vestry mins. 19 Jan. 1811.
[79] M. D. George, *Lond. Life in 18th Cent.* (1925), 115.
[80] *Langley & Belch's New Map of Lond.* (1812) (Lond. Topog. Soc. 1971).
[81] Vestry mins. 19 Jan. 1811.
[82] *Rep. from Sel. Cttee. on Educ. of Lower Orders in Metropolis, Third Rep. of Mins. of Evidence*, H.C. 495, pp. 220–1 (1816), iv.
[83] Below, econ., ind.
[84] *Rep. on Educ. of Lower Orders in Metropolis*, 220–1.

Junction Road (later Sussex Gardens): terraces along the south side were built as part of the Paddington Estate and those on the north by the canal company; beyond lay meaner streets, reservoirs, wharves, and warehouses. Paddington green, the chief 18th-century settlement, was cut off from Tyburnia and soon also, by the Regent's canal which had a few villas alongside it, from the fields to the north.[85]

The division between north and south was reinforced from the late 1830s by the G.W.R. line, with its terminus and goods station. Land was left between the railway and the canal, part of it intersected by Harrow Road, where working-class streets formed slums and where some larger canalside houses also deteriorated. Much cramped building around Paddington green and, farther west, railway stations at Royal Oak and Westbourne Park extended the belt of industry and poor housing.[86]

Although Tyburnia could not expand northward, its success, and the attractions of Kensington Gardens, encouraged building to the west, on land that was not all part of the bishop's estate. Tea gardens and other amenities flourished around the roadside settlement of Bayswatering, until in the mid 19th century they made way for the prosperous suburb of Bayswater. Paddington, like Kensington, shared in a twenty years' building boom from the mid 1830s, when rich merchants and professional men followed the aristocracy.[87] During the 1840s and 1850s loans from insurance companies, notably the London Assurance Group and Royal Exchange Assurance, enabled a few builders to plan on a more lavish scale.[88] In 1845 the G.W.R. Co.'s station was also thought to have furthered the recent and surprisingly rapid rise of a suburb which, in extent and respectability, surpassed any other.[89] North of Bayswater, middle- and upper middle-class streets, sometimes called Westbournia, reached to the southern end of Westbourne green; beyond, obliterating part of the old hamlet, lay the railway.[90]

In the 1860s growth temporarily slackened, as disputes arose among the beneficial lessees and as the upper middle class began to move farther from London.[91] By c. 1870, however, there remained open only the northern part of the parish.[92] Building activity soon revived, at least partly because of the provision of suburban and underground train services.[93] Leap-frogging the railway and canal, the Paddington Estate laid out middle-class avenues near Edgware Road, creating the greater part of Maida Vale. Humbler housing was built to the west, in St. Peter's Park, from the early 1860s. Lying north of Westbourne green, it was intended to be superior to the artisans' terraces put up from the

1870s in the northern part of Chelsea detached, which from 1900 was included in Paddington metropolitan borough as Queen's Park.[94]

Paddington was a comparatively small metropolitan borough and, for all its tree-shaded roads and squares, short of public open space.[95] Overall wealth, producing a very high rateable value, disguised wide disparities between districts,[96] as shown in residents' occupations, housing, and health. The contrast was particularly marked between the streets near Hyde Park and many of those along the canal, although even Tyburnia had pockets of poverty among its mews dwellings.[97] Further variety came from canalside industry, from hotels and lodging houses around the railway terminus, from early blocks of flats in Maida Vale, and from the shops and centres of entertainment in Westbourne Grove, Queen's Road (later Queensway), and Edgware Road.[98]

Restrictive building covenants on the Paddington Estate, although successful in attracting the well-to-do, by the 1880s were blamed for having hindered improvements, even the provision of better drains. Market values accordingly suffered when tenants wished to sell their leases, most of which had 40-50 years to run. Although the Ecclesiastical Comissioners could dissent to lettings, general management was left to the trustees. There was criticism that less desirable houses were subdivided, annual rentals were hard to ascertain, and that no land was made available for purpose-built dwellings for the poor.[99]

In the period between the World Wars, Paddington claimed to cater for people of all incomes. Publicity was given to its shops, social amenities, and good communications with the City and west end of London.[1] The areas facing Hyde Park and parallel with Maida Vale remained fashionable.[2] More flats were built, nearly all, as in Kensington and Hampstead, for private occupation.[3] While some large houses became derelict and others were split into cheap lodgings, in the smarter districts there were divisions into expensive flats, besides conversions of mews dwellings.[4]

There was a high density of 106 persons to an acre in 1921, similar to that in Holborn and Islington but much less than in Southwark, Shoreditch, Bethnal Green, Stepney, and Finsbury. The five most crowded metropolitan boroughs, however, had all reduced their densities by 1931, whereas Paddington's had very slightly risen. Old contrasts within the borough persisted, to such an extent that in 1921 there were 61 persons to an acre in Bayswater's Lancaster Gate East ward compared with 180 persons to

85 Gutch, *Plan of Paddington* (1828, 1840).
86 Ibid.; below, growth, Paddington green, Westbourne green.
87 *Study of Urban Hist.* 254-5.
88 Reeder, 'Capital Investment', 161-2, 169, 236.
89 *Illus. Lond. News*, 27 Sept. 1845, 208.
90 Below, growth, Bayswater, Westbourne green.
91 Reeder, 'Capital Investment', 237; *Study of Urban Hist.* 257-8.
92 Lucas, *Plan of Paddington* (1869).
93 *Study of Urban Hist.* 259.
94 Below, growth, Maida Vale, Queen's Pk.
95 *Plan of Paddington* (1901); *Official Guide to Paddington* [1921].
96 Mudie-Smith, *Rel. Life*, 71, 79.
97 Ibid. 79; Booth, *Life and Labour*, i (2), app. pp. 12-13;
iii (3), 122-4 and map between pp. 136 and 137. For canalside ind., below, econ., ind., and insurance plan 409 (1891, 1942, 1963).
98 Below, growth, *passim*.
99 *Rep. from Sel. Cttee. on Town Holdings, 1886*, H.C. 213, pp. 332, 359 (1886), xii; *First Rep. from Com. on Housing of Working Classes, 1884-5* [C. 4402], pp. 118, 209 (1884-5), xxx.
1 *Official Guide to Paddington* [1921, 1925]; *Paddington Past and Present* [1936].
2 *New Lond. Life and Labour*, vi (2), 431.
3 *Paddington Past and Present* [1936]; K. Young and P. L. Garside, *Metropolitan Lond.* (1982), 190, 192, 195, 197.
4 M. Fitzgerald, *Church as Landlord* (rep. of survey for housing assoc. of Ch. Union 1937), 65, 67-8.

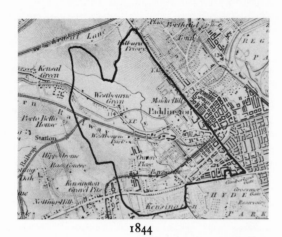

1844

1877

PADDINGTON: EVOLUTION OF SETTLEMENT, 1844–1904
(scale 1 in. to 1 mile)

an acre in Harrow Road ward; the gap had narrowed only a little, to densities of 74 and 166.5, by 1931.[5] Rising infant mortality in 1931–2, caused by patches of overcrowding, led to the designation of Paddington, Kensington, and St. Marylebone as areas of housing stress, in addition to poorer boroughs north, north-east, and south-east of the City.[6]

Failure to lessen overcrowding may have been due both to municipal inactivity[7] and to the fact that the Paddington Estate still covered c. 600 a. or roughly half of the borough. The Ecclesiastical Commissioners, who had succeeded to the bishop's interest, were criticized for drawing so much of their profits from squalor and even from vice. In defence it was pointed out that the comparatively few houses subleased on weekly or monthly tenancies were well kept up, but that most sites, including many along the canal, had been surrendered for long terms and were beyond the estate's control.[8] A steep rise in the commissioners' Paddington rental, from £23,000 in 1920 to £84,000 by 1940, was attributed by them to reletting after the expiry of the early leases. On such occasions they inserted stringent conditions; in 1943 immorality was associated mainly with properties whose long leases were nearly at an end, notably in Maida Vale.[9]

Damage during the Second World War affected only c. 5 per cent of Paddington's acreage.[10] Much rebuilding took place after the war, although more slowly than in many parts of London. Paddington's density of 92.5 persons to an acre was the highest of all the metropolitan boroughs in 1951 and at 86 persons to an acre it remained so in 1961, the most crowded area still being along Harrow Road.[11] Paddington council, the L.C.C., and their successors laid out housing estates with terraces and tower blocks, in place of slums and some canalside industry. The changes which eventually came were striking: blocks of maisonettes by the canal were claimed

to be the tallest in the country[12] and in 1967 Westminster planned what was described as the largest single comprehensive development yet seen in London, after a survey of 16,620 households had revealed that 86 per cent of the families were without their own lavatory or bath.[13] In 1985 Westminster owned 4,868 dwellings in south and central Paddington, which made up the council's housing area no. 3, and 4,166 in northern Paddington, including Queen's Park, which was housing area no. 4.[14]

Private building was more piecemeal: mainly hotels and flats on individual sites, with the exception of projects by the Church Commissioners, who succeeded the Ecclesiastical Commissioners and in 1953 bought out the beneficial lessees' interest in the Paddington Estate.[15] In order to escape the expense and embarrassment of owning decayed housing, the commissioners quickly sold much of their estate in southern Paddington or entered into partnerships with property companies. Work included the replacement of houses with office blocks in Eastbourne Terrace next to Paddington station and the rebuilding of much of stuccoed Tyburnia in the 1960s.[16] Thereafter sweeping changes were hindered by growing support for conservation. Four conservation areas were created under the Civic Amenities Act, 1967: Bayswater and Maida Vale in 1967, Westbourne in 1973, all three of which were later enlarged, and Queen's Park in 1978.[17]

Much conversion and some new building was carried out by housing associations. Mulberry Housing Trust, financed by Westminster city council and based in north Paddington, was founded in 1965, after bad conditions had received much publicity. In 1974 the trust merged with St. Marylebone Housing Association, which had been founded in 1926 and which continued to acquire properties in both Paddington and Marylebone, with funds from Westminster and from the Housing Corporation of

[5] *Census*, 1921–31.
[6] Young and Garside, *Metropolitan Lond.* 193, 195.
[7] Ibid. 190, 192, 195, 197.
[8] G. W. Currie, *Church of Eng. and her Ground Rents* (1930), *passim*.
[9] Lond. Diocesan Conference, *Paddington Estate* (rep. by special cttee. 1943), 6, 18, 28–9.
[10] Young and Garside, *Metropolitan Lond.* 225.
[11] *Census*, 1951–61.
[12] *The Times*, 11 July 1963, 16d.

[13] Ibid. 11 July 1967, 9a.
[14] Inf. from asst. dir. (policy), Westm. Planning Dept. Municipal properties are marked on *Map of Westm. Housing Est. 1985* (in Marylebone libr.).
[15] Below, manors.
[16] O. Marriott, *Property Boom* (1967), 100, 104–7; S. Jenkins, *Landlords to Lond.* (1975), 218–19; below, growth, Tyburnia, Bayswater; above, plates 41, 45.
[17] Inf. from asst. dir. (development), Westm. Planning Dept.

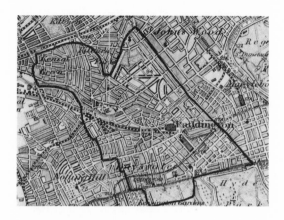

1904

the Department of the Environment. Some recon-version into larger flats was in progress in 1985, when all the homes were for renting. About one third of the association's tenants was of West Indian origin, about one third was Irish or from other immigrant groups, and the rest were mainly old people.[18]

Several other local bodies in 1974 amalgamated to form Paddington Churches Housing Association. It was financed mainly by Barnet and Camden L.B.s, Westminster, and the G.L.C., all of which continued their support in 1985, when most of the funds then came from the Housing Corporation. Converted property was solely for renting, although there were links with Sutherland Housing Association, which promoted cheap home ownership. Paddington Churches Housing Association, whose work had spread to many boroughs of north-west London, in 1985 managed 4,500 housing units, of which c. 1,800 were in Paddington.[19] Brent People's Housing Association was also active in Paddington, from 1975.[20] It was financed by Brent, Barnet, Harrow, and Westminster, and also at first by the G.L.C. and later by building societies.[21]

Although by 1983 Westbourne Grove had declined as a shopping centre and Queensway had grown more cosmopolitan, Tyburnia, including the rebuilt parts, and most of Bayswater remained expensive. The central belt, despite slum clearance, was still working-class and, with the lines of communication, separated the southern districts from the avenues of Maida Vale and the humbler streets stretching to Queen's Park. The local differences which had grown up with 19th-century Paddington thus survived.[22]

The population[23] rose from 1,881 in 1801 to 4,609 in 1811, 6,476 in 1821, 14,540 in 1831, and 25,173 in 1841. The rates of increase of more than 100 per cent from 1801 to 1811 and more than 50 per cent from 1831 to 1841 were higher than in any other

parish in the later county of London.[24] Numbers had risen to 46,305 by 1851, 75,784 by 1861, 96,813 by 1871, and 117,846 by 1891. In 1901, after the addition of Queen's Park, the population was 143,976. It reached 144,923 in 1931 but fell from 125,463 in 1951 to 116,913 in 1961, and, after the wards had been reorganized as part of Westminster L.B., 95,958 in 1971.

PADDINGTON GREEN originally consisted of waste-land occupying a central position on the estate which supported the almoner of Westminster. The name came to be applied both to the surrounding village and to a small part of the open space, east of the late 18th-century church. The area described below is larger: bounded north-east by Edgware Road, south and for much of the south-west by the Grand Junc-tion canal, and north-west by the Regent's canal, it corresponds with the north-eastern part of Church ward as created in 1901.[25]

When the green was first recorded in 1549 it spread southward across Harrow Road near its junc-tion with Edgware Road. Presumably the medieval chapel stood near the middle of the north side of the waste, as did the 17th-century church, which was farther north than its successor.[26] In 1647 a large house adjoined the northern side of the churchyard, with another to the east; one of them was the manor house, perhaps the building in use by 1582, and nearby there was also a divided vicarage house.[27] A fishpond was mentioned in 1617[28] and the lord had six ponds on the green in 1647, by which date encroachments included a tenement and two small gardens.[29]

The buildings around the green and those a little farther east, rounding the junction of Harrow and Edgware roads, constituted a single settlement. The description of properties in 1773 as in the Square or as in Paddington may have represented an attempt to distinguish the green from Edgware Road,[30] but the only distinctions made in 1552 and 1664 had been between Paddington and Westbourne.[31] 'The town of Paddington' was a term used in 1757,[32] al-though the locality was normally described as a vil-lage until the building of Tyburnia joined it to London.[33]

By 1746 there were houses from Edgware Road along Harrow Road to a little way beyond the green and along Church Street to the north. Others faced the east side of the green. A pond, perhaps formed out of several earlier ones, lay on the south side of Harrow Road.[34] Presumably it was the church pond, from which no mud or sand was to be taken in 1722.[35] Almshouses were built west of the pond, probably in 1714,[36] and throughout the 18th century other parcels of waste were taken for cottages or as additions to the gardens of larger houses.[37] Padding-ton House or its predecessor had been built on the east side of the green and was freehold by 1720, when

[18] Inf. from dir., St. Marylebone Housing Assoc.
[19] Inf. from regional dir., Camden/Westm., Paddington Churches Housing Assoc. Ltd.
[20] Below, growth, Queen's Pk.
[21] Inf. from dir., Brent People's Housing Assoc. Ltd.
[22] Below, growth, *passim*.
[23] Para. based on *Census*, 1801–1971.
[24] F. H. W. Sheppard, *Lond. 1808–70* (1971), 11, 13, 15.
[25] *Plan of Paddington* (1901).
[26] McDonald, 'Paddington', cap. 6.
[27] Below, manors; churches.

[28] Mdx. Sess. Rec. iv. 344, 366.
[29] Guildhall MS. 10464A, p. 39.
[30] Poor rate bk. (1721–74).
[31] *Mdx. County Rec.* i. 11; G.L.R.O., MR/TH/2.
[32] Vestry mins. 23 Sept. 1757.
[33] e.g. *Lond. and Its Environs Described* (1761), v. 100; *Ambulator* (1792).
[34] Rocque, *Map of Lond.* (1741–5), sheet 11.
[35] Chwdns. acct. bk. (1656–1736), f. 99.
[36] Below, charities.
[37] e.g. Guildhall MSS. 10465/45, 55.

the owner Denis Chirac, a retired jeweller, was admitted to some waste in front of it.[38] Probably it was the three-storeyed house, with elm trees and a small pond nearby, drawn by John Chatelaine in 1750.[39]

In 1753 a neighbour pulled down the fence on the green of Chirac's son and namesake, who had received permission to inclose.[40] Railings separated the green from Harrow Road by 1750[41] and the vestry, seeking ballast for road repairs, in 1757 agreed to work only a patch on the edge of the green, in order not to hamper the letting of houses.[42] In a 19th-century novel, by a resident who might have drawn on local tradition, the village in the 1750s was depicted as no more than a few houses at the eastern end of Harrow Road, with some better ones, inhabited by retired tradesmen and lady annuitants, around the green, and a church whose graveyard was shadowed by elms in the grounds of the manor house.[43]

In the later 18th century the village continued to offer a rural retreat. A 'handsome house' with walled garden near the Edgware Road junction and a new large brick house at the upper end of the green were advertised, probably in 1768 and 1783 respectively.[44] The Hon. Charles Greville (d. 1809) lived by the green with Emma Hart, the future Lady Hamilton, from 1782 to 1786 and later built a bigger house at the north-eastern corner, on the site of the modern technical college.[45] Greville's garden adjoining Church Street was stocked with imported plants, as was that of Chirac's house to the south, on the site of the children's hospital, when occupied from c. 1797 until 1826 by John Symmons, who employed the botanical nurseryman William Salisbury.[46] North of Greville's house there was a new house in 1807, together with a building called the banqueting house, in gardens which contained a small lake and an island.[47]

In contrast with gentlemen's residences were cottages, including one on the west side of the green which survived until 1896; originally a pair of cottages, of flint and rubble roughcast and with a steep thatched roof, it presumably resembled many of the 18th century or earlier.[48] A reminiscence of Paddington in the 1780s noted the alehouses, with long troughs for watering the teams of hay wagons and with signs spanning Edgware Road. Tall elms screened the inns and formed the most impressive feature of the green, drawing most of the landscape painters of London.[49]

The ultimate preservation of part of Paddington green was foreshadowed in 1753, when the lord, at the petition of several residents, granted land called the green in front of their houses to Denis Chirac. It was to be inclosed with posts and open rails, as had

been done before, and to serve as an ornament to the parish, rights of way being unaffected.[50] In 1779 land called the green, with the site of the almshouses and ground in front of them and to the east, was vested in the lawyer Francis Maseres (1731–1824) and two other trustees for the benefit of the parish.[51] Maseres had been left all the real estate of the second Denis Chirac,[52] and the trust presumably included inclosures which had been made in front of Paddington House. The rebuilding of the church between 1788 and 1791 placed it near the middle of the green, which it helped to divide, the northern section eventually being taken for burials.[53] Seats on the green and the fence around it were in bad repair in 1803, when the trustees' lessee John Symmons refused to pay for their replacement.[54] In 1805 Charles Greville submitted suggestions for improving the green.[55] A different plan was adopted in 1807, for immediate work to be financed by private subscriptions and future upkeep by the highway rates, and in 1808 Symmons formally ceded management of the green to the vestry.[56]

Meanwhile seclusion was threatened by the canals and the gradual advance of London. Obstruction in Edgware Road, by carters around the White Lion, gave rise to complaint in 1795.[57] Although industry did not spread as widely as had been expected,[58] a rising poor population, presumably around the canal basin or on building sites farther south rather than at Paddington green itself, led to demands for a school, built in Harrow Road in 1802,[59] and for a poorhouse. It was hoped that the poorhouse might replace the decayed manor house, whose grounds were needed for the overcrowded churchyard.[60] Prosecutions for dumping night-soil on the wharves by the canal had greatly increased in 1808 and petitions were sent to the bishop and parliament against the proposed Regent's canal.[61] Once the Regent's canal had been opened, however, it seems to have benefited residents: some canal traffic was diverted, select villas were built in Maida Hill West (later Maida Avenue and treated below as part of Little Venice),[62] and the canal was advertised as offering beautiful views from a house on the north side of Paddington green.[63] Along Edgware Road, there were houses in Philpott Terrace and Devonshire Place, north of Church Street, by 1811.[64] With little room towards Edgware Road or towards the basin, the bishop and his lessees inevitably decided to build west of the church. Their architect S. P. Cockerell, himself a vestryman, in 1812 submitted a plan for nearly 100 tall and closely packed terraced houses on nursery ground, in new roads which afterwards formed Park Place (later St. Mary's Terrace) and Porteus Road.[65] The road in Park Place, however,

[38] Ibid. 55.
[39] McDonald, 'Paddington', cap. 6; Marylebone libr., P 133, cuttings.
[40] Vestry mins. 2 Dec. 1753.
[41] Marylebone libr., P 133, cuttings.
[42] Vestry mins. 25 Feb. 1757.
[43] C. Ollier, *Ferrers* (1842), i. 174, 190–1, 195–6.
[44] Marylebone libr., P 133, cuttings.
[45] McDonald, 'Paddington', cap. 6; Guildhall MS. 12531 (lease of 1807 and plan).
[46] McDonald, 'Paddington', cap. 6; W. Salisbury, *Hortus Paddingtoniensis* (1797); above, plate 34.
[47] Guildhall MS. 12531 (lease and plan).
[48] Marylebone libr., P 133, cuttings.
[49] *Reminiscences of Hen. Angelo*, i. 230; below, social.

[50] Guildhall MS. 10465/68, f. 77.
[51] Ibid. 94, ff. 208–9; *D.N.B.*
[52] Guildhall MS. 10465/92, ff. 5–7.
[53] McDonald, 'Paddington', cap. 6; below, churches.
[54] Vestry mins. 25 Feb., 12 Apr. 1803.
[55] Ibid. 23 Sept. 1805.
[56] Ibid. 7 May 1807; 26 May 1808.
[57] Ibid. 22 Oct. 1795.
[58] Below, econ., ind.   [59] Below, educ.
[60] Vestry mins. 4 Apr. 1809.
[61] Ibid. 26 May 1808; 2 Mar., 5 May 1812.
[62] Below, Maida Vale.
[63] Marylebone libr., P 133, cuttings.
[64] M.L.R. 1811/4/23.
[65] Vestry mins. 3 Mar. 1812 and plan.

was not sufficiently well made for the parish to take it over in 1824[66] and only a single terrace had been built there, opposite Porteus Road, by 1828.[67]

Older village features gradually disappeared. The parish was authorized to buy the manor house in 1810 and demolished it in 1824, enabling the churchyard to be enlarged to the north.[68] The pond on the south side of Harrow Road had been used as a rubbish tip by the turnpike trustees' surveyor in 1813 when the vestry, anxious about drainage, insisted that it should not be filled up. In 1818, when there was a pumping-engine house nearby, the Grand Junction Canal Co. was allowed to fill in the western part of the pond in order to construct a short way (later Church Place) from Harrow Road to North Wharf Road. The parish in return received a strip of land east of the almshouses,[69] where a free school was built in 1822, either then or soon afterwards replacing the remains of the pond.[70] A new vestry room behind the almshouses was ready in 1823[71] and the company had constructed more ways to North Wharf Road, later Hermitage Street to the west and Green Street to the east, in 1828, by which date North Wharf and Irongate Wharf roads, serving the basin, were lined with buildings or yards. Both Hermitage Street, containing a watchhouse where the fire engine was also kept, and Church Place were taken as parish roads in 1828.[72]

Fashionable churchgoers could attend Bayswater chapel from 1818 or St. John's, Southwick Crescent, from 1832. Despite the provision of a large vicarage house at the corner of Park Place and Porteus Road, St. Mary's ceased to be the parish church in 1845. Part of the green immediately west of it, which had been bought as more burial ground in 1843, was taken instead for a new vestry hall in 1853.[73] North of the hall, a short way leading from Park Place to the church was called Stanley Place in 1846, when 6 houses were to be built there,[74] and St. Mary's Square from 1864.[75] A police station was built in Dudley Grove, the stretch of Harrow Road west of the hall, in 1864. Both the vestry hall, which became the town hall, and the police station were afterwards enlarged, giving some dignity to a run down neighbourhood at the price of being separated from many of Paddington's later public buildings in Bayswater.[76]

The building of the new vestry hall[77] reduced the open space to an area comprising the churchyard, the burial ground to the north, a four-sided plot (the modern Paddington green) east of the church, and a plot east of the free school on the south side of Harrow Road. The last was built over between 1842 and 1855, with working-class terraces in Victoria and Albert streets, which ran parallel to Church Place and Green Street, and also facing the green in Harrow Road.

West and north-west of the green, the vicarage was still the only house on the west side of Park Place in 1840, although Porteus Road and the parallel Fulham Place and Howley Place were already projected. Building agreements for some of the houses in Howley Place were made in 1841 and, with Matthew Wyatt, for some in Porteus Road in 1846-7.[78] The roads had been built up by 1855, when the vicarage itself had made way for St. Mary's Terrace, where the houses were stuccoed and had pillared porches. Porteus Road and Fulham Place were also terraced and middle-class. Nearer the Regent's canal, detached and semi-detached houses, with larger gardens, lined Park Place Villas and the north side of Howley Place.

To the north and north-east there was still open ground behind the villas of Maida Hill West and the denser housing along Edgware Road, although Hall Place, running north from Church Street parallel with Edgware Road, had been named by 1828. It was built up for Benjamin Edward Hall, a local gentleman.[79] Many large semi-detached houses stood in the northern part of Hall Place, then called Hall Park, and in and around Crompton Street, then called Elm Tree Place, by 1842.

Efforts were made to preserve some of the village's 18th-century charm. When the former manor house garden was cleared of its undergrowth in 1825, the timber and ornamental trees were to be retained.[80] The Act of 1824 authorized refencing and planting of the green,[81] which in 1839 was to be enclosed with iron railings and kerbstones.[82] Artists still lived in the neighbourhood, although Bayswater became increasingly popular.[83] They included William Sawrey Gilpin (1762-1843), first president of the Old Watercolour Society and a parish officer, in Harrow Road in 1803 and Edgware Road by 1805, Cornelius Varley (1781-1873) at Junction Place, Paddington green, before 1811, and Joshua Cristall (1767-1847) at the manor house from 1812 to 1816.[84] George Barret the younger (d. 1842), of Philpott Terrace, Edgware Road, exhibited views of the canal and the enlarged St. Mary's churchyard. Thomas Uwins (1782-1857) spent periods at Paddington green from 1834, Edward Calvert (1799-1883) lived in Park Place, where he printed his woodcuts, from c. 1832 to 1851, and William Henry Pyne (1769-1843) was briefly in Dudley Grove in 1835. The sculptor Matthew Cotes Wyatt (1777-1862), who with his sons took leases for several new houses in Tyburnia,[85] was at Dudley Grove House probably from 1843 until his death.

The green's attractions could not survive the urbanization which took place around it in the mid 19th century. Edgware Road became an increasingly

---

[66] Ibid. 17 Feb. 1824.
[67] Gutch, *Plan of Paddington* (1828); above, plate 37.
[68] Below, manors.
[69] Vestry mins. 7 Sept. 1813; 30 Apr., 22 Sept. 1818.
[70] Below, educ. The pond, although said to have gone, was shown on a plan: vestry mins. 23 Sept. 1822; 25 Feb. 1823.
[71] Below, local govt.
[72] Gutch, *Plan of Paddington* (1828); select vestry mins. 1 Apr. 1828; below, pub. svces.
[73] Below, church; local govt.
[74] Guildhall MS. 12422/2; Lucas, *Plan of Paddington* (1855).

[75] M.B.W. *Street Nomenclature* (1882), 40.
[76] Below, local govt.; pub. svces.
[77] Following three paras. based on Gutch, *Plan of Paddington* (1828, 1840); Lucas, *Plan of Paddington* (1842, 1855).
[78] Guildhall MSS. 12422/1-2.
[79] G.L.R.O., WCS 79, p. 211.
[80] Select vestry mins. 29 Mar. 1825.
[81] 5 Geo. IV, c. 126 (Local and Personal).
[82] Select vestry mins. 1 Oct. 1839.
[83] Rest of para. based on McDonald, 'Paddington', cap. 21; *D.N.B.*
[84] Below, manors.
[85] Guildhall MS. 12422/1; below, Tyburnia.

busy thoroughfare: omnibuses, causing congestion at the corner of Church Street in 1831, were blamed in 1833 by 28 residents for the depreciation of property,[86] and commercial interests prompted ambitious rebuilding, of which a noted example was the White Lion with its courtyard north of the corner of Harrow Road, a forerunner of the Metropolitan Music Hall, in 1836.[87] Shops, small warehouses, workshops, inns, and dining or coffee rooms lined Edgware Road from Star Street to Church Street by 1845. Farther north-west, Devonshire Place and Prospect Place stretched to Crompton Street; set back from the road, they consisted mainly of private residences, with a few schools or offices for professional men. The scene had changed little by 1863 but the names of the terraces in Edgware Road were abolished in 1868 and most of the houses north of Church Street had been taken for shops by 1879. There were also shops in Church Street and Hall Place and, west of the green, in Harrow Road between Porteus Road and Fulham Place.[88]

The green itself, where old trees had to be felled in 1849,[89] became less desirable. It drew disorderly crowds in 1851 and was used for games in 1856, prompting a petition for the paths to be railed in, to which the vestry replied that it was empowered only to preserve the green for general use, subject to the lord's rights.[90] There were rival open-air preachers and in 1861 a pedlar had set up a stall, 'to expose offensive anatomical drawings'.[91] After 115 inhabitants had asked for the green to be enclosed for recreation, as at Islington and Camberwell, the vestry agreed to do so in 1865, the burial ground being taken over later.[92]

By the mid 19th century the old village centre was hemmed in by Edgware Road to the east, by the canal basin, considered the worst threat to Paddington's health,[93] amid industrial and working-class premises to the south, and by the canal with the sidings and goods depot of the G.W.R. beyond it to the west.[94] Only to the north was there an adjoining middle-class area, where elegant villas survived along the Regent's canal in Maida Hill West and north-west of the green in Howley Place and Park Place. The large houses of Elm Tree Place and the northern end of Hall Place, however, made way for tightly packed terraces, presumably when the name Crompton Street was adopted in 1859. Terraces also filled the new Hethpool, Campbell, Howell, and Cuthbert streets, so named from 1858 and 1859. Adpar Street, squeezed in between Hall Place and Edgware Road, was named in 1878. Manor Place, facing the burial ground and still mostly empty in 1869, was being built up in 1885[95] and had been lined with terraced

houses by 1901. Two new houses at the corner of Church Street and the green were taken in 1883 for a children's hospital, which was later extended.[96] Housing was so dense that an iron church, St. Philip's, was sited on part of the burial ground at the northern end of Manor Place from c. 1861 until 1893.[97]

No longer the home of noted artists, the neighbourhood was better known in the 1870s for the song 'Polly Perkins of Paddington Green', published in 1863 and probably referring to Annette Perkins, who may have lived in Albert (later Consort) Street, a cul-de-sac off Harrow Road south of the green, and who entered domestic service.[98] Also well known was Ignatius Paul Pollaky (W. S. Gilbert's 'Paddington Pollaky'), the first eminent private detective. Pollaky (d. 1918) had an inquiry office at no. 13 Paddington Green from 1865 until 1882 and lived in Maida Hill West in 1865 and later in Portsdown Road.[99]

The last building spaces were taken in 1881, for a board school in Campbell Street,[1] and in the 1890s, when leases were made of a plot south of Porteus Road for a drill hall and land west of the former burial ground for St. David's Welsh church.[2] Many houses in St. Mary's Terrace were leased in reversion by the Paddington Estate for rebuilding as flats,[3] called St. Mary's Mansions. Since 1864 the name St. Mary's Terrace had applied to the whole of the road which had been called Park Place, except to the more select Park Place Villas at the northern end.[4] Three lodging houses were listed in St. Mary's Terrace, 2 in Porteus Road, and 1 in Fulham Place in 1879; the same roads had 15, 7, and 9 houses offering 'apartments' by 1901. Park Place Villas, Howley Place, and Maida Hill West had escaped such a change,[5] although nos. 4 to 6 Maida Hill West were to be demolished in 1902 and three blocks of flats, called Stafford House, Douglas House, and Aubrey House, replaced those and other villas at the Edgware Road end of Maida Hill West between 1905 and 1910.[6]

No streets in the area were considered wealthy c. 1900, unlike many in Tyburnia and Bayswater. Prosperous residents lived along Edgware Road, the Regent's canal, St. Mary's Terrace, and Howley Place, and fairly prosperous ones in Fulham Place, Porteus Road, and near the green itself in Harrow Road, Church Street, and Manor Place. The terraces between Crompton and Cuthbert streets were classified as mixed, but there was poverty in parts of Hall Place and adjoining cul-de-sacs, including Adpar Street, and more in the alleys running from Harrow Road to the canal basin.[7] In 1894–5 Kent's Place, North Wharf Road, had 16 persons to a house,

[86] Select vestry mins. 4 Oct. 1831; 3 Dec. 1833.
[87] Below, social.
[88] P.O. Dir. Lond. (1845 and later edns.); M.B.W. Street Nomenclature (1882), 95.
[89] Select vestry mins. 5 Nov. 1849.
[90] Ibid. 1 Apr. 1851; 1, 15 July 1856.
[91] Bayswater Chron. 12 Sept. 1860; metropolitan vestry mins. 16 July 1861.
[92] Metropolitan vestry mins. 19 Dec. 1865; below, pub. svces.
[93] Rep. on Health of Paddington to Lady Day 1865 (in Marylebone libr.).
[94] Rest of para. based on Lucas, Plan of Paddington (1855, 1869); Plan of Paddington (1901); L.C.C. Names of Streets (1901).

[95] Guildhall MS. 12531.   [96] Below, pub. svces.
[97] Below, churches.
[98] Marylebone libr., L 132.1, Westm. cuttings (TS. notes and songsheet).
[99] Marylebone libr., L 132.1, Westm. cuttings; The Times, 28 Feb. 1918, 3e.
[1] Below, educ.
[2] Below, social; churches.
[3] Ch. Com., Bldg. Agreements, vol. x, nos. 3, 4, 17.
[4] L.C.C. Names of Streets (1901); Plan of Paddington (1901).
[5] P.O. Dir. Lond. (1879, 1901).
[6] Ch. Com., Bldg. Agreements, vol. x, no. 23; Kelly's Dir. Paddington (1905, 1910).
[7] Booth's Map (1890), NW.

making it the third most overcrowded street in Paddington, and Church Place had 13.7 persons.[8]

Little further building took place until after the Second World War. Social decline continued, with many subdivided houses in Porteus Road having deteriorated by 1937.[9] Two large houses in Howley Place, nos. 8 and 20, were to be turned into furnished apartments under 24-year leases in 1938.[10] The borough council made its first major move towards rehousing in 1937, when it acquired *c.* 50 houses in Dudley Street, a cul-de-sac west of Hermitage Street at the corner of Harrow and North Wharf roads. Dudley House, a five-storeyed block of 50 flats for 232 people, was opened there in 1938.[11]

More extensive clearance was carried out from the 1950s, mostly among the dense streets north of the green. North of Church Street, buildings in and back from Edgware Road made way in 1954 for Gilbert Sheldon House, where 40 families occupied an eight-storeyed block of flats and a four-storeyed block of maisonettes.[12] Immediately to the west between Hall Place and Manor Place, Paddington's scheme for three blocks of fifteen storeys to be called Perkins Heights was defeated by the L.C.C., which secured the site for a technical college, finally opened in 1967.[13] Plans by the borough council to extend municipal building along Edgware Road from Gilbert Sheldon House to the Regent's canal[14] were partially realized by Westminster L.B., which replaced the terraces between Crompton and Cuthbert streets with the Hall Place estate. A small shopping precinct and 146 dwellings, in maisonettes and a tower block of twenty-one storeys, were finished by 1973.[15]

West of the green a four-storeyed range of flats, Fleming Court, was built in the 1950s by the L.C.C. at the corner of St. Mary's Terrace and St. Mary's Square. A much larger municipal scheme replaced most of the houses between St. Mary's Terrace and Harrow Road with the yellow-brick blocks of John Aird Court. The estate stretched north from Porteus Road, which became a cul-de-sac, across Fulham Place, which formed a residents' car park, to Howley Place, leaving only the Warwick hotel in Harrow Road as a Victorian survival. A later, private, scheme created Hogan Mews, a cul-de-sac off the south side of Porteus Road.[16]

South of the green, short terraces east of Hermitage Street made way for Sarah Siddons school, opened in 1961–2, and for industrial rebuilding in North Wharf Road.[17] The most striking change was the construction in the mid 1960s of the flyover across Edgware Road and its linking in 1970 with the elevated Westway, which ran parallel to a widened and realigned Harrow Road along the southern edge of Paddington green. Buildings at the junction of Harrow and Edgware roads, including the Metropolitan Theatre of Varieties, were partly replaced by the large Paddington green police station at the north corner and the towering London Metropole hotel at the south. The old town hall, police station, and houses of Dudley Grove were also demolished, to allow Harrow Road to pass closer to the church.[18]

The immediate neighbourhood of the church forms a small outlying part of Maida Vale conservation area, to which houses along the Regent's canal and around Howley Place also belong.[19] Modern road building has reinforced the separation of Paddington green from the south part of the parish, where Edgware Road, except near Praed Street, is much more imposing and uniform than it is between the flyover and Maida Vale. The stark new concrete police station and yellow-brick blocks of Gilbert Sheldon House contrast with many converted mid 19th-century houses, those of the old Devonshire Terrace having shop fronts built over their gardens, and with J. Turner & Son's former boot factory of *c.* 1865 at the corner of Cuthbert Street. Similarly the shopping parade and towers of Hall Place contrast with a late 19th-century red-brick range near Maida Avenue.

Back from Edgware Road, overshadowed by tower blocks and skirted by traffic lanes, some of them sweeping upward to the flyover and Westway, the open space around the refurbished church provides an unexpected oasis. Plane trees shade the railed paths of the green itself and a marble statue of Sarah Siddons as the Tragic Muse, by Léon-Joseph Chavalliaud, unveiled in 1897.[20] Other established trees border the former burial ground, which, with tombstones lined against its wall, stretches north to a children's playground. A few tombs stand undisturbed, including that of Sarah Siddons beneath a modern glass canopy. Some altered houses and a yellow-brick pair belonging to the children's hospital are the only reminders that Paddington green was a desirable place of residence in the earlier 19th century.

West of the church, where St. Mary's Square has been cut off from the realigned Harrow Road, a neo-Georgian vestry hall by Quinlan Terry[21] stands slightly north of the site of the demolished town hall. The east side of St. Mary's Terrace contains the 119 flats of St. Mary's Mansions, two blocks of five storeys and basements in red brick with stone dressings, shielding two less imposing blocks which back on the burial ground. The similar but slightly later flats of Alexandra House and Osborne House stand to the south. Beyond St. Mary's Mansions is a line of older houses but on the west side of St. Mary's Terrace only the refurbished nos. 1–21 (odd) survive in that or neighbouring roads from the mid 19th century. Farther north, facing John Aird Court along the north side of Howley Place and where St. Mary's Terrace gives way to Park Place Villas, are large

[8] *Rep. on Vital Statistics and San. Work 1895* (in Marylebone libr.), 11.
[9] M. Fitzgerald, *Church as Landlord* (1937), 70–1.
[10] Ch. Com., Bldg. Agreements, vol. xv, no. U. 445.
[11] Marylebone libr., P 138, cuttings; *The Times*, 30 Nov. 1938, 9*f.*
[12] Marylebone libr., P 138, cuttings.
[13] Ibid. P 133, cuttings; *The Times*, 15 Dec. 1953, 4*g*; 11 Aug. 1953, 3*b*; 14 Aug. 1953, 2*g*; 29 Apr. 1955, 12*a*; below, educ.
[14] Marylebone libr., P 133, cuttings.

[15] Ibid.; *Architect & Bldg. News*, 28 June 1967, 1147.
[16] *P.O. Dir. Lond.* (1952 and later edns.).
[17] Below, educ.; *Paddington Basin Draft Planning Brief, 1985* (in Marylebone libr.).
[18] O.S. Map 1/10,000, TQ 28 SE. (1974 edn.); above, communications; below, local govt., pub. svces.
[19] *Westm. Dist. Plan, Draft Proposals Map, 1977*; *Westm. Dist. Plan, Proposals Map, 1982* (in Marylebone libr.).
[20] *Lond. Encyc.* 821; *The Times*, 15 June 1897, 12*e*.
[21] TS. notes by vicar.

stuccoed houses of the earlier and mid 19th century. Single or in pairs, well kept and in leafy gardens, they have not shared the decline of the terraces closer to Paddington green. Together with those at the west end of Maida Avenue, they are among London's 'best examples of early Victorian domestic architecture.' In appearance and social standing they have remained part of the area which came to be known as Little Venice.[22]

TYBURNIA was a name used in the early 19th century for the south-eastern corner of the parish, the first part of the Paddington Estate to be built up.[23] It was adopted presumably because 'Tyburn' was already well known, as a reference to the gallows at Tyburn tree.[24] The old name of the execution site was itself misplaced since the *Tyburn, teo* or 'boundary' stream,[25] ran much farther east, from Hampstead across Marylebone to Oxford Street. The Marylebone manor of Lisson lay west of the stream, along Edgware Road, and that of Tyburn to the east.[26] Paddington's Tyburnia, in the angle between Edgware and Bayswater roads, stretched westward from the former gallows to merge with Bayswater. In the 1870s the name was confined to a fashionable area, bounded on the west by Westbourne and Gloucester terraces, north of Lancaster Gate.[27] The area described below extends westward only to Eastbourne Terrace and the southern end of Westbourne Terrace[28] but northward to the industrial belt beyond Praed Street, as far as the canal basin. It covers Hyde Park ward and a southerly part of Church ward, as created in 1901, and also includes St. George's burial ground.[29]

The execution site[30] was chosen presumably because there was a prominent group of trees at the parting of two main roads out of London. Some medieval references to 'the elms' may have been to those at Smithfield, but it was at Tyburn that William FitzOsbert was hanged in 1196 and at the elms there that Roger Mortimer, earl of March, died in 1330. From the 14th century many political executions took place at Tyburn, where the trees probably made way for temporary gallows before a permanent triangular frame was set up in 1571. The frame was depicted by Hogarth,[31] in whose day it was known as Tyburn tree and served as London's chief place of public execution, where 21 victims could be hanged simultaneously. Often there were triumphant processions and huge crowds, an estimated 200,000 attending the death of Jack Sheppard in 1724. A grandstand on the west side of Edgware Road was sometimes used,[32] before and after the triangular frame was replaced by a movable gallows

in 1759, until criticism led to the choice of a new site outside Newgate gaol in 1783.

The triangular gallows stood in the centre of the wide southern extremity of Edgware Road until the building of the Uxbridge road tollhouse in 1759. The approximate site has been marked by successive plaques: against the railings of Hyde Park, in 1909 in Edgware Road, and in 1964, after road widening, on a traffic island at the junction with Bayswater Road. The position of the later movable gallows was *c.* 50 yards farther north in Edgware Road and was thought in the 1870s to have been that of a house at the south-east corner of Connaught Square (formerly no. 49),[33] although several sites close by have been suggested.

Burials of corpses from Tyburn were recorded from 1689 and brought profit to the minister and churchwardens of Paddington in the late 17th and the 18th century,[34] when execution days came to be known as 'Paddington fair'.[35] Remains were also buried under the scaffold and unearthed when the area came to be built up. Among them were the presumed bones of Oliver Cromwell and fellow regicides, whose posthumous consignment to a pit at the gallows' foot in 1661 probably gave rise to William Blake's allusion to 'mournful ever-weeping Paddington'.[36]

In 1742 the whole area was farmland, part of the bishop of London's Paddington Estate. At the south-eastern tip lay Tyburn field of *c.* 16 a., bounded by other fields of the 90-a. Bell farm, whose home field lay farther north along Edgware Road. There were no buildings, the nearest being at the Harrow Road junction or at Bayswatering,[37] although in 1746 a single structure was marked at Tyburn, perhaps connected with the gallows.[38]

The earliest building between Tyburn and Bayswatering was a chapel, on part of Tyburn field which Sir Thomas Frederick sold in 1763 to the parish of St. George, Hanover Square.[39] The chapel, with its walled burial ground behind, was set back from the Uxbridge road, leaving strips of waste to east and west. St. George's vestry, hoping to recoup its expenses, took legal advice and granted the verge on a 99-years' building lease to William Scott, who by 1767 had covered part of it with seven houses, known by 1772 as St. George's Row.[40] Eventually there were 14 houses, forming two terraces in 1790, beside a footway which was maintained by St. George's.[41] No. 4 St. George's Row was from 1772 the home of the artist Paul Sandby (1725–1809), who lived next door to the marine painter Dominic Serres (1722–93) and who entertained many distinguished men.[42] A lying-in (later Queen Charlotte's maternity)

[22] *Illus. Lond. News*, 24 Apr. 1971, 19–21; below, Maida Vale.
[23] G. Mackenzie, *Marylebone* (1972), 22.
[24] Below.
[25] *P.N. Mdx.* (E.P.N.S.), 7.
[26] *T.L.M.A.S.* x, map facing p. 56; Mackenzie, *Marylebone*, 19.
[27] Walford, *Lond. Old and New*, 188.
[28] Eastbourne and Westbourne terrs. are treated below, under Bayswater.
[29] *Plan of Paddington* (1901).
[30] Following two paras. based on *Encyclopaedia of Lond.* ed. Kent; *Lond. Encyc.*; H. Phillips, *Mid-Georgian Lond.* (1964), 259, 262; Marylebone libr., P 138, cuttings.
[31] 'Industry and Idleness' [1747]: J. Burke and C. Caldwell, *Hogarth, Complete Engravings* (1968), plate 213.

[32] B.M., Crace xxx. 3, 5, 9.
[33] Walford, *Lond. Old and New*, 201.
[34] Chwdns. acct. bk. (1656–1736), ff. 52, 55, 60 et seq.
[35] D. Newton, *Lond. West of the Bars* (1951), 276.
[36] *Diary of John Evelyn*, ed. E. S. de Beer, iii. 269; D. V. Erdman, *Blake, Prophet against Empire* (1969), 474.
[37] Ch. Com., 'Map of 1742'.
[38] Rocque, *Map of Lond.* (1741–5), sheet 11.
[39] Westm. libr., C 770, ff. 204, 220; below, churches.
[40] Westm. libr., C 770, f. 288; C 771, ff. 7–8, 17, 40, 141, 157, 266–7.
[41] Ch. Com., 'Plan of 1790'; Westm. libr., C 778, ff. 49, 98.
[42] *D.N.B.*; W. Sandby, *Thos. and Paul Sandby* (1892), 48, 77–8; T. J. Mulvany, *Life of Jas. Gandon* (1846), 39–40, 191.

hospital was also in St. George's Row before moving in 1791 to Bayswater.[43] Some more buildings were put up along the Uxbridge road frontage and a few isolated ones along Edgware Road during the 1790s, while fields remained behind them.[44]

The south-eastern tip of the parish, being the closest to London, was the first part to be affected by the building Act of 1795.[45] Successful schemes for the Marylebone side of Edgware Road influenced not only the decision to build on the Paddington Estate but to some extent the layout devised by the bishop's surveyor Samuel Pepys Cockerell, who had already designed the Foundling hospital's estate in Bloomsbury.[46] The key to Cockerell's plan was a wide avenue running north-east to link the Uxbridge road with the western end of the New (later Marylebone) Road. Traffic would thus be diverted and the proposed residential area would also be separated by the avenue from the industrial belt around the new canal basin where building materials could be brought.

Many changes were made to the plans, which may have been drafted as early as 1804, but the attraction of Hyde Park always permitted a layout in the grand manner. Intended improvements of 1809 included not only the avenue from the Uxbridge road to Edgware Road, eventually completed as Grand Junction Street (later Sussex Gardens), but two focal points in the form of a large open space to the south, called the polygon, and an imposing crescent facing the park west of St. George's burial ground.[47] Presumably it was the determination of the bishop and his lessees to maintain high standards which induced them to lease small plots to local builders or other speculators, rather than call in a contractor such as Thomas Cubitt, and at first delayed the progress of building.

The first building agreement was made in 1807 between the trustees for the beneficial lessees of the Paddington Estate and John Lewis, surgeon, of St. George's, Hanover Square. Lewis took a lease for 98 years from 1806 of land with a frontage of *c.* 400 ft. along the Uxbridge road and one of 360 ft. along Edgware Road to the corner of Upper Seymour Street West, a proposed continuation of Marylebone's Upper Seymour Street. A range of substantial dwellings of the first class facing Hyde Park was to be built by 1812, with second- or third-rate houses along the south side of Upper Seymour Street West and mews between in Edinburgh (later Connaught) Place. He took a similar lease of a 56-ft. frontage in the Uxbridge road, for a 'capital mansion of the first rate', in 1808, when he was also to be granted more land nearby.[48]

Aristocratic patronage was assured from the start.

Lewis's first lease referred to a projected Connaught Street and Edinburgh Mews (built as Stanhope Place and Connaught Place),[49] named after George III's nephew and son-in-law Prince William Frederick (d. 1834), who in 1805 had succeeded as duke of Gloucester and Edinburgh and earl of Connaught.[50] The duke apparently had the first house facing Hyde Park, no. 1 Connaught Place, built for Lady Augusta De Ameland (d. 1830), who had married his royal brother-in-law, the duke of Sussex (d. 1843), without parliamentary sanction.[51] Lewis had built the house by the end of 1807, when Lady Augusta took a 96½ years' lease, and the 12 other houses of Connaught Place by 1812.[52] Lady Augusta was one of four residents listed for 1811 and one of ten for 1819, when the others included the earl of Lindsey, Viscount Barnard, Sir Charles Coote, Bt., Sir Robert Wigram, Bt., and the bishop of Exeter.[53] Her house was later occupied by her son Sir Augustus D'Este (1794–1848) and by 1855 nos. 1 and 2 Connaught Place had been united as Arklow House, named after the duke of Sussex's Irish barony of Arklow.[54] No. 7 (Connaught House) was a residence of Caroline, princess of Wales, in 1814, when her daughter Princess Charlotte briefly sought refuge there.[55] The mansions enjoyed the same prospect as St. George's Row, where the actress and writer Elizabeth Inchbald lodged from 1810 to 1816 at no. 5 and then at no. 1, in a position claimed as the finest in London.[56]

The tall stuccoed houses of Connaught Place had their principal rooms overlooking the park and were entered from a private road behind. That layout was used by Cockerell some 15 years before Nash adopted it for York Terrace, facing Regent's Park, and was later to be repeated farther west along the Uxbridge road.[57]

Connaught Place and Mews were to be lit with gas in 1819[58] but it was not until 1821 that work began on the brick houses of Tyburnia's first square, Connaught Square.[59] Meanwhile a start had been made on Connaught Terrace, along Edgware Road. Building, as elsewhere on the Paddington Estate, was piecemeal: leases, for example, were granted for no. 6 Connaught Terrace in 1818, for nos. 4, 7, and 9 in 1820, for nos. 2, 3, and 8 in 1821, and for nos. 10 and 16 in 1822. Many lessees were individuals,[60] including Sir Carnaby Haggerston, Bt. (d. 1831), and the Revd. Mr. Whalley (possibly the poet Dr. Thomas Sedgwick Whalley), but others were local builders such as Arthur Bott, who in 1829 was to take seven houses in Connaught Square.[61]

By 1824 only 36 builders had taken up contracts for *c.* 570 houses on the Paddington Estate.[62] Under Cockerell, who in 1820 was accused by Sir Frederick

[43] Below, Bayswater.
[44] R. Horwood, *Plan of Lond. and Westm.* (1792–5), sheet A 2.
[45] Following two paras. based on G. Toplis, 'Tyburnia', *Country Life*, 15 Nov. 1973 (reprint in Marylebone libr.).
[46] Colvin, *Brit. Architects*, 226.
[47] Guildhall Libr., P 1: lithograph of perspective plan by S. P. Cockerell; above, plate 37.
[48] Ch. Com., Bldg. Agreements, vol. i, p. 17.
[49] Ibid. 21.   [50] *Complete Peerage*, v. 745.
[51] Ibid. xii (1), 536; *Lond. Encyc.* 193.
[52] Guildhall MS. 12479. Similar leases for most of the Paddington Estate, with marginal plans, are in Guildhall Libr.

[53] *Boyle's Court Guide* (1811, 1819).
[54] Marylebone libr., P 138, cuttings; *P.O. Dir. Lond.* (1855).
[55] *Lond. Encyc.* 193; H. Brougham, *Life and Times*, ii (1871), 226, 233.
[56] J. Boaden, *Memoirs of Mrs. Inchbald*, ii (1833), 156–7, 171.
[57] Toplis, 'Tyburnia', *Country Life*, 22 Nov. 1973; below.
[58] Vestry mins. 21 Oct. 1819.
[59] *Country Life*, 15 Nov. 1973.
[60] Guildhall MS. 12422/1 (lease bk. 1817–46, unpag.).
[61] Ibid.; G.E.C. *Baronetage*, ii. 245; *D.N.B.*
[62] Reeder, 'Capital Investment', 234.

Morshead of mismanagement,[63] progress continued to be unspectacular.[64] By 1828 about a third of the triangular site between the Uxbridge road, Edgware Road, and Grand Junction Street had been filled in: housing extended west of St. George's burial ground to Hyde Park Street and along the entire Edgware Road frontage but did not reach far behind the main roads except along Albion Street, Upper Berkeley Street West (later Connaught Street), Sovereign (soon renamed Cambridge and later Kendal) Street, and Titchborne Street.[65]

Quicker progress was made in the humbler area farther north, where land had been leased to the Grand Junction Canal Co. and the Grand Junction Waterworks Co.[66] By 1828 there existed South Wharf Road, Praed Street as far as the beginning of Conduit Street, the three reservoirs of the waterworks company, Sale Street (later Place), most of Market (later St. Michael's) Street, and part of Star Street.[67] Praed Street had been named after William Praed, banker and chairman of the canal company.[68] Grand Junction Street itself was the joint responsibility of the canal company and the Paddington Estate. The street was built up from the Edgware Road end: leases for the first houses were granted in 1826, many there and in Titchborne Street immediately to the south being taken by Henry Augustus Capps.[69]

The vestry was asked to survey Grand Junction Street in 1827, when drainage had been provided, but refused to accept it as a parish road. The dispute turned on interpretation of Paddington's Local Act of 1824: whether the vestry was compelled to appoint surveyors for new roads and whether such appointment would automatically commit it to maintenance, a crucial question since Paddington was considered 'the most eligible parish for additional buildings of any of the out parishes near London'.[70] Judgement was given for the vestry in 1829, on the grounds that Grand Junction Street had so few inhabited houses that its maintenance by ratepayers would amount to a subsidy to private builders.[71]

Uncertainty about the responsibility for roads may have delayed progress on building Tyburnia as a whole during the 1820s.[72] Another delaying factor may have been the grandiose nature of Cockerell's plans, with their lavish use of space, although some changes were made: Connaught Square had not originally been included and Cockerell's own design for a classical church on the axis of the polygon was not put into effect. His successor George Gutch,[73] formerly surveyor to the Grand Junction Canal Co., made further changes, although he still catered for the rich, by introducing more squares and larger houses. The polygon was partly filled by the Gothic St. John's church, built 1829–32, and neighbouring houses, leaving Cambridge Square to the north and Oxford Square to the south; a projected Polygon

Street, running south-westward past a single square towards Lancaster Gate, was made to border Gloucester and Sussex squares; the proposed west end of Berkeley Street West was widened to form Hyde Park Square. A straight terrace, Hyde Park Gardens, was substituted for the crescent which was to have faced the park.

Building activity, while increasing from the late 1820s, remained fragmented.[74] In both Tyburnia and Bayswater leases, for 95 years or thereabouts, were still made to a few private individuals but more often to speculators, many of them builders, who acquired several plots in different streets. Prominent in Tyburnia was James Ponsford, who had a wharf at Paddington basin from c. 1835 to 1850 and who by 1845 was also listed as an architect.[75] Leases taken by him in Tyburnia were for houses and stabling behind Connaught Terrace in 1825, for houses in Titchborne Street in 1828, in Connaught Square, Sovereign Street, and Lower Porchester Street in 1829, for 10 on the south side of Grand Junction Street in 1834, for others in Southwick Street, Porchester Place, and Bathurst Street in 1838–9, and for two more in Grand Junction Street in 1840. Apparently unscathed by charges that he had defrauded house buyers,[76] he was building farther west on the edge of Bayswater in Gloucester Road (later Terrace), Conduit Street, and Spring Street from 1840, when Thomas and William Ponsford were also active. Thomas Ponsford, of Westbourne Terrace, was listed as a builder in 1845, as were Lionel Ponsford of Porchester Terrace and William Ponsford of Gloucester Road in 1847.[77] Also prominent was William Crake, who took leases of the first 'mansion houses' in Hyde Park Gardens in 1837 and soon acquired most of that terrace, with a few other houses nearby. He was a builder, of Old Quebec Street, Marylebone,[78] and presumably was related to John Crake, the architect of Hyde Park Gardens. Among other speculators were Matthew Cotes Wyatt and his sons Matthew, later knighted, George, and James Wyatt. Matthew Cotes Wyatt acquired many sites, beginning with four houses in Upper Hyde Park Street in 1839, when George and James also took leases, but he was apparently acting on behalf of his eldest son Matthew, a practising architect who retired in affluence to Hyde Park Square in the late 1840s.[79]

A few of the larger builders were helped by loans from the Royal Exchange Assurance, which from 1839 generally advanced up to half the estimated completion value of a house, at 5 per cent interest. Borrowers included William Kingdom, also active on the edge of Bayswater as a builder in Westbourne Terrace, George Wyatt, who by mid 1846 had received £135,400, and Matthew Wyatt, who received £25,000. Such investments, made on a smaller scale after George Wyatt's bankruptcy in 1846, was

[63] Ibid. app. A, p. viii.
[64] *Country Life*, 15 Nov. 1973.
[65] Gutch, *Plan of Paddington* (1828).
[66] Below, manors and other est.
[67] Gutch, *Plan of Paddington* (1828); select vestry mins. 2 Oct. 1827. [68] C. Hadfield, *Brit. Canals* (1979), 126.
[69] Select vestry mins. 8 Jan. 1828; Guildhall MS. 12422/1.
[70] Select vestry mins. 2 Oct. 1827; 8 June 1828.
[71] Ibid. 2 June 1829.

[72] Para. based on *Country Life*, 15 Nov. 1973; Gutch, *Plan of Paddington* (1828, 1840).
[73] Colvin, *Brit. Architects*, 369.
[74] Para. based on Guildhall MS. 12422/1.
[75] Below, econ., ind.; *P.O. Dir. Lond.* (1845).
[76] Marylebone libr., L 132.1, Westm. cuttings.
[77] *P.O. Dir. Lond.* (1845, 1847).
[78] G.L.R.O., WCS 76, p. 262; *Robson's Lond. Dir.* (1845); *Robson's Com. Dir. Lond.* (1840).
[79] Colvin, *Brit. Architects*, 944–5.

generally confined to London's west end, benefiting the fashionable parts of Paddington and, to a lesser extent, Belgravia.[80]

Gutch's final proposals, published in 1838, determined the appearance of Tyburnia for almost a hundred years.[81] Many of them had already been carried out, Grand Junction Street having been almost completed as a tree-lined avenue, bordered by carriage roads called Cambridge Terrace to the north and Oxford Terrace to the south. The whole of the area south of Grand Junction Street had been filled by 1840, except Gloucester Square, Sussex Square, and a small gap at the avenue's western end. Star Street, farther north, had also been finished.

It is not known how far Gutch was responsible for architectural details in the 1830s, as the Italianate style evolved and brick gave way to stucco. Another Gothic church, St. James's, designed partly by Gutch, was built at the end of Grand Junction Street in 1841–3.[82] Houses were generally built one storey higher than in the 1820s, the effect being sometimes to produce a verticality which strained the classical orders 'almost to breaking point': circular turrets softened the angles of the layout, and bow fronts afforded north–south terraces, such as Hyde Park Street, a glimpse of the park. The monumental Hyde Park Gardens was designed by John Crake[83] but presumably it was Gutch who decided to repeat the back-to-front principle of Connaught Place, with mews behind the entrances to the north and the main rooms facing the park across a large strip of communal garden. The same arrangement was used in Gloucester Square, where in the 1840s George Ledward Taylor's houses[84] faced the central garden, with their entrances in the approach roads behind. Taylor, who took over many sites from Crake, also built Chester (later Strathearn) Place and part of Hyde Park Square.[85] The new emphasis on gardens, marking a shift from status to amenity, was to be copied both in Kensington and Bayswater.

Several of the new houses had notable residents.[86] No. 32 Cambridge Terrace was occupied by Napoleon I's surgeon Barry O'Meara (1786–1836) from 1830 and no. 34 by the caricaturists John Doyle (1797–1868) and his son Richard (1824–83) from 1833 to 1864. Henry Buckle (1821–62), the historian, lived in Oxford Terrace from 1843 to 1846. The painter Benjamin Robert Haydon (1786–1846) lived nearby in the slightly older Burwood Place, off Connaught Square, from 1839 or earlier until his suicide. The civil engineer Robert Stephenson (1803–59) occupied no. 15 Cambridge Square and later no. 34 Gloucester Square, where he died.[87] William Makepeace Thackeray's first London return was with his mother and step-father, Maj. and Mrs. H. Carmichael-Smyth, at no. 18 Albion Street in 1836 and 1837.[88] Edwin Chadwick, the sanitary reformer,

was at no. 4 Stanhope Street from c. 1844 to c. 1850.[89]

The grandest houses, as in Bayswater immediately to the west, were those facing Hyde Park. Special vestrymen in 1843, by virtue of their rank, included the duke of Argyll, the earls of Shannon and Bandon, and Sir Charles Coote, M.P., all of Connaught Place, and Lord Sherborne, Mr. Justice Coltman, and five other M.P.s of Hyde Park Gardens or Hyde Park Terrace.[90] Unlike most of his neighbours John George Shaw-Lefevre, the future clerk of the parliaments, in 1838 took a direct lease from the Paddington Estate of his house at no. 5 Hyde Park Gardens.[91] It had passed to the earl of Ducie by 1845, when the earl of Dalhousie occupied no. 21.[92] The chief beneficial lessee of the estate, Thomas Thistlethwayte (d. 1850), by 1826 held a lease of no. 8 Connaught Place, which passed to his third son Augustus Frederick,[93] husband of the courtesan Laura Bell.[94]

Rapid building and social recognition led to some criticism. Trollope's 'Princess Royal Crescent', from one end of which a corner of Hyde Park could be glimpsed, was unfinished, chilly, and pretentious; although the houses were cramped, except their drawing rooms, and less well built than those of such areas as Fitzroy Square or Baker Street, they had the advantage of forming a 'quite correct' address.[95]

Several tradesmen served the new suburb by 1835.[96] Some were established near the southern end of Edgware Road, south of the Mitre at the corner of Upper Seymour Street West (later Seymour Street). Farther north most of Edgware Road was lined with private houses as far as Titchborne Street, but close by there were tradesmen in Berkeley (later Upper Berkeley) Street West (renamed Connaught Street by 1879) and its offshoot Lower Porchester Street (later the southern end of Porchester Place). Their numbers had grown by 1840, when, with others in the adjoining Cambridge (later Kendal) Street and Upper Frederick Street (by 1844 called Portsea Place), they formed a centre which has survived as Connaught village. Businesses included a post office in Berkeley Street West and two taverns, the Hope and the Rent Day, to which the Duke of Kendal had been added by 1845. There were also shops in Praed Street before it came to form the chief approach to Paddington station.

Tyburnia was compared with Belgravia in the 1850s.[97] An example of entertainment on the grand scale was described in 1861, when crowds watched the arrival of glittering guests of Mrs. Milner Gibson at no. 5 Hyde Park Place, where in 1870 Charles Dickens was to hold his last public meetings.[98] The two districts were considered almost equally fashionable in 1873, although Belgravia was noted more for its blue-blooded householders and Tyburnia for its 'mushroom aristocrats' and self-made millionaires.[99]

---

[80] B. Supple, *Royal Exchange Assurance* (1970), 321–3.
[81] Following two paras. based on *Country Life*, 15 Nov. 1973; Gutch, *Plan of Paddington* (1840).
[82] Below, churches.
[83] *Lond. Encyc.* 46; B.M., Crace xiv. 15.
[84] Pevsner, *Lond.* ii. 306.
[85] G. L. Taylor, *Auto-biography*, i (1870), 180–1.
[86] Para. based on *D.N.B.*
[87] L.C.C. *Indication of Hos. of Historical Interest*, i. 58.
[88] A. Monsarrat, *Uneasy Victorian* (1980), 77, 87.
[89] Kelly's *Dir. Lond.* (1844, 1850).
[90] *Lucas's Paddington Dir.* (1843).
[91] Guildhall MS. 12422/1.

[92] *P.O. Dir. Lond.* (1845).
[93] Rate bk. Feb. 1826, f. 56; *P.O. Dir. Lond.* (1842, 1852); Guildhall MS. 12479 (licence, 1887); Burke, *Land. Gent.* (1952).
[94] W. H. Holden, *They Startled Grandfather* (1950), 125.
[95] A. Trollope, *Small Ho. at Allington* (1864), ch. xi.
[96] Para. based on *Robson's Lond. Dir.* (1835); *P.O. Dir. Lond.* (1840 and later edns.).
[97] G. A. Sala, *Gaslight and Daylight* (1859), 225.
[98] *Mary Howitt, An Autobiog.*, ed. M. Howitt, ii (1889), 142.
[99] Walford, *Lond. Old and New*, 202.

In 1884 Tyburnia was 'the city of palaces north of the park'.[1]

Despite their social eminence, several houses soon came to be used for prostitution. The problem, although presumably made worse by the opening of the railway terminus, was widespread. In 1843 nine householders in [Upper] Frederick Street were prosecuted and seven convicted,[2] in 1849 neighbours complained of a brothel in Titchborne Street, and in 1851 a woman was prosecuted for keeping a disorderly house in Upper Berkeley Street.[3] Complaints in 1865 concerned, beside Moscow Road in Bayswater, Star Street and three houses in Titchborne Street.[4] By 1899 the incidence was slowly lessening, in face of a municipal policy based on dispersal, through rigorous inspection of premises, rather than prosecution.[5]

While the area south of Grand Junction Street remained select, that to the north was more varied.[6] The character of Edgware Road north of Titchborne Street was always more commercial than residential, with several shops and workshops by 1835.[7] The terraces of Star, Market, and Praed streets remained unchanged, as did the warehouses of South Wharf Road, but the three reservoirs became redundant with improvements in the water supply and were filled in during the 1840s.[8] The site of the northern one was taken for St. Mary's hospital, opened in 1851,[9] and for Francis (later Winsland) and Stanley streets and Arthur Mews. Ground to the west, between London Street and the northern part of Spring Street (later Eastbourne Terrace), both projected by 1828, was earmarked for the permanent Paddington railway station. The sites of the Southern and Lower reservoirs, by contrast, were taken for Norfolk Square, with a church from 1847 and partly built up by 1855, and Talbot Square, slightly later, whose first-class houses[10] constituted a northward extension of residential Tyburnia.[11] Leases for new houses at the western end of Grand Junction Street and in its cross-streets Spring Street and Gloucester Road had been taken by the Ponsfords and others between 1840 and 1842.[12] Sussex Gardens by 1842 constituted the westernmost stretch of Grand Junction Street, itself later called Grand Junction Road,[13] but did not give its name to the whole avenue until 1938.[14]

Tyburnia had been filled by the mid 1850s, when builders were still active in Westbournia and Maida Vale.[15] Gutch had successfully carried out the original scheme of extending the fashionable west end of London north of Hyde Park, producing what was hailed in 1851 as the capital's one example of the symmetry and variety of street planning which

Wren had vainly tried to introduce.[16] Social change had nonetheless taken place in Edgware Road, where north of the Mitre tavern Connaught Terrace, stretching to Titchborne Street, had in 1845, although containing a stables and two lodging houses, consisted mainly of private houses, some used by professional men. By 1863 most of the terrace had been taken for shops, offices, or consulting rooms[17] and in 1868 its buildings were renumbered as part of Edgware Road.[18] Another change was the conversion of many houses to apartments, at first notably in Connaught village and by the 1860s also on either side of Grand Junction Road.[19]

The residents of Bayswater Road were classified as wealthy c. 1890, and those of Edgware Road and Grand Junction Road as wealthy or well-to-do. Most of the streets and all the squares within the triangle formed by those thoroughfares were also occupied by the wealthy, although a few ways leading off the main roads, such as Cambridge, Seymour, and much of Connaught and Albion streets, contained merely the well-to-do; pockets of poverty existed only in mews alleys, such as Sovereign Mews or Titchborne Place, behind the Edgware Road frontage. North of Grand Junction Road the social pattern was more varied. Norfolk and Talbot squares were inhabited by the wealthy, as was the whole of Westbourne Terrace, and Eastbourne Terrace and much of Praed Street by the well-to-do, but Star and Market streets and their offshoots supported both the moderately comfortable and the poor; mews alleys there and in South Wharf Road were poor.[20] In 1902 Tyburnia was chiefly an area for the rich and their servants, with some high-class lodging-house keepers and shopkeepers.[21]

Eminent residents towards the end of the 19th century[22] included Lord Chief Justice Coleridge, who died at no. 1 Sussex Square in 1894,[23] the artist and writer George Du Maurier, who died at no. 17 Oxford Square in 1896,[24] the diplomatist Lord Currie (1834–1906), householder of no. 1 Connaught Place in 1902, and the contractor Sir John Aird, Bt. (1833–1911), M.P. and Paddington's first mayor, at no. 14 Hyde Park Terrace from 1874. Lord Randolph Churchill moved in 1883 to no. 2 Connaught Place, which was soon claimed to be the first private house in London to have electric lighting.[25] The distinction between plutocratic Tyburnia and aristocratic Belgravia, although always exaggerated, still held some force: Tyburnia in 1902 housed the Jewish philanthropist Frederick Mocatta (1828–1905) at no. 9 Connaught Place, Sir Joseph Sebag Montefiore at no. 4 Hyde Park Gardens, and the Armenian oil

[1] W. J. Loftie, *Hist. Lond.* ii (1884), 235.
[2] Sel. vestry mins. 4 Apr. 1843.
[3] Ibid. 7 Aug. 1849; 7 Jan. 1851.
[4] Metropolitan vestry mins. 3 Jan., 4 July, 5 Dec. 1865.
[5] Booth, *Life and Labour*, iii (3), 127.
[6] Para. based on Gutch, *Plan of Paddington* (1828, 1842); Lucas, *Plan of Paddington* (1869).
[7] *Robson's Lond. Dir.* (1835).
[8] Below, pub. svces.
[9] Ibid.
[10] Below, churches; *P.O. Dir. Lond.* (1855, 1863); *Bldg. News*, 10 July 1857, 712.
[11] Norfolk Sq. was advertised as near Hyde Pk.: Guildhall Libr., P 1/NOR (coloured lithograph).
[12] Guildhall MS. 12422/1.
[13] Ibid.; Bacon, *Atlas of Lond.* (1886, 1910).
[14] *Lond. Encyc.* 848.   [15] Guildhall MS. 12422/1.

[16] J. Weale, *Lond. Exhibited* (1851), 770.
[17] *P.O. Dir. Lond.* (1845, 1853).
[18] M.B.W. *Street Nomenclature* (1882), 95.
[19] Below, econ., trade and ind.
[20] *Booth's Map* (1889), NW.
[21] Booth, *Life and Labour*, i (2), app. p. 12. Booth's 'Tyburnia' stretched beyond the area treated here, north to Paddington green and west to Porchester Terr. in Bayswater.
[22] Para. based on *D.N.B.*; *P.O. Dir. Lond.* (1902).
[23] *Complete Peerage*, iii. 372.
[24] *The Times*, 9 Oct. 1896, 6a.
[25] *Reminiscences of Lady Randolph Churchill* (1908), 101–2. An earlier experiment in electric lighting had been tried, at no. 23 Porchester Gdns.: below, Bayswater. A ho. in Highgate was claimed in 1884 to be the first to be lighted throughout by electricity: *V.C.H. Mdx.* vi. 135.

millionaire and art collector Calouste Sarkis Gulbenkian, who from 1900 until 1925 was lessee of no. 38.[26]

Only slight changes were made to the Regency or Italianate streets before the First World War. In Edgware Road houses on the south corner of Seymour Street in 1898 were to be replaced by flats and shops before 1905.[27] Connaught House, dated 1906, was built under that or a revised agreement; most of its Seymour Street frontage was taken up by the Connaught club, first established for young men of limited means, which was bombed in 1940, taken over by the American Red Cross, and in 1948 leased to the Victory (Ex-Services) club.[28] In Bayswater Road the replacement of St. George's chapel by the Ascension chapel[29] was followed by the sale in 1900 of the former St. George's Row (in the mid 19th century called St. George's Terrace and from 1866 Hyde Park Place).[30] The houses made way for blocks of flats, which survived in 1984 as no. 12 Hyde Park Place, called Hampshire House, and nos. 18 to 23.[31]

Piecemeal rebuilding began in the late 1920s, as the first leases fell in, and gathered pace until halted by the Second World War. Although most noticeable along Edgware Road, rebuilding occurred on widely scattered sites, as some large houses were replaced by flats, shops, hotels, or smaller houses, others were subdivided, and mews dwellings converted into 'bijou residences'.[32] Changes in appearance were carefully controlled by the Paddington Estate, through leases which often specified the height and materials of the new buildings.[33] The population density of Hyde Park ward, covering fashionable Tyburnia, was 91 persons to an acre in 1921 and 97.3 in 1931, already higher than that of the Lancaster Gate wards or Maida Vale; by 1951, at 102.5, it was much higher,[34] presumably in consequence of changes in the 1930s. On the whole, however, the area remained upper- or middle-class. In 1937 the mews alleys north of Hyde Park and west of Edgware Road held a few old working-class tenants and some chauffeurs, lodged over garages near their employers, but many of the conversions had been into studios for a rising number of 'well-to-do people who have a fancy for living in queer places'.[35]

An early agreement for conversions in 1927 provided for three houses on the north-west side of Gloucester Square, nos. 26 to 28, to be turned into five self-contained flats and for their three abutments behind, nos. 38 to 40 Devonport Mews, to become garages with living rooms overhead.[36] Similar agreements of 1927 were for nos. 13 and 14 and nos. 15 and 16 Hyde Park Terrace, each pair to form five flats, and for nos. 5 and 6 Chester Mews, behind them, to be replaced by two small private houses. In all those instances the lease was renewed for 61 years or less, although the most common term was still to be 98 years.[37]

The most thorough-going changes were along Edgware Road, where almost all the four-storeyed terraced houses were demolished as far north as Praed Street. Nos. 13 to 43 odd, from Seymour Street to Connaught Street, in 1928 were to be replaced by shops with flats overhead, built in 1932 as Westchester House and Grosvenor Mansions,[38] and mews buildings were to make way for a garage.[39] Between Connaught and Cambridge (later Kendal) streets, a block formed by nos. 51 to 79 Edgware Road, with the buildings behind it in Berkeley Mews and Portsea Place, in 1935 was to be replaced by shops and flats, completed in 1938 as Connaught Mansions and Portsea Hall. Immediately to the north, the block from Cambridge Street to Burwood Place in 1935 was likewise to be replaced; Bell Properties Trust in 1936 built the shops and flats of Park West, which had its main entrance in Cambridge Street and a private club with sports facilities for its residents.[40] Farther north, between Sussex Gardens and Star Street, the flats and shops of Cambridge Court had been built on the Grand Junction Co.'s estate in 1932.[41]

Bayswater Road, more desirable residentially and with no shops, underwent little rebuilding. A few of the largest houses became offices or institutions and others were subdivided; in Connaught Place a lease of no. 1 was taken in 1920 by Schweppes, which acquired no. 2 c. 1922 and the next four houses before and after the Second World War,[42] and nos. 13 and 14 were being gutted for flats in 1923.[43] Demolition took place only at the two corners of Bayswater Road and Albion Street, where houses in Hyde Park Terrace in 1934 and 1935 were to be replaced by expensive flats, built as two blocks called Albion Gate in 1936.[44] Away from the main thoroughfares there were major changes in Gloucester Square, whose north-east and south-west sides were rebuilt with smaller 'high-class' houses, in Sussex Place, where eight houses and their adjoining mews made way for flats called Sussex Lodge, built in 1937, and in and around Southwick Crescent, the south-western end of the polygon, where many of the five-storeyed houses with deep basements were replaced by houses of three storeys between 1934 and 1939.[45] Works of modernization included the conversion of nos. 215, 217, and 219 Sussex Gardens, with buildings behind in Bathurst Mews, into flats.[46]

North of Sussex Gardens there was also some scattered rebuilding, although not enough to alter the character of the area. New buildings included a telephone exchange of 1935[47] in Market (later St. Michael's) Street, London University's Lillian

[26] R. Hewins, *Mr. Five Per Cent* (1957), 89, 92.
[27] Ch. Com., Bldg. Agreements, vol. x, no. 16.
[28] H. P. Clunn, *Face of Lond.* (1951), 271; inf. from gen. manager, Victory (Services) Assoc.
[29] Below, churches.
[30] Westm. libr., C 819; C 819A.
[31] Clunn, *Face of Lond.* 436.
[32] Ibid. 435–6; M. Fitzgerald, *Church as Landlord* (rep. of survey for housing assoc. of Ch. Union, 1937), 65–6.
[33] e.g. Ch. Com., Bldg. Agreements, vol. xiii, no. 13; xv, no. U. 287.   [34] *Census,* 1921–51.
[35] Fitzgerald, *Church as Landlord,* 68–9.
[36] Ch. Com., Bldg. Agreements, vol. xiii, no. 2.
[37] Ibid. nos. 3–4.

[38] Ibid. no. 6; Clun, *Face of Lond.* 271n.
[39] Ch. Com., Bldg. Agreements, vol. xiii, no. 5.
[40] Ibid. xiv, nos. 2, 1; Clunn, *Face of Lond.* 271–2.
[41] Grand Junction Co. min. bk. i. 245, 324, 357; ii. 72, 284; Clunn, *Face of Lond.* 272.
[42] Inf. from group admin. manager, Cadbury Schweppes plc.
[43] Marylebone libr., P 138, cuttings.
[44] Ch. Com., Bldg. Agreements, vol. xiii, no. 13; xiv, no. 4; Clunn, *Face of Lond.* 436.
[45] Ch. Com., Bldg. Agreements, vol. xiii, nos. 15, 19; xiv, nos. U. 287–8, 369, 408, 415; Clunn, *Face of Lond.* 437.
[46] Ch. Com., Bldg. Agreements, vol. xv, no. U. 434.
[47] Datestone.

Penson hall of residence in Talbot Square, and projects carried out for St. Mary's hospital.[48] Overcrowding persisted close to Praed Street, where Star Street was 'not without a criminal element'.[49]

Haphazard rebuilding and conversions had destroyed the uniformity of Gutch's Tyburnia before the Second World War. Although disfigured and with many neglected properties, particularly along its borders, an area so close to Hyde Park and Edgware Road remained desirable.[50] It did not therefore figure among those parts of the Paddington Estate which the Church Commissioners, having bought out the interest of the beneficial lessees,[51] began to sell in 1954. The name Paddington Estate was then dropped in favour of Hyde Park estate for the area south-east of Sussex Gardens, Maida Vale estate for the area north of the Regent's canal, and Lancaster Gate for most of the remaining property, in Bayswater or around Westbourne green, which was to be sold.[52]

Early rebuilding on a bombed site at the corner of Edgware Road and Seymour Street was carried out by the Victory (Ex-Services) club, which opened its Memorial wing, with shops below, in 1956. The club, renamed the Victory Services club in 1970 in order to accommodate both serving and former members of the armed forces, remained leaseholders from the Church Commissioners in 1985.[53]

In perhaps the most ambitious project for private housing attempted in London since the Second World War, the Church Commissioners entered into partnership with Wates, property companies controlled by Max Rayne, and Basil & Howard Samuel to restore the prestige of what had become the 90-a. Hyde Park estate.[54] Under a general plan by Anthony Minoprio, begun in 1957 with demolition in Hyde Park Square,[55] many early 19th-century terraces disappeared, notably in the central area around the polygon. Rebuilding was to a high density yet expensive: 930 flats and 68 houses, with shops, showrooms, and offices, were to accommodate c. 4,000 people on 27 a. around Oxford and Cambridge squares in 1962, and over 1,000 garages were to be provided, many underground.[56] A corner of the estate between Sussex Gardens and Norfolk Crescent was reserved for total control by the Church Commissioners, who started demolition in 1961 and finished building the luxurious development called Water Gardens in 1966.[57] It covered 3 a. and consisted chiefly of 250 flats, most of them to be offered on short leases, with 6 penthouses, 15 houses, and shops and offices.[58] In Norfolk Crescent 139 flats in 3 blocks, called Castleacre, Southacre, and Rainham, were finished jointly by the Church Commissioners and London Merchant Securities in 1969 and later

passed to the commissioners.[59]

Rebuilding by the Church Commissioners and their associates proved successful, in that the expensive new dwellings were quickly occupied.[60] In 1972, however, when conservation was more acceptable, a fifteen-year plan modified the proposals of 1957 by providing for the renovation rather than the rebuilding of Connaught village and, on the western side of the estate, of Westbourne Street and a terrace at the end of Sussex Gardens.[61] Meanwhile the former St. George's burial ground and the site of the bombed Ascension chapel had been taken in 1967 for flats by the Utopian Housing Society (Group One), which exchanged a strip at the northern end with the Church Commissioners, in return for freehold access from Albion Street, and later passed the ownership to St. George's Fields Ltd.[62] By 1981 restoration had begun on most of Connaught Place.[63] Thus, after widespread rebuilding between c. 1930 and c. 1970, the early 19th-century suburb emerged with its social status ensured.[64] In 1985 the Church Commissioners, having decided to sell their Maida Vale property,[65] intended to retain their freehold interest in the Hyde Park estate bounded by Sussex Gardens and Edgware and Bayswater roads. The area, excluding St. George's Fields and some freeholds which had been sold around Albion Street and Hyde Park Gardens Mews, covered c. 80 a.[66]

Tyburnia, the first part of the Paddington Estate to have been built up, has lost more of its original buildings than has Bayswater. Most of those that remain have been included in Bayswater conservation area since 1967 or 1978.[67] The elaborate grouping of squares and crescents, considered second only to Edinburgh's,[68] survives, however, in the street plan, despite changes of name and the disappearance of some mews alleys. Moreover, the stages of growth can be seen in contrasts between restrained brick houses, as in Connaught Square, and taller, stuccoed ranges in a more opulent Italianate style.[69] Equally striking are the contrasts between those and the shops and flats of the 1930s, or between small modern town houses and tower blocks. Architecturally varied, the district south-east of Sussex Gardens is socially homogeneous: within the triangular Hyde Park estate there is little but private housing, although the roads forming that triangle bear separate characters.

Edgware Road as far north as Praed Street remains largely as it has been rebuilt in the 1930s, with flats over shops. The blocks, which stretch along the side streets, are mostly faced in red or yellow brick, with stone dressings, and include Portsea Hall, designed by T. P. Bennett.[70] In 1951 they were thought to

48 Below, pub. svces.
49 New Lond. Life and Labour, vi (2), 431.
50 Clunn, Face of Lond. 436.
51 Below, manors.
52 The Times, 22 Sept. 1954, 8g.
53 Inf. from gen. manager, Victory (Services) Assoc.
54 O. Marriott, Property Boom (1967), 106–7.
55 Marylebone libr., P 138, cuttings (Paddington Mercury).
56 The Times, 23 Oct. 1962, 12d.
57 Paddington Mag. July 1961; Marylebone libr., P 138, cuttings; Marriott, Property Boom, 107.
58 Country Life, 27 May 1965, 1309.
59 Business Observer, 21 Oct. 1973.
60 e.g. flats under construction in Sussex Sq.: Paddington

Mag. Dec. 1960.
61 Marylebone libr., P 138, cuttings.
62 Inf. from Mr. M. S. Fry (architect).
63 Marylebone libr., P 138, cuttings.
64 L. Lane, 'Restoration of Tyburnia', Country Life, 6 Dec. 1973, 10.
65 Below, Maida Vale.
66 Inf. from Chestertons (estate agents).
67 Westm. Dist. Plan, Draft Proposals Map, 1977; Westm. Dist. Plan, Proposals Map, 1982 (in Marylebone libr.); inf. from asst. dir. (development), Westm. Planning Dept.
68 S. Muthesius, Eng. Terraced Ho. (1982), 167.
69 Country Life, 6 Dec. 1973.
70 Pevsner, Lond. ii. 307.

have given greater dignity to one of London's broadest approach roads, making it seem typical of modern Paris.[71] Many of the tall blocks are at right angles to the road and linked by a continuous street elevation of two or three storeys. The pattern is continued by three 17-storeyed towers faced with bands of white tiles, designed by Trehearne & Norman, Preston & Partners,[72] rising out of a shopping range as part of the Water Gardens estate. Only between Star Street and St. Michael Street does an older brick terrace with shop fronts (nos. 195–203), survive. Edgware Road's shops and restaurants, many of good quality, form a north-westward offshoot of the commercialism of Oxford Street.

Bayswater Road, although a direct continuation of Oxford Street, marks an abrupt transition from trade to residential occupation,[73] interspersed with institutions and prestigious offices in converted houses. New buildings have more storeys but in general are no taller than the older ones. From Marble Arch to Stanhope Place stretch the stuccoed terraces of Connaught Place, of five storeys over basements and with first-floor verandahs. The houses still appear residential: after refurbishment nos. 1–6 consist of offices and flats for Cadbury Schweppes, no. 1 having lost its porch on the Edgware Road frontage,[74] and nos. 7–10 of expensive flats. The next range, Hyde Park Place, begins with stuccoed Italianate frontages (nos. 1–3), brown-brick flats (nos. 4–5), dated 1953, and the more recent Tyburn shrine, with houses converted for the convent of the Sacred Heart and other Roman Catholic bodies,[75] including the former no. 10, barely 6 ft. wide and sold in 1946 as London's smallest house. Hampshire House (no. 12), ornate and in golden stone, advertised in 1981 as luxurious flats, stands at the eastern corner of a gap formed by part of the garden of St. George's Fields. The estate, planned by Design 5, was first occupied in 1973; 300 flats or maisonnettes are contained in four large stepped blocks and three smaller blocks, white-brick and seven-storeyed or less, in a landscaped setting and with a car park beneath.[76] Beyond the gap is another block of c. 1900, neo-Jacobean and in red brick and terracotta, including Oranjehaven (no. 23), a former Dutch club. Albion Gate, the only flats of the 1930s resembling those in Edgware Road, consists of taller buff-brick and Portland stone blocks designed by Septimus Warwick[77] on each corner of Albion Street. Beyond is the imposing classical Park Towers at the east corner of Hyde Park Street and a similar building at the west corner, both converted from pairs of houses to flats under a lease of 1927,[78] and the brown-brick flats called Falmouth House, built c. 1960.[79] From Clarendon Place to Brook Street stretches the ornate stuccoed terrace of Hyde Park Gardens, set back from the road behind thick shrubs and still entered only from behind. There is a similar, shorter, range,

built at an angle to meet the road, on the west side of Brook Street. Together with the slightly later terraces immediately west of Lancaster Gate,[80] Hyde Park Gardens has been acclaimed as '19th-century building at its most assured'.[81]

Sussex Gardens, forming the third boundary of the Hyde Park estate, retains more of its 19th-century appearance than do the other sides. Stock brick terraces, of four storeys and basements, with stuccoed ground floors, line the north-west side, on the former Grand Junction Canal Co.'s land, as private hotels, having survived presumably because plans for their rebuilding were not put forward until the 1970s.[82] The south-eastern side is less uniform, with the flats of the Water Gardens, built around a courtyard with fountains, and the Quadrangle, six-storeyed, with a 24-storeyed tower behind, having replaced Oxford Terrace in the 1960s.[83]

The Water Gardens and the Quadrangle stretch south from Sussex Gardens to where modern town houses surround the former polygon, the heart of Cockerell's layout, which has lost all its original buildings except St. John's church in the centre. Three tower blocks also share the central island, overshadowing Oxford and Cambridge squares and Norfolk Crescent, and a still taller block of 22 storeys occupies the corner of Oxford Square and Porchester Place. West of the church there has been extensive rebuilding, although more modest in height. Hyde Park Crescent contains neo-Georgian houses of the 1930s, in greyish brick and 'far too like Dagenham'.[84] Neighbouring streets have similar small but expensive houses, such as those by S. Warwick in Radnor Place,[85] or later ones in brownish brick. Gloucester Square on its north side has Chelwood House, built c. 1963,[86] and on the east and west sides flats of the 1930s, red-brick with stone dressings and in 1951 thought more attractive than the houses in Hyde Park Crescent.[87] To the west in Sussex Place the seven-storeyed Sussex Lodge is another example of piecemeal rebuilding, from 1937.[88] Beyond is Sussex Square, rebuilt with three-storeyed houses on its east and west sides, including one bearing a plaque commemorating the residence of Winston Churchill 1921–4, and with modern flats to the north. Hyde Park Square in contrast has a stuccoed 19th-century range to form its long north side and similar survivals along part of its south side, stretching westward along Strathearn Place to Sussex Place. Mews dwellings behind the terraces have likewise met varied fates: Hyde Park Mews retains its original buildings while the neighbouring Clarendon Mews has been rebuilt, as has Sussex Mews between Sussex Square and Sussex Place.

Nineteenth-century buildings survive mainly near the perimeter of the Hyde Park estate, notably in Stanhope Place, Albion Street, and Westbourne Street, all leading off Bayswater Road, in Strathearn

[71] Clunn, *Face of Lond.* 270.
[72] *Country Life,* 27 May 1965, 1309.
[73] *Country Life,* 6 Dec. 1973. Rest of para. based on Marylebone libr., P 138, cuttings.
[74] Inf. from group admin. manager, Cadbury Schweppes plc.
[75] Below, Rom. Cathm.
[76] Inf. from Mr. M. S. Fry (architect).
[77] Pevsner, *Lond.* ii. 307.
[78] Above.

[79] *P.O. Dir. Lond.* (1960, 1961).
[80] Below, Bayswater.
[81] *Lond. Encyc.* 47.
[82] *The Times,* 31 Jan. 1974, 4g; 28 Aug. 1974, 15e; below, econ.
[83] Above.
[84] Clunn, *Face of Lond.* 437.
[85] Pevsner, *Lond.* ii. 307.
[86] *P.O. Dir. Lond.* (1962, 1964).
[87] Clunn, *Face of Lond.* 437.   [88] Ibid.

Place, and in the south-eastern corner, around Connaught Street. Connaught Square retains nearly all of its brown-brick terraced houses of four storeys over basements, with their ground floors stuccoed and rusticated and first-floor balconies, remarkable for their contrast with the nearby blocks in Edgware Road.[89] Connaught Street is of similar date, as is the south side of much of Kendal Street, which meets it at the Duke of Kendal. Renovated shops near the corner and in Porchester Place, which links the two streets, here make Connaught village a busy centre,[90] with whose preservation there is little likelihood of further demolition in fashionable Tyburnia.

Scattered rebuilding has also taken place farther north around Norfolk and Talbot squares. A five-storeyed block of flats, Edna House, has replaced All Saints' church on the east side of Norfolk Square, and the seven-storeyed Lillian Penson hall of residence, in pale concrete, fills the north side of Talbot Square. Mid 19th-century stuccoed terraces, used mainly as hotels, form most of the other sides of the squares and contain shops in London and Spring streets. To the east the much humbler Star and St. Michael's streets, between Sussex Gardens and Praed Street, retain most of their brick terraces, those in Star Street being of three storeys and a basement and those in the narrower St. Michael's Street being a storey lower. St. Michael's Street is the more altered, with the site of the church used as a playground, a few rebuilt town houses, and business premises backing on to it at the Edgware Road end. In both streets and in Sale Place and other cross-streets there are shops and public houses, often on corner sites. Praed Street, lined with shops and with St. Mary's hospital taking up much of its north side, presents a mixture of styles. There are modern blocks near the Edgware Road corner, including British Telecom's depot of the 1960s at nos. 12-20 (even),[91] and a new red-brick range containing the post office at nos. 128-42 between the hospital and the Great Western hotel. Much of the south side is down-at-heel, with four-storeyed shopping parades of the late 19th century and, between Sale Place and Junction Place, a more modest row of empty shops awaiting demolition. Behind St. Mary's a massive block faced with creamy yellow brick is under construction for the hospital in South Wharf Road, next to the five-storeyed Paterson wing, recently completed.[92]

WESTBOURNE GREEN was, with Paddington green, one of the parish's earliest settlements. It was obliterated by mid 19th-century building, much of which consisted of streets with the prefix Westbourne and was sometimes known as Westbournia.[93] The area treated below covers central Paddington west of the

G.W.R. terminus, along Harrow Road, the Grand Junction canal, and the railway; it formed Westbourne ward and a western projection of Church ward in 1901.[94] The northern boundary is taken to be Harrow Road north-west of the Lock bridge, where it curves and crosses the canal, and Amberley Road, formerly lined by canalside wharves, to the east. The southern boundary is taken to be Bishop's Bridge Road and its continuation, Westbourne Grove, although Westbournia has been taken by some to extend south of that line[95] just as Bayswater has been assumed to reach as far north as the railway.[96]

The name Westbourne is thought to have originated not as the west *burna* or stream but as a place on the west side of the stream which came to be called after it.[97] As one of three vills in St. Margaret's, Westminster, in 1222,[98] Westbourne presumably owed its origin to the need to administer Westminster abbey's estates.[99] Westbourne green was mentioned in 1548[1] and became a common name from the 1660s for both Westbourne manor and the western half of Paddington parish,[2] only to go out of use in the later 19th century.[3]

The settlement long remained small, with a single alehouse in 1552.[4] Eighteen residents of Westbourne green were assessed for hearth tax in 1664, compared with 52 for Paddington.[5] There were only a few houses in 1745, mostly south of the point where Harrow Road running westward from Edgware Road was joined by Westbourne Green (later Black Lion) Lane running northward from the Uxbridge road. From the southern end of the hamlet, a footpath later called Bishop's Walk (eventually Bishop's Bridge Road) provided a short cut to Paddington green.[6] The Red Lion, where Harrow Road bridged the Westbourne, and another inn were recorded in 1730.[7] The second inn was probably one called the Jolly Gardeners in 1760 and the Three Jolly Gardeners in 1770,[8] near the Harrow Road junction, where it probably made way for the Spotted Dog.[9] Harrow Road *c.* 1745 there turned northward and was bordered by waste, not yet built upon, as far as solitary buildings probably on the sites of Westbourne Farm and Westbourne Manor House.[10] Westbourne green, including those houses, thus extended for *c.* 1 km. from south to north. It did not form one of Paddington's wards in 1773, when it was apparently assessed as part of Bayswater.[11]

There were large houses by 1664, when Sir Thomas Cox was assessed on 14 hearths and John Townsend on 11.[12] Possibly they included the house rebuilt in the 1740s as Westbourne Place (later called Westbourne Park or House),[13] whose garden was enlarged with parcels of roadside waste,[14] and Westbourne Manor House. The early 19th-century

[89] I. Nairn, *Nairn's Lond.* (1966), 93.
[90] *Country Life*, 6 Dec. 1973.
[91] *Paddington Basin Draft Planning Brief, 1985* (in Marylebone libr.).   [92] Ibid.
[93] Marylebone libr., P 138, cuttings.
[94] *Plan of Paddington* (1901).
[95] e.g. Marylebone libr., P 138, cuttings (*Builder*, 1862).
[96] e.g. *Study of Urban Hist.* ed. Dyos, 263.
[97] *P.N. Mdx.* (E.P.N.S.), 133.
[98] Harvey, *St. Marg. Westm.* 45.
[99] Below, local govt., manorial.
[1] *Cal. Pat.* 1548-9, 59.
[2] Below, local govt., manorial; G.L.R.O., MR/TH/2, m. 30d.

[3] *Home Counties Mag.* ii. 17.
[4] *Mdx. County Rec.* i. 11.
[5] G.L.R.O., MR/TH/2, m. 30d.
[6] Rocque, *Map of Lond.* (1741-5), sheet 11; *Home Counties Mag.* ii. 21.
[7] McDonald, 'Paddington', cap. 15; G.L.R.O., MR/LV5/22.
[8] G.L.R.O., MR/LV7/45; MR/LV8/64.
[9] McDonald, 'Paddington', cap. 15.
[10] *Home Counties Mag.* ii. 22 and map facing p. 17; Rocque, *Map of Lond.* (1741-5), sheet 11; below, manors.
[11] Poor rate bk. (1721-74).
[12] G.L.R.O., MR/TH/2, m. 30d.   [13] Below, manors.
[14] e.g. W.A.M. 16460 (1757); W.A.M. 16463 (1771).

village contained five notable residences: Westbourne Place, west of Black Lion Lane at its junction with Harrow Road, and, from south to north on the east side of Harrow Road, Desborough Lodge, Westbourne Farm, Bridge House, and Westbourne Manor House.[15] Bridge House was built *c.* 1805 by the architect John White, owner of Westbourne Farm.[16]

Westbourne green had a very refined air in 1795 and was still considered a beautiful rural place in 1820.[17] Encroachments on the waste apparently were made only for the grounds of gentlemen's seats, by S. P. Cockerell of Westbourne Park and John White of Westbourne Farm in 1801, by a Mr. Harper in 1802, and by John Braithwaite of Westbourne Manor House in 1815.[18] The Grand Junction canal, passing north of the village between the grounds of Westbourne Farm and Bridge House,[19] was a scenic enhancement, later used to attract expensive building to the area.[20] Although housing was spreading along Black Lion Lane, it had not reached Westbourne green by 1828, when a house later called Elm Lodge stood north-west of Westbourne Manor House. There was also a short row, later called Belsize Villas, alone to the west on the south side of Harrow Road at Orme's green,[21] with 3 ratepayers in 1826 and 7, mostly on empty houses, by 1830.[22] The main addition was at the southern end of the village, opposite Bishop's Walk, where Pickering Terrace (later part of Porchester Road), backed by a double row called Pickering Place, formed a compact block of cottages amid the fields.[23] Seven ratepayers had been assessed at Pickering Terrace in 1826[24] but some of the houses were still unfinished and others empty in 1837.[25]

The cutting of the G.W.R. line across the middle of Westbourne green was begun in 1836, necessitating a slight northward realignment of Harrow Road east of its junction with Black Lion Lane, where a turnpike gate was moved. Since the railway obstructed the Paddington green end of Bishop's Walk, the footpath was replaced by Bishop's Road, soon extended westward as Westbourne Grove.[26] Although no large houses were demolished, the railway passed close to Westbourne Park, from which Lord Hill moved out, and still closer to a house to the east,[27] whose owner William Penney claimed compensation for 10 a. based on their value as building land.[28] By 1840 several new roads were projected, including Westbourne Grove.[29] Houses had been built there by 1842, when the Lock hospital, giving

its name to the Lock bridge where Harrow Road crossed the canal, stood opposite Westbourne Manor House to the north. The centre of the area, however, along Harrow Road and on either side of the railway, remained empty.[30]

Housing spread in the 1840s, mainly south of the railway. The eastern end of Bishop's Road was built up and at first called Westbourne Place,[31] where the publisher George Smith was visited by Charlotte Brontë in 1848 and 1849.[32] Farther north, residential growth was banned by the G.W.R. depots and sidings.[33] Immediately to the west, where the Paddington Estate straddled the Westbourne,[34] roads were laid out, with bridges over the railway to link them with Harrow Road.[35] Holy Trinity church was finished in 1846[36] and Orsett Terrace, Gloucester Crescent (later the northernmost part of Gloucester Terrace), and Porchester Square had been planned by 1851.[37] No. 37 Gloucester Gardens, Bishop's Road, was the London home of the architect Decimus Burton by 1855.[38] Most of the area between Bishop's Road and the railway had been filled by 1855, except the site of Penny's house, which was to be taken in 1871 for Royal Oak station.[39]

As elsewhere on the Paddington Estate, building agreements were made with several individuals for every street. Some were speculators, including the Revd. Simon Sturges,[40] who took leases for 12 houses on the north side of Bishop's Road in 1847, Thomas Dowbiggin of Mayfair, who took leases for 19 houses in Orsett Terrace in 1850, or Lieut. Edward Thomas Dowbiggin, a lessee nearby in 1853.[41] Other lessees were builders, including William Scantlebury, who probably had worked from Albany Street, Marylebone, in the mid 1830s, had taken leases of plots in Grand Junction Street and elsewhere in Tyburnia from 1839 and, after moving to Eastbourne Terrace, had settled as a gentleman in Porchester Terrace North (later part of Porchester Terrace) by 1849.[42] He built much of the neighbourhood around Orsett Terrace and Gloucester Crescent, where he took leases in 1849–50 and 1852 respectively.[43] John Scantlebury of Porchester Terrace North built part of Porchester Square, where many plots were subleased by George Wyatt between 1853 and 1855,[44] and was presumably the John Vandersluys Scantlebury who often occupied premises close to or the same as those of William and who was active on the Ladbroke estate in North Kensington.[45] William Oliver Scantlebury, of Gloucester Crescent in 1854, was also a local builder.[46]

[15] *Home Counties Mag.* ii, map facing p. 17.
[16] Ibid. 17; Colvin, *Brit. Architects*, 883.
[17] Lysons, *Environs*, iii. 330; *Ambulator* (1807, 1820).
[18] Vestry mins. 15 July, 11 Nov. 1801; 20 Oct. 1802; 3 Jan. 1815. Encroachments are marked on 'Map of Man. of Westbourne Green in 1811' (in Marylebone libr.).
[19] *Home Counties Mag.* ii, map facing p. 17.
[20] Guildhall Libr., P1/HAR (view by G. E. Lee, 1847).
[21] Gutch, *Plan of Paddington* (1828); *P.O. Dir. Lond.* (1855); Stanford, *Libr. Map of Lond.* (1862 edn. with additions to 1865).
[22] Rate bk. July 1826, f. 2; rate bks. sel. transcripts, 1830.
[23] Gutch, *Plan of Paddington* (1828); above, plate 36.
[24] Rate bk. Feb. 1826, f. 7; rate bks. sel. transcripts, 1830.
[25] *The Times*, 2 Dec. 1837, 7a.
[26] Above, communications.
[27] Lucas, *Plan of Paddington* (1842); below, manors.
[28] *The Times*, 2 Dec. 1837, 7a.
[29] Gutch, *Plan of Paddington* (1840).
[30] Lucas, *Plan of Paddington* (1842).

[31] Lucas, *Plan of Paddington* (1869).
[32] Shakespeare Head Brontë, *Life and Letters* (1932), ii. 253; iii. 52.
[33] Lucas, *Plan of Paddington* (1869).
[34] Guildhall Libr., boro. maps P1: Gutch, *Plan of Paddington* (1828, coloured to show estates).
[35] Gutch, *Plan of Paddington* (1840).
[36] Below, churches.
[37] J. Weale, *Lond. Exhibited* (1851), map at back.
[38] *P.O. Dir. Lond.* (1855, 1863).
[39] Lucas, *Plan of Paddington* (1855); above, communications.
[40] *Alum. Oxon. 1715–1886*, iv. 1370.
[41] Guildhall MS. 12422/2.
[42] *Robson's Lond. Dir.* (1833, 1835); *P.O. Dir. Lond.* (1845 and later edns.); Guildhall MS. 12422/1.
[43] Guildhall MSS. 12422/1; 12535; 12505.
[44] Ibid. 12545.
[45] *P.O. Dir. Lond.* (1850 and later edns.); *Survey of Lond.* xxxvii. 220.   [46] Guildhall MS. 12505.

Farther west building had already begun for William Kinnaird Jenkins, of Nottingham Place, Marylebone, and later of Paddington, a lawyer who also acquired part of the Ladbroke estate from W. H. Jenkins and was responsible for laying out Kensal New Town.[47] Houses were planned for W. K. Jenkins along both sides of Westbourne Grove, west of Pickering Place, in 1838 and along an extension of Westbourne Grove in 1840.[48] They were detached villas,[49] like those to be built for him in Newton Road in 1846, when he also had plans for Hereford Road.[50] More land in Hereford Road was leased out by the Paddington Estate between 1853 and 1855, much of it for terraces by J. P. Waterson, a Bayswater builder, who assigned his interest in several sites to John Wicking Phillips.[51] To the north, Westbourne Park and its grounds made way for large semi-detached villas in Westbourne Park Road and, beside the railway, Westbourne Park Villas.[52] No. 16 Westbourne Park Villas from 1863 to 1867 was the intermittent home of Thomas Hardy, who also lived briefly at no. 4 Celbridge Place (later Porchester Road) and in Newton Road.[53] Fields survived between Westbourne Park Road and Newton Road in 1851[54] but had been covered with modest terraces by 1855, when St. Stephen's church was being built.[55]

Between the railway and the canal, the pace of building and the social pattern were more varied. The eastern part, where Delamere Terrace lined the canal and Warwick Crescent overlooked the pool, was begun as an extension of Little Venice. Leases for 13 houses in Westbourne Terrace Road were taken in 1847 by G. L. Taylor, architect of some of the grandest houses in Tyburnia and Maida Vale, who also built in Blomfield Terrace, along Harrow Road. Other lessees included William Buddle, for 19 houses in Blomfield Street (later Villas) and Delamere Terrace in 1851 and 12 in Warwick Crescent, where plots were assigned to him by G. L. Taylor in 1852.[56] Early residents included Elizabeth Barrett Browning's sister Arabel Barrett in Delamere Terrace; in order to be near her Robert Browning moved from lodgings at no. 1 Chichester Road and made his English home at no. 19 Warwick Crescent from 1862 until 1887.[57]

Farther west, beyond Ranelagh (from 1938 Lord Hill's) Road,[58] building was slightly delayed by the survival until after 1855 of Desborough Lodge and Westbourne Farm, although between the first and Harrow Road a short terrace had been built. Brindley Street, Alfred Road, and their neighbours already formed densely packed terraces west of the Lock bridge and Harrow Road. By 1861 Desborough Lodge and Westbourne Farm had made way for Clarendon, Woodchester, and Cirencester streets, whose small houses resembled those around Brindley Street rather than the stately terraces to the east.[59]

North of the canal, the workhouse was built next to the Lock in 1846-7.[60] Building, although not the imposing crescent planned in 1847,[61] stretched from there along the south side of Harrow Road to Woodfield Road at Orme's green by 1855. Opposite the Lock, however, Bridge House and Westbourne Manor House stood alone in their grounds in 1861.[62]

The 1860s[63] saw housing, which had ended in 1855 at St. Stephen's church and Hereford Road, spread to the Kensington boundary. By 1865 terraces lined westward extensions of Westbourne Grove and Westbourne Park Road, Artesian Road, and an eastward extension of the Portobello estate's Talbot Road.[64] Westbourne Grove West lay in Kensington until 1900, when its north side was transferred to Paddington; it included Norfolk Terrace west of Norfolk (later Needham) Road, where Prince Louis Lucien Bonaparte, a philologist and nephew of Emperor Napoleon III, had a house.[65] Building also stretched north-westward along Great Western Road past Westbourne Park station, opened in 1866, towards the canal. Small terraced houses and shops stood by 1867 along the south side of Kensal Road, in both Paddington and Kensington, and by 1869 along the north side, backing the canal.[66] They were the work of several local builders, lessees from W. K. Jenkins's successors the Revd. Robert Charles Jenkins and George Thomas Jenkins.[67] The only large space without houses south of the canal lay east of Westbourne Park station, where the G.W.R. lines passed between a train depot by the canal and a coal and stone depot at the end of Westbourne Park Road.

North of the canal the site of Westbourne Manor House was built over from c. 1867[68] and Amberley Road with its timber wharves was built along the canal bank.[69] The whole of Westbourne green thus came to be built up, except some gaps in Amberley Road and, in the north-west, the sites of Fermoy and Hormead roads, between Harrow Road and the canal.[70] Fermoy Road was named in 1883 and partly built up by 1884. Hormead Road was named in 1885,[71] although its site was still nursery ground in 1891.[72]

The southern part of Westbourne green at first was sometimes known as Westbournia. The name, however, also applied to streets south of Westbourne

[47] Survey of Lond. xxxvii. 260.
[48] G.L.R.O., WCS 77, p. 163; WCS 78, p. 543.
[49] Weale, Lond. Exhibited, map at back.
[50] G.L.R.O., WCS 79, pp. 82-3; WCS 80, p. 248.
[51] Guildhall MS. 12511.
[52] H.-R. Hitchcock, Early Victorian Archit. in Britain, i. 486.
[53] R. Gittings, Young Thos. Hardy (Penguin 1978), 100, 129, 224; F. E. Hardy, Early Life of Thos. Hardy (1928), 135.
[54] Weale, Lond. Exhibited, map at back.
[55] Lucas, Plan of Paddington (1855); below, churches. Second-class hos. in Sunderland Terr. and Alexander Street 1855: Bldg. News, 9 Oct. 1857, 1056.
[56] Guildhall MSS. 12422/2; 12484; 12592.
[57] D.N.B.; New Letters of Rob. Browning, ed. W. C. DeVane and K. L. Knickerbocker (1950), 144.
[58] L.C.C. Names of Streets (1955).
[59] Lucas, Plan of Paddington (1855, 1861).

[60] Below, local govt.
[61] Guildhall Libr., P1/HAR (view by G. E. Lee).
[62] Lucas, Plan of Paddington (1855, 1861).
[63] Para. based on ibid. (1855, 1861, 1869); Stanford, Libr. Map of Lond. (1862 edn. with additions to 1865), sheets 5, 9.
[64] Survey of Lond. xxxvii, map at end.
[65] Dictionnaire de Biographie Française, vi (1954), 922-3; P.O. Dir. Lond. (1855, 1863, 1879).
[66] M.L.R. 1867/18/415-25; 1869/25/75, 212-14, 376-8.
[67] G.L.R.O., WCS 79, p. 82; Alum. Cantab. 1752-1900, iii. 562.
[68] Below, manors.
[69] Below, econ., ind.
[70] Stanford, Libr. Map of Lond. (1862 edn. with additions to 1865), sheets 5, 9.
[71] L.C.C. Names of Streets (1901), 190, 262; Marylebone libr., Acc. 1468.
[72] Stanford, Libr. Map of Lond. (1891), sheet 5.

Grove which might have been described more cor-
rectly as in Bayswater: Trollope's Westbournia of
1858 was the fashionable neighbourhood of Westbourne Terrace,[73] and c. 1860 Westbourne Grove
was recorded as Westbournia's main thoroughfare
rather than its boundary.[74] By 1900 Bayswater was
thought to end at Westbourne Grove, leaving the
district to the north, whose status had fallen, without
a general name.[75]

A striking change soon took place in the character
of Westbourne Grove. It had been so named by
1842, when it was still empty, and contained many
cottages and semi-detached villas by 1846, as did
such offshoots as Newton and Monmouth roads,[76]
which were developed for W. K. Jenkins.[77] It was
still lined with trees and front gardens in 1850[78] but
the first shop was opened in 1854[79] and by 1859
villas were rapidly making way for shops, 'unsurpassed by any in London'.[80] The growth of Bayswater attracted tradesmen from London and led
William Whiteley to open his first shop in 1863,
when he may also have hoped to profit from the
arrival of the Metropolitan railway. Under Whiteley,
who bought and rebuilt much neighbouring property, Westbourne Grove became one of the capital's
leading shopping centres. By 1879 it was considered
economically so self-sufficient that it could have declared itself an independent republic. In 1887 it was
'the Bond Street of the west'.[81]

The rising commercial prosperity of Westbourne
Grove contrasted with a rapid social decline in
streets farther north, between the railway and the
canal. Subletting to weekly lodgers had made
Brindley Street the most overcrowded in Paddington, with 3.5 persons to a room, by 1865, although
conditions had improved slightly by 1869, when the
worst areas were near the canal basin at Paddington
green.[82] Clarendon Street (later Crescent), with 17
persons to a house, and the parallel Woodchester
Street, with 16.4 persons, were the most overcrowded in 1894–5, when Cirencester Street and
Waverley Road were also among the eleven worst in
the parish.[83] The Lock bridge area west of Ranelagh
Road, bounded north by the canal bend and south
by Westbourne Terrace North (later Bourne Terrace) and Marlborough (later Torquay) Street, was
singled out as one of six poor patches amid the
general affluence of north-west London. Clarendon
Street and its neighbours, however, were poorer than
the cul-de-sacs off the south-west side of Harrow
Road, where poverty and comfort were mixed and
where Alfred Street, like Harrow Road itself, was
considered fairly comfortable. In Clarendon Street,
where the more respectable women did laundry
work, there were thieves and prostitutes. Subletting,

which had gone so far that a room might have different tenants by day and by night, could be controlled only by declaring buildings to be lodging
houses, as had been done for one whole side of the
street. Such decay was unexpected, in that the
houses were 'cast-off clothes of the rich'. It was
attributed in 1899 to the canal, as elsewhere in London, to isolation arising from a lack of through
traffic, and to the density of building.[84] If Woodchester Street had not been crammed in, it was possible that the decline, on land which had largely been
held by the Grand Junction Canal Co., would not
have taken place.[85]

East of Ranelagh Road, partly on the Paddington
Estate, the inhabitants were classified in 1899 as
mostly well-to-do and those in Westbourne Square
as wealthy. Delamere Terrace, with Blomfield Road
opposite it in Maida Vale, represented, exceptionally, a successful effort to utilize the canal as ornamental water.[86]

South of the railway, Westbourne green shared
the social characteristics of adjoining parts of Bayswater. The eastern end of Westbourne Gardens,
with Porchester Square, and Gloucester, Porchester,
and Orsett terraces, was wealthy, as was Bishop's
Road. Westbourne Park Villas and Road, with Hereford Road and other streets running south, were
well-to-do, as was Westbourne Grove. Talbot Road
and other streets running to the Kensington boundary were well-to-do or fairly comfortable, with
poverty in some mews dwellings. There were also
some poor alleys north of the canal, off Harrow Road
near the workhouse.[87]

The early 20th century saw a more general, if
slow, decline. Whiteley's opened new buildings in
Queensway rather than in Westbourne Grove, which
lost much of its appeal.[88] By 1919 many large houses
on the western edge of the borough around Talbot
Road were empty or subdivided[89] and by c. 1929 the
area between Westbourne Grove and the railway,
with many cheap boarding houses, had an air of
neglect. Slums still lay farther north, where the
neighbourhood of Brindley, Clarendon, and Cirencester streets had Paddington's highest density, of
1.75 or more persons to a room,[90] and was 'one of the
most discreditable in London'.[91] There were 1.50 to
1.75 persons to a room along Amberley Road, as at
Kensal New Town and near the canal basin at
Paddington green, and overcrowding of 1.25 to 1.50
persons to an acre had spread south-eastward from
Cirencester Street along Harrow Road and behind
Delamere Terrace to Chichester Road and also
existed north-west of the former workhouse around
Woodfield Street. Delamere Terrace and Warwick
Crescent had begun to deteriorate, with 1 to 1.25

[73] A. Trollope, *The Three Clerks* (1858), cap. xvi.
[74] Marylebone libr., P 138, cuttings.
[75] *Home Counties Mag.* ii. 279.
[76] G.L.R.O., TA/10 (tithe map, 1842, and plan of
Westbourne Grove, 1846).
[77] G.L.R.O., WCS 79, pp. 82–3.
[78] Herbert Spencer, *Autobiog.* (1904), i. 349.
[79] R. S. Lambert, *Universal Provider* (1938), 60.
[80] Marylebone libr., P 138, cuttings; *Paddington News*,
10 Dec. 1859; Spencer, *Autobiog.* i. 349.
[81] Lambert, *Universal Provider*, 107; A. Adburgham,
Shops and Shopping (1964), 150, 156; below, econ., ind.;
above, plate 53.
[82] *Paddington San. Rep. 1869–70* (in Marylebone libr.),
7.

[83] *Rep. on Vital Statistics and San. Work 1894* (in
Marylebone libr.), 11.
[84] Booth, *Life and Labour*, i (1), 246; iii (3), 120, 122–4;
Booth's Map (1889), NW.
[85] Booth, *Life and Labour*, iii (3), 124; Gutch, *Plan of
Paddington* (1828, coloured to show estates).
[86] Booth, *Life and Labour*, iii (3), 124, map facing p.
135.
[87] Ibid. map facing p. 135.
[88] H. P. Clunn, *Lond. Rebuilt 1897–1927* (1927), 285;
below, econ., ind.
[89] *The Times*, 19 Jan. 1935, 9e.
[90] *New Lond. Life and Labour*, iv, maps; vi. 431.
[91] G. W. Currie, *Ch. of Eng. and Her Ground Rents*
(1930), 9.

persons to a room, whereas there were less than 1 on the Maida Vale side of the canal pool and elsewhere in Westbourne green.[92] In 1937 some imposing but shabby houses in Delamere Terrace were subdivided and rapidly decaying.[93] A similar threat was seen around Talbot Road.[94]

In the period between the World Wars the building of Porchester hall, with its adjacent library and baths, gave the north end of Porchester Road the appearance of a modest civic centre.[95] Nearby rebuilding produced blocks of private flats, all north of Westbourne Grove. Hatherley Court of 1936 was advertised as 'one minute from Whiteley's' and, in spite of its position behind Owen's former drapery store between Hatherley Road and Westbourne Grove Terrace, as being in Bayswater. New London Properties in 1939 offered flats in four blocks nearby: Arthur Court, at the north-west end of Queensway, and, facing it, Ralph Court, which backed Peter's Court in Porchester Road, and Claremont Court.[96] Father east Westbourne Court stood at the corner of Orsett Terrace and Westbourne Terrace by 1938.[97] The few new commercial buildings included the G.W.R. parcels depot at nos. 14, 16, and 18 Bishop's Road and its estate and other offices at the north-eastern end of Westbourne Terrace by 1934.[98] There was no slum clearance, although the borough council in 1938 had plans to clear Clarendon Road.[99]

The worst slums, between the railway and the canal from Warwick Crescent to Clarendon Crescent, were transformed by the L.C.C. In 1957 it had bought 206 properties from the borough council and 266 from the Church Commissioners, and hoped to acquire 400 more.[1] Under a scheme of 1958, for 44 a. and affecting 6,700 residents, half of the land was to be used for 1,127 dwellings, of which 946 were to be in new blocks and the others in renovated houses; the rest was to be used for shops, garages, schools and other institutions, and a canalside walk and 8 a. of badly needed open space.[2] The Warwick estate, as it came to be called, was opened in 1962[3] and soon extended west of Harrow Road over the site of Brindley Street. The scheme, together with the alignment of Westway along part of Harrow Road, involved the disappearance of nearly all the streets from Delamere Terrace and Blomfield Villas westward to Waverley Road.[4] As a further extension, the G.L.C. in 1967 acquired 4 a. north of the canal in Amberley Road, for 375 new dwellings. Westminster took over the main Warwick estate in 1971, the Brindley extension in 1972, and the Amberley Road extension in 1973.[5]

Immediately south of the railway, the yard bounded by Great Western and Westbourne Park roads was being built up in 1970 as the 10-a. Brunel estate.[6] The first blocks were finished in 1971, containing 80 dwellings out of the 417 intended for

1,500 people. Nearby it was planned in 1973 to replace a segment of housing between Tavistock Crescent, Tavistock Road, and St. Luke's Road with the 148 dwellings called Westmead, which were under construction in 1974.

On the south side of Westbourne Park Road there was much dereliction around St. Stephen's Gardens, where no. 32 was probably the first of many subdivided houses to be acquired by the notorious landlord Peter Rachman (d. 1962). Rachman, who favoured West Indian tenants, had an office at the corner of Westbourne Grove and Monmouth Street and acquired several properties near by, although by 1955-6 he had extended his activities beyond Paddington.[7] In 1965 Westminster council bought 108 houses, most of them subdivided or empty, in the hope of preventing further decay.[8] The houses, west of Porchester Road, were the first of those later known as the Westbourne Gardens estate. In 1969 the council bought property around St. Stephen's Gardens between Shrewsbury and Ledbury roads. The area was later rebuilt as the Wessex Gardens estate, named after Thomas Hardy,[9] where the first of 300 dwellings planned for 1,116 people were ready in 1978.

North of the canal, next to the hospital in Harrow Road, the G.L.C.'s small Windsor estate had been built by 1965.[10] Later there was wholesale clearance farther east, along most of Amberley Road by the canal, where Aldsworth Close and other flats were finished in 1977, and behind in Amberley Mews and Shirland Road, where Charfield and Ellwood courts were finished in 1972.[11]

In the south-eastern part of the district, adjoining Bayswater, the houses were mostly refurbished. The L.C.C. began in 1964 to rehabilitate the 8½-a. Porchester Square estate, which had been sold by the Church Commissioners in 1955. Garden walls and outbuildings made way for a play area over garages in the triangle behind Gloucester and Orsett terraces and the east side of Porchester Square, while 150 houses in those rows were converted into over 500 flats and 114 maisonettes by 1971.[12] The south-west part of Porchester Square, with Porchester Mews and buildings stretching down Porchester Road to Bishop's Bridge Road, was taken for the Colonnades, a scheme embracing shops and private flats, completed in 1975.[13]

New lines of communication and the spread of terraced housing have destroyed not only the buildings but the road pattern of the 18th-century village of Westbourne green. The suburb, divided by canal and railway, has no overall character, with an overcrowded centre and many peripheral streets resembling those of neighbouring districts. Victorian housing predominates south of the railway, although

[92] New Lond. Life and Labour, iv, maps.
[93] M. Fitzgerald, Ch. as Landlord (1937), 69-71.
[94] The Times, 19 Jan. 1935, 9e.
[95] Below, pub. svces.
[96] Clunn, Face of Lond. 444; Paddington Past and Present [1939], 33, 82-3, 85.
[97] P.O. Dir. Lond. (1938).
[98] Ibid. (1934 and later edns.).
[99] Marylebone libr., P 138, cuttings.
[1] Ibid.
[2] The Times, 17 Oct. 1958, 4e.
[3] G.L.C. Home Sweet Home (1976), 12, 62.
[4] Bartholomew's Ref. Atlas of Gtr. Lond. (1963, 1968).

[5] Marylebone libr., P 138, cuttings; Map of Westm. Housing Est. 1985 (in Marylebone libr.).
[6] Following two paras. based on ibid.
[7] S. Green, Rachman (1979), 42, 49-51, 53-5, passim.
[8] Inf. from asst. dist. offr. (management), Westm. Dist. Housing Office 3.
[9] Lond. Encyc. 941.
[10] P.O. Dir. Lond. (1964, 1965).
[11] Map of Westm. Housing Est. 1985; inf. from asst. dist. offr. (management), Westm. Dist. Housing Office 3.
[12] Marylebone libr., P 138, cuttings; Illus. Lond. News, June 1973, 45-9; G.L.C. Home Sweet Home, 12, 75.
[13] Marylebone libr., P 138, cuttings; Lond. Encyc. 46.

replaced by municipal estates near Westbourne Park station and interspersed elsewhere with much rebuilding. The older streets west of Porchester Road form Westbourne conservation area, which stretches to the boundary, and those to the east lie in the Bayswater area.[14] North of the railway, rebuilding has been widespread.

The southern boundary, along Bishop's Bridge Road and Westbourne Grove, is lined by many types of building. Westward from the railway bridge they include the former G.W.R. parcels depot, the six- and seven-storeyed block of municipal flats called Brewers' Court, finished in 1976,[15] and the empty site of Holy Trinity church, which was a subject of controversy in 1984[16] and was being prepared for flats called Trinity Court in 1986. Stuccoed pairs and a recessed terrace, undergoing renovation, make up Gloucester Gardens, an imposing mid 19th-century survival in contrast with the Hallfield estate, on the south side of the road in Bayswater. To the west are Clifton nurseries and shops forming part of the Colonnades, a yellow-brick and brown-tiled development for Samuel Properties, designed by Farrell Grimshaw Partnership and officially commended in 1977.[17] More shops and a cinema extend to the corner of Queensway. Westbourne Grove has some new buildings, including the red-brick Westbourne House (no. 16) and T.S.W. House on either side of Westbourne Grove Terrace, but consists mainly of three- or four-storeyed Victorian parades. The shops are smaller towards the west, reaching along the north side as far as the corner of Chepstow Road and along the boundary on the south side to Ledbury Road, on the fringe of the antique dealers' area of northern Kensington.

The area between the line of Bishop's Bridge Road and Westbourne Grove and the railway is residential. Restoration of the tall Italianate houses in the eastern part, around Gloucester Terrace and Porchester Square,[18] has enabled it to retain its original resemblance to Bayswater. The eastern end of Orsett Terrace (formerly Orsett Place), although much altered, contains two detached villas whose ornate features include Egyptian pillars and boldly projecting cornices; they were designed by G. L. Taylor as comparatively low buildings, in order not to hide Holy Trinity church.[19] Orsett House bears a plaque to the political thinker Alexander Herzen, who lived there from 1850 to 1863. At the south-west corner of Porchester Square the flats of the Colonnades are in scale with the seven- or eight-storeyed red-brick blocks of Peter's, Ralph, and Arthur courts to the west. Off Westbourne Grove there are tall cramped terraces of the 1860s or 1870s in Hatherley Road and Westbourne Grove Terrace, in addition to the eight-storeyed Hatherley Court, and in part of Newton Road. Another stretch of Newton Road, parallel with Westbourne Grove, has several grouped and single villas, of two storeys and basements, in small gardens, serving as reminders of the appearance of Westbourne Grove before it became a shopping centre. No. 32 has been rebuilt as a four-storeyed

rectangular block and, dating from 1937–8, is the earliest individual work of Sir Denys Lasdun.[20]

Slightly farther north the area around Westbourne Gardens and St. Stephen's church is one of mid 19th-century terraces, many still run down but others recently restored, with infilling in the form of small blocks of flats. Some of the terraces, in Westbourne Gardens and west of St. Stephen's church, are in the imposing style of Bayswater and Tyburnia, having four storeys and basements, with first-floor balconies and pillared porches. A few pairs, lower and possibly earlier, are north of the church in Westbourne Park Road. Modern flats in Westbourne Park Road are to scale and mostly five-storeyed. They include Swanleys (no. 45), built east of the church by 1978,[21] adjoining municipal flats at no. 41, and others opposite at no. 56, whose site was bought by Paddington council in 1961.[22]

Better preserved streets stretch westward to the Kensington boundary, in a block between Westbourne Grove and Talbot Road. Hereford Road is lined by terraces with pillared porches like those in Westbourne Gardens, stuccoed and perhaps slightly grander than similar brick ones in Alexander Street. Chepstow Road, the quieter Northumberland Place, and parallel streets to the west have mostly three-storeyed terraces, both brick-faced and stuccoed, with balconies and a few with verandahs and trellises. A terrace on the east side of Ledbury Road has a centrepiece of 8 bays divided by Corinthian pilasters.

North of Talbot Road there has been extensive rebuilding. The west side of Shrewsbury Road is lined with waste ground, behind which the streets stretching as far as Ledbury Road have been replaced by Casterbridge and six other purplish brick blocks, of three to seven storeys, forming the Wessex Gardens estate. Around it, older terraces are being renovated. The larger Brunel estate to the north covers the former railway depot and consists of 21 blocks; mostly six- or seven-storeyed, they include a few lower ones and a solitary tower block, the twenty-storeyed Keyham House in Westbourne Park Road. Facing the Brunel estate along Great Western Road are the new four-storeyed buff-brick ranges of Dorchester House and Hardy House. Victorian terraces survive to the west, interspersed with four- or five-storeyed blocks of flats including Westbury House, built on the corner of Westbourne Park Road and Aldridge Road Villas by 1965, Aldridge Court, in Aldridge Road Villas by 1962, and, in Tavistock Road, Leamington House, built by 1962, and Fallodon House, built by 1976.[23] Westmead day centre, in Tavistock Road, serves the estate immediately to the north, where a five-storeyed yellow-brick range stretches along the north side of Tavistock Crescent into Kensington. A few large villas survive in Tavistock Road: they include, at the north-west corner of St. Luke's Road on the Kensington side of the boundary, the former Tower House, a gaunt Italianate building where W. H. Hudson spent his last years.[24]

[14] Westm. Dist. Plan, Proposals Map, 1982 (in Marylebone libr.).
[15] Inf. from asst. dist. offr. (management), Westm. Dist. Housing Office 3.
[16] Observer, 2 Dec. 1984.
[17] Marylebone libr., P 138, cuttings; inf. from Chestertons.   [18] Illus. Lond. News, June 1973, 45–8.

[19] Taylor, Auto-biog. i. 181.
[20] A. Service, Architects of Lond. (1979), 193.
[21] P.O. Dir. Lond. (1977, 1978).
[22] Paddington Mag. Apr. 1961.
[23] P.O. Dir. Lond. (1961 and later edns.); Map of Westm. Housing Est. 1985.
[24] R. Tomalin, W. H. Hudson (1954), 95, 97.

The area between the railway, skirted by Westway, and the canal is filled mostly by the Warwick estate and, around Alfred Road, its Brindley extension. At the western end, north of Westbourne Park station, council housing is continued into Kensington as part of the Cheltenham estate. Very few buildings survive from before the 1960s on the Warwick estate except St. Mary Magdalene's church, its neighbouring primary school, Edward Wilson school to the south, and some of the grander terraced housing farther east. Most of the old street names have disappeared, including Clarendon, Woodchester, and Brindley, although a few have been given to rebuilt roads or cul-de-sacs.

The Warwick and Brindley estate has a wide range of buildings[25] and consists of 23 numbered blocks or ranges, including six 21-storeyed towers faced in brown roughcast, all of which are in the western half. On the estate only the shopping parade called Oldbury House lies along Harrow Road, the other buildings being dispersed across a landscaped slope. In the centre a large open space, with playing fields at the Harrow Road end, has been left along the line of the former Lord Hill's Road, rising to a footbridge over the canal. Farther east the estate contains some Italianate terraces in Blomfield Villas and Westbourne Terrace Road, where their restoration has been commended by the Civic Trust.[26] Both Delamere Terrace, beside the canal, and Warwick Crescent, beside the pool, have been rebuilt, as four- and five-storeyed brick ranges of maisonettes and old people's dwellings. Warwick Crescent, designed by the G.L.C.'s architect Hubert Bennett, is painted on its north-eastern side to match the stuccoed houses of Little Venice across the water.[27]

Outside the estate, alone on a corner site between the pool and Harrow Road, is Beauchamp Lodge. A community centre, it is an ornate building of 1854[28] and has five storeys and basement, with balconies, bays, and a Corinthian porch. The new Paddington fire station and, farther west beyond Torquay Street, some nondescript office blocks also face Harrow Road. Torquay Street leads to Westbourne Green sports complex, opened c. 1976 in the shadow of Westway.[29] Part of the concrete supports of Westway has a large mural, 'Man and Mechanical Energy', of 1977.[30]

North of the canal, the curving strip facing the Warwick estate, from Lord Hill's footbridge to the former Amberley school, is lined by the pale buff-brick terraces called Barnwood Close and Aldsworth Close, of three storeys along the canal and over garages on the landward side. Behind run the two-storeyed Ellwood Court and the parallel seven-storeyed Charfield Court, bordering Shirland Road, with Downfield Close to the west. The western end of Amberley Road retains a Victorian terrace. West

of the Lock bridge, the hospital and other institutional buildings line the south side of Harrow Park as far as the three- and four-storeyed yellow-brick blocks of the Windsor estate. Beyond are shops around the junction with Great Western Road and late 19th-century terraces parallel with the canal in Fermoy and Hormead roads.

BAYSWATER has come to be the name for the whole of the former Paddington metropolitan borough south of the railway.[31] The area described below, however, is the south-western part of Paddington, from the Kensington boundary eastward to Lancaster Gate Terrace and Eastbourne Terrace and from Bayswater Road northward to Bishop's Bridge Road and Westbourne Grove. It includes the two Lancaster Gate wards of 1901, besides a small part of Church ward along Eastbourne Terrace.[32] The districts to the east and north are treated separately, under Tyburnia and Westbourne green.

Bayard's Watering Place, recorded in 1380,[33] was where the stream later called the Bayswater rivulet or Westbourne passed under the Uxbridge road. The name presumably denoted a place where horses were refreshed, either from the stream itself or from a spring such as the one in Conduit field which from 1439 supplied the City with water.[34] There were several variations of the name,[35] Bayswatering being common in the 18th century,[36] although the form Bayswater occurred as early as 1659.[37]

Seventeenth-century Bayswater was a small hamlet, whose inhabitants were presumably assessed with those of Westbourne green.[38] Robert Hilliard had a dwelling house at Bayard's Watering by 1646, together with 6 a. in the common fields of Westbourne.[39] In 1710 Robert Pollard held two houses called Bayard's Watering Place, with outbuildings and 6 a. in Westbourne common fields, once occupied by Alexander Bond; he also held the new brick house called the Bell, formerly the King's Head and once occupied by Edward Hilliard, with its stable which had been converted into a little house near the road.[40] Nearby in 1730 there was at least one other inn, the Saracen's Head, perhaps at other times called the Swan.[41] To the west were the buildings of Upton farm, well back from the highway at the end of a tree-lined lane, which were bought in 1733 by Lord Craven.[42] In 1746 there were only two buildings near the road east of the Bayswater rivulet and three on the west side. The lane still led through fields, to Lord Craven's pest house, east of which were two more buildings, presumably barns, beside the rivulet.[43] The location in 1742 was 'intended to be called Craven Hill'.[44]

To the west the Oxford Arms stood alone by 1729 at the east corner of the lane leading from the Uxbridge road to Westbourne green. A gravel pit

[25] G.L.C. *Home Sweet Home*, 62 and illus.
[26] Marylebone libr., P 138, cuttings.
[27] Ibid.
[28] Inf. from dir., Beauchamp Lodge Settlement; below, social.
[29] Marylebone libr., P 132.2, cuttings.
[30] *Lond. Encyc.* 942.
[31] *Lond. Encyc.*, 46.
[32] *Plan of Paddington* (1901).
[33] J. Tanner, *Notitia Monastica* (1787), Mdx. xii.
[34] *Lond. Encyc.* 46; below, pub. svces.
[35] *P.N. Mdx.* (E.P.N.S.), 132–3.

[36] e.g. Rocque, *Map of Lond.* (1741–5), sheet 11; Ch. Com., 'Map of 1742'.
[37] P.R.O., PROB 11/292 (P.C.C. 330 Pell, will of John Chapman).
[38] G.L.R.O., MR/TH/2.
[39] G.L.R.O., BRA/513/6, 8, 13.
[40] M.L.R. 1710/2/99.
[41] G.L.R.O., MR/LV5/22; below, social.
[42] 'Survey of Upton Fm. by Wm. Gardner, 1729' (map in Marylebone libr.); below, manors (Craven).
[43] Rocque, *Map of Lond.* (1741–5), sheet 11.
[44] M.L.R. 1742/1/175.

bordered the lane north of the inn,[45] which was called the Black Lion by 1751 and was then considered to be at Bayswater, as was the Crown farther east.[46]

Still farther west, a large settlement on both sides of the Uxbridge road was known from the 17th until the 19th century as Kensington Gravel Pits. It may have preceded the discovery of gravel and lay mostly in Kensington, along the stretch of road which came to be known as Notting Hill Gate.[47] Part lay in Paddington, however, including a new brick house held by Peter Warren, a London carpenter, in 1709.[48] Some half a dozen buildings in Paddington stood close to the boundary in 1746, by the Uxbridge road and at the entrance to a lane which cut north-eastward to meet Westbourne Green (later Black Lion) Lane. Between Westbourne Green Lane and Kensington Gravel Pits, Shaftesbury House stood alone by the main road.[49]

Bayswater was one of four new rating divisions of the parish in 1773, when, however, most of its 56 properties were probably at Westbourne green.[50] Speculative building along the Uxbridge road was started by John Elkins, a bricklayer or brickmaker of South Street, St. George's, Hanover Square, to whom Benjamin Crompton in 1776 granted 91-year leases of 5 a. and of the adjoining Black Lion.[51] Elkins, who also acquired land near Paddington green,[52] from 1779 subleased several parcels of Black Lion field with road frontages of 18 ft., for 'double brick' houses which came to be known as Elkins's Row.[53] It was only a short row in 1790, when a Bayswater coffee house also existed. There were apparently no other new buildings between Bayard's Watering Place and Kensington Gravel Pits.[54] Undeveloped plots were conveyed by Elkins's executors to William Philpot in 1792.[55] Bayswater was only a 'small hamlet' in 1807, when it was noted for its tea gardens and water supply, and for the lying-in hospital (soon known as Queen Charlotte's) farther east.[56]

Widespread speculative building was carried out by Edward Orme, a print seller of Bond Street, who in 1809 acquired the former Bell at Bayswater, called Elms House, with two houses behind it, formerly a single house,[57] and also Bayswater tea gardens.[58] Meanwhile dwellings had replaced the pest house at Craven Hill, where Orme bought the lease of a house in 1811.[59] Soon he also held much property farther west along the Uxbridge road, where he may first have made money from gravel.[60] He paid for Bayswater chapel in 1818, to serve houses which he had presumably erected in Petersburgh (later St. Peters-

burgh) Place, leading north from the Uxbridge road to a 'street or place called Moscow Cottages', itself linked to Black Lion Lane by a road soon called Moscow Road.[61] The two new roads were said to commemorate Orme's business dealings with Russia[62] but may have been named merely in honour of Tsar Alexander I's visit to England in 1814. Orme Square, whose south side was formed by the Uxbridge road, was built between 1823, when land was bought east of Petersburgh Place, and 1826.[63] Edward Orme (d. 1848) granted leases of two new houses in Moscow Road in 1826 and himself lived from c. 1829 in Fitzroy Square.[64] He was probably responsible for building at Orme's green in Harrow Road[65] and, with Francis Orme, had filled in some spaces in Moscow Road in 1839.[66] Edward in 1842 owned all the houses in Porchester Gardens and St. Petersburgh Place.[67] Many leases, both of older houses and of new ones, as in Lancaster Terrace, Lancaster Gate, and St. Leonard's Terrace, Blomfield Road, were later sold by Francis Orme.[68]

Another builder in the south-western corner of the parish was John Bark, described at first as a coal merchant, who in 1818 lived in Marylebone and by 1821 in Bayswater Hill, where new houses faced the Uxbridge road west of Shaftesbury House. In 1818 Bark took a 98-year building lease of the Paddington Estate's Six-Acre field, 'lately in part dug out for making bricks', stretching from the Uxbridge road to Moscow Road, where in 1821 he was granted leases on small houses in Caroline Place and Poplar Place.[69] Farther east, beyond Elkins's Row, which was also known as Bayswater Terrace,[70] Porchester Terrace had been planned to run northward to Westbourne green by 1823. Single or semi-detached villas in the new road were leased to individuals by the Paddington Estate from 1823, one of the first being to the landscape gardener John Claudius Loudon (1783–1843).[71] Building along the Uxbridge road continued with four pairs called St. Agnes Villas, first leased in 1824; nos. 1 to 4 were west of the corner with Porchester Terrace, next to Elkins's Row, and nos. 5 to 8 on the east corner.[72]

By 1828 the main road, facing Kensington Gardens, had been built up between Petersburgh Place and Porchester Terrace. Houses stretched north to Moscow Road, itself nearly completed, although there was open ground near the boundary and between Petersburgh Place and Bark Place. Along the west side of Black Lion Lane there were houses as far as the corner of Moscow Road and more spacious villas, at first called Westbourne Terrace, farther north almost reaching Pickering Place at the

[45] 'Survey of Upton Fm.'.
[46] G.L.R.O., MR/LV7/3, 45, 64.
[47] Survey of Lond. xxxvii. 38; Ogilby, Map of Mdx. [c. 1672].
[48] M.L.R. 1709/1/91; 1714/6/179–80.
[49] Rocque, Map of Lond. (1741–5), sheet 11.
[50] Poor rate bk. (1721–74).
[51] M.L.R. 1776/5/308, 6/4.
[52] Ibid. 1776/6/5; 1777/4/75–6, 431–2.
[53] Ibid. 1779/5/244–5, 301; 1786/4/72–3.
[54] Ch. Com., 'Map of 1790'; G.L.R.O., MR/LV9/187.
[55] M.L.R. 1792/6/165.
[56] Ambulator (1807); below, social; pub. svces. The hosp. had been in St. Geo.'s Row, treated above as part of Tyburnia.
[57] M.L.R. 1809/4/763.
[58] Ibid. 1855/12/484.

[59] Ibid. 1811/6/283; below, manors (Craven).
[60] Paddington Soc. Newsletter, Feb. 1964.
[61] T. Faulkner, Hist. Kensington (1820), 585; Ch. Com., Bldg. Agreements, vol. i; below, churches.
[62] Lond. Encyc. 567.
[63] Paddington Soc. Newsletter, Feb. 1964.
[64] M.L.R. 1855/12/484; Boyle's Court Guide (1829); Gent. Mag. cxxiii. 553.
[65] Above, Westbourne green.
[66] G.L.R.O., WCS 78, p. 246.
[67] Ibid. TA/10.
[68] e.g. M.L.R. 1857/6/702–8; 1863/16/300–6.
[69] Ch. Com., Bldg. Agreements, vol. i; Guildhall MS. 12532.
[70] Pigot's Com. Dir. (1822–3), map.
[71] Guildhall MS. 12546; D.N.B.
[72] Guildhall MS. 12559.

southern end of Westbourne green. The east side was still open, apart from a few large houses at the Uxbridge road end, and villas lined Porchester Terrace only as far as the corner of Craven Hill, which itself had cottages only on the north side. Fields survived along the Uxbridge road from St. Agnes Villas to Bayard's Watering Place, whence Elms or Elm Lane led northward, with some houses between it and the stream, along the line of the later Craven Terrace to the east end of Craven Hill.[73]

Building in the south-west part of the parish thus almost kept pace with the growth of Tyburnia. Although housing spread inwards from the two southern corners of the parish, eventually to meet at Bayard's Watering Place half way along the Uxbridge road, the movements at first were unrelated. Only part of south-western Paddington belonged to the bishop of London, comprising in 1828 a block stretching from the Uxbridge road east of Bark Place, a larger block along Porchester Terrace to Hall field, and a stretch on the east side of Black Lion Lane. No overall plan was therefore drawn up. The larger houses were not stately terraces overlooking squares and served by mews alleys, as in Tyburnia, but villas with gardens.[74] The name Bayswater was not at first applied to the south-western corner: Black Lion Lane was described in 1803 as linking Westbourne green with Kensington Gravel Pits,[75] and Orme Square was 'a northward feeler of the Kensington Palace purlieus'.[76] By 1830, however, the area around Black Lion Lane was known as Bayswater.[77]

During the 1830s Victoria Grove (renamed Ossington Street in 1873)[78] was laid out from the Uxbridge road close to the boundary, on part of Gravel Pit field. A large house at the Moscow Road end was leased in 1831 to the architect Thomas Allason,[79] surveyor to the neighbouring Ladbroke estate; it was probably the villa, in 2½ a., on which Allason had worked since 1825 and which J. C. Loudon considered unequalled in the suburbs of London.[80] Seven terraced houses to the south were leased to William Ward, a Marylebone builder, in 1836 and six others in 1841.[81] Ward also filled a space along the Uxbridge road between Victoria Grove and the boundary with an inn and five shops, nos. 1 to 6 Wellington Terrace.[82] More villas were built along Porchester Terrace, as far as Hall field, but in 1840 Bayswater had still not been joined to neighbouring districts. There was open land south of Craven Hill,[83] including the parish's Bread and Cheese lands and land which Joseph Neeld held from the chapter of Westminster, partly in Westbourne common field and partly bordering the Uxbridge road.[84]

Artistic and literary figures were attracted to a district which was still semi-rural.[85] In 1834 the poet Sarah Flower Adams (1805–48) moved with her husband to no. 5 Craven Hill, where they were soon followed by the author and politician William Johnson Fox (1786–1864) and his housekeeper the composer Eliza Flower (1803–46), Sarah's sister. There, in her 'snug, out-of-the-world corner', Eliza entertained Thomas Carlyle and others in a literary circle familiar to the young Robert Browning.[86] The composer Vincent Novello (1781–1861) lived at no. 4, where from 1835 until 1856 the household included his son-in-law and daughter, Charles (1787–1877) and Mary Cowden Clarke (1809–98), the authors. At the Loudons' house in Porchester Terrace, Mary Cowden Clarke met the painters Charles (1799–1879) and Edward Landseer (1802–73), and John Martin (1789–1854), and the sculptor Joseph Bonomi (1796–1878). At the corner of Black Lion Lane, Ivy Cottage was the home of the engraver Samuel Reynolds (1773–1835) and later of Augustus Egg (1816–63); Egg's guests included the fellow painter William Mulready (1786–1863),[87] who claimed to have been a lifelong Bayswater resident, and Charles Dickens. Farther west Sir Rowland Hill (1795–1879), inventor of the penny post, lived at no. 1 Orme Square from 1839 until 1842[88] and the artist Frederic (later Lord) Leighton at no. 2 from 1860 to 1866. St. Petersburgh House, no. 8 Bayswater Hill, was the home of the conveyancer Lewis Duval (1774–1844) and then of his niece's husband the Vice-Chancellor Sir Charles Hall (1814–83).

By 1840 plans had been made to exploit more of the Paddington Estate as the eastern part of Bayswater, where the future Gloucester, Westbourne, and Eastbourne terraces were to lead to Bishop's Road.[89] The layout was presumably by George Gutch, whose long avenues contrasted with the interrelated squares and short streets of Cockerell's Tyburnia. Terraces were chosen, rather than villas, perhaps in order to mask the railway.[90] They were also used, however, in most of the rest of Bayswater: in further building along the former Black Lion Lane, renamed Queen's Road, in most of Inverness and Queensborough terraces, parallel avenues driven north between Queen's Road and Porchester Terrace, in Lancaster Gate, which filled the last gap along the Uxbridge road, around Cleveland Square north of Craven Hill, and around Prince's, Leinster, and Kensington Gardens squares north of Moscow Road. Detached villas were chosen only for the completion of Porchester Terrace as far as Bishop's Road and semi-detached ones only for the northern end of Inverness Terrace and, farther west, around Monmouth Road south of Westbourne Grove.[91]

During the 1840s and 1850s housing spread steadily. It was the work of several builders, many of them also active in Tyburnia, in the south part of Maida Vale, and in the east part of Westbourne

[73] Gutch, *Plan of Paddington* (1828). Called Elms Lane in dirs. but Elm Lane on many maps.
[74] Guildhall Libr., boro. maps P1: Gutch, *Plan of Paddington* (1828, coloured to show estates).
[75] M.L.R. 1803/2/533.   [76] Pevsner, *Lond.* ii. 309.
[77] Above, plate 36; J. Britton, *Topog. Surv. of Boro. of St. Marylebone, 1833* (Lond. Topog. Soc. 1962, 1963).
[78] L.C.C. *Names of Streets* (1901), 381.
[79] Guildhall MS. 12589.
[80] Colvin, *Brit. Architects*, 66; J. C. Loudon, *Encyclopaedia of Cottage, Farm, and Villa Archit.* (1836), pp. xix, 826–34.
[81] Guildhall MS. 12589.
[82] Ibid. 12595.
[83] Gutch, *Plan of Paddington* (1840).
[84] Below, manors (Westbourne green).
[85] Para. based on McDonald, 'Paddington', cap. 13; D.N.B.
[86] B. B. Miller, *Robt. Browning* (1952), 41, 47, 49.
[87] W. P. Frith, *My Autobiog.* (1887), i. 178, 180.
[88] *Blue Plaque Guide*, ed. V. Burrows (1953), 53.
[89] Gutch, *Plan of Paddington* (1840).
[90] G.L.C. Hist. Bldgs. Div., WM 174, 177.
[91] Lucas, *Plan of Paddington* (1869).

green, where some of Bayswater's long avenues were continued north of Bishop's Road. The grandest street was Westbourne Terrace, begun from the south end *c.* 1840 and finished 1856–60, whose main builders were William King and William Kingdom. The blocks north of Craven Road were by Kingdom,[92] who also built most of Gloucester Terrace between 1843 and 1852.[93] Meanwhile farther west lines of building similarly proceeded northward along Queen's Road, Porchester Terrace, the newer Inverness and Queensborough terraces, and the cross street Porchester Gardens. Builders who took several plots in Queen's Road included Edward Capps, whose sublessees included James Capps, from 1841 and Richard Yeo of Westbourne Park Road from 1851.[94] They also had land in Inverness Terrace, whose stretch north of Porchester Gardens was called Inverness Road until 1876 and which was built up between 1844 and 1856, largely by Yeo.[95] John Scantlebury was building at the south end of Inverness Terrace in 1857.[96]

Between the two groups of long north–south avenues lay an area, on either side of Craven Hill, which was built over from the 1850s with grand town houses, many enjoying communal gardens as in the newer parts of Tyburnia. The most lavish use of space was in Cleveland Square, where the block forming the north side gave directly on the gardens.[97] Houses on the other sides were leased between 1852 and 1854 to Henry de Bruno Austin, a speculator active in Paddington and later in outer suburbs.[98] Grounds were also attached to the nearby terraces of Queen's Gardens and Craven Hill Gardens.[99] In 1853 Joseph Neeld and the chapter of Westminster leased their land south of Craven Hill,[1] which soon formed part of the site of an ambitious scheme around the new Christ Church, itself begun in 1854.[2] Terraces were built on the scale of Hyde Park Gardens and were similarly, although less generously, set back from the main road.[3] They were known as Upper Hyde Park Gardens until 1865 and thereafter as Lancaster Gate, a name previously reserved for the square around the church.[4] The terraced houses were said to be the most handsome in London in 1868.[5]

Farther west, Carlyle could still remark *c.* 1855 that only a thin belt of houses to the north and west separated Orme Square from open country.[6] The earliest quarter of Bayswater, however, was soon hemmed in by building to the north. Hereford, Monmouth, and Garway roads were pushed a short way south from Westbourne Grove for William Kinnaird Jenkins.[7] Leinster and Prince's squares were begun in 1856, with Kensington Gardens Square to the east and mews alleys to the south behind Moscow Road. Both Leinster and Prince's squares had private gardens and were largely the work of an obscure speculator, George Wyatt. Leinster Square had a few residents in 1858 and was the first to be finished, by 1864.[8]

Building covered the whole of Bayswater by 1865, when the only sites for infilling were south of Moscow Road, chiefly along the east side of Victoria Grove.[9] In 1862 a 'great and aristocratic town' had grown up, faster than all other suburbs, during the past ten years. Although the description embraced far flung Westbournia, the most desirable part stretched south from Bishop's Road and Westbourne Grove to the Uxbridge road, henceforth called Bayswater Road. Houses were said to be better built and sited than before and, being near Kensington Gardens, to have a decided edge over 'the solemn and obnubilated grandeur of the ill drained Belgravian flats'.[10]

Wealthy residents, who were quick to arrive, in 1862 ranged from East India merchants to people who had moved from formerly more fashionable quarters.[11] In Westbourne Terrace the first occupants included the statesman Richard Cobden (1804–65), at no. 103 from 1848 to 1856, and Sir Richard Bethell (1800–73), later Lord Chancellor as Lord Westbury, at no. 70; other occupants included Admiral Sir Baldwin Wake Walker, Bt. (1802–76), Sir Charles Trevelyan (1807–86), governor of Madras, and Charles Manby (1804–84), the civil engineer.[12] Upper Hyde Park Gardens or Lancaster Gate housed Lord Westbury, Lord Rollo, and two M.P.s in 1863.[13] Socially Tyburnia had spread westward, providing a 'carriage trade' which William Whiteley was to exploit.[14]

During the late 19th century Bayswater's social character grew more mixed.[15] In the south-west corner a few shops had been among the first buildings in the Uxbridge road[16] and in the 1840s shops lined both Queen's Road as far as the Moscow Road junction and Moscow Road itself.[17] Queen's Road had grown even more commercial by 1863. Shops replaced Ivy Cottage[18] and there were very few private residents by 1879, when Whiteley's, expanding southward from Westbourne Grove, had already acquired premises next to the municipal baths.[19] From the first there were tradesmen in Craven Terrace and in Conduit Street, which was renamed Craven Road in 1868, when many of its shops had been newly rebuilt.[20] Hotels, boarding or lodging

[92] G.L.C. Hist. Bldgs. Div., WM 174.
[93] Ibid. WM 174, 177.
[94] Guildhall MS. 12552.
[95] Ibid. 12519/1–2; L.C.C. *Names of Streets* (1901), 268.
[96] *Building News*, 6 Mar. 1857, 239; 19 June 1857, 635.
[97] H.-R. Hitchcock, *Early Victorian Archit. in Britain* (1954), i. 487–8.
[98] Guildhall MS. 12467; *V.C.H. Mdx.* vii. 110.
[99] Hitchcock, *Early Victorian Archit.* 488.
[1] M.L.R. 1853/12/131–2.
[2] Below, churches.
[3] S. Mathesius, *Eng. Terraced Ho.* (1982), 81.
[4] L.C.C. *Names of Streets* (1901), 293; *P.O. Dir. Lond.* (1863).
[5] D. J. Olsen, *Growth of Victorian Lond.* (1976), 165.
[6] E. B. Chancellor, *Squares of Lond.* (1907), 320.
[7] *Survey of Lond.* xxxvii. 260; [untitled] Map of Paddington and Notting Hill (*c.* 1842, showing owners and

provisional street plans linking Bayswater with Ladbroke est.) (in Marylebone libr.).
[8] G.L.C. Hist. Bldgs. Div., WM 212; Hitchcock, *Early Victorian Archit.* 488. Wyatt was 'chief owner, architect, and builder': *Bldg. News*, 19 June 1857, 635.
[9] Stanford, *Library Map of Lond.* (1862 edn. with additions to 1865), sheet 9.
[10] *Builder*, 13 Sept. 1862, 663.
[11] Ibid.
[12] G.L.C. Hist. Bldgs. Div., WM 174; *D.N.B.*
[13] *P.O. Dir. Lond.* (1863).
[14] *Study of Urban Hist.* ed. Dyos, 263.
[15] Ibid. 264.
[16] Guildhall MS. 12595.
[17] Rest of para. based on *P.O. Dir. Lond.* (1845 and later edns.).
[18] Frith, *Autobiog.* iii. 218.
[19] Below, econ., ind.
[20] *Illus. Lond. News*, 10 Oct. 1868, 350.

houses, and apartments also multiplied, notably in Queen's Road and Kensington Gardens Square, perhaps partly due to the influence of Whiteley, who acquired staff dormitories in Queen's Road and dining rooms in the square. The most striking increase was in Eastbourne Terrace, the edge of the district, where railway travellers were responsible for the street's conversion into a row of apartments and hotels by 1902. The population, which by 1870 included many rich foreign born citizens, grew more cosmopolitan, with the consecration of a synagogue in St. Petersburgh Place in 1879 and of a Greek Orthodox cathedral in Moscow Road in 1882.[21]

Such changes tended to be limited to particular streets, leaving a preponderantly residential and prosperous suburb. At no. 23 Porchester Gardens the 'first instance of effective electric lighting of a private house' was provided in 1879 by the engineer Rookes Crompton (1845–1940), who lived there.[22] A few large houses were used by institutions, leading professional men, or tutors in polite accomplishments.[23] The Jewish householders were richer than those of Maida Vale;[24] they included the banker Samuel Montagu, later Lord Swaythling (1832–1911), in Cleveland Square and from 1873 at the opulently decorated no. 96 Lancaster Gate.[25] In 1879 there were seven M.P.s in Lancaster Gate,[26] which had Paddington's 'largest and showiest cluster' of residences.[27] Householders in 1902 included the marquess of Ailsa, the philanthropist Reginald Brabazon, earl of Meath (1841–1929), to whom a memorial was later erected, and the engineer Lieut.-Gen. Sir Richard Strachey (1817–1908).[28] Sir Richard's son Lytton Strachey was brought up from 1884 at no. 69 and always remembered it as a house of high, crammed rooms, 'afflicted with elephantiasis'.[29]

Nearly all the area from Westbourne Terrace to Inverness Terrace was wealthy c. 1890, although Leinster Place and Terrace and Craven Terrace were merely well-to-do, as were Eastbourne Terrace to the east and Queen's Road to the west. Prince's, Leinster, and Kensington Gardens squares were also wealthy. The only mixed areas were mews alleys, as in Tyburnia, and around Moscow Road.[30] In the smartest parts, the less affluent were mainly caretakers, policemen, and shopkeepers. Older property near Moscow Road was let for high rents to shopkeepers, artisans, and clerks, most of whom were 'pretty comfortable'.[31] Lancaster Gate East and West wards, created in 1901, had only 2.15 per cent and 2.58 of their inhabitants overcrowded, compared with 32.76 per cent in Church ward around Paddington green, and death rates were low at 7.67 and 9.08 per cent.[32]

Building activity in the late 19th century was limited mainly to the piecemeal replacement of houses whose leases had fallen in. The oldest houses were west of Lancaster Gate, along Bayswater Road and around Moscow Road. Part of Bayswater Hill was taken for the Red House of 1871, designed by J. J. Stevenson as a precursor of the 'Queen Anne' style, soon to be popular in Ealing's Bedford Park. The only new road was west of Orme Square, where Shaftesbury House disappeared and Palace Court was driven north to Moscow Road.[33] Some houses were built there in 1889 and flats called Palace Court Mansions were inhabited from 1890.[34] Many Palace Court residents had aesthetic tastes similar to those in Bedford Park; they included Wilfrid Meynell and his wife Alice, the poet (1847–1922), the artist George William Joy (d. 1925), and the furniture expert Percy McQuoid (d. 1925).[35] Nearby nos. 4 and 5 Bayswater Hill, which had been built on Bark's land and stood next to the Red House, were to make way for two or three expensive houses in 1894.[36] Houses at the Kensington end of Moscow Road had been replaced by flats called Prince Edward Mansions and Palace Court by 1890. A little to the east the flats of Pembridge Mansions were occupied from 1897 and those of Windsor and Moscow courts, filling a gap, from 1907.[37] The site of nos. 6 to 8 Bayswater Hill was advertised as suitable for high-class flats or a hotel in 1912.[38]

Elsewhere in Bayswater Road flats were built east of Queen's Road along Bayswater Terrace and east of Queensborough Terrace.[39] At the west corner of Queen's Road a range including shops and the Coburg hotel was put up, to include the new Queen's Road Underground station, in use from 1901. Changes had already taken place in Queen's Road with the provision of more modern shops, the building of Paddington's first public baths in 1874, and the opening of the forerunner of Bayswater Underground station in 1868.[40] Beaumanor Mansions, an imposing range of flats over shops north of the corner of Moscow Road, was occupied from 1904.[41] Urbanization culminated in the completion of most of Whiteley's new building, on the site of the baths, in 1911.[42]

In the period between the World Wars, most of the area remained expensive.[43] While Bayswater Road was gradually taken over for flats or hotels, including the former home of Field-Marshal Sir John French, earl of Ypres (1852–1925), at no. 94 Lancaster Gate,[44] the main north–south avenues still had distinguished residents. Samuel Montagu's nephew Sir Herbert (later Viscount) Samuel (1870–1963), the Liberal politician, had three successive

[21] *Study of Urban Hist.* ed. Dyos, 264; M. I. Robinson, 'Mid Victorian Bayswater' (TS. thesis, 1975, in Marylebone libr.); below, Judaism; Greek Orthodox.
[22] R. E. Crompton, *Reminiscences* (1928), 92; *D.N.B.*
[23] *P.O. Dir. Lond.* (1863, 1879, 1902).
[24] *Jewish Hist. Soc. Trans.* xxi. 84–5.
[25] S. Lasdun, *Victorians at Home* (1980), 106–9 (inc. illus. of Mrs. Montagu's boudoir).
[26] *P.O. Dir. Lond.* (1879).
[27] Wheatley and Cunningham, *Lond. Past and Present*, i. 133.   [28] *P.O. Dir. Lond.* (1902).
[29] M. Holroyd, *Lytton Strachey* (1971), 43, 46.
[30] *Booth's Map* (1889), NW.
[31] Booth, *Life and Labour*, i (2), app. p. 13.
[32] *Plan of Paddington* (1901); Mudie-Smith, *Rel. Life,* 79.

[33] Pevsner, *Lond.* ii. 308–9; *Archit. Rev.* Aug. 1948, 71; *V.C.H. Mdx.* vii. 65–7; *Plan of Paddington* (1901).
[34] *P.O. Dir. Lond.* (1889, 1890); below.
[35] Pevsner, *Lond.* ii. 309; V. Meynell, *Alice Meynell* (1929), 71–2; *Who Was Who, 1916–28*, 568, 689.
[36] Ch. Com., Bldg. Agreements, vol. x, no. 6.
[37] *Plan of Paddington* (1901); *P.O. Dir. Lond.* (1890 and later edns.).
[38] Marylebone libr., P 138, cuttings.
[39] *P.O. Dir. Lond.* (1902).
[40] Above, communications; below, pub. svces.
[41] *P.O. Dir. Lond.* (1904).
[42] Below, econ., ind.
[43] G. W. Currie, *Ch. of Eng. and Her Ground Rents* (1930), 11.
[44] *Paddington Past and Present* [1936], 71.

homes in Porchester Terrace,[45] whose many titled householders included the Lord Chancellor Viscount Buckmaster (1861–1934), and Field-Marshal Sir William Robertson (1860–1933) lived in Westbourne Terrace.[46] Lancaster Gate East and Lancaster Gate West wards, with respective densities of 61 and 78 persons to an acre, were less crowded even than Maida Vale in 1921 and 1931. Lancaster Gate East, with 69.5 persons to an acre, still had the borough's lowest density in 1951.[47] The Paddington Estate's cottages around Caroline Place, one of the oldest parts of Bayswater, which 'might be part of a country town', were being closed in 1937, although they had good tenants and did not constitute a slum. Poverty existed only in pockets: three derelict buildings had to be closed at the corner of Leinster Street and Porchester Mews, where a family with eight children lived in two rooms.[48]

Rebuilding and conversion continued, as leases fell in. In Porchester Terrace, with its unusually well spaced villas, nos. 6 and 8 in 1924 were to be turned into ten flats, whereas nos. 29 and 31 in 1934 were to be replaced by eight single houses.[49] Among piecemeal changes were demolitions to make way in 1935 for flats over an office at the corner of Bayswater Road and Lancaster Gate Road,[50] in 1934 for flats or offices over shops between Queen's Road and Inverness Terrace at the Bishop's Road end, where part of Inver Court had been finished before the Second World War, and in 1939 for 60 single houses with garages on a site eventually taken for the Hallfield estate.[51] A few very large blocks of flats were completed. They included Maitland Court, at the south-east end of Gloucester Terrace, in 1932,[52] Queen's Court of 1930–2 and the slightly later Princess Court, at first also called Queen's Court, in Queen's Road,[53] and Barrie House of 1936–7 and a block of 1938 later called Lancaster in Lancaster Gate.[54]

Bayswater experienced only sporadic private rebuilding, like Tyburnia, until the borough council acquired from the Church Commissioners land between Bishop's Bridge Road and Cleveland Square, an area badly damaged during the Second World War, for the Hallfield estate.[55] Plans had been made by 1948,[56] the first block of flats was ready in 1952,[57] and work was finished in 1959 on the only large municipal scheme in southern Paddington; the site had been extended westward by additional land for schools.[58] Meanwhile the L.C.C. began the Barrie estate on a bombed site at the south-west end of Gloucester Terrace, where the last block was under construction in 1957. Most of its tenants became owner-occupiers, forming the Lancaster Gate Housing Association, in the early 1970s.[59]

The Church Commissioners' decision in 1954 to reorganize the Paddington Estate involved the renaming and disposal of their Bayswater property as the Lancaster Gate estate. The holding was less compact than their Hyde Park and Maida Vale estates, being mainly residential but including shops and several hotels. Plans for its sale, with that of outlying properties farther north, were announced in 1955, to include Westbourne Terrace, Cleveland Square, most of Gloucester Terrace, part of Lancaster Gate and Inverness Terrace, and shops in Queensway.[60] An early purchaser, of 65 a. in the eastern part, was the Royal Liver Co., from which Maxwell Joseph in 1958 bought 25 a. called Hyde Park North. The area was also known as 'Sin Triangle', consisting of 680 properties, mainly divided houses, from Paddington station to Lancaster Gate.[61] Eastbourne Terrace was rebuilt as office blocks between 1957 and 1959[62] in partnership with Max Rayne. The Church Commissioners paid for the building costs and received half of the profits, in an experiment whose success encouraged them to take shares in another 25 joint companies between 1958 and 1962.[63]

Isolated changes included the building of flats called Caroline House in Bayswater Road, east of Orme Square, in the 1950s.[64] They also included the building of new hotels from 1961 and the conversion of older ones into flats.[65] Among new flats were ones in St. Petersburgh Place in 1960, at Palace Gate, Bayswater Road, and Craven Hill Gardens in 1961, in Palace Court, replacing an ornate French style house called Saxon Hall,[66] in Craven Hill in 1965–6,[67] and Hyde Park Towers, Bayswater Road, in 1977–9.[68] Shops and maisonettes were built in Moscow Road in 1961[69] and with offices and flats in Consort House, Queensway, completed by 1972.[70] There were no large-scale demolitions after that of Eastbourne Terrace, plans for the north-west end of Westbourne Terrace being frustrated by a preservation order in 1961.[71] By 1971 conservation had such support that the demolition of nos. 106–7 Bayswater Road, part of the former St. Agnes Villas, was followed by a successful campaign to save no. 100, where J. M. Barrie had written *Peter Pan* between 1904 and 1907.[72] Scattered rebuilding nonetheless continued in Bayswater Road: in 1981 Christ Church had been demolished, apart from the spire, and two sites, at the east corner of Queensborough Terrace and the west corner of Inverness Terrace, had been cleared by 1985. Renovation was then in progress in many streets to the north.

Bayswater in 1985 has retained most of its Vic-

[45] Vct. Samuel, *Memoirs* (1945), 80, 183, 196, 262.
[46] *P.O. Dir. Lond.* (1927); *D.N.B.*
[47] *Census*, 1921–1951.
[48] M. Fitzgerald, *Ch. as Landlord* (1937), 66–8.
[49] Ch. Com., Bldg. Agreements, vol. xiii, nos. 1, 12.
[50] Ibid. no. 16.
[51] Ibid. xiv, nos. U. 266, U. 340.
[52] Clunn, *Face of Lond.* 439.
[53] G.L.C. Hist. Bldgs. Div., WM 302.
[54] Clunn, *Face of Lond.* 438.
[55] Marylebone libr., P 138, cuttings.
[56] *Paddington Official Guide* [1948].
[57] *The Times*, 12 July 1952, 6d.
[58] A. Service, *Architects of Lond.* (1979), 193; below.
[59] Marylebone libr., P 138, cuttings.
[60] 'Paddington Est. Auction, 1955' (bound copies of sales parts., inc. plans, in Marylebone libr.); *The Times*,

22 Sept. 1954, 8g; 17 May 1955, 7d; 28 Oct. 1955, 10e.
[61] O. Marriott, *Property Boom* (1967), 107–8.
[62] Marylebone libr., P 138, cuttings.
[63] Marriott, *Property Boom*, 100–1, 104–5; S. Jenkins, *Landlords to Lond.* (1975), 218–19.
[64] *P.O. Dir. Lond.* (1952, 1959).
[65] *Paddington Mag.* Mar., May 1961; below, econ., ind.
[66] Pevsner, *Lond.* ii. 309.
[67] *Paddington Mag.* Nov. 1960; Apr., Aug. 1961; *The Times*, 2 Aug. 1965, 15c.
[68] Marylebone libr., P 138, cuttings.
[69] *Paddington Mag.* Mar. 1961.
[70] Marylebone libr., P 138, cuttings.
[71] G.L.C. Hist. Bldgs. Div., WM 174.
[72] Marylebone libr., P 138, cuttings; *The Times*, 25 Jan. 1971, 2g.

torian layout, since the only rebuilding on a scale large enough to destroy the street pattern has been on the Hallfield estate. It also possesses a greater variety of 19th-century housing than do the districts to the east and north, from comparatively plain villas and cottages of the 1820s and 1830s to increasingly grandiose Italianate terraces of the mid century and ornate piles of c. 1890. Stuccoed ranges, resembling those on the edge of Tyburnia, survive in great numbers near Westbourne Terrace and also, farther west, around Prince's Square. Most of the older buildings are in Bayswater conservation area, established in 1967 and enlarged in 1978, which extends into Tyburnia.[73] The length of several north–south avenues is an unusual feature; they have no counterparts from east to west, except along the edges, and have been criticized as inconvenient and monotonous. Much of the district appears to be less permanently settled than does Tyburnia, perhaps because many homes are in converted mews dwellings, whereas the main terraces have escaped rebuilding only to survive as hotels, boarding houses, and holiday flats. The eastern and western halves, moreover, are separated by Queensway, a cosmopolitan shopping street with many late-night restaurants.[74] There has been a recent rise in organized prostitution, particularly around Cleveland Square, where the wide roads have attracted kerb-crawling motorists.[75] Noise and vice have also been blamed on a growth in cheap tourism.[76]

Bayswater Road, lined with hotels, offices, and flats, has undergone more rebuilding west of Lancaster Gate than it has to the east. The triangle formed with Westbourne Street and Lancaster Terrace is wholly filled by the Royal Lancaster hotel, with the tallest tower in the area and the Bayswater Road frontage built over Lancaster Gate Underground station.[77] To the west mid 19th-century buildings, mainly offices but including the Swan, with a canopy,[78] and a modern addition to the Park Plaza hotel, stretch to the long imposing terraces of Lancaster Gate.

The layout and the size of the houses have caused Lancaster Gate to be described as Bayswater's most ambitious and successful architectural achievement,[79] although it has also earned disapproval for treating appearances as more important than the quality of life.[80] Two ranges, designed in 1857 by Sancton Wood, are set back a little from the road, with two further ranges behind, built c. 1865 to the designs of John Johnson and flanking a square which contains the tower of the former Christ Church. Built as narrow houses of five or six storeys piled on top of a basement, the ranges are stuccoed and richly ornamented in a blend of 'English Baroque and French Mannerism';[81] the earliest parts have continuous colonnades along the ground and first floors. Behind the façades, most of the houses have been united to form clubs or hotels. Their regularity has

been broken by several insertions, the most prominent being O. H. Leicester's Barrie House, raised to ten storeys, at the south-west corner of the square.[82] The body of Christ Church has been replaced by the six-storeyed Spire House, advertised in 1985 as 23 luxury flats.[83]

Isolated survivals from the early 19th century are nos. 100–101 Bayswater Road, forming a semi-detached pair of two storeys over a basement; they stand behind small gardens and no. 100, at the corner of Leinster Terrace, bears a plaque to Barrie. Beyond, with rebuilding in progress on two sites, are modern blocks: Hyde Park Towers, reaching up Porchester Terrace, the Hospitality Inn, and the eight-storeyed Porchester Gate. Buildings of c. 1900, including shops and restaurants, and the older Black Lion, with a ground-floor extension apparently of 1878, stand east of Queensway. To the west is a seven-storeyed red-brick and terracotta range by D. Joseph, who built the superstructures of several Underground stations;[84] it consists of the Coburg hotel, opened in 1907, with three cupolas, over shops and Queensway station. Next are the seven-storeyed flats of Caroline House, and the florid red-brick and terracotta Orme Court. West of Orme Square the modern white Embassy hotel contrasts with ornate late 19th-century buildings on either side of the entrance to Palace Court,[85] including the Guyana High Commission near the corner of Ossington Street. Wellington Terrace, a stock-brick survival from the 1830s, stretches to where a tiny house has been inserted over the ditch marking the former Kensington boundary.[86]

The oldest houses in Bayswater facing the main road, apart from nos. 100–1, date from the 1820s and are at Orme Square. Brown-brick town houses of three storeys and basements, originally in matching groups of three, flank the open end of the small square. An eagle on a double Tuscan column, of unknown origin, stands in front of a garden which is surrounded on three sides by a mixture of town houses and Italianate villas, on a modest scale and with some rebuilding and alterations.[87]

Palace Court, whose west side backs on Ossington Street, is 'the most interesting place in the borough for late Victorian domestic architecture'.[88] At the south-east corner King's Fund college occupies no. 2, in red brick and terracotta by William Flockhart, dated 1891. Similarly florid buildings stand next to it in Bayswater Road, although originally numbered with Palace Court, and include the yellow terracotta Westland hotel, formerly the Yellow House, no. 8, designed by George & Peto for Percy McQuoid. Set back from the east side of Palace Court are nos. 10, 12, and 14, the first two forming a pair designed by J. M. Maclaren with an elaborate stone frieze and an unusual bow window divided by rounded shafts. The west side of the road is more coherent, consisting mainly of houses of five storeys and basement,

[73] Westm. Dist. Plan, Draft Proposals Map, 1977; Westm. Dist. Plan, Proposals Map, 1982 (in Marylebone libr.); inf. from asst. dir. (development), Westm. Planning Dept.
[74] Marylebone libr., P 138, cuttings.
[75] Lond. Standard, 22 July 1985, 21.
[76] Marylebone libr., P 138, cuttings.
[77] Illus. Lond. News, 12 Aug. 1967, 30–1; below, econ., ind.
[78] 'Established 1775', although a Swan existed earlier: above.

[79] Lond. Encyc. 444.
[80] I. Nairn, Nairn's Lond. (1966), 93.
[81] Pevsner, Lond. ii. 308; above, plate 54.
[82] Ibid.; Clunn, Face of Lond. 438.
[83] Country Life, 31 May 1984; 7 Mar. 1985 (adverts.).
[84] Pevsner, Lond. ii. 308; Who Was Who, 1916–28, 568.
[85] Below. [86] Lond. Encyc. 46.
[87] Paddington Soc. Newsletter, Feb. 1964; Pevsner, Lond. ii. 309.
[88] Para. based on Pevsner, Lond. ii. 309; above, plate 33.

all in red brick with stone dressings and many with Dutch gables. They form a terrace, although some were individually planned. No. 45, formerly Palace Court House, was designed by Leonard Stokes for Wilfrid and Alice Meynell in 1889 and soon attracted architectural students; it has bands of brick and stone, small windows, and a first-floor bay.[89] No. 51, the Red Lodge, was built in 1889 for G. W. Joy.[90]

Elsewhere in south-western Bayswater there are humble survivals from *c.* 1840 on the west side of Victoria Grove (later Ossington Street and transferred to Kensington) in the form of terraced cottages of two storeys and basement, with a mews behind. On the west side of St. Petersburgh Place nos. 19 to 27 are a plain three-storeyed stuccoed range with a central pediment, next to St. Matthew's church, and the west side of Bark Place has a terrace of mid 19th-century Italianate villas of two storeys, basement, and attic. Orme Court, part of which faces Bayswater Road, also includes some ornate red-brick and yellow-tiled flats, dated 1896, at the southeast end of Bark Place. Refurbished mews dwellings survive in Chapel Side and Caroline Place Mews but many of the cramped streets nearby have been cleared for small neo-Georgian rows, as in Poplar Place, Lombardy Place, and Caroline Place. In Moscow Road the massive blocks of late Victorian and Edwardian flats are notable chiefly for their gauntness, Burnham and Windsor courts being of ten storeys over basements.

The earliest of the long avenues leading north from Bayswater Road is Porchester Terrace, which, in addition to modern flats, still has many stuccoed villas standing in their own gardens. Near the southeast end, next to Hyde Park Towers, is a stock brick pair of three storeys over a basement, built in 1823 and occupied from 1825 by J. C. Loudon, who lived in no. 3 and leased out the adjoining no. 5. Loudon illustrated the pair as an example of his 'double detached suburban villa', of which it has been seen as the prototype.[91] Villas of the 1840s, linked or in pairs, survive in Craven Hill; most are of three storeys and attic over a basement and some have been heightened.

The most spacious and dignified avenue is Westbourne Terrace, begun *c.* 1840 and 'unrivalled in its class in London or even Great Britain'. The houses form long stuccoed terraces of four storeys and attic over a basement, with pillared porches, many of them designed by T. Marsh Nelson.[92] They face carriage drives and were separated on either side from the tree-shaded roadway by screen walls surmounted by railings. The parallel Gloucester Terrace is also mostly of the mid 19th century, longer but narrower; for much of its length each house, of three storeys and a basement, has a segmental bay and a shallow porch. Part of the western side has been replaced by modest brick neo-Georgian flats, including Devonshire Court, and the southern end

consists of taller blocks: the seven-storeyed Maitland Court to the east and Garson, Gibray, and Carroll houses, from six to ten storeys, reaching to Craven Terrace, to the west. Although houses near the north-western end have made way for the Hallfield estate, Gloucester Terrace still provides a vista stretching north of Bishop's Bridge Road. In contrast Eastbourne Terrace has been entirely rebuilt by C. H. Elsom, whose higher and lower office blocks of 1957–9, 'a gaunt bit of plain speaking', have been praised as forming a sequence as unified as that of the stuccoed ranges to the west.[93]

Between Gloucester and Porchester terraces there are many tall, tree-shaded rows, stuccoed and with pillared porches, with some discreet infilling. Cleveland Square, which rivalled Lancaster Gate as the most expensive address in Bayswater,[94] has an unusually large private garden to serve the massive range of six storeys and basements on its north side. Less spacious enclosures are in Queen's Gardens and Craven Hill Gardens,[95] to the south. Leinster Gardens is noted for two sham houses, opposite no. 23, whose façades mask a surfacing of the Underground railway.[96] Beyond Porchester Terrace, part of the narrower Queensborough Terrace and much of Inverness Terrace are similarly made up of stuccoed four- or five-storeyed rows. Inverness Terrace has two symmetrical ranges facing each other, with centrepieces, Corinthian pilasters, and continuous balconies. The ornate Inverness Court hotel is a former private house, remodelled, with its own theatre, for Louis Spitzel (d. 1906) by Mewès & Davis, architects of the Ritz.[97]

Along Bishop's Bridge Road, from Gloucester Terrace westward across the end of Porchester Terrace to Inverness Terrace, stretches the Hallfield estate,[98] initiated by Sir Denys Lasdun in partnership with Tecton but developed in the 1950s by Lasdun and Lindsey Drake. Trees have been preserved among the 15 large blocks, of up to ten storeys, and some smaller blocks, varied in grouping, and a widely praised school[99] have been provided in an attempt to realize Le Corbusier's scheme for a city in a park. The materials are in a wide range, including concrete slabs, variegated brickwork, and glazed tile, but need expensive maintenance, whose lack has led Hallfield to be described as a 'graveyard of good ideas'.

Queensway, in contrast to the other north–south roads, is almost entirely commercial, although most of the premises have flats overhead. Nineteenth-century buildings survive mainly in the middle portion of the east side, as an assortment south of Inverness Place, where some are threatened with demolition, and a long four-storeyed range of *c.* 1860 from Inverness Place to Porchester Gardens. A shorter but taller Edwardian range, Beaumanor Mansions, lines part of the west side. The most prominent modern insertions include on the east side

[89] Meynell, *Alice Meynell*, 72 and illus.
[90] Datestone.
[91] G.L.C. Hist. Bldgs. Div., WM 176; *Country Life*, 23 Oct. 1969, 1054–5; plan of 1823 in Guildhall MS. 12456. A few semi-detached hos. had been built much earlier, e.g. at Highgate: *V.C.H. Mdx.* vi. 138.
[92] G.L.C. Hist. Bldgs. Div., WM 174. Nelson had built 46 hos. N. of Conduit Street (later Craven Rd.) by 1840: G.L.R.O., WCS 78, p. 600.
[93] Nairn, *Nairn's Lond.* 94; above, plate 45.

[94] Lasdun, *Victorians at Home*, 106.
[95] Hitchcock, *Early Victorian Archit.* 487–8.
[96] *Paddington Mag.* Dec. 1960. Their backs are visible from Porchester Terr.
[97] Inf. from Mewès & Davis and from Marylebone libr.
[98] Para. based on *The Times*, 12 July 1952, 6d; I. Nairn, *Modern Bldgs. in Lond.* (1964), 38–9; Service, *Architects of Lond.* 193–4.
[99] Below, educ. (Hallfield).

no. 26, Consort House, finished in 1972 and designed by Owen Luder in concrete with a red-brick facing as a ten-storeyed tower and five-storeyed podium over an underground car park.[1] Opposite are the seven-storeyed blocks of the 1930s called Queen's Court and Princess Court, the first and perhaps both designed by W. Henry White & Sons.[2] Queensway is notable for its restaurants and food shops, many of them foreign.

The tall stuccoed houses typical of eastern Bayswater are also found west of Queensway and north of Moscow Road, around Leinster, Prince's, and Kensington Gardens squares. All three squares also have a range served by private gardens.[3] Leinster Square has generally had a slightly lower rateable value than Prince's Square, perhaps because of the irregularity of its north range, which is the only terrace in either square not attributable to George Wyatt.[4] A few villas of the 1840s, erected for W. K. Jenkins,[5] survive nearby in Garway and Monmouth roads.

MAIDA VALE, covering north-eastern Paddington, derives its name from a stretch of Edgware Road[6] which forms its north-east boundary for c. 1.5 km. from the Regent's canal to Kilburn bridge. The north-west boundary, also, is that of the parish, following Kilburn Park Road along the straightened course of the Bayswater rivulet. Although the district has sometimes been taken as stretching across northern Paddington to Harrow Road,[7] the streets southwest of Shirland Road and in the north-west corner of the parish, which were built up more densely than those on the bishop of London's estate, are treated separately.[8] As described below, Maida Vale is defined on the south-west by Shirland Road and by part of Blomfield Road running beside the Grand Junction canal, and on the south-east by Blomfield Road beside the Regent's canal. It covers Maida Vale ward of 1901, less a westerly projection along Amberley Road,[9] and includes some houses around the junction of the two canals, at what came to be called Little Venice.

The whole area belonged to the bishop of London in 1647, when a Mrs. Wheatley was tenant of a wood and of 44 a. of pasture in 5 closes, which lay between the high road and the stream[10] and were probably the forerunner of Kilburn Bridge farm. In 1742, when Richard Marsh was tenant, the farmhouse and its yards stood by the road close to the stream, with c. 39 a. in 6 closes to the south and west. Farther south Paddington wood and some fields of Manor House farm abutted the road, with fields of Parsonage farm to the west.[11] There were no other buildings then[12] or in 1790.[13] Kilburn Bridge farm was 40 a. and worth £230 a year in 1795, when it supported rent charges towards the assistant curate's stipend and payments for common rights to the parish.[14]

Building was made possible by the Act of 1795 but for the northern part of the bishop's estate, as for Tyburnia, the first agreements were sealed only in 1807. The plots were strung along Edgware Road, in Hill field and Pond field and as far north as Paddington wood.[15] Francis Humbert of Marylebone and Abraham Callard of Paddington, builders, took a 61-year lease of part of Paddington wood with a frontage of 150 ft. for six detached houses, each with 15 ft. in front, 'in a regular line and of a fourth rate of building'. The houses were to be of stock brick, with slate roofs, and dimensions were carefully specified, as in later leases.[16] Another plot was leased in 1807 to Thomas Beedle, builder, for four houses. It had a frontage of 184 ft. and was bounded southeast by a 'street to Maida Hill', presumably a forerunner of Maida Hill West (later Maida Avenue).[17] Many new houses were leased from 1809 to 1814; a few were detached, others in pairs or terraces.[18] Land behind the plots was granted for short terms to nurserymen.[19]

The name Maida was first recorded in 1807, the year after Sir John Stuart's victory over the French at Maida in Calabria (Italy).[20] The Hero of Maida public house was licensed in 1810 at Maida Hill,[21] which served as the name of a short stretch of Edgware Road near the new Regent's canal. Part of that stretch, including the public house, was known in the mid 19th century as Maida Hill East. Meanwhile Maida Hill West became the name of the road along the southern bank of the canal (from 1939 called Maida Avenue). By 1828, as building had extended along Edgware Road, a short stretch beyond Maida Hill was called Maida Vale,[22] which from 1868 was the name of the whole length of the road between the Regent's canal and Kilburn.[23] The name was applied popularly to a district by the mid 1880s,[24] a fact which was recognized in the creation of Maida Vale ward in Paddington metropolitan borough.[25]

Building had been planned from the south along Edgware Road before the construction of the Regent's canal[26] marked a clear division between the projected suburb and the neighbourhood of Paddington green. Further leases were granted from 1819:[27] for two houses at Maida Hill, for two in 1820 and one in 1821 at Maida Hill West, and for two in 1820 at Maida Hill East.[28] By 1828 houses lined the main road almost to the corner of Stranraer Place, which was to lead into Sutherland Gardens (both

[1] Marylebone libr., P 138, cuttings.
[2] G.L.C. Hist. Bldgs. Div., WM 302.
[3] Hitchcock, *Early Victorian Archit.* 188.
[4] G.L.C. Hist. Bldgs. Div., WM 212.
[5] Above, Westbourne green.
[6] Below.
[7] e.g. *Lond. Encyc.* 490.
[8] Below, Queen's Pk. and St. Peter's Pk.
[9] *Plan of Paddington* (1901). The Amberley Rd. area is treated under Westbourne green.
[10] Guildhall MS. 10464A, pp. 130, 137.
[11] Ch. Com., 'Map of 1742'.
[12] Ibid.; Rocque, *Map of Lond.* (1741-5), sheet 11.
[13] Ch. Com., 'Map of 1790'.
[14] Guildhall MS. 12426; below, churches.
[15] Ch. Com., Bldg. Agreements, vol. i, p. 1; Guildhall MS. 12530/1.

[16] Ch. Com., Bldg. Agreements, vol. i, p. 1.
[17] Ibid. p. 13.
[18] Guildhall MS. 12530/1.
[19] Below, econ., nurseries.
[20] Ch. Com., Bldg. Agreements, vol. i, p. 13; *Lond. Encyc.* 489.
[21] G.L.R.O., MR/LV11/132.
[22] Gutch, *Plan of Paddington* (1828); *Lucas's Paddington Dir.* (1843); *P.O. Dir. Lond.* (1850, 1863); L.C.C. *Names of Streets* (1955).
[23] H. P. Clunn, *Face of Lond.* (1951), 277; Lucas, *Plan of Paddington* (1869).
[24] e.g. title of the novel by F. Danby [pseudonym of Julia Frankau], *Dr. Phillips: a Maida Vale Idyll* (1887).
[25] Below, local govt.
[26] Above, communications.
[27] Guildhall MS. 12530/1.   [28] Guildhall MS. 12422/1.

together forming Sutherland Avenue from 1887)[29] and was about a third of the way to Kilburn bridge. Some houses, more widely detached, also lined Maida Hill West, although Blomfield Road did not yet skirt the north-west side of the canal.[30]

Plans for the Paddington Estate[31] north of the Regent's canal were on as grand a scale as those for Tyburnia and covered a wider area. Gutch proposed long avenues, including Portsdown Road (from 1939 called Randolph Avenue), parallel with Edgware Road and crossed by Elgin Road (from 1886 called Elgin Avenue)[32] and other westerly projections of roads from Marylebone, the monotony of the grid plan to be relieved by an enormous circus, ringed with crescents, in Elgin Road. A leading builder along Edgware Road was Hugh Biers, described later as an auctioneer and surveyor. He had land by 1828 in Maida Vale, where Hugh Biers the elder, also of Marylebone, had built two houses.[33] The younger Biers, who had plans for Stranraer Place by 1832,[34] took leases for 3 houses in Maida Vale in 1834, for 8 in Canterbury Villas in 1836, and for many more farther north in Carlton Villas between 1840 and 1842.[35] By 1840 detached stuccoed villas lined most of Edgware Road, with a gap beyond the projected Elgin Road as far as Portsdown Terrace, which had replaced or been joined to Kilburn Bridge Farm[36] and where Biers had taken leases for 12 houses.[37] Very little building had apparently taken place behind the Edgware Road frontage, although part of Warwick Road (later Avenue) had been named by 1840 and Blomfield Road by 1841.[38]

Progress over the fields north of the canal continued to be slow. In 1851 there were buildings only in Blomfield Road and in the quadrangle between that road, Clifton Place (later Villas), and the south end of Warwick Road enclosing Warwick Place.[39] In 1857 Bristol Gardens still commanded uninterrupted country views to the north and west.[40] Leases for 7 houses in Blomfield Road had been granted to John Pink, 6 of them in partnership, in 1840–2 and of 14 houses there or in Warwick Road to John Taft, who also took several in Maida Hill West, beside the canal west of Park Place, between 1840 and 1851.[41] All the houses were stuccoed, those in Warwick Road being grander than those in Blomfield Road.[42]

Growth was quicker in the 1850s, when a lease for 32 a. around Warwick Road and Warrington Crescent required building to be finished within eight years.[43] An Italianate style was maintained, 16 of the 32 a. were set aside for gardens, and Warwick Road was widened to create a majestic approach to the new St. Saviour's church. Roads with stuccoed houses included Randolph, Clarendon (later Clarendon Terrace and Gardens), and Clifton roads by 1855, Warwick Road West (renamed Warrington Terrace and later part of Warwick Avenue leading

north-west past the church) by 1863,[44] and the southern parts of Warrington Crescent, Randolph Crescent, and Castellain Road by 1869.[45] The south end of the bishop's Maida Vale estate thus came to resemble Tyburnia, even to the extent of being served by clusters of shops, around the Warwick Arms in Warwick Place and the Eagle in Clifton Road, and soon also in Formosa Street.[46]

Meanwhile buildings had filled the entire Edgware Road frontage by 1851[47] and had started to form a humbler line behind, although only Andover Place, at the north end backing Portsdown Terrace, was complete by 1855. Park Road, begun by 1855, was projected to run along the Willesden boundary to meet the future Chippenham Road by 1861 and renamed Kilburn Park Road in 1862.[48] Edward James Hewett, of Kilburn Park Road, built pairs of houses along the east side of Randolph Gardens, which were leased from 1864 and 1865.[49]

The first line of housing behind Edgware Road had been completed by 1869, forming, from the south, Lanark, Canterbury, and Elgin terraces, Carlton Place (by 1901 called Carlton Mews), and Andover Place. Behind them the wider Portsdown Road (later Randolph Avenue) ran north to Randolph Gardens, with terraces on both sides as far as the corner with Sutherland Gardens but with open ground to the west as far north as Carlton Road (later Carlton Vale), which cut across the largely built-up land of Kilburn Bridge farm.[50] A new type of building, in red or multi-coloured brick, was used from the 1860s[51] in the avenues parallel with Edgware Road and their cross-streets. It was soon to spread over the remaining land, giving most of Maida Vale an appearance very different from that of its southern, Italianate quarter.

Piecemeal building in many parts was planned in 1880, when the Paddington Estate made ten agreements, with different builders. Three agreements were for 91 or 92 terraced houses on the Paddington side of Kilburn Park Road, the largest being with George Godson for 50 or 51 houses, three were for between 50 and 61 in Sutherland Gardens, and the others were for 37 in Portsdown Road, 20 in Shirland Road, and a few in Formosa Street and Warwick Road West. The most expensive houses, to be worth at least £1,000 each, were to be in Sutherland Gardens and the cheapest, 17 at £200 and others at £500, in Kilburn Park Road. Their construction, including drainage and paving, and appearance were specified in detail: in Sutherland Gardens trees were to be planted and builders were to help purchasers in laying out general gardens behind, which eventually would be enclosed on all sides by new ranges. The leases were all for 98 years and the rents, as elsewhere, were to be divided between the Ecclesiastical Commissioners and the beneficial lessees' trustees.[52]

[29] Gutch, *Plan of Paddington* (1828); L.C.C. *Names of Streets* (1901).
[30] Gutch, *Plan of Paddington* (1828).
[31] Para. based on ibid. (1840).
[32] L.C.C. *Names of Streets* (1901).
[33] Guildhall MS. 12530/1.
[34] G.L.R.O., WCS 78, pp. 43–4.
[35] *P.O. Dir. Lond.* (1847, 1850); Guildhall MS. 12422/1.
[36] Lucas, *Plan of Paddington* (1842).
[37] Guildhall MS. 12422/1.
[38] Ibid.
[39] J. Weale, *Lond. Exhibited* (1851), map at back.
[40] *Bldg. News*, 16 Jan. 1857, 72.

[41] Guildhall MSS. 12422/1; 12530/1.
[42] Pevsner, *Lond.* ii. 312.
[43] *Bldg. News*, 21 Aug. 1857, 885.
[44] *P.O. Dir. Lond.* (1855, 1863).
[45] Lucas, *Plan of Paddington* (1869).
[46] *P.O. Dir. Lond.* (1855, 1863, 1879).
[47] Weale, *Lond. Exhibited*, map at back.
[48] Lucas, *Plan of Paddington* (1855, 1861); L.C.C. *Names of Streets* (1901).
[49] Guildhall MS. 12556.
[50] Lucas, *Plan of Paddington* (1869).
[51] *Lond. Encyc.* 490.
[52] Ch. Com., Bldg. Agreements, vol. viii, *passim.*

The range of house prices maintained a wide variety of accommodation, for which the area west of Maida Hill was already noted.[53] Although the district was nearly all residential, a new shop was permitted near some existing ones in Formosa Street in 1880. The first rebuilding was planned in 1881, when three large villas in Edgware Road (nos. 47, 49, and 51 Maida Vale) were to be replaced with nine houses and shops facing Clifton Road, a single villa in Maida Vale, and a house or office and another house facing Lanark Villas. At the opposite corner of the estate up to 34 houses were planned in 1881 in Shirland Road, between Elgin and Kilburn Park roads, where the eight most northerly ones could be built as shops.[54]

Building continued steadily in the late 19th century but not very fast. Behind the frontages, built up except for a stretch of Portsdown Road, the area enclosed by Shirland, Kilburn Park, and Portsdown roads and Sutherland Avenue was empty in 1886,[55] allowing time for c. 26 a. in the north part to be saved for public use as Paddington recreation ground.[56] Essendine Road in 1895 was to be built up with 60 or more houses by William Henry Pearce, who had made the agreement of 1881 for Shirland Road. Morshead and Grantully roads, bordering the recreation ground, were to have flats in 1898 and 1899, as were the nearby Widley and Wymering roads in 1901.[57] There remained gaps in the smarter area to the south, between Elgin and Sutherland avenues,[58] although most of Lauderdale Road had been finished under an agreement of 1897. Infilling was carried out under agreements made between 1900 and 1902 for the rest of Elgin Avenue and for part of Castellain Road, although Delaware, Ashworth, and the west side of Castellain roads were still empty in 1910.[59] Most infilling was with flats,[60] which also replaced many villas along Edgware Road (below).

For all its wealth, Maida Vale was never as fashionable as the districts which overlooked Hyde Park. Titled residents were rare, although in 1858 the ex-queen of Oudh lived in Warwick Road West and another Indian, the rajah of Coorg, nearby in Clifton Villas.[61] Charles Ollier (1788–1859), publisher of Shelley and Keats, and Thomas Jefferson Hogg (1792–1862), Shelley's biographer, both lived in Maida Place,[62] the mid-century name for Edgware Road immediately north of Maida Hill.[63] Sir John Tenniel (1820–1914), the artist and cartoonist, lived from c. 1854 in Portsdown Road, where the change of his address from no. 3 to no. 10 probably signified no more than a renumbering of the houses.[64] The boys' story writer Thomas Mayne Reid (1818–83) died at no. 12 Blomfield Road,[65] the poet John Davidson was at no. 19 Warrington Crescent from 1889 until 1909, the radio engineer Sir Ambrose Fleming at no. 9 Clifton Gardens from 1890 to 1896, and John Masefield at no. 30 Maida Avenue from

1907 until 1909.[66]

Maida Vale was notable in the late 19th century for its large number of Jews.[67] The first influx had been into Bayswater, where a synagogue had opened in 1863,[68] but thereafter Jews settled both farther west and to the north, as Portsdown Road and its neighbourhood were built up. In the 1880s at least 1,000 and possibly 2,000 out of Maida Vale's estimated 10,000 residents were Jewish and by 1890 the area supplied more than half the members of Bayswater synagogue. Novelists of the 1880s, with some exaggeration, portrayed an exclusive and materialist society, whose leaders traded profitably in the City before returning to their wives' rounds of card parties in stifling drawing rooms.[69] Another fictional character 'practised painless dentistry with great success in the heart of Maida Vale', where he enjoyed prestige from having grander relatives in Lancaster Gate.[70] A movement farther out to newer suburbs began in the 1890s but was partly counteracted by the building of flats, which appealed to many older Jews.

The comparatively slow spread of building over the heart of Maida Vale, in contrast to the building of St. Peter's Park south-west of Shirland Road,[71] was presumably due to the ambition to maintain the character of a largely upper middle-class district. Although in time the plan was broadly realized, a few modifications were made: in 1897 land at the corner of Lauderdale and Castellain roads was intended for a church and in 1900 it was hoped to replace nos. 63–73 (odd) Maida Vale with a theatre,[72] but neither was built. In the extreme north-east the densely built up area beyond Carlton Vale included St. Augustine's church and the Kilburn Sisters' orphanage and, where the boundary extended to include a stretch of the far side of Kilburn Park Road, a school and omnibus depot.[73] That corner of the parish resembled neighbouring Kilburn.

Much of Maida Vale was classified as wealthy c. 1890, including the Edgware Road frontage from Stranraer Place (leading to Sutherland Avenue) to slightly north of Carlton Vale, and the whole of Sutherland Avenue east of Shirland Road, with Warrington and Randolph crescents and Clifton Gardens. Most of the southern portion, including Blomfield, Warwick, and Randolph roads, was well-to-do, as were the whole of Portsdown Road, part of Carlton Vale, and, so far as they had been completed, Elgin Avenue and Lauderdale Road. The long terraces between Edgware and Portsdown roads were 'comfortable' and the houses fringing the area along Kilburn Park and Shirland roads were of mixed poverty and comfort. Most of the tradesmen and artisans in the south part, off Clifton Road and Formosa Street, were considered 'pretty comfortable', although there were a few poor cabmen, sweeps, and ostlers. Only in the northern corner

[53] [W. S. Clarke] *Suburban Homes of Lond.* (1881), 313.
[54] Ch. Com., Bldg. Agreements, vol. viii.
[55] Bacon, *Atlas of Lond.* (1886).
[56] Below, pub. svces.
[57] Ch. Com., Bldg. Agreements, vol. x.
[58] *Plan of Paddington* (1901).
[59] Bacon, *Atlas of Lond.* (1910).
[60] Ch. Com., Bldg. Agreements, vol. x.
[61] *P.O. Dir. Lond.* (1858).
[62] McDonald, 'Paddington', cap. 13; *D.N.B.*
[63] Weale, *Lond. Exhibited*, map at back.

[64] Paddington Soc. *Newsletter*, Jan. 1963.
[65] McDonald, 'Paddington', cap. 13; *D.N.B.*
[66] *Lond. Encyc.* 489.
[67] Para. based on *Jewish Hist. Soc. Trans.* xxi. 82–102.
[68] Below.
[69] Danby, *Dr. Phillips: A Maida Vale Idyll.* The doctor had a four-storeyed ho. in Portsdown Rd.
[70] A. Levy, *Reuben Sachs* (1888), 98.
[71] Bacon, *Atlas of Lond.* (1886); below, Queen's Park and St. Peter's Pk.
[72] Ch. Com., Bldg. Agreements, vol. x, nos. 11, 18.
[73] *Plan of Paddington* (1901).

were there many poor,[74] notably in Carlton Mews and Andover Place. The two streets, with 17 and 19 houses respectively and densities of 7.8 and 6 persons to a house, were among the eleven most overcrowded in Paddington, although much better than some near the canal.[75]

Middle-class flats, including many of the earliest in London, were built from the 1890s, perhaps partly because buyers of large houses were tending to settle farther out. Some blocks replaced older villas, particularly along the stretch of Edgware Road called Maida Vale, and others filled empty sites. Building also took place on the Marylebone side of the road and continued in the 20th century, giving the area much of its later character.

The first flats were planned in 1890, when nos. 1 and 3 Maida Vale, at the corner of Blomfield Road, were to be replaced by one or two buildings before the end of 1891.[76] As Maida Vale Mansions (later Cunningham Court) the block had 22 flat-holders in 1902, when it was the only one on that side of the road.[77] The adjoining site of nos. 5 to 35 (odd), however, had been leased for rebuilding in 1895[78] and was filled with Aberdeen and Blomfield courts in 1903, with Clarendon Court between them.[79] Clarendon Court was claimed in 1917 as the first and most up-to-date of its kind in London, with flats, single chambers, a restaurant, and a booking office for theatres.[80] Farther north, beyond Clifton Avenue, nos. 63–73 Maida Vale in 1900 and nos. 95–103 in 1902 were to make way for flats,[81] built as Alexandra Court by 1906 and Sandringham Court by 1908.[82] Much of the open land south-west of the main road had likewise been filled with blocks: Carlton Mansions, for 90 flat-holders, at the north-west end of Portsdown Road, and Elgin Mansions, for 80, and Ashworth Mansions along the north side of Elgin Avenue, all by 1902,[83] and the nearby Biddulph Mansions in 1907 and Delaware Mansions in 1908.[84]

Early flat-holders needed to be able to pay a large premium or invest in an estate company.[85] The period immediately before the First World War was also that of the 'almost Corinthian days of Maida Vale', when jokes were made about mistresses kept there in discreet apartments.[86] During the war unprecedented damage was caused by a bomb in Warrington Crescent, where the king and queen came after four houses had been destroyed and 140 affected nearby in 1918.[87]

In the 1920s and 1930s Maida Vale continued to be described as one of London's most desirable suburbs, with 'handsome piles of residential mansions' and superior detached houses.[88] Maida Vale

ward retained a lower density than any other in Paddington except the two Lancaster Gate wards, having only 81 persons to an acre in 1921, 85.9 in 1931, and 85.3 in 1951.[89] Some large houses were subdivided, notably in Portsdown Road, where two had been listed as lodging houses in 1902 and 13 offered apartments in 1927.[90] Since no fresh building land was available, the main change was the replacement of houses by more flats. In Edgware Road Clive Court was inserted between Alexandra and Sandringham courts, in the style of its neighbours, in 1923 and Hamilton Court was built south of Elgin Avenue in 1937.[91] In the far north, where some of the earliest leases fell in, an agreement of 1935 provided for roadside villas and the poor housing behind in Andover Place to make way for 250 working-class flats, opened in 1937 as Dibdin House. The flats were the first on the estate to be in the direct control of the Ecclesiastical Commissioners, who acquired a long lease from the beneficial lessees.[92]

Flat-building along both sides of Edgware Road had made the Maida Vale section 'typical of suburban arterial roads in fairly well-to-do districts' by the time of the Second World War.[93] There were few further changes for another twenty years, since the Church Commissioners, while retaining control in the 1950s, did not draw up an ambitious rebuilding scheme like that for the Hyde Park estate. Isolated projects included Melbourne Court at the south end of Randolph Avenue, built by Blomfield Development Corporation in 1960, of which the Church Commissioners bought the leasehold,[94] and the adjacent Browning, Elizabeth, and Robert closes. Along Edgware Road many more villas made way for flats after 1964: Stuart Tower, a joint venture by the Church Commissioners and George Wimpey & Co.,[95] south of Sutherland Avenue, the G.L.C.'s Atholl, Braemar, and Dundee houses to the north, and Edinburgh, Falkirk, and Glasgow houses between Elgin Avenue and Carlton Vale were all built by 1975. The G.L.C.'s flats were part of its Maida Vale housing estate, for which more room was made by widespread clearance south of St. Augustine's church: Helmsdale, Invergarry, Keith, and Melrose houses occupied the south side of Carlton Vale, and Thurso, Renfrew, Strome, and Peebles houses, and an old people's home called Carlton Dene, the north side. Farther north the G.L.C. built Torridon House at the corner of Randolph Gardens and Kilburn Park Road.[96] Paddington Churches Housing Association had converted 21 houses in Randolph Avenue into 123 units by 1985.[97]

Improvements took place in parts of Little Venice after the Second World War. It was then that the

[74] Booth, *Life and Labour*, i (2), app., p. 13, where part of Maida Vale is described under St. Peter's Pk.; *Booth's Map* (1889), NW.
[75] *Rep. on Vital Statistics and San. Work 1895* (in Marylebone libr.), 11.
[76] Ch. Com., Bldg. Agreements, vol. x, no. 1.
[77] *P.O. Dir. Lond.* (1902).
[78] Ch. Com., Bldg. Agreements, vol. x, no. 5.
[79] Pevsner, *Lond.* ii. 313.
[80] Bingham, *Official Guide to Paddington* [1917], advert.
[81] Ch. Com., Bldg. Agreements, vol. x, nos. 18, 24.
[82] *P.O. Dir. Lond.* (1906, 1908).
[83] Ibid. (1902).
[84] Pevsner, *Lond.* ii. 313.
[85] Clunn, *Face of Lond.* 278.
[86] e.g. A. G. Macdonell, *Autobiog. of a Cad* (1938), 63.

[87] F. Morison, *War on Great Cities* (1937), 165–6 and illus. facing p. 162.
[88] Bingham, *Official Guide to Paddington* [1921, 1936]; *New Lond. Life and Labour*, vi (2), 431.
[89] *Census*, 1921–51.
[90] *P.O. Dir. Lond.* (1902, 1927).
[91] Pevsner, *Lond.* ii. 313; Ch. Com., Bldg. Agreements, vol. xiv, no. 11.
[92] Ch. Com., Bldg. Agreements, vol. xiv, no. 5; Pevsner, *Lond.* ii. 313; M. Fitzgerald, *Church as Landlord*, 73–4.
[93] Pevsner, *Lond.* ii. 313.
[94] Marylebone libr., P 138, cuttings.
[95] Inf. from Chestertons.
[96] *P.O. Dir. Lond.* (1964, 1975).
[97] Inf. from regional dir., Camden/Westm., Paddington Chs. Housing Assoc. Ltd.

name came into general use for the immediate vicinity of the pool, with its island, where the Grand Junction and Regent's canals met and for the banks of the Regent's canal leading to Edgware Road. Byron, however, had briefly compared the canal at Paddington with Venice, to which further reference had been made by Browning,[98] whose house in Warwick Crescent had overlooked the pool from the south-west,[99] and by 1925 Blomfield Road had been publicized as 'Venice in Paddington'.[1] Browning was credited with having the island planted with trees,[2] although apparently it had always been wooded.[3] Plentiful foliage, together with the mists, have often been thought to give the canal side a Dutch rather than a Venetian air.[4] The scene inspired Paul Verlaine and also contributed to the autumnal recollections of Katherine Mansfield who in 1908-9 stayed as a music student at Beauchamp Lodge (no. 2 Warwick Crescent).[5]

The tree-lined avenues beside the Regent's canal had always remained smart but the area south-west of the pool, hemmed in farther south by railway lines, had decayed in the later 19th century. Much of it was rebuilt in the 1960s, although Beauchamp Lodge survived.[6] By 1950 large derelict houses and some artists' studios stood on the east side of the pool,[7] which in 1952 was 'surrounded by a good deal of sordidness', with slums on the west side and more to the north.[8] Municipal plans to demolish the studios, one of which was occupied by Feliks Topolski, with flats, were successfully resisted by the Labour party, some eminent residents, and the L.C.C. A waterside garden was laid out instead,[9] finally named Rembrandt gardens in 1975 to mark a new link between Westminster and Amsterdam.[10] Meanwhile Blomfield Road and its neighbourhood became increasingly fashionable: in 1960 'new Venetians' included Lord Norwich, and in 1961 Lady Diana Cooper, the playwright Christopher Fry, the novelist Elizabeth Jane Howard, and many figures active in the arts or entertainment.[11] In 1968 plans by the British Waterways Board to build on the canal pool were defeated[12] and in 1974 the increasing popularity of Little Venice as a tourist centre served as an argument against the proposed infilling of Paddington basin.[13]

In 1981 it was decided to sell the entire Maida Vale estate, consisting of c. 200 a. with more than 2,000 properties. The sale was the most valuable yet undertaken by the Church Commissioners, who offered tenants a 20 per cent discount on the assessed market value of their houses and flats. Disagreement over the valuations, particularly in Little Venice, 'Maida Vale's most desirable part', was such that less than a quarter of the properties had been sold by

mid 1982. In 1985 it was expected that two thirds would be sold by the end of the year.[14] There were, however, complaints about gentrification, after a steep rise in the value of houses bought by companies for conversion into flats.[15]

Maida Vale is a residential suburb, served by some small groups of shops. Houses in the southern quarter are expensive, as are most of the private flats along Edgware Road. The large central area, around Sutherland and Elgin avenues, is less fashionable but well cared for. Municipal tenants are nearly all in the north. Each part bears its own character, with stuccoed villas, ornate blocks beside the main road, red-brick avenues, and austere council housing. A conservation area, created for the oldest streets in 1967, has been extended northward along Randolph Avenue as far as Elgin Avenue.[16]

The southern part begins at Little Venice, a 'unique combination of white stucco, greenery, and water.'[17] The rest of the stuccoed area is spaciously laid out, like most of Maida Vale, and has perhaps the broadest road in London where Warwick Avenue leads up to St. Saviour's church.[18] Most of the original houses survive, and the limited rebuilding, as at the east end of Blomfield Road and the closes at the south-east end of Randolph Avenue, has been in brick in a subdued neo-Georgian style. Some of the roads, including Blomfield Road and Warwick Avenue, have a variety of detached and semi-detached villas, a few of those at the southern end of Warwick Avenue being very large.[19] Other roads are lined with uniform pairs, such as those with three storeys and a basement in Randolph Road and the south side of Clifton Villas. Others have linked pairs, as those with four storeys and a basement in Randolph Crescent, and others have terraces, as in Clarendon Gardens. Small details often vary, notably the pillar capitals in the porches. The area is served by shops in Formosa Street, part of it briefly made a pedestrian precinct in 1975,[20] and Clifton Road. St. Saviour's church, rebuilt with the flats of Manor House Court in pale brown brick on an island site, is thought to blend well with its surroundings. To the north the Colonnade hotel, linking the end of Castellain Road with Warwick Avenue and first leased as a pair of houses in 1863, is particularly ornate, with mouldings and a continuous first-floor balustrade.[21]

The stuccoed area goes no farther north than Clifton Road and Formosa Street, each with its local shops, and Clifton Gardens between them. It once stretched along the main road to Kilburn and still stretches northward along Randolph Avenue and

[98] *Lond. Encyc.* 463; H. B. Wheatley and P. Cunningham, *Lond. Past and Present*, iii (1891), 3.
[99] Above, Westbourne green; *D.N.B.*; McDonald, 'Paddington', cap. 13.
[1] Bingham, *Official Guide to Paddington* [1925], 47.
[2] *Lond. Encyc.* 926.
[3] Guildhall Libr., Pr P1/BAY (engraving 1828, from drawing by T. Shepherd).
[4] Pevsner, *Lond.* ii. 312; Clunn, *Face of Lond.* 447.
[5] McDonald, 'Paddington', cap. 13; V. P. Underwood, *Verlaine et l'Angleterre* (1956), 104; A. Alpers, *Life of Kath. Mansfield* (1980), 66, 403-4.
[6] Above, Westbourne green.
[7] *The Times*, 5 Aug. 1950, 5g.
[8] Pevsner, *Lond.* ii. 313.
[9] *The Times*, 8 Aug. 1950, 5d; 12 Sept. 1950, 3c; 19 Dec.

1952, 7e; 20 Dec. 1952, 8g.
[10] *Lond. Encyc.* 463.
[11] *Paddington Mag.* Nov. 1960; Jan., Feb. 1961.
[12] Paddington Soc. *Newsletter*, Dec. 1967; Jan., Feb. 1968.
[13] *The Times*, 27 Aug. 1974, 3d.
[14] *Sunday Times*, 31 Jan. 1982, 15; Marylebone libr., P 138, cuttings; inf. from Chestertons.
[15] *Lond. Standard*, 10 June 1985, 22-3.
[16] *Westm. Dist. Plan, Draft Proposals Map, 1977*; *Westm. Dist. Plan, Proposals Map, 1982* (in Marylebone libr.).
[17] *Illus. Lond. News*, 24 Apr. 1971, 19.
[18] Marylebone libr., P 131.1, cuttings.
[19] Pevsner, *Lond.* ii. 312.
[20] Marylebone libr., P 138, cuttings.
[21] *Lond. Encyc.* 489; inf. from Mr. A. R. Richards.

Warwick Avenue (but not along Castellain Road between them) almost to Sutherland Avenue, and in grand terraces about half way along Warwick Crescent, where there is an abrupt change to more modest brick housing. A few more buildings with stucco, including the Warrington hotel, stand at the junction of Warrington Crescent with Sutherland Avenue and Lauderdale Road, as outlying reminders of Gutch's plans for an extensive suburb in the style of Tyburnia.

Most of the Maida Vale section of Edgware Road is dominated on both sides by blocks of flats.[22] Cunningham Court is five- or six-storeyed, faced with red brick and stone or terracotta dressings, opposite the mock-Tudor of Clifton Court in Marylebone. The Clarendon Court hotel, Boehmer & Gibbs's Blomfield Court, and Alexandra, Clive, and Sandringham courts are also red-brick and ornate, overshadowing the last of the 19th-century villas which survive as pairs on either side of the ends of shopping ranges which extend down Clifton Road. The pairs, from nos. 37/39 to 57/59 Maida Vale, are of four storeys and basement; although converted into banks, shops, and offices, some still have their pillared porches. North-west of Sandringham Court the buildings are more modern, many of them set back amid lawns and bearing the numbers of some of the villas which they have replaced: the seventeen-storeyed Stuart Tower (no. 105 Maida Vale), the six-storeyed brown-brick Atholl, Braemar, and Dundee houses (nos. 125, 135, and 145), part of the G.L.C.'s Maida Vale housing estate and in scale with the private Hamilton Court (no. 149) by Beresford Marshall, and the taller Edinburgh, Falkirk, and Glasgow houses (nos. 155, 165, and 175), also municipal. From Carlton Vale stretch the five-storeyed brick blocks of Dibdin House by Caroë & Passmore, incorporating a shopping parade near Kilburn Park Road.

The heart of Maida Vale, south of Paddington recreation ground, is residential, containing mostly brick terraces of the 1860s and later. There are a few shops at the east end of Sutherland and Elgin avenues, at the north end of Lauderdale Road, and, to the west, in Shirland Road. The earlier terraces include one of 21 bays at nos. 124–64 Randolph Avenue, containing houses of five storeys above a basement, and nos. 237–55 and 290–304 Elgin Avenue. The Randolph Avenue terrace, a symmetrical composition, with its mews to the north, is the most elaborate: grey brick with red-brick or polychrome dressings, it shows the impact of Ruskin's *Stones of Venice* on the decoration of standard London housing.[23] Most of the later buildings are red-brick, in wide roads lined with plane trees. Middle-class flats predominate from c. 1900, often in very long ranges, which are, however, less massive than the blocks in Edgware Road, being mainly four-storeyed in keeping with the neighbouring terraced houses. An example of such blending is Carlton

Mansions at the north-west end of Randolph Avenue, backing on to the recreation ground and facing a slightly older brick terrace. Some of the last roads to be built up have nothing but flats: the central section of Elgin Road has Elgin Mansions and Ashworth Mansions facing Biddulph Mansions, by Boehmer & Gibbs who also designed Delaware Mansions in Delaware Road;[24] Lauderdale Road is lined on both sides by Lauderdale Mansions, and the northern stretch of Castellain Road by Castellain Mansions. The only buildings later than 1920 are in Biddulph and Ashworth roads, where two-storeyed houses have filled the last empty sites.[25]

The northernmost tip of Maida Vale, partly cut off from the avenues of mansion flats by Paddington recreation ground, is a comparatively bleak area of council housing. It is dominated by the nine-storeyed Torridon House, built for the G.L.C., and St. Augustine's church, which retains a rough, tree-ringed enclosure. Most of the old housing has made way for blocks belonging to the Maida Vale housing estate, lower than the tallest ones in Edgware Road but in a similar style: Helmsdale House and other buildings of six storeys or less, on either side of Carlton Vale. Nos. 2, 4, and 6 Kilburn Park Road, with four storeys and basements, remain from the terrace on the north side, next to St. Augustine's primary school. A few other tall houses of the 1860s, in pairs and with pillared porches, survive in Randolph Gardens, towards the east end of Carlton Vale, and at the top of Randolph Avenue, most of them in bad condition. Humbler houses stretch in a long terrace south-westward from Carlton Vale along the Paddington side of Kilburn Park Road, where renovation is under way, in contrast to the open spaces and tower blocks on the Willesden side.

QUEEN'S PARK and ST. PETER'S PARK. The districts described below covered respectively the north-west corner and the middle of the north part of the metropolitan borough of Paddington, constituting Queen's Park and Harrow Road wards in 1901.[26] Queen's Park had no administrative connexion with the nearby open space of that name, in Willesden,[27] and until 1900 lay within Chelsea detached. St. Peter's Park was formerly the name of a characterless suburb around Walterton Road[28] and has often been considered part of Maida Vale,[29] from which, however, it differed in both origins and social status.

Until the spread of building in the mid 19th century, the area consisted of fields stretching westward from the Bayswater rivulet, bounded by Harrow Road to the south and by Kilburn Lane to the west and north-west.[30] Westbourne green lay along Harrow Road to the south-east. Whereas the eastern part of Paddington, including the area treated above as Maida Vale, belonged to the bishop of London, most of the parish west of the rivulet lay within Westminster abbey's Westbourne manor.[31] The northern part of Chelsea detached belonged to All Souls'

[22] Para. based on Pevsner, *Lond.* ii. 313, where both sides of the road are treated under Paddington.
[23] G.L.C. Historic Bldgs. Div., WM 224.
[24] Pevsner, *Lond.* ii. 313.
[25] O.S. Map 6", Mdx. XVI. NE. (1920 edn.).
[26] *Plan of Paddington* (1901).
[27] *Lond. Encyc.* 634; *V.C.H. Mdx.* vii. 235.
[28] *Lond. Encyc.* 489. St. Peter's Pk. was listed as a

separate suburb west of Walterton Rd. in Post Office suburban dirs. of the 1880s and 1890s.
[29] e.g. *Jewish Jnl. of Sociology*, vi (1), 71. Booth, on the other hand, defined St. Peter's Pk. much more widely, to include the northern part of Maida Vale: *Life and Labour*, i (2), app. p. 13.
[30] Rocque, *Map of Lond.* (1741–5), sheet 11.
[31] Below, manors; Ch. Com., 'Map of 1742'.

College, Oxford.[32]

In the 1740s all the fields were pasture, except a wooded enclosure beside Kilburn Lane almost opposite Kilburn wood, and the few farm buildings were all on the Willesden side of the lane.[33] The Grand Junction canal was later cut just south of Harrow Road, leaving much less than half of Chelsea detached to the south. Between the road and the canal there was a small triangle of land in the west, a narrow strip across most of Chelsea detached, and a much wider piece farther east towards Westbourne green. In 1828, apart from a short row of houses at Orme's green, constituting an outpost of Westbourne green, the countryside remained open.[34]

In the triangle between the canal, Harrow Road, and Kilburn Lane along the boundary, a new Italianate villa stood by 1835. Called Kensal House and occupied by Alfred Haines in 1841,[35] it was unusually large for its position, hemmed in by 1865 between housing along Kilburn Lane to the west and canalside buildings to the east. The houses along Kilburn Lane amounted to an extension of Kensal New Town,[36] which had been built between 1835 and 1850 over the southern part of Chelsea detached[37] and which in 1900 was transferred to Kensington metropolitan borough.[38] The new town was served from 1843–4 by St. John's church,[39] which in 1865 stood with only two nearby houses and the National school on the east side of Kilburn Lane north of Harrow Road, although there was much more building along the west side. The rest of Chelsea detached was fields, apart from a wharf near the south-east corner, with buildings opposite on the north side of Harrow Road, and a single building on the northern boundary in Kilburn Lane.[40]

The north-western part of Paddington parish was still rural in 1840, although there was a plan to extend Elgin Road (later Elgin Avenue) from Maida Vale across the lands of Westbourne manor to the later junction with Harrow Road.[41] Building spread northward from Westbourne green during the 1860s, as the Neeld family followed the example of the lessees of the Paddington Estate.[42] Growth was matched by a westward spread along the south side of Harrow Road, from the Lock hospital beyond Orme's green to Carlton Crescent (later Terrace).[43]

St. Peter's Park was by 1865 the name, commemorating the lordship of Westminster abbey, of a projected suburb north of Harrow Road, from the Bayswater rivulet to Chelsea detached. A few straight avenues leading from Harrow Road had been planned, although not yet built up: Malvern (soon renamed Chippenham) Road and, from a convergence farther west, an extension of Elgin Road, St.

Peter's (renamed Walterton) Road, and the southernmost stretch of the future Fernhead Road; to the west, part of Ashmore Road, also as yet unnamed, had been begun.[44]

The first leases, for 99 years, were made in 1865 by Sir John Neeld, on the nomination of Edward Vigers, a builder or timber merchant of Tavistock Lodge, Great Western Road. They were mostly to Thomas or Luke Muncey, for terraced houses of three storeys over a basement along the north side of Harrow Road, forming Chippenham Terrace, and in Marylands Road, and for two-storeyed houses in Chippenham Mews.[45] Neeld thereafter made leases to many local builders, often in association with Vigers, who in turn subleased.[46] The Goldney family, some of whom were Wiltshire neighbours of the Neelds, was also involved:[47] in 1869 land between Edbrooke and Goldney roads was leased by Neeld to Vigers and mortgaged by Vigers to Francis Hastings Goldney of Chippenham.[48]

By 1869 there were houses along much of Chippenham Road and at the west ends of Elgin Road, where St. Peter's church had been allotted its existing site, Marylands Road, and Sutherland Gardens. All three roads led towards Shirland Road, which approximately followed the line of the Bayswater rivulet bounding the bishop's estate. Most of Goldney Road had been built up and some other short linking roads had been named. Neither Fernhead nor Ashmore roads stretched very far, but Saltram Crescent had been planned to run north to Kilburn Lane.[49] There were houses on the west side of Shirland Road, at the south end, by 1870.[50]

Vigers, who had been speculating in land in north Kensington at the west end of Westbourne Park Road since 1860,[51] found the building of St. Peter's Park a risky enterprise. He had to construct roads and sewers, besides a bridge over the canal (Carlton bridge), which would provide access by omnibus but which caused a dispute with the vestry about rights of way. Some of the small builders to whom he had subleased were in trouble from 1868, Vigers himself was forced to negotiate a further loan in 1870, and over a quarter of the builders on the estate failed between 1870 and 1872.[52]

Building activity revived in the mid 1870s, after Vigers's bankruptcy had been averted by the Neeld trustees.[53] In 1886 the northern parts of Ashmore and Fernhead (then to be called Neeld) roads had no buildings, except St. Luke's church between them by Kilburn Lane, and neither had Saltram Crescent.[54] There were still gaps along the middle stretch of Saltram Crescent and to either side of Marban Road, leading west from Fernhead Road,

[32] T. Faulkner, *Hist. Chelsea*, i (1829), 10–11.
[33] Rocque, *Map of Lond.* (1741–5), sheet 11.
[34] Gutch, *Plan of Paddington* (1828); above, Westbourne green.
[35] Inf. from Chelsea branch libraries at Marylebone libr.; G.L.C. Historic Bldgs. Div., WM 184.
[36] O.S. Map 1/2,500, Lond. XXIII (1870 edn.); Stanford, *Libr. Map of Lond.* (1862 edn. with additions to 1865), sheet 5.
[37] F. M. Gladstone, *Notting Hill in Bygone Days* (1969), 197; *Survey of Lond.* xxxvii. 333.
[38] Marylebone libr., P 138, cuttings.
[39] Below, churches.
[40] Stanford, *Libr. Map of Lond.* (1862 edn. with additions to 1865), sheet 5.

[41] Gutch, *Plan of Paddington* (1840).
[42] *Lond. Encyc.* 489.   [43] Above, Westbourne green.
[44] Stanford, *Libr. Map of Lond.* (1862 edn. with additions to 1865), sheet 5.
[45] M.L.R. 1865/17/317–29.
[46] e.g. ibid. 1868/17/557–70.
[47] e.g. ibid. 1867/15/6–7.
[48] Ibid. 1869/14/9–10.
[49] Stanford, *Libr. Map of Lond.* (1862 edn. with additions to 1865), sheet 5; Lucas, *Plan of Paddington* (1869).
[50] M.L.R. 1870/20/282–4.
[51] *Survey of Lond.* xxxvii. 299 (map), 304, 306.
[52] Reeder, 'Capital Investment', 313–14, 318–21.
[53] Ibid. 321–2.
[54] Bacon, *Atlas of Lond.* (1886).

in 1891,[55] although they had been filled by 1901.[56] Housing was put up mostly by small builders,[57] to whom the Ecclesiastical Commissioners at Vigers's direction granted terms of *c.* 98 years. Between 1882 and 1895 there were many leases of houses in Saltram Crescent and Fernhead Road, and from 1890 in their connecting roads, Croxley and Denholme roads.[58]

St. Peter's Park was begun with some substantial terraces near Harrow Road. Parts came to suffer from a cramped layout, however, and much housing was soon neglected.[59] Walterton Road in the 1880s was a 'dreary thoroughfare', where small grey houses were approached by tall flights of steps and had bay windows, many with cards advertising services 'from the letting of lodgings to the tuning of pianos'. Although the description was aimed at stressing the superiority of Bayswater,[60] St. Peter's Park in general retained a reputation for being dismal, or at least dull.[61] It made a fit setting for the plight of the poet Francis Thompson (1859–1907), who lodged briefly in Fernhead Road and, from 1897, with different landladies in Elgin Avenue and its neighbourhood.[62]

Subletting had led to deterioration throughout the area by the 1890s, although there was little real hardship. In the eastern part well-to-do households lined Sutherland and Elgin avenues, as in the Maida Vale stretches of those roads, and Harrow Road and Grittleton Road. There were also some well-to-do residents in Marylands Road and its southern off-shoots, and in Chippenham and Walterton roads. Elsewhere, including the slightly newer part west of Chippenham Road, residents were 'fairly comfortable'. Houses were mostly of nine rooms and might be let to two or three families, often clerks, agents, or well paid artisans. Poverty was confined to the long Chippenham Mews behind Harrow Road, to Barnsdale Mews, to the angle between Chippenham and Walterton roads, and to Shirland Mews, and in those places some residents were comfortable.[63]

Meanwhile Queen's Park had been built up, comparatively quickly, by the Artizans', Labourers', and General Dwellings Co. Two adjoining blocks of land, 49½ a. and *c.* 24 a., were bought in 1874–5 from All Souls' College.[64] Presumably they accounted for the 80 a. whose purchase was announced, together with the name of the estate and plans to accommodate 16,000 people, in 1874. The site, chosen partly for its accessibility by road and rail, was to have tree-lined roads, with 4 a. in the centre reserved for recreation. Gardening was to be encouraged and there was to be provision for an institute, co-operative stores, coal depot, dairy farm, baths, and reading rooms, but no public house.[65] Avenues numbered from 1 to 6 were laid out leading north from Harrow Road and were joined by long cross-streets, at first called merely by the letters A to P

but soon given names in alphabetical order.[66]

Building took place in several roads at the same time. Houses were dated 1873 and 1874 on the east side and 1876 on the west side of Sixth Avenue, 1880 in Fifth Avenue, 1875 in Caird Street at the east end of the estate, and 1876 in Oliphant Street at the far end and in a nearby shopping parade in Kilburn Lane.[67] Financial difficulties in 1877 brought delays, rent increases, and building on the intended open space, but renewed progress had led to the completion of 1,571 houses by 1882, when a further 449 were under construction.[68] The whole area west of First Avenue had been built up by 1886.[69]

Queen's Park, like the company's other four residential parks in London, was the result of a well supported effort to improve working-class conditions. It came to be seen as a success, both in encouraging the company to buy land for the Noel Park estate in Tottenham[70] and in comparison with the squalor of much canalside housing, including Kensal New Town, and with the dinginess of St. Peter's Park.[71] All 2,200 houses at Queen's Park were occupied in 1887, when the rents were much lower than those nearby.[72] In 1899 the estate was 'carefully sustained in respectability', there was a waiting list for tenancies, and rents were never in arrear. Tenants were church or chapel goers and in regular work, as artisans, clerks, policemen, or railwaymen. Only a fifth of the inabitants lived in poverty, compared with more than 55 per cent in Kensal New Town, and those that did so may have lived outside the company's estate, around Herries Street.[73]

The north-east corner of Chelsea detached had been acquired by 1874 by the United Land Co.,[74] which eventually laid out Beethoven, Mozart, Herries, and Lancefield streets. The terraced houses were tightly packed: a few, facing Kilburn Lane, were to be worth £500 and the rest £300. Less than half of the plots, towards the northern end, had been numbered by *c.* 1883[75] but Beethoven and Mozart streets had been built up by 1886.[76] Both poor and comfortable households existed *c.* 1899 in Beethoven, Herries, and Lancefield streets.[77]

In the period between the World Wars Queen's Park changed very little, its rented houses continuing to be in demand,[78] while the name St. Peter's Park apparently fell into disuse. A statement made in 1931, that housing westward from Maida Vale deteriorated until it finally became working-class in the north-west corner of the borough,[79] implied that St. Peter's Park was superior. Subletting had presumably continued, however, since in 1931 there was a density of from 1 to 1.25 persons to a room between Chippenham Road and Bravington Road, whereas the whole of Queen's Park had less than one person to a room; only the eastern part of St. Peter's

[55] Stanford, *Libr. Map of Lond.* (1891).
[56] *Plan of Paddington* (1901).   [57] *Lond. Encyc.* 490.
[58] Marylebone libr., Acc. 1468 (Westm. est. deeds).
[59] *Study of Urban Hist.* ed. H. J. Dyos (1968), 265.
[60] A. Levy, *Reuben Sachs* (1888), 33, 72.
[61] *Lond. Encyc.* 490.
[62] E. Meynell, *Life of Francis Thompson* (1926), 211; P. van K. Thomson, *Francis Thompson* (1961), 151–2; *D.N.B.*
[63] *Booth's Map* (1889), NW.; Booth, *Life and Labour,* i (2), app. p. 14.   [64] M.L.R. 1875/8/117–18.
[65] *The Times,* 16 Sept. 1874, 10*e*; 9 Oct. 1874, 5*f.*
[66] *Lond. Encyc.* 634.   [67] Datestones.
[68] [M. Bond] *Artizans' Centenary, 1867–1967,* 15–17.

[69] J. Reynolds, *Map of Lond.* (1886).
[70] *Artizans' Centenary,* 17; *V.C.H. Mdx.* v. 320–1.
[71] *Study of Urban Hist.* ed. Dyos, 265.
[72] *Rep. Sel. Cttee. on Town Holdings,* H.C. 260, pp. 419, 421–2 (1887), xiii.
[73] Booth, *Life and Labour,* i (2), app. p. 9; iii (3), 142–4, and map facing p. 162.
[74] M.L.R. 1875/8/117–18 (plan).
[75] Utd. Land Co. *Kilburn and Harrow Rd. Est.* (maps, *c.* 1883 and *c.* 1885, in Marylebone libr.).
[76] J. Reynolds, *Map of Lond.* (1886).
[77] Booth, *Life and Labour,* iii (3), map facing p. 162.
[78] *Official Guide to Paddington* [1921, 1936].
[79] *New Lond. Life and Labour,* vi. 431.

Park and an area in the north between Saltram Crescent and Fernhead Road had a density as low as that of Queen's Park.[80]

Damage to Queen's Park during the Second World War included destruction by a land mine at the corner of Ilbert and Peach streets, where Paddington council was building Queen's Park Court in 1951.[81] The company changed its name to the Artizans' and General Properties Co. in 1952[82] and, having already sold to the council more than 200 houses and sites cleared during the war, disposed of its remaining Queen's Park properties in 1964. Willesden acquired 146 maisonettes and Paddington the rest of the estate, including 1,800 weekly rented houses and flats, 80 shops, 2 halls, and 32 ground rents.[83] In 1978 the houses along most of the southern edge of the estate, between Droop Street and Harrow Road from Sixth Avenue almost to Third Avenue, made way for Westminster's Avenue Gardens,[84] consisting of 11 blocks named after trees. Widespread improvements to the older houses in Queen's Park were planned in 1982.[85]

Greater changes took place farther east, with the clearance of parts of St. Peter's Park for municipal housing.[86] The triangle between Harrow Road, Elgin Avenue, and Chippenham Road, containing some of Paddington's worst housing, was earmarked in 1966 for 300 maisonettes and flats by the G.L.C. It was rapidly built up with the Elgin (originally called Walterton Road) estate, whose first tenants arrived in 1968. On the border of Queen's Park, between Lancefield Street and Third Avenue, Westminster council in 1970 began work on the Mozart estate, where 172 dwellings housed 646 people by 1972. The estate was intended for 3,450 residents and was later extended northward as far as Kilburn Lane. The completed estate formed a rectangle bisected by Dart Street, St. Jude's church having been demolished and the north–south Lancefield and Herries streets reduced to short cul-de-sacs. It was served by new shops and the Magic Flute public house, and on the south adjoined the Jubilee sports centre. A little to the south-east the 225 homes of the G.L.C.'s Lydford estate were built by 1977. They too formed a rectangle, south of Shirland Road between Fernhead and Ashmore roads, superimposed on older streets.

Renovation was carried out from 1965 by Mulberry Housing Trust, which had converted c. 270 properties into c. 950 flats by 1973,[87] when it also opened a children's centre at the junction of Shirland and Fernhead roads.[88] Work was continued by St. Marylebone Housing Association, whose programme in 1984 provided for the eventual provision of 914 flats in north Paddington, forming its Mulberry estate. The largest numbers were in the area comprising Ashmore Road (140 flats), the parallel Portnall (88), Fernhead (84), and Bravington (63) roads, Saltram Crescent (63), and their cross-roads, but there were many to the south-east in Sutherland Avenue (63), Marylands Road (61), and their neighbourhood. A four-storeyed block of 10 flats and a headquarters for the association were being built at no. 103 Fernhead Road in 1984.[89]

Other conversions into flats around Bravington, Portnall, and Ashmore roads were carried out from 1975 by Brent People's Housing Association. All the association's properties in Paddington were for rent except 40 in Shirland Mews, which passed into shared ownership. In 1985 it had c. 490 housing units in that area, with other houses awaiting conversion, and planned to build on the sites of a school, the Kensal Road baths, and the gardens in Warlock Road.[90] Paddington Churches Housing Association opened Ernest Harriss House, with a day centre and 61 housing units for old people, next to St. Peter's church in 1977.[91]

Smaller projects included the flats of the 1950s called Sutherland Court in Marylands Road,[92] the building of Paddington (later part of North Westminster) school nearby in Oakington Road, and the rebuilding of St. Luke's and St. Peter's churches.[93] Abinger Mews replaced older houses at the north-east end of Walterton Road, behind which terraces in the triangle between Walterton, Chippenham, and Warlock roads were to be cleared in 1982 by the G.L.C.[94] A private estate called Marble House was built between Walterton Road and Elgin Avenue, cutting off the eastern end of Barnsdale Road.

Most of Queen's Park, declared a conservation area in 1978,[95] remains as it was built for the Artizans', Labourers', and General Dwellings Co. by Hubert Austin and then by Roland Plumbe. The houses are two-storeyed terraces of red and yellow brick in 'minimum Gothic',[96] enlivened by turrets at some of the street corners, and many bear a date or the company's monogram. Their simple design derives from that of the smaller Shaftesbury Park estate at Battersea.[97] Although pollarded plane trees survive, the wider and longer streets have been criticized as monotonous.[98]

Rebuilding in Queen's Park has consisted chiefly of Queen's Park Court, red-brick blocks of six storeys or less, and Avenue Gardens, pale brown-brick ranges of three or four storeys surrounding the Victorian library and for most of their length facing a strip which has been cleared along the canal bank between nos. 487 and 525 (the Flora hotel) Harrow Road. East of St. John's church at no. 742 Harrow Road is the London Telecommunications Region's Ladbroke Exchange, opened in 1939.[99] Almost opposite is Kensal House, the only former gentleman's residence in the area. The original Italianate house

[80] Ibid. iv, maps 1.
[81] *Artizans' Centenary*, 30; Clunn, *Face of Lond.* 449.
[82] *Artizans' Centenary*, 32.
[83] Ibid. 42; *The Times*, 23 May 1964, 8g.
[84] *Lond. Encyc.* 634.
[85] *Westm. Dist. Plan, 1982*; *Westm. Dist. Plan, Proposals Map, 1982* (in Marylebone libr.).
[86] Following para. based on Marylebone libr., P 138, cuttings.
[87] Inf. from dir., St. Marylebone Housing Assoc.
[88] Marylebone libr., P 138, cuttings.
[89] St. Marylebone Housing Assoc. *Ann. Rep.* (1984), 5, 9; inf. from dir.

[90] Marylebone libr., P 138, cuttings; inf. from dir., Brent People's Housing Assoc. Ltd.
[91] Marylebone libr., P 138, cuttings; inf. from regional dir., Paddington Churches Housing Assoc. Ltd.
[92] *P.O. Dir. Lond.* (1952, 1959).
[93] Below, educ.; churches.
[94] *Westm. Dist. Plan, 1982* (in Marylebone libr.).
[95] Inf. from asst. dir. (development), Westm. Planning Dept.; *Westm. Dist. Plan, Proposals Map, 1982* (in Marylebone libr.). [96] Pevsner, *Lond.* ii. 314.
[97] *The Times*, 16 Sept. 1874, 10e.
[98] *Artizans' Centenary*, 17.
[99] Inf. from Telecom Technology Showcase.

contains three storeys over a basement and is of brick and stucco, the main façade having seven bays, a prominent cornice, and a Corinthian porch. A 19th-century wing has been added to the east and a modern one to the west.[1] After serving as a school, the house was occupied by the Metropolitan Railway Surplus Lands Co. by 1949,[2] stood empty when owned by the United Church of God in Christ by 1965,[3] and was owned by the I.C.E. Group in 1985.

Greater change has taken place immediately east of Queen's Park,[4] most notably with the construction of the Mozart estate, 40 buildings of two to six storeys, faced with red brick, whose design won a government award in 1973. The nearby Lydford estate, 20 three-storeyed ranges around four closes and also in red brick, received a similar award in 1977. Farther east, in contrast, the Elgin estate includes the 21-storeyed tower blocks called Chantry Point and Hermes Point, built of storey-high light-weight glass reinforced plastic panels, with distinctive round-cornered windows. Although the panels were 'unprecedented in lightness and elegance',[5] the windows quickly needed to be replaced and the blocks showed signs of wear in 1985. Other modern buildings include the four-storeyed brown-brick ranges of Marble House, the yellow-brick terrace called Abinger Mews, the six-storeyed brown-brick block of Ernest Harriss House, and the striking red-brick Mulberry Centre.

Most of the former St. Peter's Park, which has a large coloured population, still consists of 19th-century terraces, served by shops in Harrow Road and smaller groups in Shirland Road around its junctions with Elgin Avenue and Fernhead Road. Houses at the west ends of Sutherland Avenue, Marylands Road, and Elgin Avenue are mainly in Italianate terraces of three or occasionally four storeys over basements, with pillared porches, in the style of Westbournia. A few cross-streets, including Goldney Road, Surrendale Place, and Sevington Street, have similar terraces; some, including Ed-brooke Road, have less imposing ones without porches, and others, including Oakington and Thorngate roads, have only two-storeyed rows. The avenues leading towards Maida Vale are straight, wide, and still partly tree-lined. Walterton Road, whose Italianate terraces are without porches, is bleaker and more in need of refurbishment. Its houses are of three storeys over basements, whereas surviving houses in the cross-streets Errington, Barnsdale, and Warlock roads are all one storey lower. Shirland Road consists mainly of 19th-century terraces and shops. The north-west end of the area is packed with late 19th-century three-storeyed terraces, the earlier ones with basements and the later ones with bay windows; in Saltram Crescent, St.

Simon's church has been converted into private flats.

SOCIAL AND CULTURAL ACTIVITIES.

There were four alehouses, including one in the Westbourne part of the parish, in 1552[6] and three after some had been suppressed by the justices in 1830.[7] Ben Jonson's *A Tale of A Tub* of c. 1596 mentioned a Red Lion, presumably in Edgware Road,[8] and John Taylor the 'water poet' in 1636 noted a tavern kept by Walter Whitlock,[9] who may have been Walter Whittock, a vintner presented for recusancy.[10] Orders against Sunday drinking were made against alehouse keepers in 1641 and 1647.[11] The stabling of the White Lion in Edgware Road was probably painted by George Morland c. 1790;[12] the 19th-century White Lion was said to date from 1524 and an inn of that name existed by 1644.[13]

Despite changes of site and name, the number of inns varied little from the early 18th century to the early 19th. Eleven alehouse keepers were licensed in 1723 and 1730, 15 in 1760, 12 in 1790, and 14 in 1815.[14] In 1730 two of the inns, the Bell and the Saracen's Head, were at Bayard's Watering,[15] where in 1710 the Bell had been a new building, formerly the King's Head.[16] The Saracen's Head may have been a short-lived name for the late 18th-century Swan inn, since a Swan field bordered the Uxbridge road in 1729.[17] A third inn beside the road was the Oxford Arms, in 1751 called the Black Lion. Two more inns were at Westbourne green, one of them the Red Lion, near the bridge carrying Harrow Road across the Westbourne stream and later rebuilt after the road's realignment. All the other inns in 1730, including another Red Lion, were presumably in Edgware Road or close by, at Paddington green.[18] In 1760 there were three Red Lions, described as at Paddington, Westbourne green, and the road to Westbourne green. A second inn at Westbourne green, the Jolly Gardeners,[19] had become the Three Jolly Gardeners by 1770 and had made way for the Spotted Dog by 1790.[20] Of 13 inns licensed in 1810, 4 were considered to be in Bayswater, 2 in Edgware Road, 3 in Harrow Road, 1 in Maida Hill, 1 at Paddington green, and 2 at Westbourne green.[21] Numbers rose steeply with the spread of housing: 49 taverns were listed in 1862, a few of them serving hotels, and 138 on-licensed premises, including 104 public houses and 23 beerhouses, in 1906. There were 95 public houses and 16 beerhouses, besides 19 licensed hotels, by 1935 and 73 public houses c. 1960.[22] At no. 93 Warrington Crescent the Warrington hotel of c. 1900, despite its description, was built and used only as a public house; it became popular with racing men and in 1984 was a striking example of an ornately furnished gin palace.[23]

[1] G.L.C. Hist. Bldgs. Div., WM 184.
[2] Below, educ.; Marylebone libr., P 137, cuttings.
[3] G.L.C. Hist. Bldgs. Div., WM 184.
[4] Para. based on Marylebone libr., P 138, cuttings.
[5] G.L.C. *Home Sweet Home* (1976), 64, 66 (illus.).
[6] *Mdx. County Rec.* i. 11.
[7] *Cal. S.P. Dom.* 1631–3, 525; 1634–5, 106.
[8] *Tale of A Tub*, II. iii. 29–30.
[9] *Mdx. & Herts. N. & Q.* iv. 78.
[10] *Mdx. County Rec.* iii. 42, 58, 130.
[11] G.L.R.O., Cal. Mdx. Sess. Bks. i. 87; ii. 96.
[12] G. C. Williamson, *Geo. Morland* (1907), 48, 129; D.N.B.
[13] Robins, *Paddington*, 181; G.L.R.O., Q/HAL/199.

[14] G.L.R.O., MR/LV3/104; MR/LV5/22; MR/LV7/45; MR/LV9/187; MR/LV15/3.
[15] Ibid. MR/LV5/22.
[16] M.L.R. 1710/2/99; G.L.R.O., BRA/329/24.
[17] 'Survey of Upton Fm. by Wm. Gardner, 1729' (map in Marylebone libr.).
[18] G.L.R.O., MR/LV5/22.
[19] Ibid. MR/LV7/45.
[20] Ibid. MR/LV8/64; MR/LV9/81.
[21] Ibid. MR/LV11/132.
[22] Marylebone libr., P 137, cuttings (lists); L.C.C. *Lond. Statistics*, xvi. 210; xxxix. 198, 206.
[23] Inf. from director, Warrington Hotel Ltd.; *Lond. Encyc.* 925.

Pleasure gardens were often attached to inns in the late 18th and early 19th centuries. The earlier and more fashionable were at Bayswater, relatively accessible from London's west end and well known for its fresh-water springs, where medicinal plants were grown by John Hill (1716?–1775).[24] Hill's former establishment was a tea garden by 1795,[25] with boxes and arbours in 1796.[26] It was painted by Sandby[27] and later, when less exclusive, it was called the Flora and finally the Victoria tea gardens.[28] The scene of balloon ascents in 1836 and 1839, of a foot-race in 1851,[29] and of nightly concerts and vaudevilles,[30] it closed in 1854, when the adjoining nursery grounds were to be sold for building.[31] Another tea garden lay a little to the east, behind the Crown.[32] As Bayswater coffee house, in 1790 and 1810[33] it had a different licensee from that of the Crown, which had been so named at least since 1751; there had been a licensed coffee house, of unknown location, in 1751 and 1760.[34] As Bayswater tea gardens, the premises drew custom from their proprietor's lease of 4 a. to the Toxophilite Society from 1821 until 1834[35] and were united with the Crown, a music and dancing licence being received for the tavern and tea gardens in 1840.[36] Probably it was the same resort, called Wale's Bayswater tavern or the Royal Albert saloon, which was licensed in turn to William, Frances Sarah, and John David Wale from 1848 until 1860.[37] Also at Bayswater, the Black Lion had gardens which included a skittle ground in 1802 and was later licensed for music and dancing.[38] At Westbourne green, there were pleasure gardens at the Royal Oak which were described in Charles Ollier's *Ferrers* of 1842.[39] What were perhaps the last tea gardens were opened by James Bott at the Princess Royal, Hereford Road, *c.* 1842.[40]

'The Old Platform near Paddington', an unidentified site, was the scene of a theatrical performance advertised probably in 1762.[41] In Edgware Road the White Lion was rebuilt in 1836,[42] licensed for music and dancing in 1840, and advertised as a music hall in 1859.[43] In 1862 John Turnham incorporated it in his new Turnham's Grand Concert Hall, which, on changing hands, was further altered and renamed the Metropolitan Music Hall in 1864. After its acquisition by a company under G. A. Payne it was rebuilt in 1897 to the design of Frank Matcham, to hold 2,800, and renamed the Metropolitan Theatre of

Varieties Ltd. Widely and affectionately known as the Met, it was familiar to nearly every leading music hall star from the late 19th century until its decline in the 1950s. Matcham's theatre had a long street front of terracotta, with a central pediment, balustrades, and domed minarets, and was decorated internally in the Flemish Renaissance style. After serving as a wrestling booth,[44] it finally closed in 1962 to make way for road widening.

In Market (later St. Michael's) Street 'nightly balls and concerts' were suppressed as unlicensed in 1857[45] and in Harrow Road the King and Queen was licensed for entertainment from 1850 to 1868 and the Running Horse from 1855 to 1881.[46] Westbourne hall in Westbourne Grove could hold 400 people for lectures and entertainments in 1860, when its lessee opened adjoining premises in Havelock Terrace as Bayswater Athenaeum and Literary Institution.[47] An ornate four-storeyed building[48] with a hall for 1,000, designed by A. Billing, was built on the site of the first hall in 1861 and licensed for music alone by T. E. Whibley in 1863.[49] The Athenaeum, although welcomed for its educational value, had become the Athenaeum divan by 1865 and may have closed soon afterwards.[50] Westbourne hall continued to be used for concerts, plays, and public meetings until 1875 or later and survived in 1952.[51] The Phoenix coffee tavern at no. 254 Harrow Road, in existence by 1879, had a stage which was licensed for music from 1890 to 1892.[52] Queen's Park hall, at the corner of First Avenue and Harrow Road by 1888, seated 400 and was licensed for music and dancing by 1905 and until 1911 or later, as were the municipal baths in Queen's Road until 1910.[53] The council's Porchester hall, opened in 1929 with seating for 800–1,000, was sometimes used for concerts; part was known as the Porchester theatre in 1952. Several private theatre clubs, performing in halls or public houses, existed in the 1960s and 1970s.[54]

The earliest cinema[55] was probably the Bayswater cinematograph theatre at nos. 162 and 164 Queen's Road, licensed for 350 in 1910 and 1911 and called the El Dorado in 1913.[56] The Universal Co.'s bioscope theatre was at no. 5 (afterwards 5A) Praed Street by 1911; its later names included the Electric theatre in 1921, the Gaiety cinema in 1923, the New Gaiety kinema in 1927, the World's News theatre in 1938, and the Classic Cartoon cinema from 1959.

[24] *D.N.B.*
[25] Lysons, *Environs*, iii. 331.
[26] W. Wroth, *Lond. Pleasure Gdns. of 18th Cent.* (1896), 118–19. Illus. of 1796 in G. M. Woodward, *Eccentric Excursions* (1807), 18–19.
[27] Guildhall libr., Pr P1/BAY. For a watercolour of *c.* 1840, presumably of the same premises, ibid. W P1/BAY.
[28] Wroth, *Pleasure Gdns.* 119; *Country Life*, 11 Nov. 1976, 1388.
[29] *Gent. Mag.* cvi (1), 422; Marylebone libr., P 136, cuttings. [30] Marylebone libr., P 137, cuttings.
[31] Wroth, *Pleasure Gdns.* 119.
[32] McDonald, 'Paddington', cap. 15.
[33] G.L.R.O., MR/LV9/187; MR/LV11/132.
[34] Ibid. MR/LV7/3; MR/LV7/45.
[35] McDonald, 'Paddington', cap. 15; below.
[36] G.L.R.O., LMD 2/30.
[37] D. Howard, *Lond. Theatres and Music Halls 1850–1950* (1970), no. 55.
[38] G.L.R.O., MR/LV7/3; Paddington Soc. *Newsletter*, May 1966.
[39] McDonald, 'Paddington', cap. 15; *Bayswater Annual* (1885), 42–3. [40] McDonald, 'Paddington', cap. 15.
[41] Marylebone libr., P 134, cuttings.
[42] Rest of para. based on *Some Account of New Metro-politan Theatre of Varieties* (booklet 1898 in Marylebone libr.); Howard, *Lond. Theatres*, no. 493; Marylebone libr., P 134, cuttings.
[43] G.L.R.O., LMD 2/68; *Paddington News*, 26 Feb. 1859.
[44] *Paddington Mag.* i (Nov. 1960).
[45] Select vestry mins. 3 Mar., 7 July 1857.
[46] Howard, *Lond. Theatres*, nos. 418, 700.
[47] *Bayswater Chron.* 20, 27 June, 4 July, 4 Sept. 1860.
[48] *Archit. Rev.* cv. 72 (illus.).
[49] *Bayswater Chron.* 13, 20 Mar. 1861; G.L.R.O., LMD 25/7.
[50] *Bayswater Chron.* 11 July 1860; 7 Jan. 1865.
[51] *Paddington, Kensington and Bayswater Chron.* 9 Jan., 13 Mar. 1875; Pevsner, *Lond.* ii. 310.
[52] *P.O. Dir. Lond.* (1879); Howard, *Lond. Theatres*, no. 575.
[53] Bacon, *Atlas of Lond.* (1888); L.C.C. *Lond. Statistics*, xvi. 199–200; xxi. 243; xxii. 245.
[54] Marylebone libr., P 134, P 137, cuttings.
[55] Following two paras. based on *Kelly's Dir. Paddington* (1912 and later edns.); *P.O. Dir. Lond.* (1911 and later edns.); *Paddington Mag.* i–ii (1960–1).
[56] L.C.C. *Lond. Statistics*, xxi. 237; ibid. xxii. 242.

The Prince of Wales picture playhouse, the Grove picture palace, and a large cinema later called the Grand were all licensed from 1912.[57] The Prince of Wales, at no. 331 Harrow Road, survived in 1969 and served as a bingo hall, Mecca social club, from 1970. The Grove, at nos. 90 and 92 Westbourne Grove, was later called the Roxy and c. 1960 was renamed the International film theatre, which survived until 1964 or later. The Grand occupied no. 26 Great Western Road in 1915 and nos. 22 and 24, formerly a police station, from 1916. Closed during the Second World War, it was reopened as the Savoy in 1957, renamed the Essoldo in 1961, and again closed in 1966, thereafter serving as a bingo club.[58] By 1914 the Electric, later Select Electric, theatre was at no. 413 Edgware Road, where it remained until the Second World War, and there were also cinemas on the Marylebone side of the road. The Ritz was at no. 324 Harrow Road in 1915; renamed the British cinema by 1919 and the Coliseum by 1920, it closed c. 1960.

Later cinemas included the Queen's near the corner of Bishop's and Queen's roads by 1936, converted into the triple ABC cinema in 1975,[59] the Odeon at the east end of Harrow Road by 1939, soon renamed the Regal and by 1975 the ABC, the Odeon at nos. 319 and 321 Edgware Road by 1939, closed in 1975,[60] and the Royal at no. 53 Edgware Road by 1947, called the Gala Royal by 1960. Another Odeon, at the corner of Westbourne Grove and Chepstow Road, was under construction in 1939 but opened only in 1955;[61] it was converted into a triple cinema in 1978 and remained open, as the Coronet, in 1985. Other cinemas open in 1982 were the ABC in Bishop's Bridge Road, the Classic, and the former Gala Royal, which was an Arabic film club. The Bishop's Bridge Road triple cinema, renamed the Cannon, alone survived in 1986.

A bowling green lay on the south side of Alderman Bide's house at Paddington green in 1647[62] and another abutted Edgware Road, opposite Upper Berkeley Street, in the 1790s.[63] One behind the Princess Royal was converted into a skating rink in 1875.[64] Paddington Bowling and Sports Club was founded in 1905 and occupied land behind the houses along the west side of Castellain Road. An indoor bowls pavilion, claimed to be the largest in existence, was finished in 1935, when there were also squash and outdoor tennis courts. By 1956 the club was the headquarters of the English Bowling Association.[65]

Fishing in the canal was the subject of a cartoon c. 1800.[66] A roller skating rink, said to be the first in London, was opened on the west side of Portsdown Road (later Randolph Avenue) in 1875; it filled a gap in the line of houses in 1880[67] and was called Kilburn and St. John's rink in 1886.[68] The concrete rink, in an iron building, was later turned into winter tennis courts for Paddington recreation ground.[69] Maida Vale Roller Skating Palace & Club was licensed from 1909 until 1912. The building, seating 2,620,[70] occupied much of the south-west side of Delaware Road. By 1925 it was used as National Insurance offices by the Ministry of Health and from 1934 by the B.B.C., which built a studio there for operatic and orchestral broadcasts.[71] Bayswater skating rink survived behind the Princess Royal at no. 47 Hereford Road in 1879.[72] Queen's Ice-Skating Club opened in Queen's Road in 1930 as London's only private skating club; with low subscriptions, it aimed at a large membership and survived in 1986.[73]

After the departure of the Toxophilite Society in 1834 to Regent's Park, archery continued on a small ground provided by James Bott until 1839 and was commemorated in the new Archery tavern in Bathurst Street, of which Bott was licensee in 1840.[74] On leaving Regent's Park the society, by then the Royal Toxophilite Society, returned to rent St. George's burial ground, which it used from 1924 until 1968, together with successive clubhouses in Albion Mews.[75]

Cricket was played by boys on Paddington green, to the vestry's annoyance, in 1815.[76] Maida Vale cricket club was formed in 1846 and Westbourne cricket club, with help from W. C. Carbonell, in 1852. The Westbourne club's field was in Harrow Road opposite the workhouse in 1857.[77] There were several local teams in 1870, including the Goldbourne and Nonsuch clubs, both from Upper Westbourne Park, Greville House from Paddington green, and groups of workers such as the Bayswater bakers and, by 1875, employees of Whiteley's. Throughout the 1870s home matches were usually played outside the parish, at Shepherd's Bush or Kensington Park,[78] until shortage of land prompted R. (later Sir Richard) Melvill Beachcroft, as treasurer of Paddington cricket club, to start his campaign for the purchase of Paddington recreation ground.[79] In 1890 the ground was used by Paddington and six other cricket clubs.[80] At football both the Bayswater Ramblers and the Bayswater Hornets played against school sides in 1875[81] and Paddington was an early rival of Queen's Park Rangers, established in 1886 with its headquarters at St. Jude's church. Although Queen's Park Rangers soon began to play in other

[57] Ibid. xxiii. 267.
[58] H. A. F. Webb, *Lond. Suburban Cinemas, 1946–80.*
[59] Marylebone libr., P 134, cuttings.
[60] Ibid.
[61] Ibid.; D. Atwell, *Cathedrals of the Movies* (1980), 162.
[62] Guildhall MS. 10464A.
[63] R. Horwood, *Plan of Lond. and Westm.* (1799), sheet 3; *N. & Q.* 8th ser. vii. 285.
[64] *Paddington, Kensington and Bayswater Chron.* 23 Oct. 1875; below.
[65] *Paddington Past and Present* [1936]; Paddington Chamber of Commerce, *Official Guide* (1956).
[66] Guildhall Libr., W P1/BAY.
[67] *Paddington, Kensington and Bayswater Chron.* 14 Aug. 1875; Ch. Com., Bldg. Agreements, vol. xiv, pp. 37 sqq.
[68] Bacon, *Atlas of Lond.* (1886).
[69] J. Bates, *Playground of Paddington* (1902), 26.
[70] L.C.C. *Lond. Statistics*, xx. 213; xxiii. 267.
[71] *Kelly's Dir. Paddington* (1911 and later edns.); *Paddington Past and Present* (1936).
[72] *P.O. Dir. Lond.* (1879).
[73] *Paddington Past and Present* (1939).
[74] C. B. Edwards, *The 'Tox' Story* (1968), 13; G.L.R.O., LMD 2/48.
[75] Edwards, *'Tox' Story*, 20–1.
[76] Vestry mins. 6 Sept. 1815.
[77] *Lillywhite's Guide to Cricketers* (1856), 101, 103; *Western and Suburban Intelligencer*, 10 Sept. 1857; *Paddington News*, 17 Sept. 1859.
[78] *Paddington Times*, 2 July, 20, 27 Aug. 1870; *Paddington, Kensington and Bayswater Chron.* 10 July 1875.
[79] Bates, *Playground of Paddington*, 18; below, pub. svces.
[80] *Cricket and Lawn Tennis Clubs Dir.* (1890–1).
[81] *Paddington, Kensington and Bayswater Chron.* 6, 13 Nov. 1875; *Football Calendar* (1875–6).

parishes, they still met at St. Jude's church institute in 1898, when the club decided to turn professional.[82]

Roman or Turkish baths were briefly open from *c.* 1860 until 1863 in Newton Road. A 'hydropathist', Richard Metcalfe, kept Turkish baths at no. 11 Paddington Green by 1860 and still did so in 1879, by which date there were also public baths.[83] There was a riding school in Garway Road, first under Edwin Barnett and by 1879 under George Edgson, from *c.* 1863 until 1902 or later. William Pearce, a riding master in Kensington Gardens Square in 1863,[84] may have owned Pearce's riding school in Green's Road, where special constables were drilled in 1868.[85] A gymnasium and fencing academy was kept in 1870 by Capt. James Chiosso at no. 48 Norfolk Terrace, where a Mrs. Chiosso had lived since 1867 or earlier, and also at no. 123 Oxford Street. In 1885 both establishments were called Capt. Chiosso's London Gymnasium and School of Arms, the Bayswater one being under Antonio Martino Chiosso and the Oxford Street one under J. T. and P. J. Chiosso, who claimed that it had been founded in 1835. A. M. Chiosso's gymnasium continued at no. 48 Norfolk Terrace, renamed no. 160 Westbourne Grove, until 1940.[86]

A volunteer corps was to be raised in 1803, with membership at first restricted to householders or their nominees. Numbers in consequence rose slowly and later in the year the parish heard that its force would not be needed, whereupon the expenses of recruitment had to be met from the poor rate.[87] The 36th Middlesex (Paddington) Rifle Volunteer Corps was formed in 1860, with a practice ground at Wormwood Scrubs and its armoury and drill ground at the engine house in Hermitage Street.[88] The headquarters was at Greville House, Paddington green, by 1875 and continued there until after the corps's numbering had been changed to the 18th Middlesex in 1879,[89] moving to nos. 207–9 Harrow Road by 1900.[90] The corps was superseded on the establishment of the Territorial Army in 1908 by the 10th Battalion, the County of London Regiment (Paddington Rifles), which was disbanded in 1912, when its remnant was incorporated into the 3rd City of London, the London Regiment, the Royal Fusiliers.[91] The drill hall, renamed the Paddington armoury, was thereafter used by the City of London Territorial Force Association, until the building of the elevated section of Westway.[92] The 3rd Middlesex Artillery (3rd division) had its headquarters by 1893 at Porteus House, once St. Mary's Vicarage, where a drill hall was erected and where it was followed by the 5th London Brigade R.F.A. (14th County of London Battery).[93]

A parochial savings bank had been established by 1832[94] and presumably was the one at the National school in Church Place in 1858 and 1875.[95] In 1853, however, the bank was one of several institutions said to have arisen from the work of the Paddington Visiting Society, founded in 1838 to effect material and moral improvement.[96] Many friendly societies served a wider area than Paddington. The earliest were probably Paddington Benevolent Whip club and Paddington and Marylebone Loan Society, recorded respectively in 1836 and 1838 and meeting at public houses in Edgware Road.[97] They were followed by the Junction Loan Society at the Grand Junction Arms, Praed Street, from 1839, the G.W.R. Provident Association at Paddington station by 1843,[98] and the Prince of Wales Loyal Union Paddington Benefit Society at the Archery tavern from 1844.[99] Paddington and Marylebone Mutual Association met from 1844 at the Fountains Abbey in Praed Street, Bayswater and Kensington Mutual Association met from 1845 at the Princess Royal; Marylebone and Paddington Mechanics' Institute also met from 1845 and Paddington and Bayswater Mutual Association from 1846.[1] Thereafter friendly societies, many of them building societies, multiplied with the spread of housing.[2]

Paddington building society, established as a mutual benefit society for St. Peter's Park in 1879, was in Great Western Road as the North Paddington building society from the 1920s, assumed its modern name in 1957, and was at no. 125 Westbourne Grove from 1971. Westbourne Park building society, founded in 1885, moved to Porchester Road in 1889 and Westbourne Terrace in 1899. Adjoining buildings were acquired and in 1932 opened as new offices called Westbourne House. The society merged with the Leek & Moorlands building society to form the Leek & Westbourne in 1965, opened new premises in Queensway in 1972, and later became part of the Britannia building society.[3]

Benevolent institutions not primarily educational, medical, or religious included by 1862 a nightly refuge, an annuitants' home for ladies, an institution for employment of needlewomen, and Anglican and Wesleyan girls' orphanages.[4] The annuitants' homes had originated in 1855 in a house in Victoria Grove Terrace (later Ossington Street) near the Kensington boundary; by 1865 there were six houses, one of which remained open until *c.* 1930.[5] At no. 65 Walterton Road an old people's home existed from *c.* 1884, becoming a Harrison Home in the 1950s. A branch of the Y.M.C.A. which had opened in

[82] Paddington Soc. *Newsletter*, Sept. 1968; R. J. Hayter, *Queen's Pk. Rangers* (1948), 8–10.
[83] *Bayswater Chron.* 26 Dec. 1860, 16 Jan. 1861; *P.O. Dir. Lond.* (1863, 1879); below, pub. svces.
[84] *P.O. Dir. Lond.* (1863 and later edns.).
[85] *Illus. Lond. News*, 18 Jan. 1868, 65–6.
[86] *P.O. Dir. Lond.* (1867 and later edns.). Jas. Chiosso had described himself as 'superintendent of gymnastic exercises' at University Coll., Lond., in his *Remarks on Physical Educ.* (1845).
[87] *Paddington Civil Defence Corps Newsletter*, Mar. 1962 (in Marylebone libr.); vestry mins. 3 Aug., 22 Dec. 1803; 10 May 1804.
[88] *Bayswater Annual* (1885); *Bayswater Chron.* 20 June 1860; *P.O. Dir. Lond.* (1863).
[89] *Bayswater Annual* (1885); *P.O. Dir. Lond.* (1879); Hutchings and Crowsley, *Paddington Dir.* (1875).
[90] *Kelly's Dir. Paddington* (1900).

[91] J. P. Kelleher, *Paddington Rifles, 1908–12* (booklet 1982 in Marylebone libr.), 1–2, 13, 16.
[92] Idem, *Paddington Cos. of 3rd City of Lond. Bn., Royal Fusiliers* (booklet 1982 in Marylebone libr.), 2.
[93] *Kelly's Dir. Paddington* (1893 and later edns.); Ch. Com., Bldg. Agreements, vol. x, no. 2.
[94] Select vestry mins. 2 Oct. 1832.
[95] *P.O. Dir. Lond.* (1858, 1875).
[96] Robins, *Paddington*, 170.
[97] G.L.R.O., MC/R 1, ff. 18, 62, 68.
[98] Ibid. ff. 63, 73.
[99] G.L.R.O., MC/R 2, ff. 12, 17.
[1] Ibid. ff. 36, 42, 72–3, 88.
[2] G.L.R.O., MC/R 3.
[3] Marylebone libr., P 138, cuttings.
[4] Dolling's Paddington Dir. (1862).
[5] *Bayswater Chron.* 20 June 1860; 1 July 1865; *P.O. Dir. Lond.* (1875 and later edns.).

Titchborne Street by 1872 was constituted a metropolitan district centre in 1882, from which branches were founded in several neighbouring parishes.[6] Few other such organizations, apart from those of the Kilburn Sisters, survived for long at the same address.

The Kilburn Sisters,[7] who had housed orphans in Kilburn Park Road since 1875,[8] were granted a lease of nearby building land in Randolph Gardens 1874 and of their new Orphanage of Mercy there in 1884.[9] It was a red-brick building of c. 1880,[10] holding 300 girls in 1886 and 500 by 1892,[11] and came to be known also as St. Michael's home.[12] A neighbouring building in Rudolph Road was completed c. 1890, as St. Augustine's home of rest, immediately south of the church, and later joined to the orphanage. Victoria orphanage was built in 1887 at no. 111 Shirland Road, where younger children at first shared the building with Wordsworth ladies' college,[13] and leased to the sisters from 1893.[14] The home of rest apparently had closed by 1905, perhaps to make way for the resited Wordsworth college,[15] Victoria orphanage had closed by 1938, and the Orphanage of Mercy was evacuated in 1939.[16] The community also had depots for the sale of clothing at no. 227 Edgware Road from 1884 until 1900 or later, briefly also at no. 229, at no. 229 Maida Vale from c. 1890 until 1935 or later, briefly at no. 231, and finally in Kilburn High Road.[17]

Westbourne working men's institute, with W. C. Carbonell as president, had been recently founded in 1857.[18] A reading room for working men was opened off Moscow Road in 1862 and there was one at Greville House, Paddington green, in 1872; another was maintained by St. John's church in Oxford Mews in 1872 and 1875.[19] The Kildare library was opened in 1875 in Westbourne Grove by William Whiteley for employees who paid 6d. a month.[20] The West London Auxiliary Sunday School Union by 1878 occupied no. 133 Edgware Road, which served as a booksellers for the National Sunday School Union in 1927.[21] The National Lending Library for the Blind was in Queen's Road in the early 1920s.[22] There were musical societies for Bayswater in 1861 and Westbourne Park in 1875,[23] and Bayswater orchestral society was at Craven Terrace from c. 1896 until 1925 or later.[24]

A wide range of clubs, all with the prefix 'Kildare', was provided for Whiteley's staff. Earliest was the Kildare athletic club, founded in 1870, followed by the library, a volunteer corps, band, and dramatic

club by 1875; a rowing club was started in 1877, a musical union in 1885, and a choral society in 1896. Sports grounds were provided at Acton. Some 600 employees belonged to Whiteley's clubs by 1888, when their activities were brought together in the new Hatherley institute, with Whiteley as president.[25] The G.W.R. Co. had a literary society, apparently with its own rooms at Paddington station in 1859 and 1865 and with its address as no. 44 Eastbourne Terrace in 1902 and 1934.[26]

Paddington Waterways Society was founded soon after the Second World War and followed in 1957 by the Paddington Society, which later published a monthly newsletter.[27]

Three political clubs, which also acted as social centres, were founded in 1884: a Liberal club, with winter meetings at the Great Western hotel, was followed by the John Bright Working Men's club and by a Conservative club, which leased premises in Sheldon Street off Bishop's Road in order to continue the work of an older Conservative association.[28] By 1888 there were the North and South Paddington Liberal association in Porchester Road, Queen's Park Liberal club, the Whitmore Conservative club, and the John Bright Working Men's club all in Harrow Road, and Salisbury Working Men's Conservative club in Edgware Road.[29] Most late 19th-century political clubs moved or were re-formed within a very few years. Paddington Radical Working Men's club, as the John Bright club had been renamed by 1890, retained its institute at nos. 11 and 12 Paddington Green until 1952 or later.[30] The Cobden club and Working Men's institute opened at nos. 170 and 172 Kensal Road in 1880 and remained there, as a social centre with 430 members, in 1983.[31]

Beauchamp Lodge Settlement was founded in 1939 and later became a member of the British Association of Settlement and Social Action Centres. In 1985 it provided a wide range of social and educational services, mainly during the day but including a youth club and some classes for adults in the evenings. It was financed by Westminster council and private donations, supplemented by funds for individual projects from the G.L.C., I.L.E.A., and the government.[32]

The *Ratepayers' Journal for St. Pancras, Marylebone, and Paddington*, later the *Ratepayers' Journal and Local Management Gazette*, appeared monthly from 1854 to 1857 and was concerned mainly with parish government in St. Pancras and Marylebone.[33] The *Western and Suburban Intelligencer*,[34] soon

[6] *Bayswater Annual* (1885); Hutchings and Crowsley, *Paddington Dir.* (1872, 1882, 1884); *Kelly's Dir. Paddington* (1888 and later edns.).
[7] Below, churches.
[8] *The Times*, 9 Dec. 1895, 13a.
[9] M.L.R. 1875/8/16; Guildhall MS. 12556.
[10] Besant, *Lond. N. of Thames*, 152.
[11] *Official Year Bk. of Ch. of Eng.* (1886, 1892).
[12] *P.O. Dir. Lond.* (1900 and later edns.).
[13] Besant, *Lond. N. of Thames*, 151–2; Stanford, *Libr. Map of Lond.* (1891 edn.), sheet 5; below, educ.
[14] Guildhall MS. 12566.
[15] *P.O. Dir. Lond.* (1903, 1905); Bacon, *Atlas of Lond.* (1910).
[16] *P.O. Dir. Lond.* (1938); inf. from Sisters of the Ch., Richmond, Surr.
[17] *P.O. Dir. Lond.* (1884 and later edns.).
[18] *Western Chron. and Suburban Intelligencer*, 8 Oct. 1857.
[19] *Bayswater Chron.* 24 June 1865; Hutchings and Crowsley, *Paddington Dir.* (1872, 1875).
[20] Lambert, *Universal Provider*, 151.
[21] Hutchings and Crowsley, *Paddington Dir.* (1878); *P.O. Dir. Lond.* (1902, 1927).
[22] *Official Guide to Paddington* [1921, 1925].
[23] *Bayswater Chron.* 13 Feb. 1861; *Paddington, Kensington and Bayswater Chron.* 24 Apr. 1875.
[24] *Kelly's Dir. Paddington* (1896 and later edns.).
[25] Lambert, *Universal Provider*, 91, 150–1.
[26] Marylebone libr., P 135, cuttings; *Bayswater Chron.* 28 Nov. 1860; 6 May 1865; *P.O. Dir. Lond.* (1902, 1934).
[27] Paddington Soc. *Newsletter*, Dec. 1970.
[28] *Bayswater Annual* (1885).
[29] *Kelly's Dir. Paddington* (1888).
[30] Ibid. (1890 and later edns.); *P.O. Dir. Lond.* (1952).
[31] Inf. from sec.
[32] Inf. from dir.; below, educ.
[33] Bound copies in Marylebone libr.
[34] Rest of para. based on B.L. Newspaper Cat.; *Willing's Press Guide* (1980).

renamed the *Western Chronicle*, circulated in Paddington and neighbouring areas in 1857–8. The *Paddington News*, also known for a few months as the *Paddington Newsman*, was published from 1859 to 1861. The longest lived newspaper was the weekly *Paddington Times*, established in 1859; combined with the *Kilburn Times* in 1918, it was revived under its old title in 1973[35] by North West London Press of Newspaper House, Kilburn Lane. The *Bayswater Chronicle*, published from 1860, continued under various names until 1949, when, as the *West London Chronicle*, it was amalgamated with the *Indicator*, which had been founded *c.* 1870 for the west end of London; for a time during the 1920s and 1930s the *Indicator* came out daily.[36] Another long established newspaper was the *Paddington Mercury*, which appeared from 1881, also with slight variations of name, and in 1981 was owned by London & Westminster Newspapers. The *Paddington Weekly Register*, for house sales, was founded in 1893 and, after a second renaming, continued as the *Paddington Gazette and Weekly Register* from 1895 until 1939. The *Marylebone Record* appeared with that or similar titles, including that of the *St. Marylebone and Paddington Record*, from 1914 until 1971. The *Paddington News* was published from 1919, becoming the *Westminster and Paddington News* in 1963 and merging with the *Hackney Gazette* in 1975. Shorter lived newspapers, most of them weekly, included the *Paddington Advertiser* from 1861 to 1866, the monthly *Christian Messenger* from 1874 to 1875, the *Weekly Advertiser*, renamed the *Paddington Star*, from 1878 to 1880, the *West London Gazette* in 1882, the *Bayswater Fiction Press* from 1893 to 1895, the *Advertiser* from 1893 to 1909, and the *Paddington Echo* from 1948 to 1949. William Whiteley's unsuccessful publication of the *Westbourne Gazette and Belgravia Herald* in 1877 increased the hostility shown to him by the *Bayswater Chronicle*.[37]

MANORS AND OTHER ESTATES. The monks of Westminster claimed to have been granted a small farm at Paddington in 959 and to have held 2 hides there in 1042. Although the early charters were spurious,[38] Paddington, Knightsbridge, and Westbourne were probably part of the abbey's ancient endowment and among the 13½ hides at Westminster attributed to it in Domesday Book.[39] Paddington presumably formed a separate estate by 1135 × 1152 when, with Fanton (Essex) and Claygate (Surr.), it supported the almoner of Westminster.[40] Before 1185 the abbot bought from Richard of Paddington and his brother William the whole tenement which they held in Paddington of his church.[41] The manor

of *PADDINGTON*, so described *c.* 1266,[42] was treated with Knightsbridge as a single unit in a custumal of *c.* 1225.[43] Paddington, however, may have had its own courts or have been served by those for Westminster, whereas by the 14th century Knightsbridge formed a manor with Westbourne.[44] In 1647 and later Paddington was said to lie east of Westbourne stream, with a few outlying fields to the west.[45]

Paddington remained in the abbey's lordship until the Reformation. The almonry, to which the tenement of Richard and William of Paddington was assigned, later shared the issues with the abbey's new work, which took the bulk in 1535, and the Lady chapel.[46] After passing to the Crown the manor was granted in 1550 to the bishop of London,[47] whose successors held it until the Interregnum, when it was sold to Thomas Browne.[48] At the Restoration the bishop regained it and in 1868 his rights passed to the Ecclesiastical Commissioners.[49] His lands covered almost the entire eastern half of the parish, the exceptions being mainly around Paddington green. They also stretched across the Westbourne to include a field called Desboroughs north of Harrow Road, Upper and Lower Readings and other plots beyond Westbourne green, Hall field farther south reaching to Black Lion Lane, and separate fields abutting on the Uxbridge road.[50]

The manor was let at farm by 1422, when Edmund Bibbesworth was to pay a rent which had scarcely changed by 1514. Leases were made to Thomas Parnell, a London butcher, in 1489 for 21 years, to William Parnell in 1499 for 11 years, and to Thomas Kempe, sergeant of the refectory at Westminster, in 1514 for 40 years.[51] The lease had passed to Sir Edward, later Lord, North, by 1541, when the Crown acquired it from him. The Crown granted the lease to Sir Edward Baynton and in 1543, on Baynton's surrender, to Richard Reade, salter of London, whose term was extended for another 40 years in 1544.[52] Richard Reade died in 1550, when his beneficiaries included the children of the late John Browne, salter, who was probably his son-in-law.[53] Reade's widow Anne (d. 1558) was said to have conveyed her interest both to Robert Vaughan and, by will, to his brother-in-law Richard Browne, her grandson. Litigation arose after new leases were obtained from the bishop in 1595 on behalf of Matthew Smale, who, directly or through his mother Jane Parkinson, had already acquired Browne's interest, and in 1605 to Sir Fulk Greville, who asserted the right of Vaughan's assignee.[54] A lease for three lives was made in 1626 to Sir Rowland St. John (d. 1645), whose term expired with the death of his son Sir Oliver St. John, Bt., in 1662.[55]

35 Paddington Soc. *Newsletter*, Sept. 1974.
36 Ibid. Oct. 1969.
37 Lambert, *Universal Provider*, 92–3.
38 *Cart. Sax.* ed. Birch, iii, p. 265; F. E. Harmer, *A.-S. Writs* (1951), 338; *V.C.H. Mdx.* i. 107.
39 Harvey, *Westm. Abbey*, 45; *V.C.H. Mdx.* i. 122.
40 *Reg. Regum Anglo-Norm.* iii, no. 936.
41 Besant, *Lond. North of Thames*, 137; W.A.M. 16194.
42 *Customary of St. Peter's, Westm.* ed. E. M. Thompson (Henry Bradshaw Soc. 1904), 94.
43 Harvey, *Westm. Abbey*, 105; B.L. Add. Ch. 8139.
44 Below, local govt.
45 Guildhall MS. 10464A; Ch. Com., 'Map of 1742'; W.A.M. 12480.
46 Harvey, *Westm. Abbey*, 353; *Valor Eccl.* (Rec. Com.),

i. 413–14.
47 *Cal. Pat.* 1549–51, 171, 262.
48 Lysons, *Environs*, iii. 329; *Home Counties Mag.* i. 222.
49 Ch. Com., 'Paddington Estate 1895' (MS. notebook).
50 Ibid. 'Map of 1742'; 'Plan of 1790'; Guildhall Libr., boro. maps P1: Gutch, *Plan of Paddington* (1828, coloured to show estates).
51 Harvey, *Westm. Abbey*, 152, 158; W.A.M., Reg. Bk. i, ff. 39v.–40, 115–16; ii, ff. 36v., 62v.–64.
52 *L. & P. Hen. VIII*, xvi, pp. 245, 729; xix (1), pp. 644, 650; P.R.O., STAC 8/5/8.
53 P.R.O., PROB 11/33 (P.C.C. 27 Coode).
54 Ibid. PROB 11/41 (P.C.C. 48 Noodes); ibid. STAC 8/5/8; 8/74/17.
55 Guildhall MS. 10464A; G.E.C. *Baronetage*, iii. 68.

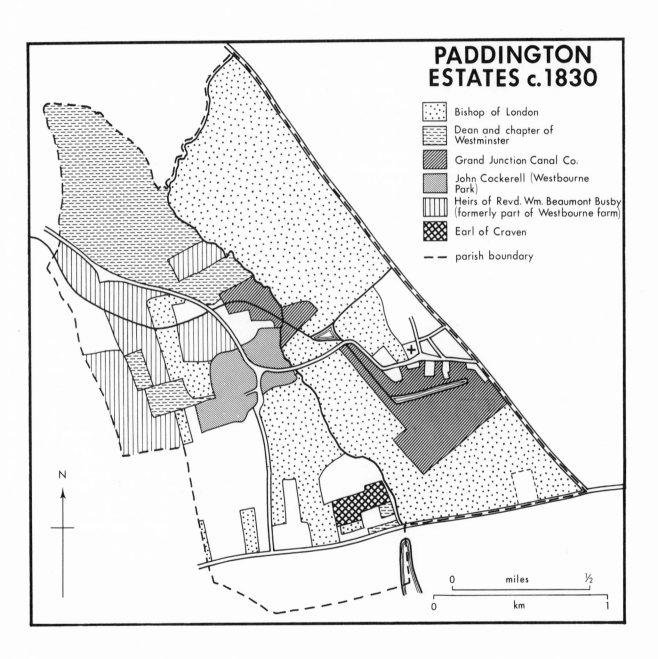

PADDINGTON ESTATES c.1830

- Bishop of London
- Dean and chapter of Westminster
- Grand Junction Canal Co.
- John Cockerell (Westbourne Park)
- Heirs of Revd. Wm. Beaumont Busby (formerly part of Westbourne farm)
- Earl of Craven
- – – parish boundary

N

| 0 | miles | ½ |

| 0 | km | 1 |

Bishop Gilbert Sheldon in 1662 made leases of the manor for three lives to the attorney-general Sir Geoffrey Palmer, Bt. After further transactions by the bishop's successor the manor was temporarily transferred back to Sheldon in 1668, when he was archbishop of Canterbury, and was leased by the bishop of London in 1678 to Sheldon's nephews Sir Joseph (d. 1681), a former lord mayor of London, and Daniel Sheldon (d. 1699).[56] On the death by 1721 of Daniel's son Gilbert the lease was renewed for Gilbert's sisters Judith and Mary.[57] Judith's son Paul Jodrell and Mary's son Sheldon Craddock in 1741 conveyed their freshly renewed term to Sir John Frederick, Bt. (d. 1755), of Hampton,[58] who was succeeded by his sons Sir John (d. 1757) and Sir Thomas (d. 1770).[59]

Sir Thomas Frederick's successors were his daughters Elizabeth and Selina, who in 1778 respectively married Sir John Morshead, Bt. (d. 1813) and Robert Thistlethwayte (d. 1802).[60] Both moieties were mortgaged in the 1780s, the lease having been vested in trustees.[61] In 1795 the bishop made a new lease to the trustees of the former lessees for 99 years, renewable after 50 years, in accordance with the recent Act to promote building on the bishop's estate.[62] Renewed by the bishop in 1845[63] and by the Ecclesiastical Commissioners from 1895, the lease was converted into one for 2,000 years under the Law of Property Act, 1925, and was surrendered by the trustees to the Church Commissioners in 1953.[64]

From 1795[65] the trustees of what came to be called the Paddington Estate paid modest sums for the traditional rent of the manor, for the curate's stipend, for compensation to the parish for waste lands,[66] and for the land tax; in return they took two thirds of the ground rents from new building, until in 1892 the Ecclesiastical Commissioners insisted that future ground rents should be divided equally. During the 19th century parts of the estate were subleased to the Grand Junction Canal Co.,[67] the Grand Junction Water Works Co., and the G.W.R. Co. Alienations included the sale of c. 7 a. for the purchase of the City of London's conduit system under an Act of 1812, smaller sales to redeem the land tax, and grants of land for new churches.[68] In 1985 the Church Commissioners still had c. 4,500 lettings in Paddington, mostly on the Hyde Park estate but including some which they hoped to sell in Maida Vale.[69]

The beneficiaries of the trust established in 1795[70] were Elizabeth Morshead (d. 1845), Selina Thistlethwayte (d. 1817), and their heirs. Their interests, affected by many family settlements, passed chiefly to the Thistlethwaytes. Selina's son Thomas Thistlethwayte of Southwick Park (Hants) was himself a trustee in 1845 and was entitled to seven eighths of the interests, estimated to be worth £430,000 as a capital sum, at his death in 1850.[71] In 1868 the rental of the Paddington Estate, including the third paid to the Ecclesiastical Commissioners, was £33,175.[72] Thomas Thistlethwayte's eldest son Thomas (d. 1900) and grandson Alexander Edward Thistlethwayte (d. 1915), of Southwick Park, between them held seven eighths in 1895, when, however, the trustees included Walter Morshead and the other beneficiaries· Elizabeth's grandson Sir Warwick Morshead, Bt. (d. 1905), of Tregaddick (Cornw.) and his wife. A. E. Thistlethwayte's successive heirs, his brothers Capt. Arthur (d. 1924) and Lt.-Col. Evelyn William Thistlethwayte (d. 1944) both acted as trustees, as did the latter's nephew and heir F. H. P. Borthwick-Norton (d. 1950).[73]

The building called the manor house may have been the parsonage house[74] and was presumably the one occupied by Matthew Smale,[75] where he allowed the Lord Chief Justice Sir John Popham to stay c. 1582.[76] Apparently it was always subleased after Sir Rowland St. John's time. In 1647 when Sir Rowland's 624-a. estate, consisting mainly of the demesne lands and Paddington wood, had been divided among 16 undertenants, a 'capital messuage of three bay of building' was held with 6 a. and a further 40 a. by James Hall. It abutted on the churchyard, itself bordered on the east by a 'great house' occupied with a 4-a. close and a further 90 a. by a London brewer, Alderman John Bide. Sir Rowland St. John had lived in Bide's house, formerly occupied by Edward North;[77] it may have been the larger and newer building, as 17th- and 18th-century leases of the manor always specified both the capital messuage and North's house.[78] The 'great house' may have been occupied by Arthur Blyth, the third largest ratepayer in 1670 and an overseer from 1681 to 1683.[79] St. John's great house on Paddington green, with a barn of five bays, was subleased with over 100 a. in 1697 to Sarah Blyth for 16 years and in 1709 to her son Charles for 21 years.[80] It was mortgaged by Charles, whom Gilbert Sheldon accused of non-payment of rent, and in 1714 by Ralph Hide, clothworker of London.[81] Probably it was the 'manor house' or 'old house' of Manor House farm, held in 1742 and 1751 by William Godfrey.[82]

In 1810 the trustees of St. Mary's church, appointed under Acts of 1778 and 1793,[83] were empowered to buy 2 a., including the manor house, in order to enlarge the churchyard which lay to the

[56] Guildhall MS. 12426; Beaven, *Aldermen*, ii. 99, 109; P.R.O., PROB 11/453 (P.C.C. 200 Pett).
[57] Guildhall MS. 12426.
[58] M.L.R. 1740/3/40; 1741/2/102.
[59] G.E.C. *Baronetage*, v. 57.
[60] Burke, *Land. Gent.* (1952), 1831–2, 1906–7.
[61] M.L.R. 1779/2/426–7; 1783/4/423; 1787/4/317–18, 5/296–7, 353; Guildhall MS. 10234/6, ff. 246–8.
[62] Guildhall MS. 10234/8, ff. 171–8; above, growth, bldg. after c. 1800.
[63] Guildhall MS. 10234/12, ff. 463–83.
[64] Ch. Com., deed 26 Mar. 1953.
[65] Para. based on Ch. Com., 'Paddington Estate 1895'.
[66] Below, econ.; churches.
[67] Below.
[68] 34 & 35 Vic. c. 5 (Private).
[69] Above, growth, Tyburnia; inf. from Chestertons.
[70] Para. based on 'Paddington Est. 1895'; Burke, *Land.*

Gent. (1952).
[71] *The Times*, 5 May 1852, 7b.
[72] Reeder, 'Capital Investment', 266.
[73] Ch. Com., Bldg. Agreements, vols. xiii–xv; *The Times*, 15 Mar. 1950, 2f.
[74] Robins, *Paddington*, 125–6.
[75] P.R.O., PROB 11/132 (P.C.C. 112 Meade).
[76] Ibid. STAC 8/5/8.
[77] Guildhall MS. 10464A.
[78] Ibid. 10464A, 12426. Presumably neither ho. was the one with only six hearths, occupied by Ralph Snow, a trustee of the Sheldons, in 1664: G.L.R.O., MR/TH/2, m. 30d.
[79] Marylebone libr., overseers' acct. bk. (1670–90).
[80] P.R.O., C 5/358/29.
[81] Ibid.; M.L.R. 1712/3/99; 1719/1/9.
[82] M.L.R. 1751/1/456; Church Com., 'Map of 1742'.
[83] Below, churches.

south.[84] Part of the purchase money was advanced by John Parton, the vestry clerk, who from 1811 held the house with 1 a. as security and kept separate accounts of the rents.[85] Repairs were needed in 1813, including iron bars to strengthen the first floor, which was 'much pressed outwards'. The house was leased for seven years in 1813, to the painter Joshua Cristall, and annually from 1820.[86] After serving as a girls' school, it was suggested as a parsonage and as a watch house before the vestry finally ordered demolition in 1824.[87] Only timber and ornamental trees were to be preserved in 1825, when the site was added to the churchyard.[88] In a novel about the mid 18th century the haunted Manor House was described by Charles Ollier, himself a vestryman in 1820, as a plain, square, red-brick building, in a walled garden with elm trees.[89]

Paddington *RECTORY* was always leased with the manor from 1489,[90] the rent being payable separately to the sacrist of Westminster in 1514[91] but included in the rent for the manor after the Reformation.[92] When subleased by Matthew Smale to John Chirme for eight years in 1591, the rectory estate included the churchyard, two tenements, two closes called Church fields, and a close called the Five Acres.[93] Smale later resumed the rectory and in 1604 compounded for an undertenant's tithes, for a term which was disputed.[94] Great Church field and Five Acres were held in 1644 by Elizabeth Kenwrick,[95] a widow who in 1647 lived in a house lately built by Edward Kenwrick. By 1647 the rectory had been subleased to John Lisle and consisted mainly of great and small tithes on all freehold land in the parish, of both Paddington and Westbourne manor, but not on the demesne lands the tithes of which had been demised to particular tenants.[96] John Lisle or a namesake was later churchwarden and, in 1670, the largest ratepayer.[97] Property in Paddington, previously leased to George Starkey, was released in 1712 by Thomas Lisle of Lambeth (Surr.), son of Thomas Lisle of Paddington (d. 1678).[98] In 1742 the rectory lands, which did not include Great or Little Church fields, amounted to c. 30 a., mostly at Westbourne green.[99] A 'new house' called Chirme's house at Westbourne green was mortgaged in 1714 by George Starkey, the house itself being in the possession of the Huguenot marquise de Gouvernet (d. 1722).[1] Mrs. Elizabeth Starkey paid the highest rates in the parish from 1721 to 1723 and Thomas Starkey was

also a substantial ratepayer from 1725 until 1745.[2] All the tithes were commuted in 1844 for a rent charge of £154 11s. 5d., payable to the trustees of the Paddington Estate.[3] Chirme's house had been divided by 1758, when it was sold by John Starkey to William Pickering.[4] In 1771 it was sold, with other property, by Pickering's executors to Jukes Coulson and by 1801 it had been demolished, the site forming part of the grounds of Coulson's Westbourne Place.[5]

Lands in the west part of the parish belonged in the Middle Ages to Westminster abbey's manor of *KNIGHTSBRIDGE WITH WESTBOURNE*, most of which lay in Westminster. Although Westbourne tenants remained subject to courts at Knightsbridge,[6] lands in Westbourne were not named in late 15th-century leases of Knightsbridge manor.[7] The lordship of Knightsbridge with Westbourne was granted in 1542 to the short-lived see of Westminster, from which it passed to the dean and chapter of the collegiate church.[8] The manor was sold by parliamentary commissioners in 1650 to Thomas Evans, who in 1652 conveyed it to Sir George Stonhouse, beneficial lessee of the Westbourne estate described below, but it reverted to Westminster at the Restoration.[9] In 1821 Joseph Neeld (d. 1856), later of Grittleton Hall near Chippenham (Wilts.),[10] obtained a lease of Westminster's manorial rights, in order to inclose all the remaining waste. He also obtained a lease of the Westbourne estate, for three lives, in 1832 and again in 1850.[11] Neeld's proposals for building leases were treated with caution by the dean and chapter, who felt that the lessees of the bishop of London's estate had been treated too favourably. Arbitrators, appointed in 1859, in 1862 allotted 74 a. in a single block to Westminster and the same acreage in two blocks to trustees for Joseph's brother Sir John Neeld, Bt., whose lands were thereupon enfranchised and soon afterwards built over.[12]

The estate known in the 19th century as the manor of *WESTBOURNE* or *WESTBOURNE GREEN*[13] formed part of the abbey's lands in the parish. Abbot Walter of Wenlock (d. 1307) was found in 1316 to have acquired property without licence in Knightsbridge, Paddington, Westbourne, and Eye, the Westbourne lands totalling 26 a. and including 2 a. received from Maud Arnold.[14] By the time of Henry VIII the warden of the abbey's new work had been assigned much land in Westbourne,

[84] 50 Geo. III, c. 44 (Local and Personal); Robins, *Paddington*, 89; M.L.R. 1811/5/29 (plan).
[85] M.L.R. 1811/5/30; Vestry mins. 11 Aug. 1820; accts. by Parton at back of vestry min. bk. (1812–20).
[86] Vestry mins. 22 Sept., 2 Nov. 1813; 11 Aug., 22 Sept. 1820; 30 Mar. 1821; *D.N.B.*; McDonald, 'Paddington', cap. 6.
[87] Marylebone libr., Westm. cuttings L. 135; select vestry mins. 10 Aug., 14 Sept. 1824.
[88] Robins, *Paddington*, 142; sel. vestry mins. 1, 29 Mar. 1825.
[89] C. Ollier, *Ferrers*, i (1842), 195–8; vestry mins. 4 Apr. 1820.
[90] W.A.M., Reg. Bk. i, ff. 39v.–40.
[91] W.A.M. 16200; *Valor Eccl.* (Rec. Com.), i. 413.
[92] e.g. Guildhall MS. 12426.
[93] P.R.O., STAC 8/5/8.
[94] P.R.O., C 2/Jas. I/T 7/40.
[95] P.R.O., C 8/59/34.
[96] Guildhall MS. 10464A.
[97] Chwdns. acct. bk. (1656–1736); overseers' acct. bk. (1670–90).

[98] M.L.R. 1712/3/80; P.R.O., PROB 11/358 (P.C.C. 129 Reeve).
[99] Church Com., 'Map of 1742'.
[1] M.L.R. 1714/6/14; Marylebone libr., ch. and poor rates bk. (1721–74) (unpag.); D. C. Agnew, *Prot. Exiles from France*, ii (1886), 194.
[2] Ch. and poor rates bk. (1721–74).
[3] G.L.R.O., TA/10.
[4] M.L.R. 1758/1/423; 1759/1/66–7.
[5] Ibid. 1771/1/476; below.
[6] Below, local govt.
[7] e.g. W.A.M., Reg. Bk. i, ff. 20, 34.
[8] *L. & P. Hen. VIII*, xvii, p. 392; W.A.M., Reg. Bk. iii, f. 144v.
[9] W.A.M. 16322–3; below, local govt.
[10] Burke, *Peerage, Baronetage, and Knightage* (1890). 1017.
[11] W.A.M., Reg. Bk. lxi, f. 342; box RCO 34; M.L.R. 1851/4/91–3 (inc. plans).
[12] W.A.M., Reg. Bk. lxi, f. 342; box RCO 34.
[13] W.A.M., box RCO 34.
[14] Robins, *Paddington*, 23; W.A.M. 16247.

including Arnold's and William's fields north of Harrow Road and Knight's field to the south.[15] Together with all the lands in Paddington formerly devoted to the Lady chapel, they were leased for 99 years in 1542 to Sir Edward North.[16] Thereafter the estate consisted mainly of the three fields in Westbourne, 6 a. farther south in the common fields near the Uxbridge road, and five closes west of Arnold's field, formerly of St. Mary's chapel and known by 1669 as Ashgroves. They were leased in 1631 for three lives to George Stonhouse,[17] who in 1632 succeeded as Sir George Stonhouse, Bt., of Radley (Berks.).[18] Sir George (d. 1675) settled the lease on his third son James,[19] for whom and for whose heirs it was repeatedly renewed for lives. In 1725 the lessee was James's son Richard Stonhouse (d. 1776) of Tubney (Berks.) and in 1742 Richard's son James (d. 1795),[20] physician and divine, who later inherited the baronetcy,[21] and in 1796 the Revd. Timothy Stonhouse Vigor and George Vansittart were trustees for Sir James Stonhouse's son Sir Thomas (d. 1810). Their interest was conveyed in 1805 to the engineer John Braithwaite (d. 1818), who obtained a new lease in 1811.[22]

The Stonhouses probably always divided and subleased their estate: Ashgroves and William's field were subleased in 1634 and Ashgrove,[23] Ash field, and Knight's field were part of the large Westbourne Green farm in 1776.[24] No house was recorded in leases by Westminster until the early 19th century, when Westbourne Manor House stood north-east of Harrow Road and north of the Grand Junction canal, with William's field to the north-east.[25] There was, however, a building on or near that site by 1746.[26] John Braithwaite's residence in 1814, with two storeys and a steeply pitched roof, was perhaps of c. 1700; the main front was of five bays, with a single-storeyed extension of three bays, beyond which it was proposed to build new stables and offices. Extensive improvements were reported in 1815, including the inclosure and planting of ground between the house and Harrow Road and probably a tree-lined walk which ran from the rear alongside William's field to the Westbourne.[27] Braithwaite died at Westbourne Manor House, which his son John (1797–1870), also a noted engineer,[28] retained until c. 1840. Later tenants were William Charles Carbonell, a wine merchant, who held it with 14 a. in 1846, and from 1854 John, afterwards Sir John, Humphreys. The house probably survived in 1866 but had been replaced by the western end of Sutherland Avenue in 1867.[29]

The estate known c. 1800 as *WESTBOURNE*

PLACE[30] and later as *WESTBOURNE PARK*[31] probably represented lands in Westbourne which had been left to Westminster abbey by Margaret Beaufort, countess of Richmond (d. 1509).[32] Her gift consisted of the Kensington manor of Notting Barns, which she had bought from feoffees who included Sir Reginald Bray and to which the Westbourne lands may have been added as the result of a separate purchase. Perhaps they were Stonyland and Herryland in Westbourne, sold to Bray in 1492 by Thomas and Robert Stillington, cousins and heirs of the Lord Chancellor Robert Stillington, bishop of Bath and Wells (d. 1491).[33] Westminster abbey leased lands in Westbourne and Chelsea detached, with Notting Barns manor, to Alderman Robert Fenrother, a goldsmith, who by will of 1524[34] left them to his son-in-law Henry White, whose son Robert in 1543 was forced to exchange them with the Crown. Robert White's house and lands at Westbourne had been subleased to Thomas Dolte[35] and in 1554 were occupied by William Dolte. In that year, having been separated from Notting Barns which had gone to Sir William Paulet, the reversions were granted in fee to the queen's doctor Thomas Hughes.[36]

Alderman Benedict Barnham died in 1598, seised of a house called Westbourne and 70 a. in Paddington, Kensington, and Chelsea detached, held of the Crown by $\frac{1}{40}$ knight's fee, and a further 66 a. there, of unknown tenure, including 40 a. occupied by William Lisle.[37] Of Barnham's five daughters Alice married Francis Bacon, Viscount St. Alban, and in 1626 John, later Sir John, Underhill, and Bridget, who married Sir William Soame of Thurlow (Suff.).[38] Westbourne farm in Paddington, Kensington, and Chelsea was the subject of a recovery executed by the Underhills on their marriage and was among the lands to which Underhill renounced all claim, in return for £400 a year, on separating from his wife in 1639.[39] Alice (d. 1650) apparently settled her interest on her nephew and executor Stephen Soame, who in his will proved in 1658 stated that she had left him a moiety. The lands may have been sold to meet bequests[40] but in 1673 were named in a claim by Underhill against Stephen's son William Soame (later a baronet, d. 1686) for the full payment of his annuity.[41] Their ownership in the late 17th century is obscure.

Elizabeth, widow of Thomas Allam of Westbourne green, and her children Jane and Thomas Allam mortgaged a capital messuage with 4 a. in 1715 to William Gilbert, by which time it had been divided from a brick house belonging to Catherine Whitcomb

[15] W.A.M. 16321.
[16] Ibid. Reg. Bk. iii, f. 144v.
[17] Ibid. xiv, ff. 131–2; xix, ff. 5v.–7.
[18] G.E.C. *Baronetage*, ii. 37.
[19] P.R.O., C 7/528/31.
[20] W.A.M., Reg. Bk. xx, ff. 35v.–37; xxx, f. 147; xxxii, f. 109; xxxvii, f. 141v.
[21] *D.N.B.*; G.E.C. *Baronetage*, ii. 38.
[22] W.A.M., Reg. Bk. liii, ff. 218–19; lviii, f. 43; *D.N.B.*; M.L.R. 1812/3/145–7.
[23] P.R.O., C 8/290/119.
[24] W.A.M. 16339.
[25] W.A.M., box RCO 34; Gutch, *Plan of Paddington* (1828).
[26] Rocque, *Map of Lond.* (1741–5), sheet 11.
[27] W.A.M., box RCO 34 (inc. sketch, 1814); Gutch, *Plan of Paddington* (1828); *Home Counties Mag.* ii, illus. facing p. 277.

[28] *D.N.B.*
[29] *Home Counties Mag.* ii. 276–7; G.L.R.O., TA/10; N. & Q. 8th ser. vi. 42; Lucas, *Plan of Paddington* (1869).
[30] Lysons, *Environs*, iii. 330; *Ambulator* (1807).
[31] Gutch, *Plan of Paddington* (1828).
[32] Para. based on F. M. Gladstone, *Notting Hill in Bygone Days* (1969), 9–16.
[33] W.A.M. 16181–2.
[34] *Cal. Wills in Ct. of Husting*, ii (2), 630.
[35] P.R.O., SC 6/Hen. VIII/2105.
[36] *Cal. Pat.* 1553–4, 487–8.
[37] *Inq. p.m. Lond.* iii (Brit. Rec. Soc. 1908), 259–62.
[38] *Complete Peerage*, xi. 284–5; *Visit. Lond.* (Harl. Soc. xvii), 251.
[39] P.R.O., C 10/168/128; C 10/174/123.
[40] Ibid. PROB 11/213 (P.C.C. 123 Pembroke); PROB 11/287 (P.C.C. 52 Pell).
[41] Ibid. C 10/168/128; G.E.C. *Baronetage*, iv. 136.

and her three half-sisters, the daughters of John Scudamore.[42] Jane Allam in 1730 conveyed her interest to Reginald Heber of the Middle Temple,[43] who had been resident from 1725[44] and whose son Reginald, with William Gilbert's brother Edward, in 1742 conveyed the house in trust for the architect Isaac Ware (d. 1766). Ware sold it in 1764 to Sir William Yorke, Bt.,[45] who in turn sold it in 1768 to Jukes Coulson, a London anchorsmith.[46] In 1771 Coulson also bought, from the son-in-law and daughter of William Pickering, Chirme's house at Westbourne green, with the nearby brick house called Mr. Scudamore's, which Pickering had bought from John Ewens in 1759 and which had been allotted in 1731 to Catherine Whitcomb by her half-sisters.[47] Westbourne Place was the seat of Coulson's widow in 1795 and was sold by his nephew and namesake in 1801 to the architect Samuel Pepys Cockerell (1753–1827), who died there.[48] Samuel's eldest son John held a compact estate west of the Westbourne stream, on either side of Harrow Road, in 1828.[49] As Westbourne Park or House the main residence was leased from c. 1829 to 1837 to Gen. Lord Hill (1772–1842), while John Cockerell lived at a smaller house to the east, Little Westbourne. Sir Charles Rushout Cockerell, Bt., Samuel's nephew, conveyed his interest in the estate in 1844 to John Pink, who already had started to build there.[50]

Isaac Ware rebuilt Westbourne Place and Coulson presumably demolished Chirme's and Scudamore's houses, both of which had gone by 1801. Allegedly incorporating materials from Lord Chesterfield's former London residence,[51] Ware's seat had a stuccoed entrance front of nine bays; three, between canted bows, rose above the cornice to form a third, attic, storey with a central pediment.[52] Coulson enlarged the house and laid out park-like grounds, to which Cockerell added from the waste. The pleasant situation was widely admired,[53] and during Lord Hill's tenancy visitors included William IV, Queen Adelaide, and the duke of Wellington. The house partially survived, a little south of the railway, in 1846 but its site had been covered by nos. 6–18 Westbourne Park Villas by 1847.[54]

Half of a large estate called *WESTBURY* or *WESTBOURNE FARM*, in Paddington, Kensington, and Chelsea detached, was held in 1724 by Thomas Folkes of Great Barton (Suff.), a lawyer.[55]

Then or lately occupied by Mrs. Starkey, the moiety was settled on Folkes's only child Elizabeth (d. 1741),[56] who married the Speaker Sir Thomas Hanmer, Bt. (1677–1746), but eloped with Thomas Hervey (d. 1775). Elizabeth left Hervey her moiety of Westbourne farm,[57] which was included in marriage settlements for Capt. Thomas Hervey in 1774 and for his son William of Bodvel (Caern.) in 1802.[58] Folkes may have held the other moiety also, since in 1759 William and Henry Folkes conveyed it to Tomlinson Busby of Gray's Inn.[59] Lt.-Col. Tomlinson Busby secured a rent charge on Westbourne farm in 1803 and he and William Hervey jointly sold some land to S. P. Cockerell and another piece to John White, the tenants, in 1810.[60] Partition of the estate was regulated by an Act of 1816 for the Revd. William Beaumont Busby, dean of Rochester (d. 1820), and William Hervey.[61] Some 10 a. with a house east of Westbourne Park were sold by Hervey in 1817 to William Penney, varnish maker.[62] Busby's heirs retained a substantial estate in 1828, west of the village and south of Harrow Road.[63]

In the 18th century the farmhouse of Westbourne farm was divided. In 1803 it had been occupied by Jacob Simmons, tenant of Hervey's moiety, and by the marquess of Buckingham,[64] who had had a country retreat there in 1792.[65] From 1805 until 1817 the actress Sarah Siddons (1755–1831) also had a retreat at Westbourne Farm, described by her husband William as 'a thing so pretty and so small', where she received several famous visitors.[66] It was later called Desborough Cottage and finally Desborough House,[67] taking its name not from the Westbourne farm estate but from a neighbouring meadow called Derborough in 1647 and Desboroughs in 1742, leased by the bishop as part of the demesne of Paddington manor.[68] A sketch by the actor Charles James Mathews, who lived there with his wife Mme. Vestris from 1845 until c. 1849, showed a building with three gables facing Harrow Road. In 1856 it survived, south of the canal, but by 1861 it had been replaced by Cirencester and Woodchester streets. A few yards to the south Desborough Lodge, recently completed by Sarah Siddons's brother Charles Kemble, who soon moved nearer Paddington green,[69] was advertised with 4 a. in 1813.[70] Occupied with nearly 2 a. in 1846 by James Oliver,[71] it made way for Desborough Mews between 1855 and 1861.[72]

William Craven, Lord (later earl of) Craven (d.

[42] M.L.R. 1715/6/29; 1731/3/143.
[43] Ibid. 1730/5/25; *Middle Temple Adm. Reg. 1501–1781*, i. 273, 309.
[44] Ch. and poor rates bk. (1721–74).
[45] M.L.R. 1742/4/286–8; Colvin, *Brit. Architects*, 865; *D.N.B.*; G.E.C. *Baronetage*, v. 367.
[46] M.L.R. 1768/4/173; *Ambulator* (1792).
[47] M.L.R. 1731/3/143; 1759/2/108; 1771/1/476.
[48] Lysons, *Environs*, iii. 330; M.L.R. 1801/2/67; *D.N.B.*; Colvin, *Brit. Architects*, 227.
[49] Guildhall Libr., boro. maps P1: Gutch, *Plan of Paddington* (1828, coloured to show estates).
[50] *Home Counties Mag.* ii. 125–6, 280; *D.N.B.*; M.L.R. 1845/5/698.
[51] Lysons, *Environs*, ii. 330; Colvin, *Brit. Architects*, 865; M.L.R. 1801/2/67.
[52] Grangerized copy of Lysons, *Environs*, iii (2), at pp. 330–1; above, plate 32. Plan by C. R. Cockerell, probably with 19th-cent. additions, in *Archit. Hist.* xiv, fig. 14b.
[53] Lysons, *Environs*, iii. 330; *Ambulator* (1807); *Home Counties Mag.* ii. 123.
[54] *Home Counties Mag.* ii. 123–7, 279.
[55] M.L.R. 1724/1/438–9; W. A. Copinger, *Manors of*

Suff. vi. 252.
[56] M.L.R. 1724/1/438–9; 1733/5/67.
[57] *D.N.B.*; *Hist. Parl., Commons*, 1715–54, ii. 135.
[58] M.L.R. 1774/3/457; 1802/1/504.
[59] Ibid. 1759/2/469–70.
[60] Ibid. 1803/6/415; 1810/6/613, 736.
[61] 56 Geo. III, c. 9 (Private Act); Le Neve, *Fasti, 1541–1857, Rochester*, 57.
[62] M.L.R. 1817/4/601.
[63] Guildhall libr., boro. maps P1: Gutch, *Plan of Paddington* (1828, coloured to show estates).
[64] M.L.R. 1803/6/415.
[65] *Ambulator* (1792).
[66] *Home Counties Mag.* ii. 190, 197; R. Manvell, *Sarah Siddons* (1970), 289, 338; *D.N.B.*
[67] *Home Counties Mag.* ii. 190, 270, 273.
[68] Guildhall MS. 10464A; Ch. Com., 'Map of 1742'.
[69] *Home Counties Mag.* ii. 190, 269–74, 279; Lucas, *Plan of Paddington* (1861).
[70] Marylebone libr., P 132.2, cuttings.
[71] G.L.R.O., TA/10.
[72] *Home Counties Mag.* ii. 279; Lucas, *Plan of Paddington* (1855, 1861).

1697), was a modest ratepayer in Paddington from 1670 to 1672.[73] In 1671 he rented land near Marshall Street, Westminster, to which he later added and which he settled in trust in 1687 for a pest house and burial ground to serve the parishes of St. Clement Danes, St. Martin-in-the-Fields, St. James, and St. Paul, Covent Garden.[74] The spread of building nearby impelled William, Lord Craven (d. 1739), in 1733 to buy two houses at Bayswater, forming an outlying parcel of Tyburn manor, with 6 a. and a further 3 a. in the common fields of Westbourne, from Jane, widow of Thomas Upton, and her son John Davis Upton.[75] Thomas Upton had bought the property in 1725 from Robert Pollard.[76] The pest house was moved there under an Act of 1734[77] and existed as a long building with several enclosures, amid fields and well back from the Uxbridge road, in 1746.[78] Presumably it was no longer used as a pest house in 1795, when the *CRAVEN* estate was 'very pleasantly situated' on a slight eminence known as Craven Hill.[79] In 1811 Robert Shirley, Earl Ferrers (d. 1827), granted a lease of no. 3 Craven Hill,[80] presumably one of a terrace of 6 houses, varying in size, which in 1829 stood on the site of the pest house, east of a detached house and along the north side of a lane called Craven Hill. The estate then formed a rough rectangle, bisected by the lane which ran from behind Porchester Road (later Terrace) eastward almost to the Westbourne stream.[81] The vestry was told in 1833 that an outbreak of plague, rather than cholera, would be needed before the land could be claimed for charitable purposes.[82] Detached and terraced houses were built along both sides of Craven Hill, and in mews to the north, between 1840 and 1854. Leases were granted by William, earl of Craven (d. 1866) to several builders,[83] including Charles Claudius Cook for no. 23 in 1840,[84] and James Ponsford.[85]

The *GRAND JUNCTION CANAL CO.*, whose negotiations were exempted from the restrictions of the bishop's building Act of 1795,[86] in 1798 took a lease until 1894 of *c.* 48 a. between Westbourne green and Edgware Road. The land consisted mainly of a strip along the canal but from North Wharf Road by the basin it stretched southward to the intended Grand Junction Street,[87] where 8 a. were subleased under an Act of 1812 to the new Grand Junction Waterworks Co. for a peppercorn rent.[88] The canal company, represented on the select vestry from 1825, shared the building up of Grand Junction Street with the bishop and his lessees.[89] More

lands were acquired from the Paddington Estate, including 14 a. of Desboroughs, in 1825, when some parcels were exchanged.[90] The company had 81 a. in 1845[91] and was granted a renewal of its lease for 99 years in 1846.[92] In the late 19th century a third of all its income came from rents from property in Paddington.[93]

A new term was secured in 1899 and converted to 2,000 years under the Law of Property Act, 1922.[94] Having purchased the Grand Union Canal Co. in 1894,[95] the Grand Junction Canal Co. with effect from 1929 transferred all its canal undertakings to the Regent's Canal and Dock Co., which was reconstituted as the Grand Union Canal Co.[96] Subleases were made to the new canal company of extensive property including most of North and South wharves, canalside sites in Harrow Road between Bishop's Road and Harrow Road bridges, and Amberley wharves.[97] The Grand Union Canal Co.'s title passed under the Transport Act, 1947, to the British Transport Commission and under the Transport Act, 1963, to the British Waterways Board. The freehold nos. 431 to 523A (odd) Harrow Road, along the canal, were sold in 1937 to the Artizans' and General Dwellings Co., which owned the neighbouring Queen's Park estate, houses farther east in Harrow Road were sold in 1966 to the G.L.C. for the Western Avenue extension, and part of Amberley wharves was also sold in 1969 to the G.L.C., whose interest passed in 1980 to Westminster council. In 1983 the British Waterways Board had agreed to sell *c.* 4 a. to the Department of Health and Social Security for an extension to St. Mary's hospital. The sale was to include nos. 6–16 South Wharf Road and access over the canal to North Wharf Road, leaving the British Waterways Board with *c.* 11 a. around the east end and along the north side of the basin, together with an option to buy the former Lock hospital in Harrow Road.

Land and buildings not used for the canal undertaking remained after 1929 with the renamed Grand Junction Co., which functioned as a property company.[98] While retaining its own name, it was taken over in 1972 by the Amalgamated Investment and Property Co., which went into liquidation in 1976.[99]

The Grand Junction Co.'s extensive Paddington holdings were reduced by sales, including those of houses in Shirland Road, Formosa Street, Amberley Road, and Abourne Street in 1956 and by the L.C.C.'s compulsory purchase in 1960 of property

[73] Overseers' acct. bk. (1670–90).
[74] *Survey of Lond.* xxxi. 196.
[75] M.L.R. 1733/2/388; 1735/2/17–19.
[76] Ibid. 1725/4/6; above, growth, Bayswater. For the surrounding fields, see 'Surv. of Upton Fm. by Wm. Gardner, 1729 (map in Marylebone libr.).
[77] 7 Geo. II, c. 11 (Private Act).
[78] Rocque, *Map of Lond.* (1741–5), sheet 11.
[79] Lysons, *Environs*, iii. 331.
[80] M.L.R. 1811/6/283.
[81] Guildhall libr., boro. maps P1: Gutch, *Plan of Paddington* (1828, coloured to show estates); Westm. libr., Acc. 1307 (plans of Craven est. by Thos. Finden, 1829).
[82] Marylebone libr., McDonald, *Short Hist. Paddington*, no. 33 (Craven Est.), p. 79.
[83] M.L.R. *passim*.
[84] Ibid. 1845/3/365.
[85] Ibid. 1849/10/103–5; 1850/8/601–4; 1851/12/652–4.
[86] 35 Geo. III, c. 83 (Private Act); Robins, *Paddington*, 83.

[87] Guildhall MS. 12601 (lease of 1798, with plan).
[88] Robins, *Paddington*, 90–1.
[89] 5 Geo. IV, c. 126 (Local and Personal); above, communications; below, local govt.
[90] Guildhall MS. 12601 (leases of 1825 and 1846, with plans showing surrenders and acquisitions); Guildhall libr., boro. maps P1: Gutch, *Plan of Paddington* (1828, coloured to show estates).
[91] G.L.R.O., TA/10 (supplementary award).
[92] Guildhall MS. 12601.
[93] *Jnl. Transport Hist.* ii. 85.
[94] Following 2 paras. based on inf. from Estate Office (South East), British Waterways Bd.
[95] *Brit. Transport Com. Historical Rec.* (List & Index Soc. cxlii, 139).
[96] 18 & 19 Geo. V, c. 98 (Local and Personal).
[97] Plan in bound copy of agreement, 1928, *penes* Brit. Waterways Bd.
[98] 20 & 21 Geo. V, c. 22 (Local and Personal).
[99] Inf. from Mr. A. J. Barrett, liquidator.

in North Wharf Road and between Delamere Terrace, Chichester Road, Westbourne Square, and Lord Hill's Road.[1] More houses in Formosa Street and Warwick Avenue, still held in 1965, had been sold by 1973.[2] The company nonetheless took leases of some of the British Waterways Board's premises for rebuilding, including land in Irongate Wharf (later Harbet) Road from 1970 and in North Wharf Road from 1971. In 1973 the Grand Junction Co.'s Paddington estate was mainly freehold and lay north of the canal basin or in blocks from Praed Street across St. Michael's and Star streets to Sussex Gardens, with an estimated capital value of £9,727,950, half that of all its properties. Major assets included new factories at nos. 55–6 North Wharf Road, on land leased from the British Waterways Board, the new London Metropole hotel, freehold but with access across leasehold ground in Harbet Road, the flats of Siddons House, at the corner of Harrow and Harbet roads, and of Cambridge Court, with shops beneath, in Edgware Road, and most of the houses which had been converted into hotels along the north side of Sussex Gardens.[3] The estate had been broken up and sold by 1984,[4] when the London Metropole was owned by Lonrho.[5]

ECONOMIC HISTORY. AGRICULTURE. Paddington, with Knightsbridge and Westbourne, was probably included in the 13½ hides in the vill of Westminster which were attributed to St. Peter's abbey in Domesday Book.[6] The manor was not subinfeudated, and was still in the hands of a monk warden in Stephen's reign.[7] A custumal of c. 1225 treated Knightsbridge and Paddington together, listing 29 villein holdings and one holding of both free and customary land; free holdings, known to have existed, were not recorded. All but one of the 30 customary tenants held ½ virgate (probably 7 a.) or more; thirteen holdings were of up to 10 a., seventeen were of between 10¼ and 20 a. Services owed were manuring, hoeing, ploughing, harrowing, mowing, and carting hay.[8] Hoeing, ploughing, reaping, and carting services were recorded in Knightsbridge and Paddington in 1316.[9]

In the early 14th century the Paddington demesne, separated from Knightsbridge but including Paddington rectory, comprised 155 a. of arable, 10 a. of meadow, and no pasture. By that time there was no customary land. The demesne was leased out with the rectory from the early 15th century, the rent in 1514 being slightly less than it had been in 1422–3.[10] In 1647 the bishop of London's lands in Paddington

were estimated at 641 a.,[11] slightly more than half of the parish, consisting of 12 houses, 20½ a. of arable, 576½ a. of meadow or pasture, and 44 a. of woodland. The manor had been leased to Sir Rowland St. John and the lands subleased to 15 tenants, the most substantial being William Kenwrick with 117 a. and Mrs. Kenwrick with 60 a., Alderman Bide with 94 a., Mrs. Wheatley with 90 a., and William Browncar with 54 a.[12] In 1742, when the bishop's estate was leased to Sir John Frederick, it was estimated at 612 a. in 12 holdings, besides 20 a. divided into 9 lots in the common fields. The chief tenants were William Godfrey with c. 127 a., John Pruce and John Baker jointly with c. 123 a., Bartholomew Wetherall with 94 a., and John Geayes with c. 73 a. and Martin Geayes with c. 40 a.[13]

Early field names included Hundeshalle[14] from the early 14th century, and South field,[15] the Downe (later Downes), Westbourne field, the Half Hide, and the Westland in 1360.[16] North field, South field, Bush field, and Oxleas were mentioned in 1489 and Bridge field in 1530.[17] Few medieval names were used after the 16th century, presumably because of subdivision, although 4 a. were called Little Hounshill in 1647[18] and Bridge field survived in the 18th century. The Paddington Estate had c. 70 fields in 1742, many of them upper or lower portions of older areas; the largest was nearly 25 a. comprising one of three divisions of Pond field, abutting Edgware Road south of Paddington wood. The common field, a mere 20 a. beside the Uxbridge road between the Westbourne and Black Lion Lane in 1742, had disappeared by 1790.[19] Westbourne manor had c. 30 fields in 1790. They were of similar size to those of Paddington manor, the largest being Great Marylands and Oak Tree field, each of 27 a. in the northwest corner of the parish.[20] Great Marylands was presumably so named because it had been assigned to the upkeep of St. Mary's chapel in Westminster abbey; the nearby Arnold's field in Henry VIII's reign belonged to the warden of the abbey's new work.[21] The 18th-century fields of both Paddington and Westbourne manors survived until building spread over them from the south and east.[22]

Encroachments on the commons of Westbourne manor were presented from 1566. Inhabitants of Kensington were not to seek pasture in Westbourne in 1584 and heavy fines were ordered for unlicensed inclosures in 1616.[23] Encroachments on the waste of Paddington manor in 1647 amounted to only two tenements, one of them on Paddington green, in addition to two small gardens occupied by Mrs. Kenwrick.[24] Several petty infringements of the waste

---

[1] Grand Junction Co. min. bk. vi, ff. 37v., 49v., 54, 56, 76; ibid. vii, f. 6v. In 1984 the min. bks. 1929–75 and valuations (below) were held by the liquidators Deloitte, Haskins & Sells.

[2] 'Grand Junction Revaluation, 1965' (TS. photocopy).

[3] 'Grand Junction Co., Valuation 1973' (TS. photocopies, with details of properties).

[4] Inf. from liquidator.

[5] Inf. from hotel manager.

[6] Harvey, *Westm. Abbey*, 353; *V.C.H. Mdx.* i. 122.

[7] Harvey, *Westm. Abbey*, 78, 353; *Reg. Regum Anglo-Norm.* iii, no. 936.

[8] Harvey, *Westm. Abbey*, 104–5, 205, 433–5; B.L. Add. Ch. 8139.

[9] Robins, *Paddington*, 23.

[10] Harvey, *Westm. Abbey*, 152, 158, 428, 430.

[11] Revised figure in third parliamentary survey, 1647,

correcting slightly earlier estimate: Guildhall MS. 10464A.

[12] Ibid.

[13] Ch. Com., 'Map of 1742'.

[14] e.g. W.A.M. 16169, 16175–6.

[15] W.A.M. 27223B.

[16] W.A.M. 16446.

[17] W.A.M., Reg. Bk. i, ff. 39v.–40; ii, f. 264.

[18] Guildhall MS. 10464A.

[19] Ch. Com., 'Map of 1742'; ibid. 'Plan of 1790'.

[20] Ibid. 'Plan of 1790'.

[21] Harvey, *Westm. Abbey*, 353; W.A.M. 16321.

[22] Many of the fields are shown, with the lines of projected roads superimposed, on Gutch, *Plan of Paddington* (1828, 1840).

[23] W.A.M. 16452–3.

[24] Guildhall MS. 10464A.

were presented in 1678[25] and admissions to wastehold parcels of both manors took place throughout the 18th century.[26] Often inclosures were made by the occupants of large houses around the greens, such as Denis Chirac and Isaac Ware.[27] In 1801 the vestry agreed to inclosures by S. P. Cockerell for £3 an acre, apparently the usual rate, and by a neighbour on payment of £100, the money to be invested for the poor. The vestry, however, refused another applicant leave to inclose, since he had no adjoining property,[28] and in 1814 threatened to demolish the fences of those who had inclosed more than the agreed amount of land or had not paid. In 1819 Cockerell himself claimed that inclosures had always been restricted to freeholders, who might take in only strips along public roads in order to preserve their frontages.[29] Although responsibility for the commons in practice had passed to the vestry, the chapter of Westminster, as lord of Westbourne manor, was asked to prevent the removal of turf in 1817.[30]

Enclosed meadows covered most of the parish east of the Bayswater rivulet in the 1740s, stretching across the north part into Chelsea detached and also south of Westbourne green along the west side of the later Black Lion Lane to the Uxbridge road. There were arable fields in the south-western corner of the parish, adjoining those of northern Kensington, and the common field east of Black Lion Lane was also arable, as were two large fields of Paddington manor in the south-eastern corner, away from the main roads. Also on Paddington manor, apparently converted to grass, were the Parsonage farm's Wheat and Rye Grass fields, abutting the parish's northern boundary formed by the Bayswater rivulet.[31] By 1800 the arable had been reduced to a small field at Westbourne green and another on the east side of Black Lion Lane.[32] Of c. 430 a. subject to tithes in 1844, 310 a. were under grass and only 10 a. arable, the rest being covered by gardens, roads, or buildings.[33]

Orders were made in 1595 for controlling cattle and ringing swine.[34] The conversion of arable to grassland, arising from London's demand for dairy produce and hay, was to meadow rather than pasture. In 1798 cowkeepers were said to engross every inch of available land around Paddington and similarly placed villages. The cows were kept in stalls and yards, while the fields were mown two or three times every summer to supply a rich diet of soft hay, supplemented by grain and green vegetables.[35] There were still 99 a. of permanent grassland for hay in 1867, besides 20 a. of clover and ½ a. of potatoes.

Three farms of under 50 a. survived in 1870, when there were 57 a. of permanent grass.[36] Confined to the north part of the parish, grassland had shrunk to 33½ a. by 1880 and 7 a. by 1890, after which date the only agricultural land consisted of allotments, numbering 200 in 1895.[37]

Cowsheds in unhealthy proximity to dwellings, together with adulteration of milk, formed a major preoccupation of the medical officer of health in 1856, when 314 cows were kept by 27 keepers.[38] Many families lived under the same roof as livestock in 1862[39] and an outbreak of cattle plague led to the appointment of a temporary assistant inspector of nuisances in 1865.[40] The number of cows in milk fell more slowly than the acreage of grassland: there were 157 cows in 1867, 133 in 1870, 86 in 1880, when 2 people were returned as occupying farmland and 7 as keeping livestock but not occupying land, and 83 in 1890.[41] Three cowhouses survived in 1894, in Elgin Avenue, Chichester Mews, and Star Street; only the one in Star Street, licensed for 10 cows, remained in 1904, surviving until 1927.[42]

Welford & Sons,[43] dairymen to the queen from 1876, was founded by Richard Welford, who took over Warwick farm between Harrow Road and Warwick Crescent in 1845 and opened his first dairy shop at no. 4 Warwick Place in 1848. The cowsheds were soon removed to Wembley but much land was acquired in Willesden[44] under Richard (d. 1858), his widow, and their three sons, and dairy shops were opened in Queen's Road, by 1879, and elsewhere. A new model dairy, with workmen's flats, was opened in 1882 on 2 a. at the north corner of Elgin Avenue and Shirland Road, where in 1891 the processing of produce from over 100 farms employed 400 men, besides 50 girl clerks. After forming subsidiary companies in the 1890s, Welford's in 1915 joined United Dairies, which from 1959 was part of Unigate.[45] United Dairies retained a depot at Welford House, part of the Shirland Road building, where the Church Army Housing Trust had its headquarters in 1983.[46] United Dairies also had offices in St. Petersburgh Place which had been built for the Kensington-based Belgravia Dairy Co., most of whose outlets had been in Bayswater.[47]

Livestock other than dairy cattle were both kept in and driven through the parish. A slaughter house for horses and other beasts was to be inspected in 1798.[48] Styes and slaughter houses could be removed under the Local Act of 1824, which also authorized fines to curb the driving of great numbers of sheep and cattle during churchgoing hours on Sunday.[49] Stray animals were to be taken in 1830 to

---

25 Ibid. 10312/113, m. 11.
26 Ct. rolls, *passim.*
27 Guildhall MS. 10465/55; W.A.M. 14640.
28 Vestry mins. 15 July, 11 Nov. 1801; 20 Oct. 1802.
29 Ibid. 11 Apr. 1814; 22 Sept. 1819.
30 Ibid. 5 Aug. 1817.
31 Rocque, *Map of Lond.* (1741–5), sheet 11; Ch. Com., 'Map of 1742'.
32 T. Milne, *Land Use Map of Lond.* (1800) (Lond. Topog. Soc. 1975–6).
33 G.L.R.O., TA/10. The bp.'s and part of the Grand Junction Canal Co.'s estates were tithe free.
34 W.A.M. 16453.
35 Middleton, *View of Agric.* 225, 329–32.
36 P.R.O., MAF 68/136; MAF 68/250.
37 Ibid. MAF 68/706; MAF 68/1276; MAF 68/1561.
38 *Paddington San. Rep. 1856* (in Marylebone libr.), 14–17.

39 *Rep. on Health of Paddington to Lady Day 1862* (in Marylebone libr.).
40 Sanitary cttee. mins. 3 Aug. 1865.
41 P.R.O., MAF 68/136; MAF 68/250; MAF 68/706; MAF 68/1276.
42 *Rep. on Vital Statistics and San. Work, 1894,* 129; ibid. *1904,* 70 (in Marylebone libr.); L.C.C. *Lond. Statistics,* xxxiii. 85.
43 Para. based on S. Welford, 'Hist. Welford & Sons' (pamphlet 1983 in Marylebone libr.); Marylebone libr., P 137, cuttings.
44 *V.C.H. Mdx.* vii. 224.
45 Marylebone libr., P 138, cuttings.
46 Plaque on bldg.
47 Marylebone libr., P 138, cuttings; *Kelly's Dir. Paddington* (1888 and later edns.).
48 Vestry mins. 18 Dec. 1798.
49 5 Geo. IV, c. 126 (Local and Personal).

the parish's green yard, which adjoined the infants' school and which in 1835 was to be attended by the engine keeper.[50] Livestock in an increasingly built up area gave rise to many complaints, including those about a slaughter house behind the late Earl Ferrers's residence at Craven Hill in 1831 and one behind St. Petersburgh Place in 1845,[51] and about sheep crowded into a stable in Porchester Square Mews in 1859 and pigs being killed in Cirencester Mews in 1861.[52] Thirty-nine slaughter houses were inspected in 1856, of which 8 were found satisfactory and all but one of the others were improved, often by finding better premises.[53] There were 32 licensed slaughterers in 1865,[54] 12 in 1894, 8 in 1904, and 3 in 1925; one survived in 1937.[55] A three-storeyed stable block was built in Winsland Street east of Paddington station in 1878 and still held 500 horses of the G.W.R. Co., mainly for deliveries to London markets, in 1938. British Railways later converted the building into offices.[56]

NURSERIES AND MARKET GARDENS. Nurserymen called Latin, in Edgware Road, and Prior were listed as at Paddington in 1786. Both may have been on the Marylebone side of the road, which had nurseries at Pine Apple Place and elsewhere[57] and where John Prior was in business as a florist in 1802.[58] At Bayswater John Hill (1716?–1775), miscellaneous writer and superintendent of the royal gardens at Kew, prepared medicines from herbs grown in his own physic garden, later the Flora and finally the Victoria tea gardens.[59] Nursery or market gardens, mostly set back from the Uxbridge road, stretched eastward from Black Lion Lane to the Bayswater rivulet in 1800.[60] Irrigated from the stream, the neighbourhood supported several nurseries, including those of the Greig family, with watercress beds,[61] and by 1812 of Thomas Hopgood. The Craven Hill nursery of Francis Hopgood, next to the Flora tea gardens, survived until 1855 or later.[62]

As housing spread along the Maida Vale section of Edgware Road, much land behind the main road, north of Paddington green, was leased to nurserymen for 21 years. George Hogg, who had been a gardener at Pine Apple Place in 1802, took a lease in 1808 of 3½ a. of Pond field, bounded north by the field called Paddington wood.[63] Thomas Hogg was a florist at no. 55 Harrow Road, Paddington green, by 1826,[64] and a younger Thomas and James Hogg re-

mained in business until c. 1842.[65] The elder Thomas raised a pink called 'Paddington' and in 1820 published a successful gardening treatise, dedicated to the dowager Lady de Clifford, a Paddington resident.[66] Parts of Lower Pond field were leased in 1809 to William Hill and to John Dobson and Henry Heyward, to be used only as nursery ground and not for market vegetables except during the first three years. William Calder, a nurseryman of Edgware Road, was leased a nearby plot in 1815.[57] Both George Hogg and William Hill built houses facing Edgware Road.[68] James Stephens had a nursery at Paddington green in 1826 and 1836,[69] and T. Pearman had nurseries in Queen's and Blomfield roads in 1863.[70] The 430 a. not subject to tithe included c. 28 a. of 'garden ground' in 1844.[71] The parish contained 5½ a. of market garden in 1880 but none in 1890.[72] Clifton nurseries was established in Warwick Avenue in 1941 and acquired further premises in Bishop's Bridge Road in 1977.[73]

WOODS. Richard the forester was among the customary tenants of Knightsbridge and Paddington c. 1225.[74] Woodland was not fully recorded in the early 14th century but was extensive, to judge from sales of faggots,[75] as in 1321–2, and the use of timber from Paddington for rebuilding the nave of Westminster abbey, including the provision of 22 cartloads in 1460–1 and 42 loads in 1478–9.[76] When Paddington manor paid £19 to the warden of the new work in 1535, both the almoner and the keeper of St. Mary's chapel received £1 in wood.[77]

Paddington wood, in Paddington manor, in 1647 amounted to 44 a.,[78] although 17th- and 18th-century leases routinely described it as 30 a.[79] In 1742 it was the name of c. 48 a. abutting Edgware Road, half way between Paddington village and Kilburn bridge.[80] Westbourne manor's Ash Groves survived into the 19th century as a name for the land along the north side of Harrow Road in the parish's north-western corner.[81]

Woods, underwoods, and hedgerows were reserved when Paddington manor was leased in 1489,[82] as were the great trees and woods in 1543.[83] In leases by the bishop of London from 1626 Paddington wood, with the right to take timber and herbage and pannage there, was included with the rest of the estate for an additional 40s. a year. Great trees and saplings were noted in 1647[84] but Paddington wood

[50] Guardian bd. mins. 16 July 1830; 23 Oct. 1835; select vestry mins. 4 Mar. 1834.
[51] Select vestry mins. 2 Aug. 1831; 4 Nov. 1845.
[52] San. cttee. mins. 16 June 1859; 6 June 1861.
[53] Ibid. 16 Oct. 1856; Paddington San. Rep. 1856, 23.
[54] Metropolitan vestry mins. 3 Jan. 1865.
[55] Rep. on Vital Statistics 1894, 129; 1904, 70; L.C.C. Lond. Statistics, xxiii. 83; xlii. 87.
[56] A. Wilson, Lond.'s Industrial Heritage (1967), 90; Marylebone libr., P 135, cuttings.
[57] T.L.M.A.S. xxvi. 303–4.
[58] Holden's Triennial Dir. (1802–4).
[59] D.N.B.; above, social.
[60] Milne, Land Use Map of Lond. (1800).
[61] McDonald, 'Paddington', cap. 16.
[62] Rate bks. select transcripts, 1812, 1817, 1820 (TS. in Marylebone libr.); Pigot's Com. Dir. (1832–4); P.O. Dir. Lond. (1855).
[63] Guildhall MS. 12428; Holden's Triennial Dir. (1802–4).
[64] Pigot's Com. Dir. (1826–7).
[65] Robson's Lond. Dir. (1842).

[66] R. Genders, Cottage Gdn. (1983), 110, 166, 174; T. Hogg, Concise and Practical Treatise on Culture of the Carnation (6th edn. 1839); Boyle's Court Guide (1819, 1824).
[67] Guildhall MS. 12428.
[68] Ibid. 12530/1.
[69] Pigot's Com. Dir. (1826–7); Robson's Lond. Dir. (1836).
[70] Dolling's Paddington Dir. (1863).
[71] G.L.R.O., TA/10.
[72] P.R.O., MAF 68/706; MAF 68/1276.
[73] Inf. from Clifton Nurseries Ltd.
[74] Harvey, Westm. Abbey, 105, 127.
[75] W.A.M. 18968.
[76] Refs. to timber in W.A.M. Novum Opus rolls, supplied by Mr. N. Woodward-Smith.
[77] Valor Eccl. (Rec. Com.), i. 413–14.
[78] Guildhall MS. 10464A.
[79] Guildhall MSS. 10464A, 12426, 10234/5–6.
[80] Ch. Com., 'Map of 1742'.
[81] Gutch, Plan of Paddington (1828, 1840).
[82] W.A.M., Reg. Bk. i, ff. 39v.–40.
[83] P.R.O., STAC 8/5/8.   [84] Guildhall MS. 10464A.

had been divided into four closes by 1742, when it formed part of the meadow land of William Godfrey's Manor House farm.[85] All trees were reserved when Paddington green was settled in trust from 1753.[86] Timber was similarly reserved in leases of Westbourne manor from the 16th century until the 19th.[87] Probably no woodland was left in the parish by 1746,[88] although the former wooded state of Ash Groves, five closes by 1669,[89] and the adjacent Marylands was suggested by some of the names of their later divisions: Oak Tree field, Elm field, and, south of Harrow Road, Wood field. Adjoining Wood field, west of Westbourne green and so detached from most of Paddington manor, were Upper and Lower Readings,[90] whose names recalled woodland clearings.[91]

TRADE AND INDUSTRY. Before the opening of the Paddington branch of the Grand Junction canal in 1801, only a few craftsmen were recorded. They included a tailor in 1566[92] and 1617,[93] a weaver in 1581,[94] and a carpenter and collar maker in 1615.[95] Peter Parisot, a carpet and tapestry maker, employed two French workmen at Paddington c. 1750 before moving to Fulham c. 1753.[96]

Almost equal numbers were employed in agriculture, 158, and in trade, manufacturing, or handicrafts, 160, in 1801, when as many as 1,563 people belonged to neither group. The canal so stimulated industry that by 1811 there were 95 families engaged in agriculture, 549 families in trade, manufacturing, or handicrafts, and 439 others. In 1831 there were 82 families in agriculture, 1,049 in trade, manufacturing, and handicrafts, and 2,362 others, many of them presumably residents of newly built Tyburnia with their servants.[97]

For the area around the canal basin, ambitious schemes projected docks to the north, besides wharves and warehouses stretching as far as Edgware Road and Grand Junction Street. In the event a smaller area was taken over.[98] Yards and warehouses, reached by North Wharf or South Wharf roads, lined the basin[99] where eight laden barges arrived on the canal's opening day. A market in straw, hay, and vegetables soon arose on the north side and one in cattle on the south, but the early activity dwindled when the basin was bypassed by the Regent's canal.[1] Coal from the Midlands was one of the chief commodities, although in 1805 its transport to London by canal was restricted to 50,000 tons for one year and subjected to a duty equivalent to that on north country sea coal.[2] While canal-borne supplies remained small compared with the amount shipped to the Thames or later brought by railway,[3] the Act of 1805 was repeatedly renewed; the duty was eventually reduced and finally abolished in 1890.[4] In 1844 three coal agents or merchants were listed among the 30 lessees of wharves on the north side and 12 among 38 lessees on the south side, besides two in Irongate wharf (later Irongate Wharf Road) at the eastern end of the basin. Despite competition from the railways there were still six coal merchants in 1855 beside the canal company's own coal wharf. At least 10 occupants in 1844 were described simply as wharfingers or carmen and many of the others were suppliers of builders' materials.[5]

The wharfingers were presumably engaged in general conveyance, as was the firm of Pickford & Co., which in the late 18th century had expanded with the canal trade. A warehouse at the basin was finished in 1801 and a second in 1804, and in 1817 the Paddington depot was insured for £16,000, more than a third of the company's total payments. Pickford's moved c. 1890 from South Wharf Road to no. 68 Harrow Road and c. 1930 to no. 101A, leaving no. 68 to Carter, Paterson & Co., which had controlled Pickford's since 1912.[6] Both concerns passed in 1933 to the four main railway companies and in 1947 to the British Transport Commission, which maintained a parcels office in Harrow Road until 1962.[7] Most canal boats came to be owned by companies: as many as 164 boats were registered at Paddington between 1879 and 1884, a number similar to those at Coventry or Wigan, but only 15 were steered by their owners.[8] Conveyance was the chief male occupation in Paddington in 1902, accounting for 22 per cent of the workforce.[9] Presumably the figure included those who worked for the railway companies: the G.W.R. Co. had a staff of nearly 3,000 at Paddington station in 1921.[10]

Builders and their suppliers occupied wharves both around the basin and farther west along the canal.[11] In 1844 and 1850 they included James Ponsford, who built much of Tyburnia and Bayswater, and John Mowlem, stone and granite merchants. Mowlem's business, forerunner of the modern building contractors, had started in Paddington in 1820[12] and, as Mowlem, Freeman & Burt, still had a wharf there in 1863. There were also five lime merchants or lime burners around the canal in 1844, some of them later also described as makers of tiles, bricks, and cement, besides two timber merchants, a brickmaker, and a cement maker in Irongate wharf. Building and allied trades formed the

[85] Ch. Com., 'Map of 1742'.
[86] Guildhall MS. 10465/92, f. 6.
[87] W.A.M., Reg. Bk. iii, f. 144v.; lxi, f. 342v.
[88] Rocque, Map of Lond. (1741–5), sheet 11.
[89] W.A.M., Reg. Bk. xix, f. 5v.
[90] Ch. Com., 'Plan of 1790'; Gutch, Plan of Paddington (1828, 1840).
[91] P.N. Mdx. (E.P.N.S.), 203.
[92] Mdx. County Rec. i. 59.
[93] Mdx. Sess. Rec. iv. 284.
[94] Mdx. County Rec. i. 123.
[95] Mdx. Sess. Rec. iii. 38, 100.
[96] W. G. Thomson, Hist. of Tapestry (1973), 492–3; Lysons, Environs, ii. 400.
[97] Census, 1801–31.
[98] Original Plan of the Termination of the Grand Junction Canal (undated, in Marylebone libr.); Improved Plan (1799, in Marylebone libr.).   [99] Above, plate 43.

[1] M. Heaney, 'Paddington in first half of 19th cent.' (TS. in Marylebone libr.), 3–6.
[2] Hadfield, Canals of E. Midlands, 119; R. Smith, Sea Coal for Lond. (1961), 119, 151; 45 Geo. III, c. 128.
[3] Smith, Sea Coal, 276, 335, 339.
[4] e.g. 46 Geo. III, c. 104; Hadfield, Canals of E. Midlands, 119.
[5] P.O. Dir. Lond. (1844, 1855).
[6] G. L. Turnbull, Traffic and Transport (1979), 29, 38, 156; Kelly's Dir. Paddington (1890 and later edns.).
[7] Turnbull, Traffic and Transport, 171, 178; P.O. Dir. Lond. (1962, 1963).
[8] H. Hanson, Canal Boatmen (1975), 108, 110.
[9] Mudie-Smith, Rel. Life, 82.
[10] Official Guide to Paddington [1921].
[11] Para. based on P.O. Dir. Lond. (1844 and later edns.).
[12] London John [mag. of John Mowlem & Co. Ltd.], Sept. 1949, 1.

second largest source of employment for men, 13 per cent of the workforce, in 1902.[13]

Among long-lived firms were the timber merchants Samuel Putney, who by 1879 were at Baltic wharf, no. 149 Harrow Road, where their successors Sandell Perkins opened a new warehouse in 1974.[14] Sandell Perkins was formed after 1964 by the amalgamation of Ingram, Perkins & Co. with Joseph Sandell & Co.; both of those older firms of timber merchants had started business outside Paddington, where by 1927 the premises of Ingram, Perkins had included no. 12 Praed Street, no. 1 Irongate Wharf Road, and no. 6 Amberley wharf.[15] The brickmakers Broad, Harris & Co., established in 1881, leased no. 2 South Wharf Road in 1891, supplying their depot from west Middlesex. Broad & Co. Ltd. was formed in 1896 and, after the dissolution of the original partnership and further acquisitions, Broad's Manufacturing Co. in 1948.[16] The company was taken over by Sandell Perkins in 1975 and came to be administered from the group's head office in Kent, although the traditional name was retained for Broad's showrooms in Praed Street. In 1983 Sandell Perkins occupied nos. 119 and 149 Harrow Road, no. 4 South Wharf Road, and no. 22 Praed Street, with a local workforce of c. 140.[17]

Rubbish tipping and burning added to the unhealthy state of the area around the canal basin, where in 1856 the water itself formed a fetid pool, polluted by stockyards, laystalls, dust wharves, and bargees' sewage.[18] In the face of the vestry's repeated demands for a thorough cleansing,[19] stimulated by complaints from St. Mary's hospital about effluvia,[20] the Grand Junction Canal Co. blamed careless wharfingers and the illicit dumping of manure.[21] In 1876, by which time conditions had improved, it was recalled that rubbish heaps had once towered above the house tops.[22] In 1891 yards on the north side of the basin contained piles of cinders and manure, a sifter, and mud pits.[23] In 1899, when three wharves belonged to the vestry's scavenging department,[24] the neighbourhood was described as 'the home of the dustmen'.[25] Besides the three municipal wharves of Paddington, there were six used by Marylebone council by 1927.[26] Westminster council had recently left nos. 33–37 North Wharf Road in 1985, when it retained a street cleansing depot, with c. 300 employees, at nos. 21–31.[27]

Engineering firms[28] included that of William Henry Lindsay, whose Paddington iron works was on the south side of the basin by 1879 and, as Lindsay, Neal & Co., on the north side by 1902. Described as constructional engineers and iron and steel roof manufacturers, the company remained in North Wharf Road until after 1964. James H.

Randall & Son, founded in 1851 in Marylebone, from 1904 had a tinplate works in Green Street, leading south from Paddington green (later part of North Wharf Road). As Randalls of Paddington, it employed c. 40 people in making sheet metal and in light engineering in 1984.[29] Acrow (Engineers) in 1952 moved to no. 8 South Wharf Road, where, together with Acrow (Automation), it made steel shutters and storage racks in 1975. About 100 people worked there in 1983, when it was the head office of Acrow's group of international companies, whose business was in construction equipment and general engineering.[30] Selfridges, the department store, acquired part of a building in South Wharf Road in 1947 and the rest in 1956. After a third of it had been reconstructed, the premises served in 1983 as a warehouse, despatch depot, and offices, with a total workforce of c. 200.[31] James Purdey & Sons, the gunmakers, which had been founded in 1814, took over no. 2 Irongate Wharf Road in 1900 and later also nos. 18–22, before moving into a new factory at no. 57 North Wharf Road in 1971. All the premises were used for making sporting weapons, the workforce at its largest numbering 109. The firm left Paddington for Hammersmith in 1979.[32]

By 1985 there was little need for warehousing around the basin, since the transport by water of refuse from the municipal depot and of building material by Sandell Perkins had recently ceased. Employers nearby included Sandell Perkins, British Telecom's depot at the eastern end of the basin, Westminster council, Selfridges, and varied users of nos. 47–55 North Wharf Road. There were several vacant sites in South Wharf Road, owned by St. Mary's hospital, which planned further extensions, or by the British Waterways Board.[33] The hospital was probably the biggest employer: in 1986, when catering and domestic services were done by contracts, it retained a staff of over 1,000, including c. 425 trained nurses and 250 medical and 230 technical staff.[34]

Another patch of canalside industry arose in the 1860s, as building spread around Westbourne green, in the form of a line of wharves along the south side of Amberley Road.[35] In 1879 there were 9 occupants of Amberley wharves, including Richard Marks, an ice merchant, whose firm survived there until c. 1968. There was a lime and cement merchant at the neighbouring Westbourne Bridge wharf and a timber merchant at St. Peter's wharf, where the Metropolitan Electric Supply Co. later had its works. In addition to Ingram, Perkins & Co., later timber merchants at Amberley wharves from c. 1927 until 1964 or later included A. J. Ferguson & Co., which was succeeded by H. W. Daniells.[36] Industry had

[13] Mudie-Smith, *Rel. Life*, 82.
[14] *P.O. Dir. Lond.* (1863 and later edns.); Marylebone libr., P 138, cuttings.
[15] *P.O. Dir. Lond.* (1927 and later edns.); inf. from Mr. D. C. W. Perkins, director.
[16] *Paddington Mag.* July 1961; Marylebone libr., P 136.2, cuttings.
[17] Inf. from co. sec.
[18] *Paddington San. Rep. 1856*, 11.
[19] e.g. San. cttee. mins. 17 Apr., 5 June 1856; 7 Jan., 9 July 1858; vestry mins. 21 June 1859.
[20] San. cttee. mins. 7 July 1859; 15 June 1865.
[21] Ibid. 5 July 1860; 18 Aug. 1864.
[22] J. Timbs, *Curiosities of Lond.* (1876), 624.
[23] Insurance plan 409 (1891).
[24] Below, pub. svces.

[25] Booth, *Life and Labour*, iii(3), 120.
[26] *P.O. Dir. Lond.* (1902 and later edns.).
[27] *Paddington Basin Draft Planning Brief, 1985* (in Marylebone libr.).
[28] Para. based on *P.O. Dir. Lond.* (1879 and later edns.); *Kelly's Dir. Paddington* (1888 and later edns.).
[29] Inf. from Mr. M. Rothstein.
[30] Inf. from group publicity manager.
[31] Inf. from co. sec.
[32] Inf. from asst. sec.; Marylebone libr., P 138, cuttings.
[33] *Paddington Basin Draft Planning Brief, 1985* (in Marylebone libr.).
[34] Inf. from gen. manager, St. Mary's hosp.
[35] Lucas, *Plan of Paddington* (1869).
[36] Hutchings and Crowsley, *Paddington Dir.* (1878); *P.O. Dir. Lond.* (1879 and later edns.).

left the wharves by 1975, the departure of Matthew Hall & Co., heating engineers, in 1968 being seen as part of a general movement out of London.[37]

Away from the canal, there were few industrial firms of large size or long duration. The Sovereign brewery, north of the Black Lion on the east side of Black Lion Lane (later Royal Hill, Queen's Road) c. 1830, was under Christopher Alexander by 1843,[38] Mrs. Ann Alexander by 1857, and A. and G. Alexander in 1876. It retained its old name in 1895 but belonged to Usher's Wiltshire Brewery by 1900 and was merely an off-licence by 1923. Among other businesses in Queen's Road by 1888 was a parquet floor maker's and an early ice cream company, Horton Ices, which survived until c. 1912 and c. 1929 respectively.[39] The residential nature of much of the parish placed industry at a disadvantage: there were complaints about nuisances from a carpet-beating yard in 1831,[40] from brick burning near Talbot Road in 1861,[41] and from a veterinary college and from a cocoa mill in White Lion Place in 1866.[42]

Much work was done on a small scale. Paddington had 149 factories and 579 workshops in 1904, employing 7,442 people.[43] More than 500 girls had been identified as seamstresses in 1869, when there were thought to be many more in unidentified private houses around Westbourne Grove,[44] and dress-making was by far the biggest industrial employer, with 47 per cent of the workforce, in 1904.[45] Laundries, of which there were many in former dwellings in northern Paddington,[46] employed c. 10 per cent of the industrial workforce, while men worked mainly in making articles of wood or metal, accounting for 13.5 and 10.5 per cent of the industrial workforce respectively.[47]

Many more men came to be employed in public transport. In 1901 they included over 2,500 workers on the railways, over 2,200 cabmen or non-domestic coachmen and grooms, and over 1,800 carriers.[48]

Domestic service was a still greater source of employment in the late 19th century, when there were also increases in the hotel or boarding house and catering trades and the retail trade in general. In Tyburnia, where special services for servants in 1879 preceded the opening of Ascension chapel,[49] the population c. 1902 consisted mainly of rich families, their servants, and a few good-class lodging house keepers and shopkeepers.[50] Paddington had 16,881 indoor servants, most of them women and excluding those in hotels or lodging houses, in 1901. With 50.2 servants to every 100 families or separate occupiers, it ranked sixth among the London boroughs with the

highest proportion of servants and, with its aristocratic quarters, fifth among those with men servants.[51] In 1902 nearly 7 per cent of the total male workforce and 61 per cent of the female worked in domestic offices and services.[52]

In addition to the Great Western hotel,[53] the opening of the railway terminus gave rise to many small hotels and boarding houses in Paddington,[54] as did the opening of Victoria station in Pimlico.[55] John Pearson kept the Warwick Arms hotel in Bridge Terrace, Harrow Road, in 1847. It was called Pearson's Warwick hotel in 1855, when there were also hotels in Chichester Place and Westbourne Villas, Harrow Road, in Eastbourne Terrace, and in Queen's Road. By 1863 there was a second hotel in Queen's Road and there were others in Gloucester Crescent, Sutherland Gardens, London Street, and Conduit Street. By 1902 there were at least 26 hotels, many of them private. Establishments classed as boarding or lodging houses[56] numbered at least 30 by 1850 and over 120 by 1863 and had further multiplied by 1902, when many were described simply as apartments. In the poorer areas the subletting of houses to weekly lodgers made it hard to enforce sanitary standards in 1869.[57] The need to cater for both travellers and lodgers perhaps accounted for the employment of 10 per cent of the male workforce in food and drink trades in 1902.[58] There were 851 houses registered as being let in lodgings in 1902 and 1,326 by 1910, when Paddington, although only the fourteenth most populous metropolitan borough, had the sixth highest total of such houses. In 1937 there were 2,031 houses let in lodgings.[59]

Most of the early boarding houses were in Tyburnia, where in 1850 there were 9 in Portsea Place off Connaught Square and 3 in Upper Berkeley Street West (later Connaught Street). Cambridge and Oxford terraces, along the northern and southern sides of Grand Junction Road (later Sussex Gardens) contained 1 each. By 1863 the lodging houses in Tyburnia included as many as 14 in Cambridge Terrace, 7 in Oxford Terrace, 10 in Cambridge (later Kendal) Street, and 5 in Albion Street. Another large group existed in the recently built area bordering Bayswater and Westbournia: Cumberland Place (later Courtnell Street) and Northumberland Place, both running north from Artesian Road, had 8 each. The tendency for such establishments to form concentrations continued with the conversion of large houses in Bayswater. There were 8 boarding house keepers, some at more than one number, in Kensington Gardens Square but only two in the

[37] *The Times*, 12 Feb. 1968, 15a.
[38] C. and G. Greenwood, *Map of Lond.* (c. 1830); *Lucas's Dir. Paddington* (1843).
[39] *P.O. Dir. Lond.* (1857 and later edns.); *Kelly's Dir. Paddington* (1888 and later edns.).
[40] Select vestry mins. 1 Feb. 1831.
[41] Metropolitan vestry mins. 6 Aug. 1861.
[42] San. cttee. mins. 21 June, 13 Sept. 1866.
[43] L.C.C. *Lond. Statistics*, xix. 42–3. The figures below for 1904 refer only to employees in factories or workshops and so to a smaller workforce than that for 1902 described by Mudie-Smith.
[44] *Paddington San. Rep. 1869–70*, 25.
[45] L.C.C. *Lond. Statistics*, xvii. 55, 59. Dress trades accounted for 17 per cent of the workforce in Mudie-Smith, *Rel. Life*, 82.
[46] *Rep. on Vital Statistics and San. Work, 1902*, 58.
[47] L.C.C. *Lond. Statistics*, xvii. 55, 59.
[48] *Census*, 1901, table 35.

[49] Below, churches.
[50] Booth, *Life and Labour*, i (2), app. p. 12.
[51] *Census*, 1901, table 35; Thompson, *Hampstead*, 50–1.
[52] Mudie-Smith, *Rel. Life*, 71, 82.
[53] Above, communications.
[54] Following 6 paras. based on *P.O. Dir. Lond.* (1847 and later edns.). There were separate lists for boarding ho. keepers, hotels and taverns, private (unlicensed) hotels, lodging ho. keepers (by 1902 letters of apartments), and publicans. A few establishments not entered under trades are to be found under streets.
[55] J. R. Kellett, *Impact of Rlys. on Victorian Cities* (1969), 319.
[56] Lodging hos. were presumably more rudimentary than boarding hos., although some establishments were listed under both categories.
[57] *Paddington San. Rep. 1869–70*, 6.
[58] Mudie-Smith, *Rel. Life*, 82.
[59] L.C.C. *Lond. Statistics*, xvi. 99; xxii. 129; xlii. 87.

nearby Leinster Square in 1902. Paddington station lay between Eastbourne Terrace, with 3 hotels and 28 apartment houses, and the more commercial London Street, with 7 hotels. Most of the houses in Grand Junction Road, including 47 of the 83 numbers in Cambridge Terrace and 35 of the 93 numbers in Oxford Terrace, were described as apartments; Cambridge Street had 22 apartment houses, besides a private hotel, and Albion Street had 13.

Several of the earliest hotels had a long existence. Pearson's Warwick hotel was called simply the Warwick hotel in 1879 and survived at no. 106 Harrow Road in 1985. The Prince of Wales, at no. 1 Eastbourne Terrace by 1855, was owned by Cope's Taverns in 1947 and closed by 1952. In Harrow Road the Maze hotel was open in Chichester Place from c. 1855 until 1959 or later and the Stafford at no. 1 Westbourne Villas from c. 1855 until 1964 or later. The Norfolk Square hotel was in Norfolk Square by 1863 and also in London Street by 1879; it was called the New Norfolk hotel by 1917[60] and the Royal Norfolk by 1975, surviving in 1985. The Warrington hotel was in Sutherland Gardens (later Avenue) in 1863 and 1879; a later establishment of that name, however, at no. 93 Warrington Crescent, was no more than a public house.[61] In London Street a private hotel at no. 29 by 1879 was kept by Richard Ashton in 1902, still open as Ashton's hotel in 1959, and refurbished as the Grosvenor Court in 1975,[62] while the Sussex, at no. 21 by 1902, had become the Sussex Arms by 1975. The purpose-built Coburg Court hotel was opened in 1907 and renamed the Coburg in the 1960s; it was built over an Underground station and part of the freehold remained with the London Transport Executive in 1985.[63] The Inverness Court hotel was open by 1912.[64] The Court Royal opened at nos. 105–6 Lancaster Gate in 1927 and was renamed the Lancaster Gate hotel in 1964.[65] The former Warrington Lodge nursing home was opened as the Esplanade hotel in 1936 and, under the management of Austrian emigrés, offered a temporary home in 1938 for Sigmund Freud.[66] It was renamed the Colonnade in 1947 and from 1948 was run by the Richards family, which bought the freehold in 1983.[67]

The philosopher Herbert Spencer (1820–1903) lived permanently at a private hotel at no. 37 (later also no. 38) Queen's Gardens from 1866 for more than 20 years. The writer W. H. Hudson (1841–1922) in 1876 married Emily Wingrove, who kept a boarding house in Leinster Square and, on its failure in 1884, another in Southwick Crescent.[68]

After the Second World War, the movement of industry away from London was counterbalanced by an increase in tourism, enhancing the importance of the hotel and catering trades. Many new hotels were built, beginning with the 10-storeyed Hertford hotel (later the Post House hotel and from 1982 the Hospitality Inn)[69] in Bayswater Road in 1961. They included such landmarks as the 19-storeyed Royal Lancaster, designed by T. P. Bennett & Son as the Rank Organization's largest hotel and opened in 1967,[70] and the 24-storeyed London Metropole, designed by R. Seifert & Partners and opened in 1973,[71] in Harbet Road. The seven-storeyed London Embassy hotel of 1972, in Bayswater Road, was also by Seifert.[72] A large but less obtrusive building, in scale with the neighbouring houses in Queensborough Terrace, was the Central Park hotel of 1973, designed by Zakaria & Associates.[73] Many enlargements and amalgamations also took place: in Lancaster Gate, Strand Hotels extended the Park Court hotel from no. 75 to include hotels and flats as far as no. 89 in 1970–2 and Mount Charlotte Hotels remodelled White's hotel, opened c. 1925 as the Whitehall and renamed c. 1949, at nos. 90–2 in 1984–6.[74]

Smaller hotels, many offering only bed and breakfast, were threatened by rebuilding schemes. Some disappeared with work on the Hyde Park estate, and in 1974 Tandlewell Trading Co. proposed to replace as many as 54 hotels on the north side of Sussex Gardens, either with 6 larger hotels or with flats: the company, which had bought the freehold from the Grand Junction Co., was refused planning permission by Westminster city council.[75] In 1961 a review of local industry admitted that Paddington was known chiefly for its station and as an area of hotels and furnished rooms.[76] Some 150 hoteliers were among the 500 members of the chamber of commerce in 1972.[77]

The retail trade flourished from the mid 19th century, particularly in and around Queen's Road and Westbourne Grove. Although it came to be linked with hotels and boarding houses, it first arose from the building up of Tyburnia, Bayswater, and Westbournia, whose residents needed shops that were nearer than those in the increasingly congested Oxford Street. The Metropolitan railway could bring customers from other areas from 1863, while William Whiteley successfully attracted the 'carriage trade' of southern Bayswater, of Tyburnia, and eventually of much of fashionable London.[78]

The first shop in Westbourne Grove, a chemist's, was opened in 1854. So many early ventures failed that the road was nicknamed 'Bankruptcy Avenue'[79] but by 1859 the older semi-detached villas were giving way to shopping terraces; the shops at its eastern end were claimed as unsurpassed by any in London and still more premises were needed as middle-class housing spread farther west.[80]

William Whiteley[81] opened a fancy goods' shop in 1863 at no. 63 (later no. 31) Westbourne Grove,

[60] Bingham, *Official Guide to Paddington* [1917], advert.
[61] Inf. from director; above, social.
[62] Marylebone libr., P 137, cuttings.
[63] Inf. from managing dir.
[64] *Kelly's Dir. Paddington* (1912).
[65] Inf. from managing dir., Newlands Hotel Ltd.
[66] Inf. from Mr. A. R. Richards; *Sigmund Freud, His Life in Pictures and Words*, ed. E. Freud and others (1978), 303.
[67] Inf. from Mr. A. R. Richards.
[68] H. Spencer, *Autobiography* (1926), ii. 145–6; J. Duncan, *Life of Herb. Spencer* (1908), 125, 289; R. Tomalin, *W. H. Hudson* (1954), 90; *D.N.B.*

[69] *Paddington Mag.* Sept. 1961; inf. from gen. manager.
[70] Marylebone libr., P 137, cuttings.
[71] Inf. from hotel manager.   [72] *Lond. Encyc.* 47.
[73] Inf. from executive sec.
[74] Inf. from manager, White's hotel.
[75] *The Times*, 31 Jan. 1974, 4g; 28 Aug. 1974, 15e.
[76] *Paddington Mag.* Apr. 1961.
[77] Marylebone libr., P 138, cuttings.
[78] Lambert, *Universal Provider*, 61; *Study of Urban Hist.* ed. H. J. Dyos (1968), 263.
[79] Lambert, *Universal Provider*, 60–1.
[80] *Paddington News*, 10 Dec. 1859.
[81] Para. based on Lambert, *Universal Provider, passim.*

which he had leased for 15 years. Originally describing himself as hosier, glover, laceman, and florist, he had 17 departments by 1867, when he leased the later nos. 41 and 43A, which soon formed part of a long row in Westbourne Grove. Dressmaking was started in 1868 and a house agency and refreshment room, the first ventures outside drapery, opened in 1872, when it was claimed that 622 people were employed on the establishment and a further 1,000 outside. New enterprises quickly followed, a building and decorating department from 1876 proving particularly profitable because the large stuccoed houses of Tyburnia and southern Bayswater needed regular repainting. A slight fall in profits from 1877 to 1880 preceded further expansion, when Whiteley, as self styled 'universal provider', claimed to be able to meet any demand, even for the hire of an elephant. He met strong opposition from smaller tradesmen, especially for starting to supply foodstuffs in 1875, and from the vestry over building plans;[82] several bad fires in the 1880s may have been caused by incendiarism. Business nonetheless prospered, aided by a delivery service extending up to 25 miles, and in 1887 the store was described as 'an immense symposium of the arts and industries of the nation and of the world'.[83] Whiteley also gained royal patronage and, by 1892, some local popularity as an economic benefactor. By 1906 his stores, with farms and factories elsewhere, covered 250 a. and employed 6,000 people.

Whiteley's, while still trading under its old name, was acquired by Gordon Selfridge in 1927 and by United Drapery Stores in 1961. After the Second World War Bayswater became less fashionable and more cosmopolitan as a shopping district, until in 1973 it was decided to close Whiteley's food halls as a result of competition from smaller shops. The main store was refurbished but trading was eventually restricted to two floors. High rates and the cost of travel from central London, together with falling sales to tourists after 1978, were blamed for the store's closure in 1981.[84]

The physical expansion of Whiteley's was so rapid that by 1879 it consisted of a long row along the south side of Westbourne Grove, nos. 31 to 53 (odd), which was remodelled and ultimately acquired as freehold. In addition there was a provision warehouse at no. 14A Westbourne Grove, and there were premises at nos. 50, 51, and 53 Kensington Gardens Square, where a restaurant was to be opened in 1881, and shops at nos. 147, 149, 151, and 157 on the west side of Queen's Road, where the first premises had been taken in 1875. Several houses in the cul-de-sacs of Hatherley Grove and Westbourne Grove Terrace accommodated male and female staff. The conversion of nos. 147 and 149 Queen's Road, which overlooked the municipal baths, had already proved controversial, as did further work on property in Queen's Road, where two new buildings were ready in 1880 and four more in 1881.[85] Property was also

secured on either side of Douglas (later Redan) Place, in the hope of joining the block in Westbourne Grove with that in Queen's Road, although attempts to have the lane widened were defeated. Much rebuilding took place in the 1880s, partly as a result of fires.[86] Male employees eventually slept in big dormitories at nos. 139 and 141 Queen's Road, while women lived in Hatherley Grove and Westbourne Terrace.[87]

Westbourne Grove, where electric lighting outside Whiteley's windows attracted sightseers in 1878,[88] remained the principal frontage in the 1890s. It was, however, for the Queen's Road frontage between Porchester Gardens and Redan Place that plans were drawn up by Belcher & Joass in 1910. Their last major work, it was a steel-framed building with a cladding of Cornish granite and Portland stone and with three gilt domes, the central one modelled on that of the Venetian church of Santa Maria della Salute. The southern two-thirds was built and opened in 1911, a roof garden made way for a restaurant in 1922, and the main façade was finished by William Curtis Green to the original design in 1925. Three of the five floor served as offices in 1981.[89] Whiteley himself, having moved from above his shop to no. 2 Kildare Terrace and in 1885 to no. 31 Porchester Terrace, was shot while at work at no. 43 Westbourne Terrace in 1907.[90]

Other fashionable retailers in Westbourne Grove included the bootmaker A. Abrahams from 1851, S. Bradley & Co., which was probably connected with an earlier Arctic Fur Store in Chepstow Place, from 1871, and William Owen, who opened his Bayswater Trimming Shop opposite Whiteley's in 1873. Bradley's, one of the first firms to have cold storage for raw skins, expanded into tailoring and dressmaking, with showrooms covering nearly 6 a., and was managed by the same family until 1953. Owen, with 2 shops in Westbourne Grove and 15 in Hatherley Grove, employed 350 assistants by 1888; he was perhaps Whiteley's main rival, although the two cooperated in trying to attract more custom to the neighbourhood. Drapers' shops were also opened in Westbourne Grove in 1873 by T. H. Ponting, whose business was later concentrated with that of his brothers in Kensington High Street, and in 1894 by the brothers-in-law Bourne and Hollingsworth, who in 1902 moved to Oxford Street. Personnel who left Whiteley's included John Barker, who opened his own store in Kensington in 1870, and Richard Burbidge, the founder of Harrods.[91]

More recent firms included William Perring & Co., house furnishers, which opened in 1892 at no. 382 Harrow Road. A new building, one of 15 Perring stores, was opened there in 1940 and retained by the firm until c. 1961. Frederick Lawrence, another furnisher, had taken over nos. 47 and 49 Westbourne Grove by 1923 and later expanded, occupying eleven former Whiteley's shops, nos. 33 to 53 (odd) in 1964, besides four showrooms opposite at nos. 18–24. In

[82] Below, local govt.
[83] Adburgham, *Shops and Shopping*, 156.
[84] Marylebone libr., P 137, cuttings.
[85] *P.O. Dir. Lond.* (1879); Lambert, *Universal Provider*, 68–9, 74–5, 76, 110–11.
[86] Lambert, *Universal Provider*, 99–100, 110–11, 164–5, 168, 174, 187, 197–205.
[87] Ibid. 153; insurance plan B 23 (1892).

[88] Lambert, *Universal Provider*, 99.
[89] G.L.C. Historic Bldgs. Div., WM 290; Marylebone libr., P 137, cuttings; above, plate 44.
[90] Lambert, *Universal Provider*, 70, 192, 244–6; *D.N.B.*
[91] Adburgham, *Shops and Shopping*, 151–3, 157–9; Lambert, *Universal Provider*, 135; *P.O. Dir. Lond.* (1879 and later edns.).

1975 Lawrence's was described as the new king of Westbourne Grove, in succession to Whiteley's.[92] Both William Perring and Frederick Lawrence served as mayor of Paddington and were knighted.[93]

A few small businesses traded under the same name for several generations: John A. Leuty, an undertaker's established in 1842, was in Queen's Road and later at no. 312 Harrow Road until c. 1936. William Rayners, grocer's and wine merchant's, was established in 1858 and survived in Leinster Terrace until c. 1926; part of its premises continued as a grocery under Oakeshotts. John Wise, a bootmaker's established in 1861, was still in Craven Terrace in 1929.[94] Thomas Smith, a grocer's established at no. 17 Cambridge (later Kendal) Street by 1839, also survived in 1929 and was succeeded by Oakeshotts, which closed c. 1962.[95]

LOCAL GOVERNMENT. MANORIAL GOVERNMENT. The almoner of Westminster abbey was granted widespread fiscal exemptions for his lands, including Paddington, in 1103–4 and later.[96] Paddington, Knightsbridge, and Westbourne, as members of the vill of Westminster, belonged to the extensive liberty for which the abbot claimed infangthief, outfangthief, view of frankpledge, and most of the sheriff's pleas in 1294.[97]

There are no medieval court rolls for Paddington manor. It does not appear that jurisdiction lay with the courts for Eye (Ebury) or, after its acquisition by the abbey in the mid 14th century, with those for Hyde. The almoner was supposed to make periodic visits to Paddington c. 1270[98] and he or some other official may have held courts there. It is also possible that Paddington, having belonged to St. Margaret's parish, was served by courts for the vill of Westminster.[99] Presumably courts were held for the bishop of London after the Reformation, although the first surviving proceedings are of 1678[1] and courts are recorded regularly only from 1720. Thereafter a court baron was held by the steward of the manor or his deputy, usually between April and June. It met in Paddington, at an inn from 1815 or earlier until 1840, after which date a few transactions 'out of court' were noted.[2]

Paddington had a headborough, in charge of the watch, in 1615.[3] No manorial officers were elected at later courts, although homagers were always sworn. In the mid 18th century a headborough and a constable for the whole parish were chosen in vestry, the bishop's courts being almost wholly concerned with property.[4] The steward of the manor was asked by

the vestry to appoint a pound keeper in 1817, but was not recorded as having done so.[5]

Westbourne was served by courts for Knightsbridge, which were recorded from 1358 and for the next 200 years were normally held with a view of frankpledge at Whitsuntide. From 1587 courts of the dean and chapter of Westminster were held for Knightsbridge with Westbourne, by 1661 called Westbourne green. Presided over by the steward or his deputy, most courts were at Knightsbridge in the 17th and 18th centuries and from the 1670s were either customary or special courts baron.[6]

Fines and presentments for Westbourne were entered separately from those for Knightsbridge in 1440–3, although both places apparently were served by the same constable and aletasters.[7] By 1511 or earlier Westbourne had its own homagers and, until 1590, its own constable,[8] whose place thereafter seems to have been taken by a chief pledge. Homagers only were sworn after the Restoration, when courts were concerned mainly with property transactions.[9]

PARISH GOVERNMENT TO 1837. There were normally two churchwardens, elected in vestry at Easter, by 1655. They were said to be the joint choice of the minister and inhabitants in 1663[10] but later both offices were always filled by a majority vote; in 1827 there were protests, apparently successful, after one of the churchwardens had been chosen by the minister alone.[11] Two overseers of the poor, who occasionally were the same persons as the churchwardens, two surveyors of the highways, and a constable were recorded from 1663 and a clerk was paid in 1693.[12] There was a beadle by 1774, a woman pew-opener by 1800,[13] a second constable by 1802, and a collector of poor rates, who acted under the overseers, from 1808.[14] The assistant curate John Shepherd acted as vestry clerk, sexton, and parish clerk before his dismissal in 1798, whereupon the offices were separated.[15] An assistant overseer was appointed on the first attempt to establish a select vestry in 1820 and held one of seventeen posts under the Paddington vestry which carried a salary or gratuities in 1826. By that date the vestry had created three boards, each of them with a clerkship which was held by the vestry clerk.[16] Parish records include churchwardens' accounts for 1656–1736 and from 1774,[17] payments to the poor and overseers' accounts from 1670, highway surveyors' accounts from 1738, vestry minutes for 1753–9 and from 1793, and (statutory) select vestry minutes from 1824.[18]

The vestry met at Easter and irregularly, less

[92] Kelly's Dir. Paddington (1893 and later edns.); Marylebone libr., P 138, cuttings.
[93] Who Was Who, 1929–40; Who's Who, 1981.
[94] Official Guide to Paddington [1917], adverts.; P.O. Dir. Lond. (1855 and later edns.).
[95] P.O. Dir. Lond. (1839 and later edns.).
[96] Reg. Regum Anglo-Norm. ii, nos. 667–8; iii, nos. 936–7.
[97] Plac. de Quo Warr. (Rec. Com.), 480.
[98] Customary of St. Peter's, Westm. ed. Thompson, 94.
[99] Inf. from Miss Barbara Harvey.
[1] Guildhall MS. 10312/113, m. 11.
[2] Ct. bks. for bp. of Lond.'s manors, inc. Paddington: Guildhall MSS. 10465/36–228.
[3] Mdx. Sess. Rec. ii. 236.
[4] Guildhall MSS. 10465/36–228; vestry mins. 16 Apr. 1754.
[5] Vestry mins. 5 Aug. 1817.

[6] Ct. rolls for 1358–77, 1380–1411, 1437–43, 1511–29: W.A.M. 16446–9; ct. rolls for most years 1564–1797: ibid. 16452–16463.   [7] Ibid. 16448.
[8] Ibid. 16453.   [9] Ibid. 16454.
[10] Chwdns. acct. bk. (1656–1736), ff. 1, 10.
[11] Vestry mins. 17 Apr. 1827.
[12] Chwdns. acct. bk. (1656–1736), ff. 10, 57.
[13] Ibid. (1774–1833) [unpag.].
[14] Vestry mins. 20 Apr. 1802; 19 Apr., 26 May 1808.
[15] Ibid. 24 Sept., 9 Oct. 1798; 20 Oct. 1801.
[16] Vestry mins. 11 May 1820; select vestry mins. 19 Dec. 1826; below.
[17] Full transcription of accts. for 1655–6, 1729–30, 1779–80, and 1829–30 in J. Booth, 'Archives of Paddington' [TS. 1930 in Marylebone libr.].
[18] All par. rec. are in Marylebone libr.; listed in Booth, 'Archives', and Subject Index to Rec. of Paddington [duplicated in 1961].

frequently than monthly, in the 1750s and 1790s. Average attendance was barely a dozen, a figure of 27 recorded in 1757 perhaps not being exceeded until the early 19th century. Dr. Morell, probably an assistant curate, was often present from 1753 until 1757, as later were John Shepherd and, from 1803, successive ministers. Meetings took place at the church and, from 1823, at a new vestry room adjoining the schoolhouse in Harrow Road.[19]

The vestry petitioned in favour of Sturges Bourne's first Act and in 1819, hampered by a constant 'spirit of irritation' at its meetings, it resolved that the general public was not concerned with many of the proceedings, which therefore should not be advertised.[20] In 1820 a large meeting under the new minister, Charles Theomartyr Crane, set up a select vestry consisting of the parish officers and 20 members. The new body, reporting four times a year to the full vestry, was renewed in 1821 but not in 1822.[21] A local Act for the general government of Paddington was then secured, under which a select vestry was re-established in 1824. Voters were restricted to residents assessed to poor rate at £10 a year or more and candidates to those assessed at £30; 36 vestrymen were elected, the Grand Junction Canal Co. and the trustees of the Paddington Estate nominated one member each, and other members included the minister, churchwardens, and overseers, the lord of the manor, and resident peers, privy councillors, judges, and Middlesex J.P.s.[22] S. P. Cockerell and Edward Orme were among early attenders and in 1829 the bishop himself was present, when building plans were discussed.[23]

From 1824 the full vestry met only once a year, to elect officers and auditors and inspect books.[24] Administration was left to the select vestry, which appointed three standing committees: the guardian board, the highway, paving, and cleansing board, and the watching and lighting board, to which three a finance committee was added in 1825.[25] By 1831 the functions of the watching and lighting board had been divided between the highway board and the new metropolitan police.[26] Permanent salaried appointments were not to be made by the boards without the vestry's approval.[27] Other committees, as before, dealt with specific problems, including the scrutiny of parliamentary Bills.[28]

Auditors complained in 1828 that accounts were badly kept and that the vestry clerk, who received nearly 5 per cent of the parish's £10,000 income besides fees for legal work, was overpaid.[29] In 1833, after charges of extravagance had repeatedly been denied, the auditors consulted a wider body of ratepayers, who formed a Paddington association but were refused use of the vestry room.[30] It was later alleged that the select vestry, which could be enlarged to match rises in the parish's rateable value,[31] was dominated by men who hoped to profit from the building up of the Paddington Estate.[32] The select vestry in 1830 petitioned against Hobhouse's proposed Act to abolish plural voting. Representing the 'respectable party', it was narrowly supported by a local poll in resisting the Act's adoption in 1836, when it also succeeded in securing the election of its own candidates as churchwardens and vestrymen, in opposition to the Paddington association's list.[33] The old vestry in 1815 had petitioned parliament in favour of free trade but the select vestry in 1835, considering itself elected solely for parochial purposes, declined to join Marylebone in supporting a 'liberal' candidate.[34]

The vestry clerk's high salary was presumably a recognition of the large amount of legal work involved in dealing with such powerful bodies as the trustees of the Paddington Estate, the Grand Junction Canal Co., and, from the 1830s, the G.W.R. Co. As early as 1800 there were disputes with the Grand Junction Canal Co. over threatened rights of way[35] and from 1806 complaints were made to the bishop and his lessees over their responsibility for the spread or subdivision of poor tenements.[36] The bishop's liability to poor rate in respect of the great tithes, which were let on lease, and the amount for which the canal company should be assessed were both referred to arbitration in 1810.[37] Reluctance by the select vestry to assume the upkeep of new roads led to an action in King's Bench in 1829 by the bishop, his lessees, and the company, who were jointly responsible for laying out Grand Junction Street. The Lord Chief Justice refused to order the appointment of a surveyor, since few houses had been built and the parish, lacking an income from new occupiers, would be forced to maintain the road for the benefit of the builders.[38]

Income in the late 17th century came mainly from rent for the parish properties and from poor rates. A church rate was occasionally levied, as in 1679 on 38 inhabitants and 8 non-residents,[39] while smaller sums included several for the burial of people hanged at Tyburn[40] and in 1717 the minister's gift of his offerings to buy coal for the poor.[41] The parish's half share in fees for burials in the church or churchyard rose considerably in the 18th century and was probably responsible for a note in 1786 that no church rates had been made since 1712,[42] although poor rates were levied by the 1750s.[43] Rents were later raised and supplemented by fines for inclosures, the churchwardens' receipts of c. £142 in 1774–5 including £50 for a trespass on the bread and cheese lands. In 1814–15 their receipts of c. £728 consisted largely

[19] Vestry mins. 1753–9, 1793–1812, *passim*; 17 Oct. 1823.
[20] Ibid. 7 Apr. 1818; 13 Apr. 1819.
[21] Ibid. 4, 11 Apr. 1820; 30 Mar., 24 Apr. 1821; 30 Mar. 1822.
[22] Ibid. 1 July 1824; 5 Geo. IV, c. 126 (Local and Personal).
[23] Select vestry mins. 6 July 1824; 5 May 1829.
[24] Select vestry mins. *passim*.
[25] Ibid. 6 July 1824; 1 Mar. 1825.
[26] Ibid. 1831–6, *passim*.
[27] Ibid. 1 Aug. 1826.
[28] e.g. ibid. 4 Aug. 1829.
[29] Ibid. 5 Aug. 1828.
[30] Ibid. 6 Aug., 17, 22 Oct. 1833; 10 Dec. 1834.

[31] *Lucas's Paddington Dir.* (1843).
[32] Robins, *Paddington*, 185–6, 196–9.
[33] Select vestry mins. 25 May 1830; 5 Apr. 1836; *The Times*, 12 Apr. 1836, 7e; 2 May 1836, 6b.
[34] Vestry mins. 7 Mar. 1815; select vestry mins. 6 Jan. 1835.
[35] Vestry mins. 30 June 1800; 14 May 1801; 4 Feb., 27 May 1802.
[36] Ibid. 19 Jan. 1811; 2 Dec. 1808; 4 Aug. 1812.
[37] Ibid. 27 Oct. 1807; 3 Nov. 1810.
[38] Select vestry mins. 8 Jan. 1828; 2 June 1829.
[39] Chwdns. acct. bk. (1656–1736), ff. 32–3.
[40] e.g. ibid. ff. 52, 55.   [41] Ibid. f. 87.
[42] Ibid. note at front of vol.; below, churches.
[43] e.g. vestry mins. 26 Oct. 1753.

of £555 for burials and £105 rents.[44] The local Act of 1824 enabled money to be borrowed on the security of the rates,[45] and the select vestry's establishment of standing committees was followed by the levying of separate rates for the poor, for highways, and for lighting and watching.[46] Rates were assessed by wards from 1773, when 56 properties were listed in Bayswater ward, 37 in Paddington ward, probably in or near Edgware Road, 50 in the Square, probably around Paddington green, and 16 in Kilburn.[47]

Poor relief, in the form of individual payments in money or in kind, was recorded from 1657.[48] Regular allowances were presumably made by 1670, when casual payments were listed separately.[49] The vestry in the 1750s still decided in detail the weekly sums to be paid to the 'pension poor', numbering 10 or 11 recipients in the summer of 1754; pensioners were paid by the overseers and casual recipients by the churchwardens.[50] By the 1790s the vestry merely gave general approval to the actions of its officers. Parish property was leased rather than used for paupers,[51] although in 1757 the vestry decided to provide beds in one of its houses and in 1801 to furnish and warm an almshouse hitherto reserved for the casual poor.[52] S. P. Cockerell urged the provision of a proper place in 1809, when the needy were 'kept by contract like animals at a distance of 5 miles'. A house had recently been taken for the sick poor in 1815 and it was proposed to take a larger one, to relieve the heavy burden of weekly allowances, in 1818.[53] That or some other converted building was described as a workhouse from 1820, when the first select vestry decided on admissions, leaving its daily supervision to the assistant overseer and a matron. It was rented from the charity estates and may have been enlarged by the addition of a house on either side following a recommendation of 1833;[54] in 1838 the poor were said to have occupied three buildings in Harrow Road.[55] Admissions from 1824 were decided by the guardian board, which managed tenders for supplying the workhouse.[56] There were 23 inmates, including 14 children, in 1821, when 154 paupers with 89 children were on the pension list, and 47 inmates, of whom 17 were children, in 1833; the adults were mostly old.[57] The guardian board also maintained a few refractory and other paupers at William Perry's farmhouse in Islington, besides lunatics at private establishments.[58]

The cost of maintaining the poor was £165 in 1776 and an average of £289 during the three years

1783–5.[59] It was said in 1802 to have greatly increased[60] and rose from £694 in 1803 to £4,376 by 1831, although in the later years it did not match the growth in population: the expense for each inhabitant was 7s. 4d. in 1803, 9s. 5d. in 1813, and only 6s. in 1831.[61] The guardian board in 1826 took pride in an unprecedentedly low poor rate and in 1836 attributed further economies to greater vigilance and a move towards relief in kind rather than in money.[62] Auditors commended the management of the workhouse in 1828 but complained of extravagance, which a select vestry committee denied, in 1833. Newspaper stories about callous treatment led the vestry to admit reporters to its meeting in 1836, when it resolved to allow less discretion to the assistant overseer.[63]

LOCAL GOVERNMENT AFTER 1837. Paddington in 1837 became the largest financial contributor to Kensington poor law union, which also contained Chelsea, Fulham, Hammersmith, and Kensington.[64] Having opposed the Poor Law Amendment Act in 1834 and later requested sole responsibility for its own poor, the vestry remained hostile to the union, with the support of legal advice.[65] Claims for independence were renewed after the secession of Chelsea in 1841, when plans for a central workhouse for the remaining parishes were resisted,[66] until both Paddington and Kensington became separate poor law districts in 1845.[67]

The poor had left the houses in Harrow Road by 1838, when the property was to be leased out.[68] When Paddington resumed control of its poor, it continued to pay Kensington union for housing the adults until 1846, when they were moved to the establishment of Mr. Drouet at Brixton (Surr.), where children had already been lodged by the late union.[69] The new board of guardians also bought provisions by contract for its relieving officer to give to the outdoor poor and hired a house at the corner of Hermitage Street as a temporary relief centre.[70] Meanwhile c. 5 a. on the south side of Harrow Road next to the Lock hospital were bought from the Paddington Estate and an adjoining strip along the canal was leased from the Grand Junction Canal Co. A workhouse was built there in 1846–7[71] and staffed with officers who included a master, matron, medical officer, chaplain, schoolmaster, and schoolmistress.[72] Paddington maintained 211 indoor and 627 outdoor paupers, 18 for every 1,000 inhabitants, in 1850, and

44 Chwdns. acct. bk. (1774–1833) [unpag.].
45 Select vestry mins. 7 Sept., 5 Oct. 1824.
46 e.g. ibid. 21 Sept., 5 Oct. 1824.
47 Poor rate bk. (1721–74).
48 Chwdns. acct. bk. (1656–1736), f. 5.
49 Overseers' acct. bk. (1670–90).
50 Vestry mins. 22 May, 27 Sept. 1754; 11 Oct. 1759.
51 Chwdns. acct. bk. (1656–1736), passim.
52 Vestry mins. 9 Oct. 1757; 11 Nov. 1801.
53 Ibid. 20 Oct. 1809; 5 Dec. 1815; 3 Feb. 1818.
54 Ibid. 11 Aug. 1820; Guardian bd. mins. 25 Jan. 1833; 30 June 1837.
55 Select vestry mins. 6 Feb. 1838.
56 Select vestry mins.; guardian bd. mins. passim.
57 Rep. Com. Poor Laws, H.C. 44, p. 166g (1834), xxxv; vestry mins. 30 Mar. 1821; select vestry mins. 5 Mar. 1833.
58 Weekly figures for all paupers accommodated at par. expense were supplied by the asst. overseer: guardian bd. mins. passim; below, pub. svces.
59 Abstract of Returns by Overseers, 1787, H.C. 1st ser. ix.

60 Vestry mins. 22 Sept. 1802.
61 Rep. Com. Poor Laws, 166f.
62 Guardian bd. mins. 6 Apr. 1826; 26 June 1835.
63 Select vestry mins. 5 Aug. 1828; 6 Aug. 1833; 29 Jan., 11 Feb. 1836; The Times, 30 Jan. 1836, 5c; 12 Feb. 1836, 6c.
64 Poor Law Com. 4th Rep. H.C. 147, App. D, p. 98 (1840), xviii.
65 Select vestry mins. 28 July 1834; 4 Oct. 1836; 7 Mar. 1837.
66 Ibid. 5 Jan., 1 June 1841; 5 Apr. 1842.
67 Poor Law Com. 11th Rep. H.C. 624, p. 14 (1845), xxvii.
68 Select vestry mins. 6 Feb. 1838.
69 G.L.R.O., Pa. B.G. 1/1 (guardians' min. bk. 1845–7), ff. 37–8, 66, 211, 222. Wm. Drouet kept an inf. sch. at Brixton Hill: P.O. Dir. Six Home Counties (1845).
70 G.L.R.O., Pa. B.G. 1/1, ff. 11, 44, 194, 322.
71 Ibid. ff. 13, 20, 31, 37, and passim; Lucas, Plan of Paddington (1855).
72 G.L.R.O., Pa. B.G. 1/1, f. 373 and passim; Pa. B.G. 79/1, list of appts. at end.

proportionately fewer in 1860; after extensions for the sick, there were 605 indoor and 2,108 outdoor paupers, 28 for every 1,000 inhabitants, in 1870.[73] Despite the subsequent opening of a separate infirmary[74] the workhouse continued to receive infirm and lying-in patients and was certified for 703 inmates by 1884.[75]

The guardians greatly reduced out relief in the 1880s and 1890s, when they provided more accommodation.[76] Paupers were maintained at the workhouse until the First World War, when Paddington and other districts transferred their poor to Marylebone.[77] A chapel to seat 300, with an apsidal chancel and aisled and clerestoried nave, was built over the workhouse's remodelled dining hall by the guardians' architect H. H. Collins in 1875.[78]

The highway board and the finance committee continued to be renewed annually after 1837, it being reaffirmed in 1850 that each should have 18 members besides the minister, church officers, and resident J.P.s.[79] A committee for new churches existed from 1837 and became virtually a standing body, although in 1847 it was not required to report regularly.[80] The highway board had been charged with abating nuisances, but in 1849 a sanitary committee was appointed to enforce the Nuisances Removal Act.[81] A burial board was set up in 1853, when the vestry renewed for another year the highway board and the finance, sanitary, church, almshouse ground, and parliamentary committees.[82]

Paddington vestry was unusual in its readiness to raise bank loans, whether for new churches or, in the 1850s, for road and sewage works. In other respects it was a conservative body, opposed to all early plans for railway links with the City and to spending on lodging houses or baths for working men.[83] Continuing to resist the introduction of Hobhouse's Act, the vestry in 1849 printed a reply to complaints by the Paddington association and in 1853 was required to send to the Home Secretary the names of supporters of the Act who had been struck off the voters' lists.[84] Among the critics was William Robins, who opposed large grants towards churches which he thought should have been built by the bishop and his lessees; in his history of Paddington he lamented that the parish enjoyed less representative government than its neighbours.[85]

A new vestry hall was built in 1853, by means of a loan to be repaid by a special rate.[86] A faculty was obtained for appropriating the site, on the north side of Harrow Road west of the church, which had been bought from the Paddington Estate in 1843 in order to enlarge the burial ground and accordingly had

been vested in the incumbent.[87] The building, designed by James Lockyer, was two-storeyed with projecting pedimented wings connected by a Tuscan colonnade forming a porch; the front was faced with white brick, the colonnade was of Portland stone, and other details were of Portland cement. It was enlarged in 1900, as the town hall, and again in 1920, the additions including an eastern projection in the original style and an entrance canopy; panels in the outer hall were unveiled as a war memorial in 1924. The hall was closed in 1965, to make room for Westway, and the war memorial removed to St. James's church, with other fittings. When it was found that the vestry had paid no money for the site, the Church rather than Westminster city council obtained compensation from the G.L.C. and spent the large sum in the 1970s on restoring St. Mary's church.[88]

A metropolitan vestry was elected under the Metropolis Local Management Act, 1855, a measure which the select vestry's parliamentary committee had opposed.[89] Paddington elected one member of the Metropolitan Board of Works. Parish government was left to a metropolitan vestry, consisting of the vicar, churchwardens, and overseers, a representative of the M.B.W., and 72 vestrymen, at first including William Robins; the members, one third of whom were to retire every year, represented four unnamed wards. Highway and finance committees were each to consist of the minister, parish officers, and 18 members, as before, and a standing sanitary and public health committee followed in 1856.[90]

The new metropolitan vestry continued to protect local interests against the G.W.R. Co. and the Grand Junction Canal Co., particularly over rate assessments, rights of way, and pollution.[91] It asked to be allowed to rate new buildings on part of St. George's burial ground and that Paddington should form a separate parliamentary borough,[92] it complained of inadequate policing and of the M.B.W.'s extravagance, and it opposed Bills for tramways through Bayswater and for equalization of the rates.[93] In 1868 it claimed that the lighting, general, church, vestry premises, and sewer rates, all for expenditure within the vestry's control, had not increased faster than new property had been brought into rating.[94]

In the 1870s Paddington achieved a reputation for progressive policies, exemplified in spending on a public laundry and baths and on street improvements. They were the work of a 'shopocracy' largely composed of rivals of William Whiteley and led by James Flood, chairman of the baths commissioners,

[73] Return of Paupers in each Union, H.C. 214, p. 1 (1876), lxiii; G.L.R.O., Pa. B.G. 79/1, 27 Jan. 1869 and passim.
[74] Below, pub. svces.
[75] Return relating to Accn. in Workhos. and Infirmaries in Metropolis, H.C. 93, pp. 2–3 (1888), lxxxvii.
[76] Booth, Life and Labour, iii (3), 128–9.
[77] A. R. Neate, Marylebone Workho. (1967), 33.
[78] Paddington, Kensington and Bayswater Chron. 20 Mar. 1875.
[79] Select vestry mins. 4 Apr. 1837; 9 Apr. 1850.
[80] Ibid. 5 Dec. 1837; 3 Dec. 1839; 2 Mar. 1847.
[81] Ibid. 1 Aug. 1848; 4 Dec. 1849.
[82] Ibid. 15 July 1853; 25 Apr. 1854.
[83] Reeder, 'Capital Investment', 153–4.
[84] Select vestry mins. 6 Feb., 6 Mar. 1849; 1 Mar., 7 June 1853.
[85] Ibid. 28 June 1853; 3 Jan. 1854; Robins, Paddington, 199.
[86] Select vestry mins. 4 Jan., 3 May, 1 Nov. 1853.
[87] Ibid. 5 Feb., 23 Mar. 1850.
[88] Pevsner, Lond. ii. 303; Official Guide to Paddington [1921]; Marylebone libr., P 131.1, cuttings s.v. St. Mary's; P 137; below, churches.
[89] 18 & 19 Vic. c. 120; select vestry mins. 17 Apr. 1854; metropolitan vestry mins. 27 Nov. 1855.
[90] Metropolitan vestry mins. 4 Dec. 1855; 26 Feb. 1856. Wards in Lond. Gaz. 20 Oct. 1855, p. 3880, and Lucas, Plan of Paddington (1869).
[91] e.g. metropolitan vestry mins. 15 Jan. 1856; 21 June, 18 Oct. 1859; 19 June 1860; The Times, 5 July 1858, 11a; ibid. 14 Apr. 1859, 11c; Dolling's Dir. Paddington (1862, 1863).
[92] Metropolitan vestry mins. 7 Dec. 1858; 8 Feb. 1859.
[93] Ibid. 15 July, 16 Dec. 1856; 16 Mar., 20 Apr. 1858.
[94] Ibid. 17 Mar. 1868.

whose estate agency may have been threatened by Whiteley's expansion into that field. Whiteley, with whom the vestry was often in dispute, chiefly over his plans to rebuild premises in Queen's Road next to the baths, had an ally in his own solicitor Charles Mills Roche, who was influential both in the vestry and the M.B.W. Flood's party was accused of penalizing the richest residents, Whiteley's best customers, through rate assessments. By supporting an existing ratepayers' association, Whiteley attacked fiercely in the vestry elections of 1879, with only partial success. Further struggles took place in 1880 and 1881, after Roche's suspension by the Law Society, although they did not prevent Whiteley from putting up more buildings in Queen's Road. Flood retired in 1883 and thereafter municipal spending was more restrained.[95]

Under the London Government Act, 1888, two members represented Paddington North and two represented Paddington South on the new L.C.C.[96] There were still 72 vestrymen elected by four wards in 1890, with finance, works, sanitary, legal, assessment, and electric lighting committees, besides a burial board and commissioners for public baths. From 1895 there were six wards: Harrow Road, Maida Vale, Church, Westbourne, Lancaster Gate, and Hyde Park.[97]

BOROUGH OF PADDINGTON. *Azure, in chief two wolves' heads argent and in the base two swords proper pommelled and hilted or, crossed saltirewise and passing through a mural crown or*
[Granted 1902]

Paddington metropolitan borough was created under the London Government Act, 1899.[98] The borough council, incorporated in 1902,[99] consisted of a mayor, 9 aldermen, and 60 councillors for 8 wards: Queen's Park and the wards of the 1890s, Lancaster Gate having been divided. The first mayor was the contractor John Aird (1833–1911), who was created a baronet and who had moved in 1874 to no. 14 Hyde Park Terrace.[1] In 1903 the town hall, formerly the vestry hall, was the meeting place of the council twice monthly, and also of finance, works, public health, legal and parliamentary, assessment, cemetery, public baths, and libraries committees.[2] A new ward, Town, had been created by 1919;[3] thereafter, except during the 1920s when Westbourne was temporarily divided, the borough council

always had 9 wards with 70 representatives until 1965,[4] when Paddington, under the London Government Act, 1963, joined Westminster and St. Marylebone in the new city of Westminster.[5]

CITY OF WESTMINSTER. *Azure, between two wolves' heads argent and on a base wavy argent and azure, a female figure vested and mantled and on her sinister arm a child vested, around the head of each a halo, all or; on a chief or charged with a pale azure a cross flory between five martlets or, between two united roses argent upon gules*
[Granted 1964]

Conservatives, at first called Moderates and from 1906 Municipal Reformers, controlled the council until 1945.[6] Often returned unopposed in Hyde Park, Lancaster Gate, and Maida Vale wards,[7] they won all 60 seats in 1922 and 1931 and never held less than 37, the number held in 1937.[8] Labour gained control with 34 seats in 1945 but lost it to the Conservatives in 1949 and thereafter remained in opposition.[9]

In the first metropolitan borough elections, of 1900 and 1903, a smaller percentage of the electorate voted in Paddington than in any other London borough. In 1906 41.3 per cent voted, more than in two other boroughs, in 1919 only 23.1 per cent, and in 1931 28.8 per cent. The turnout was close to London's average after the Second World War.[10]

The parliamentary borough of Marylebone included Paddington from 1832 until the constituencies of Paddington North and Paddington South were created under the Redistribution of Seats Act, 1885. The northern division, originally covering no. 2 ward,[11] was united with the southern before the general elections of 1974. Except in 1906 Paddington North returned a Conservative or Unionist until 1945, after which it remained a Labour seat. Members included Sir John Aird from 1887 to 1905 and Brendan, later Viscount, Bracken (1901–58) from 1929 to 1945. Paddington South always returned a Conservative, from 1885 until 1892 Lord Randolph Churchill (1849–95),[12] who lived at no. 2 Connaught Place.[13] The united Paddington constituency returned a Labour member in 1974 and a Conservative in 1979.[14] The same Conservative was returned for a new seat, Westminster North, which included Paddington except its south-eastern corner and stretched eastward over much of Marylebone, in 1983 and 1987.[15]

In 1906 a comparatively modest 73.7 per cent of

[95] Lambert, *Universal Provider*, 80–3, 101, 108–9, 114; Reeder, 'Capital Investment', 389–91.
[96] *Paddington, Bayswater, and Kensal Green Dir.* (1890).
[97] *Kelly's Dir. Mdx.* (1895).
[98] A. Bassett Hopkins, *Boros. of the Metropolis* (1900), 48.
[99] Scott Giles, *Civic Heraldry*, 257.
[1] *Kelly's Dir. Mdx.* (1903); *D.N.B.*
[2] *Kelly's Dir. Mdx.* (1903).
[3] *The Times*, 4 Nov. 1919, 14b.
[4] *Official Guide to Paddington* [1921, 1925]; *Paddington Past and Present* [1936]; *The Times*, 12 May 1956, 10d.
[5] City of Westm. *Official Guide* [1980–1].
[6] Election results in *The Times*, 3 Nov. 1900, 14c; 3 Nov. 1906, 5c; and *passim*.

[7] e.g. ibid. 2 Nov. 1912, 11b; 4 Nov. 1925, 9c; 3 Nov. 1928, 7f.
[8] Ibid. 3 Nov. 1922, 14d, 16c; 4 Nov. 1931, 12d; 3 Nov. 1937, 19b, c.
[9] Ibid. 3 Nov. 1945, 12d; 14 May 1949, 2b; and *passim*.
[10] L.C.C. *Lond. Statistics*, xvii. 19, 22; xxv. 17; N.S. i. 26, 31.   [11] *V.C.H. Mdx.* ii. 58; 48 & 49 Vic. c. 23.
[12] *British Parl. Election Results, 1885–1916*, ed. F. W. S. Craig (1974); *1918–49* (1969); *1950–70* (1971); *D.N.B.*
[13] *Royal Blue Bk.* (1883, 1892).
[14] *Whitaker's Almanack* (1975, 1980).
[15] Ibid. (1984); *Boundary Com. for Eng. 3rd Rep.* ii, maps [Cmnd. 8979-II] (1983); *The Times*, 13 June 1987, 19c.

the electorate voted in Paddington North and 72.1 per cent in Paddington South. The proportions fell to 60.3 and 55.7 per cent in 1935. Paddington North always had the larger turnout, the numbers differing as widely as 81 and 71.7 per cent in 1951.[16]

PUBLIC SERVICES. In 1440 Westminster abbey allowed the City of London to draw water from a close in Bayswater called Oxleas, which probably was bounded on the west by Bayswater brook.[17] In 1471 works were completed whereby the water, from springs rather than from the brook, was channelled east-south-east past Tyburn gallows to supplement an earlier supply from Marylebone. The whole Paddington conduit system was sold by the City to the bishop of London and his lessees under an Act of 1812.[18] A conduit house known as the Roundhead, probably 15th-century but later repaired, survived in 1835 and perhaps in 1844.

A regular water supply for Paddington itself[19] was first authorized in 1798, when the Grand Junction Canal Co. was to provide drinking water from its abundant canal water.[20] Nothing was done until after the West Middlesex Water Co., established in 1806, had been empowered to extend its supply to Paddington in 1810.[21] The Grand Junction Waterworks Co. was thereupon set up by an Act of 1811, under which tenants of the Paddington Estate were to pay 10 per cent less than the company's consumers elsewhere. A pumping station was built between the new Grand Junction Street (later Sussex Gardens) and Conduit Street, its position and the height of its furnace chimney being laid down in the Act.[22] Canal water having proved impure, the company bought a site at Chelsea in 1820 and pumped Thames water to three reservoirs in Paddington.[23] After sediment had settled in the Northern reservoir, water passed to the Southern, whence a low-level service supply was drawn, and finally to the Engine reservoir, for a more expensive high-level service. Both the Paddington and Chelsea works were closed after the company moved its intake point to Kew under an Act of 1835. Between 1842 and 1851[24] the Northern, Southern, and Engine reservoirs made way for the first block of St. Mary's hospital and for Norfolk Square and Talbot Square respectively. Meanwhile the West Middlesex Waterworks Co. continued its supply, despite having been attacked in 1819 for overcharging,[25] and from 1855 both companies supplied adequately filtered water from near Hampton.[26] In 1888 part of Bayswater and houses by Edgware Road near Paddington green were served by the West Middlesex, leaving Tyburnia and most of the

parish to the Grand Junction Canal Co.[27] Under the Metropolis Water Act, 1902, both companies were superseded by the Metropolitan Water Board, on which the borough councils were represented. In 1859 the Metropolitan Free Drinking Fountains Association was paid to provide five public fountains.[28]

Sewerage probably first became a problem with the construction of the canal basin and nearby buildings. The shooting of night soil on the wharves had greatly increased in 1808, when prosecutions were ordered, and again in 1817, when the vestry resisted a demand for a rate by the commissioners of sewers for Westminster. The demand was said to be unprecedented and not justified by any services,[29] presumably because the commissioners were concerned with drainage of surface water rather than sewerage. In 1825 they fined the parish's highway surveyor for filling in a pond near the church.[30]

Meanwhile the Westbourne had also become known as the Ranelagh sewer; part of the stream had been straightened north of the Uxbridge road[31] and a branch had been built across Hyde Park in 1810 to drain the Paddington Estate.[32] The Grand Junction Canal Co. was paid by the parish in 1826 for constructing an outfall under its canal and was also asked to build a sewer in Harrow Road. In view of Paddington's rapid growth, eight names were put forward in 1834 for inclusion on the Westminster commission, on which there had previously been only three representatives.[33] Under an Act of 1834 soil drainage from new houses into the Westbourne was to be diverted from the Serpentine by a new sewer along the Uxbridge road, which would connect near the end of Albion Street with a sewer representing the small stream once sometimes called Tyburn brook.[34] A stretch of the Westbourne south-west from Kilburn bridge, part of the main Ranelagh sewer, was straightened by the commissioners c. 1840.[35]

The Metropolitan Commissioners of Sewers replaced the commissions for Westminster and six other areas in 1847 and themselves made way for the Metropolitan Board of Works under the Metropolis Management Act, 1855. The vestry thereupon became responsible for enforcing house drainage, abating nuisances, and building local sewers with the approval of the M.B.W., which, after the Metropolis Local Management Amendment Act, 1858, was free to concentrate on the main 'intercepting' sewers which were to convey sewage outside the London area.[36] Paddington's new medical officer of health found that the sewers were unsatisfactory, having been made piecemeal:[37] among the worst nuisances were cesspools to cottages in Elms Lane,

[16] L.C.C. *Lond. Statistics*, xvii. 12; xli. 19; N.S. iii. 12–13.
[17] Para. based on *T.L.M.A.S.* viii. 9–59; H. W. Dickinson, *Water Supply of Gtr. Lond.* (1954), 11.
[18] 52 Geo. III, c. 193 (Local and Personal).
[19] Para. based on Dickinson, *Water Supply*, 98–100.
[20] 38 Geo. III, c. 33 (Local and Personal); Hadfield, *Canals of E. Midlands*, 118.
[21] 46 Geo. III, c. 119 (Local and Personal); 50 Geo. III, c. 132 (Local and Personal).
[22] 51 Geo. III, c. 169 (Local and Personal).
[23] Gutch, *Plan of Paddington* (1828, 1840); Lucas, *Plan of Paddington* (1842).
[24] Lucas, *Plan of Paddington* (1842, 1855); J. Weale, *Lond. Exhibited* (1851), map.
[25] Vestry mins. 13, 29 Apr. 1819.

[26] *Paddington San. Rep. 1856* (in Marylebone libr.), 20.
[27] P. A. Scratchley, *Lond. Water Supply* (1888), maps.
[28] [Metropolitan] vestry mins. 5 July 1859.
[29] Vestry mins. 26 May 1808; 2 Sept. 1817.
[30] Ibid. 6 Sept. 1825.
[31] *Westm. Sewers*, H.C. 156, p. 5 (1841), xxvii; Gutch, *Plan of Paddington* (1828).
[32] G. W. Humphreys, *Main Drainage of Lond.* (L.C.C. rep. 1930), 9.
[33] Vestry mins. 4 July 1826; 26 Sept. 1834.
[34] 4 & 5 Wm. IV, c. 96.
[35] Select vestry mins. 5 Oct. 1841, with plan by Geo. Gutch.
[36] Humphreys, *Drainage of Lond.* 5–6, 12.
[37] H. Jephson, *San. Evolution of Lond.* (1907), 100.

Bayswater, the subject of repeated complaints.[38] After 2,201 house inspections in 1856, the vestry advertised for builders and executed over 1,600 works through its sewerage department, suggesting that two out of every three houses had been sanitarily defective.[39] Although the canal basin, the slaughter houses, and other nuisances remained, the sewers were reported satisfactory in 1858.[40] Problems increased again, with a rising population: the inspector of nuisances appointed in 1856 was given an assistant in 1866 and nearly 1,000 sanitary orders a year were issued in 1870. Meanwhile the Ranelagh sewer was covered in by the M.B.W.,[41] whose middle-level 'intercepting' sewer, running eastward along Bayswater Road with a storm relief sewer branching south through Hyde Park, was built between 1861 and 1864. The L.C.C., succeeding the M.B.W. in 1889, built a second middle-level sewer across the north part of the parish and Marylebone between 1906 and 1911.[42]

Medical expenses met by the churchwardens included payments for nursing from 1722, to a midwife from 1728, and for an apothecary from 1731.[43] A salaried apothecary was chosen in 1794 and a successor, who was allowed extra expenses, in 1799, another being dismissed in 1807. A higher salary, to cover midwifery and medicines, was granted in 1810 and was doubled in 1816.[44] In 1824 the parish surgeon and apothecary was considered an officer of the select vestry's guardian board, which appointed a midwife at a fixed rate for cases outside the workhouse.[45]

Subscriptions to a hospital were urged in 1816, shortly after the equipping of a house for the sick poor, and to a lunatic asylum in 1817.[46] Concerned at drownings in the canal, the vestry sought resuscitatory apparatus from the Royal Humane Society in 1814 and paid an annual subscription in 1824.[47] Use of the Royal Sea-Bathing infirmary at Margate was discussed in 1825.[48] Lunatics were boarded at private asylums outside the parish at least from 1826 and at the county asylum at Hanwell after its opening in 1831.[49] Paddington's Act of 1824 permitted patients to be sent up to 10 miles away and a parochial infirmary to be provided.[50] Annual payments were made to the smallpox, St. George's, and Middlesex hospitals in 1826, and also to the London fever hospital in 1827 and Queen Charlotte's lying-in hospital in 1828.[51]

Two non-parochial institutions had existed for a time in Bayswater. The first was the pest house which had been transferred from Westminster to 9 a. in Westbourne common fields by 1746. The land was leased for building on the death of William, earl of Craven, in 1825, Paddington vestry learning that it might be recovered only if there should be an outbreak of plague rather than of cholera,[52] and the ground rents were assigned in 1864 to two London hospitals.[53] The second was the kingdom's earliest lying-in hospital, which after several moves had been accommodated in 1773 in St. George's Row[54] and had moved again in 1791 a little to the west. The singer Mrs. Kennedy, whose husband was one of the physicians, died there in 1793. Known from 1791 as Bayswater, the Queen's, or Queen Charlotte's lying-in (later maternity) hospital, it had moved to Marylebone Road in 1813.[55] At Paddington green, the Royal Naval asylum occupied a rented house for at least 4 years before its removal to Greenwich in 1807.[56]

The London Lock hospital,[57] founded in 1746 for treatment of venereal disease, moved in 1842 from Grosvenor Place, Westminster, to Harrow Road. The site, 4 a. at the north-west end of the canal bridge near Westbourne Manor House, was bought from the G.W.R. Co. An asylum, which had been attached to the hospital since 1787, also moved to the new building, for which additional wings were opened in 1849 and 1867.[58] Although it served a wide area, the Lock gave rise to several parish societies[59] and at first derived pew rents from its chapel, which by 1890 was virtually a district church.[60] From the 1860s a government subsidy was received in return for the treatment of naval and military patients. A branch for men and for out-patients was opened in Dean Street, Soho, in 1862.[61] At Paddington there were 140 beds for women and 40 places in the asylum in 1890, when the two departments together constituted the only such specialist hospital in London,[62] supported by gifts and payments for paupers sent there from many workhouses. From 1893 the asylum was called a rescue home. The number of beds was reduced from 1932[63] but both hospital and home survived in 1935 at no. 283 Harrow Road. In 1938 a

[38] Select vestry mins. 1 Dec. 1846; 6 Apr. 1847; P.R.O., MH 13/261, nos. 6083/49, 2733/53, 5453/53.
[39] Select vestry mins. 20 Oct. 1857; Jephson, *San. Evolution of Lond.* 123. Inspection procedure described in *Paddington San. Rep. 1856*, 21–3.
[40] Select vestry mins. 2 Feb. 1858.
[41] *Replies from Vestries relative to San. Improvements*, H.C. 298, p. 16 (1872), xlix.
[42] Humphreys, *Drainage of Lond.* 6, 12, 30, and plan 2.
[43] Chwdns. acct. bk. (1656–1736), ff. 102, 118, 136–7, 152–4.
[44] Vestry mins. 22 Apr. 1794; 2 May 1799; 31 Mar., 7 May 1807.
[45] Guardian bd. mins. 16 Sept., 25 Nov. 1824; select vestry mins. 19 Dec. 1826.
[46] Vestry mins. 2 Jan., 2 July 1816; 4 Nov. 1817.
[47] Ibid. 2 Aug. 1814; 17 Jan. 1823.
[48] Guardian bd. mins. 2 June 1825.
[49] Ibid. 30 Mar. 1826; 23 Sept. 1831; *V.C.H. Mdx.* iv. 42.
[50] 5 Geo. IV, c. 126 (Local and Personal).
[51] Guardian bd. mins. 4 May, 3 Aug., 19 Oct. 1826; 3 May 1827; 20 Mar. 1828.
[52] *T.L.M.A.S.* viii. 29; Rocque, *Map of Lond.* (1741–5), sheet 11; McDonald, *Short Hist. Paddington*, no. 33,

pp. 78–80; above, manors (Craven).
[53] *Survey of Lond.* xxxi. 197.
[54] The hosp. is sometimes said to have been in St. George's Row in the 1750s, before the row was built, and even to have been founded there, but apparently it started in Jermyn Street (Westm.): Lysons, *Environs*, iii. 332; ibid. (Suppl.), 243; *Lond. and Its Environs Described* (1761), iii. 222; *Lond. Encyc.* 628.
[55] Lysons, *Environs*, iii. 332; ibid. (Suppl.), 243–4; Brewer, *Beauties of Eng. & Wales*, x (5), 166; *D.N.B.*; Marylebone libr., P 139.3, cuttings.
[56] Lysons, *Environs* (Suppl.), 244; M.L.R. 1803/4/451; *Accounts relating to the Royal Naval Asylum*, H.C. 227, p. 6 (1809), x.
[57] Para. based on Weale, *Lond. Exhibited*, 521, and *2nd Rep. Cttee. of H.L. on Metropolitan Hosps.* H.C. 457, pp. 325–35 (1890–1), xiii; *Short Hist. Lond. Lock Hosp. 1746–1906* (in Marylebone libr.); *Lond. Jnl.* x (2), 167–75.
[58] L. Slade, *Paddington As It Was and Is* (1877), 172–3.
[59] Robins, *Paddington*, 175.
[60] Below, churches (Christ Ch.).
[61] *Survey of Lond.* xxxiii. 140–1.
[62] *Rep. Cttee. of H.L. on Metrop. Hosps.* H.C. 392, pp. 198–9 (1890), xvi.
[63] L.C.C. *London Statistics*, xxxvii. 99.

new maternity centre was opened at no. 283A.[64] On the establishment of the N.H.S. in 1948, the premises served as an out-patients' department of Paddington hospital until 1952.[65]

The first buildings of the Lock hospital in Harrow Road were designed by Lewis Vulliamy, who intended others to be put up when funds should permit. The east wing of 1867 was designed by his pupil F. W. Porter, who also heightened the main block, and a nurses' home by Porter's son Horatio was added to the east wing c. 1909. Of extensive additions planned by A. Saxon Snell in 1918, only an out-patients' department was built. The chapel and Vulliamy's west wing were demolished soon after closure in 1952 but other buildings were used as offices or for record storage by the St. Charles group of hospitals until 1968, after which they stood empty.[66]

A house beside a canal wharf was used as a cholera hospital by a temporary board of health in 1832 but was soon returned to the Grand Junction Canal Co.[67] In 1844 a Marylebone coroner expressed surprise that so rich a parish as Paddington should have no infirmary of its own.[68] Beds for the sick poor were soon provided in the new workhouse,[69] for which a medical officer was appointed; the guardians also created two districts in 1845, although the medical officer for the western district was also the one who attended the workhouse until 1864.[70] The workhouse had fever and smallpox wards and could hold 131 patients, including 12 children and 10 lying-in women, in 1867, shortly before it was extended as a forerunner of Paddington infirmary.[71]

A free dispensary for women and children in 1853 was presumably Paddington provident dispensary, to which families contributed 1d. or 1½d. a week in 1851. Founded in 1838,[72] it remained at no. 104 Star Street until 1919.[73] Westbourne provident dispensary, founded in 1855, was in Bishop's Road by 1857, Westbourne Park Crescent by 1888, and at no. 244 Harrow Road until 1919. Kilburn general dispensary, founded in 1862 and also serving Maida Vale and St. John's Wood, was still at no. 13 Kilburn Park Road in the 1930s.[74] Paddington dispensary for the prevention of consumption was opened at no. 20 Talbot Road in 1909 and survived, with help from private donors, until 1941.[75]

A carriage for smallpox patients was provided by the guardians; it was discarded after the vestry, as sanitary authority, in 1863 had bought a new one, which was maintained by a contractor.[76] Lunatics were lodged at first both in private asylums and at Hanwell by the guardians, who obtained further accommodation by contributing to St. Mary's

hospital, besides the Lock and later the Royal Sea-Bathing infirmary and other specialized institutions.[77]

St. Mary's[78] was founded in 1845 as a general hospital, taking all except infectious cases, for the growing suburbs of north-west London. A building designed for 150 patients was opened, with 50, in 1851 between Praed Street and South Wharf Road, on part of the site of the Northern reservoir.[79] The governors were the subscribers of 3 gns. a year or donors of £30 and, with other contributors, were entitled to recommend people for treatment. Admission was practically free by 1890, when there was criticism of continued government by an open board. Further wings had been built, producing a total of 281 beds, and St. Mary's was then more advanced than the older metropolitan hospitals in that it accepted medical staff without degrees of the colleges of Physicians and Surgeons of London.[80] Still dependent mainly on subscriptions, it had in 1888 bought the reversion to a row of shops which separated the main building from Praed Street, the freehold of which site was soon given by the Ecclesiastical Commissioners. The construction there of the Clarence wing was followed in the 1920s by the conversion of nurses' dormitories into wards and the acquisition of land to the east for further building. There were 384 beds, all free, in 1935 and 475, including 66 private and mainly for acute cases, in 1949. The hospital was made directly responsible to the Ministry of Health on the establishment of the N.H.S. in 1948, when it was linked with five specialist hospitals near by.[81] St. Mary's, Praed Street, had 450 beds, of which 54 were private, in 1986, when it was administered by Paddington and North Kensington health authority.[82]

Teaching was from the first contemplated at St. Mary's, whose foundation was supported not only by local subscribers but by Samuel Lane, a surgeon with his own school of anatomy next to St. George's hospital. A school for 300 was completed behind St. Mary's and fronting South Wharf Road in 1854, when Lane joined the staff, and in 1890 some houses had recently been bought to establish a residential college. It was one of nine medical schools included in the university of London under the Gresham report of 1894 and consequently was later financed by grants made through the university. Affiliation with specialist hospitals, together with access to 200 beds at Paddington general hospital, had placed c. 1,000 beds at the school's disposal by 1965. St. Mary's is also distinguished for its inoculation department, in particular for the therapeutic work of Sir Almroth Wright,[83] who installed laboratories in

[64] Marylebone libr., P 139.3, cuttings.
[65] *Hosp. Year Bk.* (1935, 1949–50); below, Paddington infirmary.
[66] *Lond. Jnl.* x (2), 167–75 (inc. illus.).
[67] Marylebone libr., bd. of health mins. (1832) at back of watching and lighting sub-cttee. min. bk. (1830).
[68] Select vestry mins. 7 May 1844.
[69] G.L.R.O., Pa. B.G. 1/1, ff. 146–7.
[70] Ibid. ff. 6, 8; Pa. B.G. 79/1, f. 97 and list of offrs.
[71] Ibid. Pa. B.G. 79/1, ff. 125, 134 sqq.; below.
[72] Robins, *Paddington*, 173; Weale, *Lond. Exhibited*, 515.
[73] *P.O. Dir. Lond.* (1879, 1919).
[74] Ibid. (1857 and later edns.); *Kelly's Lond. Medical Dir.* (1892).
[75] *The Times*, 18 Mar. 1910, 21e; 1 Jan. 1931, 8c; *P.O.*

Dir. Lond. (1910, 1941).
[76] G.L.R.O., Pa. B.G. 79/1, f. 98; san. cttee. mins. 5 Mar., 16 July 1863; 27 Aug. 1867.
[77] G.L.R.O., Pa. B.G. 1/1, f. 157; Pa. B.G. 79/1, list of subscriptions.
[78] Following two paras. based on *2nd Rep. Cttee. on Metrop. Hosps.* 197–219; *Official Guide to Paddington* [1921]; *St. Mary's Hosp.* (booklet pub. for hosp. 1965), *passim.*
[79] Robins, *Paddington*, 171–3; *Illus. Lond. News*, 5 July 1845, 5; O.S. Map 1/2,500, Lond. XXXIII (1869 edn.).
[80] *Rep. Cttee. on Metrop. Hosps.* 242, 255, 290.
[81] *Hosp. Year Bk.* (1935, 1949–50); below.
[82] Inf. from gen. manager, St. Mary's hosp.
[83] *The Times*, 12 Dec. 1933, 15d; *D.N.B.*

the Clarence wing in 1907 and research wards in 1909, and of Alexander Fleming, who discovered penicillin there in 1928.[84]

The buildings of St. Mary's[85] include the original block, with its main entrance to the north-east in Norfolk (formerly Cambridge) Place. Designed for no fee by Thomas Hopper (1776–1856), who lived in Bayswater,[86] it is four-storeyed and of red brick with painted stone dressings, in a vaguely classical style. The south-west side is hidden from Praed Street by the florid Clarence wing of red brick and stone, begun in 1892 to the designs of William Emerson and finished in 1904. To the north-east are the combined medical school and pathological institute (later the Wright-Fleming institute of microbiology) of 1933[87] and, beyond, the nurses' home, of which the first part was opened in 1936.[88] Both are restrained neo-Georgian buildings by Sir Edwin Cooper, as is a private patients' wing north-west of the old block and opened in 1937; called after its donor F. C. Lindo, it was the birthplace of Prince William of Wales in 1982.[89] To the south-west in Praed Street is the Winston Churchill wing, in a contemporary style and opened in 1959,[90] with the yellow-brick 19th-century Mint wing behind. In the 1970s there were students' hostels at no. 32 Southwick Street and no. 54 Sussex Gardens. In 1985 the hospital planned another building, east of the block already under construction in South Wharf Road.[91]

Paddington infirmary,[92] later hospital, was built under the Metropolitan Poor Act, 1867. The name originally applied to the sick wards of the workhouse, which were extended in 1868, when a parochial dispensary and relief offices were also built, and again in 1874.[93] A new infirmary, a long north–south building between the workhouse and the Lock hospital, was opened in 1886.[94] Pavilions for men and for women held a total of 284 beds in 1890, when the medical superintendent was also responsible for 295 sick beds, including lying-in beds, in the workhouse. A course of lectures there allowed it to be claimed that Paddington's was the only metropolitan infirmary where clinical instruction, normally restricted to general hospitals, had recently been attempted. The infirmary's staff were better qualified than the medical staff of the workhouse, where the union guardians insisted on keeping overall control. The infirmary was transferred to the L.C.C. under the Local Government Act, 1929,[95] and, as Paddington hospital, had 603 beds at no. 285 Harrow Road in 1935. It was called Paddington General hospital from 1954 until 1968, when it became the

Harrow Road branch of St. Mary's. There were 431 beds, mainly for acute cases, in 1981 and 166 in 1985. The branch was due to close in 1986.[96]

Paddington Green children's hospital[97] was established in 1883 as the successor to a dispensary which had been opened in 1862 in Bell Street, Marylebone. The hospital occupied two new houses at the north-east corner of Paddington green, to which an iron waiting room and an out-patients' department were added, until it was rebuilt on the same site in 1894–5.[98] It was financed by gifts, which included £5,000 bequeathed in 1907 by Samuel Lewis, and in 1911 opened a new out-patients' department, which was extended in 1934.[99] There were 27 beds in 1892, 46 in 1920, 51 in 1935, and 16 in 1985.[1] From 1948 it was affiliated to St. Mary's. A convalescent home for the children's hospital was opened at Lightwater (Surr.) in 1931.[2]

St. Luke's hospital for advanced cases was opened in Osnaburgh Street, St. Pancras, in 1893 as a branch of the West London Mission. It moved to Hampstead in 1901, to Pembridge Square, North Kensington, in 1903, and to a new building with 48 beds in Hereford Road in 1923. Affiliated to St. Mary's in 1948, it had 42 beds for pre-convalescence and terminal care in 1981.[3] After being renamed Hereford Lodge, its functions were divided between St. Charles hospital, North Kensington, and Paddington Community hospital.[4]

Three other specialist hospitals were affiliated to St. Mary's in 1948: the Samaritan hospital for women and the Western Ophthalmic hospital, both in Marylebone Road, and Princess Louise's children's hospital, Kensington.

Chepstow Lodge, four converted houses in Chepstow Road, backing on St. Luke's hospital, was opened as a pre-convalescent annexe of St. Mary's by 1965 and had 47 beds in 1981 and 24 in 1985.[5] Joyce Grove in Nettlebed (Oxon.) was given to the hospital in 1938 and converted into a convalescent home in 1955. Chepstow Lodge had been superseded by Paddington Community hospital in 1986.[6]

Paddington Community hospital took over part of St. Marys' former premises in Harrow Road. It contained Chepstow unit, the first to open, in 1982, attended by general practitioners and with 24 beds, and Pembridge unit, for continuing care, with 22 beds. Maternity and mental health clinics had also been brought to Harrow Road by 1986, when other parts of the site were to be sold.[7]

Warrington Lodge was opened as a private hospital in a former girls' school, originally two houses,

[84] Plaque on bldg.; *D.N.B.*
[85] Para. based on Pevsner, *Lond.* ii. 304; Marylebone libr., P 139.3, cuttings.
[86] Robins, *Paddington*, 171; Colvin, *Brit. Architects*, 433; above, plate 46.
[87] *St. Mary's Hosp.* 22, 29.
[88] *The Times*, 12 Dec. 1933, 11*f*; 19 Nov. 1936, 11*b*.
[89] Ibid. 11 Nov. 1937, 11*c*; 2 Mar. 1938, 19*c*; 22 June 1982, 1*b*.
[90] Ibid. 29 May 1959, 17*e*.
[91] *Paddington Basin Draft Planning Brief, 1985* (in Marylebone libr.).
[92] Para. based on *Second Rep. Cttee. on Metrop. Hosps.* 647–57.
[93] *Return relating to Bldgs. for Paupers (Metropolis)*, H.C. 86, p. 3 (1876), lxiii.
[94] *Return relating to Accn. in Workhos.* 2–3; Bacon, *Atlas of Lond.* (1886).
[95] L.C.C. *London Statistics*, xxxv. 98.

[96] *Hosp. Year Bk.* (1935, 1981, 1985); *Paddington Group, 5th Ann. Rep. of Hosp. Management Cttee. 1953–4*; Marylebone libr., P 139.3, cuttings; inf. from gen. manager.
[97] Following four paras. based on *St. Mary's Hosp.* 43, 50, 54–5.
[98] Marylebone libr., P 139.3, cuttings.
[99] *Official Guide to Paddington* [1921, 1936]; *The Times*, 17 Nov. 1911, 11*a*.
[1] *Kelly's Lond. Medical Dir.* (1892); L.C.C. *Lond. Statistics*, xxvii. 86; *Hosp. Year Bk.* (1935, 1985).
[2] *The Times*, 26 Oct. 1933, 16*c*.
[3] *Hosp. Year Bk.* (1981).
[4] Ibid. (1985); inf. from gen. manager, St. Mary's hosp.
[5] *Hosp. Year Bk.* (1981, 1985); inf. from gen. manager, St. Mary's hosp.
[6] Inf. from gen. manager, St. Mary's hosp.
[7] Inf. from Mrs. Meacher, Paddington community hosp.

in 1886 by Dr. Heywood Smith. The event was hailed as marking the rehabilitation of Smith, a gynaecologist of Harley Street, who had been censured for his examination of a girl who had figured in a widely publicized abduction case. Warrington Lodge was equipped with an operating theatre and was intended for 36 women, both free and fee-paying. As a nursing home it remained open until the 1920s, later becoming a hotel.[8]

A stocks was repaired by the vestry in 1724 and there was a salaried beadle by 1774.[9] In 1778, after several bodies had been stolen, St. George's, Hanover Square, appointed a man to watch the chapel and St. George's Row.[10] In 1808 the constable was rewarded for detecting a servant shooting night soil and in 1815 the beadle was ordered to keep the green and streets peaceable, in particular from boys playing cricket.[11] A reward had been offered in 1801 to curb vandalism in the churchyard and the magistrates had been asked in 1803 to take steps against burglars.[12] Watchmen were employed by 1815, when four of them were proposed as special constables and when a patrol was instituted from Edgware Road along Harrow Road to the west side of Paddington green.[13] Under the local Act of 1824 the select vestry could appoint up to 52 parishioners as constables for a year, acquire a watchhouse, and police the parish.[14] The new watching and lighting committee (board from 1825) thereupon ordered the building of a watch house in Hermitage Street and of 26 watch boxes, employing 31 watchmen, with supernumeraries, for both early and late watches.[15] After Marylebone watchmen had been accused for frequenting Paddington alehouses, it was agreed that residents might report them and that Paddington's patrols might arrest vagrants on either side of Edgware Road.[16] In 1828 policing was by 59 officers: the watch house keeper and his assistant, 4 night sergeants, 2 day sergeants, 36 watchmen, the beadle, his assistant, a combined assistant and messenger, and 12 constables.[17]

Paddington was part of the Metropolitan Police Area from 1829. The watch was disbanded and the watch boxes were removed in 1830,[18] although constables continued to assist prosecutions by the vestry.[19] Complaints that the new force was expensive and undermanned began in 1831 and persisted for many years.[20] The police station continued in Hermitage Street south of the almshouses[21] until 1864, when a new one was built on the north side of Dudley Grove, later no. 62 Harrow Road.[22] Called Paddington Green police station, it survived as part of Paddington and, by 1942, Marylebone divisions and formed a setting for the film 'The Blue Lamp'. The building contained married quarters, converted to single rooms in 1887, and was extended on the acquisition of houses in St. Mary's Square in 1902. It was demolished as part of the road improvements for Westway after the opening of a station at the north corner of Harrow and Edgware roads in 1971. The new station formed part of London's largest group of police buildings, which included a selection centre in a tower block in Harrow Road, a divisional headquarters, and a residential fourteen-storeyed block above a three-storeyed podium in Edgware Road.[23] By 1872 there was also a police station at the corner of Fermoy Road and Carlton Terrace (later a stretch of Great Western Road), between Harrow Road and the canal. The station remained in the Kilburn division after its move c. 1913 to a new building at no. 325 Harrow Road, at the corner of Woodfield Road, where it survived in 1986.[24] Britain's first combined neighbourhood law centre and citizens' advice bureau, financed mainly by Westminster council, was opened at no. 465 Harrow Road in 1973 and reopened at nos. 439–41 in 1977.[25]

The parish had a fire engine in 1776 and hosepipes in 1806. An engine keeper was to test the equipment regularly in 1808 and the Chelsea Waterworks Co. was asked to provide six fire plugs in 1809. There was an engine house near the pond at Paddington green in 1818.[26] The select vestry's watching and lighting subcommittee in 1825 installed the engine in its new watch house, whose keeper was also the engine keeper[27] and who continued in the second post after the watch had been superseded.[28] In 1838 the engine keeper was reprimanded for having lent the hose for a fire outside the parish. The spread of housing had made better equipment necessary by 1843, when it was suggested that a new engine be bought for Hermitage Street and the old one be moved to Bayswater to replace another already there. A driver to transport the engines was to be retained by contract in 1855 and a trained fireman to have charge of the larger engine in 1860.[29] Two men attended three engines in 1863.[30] Under the Metropolitan Fire Brigade Act, 1865, fire fighting was the responsibility of the M.B.W.,[31] whose brigade later passed to the L.C.C. The station in Bayswater apparently had closed by 1872,[32] leaving only the one in Hermitage Street until a station was opened in 1900 at no. 494 Edgware Road, on the Marylebone side, where a site had been bought by 1890. A sub-station remained at Hermitage Street until the

[8] *Pall Mall Gaz.* 21 Apr. 1886; *The Times,* 28 Dec. 1885, 5e; inf. from Mr. A. R. Richards; above, econ.
[9] Chwdns. acct. bk. (1656–1736), f. 106; (1774–1833).
[10] Westm. libr., C 772, ff. 244, 252–3.
[11] Vestry mins. 26 May 1808; 6 Sept. 1815.
[12] Ibid. 14 May 1801; 6 July 1803.
[13] Ibid. 7 Nov., 5 Dec. 1815.   [14] 5 Geo. IV, c. 126.
[15] Marylebone libr., watching and lighting sub-cttee. min. bk. (1824–30), *passim.* For watch ho. kpr.'s duties, ibid. 17 Feb. 1826.
[16] Ibid. 21 Jan., 18 Feb. 1825.
[17] *Rep. Cttee. on Police of Metropolis,* H.C. 533, p. 406 (1828), vi.
[18] 10 Geo. IV, c. 44; watching and lighting sub-cttee. min. bk. 19 May 1830.
[19] Select vestry mins. 4 Apr. 1843.
[20] Select vestry mins. 1 Feb., 2 Aug. 1831; 6 Oct. 1840; [metropolitan] vestry mins. 15 July 1856.
[21] Guildhall MS. 10465/186, p. 455.

[22] Vestry mins. 21 June 1864.
[23] *P.O. Dir. Lond.* (1879 and later edns.); Marylebone libr., P 137, cuttings.
[24] Hutchings and Crowsley, *Paddington Dir.* (1872); Bacon, *Atlas of Lond.* (1886); *P.O. Dir. Lond.* (1879 and later edns.).
[25] *The Times,* 1 Feb. 1973, 3a; Marylebone libr., P 137, cuttings.
[26] Chwdns. acct. bk. (1774–1833); vestry mins. 20 Dec. 1806; 19 Apr. 1808; 4 Apr. 1809; 30 Apr. 1818.
[27] Watching and lighting sub-cttee. min. bk. 25 Mar., 22 Apr., 9 Dec. 1825.
[28] Select vestry mins. 6 July 1830.
[29] Ibid. 6 Mar. 1838; 3 Oct. 1843; [metropolitan] vestry mins. 2 Oct. 1855; 3 Apr. 1860.
[30] *Return of Amounts paid to Maintain Fire Engines,* H.C. 322, p. 6 (1864), l.
[31] 28 & 29 Vic., c. 90; vestry mins. 1, 21 Nov. 1865.
[32] Hutchings and Crowsley, *Paddington Dir.* (1872).

opening of another in Pickering Place (later no. 210 Queen's Road), Bayswater, in 1904.[33] The Bayswater sub-station was closed in 1935, leaving the Edgware Road station to serve Paddington until its closure on the opening of one in Harrow Road in 1969.[34] The new station initially had a staff of 69, whose work was described in *Red Watch*, published after a hotel fire in 1974.[35]

Lamp lighting was paid for in 1773 and 1793 and regularly from 1800, the lamps numbering 17 by 1801.[36] Street lamps, presumably still oil lamps, were to be lit by contract in 1816 and by the surveyors in 1819, when the total number might be increased to 50. Three of the lamps were to be in Harrow Road, whose turnpike trustees had declined to light or watch it in 1816.[37] The Imperial Gas Light & Coke Co. asked permission to lay pipes in 1823 and it was decided to light the parish with gas in 1824, after the Marylebone turnpike trustees had agreed to light part of Edgware Road.[38] Lighting became the responsibility of the highway board's watching and lighting sub-committee, which extended lighting in Edgware Road north of Maida Hill and had been provided with 120 lamps by the Imperial Gas Light & Coke Co. by 1825, when 10 more were ordered and a seven-year contract was agreed.[39] The parish was to have lighting for the whole year, instead of nine months, in 1832.[40] In 1838 Marylebone was asked to light its side of the northern part of Edgware Road, Paddington having lit the south-west side as far as Kilburn bridge. The metropolis roads commissioners ceased to light their turnpike roads in 1841, whereupon Paddington, on legal advice, reluctantly paid for lighting the Uxbridge road.[41] Despite arguments over the terms,[42] the parish continued to be supplied by the Imperial Gas Light & Coke Co., which was taken over in 1876 by the Gas Light & Coke Co., itself nationalized in 1949.[43]

Under a local Act of 1890 electricity mains were to be laid within two years in the principal streets by the Metropolitan Electric Supply Co.[44] By 1892 the company's works was at St. Peter's wharf, Amberley Road, where in 1985 the London Electricity Board had a depot.[45]

Dust and ashes were collected by contractors, who were appointed annually, from 1824. Rates for watering certain roads were ordered in 1836[46] and the Grand Junction Canal Co.'s offer to water all streets was accepted in 1845. There were separate contracts for watering, cleansing, and dust collection in 1856 and 1865.[47] Refuse was collected in 1888 by

the vestry, without the aid of contractors.[48] A parish wharf had long been leased from the canal company, on the north side of the basin, and Paddington council's scavenging (later cleansing) department remained there until succeeded by Westminster in 1965.[49]

Public baths and washhouses[50] in Queen's Road were opened by the vestry in 1874. They stood north of Porchester Gardens and came to be overlooked on either side by the premises of William Whiteley, whose building plans were strongly opposed and to whose firm the site was sold in 1910.[51] The construction of new baths at the north end of Queen's Road (formerly Pickering Place) was delayed by the First World War and started only in 1923. Two swimming baths and a laundry were opened there in 1925, followed by Turkish and Russian baths beneath the neighbouring Porchester hall in 1929. By 1977 Paddington's were the only surviving Turkish baths in London.[52] Baths and a laundry to serve Queen's Park had been built in 1898, where the boundary with Kensington ran slightly south of the canal along Wedlake Street to Kensal Road, and were closed in 1980.[53] Work began in 1982 on a swimming pool west of the council's new Jubilee sports hall in Caird Street.[54] Baths were also planned for Clarendon Street and Hall Park in 1912 but apparently not built. A disused laundry at the workhouse was temporarily reopened in 1920.

A public library[55] at the corner of Harrow Road and Fourth Avenue was opened in 1890, after Chelsea had adopted the Public Libraries Act, and was transferred to Paddington with Queen's Park in 1900. Its use was restricted to Queen's Park ward since Paddington's ratepayers, said to be well served by reading rooms or circulating libraries,[56] had rejected proposals to adopt the Public Libraries Act in 1887 and 1891. Some residents had nonetheless financed the opening in 1888 of 'Paddington free public library', whose stock of books at no. 7 Bishop's Road was offered in vain to the borough council in 1901. The council in 1903 also rejected a grant from Andrew Carnegie, which was conditional upon levying a full library rate, and it was only in 1920 that the Public Libraries Acts were adopted. A small lending library opened at no. 4 Hatherley Grove in 1924 and was superseded in 1930 by Paddington's main public library on the north side of Porchester hall. A temporary reading room for the main library was opened in Westbourne Gardens in 1938 and a lease of Clifford memorial hall was acquired in 1962. Maida Vale branch library, in the former Methodist church in

[33] *Rep. of L.C.C. for 1900–1*, 121, 123; *1904–5*, 175.
[34] L.C.C. *Ann. Rep. for 1935*, i. 71; Marylebone libr., P 137, cuttings.
[35] G. Honeycombe, *Red Watch* (1976).
[36] Highway surveyors' acct. bks. (1738–73, 1774–1822).
[37] Vestry mins. 1 Oct., 5 Nov. 1816; 21 Oct. 1819.
[38] Ibid. 8 May 1823; select vestry mins. 17 Aug. 1824.
[39] Watching and lighting sub-cttee. min. bk. 27 Sept., 18 Oct. 1824; 18 Feb., 6 June 1825.
[40] Select vestry mins. 1 May 1832.
[41] Ibid. 4 Sept. 1838; 1 June, 2 Nov. 1841.
[42] Ibid. 2 Oct. 1849; [metropolitan] vestry mins. 1 Aug. 1865.
[43] *Kelly's Dir. Paddington* (1888 and later edns); S. Everard, *Gas Light & Coke Co.* (1949), 247, 282.
[44] 53 & 54 Vic. c. 198 (Local).
[45] *P.O. Dir. Lond.* (1891 and later edns.).
[46] Select vestry mins. 20 July 1824; 7 June 1836.

[47] [Metropolitan] vestry mins. 12 Apr. 1845; 29 Jan., 26 Feb. 1856; 21 Feb., 7 Mar. 1865.
[48] *Kelly's Dir. Paddington* (1888).
[49] Select vestry mins. 24 Apr. 1838; *P.O. Dir. Lond.* (1850 and later edns.).
[50] Para. based on Bingham, *Official Guide to Paddington* [1921, 1925] and *Plan of Paddington M.B.* (1901).
[51] Lambert, *Universal Provider*, 80–3, 112–14; insurance plan B 23 (1892); above, local govt.
[52] *The Times*, 26 Nov. 1923, 11g; 27 June 1925, 11g; 31 Oct. 1927, 11g; Marylebone libr., P 137, cuttings.
[53] *P.O. Dir. Lond.* (1902 and later edns.); Marylebone libr., P 137, cuttings; G.L.C. Hist. Bldgs. Div., file WM 314.
[54] Marylebone libr., P 137, cuttings.
[55] Para. based on A. C. Jones, 'Paddington Public Librs.' (duplicated hist. 1965 in Marylebone libr.); souvenirs of openings in Marylebone libr., P 137, cuttings.
[56] *Bayswater Annual* (1885); above, social.

Sutherland Avenue, opened in 1948. Paddington, Maida Vale, and Queen's Park libraries survived in 1985.

St. Mary's churchyard having been closed,[57] the burial board in 1855 opened a 25-a. cemetery in Willesden, two-thirds of the ground being reserved for Anglicans and with both Anglican and nonconformist chapels. A second Paddington cemetery, of 26 a., was acquired at Milespit Hill, Hendon, in 1931 and opened in 1938.[58] There was a dead house near the main entrance to St. Mary's churchyard in 1861. Its state and location were criticized by a coroner in 1865[59] and it was to be altered in 1884.[60] A new coroner's court, with a mortuary, had been built in St. Mary's Square by 1921.[61]

While Paddington had easy access to Hyde Park and Kensington Gardens, which the houses in Bayswater Road faced, the spread of 19th-century building left comparatively little open space within the area of the parish. Paddington green, long preserved as an amenity,[62] was finally opened to the public in 1864, when it covered 1½ a. east of the churchyard. The northern part of the churchyard, formerly the manor house grounds, was opened by the vestry as a 3¼-a. public garden, known as the old burial ground, in 1885. The southern part, 1 a., was opened as St. Mary's churchyard in 1892.[63] By far the largest open space was the 26-a. Paddington recreation ground[64] between Elgin Avenue and Carlton Vale, where R. Melvill Beachcroft, treasurer of Paddington cricket club, tried to buy land in 1882. After delays arising from disagreement between the Ecclesiastical Commissioners and the trustees of the Paddington Estate, Beachcroft took a lease of 9 a. and organized a festival for the queen's jubilee; eventually, aided by a royal visit and a matching grant from the vestry, money was raised to permit the purchase of a larger area under an Act of 1893. At least 4 a. were reserved for general use, the leasing out of the rest for sports being vested in a committee of 15 members, of whom 9 represented Paddington and the others Marylebone, Hampstead, and Willesden.[65] A contribution from the L.C.C. was later authorized[66] and facilities were provided for many sports, including running and cycling tracks. Paddington metropolitan borough thus contained 100 a. of public open space: 67 a. were maintained by the government as part of Kensington Gardens and 33 a., consisting of the recreation ground, Paddington green, the old burial ground, and the churchyard, were maintained by the council.[67] Much of the rest of the 132 a. which the

borough was said to contain in 1921 consisted of residential squares.

CHURCHES. A chapel at Paddington was declared in 1222 to belong to the parish of St. Margaret, Westminster,[68] of which the rectory had long been held by Westminster abbey. The rectory of Paddington, so called only from the late Middle Ages, was appropriated to Westminster[69] and afterwards to the bishop of London.[70] A vicar was mentioned in 1324[71] and a vicarage c. 1485,[72] although later Paddington was usually styled a perpetual curacy until 1868.[73] In 1708 Paddington was said to be a donative, the curate being licensed by the bishop,[74] and to be exempt from the archdeacon's jurisdiction and subject wholly to the bishop.[75] A single chapel or church at Paddington green, twice rebuilt, served the parish until 1818. In 1845 its function as the parish church was transferred to St. James's, Sussex Gardens.[76]

The vicar or perpetual curate was presumably nominated by the holder of the rectory, which from 1489 was leased with Paddington manor.[77] In 1650, when Sir Rowland St. John, lessee of the manor, was said to have formerly had a reading minister, the patronage lay with Thomas Browne as purchaser of the manor.[78] Patronage was specifically reserved to the bishop in leases of the manor and rectory from 1795.[79] When the incumbent moved to the new parish church as vicar of Paddington in 1845 he presented a successor to the old church, but thereafter patronage lay with the bishop.[80]

Early valuations were not those of the incumbent's living, since the chapel was valued with St. Margaret's, Westminster, in 1291[81] and at the same sum as the leasehold rent for the rectory in 1535.[82] The minister was paid £28 a year, representing the rent of the tithes, in 1650 when it was thought that the tithes might be let for £100 and that the parish ought to be united with Marylebone.[83] The curate's stipend was fixed at £80, to be paid by the bishop's lessee, in 1668[84] and confirmed by the Augmentation of Benefices Act, 1677.[85] Increases to £120, chargeable on the tithes and on Kilburn Bridge farm, and to £200 were authorized in the building Acts of 1795 and 1825.[86] Lessees of the manor were discharged from payments under the Paddington Estate Act, 1871, which provided for the purchase of stock to produce £200 a year.[87]

Burial fees, apparently divided between the minister or assistant curate and the parish officers, rose

[57] Below, churches.
[58] Marylebone libr., file 131.1 (cuttings); *Paddington Cemetery, Milespit Hill* (booklet).
[59] [Metropolitan] vestry mins. 16 Apr. 1861; san. cttee. mins. 19 Jan. 1865. Five vols. of coroners' inquests, 1840–65, are in Marylebone libr.
[60] *Boro. of Paddington Faculties* (bound colln. of faculties 1901, in Marylebone libr.), 17–20.
[61] *Official Guide to Paddington* [1921].
[62] Above, growth.
[63] Marylebone libr., file 131.1; *Paddington Faculties*, 17–41; McDonald, 'Paddington', cap. 16; L.C.C. *Lond. Statistics*, xvi. 155.
[64] Rest of para. based on J. Bates, *Playground of Paddington* (1902); McDonald, 'Paddington', cap. 16; *Official Guide to Paddington* [1921]. Paddington recreation ground was later estimated at 27 a.
[65] 56 & 57 Vic. c. 67 (Local).
[66] 57 & 58 Vic. c. 212 (Local).
[67] L.C.C. *Lond. Statistics*, xvi. 155, 157.

[68] Westlake, *St. Marg. Westm.* 231.
[69] Harvey, *Westm. Abbey*, 407–8.
[70] Hennessy, *Novum Rep.* 367.
[71] *Ft. of F. Lond. & Mdx.* i. 101.
[72] W.A.M., Reg. Bk. i, f. 5v.
[73] *Rep. Com. Eccl. Revenues*, 666.
[74] Newcourt, *Rep.* i. 704.
[75] Newcourt, *Rep.* i. 704.   [76] Below.
[77] Above, manors (Rectory).
[78] *Home Counties Mag.* i. 222.
[79] Robins, *Paddington*, 83; Guildhall MS. 12426.
[80] Hennessy, *Novum Rep.* 369; *Crockford* (1977).
[81] *Tax. Eccl.* (Rec. Com.), 17.
[82] *Valor Eccl.* (Rec. Com.), i. 413; Harvey, *Westm. Abbey*, 409.
[83] *Home Counties Mag.* i. 222.
[84] Guildhall MS. 12426.
[85] Newcourt, *Rep.* i. 704; 29 Chas. II, c. 8.
[86] Robins, *Paddington*, 79, 93.
[87] 34 & 35 Vic. c. 5 (Private).

considerably during the 18th century.[88] In 1796 the vestry on legal advice rejected a claim by the bishop and his lessees for half of the fees; the bishop's table of fees was rejected and in 1798 the assistant curate was deprived of his parish offices (see below) for withholding payments on the bishop's orders, burials of all non-parishioners being temporarily forbidden by the vestry until a new table was agreed.[89] Such burials were estimated to add £250 a year to an otherwise poor living in 1809 and were admitted by the minister to have reached £370 a year by 1811.[90] A further dispute then arose, when the vestry proposed to pay for enlarging the burial ground by allowing the minister only one third of the fees; the bishop, in support of the minister, declined to consecrate the new ground until agreement had been reached.[91] The gross income of the benefice was £500 in 1851, having been estimated to average £930 a year between 1829 and 1832.[92]

The parsonage house mentioned in 1581 may have belonged to Matthew Smale, lessee of Paddington manor and rectory, whose house was also referred to as the manor house,[93] and it may have been one of two large residences in 1647. At that date there was also a vicarage house, but it too had been appropriated by the lessee, divided into two, and in 1642 leased to Thomas Satterchott, with 12 a. and the herbage of the adjoining chapel yard.[94] Paddington probably had no house for the incumbent in the early 18th century and certainly had none in the early 19th.[95] In 1820 the new incumbent offered to contribute towards the purchase of the manor house, which the vestry refused to sell. A building Act of 1825 empowered the bishop to grant up to 1 a. for a parsonage house, for which the parish borrowed money in 1830,[96] and one was built in 1831[97] at the south corner of Park Place and Porteus Road. When St. Mary's ceased to be the parish church the house was sold to George Gutch (d. 1875), whose widow stayed there until 1891. As Porteus House it served as a home for the Church Extension Association and after 1916 for the Territorial Army until it was converted into flats in 1927. The new glebe house for St. Mary's was no. 1 St. Mary's Terrace, which had been built in Park Place,[98] and from c. 1964 no. 6 Park Place Villas.[99]

Bernard Sandiford or Sandiforth (d. 1559) may have been resident while perpetual curate, since he made his will as of Paddington after deprivation as vicar of Canewdon (Essex) and canon of West-

minster.[1] John Aylmer, bishop of London 1577–94, was said to have appointed his blind gatekeeper to Paddington. Although the story was exaggerated, in that the man lost his sight only later, it illustrated the insignificance of the living.[2] It was at Paddington that John Donne gave his first sermon in 1615.[3] Anthony Dodd, minister in 1650, conducted several irregular marriages which were declared void in 1655–6.[4]

Peter Lane was apparently resident in the 1670s, when he signed the churchwardens' accounts,[5] but thereafter many perpetual curates combined Paddington with other preferments. Philip Atkinson, 1688–98, may also have had a vicarage in Cornwall[6] and his successor Daniel Amiand had a rectory in Northamptonshire.[7] Samuel Dunster, translator of Horace and a canon of Salisbury and Lincoln, held the perpetual curacy but apparently surrendered it while holding a vicarage in Lancashire, where he died in 1754.[8] Joseph Smith (d. 1756), writer and provost of Queen's College, Oxford, in 1730 added Paddington to other preferments, which included prebends of Lincoln and St. Paul's and a lectureship at St. George's, Hanover Square.[9] Richard Brown, appointed in 1756, was a canon of St. Paul's who remained Lord Almoner's Professor of Arabic and later became Regius Professor of Hebrew at Oxford.[10] Thomas Hayter, licensed in 1780, was probably the Whitehall preacher and fellow of King's College, Cambridge, who died at Cambridge in 1799.[11] His successors Joseph Pickering (d. 1820)[12] and Charles Theomartyr Crane apparently resided, since they often chaired vestry meetings.[13] Archibald Montgomery Campbell, 1829–59, was resident,[14] although he held Paddington with a rectory in Lincolnshire and later also became a canon of St. Paul's.[15]

An assistant curate normally resided in the 18th and early 19th century, when incumbents lived elsewhere.[16] Amiand's assistant curate was Daniel Debat, who in 1730 succeeded him in Northamptonshire, and Joseph Smith's assistant was paid £40 a year.[17] Another assistant curate may have been Dr. Morell, who sometimes presided over the vestry in the 1750s and paid rates between 1762 and 1764.[18] In 1795 the vestry asked the bishop to raise the stipend of the assistant curate, the author John Shepherd (1759–1805).[19] In 1800, assuming that Hayter's successor would not reside, it asked for the retention of Shepherd, who had served since 1785[20] and variously acted as vestry clerk, parish clerk, clerk to the

[88] The par. offrs.' share was £11 7s. in 1712 and £49 10d. in 1724: chwdns. acct. bk. (1656–1736), ff. 78, 107.
[89] Robins, Paddington, 139; Booth, 'Archives', 181–5; vestry mins. 21 June, 4 Aug. 1796; 23 Mar. 1797; 27 June to 24 Dec. 1798.
[90] Vestry mins. 20 Oct. 1809; 31 Dec. 1811.
[91] Ibid. 17, 31 Dec. 1811; 7 Jan., 31 Mar. 1812 to 9 Jan. 1813.
[92] P.R.O., HO 129/1/1/1/1; Rep. Com. Eccl. Revenues, 667.
[93] Acts of P.C. 1581–2, 107.
[94] Above, manors; Guildhall MS. 10464A, pp. 125, 130, 137. [95] Guildhall MSS. 9558, 9560.
[96] Robins, Paddington, 141–3; 6 Geo. IV, c. 45 (Private).
[97] Inf. from G.L.C. Hist. Bldgs. Div.
[98] Ibid.; Robins, Paddington, 143; Lucas, Plan of Paddington (1842, 1855). [99] Inf. from V.
[1] Alum. Cantab. to 1751, iv. 18; P.R.O., PROB 11/42 B (P.C.C. 14 Chaynay).
[2] J. Strype, Life of John Aylmer (1821), 142.
[3] D.N.B.; R. C. Bald, John Donne (1970), 311.

[4] Mdx. County Rec. iii. 234; G.L.R.O., Cal. Mdx. Sess. Bks. 1652–7, 112, 116, 170.
[5] Chwdns. acct. bk. (1656–1736), ff. 20, 27, 29, 31.
[6] Alum. Cantab. to 1751, i. 53.
[7] Guildhall MS. 9550.
[8] D.N.B.; Hennessy, Novum Rep. p. cxlix.
[9] D.N.B.; Guildhall MSS. 9550, 9556.
[10] Hennessy, Novum Rep. p. xlvi; Alum. Oxon. 1715–1886, i. 175.   [11] Eton Coll. Reg. 1753–90, 261.
[12] Gent. Mag. xc (1), 566. Wrongly called John in Hennessy, Novum Rep. 367.
[13] Vestry mins. 15 Mar. 1802; 12 Apr. 1803; passim.
[14] Guildhall MS. 9560.
[15] Alum. Cantab. 1752–1900, i. 497; Le Neve, Fasti, 1541–1857, St. Paul's, Lond. 23.
[16] Guildhall MS. 9550.
[17] Ibid.; G. Baker, Hist. Northampton, i (1822–30), 208.
[18] Vestry mins. 12 Oct. 1753; 25 Feb. 1757; rate bk. 1762, 1767.
[19] Vestry mins. 11 Mar. 1795; D.N.B.
[20] Booth, 'Archives', 186–7; vestry mins. 14 Feb. 1800.

trustees of the rebuilt church, and sexton, presumably to augment his stipend.[21] In 1835 the assistant curate was paid £150.[22] Thereafter there were normally one or two assistant curates until the Second World War.[23]

Gifts of property to the chapel yielded 8s. a year in 1548, when there were 74 communicants.[24] The minister preached twice on Sundays in 1650.[25] There were two Sunday services in the 18th century, with communion probably quarterly in the early years and monthly, for 20, by c. 1800.[26] An afternoon lecture was given during the summer in 1795 by Shepherd, who had been chosen by the vestry, and was continued in 1803 after he had left the parish.[27] A. M. Campbell was thanked in 1832 for having instituted full afternoon and evening services throughout the year.[28] In 1851, when 100 of the 600 sittings were free, Sunday attendances were estimated at 600 in the morning, 100 in the afternoon, and 400 in the evening.[29] In 1886 there were attendances of 270 in the morning and 356 in the evening.[30] In 1902 they had fallen to 191 in the morning and 202 in the evening.[31]

The medieval church of St. Nicholas was thought by Newcourt to have been dedicated to St. Catherine, whose picture he saw in the east window.[32] Nothing else is known of the appearance of the building. It was replaced in 1678 at the expense of Sir Joseph and Daniel Sheldon,[33] whose church was later described as St. James's and, in 1788, as St. Mary's.[34] A modest building in a Gothic style, containing a nave with one aisle, chancel, south porch, west bell turret, and rustic west porch, it was the scene of William Hogarth's runaway marriage in 1729.[35] After its demolition, some floor stones were still visible north of its successor c. 1828.[36]

The existing church of *ST. MARY*, Paddington green,[37] was built under an Act of 1788, which authorized national collections and appointed 45 trustees, headed by Sir John Morshead and Robert Thistlethwayte.[38] A small building of yellow brick with white stone dressings, its plan is that of a Greek cross, whose square centre lies beneath a shallow dome carried by four columns and whose four short arms have low segmental vaults. The eastern arm forms a chancel, with a venetian window, and the other arms hold sections of a three-sided gallery. The south front forms the main façade, whose pedimented Tuscan portico is grander than the semicircular entrance porch to the west. A small clock tower and cupola surmount the dome. Designed by John Plaw, the church was begun in 1788 and consecrated in 1791, when it was widely admired.[39] It is notable as Plaw's only surviving building, apart from a house on Belle Isle (Westmld.). Restoration under Raymond Erith and Quinlan Terry was carried out in 1972–3, with money from the sale of the site of the town hall. Bodies in the vaults were reburied more compactly[40] and many original fittings were reinstated. The chief innovation was reflooring in coloured marbles and in York and Portland stone.

The body of the church was reseated with new box pews in 1972–3, when the original panelling, font, pulpit, altar, and altar rails were restored. A new organ with an 18th-century tone was installed in 1978.[41] Among the many wall monuments are those to Eleanor Boucher (d. 1784) and the Revd. John James (d. 1786) by Thomas Scheemakers, Frances Aust (d. 1794) by John Bacon the elder, Gen. Charles Crosbie (d. 1807) by John Bacon the younger, Elizabeth Kent (d. 1810) by Thomas Sealey, Lt.-Col. Thomas Aubrey (d. 1814) and his son Capt. Thomas Aubrey (d. 1806) by Henry Rouw, Charlotte Cumberbatch (d. 1818) by William Cramphorn, and the sculptor Joseph Nollekens (1737–1823) by William Behnes.[42]

The burial ground was extended northward under an Act of 1732, the bishop to receive rent of 5s. a year, and eastward under an Act of 1753,[43] the bishop to receive 40s. rent and Sir John Frederick £10.[44] Further enlargement took place under the rebuilding Act of 1788,[45] but more space was urgently needed by 1807[46] and obtained under an Act of 1810 when the manor house was acquired, its site finally being consecrated in 1825.[47] Burials close to the church ceased in 1853 and those farther away in 1857, most of the churchyard later being laid out for recreation.[48]

Among memorials in the enclosure around the church is the table tomb of the hymn writer Basil Woodd (1760–1831) by J. C. F. Rossi. A few tombs also survive in the public garden to the north, where many stones have been lined against the wall and where a modern glass canopy covers the grave of Sarah Siddons.[49] Other people buried in the church or churchyard[50] included the sculptor George Bushnell (d. 1701), the painter Joseph Francis Nollekens (1702–48), the violinist Matthew Dubourg (1703–67), the landscape painter George Barret the elder (1728?–1784), the line engraver John Hall (1739–97),

[21] Booth, 'Archives', 186–7; vestry mins. 24 Sept. 1798; 27 May, 22 Sept. 1802.
[22] *Rep. Com. Eccl. Revenues*, 667.
[23] *Clergy List* (1859 and later edns.); *Crockford* (1926 and later edns.).
[24] *Lond. Rec. Soc.* xvi. 73.
[25] *Home Counties Mag.* i. 222.
[26] Guildhall MSS. 9550; 9557, f. 40.
[27] Lysons, *Environs*, iii. 336; vestry mins. 22 Dec. 1803.
[28] Select vestry mins. 2 Oct. 1832.
[29] P.R.O., HO 129/1/1/1/1.
[30] *Brit. Weekly*, 26 Nov. 1886, 16.
[31] Mudie-Smith, *Rel. Life*, 101. The census was taken in 1902–3, the Paddington figures being for Dec. 1902.
[32] Newcourt, *Rep.* i. 703; Hennessy, *Novum Rep.* 367.
[33] Hennessy, *Novum Rep.* 367.
[34] Paddington Soc. *Newsletter*, Jan. 1964; Jan. 1970.
[35] Bingham, *Guide to Paddington* [1921], 136; *D.N.B.*; above, plate 49.
[36] Paddington Soc. *Newsletter*, Jan. 1970; *Reminiscences of Hen. Angelo*, i. 230.
[37] Para. based on Clarke, *Lond. Chs.* 113; Pevsner, *Lond.*

ii. 296; notes supplied by V. Illus. in *Country Life*, 1 Nov. 1973, 1358–60.
[38] 28 Geo. III, c. 74.
[39] e.g. Lysons, *Environs*, iii. 332; Bingham, *Official Guide to Paddington* [1921], 136–7; above, plate 48.
[40] Marylebone libr., P 131.1, cuttings; inf. from V.
[41] Inf. from V.
[42] Pevsner, *Lond.* ii. 296; Gunnis, *Sculptors, passim*.
[43] 5 Geo. II, c. 10 (Private); 26 Geo. II, c. 43.
[44] Chwdns. acct. bk. (1656–1736), f. 148; Robins, *Paddington*, 72–3.
[45] 28 Geo. III, c. 74.
[46] Vestry mins. 31 Mar. 1807; 4 Apr. 1809.
[47] 50 Geo. III, c. 44 (Local and Personal); Robins, *Paddington*, 89, 139–42; above, manors.
[48] Marylebone libr. *Boro. of Paddington, Faculties* (1901), 3–5, 8–12, 42, 48–52; *Lond. Gaz.* 9 Aug. 1853, p. 2192; 28 Aug. 1857, p. 2913; above, social; pub. svces.
[49] *D.N.B.*; Gunnis, *Sculptors*, 327; inf. from V.
[50] Rest of para. based on Wheatley and Cunningham, *Lond. Past and Present*, iii. 2–3; *D.N.B. passim*; notes supplied by V.

the sculptor Thomas Banks (1735–1805), the biblical critic Alexander Geddes (1737–1802), the diplomatist Caleb Whitefoord (1734–1810), the line engraver Luigi Schiavonetti (1765–1810), the Irish judge John Philpot Curran (1750–1817) until 1840, the connoisseur Michael Bryan (1757–1821), Napoleon I's surgeon Barry O'Meara (1786–1821), and the painters Sir William Beechey (1753–1839), Benjamin Robert Haydon (1786–1846), and William Collins (1788–1847). Immediately west of the church are the parish assembly rooms, built in 1981 to the design of Quinlan Terry.[51]

The church has a silver headed beadle's staff of 1774 and two bells of 1790 but no plate that is earlier than the 19th century,[52] older silver pieces having disappeared when the church was rebuilt.[53] The registers, which were transferred to St. James's, Sussex Gardens, begin in 1655.[54]

Under an Act of 1763 an almost square plot of 5 a., abutting Bayswater Road, was rented for burials by the churchwardens of St. George's, Hanover Square.[55] The chapel which they built there, although treated below, was not considered to lie within Paddington. In consequence St. Mary's remained the parish's only Anglican place of worship until the opening of Bayswater chapel in 1818.[56] Charles Theomartyr Crane, incumbent of St. Mary's 1820–9, and his successor A. M. Campbell actively promoted the building of new churches.[57] One district chapelry, that of St. John, Hyde Park Crescent, was created in 1834,[58] before St. James's replaced St. Mary's as the parish church in 1845.[59] The select vestry, believing that churches would attract the well-to-do, contributed heavily to building funds. More than £20,000 were voted over eleven years towards All Saints and six other churches, the sums being borrowed on the security of the rates.[60] Criticism mounted, largely through the revitalized Paddington association,[61] and in 1853–4 there was strong opposition to continuing such expenditure. The vestry petitioned against the re-establishment of the Roman Catholic hierarchy in 1851.[62]

Although Paddington consisted of six ecclesiastical districts by 1852, its churches provided no more than 9,400 sittings for a population four times that number; the most neglected district was St. Mary's, the oldest and poorest, with sittings for less than one person in ten.[63] In 1902, when Paddington had 26 Anglican churches or missions, attendance was relatively low for west London: 16.7 per cent of the inhabitants attended a place of worship, 9.6 being

Church of England.[64] No more parishes were created in the 20th century, and two Victorian churches closed in the period between the World Wars. As a result of bomb damage and, in the 1960s and 1970s, of decaying stonework, ten more churches closed between the Second World War and 1982, although three were rebuilt.[65]

The London Diocesan Deaconess Institution, established near King's Cross in 1861 as the North London Deaconess Institution, moved in 1873 to St. Andrew's House, no. 12 Tavistock Crescent, where members ran a nursing home until 1881. No. 12A Tavistock Crescent was then acquired and, as St. Gabriel's home, used for training destitute girls for domestic work until 1897, when it was converted to extra accommodation for the sisters. Officially renamed the Deaconess Community of St. Andrew in 1943, the sisters opened a new building for 30, including a chaplain and 14 students, in 1974.[66]

The Church Extension Association was founded in 1863 by Miss Emily Ayckbourn, who in 1870 also founded the Sisters of the Church, commonly called the Kilburn Sisters,[67] of whom she became mother superior for life.[68] Property was held and charities were administered in the name of the association, which was under the sisterhood's management and at first was concerned chiefly with religious instruction.[69] It was high church, being connected with St. Augustine's, and in the 1870s it occupied two houses in Kilburn Park Road.[70] Financed largely by the income of individual sisters, each of whom controlled her own capital,[71] and with many aristocratic patrons,[72] it had undertaken a wide range of work in the immediate neighbourhood, London's east end, and the provinces by 1886. Teaching was carried out in local schools, and visiting clergy were accommodated and retreats were held at St. Augustine's home of rest.[73] The archbishop of Canterbury was made visitor in 1892 but removed in 1894, when external supervision was resisted, despite charges ranging from financial mismanagement to cruelty.[74] The community secured public defenders[75] and remained prosperous in 1911 with c. 160 sisters, many of them overseas.[76] After war damage the Randolph Gardens premises were taken over by the government in 1941. A few sisters remained in Kilburn Park Road until, its other institutions nearby having closed, the association moved its offices to Richmond (Surr.) in 1955.[77]

Other C. of E. churches were:[78]

ALL SAINTS, Norfolk Sq. Dist. formed 1848 from

[51] Inf. from V.
[52] Ibid.; Freshfield, *Communion Plate*, 53.
[53] Vestry mins. 10, 14 Feb. 1800.
[54] In 1982 the regs. were at G.L.R.O., P87/JS.
[55] 3 Geo. III, c. 50.   [56] Below.
[57] e.g. select vestry mins. 2 May 1826 et seq.
[58] *Lond. Gaz.* 23 Sept. 1834, pp. 1717–18.
[59] J. Wittich, *St. John's Ch., Hyde Pk. Cres.* (booklet 1980), 4.   [60] Reeder, 'Capital Investment', 335–6.
[61] Ibid. 337; above, local govt.
[62] Select vestry mins. 7 Jan. 1851; 28 June 1853; 3 Jan. 1854.
[63] Marylebone libr., P 131.1 (rep. of vestry cttee.).
[64] Mudie-Smith, *Rel. Life*, 88–9, 101.
[65] For 19th- and 20th-cent. chs., below.
[66] Marylebone libr., P 138, cuttings; inf. from mother superior.
[67] *Official Year Bk. of C. of E.* (1921).
[68] *The Times*, 12 Nov. 1895, 12a.
[69] Inf. from Sisters of the Ch.; *Official Year Bk. of C. of*

[70] *P.O. Dir. Lond.* (Suburban North 1880).
[71] Besant, *Lond. N. of Thames*, 152.
[72] *The Times*, 12 Nov. 1895, 12a.
[73] *Official Year Book of C. of E.* (1886, 1892).
[74] *The Times*, 28 Sept. 1895, 7d; 12 Nov. 1895, 12a; 9 Dec. 1895, 13a; 17 Dec. 1895, 15a; 30 Jan. 1896, 15a.
[75] *Kilburn Sisters and their Accusers* (rep. by *Church Bells* magazine, 1896).
[76] Besant, *Lond. N. of Thames*, 152.
[77] Inf. from Sisters of the Ch.; above, social.
[78] Inf. about patrons and asst. curates is from *Clergy List, Crockford*, and *Lond. Dioc. Bk.* (various edns.). Attendance figs. 1886 are from *Brit. Weekly*, 26 Nov. 1886, p. 16; figs. 1902 from Mudie-Smith, *Rel. Life*, 101. Liturgical directions are used in all architectural descriptions. The following abbreviations are used, in addition to those in the index: asst., assistant; Dec., Decorated; demol., demolished; Eng., England or English; mtg., meeting; Perp., Perpendicular; temp., temporary; V., vicar.

E. (1921).

St. Jas. and St. John, Hyde Pk. Cres.[79] Patron bp. of Lond. Attendance 1851: *c.* 1,000 a.m.; 150 aft.; 500 evg.;[80] 1886: 150 a.m.; 148 evg. Bldg., on site of part of Grand Junction Waterworks Co. reservoir, of Kentish rag and Bath stone in Early Pointed style, seating *c.* 1,200 (500 free),[81] by Hen. Clutton 1847:[82] aisled nave, chancel, SE. turret and spirelet; alterations, inc. W. porch and choir in E. bay of nave by Jas. Brooks 1872. Replaced after fire by bldg. of red brick with terracotta detail, seating 1,400,[83] by R. Nevill 1895; plan as before but with S. chancel aisle and N. transeptal organ chamber. Attendance 1902: 263 a.m.; 106 p.m. Closed 1919 on union with St. Mic. and All Angels.[84] Bldg. sold to Royal Assoc. for Deaf and Dumb 1923; used as offices and for worship by soc. and again for worship by par. after bombing of St. Mic. Demol. and replaced by Edna Ho. 1961.[85]

ASCENSION chapel, Bayswater Rd. Chapel for meditation built at expense of Mrs. Emilia Russell Gurney, replacing chapel of St. Geo.'s burial ground (q.v.); to be equipped for services by St. Geo.'s 1911.[86] Bldg. of red brick with stone dressings in 'chastest Italian Quattrocento' style by H. P. Horne and probably A. H. Mackmurdo 1890–3;[87] internal frescoes by Frederic Shields.[88] Gutted during Second World War and demol. after 1952.[89]

BAYSWATER chapel, see ST. MATTHEW.

CHRIST CHURCH, Harrow Rd. Originally chapel of Lock hosp. and founded to provide income for hosp., chaplains being noted preachers. Institution moved with hosp. to Westbourne green 1842.[90] Patron trustees. Known as Christ Ch. by 1902.[91] Called vicarage 1905, 1915, but perpetual curacy served by hosp. chaplain 1925, 1935. Attendance 1886: 480 a.m.; 378 evg.; 1902: 248 a.m.; 271 p.m. Bldg., abutting N. side of hosp., of yellow brick in Perp. style by Lewis Vulliamy 1845–7.[92] Closed by 1940 and demol. 1953.[93] Robt. Wm. Forrest, chaplain 1865, became canon of St. Paul's and dean of Worcester.[94] Mission ho. in Amberley Rd. 1878, 1886.[95]

CHRIST CHURCH, Lancaster Gate. Dist. formed 1856 from St. Jas.[96] Patron bp. of Lond. Attendance largest in Paddington 1886: 1,593 a.m.; 1,295 evg.; largest 1902: 1,383 a.m.; 442 p.m. Bldg. of Kentish ragstone with Bath stone dressings in Dec. style, seating 1,800, by F. & H. Francis 1854–5: chancel flanked by chapels with vestry to N., transepts, aisled and clerestoried nave, S. porch 1854–5; NW. tower

with tall thin spire, originally crocketted, completed later. Not oriented. Fittings inc. glass by Wailes and Powell[97] and fine organ by Norman & Beard.[98] Demol. after closure 1977, tower surviving 1985. Par. united with St. Jas., Sussex Gdns., 1978.[99] Wm. Boyd Carpenter, V. 1879–84, became bp. of Ripon 1884;[1] C. J. Ridgeway, V. 1884–1905, became dean of Carlisle; F. Gurdon, V. 1906–13, became bp. of Hull; H. N. Bate, V. 1913–21, became dean of York; R. W. de la Poer Beresford-Peirse, V. 1921–48, and O. Hardman, V. 1948–57, both became canons of St. Paul's; A. C. Bridge, V. 1958–68, became dean of Guildford.[2]

EMMANUEL, Harrow Rd. Dist. formed 1886 from St. Jude and St. Peter.[3] Patron trustees. Attendance 1886: 280 a.m.; 362 evg.; 1902: 193 a.m.; 137 p.m. Bldg. of yellow brick with freestone and red-brick dressings in Early Eng. style, seating 626, by J. T. Lee 1885–6; chancel with N. vestries and S. organ chamber, aisled and clerestoried nave, W. narthex, low SW. tower with broach spire. Not oriented. Adjoining Burrage institute built 1886 and used for mission svces. by 1888, seating 500.[4] Attendance 1902: 27 a.m.; 50 p.m.

HOLY TRINITY, Bishop's Bridge Rd. Ch. and Vicarage built partly at expense of John Miles, first V.[5] Dist. formed 1846 from St. Jas.[6] Patron bp. of Lond. Attendance 1851: 1,380 a.m.; 500 aft.;[7] 1886: 1,205 a.m.; 1,081 evg.; 1902: 449 a.m.; 265 p.m. Bldg. of Kentish rag with Bath stone dressings in Perp. style, seating *c.* 1,600,[8] by Thos. Cundy 1844–6: short chancel, formed late 19th cent. from E. bays of nave, N. organ chamber and vestry, clerestoried nave with plaster vaults and flat ceilinged aisles. Tall W. tower, on site of reservoir, with pinnacles and octangular crocketted spire, completed after rest of ch.; pinnacled buttresses. Criticized when new for 'misapplied ornament'.[9] Crypt converted for youth club by 1967. Closed 1971, when svces. moved to community hall recently built by ch. with old people's flats on site of original Vicarage at no. 170 Gloucester Terr. Spire demol. 1972 and rest of bldg. 1984.[10]

ST. AMBROSE, see ST. MARY MAGDALENE.

ST. AUGUSTINE, Kilburn Pk. Rd. Dist. formed 1870 from St. Mary, Kilburn,[11] St. Mark, Marylebone, and St. Saviour. Patron trustees, inc. V. of St. Mary Magdalene, 1870,[12] Soc. for Maintenance of Faith by 1973–4. Four asst. curates 1881, eight in 1892, six in 1905. High Ch. svces. held first in iron

[79] *Lond. Gaz.* 21 Apr. 1848, p. 1564.
[80] P.R.O., HO 129/1/2/1/1.
[81] Ibid.; Robbins, *Paddington*, 156–8.
[82] Rest of para. based on C.C.C., Clarke MSS. xii. 1; ibid. 'Demol. chs.'.
[83] *Mackeson's Guide* (1889).
[84] Regs. in G.L.R.O., P87/ALL.
[85] Wittich, *St. John's Ch.* 4, 6, 16.
[86] Marylebone libr., P 131.1, cuttings.
[87] Pevsner, *Lond.* ii. 297.   [88] *D.N.B.*
[89] Paddington Soc. *Newsletter*, Feb. 1971.
[90] J. Weale, *Lond. Exhibited* (1851), 521; above, pub. svces.
[91] Mudie-Smith, *Rel. Life*, 101.
[92] Lucas, *Map of Paddington* (1855); Pevsner, *Lond.* ii. 304; Marylebone libr., P 139.3 Lock hosp.
[93] *Crockford* (1935, 1940); Paddington Soc. *Newsletter*, Oct. 1970.
[94] Hennessy, *Novum Rep.* pp. xliv, 369.
[95] Hutchings and Crowsley, *Paddington Dir.* (1878, 1886).   [96] *Lond. Gaz.* 7 Mar. 1856, p. 957.

[97] *Mackeson's Guide* (1889); Pevsner, *Lond.* ii. 298; Clarke, *Lond. Chs.* 116; C.C.C., survey files; Marylebone libr., P 131.1, cuttings.
[98] Bingham, *Official Guide to Paddington* [1921], 145.
[99] Marylebone libr., P 131.1, cuttings; regs. in G.L.R.O., P87/CTC.
[1] Hennessy, *Novum Rep.* pp. cix, 368; *D.N.B.*
[2] *Crockford* (1907 and later edns.).
[3] *Lond. Gaz.* 13 Aug. 1886, p. 3949.
[4] *Mackeson's Guide* (1889); C.C.C., Clarke MSS. xiv. 91; inf. from Mr. C. Hewer.
[5] Robins, *Paddington*, 154, 156; *Clergy List* (1859).
[6] *Lond. Gaz.* 17 Nov. 1846, p. 4659.
[7] P.R.O., HO 129/1/1/1/4.
[8] Ibid.; 1,400 according to *Mackeson's Guide* (1889).
[9] Robins, *Paddington*, 153–6; Pevsner, *Lond.* ii. 301; Clarke, *Lond. Chs.* 115; C.C.C., survey files; *Illus. Lond. News*, 27 Sept. 1845, 208; above, plate 51.
[10] Marylebone libr., P 131.1, cuttings.
[11] Above, Hampstead, churches.
[12] *Lond. Gaz.* 25 Feb. 1870, pp. 1013–14.

chapel by seceders from St. Mary, Kilburn, under Ric. Carr Kirkpatrick 1871. Attendance 1886: 866 a.m.; 785 evg.; 1902: 613 a.m.; 583 p.m. Bldg. of dark red brick with Bath stone dressings,[13] internally of yellow brick and vaulted throughout, in Norman French style, seating 1,800, by J. L. Pearson, consecrated 1880: square 3-bay chancel 1871–2; apsidal SE. chapel; transepts; nave with internal buttresses, perhaps copied from cathedral at Albi (France), creating lofty triforium and low double aisle 1877; turrets at 4 angles; flèche at crossing; NW. tower with pinnacles and 254-ft. high spire, tallest in Lond., 1897–8. Fittings in stone in Early Eng. style, inc. reredos by Nicholls; murals and glass by Clayton & Bell; Lady chapel reredos and Stations of the Cross by Sir Giles Gilb. Scott. Plate inc. 13th-cent. censer and 17th-cent. Spanish processional cross. Italian paintings, given by Vct. Rothermere 1935, sold 1973.[14] Pearson's masterpiece: architecture, especially spatial composition, and acoustics widely admired.[15]

St. David's Welsh ch., St. Mary's Terr. Originated in West End Welsh Ch. mission, which met in Shaftesbury schs., Salisbury Street, Marylebone 1885 and moved to St. Mary's sch., Harrow Rd., 1887. Iron ch. in St. Mary's Terr., with full-time priest-in-charge, 1890.[16] Patron bp. of London. Attendance 1902: 35 a.m.; 122 p.m. Bldg., approached through Gothic arch from St. Mary's Terr., of stock brick with stone dressings in Perp. style by C. Evans Vaughan 1896: open ch., with hall beneath.[17] Priest-in-charge also V. of Metropolitan Welsh ch. of St. Benet, Paul's Wharf (Lond.) from 1964, each benefice retaining separate officials.[18]

St. George's chapel, Bayswater Rd. Consecrated with new burial ground for St. Geo., Hanover Sq., 1765.[19] Disused after closure of burial ground 1854[20] until renovated with private gifts 1880, for svces. for domestic servants begun in St. Geo.'s sch. 1879.[21] Wednesday evg. svces. and monthly communion 1888.[22] Bldg. with cupola[23] and round-headed windows; many monuments.[24] Replaced by Ascension chapel (q.v.). Burials beneath chapel, where vaults held 1,120 coffins 1851, and in ground said to have reached 1,000 a year.[25] Graves included those of Laur. Sterne (1713–68), whose body was stolen for dissection, Sir John Parnell, Bt., Chancellor of the Irish Exchequer (1744–1801), Paul Sandby, R.A. (1725–1809), Lt.-Gen. Sir Thos. Picton (1758–1815), later reburied in St. Paul's cathedral, novelist

Ann Radcliffe (1764–1823), antiquary John Thos. Smith (1766–1833), and Hen. Brooke Parnell, created Ld. Congleton (1776–1842).[26]

St. James, Sussex Gdns. Consecrated as additional ch. 1843 and replaced St. Mary as par. ch. 1845.[27] Patron bp. of Lond. Two asst. curates in 1979, after union with Christ Ch., Lancaster Gate. Attendance 1851: 1,300 and 200 Nat. sch. a.m.; 400 aft.; 500 evg.;[28] 1886: 697 a.m.; 518 evg.; 1902: 415 a.m.; 240 p.m. Bldg. of yellow brick in Gothic style by John Goldicutt and Geo. Gutch[29] 1841–3: nave, chancel at base of E. tower with tall Early Eng. spire, flanked by porches. Rebuilt, except tower and porches, in grey brick with stone dressings in mixed Gothic style, seating 1,300, by G. E. Street 1881–2: orientation reversed, with W. chancel, NW. chapel, SW. organ chamber, aisled and clerestoried nave, and mem. chapel beneath tower. Much internal facing in marble; glass by Clayton & Bell.[30] Archibald Boyd, V. 1859–68, became dean of Exeter 1866.[31] Jas. Moorhouse, V. 1868–76, became bp. of Melbourne 1876 and bp. of Manchester 1886.[32]

St. John the Evangelist, Hyde Pk. (formerly Southwick) Cres. Dist. formed 1832 from St. Mary.[33] Patron V. of Paddington until c. 1965–6, diocesan bd. of patronage by 1973–4. 'Tolerably full' 1851.[34] Attendance 1886: 727 a.m.; 593 evg.; 1902: 531 a.m.; 283 p.m. Bldg., intended to be called Connaught chapel, of yellow brick with stone dressings in Perp. style, seating c. 1,500 (500 free), by Chas. Fowler 1829–32:[35] square chancel; aisled and clerestoried nave with plaster vault; angle pinnacles. External W. porch and new E. and W. windows by A. Blomfield 1881.[36] Edw. Meyrick Goulburn, min. 1859–67, had been headmaster of Rugby sch. 1850–7 and became dean of Norwich 1866.[37]

St. John the Evangelist, Kensal Green. Dist. formed 1845 from Chelsea detached and contiguous parts of Kensington, Paddington, Hammersmith, and Willesden pars.[38] Patron bp. of Lond. Attendance 1851: 201 and 181 Sunday sch. a.m.; 243 and 74 Sunday sch. p.m.;[39] 1902: 151 a.m.; 272 p.m. Bldg. of white and yellow brick with black flint dressings in Romanesque style, seating 600 (300 free),[40] by H. E. Kendall the yr. 1843–4: shallow apse, nave, twin W. towers with pinnacles and short spires flanking 3-order portal. Chancel in Gothic style, replacing apse, by A. Billing 1903. Architecture often criticized.[41]

St. Jude, Lancefield Street, Kensal Green. Dist.

[13] Rest of para. based on *Mackeson's Guide* (1889); T. F. Bumpus, *Lond. Chs.* ii (1908), 343–7; Pevsner, *Lond.* ii. 297–8; Clarke, *Lond. Chs.* 119–20; G. Stamp and C. Amery, *Victorian Bldgs. of Lond. 1837–87* (1980), 116–17; A. Quiney, *John Loughborough Pearson* (1979), 104–14; Marylebone libr., P 131.1, cuttings; above, plate 50.
[14] Marylebone libr., P 131.1, cuttings (where letter, like some other sources, says that paintings were given by Ld. Northcliffe); inf. from Revd. R. J. Avent.
[15] Hen. Wood Promenade Concerts held there in 1970s: *Paddington Times*, 14 June, 2 Aug. 1974; inf. from Revd. R. J. Avent.
[16] Inf. from Revd. T. J. Thomas.
[17] Datestone; C.C.C., survey files; Clarke MSS. vii. 82.
[18] Inf. from Revd. T. J. Thomas.
[19] Westm. libr., C770, f. 301.
[20] *Lond. Gaz.* 10 Mar. 1854, pp. 783–4.
[21] C. Moore, *St. Geo.'s Chapel* (1883), 17, 19.
[22] *Kelly's Dir. Paddington* (1888).
[23] Westm. libr., C771, f. 291.
[24] Moore, *St. Geo.'s Chapel*, 8.
[25] Wheatley and Cunningham, *Lond. Past and Present*, i. 135.   [26] Ibid. 134; *D.N.B.*
[27] Bingham, *Official Guide to Paddington* [1921], 133–4.
[28] P.R.O., HO 129/1/2/1/2.
[29] Gutch's appt. by the vestry led to charges of favouritism from Lewis Vulliamy: select vestry mins. 6 July, 3 Aug. 1841.
[30] Robins, *Paddington*, 147–9; *Mackeson's Guide* (1889); Pevsner, *Lond.* ii. 299; Clarke, *Lond. Chs.* 114.
[31] Hennessy, *Novum Rep.* pp. cl, 368; *D.N.B.*
[32] Hennessy, *Novum Rep.* pp. xxvi, 368; *D.N.B.*
[33] *Lond. Gaz.* 23 Sept. 1834, p. 1718.
[34] P.R.O., HO 129/1/2/1/4.
[35] Wittich, *St. John's Ch.* 3–4; Robins, *Paddington*, 146; P.R.O., HO 129/1/2/1/4.
[36] Wittich, *St. John's Ch. passim*; Pevsner, *Lond.* ii. 299; Clarke, *Lond. Chs.* 113.
[37] Hennessy, *Novum Rep.* pp. xxv, 368; *Rugby Sch. Reg.* i, p. xviii.   [38] *Lond. Gaz.* 4 July 1845, p. 1979.
[39] P.R.O., HO 129/2/3/1/3.   [40] Ibid.
[41] Clarke, *Lond. Chs.* 114–15; Pevsner, *Lond.* ii. 299.

formed 1879 from St. John, Kensal Green.[42] Patron trustees. Attendance 1902: 243 a.m.; 361 p.m. Bldg. of brown and red brick with stone dressings in Early Eng. style, seating 800, by J. T. Lee 1878: apsidal chancel, transepts, wide aisled and clerestoried nave, NW. tower with spire.[43] Par. united with St. Luke, Fernhead Rd., and St. Sim., Saltram Cres., 1952.[44] Ch. closed 1959, demol. c. 1960–1.[45] Mission at St. Jude's hall, Lancefield Street. Attendance 1902: 59 a.m.; 94 p.m. Mission at St. Jude's institute, Ilbert Street. Attendance 1902: 111 a.m.; 66 p.m.[46]

ST. LUKE THE EVANGELIST, Fernhead Rd. Dist. formed 1877 from St. John, Kensal Green, and Holy Trinity, Kilburn.[47] Patron trustees until 1921, Ch. Pastoral Aid Soc. thereafter.[48] Attendance 1886: 256 a.m.; 280 evg.; 1902: 155 a.m.; 204 p.m. Bldg. of stone in Early Eng. style, seating 800, by J. T. Lee 1876–7;[49] aisled and clerestoried nave, bellcot. Bombed 1940, svces. moving to temp. chapel and later to St. Sim., Saltram Cres. (q.v.). United par. of St. Luke with St. Sim. and St. Jude formed 1952. New yellow-brick St. Luke's ch. centre by Mic. Farey opened c. 1959: low octagonal bldg. with square central chapel, flanked by hall and classrooms, beneath aluminium spire.[50]

ST. LUKE, Tavistock Rd. Served from St. Steph., Westbourne Pk., 1866. Dist. formed 1868 from St. Steph.[51] Patron Revd. H. W. Brooks, V. of St. Steph., then his trustees for 2 turns, then bp. of Lond. Attendance 1886: 354 a.m.; 395 evg.; 1902: 199 a.m.; 174 p.m. Bldg. of white brick, internally of white striped with red and black, in Middle Gothic style, seating 900, by F. & H. Francis 1867–8: apsidal chancel, NE. vestry, N. transept, nave, wide N. aisle. Chancel alone used for worship 1959.[52] Demol. by 1963.[53] Par. united with St. Steph. 1952.[54]

ST. MARTHA, Cirencester Street. Mission ch., served from St. Mary Magdalene and used by servants. Attendance 1902: 154 p.m. Bldg., adjoining St. Mary Magdalene schs. and seating 200, consecrated 1880. Disused by c. 1957.[55]

ST. MARY MAGDALENE, Woodchester Street. Dist. formed 1864 from Holy Trinity and St. Saviour.[56] Patron trustees until c. 1892, Keble Coll., Oxf., by 1905. Seven asst. curates 1881, eight in 1892, five in 1905. High Ch. services held first in temp. ch. of St. Ambrose by Ric. Temple West, former asst. curate of All Saints', Margaret Street (Westm.), 1865.[57]

Attendance 1886: 1,005 a.m.; 1,100 evg.; 1902: 448 a.m.; 415 p.m. Bldg. of red brick and white stone in N. German Gothic style, seating 900, by G. E. Street consecrated 1878: tall apsidal chancel and aisled nave with temp. roof, over vestries, 1868; clerestory and nave roof under construction 1872; thin tower with octagonal upper stage and spire, in angle between S. transept and chancel, 1873. Fittings inc. Stations of Cross, glass by Hen. Holiday and, in crypt, Sir Ninian Comper, reredos by T. Earp. Not oriented. Remarkable for use of cramped and uneven site.[58]

ST. MATTHEW, St. Petersburgh Pl. Proprietary chapel built at expense of Edw. Orme, as first Anglican place of worship apart from par. ch. Min. licensed by bp. and supported by proprietor and from pew rents. Average attendance 1850–1: 800 a.m.; 500 p.m. Bldg. on W. side of rd., seating 1,200, by T. Cooper 1818: plain and square, with round-headed windows, pillared porch, and cupola.[59] Renamed St. Matthew's 1858.[60] Patron Revd. Cornwall Smalley, incumbent and father of succeeding incumbent, 1859,[61] J. D. Allcroft 1881, Lady Magnus-Allcroft by 1973–4. Chapel altered, with Italianate front by F. & H. Francis c. 1858 and Italianate NW. tower 1871.[62] Attendance 1886: 1,342 a.m.; 1,182 evg.; 1902: 945 a.m.; 656 p.m. New bldg. of rag with freestone dressings in Middle Gothic style, seating 1,550, by J. Johnson 1881–2: chancel with triple chancel arch, transepts, spacious clerestoried nave with passage aisles, apsidal S. baptistery, richly decorated main W. doorway, tall SW. tower with spire. Not oriented. Glass by Clayton & Bell.[63]

ST. MICHAEL AND ALL ANGELS, Star Street. Dist. formed 1864 from St. John, Hyde Pk. Cres.[64] Patron Wm. Gibbs, who left endowment for clergy,[65] 1866, G. A. Gibbs 1926, bp. by 1935. Attendance 1886: 975 a.m.; 663 evg.; 1902: 416 a.m.; 237 p.m. Bldg. of brick with Portland stone dressings and Bath stone interior in 14th-cent. French style, seating 900, by Rohde Hawkins 1860–1:[66] short chancel, transepts, aisled and clerestoried nave, conspicuous W. tower with slate spire terminating in ridge. Flanked by terraced hos. and therefore lit mainly from E. and W. Not oriented. Damaged 1941, closed 1964, demol. 1967,[67] when site taken for playground. Anglo-Cath. and musical tradition.[68] Par. united with All Saints and St. John 1965.[69]

[42] Lond. Gaz. 23 May 1979, p. 3536.
[43] Mackeson's Guide (1889); C.C.C., survey files; ibid. Clarke MSS. xiv. 90; Marylebone libr., P 131.1, photos.
[44] Youngs, Local Admin. Units of Eng. 331.
[45] Inf. from V., St. Luke with St. Sim. and St. Jude; Kilburn Times, 18 Oct. 1960.
[46] Mudie-Smith, Rel. Life, 101; Kelly's Dir. Mdx. (1888); Kelly's Dir. Paddington (1930).
[47] Lond. Gaz. 21 Dec. 1877, p. 7339.
[48] Inf. from V.
[49] Mackeson's Guide (1889).
[50] Marylebone libr., notes; P 131.1, cuttings; C.C.C., Clarke MSS. xxiii. 79.
[51] Lond. Gaz. 4 Aug. 1868, p. 4322.
[52] Mackeson's Guide (1889); C.C.C., survey files (photo. 1944); ibid., Clarke MSS. xiv. 91–2.
[53] P.O. Dir. Lond. (1962, 1963).
[54] Youngs, Local Admin. Units of Eng. 337 (which, however, confuses St. Luke, Tavistock Rd., with St. Luke, Fernhead Rd.).
[55] Bacon, Atlas of Lond. (1886, 1910); Mackeson's Guide (1889); Marylebone libr., P 131.1, cuttings (St. Mary Magdalene).

[56] Lond. Gaz. 4 Nov. 1864, p. 5179.
[57] Clarke, Lond. Chs. 118.
[58] Ibid. 118–19; Mackeson's Guide (1889); T. F. Bumpus, Lond. Chs. i. 43; ii. 318–25; Pevsner, Lond. ii. 300; above, plate 52.
[59] P.R.O., HO 129/1/2/1/3; Robins, Paddington, 143; Clarke, Chs. of Lond. 120; Marylebone libr., P 131.1, photos.; above, plate 47.
[60] McDonald, Short Hist. Paddington, no. 46, p. 111.
[61] Clergy List (1859); Hennessy, Novum Rep. pp. cl, 370.
[62] C.C.C., survey files (leaflet).
[63] Mackeson's Guide (1889); C.C.C., Clarke MSS. xv. 83; Pevsner, Lond. ii. 300; Clarke, Lond. Chs. 120–1.
[64] Lond. Gaz. 2 Aug. 1864, p. 3827.
[65] Wittich, St. John's Ch. 6.
[66] Rohde is the spelling adopted in D.N.B., s.v. Edw. Hawkins; alternative spellings are Rodhe and Rhode(s).
[67] Mackeson's Guide (1889); C.C.C., survey files; ibid. Clarke MSS. ia. 180, demol. chs.; Pevsner, Lond. ii. 300; Clarke, Lond. Chs. 118; Marylebone libr., notes and P 131.1, photos.
[68] Wittich, St. John's Ch. 16.
[69] Regs. in G.L.R.O., P87/MAA.

ST. PAUL, Harrow Rd. Dist. formed 1874 from Holy Trinity.[70] Patron V. of Holy Trinity. Attendance 1886: 590 a.m.; 680 evg.; 1902: 237 a.m.; 221 p.m. Cramped site by railway, approached from Marlborough (later Torquay) Street.[71] Bldg. of yellow brick in Early Eng. style, seating 761, by E. L. Blackburne 1873: chancel with apsidal chapel, aisled and clerestoried nave, narthex, base of NW. tower.[72] Closed after bomb damage 1944 but vestry used for svces. until 1947; replaced by Copydex factory by 1959. Par. united with Holy Trinity 1952.[73]

ST. PETER, Elgin Ave. Dist. formed 1871 from Holy Trinity.[74] Patron trustees until c. 1905, Ch. Patronage Soc. (later Trust) by 1926. Attendance 1886: 604 a.m.; 578 p.m.; 1902: 456 a.m.; 472 p.m. Bldg. of Kentish rag with Bath stone dressings in mixed Gothic style, seating 940, by Newman & Billing 1867–70: apsidal chancel with N. vestry and S. organ chamber, transepts, aisled and clerestoried nave, tall SW. tower with pinnacles and short spire. Svces. only in crypt from 1971. Demol. 1975. New brick bldg. in contemporary style on part of site, adjoining flats and community centre, 1975–7.[75] Not oriented.

ST. PHILIP, Manor Pl. (later St. Philip's Pl.). Served from St. Mary's.[76] Attendance 1886: 165 a.m.; 89 evg. Iron bldg., seating 400, erected at N. end of recently closed burial ground under faculty of 1861. Demol. under faculty of 1893, site being added to recreation ground.[77]

ST. SAVIOUR, Warwick Ave. Dist. formed 1856 from St. Jas. and Holy Trinity.[78] Patron bp. of Lond. Attendance 1886: 1,350 a.m.; 700 evg.; 1902: 702 a.m.; 352 p.m. Bldg. of Kentish rag and Bath stone in Dec. style, seating 1,670, by Thos. Little 1855–6: tall aisleless flat-roofed nave lit by double range of windows, chancel rebuilt on larger scale by F. Wade-Farmer 1884, tall W. entrance tower with pinnacles, buttresses. Not oriented.[79] Reredos and other fittings by W. Farmer, glass by Messrs. Gibbs and by Clayton & Bell. Demol. 1972, when svces. moved to Sutherland Ave. Meth. ch. New pale brown brick bldg. in contemporary style, seating c. 250, by Biscoe & Stanton, 1974–6: ch., with hexagonal roof and fibre-glass spire, built over hall or theatre and adjoined flats of Manor Ho. Ct.[80]

ST. SIMON, Saltram Cres. Dist. formed 1899 from St. Jude and St. John, Kilburn.[81] Patron trustees.

Attendance 1902: 201 a.m.; 245 p.m. Mission ch. at SE. corner of Croxley Rd. by 1896.[82] Bldg. of red brick with stone dressings in Middle Gothic style by J. S. Alder 1898–9: apsidal sanctuary, aisled and clerestoried nave, N. and S. vestries, small NW. bell turret. Not oriented. Closed 1978 but bldg. survived 1985.[83] Par. united with St. Luke, Fernhead Rd., and St. Jude 1952. Vicarage by J. S. Alder 1904 served united par. 1982.[84]

ST. STEPHEN, Westbourne Pk. Rd. Dist. formed 1856 from St. Jas. and Holy Trinity,[85] after benefaction from Revd. Harvey Wm. Brooks. Patron Revd. H. W. Brooks (incumbent until 1872), then son Revd. T. B. H. Brooks (V. 1883–94)[86] and trustees, bp. of Lond. by 1935. Attendance 1886: 1,490 a.m.; 1,115 evg.; 1902: 956 a.m.; 620 p.m. Bldg. of Kentish rag with Bath stone dressings in 13th-cent. style, seating 1,600 with galleries, by F. & H. Francis 1855–6: apsidal chancel with N. organ chamber and S. chapel, transepts, lofty aisled and clerestoried nave, W. tower with pinnacles and spire; alterations inc. apsidal end to chancel and choir vestry off S. transept 1900; baptistery 1911. Not oriented. Glass by Messrs. Gibbs and by Clayton & Bell. Spire demol. early 1950s. Bldg. decayed 1971 but still in use 1982.[87]

ST. THOMAS, Newton Rd.[88] Proprietary chapel served, with St. Luke, Tavistock Rd., from St. Steph. 1866, with own min. 1881. Attendance 1886: 288 a.m.; 199 evg. Iron bldg. E. side of Newton Rd., leased to grammar sch. c. 1904.[89]

ROMAN CATHOLICISM. Matthew Smale, presumably the lessee of the manor, was absent from church in 1589.[90] Five residents or former residents of Paddington were charged with recusancy between 1628 and 1640,[91] one of them being Dame Anne Conway (d. 1647), a relative of the St. Johns.[92] Mass was said to be celebrated at a lone farmhouse c. 1780[93] and a few papists were reported c. 1800 but they had no regular meeting place until the mid 19th century.[94] Despite the presence of several religious orders and a very large attendance in Bayswater, the total number of Roman Catholic worshippers in 1902, at 2,071, was less than that of either Baptists or Methodists.[95] The churches, with other places of worship, are described below.[96]

[70] Lond. Gaz. 30 Jan. 1874, p. 412.
[71] O.S. Map 1/2,500, Lond. LX (1897 edn.); ibid. Lond. IV. 12 (1916 edn.).
[72] Mackeson's Guide (1889); C.C.C., Clarke MSS. iii. 36; Bingham, Official Guide to Paddington [1921], 138; Marylebone libr., P 131.1, photos.; inf. from Revd. F. G. W. W. Heydon.
[73] Inf. from Mr. Heydon; P.O. Dir. Lond. (1959).
[74] Lond. Gaz. 17 Jan. 1871, p. 166.
[75] Mackeson's Guide (1889); Clarke, Lond. Chs. 120; C.C.C., survey files; Marylebone libr., P 131.1, cuttings and photos.   [76] Clergy List (1866, 1892).
[77] Mackeson's Guide (1889); Lucas, Plan of Paddington (1869); Marylebone libr. Paddington Faculties, 41–8.
[78] Lond. Gaz. 1 Aug. 1856, p. 2662.
[79] Pevsner, Lond. ii. 301; Clarke, Lond. Chs. 116–17; Illus. Lond. News, 19 Apr. 1856, 405; Marylebone libr., P 131.1, cuttings. Late example of open auditorium: Ecclesiologist, xvii. 425.
[80] Marylebone libr., P 131.1, cuttings; inf. from V.
[81] Lond. Gaz. 11 Aug. 1899, p. 4989.
[82] O.S. Map 1/2,500, Lond. XLVII (1894–6 edn.).
[83] Above, growth, Queen's Pk. and St. Peter's Pk.

[84] Clarke, Lond. Chs. 121; Marylebone libr., notes; C.C.C., survey files; inf. from V., St. Luke with St. Sim. and St. Jude.   [85] Lond. Gaz. 1 Aug. 1856, p. 2662.
[86] Hennessy, Novum Rep. 371; Alum. Oxon. 1715–1886, i. 169.
[87] Clarke, Lond. Chs. 117; C.C.C., survey files; Illus. Lond. News, 26 Jan. 1856, 102; Marylebone libr., P 131.1, cuttings; inf. from V.
[88] The incumbent and patrons listed for 1889 in Hennessy, Novum Rep. 371, were those for St. Thomas's, Kensal Rd., Kensal New Town.
[89] Mackeson's Guide (1889); Clergy List (1881); Bacon, Atlas of Lond. (1886, 1910); Marylebone libr., P 131.1, cuttings, St. Steph.   [90] Mdx. County Rec. i. 187.
[91] Ibid. iii. 20, 42, 58, 66, 130, 135, 139, 143, 154.
[92] P.R.O., C 6/132/34; C 8/133/31.
[93] J. Harting, Cath. Lond. Missions (1903), 212.
[94] Guildhall MS. 9557, f. 40; below.
[95] Mudie-Smith, Rel. Life, 103.
[96] For abbreviations used in the following accounts see above, p. 152. Attendance figs. 1886 are from Brit. Weekly, 26 Nov. 1886, p. 16; figs. 1902 (Dec.) are from Mudie-Smith, Rel. Life, 103.

St. Mary of the Angels, Westmoreland (later Moorhouse) Rd., Bayswater, originated in svces. *c.* 1849 at no. 4 Sutherland Pl.[97] Ch. begun 1851 under Revd. A. Magee, with private benefactions; called St. Helen's and St. Mary's *c.* 1854,[98] opened 1857 under Hen. Edw. (later Cardinal) Manning, first superior of Oblate Fathers of St. Chas. Borromeo.[99] Attendance 1886: 548 a.m.; 475 evg.; 1902: 1,352 a.m.; 193 p.m. Chief ch. of Oblates of St. Chas., serving par., schs., and wider missionary work; acquired by archdiocese of Westm. 1974. Grey-stone bldg. in Early Eng. style by Thos. Meyer: nave, N. and S. aisles, sanctuary. Outer N. aisle added 1869, extended 1887, outer S. aisle and Lady chapel 1872 by J. F. Bentley;[1] unfinished SW. tower. Seating for 500 in 1982. Glass by Bentley. Community ho. *c.* 1857.

Our Lady of Lourdes and St. Vincent de Paul, Harrow Rd. No. 337 on S. side near Woodfield Rd. bought by Revd. Ld. Archibald Douglas for St. Vincent's boys' home 1877. Chapel dedic. to Our Lady opened 1882.[2] Reg. as mission ch. of Our Lady Immaculate 1893[3] but dedic. soon changed, perhaps to inc. that of home, which closed 1912.[4] Attendance 1886: 171 a.m.; 255 evg.; 1902: 340 a.m.; 97 p.m. Bldg. in French Gothic Transitional style by J. Hall 1882: nave, apsidal sanctuary, steep wooden roof.[5] Demol. 1970 and replaced with concrete ch. in contemporary style, seating 500 and adjoining halls and priest's ho., consecrated 1976.[6]

Our Lady of Sorrows, Cirencester Street. Chapel on ground floor of sch. Attendance 1903: 89 a.m. Chapel of ease to St. Mary of the Angels until 1912, thereafter mission ch. served by Oblates of St. Chas. until 1970, when acquired by archdiocese of Westm. Plain yellow-brick bldg., with hall and classrooms later added overhead, 1912; remodelled after fire 1965. Seating for 325 in 1982.[7]

St. Katharine's chapel of ease reg. at no. 20 Paddington Green 1920. Closed by 1954.[8]

Our Lady Queen of Heaven opened 1954 by Oblates of St. Chas. as chapel of ease to St. Mary of the Angels. Separate par. 1973, after disbanding of Oblates of St. Chas. Bldg., no. 46 Queensway, bought from Ethical ch. and originally used by Meths. (qq.v.). Internal alterations left seating for *c.* 400 in 1982.[9]

Sisters of Notre Dame de Bon Secours came to Eng. at invitation of Cardinal Manning 1870, stayed temporarily in Kentish Town (St. Pancras), and occupied ho. in Norfolk Terr. (later no. 166 Westbourne Grove) by 1875. Order originally cared for sick at home but later acquired own nursing homes;

doctor was writer A. J. Cronin, who lived nearby at corner of Norfolk (later Needham) Rd. 1927. All sisters at Bon Secours convent were state reg. nurses 1984.[10]

Sisters of the Adoration of the Sacred Heart of Jesus of Montmartre,[11] having left France and stayed briefly in Notting Hill, moved into no. 6 Hyde Pk. Pl., Bayswater Rd., 1903.[12] Known as Tyburn convent, in memory of martyred Rom. Caths., premises inc. chapel called Tyburn shrine for relics and continuous public worship. Gdn. of no. 9 acquired *c.* 1913. No. 6 bombed 1944 but worship soon resumed at no. 9,[13] rented 1944 and bought with no. 10 in 1946. Damaged no. 7 acquired 1945 and no. 8 in 1948. New shrine, comprising chapel and crypt of martyrs, built at nos. 6 and 7 1961–3,[14] replacing no. 9. Mother ho. of Adorers of Sacred Heart, except 1933–45; Benedictine rule adopted 1914. Tyburn Assoc. of Lay Adorers formed for night watches 1964.[15] Convent adjoined offices of Our Lady's Missionary League and of International Cath. Soc. for Girls 1981.

Old Roman Caths., established 1704 after excommunication in Holland, reg. chapel of Sacred Heart, no. 119 Gt. Western Rd., 1952 to 1957. Bldg., a single room formerly used as coal merchant's office, reputedly Lond.'s smallest ch. Chapel of Holy Cross at no. 60 Herries Street also reg. 1953 to 1964.[16]

PROTESTANT NONCONFORMITY. An otherwise unknown minister called Arnhall or Arnold was said to have been ejected at Paddington in 1662.[17] Rooms were registered for worship by Baptists in 1791 and 1794, the first of them being in Star and Garter Mews,[18] but probably were not used for long. Dissenters had no meeting house in 1810, when several who were resident worshipped outside the parish and some Methodists were reported.[19] Independents, who registered houses near St. George's burial ground in 1812 and 1815,[20] presumably could attend Marylebone's Paddington chapel from 1813. Bishop Blomfield and his predecessors were accused in 1853 of having obstructed Dissent by restrictive leasing: although some chapels stood on sites which had been leased without restrictions, many people still worshipped in Marylebone.[21] Later the most flourishing chapels served shopkeepers, clerks, and artisans who lived north or west of the Paddington Estate;[22] the Baptist leader John Clifford, who secured a site in Westbourne Park Place in 1872, recalled that the Ecclesiastical Commissioners had denied him land at Paddington green.[23]

From the opening of the canal boatmen's chapel

[97] Para. based on A. Rottmann, *Lond. Cath. Chs.* (1926), 93–6; F. J. Kirk, *Reminiscences of an Oblate of St. Chas.* (1905), 1–12; inf. from par. priest.
[98] *Cath. Dir.* (1854–7).
[99] E. S. Purcell, *Life of Card. Manning*, ii (1895), 71–2.
[1] Pevsner, *Lond.* ii. 300.
[2] Para. based on *Kilburn Times* (centenary edn.), 15 Mar. 1968, and inf. from par. priest.
[3] G.R.O. Worship Reg. no. 34059.
[4] *Kelly's Dir. Paddington* (1888, 1894).
[5] Rottmann, *Lond. Cath. Chs.* 92.
[6] Marylebone libr., P 131.1, cuttings.
[7] Rottmann, *Lond. Cath. Chs.* 91; G.R.O. Worship Reg. no. 45548; inf. from par. priest.
[8] G.R.O. Worship Reg. no. 47977.
[9] Ibid. no. 64749; inf. from par. priest.
[10] Inf. from Sister Columcille; *P.O. Dir. Lond.* (1875

and later edns.); *Cath. Dir.* (1900).
[11] Para. based on Nuns of Tyburn, *Tyburn Hill of Glory* (1952), 77, 83, 153–4; inf. from Mother John Baptist, sec. gen.
[12] G.R.O. Worship Reg. no. 41130.
[13] Ibid. nos. 60996, 62859.
[14] Ibid. no. 69602; datestone.
[15] *Montmartre to Sydney* (A.C.T.S. booklet, Melbourne, 1975), 25–6, 28.
[16] G.R.O. Worship Reg. nos. 63620, 64159; Marylebone libr., P 131.1, cuttings.
[17] *Calamy Revised*, 15.
[18] Guildhall MS. 9580/1, pp. 11, 78.
[19] Ibid. 9557, f. 40; 9558, f. 468.   [20] Ibid. 9580/4.
[21] Robins, *Paddington*, 162–3.
[22] *Study of Urban Hist.* ed. H. Dyos (1968), 264.
[23] J. Marchant, *Dr. John Clifford* (1924), 42–3.

in 1828, much nonconformity was closely linked with social welfare. John Clifford's work in the early 1860s gave rise to a claim that his Praed Street chapel was London's first 'institutional' church and later his activities were multiplied at Westbourne Park.[24] Nonconformity was considered relatively weak in the wealthy southern part of Paddington in 1899, although Clifford's Baptists rivalled the Anglicans in the middle-class parishes of St. Matthew's and St. Stephen's. Congregationalists, following Clifford's example, were most active in Queen's Park, where the Wesleyans' following was made up largely of immigrants from the country.[25] In 1902 Baptists formed the leading sect with 3,398 attendances, followed by Methodists with 2,223, Congregationalists with 1,991, and Presbyterians with 552.[26] Some chapels closed soon after the First World War and others after the Second, a few bomb-damaged ones being rebuilt.[27]

BAPTISTS. Praed Street chapel began with mtgs. in ho. in Praed Street at expense of Mrs. Alice Ludford 1827. Moved to Church Street, Marylebone, 1831, where admitted to New Connexion 1832.[28] Seceders joined cong. from Edward Street c. 1840 and bought lease of tabernacle built c. 1818 by Inds. near E. end of Praed Street.[29] Attendance 1851: 264 and 150 Sun. sch. a.m.; 498 p.m.[30] John Clifford (1836–1923), pastor from 1858,[31] increased seating 1872 but moved main ch. to Westbourne Pk.[32] below. Attendance 1886: 191 a.m.; 317 evg.; 1902: 101 a.m.; 129 p.m. Closed by 1910.[33]

Bapts. in Charles Street 1838 moved to Crawford Pl., Marylebone, 1845.[34] Bapt. chapel reg. at no. 5B Newcastle Pl., Edgware Rd., former dancing academy, 1838.[35] Perhaps used by Inds. 1851.[36]

Westbourne Grove Bapt. ch. moved from Silver Street, Kensington, to NE. corner of Westbourne Grove and Ledbury Rd. 1853; new site on Kensington side of boundary until 1900.[37] Bldg. of Kentish ragstone with Bath stone dressings in Early Eng. style; twin towers with spires. Enlarged by galleries 1859 and extended 1866 to seat 2,000. 'Largest chapel yet seen in London' and one of most influential 1872.[38] More traditional than Westbourne Pk. ch. 1899.[39] Attendance 1886: 417 a.m.; 545 evg.; 1902: 228 a.m.; 344 evg.

Beulah chapel, Paddington green, although said to have begun in Marylands Rd. 1853,[40] was presumably freehold chapel recorded at entrance to green 1853.[41] In Grove Street, Marylebone, 1857 and Marylebone Rd. 1859, but at no. 29 Harrow Rd. by 1862.[42] Attendance 1886: 65 a.m.; 97 evg.; 1902: 33 a.m.; 46 p.m. Moved to Cornwall Rd. (later part of Westbourne Pk. Rd.), Notting Hill, c. 1911. Strict Bapt. 1912.[43] Closed after 1951.[44]

St. Peter's Pk. ch., perhaps chapel in Marylands Rd. 1875,[45] reg. for Particular Bapts. S. corner of Shirland Rd. and Elgin Ave. 1876.[46] Attendance 1886: 100 a.m.; 96 evg.; 1902: 38 a.m.; 60 p.m. Small brick bldg. below rd. level 1911,[47] when recently closed.[48]

Westbourne Park chapel opened at S. corner of Porchester Rd. and Westbourne Pk. Villas 1877. Site acquired by John Clifford, who moved to no. 51 Porchester Rd. from Praed Street (q.v.). Bldg. of red brick with stone dressings in Early Eng. style by J. Wallis Chapman, deacon; 15 rooms for numerous mtgs.[49] Attendance 1886: 1,023 a.m.; 1,456 evg. Total Sun. attendance 1902 much the largest at any place of worship in Paddington: 910 a.m.; 1,303 p.m. Church, seating 1,050 in 1928,[50] bombed 1944, when svces. moved to Clifford memorial hall, built 1928. New ch. of pale brick with Portland stone dressings in contemporary style, seating 300 and with rooms beneath, opened 1962.[51] Besides nearby institute[52] and girls' home,[53] Clifford opened mission in Bosworth Rd., Kensal New Town, and helped to found other suburban chs.[54] Mission in Hall Pk., Edgware Rd., survived 1928.[55] Attendance 1902: 42 p.m.

Queen's Pk. tabernacle, Herries Street, was reg. as evangelistic mission from 1887 until 1925.[56] Presumably on E. side between nos. 96 and 98, called Wycliffe Union tabernacle 1888–91 and 1910 and listed as Bapt. 1888–93.[57] Attendance 1902: 75 a.m.; 167 p.m.

METHODISTS. Room in Poplar Pl., S. of Moscow Rd., reg. for dissenters 1823,[58] may have been preaching room opened for Primitive Meths. 1850. Attendance 1851: 12 a.m.; 18 aft.; 29 evg.[59] Probably closed by 1863.[60]

Bayswater Wes. chapel, with 150 free sittings and

[24] Ibid. 42; above, social.
[25] Booth, *Life and Labour*, iii (3), 104–5, 143–4.
[26] Mudie-Smith, *Rel. Life*, 103.
[27] For abbreviations used in the following accounts see above, p. 154. Attendance figs. 1886 are from *Brit. Weekly*, 26 Nov. 1886, p. 16; figs. 1902 are from Mudie-Smith, *Rel. Life*, 101–2.
[28] Marchant, *Clifford*, 38; W. T. Whitley, *Bapts. of Lond.* (1928), 159; Guildhall MS. 9580/6, p. 154.
[29] Whitley, *Bapts. of Lond.* 159, 161; Bacon, *Atlas of Lond.* (1886). Built 1816, according to P.R.O., HO 129/1/2/1/8.
[30] P.R.O., HO 129/1/2/1/8.   [31] *D.N.B.*
[32] Marchant, *Clifford*, 43.
[33] *Kelly's Dir. Paddington* (1909, 1910); G.R.O. Worship Reg. no. 13604.
[34] Whitley, *Bapts. of Lond.* 163.
[35] Guildhall MS. 9580/6, p. 306.   [36] Below, Cong.
[37] Bacon, *Atlas of Lond.* (1886); *Plan of Paddington* (1901).
[38] W. Pepperell, *Church Index*, i (1872), 48–9.
[39] Booth, *Life and Labour*, iii (3), 125.
[40] Whitley, *Bapts. of Lond.* 179.
[41] Robins, *Paddington*, 162.
[42] Whitley, *Bapts. of Lond.* 180.

[43] *Kelly's Dir. Paddington* (1910, 1912).
[44] S. F. Paul, *Further Hist. of Gospel Standard Bapts.* i (1951), 97.
[45] Hutchings and Crowsley, *Paddington Dir.* (1875); Whitley, *Bapts. of Lond.* 212.
[46] G.R.O. Worship Reg. no. 23030; Bacon, *Atlas of Lond.* (1886).
[47] Besant, *Lond. N. of Thames*, 152.
[48] *Kelly's Dir. Paddington* (1910, 1912); G.R.O. Worship Reg. no. 23030.
[49] Marchant, *Clifford*, 43–5; Marylebone libr., P 131.1, cuttings.
[50] Whitley, *Bapts. of Lond.* 289.
[51] Marylebone libr., P 131.1, cuttings; G.R.O. Worship Reg. nos. 59519, 68823.
[52] Below, educ.   [53] Above, social.
[54] Marchant, *Clifford*, 71–2; *Brit. Weekly*, 14 Jan. 1887, 11a.
[55] Whitley, *Bapts. of Lond.* 289.
[56] G.R.O. Worship Reg. no. 30327.
[57] *Kelly's Dir. Paddington* (1888, 1890–3); Bacon, *Atlas of Lond.* (1910).
[58] Guildhall MS. 9580/5.
[59] P.R.O., HO 129/1/2/1/6.
[60] *Dolling's Paddington Dir.* (1863).

158 others 1851, probably originated in Poplar Pl. bldg. reg. 1824. By 1843 chapel was next to orphanage in Royal Hill, Queen's Rd. (later Queensway), perhaps where bldg. was reg. 1861.[61] Attendance 1851: 163 and 98 Sun. sch. a.m.; 128 and 26 Sun. sch. p.m.[62] New bldg. in Queen's Rd., of white brick with stone facings in Dec. style, and seating c. 900 in semicircular interior with galleries, reg. for United Meth. Free Ch. 1868.[63] Attendance 1886: 113 a.m.; 125 evg.; 1902: 110 a.m.; 137 p.m. Bldg. bought for conversion to Ethical ch. (below) 1909.[64]

United Meth. Free ch. on N. side of Brindley Street, backing canal, recorded 1879 and 1886.[65]

Sutherland Ave. Wes. ch., at W. corner of Shirland Rd. and Sutherland Gdns. (later part of Sutherland Ave.), opened between 1872 and 1875.[66] Large red-brick bldg. over schs. 1876.[67] Sent mission teams to Queen's Pk., with svces. in Moberley sch. and Kilburn Lane.[68] Attendance 1886: 641 a.m.; 702 evg.; 1902: 245 a.m.; 295 p.m. Replaced by room on ground floor of ho. in Sutherland Ave. reg. 1948. Closed 1979.[69]

Harrow Rd. Primitive Meth. ch., at W. end of Blomfield Terr. at corner of Chichester Pl. and Harrow Rd., reg. 1878. Bldg., perhaps former Presb. ch. (q.v.), of contrasting bands of brick.[70] Attendance 1902: 137 a.m.; 91 p.m. Closed c. 1940.[71]

Kilburn Lane Primitive Meth. ch., at W. corner of Herries Street and Kilburn Lane, reg. 1884. Iron bldg. 1886, 1910. Attendance 1902: 197 a.m.; 219 p.m. Closed by 1937.[72]

Trinity Wes. ch.,[73] at S. corner of Croxley and Fernhead rds., opened 1886. Bldg. of brick with stone dressings 1885; round-headed windows, pedimented entrance flanked by 3-stage towers with corner pinnacles. Attendance 1902: 329 a.m.; 463 p.m. Ch. bombed 1941, svces. moving to lecture hall of 1888 and then to reopened Sun. sch. hall 1944. Joined by former Percy Rd. (Bible Christian) Meth. ch.[74] 1947. New ch. of yellow brick in contemporary style, adjoining hall of 1949 and seating 200, opened 1959.[75]

Meth. International Ho., mother ho. of several homes, opened at no. 4 Inverness Terr. 1950. Chapel in room on ground floor reg. 1951 but svces. held in lounge from c. 1975.[76]

CONGREGATIONALISTS. Providence chapel, Newcastle Pl., called Ind. 1851, may have been chapel reg. for Bapts. 1838 (q.v.). Part of bldg. of 1820, with 50 free sittings and 100 others. Attendance 1851: 30 a.m.; 50 p.m.[77] Closed by 1862.[78]

Craven Hill Cong. ch., E. side Craven Terr., formed 1846.[79] Bldg. in Dec. style, seating c. 700, reg. 1862.[80] Attendance 1886: 286 a.m.; 361 evg.; 1902: 112 a.m.; 105 p.m. Closed 1911, opening new chapel in Wrentham Ave., Brondesbury Pk., 1912.[81] Craven Hill chapel sold to Jehovah's Witnesses (below).

Queen's Pk. Cong. ch., at W. corner of Third Ave. and Harrow Rd., formed 1884.[82] Bldg. reg. 1887, later used as hall. Adjoining ch. of brick with stone dressings in Gothic style reg. 1890.[83] Largest and most active ch. in Queen's Pk. 1902.[84] Attendance 1902: 547 a.m.; 1,227 p.m. Utd. Ref. ch. from 1972. First bldg. demol. by 1982, when ch. seated 925.[85]

CATHOLIC APOSTOLIC CH. Bldg. of 1835 SE. of Paddington green, later said to be between nos. 62 and 63 or 65 and 67 Harrow Rd., used as Cath. Apostolic ch. from c. 1845. Attendance 1851, when 300 free sittings: 200 a.m.; 100 p.m.;[86] 1886: 260 a.m.; 200 evg. Replaced by large new ch. in Maida Hill West, reg. 1894.[87] Bldg. of red brick with stone dressings in Early Eng. style by J. L. Pearson begun 1891: aisled and clerestoried nave, polygonal apse with ambulatory, apsidal SE. chapel with ambulatory, apsidal W. baptistery beneath W. gallery; 2 W. porches; stump of SW. tower. Pearson's only Eng. ch. built for non-Anglicans.[88] Attendance 1902: 245 a.m.; 244 p.m. One of 22 Cath. Apostolic chs. open 1962; sole survivor 1981.[89]

PRESBYTERIANS. Harrow Rd. ch., Blomfield Terr., was reg. by Presb. Ch. of Eng. from 1861 until 1878.[90]

Westbourne Grove ch., N. end of Westbourne Grove Terr., was reg. by United Presb. Ch. 1863 and, as St. Paul's ch., by Presb. Ch. of Eng. 1877.[91] Bldg. in Gothic style by W. G. Habershon.[92] Attendance 1886: 189 a.m.; 300 evg.; 1902: 168 a.m.; 116 p.m. Built 4-storeyed ch. ho. in Newton Rd. c. 1903.[93] Reg. as Bayswater Presb. ch. (Trinity and St. Paul's) 1919, on union with Trinity ch.,

[61] Guildhall MS. 9580/5; P.R.O., HO 129/1/2/1/5.
[62] *Lucas's Paddington Dir.* (1842–3); *P.O. Dir. Lond.* (1844); G.R.O. Worship Reg. no. 14424.
[63] Besant, *Lond. N. of Thames*, 141; G.R.O. Worship Reg. no. 18633.
[64] Marylebone libr., P 131.1, cuttings.
[65] *P.O. Dir. Lond.* (1879); Bacon, *Atlas of Lond.* (1886).
[66] Bacon, *Atlas of Lond.* (1886); Hutchings and Crowsley, *Paddington Dir.* (1872, 1875); G.R.O. Worship Reg. no. 22880.
[67] Besant, *Lond. N. of Thames*, 151.
[68] Marylebone libr., P 131.1, cuttings, s.v. Fernhead Rd.
[69] G.R.O. Worship Reg. no. 61891; inf. from Revd. Mrs. Denise M. Greeves.
[70] Bacon, *Atlas of Lond.* (1886); G.R.O. Worship Reg. no. 24241; Besant, *Lond. N. of Thames*, 150.
[71] *Kelly's Dir. Paddington* (1939); G.R.O. Worship Reg. no. 24241.
[72] G.R.O. Worship Reg. no. 27981; Bacon, *Atlas of Lond.* (1886, 1910); *Kelly's Dir. Paddington* (1936, 1937).
[73] Para. based on F. Hayman, *Fernhead Arise* (pamphlet 1959).
[74] *V.C.H. Mdx.* vii. 243.
[75] Inf. from Revd. Mrs. Denise M. Greeves.
[76] G.R.O. Worship Reg. no. 63255; inf. from warden.

[77] P.R.O., HO 129/1/1/1/2.
[78] *Dolling's Paddington Dir.* (1862).
[79] Bacon, *Atlas of Lond.* (1886); *V.C.H. Mdx.* vii. 243.
[80] Besant, *Lond. N. of Thames*, 140; G.R.O. Worship Reg. no. 15196.
[81] Note on rec. at G.L.R.O.; *V.C.H. Mdx.* vii. 243.
[82] Bacon, *Atlas of Lond.* (1886); *Cong. Year Bk.* (1894).
[83] Inf. from ch. sec.; Marylebone libr., P 131.1, photographs; G.R.O. Worship Reg. nos. 29941, 32131.
[84] Booth, *Life and Labour*, iii (3), 143–4.
[85] Inf. from ch. sec.
[86] *P.O. Dir. Lond.* (1845, 1850, 1863); P.R.O., HO 129/1/1/1/3.
[87] G.R.O. Worship Reg. no. 34468.
[88] Pevsner, *Lond.* ii. 301–2; Quiney, *Pearson*, 206–8. Early design, by J. Belcher, in *Architect*, 27 Feb. 1891.
[89] Inf. from lecture by Dr. D. J. Tierney.
[90] G.R.O. Worship Reg. no. 13549; *P.O. Dir. Lond.* (1863).
[91] Lucas, *Plan of Paddington* (1869); G.R.O. Worship Reg. nos. 15645, 23198.
[92] Marylebone libr., P 138, cuttings, where described as Scotch ch.
[93] Marylebone libr., P 131.1, cuttings.

PADDINGTON PROTESTANT NONCONFORMITY

Kensington Pk. Rd., Kensington. Ch. closed 1970, when ch. ho. reg. with seating for 100. Called Bayswater Utd. Ref. ch. from 1972.[94]

Welsh Calvinistic Meths. reg. ch. at N. corner of Braden Street and Shirland Rd. 1874.[95] Called Presb. Ch. of Wales 1981 and earlier,[96] although sometimes listed as Meth.[97] Bldg. of brick, stuccoed front with pedimented centre.[98] Attendance 1886: 125 a.m.; 200 evg.; 1902: 70 a.m.; 198 p.m.

FRENCH PROTESTANTS. French Evangelical Reformed ch., Monmouth Rd., Westbourne Grove, formed 1861 and reg. 1866. Attendance 1886: 73 a.m.; 52 evg. Supported day sch. in Bedford Passage, St. Pancras, and home for governesses 1914.[99] Closed between 1949 and 1952.[1] Brick bldg., with stuccoed and pedimented front, acquired by Jehovah's Witnesses (below).

SALVATION ARMY. No. 5 Newcastle Pl. (formerly Bapt. q.v.) reg. 1884 to 1886.[2]

Gt. Western hall, no. 55 Harrow Rd., reg. 1895. Beds for 200 men 1901.[3] Attendance 1902: 95 a.m.; 265 p.m. Replaced 1938 by hall at no. 3 South Wharf Rd., closed by 1954.[4]

No. 93 Lancefield Street, Kensal Town, reg. 1901 to 1926. Attendance 1902: 33 a.m.; 74 p.m. Perhaps replaced by Ranelagh hall, part of nos. 34–8 Cirencester Street, reg. 1932 and replaced by no. 228 Harrow Rd., reg. 1962 to 1965.[5]

BRETHREN. Plymouth Brethren used Moscow hall at no. 23 Moscow Rd. 1872, 1888.[6] Presumably different group used New Providence hall. Attendance 1902: 43 a.m.; 49 p.m.

Hope hall, Kilburn Lane, reg. by Open Brethren 1903, was presumably Hope hall, Kilburn Pl., reg. 1967.[7] Attendance 1902: 46 a.m.; 110 p.m.

No. 593 Harrow Rd., Queen's Pk., was reg. for Brotherhood Ch. 1898. Assembly rooms at no. 742 Harrow Rd. were reg. for Plymouth Brethren 1912, replaced by Hermon hall at no. 598 in 1914, and by Prospect hall at no. 593 in 1926.[8]

OTHER DENOMINATIONS AND UNSPECIFIED MISSIONS. Boatmen's chapel,[9] Junction Mews, Sale Street (later Pl.), opened by Paddington Soc. for Promoting Christian Knowledge among Canal Boatmen and Others 1828. Interdenominational but said to be connected with Inds.' Paddington chapel, Marylebone, 1853 and sometimes listed as Wes. Meth.[10] Bldg. a converted coach ho. leased and in 1832 bought from Grand Junction Canal Co. Attendance 1851, when 240 free sittings: 33 afternoon; 30 and 5 Sun. sch. evg. Later, as Boatmen's institution, administered by Lond. City Mission.[11] Attendance 1902: 52 p.m. Closed by 1921.[12]

Unspecified Protestants reg. rooms at no. 4 North Wharf Rd. 1829.[13]

Latter-day Saints reg. bldg. in Queen's Rd. from 1853 to 1866 and Gt. Western hall, Market Street, from 1857 to 1866.[14]

Cabmen's mission hall was at no. 7 Burwood Mews 1878.[15]

Coachmen's mission was at no. 18 Conduit Pl., London Street, 1878, 1886.[16]

Railway Mission had hall at no. 88 Kensal Rd. by 1888 and reg. no. 92 Kensal Rd. 1906.[17] Attendance 1902: 45 p.m.

London City Mission at no. 2 Cuthbert Street, Edgware Rd., 1882, 1902[18] and Amberley Rd. 1903. Attendance 1902: 70 p.m.

Established Paddington Wharves mission reg. by Lond. City Mission at Church Pl. (later Unwin Pl.)[19] 1930, moved to nearby no. 95 Harrow Rd. by 1941,[20] and back to Unwin Pl. by 1951, closing between 1959 and 1964.[21] Attendance 1902: 43 p.m.

West Lond. Ethical Soc., formed 1892 and called Ethical Ch. from 1914, reg. former Meth. ch. in Queen's Rd. 1909. Eclectic beliefs, bldg. being fitted with stained glass windows of Joan of Arc, Elizabeth Fry, and Bernard Shaw.[22] Ethical Ch. reg. basement of min.'s ho. no. 4A Inverness Pl. from 1946 to 1954, Queensway bldg. being reg. by undesignated Christians 1946 and later as Rom. Cath. ch. of Our Lady of Heaven (q.v.).[23]

Jehovah's Witnesses[24] used nos. 34 and 36 Craven Terr. as headquarters in Britain from 1911 until move to Mill Hill 1958.[25] No. 34 accommodated staff and no. 36, previously Craven Hill Cong. chapel, served as Lond. tabernacle, later Kingdom hall. Former French Prot. ch. in Monmouth Rd. used as Kingdom hall from 1977.[26]

Paddington hall, Church Street, reg. for unsectarian worship 1904 to 1954. Attendance 1902: 68 p.m.[27]

94 G.R.O. Worship Reg. nos. 47627, 72154; inf. from Mr. E. A. Lawson.
95 Bacon, Atlas of Lond. (1886); G.R.O. Worship Reg. no. 21637.
96 e.g. Kelly's Dir. Paddington (1888, 1912).
97 Ibid. (1930, 1939).
98 Marylebone libr., P 131.1, photos.
99 W. H. Harris and M. Bryant, Chs. and Lond. (1914), 303; G.R.O. Worship Reg. no. 17349.
1 P.O. Dir. Lond. (1949, 1952).
2 G.R.O. Worship Reg. no. 28088.
3 Ibid. 35137; G. R. Sims, Lond. Life, ii (1901), 156.
4 G.R.O. Worship Reg. no. 57849.
5 Ibid. nos. 38286, 53593, 68622.
6 Hutchings and Crowsley, Paddington Dir. (1872); Kelly's Dir. Paddington (1888).
7 G.R.O. Worship Reg. nos. 40778, 71103.
8 Ibid. nos. 36707, 45505, 45993, 50464.
9 Para. based on Canal Boatman's Mag. (1829–32); P.R.O., HO 129/1/2/1/9.
10 Robins, Paddington, 163; Dolling's Paddington Dir. (1862).
11 Kelly's Dir. Paddington (1888).
12 Ibid. (1921–2).

13 Guildhall MS. 9580/6, pp. 238–9.
14 G.R.O. Worship Reg. nos. 964, 7803.
15 Hutchings and Crowsley, Paddington Dir. (1878).
16 Ibid. (1878, 1886).
17 G.R.O. Worship Reg. no. 41902; Kelly's Dir. Paddington (1888).
18 Hutchings and Crowsley, Paddington Dir. (1882); P.O. Dir. Lond. (1902).
19 G.R.O. Worship Reg. no. 52405; Kelly's Dir. Paddington (1939).
20 G.R.O. Worship Reg. no. 59865; P.O. Dir. Lond. (1942).
21 G.R.O. Worship Reg. no. 63226; P.O. Dir. Lond. (1959, 1964).
22 Marylebone libr., P 131.1, cuttings (Ethical Message, Nov.–Dec. 1917); G.R.O. Worship Reg. no. 43878.
23 G.R.O. Worship Reg. nos. 61532, 61533; inf. from Father P. J. H. Carpenter.
24 Para. based on inf. from branch manager, Watch Tower Soc.
25 G.R.O. Worship Reg. no. 46289; V.C.H. Mdx. v. 42.
26 G.R.O. Worship Reg. no. 74793.
27 Ibid. no. 40241.

Evangelical Protestants reg. Ranelagh hall, Cirencester Street (probably Ranelagh Rd. hall 1878, 1886) 1904 to 1932. Attendance 1902: 180 p.m.[28]

Church Mystical Union was at no. 35 Norfolk Sq. 1930.[29]

Paddington Sanctuary Spiritualist ch. was at no. 252 Harrow Rd. 1939.[30]

Unity Sch. of Christianity reg. ground floor of no. 6 Stanhope Terr. as Unity Ho. 1943 to 1954.[31]

Assemblies of God reg. ground floor of no. 141 Harrow Rd., having moved from no. 184A Edgware Rd., Marylebone, 1946;[32] called Assembly of God revival centre 1975[33] and Pentecostal ch. 1986.[34]

Christians reg. Ilbert Street hall, Queen's Pk., 1951.[35]

GREEK ORTHODOX CHURCH. Following a westward movement of Greek Orthodox families in London, worshippers at the church of Our Saviour, London Wall, moved to the church of St. Sophia (Aghia Sophia), Moscow Road, on which work started in 1877. Under statutes of 1879 the new church was vested in trustees, representing the Greek Orthodox Brotherhood of London. Cathedral status was achieved in 1922, when the see of West and Central Europe was created under the metropolitan of Thyateira, and reorganization assigned it to the exarch of Western and Northern Europe in 1924.[36] There were Sunday attendances of 179 in 1886 and 141 in 1902.[37] The building, opened in 1879[38] and consecrated in 1882, is an early example of the Byzantine Revival style, designed in red brick, to seat c. 700, by John Oldrid Scott. Not oriented, it is on the plan of a Greek cross and consists of a short nave beneath a central copper dome, with apsidal sanctuary, transepts, and narthex. The interior is of bands of brick and stone, richly decorated with marble and mosaics. The mosaics covering the vaults and dome, to a design by A. G. Walker, were completed in 1893.[39]

JUDAISM. In the 19th century prosperous Jewish communities grew up as building spread along Bayswater Road and later northward to Maida Vale. Bayswater synagogue, on the northern edge of the district and perhaps more accurately described as in Westbourne Park, was established because of a drift of Jews from Bloomsbury and the City.[40] In Maida Vale the Anglican church of St. Saviour, Warwick Avenue, although in a rich area, was said to be poor because so many residents were Jews.[41] Jewish

prominence perhaps owed more to wealth than to numbers: fewer than Roman Catholics and each of the three leading protestant nonconformist sects, Jews accounted for 422 church attendances in 1886[42] and for 1,826 out of a total of 31,331 attendances in 1902.[43] There were three synagogues and several other Jewish institutions in Paddington in 1986.[44]

Bayswater synagogue, at the west corner of Chichester Place and Harrow Road, was consecrated in 1863. It was built with grants from London's Great and New synagogues, whose joint management committee made way in 1866 for a local committee, and the first seat holders included the banker Samuel Montagu, later Lord Swaythling (1832–1911), and members of the Rothschild family. In 1870 Bayswater joined the Great, New, Hambro, and Central synagogues to form the United Synagogue. The building, designed in red brick in the Gothic style by N. S. Joseph, originally held 341, with a further 334 in the ladies' gallery, but the seating was soon extended. Some of the richest members, from Tyburnia, transferred to the New West End synagogue after 1879, with the result that by 1890 more than half of those attending Bayswater synagogue came from Maida Vale. Although numbers had fallen by the time that the site was taken for the Harrow Road flyover, litigation compelled the United Synagogue to promise to rebuild on land provided by the G.L.C.[45] From c. 1965 services were held in the hall of the Lauderdale Road synagogue[46] until a flat-roofed building in contemporary style was erected in 1971–2 in Kilburn Park Road.[47] As Bayswater and Maida Vale synagogue, the congregation remained a constituent of the United Synagogue in 1981.[48] The premises were later bought for the new Jewish Preparatory School, although high holy day services were still held there in 1986.[49]

The New West End synagogue, St. Petersburgh Place, was an offshoot of Bayswater synagogue and consecrated in 1879.[50] Designed by Audesley & Joseph[51] as an imposing building of red brick with terracotta decorations, seating 800, it had an ornate west doorway flanked by twin bell-towers with copper domes. From 1957 it adjoined the Herbert Samuel centre in Orme Lane, which included a small synagogue used for children's services. The congregation, drawn from Tyburnia and its westward extension beyond Lancaster Gate, was the richest of all those belonging to the United Synagogue before 1914.[52] In 1964 the New West End synagogue challenged the authority of the United Synagogue in a vain attempt to secure a liberal scholar, Dr. Louis Jacobs, as minister. After the

[28] Ibid. no. 40485; Hutchings and Crowsley, *Paddington Dir.* (1878, 1886).
[29] *Kelly's Dir. Paddington* (1930).
[30] Ibid. (1939).
[31] G.R.O. Worship Reg. no. 60628.
[32] Ibid. no. 61485.
[33] *P.O. Dir. Lond.* (1975).
[34] Notice at ch.
[35] G.R.O. Worship Reg. no. 63121.
[36] M. Constantinides, *Greek Orthodox Ch. in Lond.* (1933), 61, 66–7, 85, 87, 91–2, 103, 106.
[37] *Brit. Weekly*, 26 Nov. 1886, p. 16; Mudie-Smith, *Rel. Life*, 103.
[38] *Paddington, Kensington and Bayswater Chron.* 7 June 1879.
[39] *Illus. Lond. News*, 11 Feb. 1882; Pevsner, *Lond.* ii. 301; C.C.C., Clarke MSS. xv. 83; G. Stamp and C. Amery, *Victorian Bldgs. of Lond. 1837–87* (1980), 128–9; above, plate 35.
[40] *Jewish Hist. Soc. Trans.* xxi. 82; C. Roth, *Bayswater Syn.* (1938), 4.
[41] Marylebone libr., P 131.1, cuttings.
[42] *Brit. Weekly*, 26 Nov. 1886, p. 16.
[43] Mudie-Smith, *Rel. Life*, 103.
[44] *Jewish Year Bk.* (1986); *P.O. Dir. Lond.* (1986).
[45] Roth, *Bayswater Syn.* 4–7; A. Newman, *United Syn.* (1976), 169–70; *Jewish Hist. Soc. Trans.* xxi. 84.
[46] Marylebone libr., P 131.1, cuttings (Chichester Pl. syn.).
[47] Ibid.; datestone; G.R.O. Worship Reg. no. 73191.
[48] *Jewish Year Bk.* (1981).
[49] Inf. from Rabbi Dr. Abraham Levy; below, educ., private.
[50] Roth, *Bayswater Syn.* 11. Rest of para. based on inf. from Mr. Raphael Levy.
[51] Pevsner, *Lond.* ii. 302.
[52] *Jewish Hist. Soc. Trans.* xxi. 84.

board of management had been forced to resign, seceders formed the New London synagogue, which held its first service in Lauderdale Road and by 1970 had secured premises in Abbey Road, St. John's Wood.[53]

A Spanish and Portuguese synagogue was registered in 1896,[54] land at the north-east corner of Lauderdale and Ashworth roads having been leased from the Paddington Estate in 1895.[55] The building, next to a Jewish orphanage, was designed by Davis & Emanuel in red brick and white stone, with a shallow central dome and a cupola.[56] It remained a Sephardi synagogue in 1981, when the Sephardi Burial Society and Welfare Board, the Sephardi Kashrut Authority, and a religious library were at no. 2 Ashworth Road.[57]

Maida Hill Beth Hamedrash was registered on the ground floor of no. 131 Elgin Avenue in 1944.[58] Affiliated to the Federation of Synagogues in 1945, it was admitted as a constituent synagogue in 1948 and was known as Emet V' Shalom synagogue from 1949. The original premises, after internal alterations, seated 130 in 1982.[59]

EDUCATION. In 1697 and again in 1698 the overseers paid for 13 months' 'foundling schooling'.[60] In 1717 the vestry resolved that 'the children be kept to their schooling', at the churchwardens' expense,[61] and from 1723 payments were made for nursing and teaching individual boys and for their books.[62] At least one schoolmaster was paid quarterly by 1774–5 and bills from a man and a woman were met in 1779.[63] While the earliest pupils were presumably orphans, with no permanent schoolhouse, the payments in the 1770s were probably for a 'public school' recalled by some inhabitants in 1802 as having been supported by the charities' estates but having fallen into disuse.[64] Paddington in 1795 had only a Sunday school.[65]

The vestry decided to re-establish the free school, later called St. Mary's, in 1802.[66] A hundred pupils were taught in 1816, when more than 1,500 children of under 12 years of age lived on the south side of the canal alone,[67] and in 1819 the minister stated that education for the poor was insufficient.[68] Increased application of rents from the charities' copyhold estates and money from the sale of waste lands assisted the rebuilding of St. Mary's as a National school in 1822 and the building of another Church school, at Bayswater, in 1831.[69] From 1829 a school

for 50 girls was maintained by Mrs. Sutcliffe of Orme Square and from 1833 there was an infants' school for 100, also of private foundation. Fee-paying schools, smaller but much more numerous, in 1833 supported 954 children.[70]

One fifth of the income from all the charities' estates was allotted to the parochial schools in 1837.[71] By 1850 parliamentary grants were paid to the three National schools of St. Mary's, St. John's, and Bayswater, and to a fourth, St. John's, Kensal Green, in Chelsea detached.[72] Westbourne and All Saints' schools also received grants by 1855, when all six aided schools were National ones.[73] A ragged school had opened in 1848 and there were also Roman Catholic and dissenters' schools, not supported by grants, from the 1850s.[74] Church schools multiplied, eight being founded between 1859 and 1870.[75] They shared the income from the charities' estates, which in 1894 totalled £924 18s. 10d. and was divided among 15 schools according to their size.[76] The guardians employed a master and mistress to teach the workhouse children from 1847 until 1871.[77]

Under the Education Act, 1870, Paddington formed part of the Marylebone division of the London school board, together with Hampstead, Marylebone, and St. Pancras, while the adjacent area of Chelsea detached lay in the Chelsea division.[78] Three more Church schools soon opened and several others were enlarged,[79] while a mission in Ranelagh Road had been taken over as a temporary board school by 1878.[80] The board opened the first of its two schools in Queen's Park in 1877 and the second in 1881, when it also opened schools in Amberley Road and Campbell Street, Maida Vale. Two more, the Moberley and Kilburn Lane, followed in 1884 and 1885. A seventh board school, made necessary by the final building up of the northern part of Paddington, was opened at Essendine Road in 1900.[81]

The L.C.C.'s education committee succeeded the London school board in 1904, under the Education (London) Act, 1903.[82] The committee thereafter listed its Paddington schools according to electoral divisions, those in the former Chelsea detached being transferred to Paddington North.[83] In 1913 the borough contained 8 L.C.C. elementary schools, of which 7 were former board schools, and 20 non-provided schools, of which 3 were Roman Catholic and 1 was Jewish. Secondary education was provided at the County Secondary school and at Paddington and Maida Vale high school, both aided, and at St. Mary's college.[84] In 1918 North Paddington

[53] Newman, *United Syn.* 184–7; *The Times*, 24 Apr. 1964, 12d; 4 May 1964, 14e, 15b; 11 May 1964, 9a; *P.O. Dir. Lond.* (1970).
[54] G.R.O. Worship Reg. no. 35716.
[55] Ch. Com., Bldg. Agreements, vol. x.
[56] Marylebone libr., P 131.1, cuttings.
[57] *Jewish Year Bk.* (1981).
[58] G.R.O. Worship Reg. no. 60876.
[59] Inf. from sec., Federation of Synagogues.
[60] Overseers' acct. bk. (1691–1762).
[61] Chwdns. acct. bk. (1656–1736), f. 87.
[62] Ibid. ff. 104–5 sqq.
[63] Ibid. (1774–1833), *passim.*
[64] Vestry mins. 15 Mar. 1802.
[65] Lysons, *Environs*, iii. 340.
[66] Vestry mins. 15 Mar. 1802; 25 Feb. 1803; Lysons, *Environs* (Suppl.), 252. [67] Robins, *Paddington*, 164.
[68] *Educ. of Poor Digest*, 540.
[69] *14th Rep. Com. Char.* H.C. 382, pp. 182–3 (1826), xii; Robins, *Paddington*, 165.

[70] *Educ. Enq. Abstract*, 576. [71] Below, chars.
[72] *Mins. of Educ. Cttee. of Council, 1848–9* [1215], pp. ccxiii, ccxvii, H.C. (1850), xliii; *1850–1* [1357], pp. clxii, clxviii, H.C. (1851), xliv (1).
[73] Ibid. *1854–5* [1926], pp. 197, 201–3, H.C. (1854–5), xlii.
[74] Robins, *Paddington*, 169. [75] Below.
[76] *Endowed Chars. Lond.* H.C. 261, pp. 39–43 (1894), lxiii.
[77] G.L.R.O., Pa. B.G. 1/1, ff. 398–9; Pa. B.G. 79/1, list of offrs.
[78] 33 & 34 Vic. c. 75; *Final Rep. of Sch. Bd. for Lond.* (1904), 5; Stanford, *Sch. Bd. Map of Lond.* [undated].
[79] Below, s.v. individual schs.
[80] *Rep. of Educ. Cttee. of Council, 1878* [C. 2342–I], p. 955, H.C. (1878–9), xxiii.
[81] L.C.C. *Educ. Svce. Particulars* (1906–7).
[82] 3 Edw. VII, c. 24.
[83] L.C.C. *Educ. Svce. Particulars* (1906–7).
[84] Ibid. (1913–14).

MIDDLESEX: OSSULSTONE HUNDRED

was one of the metropolitan areas where poverty had produced a large number of backward pupils.[85] By 1951, apart from special and technical schools, there were 11 L.C.C. schools, 7 of them primary and 4 secondary, and 13 voluntary schools, one of which was secondary. All except one of the L.C.C.'s schools but only 5 of the voluntary schools lay within Paddington North.[86]

Under the London Government Act, 1963, Paddington was joined with the rest of Westminster and with Camden in one of ten divisions of the new I.L.E.A.[87] After amalgamations the former borough contained the whole or part of 3 mixed secondary schools, one being Anglican and one Roman Catholic, and 20 primary schools, of which 7 were Anglican and 3 Roman Catholic.[88]

Public schools. The general sources are those indicated above, p. 160, with the addition of *Endowed Chars. Lond.* H.C. 261, pp. 39–43 (1894), lxiii, for 19th-century Church of England schools, and *Kelly's Dir. Paddington*, and the same abbreviations are used. Primary sch. roll nos. for Jan. 1986 supplied by I. L. E. A. Research and Statistics Dept.

ALL SAINTS C.E., Francis Street. Opened 1852 as Nat. sch. for GBI.[89] Financed by parl. grant, vol. contributions, and sch. pence (2d.). 1893 accn. 389 BGI, a.a. 200; 1899 accn. 259 BI, a.a. 125. Closed by 1903.

AMBERLEY RD., Harrow Rd. Opened 1881 as bd. sch. for 603 BGI. Enlarged 1906 for 600 M, 393 I; 1910 for 520 B, 570 I. 1932 accn. 360 B, 480 G, 546 I, a.a. 262 B, 254 G, 281 I. JB, JG, I by 1936. Senior dept. by 1951, when renamed Kemble (q.v.); junior dept., called Amberley primary, closed 1954.[90]

BAYSWATER JEWISH, St. James's Terr., Harrow Rd. Opened 1867 at no. 1 Westbourne Pk. Villas. Moved to new bldg. in Harrow Rd., provided in compensation by G.W.R. Co., 1879.[91] Parl. grant by 1880. 1889 accn. 267, a.a. 175. 1906 accn. 152 B, 154 G, 113 I, a.a. 115 B, 90 G, 65 I. Name changed from Paddington Bayswater Jewish sch. to Kensington Bayswater Jewish sch. on move to Lancaster Rd. 1930. Later called Solomon Wolfson.

BAYSWATER NAT., see St. Matthew C.E.

BAYSWATER RAGGED, see St. Matthew parochial I.

BAYSWATER R.C., see St. Mary of the Angels, St. Mic.

BEETHOVEN STREET, Queen's Pk. Opened 1881 as bd. sch. for 1,166 MI in Chelsea detached. Higher grade by 1906. 1927 accn. 675 M, 382 I, a.a. 665 M, 340 I. 1932 accn. 548 SM, a.a. 457. SM 1958; SB by 1961, when closed.[92]

CAMPBELL STREET, Maida Vale. Opened 1881 as bd. sch. for 802 BGI. 1906 accn. 312 B, 312 G, 348 I, a.a. 277 B, 252 G, 287 I. 1932 accn. 598 JM, 330 I, a.a. 303 JM, 294 I. Name changed to Paddington Green primary 1962. Roll 1986: 218 JMI.

CIRENCESTER STREET, see St. Mary Magdalene.

CIRENCESTER STREET R.C., see Our Lady of

Dolours.

CLARENDON STREET, see St. Mary Magdalene.

CRAVEN HILL CONG. CH. Opened 1862 in rooms beneath ch. Financed by sch. pence (2d.–6d.) from 31 B and 76 G in 1874. Closed soon after 1874.

DROOP STREET, see Queen's Pk. primary.

EDWARD WILSON PRIMARY, Senior Street, Harrow Rd. Opened 1915 as Senior Street council sch. for BGI, replacing Harrow Rd. temp. council sch. (q.v.). 1919 accn. 320 B, 320 G, 384 I, a.a. 191 B, 191 G, 203 I. SB, SG, I between 1932 and 1936. Primary sch. alone, called Edw. Wilson, by 1951. Roll 1986: 249 JMI.

ESSENDINE PRIMARY. Temp. bd. sch. for GBI in iron bldgs. by 1898. Opened 1900 as Essendine Rd. bd. sch. for 422 SM, 422 JM, 438 I. Enlarged 1910 for 550 B, 550 G, 595 I. 1932 accn. 560 B, 480 G, 516 I, a.a. 495 B, 456 G, 432 I. Name changed to Essendine council sch. by 1938. Primary and SM schs. until 1958, then primary and SG.[93] SG closed 1962 on opening of Sarah Siddons (q.v.).[94] Roll 1986: 163 JMI.

HALLFIELD PRIMARY, Porchester Gdns. Opened 1953 for JM & I, on site provided by Paddington M.B., in linked bldgs. of precast concrete whose design led to growth of Denys Lasdun's reputation.[95] Rolls 1986: 235 JM, 234 I.

HARROW RD., see Moberley.

HARROW RD. VINE COURT R.C., see Our Lady of Dolours.

HARROW RD. TEMP. Opened 1911 for 324 JM in iron bldgs. Closed 1915 on opening of Edw. Wilson (q.v.).

HOLY TRINITY, see Trinity.

KEMBLE, Amberley Rd., Harrow Rd. Opened as senior dept. of Amberley Rd. sch. by 1951, when renamed Kemble. Allotted whole of Amberley Rd. bldg. 1954.[96] SM 1955. Closed by 1958.

KILBURN CH. EXTENSION, see St. Augustine C.E.

KILBURN LANE, CENTRAL, see North Paddington.

KILBURN LANE, Kensal Green. Temp. bd. sch. by 1884. Opened 1885 as perm. bd. sch. in Chelsea detached for 1,583 BGI. Higher grade by 1906. 1919 accn. 480 B, 480 G, 363 I, a.a. 381 B, 323 G, 205 I. JMI from 1926. 1927 accn. 327, a.a. 232. Closed 1936.

LANCEFIELD STREET TEMP. Opened by 1881 as bd. sch. in Chelsea detached. 1881 accn. 172, a.a. 78. Probably closed by 1882.

MAIDA VALE HIGH, see Paddington and Maida Vale high.

MOBERLEY, the, Kilburn Lane. Opened as Harrow Rd. bd. sch. for 1,182 BGI. Name changed to the Moberley bd. sch. by 1899, with accn. for 1,607 BGI. 1932 accn. 387 B, 392 G, 457 I, a.a. 290 B, 273 G, 285 I. 1936 accn. 554 JMI, a.a. 242. Closed 1957.[97]

NORTH PADDINGTON, Kilburn Lane. Opened 1925 and 1926 as separate Kilburn Lane central schs. for 400 SB and 332 SG from Kilburn Lane sch. Names

[85] L.C.C. Educ. Cttee. *Development Memo. no. 1, Backward Children* (1918).
[86] L.C.C. *Educ. Svce. Inf. 1951.*
[87] *Ann. Abstract of Gtr. Lond. Statistics* (1967).
[88] I.L.E.A. *Sec. Schs. in Westm., Camden* (1981); idem, *Primary Schs. in Paddington and Bayswater* [leaflet].
[89] Robins, *Paddington*, 165.
[90] L.C.C. *Educ. Cttee. Mins.* (1951–2), 37; (1953–4), 362.
[91] *Paddington, Kensington and Bayswater Chron.* 12 July 1879.
[92] L.C.C. *Educ. Cttee. Mins.* (1959–60), 458.
[93] Marylebone libr., P 139.2, cuttings.
[94] L.C.C. *Educ. Cttee. Mins.* (1961–2), 265.
[95] Inf. from headmaster; I. Nairn, *Modern Bldgs. in Lond.* 39; A. Service, *Architects of Lond.* 194.
[96] L.C.C. *Educ. Cttee. Mins.* (1951–2), 37; (1953–4), 362.
[97] Ibid. (1957–8), 190.

changed to North Paddington central schs. by 1932. 1938 a.a. 259 SB, 277 SG. Single sec. mod. sch. by 1951. Upper sch. in Amberley Rd. and lower sch. in Harrow Rd. by 1972. Amalg. with Paddington and Maida Vale high sch. to form Paddington sch. (q.v.) 1972.[98]

NORTH WESTMINSTER COMMUNITY. Opened 1980 on amalg. of Paddington and Sarah Siddons schs. (qq.v.) with Rutherford sch., Marylebone. Premises of former schs. used respectively for new sch.'s Paddington lower ho., upper sch., and Marylebone lower ho. Roll 1986: 1,753.

OUR LADY OF DOLOURS R.C. PRIMARY, Desborough Street, Cirencester Street. Opened 1867 as Harrow Rd. Vine Court R.C. sch. for GI and managed by priests of ch. of St. Mary of the Angels. Financed by vol. contributions and sch. pence (1d.). Moved to new bldg. in Cirencester Street 1872. Parl. grant by 1880. MI by 1893. Name changed to Our Lady of Dolours c. 1907. 1919 accn. 160 B, 240 G, 176 I, a.a. 149 B, 288 GI. Roll 1986: 305 JMI.

PADDINGTON, Oakington Rd. Opened 1972 as SM sch. on amalg. of North Paddington with Paddington and Maida Vale high sch. (qq.v.). Annexe in Elgin Ave. Part of North Westminster sch. (q.v.) from 1980.

PADDINGTON AND MAIDA VALE HIGH, Elgin Ave. Opened by 1884 as Maida Vale high in Warrington Lodge, Warrington Cres., by Girls' Public Day School Trust.[99] Moved to no. 129 Elgin Ave., as Paddington and Maida Vale high, by 1890.[1] County sch. for SG by 1913. Amalg. with North Paddington to form Paddington sch. (q.v.) 1972.[2]

PADDINGTON GREEN PRIMARY, see Campbell Street.

PADDINGTON WHARF, Church Pl. Opened 1848 as ragged schs. for GBI in Kent's Pl. Soon moved to nos. 22–4 Church Pl., where I nursery for working mothers also opened. 1853 a.a. 40 B, 30 G, 110 I.[3] Managed by cttees. of subscribers and financed by vol. contributions and sch. pence (1d. from 1873). 1878 accn. 254, a.a. 127. Probably closed by 1880.

QUEEN'S PK. HALL TEMP. Opened by 1883 as temp. bd. sch. in mission hall. 1884 accn. 185, a.a. 143. Replaced by Kilburn Lane (q.v.).

QUEEN'S PK. PRIMARY, Droop Street. Opened 1877 as D Street (later Droop Street) bd. sch. for 1,104 BGI in Chelsea detached. 1927 accn. 280 B, 264 G, 306 I, a.a. 252 B, 259 G, 217 I. 1932 a.a. 221 JM, 107 I. Name changed to Queen's Pk. primary by 1951. JM and I schs. by 1981. Rolls 1986: 165 JM, 92 I.

RANELAGH RD. Opened 1867 as mission sch. in bldg. leased from Grand Junction Canal Co. Managed by cttee. on Nat. Soc. lines. Financed by sch. pence (3d. and 4d.) and letting rooms 1867; parl. grant by 1870. Bd. sch. by 1878. 1881 accn. 258, a.a. 307. Probably closed by 1882.

ST. AUGUSTINE C.E., Kilburn Pk. Rd. GI opened 1871 as Kilburn Ch. Extension sch. and B opened

1873, both schs. at first in temp. premises. Financed by vol. contributions and sch. pence (GI 2d.–3d., B 3d.–4d.) and parl. grant by 1878. 1881 accn. 366 B, 818 GI. 1889 accn. 1,072 B, 1,347 GI, a.a. 654 B, 1,018 GI. B maintained by L.C.C. from 1909. 1919 accn. 393 B, 596 GI, a.a. 363 B, 484 GI. Primary and sec. schs. by 1951. C.E. comprehensive sch. from 1969, in new bldgs. in Oxford Rd., and C.E. primary sch. Rolls 1986: 673 SM; 177 JMI.

ST. AUGUSTINE MISSION, Kilburn Pk. Rd. Opened 1874 as mission sch. for GI on same site as Nat. schs. Managed by cttee. Financed by vol. contributions and sch. pence (1d.) 1874; parl. grant by 1878. 1880 accn. 129, a.a. 128. Probably closed by 1881.

ST. GEORGE R.C., Lanark Rd. Opened 1956 for SM in new bldg. Annexe in Linstead Street, Hampstead, acquired 1961, when sch. became comprehensive. Roll 1982: 825 SM; 1986: 575 SM.

ST. JAMES C.E., Craven Terr. Opened 1862 as Nat. sch. for BGI. Financed by vol. contributions, sch. pence (2d.), and char. estates; parl. grant by 1865. 1906 accn. 173 B, 175 G, 147 I, a.a. 86 B, 102 G, 72 I. 1919 accn. 236 M, 96 I. 1936 accn. 326 JMI. Roll 1986: 149 JM.

ST. JOHN C.E., Kensal Green. Opened c. 1850 as Nat. sch. in Chelsea detached for BGI. Financed by parl. grant. 1880 accn. 493, a.a. 267. 1900 accn. 330 GI, a.a. 194. 1919 accn. 90 G, 100 I. Closed 1930.

ST. JOHN C.E., Titchborne Street. Opened c. 1830 as Nat. sch. for BG, 1840–1 for I. Financed by vol. contributions, sch. pence (2d.), and char. estates, parl. grant by 1849. 1893 accn. 721 BGI, a.a. 428. 1919 accn. 200 M, 138 I. Closed 1940.[4]

ST. JOSEPH R.C., Lanark Rd. Opened 1959 in new bldg., replacing bombed St. John's R.C. sch. in Fisherton Street, Marylebone.[5] Roll 1986: 263 JMI.

ST. LUKE C.E., Fernhead Rd. Opened 1877 as Nat. sch. for BGI from Willesden. 1893 accn. 547 BGI, a.a. 539. Reorg. 1925. 1927 accn. 276 M, 144 I, a.a. 240 M, 144 I. Roll 1986: 122 JMI.

ST. JOHN SERVANTS' TRAINING, Gt. Western Rd. Opened by 1862 for G only, adjoining Westbourne sch. Parl. grant by 1878. 1893 accn. 326 G, a.a. 69. Called St. John's training sch. for G from c. 1890. Private sch. by 1900 and continued until c. 1933, when premises, St. John's Ho., became social club.

ST. MARY C.E., Paddington green.[6] Opened 1802 as char. sch. for 30 B, 30 G adjoining par. ho. in Harrow Rd.[7] 100 BG by 1816. Rebuilt 1822 E. of almshos., on part of pond site at corner of Harrow Rd. and Church Pl.,[8] with proceeds from waste lands and gifts from Denis Chirac, by will dated 1775, and executor. Financed by vol. contributions, char. sermon, and initially £50 a year from char. copyhold estates, receiving whole profits of copyhold estates 1823.[9] I sch. opened 1833 S. of almshos. Financed probably by char. estates,[10] parl. bldg. grant 1834, and sch. pence (2d. in 1853). Nat. schs. with parl. grants by 1851. 1853 a.a. 174 B, 98 G, 150 I. 1878 accn. 783 BGI, a.a. 413. GI premises

[98] Inf. from sec., N. Westm. sch.
[99] F. S. de Carteret-Bisson, Our Schs. and Colls. ii (1884), 429.   [1] P.O. Dir. Lond. (1890).
[2] Inf. from sec., N. Westm. sch.
[3] Robins, Paddington, 169.
[4] L.C.C. Educ. Cttee. Mins. (1940–4), 79.
[5] Ibid. (1957–8), 74; inf. from Mr. E. O'Rourke.
[6] Hist. before 1853 based on Robins, Paddington, 164–8.
[7] Lysons, Environs (Suppl.), 252; vestry mins. 25 Feb. 1803.
[8] Vestry mins. 23 Sept. 1822; 25 Feb. 1823 (plan).
[9] Ibid. 15 Mar. 1802; 1 Apr. 1823.
[10] Select vestry mins. 2 July 1833.

closed 1905.[11] 1913 temp. accn. 170 B. Closed 1917.

St. Mary Magdalene C.E., Cirencester and Clarendon streets. Built 1865 as Nat. schs. for BGI in Clarendon Street. Financed 1870 by sch. pence (2d. or 3d.), 1878 by parl. grant. Sites acquired for B 1879 in Cirencester Street, where sch. built beneath St. Martha's chapel, and for GI in Clarendon Street 1882. 1885 accn. 571 B, 774 GI, a.a. 343 B, 360 GI. 1893 accn. 1,165 BGI, a.a. 914. New I dept. opened 1914, taking some pupils from Amberley Rd. 1919 accn. 730 BGI, a.a. 542. 1936 accn. 640 BGI, a.a. 396. JMI by 1951. Roll 1986: 201 JMI.

St. Mary Magdalene Senior Street Nat. Opened 1870 for G in hired ho. Under same management as other St. Mary Magdalene schs. Financed partly by sch. pence (1d. in 1877) and 1878 by parl. grant. 1878 accn. 66 G, a.a. 38. Probably closed by 1880. Also St. Mary Magdalene penny mixed sch., probably temp., opened 1873 for BGI in ho. of vicar. Financed by sch. pence (1d.) and ch. offertory.

St. Mary of the Angels R.C., Westmoreland (later Moorhouse) Rd. Opened 1857 for G. Managed by clergy of St. Mary of the Angels. Financed by vol. contributions, sch. pence (1d.), and 1878 by parl. grant. 1900 accn. 200 M, a.a. 95. 1919 accn. 96 G, 60 I. JMI on amalg. with St. Mic.'s R.C. between 1958 and 1961. Roll 1986: 211 JMI.

St. Mary's Orphanage, Kilburn. C.E. sch. for G opened 1885 in orphanage of Sisters of the Ch. Financed by sch. pence (4d.) from 78 G 1885. Closed after 1894.[12]

St. Matthew C.E., Queen's Rd. New bldg. at NE. corner of Porchester Gdns. leased 1832[13] as Bayswater Nat. sch. for BGI. Bldg. largely financed by rents from char. estates and money from sale of waste lands.[14] Parl. grant by 1848–9, when a.a. 174. Managed by cttee. for Paddington char. (St. Mary's) schs. until placed under joint control of incumbents of St. Mat. and Holy Trinity 1860 and under cttee. for St. Mat. 1861. Name changed to St. Mat. parochial schs. 1868, when preference given to children of dist. 1878 accn. 541 BGI, a.a. 515. 1919 accn. 422 BGI, a.a. 343. 1936 accn. 316 MI, a.a. 264. Closed 1938.[15]

St. Matthew parochial I, Poplar Pl. Opened 1850 as Bayswater ragged sch. in shed,[16] replaced 1855 by 2 rooms behind nos. 23–5 Upper Craven Pl. Informally transferred to St. Mat.'s parochial schs. 1873 but received separate parl. grant 1878 and later. 1893 accn. 128 I, a.a. 45. Closed by 1900.

St. Michael C.E., Star Street. Opened 1870 as Nat. sch. for BGI in new bldg. which had replaced hos. Financed by sch. pence (2d., 4d.) and parl. grant. 1878 accn. 618 BGI, a.a. 478. 1919 accn. 466 BGI, a.a. 382. Depts. for canal boat children, 24 M and 15 I, added by 1932. 1936 accn. 143 SB, 263 SG and I. JM and I schs. by 1958. Closed between 1970 and 1972.

St. Michael R.C., Westmoreland Pl. Opened

1874 for B, on site adjoining sch. of St. Mary of the Angels. Financed by vol. contributions, sch. pence (7d.), and 1889 by parl. grant. 1889 accn. 115 B, a.a. 43. 1938 accn. 112 B, a.a. 100. JB sch. by 1955. Amalg. with St. Mary of the Angels (q.v.) as JMI by 1961.

St. Paul C.E., Waverley Rd. Opened 1868 for BGI as branch of Holy Trinity Nat. sch. Managed by cttee. for Holy Trinity until informally transferred to new dist. by 1894. Financed by sch. pence (2d.–3d.). 1893 accn. 558 MI, a.a. 456. 1919 accn. 405 MI, a.a. 338. Closed between 1951 and 1955. Premises later used for Holy Trinity with St. Paul's sec. sch. (see Trinity).

St. Peter C.E., Chippenham Mews. Opened 1867 as Nat. sch. for BGI in iron bldg. Financed by sch. pence (3d.) and parl. grant. Perm. site acquired 1872. 1880 accn. 763 BGI, a.a. 658. 1919 accn. 545 MI, a.a. 423. 1936 accn. 237 JM, 174 I, a.a. 143 JM, 107 I. Roll 1986: 94 JMI.

St. Saviour C.E., Shirland Rd. Opened as Nat. sch. for BGI in temp. accn. by 1871, when perm. bldgs. under construction. Financed by sch. pence (2d.–4d.) and 1873 by parl. grant. 1880 accn. 416, a.a. 415. 1893 accn. 632 BGI, a.a. 450. 1932 accn. 656 BGI, a.a. 491. 1936 accn. 232 SB, 232 SG, 200 I, a.a. 93 SB, 118 SG, 127 I. JMI by 1955. Roll 1986: 84 JMI.

St. Stephen C.E., Westbourne Pk. Rd. Opened 1859 as Nat. sch. for BGI. Financed by vol. contributions, sch. pence (1d.–2d.), and 1865 by parl. grant. 1893 accn. 456 BGI, a.a. 266. Bldg. enlarged 1897. 1900 accn. 866 BGI, a.a. 546. 1938 accn. 779 BGI, a.a. 589. JMI by 1955. Roll 1986: 213 JMI.

Saltram Crescent high, Kilburn. Originated 1886 in Gordon Commercial temp. sch. I classes. Opened 1891 as Nat. sch. for BGI in new bldgs. of Church Extension Assoc. Financed by sch. pence (4d.–9d.). 1893 accn. 843, a.a. 202. 1903 accn. 495. Closed c. 1913.

Sarah Siddons, N. Wharf Rd. Opened 1961–2 for SG, in bldg. of purple brick and concrete by L.C.C. Schs. Division.[17] Part of North Westm. sch. (q.v.) from 1980.[18]

Senior Street council, see Edward Wilson.

Trinity C.E., Westbourne Pk. Terr. Opened 1864 as Nat. sch. for BGI. Financed by sch. pence (2d.–3d.) and parl. grant. 1880 accn. 512, a.a. 503. 1893 accn. 547 BGI, a.a. 521. 1932 accn. 390 BGI, a.a. 294. 1936 accn. 237 JM, 124 I, a.a. 166 JM, 97 I. Closed by 1951. Holy Trinity with St. Paul's C.E. sec. sch. opened in former St. Paul's sch. by 1955. Closed between 1962 and 1964.

Westbourne C.E., Gt. Western Rd. Opened 1851 as Nat. sch. for BGI and connected with Lock hosp.[19] Financed by vol. contributions, sch. pence, and 1854 by parl. grant. 1865 a.a. 232. Middle-class dept. added by 1872 and sch. described as middle-class by 1890.[20] 1893 accn. 1,063 BG, a.a. 732. Continued as private sch. from 1905, after L.C.C.'s abolition of fees and demand for bldg. improvements.[21]

[11] L.C.C. Educ. Cttee. Mins. (1905), 4614.
[12] Endowed Chars. Lond. 42.
[13] Guildhall MS. 12552.
[14] Select vestry mins. (1831–6), ff. 7, 15, 51.
[15] L.C.C. Educ. Cttee. Mins. (1939), 187.
[16] Bayswater Chron. 24 June 1865.

[17] Nairn, Modern Bldgs. in Lond. 37.
[18] Inf. from sec., N. Westm. sch.
[19] Robins, Paddington, 169.
[20] Hutchings and Crowsley, Paddington Dir. (1872); Kelly's Dir. Mdx. (1890).
[21] L.C.C. Educ. Cttee. Mins. (1905), 4802.

Survived as Middle-Class sch. (sec.), Westbourne Pk. 1939.[22]

WILBERFORCE PRIMARY, Herries Street, Kilburn Lane. Opened 1889[23] as C.E. sch. 1906 accn. 1,037 BGI, a.a. 652 BGI. 1927 accn. 772 BGI, a.a. 300. Transferred to L.C.C. 1929. 1932 accn. 280 JM, 320 I, a.a. 241 JM, 281 I. Rolls 1986: 155 JM, 187 I.

WOODFIELD DIST., Harrow Rd. Opened by 1859, when paid parl. grant, as Nat. sch. Bldg. sold by 1870 and perhaps used as Brit. sch. 1875.[24]

Special schools. AMBERLEY RD., see John Aird.
BRAVINGTON RD., see Maryfields.
COLLEGE PK., Monmouth Rd. Opened as Kenmont Gdns. sch. for educationally sub-normal SG, Hammersmith. Renamed 1949. New bldg. in Monmouth Rd. for 100 G 1955.[25] Annexe in Bravington Rd., formerly Maryfields sch. (q.v.), by 1967.
ESSENDINE RD., see Franklin Delano Roosevelt.
FRANKLIN DELANO ROOSEVELT, Essendine Rd. Opened 1901 as Essendine Rd. sch. for physically handicapped. 1906 accn. 80. Renamed 1950,[26] when sch. for SG and primary M, with Hampstead annexe. Moved to Hampstead 1957.[27]
JOHN AIRD, Amberley Rd. Opened by 1925 as Amberley Rd. sch. for partially sighted. Renamed 1949, when sch. for SM and primary M. 1954 accn. 90.[28] Moved to Valliere Rd., Hammersmith, by 1955.
KENSAL HO., Harrow Rd. Opened 1911 as L.C.C.'s first open-air sch. for tuberculous children[29] at no. 553 Harrow Rd. Closed 1939 or later.
MARYFIELDS, Bravington Rd. Opened by 1925 as Bravington Rd. sch. for mentally defective. Renamed 1950,[30] when sch. for primary M. Closed or moved between 1958 and 1961.
MOBERLEY TEMP., Harrow Rd. Opened 1896 for mentally defective. 1906 accn. 40. Probably closed by 1925.

Adult and technical education. Evening classes were held at the National schools of St. John, Kensal Green, St. John, Titchborne Street, and St. Stephen by 1870, with average attendances of 76, 25, and 14 respectively.[31] In 1871 they were also held at St. Michael's and in 1878 they were at St. John's, Titchborne Street, St. Luke's, and St. Mary Magdalene's. By 1891 there were 183 evening attenders at Amberley Road, Harrow Road, Campbell Street, and Kilburn Lane board schools.[32]

The London school board's first manual training was at Beethoven Street, where the school keeper, a carpenter, taught woodwork to senior boys from

1885. The costs, disallowed by the local government auditor, were met by the City Guilds until the Education Department modified its code in 1890. Technical education became the responsibility of the L.C.C. in 1893, on the formation of a technical education board, which was superseded in 1904 by the council's education committee.[33]

Westbourne Park institute was established in 1885 in one of two houses in Porchester Road which had been bought by Westbourne Park Baptist church. The rooms included a library, chemistry laboratory, and, from 1888, a gymnasium, which was equipped for science teaching in 1896.[34] It received grants from the technical education board, as did the Queen's Park institute in Harrow Road.[35]

Paddington technical institute was opened in 1903 in Saltram Crescent school and soon largely superseded the older institutions.[36] By 1925, in addition to evening and Saturday classes, the institute housed a boys' day school for building and engineering and a girls' for dressmaking.[37] As Paddington technical college, it took over the Chelsea school of chiropody in 1957 and the former Beethoven Street school in 1963, before moving in 1967 into new blocks on the north side of Paddington green.[38]

Evening and commercial classes were provided by 1906 at Essendine Road school, known as Maida Vale commercial institute in 1939. Ordinary evening classes were held at the Moberley school over the same period and at Amberley Road and other former board schools for a shorter time.[39] Paddington college for further education was established in Essendine Road in 1962 and moved to Saltram Crescent and Beethoven Street in 1967. It offered less advanced courses than the technical college and was merged with it in 1974 to form Paddington college. The new institution was designed for 900 full-time and 7,000 part-time students, who could study engineering and science at Paddington green, business and general education at Saltram Crescent, or chiropody at Samford Street, Marylebone.[40]

Paddington adult education centre, after 16 years under the L.C.C. and the I.L.E.A., was given its own governing board in 1974, when it was responsible for day and evening classes at Sarah Siddons school and 11 other centres in Paddington. It was called the Marylebone–Paddington institute, at Amberley adult centre and with branches at many local schools, in 1983.[41] Adult classes in literacy and basic skills, with courses for truants and nursery classes, were provided at Beauchamp Lodge, Warwick Crescent.[42]

Private schools and colleges.[43] A ladies' school was

---

[22] *Kelly's Dir. Paddington* (1939).
[23] Inf. from headmistress.
[24] Hutchings and Crowsley, *Paddington Dir.* (1875); below, private schs.
[25] L.C.C. *Educ. Cttee. Mins.* (1949–50), 247; (1957–8), 64; Marylebone libr., P 138, cuttings.
[26] L.C.C. *Educ. Cttee. Mins.* (1949–50), 313.
[27] Marylebone libr., P 139.2, cuttings.
[28] L.C.C. *Educ. Cttee. Mins.* (1949–50), 247; (1953–4), 362.
[29] J. S. Maclure, *One Hundred Years of Lond. Educ.* (1970), 103.
[30] L.C.C. *Educ. Cttee. Mins.* (1949–50), 369.
[31] *Rep. of Educ. Cttee. of Council, 1870–1,* 499–500.
[32] Ibid. *1871–2,* 306; *1891–2,* 670, 674.
[33] Maclure, *Lond. Educ.* 48, 69, 75–6; *The Times,* 14 Oct. 1985, 3d.

[34] Marchant, *John Clifford,* 62–3.
[35] L.C.C. *Ann. Rep. of Procs. of Council* (1904–5), 50.
[36] Ibid.; *Official Guide to Paddington* [1921].
[37] *Kelly's Dir. Paddington* (1925).
[38] Marylebone libr., P 139.2, cuttings.
[39] L.C.C. *Educ. Svce. Particulars* (1906–7); *Kelly's Dir. Paddington* (1925, 1939).
[40] Marylebone libr., P 139.2, cuttings.
[41] Ibid.; inf. from principal; *Marylebone–Paddington Institute, Prospectus* (1982–3).
[42] Inf. from dir.
[43] Subsection based on: *Lucas's Paddington Dir.* (1843); *Watkins's Dir. Lond.* (1853); *Dolling's Paddington Dir.* (1862, 1863); Hutchings and Crowsley, *Paddington Dir.* (1872, 1875); Bisson, *Schs. and Colls.* (1872); ibid. i (1879); ii (1884); *P.O. Dir. Lond.* (1852 and later edns.); *Kelly's Dir. Paddington* (1888 and later edns.).

kept at the manor house, Paddington green, by the Misses Waring, who in 1820 declined to take a new lease, probably one which had been granted in 1813 to their niece's husband Joshua Cristall.[44] Of 16 private schools listed in 1828, at least 5 were at Paddington green and 5 in Bayswater; a few of the others were on the Marylebone side of Edgware Road.[45] In 1833 there were 954 pupils at 43 private schools, presumably day schools, and 11 boarding schools. Thirty-five of the day schools and four of the boarding schools had opened since 1818.[46] Although most were short-lived, the total number remained high: 50 ladies' and 19 gentlemen's schools were listed in 1863, 18 boys' schools in 1879, and over 30 girls' schools in 1884. The most popular district continued to be Bayswater, where Hyde Park was sometimes used as an address. While schools became less numerous around Paddington green, they multiplied with the building up of Maida Vale and St. Peter's Park. Few of the schools of 1879 and 1884 survived in 1902, after which time numbers declined.

Boys' establishments included Westbourne Collegiate school, in union with King's College, London, and founded in 1847. It was at Powis House, Colville Road, Kensington, in 1879, with day boys and 50 boarders. St. Charles's college was founded in 1863, under the Oblates of St. Charles Borromeo, and modelled on the great public schools. It soon moved from Sutherland Place to nearby premises adjoining the church of St. Mary of the Angels, where boarders could be taken and where a middle-class school existed in 1905, the college having moved in 1874 to St. Charles's Square, North Kensington.[47] There was a preparatory school at no. 11 Orme Square in 1879, from 1880 under Herbert Wilkinson, whose pupils included Max Beerbohm from 1881 until 1885.[48] By 1900 the school was also at no. 10; it was kept by G. H. Wilkinson from c. 1926 and by E. G. Hobhouse in 1934, closing by 1938.

A school founded in 1847 was at no. 30 Westbourne Park Villas, as Westbourne Park and Willesden educational establishment, by 1856 and also at no. 32 by 1860. Boys were taught at no. 30 and girls by Miss Mina Winch at no. 32. Despite the departure of the boys' headmaster to a school of his own at no. 9 in 1870, the departments at nos. 30 and 32 remained under Miss Winch's ownership until 1875.[49] The boys' school then continued independently as the College until after 1900, by which date Miss Winch had been succeeded by Miss Margaret Hunter, whose school continued at nos. 28 and 32 until c. 1928. Bayswater High School for girls and preparatory for boys, at no. 28 Monmouth Road between 1930 and 1935, claimed to continue Miss Winch's school. In Newton Road, where there were schools at nos. 6 and 14 c. 1870, a girls' school founded in 1856 was kept at no. 19 by Mrs. Billingham in the 1880s. Woodfield schools, at no. 502 Harrow Road in 1890 and 1910, may have existed in

1875 as Woodfield British schools, perhaps formerly a National school.[50] Westcott school, a coeducational preparatory school founded in 1898, was at no. 118 Sutherland Avenue in 1939.

Wordsworth college was presumably founded by the Kilburn Sisters, since it shared the premises of their Victoria orphanage, built in 1887 in Shirland Road. Girls were trained as teachers for low fees and there were also art students, a few of whom boarded.[51] It was not listed with other schools and colleges but was recorded as at Rudolph Road, perhaps having replaced the sisters' house of rest, in 1910.[52]

St. Mary Magdalene college for ladies existed in St. James's Terrace, at nos. 122 and 124 Harrow Road, by 1879. Called simply St. Mary's college and aided by the L.C.C. as a girls' secondary school in 1906 but not in 1913,[53] it also had premises in Warrington Crescent by 1910. It had moved to no. 34 Lancaster Gate by 1911, retaining a hostel at Warrington Crescent, and later also occupied nos. 33 and 35. In 1939 it was a training college and Anglican day school for girls up to 15 years of age and younger boys.

There were several schools of languages and secretarial schools. They included the College de Paris in Rifle Crescent and the French Institute in Clarendon Road North in 1862, the Berlitz school of languages in Queen's Road in 1910, and the Gouin school of languages at no. 60 Westbourne Grove in 1910 and 1939. Hyde Park and Bayswater school of art and science was at no. 143 Queen's Road from 1890 to c. 1895 and had been replaced before 1899 by Kensington school of shorthand and mercantile training college, which had been founded in 1887 by James Munford[54] and also had a branch in Ladbroke Grove; as Kensington college, the school had moved by 1902 to no. 34 Gloucester Gardens, where it survived until 1939. The London college of pharmacy and chemistry for young ladies was at nos. 5 and 7 Westbourne Park Road in 1899 and still at no. 7 in 1965.

The Modern Tutorial College, which had opened in Kensal Rise, Willesden, in 1966, moved to the former premises of St. John's National school, Kilburn Lane, in 1972. The buildings were still used by St. John's church for social activities in 1985, when the college offered preparation for 'O' and 'A' level examinations to c. 150 full-time students.[55]

The Jewish Preparatory School opened at no. 2 Ashworth Road in 1983 and moved into the former Bayswater and Maida Vale synagogue in Kilburn Park Road in 1985. There were 70 boys and girls on the roll in 1986, when they ranged from nursery pupils to 8-year olds and when it was planned to take them to the age of 13.[56]

King's Fund College was established in 1968 on the amalgamation of the separate staff colleges financed by King Edward's Hospital Fund for London. It occupied an ornate red-brick and terracotta building at no. 2 Palace Court in 1985, when

[44] Vestry mins. 2 Nov. 1813; 22 Sept. 1820; McDonald, 'Paddington', cap. 6.   [45] Boarding Schs. Dir. (1828).
[46] Educ. Enq. Abstract, 576.
[47] F. Kirk, Reminiscences of An Oblate of St. Chas. (1905), 72–4, 77; Survey of Lond. xxxvii. 326.
[48] Marylebone libr., P 139.2, cuttings; D. Cecil, Max (1964), 25–6.
[49] Paddington Times, 16 Apr., 25 June 1870; Paddington, Kensington and Bayswater Chron. 13 Mar. 1875.

[50] Above, pub. schs.
[51] Besant, Lond. N. of Thames, 151; Guildhall MS. 12566.
[52] Bacon, Atlas of Lond. (1910).
[53] L.C.C. Educ. Svce. Particulars (1906–7); (1913–14).
[54] Marylebone libr., P 139.2, cuttings.
[55] Inf. from principal.
[56] Inf. from Rabbi Dr. Abraham Levy, Spanish and Portuguese Jews' Congregation.

the fund's head office was at no. 14. The college aimed to raise management standards in health care through teaching, consultancy, and research, with over 20 fellows and 6,270 student days in 1984–5.[57]

CHARITIES FOR THE POOR.[58] There were 18th-century charities comprising both freehold and copyhold land and the almshouses, besides individual bequests which were mostly distributed in kind. The estates charities were first regulated in 1837, when part of their income was assigned to education, and united in 1934, after the establishment of separate educational funds.[59] The almshouse charity, which likewise had been divided between the poor and education, and the distributive charities were administered with the charitable estates from 1977.

The *Freehold Estates* was by 1894 the official name of the Bread and Cheese Lands, c. 5 a. probably acquired between 1665 and 1669 and said to have been given in gratitude by two women who had once received parish relief. The lands consisted of $2\frac{1}{2}$ a. in Bayswater common field, $1\frac{1}{2}$ a. at Westbourne green, and 1 a. by Black Lion Lane, let for a total of £6 in 1693–4 and 1715–16 when called simply the 'poor's land', £10 in 1719, and £40 18s. by 1825. In the early 19th century the chapter of Westminster disputed the boundaries of the Bayswater lands.[60] Gifts of beer, bread, and cheese were distributed on the Sunday before Christmas,[61] coal being substituted for beer from c. 1793 and the bread and cheese thrown to large crowds from the church steeple until 1834. A Chancery Scheme of 1837 allotted three fifths of the income to education, one fifth to apprenticing, and one fifth to the poor not receiving other relief as had been recommended by the vestry.[62] Some land was sold in 1838 to the G.W.R. Co. for £1,200, which was spent on obtaining a building Act,[63] under which 15 houses were built in Lancaster Gate, 2 in Westbourne Grove, and 28 in Hatherley Grove. The gross rents were £1,697 18s. in 1894, when the poor received £219 11s. 7d. in blankets and coals. A Freehold Estates educational fund was constituted in 1905 and the property was administered with the copyhold estates from 1934, as the Paddington Charitable Estates (q.v.).

The *Enfranchised Copyhold Estates* was by 1894 the official name of Dr. Compton's and Margaret Robertson's charities. Henry Compton, bishop of London (d. 1713), gave a cottage and land in Harrow Road, for unknown purposes, to which the first trustee was admitted in 1717. There were six houses by 1802, one of them the Running Horse, and rents amounting to £106, which the vestry had recently assigned to the charity school,[64] in 1825. Margaret Robertson, by will proved 1720, gave property on the corner of Edgware and Harrow roads, to which the first trustee was admitted in 1721. The buildings were to be replaced by five new houses in 1824 and were let for £15, applied to the charity school, in 1825. By a separate Scheme of 1837, the income was allotted in the same way as that of the Freehold Estates. After enfranchisement in 1845, the houses on Compton's land were rebuilt in 1846 and those on Robertson's sold under the Metropolitan Street Improvements Act, 1872. The gross income was £560 10s. 8d., half from rents and half from stock worth £10,201 6s. 11d., in 1894, when the poor received £112 2s. 1d. in gifts. An educational fund was established in 1905 and the property administered as part of the Paddington Charitable Estates (q.v.) from 1934.

Almshouse charities. In 1720 the first trustee was admitted to a strip of waste on the south side of Harrow Road at Paddington green, where there were six cottages for the poor. The plot was extended to the east in 1779. An inscription in 1825 stated that the parish had built 13 dwellings in 1714, to which S. P. Cockerell had added two more as almshouses and two for the master and mistress of the charity school. The buildings formed a single-storeyed range,[65] standing west of the school and separated from it by Church Place in 1842,[66] by which date their land immediately to the south had been taken for a vestry room, watch house, and infants' school. No compensation was paid towards the almshouses, which were not endowed and were dilapidated by 1853, when the vestry sought a building lease for the whole site. Trustees with powers to let were appointed in 1867, when the M.B.W. acquired the vestry hall for a fire station, and in 1869 the almshouses made way for five shops,[67] called Romilly Terrace, part of the proceeds being spent on the school and part invested. Almspeople probably had always been chosen by the vestry.[68] A Scheme of 1871 established the almshouse and schoolhouse charity and allotted £50 a year of its income from ground rents towards hiring accommodation for the schoolmistress and her assistants and the residue to pensions of £10–£15 for the aged poor. In 1893 the rents of £190 and dividends of £5 4s. 8d. furnished payments to 12 pensioners. A separate educational fund was established in 1904. The almshouse charity had an income of under £250 c. 1970, when it was disbursed in pensions of £25, and was included in Paddington Welfare Charities (q.v.) in 1977.

Frances King, by will dated 1845, left £200 towards coal for the inmates of the almshouses. Dividends of £4 8s. from £160 2s. 2d. stock were added to the income of the almshouses and schoolhouse charity in 1894.

[57] *King Edw.'s Hosp. Fund for Lond. Ann. Rep.* (1984); inf. from coll. administrator.
[58] Section based on Char. Com. files; *14th Rep. Com. Char.* H.C. 382, pp. 180–4 (1826), xii; *Digest of Endowed Chars.* H.C. 433, pp. 42–5 (1867–8), lii (1); *Endowed Chars. Lond.* H.C. 261, pp. 3–45 (1894), lxiii; McDonald, 'Paddington', cap. 12. 19th cent. accts. for most chars. are in Marylebone libr. Incomes c. 1970 are from list supplied by deputy clerk to trustees, Paddington Welfare Chars.
[59] Above, educ.
[60] Vestry mins. 8 Apr. 1806; select vestry mins. 14 July 1828.
[61] Expenditure was noted in the chwdns. accts. from 1669: chwdns. acct. bk. (1656–1736), ff. 17–18 and *passim.*
[62] Select vestry mins. 13 Feb. 1837.
[63] 1 & 2 Vic. c. 32 (Private).
[64] Above, educ.
[65] McDonald, 'Paddington', cap. 9; B.M., Crace xxx. 35.
[66] Lucas, *Plan of Paddington* (1842).
[67] *N. & Q.* 4th ser. iv. 407.
[68] e.g. vestry mins. 20 Oct. 1801; select vestry mins. 3 Dec. 1839.

Distributive charities. Thomas Johnson, merchant tailor, left 20s. a year by will proved 1626. The sum was chargeable on property held by John Combes (d. 1711) and in 1825 on three houses on the east side of Paddington green; payments were later reduced,[69] temporarily and probably because of rebuilding, since in 1858 it was thought that differing sums might be receivable from nos. 15–19 Paddington Green. The donor's purpose not being known, the income was paid into the churchwardens' general account in 1825 but by 1858 applied with Abourne's charity.

George Abourne, by will dated 1767, left £300 for meat and bread twice a year to poor families. The bequest, subject to life interests, was effective from 1792. Gifts worth £9, more than the income, were made in 1825 and £8 5s. in 1894.

Mary Simmonds, by will proved 1842, left £600 stock to provide pensions for 30 women not already receiving relief. The gift, subject to a life interest, was effective from 1890 and provided £16 10s. for pensions of 10s. 6d. in 1894. The income, with those of charities of Johnson and Abourne, amounted to less than £40 c. 1970, when it was distributed to c. 30 old people.

Lady Boynton (d. 1853), widow of Sir Griffith Boynton, Bt.,[70] left £500 for clothes or bedding to the minister of St. John the Evangelist's, Southwick Crescent. In 1894 the vicar spent the income with that of other charities for his own district, although it was later considered applicable to the whole of the ancient parish.

Marion Mayne, by will proved 1864, left the residue of her personal estate for the maintenance of monuments and of Paddington green and for gifts in kind. After litigation a Chancery Scheme of 1872 allotted £35 a year to the vestry for Paddington green and up to £50 for the poor not receiving parochial relief. In augmentation John Barrable (d. 1890) left £1,000, bringing the total assets to £6,427 15s. 5d. stock in 1894. A gross income of £176 15s. then provided £5 for the monuments, £35 for the green, £50 for distribution in money, and £86 15s. for pensions. The income of under £250 was disbursed in pensions of £25 c. 1970.

Augustus Frederick Smith, by will proved 1881, left the residue of his personal estate in reversion to the almshouse charity, to provide pensions of £10 to £20 to women over 60 years old. In 1894 £9,985 3s. 8d. stock yielded £274 11s. 8d. for 26 pensions of £5–£15 a year. The income of under £500 was disbursed like those of the almshouse and Marion Mayne's charities c. 1970.

Harriette Amelia Weecks Andrews, by will proved 1898, left £300, the income to be distributed by the medical officer of health to paupers not in charitable institutions.[71] The income was under £25 c. 1970.

Alicia Mary Gaselee, by will proved 1886, Thomas Kincaid Hardie, by will proved 1901, and James Toleman, by will proved 1897 and included in a Chancery Order of 1907, left money for the poor of St. John's parish. The total income, with that of Lady Boynton's charity, was under £40 c. 1970, when it was distributed among c. 30 old people.

Mary Ann Lewis left money for the poor of St. Jude's by will proved 1898. The income of £10 was paid towards the salary of a church worker c. 1970. George Haines, by will proved 1867, left £150 for his family monuments and bread and coals; it was later applied only to St. Mary's parish, as was a gift of Sarah Beach, by will proved 1899. The combined income of less than £55 was distributed among c. 10 old people c. 1970. Julia Margaret Scott, by will proved 1900, left money for the poor of St. Mary Magdalene's parish. The income of under £10 was spent on gifts and parochial expenses c. 1970.

The distributive charities were combined in Paddington Welfare Charities (q.v.) in 1977.

Paddington Charitable Estates were constituted in 1934 when trustees for both the Freehold and Enfranchised Copyhold Estates were to be appointed by Paddington metropolitan borough and the incomes reapportioned. The total income was then c. £3,000 from dividends and rents, including c. £1,400 for nos. 75–89 Lancaster Gate. Three fifths of the rents were allotted to the education funds, one fifth with half of the income from stock to apprenticing or training, and one fifth with the remaining dividends to the poor. A single education fund was set up in 1959 to receive four fifths of the income, the remaining fifth being allotted by a Scheme of 1961 to the Paddington Charitable Estates' Poor's Branch. The Lancaster Gate houses were sold in 1959, a charge thereafter being payable by Park Court Hotel Ltd., and in 1967 the total share of the Poor's Branch was £4,887 15s., spent on grants to welfare organizations and on vouchers worth 10s. 6d. distributed through the trustees, hospitals, and churches. Although the Charitable Estates were administered with Paddington Welfare Charities (q.v.) from 1977, their income was accounted for separately, amounting to a gross total of £56,963 in 1978.

Paddington Welfare Charities, under a Scheme of 1977, united the Charitable Estates with the almshouse and the distributive charities. Seven trustees named by Westminster and three by the vicars of five churches were to administer the welfare charities in two groups. Paddington Relief in Need charities were to receive a fifth of the estates' rents and some dividends, forming the Paddington Charitable Estates Non-Educational fund, with the income of the almshouse and all the distributive charities except that of Mary Ann Lewis. Paddington Relief in Sickness charities were to receive the income from Lewis's, with that of Kilburn, Maida Vale, and St. John's Wood Aid in Sickness fund, as regulated by a Scheme of 1956. In 1982 the Relief in Need charities had an income of £14,904 and the Relief in Sickness charities an income of £519.[72]

[69] Robins, *Paddington*, 70.
[70] G.E.C. *Baronetage*, i. 116.

[71] Inf. from deputy clerk to trustees, Paddington Welfare Chars.　　　　　　　　　　　　　[72] Idem.

INDEX

NOTE. An italic page number denotes a map or coat of arms on that page. A page number preceded by the letters *pl.* refers to one of the plates between pages 144 and 145.

Buildings and groups of buildings in Hampstead and Paddington parishes are indexed under their own names, without an indication of their location. Most references to roads, squares, alleys, and courtyards are to their first occurrence in the text or to buildings which do not have individual names. Proper names which occur only incidentally have not been indexed.

ASLEF, 31
Abbey (est.), 62
Abbey Farm est., 101, 106, 117
Abbey Rd., 60, 63
Abel, Jas., 55, 97
Aberdare Gdns., 38
Aberdeen Ct., 215
Abernethy Ho., 29
Abingdon, John, par. priest of Hampstead, 146
Abinger Mews, 220-1
Abourne, Geo., 272
Abrahams, A., 240
Achilles Rd., 45
Acol Ct., 50
Acol Mews, Rd., 49
Acrow cos., 237
Acton, *see* Bedford Pk.
actors and actresses, 32; *and see* Ashcroft; Booth, Barton; Chester; Cibber; Compton, Fay; Cooper, Dame Gladys; Du Maurier, Sir Gerald; Hemet; Inchbald; Kemble; Langtry; Neagle; Robson, Dame Flora; Siddons, Sarah *and* Wm.; Tree; Walbrook; Wilks; Wolfit
Acworth, Miss W. B., 40
Adams:
    Sarah Flower, 206
    Wal., min. of Hampstead, 146 n
Adamson Rd., 64
Addington, Sir Wm., 69
Addison, Revd. Mr., 53
Adelaide, queen of Wm. IV, 231
Adelaide P.H., 5
Adelaide Rd., 61, 63
Adey, Chas., 100
Adoration of the Sacred Heart of Jesus of Montmartre, Sisters of the, 260
    Tyburn shrine, 197, 260
Adpar St., 188
Æthelred, King, 2, 8, 92
Agamemnon Rd., 45
Agate, Jas., 59
Agincourt Rd., 55
Aglionby, Hen. Aglionby, 106
Aikin, Lucy, 23
Ailsa, marquess of, *see* Kennedy
Ainger, Thos., min. of Hampstead, 141, 146, 156
Ainger Rd., 64
Ainsworth (est.), 62
Aird, Sir John, Bt., 194, 245
Airey, Julius Talbot, 39
Ajax Rd., 45
Albany (flats), 29
Albert Pk., 64
Albert St., 188
Albion Cottage, 24
Albion Gate, 195, 197
Albion Grove, 25
Albion Grove Ho., 25
Albion Rd., 61
Albion St., 192, 197
Aldenham:
    Rog., 108
    Wm., 107-8

fam., 107, 115
Aldenham (Herts.), sch., 166
Aldenhams est., 16, 18, 107
Aldenhams (ho.), 18
Alder, J. S., 259
Aldred St., 44
Aldridge, Hen. (later Bliss), 98
Aldridge Ct., 203
Aldsworth Close, 202
Alexander I, tsar of Russia, 205
Alexander:
    A. & G., 238
    Mrs. Ann, 238
    Chris., 238
    Isaac, 126
Alexander St., 200 n, 203
Alexandra (of Denmark), queen of Edw. VII, 78
Alexandra Ct., 215, 217
Alexandra Ho., 189
Alexandra Mansions, 45
Alexandra Mews, 61
Alexandra Rd., 48
Alfred Rd., 200
Alice of Westm., 92
All Passion Spent, see Sackville-West
All Souls' Coll., Oxford (as landowners), 217, 219
Allaly, Thos., 116
Allam:
    Eliz., wid. of Thos., 230
    Jane, 230-1
    Thos., s. of Eliz., 230
Allason, Thos., 206
Allcroft, J. D., 258; *and see* Magnus-Allcroft
Allen:
    Edw., 99
    Lewis, 68
    Sir Thos., 99
    and see Bickerdike
Allen-Olney:
    Rita, 165
    Sarah, 165
Alliance Plating Works, 127
Allison & Foskett, 28, 39
Alpine Cottage, 23
Alulf, s. of, *see* Constantine
Alvanley, Baron, *see* Arden
Alvanley Gdns., 40
Amalgamated Investment and Property Co., 232
Amberley Rd., 200, 204
Ambridge, Wm., 69
Ambridge Cottages, 70
Amer, A. R., 74
Amiand, Dan., perpetual curate of Paddington, 253
Amis, Kingsley, 33; *and see* Howell & Amis
Amner, Ric., 154-5
Amy, Wm., 99, 113
Anderson:
    Alex., 76
    David, 76
    Jas., 39
    Wm. Dunlop, 39
Andrew:
    Jesse, 128

& Sons, 128
Andrews:
    Grace, 109
    Harriette, 272
Andrews Ho., 60
Anglo-American Brush Electric Light Corp., 179
Anglo-American Oil Co., 127
Anglo-Catholicism, *see* ritualism and High Church practices
Annesley Lodge, 74; *pl.* 17
Antrim Rd., 58
Arbuthnot, John, 83
archery, 223
Archery P.H., 223
architects, 30; *and see* Alder; Allason; Atkinson; Audesley & Joseph; Austin, Hubert; Barry; Bayes; Belcher & Joass; Bell, Chas.; Bennett, Hubert *and* T. P.; Benson; Bentley, J. F.; Bickerdike; Billing; Biscoe & Stanton; Blackburne; Blomfield, Sir Art. *and* Sir Reg.; Bodley; Boehmer & Gibbs; Boissevain & Osmond; Brawn, Mic.; Breuer; Bristow; Brook; Brooks, Jas.; Brydon; Budden; Bunney; Burton, Decimus; Butler, J. Dixon; Caroë & Passmore; Champneys; Chapman, J. Wallis; Christian; Clarke, A. *and* T. Chatfeild; Clutton; Coates; Cockerell, C. R., F. P., *and* S. P.; Collins, H. H.; Comper; Connell, Ward & Lucas; Cook, Sid.; Cooper, A. W. S., Sir Edwin, *and* T.; Cowper; Crake, John; Culverhouse, P. G.; Cundy; Davis & Emmanuel; Dawber; Dawkes; Design 5; de Soissons; Dinerman, Davidson & Partners; Dixon, W. A.; Douglas, Campbell; Douglas & Wood; Drake; Ellis; Elsom; Emerson; Emmett; Erith; Farey; Farmer; Farrell; Faulkner; Field, Horace; Fleming, O.; Flitcroft, Hen. (d. 1769); Flockhart; Forsyth, Alan; Foster, Mic.; Fowler, Chas. *and* Sir John; Francis; Fraser; Freud, E. L.; Fry, Maxwell; Garner; George & Peto; Gibberd; Goalen; Goldfinger; Goldicutt; Gowan; Gray, Alex. (fl. 1968); Green, Leslie W., T. K., *and* Wm. Curtis; Gropius; Gutch; Habershon; Hall, J.; Hall, Stan.; Hall & Waterhouse; Hare; Harrington; Hawkins, Rohde; Hesketh; Hill, Oliver; Hopkins, Mic.; Hopper; Hornblower; Horne; Horvitch; Housden; Howard, T.; Howell & Amis; Hyde-Harrison; Jackson, Thos. G.; James, C. H.; Johnson, John; Jolly; Jones, Owen; Joseph, Delissa *and* N. S.; Kendall; Kitchin; Koulermos;

architects (*cont.*)
Lasdun; Le Corbusier; Lee, J. T.; Legg; Leicester; Levy; Lutyens; Lennon; Lethbridge; Little, Thos.; Lockyer; Luder; Lyell; McInerney; Mackmurdo; Maclaren; McMorran; Manning, W. P.; Martin, Leslie; Matcham; Mather; Maufe; May; Mayer Hillman; Measures; Mew; Mewès & Davis; Meyer; Milne, Oswald; Minoprio; Mitchell, Arnold; Moore, Temple; Mumford; Munt; Murray, John; Nash, John; Neale; Nelson, T.; Nevill; Newman & Billing; Nicholson, Sir Chas.; Nickson; Nightingale, J. S.; Norman & Davison; Palgrave & Co.; Pearson, J. L.; Pite & Balfour; Plaw; Plumbe; Pollard, Thomas & Edwards; Porter, F. W. *and* Horatio; Pugin; Quennell; Roberts, John; Robson, E. R.; Rottenberg; St. Aubyn; Sanderson, John; Scarlett; Scott, Adrian, Sir Geo. Gilb., Geo. Gilb., Sir Giles Gilb., *and* John Oldrid; Searle; Seifert; Sexton; Shaw, John *and* Ric.; Simpson; Smith, F. Danby *and* T. Rog.; Snell; Soutar; Spalding; Spalding & Cross; Spence; Sprince; Stenning; Stephen; Stevenson, J. J.; Stokes, Leonard; Street, G. E. *and* W. C.; T.F.P. Architects; Tarring; Tayler, A. S. *and* Ken.; Taylor, Geo.; Tecton; Terry, Quinlan; Teulon; Thomas, J. A.; Toms; Trehearne & Norman; Vaughan, C. Evans; Ventris; Voysey; Vulliamy, Geo. *and* Lewis; Wade-Farmer; Wadmore, Jas.; Walker, Fred.; Ware, Isaac *and* Sam.; Warwick; Waterhouse; Watts; Webb, Phil.; Weedon, Harry; White, John *and* W. Hen.; Whitfield & Thomas; Williams-Ellis; Winmill; Wood, Sancton; Worthington; Wray; Wren; Wyatt, Jas. (d. 1813), Sir Mat. Digby, *and* Sir Mat.; Young; Zins
Arctic Fur Store, 240
Arden, Ric. Pepper, Baron Alvanley, 34, 89, 93, 133
Ardwick Rd., 74
Argyll, duke of, *see* Campbell, John
Ariel St., 48
Arklow Ho., 191
Arkwright Arts trust, 92, 141
Arkwright Rd., 27, 38
Arlington, earl of, *see* Bennet
Arnold:
Chris., 68
Mary, 172
Maud, 230
Arran, earl of, *see* Butler, Ric.
Artesian Rd., 200
Arthur:
Eliz., *see* Pawlett
Ric., 106
Arthur Ct., 202–3
Arthur Mews, 194
Arthur West Ho., 32
artists and designers, 13–14, 27, 31, 57, 59, 64–6, 182, 187; *and see* Barnard; Barret, Geo., sr. *and* jr.; Beaton; Beechey; Bevan; Blake; Bomberg; Boydell; Bone; Brooke, Leslie; Brown, Ford Madox; Burne-Jones; Calvert; Camden Town Group; Carline, Ric.; Clausen; Clint; Coldstream; Collier; Collins, Wm.;

Constable; Craig; Cristall; Cruikshank; Danby; de László; De Morgan; Dicksee; Dobson; Doyle, John *and* Ric.; Du Maurier, Geo.; Egg; Field, Wal.; Fry, Rog.; Frith; Gertler; Gilpin; Ginner; Grant, Duncan; Greenaway; Gunn; Hall, John; Haydon; Hayes; Herbert; Hogarth; Holl, Frank *and* Wm.; Houghton; Jackson, John; Joy; Kokoschka; Lamb, Hen.; Landseer; Leighton; Linnell; Linton, Sir Jas. *and* W. J.; Long; Low; Lucas; MARS; Macbeth; Martin, John; May, Phil.; Mondrian; Morland; Morris; Mulready; Nash, Paul; Nevinson, C. R. W.; Nicholson, Ben; Nollekens, Jos. Fras.; Oram; Orchardson; Palmer, Sam.; Pettie; Poole; Pyne; Rackham; Reynolds, Sir Josh. *and* Sam.; Romney; Rossetti, Dante Gabriel; Salisbury, Frank; Sandby; Schiavonetti; Serres; Shields; Sickert; Spencer, Sir Stan.; Stanfield; Stephenson; Stevens; Stokes, Adrian; Swinstead; Tenniel; Topham, Fras. *and* Frank; Topolski; Unit One; Uwins; Varley, John *and* Cornelius; Whistler
studios, 13, 31, 50, 65, 73; *and see* Mall studios; Steele's studios; Wychcombe studios
see also stained glass painters
Artizans', Labourers', and General Dwellings Co. (later Artizans' and General Properties Co.), 219–20, 232
Ascot Lodge, 50
Ashby, Geo. Payne, 128
Ashcroft, Dame Peggy, 42
Ashmore Rd., 218, 220
Ashton:
Hen., 108
Jos., and his wid. Mary, 108
Marg., 108
Mary, m. John Merry, 108
Ric., 239
Rob., 108
Ashton's hotel, 239
Ashurst:
Sir Wm., 103
Wm. Pritchard, 103
Ashwell, John, 57, 97
Ashworth Mansions, 215, 217
Ashworth Rd., 214, 217
Askew:
Adam, 104
Amy Anne, *see* Cary
Lucy Eliz., *see* Cary
Thos., 104
Asquith, Herb. Hen., 30, 38
Assemblies of God, 264
assize of bread and of ale, 130–1
Astley, Wm., 107
Athenaeum (flats), 73
athletics, 84, 87, 225
Atholl Ho., 215, 217
Atkinson:
Phil., perpetual curate of Paddington, 253
R., 62
Atlas line (omnibuses), 5
Atye:
Sir Art., 100, 102–3
Eleanor, m. Sir Wm. Roberts, 101
Jane, *see* St. John
Judith, w. of Sir Art., m. 2 Sir John Dormer, 100, 102–3
Rob., 101
fam., 101
Aubrey:
Lt.-Col. Thos., 254

Capt. Thos., 254
Aubrey Ho., 188
auctioneers and estate agents, 124–5; *and see* Owers; Paxon; Potter, Geo., Geo. W., *and* H. G.; Williams, W. Chas.; Williams, W. & S.
Audesley & Joseph, 264
Augustus Fred., duke of Sussex, 191
his w. Augusta, *see* De Ameland
Aust, Frances, 254
Austin:
Hen. de Bruno, 207
Hubert, 220
Australia, *see* emigrants
Austrians, *see* immigrants
authors, *see* writers
the Avenue, 55, 97, 121
Avenue Close, 62
Avenue Gdns., 220
Avenue Mansions, 45
Avenue Rd., 60
Ayckbourn, Emily, 255
Aylmer, John, bp. of Lond., 253
Ayres, John, 68

B.B.C., studios, 223
Bacon:
Alice, *see* Barnham
Edw., 101
Fras., Vct. St. Alban, 230
John, 101
John, sr., sculptor, 254
John, jr., sculptor, 147, 254
Badger:
John, 105
Thos., 105
Baesh, Anne, *see* Waad
Bagrit, Sir Leon, 73
Baileman, Jacob, 164
Baillie, Joanna, 13, 23, 36
Baines, F. E., 136
Baker:
Eliz., 103
Jas., 116, 118
John, 233
Ric. Pierce, 56
Thos., his *Hampstead Heath*, 82
Wm., 35, 118, 120
Baker Street and Waterloo Rly., 181
Bakerloo line, 7–8, 181
Balchin, Nigel, 46
Baldwin:
Eliz., 107
Jos., 170
Balfour, Geo., 137; *and see* Pite
Balogh, Thos., Baron Balogh, 33
Balta, Ric. de, 92, 93 *n*
Bandon, earl of, *see* Bernard
Banff Ho., 58
Banks, Thos., 255
Baptists, 154, 156–7, 159, 259–61
Barbauld:
Anna Letitia, 23, 123
Rochemont, 155
Barby Ave., 39
Barentyn:
Alex. de, 92, 99
Gilb. de, 145
Ric. de, 92
Thos. de, 92–3
fam., 93, 99, 102, 145
Bark, John, 205
Bark Pl., 205, 211
Barker:
John, 240
Ric. Pierce, 98
Barn Field (flats), 59
Barnard, Fred., 64
Barnard, Vct., *see* Vane, Hen.
Barne, John, 102, 113, 117, 124
Barnes:
John, & Co., 40, 129–30
R. C., & Sons, 126
Barnet, Lond. boro., 81, 185

INDEX

Barnett:
Edwin, 224
Dame Henrietta, 70, 80
Canon Sam., 70
Barnham:
Alice, m. 1 Fras. Bacon, Vct. St.
Alban, 2 Sir John Underhill,
230
Benedict, 230
Bridget, m. Sir Wm. Soame, 230
Barnsdale Mews, 219
Barnsdale Rd., 220-1
Barnwood Close, 204
Barrable, John, 272
Barratt, Thos., 29, 79, 91
Barratt Ltd., builders, 41
Barret:
Geo., sr., 254
Geo., jr., 187
Barreto, Baron, 98
Barrett:
Arabel, 200
Phil., and his w. Eliz., 99
Barrie, J. M., 209; and see Barry
Barrie (est.), 209
Barrie Ho., 209-10
Barry, E. M., 151; and see Barrie
Barton, Adm. Mat., 20, 23
Bartram Ho., 22, 26, 29, 142, 153
Bartram Pk., 22, 26
Bartrams (ho.), 18, 22, 26, 107
Bartrams (Bertrams) est., 11, 16, 22,
25, 27, 106-7
Bastard, John, par. priest of Hamp-
stead, 146
Bate:
H. N., dean of York, 256
Thos., 83
Bath (Som.), 82-3
Bath and Wells, bp. of, see Stilling-
ton, Rob.
bathing, 88
Bathurst Mews, 195
Bathurst St., 192
Batterbury:
Ric., 55
Thos., 13, 57, 64
Batterbury & Huxley, 13, 28, 38, 64
Battersea (Surr.), Shaftesbury Pk.
est., 220
Battin:
Jas., 110
Mary, see Stanwix
Baud, Rob. le, 93, 95, 102
Baugh, Lancelot, 104
Bax:
Alf. Ridley, 58
Sir Arnold, 58, 66
Clifford, 58
Bay Tree Cottage, 36
Bayard's Watering Place, see Bays-
water
Bayes, Ken., 158
Baynton, Sir Edw., 226
Bayswater (formerly Bayard's Water-
ing Place, then Bayswatering),
in Paddington, 182, 183-5, 190,
204; pl. 36
baths, 208
chapel, 205; pl. 47
chs., 187, 207, 209-10, 256-8
dom. bldgs., 206, 209-12; pl. 33
farm, 204
flats, 208-9, 211-12
gravel pit, 204
growth, 204-9
hotels and boarding hos., 207-9,
238-9
housing and council est., 196, 203,
209, 211
Jews, 208, 214, 264
King's Fund coll., 210, 270
lodging hos., 207-8
nonconf. (protestant), 261-3
office blocks, 209

Eastbourne Terr., 211; pl. 45
pest ho., 182, 204-5, 247
pop., density, 208-9
poverty, 209
pub. hos., 204-5, 221-2
retail trade, 207, 212, 240-1; and
see Whiteley
roads, 174-5, 183, 192, 205-7
Rom. Cathm., 259-60
schs., 265-8, 270
Bayswater, Paddington, and Holborn
Bridge Rly. Co., 181
Bayswater Hill, see Bayswater Rd.
Bayswater rivulet, 3, 174-5, 204
Bayswater Rd. (formerly the Uxbridge
rd.), 174, 182, 195, 197, 206-7
Bayswater Hill, 205
Bayswater Terr., 174, 205
dom. bldgs., 193, 197, 210; pl. 54
Elkins's Row, 205
flats, 195, 197, 209-10
hotels, 208-10, 239
Hyde Pk. Gdns., 192-3, 197
Hyde Pk. Pl., 174, 197
Lancaster Gate, 206-7, 210; pl. 54
lighting, 251
Oranjehaven (Dutch club), 197
St. Agnes Villas, 205, 209
St. George's Row (later Terr.),
190-1, 195, 205 n, 247
turnpike gates and tollho., 174,
190
Upper Hyde Pk. Gdns., 207
Uxbridge Pl., 174
Wellington Terr., 206
Bayswater Terr., see Bayswater Rd.
Bayswatering, see Bayswater
Bazell, Ric., 138
Beach, Sarah, 272
Beachcroft, Sir Ric. Melvill, 223,
252
the Beacon, 44
Beadle, Steph., 104
Bear P.H., 125
Beard, see Norman
Beaton, Sir Cecil, 38-9
Beauchamp Lodge, 204, 216, 225,
269
Beaufort, Marg., ctss. of Richmond,
230
Beaulieu Ave., 58
Beaumanor Mansions, 208, 211
Beaumont, Tim. Wentworth, Baron
Beaumont of Whitley, 33
Beaumont Gdns., 41
Beaumont Walk, 66
Beck & Pollitzer Contracts, 127
Becket, ——, builder, 74
Beckford:
Maria, 43, 110-11
Wm., ld. mayor of Lond., 43
fam., 43-4
Beckwith:
Eliz., m. —— Vavasor, 102; and see
Cholmeley
Frances, m. Geo. Harvey, 102
Leonard, 102
Rog., 102
Bedegar, 2
Bedford Coll., Lond., 65
Bedford Lodge, 55
Bedford Pk., in Chiswick and Acton,
208
Beecham:
Sir Jos., 31
Sir Thos., Bt., 32
Beechey, Sir Wm., 255
Beechwood, 80
Beedle, Thos., 212
Beerbohm, Sir Max, 30
Beethoven St., 219
Behnes, Wm., 254
Belcher & Joass, 240
Belgrave Gdns., 61, 63
Belgrave Rd., 61

Belgravia, see Westminster
Belgravia Dairy Co., 234
Bell:
Chas., 144, 156
Edw., 30
Ern., 30
Laura, see Thistlethwayte
P., 74
Miss, 167
Bell farm, 190
Bell P.H. (Bayswater), 205, 221
Bell P.H. (Kilburn), 47-8, 51, 83-4
Bell Properties Trust, 58, 195
Bell Terr., 48
Belle Isle (Westmld.), 254
Belle Vue, 22, 153
bell-founders, see Taylor, John, & Co.
Bellmoor (flats), 31, 81
Bellmoor (ho.), 24, 29, 31
Belsize, in Hampstead, 11, 54
chs., 55, 148, 151; pl. 27
dom. bldgs., 51-3, 55-60, 97-8
farms and farmhos., 52-3, 97, 116
flats, 58-60
growth, 51-60
hotels, 128
housing and council est., 55, 57, 98
ind., 123
Lawn Rd. community workshops,
60
man., see Belsize est.
pub. hos., 52-3, 84
retail trade, 128
roads, 3, 55-8, 60; pl. 12
Shepherd's well, 138
Belsize Ave., 14
Belsize Cottage, 52-3, 56
Belsize Ct. (flats), 59
Belsize Ct. (ho.), 53, 56, 59, 97, 119
Belsize Cres., 56
Belsize est., 11, 51-3, 95-9, 113,
115-16, 118, 121, 131-2; cts.,
131-2; grounds (Wilderness),
98; man. ho., 51, 55, 98-9
Belsize farm, 116-20
Belsize Grove (Haverstock Terr.), 55,
60
Belsize Ho. (former man. ho.), 9, 11,
52, 81-2, 97-9, 123
entertainments, 82-3
gdns. and orchards, 120
Sion chapel, 82, 98, 148, 152
Belsize Ho. (19th-cent., later Belsize
Ct.), 53, 55, 98
Belsize Lane (Village Cres.), 3, 55, 60
Belsize Lodge, 53
Belsize Pk., 55-6
Belsize Pk. Gdns., 56
Belsize Pk. Laundry Co., 126
Belsize Pk. Mews, 60
Belsize Rd., 48, 61, 63
Belsize Villas, 199
Bence, H. R., & Son, 124; and see
Gregory
Benham, Wm., 25
Benham's Pl., 24
Bennet, Hen., earl of Arlington, 103
Bennett:
Geo. Purden, 154
Hubert, 204
T. P. (Sir Thos.), & Son, 86, 130,
196, 239
Wm., 42
Benson, Gordon, 41
Bentham:
Jeremy, 35
Sir Sam., 35
Bentham Ho., 23
Bentley:
E. C., 46
J. F., 260
Bentwich:
Helen, 73
Norman, 73
Beresford, Marianne, 147

275

Beresford-Peirse, Revd. R. W. de la Poer, 256
Bergman-Osterberg, Mme., 38
Berkeley (later Upper Berkeley) Street West, 192
Berkshire, see Eton Coll.; Windsor
Bernal, J. D., 32
Bernard, Jas., earl of Bandon, 193
Bertie, Geo., earl of Lindsay, 191
Bertram:
  Steph., 106
  fam., 106, 115
Besant, Sir Wal., 39, 91
Best, Geo. Nathan, 27
Bethell, Ric., Baron Westbury, 207
Bevan, Rob., 65, 166 n
Bibbesworth, Edm., 226
Bickerdike Allen Simovic, 41
bicycle making, 127
Biddulph Mansions, 215, 217
Biddulph Rd., 217
Bide, John, 228, 233
Biers:
  Hugh, sr., 213
  Hugh, jr., 213
Billing, A., 222, 257; and see Newman
Billingham, Mrs., 270
Binfield:
  Hen., 42, 111
  Mary, 42
  fam., 111
Binnington, Fras. Thos., 58
Binns, S. H., 111
Birch, Sam., 64
Birchington Rd., 49
Bird:
  Stan., 88
  Wal., 88
Bird in Hand P.H., 5, 18
Birdall, John, 96
Bischoff, Chas., 44
Biscoe & Stanton, 259
Bishop's Bridge Rd., 175, 198
Bishop's Walk, 175, 198-9
Black Boy and Still P.H., 125
Black Death, see plague
Black Lion Lane, 174-5, 205
Black Lion P.H. (Bayswater), 205, 210, 221-2
Black Lion P.H. (Kilburn), 47, 51
Black Lion P.H. (West End), 43
Blackburn Rd., 45, 127
Blackburne, E. L., 259
Blackwood, Art. Johnstone, 55
Blake:
  Jane, 155
  W. J., 97
  Wm., 68, 190
Blakett, Ric., 73, 113
Bland:
  John, 67-9
  Thos., 113
Bland, Barnett & Co., 69
Blaquiere, John Peter, 170-1
Blashford Ho., 66
Bleak Hall, 34
Bleamire, Wm., 147
Blessington, see Stewart
Blind Lane, 3
Bliss:
  Sir Art., 32
  Baron de, 98
  Edw., 55, 97-8
  Hen., see Aldridge
  John, 83
Bliss est., 11, 116
Blomfield:
  Sir Art. Wm., 150, 257
  Chas. Jas., bp. of Lond., 260
  Sir Reg., 13, 39
Blomfield Ct., 215, 217
Blomfield Development Corp., 215
Blomfield Rd., 213, 217; pl. 40
Blomfield St. (later Villas), 200, 204

Blomfield Terr., see Harrow Rd.
Blondell:
  Eliz., 172
  Esther, 146
Blore, Ric., & Co., 177
Blount, Cath., 97
Blue Ho., 51, 53, 55
Blueh, Mat., 42
Blunden:
  Hester, see Hibbert
  Thos., 109
Blunt, Jos., 35-6
Blyth:
  Art., 228
  Chas., 228
  Sarah, 228
Boad's Corner, 17, 22
Board of Education, see Education
Bodley, G. F., 30, 151
Boehmer & Gibbs, 217
Boissevain & Osmond, 32
Bolton, Thos., 111
Bolton Ho., 20, 23
Bolton Rd., 61
Bomberg, David, 33, 50
Bonaparte, Prince Louis Lucien, 200
Bond:
  Alex., 204
  John, 107
Bone, Sir Muirhead, 73
Bonomi, Jas., 206
Boone, Thos., 110
Booth:
  Barton, 34
  Chas., 50
  Nat., Baron Delamer, 19
Boots the Chemists, 129
Borthwick, Algernon, Baron Glenesk, 70
Borthwick-Norton, F. H. P., 228
Bosanquet:
  Chas., 68
  Sir John, 68
Boswell, Jas., 34
Bott:
  Art., 191
  Jas., 222-3
Boucher, Eleanor, 254
Boundary Mews, 61
Boundary Rd., 60
Bourne & Hollingsworth, 240
Bourne Terr., 201
Bovingdon, Wm., 34 n, 95, 117
bowling, 20, 82, 89, 223
Bowyer, Chas., 100
boxing, 84, 87
'Boy George' (Geo. O'Dowd), 33
Boyd, A., 257
Boydell, Josiah, 43, 89
Boyle, Ric., earl of Shannon, 193
Boynton, Sir Griffith, Bt., and his w., 272
Brabazon:
  Reg., earl of Meath, 208
  Rog. le, 96
Bracken, Brendan, Vct. Bracken, 245
Bracknell Gdns., 39
Bracknell Gate (flats), 40
Bradley:
  S., & Co., 240
  Wm., 20, 69
Bradley's Bldgs., 20, 25 n, 28, 162
Braemar Ho., 215, 217
Bragg, Melvyn, 33
Brailsford, Hen., 30
Brain, Dennis, 42
Braine, John, 33
Braithwaite:
  John (d. 1818), 199, 230
  John (d. 1870), 230
  Warwick, 40
Bramwick, Rob., 164
Branch Hill, see Hampstead Heath
Branch Hill est., 41
Branch Hill farm, 120

Branch Hill Lodge, 34, 36-7, 41
Brandon Ho., 70
Braun, Hen., 73, 89
Bravington Rd., 219-20
Brawn:
  Fanny, 25
  Mic., 33
Bray, Sir Reg., 230
Bray Tower, 66
Brendel, Alf., 73
Brent, Lond. boro., 185
  rent office, 127
Brent, riv., 3
Brent Cross, see Hendon
Brent People's Housing Assoc., 185, 220
Brethren, 154, 157, 263
Breuer, Marcel, 59
Brewers Alley, 22
Brewers' Ct., 203
brewing, 125, 238
Briardale Rd., 74
brick and tile making, 36, 51, 76, 79, 106, 118, 123-4, 236-7
Bridge, A. C., dean of Guildford, 256
Bridge Approach Rd., 63
Bridge Ho., 199-200
Bridge Rd., 61
Brighouse, Harold, 59
Brindley St., 200
Bristol Gdns., 213
Bristow, Fred., 30
Britannia building soc., 224
Britannia P.H., 5, 84, 88
Britannia Terr., 61
British and Foreign Bible Soc., 90
British and Foreign Schs. Soc. and British schs., 159, 162-4, 269-70
British Assoc. of Settlement and Social Action Centres, 225
British Boxing Board of Control, 84, 87
British Electric Traction Co., 178
British Home Stores, 129
British Land Co., 28, 44, 48, 50, 110
British Petroleum Co., see General Petroleum Co.
British Telecommunications, 127, 198, 237
British Transport Com., 232, 236
British Waterways Board, 177, 216, 232-3, 237
Broad's Manufacturing Co., formerly Broad & Co. and Broad, Harris & Co., 237
Broadbent, Mr. (fl. 1753), 140
Broadhurst Gdns., 38, 41
Bromwich, S., 107
Brontë, Charlotte, 199
Brook, Wm., 156; and see Brooke
Brook Ho., 19
Brook St., 197
Brooke:
  Hen., Baron Brooke of Cumnor, 42, 75, 137
  Leslie, 75
Brooks:
  Revd. H. W., 258-9
  Jas., 256
  Revd. T. B. H., 259
  Wm., 68
Broomsleigh Rd., 45
Browell, Edw., 27
Brown (Browne):
  Chas. Armitage, 25
  Ford Madox, 27
  John (d. 1381), 113
  John (fl. c. 1550), 226
  Ric. (fl. 1558), 226
  Ric. (fl. 1648-81), 108-9
  Ric. (fl. 1756), perpetual curate of Paddington, 253
  Thos., 226, 252
  Wm., 45
  fam., 115

Browncar, Wm., 233
Browne, *see* Brown
Browning:
    Eliz. Barrett, 200
    Rob., 200, 206, 216
Browning Close, 215
Brunel, I. K., 178–9
Brunel (est.), 202–3
Bryan, Mic., 255
Brydon, J. M., 64
Bryston Property Group, 41, 95
Bubbington, Wm., 101
Buckhurst, Isaiah, 117
Buckingham, Jas., 61
Buckingham, marquis of, *see* Grenville, Geo.
Buckingham Mansions, 45
Buckinghamshire, *see* Eton Coll.; Hedgerley Wood
Buckland:
    Ann Seager, 125
    Eliz., 125
    Jas., 125
    John, 125
    Thos., 125
Buckland Cres., 55; *pl.* 12
Buckle, Hen., 193
Buckmaster, Stanley Owen, Vct. Buckmaster, 209
Bucknell:
    Sarah, 105
    Sarah, her dau., m. Thos. Ripley, 105
Buckner, *see* Frewen, Anne
Budd, Miss, 169
Budden, W. H., 6
Buddhists, 159
Buddle, Wm., 200
Buffar:
    Mary, *see* Regnier
    —— (d. by 1768), 109
builders and bldg. ind., 236–7; *and see* Allison & Foskett; Amer; Ashwell; Batterbury, Ric. *and* Thos.; Batterbury & Huxley; Becket; Beedle; Bell, P.; Bence; Biers, Hugh, sr. *and* jr.; Bott, Art.; Brown, Wm.; Buddle; Burford; Bursill; Callard; Capps, Edw., Hen., *and* Jas.; Carter; Cave, E. H. *and* E. J.; Clark, Thos.; Clowser; Cook, Chas.; Cossens; Crake, Wm.; Cubitt; Cuming; Davis, A.; Densham; Dixon, Jas.; Duncan, Geo. *and* John Wallace; Elkins; Estcourt; Garrett; Gelsthorp; Gibb, Jas.; Godson; Gray, ——; Gregory & Bence; Hackworth; Haines, ——; Hankin; Hart; Hewett; Humbert; Jackson, Hugh; Jay; Kellond; Kelly, Edw. *and* Herb.; Kerrison, Wm.; King, Chas. *and* Wm.; Kingdom; Laing; Leammell; Legg; Littlewood; May; Medley; Michael; Mowlem; Muncey; Oldrey; Parnell, Joshua; Pearce; Pickett; Pink; Ponsford, Jas., Lionel, Thos., *and* Wm.; Potter, Geo.; Price; Pritchard, Geo.; Pugin; Pulling; Rathbone, A. *and* ——; Rayner; Reeder; Reynolds; Roberts Bros.; Roff; Rose; Rudd; Sanders; Sanderson, John; Scantlebury, John, Wm., *and* Wm. Oliver; Sharp, Chas.; Shepherd, Wm.; Stock, Hen.; Sugden; Suttle; Taft; Tavener; Thomas & Son; Thorpe, Rob.; Tidey; Tomblin; Vigers; Wallas; Ward, Wm.; Wartnaby; Waterson; Wates; White, Hen. (fl. *c.* 1780); Willett, Wm., sr. *and* jr.;

Wimpey; Wynn; Yeo
Bull and Bush P.H., 67, 70–1, 84, 89, 125
Bunney, Mic., 30
Burbidge, Ric., 240
Burdett-Coutts, *see* Coutts
Burford, Jas., 29
Burford Ho., 18
Burgess:
    Maj. Ardwick, 103
    Hen. Weech, 73–4, 103
    fam., 74
    and see Burgeys
Burgess Hill, Pk., 74
Burgess Pk. Mansions, 74
Burgeys, Thos., 121; *and see* Burgess
Burgh, Revd. Allatson, 26
Burgh Ho., 18, 26, 29, 31–3
Burke, Edm., 69
Burne-Jones, Sir Edw., 155
Burnet, Sir Thos., 53
Burney, Dr. Chas. and Fanny, 69
    Evelina, 83
Burnham (flats), 66
Burnham Ct., 211
Burrard Rd., 45
Bursars Rd., 64
Bursill, Julia, 44, 49
Burton, Decimus, 199
Burton, Montague, & Co., 129
Burwood Pl., 193
Busby:
    Tomlinson, 231
    Lt.-Col. Tomlinson, 231
    Revd. Wm. Beaumont, 231
Bushell:
    Anne, *see* Waad
    Col. Thos., 96
Bushnell, Geo., 254
Bussee, Geo., 23
Butler:
    Eliz., dchss. of Ormond, 9
    J. Dixon, 29
    Jas., bp. of Durham, 18, 109
    Ric., earl of Arran, 9
    Thos., 51
Butt, Dame Clara, 65
Buxton, Sir Thos., and his w. Hannah, 68
Bycock, fam., 115
Byron:
    Fanny Lucy, Lady Byron (later Lady Houston), 70
    Geo. Gordon, Baron Byron, 72, 77, 216
    Anne Isabella, Lady Noel-, wid. of Geo. Gordon, Baron Byron, 36
    Wm., Baron Byron, 69
Byron Cottage, 67–8, 70–1
Byron Villas, 73

C.P.A.S., *see* Church Pastoral Aid Soc.
Cadbury Bros., 127; *and see* Schweppes
Caen Wood Towers, 80
Cage:
    Jas., 103
    Phil., 103
Caine, Sir Hall, 70
Caird St., 219
Calder, Wm., 235
Callard, Abraham, 212
Calvert, Edw., 187
Cambridge, *see* King's Coll.
Cambridge Ct., 195, 233
Cambridge Sq., 192, 196–7
Cambridge St., 192
Cambridge Terr., 193
Camden, Lond. boro., 3, 41, 81, 85, 130, 136–7, 155
    ambulance sta., 126
    arms, *137*
    arts centre, 92, 141

as housing authy., 60, 185
    schs., 160, 266
    town hall, 137
    vehicle maintenance depot, 126
    wards, 137
    workshops, 127
Camden History Review, 92
Camden History Soc., 92
Camden Town Group, 32
Camelford, Baron, *see* Pitt, Thos.
Camelford Cottage, 69–70
Campbell:
    Archibald Montgomery, perpetual curate of Paddington, 253–5
    E. J., 165
    Geo., 120
    Jas., 97
    John, 120
    John, duke of Argyll, 193
Campbell St., 188
Campden, Vct., *see* Hicks, Baptist; Noel, Baptist *and* Edw.
Campden Bldgs., 28
Canada, govt. of, exhibition com., 127
Canadian & English Stores, 129
canals and canal transport, *see* Grand Junction canal; Paddington canal; Regent's canal
Cane Wood, *see* Kenwood
Canewdon (Essex), vicar of, 253
Canfield Gdns., Pl., 38
Canfield Rd., 37, 49
Canning, Geo., 69
Cannon, Chas., 44, 104
Cannon Cottage, 19, 32
Cannon Hall, 19, 26, 32, 140
Cannon Hill, 44
Cannon Lane, 17
Cannon Lodge, 19
Cannon Pl., 17, 28
Canons Pk., *see* Edgware
Canterbury, abp. of, 255
    and see Sheldon, Gilb.
Canterbury Ho., 43, 46, 111
Canterbury Mansions, 46
Canterbury Terr., 213
Canterbury Villas, *see* Maida Vale (part of Edgware Rd.)
Capo di Monte, 20, 33
Capps:
    Edw., 207
    Hen. Augustus, 192
    Jas., 207
Carbonell, Wm. Chas., 223, 225, 230
Carlile:
    Edw., 25, 110
    Eliz., w. of Edw., 110
    Janette Anne, m. Benj. Edw. Willoughby, 110
    Jas., 110
    and see Carlyle
Carlile est., 16, 30, 110
Carlile Ho., 16, 26, 28, 110
Carline:
    Hilda, m. Sir Stan. Spencer, 31
    Ric., 31
    fam., 31
Carlisle, dean of, *see* Ridgeway
Carlton Dene, 215
Carlton Mansions, 215
Carlton Mews, Pl., Rd., 213
Carlton Vale, 213, 217
Carlton Villas, *see* Maida Vale (part of Edgware Rd.)
Carlyle, Thos., 206–7; *and see* Carlile
Carmichael-Smyth, Maj. H. and his w., 193
Carnegie:
    And., 251
    H. T., vicar of Hampstead, 145
Carnegie Ho., 32, 156
Caroë & Passmore, 217
Caroline Ho., 18
Caroline Ho. (flats), 209–10
Caroline Pl., 205, 211

Caroline Pl. Mews, 211
Carpenter, Wm. Boyd, bp. of Ripon, 256
Carr:
  Hen., 118
  Sam., 118
  Wm., 35–6
  fam., 36
Carroll Ho., 211
Cart and Horses P.H., 52, 184
Carter, Jas., 48
Carter, Paterson & Co., 236
cartridge making, 126
Cartwright:
  Chas., 22, 107
  Mr. (fl. 1723), 52
Cary:
  Amy, 23
  Amy Anne, m. Adam Askew, 104, 109
  Lucy Eliz., m. Thos. Askew, 104, 109
  Mary, 104, 109
  Rob., 104, 109
Casa Maria, 71
Castellain Mansions, 215
Castellain Rd., 213
Casterbridge (flats), 203
Castleacre, 196
Castleden, Jas., 156
Cate Mead farm, 105
Cater, Phil., 119, 122
Catholic Apostolic Church (Irvingites), 157, 262
Cave:
  E. H. & H. T., 39
  E. J., 13, 28, 45
Cavendish:
  Hon. Hen., 133
  Hon. Hen. Fred. Compton, 43
Cavendish Ho., 90
Cavendish Mansions, 45
Cayford Ho., 60
Cecilia Rd., 74
Cedar Lawn, 69, 71, 143
the Cedars, 44–5
cement merchants, 127
Central Council for the Promotion of Public Morality, 137
Central London Rly., 181
Central Pk. hotel, 239
Centre Heights, 62
Chadwick, Sir Edwin, 193
Chalcot Gdns., 64
Chalcots, in Hampstead:
  chs., 64, 150–1; pl. 24
  dom. bldgs., 63–6
  est., see Eton Coll.; Wyldes
  farms and farmhos., 100, 116, 118
  flats, 65–6
  growth, 63–6
  halls and institutes, 65
  hotels, 66, 128
  housing and council est., 64, 66
  Jews, 158
  pub. hos., 65, 84
  roads, 63–6
  schs., see the Hall
Chalk Farm, in Hampstead (part), 5, 100
Chalk Farm P.H., 81
Chambers, Sir Paul, 73
Champneys, Basil, 13, 37–8, 74, 150
Chandler, Chas., 154
the Chantry, 71
Chantry Point, 221
Chapel Side, 211
Chapman:
  Dan., and his dau. Ann, 101
  J. Wallis, 261
Charfield Ct., 202, 204
Charing Cross, Euston, & Hampstead Rly., 8
Charity of St. Vincent de Paul, Sisters of, 153

Charity Organization Soc. Pensioners, Adelaide Home, 65
Charles II, 103
Charles:
  Eliz. Rundle, 37
  Thos., 171–2
Charlotte Augusta, princess of Wales, 191
Charlton (Kent), 93
Chatelaine, John, 82, 186
Chater, Geo., 35
Chavalliaud, Léon-Jos., 189
Cheeseman, Rob., 113
Chelsea, 182, 243, 246, 251
  (detached), 173, 218–19, 230–1, 257
  Kensal New Town, q.v.
  Queen's Pk., q.v.
  schs., 265–7
Cheltenham (Gloucs.), 83
Chelwood Ho., 197
Chepstow Lodge hosp., 249
Chepstow Rd., 203
Chesnut Ho., 144
Chestnut Cottage, 71, 73
Chestnut Lodge, 19, 29
Chester, Eliza, 26
Chester Mews, 195
Chester Pl., 193
Chesterfield, earls of, see Stanhope
Chesterford Gdns., 39
Chevalier, Alb., 78
Chichester, Joscelin of, see Joscelin
Chicken Ho., 16, 22, 26, 28, 36, 110, 162
Chicken Ho. P.H., 81
Child, Ric. le, 73, 113
children's hosps.:
  Hampstead, 143
  Paddington, 188, 249
Childs Hill, in Hampstead (part), 13, 103, 113
  Blacketts well, 73, 113, 138
  chs., 74, 150
  dom. bldgs., 73–4; pl. 17
  est., 103–4
  farms and farmhos., 73, 103
  flats, 74
  growth, 73–5
  housing and council est., 74
  New West End, 74
  roads, 73–4
Childs Hill Ho., 74
the Chimes, 49
Chiosso:
  Antonio Martino, 224
  J. T., 224
  Capt. Jas., 224
  P. J., 224
  Mrs., 224
Chippenham Mews, Rd., 218
Chippenham Terr., see Harrow Rd.
Chirac:
  Denis, 186
  Denis, his s., 186, 234, 267
Chirme, John, 229
Chislett Rd., 49
Chiswick, see Bedford Pk.
Cholmeley:
  Eliz., m. 1 Leonard Beckwith, 2 Chris. Kenn, 102
  Frances, m. —— Russell, 102
  Sir Rog., 102
Cholmley Lodge, 43, 46
Christian, Ewan, 13, 28, 64, 149, 151–2
Christian Community, 154, 158
Christian Scientists, 90, 154, 158
Christian Social Union, 65
Christie, Dame Agatha, 59
Church Army Housing Trust, 234
Church (formerly Ecclesiastical) Commissioners, 58, 96, 98, 149, 157, 183–4, 196, 202, 209, 213, 215–16, 219, 226, 228, 252, 260

Church Extension Assoc., 148, 253, 255, 268
Church Lane, 16
Church Missionary Assoc., 90
Church Mystical Union, 264
Church Pastoral Aid Soc. (C.P.A.S.), 150, 258
Church Path farm, 105
Church Patronage Soc., 150, 259
Church Pl. (Hampstead), 27
Church Pl. (Paddington), 187
Church Rd. (Belsize), 55
Church Rd. (Chalcots), 64
Church Row, 11, 20, 23, 27, 30, 104; pl. 20
Church St., 185
Churchill:
  Ld. Randolph, 194, 245
  Sir Winston, 197
Cibber, Colley, 34
Cicely Davies housing assoc., 51
Cincello, marquis de, 69
cinemas, 62, 84–6, 222–3
Cirencester St., 200
Civic Trust, 204
Clare, Osbert de, prior of Westm., 92
Claremont Ct., 202
Clarendon, earl of, see Villiers
Clarendon Ct., 215
Clarendon Ct. hotel, 217
Clarendon Gdns., 213, 216
Clarendon Mews, 197
Clarendon Rd., Terr., 213
Clarendon St. (later Cres.), 200
Clarissa Harlowe, see Richardson
Clark:
  F. J., 36–7
  Ken., Baron Clark, 33
  Ric., 105
  Thos., 60
  Wm. (d. 1630), 105
  Wm. (d. 1651), 105
Clarke:
  A., 62
  Chas. Cowden, 206
  John (fl. 1802), 128
  John (d. by 1861), 172
  Jos., 128
  Mary Cowden, 206
  Ramsay Robinson, 100
  T. Chatfeild, 155
  Sir Thos., 34, 116
  Thos., 100
Clausen, Sir Geo., 57
Claygate (Surr.), 226
Clayton & Bell, 152, 257–9
Cleave, Thos., 171–2
Cleaver Ho., 66
Cleeve, Sir Wm. of, see William
Clerkenwell:
  bailiwick, 102, 113
  est., see Hampstead, mans. and other est., Temples
  Knights of the Hospital of St. John of Jerusalem, 100–3, 113, 124
  schs., 164
Cleve Ho., 50
Cleve Rd., 49
Cleveland Sq., 206–7, 211
Cliff:
  Hen., 99
  Wm. de, 113
Clifford, Revd. John, 260–1
Clifton Ct., 217
Clifton Ho., 28
Clifton nurseries, 203, 235
Clifton Pl., Rd., 213
Clifton Villas, 213, 216
Clint, Alf., 57
Clive Ct., 215, 217
Clive (formerly Clive Hall) hotel, 66, 128
Clorane Gdns., 74
Cloth Hill, 9, 17, 19
Clowser, Thos., 13, 29, 36, 70

Clutton, Hen., 256
Coach and Horses P.H., 22, 125
coal merchants, 127, 236
Coates, Wells, 59
Cobden, Ric., 207
Cobden-Sanderson, Thos., 39
Coburg hotel, 208, 210, 239
Cock P.H., 20, 125
Cock and Hoop P.H., 43, 45, 84, 123, 125
Cockburn, Thos., 152
Cockerell:
    Sir Chas. Rushout, Bt., 231
    Chas. Rob., 79
    Fred. Pepys, 147
    John, 231
    Sam. Pepys, 186, 191–2, 197, 199, 206, 231, 234, 242–3, 271
Cockram (or Cokerham), Phil., 51, 116, 121
cocoa mill, 238
Cogel, John, 122
Coggs, John, 51
Cohen, Dr. David, 167
Cokerham, see Cockram
Coldstream, Sir Wm., 73
Cole, Sir Hen., 29
Cole Lane, 3, 42
Coleman, Wm., 25, 108, 110
Coleridge:
    John, Baron Coleridge, 194
    Sam. Taylor, 72
College Cres., 55, 60
Collier, John, 65
Collins:
    H. H., 244
    John, 103
    Wilkie, 61, 68
    Wm., 34, 61, 68, 77, 255
Colls, see De Cols
Colonnade hotel, 216, 239
Colonades (flats), 202–3
Coltman, Sir Thos. (Mr. Justice), 193
Combe Edge, 37
Combes, John, 272
Combrune:
    Eleanor, m. —— Gardner, 125
    Gideon, 125
    Mic., and his wid. Mary, 125
    Susanna, 125
Commonwealth, see immigrants
Commonwealth Holiday Inns, 128
Communist party and voters, 33, 62
Compayne Gdns., 38, 42, 49
Comper, Sir Ninian, 258
composers, see musicians
Compton:
    Fay, 32
    Hen., bp. of Lond., 271
Conduit Ho., 23
Conduit St., 192, 207
Congleton, Baron, see Parnell, Hen.
Congregationalists (Independents), 105, 153–4, 157, 261–2
Connaught, earl of, see William Fred.
Connaught Ho., 191, (another), 195
Connaught Mansions, 195
Connaught Mews, 191
Connaught Pl., 191, 193, 197
Connaught Sq., 191, 198
Connaught St., 192–3, 198
Connaught Terr., see Edgware Rd.
Connaught village, see Tyburnia
Connell, Ward & Lucas, 40
Conron, P. R., 88
Conservative party and voters, 91, 137, 225, 245
Consort Ho., 209, 212
Consort St., 188
Constable:
    Isabel, 172
    John, 13, 23–5, 63, 68, 76–7, 148
Constable Ho., 66
Constantine, s. of Alulf, 92
Constantine Rd., 58

conveyance, 236
Conway:
    Dame Anne, 259
    John, 103
Conyers:
    Gerald, 105
    Tristram, 105
Cook:
    Chas. Claudius, 60, 232
    Sid., 50, 62, 66
Cooke, Hen., 152
Cooper:
    A. W. S., 144
    Lady Diana, 216
    Sir Edwin, 249
    Dame Gladys, 66
    John Julius, Vct. Norwich, 216
    T., 258
Coorg (India), rajah of, 214
Coote, Sir Chas., Bt., 191, 193
Cope, Wm., 109
Cope's Taverns, 239
Copydex Ltd., 259
Corbusier, see Le Corbusier
Cort, Hen., 148
Cory, W. J., 29
Cossens, G. W., 44–5
Cotleigh Rd., 44
Cotton, Col. Hen., 37, 49, 101; and see Powell-Cotton
Coulson:
    Jukes, 229, 231
    Jukes, his nephew, 231
Countess of Huntingdon's Connexion, 154
Court Royal hotel, 239
Coutts, Angela Burdett-, 79
Coward, Sir Noel, his Vortex, 85
Coward Coll., 154
Cowherd, see Herd
cowkeeping, 120, 234
Cowper, J. B. K., 50
Cox, Sir Thos., 198
Crabbe, Geo., 69, 72
Craddock:
    Mary, see Jodrell
    Sheldon, 228
Craig, Sir Gordon, 30
Craik, Mrs., see Mulock
Crake:
    John, 192–3
    Wm., 192
Cramphorn, Wm., 254
Crane:
    Chas. Theomartyr, perpetual curate of Paddington, 242, 253, 255
    Geo., 55
Cranfield, Jos., 123
Craven:
    Wm., earl of Craven (d. 1697), 231–2
    Wm., earl of Craven (d. 1825), 247
    Wm., earl of Craven (d. 1866), 232
    Wm., Baron Craven (d. 1739), 204 232
Craven est., 232
Craven Hill, 204, 211
Craven Hill Gdns., 207, 211
Craven Rd., 207
Craven Terr., 206
Craxton, fam., 75
Cranleigh (Surr.), sch., 165
Crediton Hill Rd., 46
Crediton Mansions, 46
Creed, fam., 107
Cressy Rd., 57–8
Cresta Ho., 62
Creswick, Thos., and his sis., 156
Crew, Anne, ctss. of Torrington, 19
Crewe, John, Baron Crewe, and his w. Frances, 69
Crewe Cottage, 69–70
Crewes, Wm., 116 n
cricket, 86–7, 223, 250
    Eton and Mdx. cricket ground, 65,

86–8
Cricklewood, in Hampstead (part), 48, 50–1
    housing est., 50
    ind., 127
    nonconf. (protestant), 155
    roads, 49
    schs., 162–3, 165
Cripps, Rob., 101
Crispin, Geo., 27
Cristall, Joshua, 187, 229, 270
Crockett's Ct., 23, 25 n
Crokesley, Richard of, see Richard
Crompton:
    Benj., 205
    Rookes, 208
Crompton St., 187–8
Cromwell, Oliver, 190
Cronin, A. J., 260
Crosbie, Gen. Chas., 254
Cross, see Spalding
Crossfield Rd., 64
Crown P.H. (Bayswater), 205, 222
Crown P.H. (Hampstead town), 17, 108
Croxley Rd., 219
Cruikshank, Geo., 77
Cubbidge, John, 108–9
Cubitt, Thos., 63, 191
Cuchow, John, ? par. priest of Hampstead, 146
Cullum, Wm., 48
Culverhouse:
    Alf., 124
    Edw., 124
    Fred., 124
    John, 28, 37–8, 72, 118, 120, 124, 127, 139 n
    P. G., 179
    fam., 118
Cumber:
    Susannah, 107
    Thos., 107
Cumberbatch, Charlotte, 254
Cumberlege, Chas. Nat., 106
Cuming, Sam., 63–4, 86
Cundy, Thos., 256
Cunningham Ct., 215, 217
Curran, Phil., 255
Currie, Baron, see Wodehouse
Curry:
    Ena, 168
    Revd. John, 150
Curwen, T. T., 157
Cuthbert St., 188
cycling, 88

Daleham Gdns., 38
Dalhousie, earl of, see Ramsay
Dallas, Sir Rob., 68
Dames Anglaises of the Institute of the Blessed Virgin Mary, 153, 167
Danby, Thos., 57
Dandelion Rd., 49
Daniells, H. W., 237
Dart St., 220
Davidson:
    Frances Mary, 143
    Hen. (d. 1827), 97
    Hen. (fl. 1850), 56, 97
    John, 214
    and see Dinerman
Davies:
    Sir Hen. Walford, 29, 46
    Isabel, see Sparkes
    Mary Llewelyn, 32
    Rob., 109
Davies Tutors, 166, 168
Davis:
    A., 46
    Joe, 84
    Mrs., laundress, 125
    and see Mewès
Davis & Emmanuel, 265

Davison, *see* Norman
Dawber, Sir Guy, 74
Dawes, Rosa Money, 165
Dawkes, S. W., 149
Dawson:
    Martin, 110
    Susan, w. of Martin, 110–11
Day, Alan, 130
Deaconess Community of St. And., 255
De Ameland, Lady Augusta, m. Augustus Fred., duke of Sussex, 191
de Clifford, Sophia, Baroness de Clifford, 235
De Cols (or Colls), Eliz., 109
De Gaulle, Gen. Chas., 41
De La Fountayne:
    Frances, *see* Palmer
    John, 110
de László, Phil., 41, 153
De La Warr, Baron, *see* West
De Morgan, Wm., 65
De Roure (or Rowe), John Peter, and his w. Mary, 109
De Rowe, *see* De Roure
de Soissons, Louis, 66
Dearmer, Revd. P., 151
Debat, Dan., asst. curate of Paddington, 253
Dee:
    John, 102, 107
    Marg., w. of John, 107
Defoe, Dan., 9, 77, 82, 158
Delamer, Baron, *see* Booth, Nat.
Delamere Terr., 200, 204; *pl.* 40
Delaware Mansions, 215, 217
Delaware Rd., 214
Delius, Fred., 59, 65
Dene Mansions, 45
Denholme Rd., 219
Denman, Thos., Baron Denman, 77
Denning Rd., 28
Dennington Pk. Rd., 45
Densham, Ric., & Sons, 124
Deormod, 2, 8
Desborough Cottage, Ho., 231
Desborough Lodge, 199–200, 231
Design 5 (firm), 197
D'Este, Sir Augustus, 191
Deutsch, Oscar, 86
Devonshire Ct., 211
Devonshire Ho., 55
Devonshire Pl., *see* Edgware Rd.; Haverstock Hill
Devonport Mews, 195
Diaghilev, Tamara Karsavina, 42
Dibdin Ho., 215, 217
Dickens, Chas., 76, 84, 86, 193, 206
Dickens & Jones, 129
Dickenson, Marsh, 107
Dicksee, Sir Frank, 50
Dilke:
    Sir Chas., Bt., 141
    Chas. Wentworth, 25
Dimsdale:
    John, Baron Dimsdale, 22
    Thos., 22 n
Dinerman, Davidson & Partners, 32
Dingley:
    Chas., 67
    Rob., 67
Disney, Lt.-Gen. Sir Moore, 55, 97
District Rly., *see* Metropolitan District Rly.
Ditchfield, ——, deputy steward of man., 9
Dixon:
    Jas., 38
    Mary, *see* James
    Rob., 17
    W. A., 156
Dobson:
    Wm., 56, 64
    John, 235

Dodd, Ant., min. of Paddington, 253
Dolte:
    Thos., 230
    Wm., 230
domestic servants, 13–14, 126–7, 238
    ch. svces. for, 257–8
    Domestic Science Coll., 46–7
    training sch., 267
Dominican Sisters, 153
Donne, John, 253
Donningtons est., 17
Dorchester Ho., 203
Dormer:
    Sir John, 100–1
    Judith, *see* Atye
Dorney, Dorney Towers, 66
Dornfell Rd., 45
Douglas:
    Ld. Alf., 30
    Ld. Archibald, 260
    Campbell, 154
Douglas & Wood, 50, 66
Douglas Ho., 188
Douglas Mansions, 49
Dowbiggin:
    Lt. Edw. Thos., 199
    Thos., 199
Down Barns, *see* Northolt
Downes, Col. ——, 96
Downfield Close, 204
Downshire Cres., 58
Downshire Hill, 25, 32
Doyle:
    John, 193
    Ric., 193
Dr. Williams's Libr., 154
Drage:
    Theodore, 107
    Dr. Wm., 107–8
Drake, Lindsey, 211
dramatists, *see* writers
Draper:
    John, 102, 107
    Thos., and his w. Eliz., 102, 107
Dresden Close, 41
dressmaking, 126, 238
Drew, John, 122
Drinkwater, John, 50, 58
Droop St., 220
Drouet, Mr., 243
Dryhurst, Sylvia, 31
Dubourg, Mat., 254
Ducie, earl of, *see* Moreton
Duddeley, Steph. de, 145
Duddingtons est., 17, 108, 118
Dudley, John, earl of Warwick, 100–1
Dudley Grove, 187
Dudley Grove Rd., 187
Dudley Ho., 189
Dudley St., 189
Dudman, John, 129
Dufferin, ctss. of, *see* Sheridan, Helen
Duffield:
    Jas., 169
    John, 5, 19, 82, 169
Duke of Cumberland's Head P.H., 34
Duke of Hamilton (Duke of Hamilton's Head) P.H., 17, 22, 84, 125
Duke of Kendal P.H., 193
Du Maurier:
    Daphne, 32
    Geo., 27, 29–30, 148, 194
    Sir Gerald, 31–2, 85
Du Maurier Ho., 60
Dunbar, Revd. Wm., 44
Duncan:
    Chas., 147
    Geo., 48
    John Wallace, 48
Dundee Ho., 215, 217
Dunlop Rubber Co., 126
Dunrobin Ct., 40
Dunster, Sam., perpetual curate of Paddington, 253

Durants, in Enfield, 93
Durham, bp. of, *see* Butler, Jos.
Dutch club, *see* Bayswater: Oranje-haven
Dutton, John, Baron Sherborne, 193
Duval, Lewis, 206
Duveen, Sir Jos. Joel, 70
Dynham Rd., 44

Earle:
    Eleanor, 100
    Eliz., *see* Rawlinson
    Giles (d. 1759), 99
    Giles (d. 1811), 100
    Giles Clarke, 100
    Marg., wid. of Giles (d. 1811), 100
    Wm. Rawlinson, 100
Earlsfield(s) est., 42 n, 106
Earlsmead, 69
Earp, T., 258
East, Alf., 157
East & West India Docks & Birmingham Junction Rly., 7
East End (Ostend), 9, 17
East Heath Lodge, 24, 32
East Heath Rd., 24
East Middlesex Militia, 89
East Pk., *see* Hampstead Heath
Eastbourne Terr., 206; *pl.* 45
Easton, *see* Hall, Stan.
Ebbsfleet Rd., 49
Ebury, *see* Eye
Ecclesiastical Commissioners, *see* Church Commissioners
Edbrooke Rd., 218, 221
Edgar, King, 1, 92
Edgeworth, Maria, 36
Edgware, Canons Pk., 148
Edgware Rd. (Watling Street), 3, 47–8, 51, 173–4, 182, 185, 195–6, 212
    Connaught Terr., 191, 194
    Devonshire Pl., 186, 188
    flats, 195–7
    gallows, *see* Tyburn
    lighting, 251
    Maida Hill, 174, 212
    Maida Hill East, 212
    Maida Pl., 214
    Maida Vale (part of Edgware Rd.), *q.v.*
    Marylebone flyover, 175, 189
    Philpott Terr., 186
    Prospect Pl., 188
    pub. hos., 221
    turnpike gates, 174
    turnpike trust, 3
Edinburgh, duke of, *see* William Fred.
Edinburgh Ho., 215, 217
Edinburgh Pl., 191
Edmonton poor law union, wkho., 135–6
Edmund (Crouchback), earl of Lancaster, and his w. Blanche, 96
Edna Ho., 198, 256
Education, Board or Dept. of, 159–60, 163, 269
Edward the Confessor, King, 92
Edward VII, *see* Wales, prince of
Edwards, *see* Pollard
Effingham, earl of, *see* Howard, Ric.
Egg, Augustus, 206
Eldon Grove, Rd., 56
Eldon Ho., 56, 60
elections:
    local, 136, 245
    parliamentary, 77, 137–8, 245–6
Eley:
    Bros., 126
    Wm., 126
    fam., 45, 126
Elgar, Sir Edw., 40
Elgin (est.), 220–1
Elgin Ave., 213, 217, 221
Elgin Mansions, 215, 217

Elgin Rd., Terr., 213
Elizabeth I, 35, 96
Elizabeth Close, 215
Elkins, John, 205
Elkins's Row, see Bayswater Rd.
Ellerdale Close, 31
Ellerdale Rd., 27, 153
Ellis, Edw., 26, 167
Ellwood Ct., 202, 204
Elm Ho., 53, 56, 58
Elm(s) Lane, 206
Elm Lodge (Hampstead town), 19
Elm Lodge (Westbourne green), 199
Elm Row, 19
Elm Tree Pl., 187
the Elms (Chalcots), 65
the Elms (Kilburn), 49
the Elms (Spaniard's End), 68, 70–1,
   79–80, 143
the Elms (West End), 44, 126
Elms Ho., 205
Elsom, C. H., 211
Elsworthy Ct., 65
Elsworthy Rd., 64, 66
Embassy Ho., 50
Emerson, Wm., 249
Emmanuel, see Davis
Emmett, J. T., 61, 157
emigrants, to Australia, 135
Empson, Sir Wm., 59
Enfield, see Durants
Enfield Ho., 120
engineering, 237–8
England's (formerly Upper Chalcot)
   Lane, 3, 51, 100
English Bowling Assoc., 223
Environment, Dept. of, Housing
   Corporation, 184–5
Eresby Rd., 49
Erith, Raymond, 84, 254
Ernest Harriss Ho., 220–1
Errington:
   Geo. (d. 1769), 53, 109
   Geo. (d. 1796), 109
   Geo. Hen. (d. 1843), 109
   Geo. Hen. (fl. 1845), 104, 109
   fam., 27
Errington Rd., 221
Erskine:
   Hon. Frances, 147
   Thos., Baron Erskine, 68, 93, 133
Erskine Ho., 68, 70–1
Esplanade hotel, 239
Essendine Rd., 214
Essex, see Canewdon; Fanton; Rom-
   ford
estate agents, see auctioneers and
   estate agents
Estcourt, Ern., 38
Esterhazy, Prince, 72
Ethical Church (formerly West Lon-
   don Ethical Soc.), 263
Eton, John of, 47
Eton Ave., 64–5
Eton Coll. (Berks., formerly Bucks.),
   11, 63–5, 99–100, 122, 146, 151,
   164; as patron, 151
   est., 11, 63–5, 99–100, 111, 113,
   115, 117–20, 122, 132; and
   see Wyldes
Eton Ct., 65
Eton Hall, Rise, 66
Eton Pk., 64
Eton Pl., 65–6
Eton P.H., 84
Eton Rd., 64
Eton Villas, 63, 66
Evangelicalism, 148–50
Evans:
   Benj. Beardmore, 129
   Dan., 154
   Joshua, 99
   T. A., & Sons, 128
   Thos., 229
Evans Row, 20

Evelina, see Burney
Evelyn, John, 98
Everett:
   Mary, see Clark
   Ralph, 105
Evergreen Hill, 68, 71
Ewens, John, 231
Exeter:
   bp. of, see Pelham
   dean of, see Boyd
Express Dairies, 28
Express Mansions, 28
Eye (or Ebury), in Westm., man.,
   229; cts., 241
Eyles, B., 103
Eyre:
   Geo. John, 103
   Hen. Sam., 103
   Col. Hen. Sam., 60, 103
   Revd. Hen. Sam., 103
   Walpole, and his wid. Sarah, 103
   Walpole, s. of Walpole, 103
   fam., 48, 60, 103
Eyre est., in Marylebone, 60

Faber, Sir Geof., 40
Fairfax Mews, Pl., Rd., 61
Fairhazel Gdns., 38, 42, 61
Faith Christian Fellowship, 158
Falkirk Ho., 215, 217
Fallodon Ho., 203
Falmouth Ho., 197
Fanton (Essex), 226
Farby, Rachel, 105
Farey, Mic., 258
Farjeon, Eleanor, 32
Farmer, Alb., 40
Farrell Grimshaw Partnership, 203
Faulkner, Amos F., 57, 65
Fawley Mansions, 46
Fawley Rd., 46
Fearn, David, & Co., 129
Fearon, Hen. B., 35
Fellows:
   Wm., 52
   fam., 52
Fellows Rd., 64, (est.), 66
fencing, 224
Fenrother, Rob., 230
Fentham:
   John Thos., 102
   Thos., 102
Fenton:
   Jas., 23
   Phil., 23
Fenton Ho., 17, 23, 27, 33
Ferguson:
   A. J., & Co., 237
   Wm., Jas., 36
Fermoy Rd., 200, 204
Fern Lodge, 69–71, 80
Ferncroft Ave., 74
Fernhead Rd., 218, 220
the Ferns, 39
Ferrers, Earl, see Shirley
Ferrier, Kath., 42
Field:
   Horace, 28–9, 37
   Wal., 29
Field Ct., 32
Fields, Gracie, 40
Fifth Ave., 219
Fiennes, Celia, 82
Finch, Edw., 117
Finchley, metropolitan boro., 84
Finchley Rd., 5, 11, 36, 39, 60–1
   retail trade, 129–30
the Firs, 68, 71, 75
First Ave., 219
Fisher, Geo., 70
fishing, 223
Fitzjohn's Ave., 27, 36–7
FitzOsbert, Wm., 190
Flecker, Jas. Elroy, 169
Fleet, riv., or Holborn, 3, 5, 138

Fleet laundry, 126
Fleet Rd., 55
Fleetwood, Hen., 108
Fleming:
   Sir Alex., 249
   Ian, 70
   John, 26
   O., 45
   Peter, 70
   Valentine, 70
Fleming Ct., 189
Fletcher:
   J. S., 137
   John (fl. 1694), 103
   John (fl. 1711), 67
   Mary, 103
   Nic., 110
Flitcroft:
   Hen. (d. 1769), 34, 105
   Hen. (d. 1826), 105
Flitcrofts est., 45–6, 105, 117
Flitcroft's farmho., 43
Flockhart, Wm., 210
Flood, Jas., 244–5
Flora hotel, 220
Florence Cayford (est.), 50
Flower, Eliza, 206
Foley Ho., 24, 26, 170
Folkes:
   Eliz., m. Sir Thos. Hanmer, 231
   Hen., 231
   Thos., 231
   Wm., 231
football, 88, 223–4
Ford:
   Christine, 104
   Florrie, 84
   Wm., 104
Fordwych Ct., 50
Fordwych Rd., 49
Forester, fam., 115
Formosa St., 213
Forrest, Revd. Rob. Wm., 256
Forster, Mat., 53, 96 n
Forsyth:
   Alan, 41
   Jane, wid. of Thos., 98
   Thos., 97
Fortune Green, see West End
Fortune Green Rd., 74
Foskett, see Allison
Foster:
   Jas., 128
   John, 34, 95, 106
   Mic., 169
   Rob., 110
Fountains Abbey P.H., 224
Fowler:
   Chas., 257
   Chris., 110
   Geof. le, 111
   Sir John, Bt., 181
Fox:
   Chas. Jas., 69
   Wm. Johnson, 206
Fox P.H., 22
Fox and Goose P.H., 18, 24, 125
Foxhanger, see Haverstock Hill
Francis, F. & H., 150, 256, 258–9
Francis St., 194
Francklin, Wm., and his sis. Martha,
   97
frankpledge, views of, 130–1, 241
Fraser:
   Maj.-Gen. Sir C. Cranford, 46
   Ian, 32
Frederick V, count palatine, 16
Frederick:
   Eliz., m. Sir John Morshead, 228
   Sir John, Bt. (d. 1755), 228, 233,
      254
   Sir John, Bt. (d. 1757), 228
   Selina, m. Rob. Thistlethwayte,
      228
   Sir Thos., Bt., 190, 228

Freeling, Sir Fras., 53
Freelove, Wm., 124
Freemasons' Arms P.H., 25, 89
French:
    Revd. J. B., 157
    John, earl of Ypres, 208
French:
    immigrants, q.v.
    schs., 270
French Protestant Ch., 263
Freud:
    Anna, 41, 66
    E. L., 40
    Sigmund, 41, 66, 239
Frewen:
    Anne, m. —— Buckner, 170
    Chas., 170
Friedenheim hosp., 61, 143
Frith, W. P., 179
Frobisher, Sir Martin, w. of, 9
Froggart, fam., 117
Frognal, in Hampstead, 8–9, 11, 21
    chs., 36, 41; pl. 25
    dom. bldgs., 34–42, 122; pls. 16,
        18, 28, 30
    farms and farmhos., 38, 115–20
        Snoxell's, 116–19
    flats, 39–41
    growth, 33–42
    halls and institutes, 41
    hotels, 128
    housing and council est., 41
    pub. hos., 34
    retail trade, 128
    roads, 36–42, 48–9
    Sailors' Orphan Girls' Home, 38
    workho., 34, 36
Frognal (rd.), 33, 38–40
Frognal Close, 40
Frognal Ct., 40
Frognal End, 39
Frognal Gdns., 39
Frognal Grove, 34
Frognal Hall, 34, 39–40, 110–11, 119;
    pl. 30
Frognal Ho., 33–4, 39, 167
Frognal Lane, 3
Frognal Mansions, 39
Frognal Pk., 35, 39–40
(Frognal) Priory, 35, 38; (another),
    38, 40
Frognal Way, 40
Fry:
    Chris., 216
    Eliz., 263
    Maxwell, 40
    Rog., 31
Fulham, 243
    sch., 165
Fulham Pl., 187
Fuller, Chas. Jas., 150
Fust:
    Edw., 111
    Jane, see Weeks
    Ric., 111
    —— (fl. 1660), 111

G.L.C., see Greater London Council
G.W.R., see Great Western Rly.
the Gables, 73
Gabo, Naum, 46, 59
Gainsborough, earls of, see Noel,
    Baptist, Edw., and Wriothesley
Gainsborough Gdns., 28
Gairdner, Jas., 30
Gaitskell, Hugh, 42
Gale, Sam., 22
Galloway, ctss. of, see Stewart
Galsworthy, John, 32
Gambier, Sam., 25, 108, 110
    his wid., 25
Games, Wm. Langhorne, 93
Gangmoor, 19, 24, 27
Gardner:
    Eleanor, see Combrune

Thos., 125
Gardnor, Thos., 18, 24
Gardnor Ho., 27, 29
Gardnor Mansions, 28
Gardnor Rd., 27
Gardnor's Pl., 24
Garlinge Rd., 49
Garner, Thos., 29–30
Garnett:
    J. C. M., 32
    Ric., 57
    Wm., 39
Garnett Rd., 55, 59
Garrett, E., 45
Garson Ho., 211
Garway Rd., 207, 212
Gas Light & Coke Co., 140, 251
Gascony Ave., 49
Gaselee, Alicia Mary, 272
Gate:
    Dorothy, m. Sir Thos. Jocelyn,
        100 n
    Edw., 100
    Sir Hen., and his w. Kath., 100
Gayton Cres., 27
Gayton est., 30
Gayton Rd., 27
Geayes:
    John, 233
    Martin, 233
Geddes, Alex., 255
Gee, Osgood, 106
Gelsthorp, John, 47
General (later British) Petroleum Co.,
    127
George III, 68
George V, 80
George, Ern., & Peto, 29, 210
George P.H., 16, 20, 22, 26, 125
Gerard, John, 75–6
Gerin of St. Giles, 95
Gerin (the) linendraper, 95
Germans, see immigrants
Gers, Gilb., 105
Gertler, Mark, 31, 66
Gibb:
    Alice, 104, 110
    Jas., 45
    John (fl. 1459), 110
    John (d. c. 1516), 110
    Thos. E., 57–8, 96
    Wm., 104, 110, 113
Gibberd, Sir Fred., 33
Gibbet Hill, see North End
Gibbon, Dr. Wm., 19, 83, 152
Gibbons:
    Grinling, 52
    Stella, 41, 59, 73
Gibbs:
    G. A., 258
    Hen. Huck, 35
    John, 111
    Ric., 42
    Thos., 111
    Wm., 258
    Messrs., 258
    and see Boehmer
Gibray Ho., 211
Gibson, Mrs. Milner, 193
Gilbert of Hendon, 93
Gilbert:
    Edw., 231
    Sir W. S., 188
    Wm., 230–1
Gilbert Sheldon Ho., 189
Gilberts est., 42 n, 47–8, 105, 117–18
Giles:
    Jas. Sharp, 98
    Peter, 98
Gilling:
    John, 110–11
    Thos., 110–11
Gilling Ct., 58
Gilling Lodge, 55
Gilpin, Wm. Sawrey, 187

Ginner, Chas., 32
Ginsberg, Morris, 40
Girls' Public Day School Trust, 168
Glastone, R. T., 166
Gladys Rd., 44
Glasgow Ho., 215, 217
Glastonbury St., 45
Glenbrook Rd., 45
Glendyne, Baron, see Nivison
Glenesk, Baron, see Borthwick
Glenilla Rd., 58
Glenloch Ct., 58
Glenloch Investment Co., 58
Glenloch Rd., 58
Glenmore Rd., 58
Gloucester, duke of, see William Fred.
Gloucester Cres., 199
Gloucester Gdns., 203
Gloucester Rd., 192
Gloucester Sq., 192
Gloucester Terr., 192, 201, 206–7,
    211
Gloucestershire, see Cheltenham
Goalen, Gerard, 153
Godfrey, Wm., 228, 233, 236
Godolphin Ho., 66
Godson, Geo., 213
Godwin (hermit), 100
Golden Spikes, 20
Golden Sq., 29
Golden Yard, 17
Golders Green, in Hendon, 155
Golders Hill, in Hendon, 75, 79–80
Goldfinger, Ernö, 31
Goldhurst Terr., 37
Goldicutt, John, 257
Goldney:
    Fras. Hastings, 218
    fam., 218
Goldney Rd., 218, 221
Goldsmith's Pl., 48
golf, 88
Gondar Gdns., 49
Goode, W. J., 29
Goodrich (Goodwike), Ric., 96
Goodwin:
    Geo., 104, 107
    Thos., 104
    Dr. Thos., 83
Gospel Oak, in St. Pancras, 14
    ch., 151
    nonconf. (protestant), 153, 156
    schs., 161
Goss:
    Art. Norman, 92
    fam., 92
Gothic Cottage, 70
Gotto, Edw., 28
Gough, Shane Hugh Maryon, Vct.
    Gough, 93
Gouldburn, Edw. Meyrick, dean of
    Norwich, 257
Goulding, Thos., 17
Gouvernet, marquise de, 229
Gowan, Jas., 41
Granary Ho., 23
Grand Junction Arms P.H., 224
Grand Junction canal, 174–5, 182,
    199, 232; pls. 40, 43; and see
    Paddington canal
Grand Junction Canal Co., 175, 182,
    232, 237, 242–4, 246, 248, 263,
    267
    est., 198, 228, 232
Grand Junction Co., 239
    est., 232–3
Grand Junction Rd., 194
Grand Junction St., 175, 191–2, 194
Grand Junction Waterworks Co., 192,
    228, 232, 246
    reservoirs, 192, 194, 246, 256
Grand Union Canal Co., 232
the Grange (Frognal), 36, 41
the Grange (Kilburn), 48–9, 85
Grange Gdns., 41

Grant:
  Revd. Chas., 34, 133
  Duncan, 65
Grantully Rd., 214
Graves, Wm., 147
Gray:
  Alex. (fl. 1889), 39
  Alex. (fl. 1968), 142
  ——, builder, 45
Great Western (later Great Western Royal) hotel, 179, 238
Great Western Rly. (G.W.R.):
  Co., 174–5, 178–9, 225, 228, 242, 244, 247, 266, 271
  line, 173, 178–9, 183, 199
  parcels depot, 202
  stas.:
    Paddington main line terminus, 178–9, 181, 183; *pl.* 39; stables, 235; workforce, 236
    Paddington suburban (Bishop's Rd.), 179, 181
    Royal Oak, 179, 199
    Westbourne Pk., 179, 200
Great Western Rd., 200
Greater London Council (G.L.C.), 84, 225, 244, 264
  as housing authy., 62, 185, 202, 215, 217, 220, 232
  dept. of mechanical engineering, 126
  pks. and open spaces, 75, 80–1
Greek Orthodox Ch., 264
  cathedral, 208, 264; *pl.* 35
Green:
  Leslie W., 8
  T. K., 27, 37
  Thos., 47, 105 *n*
  Wal., 47, 105 *n*
  Wm., min. of Hampstead, 146 *n*
  Wm. Curtis, 240
Green Hill, 18, 90
Green Lane, 175
Green Man Lane, 24
Green Man P.H., 19, 22, 82, 84, 86, 170
Green St., 187
Greenaway, Kate, 38
Greenaway Gdns., 40
Greencroft Gdns., 38
Greenhill, fam., 106
Greenhill est., 27, 30
Greenhill (flats), 28, 31, 110; *pl.* 15
Greenhill (ho.), 109
Greenhill Rd., 27
Greenwood, Ant., Baron Greenwood of Rossendale, 33
Greenwood, bros., 43
Gregory, Barnard, 35
Gregory & Bence, 124
Greig, fam., 235
Grendon, And. de, and his w. Sibyl, 92–3, 95
Grenfell, J. S. Granville, 166
Grenville:
  Geo. Nugent-Temple-, marquess of Buckingham, 231
  Wm. Wyndham, Baron Grenville, 69
Greville:
  Hon. Chas., 186
  Sir Fulk, 226
Greville Estates, 50
Greville Ho., 224–5
Greville Mews, 48
Greville Pl., 47, 51
Greville Rd., 48, 51
Grew's hotel, 128
Griffen, Wm., 113
Grigson, Geof., 32, 71
Grittleton Hall (Wilts.), 229
Gropius, Wal., 59
Grosvenor, Hugh Lupus, duke of Westm., 79–80
Grosvenor Ct. hotel, 239

Grosvenor Mansions, 195
Grove:
  Ant., 116
  Thos., 116
the Grove, 20, 23, 27
Grove Cottage, 34
Grove Ho. (Belsize), 52
Grove Ho. (Hampstead town), 19, 23, 26–7
Grove Lodge, 20, 23, 32
Grove Pl., 29
Guildford, dean of, *see* Bridge
Guinness:
  Edw. C., earl of Iveagh, 70, 80
  Wal. Edw., Baron Moyne, 70
Gulbenkian, Calouste Sarkis, 195
gunmaking, 237
Gunn, Jas., 75
Gurdon, F., bp. of Hull, 256
Gurney, Emilia Russell, 256
Gutch, Geo., 192–4, 206, 213, 217, 253, 257
Guyana, high commission of, 210
Guyon, Steph., 34
Guyon Ho., 18, 23
gymnastics, 224

H.J.R., *see* Hampstead Junction Rly.
Haberdashers' Aske's Sch., 160, 162, 165–6
Habershon, W. G., 262
Hackney Coll., 154, 157
Hackworth, Alf., 28
Haggerston, Sir Carnaby, Bt., 191
Haines:
  Alf., 218
  Geo., 272
  ——, builder, 44
Haley, John, 117; *and see* Hawley
Hall:
  Benj. Edw., 187
  Sir Chas., 206
  J., architect, 260
  Jas., 228
  John, 254
  Mat., & Co., 238
  Mrs., 52
Hall, Stan., Easton & Robertson, 62
Hall & Waterhouse, 29
Hall Oak farm, 38, 95, 116–19
Hall Pl. (formerly Pk.), 187
the Hall sch., 65, 166
Hallfield (est.), 203, 209, 211
Hamilton:
  Alex., 5
  Lady, *see* Hart, Emma
Hamilton & Clarke, 5
Hamilton Ct., 215, 217
Hammersmith, 243
  schs., 269
Hammersmith and City Rly., 179
Hammond, J. L., and his w. Barbara, 73; *and see* Wilson
Hamon, s. of Roger, 102
Hampshire, *see* Southwick Pk.
Hampshire Ho., 195, 197
Hampstead, **1–172**, 252, *10, 12, 14–15*
  adv., 145
  agric., 111–21
  bailiwick, 130
  baths, 87, 136, 144
  boro., *see* Hampstead, metropolitan boro.
  boundaries, 1–3, 60, 67
  bridges, 5
  burial bd., 136, 144
  cage, 139
  cemeteries, 44–5, 74, 105, 144
  Chalcots, *q.v.*
  Chalk Farm, *q.v.*
  chars., 28, 169–72
    Wells char., 28, 144, 161–2, 169–71
  charters, 1–3, 8, 92–3
  Childs Hill, *q.v.*

  chs., 145–52; *pls.* 19–27
  coach svces., 5
  common pasture, 112
  communications, 3–8, *4*
  conservation areas, 33, 60, 66
  Cricklewood, *q.v.*
  dispensaries, 141
  drainage, 3
  electricity, 140
    power sta., 127, 140
  fairs, 78, 123, 131
  fire, 140–1
  friendly socs., 89–90
  Frognal, *q.v.*
  gas, 140
  gentrification, 33
  geol., 3
  Hampstead Heath, *q.v.*
  Hampstead town, *q.v.*
  hosps., 29, 71, 141–4
  inclosure, 9
  ind., 123–30
  Jews, 158–9
  lecturer, 146
  librs., 90, 136, 141
  Littleworth, *q.v.*
  magistrates' ct., 31
  man. and other est., 92–111, *94*
    Hampstead man., 92–5; cts., 130–1; customs, 114; demesne, 36, 93, 111–13, 115–16, 120; grange and hall, 95, 111; man. ho., 34–5, 95, 116, 131
  metropolitan boro., 2–3, 80, 85, 136
    as housing authy., 32, 41, 46, 50
    arms, *136*
    wards, 136
  mills, 122–3
    windmills, 17, 20, 122–3
  missions, 158; *and see* London Diocesan Home
  mkt. gdns. and nurseries, 120–1
  mortuary, 144
  nonconf. (protestant), 153–8
  North End, *q.v.*
  omnibus svces., 5–6
  par. officers, 133
  par. wards, 135
  pks. and open spaces, 144–5; *and see* Hampstead Heath
  police, 139–40
  poorhos., 71–2, 134
  poor relief, 134
  pop., 9, 11, 14–15
  pound, 131–2
  Primrose Hill, *q.v.*
  rlys. and Underground rlys., 6–8
    stas., 7–8, 36
  pub. hos., 81, 84
  Ratepayers' Assoc., 65, 136–7
  retail trade, 128–9
    chamber of commerce, 129–30
    tradesmen's assoc., 128
  roads, 3, 5
  Rom. Cathm., 149, 152–3, 159–60
    convents, 153
  Sandgate, *see* North End
  St. John's Wood, *q.v.*
  schs., 89, 159–69, 265, 267, 269; *and see* Haberdashers' Aske's; University College sch.
  sewerage, 135, 139
  soc. life, 81–92
  Spaniard's End, *q.v.*
  stocks, 131
  Swiss Cottage, *q.v.*
  tithes, 95, 145
  town hall, 136
  tram svces., 6
  vestry offices, 135
  vicarage ho., 146
  vicars, par. priests, and ministers, 145–7; as patrons, 151; *and see* Ainger; Nalton
  watchhos., 131, 139

Hampstead (*cont.*)
water, 138–9
West Hampstead, *see* Hampstead, West
wkhos., 26, 134–5, 143
woodland, 111–12, 121–2; St. John's Wood, 122; Whitebirch wood, 75, 115, 121; *and see* Kilburn: Kilburn wood
Hampstead, West, 14, 46, 126
chs., 148
Jews, 158
nonconf. (protestant), 154, 157
schs., 159
tradesmen's assoc., 129
trading centre, 127
Hampstead and Highgate Express, 32, 72, 92, 126
Hampstead Annual, 91
Hampstead Antiquarian and Historical Soc., 57, 91
Hampstead Artists' council, 141
Hampstead Brewery, 125
Hampstead brook, 76
Hampstead Conservatoire, 85, 90–1
Hampstead Ethical Institute, 65
Hampstead Football News, 88
Hampstead Garden Suburb, in Hendon and Finchley, 65, 70, 74, 80
Hampstead Gen. hosp., 142–3
Hampstead Grove, 20
Hampstead Hall, 95
Hampstead Heath, 144–5
acreage, 75, 80
Branch Hill, 76
cinema shows, 85
digging, 75–7
drainage, 75–6
ponds, 76
East Heath, 75, 77–9, 117
East Pk., 75, 78–9, 93, 115
brickfields, 79, 124
geol., 1, 75–6
gibbet, 77
Hampstead Heath Protection Fund, 79
inclosures, 75
Lower Heath, 75
military events, 77, 89
North Heath, 75, 79
origins and development, 75–81
parliamentary disputes, 78–9
popular resort, 77–8; *pl.* 8
prehistoric settlement, 75
roads and tracks, 79–80
romantic appeal, 77
Sandy Heath, 75–7, 79
Upper Heath, 75
vegetation, 75–6; *and see* Hampstead: woodland, Whitebirch wood
West Heath, 75, 79
and see Golders Hill; Hampstead Heath Extension; Kenwood; Parliament Hill; Parliament Hill Fields
Hampstead Heath, *see* Baker, Thos.
Hampstead Heath Extension, in Hendon, 75, 80, 170
Hampstead Heath Extension cttee., 79
Hampstead Heath hotel, 72–3, 128
Hampstead Heath Protection soc., 71, 80, 90
Hampstead Hill Gdns., 27
Hampstead Hill Mansions, 29
Hampstead Historical Soc., 92
Hampstead Junction Rly. (H.J.R.), 7, 43, 48, 56, 72, 96–7, 105, 107–8, 124
Hampstead Mansions, 28
Hampstead Middle Class Defence League, 137
Hampstead Model Steam Laundry, 126

Hampstead Municipal Electors' Assoc., 137
Hampstead Music Trust, 148
Hampstead Pharmacy, 128
Hampstead Plating Works, 127
Hampstead Sq., 19
Hampstead Towers hotel, 128
Hampstead town, 8, 9, 11, *21*
assembly rooms, 83, 85, 89, 91
chs., 11, 25–6, 148–51; *pls.* 19–23, 26
churchyard, 24, 148
dispensary, 26
dom. bldgs., 16–20, 22–33; *pl.* 31
Everyman cinema, 86; theatre, 28, 85, 89
farm, 104
flats, 28–32
growth, 15–33
halls and institutes, 26, 28, 83, 85
Constitutional club, 83, 91
Moreland hall, 28, 85
hotels, 127–8
ind., 124–5
nonconf. (protestant), 26, 154–8
ponds, 15, 138
pop. (hos.), 22
poverty, 29
pub. hos., 16–20, 22–4, 81–4, 125
retail trade, 20, 22, 30, 33, 128–30
roads and courts, 16–33; *pls.* 1, 2, 4, 20
Rom. Cathm., 25–6, 152
Royal Sailors' Daughters' Home, 26
Monro Ho., 26, 167
Royal Soldiers' Daughters' Home, 26–7, 32, 55, 109, 161, 167
schs., 26, 29, 159–64
Heath Mount, *pl.* 14
South End Green, 28, 30–1
well (town), 15, 82, 138
wells (spa), 5, 17, 47, 82–3
ballroom, 19, 32, 83
chapel, 19, 22, 26, 82, 146, 148, 152, 170
entertainments, 82–3
Great Room, 19, 82, 148, 152
Long Room, 18–19, 22, 24, 28–9, 32, 81, 83, 89, 133; *pl.* 3
trustees, 82
Wells Ho., 19, 22, 24, 83
and see Hampstead: chars.: Wells char.
Hampstead Volunteers, 26, 37, 89
drill hall, 28, 89
Hampstead Water Co., 71, 76, 138
Hampstead Women's Local Govt. Assoc., 137
Hancock:
Ant., 152
Wal., 178
Hancock Nunn Ho., 66
Hankin, Chas., 124
Hankins, Thos., 76
Hanmer:
Eliz., *see* Folkes
Sir Thos., Bt., 231
Hanningham, Ric., 112
Hanwell, lunatic asylum, 247–8
Harben:
Sir Hen., 136, 141
Phil., 59
Harben (est.), 62
Harben Rd., 61
Hardey:
Chas. Maddocks, 109
Eliz., *see* Regnier
Hardie, Thos. Kincaid, 272; *and see* Hardy
Hardman, Revd. O., 256
Hardy, Thos., 200, 202; *and see* Hardey; Hardie
Hardy Ho., 203
Hare, C. G., 149

Hare and Hounds P.H., 67, 70–1
Haringey, Lond. boro., 81
Harley, Rob., earl of Oxford, 9
Harley Rd., 64
Harmsworth:
Alf., 72
Alf., Vct. Northcliffe, 30, 46, 72, 92, 165–6
Cecil, Baron Harmsworth, 72
Sir Geof., Bt., 32
Harold, Vct. Rothermere, 57, 70, 72, 257
fam., 61, 72
Harper, Mr. (fl. 1802), 199
harriers, 87
Harrington, D. E., 40
Harris:
Capt. Edw., 52
Edw., 125
John, 52
Thos., 69
Harrison:
John, 148
Wm., 107
Harrison Homes, 224
Harrods Ltd., 240
Harrow, Lond. boro., 185
Harrow Rd., 174, 218
Blomfield Terr., 200
Chippenham Terr., 218
pub. hos., 221
turnpike gates, 174
Harrow Road and Paddington Tramways Co., 178
Harrow sch., 174
Hart:
Emma (later Lady Hamilton), 186
Geo. (fl. 1816), 156
Geo. (fl. 1900), 74
Sir John, ld. mayor of Lond., 76
Harvard Ct., 46
Harvey:
Edw., 97
Frances, *see* Beckwith
Geo., 102
Jas., 156
Harvist, Edw., 3
Hatch, Sam., 68, 71
Hatch's Bottom, *see* Vale of Health
Hatherley Ct., 202–3
Hatherley Rd., 203
Haunch of Venison P.H., 18, 22, 108
Havelock Hall training coll., 41
Haverstock Hill, 1, 3, 55, 60, 63
Devonshire Pl., 55
Foxhanger, 1
St. John's Pk. Villas, 55
turnpike gate, 5
Windsor Terr., 55
Haverstock Lodge, 53, 55, 57–9, 97–8, 116
Haverstock Terr., *see* Belsize Grove
Hawk P.H., 19, 22, 24
hawking, 75
Hawkins:
John Tanner, 125
Rohde, 258
Hawley (or Haley), Thos., 9, 52
Hawthorne Ho., 29
Haydon, Benj. Rob., 193, 255
Hayes, Edwin, 64
Hayter, Thos., perpetual curate of Paddington, 253
Headfort, mchnss. of, *see* Taylour
Health, Min. of, 223
Health and Social Security, Dept. of, 232
the Heath (ho.), 68
Heath and Old Hampstead Protection soc., 80–1, 84, 92
Heath Brow, 70–1, 81
Heath Cottage, 31
Heath End Ho., 68, 70–1
Heath Ho. (Hampstead town), 24

Heath Ho. (Littleworth), 68–71
Heath Lodge, 68–71, 75, 80
  Hill Gdns., 80–1
Heath Mansions, 29
Heath St., 3, 17–18, 23, 25
  19th-cent. rebldg., 28
Heath View, 69
Heath Villas, 72
Heathfield Ho., 19, 27, 55, 97
Heathlands, 69–71, 80; pl. 29
Heathside, 24
Heber:
  Reg., 231
  Reg., his s., 231
Hedgerley Wood (Bucks.), sch., 168
Hedham, see Luke
Helling, Edw., 24
Helmsdale Ho., 215, 217
Hemet, Jane, alias Mrs. Lessingham, 69
Hemstel Rd., 44
Henderson:
  And., 120
  Jas. Stewart, 171–2
Henderson Ct., 32
Hendon, Gilb. of, see Gilbert
Hendon, 67, 102, 113, 169–70
  Brent Cross shopping centre, 129–30
  cemetery, 252
  ch., 95, 102, 145
  Golders Green, q.v.
  Golders Hill, q.v.
  Hampstead Garden Suburb, q.v.
  Hampstead Heath Extension, q.v.
  mans., 93; and see Hodford and Cowhouse; Wildwood; Wyldes
  nonconf. (protestant), 156–7
  schs., 160, 166
Henry I, 92
Henry VI, 99
Henry VIII, 99–100, 124
Henry, Rob., ? par. priest of Hampstead, 146
Hepworth, Dame Barbara, 59
Herbert, abbot of Westm., 100
Herbert:
  Sir Hen., 105
  John Rogers, 27, 49
Herd (or Cowherd), fam., 115
Hereford Lodge hosp., 249
Hereford Rd., 200, 203, 207
Herford, Dr. Brooke, 155
Hermes Point, 221
Hermitage St., 187
Herne:
  Basil (d. 1729), 108–9, 131
  Basil (d. 1774), 108
  Jos., 133 n
Hero of Maida P.H., 212
Herries St., 219
Herriott, Chas., 111
Hertford hotel, 239
Hertfordshire, see Aldenham
Hervey:
  Thos., 231
  Capt. Thos., 231
  Wm., 231
Herzen, Alex., 203
Hesketh, Rob., 147
Hetherington, Ann, 35
Hethpool St., 188
Hewett, Edw. Jas., 213
Heynes, Phil., min. of Hampstead, 146 n
Heysham Terr., 44
Heyward, Hen., 235
Hibbert:
  Hester, m. Thos. Blunden, 109
  (or Hubbard), John, 109
  (or Hubbert), Wm., and his w. Hester, 109
Hicks:
  Baptist, Vct. Campden, 93, 145
  Eliz., Vctss. Campden, 169

Juliana, m. Edw. Noel, Vct. Campden, 93
Hide, Ralph, 228
Higginson Ho., 66
High Close, 28
High St., 3, 15–17; pl. 2
  19th-cent. rebldg., 28
Highbury Coll., 154
Highgate, in St. Pancras (part), 78, 81, 194 n
Hilgrove (est.), 62
Hilgrove Rd., 61, 63
Hill:
  G. H., 127
  H., 73
  Jane, see Snoxell
  Jas., 164
  John, 222, 235
  Mat. Davenport, 72
  Octavia, 79–80
  Oliver, 40
  Sir Rowland, 26, 29, 143, 206
  Rowland, Baron (later Vct.) Hill, 199, 231
  Wm., 235
the Hill (ho.), 69, 144
Hill Ho. (Frognal), 40
Hill Ho. (Littleworth), 69–70
Hill View, 66
Hillcrest Ct., 50
Hillfield, 55, 59, 97
Hillfield Ct., Mansions, 59
Hillfield Estates, 59
Hillfield est., 42
Hillfield Rd., 44
Hilliard:
  Edw., 204
  Rob., 204
Hillsborough Ct., 50
Hillside Ct., 40
Hitchcock, Wm., 42
Hitchman's Bldgs., 24
Hoar, Wm., 82
Hoare:
  E. Brodie, 137
  Fras., 70, 161
  Hannah, m. Thos. Pryor, 26
  Hannah, w. of Sam. (d. 1825), 70, 162–3
  John Gurney, 69–70, 74, 79, 89–90, 135–6, 163
  Jos., 74, 106
  Juliana, 149
  Sir Sam., Bt., 70
  Sam. (d. 1825), 26, 53, 69, 162–4; his fa., 69
  Sam. (d. 1847), 68–70, 74, 106
  Sarah, 163
  Misses (fl. 1911), 70
  fam., 26–7, 69–70, 148
Hoare's bank, 68
Hobhouse, E. G., 270
hockey, 87
Hodford and Cowhouse est., in Hendon, 114
Hodges est., 27, 107
Hodgeson, see Hodgson
Hodgkinson, Enoch, 104
Hodgson (Hodgeson):
  John, 36
  Wm., min. of Hampstead, 146 n
Hodilow, Ric., 16, 33
Hogan Mews, 189
Hogarth, Wm., 67, 190, 254
Hogg:
  Geo., 235
  Jas., 235
  Thos., 235
  Thos., jr., 235
  Thos. Jefferson, 214
Hogman's farm, 103
Holborn:
  com. of sewers, 139
  metropolitan boro., 137
Holborn, riv., see Fleet

Holford:
  Chas., 23, 27
  Josiah, 23
  Mary Anne, see Toller
  Sarah, 19
  fam., 23, 27
Holford Ho., 19, 27
Holford Rd., 19
Holgate, John, 96, 103
Holiday, Hen., 30, 37, 41, 155, 258
Holiday Inn, 128
Holl:
  Frank, 37
  Wm., 65
Holly Bush Hill, 23; pl. 1
Holly Bush hotel, 127
Holly Bush P.H., 23, 83, 89
Holly Bush Vale, 28
Holly Corporation, 71
Holly Cottage, 18
Holly Hedge Cottage, 19
Holly Hill, 20
Holly Hill Ho., 17, 23, 31, 169
Holly Pl., 25
Hollybush Hill (ho.), 67
Hollycot, 73
Hollycroft Ave., 74
Holmdale Mansions, 45
Holmdale Rd., 45
Holmfield Ct., 59
Holt, Fras., 152
Holtham Rd., 61
Holyland, John, 116
Holyland farm, 52, 97, 116
Home Counties Newspapers, 92
Home Treatment of Disease by Diet, 61
Homerton Coll., 154
Honeybourne Rd., 46
Honeycombe, G., his Red Watch, 251
Honywood:
  Anne, see Pitchford
  Benoni, 34
  Edw., 110
  Fraser, 110
  Isaac (d. 1721), 16, 110, 154
  Isaac (d. 1740), 110
  Sir John, Bt., 110
  Sir John Courtenay, Bt., 110
  Ralph, 153–4
  Rebecca, see Pitchford
  —— (fl. 1762), 24
  fam., 25
Honywood est., 16, 25, 110
Hoop and Bunch of Grapes P.H., 81
Hooper, Wm., 73
Hope, Sisters of, 153
Hope P.H., 193
Hope Cottage, 68
Hopgood:
  Fras., 235
  Thos., 235
Hopkins:
  Gerard Manley, 36
  Manley, 36
  Mic., 32
Hopper, Thos., 249
Hormead Rd., 200, 204
Hornblower, Geo., 39
Horne, H. P., 256
Horrex, Edm., 107–8
horse races, 77, 82, 86
Horseley, Wm., 53
Horton, Rob. F., 157
Horton Ices, 238
Horvitch, Levy Benj., 62
Horwell, Arnold R., 127
Hospitality Inn, 210, 239
Hospitallers' est., see Temples
Houghton, Art. Boyd, 65
Houlditch:
  Edw., 106
  Ric., 106
Housden, Brian, 33
Housley, Sam. John, 150

Houston, Lady, *see* Byron, Fanny
Howard:
Eliz. Jane, 33, 216
(formerly Upton), Fulk Greville, 47–8, 101
Ric., earl of Effingham, 111
T., 74
Howell, Jas., 82
Howell & Amis, 33
Howell St., 188
Howitt, Wm., 78, 81
Howitt Ct., 58
Howitt Rd., 58
Howley Pl., 187
Hoxton, *see* Shoreditch
Hubbard, *see* Hibbert
Hubbert, *see* Hibbert
Hudson:
Emily, *see* Wingrove
W. H., 203, 239
Hügel, Friedrich von, 28
Hughes:
Ric., 20, 104
Thos., 230
Huguenot Home for French Governesses, 65
Hulbert, John S., 100
Hull, bp. of, *see* Gurdon
Humbert, Fras., 212
Hume:
Eliza Anne, 172
Jos., 136
Humez, Wal. de, abbot of Westm., 92
Humphreys:
Chas., and his wid. Sarah, 104
Sir John, 230
Hunt:
Jas. Hen. Leigh, 13, 43, 72, 77
Wal., 114
Wm., 110, 114
Hunt Cottage, 72–3
Hunter, Marg., 270
Hunter's Lodge, 53, 59
hunting, 75, 82, 122
Huntingdon, *see* Countess of Huntingdon's Connexion
Husband, Mat. Thos., 35
Hussey:
Nat., 108
Peter, 108
Sarah, 108
Thos., 16, 108
Thos., bp. of Waterford, 152
Hutchinson Ho., 66
Hutton, Barbara, 71
Huxley:
Aldous, 40
Leonard, 39–40
and see Battersbury
Hyde man., in Westm., 241
Hyde Pk., in Westm., 173, 191
Hyde Pk. Cres., 197
Hyde Pk. est. (Church Com.), 196–7, 228
Hyde Pk. Gdns., *see* Bayswater Rd.
Hyde Pk. Mews, 197
Hyde Pk. Pl., *see* Bayswater Rd.
Hyde Pk. Sq., 192, 197
Hyde Pk. St., 193
Hyde Pk. Towers, 209–10
Hyde-Harrison, David, 50
Hyndman, Hen., 30

I.C.E. Group, 221
I.L.E.A., *see* Inner London Education Authority
ice cream making, 238
ice merchant, 237
Ilbert St., 220
Ilchester, Ric., bp. of Winchester, 92
Immaculate Heart of Mary, Missionary Sisters of, 153
immigrants:
Austrian, 15, 42, 239
Commonwealth, 15

French, 14, 24, 69, 152
German, 14–15, 85
Indian, 51
Irish, 14–15, 50–1, 84, 152, 182, 185
Jewish, 14–15, 42, 50, 85
Pakistani, 51
Polish, 15, 42
Russian, 15
United States, 14
West Indian, 51, 185, 202
Imperial Gas Light & Coke Co., 140, 251
Inchbald, Eliz., 191
Independents, *see* Congregationalists
India, high commission of, 42
and see Coorg; Oudh
Indians, *see* immigrants
industry, *see* bicycle making; brewing; brick and tile making; builders; cartridge making; cement merchants; coal merchants; cocoa mill; conveyance; dressmaking; engineering; gunmaking; ice cream making; ice merchant; laboratory supplying; laundering; metal working; motor car dealers and repairers; oil depots; paper; parquet floor making; perforating machine making; piano making; pill making; printing; rubbish and manure collecting; slaughtering; stained glass artists; timber merchants; wood working; zip fastener making
Ingham Rd., 45
Inglewood Rd., 45
Inglish:
Benj. Hanson, 53
Jas., 53
Ingram, Perkins & Co., 237
Inner London Education Authority (I.L.E.A.), 160, 225, 266, 269
Innos, John, 35
Institute of Occult Social Science Religion, 158
International Catholic Soc. for Girls, 260
Inver Ct., 209
Inverforth, Baron, *see* Weir
Inverforth Ho., 71
Invergarry Ho., 215
Inverness Ct. hotel, 211, 239
Inverness Terr., 206–7, 211
Ireton, Eliz., 106
Irish, *see* immigrants
Irongate Wharf Rd., 187
Irving:
Edw., 157
Washington, 84
Irvingites, *see* Catholic Apostolic Church
Islington turnpike trustees, 76
Isokon flats, 59–60
Iveagh, earl of, *see* Guinness, Edw.
Iverson Rd., 44, 127
Ivy Bank, 53, 58
Ivy Cottage, 206–7

Jack Straw's Castle P.H., 67–9, 71, 81, 84, 90, 117, 130–1; *pl. 7*
Jacksfield est., 110–11
Jackson:
Dorothy, *see* Little
Fras., 77
Geo., 156
Hugh, 25
Sir John, 24
John, bp. of Lond., 151
John, artist, 64
John Mills, 106
Thos. Graham, 33, 147
bros. (fl. 1857), 26
fam., 33
Jacobs, Dr. Louis, 264

James I, 16, 81
James II, 81
James:
C. H., 32
Hen., 37
John (fl. 1521), 113
John (fl. 1951), 177
Revd. John, 254
Mary, m. Rob. Dixon, 17
Rob. (d. 1618), 17, 33, 119
Rob., his s., 17
Rob. (? another), 104 n
Susan, m. —— Nutting, 17
Jay, Hen., 47
Jealous, Geo. Sam., 72, 92, 126
Jehovah's Witnesses, 263
Jenkins:
Geo. Thos., 200
Revd. Rob. Chas., 200
W. H., 200
Wm. Kinnaird, 200–1, 207, 212
Jenkinson, Edw., 101
Jerome, Jerome K., 59
Jesus, Society of, 153
Jewish Domestic Training Home, 65
Jews, 14–15, 42, 50, 157–9, 264–5
schs., 163, 168–9, 264–6, 270
Spanish and Portuguese, 265
and see immigrants
Joad, C. E. M., 32, 73
Joan of Arc, 263
Joass, *see* Belcher
Jocelyn, *see* Joscelin; Josselyn
Jodrell:
Judith, *see* Sheldon
Paul, 228
John, King, 102
John, par. priest of Hampstead, 146
John, s. of Gerin of St. Giles, 96
John, Sir Wm. Goscombe, 50
John Aird Ct., 189
John St., 25
Johnson:
A. P., 103
Hilda M., 168
John, 155, 210, 258
Lancelot, 165
Dr. Sam., 34, 122
Susan, w. of Wm., 109
Thos. (d. by 1626), 272
Thos. (d. 1644), 76
Wm., 16, 109
Johnson Ho., 66
Johnson's Yard, 25 n
Jolly, J. E., 32
Jolly Gardeners P.H., 198, 221
Jones:
Alb., 128
Owen, 178
Jones Bros., 129
Jonson, Ben, 221
Joscelin of Chichester, and his w. Aubrey, 93
Joseph:
Delissa, 158, 210
Sir Maxwell, 209
N. S., 264
and see Audesley
Josselyn (Jocelyn):
Dorothy, *see* Gate
Edw., 100
Hen., 100
Mary, *see* Lamb
Sir Thos., 100
Joy, Geo. Wm., 208, 211
Joyce, Jeremiah, 155
Jubilee line, 7
Judges Bench Ho., 34
Judges' Walk, 79
Jurden, Wm., 111

Kanep, Gilb. le, 95, 113 n
Keats, John, 25, 77, 214
Keats Grove, 25, 31
Keats Ho., 25, 33, 141

Keble, Jos., 67
Keble Coll., Oxford, 258
Keck:
  Ant., 110
  Fras., 110
Keep the Aspidistra Flying, see Orwell
Keith Ho., 215
Kellond, Chas., 37
Kelly:
  Edw., 37
  Herb., 37
Kelson St., 48
Kelston, 38
Kelyng, Edw., 101
Kemble, Chas., 231
Kemp:
  Fras., 106
  John, 106
  Ric., 107–8, 121
  fam., 115
Kempe:
  Thos., bp. of Lond., 99
  Thos. (? more than one), 99, 113, 226
  Wm., 99, 113
Kemplay Rd., 28
Kendal Ct., 50
Kendal St., 192
Kendall, H. E., 135, 151, 257
Kendrick, Jos., 147
Kenn:
  Chris., 102
  Eliz., *see* Cholmeley
Kennedy:
  Archibald, marquess of Ailsa, 208
  Mrs., singer, 247
Kensal Ho., 218, 220–1
Kensal New Town, in Chelsea detached, later in Kensington, 200–1, 218–19
  nonconf. (protestant), 261
Kensington, 173, 183–4, 200, 218, 230–1, 233, 243
  ch. (St. Mary Abbot's), 181
  hosps., 249
    St. Charles, 248–9
  Kensal New Town, *q.v.*
  Kensington Palace, 173
  Kensington Palace Gdns., 173
  man. and other est., 199–200; *and see* Ladbroke; Notting Barns; Portobello
  nonconf. (protestant), 261
  poor law union, 243
  schs., 266, 270
Kensington Gdns., in Paddington and Westm., 173, 252
Kensington Gdns. Sq., 206–7, 212
Kensington Gravel Pits, in Paddington and Kensington, 205
Kent, Eliz., 254
Kent, *see* Charlton; Quex Pk.; Tunbridge Wells; Westgate-on-Sea
Kent's Pl., 188
Kenwood (Cane Wood), in St. Pancras, 3, 67, 75, 78–80, 93
Kenwood Ho., 80
Kenwood Preservation Council, 80
Kenwrick:
  Edw., 229
  Eliz., 229, 233
  Wm., 233
Kerrison:
  Rob. M., 35
  Wm., 25, 124
Kesteven, Thos., 43
Ketteridge:
  Sarah, 52
  Thos., 51–2
  —— (fl. *c.* 1740), 52
Key:
  Eliz., wid. of Jonathan, 109
  Hen. Garrett, 109
  Sir John, Bt., 109
  Jonathan, 104, 109

Jonathan Hen., 109
  Wm., 107
  Wm. Cade, 104
Keyham Ho., 203
Keys:
  Chas., 20
  Eliz., 82
Keyser, Eliezer Isaac, 158
Kidderpore Ave., Gdns., 74
Kidderpore Hall, 44, 74, 104; *and see* Westfield Coll.
Kilburn:
  John de, 47, 113
  Maud of, 113 *n*
  fam., 47
Kilburn, in Hampstead (part), 8–9, 14
  assembly rooms ('Kilburn town hall'), 83–4
  chs., 48–9, 256–7
  dom. bldgs., 48–9, 51
  farms and farmhos., 47–9, 101, 106, 117–19
  flats, 49–51
  growth, 47–51
  halls and institutes, 83–4
  housing and council est., 50–1
  ind., 124–7
  Irish, 14–15, 50–1, 152
  Jews, 50, 158
  lodging hos., 128
  nonconf. (protestant), 154–6
  pks. and open spaces, 49
  pop. (hos.), 47, 51
  poverty, 13–14, 50
  priory, 42, 47, 95, 101, 113 *n*, 122
    bldgs., 101
    priors, 175
  pub. hos., 47–9, 51, 81, 83–4
  retail trade, 51, 128–30
    chamber of trade, 128
  roads, 47–51; *pl.* 10
  Rom. Cathm., 14, 152–3
  schs., 49–50, 159, 162–5, 169
  Theatre Royal (later Kilburn Empire Theatre of Varieties), 84
  wells, 47, 83
  wood, 100–1, 106, 122
Kilburn Bon Marché, 129
Kilburn Bridge farm, 212–13, 252
Kilburn brook, 3, 5, 138
Kilburn Grange, 49, 106, 144
Kilburn High Rd., 49, 51, 126; *pl.* 10
  Priory works, 126
  St. George's Terr., 128
Kilburn Lane, 47, 219
Kilburn Pk. Rd., 213, 217
Kilburn Priory (rd.), 48
Kilburn Priory or Gate (est.), 50
Kilburn priory est., 11, 42, 47–8, 50–1, 100–1, 111, 117
Kilburn Sisters, 148, 214, 225, 255, 270
Kilburn Vale (est.), 51
Kilburn Woods est., 49–50, 101, 116–20
Killett:
  Leonard, 134
  Silvester, 67
King:
  Chas. Bean, 13, 28–9
  Frances, 271
  John, 101
  Wm., 207
King and Queen P.H., 222
King Edward's Hosp. Fund, 143, 270
King Henry's Rd., 64
King of Bohemia's Head P.H., 125, 132, 138
King William IV P.H., 16
King-Harmon, Sir Chas., 145
King's Arms P.H., 16, 22
King's Coll., Cambridge, fellow of, 253
King's College Mews, 65
King's College Rd., 64

King's Fund coll., *see* Bayswater
King's Gdns., 49
King's Head P.H. (Bayswater), 204, 221
King's Head P.H. (Hampstead town), 16, 20, 89
Kingdom, Wm., 63, 192, 207
Kingdon, Emmeline, 45
Kingdon Rd., 45
Kinghall or Kingswell est., 20, 27, 104, 111, 118
Kingscroft Rd., 49
Kingsgate (est.), 46
Kingsgate Mews, Pl., Rd., 49
Kingswell:
  Geof. de, 104, 113 *n*
  Rob. de, 104
  fam., 15
Kingswell est., *see* Kinghall
Kingswood Ct., 50
Kirkhoven:
  Chas. Hen., Baron Wotton, 96, 98, 103, 132
  Kath., his mother, *see* Stanhope
Kirkpatrick, Revd. Ric. Carr, 257
Kitchin, B., 31
Kit-Cat club, 82
Klein, Melanie, 42
Klippan Ho., 28
Knight:
  Chas., 56, 72
  Wm. (? more than one), 18, 20, 123
Knights Hospitallers, *see* Clerkenwell
Knights Templars, 2, 73, 93, 102, 113
Knightsbridge, in Westm., man., 181, 226, 229, 233, 235, 241; cts., 229, 241; customs, 233
Knollys, Edw. Geo. Wm. Tyrwhitt, Vct. Knollys, 70
Knox, E. V., 32, 42
Knyvett, Sir Hen., 103
Kokoschka, Oscar, 41, 66
Korda, Sir Alex., 62
Koulermos, Panos, 62
Kylemore Rd., 44

L.C.C., *see* London County Council
L.G.O.C., *see* London General Omnibus Co.
L.N.W.R., *see* London & North Western Rly.
laboratory supplying, 127
Labour party and voters, 91, 137, 216, 245
Ladbroke est., in Kensington, 199–200, 206
Ladywell Ct., 19, 152
Laing, John, & Co., 59
Lakis Close, 32
Lamb:
  Hen., 73
  Joan, 100
  John, 100
  Mary, m. Edw. Josselyn, 100
  Ric., 100
Lambe, Jas., and his w. Esther, 109
Lambert:
  Edw., 128
  Fras., 126
Lamboll Pl., Rd., 56
Lamerton's (shop), 129
Lampet, Revd. Barrett Edw., and his w. Rose, 104
Lanark Terr., 213
Lancaster, earl of, *see* Edmund
Lancaster (flats), 209
Lancaster Gate, *see* Bayswater Rd.
Lancaster Gate (Church Com. est.), 196, 209
Lancaster Gate hotel, 239
Lancaster Gate Housing Assoc., 209
Lancaster Grove, Rd., 56
Lancefield St., 219
Land Building Investment and Cottage Improvement Co., 45

Land Co. of Lond., 44
Landseer:
Chas., 206
Sir Edwin, 206
Lane:
John, 18
Jos., 128
Peter, perpetual curate of Paddington, 253
Sam., 248
Sir Thos., 18
Thos., 19
Lang, Jas., 53
Langford, Wm., 102, 113
Langhorne, Sir Wm., Bt., 93, 147, 169
Langland Gdns., 38
Langtry, Lillie, 61
Lansdowne, mchnss. of, see Petty-FitzMaurice
Larke, Wm., 155
Lasdun, Sir Denys, 203, 211, 266
Laski, Marghanita, 33
Lasted Lodge, 83
Latimer, Hugh, bp. of Worcester, 151
Latin, ——, nurseryman, 235
Latter-day Saints, see Mormons
Lauderdale Mansions, 217
Lauderdale Rd., 214
laundering, 9, 44, 69, 71, 125–6, 201, 238
Lauriston Lodge, 43, 45
Lavender Cottage, 73
Lavers & Westlake, 152, 155
Lavie, Germain, 43, 97, 123
the Lawn, 24, 31
Lawn Bank, 25
Lawn Cottage, 25–6
Lawn Ho., 19
Lawn Rd., 55
Lawn Rd. (flats), 59
lawn billiards, 89
lawn tennis, 87
Lawrence:
D. H., 30–1, 73
Sir Fred., 240–1
Fred., Ltd., 241
Frieda, 30, 73
——, of Bristol, 46
Le Breton, Phil., 27, 61, 79–80, 90, 136
Le Carré, John, 33
Le Corbusier (Charles-Edouard Jeanneret), 66, 211
Leamington Ho., 203
Leammell, Alf., 30
Leatherhead (Surr.), sch., 166
Leckhampton, Thos., 99, 113
Ledbury Rd., 203
Lee:
J. T., 256, 258
Lancelot, 104
Leek & Westbourne (formerly Westbourne Pk. and Leek & Moorlands) building soc., 224
Left Book Club, 32
Legg, Hen. Simpson, 28
Legge, Wal., 42
Leicester, O. H., 210
Leighton, Fred., Baron Leighton, 206
Leighton Ho., 61
Leinster Gdns., 211
Leinster Sq., 206–7, 212
Lennon, Dennis, & Partners, 66, 128
Lessingham, Mrs., see Hemet
Lethbridge, Geo., 37
Leuty, John A., 241
Lever, Wm. H., Vct. Leverhulme, 71, 80, 143
Leverhulme, Vct., see Lever
Levy, Ted, Benjamin & Partners, 32, 41
Lewis:
F. J., 127
John (fl. 1807), 191

John (d. 1928), 37
John, Partnership, 129
Mary Ann, 272
Sam., 249
Liberal party and voters, 28, 91, 225
Liddell:
Hen., 101
Mary, see Nelthorpe
Thos., 101
Liddell est., 47, 49–50, 106, 118, 120
Liddell's farm, 47
Lightwater (Surr.), convalescent home, 249
Lilley & Skinner, 129
Limbrey, Ric., 42
the Limes (flats), 70
Lincoln, canon of, see Dunster
Lindfield Gdns., 38
Lindo, F. C., 249
Lindsay, Wm. Hen., 237
Lindsay, Neal & Co., 237
Lindsey, earl of, see Bertie
Linford, A. H., 166
Lingard Rd., 27
Linnell, John, 68, 77
Linstead St., 48
Linton:
Eliza, 27
Sir Jas., 64
W. J., 27
and see Sinton
Lisburne Rd., 58
Lisle:
John, 229
Thos., of Lambeth, 229
Thos., of Paddington, 229
Wm., 230
Lisson man., in Marylebone, 102–3, 113, 122, 132, 190; bailiwick, 102
Lister, Mrs., 52
Lithos Rd., 38
Litlington, see Nicholas
Little:
Dorothy, m. John Mills Jackson, 106
John, 105–6
Ric., 106
Thos., 259
Little Dene, 45
Little est., 47–9, 105–6
Little Venice, in Paddington, 174, 200, 204, 212, 215–16
dom. bldgs., 216
island, 216
pool, 175, 177, 200, 216
Rembrandt gdns., 216
studios, 216
Little Westbourne, 231
Littles farm, 47
Littlewood, Wm., 124
Littleworth, in Hampstead, 9, 11, 66, 68–9, 71, 75
dom. bldgs., 68–71, 80–1; pl. 29
pop., 69
pub. ho., see Jack Straw's Castle
Lloyd, Marie, 65
Load of Hay P.H., 52, 84, 87
Lobb, Steph., 154
Lock hosp., 232, 247–8
chapel, 247–8, 256
Lockyer, Jas., 244
Lodington, Dan., 108
Lofte, John at, 95
Loftis:
Helen, wid. of Ric., m. 2 Bart. Quyny, 99
Ric., 99
the Logs, 25, 28
Lombardy Pl., 211
London, 81, 118
ch., St. Benet, Paul's Wharf, 257
citizens and merchants, 9, 16, 42, 51, 118
City:
Apothecaries' Co., 76

(ld.) mayors, see Beckford, Wm.; Hart, Sir John; Sheldon, Sir Jos.
hosps., 247
Newgate gaol, 190
St. Paul's cathedral, q.v.
Smithfield, gallows, 190
water supply, 76, 138, 182, 204, 228, 246; conduit ho., 246
London diocese:
bps., 145–6, 242; and see Aylmer; Blomfield, Chas.; Compton, Hen.; Jackson, John; Kempe, Thos.; Robinson, John; Sheldon, Gilb.
as lords of Paddington man., 175, 182, 186, 206, 212, 217, 226, 228, 235; and see Paddington Estate
as patrons of chs., 149, 252–4, 256–9
London Academy of Music, 65, 91
London & Birmingham Rly., 6, 63
London & City Real Estate, 62
London & North Western Rly., 6–7, 181
London and Paddington Steam Carriage Co., 178
London & Westminster Newspapers, 226
London Assurance Group, 183
London Baptist Assoc., 156
London City Mission, 263
London Congregational Union, 157
London Conveyance Co., 177
London Co-operative Soc., 129
London County Council (L.C.C.), 6, 88, 135, 216, 245, 252
as housing authy., 50–1, 62, 184, 189, 202, 209, 232
fire, 250–1
pks. and open spaces, 71–6, 80–1, 144
schs., 159–64, 167–8, 265–70
sewerage, 245
tech. educ., 269
tram depot, 126
London Diocesan Deaconess Institution, 255
London Electric Rly., 181
London Electricity Board, 127, 251
London Embassy hotel, 210, 239
London Fire Brigade, 140
London General Omnibus Co. (L.G.O.C.), 5–6, 45, 178
London Merchant Securities, 196
London Metropole hotel, 189, 233, 239
London Passenger Transport Board, 7, 178
London Permanent Building Soc., 44
London Regiment, 224
London Residuary Body, 81
London School Board, 159–60, 265, 269
London Soc. for Teaching and Training the Blind, 65
London Street Tramways Co., 6, 28
London Transport Executive, 239
Westbourne Pk. garage, 178
London Univ., 154
Lillian Penson hall, 195–6, 198
and see Bedford Coll.; University Coll. sch.; Westfield Coll.
Long, Edwin, 37–8
Longman:
Thos. Norton, 13, 35, 110, 147
Wm., 13
Lonrho (co.), 233
Lord:
Chas., 135
John le, 96
Lord Hill's Rd., 200
the Lothians, 37
Loudoun, John Claudius, 205–6, 211

Loudoun Rd., 61
Londoun Rd. Mews, 61
Loughborough, Ld., *see* Wedderburn
Love, Geo., 123
Lovel, Fras., 44
Lovell, G. W., 56
Lovelock, Thos., 83
Loveridge Rd., 48
Low, David, 32
Lower Chalcots farm, 100, 116, 118
Lower Cross Rd., 55
Lower Flask P.H., 17, 22, 24, 123
Lower Porchester St., 192
Lower Terr., 25
Lower White Ho., 18
Lowfield Rd., 44
Lownds, Louisa, 147
Loyal Hampstead Assoc., 89
Lucas:
    David, 77
    Seymour, 50
    and see Connell
Luder, Owen, 212
Ludford, Alice, 261
Luffingham, Wm., 82–3
Luke of Hedham, 95
Lund:
    John, 53, 98, 107, 136
    Wm., 55, 57, 98
Lutyens:
    Sir Edwin, 30
    Eliz., 66
Lycett, Sir Fras., 156
Lydford (est.), 220–1
Lyell, Mic., 41
lying-in hosp., *see* Queen Charlotte's
Lymington Mansions, 46
Lymington Rd., 38, 46
Lyncroft Gdns., 45
Lyndhurst Gdns., Rd., 56
Lynd, Rob., 31
Lyon:
    John (fl. 1295), 113
    John (d. 1592), 3, 174

MARS (archit. group), 59
M.B.W., *see* Metropolitan Board of
    Works
Macaulay, Dame Rose, 31
Macbeth, Rob., 57, 65
Macclesfield, earl of, *see* Parker
McCulloch, fam., 35
MacDermott, Norman, 85
MacDonald, Jas. Ramsay, 40, 59
McInerney, Thos., & Sons, 66
Mackenzie, Sir Compton, 30, 73
Mackeson Rd., 58
Mackmurdo, A. H., 37, 256
Maclaren, J. M., 210
McMillan, Misses, 168
McMorran, D. H., 66
McQuoid, Percy, 208, 210
Madariaga, Salvador de, 32
Magee, Revd. A., 260
Magic Flute P.H., 220
Magnus-Allcroft, Lady, 258
Maida, battle of, 212
Maida Ave., 186, 190, 212
Maida Hill, *see* Edgware Rd.
Maida Hill East, *see* Edgware Rd.
Maida Hill West, 186, 212
Maida Pl., *see* Edgware Rd.
Maida Vale, in Paddington, 183–5,
    212
    chs., 213–14, 216–17, 256, 259; *pl.*
    50
    dom. bldgs., 216–17; *pl.* 40
    farms and farmhos., 212–13
    flats, 183, 215–17
    growth, 212–16
    hotels, 216–17, 239
    housing and council est., 215–16
    Jews, 214, 264–5
    libr., 251–2
    pop., density, 215

poverty, 215
pub. hos., 212–13
retail trade, 213–14, 216–17
roads, 212–15
schs., 214, 265–70
Maida Vale (Church Com. est.), 196,
    216
Maida Vale (G.L.C. est.), 215
Maida Vale (part of Edgware Rd.),
    174, 212
    Canterbury Villas, 213
    Carlton Villas, 213
    Portsdown Terr., 213
    dom. bldgs., 217
    flats, 215, 217
Maida Vale Mansions, 215
Maitland Ct., 209, 211
Mall studios, 15, 57, 59, 66
Mallory, Anne, 172
Malton, earl of, *see* Watson-
    Wentworth
Malvern Rd., 218
Manby, Chas., 207
Manchester, bp. of, *see* Moorhouse
Manchester Mews, Pl., 48
Mandeville Ct., 40
Mangoda (fl. *c.* 975), 92
Manners Rd., 27
Manning, Hen. Edw., Cardinal, 260
Manning:
    Rosemary, 167
    W. P., 45, 151
Manor Cottage, 35
Manor Farm (Frognal), 38, 118–20,
    124
Manor Ho. (Hampstead man. ho.),
    34–5, 40, 95, 131
Manor Ho. Ct., 216, 259
Manor Ho. farm (Paddington), 212,
    228, 236
Manor Ho. hosp., 144
Manor Lodge, 35, 42, 118, 131
Manor Mansions, 58
Manor Pl., 188
Mansell, Hunt & Catty, 126
Mansfield, Kath., 31, 216
Mansfield, earls of, *see* Murray
Mansfield Cottage, 23
Manstone Rd., 49
Marban Rd., 218
Marble Arch Street Rail Car Co., 178
Marble Ho. (flats), 220–1
March, earl of, *see* Mortimer, Rog.
Marchant, fam., 53
Maresfield Gdns., 38
Mareys, John, 108
Marie Curie hosp., 41, 143–4
Market St., 192
Marks, Ric., 237
Marks & Spencer, 129
Marlborough Mansions, 45–6
Marlborough St., 201
Marnham, Herb., 29
Marsh:
    Ann, 101
    Blandine, 107
    Edw., 107–8
    John, 107–8, 116
    Ric. (fl. 1742), 212
    Ric. (fl. 1773), 101
    Ric. (fl. 1818), 101
    Rob., 108
    Thos. (fl. 1676), 107
    Thos. (fl. 1716), 103
    Wm., 108
    fam., 115–17
Marshall:
    Revd. D. H., 165–6
    Fras., 172
    Rosamond, w. of Fras., 172
Marston Close, 62
Martin:
    John, 206
    Kingsley, 32
    Leslie, 59

Martines, Sebastian Gonzalez, 97
Martyrs Memorial Trust, 145
Marx, Karl, 86
Mary I, Queen, 103
Mary, queen of Geo. V, 143
Mary Immaculate, Oblates of, 152–3
Mary Wharrie Ho., 66
Marylands Rd., 218, 220–1
Marylebone, 173, 181–2, 225, 244,
    251–2
    farms, St. John's Wood farmho.,
    117
    flyover, *see* Edgware Rd.
    hosps., 249
    Jews, 158
    man. and other est., *see* Eyre;
    Lisson
    New (later Marylebone) Rd., 175,
    177
    nonconf. (protestant), 156, 260
    nurseries, 265
    pk., 122
    pub. ho., Eyre Arms, 87
    St. Marylebone, metropolitan
    boro., 184, 237, 245
    schs., 265, 267, 269–70
    turnpike trust, 174, 251
    Tyburn, *q.v.*
Maryon:
    John, 93, 148
    Jos., and his wid. Marg., 93
Maryon Hall, 39
Maryon Mews, 32
Maryon Terr., 28
Maryon-Wilson, *see* Wilson
Masaryk, Thos., 75
Mascall, John, 51
Masefield, John, 30, 214
Maseres, Fras., 186
Mason, Fras., 128
Masters:
    John, 133
    Wm., 133–4
Matcham, Frank, 222
Mather, And., 85
Matheson, Hugh M., 70
Mathews, Chas. Jas., and his w.
    (Mme. Vestris), 231
Maufe, Sir Edw., 30, 40
Maurice, C. E., 79; *and see* Morice;
    Morris
M'SEX--27--
Mawson, Thos., 71
May:
    E. J., 28
    Phil. Wm., 78
Mayer Hillman, 32
Maygrove Motors, 127
Maygrove Rd., 48, 127
Mayne, Marion, 272
Maze hotel, 239
Mazenod Ave., 49
Mead:
    Harriet, *see* Parkinson
    Revd. Thos. Wynter, 104
    —— (fl. 1770s), 103
Meadowbank, 66
Mears, Mrs., 43
Measures, Harry B., 57, 65, 181
Meath, earl of, *see* Brabazon, Reg.
Medical Research Council, 41, 143
Medley, John Edw., 48
Medley Rd., 48
Melbourne (Australia), bp. of, *see*
    Moorhouse
Melbourne Ct., 215
Melbourne Ho., 215
Melville, Sir Jas. Cosmo, 19, 26
Melville Hall, 19
Menelik Rd., 49
Menet, John F., and his wid. Louisa,
    35
Mercy of the Holy Cross, Sisters of,
    153
Meredith, Geo., 37

Merry:
John, 108
Mary, *see* Ashton
Merton Rise, 64
Messina Ave., 49
metal working, 43, 126, 238
Metcalf, John, 35
Metcalfe, Ric., 224
Methe, Rog. de la, 104, 113 *n*
Methodists (or Wesleyans), 110, 154–6, 159, 259–62
Methodist International Ho., 262
Metropolitan & St. John's Wood Rly., 7, 44
Metropolitan Assoc. for Improving Dwellings of Industrial Classes, 26
Metropolitan Asylums Board, 26, 29, 107, 141–2
Metropolitan Board of Works (M.B.W.), 135, 155, 162, 170, 173, 177, 244
fire, 250, 271
open spaces, 75, 79–80, 86, 88, 95
sewerage, 139, 246–7
Metropolitan Commissioners of Sewers, 139, 246
Metropolitan District Rly. (District line), 181
Metropolitan Electric Supply Co., 237, 251
Metropolitan Electric Tramways Co., 178
Metropolitan Free Drinking Fountains Assoc., 246
Metropolitan Music Hall (later Theatre of Varieties), 188–9, 222
Metropolitan Rly., 7–8, 179, 181, 239
'Inner Circle', 181
Metropolitan Rly. Surplus Lands Co., 221
Metropolitan Theatre of Varieties, *see* Metropolitan Music Hall
Metropolitan turnpike trust, 5, 174
Metropolitan Water Board, 246
Mew, Fred., 135
Mewès & Davis, 211
Meyer, Thos., 260
Meynell:
Alice, 208, 211
Wilfrid, 208, 211
Michael, Edw., 38–9
Michell & Phillips, 125
Middlesex County Council, 144, 168
Middlesex Rifle Volunteers, 89, 152, 224
Middleton:
Ric., 101, 103
Thos., 133
Midland Rly., 7–8, 26, 37, 44, 48, 77, 105–7, 150
Miles:
Chas., 161
John, 43
Revd. John, 256
Milford, J., 155
Milford Ho., 27, 136
Mill glass works, 127
Mill Lane, 3, 42, 44
Milligan, Rob., 53
Mills, Ric., 96
Milne:
A. A., 165–6
John Vine, 165–6
Oswald, 40
Milton, Hen., 72
Minoprio, Ant., 196
Minster Rd., 49
Mitchell:
Arnold, 39, 168
John, 83, 169
Thos., 162
Mocatta, Fred., 194
Moholy-Nagy, László, 59

Mondrian, Piet, 59
Monmouth Rd., 206–7, 212
Monsarrat, Nic., 59
Montagu:
Edw., 34
Sam., Baron Swaythling, 208, 264
Montagu Grove, 34, 38–9
Montauban, G. H., 166
Montefiore, Sir Jos. Sebag, 194
Moore:
Anne, 102
Chris., 147
Edw., 102
Hen., 59
John, 22
Temple Lushington, 30, 151
Moorhouse, Jas., bp. of Melbourne (Australia) and of Manchester, 257
Mordaunt, Anne, *see* Waad
Morel, Abbé Jean-Jacques, 25, 152–3, 156
Morell, Dr., asst. curate of Paddington, 242, 253; *and see* Morrell
Moreton, Hen., earl of Ducie, 193
Moreton (ho.), 29
Morice, John, 109; *and see* Maurice; Morris
Morison, Jas. Cotter, 37
Morland, Geo., 68, 221
Morley, Hen., 57, 141
Mormons (Latter-day Saints), 263
Morrell, Zechariah, 18; *and see* Morell
Morris, Wm., 39, 155; *and see* Maurice; Morice
Morshead:
Eliz., *see* Frederick
Sir Fred., Bt., 192
Sir John, Bt., 228, 254
Wal., 228
Sir Warwick, Bt., 228
fam., 182
Morshead Rd., 214
Mortimer:
John, 42
Rog., earl of March, 190
Mortimer Cres. (est.), 51
Mortimer Rd., 48
Moscow Ct., 208
Moscow Rd., 205
Moslems, 169
Mother Huff's P.H., 67, 81
motor car dealers and repairers, 127
the Mount, 18, 29
Mount Charlotte Hotels, 239
Mount Cottage, 170
Mount farm, 104
Mount Grove, 18, 27, 35, 109
Mount Sq., 29
Mount Tyndale, 70
Mount Vernon hosp., 29, 33, 143–4
Mount Vernon Ho., 20, 23, 122
Mount Villa Cottage, 124
Mountague, Fortune, 17
Mowlem, John (formerly Mowlem, Freeman & Burt), 236
Moyne, Baron, *see* Guinness, Wal.
Mozart (est.), 220–1
Mozart St., 219
Muir, Edwin, 32
Mulberry (flats), 220; Mulberry Centre, 221
Mulberry Close, 32
Mulberry Housing Trust, 184, 220
Mulock, Dinah Maria (Mrs. Craik), 70
Mulready, Wm., 206
Mulys:
Ric., 52
Mrs. (fl. 1714), 52
Mulys (ho.), 52
Mumford, W., 151
Muncey:
Luke, 218

Thos., 218
Munford, Jas., 270
Municipal Reformers, 137, 245
Munt, Wm., 161, 167
Munyard:
Thos., 72
fam., 72
Murdoch, Jas. Gordon, 36
Mure (or Mure Warner) & Co., 125
Murray:
Sir Chas., 44
David Wm., earl of Mansfield, 78
John, 136
Wm. David, earl of Mansfield, 79, 93; as Vct. Stormont, 91
W. H., 28
Murray Ct., 25 *n*
Murry, John Middleton, 31, 73
musicians, composers, and singers, 32, 65; *and see* Bax, Sir Arnold; Beecham, Sir Thos.; Bliss; 'Boy George'; Brain, Dennis; Braithwaite, Warwick; Brendel; Butt; Chevalier; Davies, Sir Hen.; Delius; Dubourg; Elgar; Ferrier; Flower; Ford; Legge; Lloyd; Lutyens, Eliz.; Novello; Patti; Schwarzkopf; Sharp, Cecil; Shaw, Martin; Walton; Wood, Sir Hen.
Musman:
E. B., 40
E. P., 39
Mutrix Rd., 49
Myra Lodge, 65
Myrtle Cottage, 67, 70

N.L.R., *see* North London Rly.
Nag's Head P.H., 22, 125
Nalton, Revd. Sam., 138, 146
Napier, F. R., 127
Narcissus Rd., 45
Naseby Close, 62
Nash:
John, 191
Paul, 59
Ric. (Beau Nash), 82
Nassington Rd., 67
National Institute for Biological Standards and Control, 33
National Lending Library for the Blind, 225
National Soc. and National schs., 159–60, 161–3, 165, 265–70
coll. (Berridge Ho.), 44, 47
National Standard Land Mortgage and Investment Co., 45
National Sunday Sch. Union, 225
National Telephone Co., 127
Naylor, Thos., 71
Neagle, Dame Anna, 32
Neale, Jas., 39
Neave:
Sheffield, 36
Sir Thos., Bt., 36, 93, 95
Needham:
Anne, 107
Cath., 107
John (d. 1641), and his wid. Mary, 107
John (fl. 1682), 107, 152
Jos. (d. 1736), 107
Jos. (d. 1744), 107
Neeld:
Sir John, Bt., 218, 229
Jos., 206–7, 229
fam., 218
Neeld Rd., 28
Nelson:
Geo., 18
T. Marsh, 211
Nelthorpe:
Edw. (d. 1680), 101, 106
Edw. (d. 1720), 101, 106
Mary, wid. of Edw. (d. 1680), 106

Nelthorpe (*cont.*)
    Mary, m. Thos. Liddell, 101, 106
Netherhall Gdns., Terr., 38
Netherwood St., 48
Netley Cottage, 23
Nettlebed (Oxon.), convalescent
    home, 249
Nevill, R., 256
Nevinson:
    C. R. W., 31, 66
    Hen. Woodd, 31, 59
    fam., 31
New Bldgs. or Ct., 26
New Coll. of Independent Dissenters,
    60–2, 154, 157
New End, 9, 17, 22, 29
New End hosp., 143
New End Sq., 18–19, 22
New Grove Ho., 20, 25, 27, 29
New London Properties, 202
New P.H., 67
New River Co., 76, 135, 139
New West End, *see* West End
Newman, John, 51, 116
Newman & Billing, 259
Newman Hall, 19
Newport, John de, 146
Newton, E. E., 136
Newton Rd., 200, 203
newspapers, 92, 225–6; *and see*
    Hampstead and Highgate Express
Nicholas of Litlington, 96
Nicholls, ——, sculptor, 257
Nicolson:
    Ben, 33, 59
    Sir Chas., Bt., 149
Nickson, Ric., 41
Nicol, s. of, *see* Robert
Nicoll:
    Don., 43–4, 48, 72
    Edw., 106
    Jenny, 106
Nicoll Rd., 44
Nightingale:
    Florence, 36
    J. S., 25
Nihell (or Nihill):
    Felicity, 152
    Lucy, 152
    fam., 152
Nivison, John, Baron Glendyne, 41
Noble, F. W., 127
Noble Art P.H., 84
Noel:
    Baptist, Vct. Campden, 93, 145–6
    Baptist, earl of Gainsborough, 93,
        169
    Edw., Vct. Campden, 93
    Edw., earl of Gainsborough, 93,
        132, 138
    Juliana, *see* Hicks
    Susannah, mother of Baptist, earl
        of Gainsborough, 82, 169
    Wriothesley Baptist, earl of Gains-
        borough, 93
Noel Pk., *see* Tottenham
Nollekens:
    Jos., 254
    Jos. Fras., 254
    Mary, w. of Jos., 71
nonconformity (protestant), *see*
    Assemblies of God; Baptists;
    Brethren; Catholic Apostolic
    Ch.; Christian Community;
    Christian Scientists; Church
    Mystical Union; Congrega-
    tionalists; Countess of Hunting-
    don's Connexion; Ethical Ch.;
    French Protestant Ch.; Jehovah's
    Witnesses; Methodists; Mor-
    mons; Pentecostalists; Presby-
    terians; Salvation Army;
    Seventh-day Adventists; Society
    of Friends; Spiritualists; Uni-
    tarians; United Ch.; Welsh

Presbyterian Ch.
Norfolk Cres., 196
Norfolk Mansions, 41
Norfolk Sq., 194, 198
Norman & Beard, 256
Norman & Davison, 62; *and see*
    Trehearne
Norris:
    Chris., 107
    Ric. (fl. *c.* 1762), 107
    Ric. (fl. after 1800), 107
North:
    Anne, 103
    Edw., Baron North, 226, 228, 230
    Fountain, 20, 23, 133
    Rob., 102–3, 117
North End, in Hampstead, 9, 11;
    pl. 6
    dom. bldgs., 67–71
    flats, 70
    Gibbet Hill, 69
    growth, 68–71
    Parkgate, *see* Spaniard's End
    pop., 69
    pub. hos., 67, 69–71, 81, 84
    Sandgate, 1, 66
    sch., 69, 159, 163
    Wildwood Corner, 67
    woodland, 6–7
    and see Littleworth; Spaniard's End
North End (ho.), 67
North End Hill, Rd., Way, 3, 67, 70–1,
    80
North End Ho., 70
North End Lodge, 69–70
North End Rd. (later Fairhazel
    Gdns.), 61
North Hall Cottage, 100 *n*, 120
North London Rly. (N.L.R.), 6
North Metropolitan Rly., 179, 181
North Star P.H., 60, 84
North Villa, 73
North West London Press, 226
North Wharf Rd., 187
Northcliffe, Vct., *see* Harmsworth,
    Alf.
Northcote Ho., Mansions, 29
Northcourt, 61, 143
Northern line, 8
Northolt, 93
    Down Barns, 93
Northumberland, *see* Woodhorn
Northumberland Pl., 203
Northways, 62
Northwood, in Ruislip, 143
Northwood (later Norwood) farm,
    115–16
Norway Ho., 18, 31
Norwich, Vct., *see* Cooper, John
    Julius
Norwich, dean of, *see* Goulburn
Notre Dame de Bon Secours, Sisters
    of, 260
Notting Barns man., in Kensington,
    230
Nottinghamshire, *see* Welbeck Abbey
Novello, Vincent, 206
Nunn, Thos. Hancock, 141, 171
Nutting, Susan, *see* James
Nutley Terr., 38

Oak Hill Ho., 36
Oak Hill Lodge, 36
Oak Hill Pk., Way, 37
Oak Hill Pk. (est.), 36–7, 41
Oak Lodge (Belsize), 55
Oak Lodge (Kilburn), 48–9, 85
Oak Tree Ho., 37, 41
Oakeshotts grocery, 241
Oakhill Ave., 39
Oakington Rd., 221
Oaklands Hall, 43–4
the Oaks, 39
Oakwood Hall, 37; *pl.* 18
Ogden, Hen. Jos., 171

Ogilvie, John, 35
oil depots, 127
Old Brewery Mews, 32, 125
Old Cottage, 73
Old Court Ho., 69–71, 81
Old Grove Ho., 20, 23, 27
(Old) Mansion, 11, 33, 39, 122; *pl.* 28
Old Roman Catholics, 260
Oldrey, H. B., 49
Oliphant St., 219
Oliver, Jas., 231
Ollier, Chas., 214, 222, 229
O'Meara, Barry, 193, 255
O'Neill:
    Dan., 9, 96, 98
    Kath., his wid., *see* Stanhope
One Oak, 37
Oppidans Mews, Rd., 64
Oram, Wm., 68
Oranjehaven, *see* Bayswater Rd.
Orchardson, Chas., 65
Oriel Ct., 20
Oriel Ho., 20, 23, 25–6, 28, 152
Oriel Pl., 28
Orme:
    Edw., 205, 242, 258
    Fras., 205
Orme Ct. (flats), 210
Orme Ct. (rd.), 211
Orme Sq., 205, 210
Orme's green, *see* Westbourne green
Ormond, dchss. of, *see* Butler, Eliz.
Ormonde hotel, 128
Ornan Ct., 55
Ornan Rd., 56
Orsett Ho., 203
Orsett Terr. (formerly Pl.), 199, 203
Orton:
    Anne, m. John Little, 105
    Wm., 105
Orwell, Geo., 14, 31; his *Keep the*
    Aspidistra Flying, 31
Osborn Terr., 48
Osborne:
    Ld. Sidney Godolphin, 26
    Thos., 18
Osborne Ho., 189
Osgood, Rebecca, 106
Osmond, *see* Boissevain
Ossington St., 206, 211
Ossulstone hundred, *1*
    Holborn division, *2*
Otes, s. of William, 102
Oudh (India), queen of, 214
Our Lady's Missionary League, 260
Owen:
    Col. John, 11, 16, 109
    Wm., 240
Owers:
    Ern., 125
    Ern. & Williams, 125
Oxford, earl of, *see* Harley
Oxford, Regius Professor of Hebrew,
    253; *and see* All Souls' Coll.;
    Keble Coll.; Queen's Coll.
Oxford Arms P.H., 204, 221
Oxford Sq., 192, 196–7
Oxford Terr., 193, 197
Oxfordshire, *see* Nettlebed

Paddington:
    Ric. of, 226
    Wm. of, 226
Paddington, 63, 131, **173–272**, *180*,
    184–5
    adv., 252
    agric., 233–5
    almshos., 185, 271
    asst. curates, 242, 253–4
    baths, 208, 222, 251
    Bayswater, *q.v.*
    boundaries, 173
    bridges, 175, 177
    burial bd., 244, 252
    cemeteries, 252

Paddington (*cont.*)
  chars., 271–2
  charters, 226
  chs., 181, 185, 228, 244, 252–9;
    pls. 48–52
  coach svces., 177
  common fields (Westbourne man.),
    204, 206, 230, 233, 271
  common pasture, 233
  communications, 174–81, *176*
  conservation areas, 184, 189, 196,
    203, 210
  dispensaries, 248
  drainage, 173–4
  electricity, 194, 251
  engine ho., 187, 224, 250
  fire, 250–1
  friendly socs., 224
  gas, 251
  geol., 173
  hosps., 247–50
  inclosure, 234
  ind., 236–41
  Jews, 208
  Kensington Gdns., *q.v.*
  lecturer, 254
  librs., 251–2
  Little Venice, *q.v.*
  lodging hos., 238
  Maida Vale, *q.v.*
  mans. and other est., 226–33, *227*
    Paddington, 226, 228, 233; cts.,
      181, 226, 241; customs, 233;
      demesne, 233; man. ho., 181,
      185–7, 228–9, 253, 270; *and
      see* Paddington Estate
    Rectory, 229
  metropolitan boro., 173, 245
    as housing authy., 189, 203, 220
    arms, *245*
    wards, 245
    wharves, 237
  missions, 263; *and see* London
    City; Railway
  mkt. gdns. and nurseries, 235
  mkts., canalside, 236
  mortuary, 252
  nonconf. (protestant), 260–4
  oil lighting, 251
  omnibus svces., 177–8
  Paddington green, *q.v.*
  par. officers, 241, 247
  par. wards, 243
  pks. and open spaces, 223, 252
  police, 250
  poor relief, 243
  poorhos., 186, 243
  pop., 181–2, 185
    density, 183–4
  pub. hos., 81, 221
  Queen's Pk., *q.v.*
  rectory, 229, 252
  retail trade, 238–41
  rlys. and Underground rlys., 178–
    80; *and see* Great Western
    Rly.
  roads, 174–5
  Rom. Cathm., 259–60
    convents, 260
  St. Peter's Pk., *q.v.*
  schs., 160, 162, 164, 186, 265–71
  select vestry, 242
  sewerage, 246–7
  soc. life, 221–6
  steam coach svces., 178
  technical coll., 189
  tithes, 229
  Tomlins Town, 182
  town hall, 187, 189, 245
  tram svces., 178
  Tyburnia, *q.v.*
  vestry offices, 242, 244
  vicarage ho., 185, 187, 224, 253
  vicars, ministers, and perpetual
    curates, 252–3; *and see* Camp-
    bell, Archibald; Crane, Chas.
  watchho., 187, 250
  water, 246
  Westbourne green, *q.v.*
  wkhos., 243–4
    chapel, 244
    infirmary, 248–9
    laundry, 251
  woodland, 235–6
    Paddington wood, 212, 235
Paddington and North Kensington
  Health authy., 248
Paddington assoc., 242, 244
Paddington canal (branch of Grand
  Junction canal), 173–5, 177, 236
  basin, 175, 236–7
  passenger transport, 177
  pool, 175, 177
  walkway, 177
  wharves, 236–7
Paddington   Churches   Housing
  Assoc., 185, 215, 220
Paddington Community hosp., 249
Paddington Estate, 182–4, 188, 190–2,
  196, 200, 205, 209, 213, 218,
  228–9, 232, 242–4, 246, 252
Paddington Gen. hosp. (formerly
  infirmary), 249
Paddington green, in Paddington,
  181, 183, 185; *pl.* 37
  almshos., 271
  chs., 181, 185, 188, 254; *pls.* 48–9
  churchyard and burial ground,
    185–9, 228–9, 252, 254, 257,
    259
  dom. bldgs., 189–90; *pl.* 34
  farms and farmhos., 228, 236
  flats, 188–9
  growth, 185–9
  hotels, 189, 238–9
  housing and council est., Hall Pl.,
    189
  lodging hos., 188
  nonconf. (protestant), 261–3
  open space (green), 185–9, 252;
    pl. 42
  police sta., 250
  ponds, 185, 187
  pop., density, 188–9
  poverty, 188
  pub. hos., 221–2
  retail trade, 188
  roads, 185–9, 212
  schs., 186–9, 265, 267–70
Paddington Ho., 185
Paddington Soc., 225
Paddington Soc. for Promoting
  Christian Knowledge among
  Canal Boatmen, 263
Paddington Volunteers, 224
Paddington Waterways Soc., 225
Padmore, John, 33
Page, Rob., 113
Paget:
  Wm., Baron Paget (d. 1678), 16
  Wm., Baron Paget (d. 1713), 51
Painter:
  Fras., 106
  Marg., *see* Pawlett
Pakistanis, *see* immigrants
Palace Ct. (flats, Bayswater), 208
Palace Ct. (flats, Frognal), 40
Palace Ct. (rd.), 208, 210–11; *pl.* 33
Palace Ct. Ho., 211
Palace Ct. Mansions, 208
Palatine, count, *see* Frederick V
Palgrave:
  Sir Fras., 26
  Fras. Turner, 26
Palgrave & Co., 39
Palgrave Ho., 60
Palmer:
  Chas. Jas., 55, 97
  Frances, m. John De La Fontayne,
    110
Sir Geof., Bt., 110–11, 228
John, 113
Sam., artist, 68
Sam., biscuit mfr., 61
Palmerston Rd., 48
Pandora Publishing Co., 46
Pandora Rd., 45
paper ind., 126
the Parade (Cricklewood), 49
Parisot, Peter, 236
Park:
  John Jas., 23, 77
  Thos., 23
Park Bldgs., 58
Park Ct. hotel, 239, 272
Park Pl., 186, 188
Park Pl. Villas, 187, 189
Park Plaza hotel, 210
Park Rd. (Belsize), 55
Park Rd. (Maida Vale), 213
Park West, 195
Parker:
  Geo., earl of Macclesfield, 36
  Thos., earl of Macclesfield, 34
Parkgate (ho.), 68; *and see* Spaniard's
  End
Parkhill Rd., 55
Parkinson:
  Emma, m. Chas. Trueman, 104
  Harriet, m. Revd. Thos. Mead, 104
  Jane, 226
Parliament Ct., 59
Parliament Hill, in St. Pancras, 75,
  79–80, 88
Parliament Hill Fields, in St. Pan-
  cras, 57, 75, 78–9
Parliament Hill Rd., 57
Parnell:
  Hen. Brooke, Baron Congleton,
    257
  Sir John, Bt., 257
  Joshua, 49
  Thos., 226
  Wm., 226
parquet floor making, 238
Parry, Sir Wm., 70
Parsifal Rd., 45
Parsonage farm, 212
Parton, John, 229
Passionist Fathers, 153
Passive Resistance League, 159
Passmore, *see* Caroë
Patmore, Coventry, 70
Patti, Adelina, 65
Paulet, Sir Wm., 230
Pavilion Cottage, 72
Pawlett:
  Eliz., m. Ric. Arthur, 106
  John (fl. 1640), 106
  John (fl. 1764), 101, 116
  Marg., m. Fras. Painter, 106
  Thos., 106, 117
Paxon:
  Fras., 124
  Geo., 124
  Hen., 124
  fam., 125
Payne:
  G. A., 222
  John, 128
Peach St., 220
Pearce, Wm. Hen., 214; *and see*
  Peirce; Pierce
Pearman, T., 235
Pearson:
  Hesketh, 42
  J. L., 257, 262
  John, 238
  and see Pierson
Peebles Ho., 215
Peel, Sir Rob., 140
Peirce, Wm., 23; *and see* Pearce;
  Pierce
Pelham, Geo., bp. of Exeter, 191
Pemberton, Sir Max, 37

Pembridge Mansions, 208
Penne, Hugh, 111
Penney, Wm., 199, 231
Penrose, Sir Roland, 31
Pentecostalists, 264
Pentland, Baron, see Sinclair
Pepys, Sam., 34, 111
Perceval, Spencer, 89, 99, 119, 133
Perceval Ave., 58
perforating machine making, 127
Perkins, Annette ('Polly Perkins'), 188
Perkins Heights, 189
Perrin, John, 20
Perring, Sir Wm., 241
Perring & Co., 240
Perrin's Ct., 20, 25 n
Perrin's Lane, 16
Perrin's Pl., 25
Perry:
  John Padmore, 33
  Wm., 243
Peter's Ct., 202–3
Peters, Thos., 48
Petit:
  Clement, 105
  Jas., 105
Peto, see George, Ern.
Petrie, Sir Flinders, 32
Pettie, John, 37
Petty-FitzMaurice, Louisa or Maria, mchnss. of Lansdowne, 68
Peverell, Ranulf, 8, 92, 95, 111
Pevsner, Sir Nikolaus, 71
Philby:
  Harry St. John, 50
  H. A. R. ('Kim'), 50
Philharmonia Orchestra, 42
Phillips:
  John, 152
  John Wicking, 200
  Sir Ric., 53, 119
  Sam. March, 111
Philo-Investigists Soc., 89, 162
Philpot, Wm., 205
Philpott Terr., see Edgware Rd.
Phyllis Ct., 74
piano making, 126
Pickering:
  Jos., perpetual curate of Paddington, 253
  Wm., 229, 231
Pickering Pl., Terr., 175, 199, 205
Pickett, Jos., 27, 30, 57, 97, 116, 120
Picketts farm, 28, 52, 97, 116
Pickford & Co., 236
Pickwick Papers, 84
Picton, Lt.-Gen. Sir Thos., 257
Pierce, Wm., 146, 153; and see Pearce; Peirce
Pierson, Peter, 67 n; and see Pearson
Pilgrim:
  Chas., 109
  Chas., his s., 109
  Jas., 23, 109
Pilgrim P.H., 34
Pilgrim's Ct., 25 n
pill making, 127
Pink, John, 213, 231
Pitchford:
  Anne, w. of Wm., 110
  Anne, m. Isaac Honywood, 16
  Rebecca, m. Isaac Honywood (d. 1721), 110
  Wm., 16, 110
  ——, m. Ric. Hodilow, 16
Pite & Balfour, 155
Pitt:
  David, Baron Pitt of Hampstead, 137
  Thos., Baron Camelford (d. 1793), and his wid. Anne, 69
  Thos., Baron Camelford (d. 1804), 69
  Wm., earl of Chatham, 67, 69

Pitt Ho., 67–71, 80
plague, 9
  Black Death, 8–9, 96, 111–12, 114, 122
  and see Bayswater, pest ho.
Platt:
  Thos., 73, 104
  Thos. Pell, 104
Platt's est., 73–4
Platt's Lane, 73
Plaw, John, 254
Pleydall:
  Sir Chas., 101
  Jane, see St. John
Plumbe, Roland, 220
Plummer:
  John, 105
  Wal., 105
  Mr. (fl. 1653), 105
Pocock, Geo., 47
poets, see Adams, Sarah Flower; Blake, Wm.; Browning, Eliz. Barrett and Rob.; Byron, Geo. Gordon; Coleridge, Sam.; Cory; Crabbe, Davidson, John; Donne; Drinkwater; Dryhurst; Empson; Flecker; Grigson; Hopkins, Gerard Manley; Keats; Knox; Masefield; Meynell, Alice; Morris; Patmore; Pope, Alex.; Radford; Read; Rogers; Shelley; Sitwell; Spender; Macneice; Tagore; Taylor, John; Tennyson; Thompson, Fras.; Verlaine; Wordsworth
Poles, see immigrants
Pollaky, Ignatius Paul, 188
Pollard, Rob., 204, 232
Pollard, Thomas & Edwards, 32
Pollexfen, Hen., 109
Polygon (flats), 62, 151
Pond:
  Asketin, 108
  Cecily, 108
  Gallota atte, 16 n, 108
  (or Ponder), fam., 16, 115
Pond Street, 16, 18; pl. 4
Ponsford:
  Jas., 192, 232, 236
  Lionel, 192
  Thos., 192
  Wm., 192
  fam., 194
Ponting, T. H., 240
Pool, Thos., 35, 69, 95, 117–19, 131
Poole, Paul Falconer, 27, 37
Pope:
  Alex., 19, 83
  Chris., 110
  fam., 110
Popes est., 16, 25, 104, 110; ho., 110
Popham, Sir John, 228
Poplar Ho., 44–5, 126
Poplar Pl., 205
Poplars (est.), 62
Popple, Hen., 34
Porchester Gate, 210
Porchester Pl., 192
Porchester Rd., 175 n
Porchester Sq., 199, 203
Porchester Sq. (est.), 202
Porchester Terr., 175 n, 201, 205, 211
Porter:
  F. W., 248
  Horatio, 248
  John Vining, and his w. Mary Ann, 105
Porteus Ho., 224, 253
Porteus Rd., 186
Portnall Rd., 220
Portobello est., in Kensington, 200
Portsdown Rd., 213
Portsdown Terr., see Maida Vale (part of Edgware Rd.)

Portsea Hall, 195
Portsea Pl., 193
Post Ho. hotel (Bayswater Rd.), 239
Post Ho. hotel (Belsize), 60, 128
Post Office:
  telephone exchanges, 127, 195, 220
  tube rly., 181
Potter:
  Geo., builder and auctioneer, 27, 29, 125
  Geo. (fl. 1864), 126
  Geo. W., 86, 91, 125
  H. G., 125
  Thos., & Sons, (fl. 1860), 43, 45, 102, 126
  Thos. (fl. 1880s), 44, 126
Potter's Bldgs., 43, 126
Povey, Chas., 82, 98, 152
Powell:
  (formerly Roberts), Art. Annesley, 101
  Edw., min. of Hampstead, 146 n
  John, 101, 103, 106
  John Powell (formerly Roberts), 101
  ——, stained glass maker, 256
Powell-Cotton:
  Maj. Percy, 49, 101
  fam., 48–51
Pownall, Geo., 64
Powys, Hen. Littleton, 109
Praed, Wm., 192
Praed St., 192, 198
Prance:
  Reg., 39
  Rob., 26, 36
Prater, Wm., 133 n
Presbyterian Church of Wales (formerly Welsh Calvinistic Methodists), 263
Presbyterians, 153–5, 262–3
Prest, Wm., min. of Hampstead, 146 n
Prestott, Peter, min. of Hampstead, 146 n
Price, Geo., 29
Pridham, Amy, 167
Priestley, J. B., 31
Primrose Gdns., 56
Primrose Hill, in Hampstead (part), 63, 87, 99, 144
  Barrow Hill, 2
  ch., 148
  gymnasium, 87
  rly. tunnel, 6; pl. 9
  schs., 160, 164
Primrose Hill Ct., 66
Primrose Hill Rd., 64
Prince Arthur P.H., 84
Prince Arthur Rd., 27
Prince Consort Rd., 56
Prince Edward Mansions, 208
Prince of Wales hotel, 239
Prince's Sq., 206–7, 212
Princess Ct., 209, 212
Princess Royal P.H., 222–4
printing, 126
Prior:
  John, 235
  ——, nurseryman, 235
  and see Pryor
Priory Ct., 49
Priory Lodge, 34, 36, 40, 122
Priory Rd., 36–7, 48–9
Pritchard:
  Geo., 74
  Jack, 59
Progressives, 137
Prospect Ho., 23
Prospect Pl. (Hampstead town), 24
Prospect Pl. (Kilburn), 48
Prospect Pl. (Paddington), see Edgware Rd.
prostitution, 184, 194, 201, 210
Providence Corner, 19

Providence of the Immaculate Conception, Sisters of, 26, 107, 153, 163
Provost & Co., 126
Provost Rd., 63, 66
Pruce, John, 233
Prudential Assurance Co., 136
Pryor:
  Hannah, *see* Hoare
  Rob., 26
  Thos. Marlborough, 26, 52, 119
  ——, m. Chas. Toller, 26
  fam., 53
  and see Prior
the Pryors (flats), 29, 81
the Pryors (ho.), 19, 26, 29
publishers, *see* writers
Pugin, E. W., 49
Pugin & Pugin, 153
Pulling, ——, builder, 45
Purdey, Jas., & Sons, 237
Purrett, Chas., 33
Putney, Sam., 237
Pye, John, 117
Pyne, Wm. Hen., 187

Quadrangle (flats), 197
Quakers, *see* Society of Friends
Queen Charlotte's (formerly lying-in) hosp., 190–1, 205, 247
Queen Eliz. Ho., 16
Queen Mary's maternity home, 31, 82, 143
Queen's Coll., Oxford, provost of, 253
Queen's Gdns., 207, 211
Queen's Head P.H., 16
Queen's Mansions, 46
Queen's Pk., in Paddington (formerly Chelsea detached), 173, 183–5, 217
  baths, 220, 251
  chs., 218, 257–8
  dom. bldgs., 220–1
  flats, 220
  growth, 217–20
  halls and institutes, 222
  hotel, 220
  housing and council est., 220–1
  libr., 251–2
  nonconf. (protestant), 261–4
  pop., density, 219–20
  pub. ho., 220
  roads, 219–20
  schs., 218, 265–7, 269
Queen's Pk. Ct., 220
Queen's Pk. Rangers football club, 223–4
Queen's Rd., 175, 183, 206–7
Queensborough Terr., 206–7, 211
Queensway, 175, 183, 185, 211
Quennell, C. H. B., 39–40, 74
Quex Pk. (Kent), 49, 101
Quex Rd., 49
Quyny:
  Bart., 99
  Helen, *see* Loftis
  fam., 99

R.S.P.C.A., 86
Rachman, Peter, 202
Rackham, Art., 57, 65
Radcliffe:
  Ann, 257
  Rob., earl of Sussex, 100
Radford, Ern., and his w. Dollie, 30
Radicals, 136, 225
Radnor Pl., 197
Railway hotel, 88
Railway Mission, 263
Rainham (flats), 196
Ralph of Yeoveney, 92
Ralph Ct., 202–3
Ramsay, Jas., earl of Dalhousie, 193
Ramsbury, Chas., 106
Randall:

Hen., 120
Jas. H., & Son (Randalls of Paddington), 237
T. Gurney, 129
Randolph Ave., 213, 217
Randolph Cres., 213, 216
Randolph Gdns., 213, 217
Randolph Rd., 213, 216
Ranelagh Rd., 200
Ranelagh sewer, 3, 139, 174, 246–7
Rank Organization, 86, 239
Ranulf Rd., 74
Ratcliff:
  Alex., 107
  Alex., his s., 107
Rathbone:
  A., 44
  ——, of Croydon, 45
Ravenshaw St., 45
Rawlinson:
  Eliz., m. Giles Earle (d. 1759), 99
  Sir Wm., 99
Rayne, Max, Baron Rayne, 196, 209
Rayner:
  H. A., 45
  Wm., 241
Raynes:
  John, 109
  Wm., 109 *n*
Read:
  Ern., 66
  Sir Herb., 59
Reade, Ric., and his w. Anne, 226
Real Property Co., 44
Red Ho., 208
Red Lion P.H. (Belsize), 3, 52–3, 97, 131
Red Lion P.H. (Kilburn), 47–9, 51, 88, 101
Red Lion P.H. (Paddington green), 221
Red Lion P.H. (Westbourne green), 198, 221
Red Lodge, 211
Red Watch, *see* Honeycombe
Redington Gdns., 39
Redington Lodge, 37; *pl.* 16
Redington Rd., 37, 40
Reeder, ——, builder, 44
Regency Lodge, 62
Regent's canal, 177, 183, 186, 236
Regent's Canal and Dock Co., 232
Regent's Villas, 60
Regent's Villa Mews, 61
Regnier:
  And., 18, 53, 109
  Eliz., m. Chas. Maddocks Hardey, 109
  John, 23 *n*, 109
  Mary, m. —— Buffar, 109
Reid, Thos. Mayne, 214
Renfrew Ho., 215
Rent Day P.H., 193
Repton, Humphry, 68
reservoirs, *see* Grand Junction Waterworks Co.
Reynolds:
  Jabez, 45
  Sir Josh., 69
  Sam., 206
Rhodes:
  Thos., 100, 108, 118
  Thos. Wm., 108
Rhys, Ern., 72
Richard of Crokesley, abbot of Westm., 93
Richard of Ware, abbot of Westm., 93, 95
Richard the forester, 235
Richards:
  Ric., 34
  fam., 239
Richardson, Sam., his *Clarissa Harlowe*, 5, 81–2
Richborough Rd., 49

Richford Lodge, 30
Richmond, ctss. of, *see* Beaufort
Riddell, Jane, wid. of Sir John Riddell, Bt., 23, 76
Riddle, John, 128
Ridgeway, C. J., dean of Carlisle, 256
riding schs., 224
rifle and pistol shooting, 18
Ripley:
  Jeremy Jepson, 43, 105
  Sarah, *see* Bucknell
  Thos. (fl. 1750), 105
  Thos. (d. 1770), 105
  Thos. E. T., 45, 105
  Revd. Thos., 105
  Revd. Thos. Hyde, 48, 105
  fam., 45
Ripleys est., 45, 105
Ripon, bp. of, *see* Carpenter
Rippin, Dorothy, 138
ritualism and High Church practices (and Anglo-Cathm.), 147–8, 150–1, 255–6, 258
Rixton, John, 146–7, 169, 172
Robarts, Abraham, 68; *and see* Roberts
Robert, s. of Nicol, 100
Robert Close, 215
Roberts:
  Art. Annesley, *see* Powell
  John, *see* Powell
  John, architect, 32
  Mary, w. of Thos. (fl. 1800), 97
  Sarah, 97
  Thos. (fl. 1672), 17
  Thos. (fl. 1800), 52–3, 55, 97
  Sir Wm., 101, 116 *n*, 117 *n*
  Mrs. (fl. 1889), 167
  fam., 55
  and see Robarts
Roberts Bros., 64
Robertson:
  Field-Marshal Sir Wm., 209
  Marg., 271
  and see Hall, Stan.
Robin, Wm., 104
Robins, Wm., 244
Robinson:
  Revd. Gerard, 152
  John, bp. of Lond., 172
  Mrs. (fl. 1767–71), 102
Robson:
  E. R., 65
  Dame Flora, 32
Roche, Chas. Mills, 245
Roebuck P.H., 88
Roff & Sons, 124
Roger, s. of, *see* Hamon
Rogers, Sam., 83
Roke (or Rook), fam., 115
Rokele, Martin de la, 96
Rolfe, Fred., 38
Rollo, John, Baron Rollo, 207
Roman Catholicism, 14, 25, 148–9, 152–3, 155, 255, 259–60
  schs., 159–60, 163–5, 167–9, 265–8
  and see Adoration of the Sacred Heart; Charity of St. Vincent de Paul; Dames Anglaises; Dominican Sisters; Hope, Sisters of; Immaculate Heart of Mary; Jesus, Society of; Mary Immaculate; Mercy of the Holy Cross; Notre Dame de Bon Secours; Old Roman Caths.; Passionist Fathers; Providence, Sisters of; St. Charles Borromeo; St. Dorothy; St. Marcellina
Romford (Essex), Dagnam Pk., 36
Romilly, Sir Sam., 72
Romney, Geo., 13, 23, 83
Romney Ho., 23, 31, 91, 167
Rondu Rd., 49
Rook, *see* Roke

the Rookery, 18
Roper:
  John Moore, 109
  Thos., 109
  Wm., 129
Rose, R., 49
Rose Cottage, 72
Rose Lodge, 27
Rose Mount, 24
Rosecroft Ave., 74
Rosemount Rd., 38
Rossetti:
  Dante Gabriel, 27
  Eliz., see Siddal
Rossi, J. C. F., 254
Rosslyn, earl of, see Wedderburn
Rosslyn Ct., 58
Rosslyn Gdns., 57
Rosslyn Grove, 52, 55, 57, 60, 97, 157
Rosslyn Hill, 18
Rosslyn Hill Ho., 31
Rosslyn Ho., 52–3, 56, 58, 97, 138–9;
  pl. 11
Rosslyn Lodge, 52, 55, 60, 152
Rothermere, Vct., see Harmsworth
Rothery, Wm., 116
Rothschild fam., 264
Rottenberg, Gerson, 32
Rous, Jos., 19, 68, 152
Rous's Bldgs., 19
Rouw, Hen., 254
rowing, 225
Royal Assoc. for the Deaf and Dumb,
  256
Royal East Middlesex Militia, 26
Royal Exchange Assurance, 183, 192
Royal Free hosp., 142–3
Royal Humane Soc., 247
Royal Lancaster hotel, 181, 210, 239
Royal Liver Co., 209
Royal Naval asylum, 247
Royal Norfolk (formerly New Nor-
  folk and Norfolk Sq.) hotel, 239
Royal Oak P.H., 222
Royal Sailors' Daughters' Home, see
  Hampstead town
Royal Sea-Bathing infirmary, 247–8
Royal Soldiers' Daughters' Home, see
  Hampstead town
Royston Hall, 48
Royston Rd., 48
rubbish and manure collecting, 237
Rudall Cres., 28
Rudd, John, 72
le Rudyng, est., 42, 100–1
rugby football, 87–8
Ruislip, see Northwood
Rumsey, Thos., 172
Rundell, Mary Eliz., 83
Running Horse P.H., 222, 271
Ruskin, John, 217
Russell:
  Anne, see North
  Frances, see Cholmeley
  Sir John, and his wid. Eliz., 102
  John (fl. 1565), 102
  John (fl. 1929), 121
  Thos., 102–3
Russell Ho., 29
Russians, see immigrants
Rutland, Benj., 51, 116
Rye:
  John (fl. 1347), 115
  John (fl. 1450), 99, 113, 115
Ryves:
  Brune, 105
  Judith, see Tyler

Sabatini, Rafael, 41
Sackville-West, Victoria, her All
  Passion Spent, 31
Safeway Food Stores, 129
Sailors' Orphan Girls' Home, see
  Frognal
Sainsbury, John, 129

St. Agnes Villas, see Bayswater Rd.
St. Alban, Vct., see Bacon, Fras.
St. Aubyn, J. P., 151
St. Charles Borromeo, Oblate Fathers
  of, 260, 270
St. Columba's hosp., 61, 71, 143
St. Crispin's Close, 60
St. Cuthbert's Rd., 49
St. Dorothy, Sisters of, 153
St. George, Hanover Sq., Westm.,
  par. of, 173, 190
  burial ground (formerly in Pad-
    dington), 173, 182, 190, 196,
    223, 244, 255, 257, 260
  chapel, 190, 255–6
  lecturer, 253
  St. George's Row, see Bayswater
    Rd.
St. George's Fields Ltd., 196
St. George's Rd., 48
St. George's Terr., see Kilburn High
  Rd.
St. Giles, Gerin of, see Gerin
St. James's Mansions, 44
St. John:
  Jane, m. 1 Rob. Atye, 2 Sir Chas.
    Pleydall, 101
  John, 101
  Sir Rowland, 226, 228, 233, 252
  Sir Oliver, Bt., 226
  fam., 259
St. John Stevas, Norman, Baron St.
  John of Fawsley, 33
St. John's Ct., 40, 130
St. John's Pk. Villas, see Haverstock
  Hill
St. John's Wood, in Hampstead
  (part), 36, 131
  baths, 62
  chs., 61–2, 148–9, 151
  dom. bldgs., 61, 63
  est., 11, 47, 102–3, 113, 116–19
  flats, 62–3
  growth, 60–3
  housing and council est., 62
  libr. (Swiss Cottage), 62, 141
  nonconf. (protestant), 155, 157
  pub. hos., 60, 84
  retail trade, 128
  roads, 60–2
  schs., 60–2
  theatre, 62
St. John's Wood Pk., 60
St. John's Wood Pk. Investment Co.,
  62
St. Jude's Cottage, 70
St. Kilda (ho.), 38
St. Luke's hosp., 249
St. Marcellina, Sisters of, 153
St. Margaret, Westm., par. of, 173,
  181, 198, 252
  rectory, 252
St. Margaret's Rd., 56
St. Martin-in-the-Fields, Westm.,
  par. of, 173
  ch., 96 n, 147 n
St. Marylebone, see Marylebone
St. Marylebone Housing Assoc., 184,
  220
St. Mary's hosp., 194, 232, 237,
  248–9
  bldgs., 198, 246, 249; pl. 46
  medical sch., 248–9
  workforce, 237
St. Mary's Mansions, 188–9
St. Mary's Sq., 187
St. Mary's Terr., 186, 189
St. Michael's St., 192, 198
St. Pancras, 75, 182, 225
  Asylum for Journeymen Tailors,
    151
  chamber of commerce, 129–30
  dom. bldgs., 80
  Gospel Oak, q.v.
  Kenwood, q.v.

metropolitan boro., 79, 137
nonconf. (protestant), 154, 156–8
Parliament Hill, q.v.
Parliament Hill Fields, q.v.
pub. hos., 81
schs., 160, 166, 263, 265
St. Paul's cathedral, Lond., 257
  canons, see Ainger; Beresford-
    Peirse; Brown, Ric.; Camp-
    bell, Archibald; Forrest;
    Hardman; Smith, Jos.
St. Peter's Pk., in Paddington, 183,
  214, 217
  chs., 218, 220–1, 258–9
  dom. bldgs., 221
  flats, 220–1
  growth, 217–20
  housing and council est., 220–1
  nonconf. (protestant), 261–2
  pop., density, 219–20
  poverty, 219
  roads, 218–20
  schs., 268–70
St. Peter's Rd., 218
St. Petersburgh Ho., 206
St. Petersburgh (formerly Peters-
  burgh) Pl., 205, 211
St. Stephen's Gdns., 202
Sale St. (later Pl.), 192
Salisbury:
  Frank, 149
  Norwich, 42
  Wm., 186
Salisbury, canon of, see Dunster
the Salt Box, 36
Salter, Jos., 57
Saltram Cres., 218, 220
Salvation Army, 73, 89, 154, 157, 263
Samuel, Herb., Vct. Samuel, 208
Samuel, Basil & Howard, 196
Samuel Properties, 203
Sandby, Paul, 174, 190, 222, 257
Sandell, Jos., & Co., 237
Sandell Perkins, 237
Sanders, John, 58
Sanderson:
  John, 147
  Ric. Burdon, 156
Sandfield Lodge, 36–7
Sandgate, see North End
Sandiford (or Sandiforth), Bern.,
  perpetual curate of Paddington,
  253
Sandringham Ct., 215, 217
Sands:
  Ant., 106–8
  Frances, m. Sir Thos. Savile, 106–
    8
  Rob., 106
  Thos., and his wid. Marg., 106
  fam., 108
Sandwell Cres., 45
Sandwell Ho., 43, 45
Sandwell Mansions, 45
Sandy Rd., 76, 80
Sansom, Wm., 41
Sappton, John, 152
Saracen's Head P.H., 204, 221
Sarah Siddons Ho., 233
Sarre Rd., 49
Sartorius, Rear-Adm. Sir Geo., 43
Sarum Chase, 40
Satterchott, Thos., 253
Saumarez, Adm. Jas., Baron de
  Saumarez, 43
Savile:
  Frances, see Sands
  Sir Thos., 106
Saxon Hall, 209
Saxon Ho., 30
Scantlebury:
  John, 199, 207
  Wm., 199
  Wm. Oliver, 199
Scarborough (Yorks.), 83

Scarlett, Frank, 50
Scarrotts Corner, 22
Scheemakers, Thos., 254
Schiavonetti, Luigi, 255
Schofield, Dr., 143
Schreiber, Chaim, 41
Schwarzkopf, Elisabeth, 42
Schweppes (later Cadbury Schweppes), 195, 197
Scott:
　Adrian Gilb., 40
　Sir Geo. Gilb., 27, 147, 149
　Geo. Gilb., 30
　Sir Giles Gilb., 257
　John Oldrid, 264
　Julia Marg., 272
　Wm., 190
Scott Cars, 130
Scrope, Hen. le, 113–14
Scudamore, John, 231
sculptors, see Bacon, John, sr. and jr.;
　Banks; Behnes; Bonomi; Bushnell; Chavalliaud; Cramphorn;
　Earp; Gabo; Gibbons, Grinling;
　Graves; Hepworth; Kendrick;
　Moholy-Nagy; Moore, Chris.
　and Hen.; Nicholls; Nollekens,
　Jos.; Rossi; Rouw; Scheemakers;
　Sealey; Skeaping; Thomas,
　John; Thornycroft; Walker,
　A. G.; Westmacott; Wyatt, Mat.
　Cotes
Sealey, Thos., 254
Searle, C. G., 156
Searsfield est., 25, 107–8
Second Covent Garden Property
　Co., 41
Sedley, Sir Chas., 63
Seifert, R., & Partners, 47, 75, 239
Selfridge, Gordon, 240
　Selfridges Ltd., 129, 237
Serman (or Surman), Wm., 120
Serres, Dominic, 190
servants, see domestic servants
Seventh-day Adventists, 154, 158
Sevington St., 221
Sewell:
　Hannah, 19
　Hen., 19
Sexton, G. A., 129
Seymour:
　Edw., duke of Somerset, 103
　Jas. Rice, 156
Seymour St., 194
Shaftesbury Ho., 205, 208
Shaftesbury Pk., see Battersea
Shakespeare's Head P.H., 67–8
Shannon, earl of, see Boyle
Sharp:
　Cecil, 30, 40, 65, 91
　Chas. Smithee, 27, 30, 38
　Horatio, 107
Sharpe:
　Revd. E. N., 149
　Hen., 27
　Revd. Hen., 149–50
Shaw:
　Bernard, 263
　John (d. 1832), 60, 63, 66
　John (d. 1870), 63–4, 66
　Martin, 30, 57
　Ric. Norman, 13, 27–8, 37–8, 65,
　　148, 153
Shaw-Lefevre:
　Geo., Baron Eversley, 79–80
　Sir John Geo., 193
Sheldon:
　Dan., 228, 254
　Gilb., bp. of Lond. and abp. of
　　Canterbury, 228
　Gilb. (fl. 1712), 228
　Sir Jos., ld. mayor of Lond., 228,
　　254
　Judith, m. —— Jodrell, 228
　Mary, m. —— Craddock, 228

Shelford Lodge, 52–3, 97
Shelley, Percy Bysshe, 72, 77, 214
Shepheard, ——, brewer, 125
Shepherd:
　J. J., 128
　John, asst. curate of Paddington,
　　241–2, 253
　Rob., 121
　Wm., 28
　fam., 115
Sheppard, Jack, 190
Sherborne, Baron, see Dutton
Sheridan:
　Helen Selina, later ctss. of Dufferin, 72
　Ric. Brinsley, 69, 72
Sheriff, Alex., 44
Sheriff Rd., 44
Shields, Fred., 256
Shillibeer, Geo., 177
Shirland Mews, 219
Shirland Rd., 213, 218, 221
Shirley, Rob., Earl Ferrers, 232
Shoot Up Hill, 3, 42
Shoot Up Hill est., 48–9, 101–3, 113,
　132
Shoot Up Hill farm, 47–9, 101, 103,
　117–19
Shooter, Eliz., 172
Shout, Rob., 111
Shuter:
　Eliz., w. of Jas., 105
　Eliz., dau. of Jas., 105
　Jas., 105, 133
　Rebecca, 105
Sibthorp, Mr. (fl. 1753), 140
Sickert, Wal., 38, 59
Siddal, Eliz. (Lizzie), m. Dante
　Gabriel Rossetti, 27
Siddons:
　Sarah, 20, 189, 231, 254
　Wm., 231
Siddons Ho., 60
Sidney, Fred., 29
Sidney Boyd Ct., 50
Sikhs, 159
Silver St., 29
Simmonds:
　Rob., 83
　Mary, 272
Simmons, John, 231; and see
　Symmons
Simovic, see Bickerdike
Simpson, Sir John, 169
Sinclair, John, Baron Pentland, 40
singers, see musicians
Sinton (or Linton), Geo., 120
Sisters of the Church, 255, 268
Sitwell, Dame Edith, 33
Sixth Ave., 219
Skardu Rd., 49
skating, 88, 223
Skeaping, John, 59
Skerrett, Hen., 67
Skinner, John, 106
Slanning, John, 99, 118, 122
Slaughter:
　Jane, see Stanwix
　Rob., 110
slaughtering, 234–5
Sleigh:
　John (fl. 1371), 106, 108, 113
　John (d. 1420), 106, 108, 113
　fam., 108
Slingsby:
　Frances, see Vavasor
　Hen., 102
Sloper, Jos., 45, (& Co.), 127
Slyes est., 11, 16, 18, 27, 108–10;
　ho., 16, 20, 109–10
Smale, Mat., 226, 228–9, 253, 259
Smalley, Revd. Cornwall, 258
smallpox hosp., 57–8, 107, 141
Smith:
　Augustus Fred., 272

Basil Woodd, 37
F. Danby, 31
Geo., 36, 199
Dr. Heywood, 250
Hugh, 104
John, 33
John Thos., 257
Jos., perpetual curate of Paddington, 253
T. Rog., 143
Thos., bricklayer, 33
Thos., grocer, 241
Wm. (fl. 1516), 110
Wm. (fl. 1774), 104
Smithfield, see London
Smyrna Rd., 49
Snelgar, Jacob, 155
Snell, A. Saxon, 248
Snelling, Ric., 123
Snow, Ralph, 228 n
Snoxell:
　Armine, 43, 106
　Edw. (fl. 1687, 1729), 116–17, 133
　Edw. (d. 1766), 18, 27 n, 34 n, 95,
　　106, 117
　Jane, m. —— Hill, 106
　Wm., 117
　fam., 116–17
Snoxell's farm, 116–19
Soame:
　Bridget, see Barnham
　John, 83
　Steph., 230
　Sir Wm., 230
　Sir Wm., Bt., 230
Society for the Diffusion of Useful
　Knowledge, 72
Society for the Maintenance of the
　Faith, 256
Society for the Propagation of the
　Gospel in Foreign Parts, 90
Society of Friends (Quakers), 154,
　157
Solent Rd., 45
Somali Rd., 49
Somerset, duke of, see Seymour
Somerset, see Bath
Soskice, Frank, Baron Stow Hill, 33
Sotheby, Sam., 69
Soutar, A. & J., 32
South End Close, 58
South End farm, 52–3, 58, 97, 116,
　119–20
South End Green, see Hampstead
　town
South End Ho., 26
South Hampstead Sanitary Laundry
　Co., 126
South Heath (ho.), 24
South Hill Pk., 27–8, 30, 32, 79, 108
South Hill Pk. Rd., 57
South Villa, 73
South Wharf Rd., 192
Southacre, 196
Southwick Pk. (Hants), 228
Southwick St., 192
Sovereign brewery, 238
Sovereign Mews, 194
Sovereign St., 192
Spain, Chas., 43–4
Spalding, Hen., 144
Spalding & Cross, 157
Spaniard's End, in Hampstead, 9,
　66–7, 70–1
　dom. bldgs., 68, 70–1
　Parkgate, 67–8
　pub. hos., 67–8, 81
Spaniard's P.H., 68, 81–2, 84
Spaniard's Rd., 3, 76, 78, 80; tollho.,
　5, 80–1, 84
Sparkes:
　Isabel, w. of Mic., m. 2 Rob.
　　Davies, 108
　Mic., 108
Spedan Tower, 37, 41

Spence, Sir Basil, 62, 136, 141, 144
Spencer:
  Herb., 61, 239
  Hilda, *see* Carline
  Sir Stan., 31, 65, 73
Spencer Ho., 73
Spencer Walk, 32
Spender, Sir Steph., 40
Spilsbury, Sir Bernard, 42
Spire Ho., 210
Spiritualists, 158, 264
Spitzel, Louis, 211
sports and recreations:
  sports centres, 204, 220, 251
  and see archery; athletics; bathing;
    bowling; boxing; cricket; cycl-
    ing; fencing; fishing; football;
    gymnastics; harriers; hawk-
    ing; hockey; hunting; lawn
    billiards; lawn tennis; riding;
    rifle and pistol shooting; row-
    ing; rugby football; skating;
    squash; trap-ball
Spotted Dog P.H., 198, 221
Sprince, Hugh, 128
Spring Cottage, 27
Spring St., 194
Springfield Lane, 48
Springfield Rd., 61
Springfield Villas, 48
Sprint, John, min. of Hampstead, 146
squash, 88–9
Squire, Joshua, 19
Squire's Mount, 19
Stacey, Geo., 35
Stafford Ho., 188
Stafford hotel, 239
Stag and Hounds P.H., 81
Staham:
  Alex., 109
  Margery, 109
stained glass artists and makers, 29–
    30, 127; *and see* Burne-Jones;
    Clayton & Bell; East; Gibbs,
    Messrs.; Hill, G. H.; Holiday;
    Lavers & Westlake; Mill glass
    works; Morris; Noble; Powell,
    —; Wailes; Wilson & Hammond
Stamp, Edw. Blanshard, 128
Stanfield, Clarkson, 18, 56
Stanfield Ho., 18, 27, 90–1, 141, 158
Stanhope:
  Kath., ctss. of Chesterfield, w. of
    Hen., Ld. Stanhope, m. 2 Jan
    van den Kerchove, 3 Dan.
    O'Neill, 96, 103
  Philip, earl of Chesterfield (d.
    1714), 82, 96, 120
  Philip, earl of Chesterfield (Ld.
    Stanhope) (d. 1726), 96–8
  Philip Dormer, earl of Chesterfield
    (d. 1773), 97, 99, 103, 122, 231
  Philip, earl of Chesterfield (d.
    1815), 97
Stanhope Pl., 191, 197
Stanley Gdns., 56
Stanley Pl., 187
Stanley St., 194
Stanton, *see* Biscoe
Stanwick, *see* Stanwix
Stanwix (or Stanwick):
  Jane, m. Rob. Slaughter, 110
  Jos., and his wid. Mary, 110
  Mary, m. Jas. Battin, 110
Star St., 198
Starkey:
  Eliz., 229
  Geo., 229
  John, 229
  Thos., 229
  Mrs. (? Eliz.), 231
Station Rd., 48
Steele, Sir Ric., 63
Steele's Cottage, 63–4
Steele's Mews, 65

Steele's Rd., 64
Steele's studios, 65–6
Steevens, Geo., 23
Stenning, A. R., 129
Stephen, King, 92
Stephen, Doug., 62
Stephens, Jas., 235
Stephenson:
  Cecil, 59
  Rob., 193
Stephenson Ho., 60
Sterne, Laurence, 257
Stevens, Alf., 64, 66
Stevenson:
  J. J., 37, 208
  Rob. Louis, 29
Stewart:
  Jane, ctss. of Galloway, 55
  Wm., earl of Blessington, 19
Still P.H., 20
Stillington:
  Rob., bp. of Bath and Wells, 230
  Rob., his cousin, 230
  Thos., 230
Stock:
  Hen., 49
  John, 159, 171
Stoke, West (Suss.), 93
Stokes:
  Adrian, 59
  John, 52
Stoll, Sir Oswald, 85
Stone, Rob., 35, 118
Stonhouse:
  Sir Geo., Bt., 229–30
  Jas., 230
  Revd. Sir Jas., Bt., 230
  Ric., 230
  Sir Thos., Bt., 230
  fam., 230
Stopes, Marie, 30
Stormont, Vct., *see* Murray, Wm.
    David
Stow Hill, Baron, *see* Soskice
Stowe Ho., 70
Strachey:
  Lytton, 57, 73, 208
  Lt.-Gen. Sir Ric., 208
Strand Hotels, 239
Strange, Dr. W. Heath, 142
Stranraer Pl., 212
Strathearn Pl., 193, 197–8
Strathray Rd., 64
Streatley (flats), 27
Streatley Pl., 22
Street:
  G. E., 39, 126, 257–8
  W. C., 150
  fam., 39
Stringfield, Thos., 51, 116
Strome Ho., 215
Stuart, Lt.-Gen. Sir John, 212
Stuart Tower, 215, 217
studios, *see* Mall; Steele's; Wych-
    combe
Sturges, Revd. Sim., 199
Sturgis (or Turgis), fam., 115
Suburban hotel, 72, 127
Sugden, Howard, 30
Sumatra Rd., 45
Summerson, Sir John, 66
Sun Ho., 40, 42
Sun P.H., 22–3
Sunderland Terr., 200 *n*
Sunnybank, 24
Sunnyside, 61
Surman, *see* Serman
Surrendale Pl., 221
Surrey, *see* Claygate: Cranleigh;
    Leatherhead; Lightwater
Sussex, duke of, *see* Augustus Fred.
Sussex, earl of, *see* Radcliffe, Rob.
Sussex, *see* Stoke, West
Sussex Arms hotel, 239
Sussex Gdns., 175, 191, 194, 197;

  pl. 41
Sussex Lodge, 196–7
Sussex Mews, 197
Sussex Pl., 197
Sussex Sq., 192, 197
Sutcliffe, Mrs. (fl. 1829), 265
Sutherland Ave., 213, 220–1
Sutherland Gdns., 212
Sutherland Housing Assoc., 185
Sutherland Paris Developments, 41
Suttle, W. H., 45
Swan P.H., 204, 210, 221
Swanleys (flats), 203
Swaythling, Baron, *see* Montagu,
    Sam.
Sweet, Hen., 30
Swinstead, Geo., 74
Swiss Cottage, in Hampstead, 42
  libr., *see* St. John's Wood
  pub. ho., 60, 63, 84
  retail trade, 129–30
  Rom. Cathm., 152–3
  sch., 164
Swiss Cottage Holiday Inn, 66
Swiss Cottage P.H., 60, 63, 84
Sybrand, Wm., 130
Sydney Ho., 25
Symmons, John, 186; *and see*
    Simmons
Symmons's ho., *pl.* 34

T.F.P. Architects, 169
T.S.W. Ho., 203
Taft, John, 213
Tagore, Sir Rabindranath, 73
Talbot Rd., 200
Talbot Sq., 194, 198
Tandlewell Trading Co., 239
Tanza Rd., 57
Taplow Ho., 66
Tarring, J., 155
Tasker, Fras., 39
Tasker Rd., 55
Tate:
  Edwin, 38
  Wm., 53
Tavener:
  C., & Son, 124
  Chas., 124
  Jas., 44
  Wal., 124
  fam., 124
Taverner:
  Ric., 100
  Rob., 100
  Rog., 100
Tavistock Clinic, 41, 144
Tavistock Lodge, 218
Tavistock Rd., 203
Tayler:
  A. S., 141
  John, 119
  Ken., 155
Taylor:
  Geo. Ledward, 193, 200, 203
  John (fl. 1765), 110
  John, 'water poet', 221
  John, & Co., 151
Taylour, Mary, mchnss. of Headfort,
    43
tea gardens, 70, 84, 183, 222
  Bayswater, 205, 222
  Flora (later Victoria), 222, 235
Tecton, architects, 211
Teil, John, 74, 104
Templar Ho., 50
Templars, *see* Knights Templars
Temple, Sir Ric., Bt., 70
Temple Pk., 73–4
Temples (later Hospitallers') est., 47,
    73, 102–3, 111, 115
Templewood Ave., 39
Tenniel, Sir John, 214
Tennyson, Alf., Baron Tennyson, 27,
    69

Tensleys, 26, 29
tenure, customary, *see* Hampstead, man.
Territorial Army, 253
Terry:
    Revd. C. J., 149
    Revd. G. F., 149
    Quinlan, 84, 189, 254–5
Ters, *see* Gers
Tesco Stores, 129
Teulon, S. S., 26, 37, 151–2
Thackeray, Wm. Makepeace, 193
theatres and concert halls, 62, 84–5, 222; *and see* Hampstead town: Everyman; Kilburn: Theatre Royal; Metropolitan Music Hall
Theatre West (co.), 85
Theists, 159
Theosophical Soc., 61
Thistlethwayte:
    Alex. Edw., 228
    Capt. Art., 228
    Augustus Fred., 193
    Lt.-Col. Evelyn Wm., 228
    Laura (Laura Bell, w. of Augustus Fred.), 45, 193
    Rob., 228, 254
    Selina, *see* Frederick
    Thos. (d. 1850), 193, 228
    Thos. (d. 1900), 228
    fam., 182, 228
Thomas:
    J. A., 149
    John, 179
    and see Pollard; Whitfield
Thomas & Son, 60
Thompson:
    Fras., 219
    John (d. 1843), 35–6
    John, physician, 154
Thorngate Rd., 221
Thornhill, John, 107
Thornton, Ric., 123
Thornycroft, Sir Hamo, 37
Thorpe:
    John (d. 1687), 101
    John, grandson of John, 101
    Rob., 58
    Mr. (fl. 1650), 101
Thorplands est., 42, 44, 101–2
Three Gables, 37
Three Horseshoes P.H., 20
Three Jolly Gardeners P.H., 198, 221
Three Pigeons P.H., 34
Three Tuns P.H., 17, 22
Thurlow, Theresa, 171
Thurlow Rd., 56
Thurso Ho., 215
Thwaitehead, 28
Thyateira, metropolitan of, 264
Tidd:
    Mary, 67 *n*
    Thos., 67, 152
    fam., 67
Tidey, Dan., 13, 55–6, 97–8
Tildesley, David, 48
Tilford (or Titford):
    Chas., and his w. Rebecca, 105
    Eliz., m. Jas. Shuter, 105
Till, Chas., 27
timber merchants, 236–7
Timms, Revd. G. B., 151
Tindal, Sir Nic. Conyngham, 68
Titchborne Pl., 194
Titchborne St., 192
Todd:
    Geo. (d. 1829), 53, 97–8, 119, 147
    Geo. (fl. 1835), 98
Toleman, Jas., 272
Toller:
    Chas., 26
    Edw., 26–7
    Mary Anne, m. Chas. Holford, 27
    Thos., 133, 135
Tomblin, Jas., 38

Tomlins Town, *see* Paddington
Toms & Partners, 66
Topham:
    Fras. (d. 1877), 65
    Frank (d. 1924), 65
Topolski, Feliks, 216
Torquay St., 201
Torridon Ho., 215, 217
Torrington, ctss. of, *see* Crew
Tottenham, Noel Pk. est., 219
Tout, T. F., 148
the Tower, 37
Tower Close, 60
Tower Ho., 203
Tower Royal works, 127
Townsend, John, 198
Towse, John, his wid., 11, 33
Toxophilite (later Royal Toxophilite) Soc., 222–3
Train, G. F., 178
trap-ball, 86
Tree, Sir Herb. Beerbohm, 36
Trehearne & Norman, Preston & Partners, 197
Treherne Croft est., 111
Treherne Ho., 42–3, 46, 111
Tremlett, Revd. F. W., 151
Trevelyan, Sir Chas., 207
Trinidad and Tobago, high commission of, 42
Trinity Close, 32
Trinity Ct., 203
Trollope, Ant., 193, 201
Trott, Wm., 67
Troyes Ho., 59
Trueman:
    Chas., 104
    Emma, *see* Parkinson
Trusthouse Forte, 128
Tudor Close, 59
Tudor Ho., 29
Tulloch, Eliz., 167
Tunbridge Wells (Kent), 82–3
Tunnard, Chris., 40
Turgis, *see* Sturgis
Turner:
    Ambrose, 51
    Geo., 164
    J., & Son, 189
    John (fl. 1734), 68, 76
    John (d. 1688), 107
    Ric., 107
    Thos., 27
Turnham, John, 222
Tyburn, in Marylebone:
    gallows ('Tyburn tree'), 174, 190, 242
    man., 190, 232
Tyburn brook, 174, 246
    stream (another), 3, 138, 174, 190
Tyburn shrine, *see* Adoration of the Sacred Heart
Tyburnia, in Paddington, 175, 182, 183, 185, 190; *pl.* 37
    chs., 187, 192–4, 197–8, 255–8
    Connaught village, 193–4, 196, 198
    dom. bldgs., 196–8
    farm, 190
    flats, 195–7
    growth, 190–6
    hotels and boarding hos., 233, 238–9
    housing est., 196–7, 228
    Jews, 264
    office blocks, 196–7
    pop., density, 195
    pub. hos., 193, 223–4
    retail trade, 193, 197–8, 241
    roads, 191–6
    schs., 266–8
Tyler:
    Jos., 105
    Judith, w. of Thos., 105
    Judith, m. —— Ryves, 105
    Thos., 105

Wm., 105

Ulysses Rd., 45
Underhill:
    Alice, *see* Barnham
    Evelyn, 32
    Sir John, 230
Unigate (co.), 234
Unit One (artists), 59
Unitarian Soc., 155
Unitarians, 74, 94, 153–5, 163
United Arab Emirates, president of, 71
United Church of God in Christ, 221
United Dairies, 234
United Drapery Stores, 240
United Land Co., 48, 50, 219
United Sanctuary of the New Day of the Nook, 158
United States, *see* immigrants
University College sch., 31, 39, 160, 168–9
    preparatory sch., 169
Unwin, Sir Stan., 40
Uplands (ho.), 37
Upper Bowling Green Ho., 17, 82
Upper Chalcot Lane, *see* England's Lane
Upper Chalcot's farm, 65, 100, 116, 118, 120
Upper Flask P.H., 17, 23–4, 31, 143
Upper Frederick St., 193
Upper Frognal Lodge, 33
Upper Hyde Pk. Gdns., *see* Bayswater Rd.
Upper Hyde Pk. St., 192
Upper Park Rd., 55, 57
Upper Seymour St. West, 191
Upper Terr., 11, 25
Upper Terr. Ho., 20, 23, 33
Upper Terr. Lodge, 30
Upton:
    Col. Art., 48, 101
    Fulk Greville, *see* Howard
    Jane, 232
    John Davis, 232
    Thos., 232
Upton farm, 204
Usher's Wiltshire Brewery, 238
Utopian Housing Soc., 196
Uwins, Thos., 187
Uxbridge Pl., *see* Bayswater Rd.
the Uxbridge rd., *see* Bayswater Rd.

Vale Cottage, 73
Vale Ho., 72–3
Vale Lodge, 72–3
Vale of Health, 9, 75, 77, 84, 134; *pl.* 5
    Anglo-German club, 73, 89
    Athenaeum club, 73, 89
    dom. bldgs., 71–3
    flats, 73
    growth, 71–3
    Hatch's Bottom, 71, 75
    hotels, 72–3, 89, 128
    ind., 125
    nonconf. (protestant), 157–8
    pond, 71, 76
    poorhos., *see* Hampstead, poorhos.
    pop., 72
Vale of Health P.H., 72–3, 128
Vallett, *see* Vaslet
Vane:
    Sir Hen. (Harry), 16; his wid., 11, 16
    Hen., Vct. Barnard (later duke of Cleveland), 191
Vane Close, 32
Vane Ho., 16, 18, 20, 22, 27, 32, 161, 167; *pl.* 31
Vansittart, Geo., 230
Varley:
    Cornelius, 187
    John, 68

Vaslet (or Vallett), Lewis, 165
Vaughan:
C. Evans, 257
Rob., 226
Vavasor:
Eliz., see Beckwith
Frances, m. Hen. Slingsby, 102
Venice:
ambassador of, 22
ch. of Santa Maria della Salute, 240
Ventris, Mic., 71
Verey:
Geo., 49, 117
Wm., 125
Verlaine, Paul, 216
Vernon, Gen. Chas., 23, 133
Vestris, Mme., see Mathews
veterinary college, 238
Victoria, Queen, 178
Victoria Grove, 206
Victoria Mansions, 45
Victoria Mews, Rd., 61
Victoria St., 187
Victory (Ex-Services) club, 195–6
Vigers, Edw., 218–19
Vigor, Revd. Tim. Stonhouse, 230
Villa Henriette, 65
Village Mount, 32
Villas on the Heath, 72–3
Villedeuil, marquis de, 23
Villiers, Geo. Herb. Hyde, earl of Clarendon, 70
Vincent:
Eliz., 170
John, 67, 125, 138, 169–70
John, his s., 169
Ric., 125
Rob., and his wid. Eliz., 125
Vine Ho., 19, 26
Vipand, Hen., 83
the Vivary, 73
Vivian, John, 68
Volta Ho., 20
volunteers, see Hampstead Volunteers
Vortex, see Coward
Voysey, C. F. A., 13, 29, 45, 65, 74; his fa., 74
Vulliamy:
Geo., 140
Lewis, 248, 256, 257 n

Waad:
Anne, m. —— Baesh, 104
Anne, w. of Sir Wm., m. 2 Thos. Bushell, 96
Armagil, 96, 103, 123
Armenegilda, m. —— Mordaunt, 96
Jas., 96, 103–4
Sir Wm., 9, 96, 103–4
Wm., 104
fam., 98
Wachter, fam., 42–3
Waddell, Helen, 66
Wade-Farmer, F., 259
Wadham Gdns., 65
Wadmore:
Revd. H. R., 149
Jas. F., 149
Wagner, John Fred., 164
Wailes, W., 269
Waite, Hen., 172
Waitrose (co.), 129
Wake, Sir Isaac, 51
Wakeford, Hen., 172
Walbrook, Anton, 42
Wale:
John David, 222
Frances Sarah, 222
Wm., 222
Wales:
prince of (later Edw. VII), 46
prince of (later Geo. II), 82, 98
princess of (Caroline of Ansbach), 82

princess of (Caroline of Brunswick), 69, 191
Prince William of, 249
and see Charlotte Augusta
Walford, Cornelius, 57
Walker:
A. G., 264
Adm. Sir Baldwin Wake, Bt., 207
Fred., 65
Thos., 34
Wallace, Edgar, 73
Wallas, J. C., 45
Walmsley, Jos., 105
Walpole:
Horatio, Ld. Walpole, later earl of Orford, 43
Hon. Ric., 43
Walter of Wenlock, 229
Walter:
Sam., 106
——, wid., 106
Walters, —— (fl. 1858), 111
Walterton Rd., 218–19, 221; (est.), 220
Walton, Sir Wm., 32
Ward:
Jas., 120
John, and his w. Isabel, 109
Wm., 206
and see Connell
Ware:
Isaac, 34, 231, 234
J., & Sons, 128
Sam., 48, 106
Ware, Richard of, see Richard
Waring, Misses, 270
Warlock Rd., 221
Warren:
Langhorn, min. of Hampstead, 146
Peter, 205
Warrington Cres., 204, 213
Warrington hotel, 217, 221, 239
Warrington Lodge hosp., 249–50
Warrington Terr., 213
Wartnaby, W., 60
Warwick, Septimus, 197
Warwick, earl of, see Dudley
Warwick Arms P.H., 213
Warwick Ave., 175, 213, 216
Warwick Cres., 200
Warwick (est.), 202, 204
Warwick farm, 234
Warwick (formerly Warwick Arms and Pears n's Warwick) hotel, 189, 238–9
Warwick Pl., Rd., 213
Warwick Rd. West, 213
washerwomen, see laundering
Water Gdns., 196–7
Waterford (Ireland), bp. of, see Hussey, Thos.
Waterhouse, Alf., 157; and see Hall
Waterlow, Sir Ern., 168
Waterson, J. P., 200
Wates Ltd., 196
Watkins, Wm., 99
Watling Street, see Edgware Rd.
Watno, John, 104, 107–8
Watson:
Thos., 109
Lady, 170
Watson's Yard, 25 n
Watson-Wentworth, Thos., earl of Malton, 34
Watts & Co., 30
Waugh:
Alec, 46
Art., 46, 166
Evelyn, 46, 166
Wavell:
Thos. Brooke, 105
Thos. Bruce, 105
Waverley Rd., 201
Weatherall, Thos., 24
Weatherall Ho., 24, 29, 83

Webb:
Beatrice, 38
Mary, 32, 65
Phil., 37
Sidney, 38
Thos., 19
Webheath (est.), 50
Wedderburn, Alex., Baron Loughborough and earl of Rosslyn, 34, 53, 89
Wedderburn Rd., 56
Wedgwood Walk (est.), 41
Weech Hall, 74
Weech Rd., 74
Weedon:
Harry, 86
Thos., and his w. Susanna, 109
Weeks:
Jane, w. of Ric., m. 2 Edw. Fust, 111
Ric., 111
Weir, And., Baron Inverforth, 71, 144
Welbeck Abbey (Notts.), 126
Welbeck Mansions, 45, 126
Welford:
Ric., & Sons, 234
fam., 234
Well Rd., 17
Well Passage, 83
Well Walk, 15, 18–19, 24–5, 30, 82; fountain, 83
Weller:
Jane, m. Sir Thos. Wilson, Bt. (d. 1798), 24, 93
John, and his wid. Margaretta Maria, 93
Wellesley, Art., duke of Wellington, 231
Wellesley Ho., 44
Wellesley Lodge, 37
Wellington, duke of, see Wellesley
Wellington Ho., 64, 151
Wellington Terr., see Bayswater Rd.
Wells:
Miss E. G., 167
H. G., 30, 50, 165–6
T. K., 38
Wells Bldgs., 28
Wells Ho., 32
Wells hotel, 127, 170
Wells P.H., 82, 84
Wellside, 28
Welsh C.E. Church, 257
Welsh Calvinistic Methodists, see Presbyterian Church of Wales
Wenlock, Walter of, see Walter
Wentworth Ho., 29
Wentworth Pl., 25–6
Wesleyans, see Methodists
Wessex Gdns., 202–4
West:
Chas., Baron De La Warr, 51
Anne, his w., see Wilde
Revd. Ric. Temple, 258
West Cottages, 43
West Croft, 65
West End, in Hampstead, 8–9, 11
chs., 44–5, 149–50
dom. bldgs., 43–6, 111, 126; pl. 13
farms and farm hos., 105
flats, 45–6, 126
Fortune Green, 43–4, 104–5
growth, 42–7
Hackney (New) Coll., 45–6
housing and council est., 44, 46
ind., 43, 126
Jews, 46
New West End, 43
nonconf. (protestant), 158
pop. (hos.), 43
pub. hos., 43, 84, 123, 125
retail trade, 128
roads, 3, 42–6
schs., 43–4, 46, 159, 161
West End est. (Kilburn priory), 42, 100

West End Hall, 42–3, 46, 161
West End Ho., 43–4
West End Lane, 3, 42, 46, 49
West End Pk., 44, 46
West Hampstead, *see* Hampstead, West
West Hampstead Mews, 49
West Heath Rd., 40–1
West Indians, *see* immigrants
West London Auxiliary Sunday Sch. Union, 225
West London Ethical Soc., *see* Ethical Church
West Middlesex Water Co., 104, 139, 246
West Stoke, *see* Stoke, West
Westbere Rd., 49
Westbourne Ct., 202
Westbourne (or Westbourne green) est., 180, 198, 217, 226, 229–30, 241; cts., 241; man. ho. 230; *and see* Knightsbridge
Westbourne farm (or Westbury), 198–200, 230–1
Westbourne Gdns., 201, 203; (est.), 202
Westbourne green, in Paddington, 181, 184, 198; *pl.* 36
  baths, 202, 251
    Turkish baths, 224, 251
  chs., 199–200, 203–4, 256, 258–9; *pls.* 51–2
  dom. bldgs., 198–200, 203–4, 230–1; *pls.* 32, 40
  farms and farmhos., 198–200, 230–1
  flats, 202–4
  growth, 198–202
  halls and institutes, 222
    Athenaeum, 222
    Porchester hall, 202, 222
  hotels, 238–9
  housing and council est., 202–4
  librs., 202, 251
  nonconf. (protestant), 261–4
  office blocks, 203–4
  Orme's green, 199–200, 205, 218
  pop., 181, 198
    density, 201
  poverty, 201
  pub. hos., 198, 221
  retail trade, 201, 203, 239–41
  roads, 175, 198–200; *pl.* 53
  schs., 265–9
Westbournia, *q.v.*
Westbourne green farm, 230
Westbourne Green Lane, 174, 205
Westbourne Grove, 183, 185, 199–200, 203; *pl.* 53
Westbourne Grove Terr., 203
Westbourne Grove West, 200
Westbourne Ho. (ho.), 198, 231
Westbourne Ho. (office block), 203
Westbourne Manor Ho., 198–200, 230
Westbourne Pk., 198–200, 231
Westbourne Pk. building soc., *see* Leek & Westbourne
Westbourne Pk. Rd., 175, 200, 203
Westbourne Pk. Villas, 200
Westbourne Pl. (later Westbourne Pk.) est., 230–1
Westbourne Pl. (ho.), 198–9, 229, 231; *pl.* 32
Westbourne stream, 3, 138, 173–5, 198, 204, 246
Westbourne St., 197
Westbourne Terr., 192, 206–7
Westbourne Terr. North, 201
Westbourne Terr. Rd., 200, 204
Westbournia, 183, 198, 200–1, 207
Westbury, Baron, *see* Bethell
Westbury Ho., 203
Westby:
  Bart., 113

Edw., 110–11, 113
Westchester Ho., 195
Westcroft (est.), 50
Western Gas Light Co., 140
Westfield, Ric., 34
Westfield Coll., Lond., 74–5, 104
Westgate-on-Sea (Kent), sch., 166
Westlake, *see* Lavers
Westland hotel, 210
Westmacott, Sir Ric., 147
Westmead (est.), 202
Westminster:
  abbey, *q.v.*
  Alice of, *q.v.*
  Belgravia, 193, 207
  city (18th-cent.), 182
  commissioners of sewers, 246
  diocese, bps., 93, 95–6, 130, 145, 229
  Eye (or Ebury), *q.v.*
  Hyde Park, *q.v.*
  Kensington Gdns., *q.v.*
  Knightsbridge, *q.v.*
  Law Courts (Strand), 126
  London. boro., *q.v.*
  man., *see* Hyde
  sch., 96
  St. George, Hanover Sq., *q.v.*
  St. James's hosp., 99, 113, 122
  St. Margaret, *q.v.*
  St. Martin-in-the-Fields, *q.v.*
Westminster, duke of, *see* Grosvenor
Westminster, Lond. boro. (City), 173, 225, 239, 244–5
  as housing authy., 184–5, 189, 202, 220, 232
  arms, *245*
  cleansing depot, 237
Westminster abbey:
  abbey and abbots, 8
    as lords of Hampstead, 95, 99, 102, 111–13, 121–3, 130, 145
    as lords of Paddington and Westbourne, 174, 181, 198, 217, 226, 230, 233–4, 241, 246
    and see Herbert; Humez; Richard of Crokesley; Richard of Ware; Walter of Wenlock
  almoner, 181, 226, 235, 241
  bailiff, 130
  (dean and) chapter, 55–6, 96–8, 122, 131, 206–7, 241
  new work, 226, 229, 235
  priors, 96, 112–14, 130
    and see Clare; Nicholas of Litlington
  sacrist, 229
Westmorland, *see* Belle Isle
Westway, 173, 175, 202, 204, 244, 250; *pl.* 38
Wetherall, Bart., 233
Whalley, Revd. Thos. Sedgwick, 191
Wharrie, Mrs. (fl. 1935), 171
Wheatley, Mrs. (fl. 1647), 212, 233
Wheatsheaf P.H., 177
Whibley, T. E., 222
the Whinns, 69
Whistler, Jas., 70
Whitcomb, Cath., 230–1
White:
  Hen. (fl. 1524), 230
  Hen. (fl. *c.* 1780), 24, 69
  John, 199, 231
  Rob., 230
  Sam., 147
  Wm., 145
  W. Hen., & Sons, 212
White Bear P.H., 17, 22, 90
White Hart P.H., 17, 22, 108, 132
White Ho. (Belsize), 52
White Ho. (Chalcots), 63
White Ho. (Hampstead town), 18
White Ho. (Spaniard's End), 71
White Ho. (West End), 42–3
White Horse P.H., 20

White Lion P.H. (Hampstead town), 16
White Lion P.H. (Paddington green), 186, 188, 221–2
White's hotel, 239
Whitefield, Geo., 153
Whitefoord, Caleb, 255
Whiteley, Wm., 201, 207, 225–6, 239–40, 244–5, 251
  employees, 208, 223, 225, 240
  shop bldgs., 201, 207–8, 240; *pl.* 44
Whitehall hotel, 239
Whitestone Ho., 24, 31
Whitestone P.H., 82
Whitfield & Thomas, 149
Whittock (? Whitlock), Wal., 221
Whitton (est.), 66
Widgett, *see* Woodgate
Widley Rd., 214
Wight, *see* Wright
Wigram, Sir Rob., Bt., 191
Wilberforce, Wm., 90
Wilcox, Revd. John, 150, 163
Wilde:
  Sjt. John, 9, 51, 96
  Anne, m. Chas. West, Baron De La Warr, 51
Wilde's ho., 51–2
the Wilderness, 82
Wildman, Thos., 110
Wildwood Corner, *see* North End
Wildwood Cottage, 70
Wildwood est., in Hendon, 67
Wildwood Grove, 70
Wildwood (ho.), 71
Wildwood Lodge, 70–1
Wildwood Terr., 70
Wildwoods, 6–7
Wilkes, John, 67
Wilkinson:
  G. H., 270
  Herb., 270
Wilks, Rob., 34
Willes:
  Sir Fras., 69, 134, 171
  Revd. Edw., 171
Willesden, 173, 252
  cemetery, 252
  ch., 148
  char., 172
  Jews, 158
  Kilburn priory lands in, 100
  nonconf. (protestant), 156
  Queen's pk. (open space), 144, 217
  schs., 160, 163
  urban dist. council, 144
    as housing authy., 220
Willett:
  Wm. (d. 1913), 13, 56, 64–5
  Wm. (d. 1915), 13, 56, 65
William IV, 231
William, s. of, *see* Otes
William Fred., duke of Gloucester and Edinburgh and earl of Connaught, 191
William of Cleeve, Sir, 102
William the linendraper, 95
Williams:
  Sir Owen, 40
  W. & S., 126
  W. Chas., 125
  Watkin, 78
Williams-Ellis, Sir Clough, 31
Willis, Fred., 118
Willoughby:
  Benj. Edw., 110
  Dobson, 53
  Janette Anne, *see* Carlile
Willoughby Rd., 28
Willow Ho., 82, 170
Willow Pl., 24–5
Willow Rd., 24–5, 31
Wilson:
  Revd. Sir Geo. Percy Maryon-, Bt., 41, 93

Sir Hubert Guy Maryon Maryon-, Bt., 93
Dame Jane, *see* Weller
Sir John Maryon, Bt., 36, 79, 93, 150
Ric., 106
Sir Spencer Maryon, Bt., 36-7, 93
Sir Spencer Pocklington Maryon Maryon-, Bt., 93, 145
Sir Thos., Bt. (d. 1798), 35, 76, 93, 95
Sir Thos. Maryon, Bt. (d. 1821), 11, 24, 36, 93
Sir Thos. Maryon, Bt. (d. 1869), 11, 25, 27, 36, 69, 77-9, 91, 93, 95, 148-9, 151
fam. (later Maryon-), 36, 79, 145, 150, 161, 163
Wilson & Hammond, 155
Wiltshire, *see* Grittleton Hall
Wimpey, Geo., & Co., 215
Winch, Mina, 270
Winchester, bp. of, *see* Ilchester
Winchester Mews, Rd., 64
Windmill Hill, 17, 20, 123
Windmill Hill Ho., 20, 23, 122
Windmill Ho., 123
Windsor (Berks.), St. Geo.'s chapel, 99
Windsor (est.), 202, 204
Windsor Ct., 208, 211
Windsor Terr., *see* Haverstock Hill
Winfield:
Anne, w. of Wm., 107
Chas. Hen., 107
Lt.-Col. Chas. Hen., 107
Wm., 22, 107
fam., 26
Wingrove, Emily, m. W. H. Hudson, 239
Winmill, C. C., 45
Winsland St., 174
Winter:
Joshua, 107
Ralph Farr, 107
Ralph, 107
Rob., 106
Wm., 113
Wise:
John, 241
Thos., 39, 57
Wiseman, Nic., Cardinal, 153
Witanhurst, 81
Wodehouse, Phil., Baron Currie, 194
Wodesour, *see* Woodsore
Wolfe, Jonas, 75
Wolfit, Sir Don., 71
Wolsey, Thos., Cardinal, 35
Women's Co-operative Guild, 30, 32
Wood:
Sir Hen., 65
Sancton, 210
Mr (fl. 1725), 152
and see Douglas
Wood Field (flats), 59
wood working, 238
Woodbine Cottage (Vale of Health), 72-3
Woodbine Cottage (West End), 126

Woodchester St., 200
Woodchurch Rd., 49
Woodd:
Revd. Basil, 254
Basil Geo., 26, 55, 96-8
Basil Thos., 57, 97
Chas. Hen. Lardner, 55-6, 58, 97
Rob. Ballard, 55, 58, 97
Woodfield Rd., 200
Woodgate (or Widgett), John, 152
Woodhorn (Northumb.), 145-6
Woodhouse, Edw., 155
Woodlands, 55, 58
Woods:
Sir Wm., 43
Wm., 25, 72, 150
Woodsore (or Wodesour):
Phil., 108
Wm,, 108
Woodward:
John, 9
Mary, 5
Wm., 146
fam., 115
Woolf:
Leonard, 30
Virginia, 30
Woolworth, F. W., & Co., 129
Worcester, dean of, *see* Forrest
Wordsworth, Wm., 69
Worthington, Thos., 155
Wotton, Baron, *see* Kirkhoven
Wragge, Theophilus, 164
Wraith, Jas., 155
Wray, C. G., 26
Wren, Sir Chris., 194
Wrench, Wm., 113
Wright:
Ada, 169
Sir Almroth, 248
John, 97-8, 118-19
Leslie, 150
Thos., 104
Violet H., 167
(or Wight) Wm., 104
Wright & Co., 97
writers and publishers, 13-14, 23, 27, 59, 65; *and see* Agate; Aikin; Amis; Baillie; Balchin; Barbauld; Barrie; Bax, Clifford; Beerbohm; Bentley, E. C.; Besant; Boswell; Bragg; Braine; Brighouse; Brontë; Buckingham; Buckle; Burney; Caine; Carlyle; Coward; Du Maurier, Daphne *and* Geo.; Charles; Christie; Clarke, Chas. Cowden *and* Mary Cowden; Collins, Wilkie; Cooper, John Julius; Cronin; Dickens; Edgeworth; Evelyn; Faber; Farjeon; Fleming, Ian *and* Peter; Fox, Wm. Johnson; Fry, Chris.; Galsworthy; Garnett, Ric.; Gibbons, Stella; Gilbert; Gregory; Hardy; Hogg; Howard, Eliz. Jane; Hudson; Hunt, Jas.; Huxley; Inchbald; Irving, Washington; James, Hen.; Jerome; Joad;

Jonson; Knight, Chas.; Knox; Laski; Lawrence, D. H.; Le Carré; Longman; Lovell; Lynd; Macaulay; Mackenzie; Madariaga; Mansfield; Martin, Kingsley; Meredith; Milne, A. A.; Monsarrat; Morison; Morley; Mortimer, John; Muir; Mulock; Murry; Nevinson, Hen.; Ollier; Orwell; Park, John Jas.; Pearson, Hesketh; Pemberton; Pepys; Priestley; Radcliffe, Ann; Reid; Rolfe; Ruskin; Sabatini; Sackville-West; Sansom; Shaw, Bernard; Sheridan, Helen *and* Ric.; Stevenson, Rob. Louis; Stokes, Adrian; Strachey, Lytton; Summerson; Thackeray; Tout; Trollope; Underhill; Unwin; Waddell; Walford; Wallace; Waugh, Alec, Art., *and* Evelyn; Webb, Mary; Wells, H. G.; Woolf, Leonard *and* Virginia
Wroth:
John, 93, 111
Sir Rob. (d. 1606), 93
Sir Rob. (d. 1614), 93
Sir Thos., 93, 121, 145
Wrottesley, Revd. Fras. John, 166
Wyatt:
Geo., 192, 199, 207, 212
Jas. (d. 1813), 69
Jas., s. of Mat. Cotes, 192
Sir Mat., s. of Mat. Cotes, 192
Mat. Cotes, 187, 192
Sir Mat. Digby, 178
Wychcombe studios, 65-6
Wylde, Wm., 101
Wyldes est., in Hendon, 67-8, 80, 99, 113
Wyldeways, 70
Wymering Rd., 214
Wynn, Wm., 63

Y.M.C.A., 85
Yale Ct., 45
Yellow Ho., 210
Yeo:
Ric., 207
Rob., 61, 64, 161
Yeoveney, Ralph of, *see* Ralph
Yeoveney, in Staines, 92
Yerkes, Chas. Tyson, 8
Yoga sch., *see* St. John's Wood, schs.
York, dean of, *see* Bate, H. N.
York Villa, 43
Yorke, Sir Wm., Bt., 231
Yorkshire, *see* Scarborough
Yorkshire Grey P.H., 20, 84, 136
Yorkshire Grey Yard, 25 *n*
Young, Keith, 28, 142
Ypres, earl of, *see* French, John

Zakaria & Associates, 239
Zins, Stefan, 32
zip fastener making, 126
Zohrab, Count Edw., 55
Zoroastrians, 159

CORRIGENDA TO VOLUMES
I, III-VI, AND VIII

Earlier lists of corrigenda will be found in Volumes I and III–VIII

Vol. I,   page 84,   line 15, *for* 'Loefwine' *read* 'Leofwine'

„   „ 110,   note 51, line 5 from end, *for* '(d. 1086),' *read* '(d. 1104).' *and delete rest of footnote*

„   „ 111,   line 13, *for* '32' *read* '31'

„   „ 114,   line 20, *for* '39' *read* '3⅓'

„   „ 114,   line 21, *for* '£12' *read* '£22'

„   „ 114,   note 95, *for* 'Bucks.' *read* 'Berks.'

„   „ 120b,   line 6, *for* 'villagers' *read* 'villeins'

„   „ 120b,   line 21, *for* '1¼' *read* '1½'

„   „ 126b,   line 25, *for* 'se' *read* 'de'

„   „ 134,   line 5 from end, *for* '1h' *read* '4h'

Vol. III,   page 240b, lines 12–14, *to read* '. . . Harefield,[77] but the record of a performance of *Othello* during the visit by Richard Burbage's company is a literary fraud.[78] Another . . .'

„   „ 240,   note 78, *for* 'This' *read* 'The alleged' *and add at end* 'For the fraud see E. K. Chambers, *Wm. Shakespeare* (1930), ii. 388.'

Vol. IV,   page 70b, line 24, *for* 'son' *read* 'younger son Hugh (d. 1098) and then to'

„   „ 70,   note 18, line 3, *for* '(d. 1086).' *read* '(d. 1104).' *and delete rest of footnote*

Vol. V,   page 261, note 34, *for* '(1757–94)' *read* '(1820–32)'

Vol. VI,   page 178a, line 3, *after* 'bombed,' *add* 'for a time'

Vol. VIII, page xiii, line 3 from end, *for* 'J.C.' *read* 'J.A.'

„   „ 17b,   line 4, *for* 'Artisans' and Labourers' Dwelling' *read* 'Artizans' and Labourers' Dwellings Improvement'

„   „ 32a,   line 14, *for* 'a Mr.' *read* 'W.E.'

„   „ 72,   note 60, *for* 'Below' *read* 'Above'

„   „ 101,   note 9, *delete* 'G. E. Turner' *and before* '(1911)' *add* 'ed. G. L. Turner'

„   „ 129a,   line 25 from end, *after* 'classrooms' *insert* '1969'

„   „ 129a,   note 55, *after* '1963' *add* '; inf. from Mr. B. K. Mann'

„   „ 148,   right-hand side of map, *for* 'Stanford' *read* 'Stamford'

„   „ 155a,   line 33, *for* 'Street' *read* 'Road'

„   „ 155a,   line 39, *for* 'Hawkesley' *read* 'Hawksley'

„   „ 160b,   line 8 from end, *for* 'Sandor' *read* 'Sandford'

„   „ 161a,   line 25, *for* 'by' *read* 'of'

„   „ 161a,   line 28, *after* 'Yorkshire Grove' *insert* ', built by the G.L.C.'

„   „ 171a,   line 12 from end, *for* '107' *read* '109'

„   „ 209b,   line 3, *for* 'Matthais's' *read* 'Matthias's'

„   „ 239c,   s.v. Riley, *for* 'Mr.' *read* 'W.E.'